Lecture Notes in Computer Science 4611

Commenced Publication in 1973
Founding and Former Series Editors:
Gerhard Goos, Juris Hartmanis, and Jan van Leeuwen

Jadwiga Indulska Jianhua Ma
Laurence T. Yang Theo Ungerer
Jiannong Cao (Eds.)

Ubiquitous Intelligence and Computing

4th International Conference, UIC 2007
Hong Kong, China, July 11-13, 2007
Proceedings

Springer

Volume Editors

Jadwiga Indulska
The University of Queensland, St. Lucia, QLD 4072, Australia
E-mail: jaga@itee.uq.edu.au

Jianhua Ma
Hosei University, Tokyo 184-8584, Japan
E-mail: jianhuamah@gmail.com

Laurence T. Yang
St. Francis Xavier University, Antigonish, NS, B2G 2W5, Canada
E-mail: lyang@stfx.ca

Theo Ungerer
University of Augsburg, 86135 Augsburg, Germany
E-mail: ungerer@informatik.uni-augsburg.de

Jiannong Cao
Hong Kong Polytechnic University, Kowloon, Hong Kong, China
E-mail: csjcao@comp.polyu.edu.hk

Library of Congress Control Number: 2007930224

CR Subject Classification (1998): H.4, C.2, D.4.6, H.5, I.2, K.4

LNCS Sublibrary: SL 3 – Information Systems and Application, incl. Internet/Web and HCI

ISSN 0302-9743
ISBN-10 3-540-73548-8 Springer Berlin Heidelberg New York
ISBN-13 978-3-540-73548-9 Springer Berlin Heidelberg New York

Springer is a part of Springer Science+Business Media

springer.com

Printed in Germany

Typesetting: Camera-ready by author, data conversion by Scientific Publishing Services, Chennai, India
Printed on acid-free paper SPIN: 12088690 06/3180 5 4 3 2 1 0

Preface

This volume contains the proceedings of UIC 2007, the 4th International Conference on Ubiquitous Intelligence and Computing: Building Smart Worlds in Real and Cyber Spaces. The conference was held in Hong Kong, July 11-13, 2007. The event was the fourth meeting of this conference series. USW 2005 (1st International Workshop on Ubiquitous Smart World), held in March 2005 in Taiwan, was the first event in the series. This event was followed by UISW 2005 (2nd International Symposium on Ubiquitous Intelligence and Smart Worlds) held in December 2005 in Japan, and by UIC 2006 (3rd International Conference on Ubiquitous Intelligence and Computing: Building Smart Worlds in Real and Cyber Spaces) held in September 2006 in Wuhan and Three Gorges, China.

Ubiquitous computers, networks and information are paving the road towards a smart world in which computational intelligence is distributed throughout the physical environment to provide trustworthy and relevant services to people. This ubiquitous intelligence will change the computing landscape because it will enable new breeds of applications and systems to be developed; the realm of computing possibilities will be significantly extended. By embedding digital intelligence in everyday objects, our workplaces, our homes and even ourselves, many tasks and processes could be simplified, made more efficient, safer and more enjoyable. Ubiquitous computing, or pervasive computing, composes these many "smart things/u-things" to create the environments that underpin the smart world. A smart thing can be endowed with different levels of intelligence and may be context-aware, active, interactive, reactive, proactive, assistive, adaptive, automated, sentient, perceptual, cognitive, autonomic and/or thinking. The field of intelligent/smart things is an emerging research field that covers many disciplines. A series of grand challenges exist to move from the world of ubiquitous computing with universal services of any means/place/time to the smart world of trustworthy services with the right means/place/time.

The UIC 2007 conference offered a forum for researchers to exchange ideas and experiences in developing intelligent/smart objects, environments, and systems. This year, the technical program of UIC drew from a very large number of submissions: 463 papers submitted from 26 countries representing four regions — Asia Pacific, Europe, North and South America. Each accepted paper was reviewed (as a full paper) by at least three reviewers, coordinated by the international Program Committee. The Program Committee accepted 119 papers out of 463 submissions, resulting in an acceptance rate of 25.7%.

The accepted papers cover a wide range of research topics that were grouped into nine conference tracks: smart objects and embedded systems, smart spaces/environments/services, ad-hoc and intelligent networks, sensor networks, pervasive communication and mobile systems, context-aware applications and systems, service-oriented middleware and applications, models and services for intelligent computing, and security/safety/privacy. In addition to the refereed papers, the proceedings include Tosiyasu L. Kunii's keynote address on "Autonomic and Trusted Computing for Ubiquitous Intelligence," and an invited paper from Norio Shiratori on "Symbiotic Computing: Concept, Architecture and Its Applications." We believe that the conference not only presented novel and interesting ideas but also will stimulate future research in the area of ubiquitous intelligence and computing.

Organization of conferences with a large number of submissions requires a lot of hard work and dedication from many people. We would like to take this opportunity to thank the numerous people whose work made this conference possible and ensured its high quality. We wish to thank the authors of submitted papers, as they contributed to the conference technical program. We wish to express our deepest gratitude to the Program Vice Chairs, Antonio Maña Gomez, Marius Portmann, Zhijun Wang, and Daqing Zhang, for their hard work and commitment to quality when helping with paper selection. We would also like to thank all Program Committee members and external reviewers for their excellent job in the paper review process, the Advisory Committee for their continuous advice, and Stephen S. Yau for organizing a panel on "Future Trends of Autonomic and Ubiquitous Computing." We are also in debt to Bin Xiao for the conference local arrangements, to the Publicity Chairs for advertising the conference, to Lin Chen and other people from the Local Organizing Committee for managing registration and other conference organization-related tasks, and to Hong Kong Polytechnic University for hosting the conference. We are also grateful to Tony Li Xu and Liu Yang for their hard work on managing both the conference Web site and the conference management system, and for their help with editing the UIC proceedings.

July 2007

Jadwiga Indulska
Jianhua Ma
Laurence T. Yang
Theo Ungerer
Jiannong Cao

Program Committee

Waleed Abdulla	University of Auckland, New Zealand
Bessam AbdulRazak	University of Florida, USA
Bernady Apduhan	Kyushu Sangyo University, Japan
Sebastien Ardon	NICTA, Australia
Juan Carlos Augusto	University of Ulster at Jordanstown, UK
Sasitharan Balasubramaniam	Waterford Institute of Technology, Ireland
Christian Becker	University of Mannheim, Germany
Paolo Bellavista	University of Bologna, Italy
Neil Bergmann	University of Queensland, Australia
Claudio Bettini	University of Milan, Italy
Han-Chieh Chao	National Dong Hwa University, Taiwan
Hao Che	University of Texas at Arlington, USA
Guanling Chen	University of Massachusetts, USA
Yuh-Shyan Chen	National Taipei University, Taiwan
Zixue Cheng	The University of Aizu, Japan
Michele Colajanni	University of Modena and Reggio Emilia, Italy
Paul Davidsson	Blekinge Institute of Technology, Sweden
Michael Ditze	University of Paderborn, Germany
Monica Divitini	Norwegian University of Science Technology, Norway
Hakan Duman	British Telecom, UK
Elgar Fleisch	University of St. Gallen, Switzerland
Michael Gardener	Chimera, UK
Paolo Giorgini	University of Trento, Italy
Frank Golatowski	University of Rostock, Germany
Tao Gu	Institute for Infocomm Research, Singapore
Jinhua Guo	University of Michigan at Dearborn, USA
Hirohide Haga	Doshisha University, Japan
Sunyoung Han	Konkuk University, Korea
Günter Haring	University of Vienna, Austria
Karen Henricksen	NICTA, Australia
Ching-Hsien Hsu	Chung-Hua University, Taiwan
Hui-Huang Hsu	Tamkang University, Taiwan
Chung-Ming Huang	National Cheng Kung University, Taiwan
Runhe Huang	Hosei University, Japan
Brendan Jennings	Waterford Institute of Technology, Ireland
Dongwon Jeong	Kunsan National University, Korea
Young-sik Jeong	Wonkwang University, Korea
Weijia Jia	City University of Hong Kong, Hong Kong
Tao Jiang	University of Michigan, USA
Achilles Kameas	Hellenic Open University, Greece
Judy Kay	University of Sydney, Australia
Tetsuo Kinoshita	Tohoku University, Japan
Mohan Kumar	University of Texas at Arlington, USA

Stan Kurkovsky	Connecticut State University, USA
Choonhwa Lee	Hanyang University, Korea
Deok-Gyu Lee	Electronics and Telecommunications Research Institute, Korea
Jae Yeol Lee	Chonnam National University, Korea
Wonjun Lee	Korea University, Korea
Vincent Lenders	Swiss Federal Institute of Technology (ETH), Zurich
Hong-Va Leong	HongKong Polytechnic University, Hong Kong
Jiandong Li	Xidian University, China
Jiang (Leo) Li	Howard University, USA
Kuan-Ching Li	Providence University, Taiwan
Weifa Liang	The Australian National University, Australia
Yinsheng Li	Fudan University, China
Shih-Wei (Steve) Liao	INTEL, USA
Seng Loke	La Trobe University, Australia
Antonio López	University of Oviedo, Spain
Philip Machanick	University of Queensland, Australia
Mary Lou Maher	University of Sydney, Australia
Francesco Marcelloni	University of Pisa, Italy
Pedro Jose Marron	University of Stuttgart, Germany
Andreas Meissner	Fraunhofer IPSI, Germany
Geyong Min	University of Bradford, UK
Tim Moors	NICTA, Australia
Soraya Kouadri Mostefaoui	Open University, UK
Max Mühlhäuser	Darmstadt University of Technology, Germany
Maurice Mulvenna	University of Ulster, UK
Amiya Nayak	University of Ottawa, Canada
Wolfgang Nejdl	University of Hannover, Germany
Daniela Nicklas	University of Stuttgart, Germany
Thomas Noel	Louis Pasteur University of Strasbourg, France
Symeon Papavassiliou	Technical University of Athens, Greece
Tom Pfeifer	Waterford Institute of Technology, Ireland
Asad Pirzada	NICTA, Australia
Rosa Preziosi	University of Sannio, Italy
Aaron J. Quigley	University College Dublin, Ireland
Andry Rakotonirainy	Queensland University of Technology, Australia
Carlos Ramos	Polytechnic of Porto, Portugal
Anand Ranganathan	IBM T.J. Watson Research Center, USA
Marc Rennhard	Zurich University of Applied Sciences, Switzerland

Ricky Robinson	NICTA, Australia
Corrado Santoro	University of Catania, Italy
Elhadi Shakshuki	Acadia University, Canada
Yuanchun Shi	Tsinghua University, China
Behrooz Shirazi	Washington State University, USA
Carsten Sorensen	London School of Economics, UK
George Spanoudakis	City University London, UK
Bala (Srini) Srinivasan	Monash University, Australia
Tsutomu Terada	Osaka University, Japan
Bruce Thomas	University of South Australia, Australia
Anand Tripathi	University of Minnesota, USA
Klaus Turowski	University of Augsburg, Germany
Javier Garcia Villalba	Complutense University of Madrid, Spain
Cho-li Wang	Hong Kong University, Hong Kong
Guojun Wang	Central South University, China
Sheng-De Wang	National Taiwan University, Taiwan
Ying-Hong Wang	Tamkang University, Taiwan
Ryan Wishart	NICTA, Australia
Hongyi Wu	University of Louisiana at Lafayette, USA
Lu Yan	Turku Centre for Computer Science, Finland
George Yee	National Research Council, Canada
Masao Yokota	Fukuoka Institute of Technology, Japan
Zhiwen Yu	Nagoya University, Japan
Arkady Zaslavsky	Monash University, Australia
Manli Zhu	Institute for Infocomm Research, Singapore
Jingyuan (Alex) Zhang	University of Alabama, USA
Krzysztof Zieliński	AGH University of Science and Technology, Poland

Additional Reviewers

Chong Wang	Jose M. Enguita	Guohua Bai
Ha Dang	Venet Osmani	Dario Maggiorini
Xiaojuan Xie	Indradip Ghosh	Neil Bergmann
Florian Michahelles	Li Gao	Shinyoung Lim
Silvia Elaluf-Calderwood	Yingxiao Xu	Dario Bottazzi
Volker Derballa	Shui Yu	Bessam Abdulrazak
Derek Corbett	Haiming Huang	Jakob Salzmann
Majid Iqbal Khan	Arno Wagner	Daniele Riboni
Kofi Boateng	Branko Celler	Mirco Marchetti
Ken C.K. Tsang	Georgios Androulidakis	Emmanuel Lochin
Henrik Petander	Nigel Lovell	Harald Widiger
Huaiguo Fu	Benoit Gaudin	Liping Shen
Alessandra Toninelli	Voker Derballa	Michelle Liang
Wilfried Gansterer	Devdatta Kulkarni	Mario G.C.A. Cimino

Mario Di Francesco
Stefano Chessa
Carlos Ramos
Stella Kafetzoglou
Jack Tsai
Yoshihiro Kawahara
Hun Jung
Vasileios Karyotis
Lei Pan
Rajesh Prasad
Zhenghao Shi
Fiona Mahon
Raghu Srinivasan
Vassilis Chatzigiannakis
Jaime Serrano-Orozco
Linda Pareschi
Riccardo Lancellotti
Su Xia
Ralf Behnke
Dominik Lieckfeldt
Haining Chen
Jan Blumenthal
Miao Ju
Alan Davy
Keara Barrett
Adrian Frei
Gianluca Dini
Borgy Waluyo
Gamel Wiredu
Mark C.M. Tsang
Yu Wang
Zhipeng Yang
Jan Kietzmann
Anil Kumar Kapu
Guillaume Jourjon
Robert Mullins
John Ronan
Yu Zhou
Claire Fahy
Peter Danielis
Hendrik Bohn
Theo Koulouris
Yasue Kishino
Aaron Harwood
Gajaruban Kandavanam
Hui Cheng
Weigang Wu
Hailun Tan
Timotheos Kastrinogiannis

	Timothy K. Shih, Tamkang University, Taiwan
	Norio Shiratori, Tohoku University, Japan
	Ivan Stojmenovic, Ottawa University, Canada
	Makoto Takizawa, Tokyo Denki University, Japan
	David Taniar, Monash University, Australia
	Jhing-Fa Wang, National Cheng Kung University, Taiwan
	Stephen S. Yau, Arizona State University, USA
	Yaoxue Zhang, Tsinghua University, China
	Albert Zomaya, University of Sydney, Australia
	Xingshe Zhou, Northwestern Polytechnic University, China
Publicity Chairs	Jiang (Linda) Xie, University of North Carolina at Charlotte, USA
	Yan Zhang, Simula Research Laboratory, Norway
	Evi Syukur, Monash University, Australia
	Wenbin Jiang, Huazhong University of Science and Technology, China
	Stephen Yang, National Central University, Taiwan
International Liaison Chairs	Giuseppe Anastasi, University of Pisa, Italy
	Mieso Denko, University of Guelph, Canada
	Jong Hyuk Park, Hanwha S & C, Korea
	Akira Namatame, National Defense Academy, Japan
Publication Chairs	Yu Hua, Huazhong University of Science and Technology, China
	Agustinus Borgy Waluyo, Institute for Infocomm Research, Singapore
Award Chairs	Vipin Chaudhary, University at Buffalo, SUNY, USA
	David Simplot-Ryl, University Lille 1, France
	Thanos Vasilakos, University of Western Macedonia, Greece
Panel Chairs	Stephen S. Yau, Arizona State University, USA
	Victor Callaghan, University of Essex, UK
Financial Chair	Lin Chen, Hong Kong Polytechnic University, Hong Kong
Web Chairs	Tony Li Xu, St. Francis Xavier University, Canada
	Liu Yang, St. Francis Xavier University, Canada
Local Organizing Chairs	Bin Xiao, Hong Kong Polytechnic University, Hong Kong
	Wei Lou, Hong Kong Polytechnic University, Hong Kong
	Kang Ying Allan Wong, Hong Kong Polytechnic University, Hong Kong

Organization

Executive Committee

General Chairs
Jiannong Cao, Hong Kong Polytechnic University, Hong Kong
Emile Aarts, Philips, The Netherlands

Program Chairs
Jadwiga Indulska, University of Queensland, Australia
Antonio Puliafito, University of Messina, Italy
Laurence T. Yang, St. Francis Xavier University, Canada

Program Vice Chairs
Antonio Maña Gomez, University of Malaga, Spain
Marius Portmann, University of Queensland, Australia
Zhijun Wang, Hong Kong Polytechnic University, Hong Kong
Daqing Zhang, National Institute of Telecommunication, France

Steering Committee
Jianhua Ma (Chair), Hosei University, Japan
Laurence T. Yang (Chair), St. Francis Xavier University, Canada
Hai Jin, Huazhong University of Science and Technology, China
Jeffrey J.P. Tsai, University of Illinois at Chicago, USA
Theo Ungerer, University of Augsburg, Germany

International Advisory Committee
Makoto Amamiya, Kyushu University, Japan
Leonard Barolli, Fukuoka Institute of Technology, Japan
Keith Chan, Hong Kong Polytechnic University, Hong Kong
Yookun Cho, Seoul National University, Korea
Sumi Helal, University of Florida, USA
Ali R. Hurson, Pennsylvania State University, USA
Qun Jin, Waseda University, Japan
Janusz Kacprzyk, Polish Academy of Science, Poland
Moon Hae Kim, Konkuk University, Korea
Beniamino Di Martino, Second University of Naples, Italy
Christian Müller-Schloer, University of Hannover, Germany

Table of Contents

Keynote Speech

Autonomic and Trusted Computing for Ubiquitous Intelligence 1
Tosiyasu L. Kunii

Smart Objects and Embedded Systems

Sensitivity Improvement of the Receiver Module in the Passive Tag Based RFID Reader 13
Seunghak Rhee, Jongan Park, and Jonghun Chun

Q^+-Algorithm: An Enhanced RFID Tag Collision Arbitration Algorithm 23
Donghwan Lee, Kyungkyu Kim, and Wonjun Lee

Surface-Embedded Passive RF Exteroception: Kepler, Greed, and Buffon's Needle 33
Vladimir Kulyukin, Aliasgar Kutiyanawala, and Minghui Jiang

Development of a Single 3-Axis Accelerometer Sensor Based Wearable Gesture Recognition Band 43
Il-Yeon Cho, John Sunwoo, Yong-Ki Son, Myoung-Hwan Oh, and Cheol-Hoon Lee

An Enhanced Ubiquitous Identification System Using Fast Anti-collision Algorithm 53
Choong-Hee Lee, Seong-Hwan Oh, and Jae-Hyun Kim

Certification Tools of Ubiquitous Mobile Platform 63
Sang-Yun Lee and Byung-Uk Choi

Dynamic Binding Framework for Open Device Services 73
Gwyduk Yeom

Design and Evaluation of Multitasking-Based Software Communications Architecture for Real-Time Sensor Networking Platforms 83
Kyunghoon Jung, Byounghoon Kim, Changsoo Kim, and Sungwoo Tak

Automatic Partitioning Technique for Flash Memory on Linux-Based Embedded Systems 93
Yunjae Lim, Young Jin Nam, Geel-Sang Yoo, and Dae-Wha Seo

Distributed Processing in Wireless Sensor Networks for Structural Health Monitoring 103
Miaomiao Wang, Jiannong Cao, Bo Chen, Youlin Xu, and Jing Li

An Improved Fusion and Fission Architecture Between Multi-modalities Based on Wearable Computing 113
Jung-Hyun Kim and Kwang-Seok Hong

Smart Spaces/Environments/Services

A Smart Space Architecture for Location-Based Spatial Audio Scenario Orchestration 123
Lila Kim, Doo-Hyun Kim, Hwasun Kwon, Dongwoon Jeon, and Keunsoo Lee

CHASE: Context-Aware Heterogenous Adaptive Smart Environments Using Optimal Tracking for Resident's Comfort 133
Navrati Saxena, Abhishek Roy, and Jitae Shin

A Methodology of Identifying Ubiquitous Smart Services for U-City Development 143
Ohbyung Kwon and Jihoon Kim

Simulated Intersection Environment and Learning of Collision and Traffic Data in the U&I Aware Framework 153
Flora Dilys Salim, Seng Wai Loke, Andry Rakotonirainy, and Shonali Krishnaswamy

Dynamic Scheduling Protocol for Highly-Reliable, Real-Time Information Aggregation for Telematics Intersection Safety System(TISS) 163
Wang Won Han, Hongjae Park, and Young Man Kim

Spontaneous Interaction Framework for Thin-Client Access to Services 173
Brian Y. Lim, Daqing Zhang, Manli Zhu, Song Zheng, and Mounir Mokhtari

Towards a Model of Interaction for Mutual Aware Devices and Everyday Artifacts 184
Sea Ling, Seng Loke, and Maria Indrawan

A Peer-to-Peer Semantic-Based Service Discovery Method for Pervasive Computing Environment 195
Baopeng Zhang, Yuanchun Shi, and Xin Xiao

Ubiquitous Healthcare Architecture Using SmartBidet and HomeServer with Embedded Urinalysis Agent 205
SungHo Ahn, Kyunghee Lee, Doo-Hyun Kim, and Vinod Cherian Joseph

Proactive Agriculture: An Integrated Framework for Developing Distributed Hybrid Systems 214
Christos Goumopoulos, Achilles Kameas, and Brendan O'Flynn

Integrating RFID Services and Ubiquitous Smart Systems for Enabling Organizations to Automatically Monitor, Decide, and Take Actions 225
Thierry Bodhuin, Rosa Preziosi, and Maria Tortorella

Towards an RFID-Oriented Service Discovery System 235
Beihong Jin, Lanlan Cong, Liang Zhang, Ying Zhang, and Yuanfeng Wen

Activity Recognition Using an Egocentric Perspective of Everyday Objects 246
Dipak Surie, Thomas Pederson, Fabien Lagriffoul, Lars-Erik Janlert, and Daniel Sjölie

A Novel Price Prediction Scheme of Grid Resources Based on Time Series Analysis 258
Yu Hua and Dan Feng

Ad-Hoc and Intelligent Networks

Adaptive Multicast Trees on Static Ad Hoc Networks: Tradeoffs Between Delay and Energy Consumption 267
Sangman Moh

Reliable Multicast MAC Protocol for Wireless Ad Hoc Networks 276
Sung Won Kim and Byung-Seo Kim

Mobility Tracking for Mobile Ad Hoc Networks 285
Hui Xu, Min Meng, Jinsung Cho, Brian J. d'Auriol, and Sungyung Lee

Handover Cost Optimization in Traffic Management for Multi-homed Mobile Networks 295
Shupeng Wang, Jianping Wang, Mei Yang, Xiaochun Yun, and Yingtao Jiang

2-Level Hierarchical Cluster-Based Address Auto-configuration Technique in Mobile Ad-Hoc Networks 309
Uhjin Joung and Dongkyun Kim

Replication in Intermittently Connected Mobile Ad Hoc Networks 321
Ke Shi

Rate-Adaption Channel Assignment and Routing Algorithm for Multi-channel WirelessMAN Mesh Networks 331
Eric Hsiao-Kuang Wu, Wei-Li Chang, and Hsuan-Hao Chan

Neighbor-Aware Optimizing Routing for Wireless Ad Hoc Networks 340
Xianlong Jiao, Xiaodong Wang, and Xingming Zhou

Gateway Zone Multi-path Routing in Wireless Mesh Networks 350
Eric Hsiao-Kuang Wu, Wei-Li Chang, Chun-Wei Chen, and Kevin Chihcheng Hsu

On Estimating Path Capacity in Wireless Mesh Networks 360
Qinqi Wang, Ming Xu, and Xingui He

A Meta Service Description Assisted Service Discovery Protocol for MANETs 370
Zhenguo Gao, Ling Wang, Mei Yang, and Jianping Wang

On Characterizing Economic-Based Incentive-Compatible Mechanisms to Solving Hidden Information and Hidden Action in Ad Hoc Network 382
Yufeng Wang, Yoshiaki Hori, and Kouichi Sakurai

A Study on USN Technologies for Ships 392
Seong-Rak Cho, Dong-Kon Lee, Bu-Geun Paik, Jae-Hoon Yoo, Young-Ha Park, and Beom-Jin Park

A New Modeling and Delay Analysis of IEEE 802.11 Distributed Coordination Function 402
Fan Zhang, Lai Tu, Jian Zhang, and Benxiong Huang

Sensor Networks

Proactive Data Delivery Scheme with Optimal Path for Dynamic Sensor Networks 412
Kwang-il Hwang, Tea-young Kim, and Doo-seop Eom

Low-Latency Routing for Energy-Harvesting Sensor Networks 422
Hyuntaek Kwon, Donggeon Noh, Junu Kim, Joonho Lee, Dongeun Lee, and Heonshik Shin

A Localized Link Quality-Aware Optimization Mechanism for Routing Protocols in Wireless Sensor Networks 434
Zhen Fu, Yuan Yang, Wen-Cheng Yang, Jung-Hwan Kim, and Myong-Soon Park

Minimum Energy and Latency MAC Protocol for Wireless Sensor Networks ... 444
Muhammad Ali Malik, Byoung-Hoon Lee, Young-Bae Ko, and Jai-Hoon Kim

An Efficient Bi-Directional Flooding in Wireless Sensor Networks ... 454
Woosuk Cha, Eun-Mi Kim, Bae-Ho Lee, and Gihwan Cho

Maximizing Network Lifetime Under Reliability Constraints Using a Cross–Layer Design in Dense Wireless Sensor Networks ... 464
Shan Guo Quan and Young Yong Kim

Adaptive Data Aggregation for Clustered Wireless Sensor Networks ... 475
Huifang Chen, Hiroshi Mineno, Yoshitsugu Obashi, Tomohiro Kokogawa, and Tadanori Mizuno

Directed Diffusion Based on Link-Stabilizing Clustering for Wireless Sensor Networks ... 485
Zude Zhou, Wenjun Xu, Fangmin Li, and Xuehong Wu

Voronoi Tessellation Based Rapid Coverage Decision Algorithm for Wireless Sensor Networks ... 495
Lei Wang, Haowei Shen, Zhe Chen, and Yaping Lin

A Clustering-Based Approximation Scheme for In-Network Aggregation over Sensor Networks ... 503
Lei Xie, Lijun Chen, Daoxu Chen, and Li Xie

Real-Time Data Delivery in Wireless Sensor Networks: A Data-Aggregated, Cluster-Based Adaptive Approach ... 514
Shao-liang Peng, Shan-shan Li, Yu-xing Peng, Wen-sheng Tang, and Nong Xiao

A Location-Unaware Connected Coverage Protocol in Wireless Sensor Networks ... 524
Yingchi Mao, Lijun Chen, and Daoxu Chen

Fuzzy-Based Reliable Data Delivery for Countering Selective Forwarding in Sensor Networks ... 535
Hae Young Lee and Tae Ho Cho

An Efficient Grid-Based Data Gathering Scheme in Wireless Sensor Networks ... 545
Shiow-Fen Hwang, Kun-Hsien Lu, Hsiao-Nung Chang, and Chyi-Ren Dow

Grid-Based Sense Schedule for Event Detection in Wireless Sensor Networks ... 557
Xianghua Hu and Xuejun Yang

An Integrated and Flexible Scheduler for Sensor Grids ... 567
Hock Beng Lim and Danny Lee

A Lightweight Scheme for Node Scheduling in Wireless Sensor Networks ... 579
Ming Liu, Yuan Zheng, Jiannong Cao, Wei Lou, Guihai Chen, and Haigang Gong

A Multi-tier, Multimodal Wireless Sensor Network for Environmental Monitoring ... 589
Carlos Eduardo R. Lopes, Fernando D. Linhares, Michele M. Santos, and Linnyer B. Ruiz

Wireless Sensor Networks, Making a Difference Tomorrow ... 599
Mohamed Khalil Watfa

Enabling Distributed Messaging with Wireless Sensor Nodes Using TinySIP ... 610
Sudha Krishnamurthy and Lajos Lange

Localization and Synchronization for 3D Underwater Acoustic Sensor Networks ... 622
Chen Tian, Wenyu Liu, Jiang Jin, Yi Wang, and Yijun Mo

An Energy-Efficient Framework for Wireless Sensor Networks with Multiple Gateways ... 632
Jinglun Shi, Taekyoung Kwon, Yanghee Choi, Junkai Huang, and Weiping Liu

Self-configurable Structure for Tracking Moving Objects in Wireless Sensor Networks ... 641
Sang-Sik Kim and Ae-Soon Park

Secure Dynamic Network Reprogramming Using Supplementary Hash in Wireless Sensor Networks ... 653
Kwangkyu Park, JongHyup Lee, Taekyoung Kwon, and Jooseok Song

Self-deployment of Mobile Nodes in Hybrid Sensor Networks by AHP ... 663
Xiaoling Wu, Jinsung Cho, Brian J. d'Auriol, Sungyoung Lee, and Hee Yong Youn

Data Synchronization in Distributed and Constrained Mobile Sensor Networks ... 673
Shuai Hao and Hock Beng Lim

Reference Interpolation Protocol for Time Synchronization in Wireless Sensor Networks ... 684
Chongmyung Park, Joahyoung Lee, and Inbum Jung

Mesh-Based Sensor Relocation for Coverage Maintenance in Mobile Sensor Networks 696
Xu Li, Nicola Santoro, and Ivan Stojmenovic

Neighbor Position-Based Localization Algorithm for Wireless Sensor 709
Yong-Qian Chen, Young-Kyoung Kim, and Sang-Jo Yoo

Location Estimation with Mobile Nodes in Wireless Sensor Networks ... 720
Ying-Hong Wang, Chien-Min Lee, Wei-Ting Chen, and Chieh-Hsin Kuo

Pervasive Communication and Mobile Systems

A Novel Architecture for Hierarchically Nested Network Mobility 730
Hye-Young Kim and Sung Hyun Cho

Route Optimization Using Scalable Cache Management for Intra-NEMO Communication 739
Hyemee Park, Moonseong Kim, and Hyunseung Choo

Content Aware Selecting Method for Reducing the Response Time of an Adaptive Mobile Web Service 748
Euisun Kang, Daehyuck Park, and Younghwan Lim

A Study of Speech Emotion Recognition and Its Application to Mobile Services 758
Won-Joong Yoon, Youn-Ho Cho, and Kyu-Sik Park

Mobility Driven Vertical Handover for Mobile IPTV Traffic in Hybrid IEEE 802.11e/16e Networks 767
Eunjun Choi, Wonjun Lee, and Joongheon Kim

An Efficient Scheme for Lifetime Setting in the MIPv6 777
Hye-Young Kim and Jitae Shin

Bridging OSGi Islands Through SLP Protocol 787
Choonhwa Lee, Jongkyu Yi, and Wonjun Lee

Selective Grid Access for Energy-Aware Mobile Computing 798
Eunjeong Park, Heonshik Shin, and Seung Jo Kim

Cognitive Computing Resource Management for a Ubiquitous Wireless Access 808
Vuk Marojevic, Nemanja Vucevic, Xavier Revés, and Antoni Gelonch

Research of UWB Signal Propagation Attenuation Model in Coal Mine 819
Fangmin Li, Ping Han, Xuehong Wu, and Wenjun Xu

Context-Aware Applications and Systems

Context Script Language and Processor for Context-Awareness in Ubiquitous Intelligent Environment 829
Jae-Woo Chang and Yong-Ki Kim

A Semantics-Based Framework for Context-Aware Services: Lessons Learned and Challenges 839
Theodore Patkos, Antonis Bikakis, Grigoris Antoniou, Maria Papadopouli, and Dimitris Plexousakis

Devising a Context Selection-Based Reasoning Engine for Context-Aware Ubiquitous Computing Middleware 849
Donghai Guan, Weiwei Yuan, Seong Jin Cho, Andrey Gavrilov, Young-Koo Lee, and Sungyoung Lee

The u-Class Based on Context-Awareness 858
Jae-Hyun Lim, Chi-Su Kim, and Yong-Woo Lee

Audio-Visual Fused Online Context Analysis Toward Smart Meeting Room 868
Peng Dai, Linmi Tao, and Guangyou Xu

An Offset Algorithm for Conflict Resolution in Context-Aware Computing 878
Min Xi, Jizhong Zhao, Yong Qi, Hui He, and Liang Liu

UCIPE: Ubiquitous Context-Based Image Processing Engine for Medical Image Grid 888
Aobing Sun, Hai Jin, Ran Zheng, Ruhan He, Qin Zhang, Wei Guo, and Song Wu

Ontology-Based Semantic Recommendation for Context-Aware E-Learning 898
Zhiwen Yu, Yuichi Nakamura, Seiie Jang, Shoji Kajita, and Kenji Mase

Deployment of Context-Aware Component-Based Applications Based on Middleware 908
Di Zheng, Jun Wang, Yan Jia, Wei-Hong Han, and Peng Zou

Identifying a Generic Model of Context for Context-Aware Multi-Services 919
Tae Hwan Park and Ohbyung Kwon

Context Privacy and Obfuscation Supported by Dynamic Context Source Discovery and Processing in a Context Management System 929
Ryan Wishart, Karen Henricksen, and Jadwiga Indulska

Service Oriented Middleware and Applications

Context-Aware Service Composition for Mobile Network Environments 941
Choonhwa Lee, Sunghoon Ko, Seungjae Lee, Wonjun Lee, and Sumi Helal

A Context-Awareness Middleware Based on Service-Oriented Architecture 953
Eunhoe Kim and Jaeyoung Choi

On the Design, Deployment and Use of Ubiquitous Systems 963
R.S. Sohan and R.K. Harle

Performance Evaluation of 3-Hierarchical Resource Management Model with Grid Service Architecture 973
Eun-Ha Song, Laurence T. Yang, Sung-Kook Han, and Young-Sik Jeong

A Study on Ubiquitous Intelligent Healthcare Systems in Home Service Aggregation Business Model 983
Mun-Suck Jang, Kwang-Sik Shin, Eung-Huyk Lee, and Sang-Bang Choi

Implementation and Quantitative Evaluation of UbiMDR Framework ... 993
Jeong-Dong Kim, Dongwon Jeong, Jinhyung Kim, Yixin Jing, and Doo-Kwon Baik

A Key-Index Based Distributed Mechanism for Component Registration 1003
Ming Zhong, Yaoxue Zhang, Pengwei Tian, Yuezhi Zhou, and Cunhao Fang

BASCA: A Business Area-Oriented Service Component Adaptation Approach Suitable for Ubiquitous Environment 1014
Pengwei Tian, Yaoxue Zhang, Ming Zhong, Yuezhi Zhou, and Cunhao Fang

A Pervasive Service Framework for Pervasive Computing Applications 1024
Yong Zhang, Shensheng Zhang, and Songqiao Han

Intelligent Computing: Models and Services

Symbiotic Computing: Concept, Architecture and Its Applications (Invited Paper) 1034
Takuo Suganuma, Kenji Sugawara, and Norio Shiratori

Multi-agent Software Control System with Hybrid Intelligence for Ubiquitous Intelligent Environments ... 1046
Kevin I-Kai Wang, Waleed H. Abdulla, and Zoran Salcic

IUMELA: A Lightweight Multi-agent Systems Based Mobile Learning Assistant Using the ABITS Messaging Service ... 1056
Elaine McGovern, Bernard J. Roche, Eleni Mangina, and Rem Collier

Towards Intuitive Spatiotemporal Communication Between Human and Ubiquitous Intelligence Based on Mental Image Directed Semantic Theory — A General Theory of Tempo-logical Connectives — ... 1066
Masao Yokota

Graph-Based Semantic Description in Medical Knowledge Representation and 3D Coronary Vessels Recognition ... 1079
Marek R. Ogiela, Ryszard Tadeusiewicz, and Mirosław Trzupek

Persistent Storage System for Efficient Management of OWL Web Ontology ... 1089
Dongwon Jeong, Myounghoi Choi, Yang-Seung Jeon, Youn-Hee Han, Laurence T. Yang, Young-Sik Jeong, and Sung-Kook Han

Prediction-Based Dynamic Thread Pool Management of Agent Platform for Ubiquitous Computing ... 1098
Ji Hoon Kim, Seungwok Han, Hyun Ko, and Hee Yong Youn

A Ubiquitous Watch-Over System Based on Environmental Information and Social Knowledge ... 1108
Takuo Suganuma, Kazuhiro Yamanaka, Yoshikazu Tokairin, Hideyuki Takahashi, Kenji Sugawara, and Norio Shiratori

Ubiquitous Intelligent Information Push-Delivery for Personalized Content Recommendation ... 1121
Ranzhe Jing, Xun Qiu, Yiyi Tao, Caifen Guo, and Zhiyun Xin

Location-Based Recommendation System Using Bayesian User's Preference Model in Mobile Devices ... 1130
Moon-Hee Park, Jin-Hyuk Hong, and Sung-Bae Cho

Fuzzy-Smith Control for QoS-Adaptive Notification Service ... 1140
Yuying Wang and Xingshe Zhou

Security, Safety and Privacy

Petri Nets for the Verification of Ubiquitous Systems with Transient Secure Association ... 1148
Fernando Rosa-Velardo

An Approach of Trusted Program Generation for User-Responsible Privacy 1159
Ken'ichi Takahashi, Zhaoyu Liu, Kouichi Sakurai, and Makoto Amamiya

Self-updating: Strong Privacy Protection Protocol for RFID-Tagged Banknotes 1171
Eun Young Choi, Su Mi Lee, and Dong Hoon Lee

Intelligent Detection Computer Viruses Based on Multiple Classifiers . . . 1181
Boyun Zhang, Jianping Yin, and Jingbo Hao

Designated Verifier Signature: Definition, Framework and New Constructions 1191
Yong Li, Willy Susilo, Yi Mu, and Dingyi Pei

Towards Secure Agent Computing for Ubiquitous Computing and Ambient Intelligence 1201
Antonio Maña, Antonio Muñoz, and Daniel Serrano

On the Analysis and Design of a Family Tree of Smart Card Based User Authentication Schemes 1213
Raphael C.-W. Phan and Bok-Min Goi

Secret Key Revocation in Sensor Networks 1222
YoungJae Maeng, Abedelaziz Mohaisen, and DaeHun Nyang

Hybrid Key Establishment Protocol Based on ECC for Wireless Sensor Network 1233
Yoon-Su Jeong and Sang-Ho Lee

A Secure Pairwise Key Establishment Scheme in Wireless Ad Hoc Networks 1243
TaeYeon Kim, HeeMan Park, and HyungHyo Lee

Author Index 1253

Autonomic and Trusted Computing for Ubiquitous Intelligence

Tosiyasu L. Kunii

IT Institute, Kanazawa Institute of Technology
1-15-13 Jingumae, Shibuya-ku, Tokyo 150-0001 Japan
kunii@iti.kanazawa-it.ac.jp

Abstract. The world of matter was understood clearly only by finding its invariants such as mass and energy. From the invariants, physics has derived theories to govern the whole material world as variants. Cyberworlds are information worlds. Hence, finding the invariants of information worlds is the key to the success. The laws of information worlds as the discipline belong to what we call mathematics. Mathematical invariants are, in most general cases, equivalence relations. The intelligent parts of cognition for conceptualization rely on induction of concepts from cumulative knowledge gathered ubiquitously on the Web from cyberworlds and also physical devices ubiquitously in the real world. Induction and deduction based on traditional logic are found to be too limited in their capability, and they are becoming topological, algebraic topological in particular to compute. Autonomy is achieved by integrating all the cyberworlds by attaching functions based on invariants autonomously, and by deducing rapidly evolving variants from invariants also autonomously, to make the results trusted. Autonomous visual computing based on differential topology, Morse theory in particular, for autonomous digital contents generation is of increasing interest in the ubiquitous information communication community.

1 Ubiquitous Intelligence

The real world we live has been expanding globally, integrating almost all local activities in business, finance, commerce, politics, industry, education and culture, via cyberworlds that attach e- to all. "e-" stands for electronic such as e-business, e-finance, e-commerce, e-politics (as typically seen in the US President elections and international politics), e-industry (as typically seen in e-manufacturing and electronic surfing of OEM sites), e-education as practiced by the top rated US graduate schools, e-culture including those to preserve historical paintings electronically, on the Web as cyberspaces. The strength of cyberworlds lies on its speed and unlimited power of reutilization supported by cyberspaces as networked computational spaces spanning the entire real world ubiquitously. It was 1968 cyberworlds in cyberspaces faced me with thrills of finding infinitely spanning worlds at light speed [1].

Physically, the intelligent ubiquity is achieved in the real world by placing the two way communicating intelligent chips literally everywhere linked with sensors for sensing optical, haptic, audio, and literal information, and necessary software for intelligent activities. Currently such chips are 0.04×0.04 mm^2 in size.

J. Indulska et al. (Eds.): UIC 2007, LNCS 4611, pp. 1–12, 2007.

For us to conduct any activities in the real world in physical spaces and cyberworlds in cyberspaces, we have to cognize them in conceptual worlds in conceptual and cognitive spaces. The intelligent parts of cognition for conceptualization rely on *induction* of concepts from cumulative knowledge gathered ubiquitously on the Web from cyberworlds and also physical devices ubiquitously in the real world, and then rely on *deduction* to apply the results of conceptualization to individual instances. Induction and deduction based on traditional logic are found to be too limited in their capability, and they are becoming *topological logic*, *algebraic topological logic* in particular to compute. It encompasses modal logic to cover spatiotemporal logic. Researches on algebraic topological logic stem on the philosophical studies of Charles Sanders Peirce [2]. It is interesting to resume my past researches on intelligent trusted system specifications based on nested tables as *recursive graphs* in 1980 [3]. A System for Interactive Design (SID) is a computer-aided visual facility for hierarchical (or recursive) design of complex systems. SID is built as a provision to make the potential of our graph theoretical design tool.

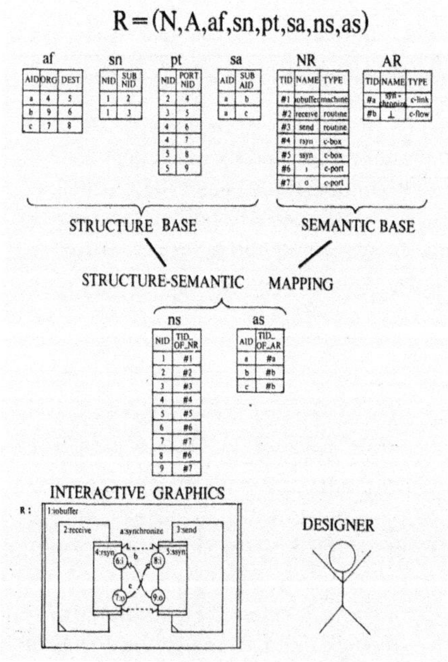

Fig. 1. Architecture of recursive graph formalism

	Type Name	Graphic Symbol	Meaning
Macro Active System	Machine		A machine represents a system which performs multiple functions and consists of routines performing those functions and data for communication among those routines.
	Routine		A routine represents a system which performs a single function.
	Communication box		A communication box represents a structured interface for communication among routines.
Primitive Active System	Routinecall		A routinecall represents an invoking of a routine.
	Assignment		An assignment represents a sequence of expression evaluations and data transfers.
	Case		A case represents a multiway control branch by a selector expression evaluation.
	Token holder		A token holder represents a place in Petri net model.
	Control port		A control port is a port for control entry and exit of a macro active system.
	Fork, Join	F J	A fork and a join represent a transition having only one incoming and one outgoing c-flow, respectively, in Petri net model.
Passive System	Data storage		A data storage represents a system holding some data.
	Parameter		A parameter represents a parameter of a machine or a routine.
	Access channel		An access channel represents a place through which a data is transferred between the inside and the outside of a macro active system.

Fig. 2. Reserved system types for concurrent system design

As shown in Figures 1, 2 and 3, RGF (the recursive graph formalism) is available to system designers. RGF [3], [4] as we initially proposed in 1978 [5], aimed at providing a logical basis for interactive design evolution from global to detailed, and/or

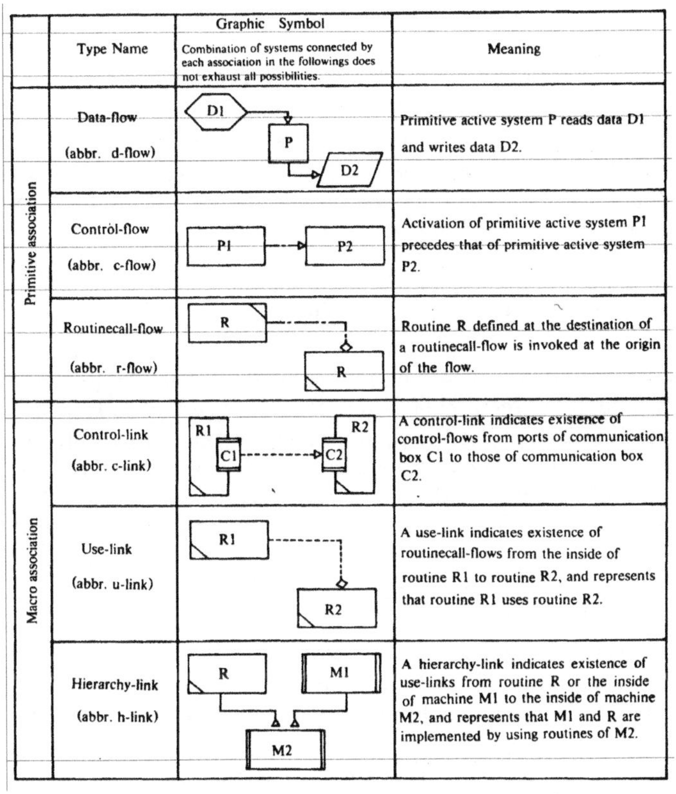

Fig. 3. Reserved association types for concurrent system design

from simple to complex [6]. RGF was actually applied to designs of hospital information systems [5] and petrochemical plants [7], and was proven useful for logically detecting and preventing human design errors and for computer-aided design evolution.

The history goes back to *primary algebra* in *Laws of Form* by George Spencer-Brown (1923-) [8], further back to Gottfried Wilhelm von Leibniz (1646-1716), to the *Leibniz praeclarum theorema* also called the *Leibniz' splendid theorem* in particular, and then to the *existential graphs* and *Peircean reduction thesis* [2] of Charles Sanders Peirce (1839-1914), that has been the core of popular Sowa's *conceptual graphs* [9] as seen at http://conceptualgraphs.org/.

Such intelligence in concepts is going to be embedded in the *intelligent two way high speed communication micro chips* to make intelligence physically ubiquitous.

For the purpose of making intelligence logically ubiquitous in a way we can manage, cognize, control, and serve intelligence ubiquitous both location wise and application wise, *fiber bundles* developed during the World War II play the central role to dynamically trace and identify ubiquitous elements and their changes. For this, fibration and *cofibration*, and *homotopy lifting property* (*HLP*, also called *covering homotopy property, CHP*) and *homotopy extension property* (*HEP*) are the keys theoretical notions of fiber bundles. Because of the physical and logical blocking of communications among mathematicians during the war time, the theories and notations on fiber bundles have been developed at various places independently of each other, lacking the consistency among the definitions until recently. The one found promising for our purpose [10] is by Jacque Feldbau (1914-1945), a Jewish French mathematician, Professor of Mathematics at the University of Strasbourg and a creative founder of fiber bundle theory. The case of him was a real tragedy. Some of his papers were even not under his name to escape from persecution.

2 Autonomous and Trusted Computing

To make ubiquitous intelligence autonomous and trusted requires further research. Autonomy of ubiquitous intelligent is achieved by automatically generating ubiquitous intelligence to manage itself without manual work. The first step to achieve it is to define cyberworlds in cyberspaces clearly based on the laws governing them. It is the same situation with the world of matter. The world of matter was understood clearly only by finding its invariants such as mass and energy. From the invariants, physics has derived theories to govern the whole material world through variants, and then the manufacturing automation of physical systems was achieved. Cyberworlds are information worlds. Hence, finding the *invariants of information worlds* is the key to the success. The laws of information worlds as the discipline belong to what is known as mathematics. For us to find the invariants, we have to look into the most general and ubiquitously applicable mathematics, generally recognized as topology. For anything to be autonomously computable, computational machines called computers are "algebraic" machines. It means we have to rely on *algebraic topology* to find autonomously computable invariants. Mathematical invariants are, in most general cases, *equivalence relations*, *homotopy equivalence* in particular to take "dynamic changes" into scope. Equivalence relations in algebraic topology derive *quotient spaces*, and then, to relate any cyberworlds and their subworlds, we attach any quotient spaces by *attaching functions* (also called *adjunction functions*, or *gluing functions*). This means, autonomous and trusted computing is automatically achieved through equivalence relations and attaching functions. Autonomous computing means we build information systems automatically without human intervention that is achieved by automatically constructing information systems by relating components via attaching functions in a valid manner. Hence, autonomic and trusted computing is achieved in *attaching spaces*. The results are trusted because they carry out only validated construction through invariant preservation. In other words, since the related worlds and subworlds are guaranteed to be equivalent, the *validation* is finished at the phase of design of cyberworlds, eliminating the current serious social problems of combinatorial explosion in testing information systems such as online mega bank systems and e-government (digital government) systems.

For intelligence to be autonomic and trusted, the invariants as explained so far play the central role. Autonomy is achieved by integrating all the cyberworlds by attaching functions based on invariants autonomously, and by deducing rapidly evolving variants from invariants also autonomously, to make the results trusted. The conclusion drawn here is extremely drastic and affects the most of the frameworks on intelligent computing as well because as seen previously, conceptual, semantic and ontological studies frameworks have been not based on information invariants including those on *existential graphs* of Peirce and conceptual graphs of Sowa. Graph theory, by definition, relates nodes by arcs without enforcing to equivalences relations to the nodes to be related.

By automatically replacing arcs by attaching functions and automatically filtering out nonequivalent nodes from the domain and codomain of the attaching functions, we can achieve autonomous trusted computing of ubiquitous and intelligent cyberworlds. We can, then, utilize the cumulative knowledge on intelligent computing by Peirce and Sowa automatically by making them autonomous and trusted.

Let us suppose that the customer C having interests I is shopping the books B_0 posted by online bookstores S_0 on the Web from the set of homepages B of online bookstore S during Web surfing. Since $Y_0 = (B_0 \times S_0)$ are a part of the properties of the online bookstore space Y, $Y_0 \subseteq Y$ holds. The processes of online book shopping on the web as e-business are analyzed and represented as shown in Figure 4. It illustrates how the customer space X becomes related to the online bookstore space Y after the shopping books Y_0 are identified for trading.

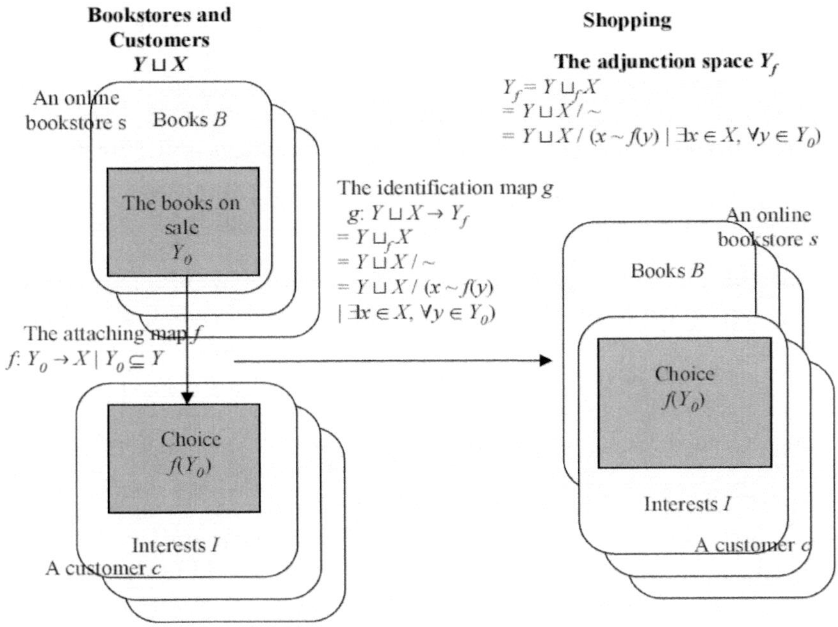

Fig. 4. An example of online book shopping as e-commerce represented in an adjunction space

This is a case of dynamic situations. The adjunction space level we present here precisely represents the *dynamic situations* by an attaching map f, and also represents the situation where "the books are identified for shopping" as the adjunction space of two disjoint topological spaces X (the customer space) and Y (the online bookstore space), obtained by starting from X (the customer space) and by attaching Y (the online bookstore space) to X (the customer space) via a continuous map f by identifying each point $y \in Y_0 \mid Y_0 \subseteq Y$ with its image $f(y) \in X$ so that $x \sim f(y) \mid \exists x \in X, \forall y \in Y_0$. Thus, the equivalence denoted by a symbol $\sim$ plays the central role to compose adjunction spaces at the adjunction space level of the incrementally modular abstraction hierarchy.

Thus, the adjunction space of online book shopping at Y (the online bookstore space) by X (the customer space) on the books of the online store Y_0 is formulated along the line explained so far as follows.

The adjunction space Y_f

$$Y_f = Y \sqcup_f X = Y \sqcup X / \sim = Y \sqcup X / (x \sim f(y) \mid \exists x \in X, \forall y \in Y_0)$$

is obtained by identifying each point $y \in Y_0 \mid Y_0 \subseteq Y$ with its image $f(y) \in X$ so that $x \sim f(y) \mid \forall y \in Y_0$. This represents the book shopping process as a *dynamic situation*. To be more precise in explaining the *dynamic situation*, from a set of books B_0 at the online bookstores S_0, the customers C having interests I select $y = (b, s) \in Y_0$ which is a pair of a book and a company. Thus, we can define a function $f: Y_0 \rightarrow X$ which specifies $y \in Y_0$ is chosen by $x \in X$. In case that there are many same books b_i in the bookstore s, there are no differences in which book a customer takes. If a customer has no preferences about bookstores, then a book is selected from any bookstore selling this book. These cases are represented as equivalence relations. Hence, $x \sim f(y)$. The customer C continues shopping in this manner to identify numbers of books B of interests I from the online bookstores S. The attaching map f and the identification map g are:

$$f: Y_0 \rightarrow X \mid Y_0 \subseteq Y, \text{ and } g: Y \sqcup X \rightarrow Y_f = Y \sqcup_f X = Y \sqcup X / \sim$$
$$= Y \sqcup X / (x \sim f(y) \mid \exists x \in X, \forall y \in Y_0).$$

The identification map (also called the quotient map) shows how the original situation where a customer having an interest in the space X and an online bookstore having a book in the space Y, namely $Y \sqcup X$, is related to the situation after the customer selects the bookstore having the book by its choice $f(Y_0)$ such that X and Y form an adjunction space $Y_f = Y \sqcup_f X = Y \sqcup X / \sim = Y \sqcup X / (x \sim f(y) \mid \exists x \in X, \forall y \in Y_0)$ relating Y_0 of the bookstores having the books to X of the customers having interests by their choice $f(Y_0)$.

As described previously, the combined fiber bundle $\xi = (E, B, F, p)$ represents customers C with interests I is going to buy books B_0 from bookstores S_0. The fiber bundle expresses every possibility of such a case such that a set of $(x = (b \in B_0, s \in S_0)$, and $y = (i \in I, c \in C))$. It shows all possibilities satisfying $x \sim f(y)$, and is expressed by the base space $(B_0 \times I)$ and the fiber $(S_0 \times C)$ of the fiber bundle ξ.

This presents one type of versatile *architectural invariance* in integrating complex and dynamic systems, including banking systems and digital government systems, automatically. The same architecture and modeling stated now applies to all of such cases. It comes from the fact that integrations are equivalent to a subset of automatically constructed all the possibilities. All the possibilities are universally automatically generated architecturally in the same way as above.

3 Technology for Autonomic and Trusted Generation of 3D Images and Animation from 2D Digital Images -Automated Generation of 3D Digital Images and Computer Animations from 2D Digital Images Taken by a Free Hand Digital Camera-

Autonomous visual computing based on differential topology for autonomous digital contents generation is of increasing interest in the ubiquitous information communication community, and we have achieved the core portion for presentation. We show that given any shapes, critical points are shape invariants, and they serve for achieving trusted autonomous computing of shapes.

3.1 Assumption

A 2D digital image with a horizontal coordinate X and a vertical coordinate Y is assumed to be a $N_X \times N_y$ grid of density map, each grid point at $(n_X, n_Y) \mid n_X \in N_X, n_y \in N_y$ being represented as $[(n_X, n_Y), D]$, where $n_X = 0, 1, \ldots, N_X$ and $n_y = 0, 1, \ldots, N_y$, and D is a density function D derived from a color value (R, G, B). Considering the D value as the height Z of each grid point and the horizontal and vertical direction to be X and Y, each 2D image is assumed to be in the Euclidean space (X, Y, Z). Then, a 2D image is turned into a shape equivalent to a terrain without any overhangs.

According to Marston Morse (1934) [11], the shape as defined above is characterized by critical points iff they are nondegenerate: peaks, pits and passes. Hence, taking the Taylor expansion, the critical points are approximated by:

A peak: $z = -x^2 - y^2$
A pit : $z = x^2 + y^2$
A pass: $z = \pm x^2 \mp y^2$.

Degenerate cases can be turned into nondegenerate ones by lifting a point of a degenerate peak $+\varepsilon$, a point of a degenerate pit $-\varepsilon$, applying the Morse theory to the shape, and then turning $\varepsilon \to 0$ [12].

Thus, the critical points are the invariants of shapes.

3.2 Reeb Graph [13]: Differential Topological Design - Morse Theoretical Model and Reeb Graph Model –

Definition. A critical point x of f is called nondegenerate if d^2f is nondegenerate at that point. This is equivalent to the condition $\det d^2f \neq 0$ at x. The index of x is the index of d^2f at x. The nullity of x is the nullity of d^2f at x.

These definitions do not depend on the choice of a local coordinate system. In this paper we will deal mostly with nondegenerate critical points.

Definition. A smooth function on a smooth manifold is called a Morse function if all its critical points are nondegenerate.

It can be proved using Sard's theorem that Morse functions exist on any smooth manifold. In fact, any smooth function on a smooth manifold can be approximated as closely as desired by a Morse function. Nondegenerate critical points are isolated (that is, there cannot be a sequence of nondegenerate critical points converging to a nondegenerate critical point); in particular, a Morse function on a compact manifold has only finitely many critical points, and they are isolated.

The fact that nondegenerate critical points are isolated follows from this result, which is proved in [14], for example.

Lemma (Morse's Lemma). If x_0 is a nondegenerate critical point of a function f on a manifold M, there is some open neighborhood of x_0 in M and a set of local coordinates $x^1, \ldots, x^n$ such that, in these coordinates, f has the form

$$f(x) = f(x_0) - (x^1)^2 - \ldots - (x^\lambda)^2 + (x^{\lambda+i})^2 + \ldots + (x^n)^2,$$

where λ is the index of the critical point.

Thus, it is always possible to choose local coordinates in the neighborhood of a nondegenerate critical point so that the function in this neighborhood is a diagonalized quadratic function when expressed in these coordinates. Note that we are dealing here with an exact equality: there are no additional higher-order terms.

A Reeb graph is defined as follows [15].

Definition. Let f: $M \to \mathbb{R}$ be a real-valued continuous function on a compact manifold M. The Reeb graph of f is the quotient space of M by the equivalence relation ~ defined by: $x_1 \sim x_2 \Leftrightarrow f(x_1) = f(x_2)$ and x_1 and x_2 are in the same connected component of $f^1(f(x_1))$.

As shown in Figures 5 and 6, the Morse lemma and the Reeb graph are powerful tools to abstract the characteristics of 3D shapes. The figures below show some examples. Kergosien [16, 17] has been pioneering researches in this area including medical applications.

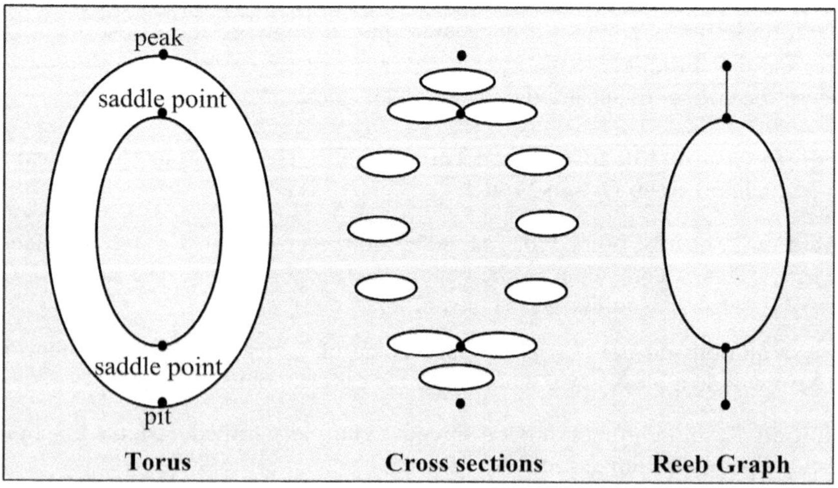

Fig. 5. Deriving the Reeb graph of a torus via foliation

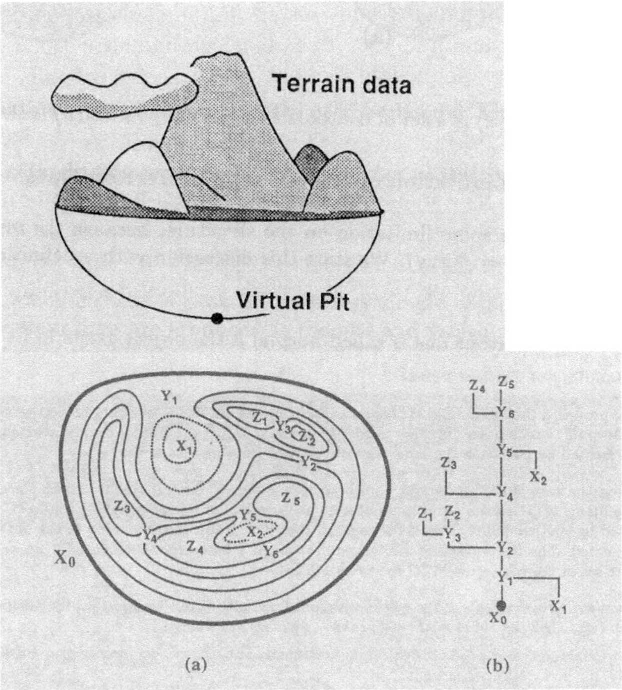

Fig. 6. Deriving the Reeb graph of a terrain via an equi height map

3.3 The Simplest 4 Neighbor Density Difference Approach

Taking the density difference of neighboring pixels, and depicting a pixel by *, the critical points are automatically detected as follows:

```
             +
a peak     + * +
             +

             -
a pit      - * -
             -

             +
a pass     - * -
             +
```

3.4 The Critical Point Filter Approach

A practical approach we have developed is to use the critical point filter (CPF) [18]. Optimal mappings between the given images are computed automatically using multiresolutional nonlinear filters that extract the *critical points of the images* of each resolution to make the computed result *trusted*. Parameters are set completely automatically to achieve the autonomy by dynamical computation analogous to human visual systems. No prior knowledge about the objects is necessary so that it truly *autonomous*. The matching results can be used to generate intermediate views when given two different views of objects. When used for morphing, our method automatically transforms the given images. There is no need for manually specifying the correspondence between the two images. When used for volume rendering, our method reconstructs the intermediate images between cross-sections accurately, even when the distance between them is long and the cross-sections vary widely in shape. A large number of experiments has been carried out to show the usefulness and capability of our method.

For example, given two frames pictures,

in-betweens are autonomously and trustily generated by applying the Morse theory in differential topology, taking the grey scale as the height function: http://www.kunii.com/HomePage/res.mpg

Thus, it autonomously generates trustworthy digital contents.

4 Conclusions

Autonomic and trusted computing for ubiquitous intelligence is the most fundamental and crucial research theme in the global societies we are facing in terms of constructing the most basic social infrastructures as well as developing applications. It is shown that almost only way we can take is pursuing the theme based on information invariants, equivalence relations in particular in adjunction spaces for information systems, and critical points for shapes. Actually there are more shape invariants in differential topology such as singularities and catastrophe signs to get you look into. The work sketched here is solely for directing working researchers to the area to think about the approaches we can share to create core of people to work together.

Acknowledgements

The work here owes a lot to Professor Jianhua Ma, and Professor Runhe Huang who have worked on the theme for a decade with me enthusiastically. Also Professor Laurence T. Yang has developed the theme areas himself as well as by founding conferences and journals with overwhelming energy to the appreciation of many researchers including myself.

References

1. Kunii, T.L.: Invitation to System Sciences – Poetry, Philosophy and Science in the Computer Age (in Japanese), October 1969. Mathematical Sciences, pp. 54–56. Science Publishing, Tokyo, Japan (1969)
2. Peirce, C.S.: Existential Graphs, MS 514 with Commentary by Sowa, J.F. http://www.jfsowa.com/peirce/ms514.htm
3. Kunii, T.L., Harada, M.: SID: A System for Interactive Design. In: Proceedings of National Computer Conference 1980, AFIPS Conference Proceedings, vol. 49, pp. 33–40. AFIPS Press, Arlington, Virginia (1980)
4. Harada, M., Kunii, T. L.: A Design Process Formalization. In: Proceedings of the IEEE Computer Societys Third International Computer Software and Applications Conference, November 1979, Chicago, pp. 367–373 (1979)
5. Harada, M., Kunii, T. L., Saito, M.: RGT: The Recursive Graph Theory as a Theoretical Basis of a System Design Tool DESIGN-TOOL- With an Application to Medical Information System Design. In: Proceedings of the International Symposium on Medical Information System, Osaka, Japan, October 1978, pp. 503–507 (1978)
6. Kunii, T. L., Weyl, S. and Tenenbaum, J.M.: A Relational Data Base Schema for Describing Complex Pictures with Color and Texture. In: Proceedings of the Second International Joint Conference on Pattern Recognition, Lyngby-Copenhagen, August 1974, 310–316 (1974)
7. Buchmann, A. P., Kunii, T. L.: Evolutionary Drawing Formalization in an Engineering Database Environment. In: Proceedings of the IEEE Computer Society's Third International Computer Software and Applications Conference, Chicago, November 1979, pp. 732–737 (1979)
8. Spencer-Brown, G.: Laws of Form, Crown Pub (September 1972) ISBN-10: 0517527766
9. Sowa, J.F.: Knowledge Representation. In: Logical, Philosophical, and Computational Foundations, 2000, Brooks Cole Publishing Co, Pacific Grove, CA (2000)
10. Feldbau, J.: Sur la loi de composition entre éléments des groupes dhomotopie, Séminaire Ehresmann. Topologie et géométrie différentielle, tome 2 (1958–960), exp. no 11, p. 017, Doctoral Dissertation (1958–1960) http://www.numdam.org/item?id=SE_1958-1960_2_A11_0
11. Morse, M.: The Calculus of Variations in the Large. American Mathematical Society Colloquium Publication 18, New York (1934)

12. Shinagawa, Y., Kunii, T. L., Fomenko, A. T. Takahashi, S.: Coding of Object Surfaces Using Atoms, In: L., Earnshaw, R. A., Encarnacao, J., Hagen, H., Kaufman, A., Klimenko, S., Nielson, G., Post, F., Thalmann, D. (eds.) Scientific Visualization: Advances and Challenges, Proc. Office of Naval Research Data Visualization Workshop, July 6-8, 1993 Darmstadt, Germany, Rosenblum, Academic Press, London, pp. 309–322 (1994)
13. Kunii, T. L.: Topological Graphics. In: Proceedings of Spring Conference on Computer Graphics (SCCG) 2001, Budmerice, Slovakia, April 25-28, 2001, IEEE Computer Society Press, Los Alamitos, California, USA, pp. 2–9 (July 2001)
14. Guillemin, V., Pollack, A.: Differential Topology (1974)
15. Reeb, B.v.G.: Sur les points singuliers d'une forme de Pfaff completement integrable ou d'une fonction numérique. Comptes Rendus Acad. Sciences 222, 847–849 (1946)
16. Kergosien, Y.L.: Generic Sign Systems in Medical Imaging. IEEE Computer Graphics and Applications 11(5), 46–65 (1991)
17. Shinagawa, Y., Kunii, T.L., Kergosien, Y.L.: Surface Coding Based on Morse Theory. IEEE Computer Graphics & Applications 66–78 (1991)
18. Shinagawa, Y., Kunii, T.L.: Unconstrained Automatic Image Matching Using Multiresolutional Critical-Point Filters. IEEE Trans Pattern Analysis and Machine Intelligence 20(9), 994–1010 (1998)

Sensitivity Improvement of the Receiver Module in the Passive Tag Based RFID Reader

Seunghak Rhee[1], Jongan Park[1], and Jonghun Chun[2]

[1] Dept of Information & Communication Engineering, Chosun University
[2] Dept. of Information & Communication,
Namdo Provincial College of Jeonnam Gwangju, Korea
stenly69@paran.com, japark@chosun.ac.kr

Abstract. In this paper, we have designed a RFID reader receiver system for improving the performance of the passive Tag based 908.5-914 MHz RFID reader, and analyzed the system performance vis-à-vis frequency, reader, and tag properties. The commercial receiver system causes a loss in sensitivity because of its 24 capacitors and 6 inductors. To improve the overall sensitivity of the receiver, we have designed a system using a circulator, LNA and a SAW filter. The experimental results show that the use of a circulator to separate the Tx/Rx paths eliminates interference, the LNA improves the sensitivity of the Rx module and SAW filter eliminates the noise and spurious components in the received signal.

1 Introduction

RFID is an electronic tag and detection system that confirms information on things and detects surrounding conditions as one of the several tasks. As RFID can exchange much more information than bar codes, it can be applied for stock management and antitheft system. Furthermore, if it is connected to smart-cards, it can be applied for more varied areas such as security control.

For standardized RFID, the world is discussing a total of fourteen standards centering on five frequency bandwidths, and most of the countries including U.S.A. and Europe are using RFID at bandwidths 13.5 KHz [1], 13.56 MHz, 433 MHz, and 2.45 MHz. In the future, 860~930MHz [2, 3] will be an appropriate frequency bandwidth for an international standard. The U.S.A. is using 902-928 MHz for RFID and Europe is reviewing to add 865-868 MHz for RFID [4]. Korea designated 918.5-914 MHz bandwidth which had been assigned to existing city phone systems for RFID in December 2004. However compatibility between EPC 0, EPC 1 and EPC Gen 2 and between EPC Gen 2 and ISO/IEC 18000-6 has been unsettled [4].

Passive RFID systems are composed of three components: an interrogator reader, a passive tag [5], and a host computer. The tag is energized by a time varying electromagnetic radio frequency (RF) wave that is transmitted by the reader [6]. This RF signal is called a carrier signal. When the RF field passes through an antenna coil, there is an AC voltage tag generated across the coil. This tag is rectified to supply power to the tag. The information stored in the tag is transmitted back to the reader. This is

J. Indulska et al. (Eds.): UIC 2007, LNCS 4611, pp. 13–22, 2007.

often called backscattering. By detecting the backscattered signal, the information stored in the Tag can be fully identified [7].

A detailed performance analysis of frequency, the features of readers and tag of the commercial receiver system were carried out. Resultantly, it was found that the existing system has loss of sensitivity due to use of 24 capacitances and 6 inductors. The study designed an improved response system with circulator, LNA, and SAW filter to improve reception of 908.5-914 MHz RFID system. The system designed by this study contributes to minimization of mutual interference due to the use of circulator and enormous improvement of reception due to LNA. The sensitivity of the system has improved as it has minimal interference in transmission and reception.

The paper is organized such that, present RFID systems and research has been discussed in section 2 and design of improved 908.5-914 MHz RFID system has been covered in section 3. Section 4 presents the analysis and discussion on results obtained through simulation and testing. Finally section 5 concludes this study.

2 RFID System

A passive RFID reader with 908.5~914MHz bandwidth attaches tags to the objects which are to be managed, recognizes information on a number of objects and surrounding conditions within 5m by wireless, collects and stores information of each object, and provides information obtained from communication with hosts. Wireless access of RFID system has been categorized into mutual induction method and electromagnetic noise method. The former is used for a short distance RFID (within 1m) and the latter is used for middle and long-distance RFID. The former uses coil antenna and the latter uses high-frequency antenna for wireless connection.

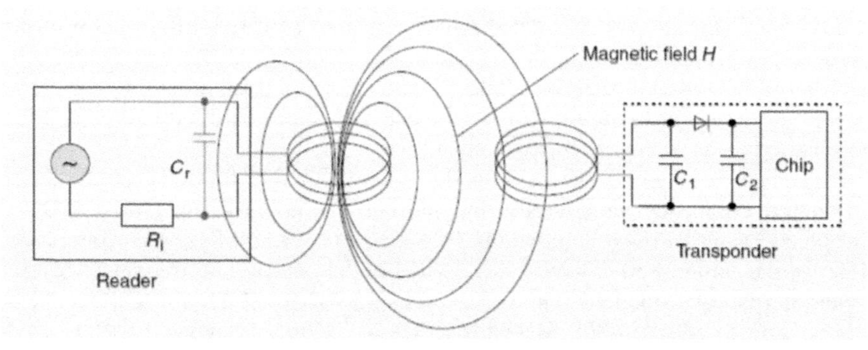

Fig. 1. Inductively coupled

The types of RFID are roughly categorized into two. Figure 1 shows active and Figure 2 shows passive [8]. The active type is characterized by transmission of RF signal [9] from tag and power should be provided from batteries. Its advantage is that long-distance transmission is possible and it can be connected with sensors. The

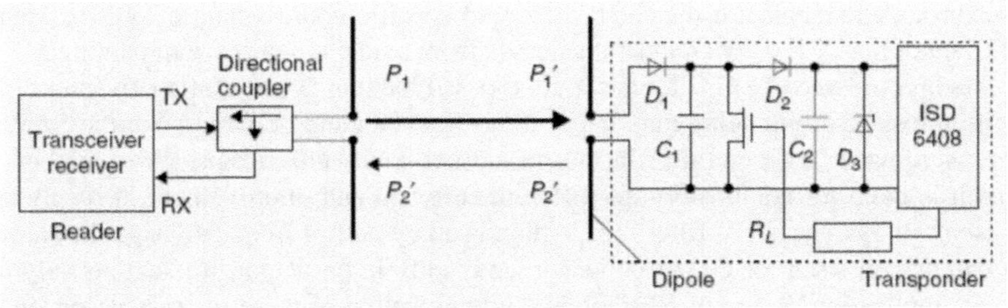

Fig. 2. Electromagnetic wave

disadvantage is a high price due to batteries and limited sweep time. However, the passive type is characterized by deformed reflection of signals from tags and its power is supplied from electromagnetic wave signals [10] from readers. As it needs no battery, low-price can be realized and no cost for battery change is needed. However, it has a limit to long distance transmission. That is why the sensitivity is low [11].

3 Design of 908.5~914 MHz RFID System

Figure 3 shows the design of improved 980.5~914MHz passive RFID reader system designed based on a circulator (MAFRIN461), RF SAW filter (SA915CM), and LNA (RF2442).

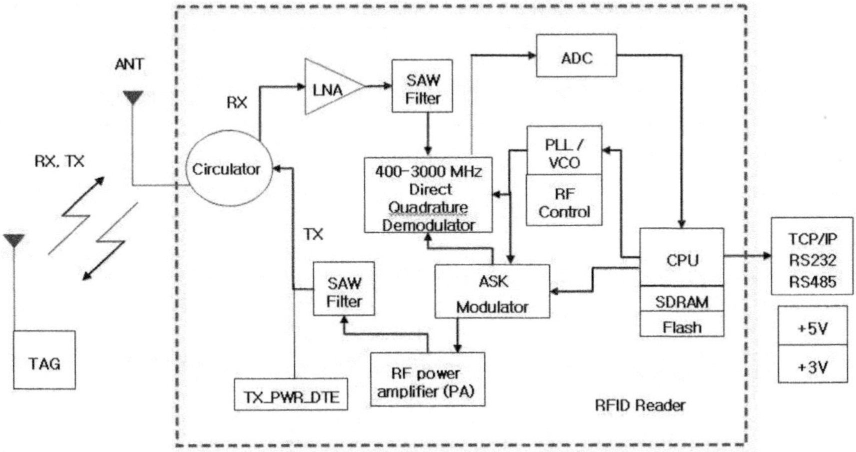

Fig. 3. Design of 980.5~914MHz passive RFID reader system

When RFID sweep receives signals from readers, tags transmits synchronized signals to adjust synchronization with readers. If synchronized signals are not matched, they transmit power signals and synchronized signals repetitively. When synchronized signals are matched, they read specific address data of tags to identify ID data of tags. The orders and data signals from readers to tags are transmitted.

As high-degree of LC filter has a good pass/blocking because of sharp filtering, insertion loss or group delay may happen and filters should be larger. So, the SAW filters were used. As it can do filtering in narrow bandwidth, frequency choice is easy and it is good for composition of different software and improvement of receivers as it is very tiny. The SAW filter [12], which is a key part of frequency signal treatment, is extensively used for GHz frequency bandwidth. In particular, it is extensively used as an application device of RF mobile communication because of its mass productivity, choice and safety. In particular, passive devices having features of a pass bandwidth filter are characterized by outstanding electricity and reliability, reproduction and micro size. So the SAW filter was used to eliminate noise. Table 1 presents characteristics of RF SAW filter (SA915CM).

Table 1. RF SAW Filter (SA915CM)

Parameter	Units
Center Frequency	915 MHz
Insertion Loss (902~928 MHz)	2.5 dB
Amplitude Ripple	0.7 dB
VSWR	1.45
Attenuation	
845 ~ 880 MHz	50 dB
950 ~ 990 MHz	31 dB

When power is input from one port, power is delivered only to either port. In Figure 4, power is input to Port 1 and a circulator has directionality as a signal rotates in one direction.

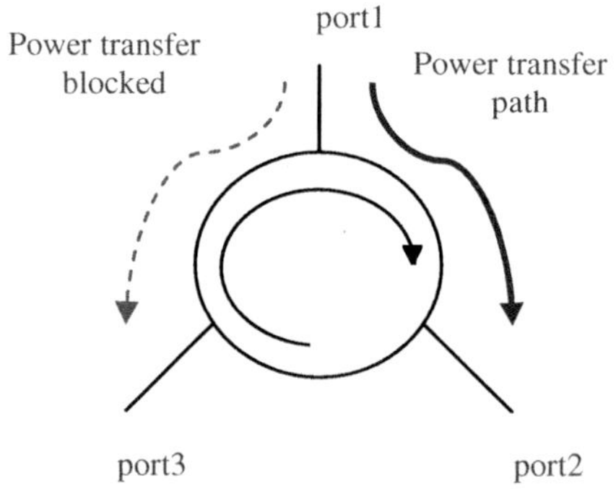

Fig. 4. Circulator signal rotates in one direction

This study used a circulator to eliminate mutual interference and unnecessary noise of RX and TX signals. That is, this study eliminated power the wrong way and prevented horn modulation using a circulator at transmission and reception of the RFID system, which improves communication modulation performance. Therefore, destruction of devices was prevented through correction of VSWR (Voltage Standing Wave Ratio) of power amp output terminal and sweep of PA was stabilized through decreasing sensitivity to the back and external duplexer. Table 2 presents characteristics of a circulator (MAFRIN461).

Table 2. Circulator (MAFRIN461)

Parameter	Units
Frequency Range	902~928 MHz
Insertion Loss	0.21 dB
Isolation	29 dB
Return Loss	28 dB

The power received from RF reception has very low power level because of attenuation and noise. So it has to be amplified and as it is a signal with much external noise, amplification to minimized noise is needed. So, LNA(Low Noise Amplifier) was used to minimize noise and maximize profits. Table 3 presents characteristics of LNA(RF2442).

Table 3. LNA (RF2442)

Parameter	Units
Gain	20 dB
OIP_3	27 dBm
Isolation	2.5 dB
Return Loss	24 dB

4 RFID Simulation and Experiment

This study used an ADS2004ARFID simulator for analysis of reception sensitivity and data analysis of readers. Figure 5 shows data received from tag by reader. Data received by reader from tag were recognized about in 0.5msec and 0.3msec when each of these is 0 and 1.

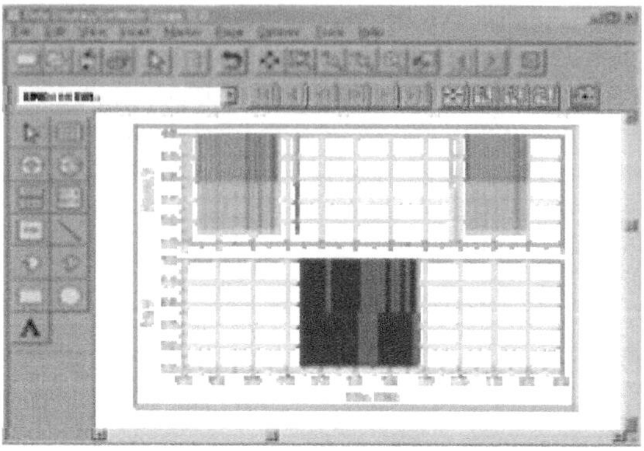

Fig. 5. RFID reader and tag simulation result

For a comparative analysis between the designed RFID reader and existing reader, this study removed existing readers ADS connected the RFID reader to middle-ware to analyze data and measure signals. It connected TX of the RFID reader with RX Local of the existing reader and measured data to identify whether existing reader responds in measuring TX data.

It is a wave of Class 0 when power of reader is on and a command of Read is given. If there is a command of Read, the first reader gives Reset (HIGH), OSC Cal signal and Data Call. Figure 6 shows the results of measuring with an oscilloscope.

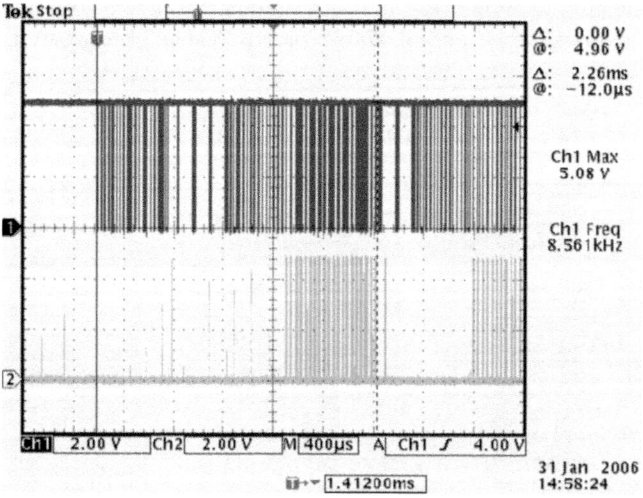

Fig. 6. Power of reader 'ON' with a 'Read' command

Figure 7 presents the wave showing the results of measuring and analyzing outputs of the RFID reader and the existing readers. To confirm whether the developed reader can be applied for other readers, this study removed TX of the existing reader, connected it to RX Local and confirmed TX data in the existing reader.

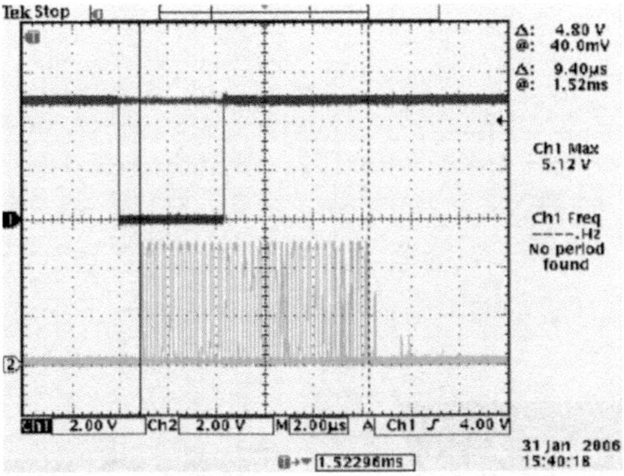

Fig. 7. The wave showing the results of measuring and analyzing outputs of the RFID reader and the existing readers

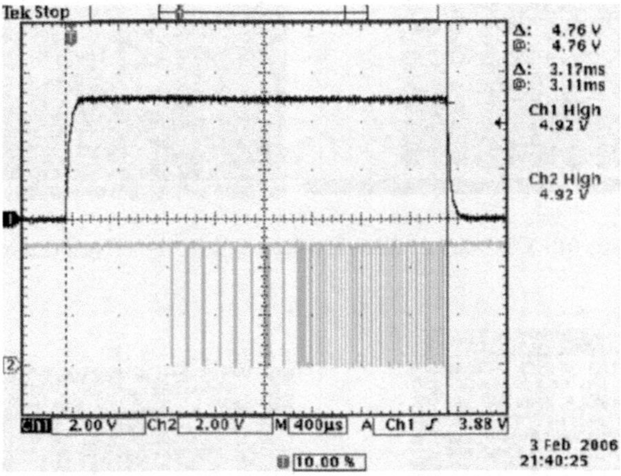

Fig. 8. Oscilloscope and TX data signal is transmitted at enable signal

Figure 8 show the wave measured with an oscilloscope and TX data signal is transmitted at enable signal.

In a Shield Room(-118dBm@3GHz), the conditions were prepared. A signal of ASK was introduced at RFID input terminal, transmitted output and received signals were measured with a spectrum analyzer and data transmitted from tag were measured with an oscilloscope. This study measured reception sensitivity by changing from +15dBm to -15dBm at 908.5~914MHz from the RF signal generated. The existing RFID has less sensitivity with a use of six inductors and 24 capacitances [13].

The measurement result in figure 9 below show that antenna RX, TX ANT matching, CTRL_ANT1, CTRL_ANT0, and Direct Quadrature Demodulator, -94.8dBm was lost in reception.

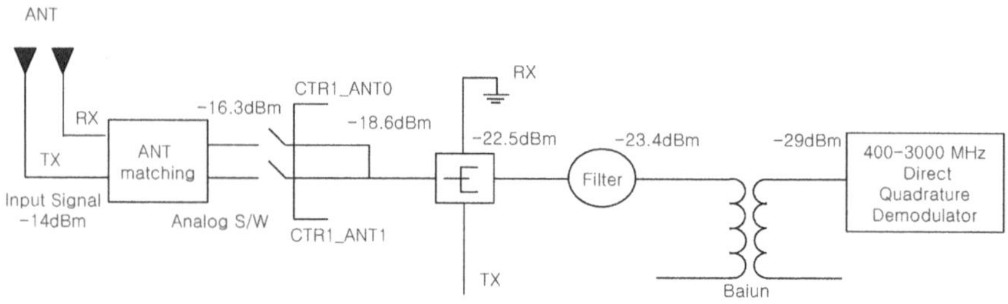

Fig. 9. RFID system block diagram (Existing product)

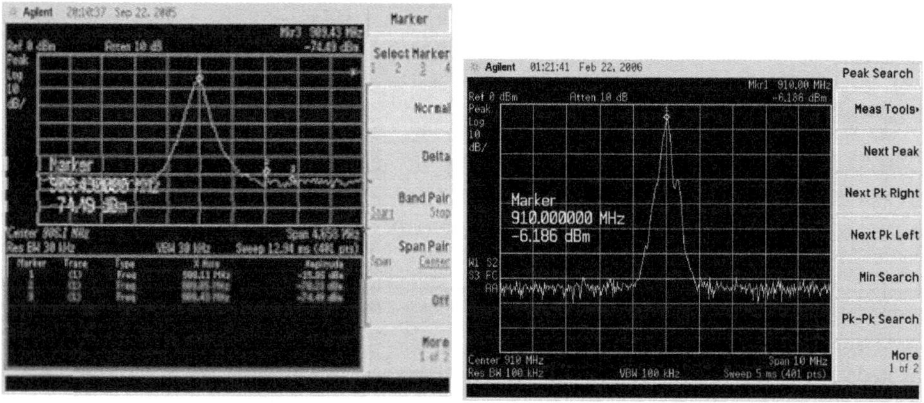

Fig. 10. VCO output data (Existing and Designed respectively)

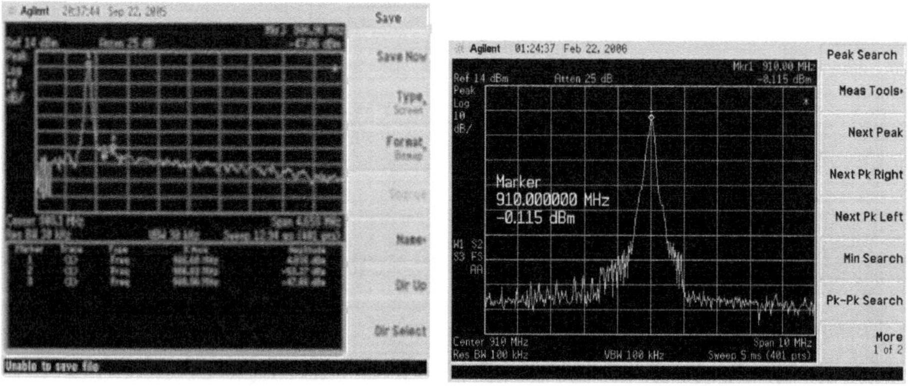

Fig. 11. Amplifier output data (Existing and Designed respectively)

Characteristics of RFID reader reception output wave were analyzed and the results for existing and designed reader are presented as RF_OUT as in Figures 10 through 13.

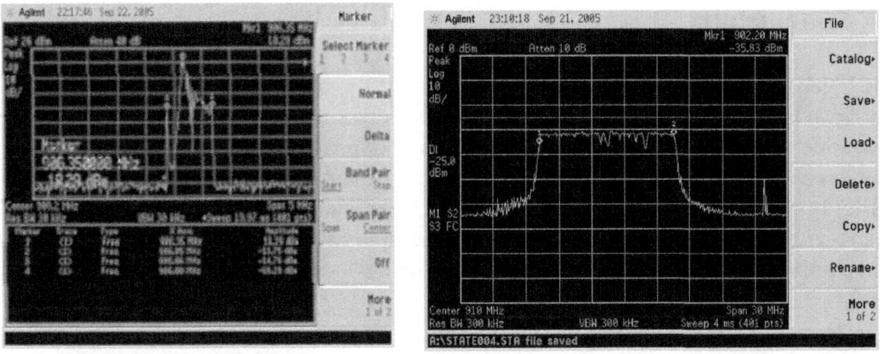

Fig. 12. Power modulate output data(Existing and Designed respectively)

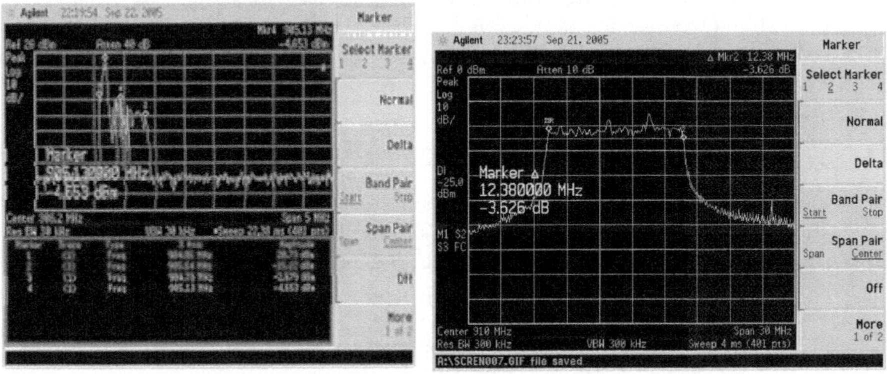

Fig. 13. Antenna output data (Existing and Designed respectively)

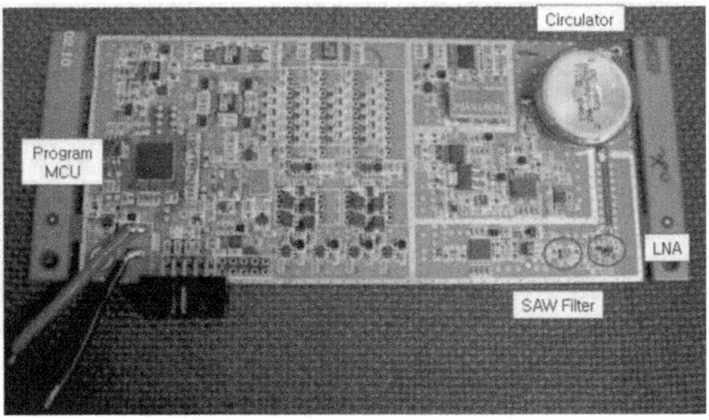

Fig. 14. The 908.5~914MHz RFID reader designed PCB

Figure 14 presents an actual PCB with a use of a circulator (MAFRIN461), RF SAW filter (SA915CM), and LNA (RF2442) at the 908.5~914MHz RFID reader designed.

5 Conclusion

This study designed a reception system to improve reception sensitivity of a passive tag-based 908.5~914MHz RFID reader. It was demonstrated that the designed system has least interference because of a circulator, improved sensitivity because of LNA and less noise in reception and transmission because of SAW filter. The designed RFID system can be applied for a variety of areas such as security system, distribution management, amusement park, libraries and ubiquitous sensor network and specifically for security and diligence and laziness management system.

References

1. Cho, J.-H., Chai, S.-B., Song, C.-G., Min, K.-W., Kim, S.: An analog front-end IP for 13.56MHz RFID interrogators. In: Proceedings of the ASP-DAC 2005, vol. 22, pp. 1208–1211 (2005)
2. De Vita, G., Iannaccone, G.: Microwave Theory and Techniques, Design criteria for the RF section of UHF and microwave passive RFID transponders. IEEE Transactions 53, 2978–2990 (2005)
3. Draft protocol specification for a 900 MHz Class 0. Radio Frequency Identification Tag. MIT Auto-ID Center (2003)
4. Avoine, G., Oechslin,: A scalable and provably secure hash-based RFID protocol. In: Third IEEE International Conference, pp. 110–115 (2005)
5. Zhou, F., Chen, C., Jin, D., Huang, C., Min, H.: Evaluating and Optimizing Power Consumption of Anti-Collision Protocols for Applications in RFID Systems. In: ISLPED, pp. 357–362 (2004)
6. Ritamaki, M., Ruhanen, A., Kukko, V., Miettinen, J., Turner, L.: Contactless radiation pattern measurement method for UHF RFID transponders. Electronics Letters 41(13), 723–724 (2005)
7. Engels, D., Sydanheimo, L., Kivikoski, M.: Planar wire-type inverted-F RFID tag antenna mountable on metallic objects. In: IEEE International Symposium, vol. 1, pp. 101–104 (2004)
8. Finkenzeller, K.: Fundamentals and Applications in Contactless Smart Cards and Identification. In: RFID handbook, 2nd edn. (2003)
9. Zhang, J., Xie, Z., Lai, S., Wu, Z.: Microwave and Millimeter Wave Technology, A design of RF receiving circuit of RFID reader. In: ICMMT 4th International Conference, pp. 406–409 (2004)
10. Qing, X., Yang, N.: A folded dipole antenna for RFID, vol. 1. IEEE Computer Society Press, Los Alamitos (2004)
11. Rappa, Michael.: Auto-ID Reader Protocol 1.0 Working Draft Version 5 Business Models on the Web (2003)
12. Hartmann, C., Hartmann, P., Brown, P., Bellamy, J., Claiborne, L., Bonner, W.: Anticollision methods for global SAW RFID tag systems. In: IEEE symposium, vol. 2 (2004)
13. UHF Multi-Protocol RFID Reader. MPE-2010BN Reader, AWID

Q^+-*Algorithm*: An Enhanced RFID Tag Collision Arbitration Algorithm*

Donghwan Lee, Kyungkyu Kim, and Wonjun Lee**

Division of Computer and Communication Engineering
Korea University, Seoul, Republic of Korea
wlee@korea.ac.kr

Abstract. Emerging applications of RFID require high efficiency of tag identification. Since passive tags have dumb functionality, the efficiency of tag identification in RFID system relies on the performance of the collision arbitration algorithm embedded in a reader. In this paper, we develop a novel collision arbitration algorithm, which is named Q^+-*Algorithm*, improving *Q-Algorithm* which is introduced in a standard, EPCglobal Class-1 Generation-2. We maximized the efficiency of tag identification by modifying and optimizing the parameters used in *Q-Algorithm*. Simulation-based performance evaluation proves that our scheme shows the best identification efficiency among the diverse solutions.

1 Introduction

RFID system has been expected to be the promising solution of manifold fields such as logistics, security, workflow management, and etc. An general RFID system is composed of a number of passive tags with their unique identifiers, i.e., tag ID, and a reader which recognizes tags within its range. A reader queries tag's ID with RF signal, and a tag is identified by the reader, backscattering its ID to the reader. As RFID application area is extended, it is required to deploy RFID networks in which multiple readers and passive tags can efficiently communicate with each other. Nevertheless, pondering the low cost of the passive tags, it has difficulties applying multiple access schemes such as FDMA and CDMA to passive tags. Therefore, it is needed to develop a new collision arbitration protocol through which can provide the efficient communicating between a reader and tags while keeping the simple structure of passive tags. According to whether the tag searching scheme is a depth first or a breadth first manner, RFID collision arbitration protocols are divided into two types; Aloha-based collision arbitration protocols [1]-[3] and tree-based collision arbitration protocols [4]-[6]. Based on proposed scheme in [4], binary tree using a random number generator and a

* This work was supported by a grant from SK Telecom, Korea [Project No. KU-R040572] and Ministry of Information and Communication, Korea under ITRC program supervised by IITA, IITA-2005-(C1090-0501-0019).

** Correspondent author.

J. Indulska et al. (Eds.): UIC 2007, LNCS 4611, pp. 23–32, 2007.

counter which are embedded in a tag has been used in ISO/IEC 18000-6 type B [7]. In [5], Siu et al. proposed query tree that uses tag's reply that matches with the prefix of tag ID. In [6], we proposed tree-based collision arbitration algorithms through which tags can be re-identified quickly with the information of the previously identified tags. In spite of the merit of tree-based protocols such as scalability, the Aloha-based protocols are widely used in RFID standards [7]-[9] now, since the tree-based approaches have lager message overheads compared with the Aloha-based ones. Recently, EPCglobal Class-1 Generation-2 [8], the standard which uses an Aloha-based protocol, is ratified as ISO/IEC 18000-6 Type C [7]. In addition, ISO/IEC 18000-6 Type C is expected to be given a big attention as a next generation standard for UHF bandwidth. In general, there are two kinds of the Aloha-based collision arbitration which are being used in RFID systems. One is pure Aloha [1] which can be regarded as that there is no-collision arbitration in it. The other one which is now broadly used is frame-slotted Aloha (FSA) which has been advanced in function by adding slotting and framing on pure Aloha. Above all, adaptive (or dynamic) frame-slotted Aloha (adaptive FSA) algorithms have been researched [2]-[3] to optimize the performance of Aloha-based protocols. They are designed to optimize the efficiency of FSA by changing the frame sizes dynamically. In general, adaptive FSA schemes proposed up to date is comprised of two parts; tag number estimation that presumes the number of unidentified tags in reader's identification range, and frame adaptation that determines the next frame size using the estimation result at that moment. In [2], Vogt first suggested a tag estimation method for adaptive FSA in RFID system. First, it came from the assumption that the number of tags at the previous frame are at least twice of the number of collision slots. Second, it came from the assumption that the expectation of the number of each slot approximates the actual number of each one. He suggested optimal frame size adaptation on the basis of a PHILLIPS I-CODE RFID system. Cha [3] proposed a tag number estimator which uses the comparison of the actual ratio of collision slots and the expected one. Cha [3] used frame size which is the same with the number of unidentified tags by assuming that frame size is an integer. However, these schemes use integer frame sizes which are not being used in the standards. Even if it is used, it leads to a lot of overheads when a reader sends messages to tags compared with the case with frame sizes are the powers of 2.

To summarize, the schemes proposed for adaptive FSA so far mainly try to optimize utilization through the estimation of the number of unidentified tags. However, in these schemes, since the estimation algorithms make a lot of estimation errors, critical throughput degradation is supposed to happen even when the optimized frame size is used. Moreover, according to our experimental research, almost of the tag number estimation algorithms have terrible computational cost, which means that it is difficult to be applied to mobile devices with low performance. On the other side, EPCglobal Class-1 Generation-2 introduced *Q-Algorithm*, which is the prototype of a collision arbitration algorithm, without specifying parameter values used in it. *Q-Algorithm* uses a heuristical

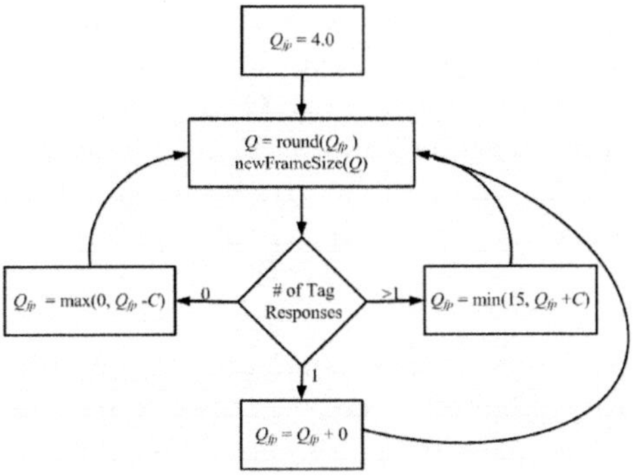

Fig. 1. The flow chart of *Q-Algorithm*: At each slot time, a reader evaluates frame size by counting the number of success, idle and collision slots

approach for converging to the optimal frame size without conducting a tag number estimation. Therefore, it wastes less computational cost than other adaptive FSA schemes.

We propose a new scheme named Q^+-*Algorithm*, which is the improvement of *Q-Algorithm*. Using this scheme, we can achieve the high recognizing efficiency with low computational cost. Although our scheme resembles the original algorithm in core structure and procedure, it is differed in optimized parameters from original one. We will show that our scheme is the optimum in terms of the efficiency of tag identification, using analytic and experimental approaches.

2 Preliminaries

In this section, we introduce *Q-Algorithm* which is introduced in EPCglobal Class-1 Generation-2 and its problems.

2.1 *Q-Algorithm*

In *Q-Algorithm*, a parameter Q denotes the exponent of frame size used in FSA. A reader using FSA sends messages to tags in order to inform the next frame size. In general, reader sends the only exponent of frame size which is denoted by 2^Q, since an integer value is not appropriate as a message format due to the overheads. Once a frame size is determined, tags choose their slot to send their ID to a reader, using a random number generator. *Q-Algorithm* is designed to evaluate tags' replies and determine the next frame size. As shown in Fig. 1, when the *Q-Algorithm* starts, it takes tags' replies slot by slot. Then, it classifies slots into three categories: success, collision and idle slot. The next frame size is updated using those three factors. Specifically, when the result of tags' replies in a slot is idle, it subtracts a constant C from Q_{fp}, because it is estimated that the used frame size is larger than ideal one. When a collision slot occurs, a constant C is added to Q_{fp}, because it means the used frame size is smaller than the number of tags. According to the standard, the range of C is from 0.1 to 0.5. Every start of each slot, it rounds Q_{fp} value. Then, new frame size Q is informed to tags. For practical uses, since messaging a size Q to tags at every slot is a redundant process, it can be omitted when Q value is not changed compared with previous one. *Q-Algorithm* has numerable advantages which are distinguished from another collision arbitration scheme using tag number estimation algorithms as follows.

- Since *Q-Algorithm* does not depend on tag number estimation method, degradation of throughput by the estimation error does not occur.
- For the same reason, even if the number of tags increases, the computation cost by tag number estimation does not increase.
- *Q-Algorithm* finds the optimal frame very quickly and does not reduce the throughput, because it evaluates the frame size in slot-by-slot manner instead of frame-by-frame one as other schemes.

In spite of these advantages, *Q-Algorithm* is not appropriate to be directly applied to RFID, since the parameters proposed in *Q-Algorithm* are not optimized. Therefore, it is required to research into this point first for the use of *Q-Algorithm*.

2.2 Optimization Problems

As stated in the previous section, *Q-Algorithm* has the advantage of the low computational cost and the property that it converges quickly to the optimal frame size. However, *Q-Algorithm* needs optimizing its parameters. The critical parameter of *Q-Algorithm* is C which determines the speed and accuracy of convergence. Before deciding the optimal value of C, we suggest several points to be considered as follows. 1) Differentiation of C: In the standard, it shows the identical C values both in collision cases and idle cases. Would this be a reasonable architecture? If it is not, we must divide the parameter C into the two different parameters and find the optimal points for each of them. 2) Scale of C: If the value of C is relatively large, the frame size converges to the optimal point very quickly. However, the oscillation will be terrible near the optimal point. On the other hand, in case of that the value of C is comparatively small, the frame size rarely changes after converging to the optimal point, but the convergence to the optimal point will be very slow. Therefore, we try to optimize *Q-Algorithm*, considering these two factors.

3 Q^+*-Algorithm*

In this section, we introduce the basic architecture of Q^+*-Algorithm*. We also introduce the optimization of the parameters used in Q^+*-Algorithm*.

Algorithm 1. Main Procedure of Q^+-*Algorithm*

```
Q_fp ← 4.0
slot number ← 0
loop
  while reader is powered
  Q ← Round(Q_fp)
  Q ← Max(Q,Q_max)
  Q ← Min(Q,Q_min)
  if Q equal to Q_old or slot number is equal to Q then
    NewFrameSize(Q)
    slot number ← 0
  else
    slot number ← slot number + 1
  end if
  Q_old ← Q
  if this slot is expired then
    slot_result ← the result of recognition in this slot.
    if slot_result == 'success' then
      Q_fp ← Q_fp + 0
    else if slot_result == 'idle' then
      Q_fp ← Q_fp − C_i
    else if slot_result == 'collision' then
      Q_fp ← Q_fp − C_c
    end if
  end if
end loop

procedure NewFrameSize(Q)
    Send a new frame size 2^Q to tags
end procedure
```

3.1 Design Rationale

Since Q^+-*Algorithm* is improved based on *Q-Algorithm*, the basic design of it is very similar to the original one. Algorithm 1 shows the main procedure of Q^+-*Algorithm*. We adopt new constants named C_i and C_c which mean the constants C for idle and collision, respectively. Specifically speaking, if a slot is diagnosed as an idle one, a reader subtracts C_i from Q_{fp}. Conversely, if a collision slot occurs, a reader adds C_c to Q_{fp}. At the end of each slot, a reader adjusts the Q value by sending a message containing a new frame size to tags. However, as we mentioned in the previous section, because the size of the message that decides a new frame size is larger than that of the message that informs the next slot, the frequent uses of new frames will bring about a lot of overheads. Therefore, in Q^+-*Algorithm*, if the value of Q is not different from that of Q_{old}, the new frame size does not be sent to tags. Optimal values of C_i and C_c will be introduced in the next section.

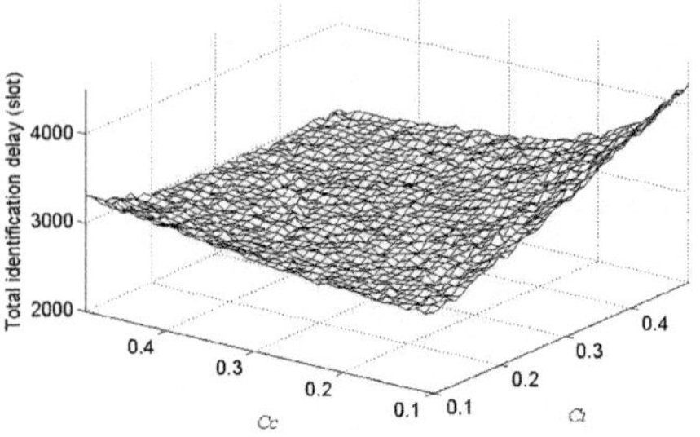

Fig. 2. Total identification delay vs. C_i and C_c when identifying 1000 tags (Test results are averaged after iterating the simulation 10 times with varying random seeds.)

3.2 Parameter Optimization

C_i and C_c are the important parameters that influence on the process of the search of the optimal frame size. Through an experiment with simulations, we analyze the effect of those parameters on the efficiency of tag identification. As shown in Fig. 2, the efficiency of tag identification, i.e., the number of consumed tags until all the tags are identified, is changed not only by the ratio of C_i to C_c but by the scale of C_i and C_c. Specifically, the plots located at relatively low delays form the shape with constant ratios, and show the different efficiencies by the scale of C_i and C_c within the identical ratios of those. Having made the above observations, we analyze and optimize C_i and C_c on these two factors: a) The ratio of C_i to C_c and b) The scale of C_i and C_c.

The ratio of C_i and C_c. To optimize the efficiency of tag identification, we conduct an analysis as follows. When the probability that a tag selects a slot in a frame is p, the distribution function which describes how many tags among m tags transmit its ID to a slot is denoted with the binomial distribution as following:

$$Pr_{m,p}(X = r) = \binom{m}{r} p^r (1 - p)^{m-r} \tag{1}$$

Using Eq. (1), the successful transmission probability of a tag, which is denoted as S, can be derived as follows.

$$S = Pr_{m,p}(X = 1) = mp(1 - p)^{m-1} \tag{2}$$

The condition under which S is maximized is given by,

$$\frac{dS}{dp} = m(1 - p)^{m-1} - m(m - 1)p(1 - p)^{m-2} = 0 \tag{3}$$

Through this, the optimal condition is derived as $p = \frac{1}{m}$. Let the frame size is L, then the relationship of p and L is given by . Therefore, under the optimal condition, the relationship of L and m is written as $L = m$. Using this optimal

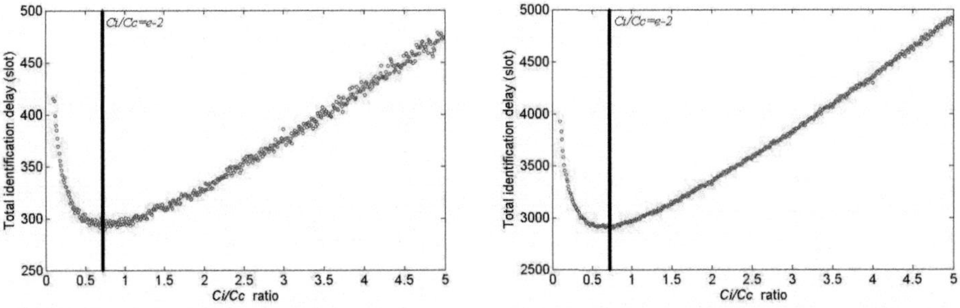

(a) (b)

Fig. 3. Total identification delay vs. C_i/C_c ratio (Test results are averaged after iterating the simulation 100 times.) (a) Total identification delay vs. C_i/C_c ratio when identifying 100 tags, and (b) Total identification delay vs. C_i/C_c ratio when identifying 1000 tags.

condition, P^*_{idle} and P^*_{coll}, which are the probabilities denoting a slot is idle and collision under the optimal condition, respectively, are derived as follows.

$$P^*_{idle|m,L} = Pr_{m,p}(X = 0|L = m) = \left(1 - \frac{1}{m}\right)^m \tag{4}$$

$$P^*_{coll|m,L} = Pr_{m,p}(X \geq 2|L = m) = \left(1 - \frac{1}{m}\right)^m \left(1 + \frac{m}{m-1}\right) \tag{5}$$

As m is taken to infinity, P^*_{idle} and P^*_{coll}, which are asymptotical proportions of idle and collision slots under the optimal condition, respectively, are given by,

$$P^*_{idle} = \lim_{m \to \infty} Pr_{m,p}(X = 0|L = m) = \frac{1}{e} \tag{6}$$

$$P^*_{coll} = \lim_{m \to \infty} Pr_{m,p}(X \geq 2|L = m) = \left(1 - \frac{2}{e}\right) \simeq 0.264 \tag{7}$$

If the Q value is the optimal, Q must not to be changed at all at that point. For this reason, by an intuitive view, it is clarified that the ratio of C_i to C_c under the optimal condition has a reciprocal relationship with the proportion of collision slots to idle slots in the same condition. Accordingly, we get the optimal ratio of C_i to C_c as the following equation.

$$\frac{C_i}{C_c} = \frac{P^*_{coll}}{P^*_{idle}} = e - 2(\simeq 0.71828) \tag{8}$$

Finally, this allows us to know that the optimal ratio of C_i to C_c is $e - 2$. The optimal ratio is verified in Fig. 3. The optimal ratio is located near $e - 2$ both in Fig. 3(a) and Fig. 3(b).

Scale of C_i and C_c. Although the optimal ratio of C_i to C_c is derived, according to Fig. 2, it shows the slight differences of efficiency by the scale of C_i and C_c within the analogous ratio of those. According to our experimental researches, the optimal ratio of C_i and C_c has a dependency on the number of unidentified tags, though there is no relationship between the optimal ratio and the number of tags. A simulation is conducted to find the optimal scale of C_i and C_c with respect to the number of unidentified tags. As the number of tags increases, Table 1 shows that the point with the optimal scale decreases while the number of tags is below 1500, but it converges to around 0.17 as the number of tags increases over 1500. Based on these observation results, we make the logarithmic approximation for the optimal scale of C_c with the least-square method. Note that this function is for the case of that the number of tags is predetermined.

$$optimal\ C_c = -0.0491 \ln(m) + 0.534 \tag{9}$$

Final solution. Having performed preceding analysis, the final solution is given as follows.

If the number of tags is known,

$$C_c = -0.0491 \ln(m) + 0.534$$
$$C_i = (e - 2) \cdot C_c$$

If the number of tags is unknown,

$$C_c = \text{set arbitrarily between 0.1 and 0.5}$$
$$C_i = (e - 2) \cdot C_c$$

As shown above, the value of C_c is not specified when the number of tags is unknown. However, according to our experimental study, even though C_c is randomly selected, it shows slight influence on the throughput. Our experiment results confirmed this with showing the fact that the difference between the maximum slot delay and the minimum slot delay is at maximum 80 slots. As a result, it is revealed that the ratio of C_i to C_c is more critical factor than the scale of those.

Table 1. Optimal C_c when C_i/C_c ratio is fixed to $e - 2$

The number of tags	The optimal C_c
100	0.35
300	0.22
500	0.21
1000	0.17
1500	0.16
2000	0.17
3000	0.18

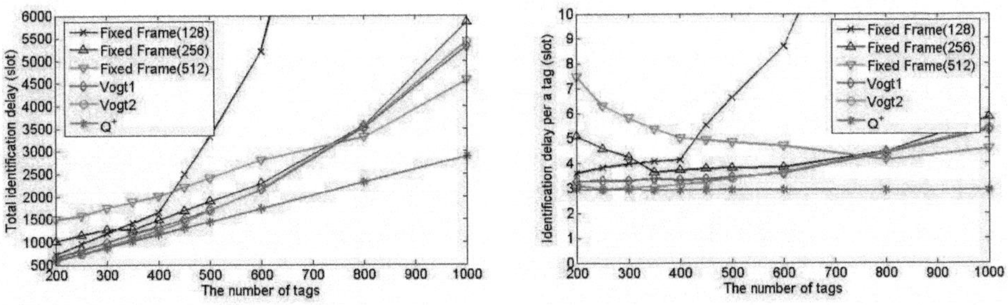

(a) (b)

Fig. 4. Simulation Results: (a) Total identification delay vs. the number of tags, and (b) Marginal identification cost vs. the number of tags

4 Performance Evaluation

In this section, we compare Q^+-*Algorithm* with other algorithms by evaluating them through the simulation which is developed with Microsoft Visual C++ 6.0. Q^+-*Algorithm* uses the final solution that is proposed in section 3.2. For the fairness with other algorithms, we assume that the initially given number of tags is unknown. For this reason, the value of C_c of Q^+-*Algorithm* is fixed as 0.35. Q^+-*Algorithm* is compared with the two adaptive FSA algorithms proposed by Vogt [2], the fixed frame size with 128(=27), 256(=28), and 512(=29). The algorithm proposed in [3] is not considered for the comparison, because they do not use the frame size with powers of 2. For the sake of convenience, we name the algorithm that uses the tag number estimator with the double of collision slots Vogt1 and the algorithm that uses the property of Chebyshv's inequality Vogt2. For the evaluation in terms of the identification efficiency, we counted the all slots consumed for identifying all given tags. In each simulation, the number of given tags is changed from 200 to 1000. All the results of the simulation are averaged after iterating it 100 times.

4.1 Total Identification Delay

The total identification delay means the number of the all consumed slots until all tags are recognized by a reader. The fewer slots consumed in an algorithm, the better algorithm it is. Fig. 4(a) describes that Q^+-*Algorithm* outperforms other algorithms in terms of total identification delay. Vogt1 and 2 show the higher total identification delay as the number of tags increases. This mainly comes from the fact that the tag number estimator does not work well with many tags. The cases with fixed frame also show low throughput as the number of tags increases, except the case of the frame size with 512. In case of frame size with 512, it shows terrible efficiency below 800 slots. These results prove that the performance of an adaptive FSA algorithm depends on its adaptability.

4.2 Marginal Identification Cost

The marginal identification cost denotes the average slots used for identifying a tag. This is a good indicator for the scalability of an adaptive FSA algorithm. To know this, we divided results on the total delay by the number of tags. As shown in Fig. 4(b). Q^+-*Algorithm* constantly shows the outstanding performance regardless the number of tags. A brilliant fact we found is that the marginal identification cost of Q^+-*Algorithm* very closely approaches e, i.e., the theoretically optimal marginal identification cost in adaptive FSA algorithms.

5 Conclusions and Future Works

In this paper, we proposed Q^+-*Algorithm*, which is an enhanced adaptive FSA algorithm for RFID tag collision arbitration. We introduced new parameters C_i and C_c in addition to the basic architecture of *Q-Algorithm*. Our performance evaluation demonstrated that proposed scheme shows predominant performance compared with other solutions. In addition, Q^+-*Algorithm* does not have drawbacks like the overheads and the errors which are generated by a tag number estimation, and it does not require the modification of tag architecture or standards. Therefore, it is expected that our scheme can be applied widely for improving the efficiency of RFID systems.

References

[1] Abramson, N.: The Aloha System-Another Alternative for Computer Communications. In: Proc. AFIP Fall Joint Computer Conf. (1970)
[2] Vogt, H.: Multiple Object Identification with Passive RFID Tags. In: Proc. Int'l. Conf. Pervasive Computing (2002)
[3] Cha, J., Kim, J.: Novel Anti-collision Algorithms for Fast Object Identification in RFID Systems. In: Proc. IEEE Int'l Conf. Parallel and Distributed Systems (2005)
[4] Capetanakis, J.I.: Tree Algorithm for Packet Broadcast Channels, Trans. on Information Theory, vol. 25, pp. 505–515. IEEE, Los Alamitos (1979)
[5] Law, C., Lee, K., Siu, K.Y.: Efficient Memory-less Protocol for Tag Identification. In: Proc. ACM Int'l. Workshop on Discrete Algorithms and Methods for Mobile Computing and Communications (2000)
[6] Myung, J., Lee, W.:Adaptive Splitting Protocols for RFID Tag Collision Arbitration. In: Proc. ACM Int'l Symposium on Mobile Ad Hoc Networking and Computing (2006)
[7] Information Technology - Radio Frequency Identification for Item Management - Part 6: Parameters for Air Interface Communications at 860-960 MHz, 18000-6, ISO/IEC (2006)
[8] EPC Radio-Frequency Identity Protocols Class-1 Generation-2 UHF RFID Protocols for Communications at 860 MHz-960 MHz, Ver. 1.0.9, EPCglobal (2004)
[9] Information Technology Radio-Frequency Identification for Item Management Part 3: Parameters for Air Interface Communications at 13.56 MHz-First Edition, 18000-3, ISO/IEC (2004)

Surface-Embedded Passive RF Exteroception: Kepler, Greed, and Buffon's Needle

Vladimir Kulyukin, Aliasgar Kutiyanawala, and Minghui Jiang

Computer Science Assistive Technology Laboratory (CSATL)
Department of Computer Science
Utah State University
Logan, UT, 84322
vladimir.kulyukin@usu.edu, {aliasgar,mjiang}@cc.usu.edu

Abstract. Surface-embedded passive radio frequency (PRF) exteroception is a method whereby an action to be executed by a mobile unit is selected through a signal received from a surface-embedded external passive RFID transponder. This paper describes how Kepler's hexagonal packing pattern is used to embed passive RFID transponders into a carpet to create PRF surfaces. Proof-of-concepts experiments are presented that show how such surfaces enable mobile robots to reliably accomplish point-to-point navigation indoors and outdoors. Two greedy algorithms are presented for automated design of PRF surfaces. A theoretical extension of the classic Buffon's Needle problem from computational geometry is presented as a possible way to optimize the packing of RF transponders on a surface.

1 Introduction

A smart environment is a regular everyday environment, e.g. a home, a store, or a community center, instrumented with embedded sensors and computer systems that that make use of the data they receive from those sensors in order to support a quality-of-life function. The University of Washington Assisted Cognition Project [17] seeks to synthesize AI and ubiquitous computing to develop solutions that help people with cognitive limitations. Japan's Ministry of Land, Infrastructure, and Transport announced its support for the Autonomous Movement Support Project [18] whose objective is to embed small electronic sensors into the pavement and street furniture to supply users with location-specific information anytime and anywhere. Willis and Helal [15] propose an assisted navigation system where an RFID reader is embedded into a blind navigator's shoe and passive RFID sensors are placed in the floor.

Mobile units that operate in smart environments utilize either *proprioception* (action is determined relative to an internal frame of reference) or *exteroception* (action is determined from a stimulus originating in the environment itself). Low power requirements, low cost, and ease of installation are among the principal reasons for a wide acceptance of RFID as an exteroceptive technology in many application domains [20]. Kantor and Singh use RFID tags for robot localization and mapping[6]. Once the positions of the RFID tags are known, their system uses time-of-arrival type of information to estimate the distance from detected tags. Tsukiyama[7] developed a navigation system for mobile robots using RFID tags under the assumption of perfect signal reception and zero

J. Indulska et al. (Eds.): UIC 2007, LNCS 4611, pp. 33–42, 2007.

uncertainty. Hahnel et al.[10] developed a probabilistic robotic mapping and localization system to analyze whether RFID can be used to improve the localization of mobile robots in office environments.

Since smart environments are composed of surfaces [16], it is natural to pose the question of how PRF sensors can be embedded into those surfaces in order to improve the point-to-point navigation and localization of mobile units operating in those environments. This paper describes how Kepler's hexagonal packing pattern is used to embed passive RFID transponders into horizontal surfaces. Proof-of-concept experiments show how such surfaces enable mobile robots to accomplish point-to-point navigation indoors and outdoors. Two greedy algorithms are presented for automated design of PRF surfaces. Simulations show that greed compares favorably to brute force and hill climbing. An extension of the classic Buffon's Needle problem from computational geometry is proposed as a possible way to optimize the packing of PRF transponders on a surface. An optimal two-column pattern of arranging transponders on the edges of a surface is briefly investigated.

2 The Problem

A RFID reader reads a RFID transponder, through it antenna, by powering it with electromagnetic waves. A factor that determines whether a tag can be read or not is the number of electromagnetic lines of force that pass through the coil of the antenna. This is a function of the proximity of the antenna to the tag and its orientation with respect to the tag.

Tag collision is another factor. If two tags are near an antenna, both may be powered up and transmit their identification codes simultaneously. Most readers do not have a collision avoidance mechanism and as a result no tags are read. Thus, the read area of an antenna is also a function of the proximity of the tags with respect to each other.

The above considerations lead to the following formulation of the problem. Given a mobile device capable of carrying a number of RFID antennas, what type of PRF surface would be needed for the device to accomplish point-to-point navigation tasks reliably. Furhermore, to what extent does surface-embedded PRF exteroception simplify on-board computational machinery and increase navigational reliability?

The above considerations lead to the following formulation of the problem. Given a mobile unit capable of carrying a number of RFID antennas, what type of PRF surface is needed for the unit to accomplish point-to-point navigation reliably. The problem can be motivated through two application scenarios. The first application is robot-assisted navigation for the blind and cognitively impaired [14,11,12]. Safety is the primary requirement. The robot's pose must be known with absolute certainty to determine the next navigation action. It is not feasible to assume, as is generally assumed in many probabilistic approaches [5,10], that there can be a period of time when the robot is not certain about its pose, but can recover from the uncertainty by navigating the environment. To be sure, the environment must be instrumented with PRF surfaces, which incurs a cost. However, the overall cost is reduced, because the on-board navigation machinery is likely to become simpler.

The second application is rapidly deployable transportation infrastructures for autonomous vehicles. In an urban disaster area, it is critical to have an infrastructure for evacuating the sick and wounded. Probabilistic approaches may be inappropriate because of the high cost of calibration: there simply may not be sufficient time to move the robot around all intended routes and let it build an adequate sensor map. In addition, other exteroceptive sensors, such as GPS, are highly suspect in urban canyons and in areas for which no GPS maps exist. On the other hand, a network of PRF surfaces can be rapidly deployed, manually or through a teleoperated vehicle, in order to establish a temporary transporation infrastructure which, after the mission is completed, can be removed and deployed elsewhere. A critical point is that the cost of calibration is equivalent to the cost of deployment, because no subsequent fine tuning is needed.

3 A Solution

3.1 Where Can a Tag Be Read?

As was mentioned above, the area where a tag can be read by the antenna, called *read area*, depends on the distance between the tag and the antenna, the orientation of the antenna with respect to the tag, and the proximity of other tags. To get a better understanding of a tag's read area, experiments were performed for four different orientations of the antenna with respect to a single tag at a fixed vertical distance of 3cm from the tag.

The RFID tag used in the experiments is the wedge shaped transponder (RI-TRP-W9WK) from Texas Instruments, Inc. The reader used in the experiments is the Series 2000 reader (RI-STU-MB2A) from Texas Instruments, Inc. It operates on 134.2 kHz. This reader was also chosen due to its small size, ease of operation and compatibility with the selected tag type. The antenna used is the Stick Antenna (RI-ANT-PO2A) from Texas Instruments, Inc.

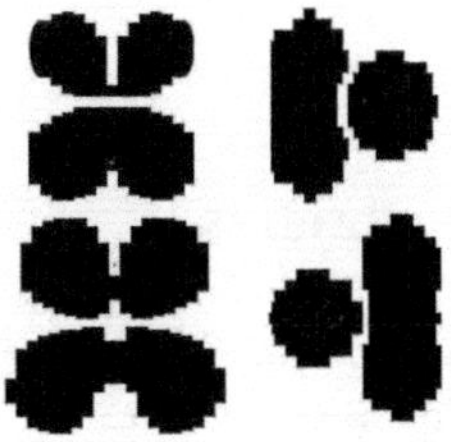

Fig. 1. Read Shapes at Four Orientations

Figure 1 shows the areas (in black) where the tag (designated by circles) can be read and areas (in white) where the tag cannot be read by the antenna raised 3cm from the tag at the following orientations: 0 degrees (upper left), 90 degrees (upper right), 180 degrees (bottom left), and 270 degrees (bottom right). The black shapes, although irregular, can be approximated with regular shapes, e.g., circles or squares, which, as discussed below, bodes well for the automated design of PRF surfaces.

3.2 PRF Suface

In his book *De Nive Sexangula* (On the Six-Sided Snowflake), Kepler asserted that in the 3D space, face-centered cubic packing, e.g., apples on a fruit stand, was the tightest possible. Approximately 200 years later, Axel Thue proved the conjecture for the 2D space. Thue's theorem states that no packing of overlapping discs of equal size in the plane has denisity higher than that of the hexagonal packing [19]. Since the read area of a tag can be approximated as a disc, Thue's theorem immediately applies.

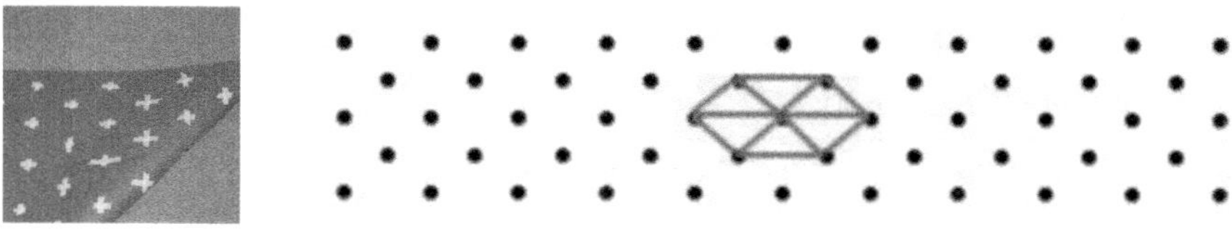

(a) Carpet (b) Pattern

Fig. 2. (a) PRF Carpet (b) Hexagonal Packing Pattern

A total of 280 tags were placed beneath a standard carpet surface, 4 meters long and 2 meters wide, in a hexagonal pattern in which each tag is 15cm from its neighbors shown in Figure 2(b). Figure 2(a) shows a small section of the carpet surface with embedded tags. The carpet forms its own 2D coordinate system where each tag is mapped to its x,y coordinates. The distance of 15cm was discovered experimentally to be the smallest distance that does not result in overlapping between the tag read areas. As the density of tag packing increases, up to a point, the localization resolution increases but so does the cost. When the packing of tags becomes too dense, many ID collisions must be resolved and the localization resolution decreases.

4 Proof-of-Concept Experiments

Figure 3(a) shows the platform used in the first experiment. This robot has a differential drive mechanism that allows it to move forward, backward as well as turn in place. It is equipped with two RFID readers and antennas and a microcontroller for interfacing them with an on-board laptop. The robot was placed on a PRF surface (2 meters by 4 meters). The navigation task was to patrol the surfaces's perimeter. The robot did a total of five 10 minute patrols without going off the mat or deviating off the planned paths that consisted sequences of tag IDs.

In the second experiment, the Pioneer 2DX robotic base from Activmedia Robotics, Inc. was used. It was also equipped with two RFID readers and antennas. The point of this experiment was to demonstrate the rapid deployability of PRF surfaces. A PRF

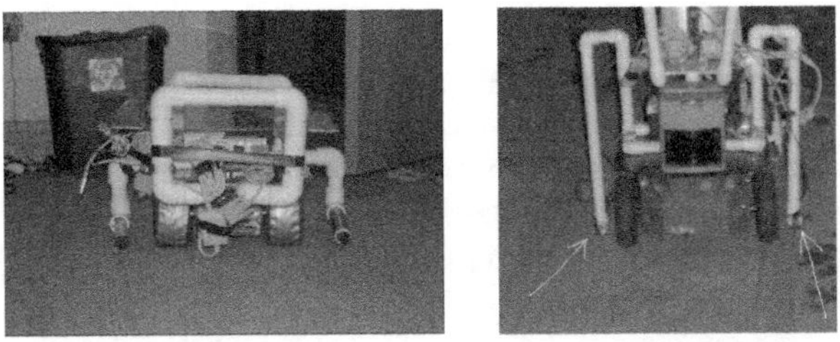

(a) Tiger Robot (b) Pioneer 2DX

Fig. 3. (a) Tiger Robot Indoors (b) Pioneer 2DX Outdoors

surface (0.75 meters by 2.5 meters) on a sidewalk on the Main Quad of Utah State University and had the robot patrol the surface. The robot did a total of five 10-minute patrols without going off the surface or deviating from the planned paths.

5 Automated Design of PRF Surfaces

It is desirable to automate the design of PRF surfaces to reduce cost and improve localization. Before describing the algorithms for automating PRF suface design, several assumptions must be explicitly stated.

5.1 Assumptions

The read area area of a tag is assumed to be a circle with a known radius centered on the tag. It is also assumed that collision resolution is not available. Thus, if the readable areas of two tags intersect, neither tag can be read in that area.

A mobile device operating on an PRF surface is assumed to have a fixed number of RFID readers and placed according to a fixed pattern. Let R be the number of RFID readers placed on the unit. The inclusion of each RFID reader should increase the probability of localization as well as the robustness of the entire system. Let n^a denote the number of available tags and n denote the actual number of tags used. Localization probability as well as robustness of the system should increase with an increase in the number of tags.

Figure 4 shows the surface into which available tags must be packed. It is discretized into N points (shown by blue colored dots) on both sides of the surface. It is assumed that the mobile device can cross the surface only along a straight line (shown by blue colored lines) connecting any two points on either side of the surface. The device is said to be moving along a *valid path* when it travels along a straight line between any two of the N points on either side of the surface.

The probability of localization, P, is defined to be the probability of a RFID reader intersecting the readable area of a tag, when the device is moving along a valid path. Let T be the total number of valid paths on the surface. Then $T = N^2$. Let S be the number of paths that intersect with the readable area of at least one tag. Then $P = \frac{S}{T}$.

5.2 Algorithms

Automated design of PRF surfaces can now be formualted as an optimization problem: Position a given number of circles on a surface of a given area in such a way that the circules do not intersect with each other but intersect with the maximum number of valid lines on the surface. By maximizing the number of lines that intersect the circles, the probability of localization is maximized. Four different algorithms were developed and implemented to solve this problem.

- **Brute-Force Algorithm:** All feasible packing patterns to position the circles on the surface are enumerated and the probability of localization is computed for each pattern by dividing the number of lines that intersect with the circles with the total number of lines on the surface. The pattern that maximizes the localization probability is chosen. Ties are broken arbitrarily. The algorithm is exponential in the number of tags. Only simluations for surfaces with 2 and 3 tags completed. Simulations for four or more tags were not observed to terminate after several days of compuation. Even though this algorithm is not practical, it can serve as a baseline to compare the results of the other algorithms for the cases of two and three tags.
- **Static Greed:** The maximum number of valid lines intersect the circles, if the circles are placed at line intersections. For example, if only one circle was available, it would be placed in the center of the surface to maximize the localization probability. Initially, all unique points where the valid lines intersect are calculated and weighed according to the number of lines that pass through them. Figure 5.3 shows the unique intersection points (represented by red colored dots) along with their weights for a surface with $N = 3$ points and $T = 9$ lines. The intersection points are sorted in descending order of their weights. The circles are placed on the highest available intersection point until the available number of tags is exhaused or it is no longer possible to place any more circles on the surface.
- **Dynamic Greed:** The static greedy algorithm chooses the weights of the points (which are computed only once at the start of the algorithm) as the basis for placing the next circle and fails to consider that a line may already be covered by a previously placed circle. This problem is rectified through dynamic recomputation of the intersection weights each time a circle is placed. After each placement, the lines that are already covered with circles are taken out.
- **Hill-Climbing Method:** All available circles are thrown randomly on the surface in such a way that their readable areas do not intersect. The probability of localization is computed. A circle is chosen at random and moved in a random direction by a random distance in such a way that the readable areas do not intersect. If the value increases, the move is accpeted, otherwise it is rejected.

5.3 Simulations

Simulation experiments were performed to compare the above algorithms. A simulated surface with $N = 15$ points was used. The results of the experiments are summarized in Figures 5(a) through 7(b). The blue colored circle represents the area where a tag can be read, green colored lines represent localized paths and red colored lines represent

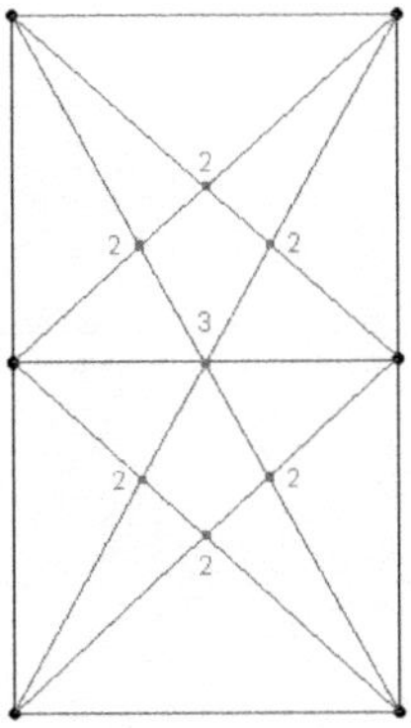

Fig. 4. RFID mat with valid paths and intersection points

unlocalized paths. The ratio of the number of green colored lines to the total number of lines gives the probability of localization.

The experiments showed that dynamic greed is the best solution of the four. Even though the brute-force method gives the provably best results, it is impractical to use. Hill-Climbing is better for relatively smaller number of tags but the results of the dynamic greed algorithm are better in real-life situations where surfaces are more densely packed.

Table 1. Probability of localization (in %) for different algorithms and number of tags

Number of Tags	Brute-Force	Greedy	Greedy with Recompute	Hill Climbing (average)
2	63.11	53.77	53.78	58.56
3	78.66	69.77	76.89	73.32
4	-	80.44	85.78	84.32
5	-	91.11	94.67	90.56
6	-	95.55	97.33	94.93
7	-	95.55	100	97.58

6 Buffon's Needle Problem Reformulated

The Buffon's Needle problem, first posed by the French naturalist Buffon in 1733 [1] is considered to be one of the best known problems in geometric probability [3,4]. Imagine that a needle is dropped at random on the plane marked by equidistant parallel lines. Let l be the length of the needle and let h be the distance between two consecutive lines. Buffon considered the case that $l < h$. For this case, the probability that the needle cuts at least one line can be shown to be $\frac{2l}{\pi h}$. The needle can be looked at as an imaginary line connecting two RFID readers placed on the robot. As the first approximation, the tag placement pattern can be a chessboard. The Buffon's Needle problem is reformulated as follows. A needle is dropped at random on a chessboard. What is the probability that

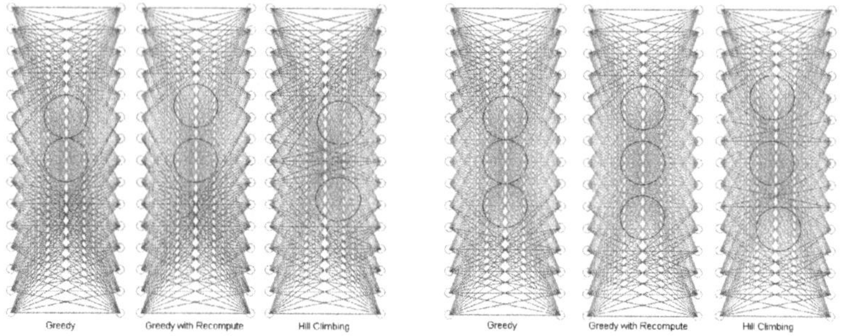

(a) 2 Tags (b) 3 Tags

Fig. 5. (a) 2-Tag Surface (b) 3-Tag Surface

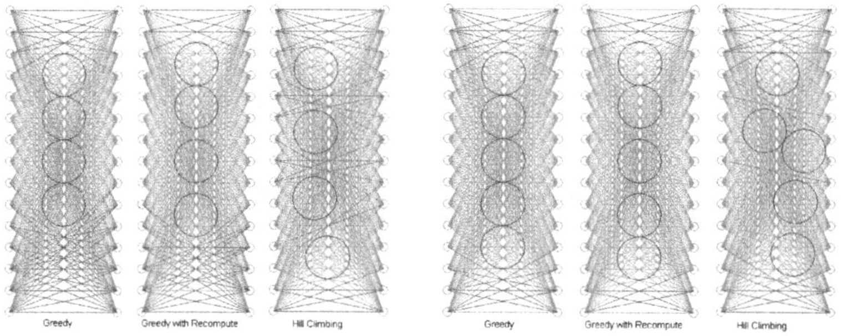

(a) 4 Tags (b) 5 Tags

Fig. 6. (a) 4-Tag Surface (b) 5-Tag Surface

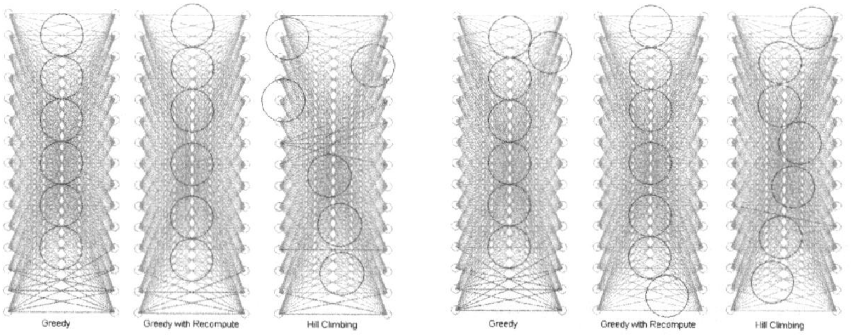

(a) 6 Tags (b) 7 Tags

Fig. 7. (a) 6-Tag Surface (b) 7-Tag Surface

the needle's two endpoints are in two cells of the same color? An interested reader is referred to [2] for the exact derivation of the formula. An optimal placement of RFID readers for a given robot is now chosen by maximizing the probability that at least two readers get valid readings.

Similar probability-theoretic formulations can be made over other placement patterns so long as each cell in the pattern is approximated with a known geometric shape: a circle, a triangle, an oval, etc. The quantification *at least two readers* in the optimization criterion should also be noted. There is nothing that prevents a robot to have more than two RFID readers. The practical considerations of cost and power consumption will act as the reality induced bounds on the probability-theoretic arguments.

7 Conclusions

In surface-embedded PRF exterocpetion, the cost of calibration is equivalent to the cost of deploying the PRF surface. Kepler's hexagonal packing pattern can be used to embed passive RFID transponders into horizontal surfaces. Proof-of-concept experiments show that such surfaces enable mobile robots to accomplish point-to-point navigation indoors and outdoors. Simulations show that dynamic greed compares favorably to brute force and hill climbing. The classic Buffon's Needle problem from computational geometry can be extended to create a feasible optimization pattern for packing PRF transponders into horizontal surfaces as long as the transponders' read areas can be respresented as circles with known radii. An optimal two-column pattern of arranging transponders on the edges of a surface occurs when the outer column is vertically shifted with respect to the inner column so that the horizontal line through each circle center in one column runs through the midpoint of two consecutive circle centers in the other column.

Acknowledgments

The first author would like to acknowledge that this research has been supported, in part, through NSF CAREER grant (IIS-0346880) and three Community University Research Initiative (CURI) grants (CURI-04, CURI-05, and CURI-06) from the State of Utah.

References

1. Buffon, G.: Editor's note concerning a lecture given 1733 by Mr. de Buffon, L.C. to the Royal Academy of Sciences in Paris. Histoire de l'Académie Royale des Sciences 1733, 43–45
2. Jiang, M., Kulyukin, V.: Connect-the-Dots in a graph and Buffon's needle on a chessboard: two problems in assisted navigation. Technical Report USU-CS-THEORY-2006-0309, Department of Computer Science, Utah State University (2006)
3. Klain, D.A., Rota, G.C.: Introduction to Geometric Probability. Cambridge University Press, Cambridge (1997)
4. Mathai, A.M.: An Introduction to Geometrical Probability: Distributed Aspects with Applications. Gordon and Breach Science Publishers (1999)
5. Fox, D.: Markov Localization: A Probabilistic Framework for Mobile Robot Localization and Navigation. University of Bonn, Germany (1998)

6. Kantor, G., Singh, S.: Priliminary Results in Range-Only Localization and Mapping. In: IEEE Conference on Robotics and Automation, May 2002, Washington, D.C (2002)
7. Tsukiyama, T.: Navigation System for Mobile Robots using RFID tags. IEEE Conference on Advanced Robotics, June-July, 2003, Coimbra, Portugal (2003)
8. Highthower, J., Want, R., Borriello, G.: SpotOn: An Indoor 3D location sensing technology based on RF signal strength. Technical Report, CSE 2000-02-02, University of Washington, Seattle, Washington (2000)
9. Khatib, O.: Real-Time Obstacle Avoidance for Manipulators and Mobile Robots. IEEE International Conference on Robotics and Automation, St. Louis, MO (1985)
10. Hahnel, D., Burgard, W., Fox, D., Fishkin, K., Philipose, M.: Mapping and localization with rfid technology. Intel Research Institute. Tech. Rep. IRS-TR-03-014, Seattle, WA (2003)
11. Kulyukin, V., Gharpure, C., Nicholson, J.: RoboCart: Toward Robot-Assisted Navigation of Grocery Stores by the Visually Impaired. In: Proceedings of the IEEE/RSJ International Conference on Intelligent Robots and Systems (IROS), July 2005 (2005)
12. Kutiyanawala, A., Kulyukin, V., LoPresti, E., Matthews, J., Simpson, R.: A Rollator-Mounted Wayfinding System for the Elderly: A Smart World Perspective. In: Proceedings of the 8th Conference on Computers and Accessibility (ASSETS 2006), Portland, Oregon (2006)
13. Kulyukin, V., Gharpure, C., Nicholson, J., Osborne, G.: Robot-Assisted Wayfinding for the Visually Impaired in Structured Indoor Environments. Autonomous Robots 21(1), 29–41 (2006)
14. Burrell, A.: Robot lends a seeing eye for blind shoppers. USA Today (Monday, July 11, 2005)
15. Willis, S., Helal, S.: A Passive RFID Information Grid for Location and Proximity Sensing for the Blind User. University of Florida Technical Report number TR04-009 (2004)
16. Orr, R.J., Abowd, G.D.: The Smart Floor: A Mechanism for Natural User Identification and Tracking. Georgia Institute of Technology, Technical Report number GIT-GVU-00-02 (2000)
17. Kautz, H., Arnstein, L., Borriello, G., Etzioni, O., Fox, D.: An Overview of the Assisted Cognition Project. In: Proceedings of the 2002 AAAI Workshop on Automation as Caregiver: The Role of Intelligent Technology in Elder Care (2002)
18. AMS Project: Autonomous Movement Support Project, `http://www.ubin.jp/press/pdf/TEP040915-milt01e.pdf`
19. Casselman, B.: Packing Pennies in the Plane: An Illustrated Proof of Kepler's Conjecture in 2D, `http://www.math.sunysb.edu/ tony/whatsnew/column/pennies-1200/cass1.html`
20. Gharpure, C., Kulyukin, V., Jiang, M., Kutiyanawala, A.: Passive Radio Frequency Exteroception in Robot Assisted Shopping for the Blind. In: Proceedings of the 3rd International Conference on Ubiquitous Intelligence and Computing (UIC 2006), September 2006, Wuhan, China (2006)

Development of a Single 3-Axis Accelerometer Sensor Based Wearable Gesture Recognition Band

Il-Yeon Cho[1], John Sunwoo[1], Yong-Ki Son[1], Myoung-Hwan Oh[1], and Cheol-Hoon Lee[2]

[1] Digital Home Research Division, Electronics and Telecommunications Research Institute Daejeon, Korea
{iycho,bistdude,handcourage,mhoh}@etri.re.kr
[2] System Software Laboratory, Department of Computer Engineering Chungnam National University, Daejeon, Korea
clee@cnu.ac.kr

Abstract. A daily-wear wearable system is one of the most convenient mediums in practical application scenario of transferring various information data or services between two users as well as between a user and a device. To implement this service scenario, we chose to develop a wearable forearm mounted accelerometer based input system. A set of gesture commands was defined by analyzing intuitive forearm movements. A hardware system and software recognition engine that utilizes the accelerometer sensor data to recognize the gesture commands were implemented and tested. This paper describes the development techniques of a wearable gesture recognition system. It also includes discussions of software and hardware design and how variations in these affected gesture recognition rate by analyzing experimental results from the actual implementations.

1 Introduction

Wearable devices are well-known for their use in specialized fields such as medicine-art, sports, gaming, and sign language recognition [1]. However, they can also be used everyday to increase the productivity and convenience of our normal life. One currently commonplace example would be when dealing with information in an electronic format. We often encounter situations where someone asks another person for a particular data file. Such files might be stored on a USB flash disk or CD-ROM and perhaps carried in our pockets or briefcases. Without accessing a computer, it is impossible to use these devices. However, wearable computers have the potential to achieve this task quickly, easily and seem lessly. For example, one user could make a pointing gesture to trigger a file transfer to another wearable system wearer. The advantage of this approach is that we do not have to look for computers to do the task; instead, the wearable system can recognize intuitive gestures to do the task for us.

We can broaden this service scenario to other diverse situations so that the wearable system can interact with various objects like multimedia appliances. Based on this scenario, we targeted the development of the wearable system that can be

J. Indulska et al. (Eds.): UIC 2007, LNCS 4611, pp. 43–52, 2007.

operated by intuitive forearm gestures using an accelerometer sensor. One advantage of using an accelerometer sensor-based wearable system is its unrestricted operating environment where extensive vision-based device for tracking gestures are not required. By developing specific and customized gesture commands for the scenario, we suggest that we can avoid using more than one accelerometer sensors, which will reduce power consumption [2]. In software, there are intelligent algorithms that utilize neural networks or Hidden Markov Model (HMM) to power gesture recognition engines [3-7]. They have been used widely for recognizing human gestures, however they require reasonable amounts of memory and processing power and are perhaps not suitable for a low-power wearable system. This prompted us to avoid the use of such algorithms and develop a light-weight robust engine customized for our service scenario defined.

The paper begins with an overview of related work discussing a number of gesture recognition devices in Section 2. The service scenario that we've targeted for our gesture recognition device is presented in Section 3 followed by the definition and evaluation process of the gesture commands in Section 4. Section 5 will discuss the development of a customized software gesture recognition engine and the hardware design process that includes the determination of optimal accelerometer sensor location. Discussions from the final evaluation process will be in Section 6 and the paper concludes in Section 7.

2 Related Work

Methods of recognizing gestures are widely investigated using various sensing devices and software implementations [1-12]. It is known that gesture recognition algorithms such as neural networks and the HMM model technique are effective. However, most of these systems deal with vision based recognition, and are subject to environmental restrictions such as that they are unsuitable in scenarios where the background environment is changing as the user moves in real world [1].

One previous system uses accelerometer sensors placed on gloves and represents the most directly relevant work. The accelerometer sensors were placed on every finger and both wrists to monitor hand shape without the use of cameras [13]. Avoiding vision-based techniques could give more mobility and robustness, however the gesture glove could also lead to problems if we want to use it for daily use because it covers all five fingers and palm area obstructing the normal use of the hand [1][9].

Rekimoto's 'GestureWrist' seemed to closely relate to our study in terms of the form factor by adopting a wristwatch type device that enables a hands-free operation on both hands [9]. The 'GestureWrist' mainly uses the cross-sectional shape of the wrist to detect hand motions, as well as a 2-axis accelerometer sensor embedded on the wristwatch to detect inclination of the forearm. It also notes other related gesture based input devices such as [10-12] are not sufficiently unobtrusive for daily wear. Unfortunately, use of a 2-axis accelerometer sensor would prevent detecting other various forearm movements other than inclination.

Similar service to what we've targeted for our study can be seen in work by Khotake [19]. The 'InfoStick' is a small handheld device that enables a drag-and-drop operation by pointing at the target objects by using a small video camera, buttons and a microprocessor [19]. Although the results demonstrated a positive interaction technique, it has environmental restrictions because it recognizes objects with the camera, and the device had to hold by one hand which prevented the hands-free operations.

In this work, we developed a wearable device using gesture defined by intuitive forearm movements that were not considered in the previous research. From these movements, we define gesture commands which result in development of a customized recognition engine. Considering mobility is also important for wearable devices. We want to ensure our device is wearable anytime, anywhere, supports hands-free operations and uses the minimal possible sensors (requires only one 3-axis accelerometer sensor in this study) that would help elongate system's run time by consuming low power.

3 Application Scenario and Wearable System

Our application scenario involves a daily-wear wearable gesture recognition system can effectively command information, data or services to be transferred to other wearers or devices by making an intuitive pointing gestures. Data or services on the targeting devices can also be controlled using intuitive gesture commands. We argue that a wearable band type of gesture recognition device would be greatly beneficial for such activities. We defined a scenario for dealing with multimedia services:

A wearer named 'Ashley' navigates through some movie icons and selects one of them to watch a movie through her Head-Mounted-Display (HMD). She can control the volume or skip chapters of the movie as she like. Ashley's friends, 'Brandon' and 'Christopher' show up to see Ashley. They get interested in what she is watching. Brandon and Christopher both ask Ashley to watch the movie with her. Ashley intuitively points the display device (such as television) near her so that everybody can watch the movie (Figure 1-a). Ashley adjusts the volume remotely by making a gesture. Brandon and Christopher have to go back home before the movie ends. Again, Ashley intuitively points at Brandon and Christopher, one at a time to transfer the movie file or the website link that directs to the movie so that they can watch it later (Figure 1-b).

Note that the scenario can be extended to handle any general file and services. Also generalized transfers between devices are possible: a television to a digital frame, a home audio to a car audio system, a display device to a photo printer. However, we have selected the scenario of dealing with a movie service for this paper in order to achieve maximum demonstration effect because a movie can be seen easily with relatively simple setup of supporting devices.

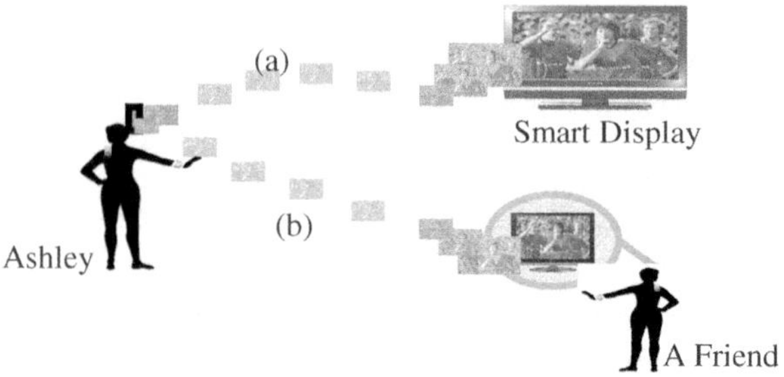

Fig. 1. Service Scenario Diagram

4 Defining Gesture Command

Based on our application scenario, we have defined 12 commands designed to be sufficient to control general multimedia appliances. Note that most of the commands can be interpreted differently according to applications they are being used to control. It is also possible that combinations of two or more gesture commands result in more complex compound commands.

Each command was then mapped to forearm gestures by considering a human's intuitive gestures used to make each operation in the real world. For example, the 'Device Selection' command is based on the act of pointing towards something, 'Select' resembles marking something important within a circle, the 'Left' gesture command is when someone tries to drag an object from right to left, 'Up' is related to how someone tries to pick up an object from ground, and 'volume up-continuously' is made by considering the gesture when we make when we adjust the volume on an audio system by rotating a circular knob. Each command was made with a counterpart; a command which resulted in the opposite action. While we were defining the gesture commands, we were also evaluating them to see how intuitive they were for various people.

Table 1. Defined gesture table

Commands	Gestures	Commands	Gestures
Device Selection /Data Transfer		Enter/Select/Play	
Device Cancel		Esc/Cancel/Stop	
Left/Rewind/previous		Volume up (1 unit)	
Right/Fast forward/next		Volume down (1 unit)	
Up/Continue		Rotate right/Menu Navigation /volume up (continuously)	
Down/Pause		Rotate left/Menu Navigation /volume down (continuously)	

5 Implementation of Hardware and Software

As we began the hardware and software implementations that could recognize the 12 gesture commands defined in the previous section, we investigated the use of an accelerometer sensor by utilizing one of the development sensor modules that includes Kionix KXM52-1050 tri-axis accelerometer sensor shown in Figure 2. The evaluation module includes one Kionix KXM52 tri-axis accelerometer sensor and an Analog-to-Digital Converter (ADC). It has the accelerometer sensor packaged in a 5x5x1.8mm that detects acceleration and generates an analog voltage which is proportional to the acceleration. The analog value then converts to a digital value resulting in vector consists of x, y, z values.

Fig. 2. Kionix KXM52 tri-axis accelerometer evaluation module [14]

In order to observe the characteristics of the sensor module and investigate how we could utilize the sensor in our development, we started to gather accelerometer sensor data from various people when they performed each of our gestures while holding the evaluation module in an upright position. We assumed that the sensor was attached in an upright position in the forearm area where it could monitor the gestures. By analyzing this sensor data, we started to implement the first version of recognition engine. We argued that if using only one sensor was sufficient for our purposes, then this would help to implement a light-weight recognition engine that would result in a fast and reliable wearable system. From this simple evaluation, we determined that we could implement the customize recognition engine that can distinguish among our 12 gesture commands.

5.1 Placement of an Accelerometer Sensor

Along with the development of the software recognition engine, we also continued our hardware design process. The most important hardware design issue we encountered was selecting the precise placement of the accelerometer sensor. We had already decided to locate it on the forearm, but the optimal position was important as it could affect the usability as well as the gesture recognition rate. For wearable design, the locations of hardware components on the body are often an important factor [16], which made us to design 3 prototypes for a experimental evaluation where the sensors were located differently as shown in Figure 3 (sensors are indicated with arrows in the figure). The locations were selected by investigating natural positions of hand and wrist area when we lift our forearm by bending the elbow until the forearm becomes perpendicular to the body as the posture seemed the most natural for making gesture command. The sensor was then placed on a flat surface resulting from the

	Type-*a*	Type-*b*	Type-*c*
Sensor locations	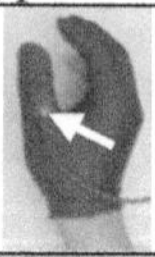		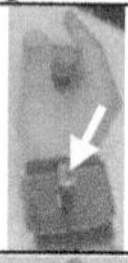
Button locations	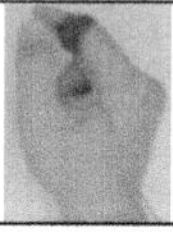	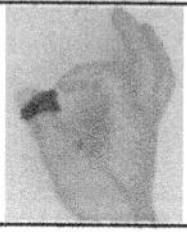	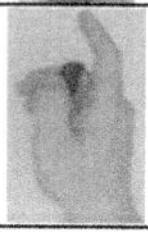

Fig. 3. Sensor and button locations (top view)

natural hand or arm posture so that the sensor can stay flat to generate robust output. The possible location of a button which can be used to signify the start and end of gesture was also considered at this time.

Although the type-c design, where the sensor was placed on the wrist, seemed the most hands-free and preferable for most wearable users, we initially speculated that the further the sensor was placed from the elbow and closer to the tip of the fingers, the greater the recognition rate would be. Note that the prototype-a and prototype-b in Figure 3 uses a glove for a stable placement of the sensor. However, wearing gloves is not ideal for everyday use and therefore it was outside of our target scenario. Instead, we wanted to see how the locations of the sensor affect our development by conducting an experiment that will be discussed in section 5.3.

5.2 Gesture Recognition Engine

First we classified each gesture command by the plane it traverses. Note that there are no gestures assigned that use only the y-axis because making gestures only traversing the y-axis did not seem natural but rather awkward. Other possible gesture commands can be added later if they seem suitable for the y-axis alone.

The gesture recognition engine classifies each of the users' movements according to the partitioning diagram shown in Figure 4. Each gesture data was preprocessed using normalizing and sub-sampling techniques and analyzed and characterized in

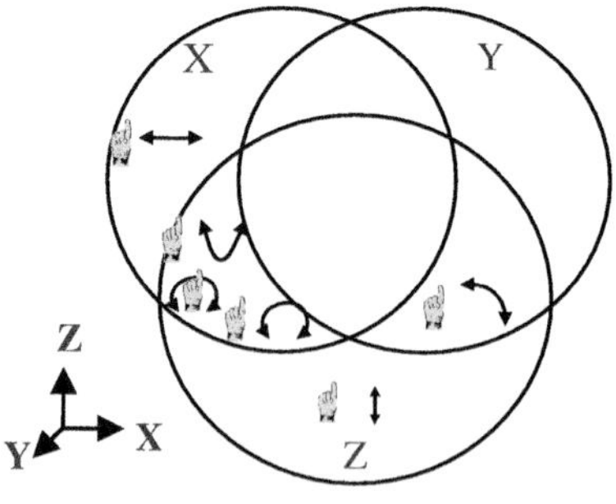

Fig. 4. Partitioning gesture commands in diagram

terms of the maximum and minimum values of the acceleration along each axis and where they occur in time-vs.-acceleration plots as well as quantitative comparison of them in order to find parameters for the software recognition engine so that it can recognize each command. In addition, as the command set increased, more geometric characteristics were considered such as the starting/end value and vertex (local maxima/minima) locations of each input vector. This method of extracting characteristic information to distinguish gesture commands was used to determine parameters to drive a rule-based recognition engine.

5.3 Experiment Determining the Sensor Location

After we implemented the first version of recognition engine, we conducted an experiment to determine the optimal location of the sensor as discussed in section 5.1. The study had 11 participants. 2 were female, 9 male, all were right-handed except one person. The mean age was 34. The goal of the experiment was to examine the relationship between the performance of the gesture recognition engine and hardware design by determining how the accelerometer sensor location affected gesture recognition rate. Each participant was asked try on our 3 different prototypes and buttons, then make every gesture command three times. All were asked to fill out a questionnaire (categorized as 'excellent', 'good', 'average', 'somewhat hard', 'poor') that asks how well the prototype device worked. The results are shown in Table 2 (with responses scored from -2 to +2).

Table 2. Questionnaire result

	Sensor locations			Button locations		
Type	*a*	*b*	*c*	*a*	*b*	*c*
Score	5	4	9	13	1	3

Table 3. Gesture recognition rate according to different sensor locations

	Type-a	Type-b	Type-c
Total %	65.2	55.9	72.6

From Tables 2 and 3, we concluded that the sensor located on the wrist as shown in Figure 3 (type-c) gave the best recognition rate. Most of the testers seemed to share these sentiments as indicated by the questionnaire results illustrated in Table 2. One of the reasons why the type-c configuration showed the best result is that the accelerometer sensor is placed on the wrist so that the data has less variance than that derived from having the sensor on the top of the hand where it also monitors independent movements of the wrist. Removing this extra degree of freedom results in cleaner and more consistent data. This led us to the conclusion that monitoring wrist action (or forearm action) is the best way to monitor broad group of users with our hard-coded gesture recognition engine which is suitable to. The recognition rate of 72.6%, which was not yet considered acceptable, showed that the software recognition engine requires additional improvement with the sensor placed on the wrist and the users need a longer training period.

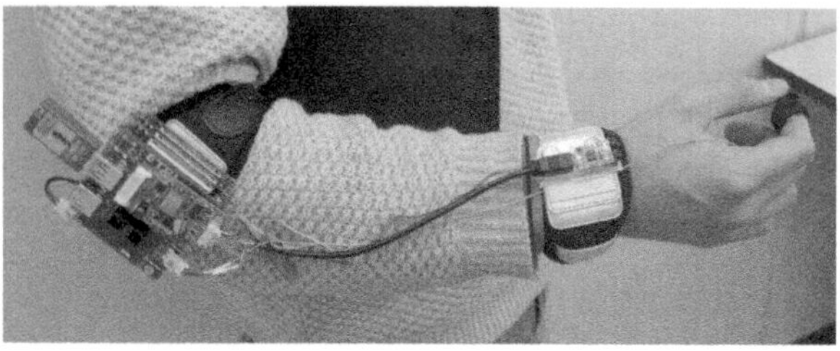

Fig. 5. Final prototype gesture band

Finally we further developed our gesture band prototype hardware design as shown in Figure 5. In this iteration, it can be worn on the forearm in order to enable the activities of controlling and transferring multimedia files. The software recognition engine was also improved to tailor it to the scenario where the accelerometer is fixed on the wrist to achieve the maximum recognition rate. Note that the gesture band has mobility as it has its own battery and processor unit (worn on elbow in Figure 5, I.MX21 on 266MHz) running an embedded operating system and supports wireless communication (IrDA transceiver, Bluetooth and Wireless LAN) [17]. The usage of the IrDA transceiver is to trigger the data transfer between the two wearers, or between one wearer and other devices.

For the future commercial production, our prototype device can be separated into two pieces depends on its usage so that it can have smaller form factor. We think the two pieces will be 1) a wristband type gesture recognition unit and 2) a portable gateway unit, and they are paired together.

6 Final Evaluation

As an evaluation stage of our development process, we needed to compare the system with an existing system that is used for similar purposes. However, to the best of our knowledge, there is no such wearable device that utilizes only one 3-axis accelerometer sensor to recognize a small group of gesture set. One part that could be compared to the existing technology was the gesture recognition software module which was one of the critical factors in this project. Since the HMM based gesture recognition technique is most commonly used and well-approved, we spent time porting an HMM based recognition engine onto our device. To do this we used the Hidden Markov Toolkit (HTK) that is available from the Cambridge University HTK home page [18].

With the gesture recognition band shown in Figure 5, we let one of our experimental participants to use the device in a regular basis (once every two weeks) and make each of our gesture commands. We observed the improvements on the recognition rate from this user after the 3 months. This is shown in Table 4. This individual user became well adapted to the wearable gesture band by achieving a recognition rate of 96.7%. The same experiment participant was asked to use the HMM based gesture recognition band as well. The resulting recognition rate of 99% was better than that of the customized engine however the recognition time (of 1.4

Table 4. Gesture recognition engine summary and performance

	Customized Engine(1)	HMM based Engine(2)	Ratio (1)/(2)
Recognition rate in %	96.7	99	0.977
Recognition time in sec	0.2	1.4	0.143
Number of lines of code	400	1170	0.342
Size of the code in byte	12K	41K	0.293
Size of compiled engine	33K	550K	0.060

second) was not as quick as the customized engine (of 0.2 second). The actual number of lines in the code of the customized engine has 400 uncommented lines of code while the HMM based engine has 1170. For the compiled engine, the customized engine is 33Kbytes in size including required drivers such as USB driver and button driver, while the HMM based system is 550Kbytes including required libraries.

Generally speaking, our customized rule-based engine has weaker expendability in terms of the recognizable gesture set compare to that of learning-based engine. However, when considering that the embedded systems usually have limited CPU power and memory, the recognition rate and the response time of the customized engine using a single accelerometer sensor attached on the top of the wrist demonstrates that our recognition engine and device can be useful.

7 Conclusions

We have presented a wearable system that can be worn on a forearm and that enables the practical application scenario of controlling and transferring various information or services.

Analyzing intuitive gestures suitable to this scenario, we defined 12 specific gesture commands. We also developed a software recognition engine that receives and recognizes the gesture commands. The method used to develop the gesture recognition algorithm was to classify gesture commands in terms of x, y, z axis and x-y, y-z, x-z planes, then design the engine such that it extracts commands by monitoring feature values of the preprocessed x, y, z data, while the x, y, z data is being cross-compared. Then we examined the relationship between the gesture recognition engines and the hardware construction design by discussing how we determined the optimal accelerometer sensor location.

After going through the evaluation process of the development considering the recognition rate compared to the existing HMM based gesture recognition engine, we conclude that the gesture recognition band with an accelerometer sensor attached to the wrist showed potential to achieve a relatively high recognition rate in real-time operation.

To summarize, we have developed a gesture recognition band that is suitable for a mobile environment with the considerations of wearability in such a way that the device could worn anytime, anywhere and supports hands-free operation. It provides a reasonable gesture recognition rate using the minimum possible sensors (requires only one 3-axis accelerometer sensor in this study). We are currently investigating how we could remove the buttons as well as to reduce the form factor to a wristwatch type wearable device.

References

1. Brashear, H., Starner, T., Lukowicz, P., Junker, H.: Using Multiple Sensors for Mobile Sign Language Recognition. In: Proc. IEEE International Symposium on Wearable Computers, pp. 45–52. IEEE Computer Society Press, Los Alamitos (2003)
2. Randell, C., Muller, H.: Context Awareness by Analyzing Accelerometer Data. In: Proc. IEEE International Symposium on Wearable Computers, pp. 175–176. IEEE Computer Society Press, Los Alamitos (2000)
3. Lee, H.K., Kim, J.H.: An HMM-based threshold model approach for gesture recognition. Transactions on Pattern Analysis and Machine Intelligence, 961–973 (1999)
4. Yamato, J., Ohya, J., Ishii, K.: Recognizing Human Actions in Time-Sequential Images Using Hidden Markov Models. In: Proc. Computer Vision and Pattern Recognition, pp. 379–385 (1992)
5. Schlenzig, J., Hunter, E., Jain, R.: Recursive Identification of Gesture Inputs Using Hidden Markov Models. In: Proc. Conference on Applications of Computer Vision, pp. 187–194 (1994)
6. Campbell, L., Becker, D., Azarbayejani, A., Bobick, A., Pentland, A.: Invariant Features for 3-d Gesture Recognition. In: Proc. International Conference on Face and Gesture Recognition, pp. 157–162 (1996)
7. Pylyanainen, T.: Accelerometer Based Gesture Recognition Using Continuous HMMs. In: Proc. International Conference on Pattern Recognition and Image Analysis, pp. 639–646 (2005)
8. Jang, I.J., Park, W.B.: A Gesture-Based Control for Handheld Devices Using Accelerometer. In: Proc. International Conference on Progress in Pattern Recognition, Image Analysis and Applications, pp. 259–266 (2004)
9. Rekimoto, J.: GestureWrist and GesturePad: Unobtrusive Wearable Interaction Devices. In: Proc. IEEE International Symposium on Wearable Computers, pp. 21–27. IEEE Computer Society Press, Los Alamitos (2001)
10. Baudel, T., beaudouin-Lafon, M.: Charade: Remote Control of Objects Using Free-hand Gestures. Communications of the ACM 36, 28–35 (1993)
11. Starner, T., Auxier, J., Ashbrook, D., Gandy, M.: The Gesture Pendant: A Self-Illuminating, wearable, Infrared Computer Vision System for Home Automation Control and Medical Monitoring. In: Proc. International Symposium on Wearable Computers, pp. 87–94 (2000)
12. Fukumoto, M., Tonomura, Y.: Body Coupled FingerRing: Wireless Wearable Keyboard. In: Proc. CHI, pp. 147–154 (1997)
13. Perng, J.K., Fisher, B., Hollar, S., Pister, K.S.J.: Acceleration Sensing Glove (ASG). In: Proc. International Symposium on Wearable Computers, pp. 178–180 (1999)
14. Kionix, Inc. USB Demo Board Kit User's Manual. User's manual, Kionix Inc. (2006)
15. Kortuem, G., Segall, Z., Bauer, M.: Context-Aware, Adaptive Wearable Computers as Remote Interfaces to Intelligent' Environments. In: Proc. IEEE International Symposium on Wearable Computers, pp. 58–65. IEEE Computer Society Press, Los Alamitos (2000)
16. Thomas, B., Grimmer, K., Mackovec, D., Zucco, J., Gunther, B.: Determination of Placement of a Body-attached Mouse as a Pointing Device for Wearable Computers. In: Proc. International Symposium on Wearable Computers, pp. 193–194 (1999)
17. Ahn, H.J., Cho, M.H., Jung, M.J., Kim, Y.H., Kim, J.M., Lee, C.H.: UbiFOS: A Small Real-Time Operating System for Embedded Systems. ETRI Journal 29(3) (submitted for publication, 2007)
18. HTK Hidden Markov Model Toolkit home page http://htk.eng.cam.ac.uk/
19. Khotake, N., Rekimoto, J., Anzai, Y.: InfoStick: an interaction device for Inter-Appliance Computing. In: Proc. International Symposium on Handheld and Ubiquitous Computing, pp. 246–258 (1999)

An Enhanced Ubiquitous Identification System Using Fast Anti-collision Algorithm

Choong-Hee Lee, Seong-Hwan Oh, and Jae-Hyun Kim*

School of Electrical and Computer Engineering
Ajou University, Suwon, Korea
{hedreams,dbosh,jkim}@ajou.ac.kr

Abstract. We analyze the tag identification procedure of conventional EPC Class 1 RFID system and propose the fast anti-collision algorithm for the performance improvement of the system. In the proposed algorithm, the reader uses information of tag collisions and reduces unnecessary procedures of the conventional algorithm. We evaluate the performance of the proposed anti-collision algorithm and the conventional algorithm using mathematical analysis and simulation. According to the results, the fast anti-collision algorithm shows greatly better performance than conventional algorithm.

1 Introduction

Object identification technology is very useful in various fields such as tracking(e.g. libraries, animals), automated inventory, stock-keeping, toll collecting, and similar tasks where physical objects are involved. The radio frequency identification (RFID) system is an important branch of the ubiquitous identification system. The RFID system identifies the unique tag ID or detailed information that saved in the tag through RF communication. Passive RFID system generally consists of three components - a reader, passive tags, and a controller. The reader interrogates tags for their ID or detailed information through RF communication link, and contains internal storage, processing power, and so on. Tags obtain processing power through RF communication link from the reader using back scattering and use this energy for on-tag computations and communication with the reader. The reader in the RFID system broadcasts the request message to the tags. Upon receiving the message, all the tags send the response back to the reader. If only one tag responds, the reader identifies the tag. However, if two or more tags respond, their responses will collide on the RF communication channel, and thus cannot be received by the reader. This problem is called "Tag-collision Problem," and the ability to resolve this collision is crucial for the performance of RFID system [1],[3].

* This research was partly supported by a grant (06-CIT-A02: Standardization Research for Construction Materials) from Construction Infrastructure Technology Program funded by Ministry of Construction & Transportation of Korean government and partly MIC, Korea, under the ITRC support program supervised by the IITA(IITA-2006-(C1090-0602-0011)).

J. Indulska et al. (Eds.): UIC 2007, LNCS 4611, pp. 53–62, 2007.

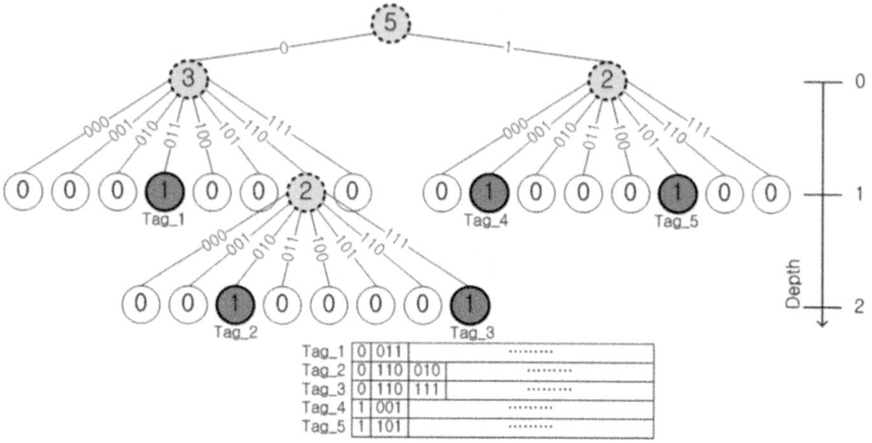

Fig. 1. An example of binary tree structure of conventional anti-collision algorithm

In this paper, we propose the fast anti-collision algorithm for EPC Class 1 systems operating in the frequency range of 860MHz-930MHz. We deduce the algorithm from experiments with conventional EPC Class 1 system since there is no detailed general anti-collision algorithm in the document [4] of the AutoID center. We observe the sending waveform on RF, convert it to the sequence of commands and then deduce the tag identification procedure of the conventional RFID system. To assess the performance of the algorithm, we derive the number of transmission, tag identification time and number of identified tags per second and validate the mathematical analysis by simulation. We also propose the fast anti-collision algorithm and compared the performance with conventional algorithm by mathematical analysis and simulation.

2 The Conventional Anti-collision Algorithm

In the EPC CLASS 1 system, the reader identifies tags in their interrogation zone with a binary tree structure which is composed of 8 branches for each node. Fig. 1 shows an example of a tag identification procedure when there are 5 tags in the RFID reader's interrogation zone. The labels on the lines between nodes represent a tag ID. And, the numbers in the nodes indicate the number of tags with same prefix. If the number is more than one, there are two or more tags in that node (with same prefix) so that the reader is not able to identify tags.

The reader requests the tags in its interrogation zone to reply by transmitting command and prefix bits. If the reader transmits request bits, the tags with matched prefix will reply. *PingID* and *ScrollID* are the most important commands in the EPC CLASS 1 system. The reader transmits *PingID* command when it concludes that there are more than one tags (collision). Then

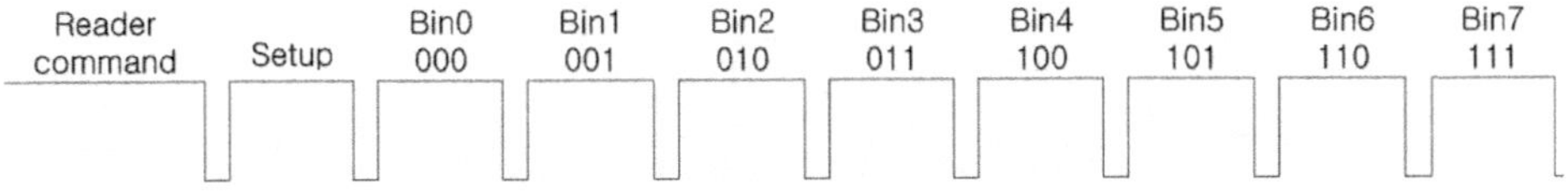

Fig. 2. *PingID* reply response period

the tags with matched prefix reply by transmitting their next 8 bits of identifier tag memory (ITM). Each replying tag transmits 8 bits in the bin slot (time slot) matched with most significant 3 bits out of 8 bits. Fig. 2 shows *PingID* reply response period [4]. Because there are 8 bin slots, the tree structure in fig. 1 has 8 branches. Another important command, *ScrollID* is transmitted when the reader requests tag's full ITM. In the conventional anti-collision algorithm, there are two confirmation procedures by transmitting *PingID* and *ScrollID* after successful identification.

We choose the ALR-9780 system of the Alien Technology Corporation as the conventional EPC CLASS 1 system. The Alien Technology Corporation system is one of leading companies in the field of RFID. We find out three main characteristics of conventional anti-collision algorithm by experiments and analysis. First, if there is a response in a bin slot, the reader request tags with the same prefix to transmit their full ITM. Second, there are two confirmation procedures after each successful identification. Third, in a tag identification procedure, ITMs have a remarkable characteristic caused by its structure. ITMs of the tags are always distributed randomly because the CRC is located in front of the tag ID, even though the IDs of tags are sequentially distributed. These three observations motivate us to propose the fast anti-collision algorithm.

3 The Fast Anti-collision Algorithm

In this paper, we assume that the reader use the collision information in bin slots of *PingID* replies. Fig. 3 shows the flow chart of the fast anti-collision algorithm. LEN and $VALUE$ are the bit length and exact value of prefix. The main ideas of the fast anti-collision algorithm is following two ideas.

1. The reader operates each bin slots with two different ways according to the collision information in bin slots.
   (a) If there is a collision in the bin slot, the reader sends *PingID* while the conventional reader sends *ScrollID*.
   (b) If there is no collision in the bin slot, the reader requests tags ITM as the same way as the conventional algorithm.
2. We reduce the additional confirmation procedures (*ScrollID* and *PingID* transmissions) after successful identification because there is not considerable performance decrease in the RFID system. Even though there are remaining or missed tags, those will be identified next identification procedure.

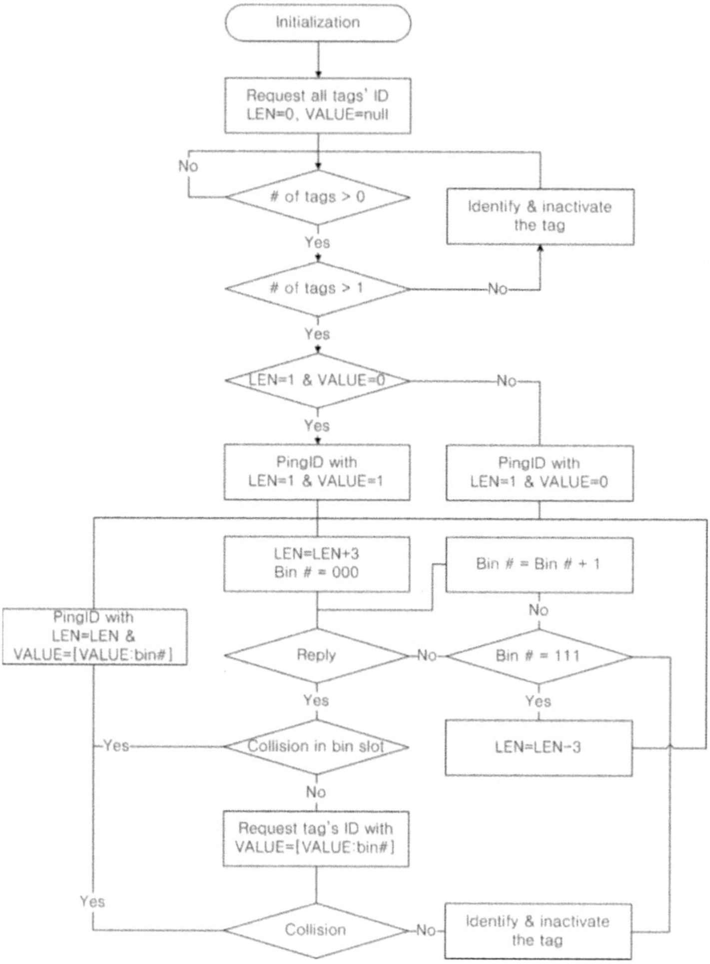

Fig. 3. *PingID* The flow chart of the fast anti-collision algorithm

4 Performance Analysis

In this section, we analyze the performance of the conventional and the proposed fast anti-collision algorithm. For the performance metrics, we consider the time to identify tags and the number of command transmission. First, we derive the time to identify tags ($T_{identification}$).

$$T_{identification} = CW \times n_{total} + \frac{b_{reader}}{DR_{reader}} + \frac{b_{tag}}{DR_{tag}}, \tag{1}$$

where CW is the time to send continuous wave, n_{tatal} is the number of total command transmissions, b_{reader} is total number of bits from a reader, DR_{reader}

is reader-to-tag data rate, b_{tag} is total number of bits from tags and DR_{tag} is tag-to-reader data rate. To derive b_{reader} and b_{tag}, we derive the number of command transmission in the following sections. The mathematical approach is similar to [5],[6].

4.1 The Conventional Anti-collision Algorithm

Let the number of transmission of *ScrollID* and *PingID* commands with k depth are IS_k and IP_k respectively (k =1,2,3,). To derive IS_k and IP_k, we calculate the probabilities of replies for each case. If there is a response in a bin slot of *PingID* reply, the reader transmits *ScrollID*. The probability that one or more tags reply in a bin slot ($P_{response}$) is

$$P_{response} = 1 - \left(\frac{r-1}{r}\right)^n, \tag{2}$$

where r is the number of bin slot and n is the number of tags to be identified. If only one tag replies in a bin slot, there is no collision in *ScrollID* reply. The reader identifies the tag and transmits additional *ScrollID*. The probability that there is only one tags reply in a bin slot(P_{no_coll}) is

$$P_{no\_coll} = n\left(\frac{r-1}{r}\right)^{n-1} \cdot \frac{1}{r}, \tag{3}$$

Let m be the total number of tags to be identified and n_{bin} be the number of leafs with k depth, the expected number of transmission of *ScrollID* with k depth (IS_k) is given by

$$\begin{aligned} p_{ij} &= n_{bin} \times P_{response} + n_{bin} \times P_{no\_coll} \\ &= 2r^k \times \left[1 - \left(\frac{r-1}{r}\right)^{\frac{m}{2r^{k-1}}} + \frac{m}{2r^{k-1}}\left(\frac{r-1}{r}\right)^{\frac{m}{2r^{k-1}}-1} \cdot \frac{1}{r}\right]. \end{aligned} \tag{4}$$

If two or moer tags replies in a bin slot, the reader transmits *PingID*. The probability that there are two or more tags replies in the bin slot (P_{coll}) is

$$P_{coll} = P_{response} - P_{no\_coll} = 1 - \left(\frac{r-1}{r}\right)^n - n\left(\frac{r-1}{r}\right)^{n-1} \cdot \frac{1}{r} \tag{5}$$

If there is no more reply in other bin slots, the reader sends additional *PingID* to search remaining tags which have same prefix with last identified tag. The number of transmissions of *PingID* commands (IP_k) is given by

$$\begin{aligned} IP_k &= [n_{bin} \times P_{coll}]_{k=k} + [n_{bin} \times P_{no\_coll}]_{k=k-1} \\ &= 2r^k \times \left[1 - \left(\frac{r-1}{r}\right)^{\frac{m}{2r^{k-1}}} - \frac{m}{2r^{k-1}}\left(\frac{r-1}{r}\right)^{\frac{m}{2r^{k-1}}-1} \cdot \frac{1}{r}\right] \\ &+ 2r^{k-1} \times \left[\frac{m}{2r^{k-2}}\left(\frac{r-1}{r}\right)^{\frac{m}{2r^{k-2}}-1} \cdot \frac{1}{r}\right]. \end{aligned} \tag{6}$$

In Eq. 6, the first part($k = k$) is with k depth and the second part($k = k + 1$) is with $k + 1$ depth. We assumed that the remaining tags are identified in the branch if the expected number of tags in the bin slot is less than 1.

4.2 The Fast Anti-collision Algorithm

In the proposed fast anti-collision algorithm, the reader sends *ScrollID* if there is a response and no collision in a bin slot. No collision means one of two cases. First case occurs when only one tag responses. Second case occurs when two or more tags transmitted *PingID* replies with the same 8 bits. The probability that there is only one tags reply in the bin slot (P_{tag_1}) is

$$P_{tag\_1} = n\left(\frac{r-1}{r}\right)^{n-1} \cdot \frac{1}{r}. \tag{7}$$

And, the probability that there are two or more tags replies in the bin slot ($P_{tag\geq 2}$) is given by

$$P_{tag\geq 2} = 1 - \left(\frac{r-1}{r}\right)^{n} - n\left(\frac{r-1}{r}\right)^{n-1} \cdot \frac{1}{r}. \tag{8}$$

Each tag transmits 8 bit reply in the bin slot matched with most significant 3 bits out of 8 bits when it replies to *PingID* command. Therefore the probability that there is no collision between tags which replied in a bin slot depends on least significant 5 bits. $P_{bin\_no\_coll}$ is derived by

$$P_{bin\_no\_coll} = \left(\frac{1}{2^5}\right)^{n} \quad , n \geq 2. \tag{9}$$

If more than two tags reply in the bin slot, the reader sends *PingID* with the probability of $P_{bin\_no\_coll}$. Here, we assume that $P_{bin\_no\_coll}$ is zero in numerical analysis since it is negligible. Therefore, the expected number of transmissions of *ScrollID* with k depth (IS_k) is

$$\begin{aligned} IS_k &= n_{bin} \times (P_{tag\_1} + P_{tag\geq 2} \times P_{bin\_no\_coll}) \\ &\approx n_{bin} \times P_{tag\_1} = 2r^k \times \left[\frac{m}{2r^{k-1}}\left(\frac{r-1}{r}\right)^{\frac{m}{2r^{k-1}}-1} \cdot \frac{1}{r}\right]. \end{aligned} \tag{10}$$

And, the number of transmission of *PingID* with k depth (IP_k) is

$$\begin{aligned} IP_k &= n_{bin} \times P_{tag\geq 2} \times (1 - P_{bin\_no\_coll}) \approx n_{bin} \times P_{tag\geq 2} \\ &= 2r^k \times \left[1 - \left(\frac{r-1}{r}\right)^{\frac{m}{2r^{k-1}}} - \frac{m}{2r^{k-1}}\left(\frac{r-1}{r}\right)^{\frac{m}{2r^{k-1}}-1} \cdot \frac{1}{r}\right]. \end{aligned} \tag{11}$$

Table 1. Simulation parameters

Parameter	Value
CW	0.064 msec
master clock interval (T_0)	0.025 msec
DR_{reader} $(1/T_0)$	40 kbps
DR_{tag} $(2/T_0)$	80 kbps
Transaction gap$(1.25T_0)$	0.3125 msec
Tag setup period $(8T_0)$	0.2 msec
Tag response period $(64T_0)$	1.6 msec

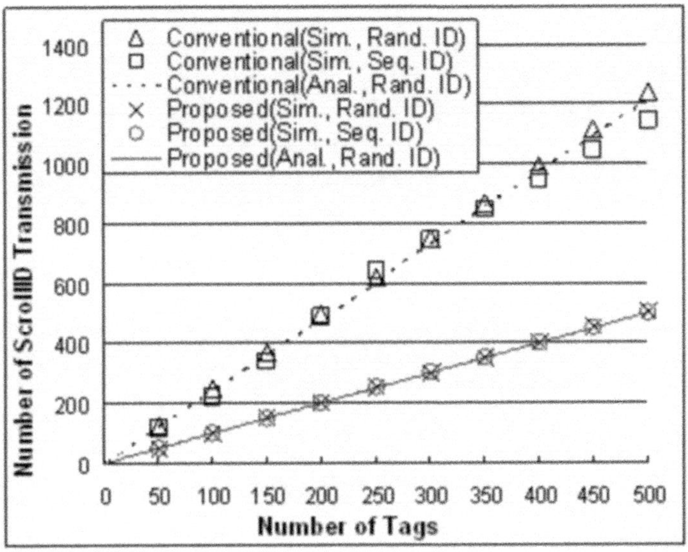

Fig. 4. Number of *ScrollID* transmission

5 Numerical and Simulation Results

We compare the performance of the proposed algorithm with that of the conventional algorithm and validate analytic results using simulation. Table 1 shows parameters used in mathematical analysis and simulation [4], [7]. The range of considered number of tags is from 50 to 500. In the mathematical analysis, we assume that ID of tags distributes randomly. However, we perform the simulation with both randomly distributed tags ID and sequentially distributed tags ID.

The results of mathematical analysis and simulations are illustrated from Fig. 4 to Fig. 7, and curves mean the mathematical results and symbols mean the simulation ones. The results of mathematical analysis are very close to the simulation ones. And, the results of simulations with randomly distributed tag IDs and sequentially distributed tag IDs are much similar. The reason is that ITMs

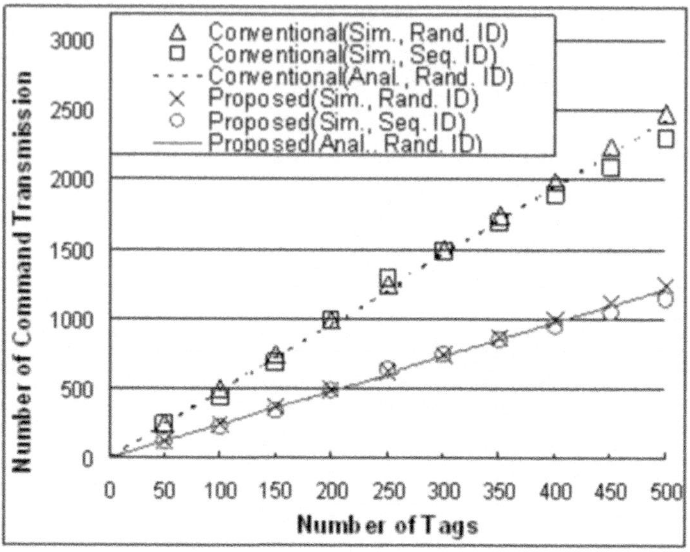

Fig. 5. Number of command transmission

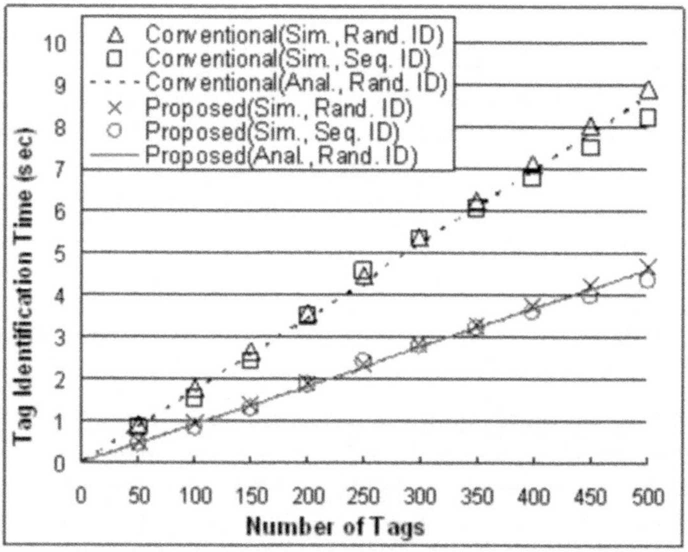

Fig. 6. Tag idnetification time

of the tags are always distributed randomly because the CRC is located in front of the tag ID, even though the IDs of tags are sequentially distributed. Fig. 4 and Fig. 5 show the number of *ScrollID* and total command transmissions for the number of tags. The transmission number of commands increases linearly as the number

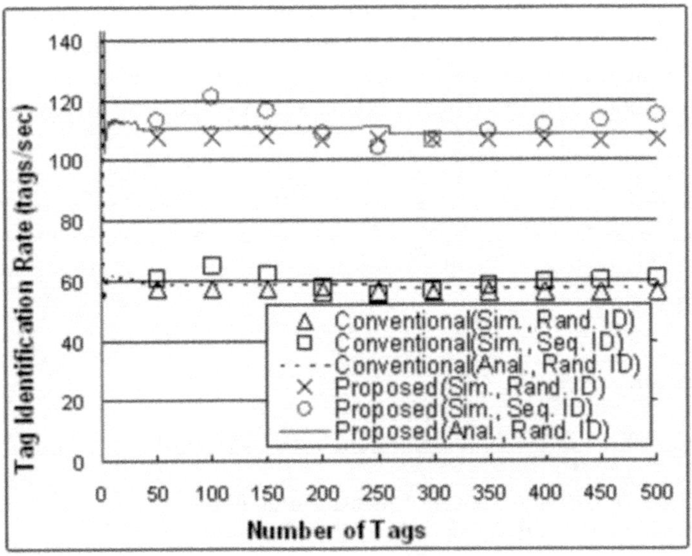

Fig. 7. Tag identification rate

of tags increases. In Fig. 4, the number of ScrollID transmission is about 1210 for the conventional algorithm and 500 for the proposed algorithm when the number of used tags is 500. It presents that using collision information in bin slots reduces number of ScrollID transmission. In Fig. 5, the number of total command transmissions is about 2400 and 1200 for the conventional algorithm and the proposed algorithm respectively. The results show 50.21% performance improvement for the proposed algorithm in terms of the total number of command transmission. Fig. 6 and Fig. 7 show the tag identification time and tag identification rate, which indicates the number of identified tags per second. In case of randomly distributed tags ID, the proposed algorithm identifies 500 tags at 4.7 second while the conventional algorithm does at 8.9 second in Fig. 6. It means that each algorithm identifies approximately 106 tags and 56 tags per second respectively as shown in Fig. 7. The proposed algorithm shows about 89.2% performance improvement compared to the conventional algorithm in the view of tag identification rate.

6 Conclusion

In this paper, we analyzed the anti-collision algorithm of the conventional EPC Class 1 RFID system and proposed the fast anti-collision algorithm. In the proposed algorithm, the number of unnecessary transmission of *ScrollID* commands is reduced by using the collision information of bin slots. Moreover, transmissions of unnecessary verification commands are eliminated. We mathematically analyzed the performance of the conventional anti-collision algorithm and the proposed anti-collision algorithm. We also validated analytic results using simulation.

According to the results, we found that the proposed algorithm shows about 89.2% performance improvement compared to the conventional algorithm in aspect of the identification rate. Consequently, if the proposed fast anti-collision algorithm applies to EPC Class 1 RFID system, the reader can identify more tags within shorter time.

The main contributions of this paper are threefold:(1) we analized tag anti-collision algorithm of the conventional EPC Class 1 RFID system, (2) proposed the fast anti-collision algorithm, and (3) evaluated the performance of both the conventional and proposed anti-collision algorithm using mathematical analysis and simulations.

References

1. Vogt, H.: Efficient Object Identification with Passive RFID tags. In: IEEE ICPC, pp. 98–113 (2002)
2. Finkenzeller, K.: Radio-Frequency Identification Fundamentals and applications. In: RFID Handbook, John Wiley & Sons Ltd, Chichester (1999)
3. Sarma, S., Brock, D., Engels, D.: Radio frequency identification and electronic product code. In: IEEE MICRO, pp. 50–54 (2001)
4. Auto-ID Center: Technical report 860MHz-930MHz Class I Radio Frequency Identification Tag Radio Frequency & Logical Communication Interface Specification Candidate Recommendation, Version 1.0.1 (2003)
5. Choi, H.S., Cha, J.R., Kim, J.H.: Fast Wireless Anti-collision Algorithm in Ubiquitous ID System. IEEE VTC 2004 26–29 (2004)
6. Choi, H.S., Kim, J.H.: A Novel Tag identification algorithm for RFID System using UHF. In: Yang, L.T., Amamiya, M., Liu, Z., Guo, M., Rammig, F.J. (eds.) EUC 2005. LNCS, vol. 3824, pp. 629–638. Springer, Heidelberg (2005)
7. EPCglobal: EPCTM Tag Data Standards Version 1.1 Rev.1.24 (2005)

Certification Tools of Ubiquitous Mobile Platform

Sang-Yun Lee[1] and Byung-Uk Choi[2]

[1] Dept. of Electronical Telecommunication Engineering, Hanyang University, Seoul, Korea
syllee@etri.re.kr
[2] Division of Information and Communications, Hanyang University, Seoul, Korea
buchoi@hanyang.ac.kr

Abstract. The Wireless Internet Platform for Interoperability (WIPI) is a wireless Internet standard platform in Korea. The WIPI is composed of four main parts including the hardware abstraction layer (HAL), a runtime engine, and two standard application programming interfaces (APIs, WIPI-C and WIPI-Java). A certification process is required to ensure the interoperability of the developed WIPI platform. In this paper, we propose the platform certification toolkit (PCT) and HAL certification toolkit (HCT) as WIPI specification certification tools. The PCT certifies the functions of the platform and standard APIs, whereas The HCT certifies the HAL API. Users can find precisely where an error occurred by using the tools, which facilitate the debugging processes and reduce development time. We describe the architecture of the PCT and the HCT and show the implementations. And, we introduce the case study applying them to the real WIPI reference implementations.

Keywords: WIPI, HAL, Platform, Certification tool, PCT, HCT.

1 Introduction

WIPI is a mobile standard platform specification established by Korea Wireless Internet Standardization Forum (KWISF) [1], [2], which provides an environment for executing a downloaded program through wireless Internet on a handset. Qualcomm's Brew and JCP's J2ME (MIDP/CLDC) are similar platforms that were used prior to development of the WIPI platform. The WIPI specification provides standard APIs for the C and Java languages widely used by developers of handset applications.

The WIPI platform must be officially certified before it is released. The Java Community Process (JCP) establishing Java standard APIs requires that the reader of a Java Specification Request (JSR) provide a Technology Compatibility Kit (TCK) certification tool [3]. The WIPI application should be written with those standard API. The application can operate only within standard APIs or can be supported by a runtime engine or a HAL layer for essential functions such as an event and a user's input.

Four main types of companies use WIPI including manufacturers of HAL, platform developers of a WIPI runtime engine, solution developers, and content providers. If an error occurs during development or application testing, these companies should cooperate to trace its cause, and under certain circumstances, share their source codes. However, companies often hesitate in sharing their source codes and instead tend to

J. Indulska et al. (Eds.): UIC 2007, LNCS 4611, pp. 63–72, 2007.

ascribe the problems to the other parties. Resolving these problems takes time, and as a result WIPI platform cannot be released to market in a timely manner [4].

We propose the Platform Certification Toolkit (PCT) and HAL Certification Toolkit (HCT) to address these problems. In addition, we describe cases in which these tools were applied to an actual WIPI platform and discuss the usefulness of the proposed certification tools. This paper is organized as follows: section 2 introduces the WIPI platform; section 3 presents the architecture of the proposed PCT and certification procedure; section 4 describes the architecture of the proposed HCT and the certification agent; section 5 demonstrates the implementation results and shows an example of applying those tools to actual WIPI platforms; and section 6 provides our conclusions.

2 Related Works

In the standard specification, the WIPI platform is defined by basic functions, a secure WIPI runtime engine, WIPI-C APIs for C-application developers, and WIPI-Java APIs for Java-application developers. A HAL API also supports various hardware devices [5], [6]. Fig. 1 shows architecture of a WIPI platform based on Qualcom's MSM chips.

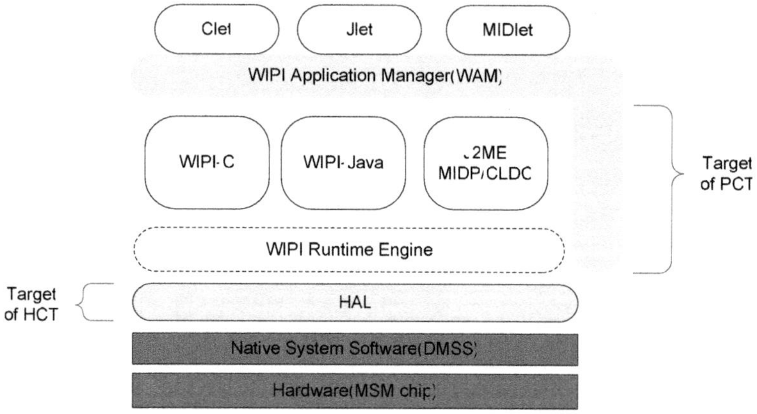

Fig. 1. The architecture of the WIPI platform

Native system software designates the Dual-Mode Subscriber Station (DMSS) software provided by Qualcomm, which includes a terminal operating system called REX, communication functions, and various device drivers.

A runtime Engine is middleware that executes a WIPI application downloaded through a code division multiple access (CDMA) network, serves as a linker and a loader, and provides memory management, resource management, and garbage collection. The WIPI Application Manager (WAM) manages WIPI applications downloaded from a server and enables us to store, delete, and retrieve those programs with it. It is possible to implement WAM with Clet or Jlet. Whereas it is unnecessary to port a runtime engine, WIPI-C API, and WIPI-Java API, regardless of the hardware or the operating system, HAL must be ported in order for it to be appropriate to the loaded terminal.

Recently, WIPI platform has been extended to Terrestrial Digital Multimedia Broadcasting (T-DMB) platform [7] and Radio Frequency Identification (RFID) platform [8]. It shows that the WIPI platform can be extended to ubiquitous platform in the future.

3 Platform Certificate Tool

3.1 System Architecture

As shown in Fig. 2, the PCT is composed of a certificate agent running on a target terminal on which the WIPI platform is loaded and the PCT server that processes the certification. The PCT server running on a desktop PC is further divided into an integrated certification toolkit to select a testcase or command testing on a GUI display and a database server to store various test data required for certification and the test results.

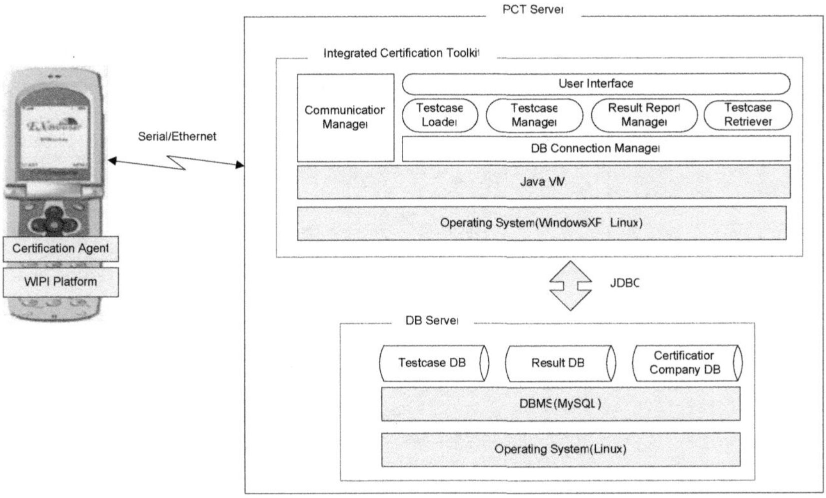

Fig. 2. The PCT system architecture

The integrated certification toolkit is further divided into the user interface, where a testcase is selected; the connection manager, which assigns a certificate agent to the communication channel; the testcase loader, which downloads a testcase to the certificate agent; the testcase manager, which creates or manages a testcase project; the report manager, which displays a test result in a summarized form; the testcase retriever, which searches for a testcase in the database server; and the database connection manager, which connects to the database server via JDBC.

3.2 Certification Procedure

Fig. 3 shows the certification procedure. The procedure of the proposed rendering algorithm is as followings: (1) We select a type of test and a testcase from the PCT server; (2) The PCT server downloads a binary code to the target terminal for the selected testcase; (3) The certification agent performs the test on the target terminal; (4) The certification agent uploads the test results to the PCT server; (5) The integrated certification toolkit certifies the results; (6) If the testcase passes, we proceed to another testcase; if it fails, we test it again after debugging the running platform; (7) The PCT server displays a report of the results, and completes the certification after all the testcases are performed.

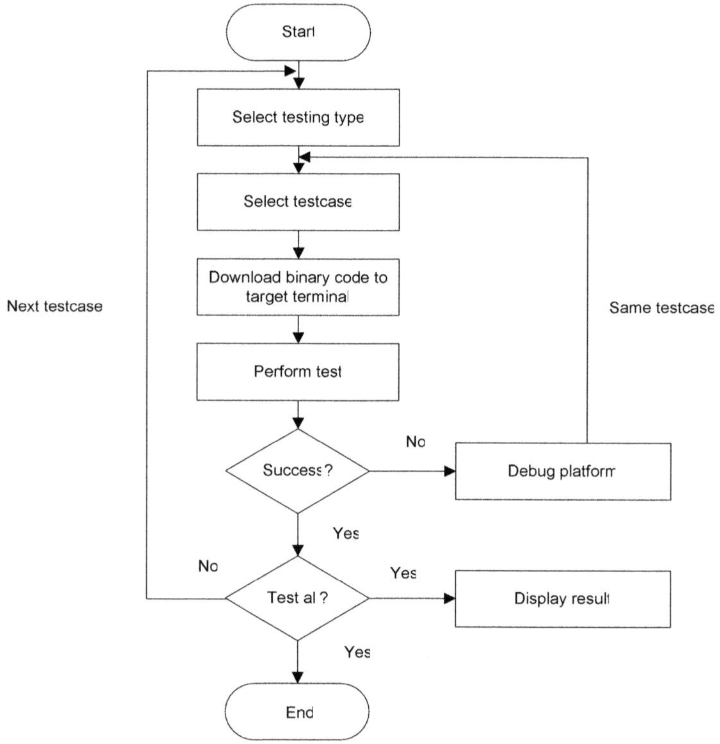

Fig. 3. Certification flow chart

3.3 Discussion of the J2ME Certification Scheme

In WIPI 2.0, the certification process is separated such that the PCT undertakes the certification of WIPI-C and WIPI-Java, and the TCK undertakes the certification of J2ME.

A WIPI platform executes the J2ME application in binary codes, whereas the TCK performs certification for byte codes. So a new certification scheme is necessary to adapt the TCK byte codes to pass the TCK. We resolved this problem by linking an

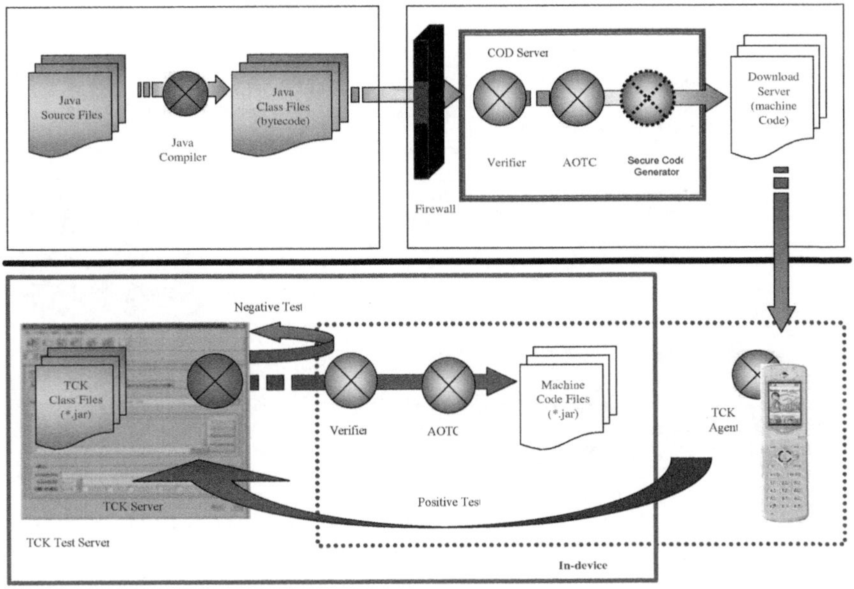

Fig. 4. The TCK certification scheme on the WIPI platform

AOTC, a byte code translator, and a WIPI terminal that executes the translated codes with a notion of an expanded in-device.

Fig. 4 shows the TCK certification scheme on the WIPI platform.

The compiled java source files are sent to a compile-on-demand (COD) server in the form of a byte code. The COD server then verifies the class files and sends the files translated by the AOTC to a target terminal in the form of a binary code.

The WIPI platform in the terminal executes Java applications with binary codes. The TCK certification agent running on the target terminal downloads test class files from the TCK server. After those files are verified, the WIPI platform executes the binary code translated by the AOTC. Finally, the TCK certification agent sends the test results to the TCK server.

The AOTC and the TCK certification agent are effectively one component running on an 'in-device' so the TCK server can certify test results whereas the test class files sent to a target terminal are translated into binary codes.

4 HAL Certification Toolkit

As shown in Fig. 5, the HCT system is composed of the HCT server that manages a testcase and a test program, as in the PCT, and the HCT agent that executes a test on a target terminal. The HCT server is further divided into an integrated certification toolkit and a database server.

The project manager manages the information on a target terminal with HAL, the HAL certification progress, and the certification results. The testcase generator binds

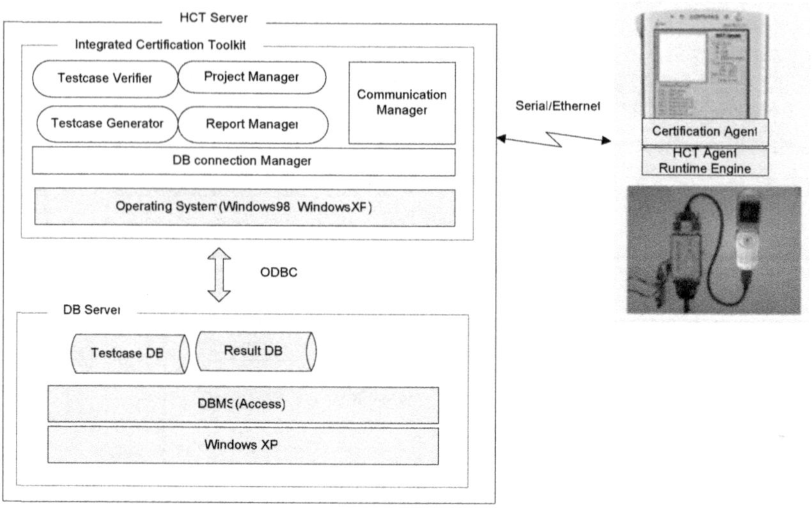

Fig. 5. The HCT system architecture

testcases with a package and enables us to enter a parameter values and the return value of a test function.

The report manager displays the results of a test on a screen or makes them Web pages. The testcase verifier determines whether the implemented APIs work normally, based on the results of a test from the HCT agent. The communication manager controls the connection to the network through an ethernet or a serial cable. The database server stores testcases or the test results.

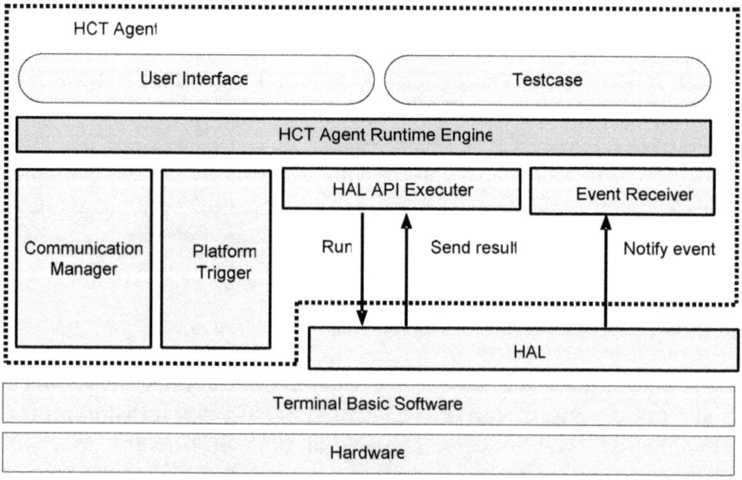

Fig. 6. Architecture of the HCT agent

Unlike the PCT agent, the HCT agent cannot use WIPI APIs because it runs without the WIPI platform. Therefore, we developed a runtime engine for the HCT agent. Fig. 6 shows the architecture of the proposed HCT agent.

The platform trigger is a module defined in the HAL specification, such as MH_pltStart() and MH_pltEvent(), which a WIPI platform should provide. This module executes the HCT agent or handles an event from a terminal's operating software. The user Interface is used in an interactive test which requests that confirming results be sent to the user when testing is taking place. The event receiver handles an event from HAL. The runtime engine for the HCT agent receives testcases from the HCT server and executes tests through the HAL API executor. Test results can be reviewed using the HAL API executor or the user interface.

5 Implementation Result

5.1 WIPI Reference Implementation

We have developed a WIPI runtime engine based on QPlus, embedded Linux developed by ETRI [9], [10], and an emulator based on Windows [11]-[13] as a WIPI reference implementation (RI). These RIs support WIPI 1.1, WIPI 2.0, and WIPI2.1 simultaneously. Additionally, we have developed Linker & Loader, core technology of WIPI runtime engine for handset [14], [15].

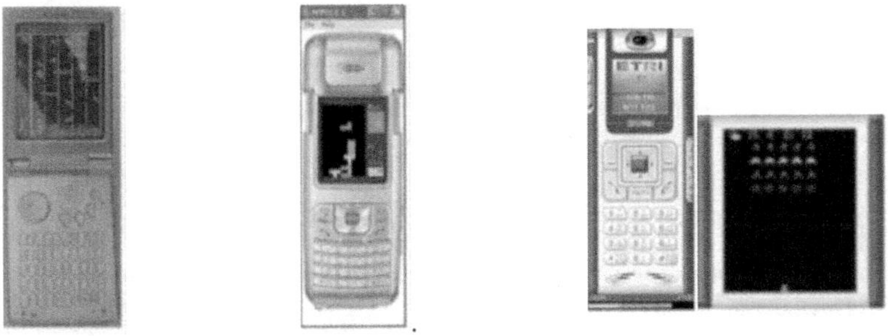

(a) RI on Yopy (b) WIPI Clet emulator (c) WIPI Jlet emulator

Fig. 7. WIPI reference implementation

Fig. 7(a) shows a Clet game running on the Yopy. Fig. 7(b) shows a Tetris game running on the WIPI Clet emulator. The WIPI Clet emulator is developed with Visual Studio 6.0 and cooperates with Visual Studio. Fig. 7(c) shows a Space Invader game running on the WIPI Jlet emulator.

5.2 PCT Implementation

The PCT integrated certification toolkit runs on all the systems with a Java Virtual Machine because that toolkit is implemented with Java. We used the MySQL server as a database server.

We implemented the certification agent with Jlet; during the job, we used a WIPI platform function that allows one application to invoke another application, and used the communicational functionality between the applications. Therefore, a WIPI platform supporting WIPI-Java API should be implemented first to execute the certification agent.

The PCT server and the certificate agent can communicate with each other through a serial cable or an ethernet. Fig. 8 shows the PCT system running. Fig. 8(a) shows the PCT integrated certification toolkit, and Fig. 8(b) shows the PCT agent on an emulator.

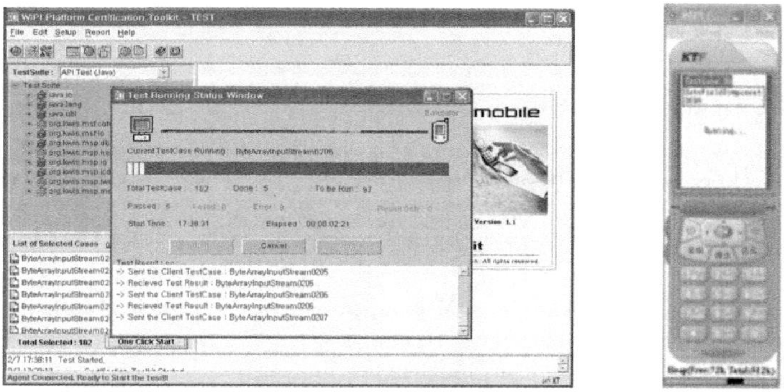

(a) PCT server (b) PCT agent

Fig. 8. The PCT system

5.3 The HCT Implementation

The HCT server as shown in Fig. 9(a) was developed with Delphi and runs on Windows 98 and above. We used the Access DB as a database server. The HCT agent should be ported according to the target terminal. We developed two agents for Qplus and Windows.

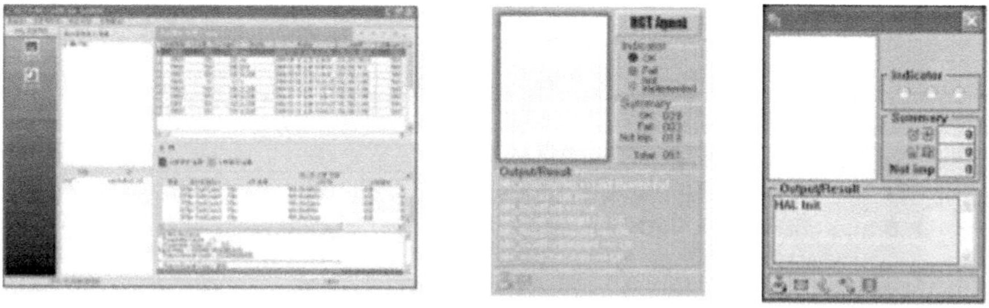

(a) HCT server (b) HCT agent for QPlus (c) HCT agent for Windows

Fig. 9. The HCT system

5.4 Case Study: Applying a WIPI Platform

Certifying the **MC_fsOpen** function with a batch test took less than 1 seconds in an environment with a Pentium-IV 2.8GHz, Windows XP, and1GB RAM. Other functions took similar times.

The **MC_grpDrawLine** function took much longer to certify because a tester must subjectively determine whether a line is drawn normally or dotted well based on a visual examination. It took more time to send testcases to the terminal than to execute the PCT by applying PCT to the mobile terminal with a WIPI platform.

There are many difficulties in certifying a WIPI platform on a handset device. It takes approximately 5-30 min according to transmission equipment. Also, each operator's strategy is different; some operator allows testing with transmission equipment whereas others do not permit it, leaving the PCT tester with no option of paying a fee for CDMA usage.

6 Conclusion and Future Work

The number of the cellular phones loaded with the WIPI was over 10,000,000 in Korea, in 2006. And the WIPI platform and WIPI contents have been exported to several countries.

We have proposed the PCT, a WIPI platform certification tool, and the HCT, a HAL certification tool in this paper. Considering hardware limitations of the terminals, we designed so that these tools are composed of the certificate agent running on a target terminal and the server running on a desktop PC. Therefore we have only to port the agent according to a target terminal without modifying the server.

The PCT that we developed earned software quality authentication from the Telecommunications Technology Association (TTA), and has been adopted as an official tool to certify WIPI platforms by major mobile communication companies such as SK Telecom, KTF, and LG Telecom. And the HCT can confirm where errors occur, thus helps debugging and makes development time short. So we expect our solutions will become useful tools for the WIPI developers.

In the future work, we will upgrade the tools according as the WIPI specification is refined, develop the agents supporting various platforms, and build a convenient test environment.

References

1. KWISF, Wireless Internet Platform for Interoperability (2006) www.wipi.org.kr
2. TTA, Wireless Internet Platform for Interoperability, TTAS.KO-06.0036/R3 (2004) www.tta.or.kr
3. JCP www.jcp.org
4. Lee, S.Y., Lee, H.G., Choi, B.U.: Design and Development of a WIPI Certification Toolkit. Korea Information Processing Society 13-D (5), 731–740 (2006)
5. Lee, S.Y., Kim, S.J., Kim, H.N.: Present standard status of WIPI and development prospects. Korean Information Science Society 22(1), 16–23 (2004)

6. Lee, S.Y., Kim, S.J, Kim, H.N.: Wireless Internet Platform for Interoperability WIPI 2.0, TTA Journal (92), 97–102 (2004)
7. Bae, B.G., Kim, W.S., Yun, J.G., Ahn, C.H., Lee, S.I., Sohng, K.I.: Verification of WIPI-based T-DMB Platform for Interactive Mobile Multimedia Services. In: Proc. of SPIE-IS&T, vol. 6074, 60740W-1-60740W-8 (2006)
8. Park, N.M., Kwak, J., Kim, S.J., Won, D.H., Kim, H.W.: WIPI Mobile Platform with Secure Service for Mobile RFID Network Environment. In: Shen, H.T., Li, J., Li, M., Ni, J., Wang, W. (eds.) Advanced Web and Network Technologies, and Applications. LNCS, vol. 3842, pp. 741–748. Springer, Heidelberg (2006)
9. Lee, J.H., Kim, S.J., Lee, S.Y., Kim, W.S., Lee, H.G.: Implementation WIPI for Linux-based Smartphone. In: 7th ICACT 2005, pp. 692–696 (2005)
10. Lee, J.H., Kim, S.J., Lee, S.Y.: Embedded Linux-based smartphone platform for sharing WIPI contents. In: IT-SOC, pp. 550–553 (2004)
11. Kim, Y.S., Kang, M.C., Yu, Y.D., Choi, H.: Design of a multi-task scheduler for a wireless Internet platform. In: Proceedings of the 22nd KIPS Fall Conference, pp. 1759–1762 (2004)
12. Lim, H.T., Jang, J., Choi, H.: Design and implementation of the API manager on wireless Internet platform. In: Proceedings of the 22nd KIPS Fall Conference, pp. 1763–1766 (2004)
13. Yoo, Y.D., Kim, Y.S., Lim, H.T., Kang, M.K., Choi, H.: Design and implementation of a memory management module for a wireless Internet platform. In: Proceedings of the 22nd KIPS Fall Conference, pp. 1783–1786 (2004)
14. Lindholm, T., Yellin, F.: The JavaTM Virtual Machine Specification, 2nd edn. Addison-Wesley, Reading (1999)
15. Lee, S.Y., Choi, B.U.: Design and Implementation of WIPI Runtime Engine. In: 2006 International Conference on Hybrid Information Technology, pp. 19–23. IEEE Computer Society, Los Alamitos (2006)

Dynamic Binding Framework for Open Device Services

Gwyduk Yeom

School of Computer Science, The University of Seoul,
Jeonnong-dong, Dongdaemun-gu, Seoul, 130-743, Korea
kdyeom@venus.uos.ac.kr

Abstract. We present a SOA-based, dynamic, extensible service binding framework that exports public services built on embedded systems' low-level capabilities. We have also implemented our framework on a small device equipped on a robot and demonstrated various interactions between our system and other services or devices. Our work is different from the SOA (Service Oriented Architecture)-based products many software vendors have announced in that our framework develops low-level device capabilities into public services that are readily integrated into existing high-level services. Recent proliferation of embedded systems made the motivation of this work.

1 Introduction

Traditionally hardware devices have been regarded as parts of the entire system. They have been dedicated to a single system and controlled by the system software. Furthermore, software for device control has been built based on vendor-proprietary technologies or specific service platforms. This restrains the interoperability between products with related or similar capabilities from various vendors.

Allowing devices to directly participate in the Web services is new direction catching many system designers' interest. Making devices into abstract services allows devices to contribute to Web services scenarios that are traditionally beyond the reach of individual devices.

Integration of different services enables seamless interoperation between services and this is one of important technical factors for building ubiquitous environments [1]. One example enabling integration of different services in enterprise application environment is SOA (Service Oriented Architecture).

However, in embedded systems application environments, the technology to devices into abstract services is not popular and platforms for service integration have not being widely used. Recently, as the interoperability of devices becomes an issue in home networks, several service platforms supporting integration of device services are being developed.

In this work, we present a component-based dynamic service binding framework that supports making devices into services and integration of standard services. This framework defines and implements standardized interfaces to support various standard service platforms in a way that service platforms can be added or removed dynamically at runtime using the dynamic component exchange technique. It supports standard C++ classes rather than alternatively defined interfaces for device services

J. Indulska et al. (Eds.): UIC 2007, LNCS 4611, pp. 73–82, 2007.

and thus allowing minimum modifications to the existing device control objects and giving maximum implementation flexibility. We have experimentally deployed our framework onto a robot and showed that it can interoperate with other services or devices.

Following this introduction, we review related work in Section 2. Our proposed framework is presented in Section 3 and its main technical characteristics are explained in Section 4. Experimental implementation is shown in Section 5 and Section 6 concludes the paper.

2 Related Work

This work puts focus on making hardware resources into abstract services taking SOA (Service Oriented Architecture) into consideration as a basic structure. SOA is the architecture that loosely-couples application units called service into a complete application [2]. In SOA, hardware resources are regarded as a kind of service. An implementation example of SOA is ESB (Enterprise Service Bus) [3, 4]. DP4WS (Device Profile for Web Service) [5] is an example that provides the operation mechanism for hardware devices using Web services.

ESB is a kind of middleware that interconnects and integrates services, applications, and resources in business environments. It is a new integration methodology that enables integration of software modules which were developed in different languages and programming models. It includes Web services and messaging-based transport and routing. Five functional layers residing at the top of ESB - user interaction service, application service, information service, process service, and community integration service – give the flexibility to it allowing various kind of integration. Especially the universal interconnection layer expands the scale and extents of integration between enterprises [5].

DP4WS[5] is one of the examples that abstract the functions of devices into a service. It defines service execution environments using the extended specification of Web services and implements UPnP model[6] based on Web services.

DP4WS comprises of definition, discovery, control, and event processing of device Web services, and uses encrypted messages. Device Web services are defined by WSDL (Web Service Description Language) [7] and found through WS-Discovery [8]. They use metadata messages conformant to WS-Metadata [9] and are controlled by SOAP (Simple Object Access Protocol) messages[10]. Device events are dispatched and processed according to WS-Eventing [11]. MTOM(Message Transmission Optimization Mechanism)[12] is a specification that enables bulk data transmission.

3 Framework Architecture

In this section we express local objects used for hardware control in various types of standard services and present a dynamic service binding framework that manages them. It focuses on making devices into abstract services based on SOA and supports dynamic service extension allowing real-time use of hardware resources.

3.1 Dynamic Service Binding Framework

Figure 1 shows the architecture of the dynamic service binding framework. It provides an extendable structure and real-time support to make internal device objects into various standardized services.

Our framework provides two types of interfaces – IAdaptor and IHandler – to support various standard services. Once service platform vendors or groups have their products implement these interfaces, our platform will support them. Adaptors and Handlers conformant to IAdaptor and IHandler interfaces can be dynamically loaded or removed by AdaptorFactory and HandlerFactory in real-time[13, 14].

There is a channel-based message delivery structure to support binding between adaptor and handler. Messages received through the adaptor are delivered to the handler through the logical transmission channel and message dispatcher. The channel takes the role of carrier to transport messages. Single channel or multiple channels are possible and channels are stored in the channel pool for later reuse.

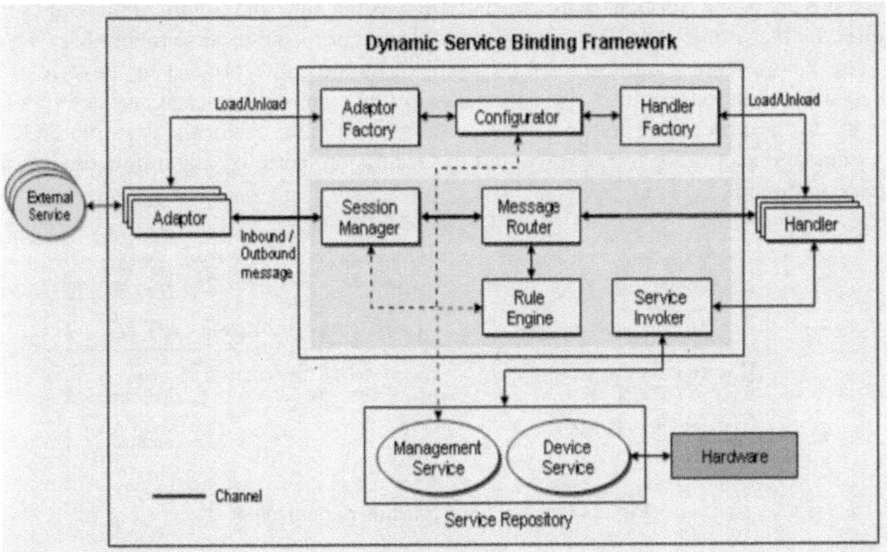

Fig. 1. Dynamic service binding framework

The message dispatcher delivers messages in the adaptor to the corresponding handler according to the mapping table. The mapping table defines message types and handler descriptors. This table is updated in real-time by the configuration manager. One can block or modify coming from some specified devices by setting the message processing rule engine. Rules used by the message processing rule engine enable the framework to process various messages changing time-to-time by defining some comparison conditions and processing sequences.

Device service objects in the framework form a dynamically loadable library built with the interface definition technology developed by GCC_XML [15] group and are loaded onto the memory by the corresponding loader as the adaptors and handlers.

For the management of the framework a web-based console is provided. It collects information or controls internal modules using the management service in the service repository.

3.2 Adaptor and Handler Architecture

Figure 2 shows the connection architecture of the adaptors and handlers. They implement the IAdaptor and IHandler interfaces respectively. Adaptors recognize messages of specific service description and transform them to have the format required by the dynamic service binding system. Handlers analyze messages delivered by the adaptors and process them according to the standard technical specification. For example, a UPnP handler processes UPnP messages coming from the message dispatcher according to the UPnP specification.

An adaptor implements the IAdaptor interface and is composed of the transmit module and receive module that communicate with the corresponding service platform. The receive module reads in messages coming through the protocol interface of the corresponding service platform and transforms into the standard messages required by the framework. The transmit module performs the reverse function.

The handlers are composed of the analysis module the processing module. The analysis module deserializes the commands in the standard message and delivers the results to the processing module. The processing module performs tasks required by the message according to the rules and the results are serialized and delivered to the next component.

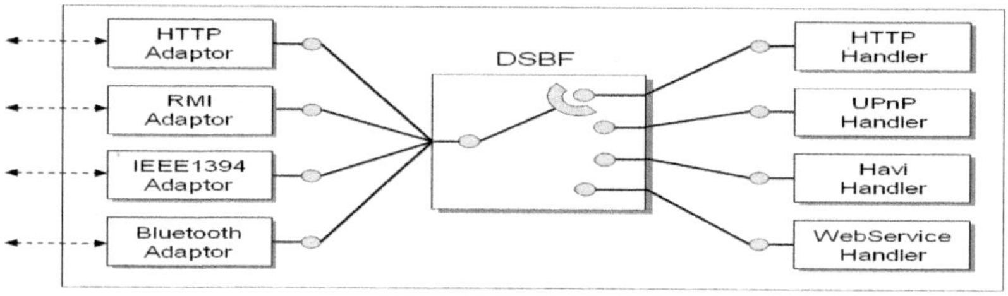

Fig. 2. The adaptor and handler architecture

4 Issues About the Architecture

Our framework converts device-dependent services into various standard service middleware platform services. It lets hardware devices be recognized as SOA-based services and supports interoperability with other standard services. Standard service platforms are implemented as adaptors and handlers in our framework and are distributed in a form than can be expanded by the configuration manager.

4.1 Making Hardware Objects into Standard Services

Our framework makes hardware objects into standard services by dynamically binding device control objects and standard services. To do this our framework implements standard service platforms in adaptors and handlers and has the architecture that binds them dynamically in the running system and can add them in real-time.

Figure 3 shows how our framework is seen as a service with a specific service platform in it to external services or devices. External devices or services can use or control internal hardware device without knowledge about it. For example, if the framework is equipped with an HTTP adaptor and Web service handler, internal devices can be exported as a Web service [16]. With the HTTP adaptor (UPnP[6] uses HTTP for message exchange) and UPnP handler the framework can export the internal devices as an UPnP service. This capability to exporting a device as several standard services increases the utility of the hardware device.

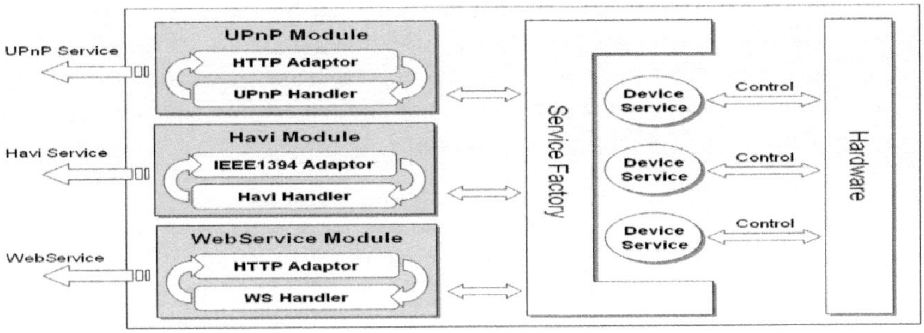

Fig. 3. Making device services into standard services

4.2 Message Processing

Messages from the adaptor are relayed to handlers through the dispatcher. The dispatcher performs its switching function referencing the routing table. The routing table maps message types to handler descriptors. This table is updated in real-time by the configuration manager. Rules generated by the rule engine can also be reflected on this table to drop or modify messages coming from specific devices.

4.3 Real-Time Module Management

AdaptorFactory and HandlerFactory dynamically load adaptors and handlers in the form of dynamic library module (.so, .dll). Adaptors and handlers are stored in the repositories embedded in each factories and are activated at the initialization stage of the framework [13, 17].

Adaptors and handlers in action can be replaced by new adaptors and handlers automatically by the update manager or manually by commands from the management console. In this case, the old adaptors and handlers take no more messages and are removed from the repositories, completing messages already in processing. New adaptors and handlers take over the role and keep processing messages without service interruptions for users.

Adaptors and handlers have the life cycle spanning from the install stage and to the uninstall stage. There are four stages in between – Starting, Active, Waiting, and Stopping stages. Parameters and configurations are initialized in the Starting stage.

The Active stage is where adaptors and handlers perform their functions, receiving messages and processing them. Waiting stage is the zombie state in which no more action is performed entered after completing current jobs. In the Stopping stage, adaptors and handlers are removed from the repositories after completing current jobs and releasing resources in use.

4.4 Device Service Transform and Export

When a new hardware control object is defined in our framework, the service manager loads it in the form of service and exports the device service to other devices or services. Hardware control objects are dynamically loadable libraries implemented based on the interface definition technology provided by GCC_XML [15] group. In order to export the loaded devices service in various standard service forms, the reflector extracts the object interface information and hands it over to the handlers of interest. With this information handlers register and export this new service following mechanism defined in each platform as in Figure 4.

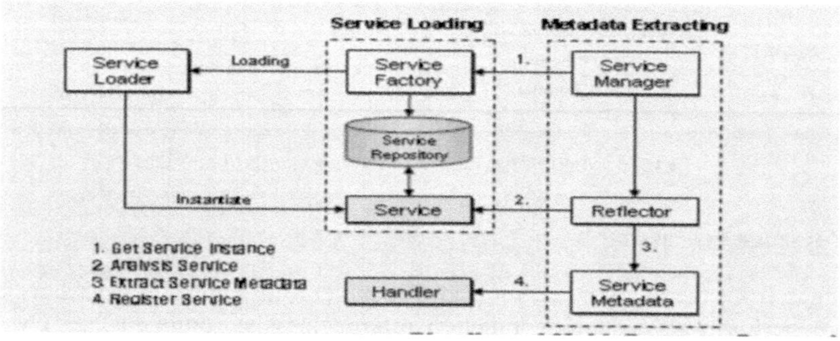

Fig. 4. Device service transformation

The reflector used in the service export process extracts the interface information from the newly loaded object using the reflection technology developed by the Seal project [17] and GCC_XML [15] technology. With this information the reflector processes dynamic calls on the device services.

5 Experimental Implementation

We had built a prototype system of the proposed framework. The implementation details of our framework and experimental deployment on a hardware device are presented with some results in this section.

5.1 Experimental Environments

We used C++ language on embedded Linux and WinCE.NET, Xerces-C library for XML parsing, POSIX thread library. We implemented and deployed our framework

Table 1. Specifications of the embedded board

H/W Specification	OS Specification
X-Hyper255B - Intel XScale PXA255 - 64MB SDRAM - 32MB Flash - 10Base-T CS8900A - PCMCIA 1 slot	Embedded Linux - kernel 2.4.18 WinCE .NET - 4.2

on a robot device equipped with the X-Hyper255B embedded board. Specifications of the robot embedded board are shown in Table 1.

We also implemented a deploy server to load new modules on our framework. The robot device provides all-direction movement and visual monitoring services and accepts control commands for the web camera and driving motor. Figure 5 shows the robot device used in our experiment.

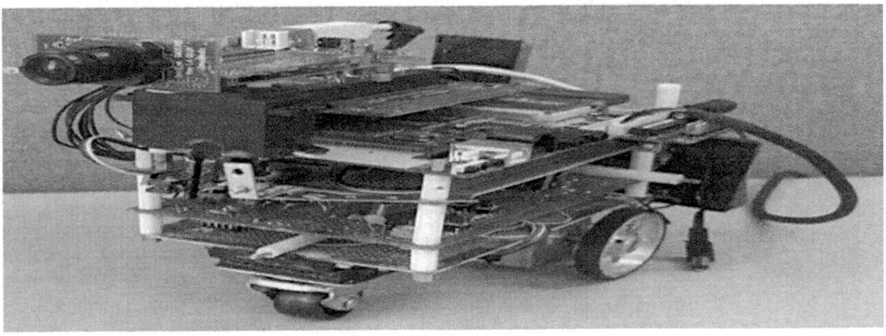

Fig. 5. The robot device loaded with our implementation of the framework

5.2 Experiment and Results

The experimental implementation of our framework supports two standard service platforms – UPnP and Web services with HTTP adaptor, RMI adaptor, UPnP handler, and Web service handler. With this implementation we demonstated that the robot with our experimental framework could dynamically interoperate with other devices or applications with UPnP or Web service platform. Dynamic interoperation means that when the robot discovers a new device with a platform currently not supported by the robot, it downloads an approated handler from the deployment server and begin to interoperate with the new device.

To demonstate the dynamic binding framework we tested two cases. In each test case, the robot was started without any service platform loaded. Once a device is discovered, an appropriate platform supporting modules were loaded at runtime to provide the corresponding services.

In the first test scenario we demonstrated that the robot, discovering the UPnP control point on the PDA, downloads the UPnP handler module from the deployment server to interoperate with it. The PDA was located on the local wireless network and could monitor views transmitted from the camera on the robot and drive the robot, once the robot completes the loading of the UPnP handler.

In the second test scenario we demonstrated that a Web service application out of the local network can use the Web services exported by the robot. With these Web services outside applications can control devices discovered inside the local network. The robot downloads the Web service handler module in order to support the Web services.

Figure 6 shows the overall experimental settings modeling the home security system. Door lock and warning device having UPnP interface is emulated on the notebook computer. Users can use PDA in house and use Web service applications out of house to monitor and control the house.

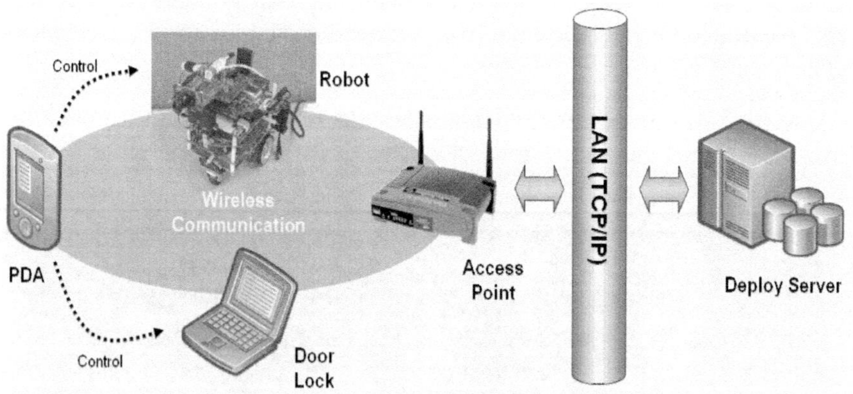

Fig. 6. Experimental setting

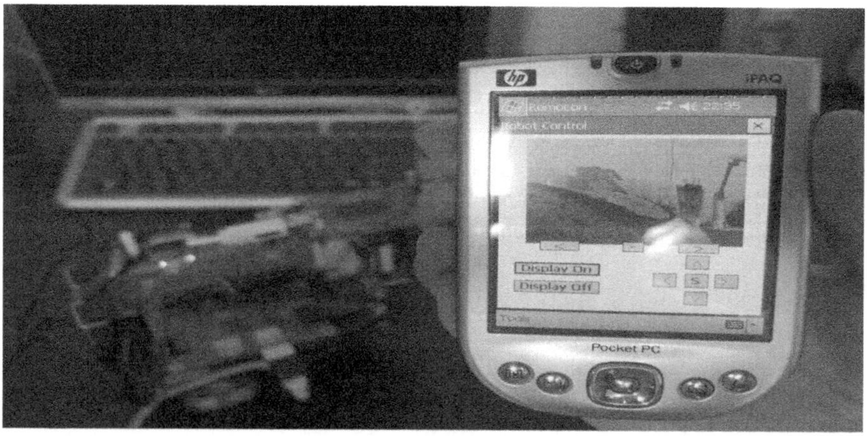

Fig. 7. PDA controls the robot on UPnP platform

In each test case, the robot device started without any service platform loaded. Once the device started, service platforms were loaded at runtime to provide the corresponding services and supporting modules in the platform were replaced by others without interruption in the ongoing services. Replacement of the supporting modules was controlled through the management console. Figure 7 is a picture of the PDA that is used to monitor and control the robot.

6 Conclusions

We have presented a dynamic service binding framework that enables existing devices to support various standard service platforms. Existing devices can interoperate with other devices or services, once they are promoted to a service by our framework. They do not need any technical development for interoperation with others. Adding new service platform modules conformant to the interfaces specified by the framework is the only thing to do for the interoperation with outside world. If the service objects of the existing device were implemented in the standard C++ classes, they can be added to the framework without any modification to the source code.

This framework allowing dynamic change of supporting service platforms at runtime can be applied to other service areas as well as the embedded device applications. For example, it can be used to replace the software-defined radio [19] technology that replaces wireless communications circuits with software logic. It can also be used for integration of home appliances from different vendors.

References

1. Iwao, T., Amamiya, S., Zhong, G., Amamiya, M.: Ubiquitous computing with service adaptation using peer-to-peer communication framework. In: Distributed Computing Systems. The Ninth IEEE Workshop (2003)
2. IBM: Implementing an SOA using an Enterprise Service Bus, Martin Keen (2004)
3. Gilpin, M.: What Is An Enterprise Service Bus?, Integration Landscape (2004)
4. Thomas, N.: Extending Web Services with Asynchronous Message Delivery and Intelligent Routing (2004)
5. A Technical Introduction to the Devices Profile for Web Services, http://msdn-microsoft.com/
6. UPnP^{TM} Device Architecture (2000) http://www.upnp.org/ download/
7. W3CNote, WSDL(WebServices Description Language)1.1 (2001) http://www.w3c.org/ TR/WSDL/
8. Beatty, J., Kakivaya, G., Kemp, D., Kuehnel, C.T.: Web Services Dynamic Discovery, MSDN (2004)
9. WS-Metadata Exchange 1.1 (2006) http://www.sdn.sap.com/
10. W3C, SOAP(Service Object Access Protocol) (2000) http://www.w3c.org/
11. Web Services Eventing, http://www-128.ibm.com/
12. SOAP Message Transmission Optimization Mechanism, http://www.w3.org-/
13. Ning EFNG, M. Eng: S-Module Design for Software Hot-Swapping (1999)
14. Ning, F.: S-Module Design for software Hot Swapping Technology, Technical Report SCE-99-04, Systems and Computer Engineering, Carleton University (1999)

15. GCC_XML, http://www.gccxml.org/
16. Mule's Architecture Guide, http://mule.codehaus.org/Architecture+Guide
17. Gang, A.: Software Hot Swapping Techniques, Technical Report SCE-98-11, Systems and Computer Engineering, Carleton University (1998)
18. Roiser, S.: The SEAL C++ Reflection System, CHEP'04, Interlaken, Switzerland (2004)
19. Cook, P.G.: Overview and Definition of Radio Software Download for RF Reconfiguration in a Technical and Regulatory Context, Base Station Working Group (2002)

Design and Evaluation of Multitasking-Based Software Communications Architecture for Real-Time Sensor Networking Platforms

Kyunghoon Jung[1], Byounghoon Kim[1], Changsoo Kim[2], and Sungwoo Tak[1,*]

[1] School of Computer Science and Engineering, Pusan National University, San-30, Jangjeon-dong, Geumjeong-gu, Busan, 609-735, Republic of Korea
swtak@pusan.ac.kr

[2] Pukyong National University, Dept. of Computer Science, Busan, Republic of Korea
cskim@pknu.ac.kr

Abstract. Real-time wireless sensor networking platform should satisfy requirements of sensor networking features - efficient exploitation of limited resources and energy efficiency, real-time characteristics and scalability. Existing studies on sensor networking platforms, such as TinyOS and DCOS, have been focused on solving the maximization problem of exploitation of limited resources and the energy efficiency. Envisioned application scenarios applied in sensor networking platforms need to perform real-time sensing activity as well as provide good response time with task communication, and support the scalability to improve productivity. The proposed method is able to support task scheduling which meets deadlines of all the periodic tasks and provides aperiodic tasks with good average response time. It also supports the scalability by dividing the functionalities in sensor node into periodic and aperiodic tasks. Experimental results show that our method improves real-time characteristics of sensor networking platforms by means of guaranteeing to complete the execution of all the periodic tasks within their deadlines and having a good response time for aperiodic tasks.

1 Introduction

To develop real-time wireless sensor networking platforms, the requirements for sensor networking platform, real-time processing and scalability should be considered. One is to maximize the lifetime of hardware resources with low processing power, and limited memory and battery capacities in sensor node. In order to satisfy this, the miniaturization and low power technology of hardware, and the lightweight of software modules have been studied. Another is to provides deterministic and responsibility of real-time tasks. The deterministic and responsibility of tasks mean guaranteeing the completion of a task within a specific period and responding as fast as possible to an asynchronous event, which should be processed immediately, for the external stimuli respectively. In general, since the problem of optimizing the real-time task scheduling

* Corresponding author.

J. Indulska et al. (Eds.): UIC 2007, LNCS 4611, pp. 83–92, 2007.

proved to be NP-hard, heuristic methods which guarantee the deadlines of all the periodic tasks and provide aperiodic tasks with good average response time have been studied. The other is to optimize components of the sensor node to suit to the features and environment of sensor network platform. The support of the component based structure can be achieved through software modularity which divides tasks and functionalities in a sensor node such as kernel, communication protocol stacks and user applications. Existing studies on sensor networking platforms, such as TinyOS[1] and DCOS[2], have been focused on solving the maximization problem of exploitation of limited resources and the energy efficiency. Envisioned application scenarios applied in sensor networking platforms need to not only perform real-time sensing activity but also provide good response time with task communication, and support the scalability to improve productivity. In this paper, we propose task scheduling technique, meeting deadlines of all the periodic tasks and have a good response time for aperiodic tasks, for real-time sensor networking platforms. This paper is organized as follows. Section 2 presents the real-time sensor networking platform incorporating an efficient periodic and aperiodic task decomposition technique. In Section 3, the proposed technique is evaluated in terms of two significant, objective goals: average response time and processor utilization of periodic and aperiodic tasks. Section 4 concludes this paper.

2 Real-Time Sensor Networking Platform

Fig 1 shows work-flow of task sets composed of periodic and aperiodic tasks in the proposed real-time sensor networking platform. In fig.1, the proposed task scheduling technique consists of a set of periodic and aperiodic tasks and PATS (Periodic and Aperiodic Task Scheduler). The periodic task set consists of Sensing tasks, Application tasks and ARP Update task. Sensing tasks sense the environmental stimuli, send and receive the sensing data periodically. Application tasks perform their specific operations. In case of Application tasks, their properties may be periodic or aperiodic according to their own specific operations. ARP Update task, one of network protocol layer, updates the ARP table every 20 minutes. Aperiodic task set is made up of Application tasks, and the network tasks divided into TCP, UDP, IP and ARP tasks. Since these network tasks do not have their execution periods, they are included in aperiodic task set. In order to support bi-directional communication, the TCP task is decomposed into TCP-IN and TCP-OUT subtasks. The UDP task also is divided into UDP-IN and UDP-OUT tasks for the same purpose as the TCP task. The TCP-IN and the UDP-IN tasks receive packets, and the TCP-OUT and UDP-OUT tasks transmit packets. TCP timer operation that handles the packet retransmission and channel connection management is incorporated in the timer interrupt service routine since its time is much less than the context switching time of tasks. Since the ARP itself does not have real-time constraint except the ARP Update task, it can be included in a set of aperiodic tasks without the deadline of execution. Although TCP/IP protocol suite is heavy to be exploited to sensor nodes with limited resources, its architecture is well-known layered communication architecture and its layer functionality has been exploited to sink nodes which played a role in gateway connecting between sensor network and TCP/IP internet. Therefore, if our real-time task scheduling technique achieves good performance under the TCP/IP protocol suite environment, the performance of our technique will be acceptable under sensor node in which lightweight software communication architecture standardized is incorporated. The PATS is made up of SV (Schedulability Verifier), STM (Slack Time Manager), ATS (Aperiodic Task Scheduler), and PTS (Periodic Task Scheduler). In case of the STM, it is composed of STC (Slack Time Creator for aperiodic task) and STA (Slack Time Allocator) sub-functions for computing and allocating the processor idle time called the slack time. The PATS scheduling steps are as follows. Given a set of periodic tasks, the SV determines if it is schedulable. If the periodic task set is decided to be schedulable, the STC of the STM performs the computation of the slack time and stores it in the STT (Slack Time Table). Then, if the aperiodic tasks waiting for execution exist, the STA assigns the available slack time to an aperiodic task chosen by the ATS. The ATS schedules the aperiodic task after evaluating the slack time of the aperiodic task assigned by the STA. aperiodic tasks are scheduled in the FIFO (First-IN First-Out) policy. The PTS schedules a set of periodic and aperiodic tasks by the priority-driven policy. We make full use of the RM (Rate Monotonic) algorithm for periodic tasks and the Slack Stealing algorithm for aperiodic tasks [3-4].

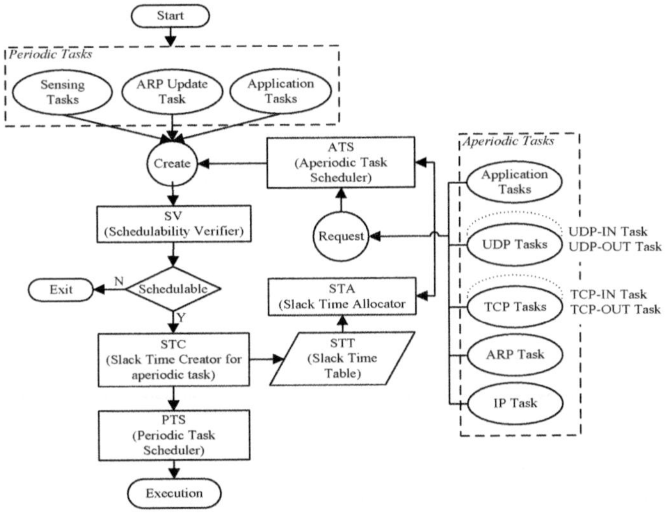

Fig. 1. Work-flow of periodic and aperiodic task sets in real-time sensor networking platform

SV (Schedulability Verifier) Module

The SV module determines whether each of periodic tasks can be schedulable or not to meet its deadline. Here are parameters used in the SV module. From our point of view, a task τ_i, is described by four nonnegative numbers: R_i *release time* or time that the task waits till its first request, C_i the *execution time*, T_i the *period* (time between τ's successive requests), and D_i the *deadline* (relative to a request time). A task set $\mathcal{T}$ is a collection of tasks $\mathcal{T} = \{\tau_1,\ldots,\tau_n\}$. Let n be the cardinal of $\mathcal{T}$. $\tau_i = (R_i, C_i, D_i, T_i)$. $W_i(t)$ denoted in equation (1) stands for the cumulative demands on the processor made by periodic tasks over $[0, t]$, where the value of t is derived from equation (5). We define $L_i(t)$ as the processor utilization of task τ_i. The condition of $L \le 1$ implies that given periodic tasks are schedulable.

$$W_i(t) = \sum_{j=1}^{i} C_j \cdot \lceil t/T_j \rceil \tag{1}$$

$$L_i(t) = W_i(t)/t \tag{2}$$

$$L_i = \min_{\{0<t\le T_i\}} L_i(t) \tag{3}$$

$$L = \max_{\{1\le i\le n\}} L_i \tag{4}$$

$$t = S_i = \{k \cdot T_j \mid j = 1,\ldots,i; k = 1,\ldots,\lfloor T_i/T_j \rfloor\} \tag{5}$$

Table 1. Processor utilization of periodic tasks

i	$\tau_i(T_i, C_i)$	t	$W_i(t)$	$L_i(t)$	L_i	L
1	$\tau_1(5, 2)$	5	$C_1 = 2$	0.40	***0.40***	
2	$\tau_2(10, 3)$	5	$C_1 + C_2 = 5$	1.00	1.00	
		10	$2C_1 + C_2 = 7$	0.70	***0.70***	
3	$\tau_3(40, 4)$	5	$C_1 + C_2 + C_3 = 9$	1.80	1.80	
		10	$2C_1 + C_2 + C_3 = 11$	1.10	1.10	
		15	$3C_1 + 2C_2 + C_3 = 16$	1.06	1.06	
		20	$4C_1 + 2C_2 + C_3 = 18$	0.90	0.90	
		25	$5C_1 + 3C_2 + C_3 = 23$	0.92	0.90	
		30	$6C_1 + 3C_2 + C_3 = 25$	0.83	0.83	
		35	$7C_1 + 4C_2 + C_3 = 30$	0.85	0.83	
		40	$8C_1 + 4C_2 + C_3 = 32$	0.80	***0.80***	***0.80***

For example, given a set of periodic tasks $\mathcal{T} = \{\tau_1:(0, 5, 2, 2), \tau_2:(0, 10, 3, 3), \tau_3:(0, 40, 4, 4)\}$, values of L_1, L_2, and L_3 calculated by equations (1) through (5) are 0.4, 0.7, and 0.8 respectively. Since the condition of $L \le 1$ is satisfied according as $L = \max(L_1, L_2, L_3) = (0.4, 0.7, 0.8) = 0.8$, the task set $\mathcal{T}$ is schedulable. In $\mathcal{T} = \{\tau_1:(0, 5, 2, 2), \tau_2:(0, 10, 3, 3), \tau_3:(0, 40, 4, 4)\}$, all possible values of $L_i(t)$ calculated by equation(1), (2), and (5) over i [1,3] are shown in Table 1. The values of L_1, L_2, L_3 described in equation (3) are as follows. $L_1 = \min(0.40) = 0.40$, $L_2 = \min(1.00, 0.70) = 0.70$, $L_3 = \min(1.80, 1.10, 1.06, 0.90, 0.83, 0.83, 0.80) = 0.80$. Since the condition of $L \le 1$ is satisfied according as $L = \max(L_1, L_2, L_3) = (0.40, 0.70, 0.80) = 0.80$, the task set $\mathcal{T}$ is schedulable.

STM (Slack Time Manager) Module

Here are parameters used in the STM module. Each task τ_i is a periodic stream of identical requests, and we denote the j-th request of τ_i by τ_{ij}. Consider a periodic request τ_{ij} which has $(j-1)T_i$ the ready time, D_{ij} the deadline, and C_{ij} the execution time. $\alpha_i(t)$ represents the total execution time of aperiodic tasks of which priorities are higher than or equal to priority i, where $0 \leq t \leq D_{ij}$. $P_i(t)$ represents the ready time of periodic tasks over $[0, t]$. $I_i(t)$ denotes the processor idle time or the execution time of tasks of which priorities are lower than priority i. A_{ij} represents the maximum slack time over $[0, C_{ij}]$, where $A_i(t) = A_{ij}$ and $C_{ij-1} \leq t \leq C_{ij}$. The maximum slack time over $[0, C_{ij}]$, $A^*(t)$, is estimated by equations (6) through (8).

$$W_i(t) = \alpha_i(t) + P_i(t) + I_i(t) \tag{6}$$

$$\min_{\{0 \leq t \leq D_{ij}\}} \{(A_{ij} + P_i(t))/t\} = 1 \tag{7}$$

$$A^*(t) = \min_{\{1 \leq i \leq n\}} A_i(t), \ C_{ij-1} \leq t < C_{ij} \tag{8}$$

For example, given a set of periodic tasks $\tau = \{\tau_1$:(0, 5, 2, 2), τ_2:(0, 10, 3, 3), τ_3:(0, 40, 4, 4)}, τ 's hyper period which implies the least common multiple is 40. Fig. 2 shows the slack time table of given τ including the value of $A^*(t)$. In Fig. 2, cells shaded in black represents that the processor is busy.

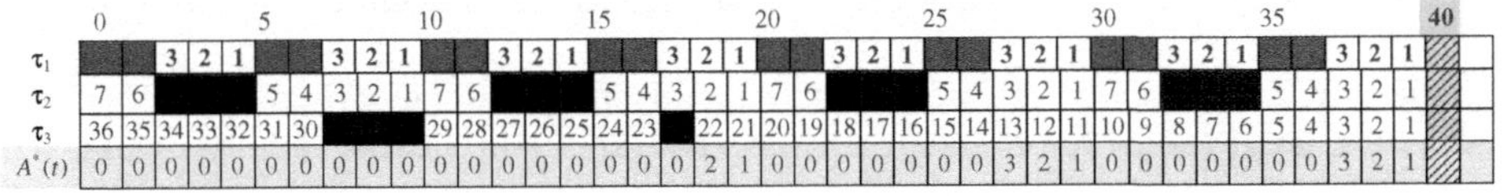

Fig. 2. STT (Slack Time Table) generated by the STM

ATS (Aperiodic Task Scheduler) Module

The ATS module schedules one of aperiodic tasks with their positive values in the STT. Suppose a set of periodic tasks $\tau = \{\tau_1$:(0, 5, 2, 2), τ_2:(0, 10, 3, 3), τ_3:(0, 40, 4, 4)}, an aperiodic task AT with 9 of its execution time. The priority of AT is assumed to be higher than that of τ_3. Fig. 3 shows the task allocation table generated by scheduling tasks in the priority-driven policy. In case of the priority-driven policy, τ_3 misses its deadline because of the interference execution of the aperiodic task AT. Fig. 4 shows the task allocation table generated by the STM modules, which are proposed in this paper. In Fig. 4, since the AT executes in the slack time assigned to the STT, τ_3 meets its deadline and the AT completes its execution in the next hyper period.

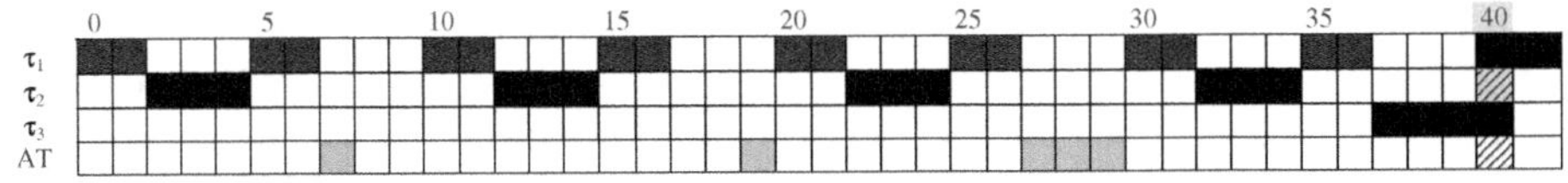

Fig. 3. Task allocation table without based on the priority-driven policy

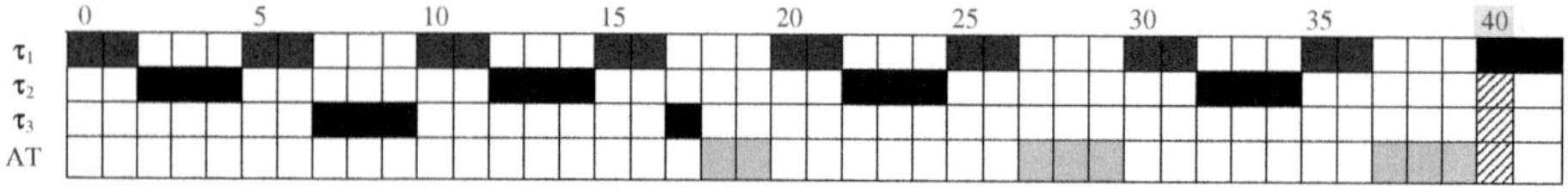

Fig. 4. Task allocation table based on the STM

PTS (Periodic Task Scheduler) Module

The PTS module schedules periodic and aperiodic tasks according to follows: The priority of periodic tasks is assigned by the RM algorithm and that of aperiodic tasks is specified according to its urgency and criticality. The PTS module elects the task with highest priority from a set of periodic and aperiodic tasks passed successfully through SV, STM, and ATS modules.

3 Experiments

We experimented on our proposed technique with the CC2420DB sensor mote for hardware platform, and the version 2.52 of uC/OS[5] and the version 0.9 of uIP[6] for software platform. The CC2420DB sensor mote contains CC2420 which is the IEEE802.15.4 compliant RF transceiver, 8-bit microcontroller, one internal sensor and two external sensors, a temperature sensor, a light sensor, and a humidity sensor, we installed. uC/OS and uIP has been well-known for a micro embedded operating system and full TCP/IP software communication architecture for 8-bit micro-controllers respectively although they are not designed for full real-time processing. Hence, uC/OS and uIP is implemented in this paper are modified to support the software architecture for efficient periodic and aperiodic task scheduling using our task scheduling and decomposition method. In this section, we compare the Case-I, original version 2.52 of uC/OS incorporating original version of uIP, with two versions of experimental models, the Case-II and the Case-III, developed in this paper so as to evaluate the performance of our task scheduling method. The Case-II is original version of uC/OS incorporating the TCP/IP protocol which is decomposed into tasks. We develop the multi-task based TCP/IP software communications architecture by exploiting the version 0.9 of uIP. The Case-III is the modified version of uC/OS incorporating the proposed real-time task scheduling method and supporting the multi-task based TCP/IP software communications architecture (See Fig. 1). In case of the Case-III model containing the technique described in Section 2, it guarantees that all the periodic tasks are able to complete their executions within their deadlines and aperiodic tasks make a good average response time. In addition, Case-II and Case-III unlikely Case-I are able to provide multiple TCP/UDP connections simultaneously. To evaluate the performance of Case-I, Case-II and Case-III, we measure the code size of modules, response times and processor utilizations of the sets of periodic and aperiodic tasks by executing each one of them on two CC2420DB motes communicating with each other. Table 2 presents the basic information set for scheduling application and networking tasks, either periodic or aperiodic task, running on the Case-I/II/III models. Application tasks are composed of three sensor tasks and one Big_AP task having a big execution time. The Big_AP has 200ms of execution time and its request occurs every 300ms in order to give a harmful influence on the remaining aperiodic tasks and all the periodic tasks. In experiments, Case-I that has no function of real-time task management excludes the Big_AP task on its execution environment. Sensor Task 1 which senses the temperature blinks a LED when the temperature exceeds the specified threshold. Sensor Task 2 transmits the strength value of current light to the remote CC2420DB mote via the TCP protocol. Sensor Task 3 performs the transmission of the value of the current humidity via the UDP protocol. The transmitted or received sensing data frame has the format of 1-byte ID field and 4-byte data field. In case of Sensor Task 2, 45 bytes made up of 40-byte TCP/IP header and 5-byte sensing data frame are transmitted. In case of Sensor Task 3, the size of the sensing data frame transmitted is 33 bytes consisting of 28-byte UDP/IP header and 5-byte sensing data frame. The priority of each task is assigned as in Table 2. Table 3 shows the code and data size of Case-I, Case-II, and Case-III as well as those of periodic and aperiodic tasks.

Table 2. Task set of application and networking protocol tasks running on the Case-I/II/III

Task Name		Priority	Period (ms)	Execution Time (ms)		
				Case-I	Case-II	Case-III
Application Tasks	Sensor Task 1	16	200	40	40	40
	Sensor Task 2	17	300	10	10	10
	Sensor Task 3	18	400	10	10	10
	Big_AP Task for Case-II/Case-III	10	*Aperiodic*	*None*	20	20
Networking Protocol Tasks	ARP Task	9	*Aperiodic*	10	10	10
	IP Task	10	*Aperiodic*	2.7	2.7	2.8
	TCP-OUT Task	11	*Aperiodic*	3.1	3.3	3.3
	TCP-IN Task	12	*Aperiodic*	3.0	3.0	3.0
	UDP-OUT Task	13	*Aperiodic*	3.0	3.0	3.0
	UDP-IN Task	14	*Aperiodic*	3.0	3.0	3.0
	ARP Update Task	19	500	10	10	10

Table 3. Code and data size of periodic/aperiodic tasks and Case-I / II / III

Task Type	Code Size (Bytes)	Data Size (Bytes)	Experimental Model	Code Size (Kbytes)	Data Size (Kbytes)
Sensor Task 1	164	*None*	Case-I	2.94	19.18
Sensor Task 2	556	*None*			
Sensor Task 3	152	*None*			
Big_AP Task	192	*None*	Case-II	7.08	25.69
ARP Update Task	178	*None*			
ARP Task	56	*ARP Table: 44*			
IP Task	594	*IP Input Queue: 544*			
TCP-IN Task	2808	*Control Block: 124* *Listen Block: 16*	Case-III	11.52	27.25
TCP-OUT Task	600				
UDP-IN Task	248	*UDP Packet Buffer: 40*			
UDP-OUT Task	248				

Total execution time is 10,000s from Fig. 5 to Fig. 9. Fig. 5 shows the average response time of Case-I, Case-II, and Case-III models where only Sensor Tasks 1, 2, and 3 executes in the application layer. The average response time of networking protocol tasks in the Case-III model is close to that of Case-I and Case-II. Besides, the Case-III meets deadlines of all the periodic tasks and simultaneously providing multiple communications via TCP and UDP protocols. Note that the Case-III requires additional overheads of both context switching of networking protocol tasks and real-time task management. Fig. 6 shows average response time of user and networking tasks. The performance of Sensor Tasks 1, 2, 3, and the ARP Update Task that run the Case-III is better than that of the Case-II. The Case-III meets deadlines of periodic tasks at any time at the cost of minimizing any interference from the Big_AP task. In the Case-III, STM and ATS modules described in Fig. 1 prevent aperiodic tasks from preempting periodic tasks. Therefore, the Big_AP Task in the Case-III produces the poor quality of performance. The deadline miss ratio of Sensor Task 1 and Sensor Task 2 are 1.6% and 0.01% respectively in the Case-II.

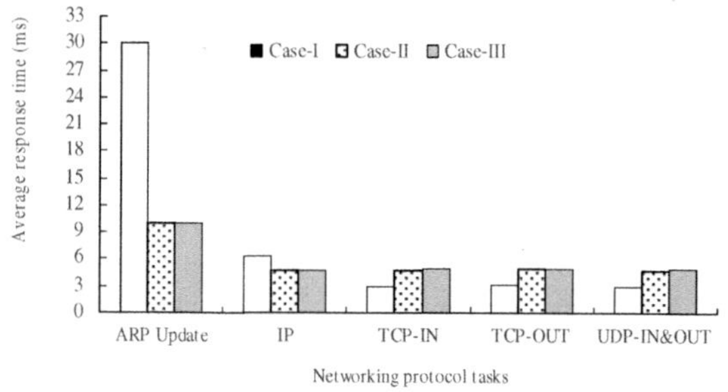

Fig. 5. Average response time of networking protocol tasks without the Big_AP Task

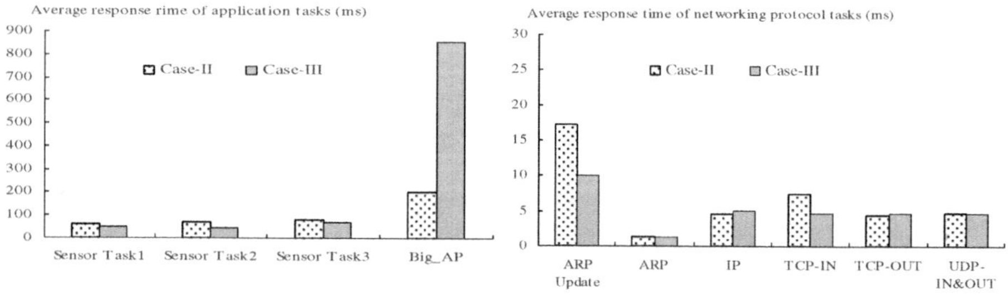

(a) Application tasks (b) Networking protocol tasks

Fig. 6. Average response time of periodic and aperiodic tasks

Fig. 7 shows the processor utilization of Case-II and Case-III models where Sensor Tasks 1, 2, 3, and the Big_AP Task run. The value of x axis represents 100 ticks per 1ms. The maximum processor utilization of Case-III is lower than that of Case-II since aperiodic tasks in the Case-III run only when the processor is idle. Therefore, Case-III would achieve lower electronic power than Case-II.

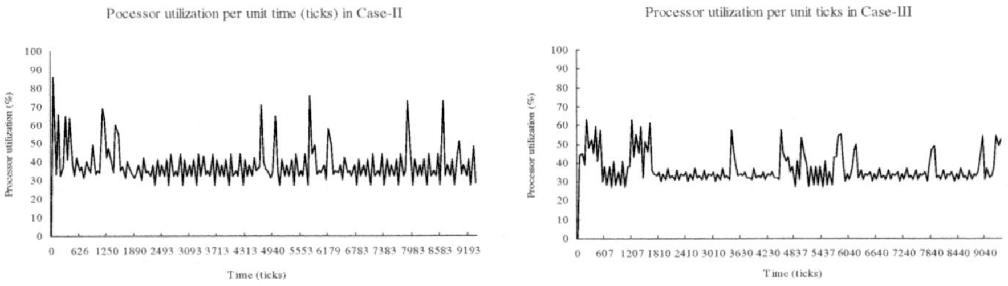

Fig. 7. Processor utilization of Case-II and Case-III with the Big_AP Task

Fig. 8 shows the processor utilization of Case-II and Case-III models where Sensor Tasks 1, 2, and 3 run. The processor utilization of Case-III is very close to that of Case-I.

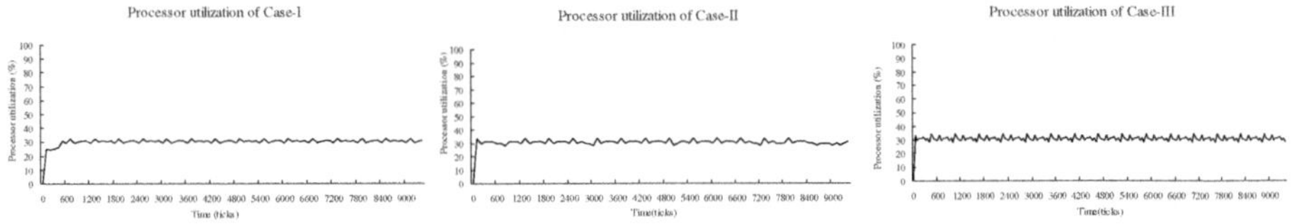

Fig. 8. Processor utilization of Case-I, Case-II, and Case-III without the Big_AP Task

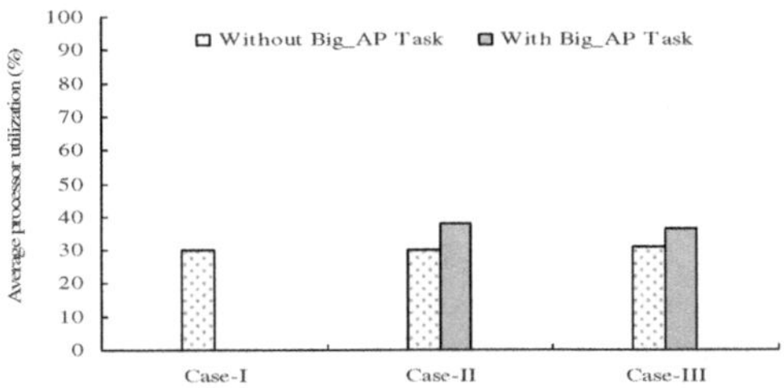

Fig. 9. Average processor utilization of Case-I, Case-II, and Case-III

Fig. 9 shows the average processor utilization. The average processor utilization of Case-III, where Sensor Tasks 1, 2, 3, and the Big_AP Task run, is a bit higher than that of Case-II due to the execution of the ATS module described in Fig. 1. However, the average processor utilization of Case-III is close to that of Case-I and Case-II when only Sensor Tasks 1, 2, and 3 execute. Besides, the packet loss ratio of Case-I, Case-II, Case-III amounts to less than 1%. Through extensive experiments, we show that the proposed approach is a feasible approach to assigning system components to a set of hybrid task set containing periodic and aperiodic tasks in real-time sensor networking platforms.

4 Conclusion

We propose task scheduling technique meeting deadlines of all the periodic tasks and providing aperiodic tasks with good average response time in real-time sensor networking platforms. Existing studies on real-time sensor networking platforms are mainly focused on solving the maximization of exploitation of limited resources and the energy efficiency instead of efficient task management of periodic and aperiodic task sets. Experimental results show that our task scheduling technique improves real-time characteristics of sensor networking platforms by means of guaranteeing to complete the execution of all the periodic tasks within their deadlines and having a good response time for aperiodic tasks. And our method supports scalability by decomposing functionalities of sensor nodes into periodic or aperiodic tasks.

Acknowledgement

This work was supported by the Korea Research Foundation Grant funded by the Korean Government (MOEHRD) (The Regional Research Universities Program/Research Center for Logistics Information Technology).

References

1. Hill, J., Szewczyk, R., Woo, A., Hollar, S., Culler, D., Pister, K.: System architecture directions for networked sensors. In: Proc. of 9th International Conference on Architectural Support for Programming Languages and Operating Systems (ASPLOS 2000), Massachusetts, USA, November 2000, pp. 93–104 (2000)
2. Hofmeijer, T.J., Dullman, S.O., Jansen, P.G., Havinga, P.J.: DCOS, A real-time light-weight data centric operating system. In: Proc. of International Conference on Advances in Computer Science and Technology, St. Thomas, USA, November 2004, pp. 259–264 (2004)
3. Lehoczky, J., Sha, L., Ding, Y.: The rate monotonic scheduling algorithm: exact characterization and average case behavior. In: Proc. of 10th Real Time Systems Symposium, California, USA, December 1989, pp. 166–171 (1989)
4. Lehoczky, J.P., Ramos-Thuel, S.: An optimal algorithm for scheduling soft-aperiodic tasks in fixed-priority preemptive systems. In: Proc. of 13th Real-Time Systems Symposium, December 1992, pp. 110–123 (1992)
5. Labrosse, J.J.: Micro C/OS-II. CMP Books, Kansas (2002)
6. Dunkels, A.: Full TCP/IP for 8Bit architectures. In: Proc. of the First ACM/Usenix International Conference on Mobile Systems, Applications and Services (MobiSys 2003), San Francisco, USA, May 2003, pp. 85–98 (2003)

Automatic Partitioning Technique for Flash Memory on Linux-Based Embedded Systems

Yunjae Lim[1], Young Jin Nam[2], Geel-Sang Yoo[1], and Dae-Wha Seo[1,*]

[1] School of Electrical Eng. & Computer Science, Kyungpook National University
{launius,love6140,dwseo}@ee.knu.ac.kr
[2] School of Computer & Information Technology, Daegu University
yjnam@daegu.ac.kr

Abstract. This paper proposes an automatic partitioning technique for flash memory in Linux-based mobile embedded systems. The proposed technique creates a set of flash memory partitions whose sizes are exactly the same as the software modules stored in the flash memory, resultantly maximizing the space for user applications. When updating software modules, the proposed scheme automatically reconfigures the partitions by moving the unchanged software modules and replacing the updated modules with the old ones. Moreover, it can facilitate software updates in flash memory by removing the need for human intervention. Our performance evaluations reveal that the proposed technique not only guarantees about 10% more space for the user area in the flash memory, but also increases the speed of the software module updates by eight times, as compared with a manual update.

1 Introduction

Linux has been used in many embedded systems because it offers excellent stability and great developmental facilities. Recently, due to the growth of hardware technology, developers came to use denser IC memories and more powerful microprocessors at low cost. As a result, a scaled-down version of a standard OS such as Linux, has been used widely in the embedded operating systems market [1]. Linux-based embedded systems require relatively less storage capacity than desktop PCs, and they usually employ flash memory as data storage for embedded OSs and applications. Since flash memory has advantages; smaller size, lower power usage, less noise and vibration, and greater durability, it is suitable for embedded systems [2].

Flash memory, as a type of electrically erasable programmable read-only memory (EEPROM), is non-volatile memory that maintains its stored data even after power is turned off. In a flash action, the memory systems can write pages of data containing multiple bits or erase blocks of data containing multiple pages. This is different than both hard drives and the earlier types of EEPROM that can write and erase data one byte at a time [3]. Flash memory, however, has a constraint that the erase operation of block units should be performed before the write operation of page units, because of its hardware feature.

* Corresponding Author.

J. Indulska et al. (Eds.): UIC 2007, LNCS 4611, pp. 93–102, 2007.

The hardware platform of embedded systems that use flash memory as a data storage, is very restrictive, as compared with desktop PCs. As shown in Tab. 1 that compares the hardware platforms of a set top box, a cellular phone, and a desktop PC, embedded systems use far less memory [4]. Moreover, flash memory's price per Mbyte is even higher than that of hard drives. In fact, flash memory per Mbyte currently costs three times as much as mini-drives' and 100 times as much as large-capacity drives'. Therefore, the efficient use of flash memory storage, which is costly and restrictive, is important in embedded systems.

Table 1. Comparisons of hardware platforms of embedded systems and a desktop PC

	Set Top Box (STB)	Cellular Phone	Desktop PC
CPU(frequency)	MIPS(30MHz)	ARM(50MHz)	Pentium(2,200MHz)
RAM size	32Mbyte	8Mbyte	512Mbyte
Flash/ROM	16Mbyte	4Mbyte	-
Storage HDD	15Gbyte	none	HDD 80Gbyte

In this paper, we present an automatic flash memory partitioning optimization technique for the efficient use of flash memory storage in Linux-based embedded systems. The proposed technique configures embedded Linux partitions to the exact data size of a bootloader, a kernel and a root filesystem without concerning the block size of flash memory, so that the amount of wasted space is minimized and user area is maximized. When flash memory partitions are modified by data updating, it reconfigures automatically each partition to optimal conditions without user's intervention for flexible updating. In addition, by resizing the JFFS2 user partition along with maintaining its stored data, the technique not only preserves user data in the user partition, but also reduces the update time of the modified embedded Linux and applications.

The remainder of this paper is organized as follows. Section 2 explains the configuration of flash memory partitions in common Linux-based embedded systems and analyzes problems in those systems. Section 3 describes the proposed automatic partitioning optimization technique for flash memory, and Section 4 evaluates the proposed technique. Finally, this paper concludes with Section 5.

2 Background

We, in this section, present the flash memory partitions and describe the design techniques of flash memory partitioning used in common Linux-based embedded systems. Next, the issues that are caused by the design techniques are analyzed.

2.1 Flash Memory Partitions

The flash memory of *N*MB size is usually partitioned, as shown in Tab. 2 [5]. The bootloader, kernel, root filesystem, user filesystem and parameters are stored in flash memory, and areas for each data are partitioned as software in the memory technology device (MTD) driver. The partitions can be accessed with device files such as **dev/mtdblock0**, **dev/mtdblock1**, and etc. Flash memory partitioning in the common design, is always set up as the values of a fixed address and size in the code of a bootloader and in the MTD driver of a kernel. The design technique allocates the partition size of bootloader, kernel, and root filesystem into the stored data size and configures the rest of the area to a user filesystem partition.

Table 2. Flash memory partitions in common Linux-based embedded systems

Partition Name	Description	Filesystem Type	Size
MTD0	Bootloader	none	256K
MTD1	Linux kernel	none	1~2M
MTD2	Root filesystem	Initrd, jffs, jffs2, cramfs	2.5~8M
MTD3	/usr/local and home directories	jffs2	($N-10.5$)~ ($N-4$)M
MTD4	Parameter	none	256K

Each partition size is allocated to block units, which are standard units of the erase operation in flash memory. This enables the read/write operations in those partitions, since flash memory has constraint in that an erase operation should precede a write operation in the area of flash memory. After all, flash memory partitions are aligned to the sizes of block units, so it is possible to calculate the minimum size of each partition as in Equation (1). In this equation, S_{data} is the stored data size and S_{align} is the partition alignment unit size. Flash memory block size, which is the partition alignment unit size, is determined by hardware structure, depending on each manufacturer or product. At this time, most flash memory has a block size between 64~256KB.

$$P_{\min} = \left\lfloor \frac{S_{data}}{S_{align}} \right\rfloor \times S_{align} \tag{1}$$

Embedded Linux and applications, which are stored in flash memory, can be updated to the modified size according to the needs of the system. Therefore, when configuring the other partitions, which exclude user area in flash memory, the partitioning technique is commonly used, which allocates additional blocks for larger partitions than the minimum-sized ones' (P_{min}). As a result, each partition acquires extra space.

2.2 Issues Related to Common Partitioning Techniques

Common partitioning techniques for flash memory, in Linux-based embedded systems, can be summarized in two cases; a technique that allocates the minimum number of flash memory blocks and a technique that allocates additional blocks. The first technique, which allocates flash memory partitions to the minimum size of block units depending on the data size, can reduce wasted memory space, but there exists a risk by performing data updates. Meanwhile, the second technique, which allocates the partitions to sizes larger than data size, can perform a flexible data update, but there exists the problem of an increase in wasted space.

Moreover, both cases have fragmentation issues in each partition, as shown in Fig. 1, so wasted space always occurs in flash memory. This fragmentation causes lower efficiency in flash memory. In addition, if the update data size is larger than the previous partition size, all flash memory area should be reconfigured. Then, the data loss of a user area is inevitable, and the execution time for the updates needs much more. Therefore, the next section describes the automatic partitioning optimization technique for flash memory, which not only minimizes wasted space, but supports each data update efficiently. The proposed technique also includes the function that is able to adjust the size of the JFFS2 user partition along with maintaining its stored data. From this, the technique derives the effect to reduce update time.

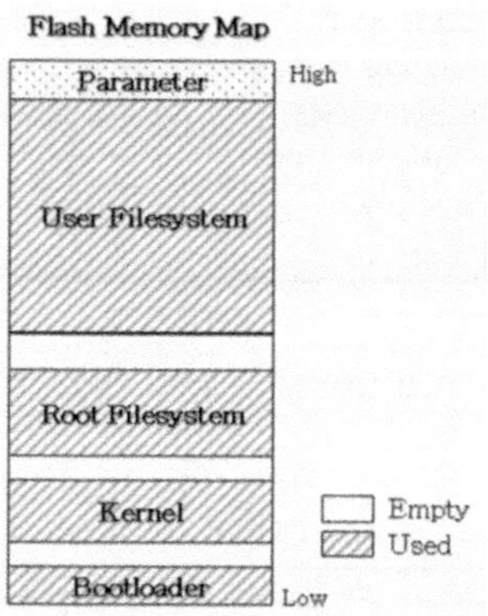

Fig. 1. Fragmentation of flash memory partitions

3 The Proposed Technique

This section describes the proposed automatic partitioning optimization technique for flash memory. Fig. 2 shows the software architecture (Partitioning-Optimizer) that executes automatic flash memory partitioning optimization. The Partitioning-Optimizer is implemented in the bootloader, and it consists of the Configuration Agent (CA) that configures the bootloader, kernel and root filesystem in SDRAM temporarily, the Partitioning-Planner that determines the address and size plan of the partitions, and the JFFS Scaler (UA-JS) and the Image Mover (UA-IM) of the Update Agent, which configures the user filesystem partition and the partitions of the bootloader, kernel, and root system in flash memory.

3.1 Image Downloader

In embedded systems that run a bootloader, bootloader images, kernel images, root filesystem images and user filesystem images are downloaded from host PCs to the target systems, and these images are stored in flash memory. In the Partitioning-Optimizer, these roles are performed by the Image Downloader that downloads an updated image to the SDRAM of a target system through TFTP. The file name of the updated image and the SDRAM address that is to be stored, are offered to the Image Downloader.

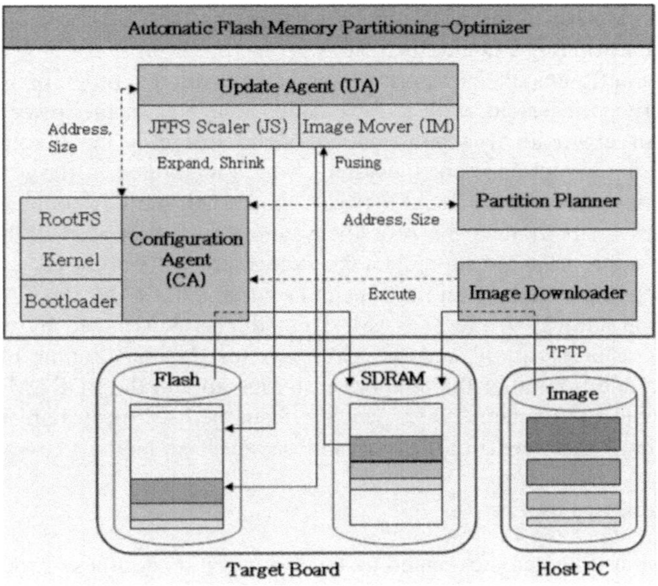

Fig. 2. Software architecture of the Partitioning-Optimizer

3.2 Configuration Agent (CA)

The image that is updated to a target system is downloaded first in the SDRAM. In the SDRAM, we can configure partitions by using the alignment units of byte size, without having to consider the block size of flash memory. The Configuration Agent (CA) carries out the configuration in such a manner. Fig. 3 shows the CA actions of the Partitioning-Optimizer. In other words, the CA configures the temporary storage area in the SDRAM before writing the updated image into flash memory. For the configuration, the CA processes each update action of the bootloader, kernel or root

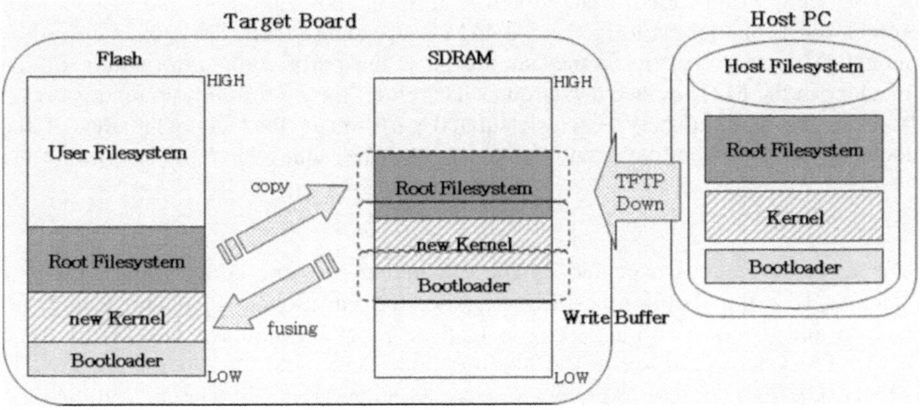

Fig. 3. Execution of the Partitioning-Optimizer

filesystem separately. To the CA, the updated image size is offered and it is used to execute the Partitioning-Planner by the CA.

The CA configures the temporary storage area to the order of the bootloader, kernel, and root filesystem, with a downloaded image from the lower address in the SDRAM. For example, if a newly downloaded image is the bootloader, the CA should copy the kernel and root filesystem, which are stored in flash memory, to the appropriate position in the SDRAM. If it is the kernel, the CA copies the bootloader and root filesystem. If it is the root filesystem, the CA copies the bootloader and kernel to the appropriate position, then the storage area is configured.

For the copying of data from flash memory into the SDRAM, the CA should assign the destination address in the SDRAM. This address is assigned by considering the data size of each partition, and the CA executes the Partitioning-Planner for the assigning. In addition, after the temporary storage area in the SDRAM is configured, the CA executes an Update Agent, which adjusts the user filesystem size and moves the bootloader, kernel and root filesystem areas into flash memory.

3.3 Partitioning-Planner

The Partitioning-Planner is executed by the CA and it determines the address and size plan of the partitions, which are modified after update action, by using hexadecimal calculations. Calculations are performed using the size of the new update image, the sizes of other partitions except for the updated partition, and the size of the partition alignment unit. The addresses for each partition are calculated to two values of the temporary storage area address in the SDRAM and the stored address in flash memory. The size of each partition is determined by the size of the stored data and the partition alignment unit.

Since each partition was configured in the temporary storage area of the SDRAM before fusing into flash memory, theoretically the alignment unit can be any size over 1Byte. When we use the alignment unit of S_{align}, the minimum size of partition (P_{min}) is determined by a prior Equation (1). In Equation (1), if we use a smaller S_{align}, we can acquire more exactly same area size with data size. It, however, is appropriate to use more than 1KB for the simplicity of memory address calculations.

For booting embedded Linux stored in flash memory, the bootloader should copy kernel and root filesystem to the SDRAM and execute them. Moreover, in order to mount flash memory, the kernel should have the partitioning information of flash memory in the MTD device driver code. Therefore, the Partitioning-Planner stores the address and size values of each calculated partition in the parameter area of flash memory, then the bootloader and kernel can read the values when they are performed.

3.4 Update Agent

The Update Agent is executed by the CA and it uses the address and size values calculated by the Partitioning-Planner. After the Partitioning-Planner calculates the address and size of partitions, first, the Update Agent JFFS Scaler (UA-JS) configures a user filesystem partition to the modified size, and then, the Update Agent Image Mover (UA-IM) configures the bootloader, kernel and root filesystem partitions.

The Update Agent JFFS Scaler (UA-JS) expands or shrinks the user filesystem partition, which was designed by JFFS2, while maintaining its stored data, as shown in Fig. 4. A JFFS2 file system operates with a scheme that scans the entire physical medium of flash memory, allocates inode cache structures, and builds the full map of data for each inode, when a kernel mounts the flash memory [6]. Therefore, the UA-JS allocates additional free blocks for the expansion of the partition. The free blocks are created by executing an erase operation at the additional blocks for expansion. When the partition shrinks, the data stored in the removed blocks moves into other free blocks in the partition. To find free blocks in the partition, the UA-JS sequentially scans the partition of flash memory with an examination of the JFFS2 common node header, as shown in Fig. 5. After that, the UA-JS determines whether the node is free or used.

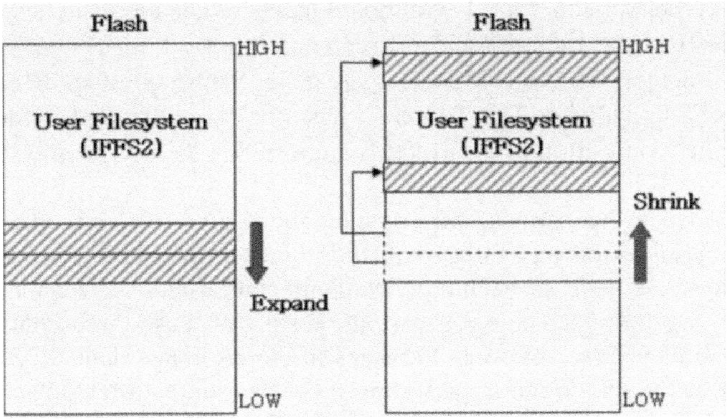

Fig. 4. Expansion and shrinkage of a user filesystem partition

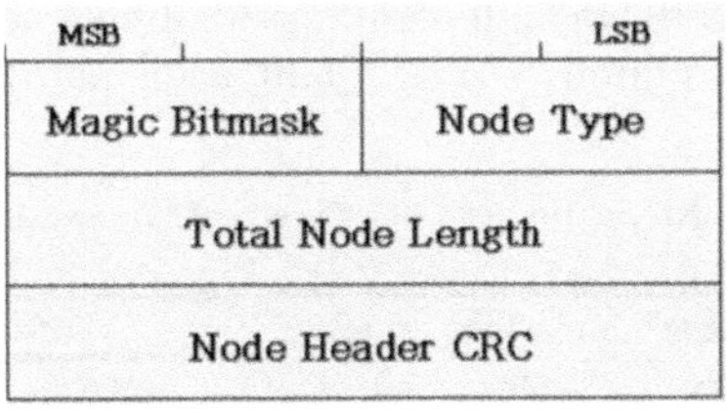

Fig. 5. JFFS2 Common node header [7]

The Update Agent Image Mover (UA-IM) performs a fusing action, which writes the data of the temporary storage area in SDRAM into flash memory. From this, the UA-IM configures the partitions of the bootloader, kernel, and root filesystem in flash memory, as shown in Fig. 3. The write operation uses the write buffer of the same size with a block of flash memory. Since the UA-IM is executed on a bootloader, it writes sequentially the data from the lower address parts, except bootloader blocks of the flash memory. In the end, the UA-IM performs a write operation into the boot blocks. When the UA-IM writes data into the boot blocks, it takes several steps. First, the UA-IM unlocks the write protection of the boot blocks. Second, it writes the data, and finally, locks the write protection again.

If all partitions are updated in flash memory, a kernel can mount flash memory through the known information of the partitions in the MTD device driver. Therefore, the MTD device driver is modified to load the values of `struct mtd_partition` from the parameter area of flash memory, when the kernel is executing.

4 Performance Evaluation

In this section, we evaluate the performance of the proposed automatic partitioning optimization technique for flash memory. To implement and evaluate the proposed technique, we used a T-Box Xt embedded board, a bootloader based on BLOB [8], and a Linux kernel version 2.6.8.1 with board patches. The hardware specifications of the T-Box Xt include Intel PXA255 Xscale processor, Intel StrataFlash E28F128 NOR flash memory 32M(16MB×2) [9], and Samsung K4S561632 SDRAM 64M(32MB×2). In addition, The T-Box Xt has a block unit size of 256KB because it uses the parallel connection of two Intel Starata E28F128 flash memories for a 32bit bus.

For performance evaluations, we compare the results of the proposed automatic partitioning optimization technique with the common partitioning of the embedded platform that is used for the technique implementation and the manual partitioning optimization, one by one. Table 3 shows the results of these three configurations. In Table 3, the "Image Size" presents the sizes of stored image data, "Common" is the size of partitions in the common partitioning configuration, "Manual" shows the size of partitions in manual partitioning, "Automatic" represents the size of partitions in automatic partitioning, and "Offset" gives the address of flash memory partitions.

First, the common partitioning of the embedded platform that is used for performance evaluation, is the design technique that allocates additional blocks to the larger, rather than the minimum size(P_{min}) of each partition in general embedded

Table 3. Size comparison of flash memory partitioning

Partition Name	Descrip-tion	Image Size	Common Size	Manual Size	Automatic		Efficiency (Size, Rate)
					Offset	Size	
MTD0	Boot-loader	36K (+2K)	256K	256K	0x00000000	38K	−218K (85%)
MTD1	Linux kernel	1330K	2048K	1536K	0x00009800	1330K	−(206~718K) (13~35%)
MTD2	Root filesystem	2442K	4096K	2560K	0x00156000	2442K (+30K)	−(88~1624K) (3~40%)
MTD3	User filesystem	13056K	26112K	28160K	0x003B8800 (+0x00007800) 0x003C0000	28672 K	+ (512~ 2560K) (2~10%)
MTD4	Parameter	–	256K	256K	0x01FC0000	256K	0
Total	–	16866K	32768K	32768K	–	32768 K	–

systems. In this case, each partition has extra space and it can support a flexible data update, however, the problem is that wasted space is increased among the partitions.

Second, the manual partitioning optimized manually by a user, is the design technique that allocates each partition to the P_{min} of the block units depending on data size. In this case, with a decrease in the wasted areas among partitions, we could derive the effects of increasing user areas by as much as 2048K(28160K - 26112K). The problem, however, is that high risk is associated with data updates. If update data are larger than the pre-defined partitions, all areas of flash memory should be reconfigured.

The automatic partitioning that employs the proposed optimization technique, configures partitions using a 1KB alignment unit(S_{align}). In this case, we configured the partitions of the bootloader, kernel and root filesystem to the smallest size, for other design techniques, and we could increase the user area by as much as the decreased area of those partitions. As partitioning design techniques, we derived the effects by increasing the user area from the minimum 512KB to more than 2.5MB. Between the root filesystem and user filesystem, there is an empty area of 30KB. This is because we set the start address of the user partition to the alignment of block units for a readable and writeable user partition. The automatic partitioning optimization technique module, which is implemented on the bootloader, is a little overhead in size. However, the increased bootloader image, as a result of implementation, about 2KB, was well within an acceptable level and could be ignored.

Moreover, since the automatic partitioning optimization technique maintains the stored data in the JFFS2 user partition, it does not have the loss of user data and it significantly reduces update time. Table 4 compares the execution times for the configuration of all partitions in flash memory. To update data and configure partitions by executing the automatic partitioning optimization technique, a constant period of about 50 seconds is needed. When we consider that the manual update for all area of flash memory requires more than 6 minutes, the amount of time has been significantly reduced. This is because partitioning time in flash memory depends on the writing data size. The automatic partitioning optimization technique requires only 4M of writing, on the other hand, the partitioning for all areas of flash memory requires 32M of writing.

Table 4. Execution time of flash memory partitioning

	Manual	Automatic
Execution Time	> 400 sec	50 sec

5 Concluding Remarks

In this paper, for the efficient use of flash memory in Linux-based embedded systems, we implemented an automatic flash memory partitioning optimization technique and evaluated its performance. The proposed technique allocates the size of each partition to the exact data size without concerning block size in flash memory. As a result, we could derive the effects of increasing user area from a minimum of 512KB to more than 2.5MB in large quantities, as compared with others partitioning design techniques; that is, 10% more space for the user area in the flash memory. Moreover, the proposed scheme could speed up the software module updates by eight times, as compared with a manual upgrade.

Acknowledgements. This research was in part supported by the Center for Embedded Software Technology, and by the MIC(Ministry of Information and Communication), Korea, under the ITRC(Information Technology Research Center) support program supervised by the IITA(Institute of Information Technology Assessment) (IITA-2006-C1090-0603-0045), and by the Daegu University Research Grant, No. 20060242.

References

1. Santo, S.: Embedded Battle Royal. IEEE Spectrum 38, 36–41 (2001)
2. Chiang, M., Lee, P., Chang, R.: Managing Flash Memory in Personal Communication Devices. In: Proc. of IEEE Symposium on Consumer Electronics, pp. 177–182. IEEE Computer Society Press, Los Alamitos (1997)
3. Lawton, G.: Improved Flash Memory Grows in Popularity. IEEE Computer 39, 16–18 (2006)
4. CE Linux Forum: SystemSizeSpec_R2. http://tree.celinuxforum.org/pubwiki/moin.cgi/SystemSizeSpec_5fR2
5. Brake, C., Sutherland, J.: Flash Filesystems for Embedded Linux Systems. ELJOnline (2001)
6. JFFS2: The Journalling Flash File System, version 2. http://sourceware.org/jffs2/
7. Woodhouse, D.: JFFS: The Journalling Flash File System. Ottawa Linux Symposium (2001)
8. SourceForge.net: Blob, a StrongARM Boot Loader, http://sourceforge.net/projects/blob/
9. Intel Corporation: 3 Volt Intel StrataFlash Memory, http://www.intel.com/

Distributed Processing in Wireless Sensor Networks for Structural Health Monitoring

Miaomiao Wang[1,2], Jiannong Cao[2], Bo Chen[3], Youlin Xu[3], and Jing Li[1]

[1] Department of Computer Science,
The University of Science and Technology of China, Hefei, Anhui, China
[2] Internet and Mobile Computing Lab, Department of Computing,
The Hong Kong Polytechnic University, Kowloon, Hong Kong
[3] Department of Civil and Structural Engineering,
The Hong Kong Polytechnic University, Kowloon, Hong Kong
{csmmwang,csjcao}@comp.polyu.edu.hk,
{02902410r,ceylxu}@polyu.edu.hk, lij@otcaix.iscas.ac.cn

Abstract. Wireless Sensor Networks (WSNs) have found many applications in a variety of ubiquitous computing environments. One of the key applications is Structural Health Monitoring (SHM) which seeks to monitor the functionality and detect the possible damages of large civil engineering structures, by measuring the structural responses to ambient or forced excitation. WSNs are a promising new technique for SHM, but the contradicting considerations on the unique characteristics of WSNs and the inherent requirements of SHM pose challenges for practical implementation. Distributed processing in WSNs can help reduce energy consumption, make efficient use of network bandwidth, and improve system response time. In this paper, we analyze the design issues of WSN-based SHM, and propose distributed processing architecture with algorithms. Results of performance the evaluations using both simulation and emulation demonstrate the effectiveness of our proposed approach.

Keywords: Ubiquitous Computing, Wireless Sensor Network, Distributed processing, Structural Health Monitoring.

1 Introduction

In recent years, the emerging wireless sensor networks (WSNs) have attracted a lot of attentions from both academic and industrial communities [1]. In this paper, we focus on WSN applications in advanced structural health monitoring (SHM), where WSNs can be used to monitor the functionality and safety and detect the possible damages of large civil engineering structures, such as tall buildings and long distant span bridges, under harsh environments [2].

Traditionally, structural engineers use wired data acquisition systems to collect data to the back end-server for centralized processing. Compared with traditional wired structural monitoring system, WSN-based SHM offers several advantages. First, low cost WSN instrumentation promises dense deployment of wireless sensors, which can increase the accuracy of the collected SHM data. Second, there is no need for fixed system infrastructure, bring with fast and flexible deployment, and easier maintenance.

J. Indulska et al. (Eds.): UIC 2007, LNCS 4611, pp. 103–112, 2007.

Inspired by these advantages, WSN-based SHM has attracted considerable attentions in the recent years [2-6]. Although existing works have demonstrated the feasibility of structural data collection using WSNs, research is still in a preliminary stage. In addition to the issues in ordinary WSN-based monitoring applications, SHM involves a larger amount of data with the requirements on high quality and reliability. Consequently, how to transmit and process the data yet taking into consideration the unique characteristics of WSNs is a challenging problem to solve.

Distributed in-network processing by collaborative sensor nodes is a paramount approach to solving the above problem. First, SHM applications always involve with a large amount of raw data. Distributed processing can help minimize the amount of data to be transmitted for system maintenance by only yielding and storing interesting information. Second, wireless radios generally consume the greatest amount of energy from portable batteries. Distributed processing can be seen as a means of minimizing energy consumption by transmitting only the partially processed results so as to prolong the network life. Third, SHM requires on-line damage alarming. Distributed processing can help reduce the system response time by processing the collected data in-time rather than delaying the processing to the back-end computing. It can also help improve the reliability by reducing the amount of data to be transmitted.

However, design of efficient distributed processing algorithms for SHM is not trivial. Above all, many traditional SHM algorithms are inherently centralized. How to adapt these algorithms to a distributed context requires a careful consideration. Next, many SHM algorithms are resource consuming. Distributed processing may need more computation on sensor nodes as well as information exchange between the nodes, which can decrease or even counteract the benefits it could bring. How to design capable and lightweight distributed algorithms to run on sensor nodes poses new challenges.

In this paper, we analyze the design requirements of WSN-based SHM applications and discuss the corresponding challenges in distributed processing. We propose a generic classification of processing techniques in WSNs, and a distributed processing framework for SHM. We also develop two algorithms based on our framework. The first algorithm, *distributed damage index detection (DDID)*, is based on a centralized algorithm proposed in our previous work [7]. We revise the centralized algorithm into a distributed version which is light-weight yet producing sufficiently accurate results. The second algorithm, *collaborative damage event detection (CDED)*, is based on the DDID algorithm to improve the reliability and accuracy of the damage report by exchanging the information between the sensor nodes. We have also evaluated our approach by both simulation and emulation. Results show that our approach can precisely detect the damages with lower energy consumption and acceptable time delay.

The remainder of this paper is organized as follows. Section 2 proposes a classification of processing techniques in WSNs and reviews the related works based on the classification. Section 3 proposes the distributed processing framework for SHM using WSN and, based on the framework, describes the design of the DDID and CDED algorithms. Section 4 reports the simulation and emulation results. Finally, Section 5 concludes the paper with a discussion of our future works.

2 Related Work

Generally speaking, processing in WSNs can be divided into three categories: 1) Centralized processing by which all the data are collected and then sent to a central node for processing, 2) Node level distributed processing by which raw data collected in the sensor nodes are pre-processed to obtain partial decisions, which are collected by the sink node for further processing to get a final decision, 3) Network level distributed processing by which final decisions are made in network through both node-level distributed processing and information exchange between the sensor nodes, and between the sensor nodes and the sink node. The following review of the existing related work is based on the above classification.

Research on applying WSN to SHM has been carried out for several years. Allen [8] described a dynamic software architecture that empowers the data repository to manage the processing of the response data collected by remote wireless sensors. Wong et al. [9] presented another approach to the software design of a data repository driven structural monitoring system. Both approach are based on centralized processing techniques.

Distributed processing for SHM at the node level includes compressing and pre-processing of raw data. Xu [6] studied the applicability of the wavelet-based compression techniques. Lynch [10] implemented the Fast Fourier Transform (FFT) algorithm in the wireless sensing unit. In both approaches, results are transmitted to the back-end server which performs damage detection and damage location separately by using modular analysis [11]. In this paper, we present the design of the distributed damage index detection (DDID) algorithm which is at the node level. Compared with the existing work, DDID is simpler and thus can save more resources. Furthermore, it is an online method and can detect multiple damages simultaneously. It can also determine the local damage extent by the index value.

Distributed processing at the network level has attracted attentions in the recent years. Wang [12] proposed the AR-ARX approach for SHM using pattern recognition techniques. The approach involves with the node level processing as well as collaboration between the sink node and the sensor nodes. However, it is somewhat resource consuming and has low scalability. Closest in spirit to our work, Cao [13] presented a de-centralized processing strategy for SHM. A two-tier hierarchical strategy is proposed in which adjacent sensors are grouped together to form sensor communities, and a damage detection method is employed to evaluate the condition of local elements within the communities by utilizing locally measured information. The nodes at the lower tier transmit information to the nodes at the higher tier in a single hop. Compared with this work, our algorithms also use a two-tier structure, but at the lower tier within a group, our CDED algorithm supports multi-hop information exchange between nodes. Owing to the use of multi-hop mechanism, our system can achieve more flexible and dense deployment. Furthermore, CDED makes use of the damage candidates produced by DDID, and can help eliminate false damage reports through the negotiation between the nodes and locate the damage by using related sensor node IDs. The higher tier of our system is organized into a mesh overlay, through which damage reports can be consolidated and transmitted efficiently and reliably even in a large scale network.

3 Distributed Processing for SHM in WSN

In this section, we first introduce our framework of distributed processing for SHM, and then describe the proposed distributed algorithms in detail. Our intention is not to devise novel SHM techniques but to show how to redesign exiting SHM techniques to leverage a distributed processing approach in WSN.

3.1 Framework of Distributed Processing for SHM

The design of our distributed algorithms is based on a two-tier system model. The first tier consists of sensor nodes clustered into groups, and the second tier is an overlay consisting of the master nodes of the groups. The main function of this overly layer is for large scale data transmission and reliable data delivery.

Figure 1 shows our distributed processing framework for SHM. Every sensor node inspects the raw data and determines the damage candidates by using the DDID algorithm. Once the candidates are captured, the sensor nodes in a group will use the CDED algorithm to cooperatively decide the damage report containing the information about the location, scale, and index of the damage. Then, the master nodes of all the groups will exchange their damage reports to obtain a consolidated damage report, which will be transmitted to the back-end server, where damage alarm or other applications will be executed.

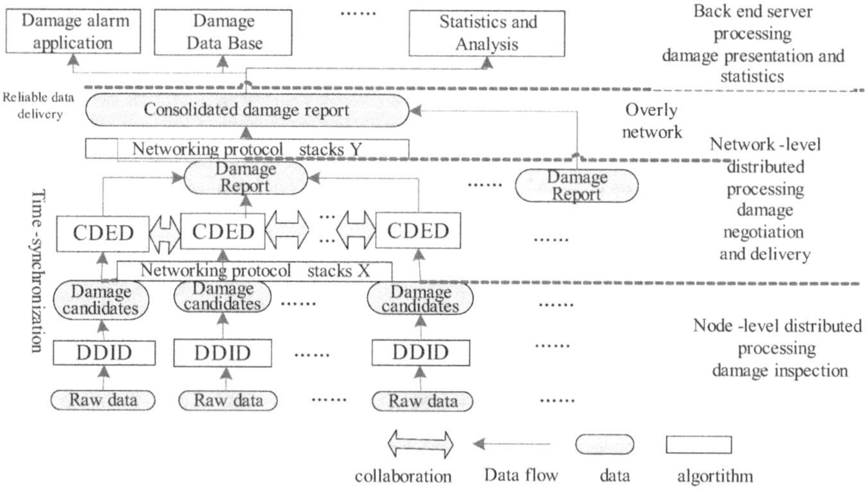

Fig. 1. Distributed processing framework for SHM

The time synchronization and reliable data delivery mechanisms in the framework can be implemented respectively by using suitable existing techniques. Within a group, a dense deployment with a multi-hop mechanism is needed since damage negotiation needs redundant data. For cooperation among the groups, large scale, timely and reliable data delivery is needed for delivering the consolidated damage report.

3.2 Distributed Processing Algorithms for Damage Detection

The design of distributed processing algorithms is based on our previous work [7], where a centralized algorithm is used in the wired SHM system for damage detection. The basic idea of the centralized algorithm is that the sudden changes of structural stuffiness associated with the events, such as weld fracture and brace breakage, will cause a discontinuity in the acceleration response time histories recorded in the vicinity of damage location at the damage time instant. Processing of the algorithm includes three phases: (1) the server continuously collects acceleration values from all the sensors, (2) the server calculates the damage indexes of all the sensors based on the acceleration values, and (3) the operator compares the index values of all the sensors and determines the damage location.

To develop the distributed version of this algorithm, we let the wireless sensor nodes to compute the damage indices. Two issues need to be considered: how much information should still be sent back to the server in order to ensure the energy efficiency as well as result precision, and how to automate the decision on the existence, location, and extent of damages which is originally made through human interference.

The distributed version of the algorithm consists of two algorithms: DDID and CDED. To address the first issue, DDID is used by individual sensor nodes to identify the damage candidates, which are the only information that might be sent back to the server. Considering the constraints in the processing and the storage capabilities of the sensor nodes, we divide the processing into consecutive windows in time. Each window is of size *m* which defines the number of sets of raw data to be used for computing the candidates. We also define *n* as the steps to slide the window. m and n

```
m is the size of computing window; n is the size of sliding
step; T is the time between two samples; Candidate-num is
the candidate number;
Yi=< timeStep, acceleration >;
Candidate=< timesStep, damageIndex>;
Initialize: Set the Threshold to the nodes, set the value
    of m; Every node reports its positions relative to its
    master; Set as inspection_state;
Inspection:
    For (data (y_i) in computing window )
    {  T= timeStep of y_{i+1} - timeStep of y_i
       K_i=(y_{i+1} - y_i )/ T;
       DI_i=| (2K_i - K_{i-1} - K_{i+1}) |
       if (DI_i > Threshold) Candidate_num++;}
       if  (Candidate_num>=1)
          {  Turn to suspection_state;
             Silde the window by n steps;
             New round Inspection }
             Else { Slide the window by n steps;
                    New round Inspection;}
```

Fig. 2. DDID algorithm

```
proposal_msg = <Candidtate, NodeId>;
replay_msg = <disgree_msg|agree_msg>;
agree_msg= <index,NodeId>;
damage_report= array of <time_stamp,nodeId,index>;
While in suspection_state:
Prepare for decision Negotiation:
if(no proposal_msg queue)create a  proposal_msg queue;
if(no reply_msg queue)create a  reply_msg queue;
create a  proposal_msg;
Put the  proposal_msg into proposal_ queue;
Negotiation initialization:
if(message  in  proposal  queue)  send  proposal_msg  to
neighbors;
Set smelled as ture; timer setup;
Negotiation:
if(receive proposal_msg) {
       if (not smelled) set smelled as ture;
       Check  the Candidates in the proposal_msg queue;
       if  (corresponding  candidates is found)
       { send Agree_msg as replay_msg;
         Relay the proposal to un-smelled neighbors;}
       if (no corresponding  candidates is found)
        { send Disgree_msg as relay_msg;}}
  if (receive disgree_msg from all neighbors)
   {Discard the proposal; Turn to Inspection_State;}
  if (receive agree_msg from some neighbors)
    {consolidate the agree-messages to damage report;
    deliver   damage_report   to   sink;   Turn   to
    Inspection_State; }
  if (time_out) {reset timer; Turn to Inspection_State;}}
```

Fig. 3. CDED algorithm

will affect the response time of the system. The pseudo-code of the DDID algorithm is shown in Figure 2.

To address the second issue, the CDED algorithm is used by the sensor nodes to collaboratively determine the damage locations and indices without requiring human interference. The pseudo-code of the CDED algorithm is shown in Figure 3.

Each sensor node in our distributed algorithm has two states: *Inspection* and *Suspicion*. In the Inspection state, a sensor node executes DDID to inspect the candidates and, if found, changes to the Suspicion state. It then executes the CDED algorithm. First, it will set up a proposal message queue and a reply message queue for later use in negotiation. Then, it will wrap the candidates with its node id into a proposal message, and send the message to the neighboring sensor nodes in the group. When a sensor node receives a proposal message, it will mark itself as smelled, and check its proposal message queue. If it finds in the queue a candidate whose timestamp is close to the timestamp of the candidate in the proposal message, it will replies with an agree message and relays the negotiation process to its un-smelled neighbors so as to enlarge the detection scope and to determine the damage boundary. If no such candidate is found, the node will reply with a disagree message.

If a sensor node receives disagree messages from all its neighbors, it will discard its proposal as it has a false detection. This is because the sensor nodes are densely deployed and the sensing ranges of the neighbor nodes overlap, so when damage occurs, it should be detected by at least two sensors. When a node receives disagree messages from some of its neighbors and all neighbors are smelled, the node knows that it is on the boundary of the damaged area.

Since the communication may not be reliable, messages can get lost during transmission. To handle message loss, a timer is used to help decide the termination of the algorithm. Upon timeout, a new round of the algorithm execution starts.

In addition, DDID and CDED can support the detection of multiple damages. Since all the nodes can propose damage candidates, for non-overlapping damages, the damage negotiation process can be carried out independently at the same time. However, if two or more damages overlap, the compound effect of the damage can be detected.

4 Experiments and Evaluation

To evaluate our approach, we have performed both emulation using a prototype system and simulation using the Power TOSSIM simulation platform. The goal of emulation is to demonstrate the effectiveness of our design and lay the basis for the practical deployment. The goal of simulation is to gain insight of the benefits of distributed processing and the performance of the distributed algorithms in large-scale deployment.

4.1 Emulation

We have been developing a prototype of our system design. Following the design, the prototype also uses two-tier architecture. On the first tier, we use Berkeley's Motes as the sensor nodes. In the second layer we use TFAD-901 as the master nodes. TFAD-901 is our custom-made processing node which has higher capability for processing and communication. To evaluate the feasibility of the proposed approach, we conducted several sets of experiments with a five-story shear building model. The external excitation used is the first 20 second portion of the El-Centro 1940 earthquake ground acceleration (S-N component) with a peak amplitude 1.0m/s2.

Let us look at an example of a five-story building under seismic excitation. There are two groups of sensor nodes. The first group contains nodes #1, #2, and #3, and the second group contains nodes #4 and #5. Figure 4 shows the output of the DDID algorithm in each of the five sensor nodes. Damage candidates can be identified by monitoring the obviously high values. It is worth notice that Figures 4 (a) and 4(b) both describe the Index values of the sensor node #1. Figure 4(b) is a partial enlargement of Figure 4 (a). In fact, at the time around the 6th second, sensor node #1 proposed three candidates (using 1 as the threshold valve): 158.970 (6.000 sec), 315.090 (6.001 sec), 152.480 (6.002 sec). By using the CDED algorithm, the node sends messages to its neighbor sensor node #2 as shown in Figure 4(c). In the corresponding time interval, sensor node #2 also found three candidates: 1.04283 (6.000 sec), 2.25399 (6.001 sec), 2.24670 (6.002 sec). It relays the proposal to node #3, which refuses the proposal because it has found no candidate in the corresponding time interval see Figure 4(d). So sensor nodes #1 and #2 figure out that places near sensor node #1 has been damaged. Since in the same time interval sensor nodes #5 and #6 did not detect any candidate see Figure 4(e, f), the final report transmitted to the base station through the masters is the one from the nodes #1 and #2.

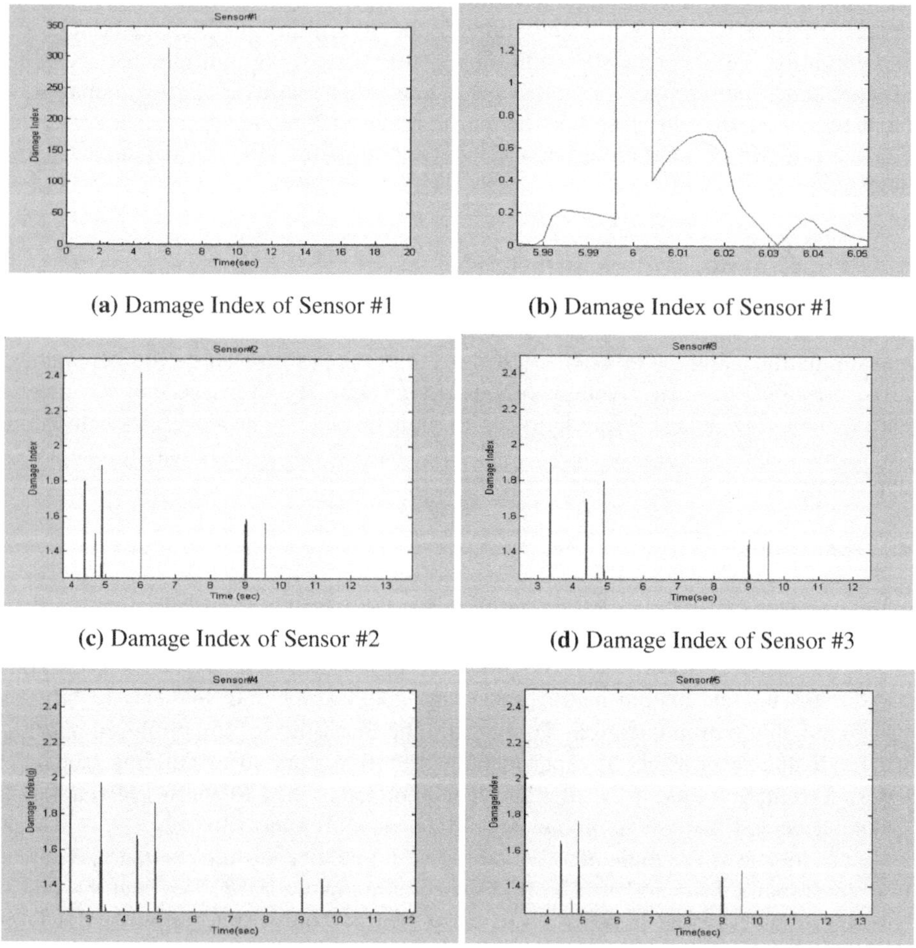

(a) Damage Index of Sensor #1

(b) Damage Index of Sensor #1

(c) Damage Index of Sensor #2

(d) Damage Index of Sensor #3

(e) Damage Index of Sensor #4

(f) Damage Index of Sensor #5

Fig. 4. Damage Index results of Sensor #1 to #5 by DDID algorithm under Seismic excitation

4.2 Simulations

Two performance metrics are used in the simulation. *Detection delay* is the time interval from the moment the damage occurs to the time when the damage report is generated at the master node. *Total energy consumption* is the sum of the energy consumption at all the sensor nodes. Since in our framework the overlay is considered to be powerful enough, we only consider the delay and energy consumption at the sensor nodes within one group.

The simulation is done using the Power-TOSSIM simulator. We have used the Mica2 communication stacks and energy model. In the simulation, the terrain size is set to 200m*200m, and the transmission range is set to 20m. The locations of the damages are assumed to be evenly distributed across the network. We performed 20 times of the simulation. The results shown here is the average of the results of all the simulation runs.

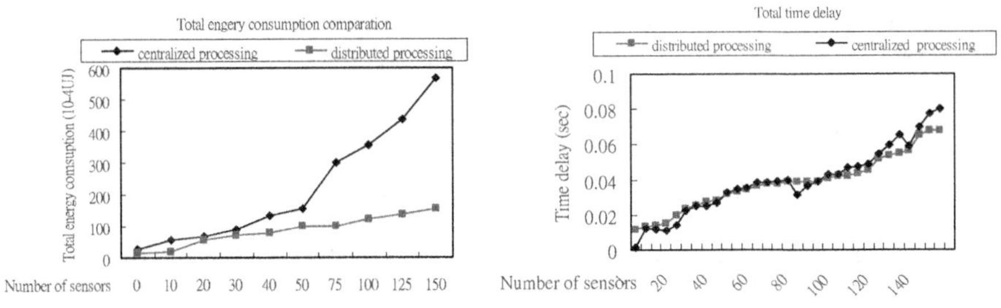

(**a**) Total energy consumption vs. Number of nodes (**b**) Time delay vs. Number of nodes

Fig. 5. Performance simulation results

Figure 5(a) shows the comparison of the performance of the centralized and distributed algorithms on the total energy consumption. Figure 5(b) shows the result on the time delay. We can see that, when the number of sensor nodes is small, the centralized method performs well, but when the network becomes large in scale, the distributed approach saves much more energy due to the decrease in the amount of data transmitted in the network. Also, the distributed approach leads to shorter detection delay, mainly because of the better use of bandwidth by transmitting only the useful damage report information rather other than the huge amount of raw data.

5 Conclusions and Future Works

Although WSN-based SHM is still in its infancy, it has been believed that wireless sensor networks are a very promising technology for structural health monitoring applications. In this paper, we proposed a distributed processing framework and the corresponding algorithms for WSN-based SHM. Results of the evaluation, including simulation and emulation, demonstrate the effectiveness of the proposed distributed approach.

In our future work, we will enhance the proposed distributed processing framework by carrying out real in-field deployment and conducting performance testing to further improve our existing methods and algorithms, and find new research issues.

Acknowledgement

This work is supported by Hong Kong Polytechnic University under the ICRG grant G-YE57and the large equipment fund G.61.27.D01B, and the National Hi-Tech Research and Development 863 Program of China under Grant No. 2006AA01Z231.

Reference

1. Akyildiz, I.F., et al.: Wireless Sensor Networks: A Survey. Computer Networks 38, 393–422 (2002)
2. Sohn, H., et al.: A Review of Structural Health Monitoring Literature: 1996-2001. Los Alamos National Laboratory Report, LA-13976-MS (2003)
3. Lynch, J.P., Loh, K.J.: A Summary Review of Wireless Sensors and Sensor Networks for Structural Health Monitoring. The Shock and Vibration Digest 38(2), 91–128 (2006)
4. Kottapalli, V.A., et al.: Two-Tiered Wireless Sensor Network Architecture for Structural Health Monitoring. In: Proc. SPIE International Symposium on Smart Structures and Materials (2003)
5. Paek, J., et al.: A Wireless Sensor Network for Structural Health Monitoring: Performance and Experience. In: Proc. IEEE Workshop on Embedded Networked Sensors, IEEE Computer Society Press, Los Alamitos (2005)
6. Xu, S.N. et al.: A Wireless Sensor Network for Structural Monitoring. In: Proc. ACM Conference on Embedded Networked Sensor Systems, November 2004, Baltimore, MD (2004)
7. Chen, B., Xu, Y.L.: A new damage index for detecting sudden stiffness reduction. Special session paper. In: Proc.1st International Conference on Structural Condition Assessment, Monitoring and Improvement, Perth, Western Australia, pp. 63–70 (2005)
8. Allen, D.W.: Software for Manipulating and Embedding Data Interrogation Algorithms into Integrated Systems. M.S. Thesis. Department of Mechanical Engineering, Virginia Polytechnic Institute and State University, Blacksburg, VA (2004)
9. Wong, J-M., Goethals, J., Stojadinovic, B.: Wireless Sensor Seismic Response Monitoring System Implemented on Top of NEESgrid. Health Monitoring and Smart Non-destructive Evaluation of Structural and Biological Systems IV, San Diego, CA, March 6–10, 2005, pp. 74–84 (2005)
10. Lynch, J.P., et al.: Embedding Damage Detection Algorithms in a Wireless Sensing Unit for Operational Power Efficiency. Smart Materials and Structures 800–810 (2004)
11. Chintalapudi, K., Paek, J.: Structural Damage Detection and Localization Using NetSHM. IPSN'06, April 19–21, 2006, Nashville, Tennessee, USA (2006)
12. Wang, Y., Lynch, J.P., Law, K.H.: A Wireless Structural Health Monitoring System with Multithreaded Sensing Devices: Design and Validation. In: Struct. Infrastructure Eng., Taylor & Francis, Abington (2006)
13. Gao, Y., Spencer Jr, B.F., Ruiz-Sandoval, M.: Distributed computing strategy for structural health monitoring. Structural control and health monitoring 488–507 (2006)

An Improved Fusion and Fission Architecture Between Multi-modalities Based on Wearable Computing

Jung-Hyun Kim and Kwang-Seok Hong

School of Information and Communication Engineering, Sungkyunkwan University, 300, Chunchun-dong, Jangan-gu, Suwon, KyungKi-do, 440-746, Korea
kjh0328@skku.edu, kshong@skku.ac.kr
http://hci.skku.ac.kr

Abstract. This paper introduces improved fission rule depending on SNNR (Signal Plus Noise to Noise Ratio) and fuzzy value for simultaneous multi-modality, and suggests the Fusion User Interface (hereinafter, FUI) including a synchronization between audio-gesture modalities, based on the embedded KSSL (Korean Standard Sign Language) recognizer using the WPS (Wearable Personal Station for the next generation PC) and Voice-XML. Our approach fuses and recognizes 65 sentential and 157 word language models that are represented by speech and KSSL, then translates the recognition result into synthetic speech and visual illustration (graphical display by HMD-Head Mounted Display) in real-time.

1 Introduction

Multi-modal interaction with Ubiquitous Computing needs to be carefully examined for its appropriate use within systems. The importance of this analysis is highlighted through the presentation of an experimental study that demonstrates that one modality could be implicit within another [1], and the functionality of a multi-modal interface can be fairly extensive, and applications may be found in a number of fields. In addition, wearable computers, which are worn on the body, have been applied to areas such as behavioral modeling, health monitoring systems, information technologies and media development. Government organizations, military, and health professionals have all incorporated wearable computers into their daily operations. Wearable computers are especially useful for applications that require computational support while the user's hands, voice, eyes or attention are actively engaged with the physical environment. One of the main features of a wearable computer is consistency. There is a constant interaction between the computer and user, ie. there is no need to turn the device on or off. Another feature is the ability to multi-task. It is not necessary to stop what you are doing to use the device; it is augmented into all other actions. These devices can be incorporated by the user to act like a prosthetic. It can therefore be an extension of the user's mind and/or body [2].

Consequently, we introduces improved a weight decision rule that fission the handling of haptic and aural modalities by coupling the WPS-based embedded KSSL recognizer with a remote Voice-XML user using SNNR and fuzzy value, for clear language processing in noisy environments, and suggests the FUI including a synchronization between audio-gesture modalities. In contrast to other proposed

J. Indulska et al. (Eds.): UIC 2007, LNCS 4611, pp. 113–122, 2007.

Multi-Modal interaction approaches, our approach is unique in two aspects: First, because the FUI provides different weight and feed-back function in individual (speech or gesture) recognizer, according to SNNR and fuzzy value, it may select an optimal language processing interface under a given situation or noisy environment, and can allow more interactive (natural) communication functions in noisy environment. Second, according as the FUI fuses and recognizes 62 sentential and 152 word language models that are represented by speech and KSSL, then translates the recognition result into synthetic speech and visual illustration (graphical display by HMD-Head Mounted Display) in real-time, it provides a wider range of personalized and differentiated information more effectively.

2 Web-Based Speech Recognition and Synthesis Using Voice-XML

Voice-XML is the W3C's standard XML format for specifying interactive voice dialogues between a human and a computer. For ASR-engine in architecture [3] of W3C's VXML 2.0, we used the HUVOIS solution that is Voice-XML-based voice software developed by KT Corp. in Korea for those with impaired sight that converts online text into voice and reads out the letters and words punched in through the computer keyboard, thus enabling them to use computers and the internet. The HUVOIS solution consist of HUVOIS-ARS based on HMM, TTS using Tri-phone unit and HUVOIS Voice-XML, and supports client-sever network, LSS(Load Share Server) and modular structure.

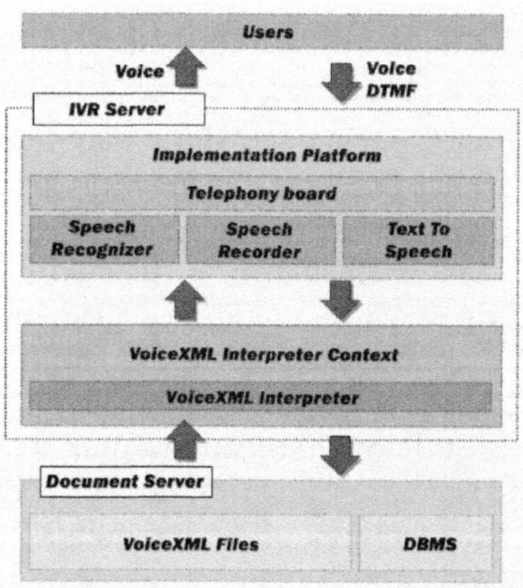

Fig. 1. The Voice-XML's architectural model

The Voice-XML's architectural model is shown in Fig. 1. A document server (e.g. a web server) processes requests from a client application, the Voice-XML interpreter, through the VXML interpreter context. The server produces Voice-XML documents in reply, which are processed by the Voice-XML interpreter. The Voice-XML interpreter context may monitor user inputs in parallel with the Voice-XML interpreter. For example, one Voice-XML interpreter context may always listen for a special escape phrase that takes the user to a high-level personal assistant, and another may listen for escape phrases that alter user preferences like volume or text-to-speech characteristics. The implementation platform is controlled by the Voice-XML interpreter context and by the Voice-XML interpreter.

3 WPS-Based Embedded KSSL Recognizer

For an improved KSSL recognition based on WPS and ubiquitous computing, we used 5DT company's wireless data gloves and Fastrak® which are popular input devices in the haptic application field, and utilized blue-tooth module for the wireless sensor network.

Wireless data gloves are basic gesture recognition equipment that can capture various haptic information (e.g. hand or finger's stooping degree, direction) using the fiber-optic flex sensor. In addition, the Fastrak® is a solution for the position/orientation measuring requirements of applications and environments, and is a 3D digitizer and a quad receiver motion tracker, making it correct for a wide range of applications requiring high resolution, accuracy, and range [4].

3.1 WPS

The wearable computer is a small portable computer designed to be worn on the body during use, and it differs from PDAs, which are designed for hand-held use, although the distinction can sometimes be blurry. In this paper, as the WPS (a wearable platform for the next-generation PC), the i.MX21 test board was selected, which is a next-generation PC platform in the Rep. of Korea, for application to our system. The i.MX21 test board consists of an ARM926EJ-S (16KB I-Cache, 16KB D-Cache) CPU, and includes ARM Jazelle technology for Java acceleration and MPEG-4 and H.263 encode/decode acceleration. The i.MX21 provides flexibility for software implementation, for other video encoders, such as packet-video, real-networks and windows media. The i.MX21 not only enables smart LCD displays and exceptional video, it also powers versatile multitasking capabilities [5].

3.2 Feature Extraction and Language Recognition Models Using RDBMS

Statistical classification algorithms such as K-means clustering, QT (Quality Threshold) clustering, the fuzzy c-means clustering algorithm and the Self-Organizing Map (SOM), have been applied universally in traditional pattern recognition systems with unsupervised training, such as machine training, data mining, pattern recognition, image analysis and bioinformatics [6], [7], [8]. However, such classification algorithms have certain restrictions and problems, such as the necessity of complicated mathematical computation according to multidimensional features, the difficulty of applications in distributed processing systems, relativity of computation costs by pattern size, and minimization of memory swapping and assignment.

In this paper, we prescribed 32 basic KSSL motion gestures and 28 hand gestures connected with a travel information scenario, according to "Korean Standard Sign Language Tutor (KSSLT) [9]". KSSL gestures and hand gestures are classified by an arm's movement, hand shape, pitch and roll degree. Consequently, we constructed 65 sentential and 1572 word language models according to associability and presentation of hand gestures and basic KSSL motion gestures. In addition, for a clustering method to achieve efficient feature extraction and construction of training / recognition models based on distributed computing, we suggest and introduce an improved RDBMS (Relational Data-Base Management System) clustering module, to resolve such restrictions and problems.

3.3 Fuzzy Logic: Max-Min Composition of Fuzzy Relation

As the fuzzy logic for KSSL recognition, we applied trapezoidal shaped membership functions for representation of fuzzy numbers-sets, and utilized the fuzzy max-min composition. Two fuzzy relations *R* and *S* are defined in sets *A, B* and *C* (we prescribed the accuracy of hand gestures and basic KSSL gestures, object KSSL recognition models as the sets of events that occur in KSSL recognition with the sets *A, B* and *C*). That is, $R \subseteq A \times B$, $S \subseteq B \times C$. The composition $S{\cdot}R = SR$ of two relations *R* and *S* is expressed by the relation from *A* to *C*, and this composition is defined in Eq. (1) [10], [11].

$$\textit{For } (x, y) \in A \times B,\ (y, z) \in B \times C,$$
$$\mu_{S \bullet R}(x, z) = \underset{y}{Max}\,[Min(\mu_R(x, y), \mu_S(y, z))] \tag{1}$$

$S{\cdot}R$ from this elaboration is a subset of $A \times C$. That is, $S{\cdot}R \subseteq A \times C$. If the relations *R* and *S* are represented by matrices M_R and M_S, the matrix $M_{S \bullet R}$ corresponding to $S{\cdot}R$ is obtained from the product of M_R and M_S; $M_{S \bullet R} = M_R{\cdot}M_S$. For example, by matrices M_R, the possibility of "Best" $\in B$ after "Best" $\in A$ is 0.9. Also, by matrices M_S, the possibility of "Good_YOU" after "Best" is 0.6. The matrix $M_{S \bullet R}$ in Table 1 represents max-min composition that reason and analyze the possibility of *C* when *A* occurs, and it is also given in Fig. 2. In addition, the flowchart of KSSL recognizer is shown in Fig. 4 (in section 4) together with an outline and flow-chart of the FUI.

Table 1. The matrix $M_{S \bullet R}$ corresponding to the relations $S \bullet R$

S • R	KSSL recognition model : "YOU"				
Accuracy of basic KSSL gestures	Insignificance	Bad_YOU	Normal_YOU	Good_YOU	Best_YOU
Very_bad	0.9	0.6	0.3	0.2	0.1
Bad	0.6	0.7	0.4	0.2	0.2
Normal	0.3	0.4	0.4	0.3	0.3
Good	0.3	0.3	0.5	0.8	0.7
Best	0.2	0.3	0.4	0.6	0.9

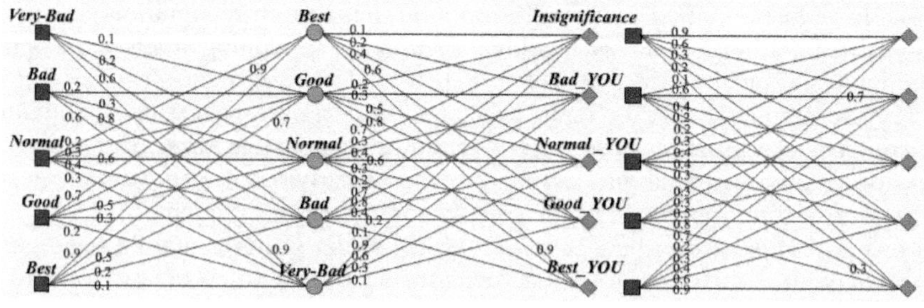

Fig. 2. Composition of fuzzy relation

4 Fusion and Fission Between Modalities

4.1 Fusion Scheme Between Audio-Gesture Modalities

The fusion scheme consists of seven major steps: 1) the user connects to Voice-XML server via PSTN and internet using telephone terminal and WPS based on wireless networks (including middleware), and then inputs prescribed speech and KSSL, 2) the user's speech data, which are inputted into telephone terminal, is transmitted to ASR-engine in Voice-XML, then ASR results are saved to the MMDS (Multi-Modal Database Server; The MMDS is the database responsible for synchronizing data between speech and KSSL gesture), 3) user's KSSL data, which are inputted into WPS, are recognized by embedded KSSL recognizer, then the WPS transmits and saves recognition results to the MMDS, using middleware over TCP/IP protocol and wireless an optional language processing interface. We used an average speech recognition rate as speech probability value for weight decision, and to define speech probability value networks(blue-tooth module), 4) at this point, the user's KSSL and speech data run the synchronization session using internal SQL logic of the MMDS, 5) while suggested

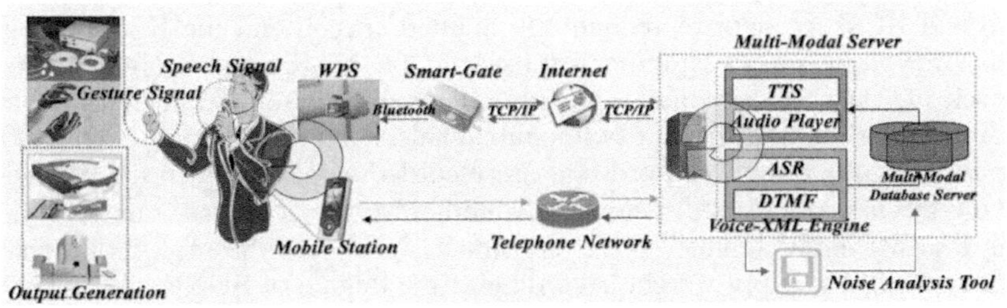

Fig. 3. The components and architecture of fusion architecture

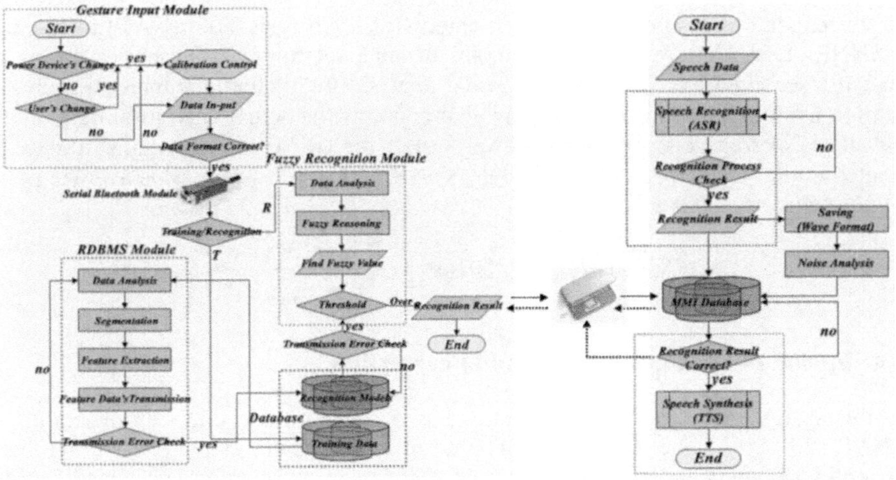

Fig. 4. The flowchart of the FUI integrating 2 sensory channels with speech and gesture

the FUI runs comparison arithmetic (validity check) on ASR and KSSL recognition results with pre-scribed language models by internal SQL logic, the NAT(Noise Analysis Tool) analyzes noise for user's speech data (wave file) which is recorded by Voice-XML, 6) According to analyzed noise and arithmetic result, the FUI gives weight into an individual (gesture or speech) recognizer, 7) finally, user's intention is provided to the user through TTS and visualization. The suggested architecture and flowchart of FUI are shown in Fig. 3 and Fig. 4.

4.2 Synchronization Between Audio-Gesture Modalities

Human's utterance and gesture representation usually have some time difference and such asynchronous control should occur necessarily in speech synthesis processing of recognition results. All multi-modal inputs are synchronized, because while speech recognizer generates absolute times for words, gesture movements generate *{x, y, t}* triples, and initial work identifies an object or a location from gesture inputs accordingly, as speech understanding constrains gesture interpretation. This paper solves the asynchronous control problems between speech and gesture signals using a web-logic and word-unit input method based on the database (the MMDS in section 4.1). In other words, for synchronization between speech and gesture signals, after individual speech and KSSL recognizer recognizes inputted speech and the KSSL recognition models, they transmit recognition results into the MMDS for weight application. However, the transmission time of recognition results has some time delay because of asynchronous communication of two input signals. As a result, the speech and KSSL recognition results based on word-unit are recorded sequentially to the MMDS, and while the DB is kept in standby mode via internal web-logic in case one was not input among the two input signals (where, two input signals are the recognition results of speech and KSSL), apply weight according to the degree of SNNR and fuzzy value, in the case where all input values are recorded.

4.3 Noise Analysis

In this paper, we designed and implemented Noise Analysis Tool (NAT) to calculate a SNNR. The NAT extracts data samples in mute section (1,000 samples during the first 0.1 seconds) as a noise domain, and analysis total sample frames; speech data section from the 'waveformData array' that contains the actual waveform data, then it calculates average energy (mean power; [dB]) for two types of sample frames extracted in the first step, finally, calculate SNNR by Eq. (2), where, P is average power of noise and speech data.

$$SNNR(dB) = 10\log_{10} \frac{P_{signal + noise}}{P_{noise}} \tag{2}$$

4.4 Fission Depending on SNNR and Fuzzy Value

In this section, we describe a web logic-based a weight decision rule depending on SNNR and fuzzy value for the fission between audio-gesture modalities, in FUI that is an optional language processing interface. We used an average speech recognition rate as speech probability value for weight decision, and to define speech probability value depending on SNNR, we achieved repeatedly speech recognition experiments 10 times with the 20 test speech recognition models in noisy and clean environments, for every 5 reagents. In addition, speech recognition rate does not usually change to a SNNR of 25 dB, but if the rate lowers, the speech recognition rate falls rapidly. Therefore, the FUI provides feed-back function according to SNNR critical value. In case SNNR critical value for weight decision is ambiguous (We applied SNNR critical value that the difference between each average speech recognition rates is max value; 15[dB] ≤ SNNR < 20[dB] in Table 2), according as feed-back function requests re-inputto user for clear a declaration of intention, more improved language processing is available. The average speech recognition rates as speech probability value are given Table 2, together with weight values that are defined depending on SNNR between actual waveform data and SNNR critical value for feed-back function.

Table 2. Weight value according to the SNNR and critical value for the feed-back function

SNNR Critical value	Weight value (%)		Average speech recognition rate for the 20 test recognition models (%)						
	Speech (W_S)	KSSL(W_G)	Reagent 1	Reagent 2	Reagent 3	Reagent 4	Reagent 5	Average(S)	Dif.
more than 40 [dB]	99.0	1.0	98.2	98.4	97.9	98.5	98.2	98.2	0.9
35 [dB] ≤ SNNR < 40 [dB]	98.0	2.0	97.8	97.3	96.6	97.1	97.5	97.3	0.3
30 [dB] ≤ SNNR < 35 [dB]	96.0	4.0	97.5	96.5	96.6	97.0	97.4	97.0	0.2
25 [dB] ≤ SNNR < 30 [dB]	94.0	6.0	97.2	96.5	96.5	96.9	96.9	96.8	0.2
20 [dB] ≤ SNNR < 25 [dB]	92.0	2.0	96.9	95.9	96.4	96.8	96.8	96.6	2.2
15 [dB] ≤ SNNR < 20 [dB]	*Feed-Back*		*92.4*	*96.2*	*93.8*	*95.2*	*94.1*	*94.3*	*11.1*
10 [dB] ≤ SNNR < 15 [dB]	6.0	94.0	83.6	83.4	83.5	82.6	83.2	83.3	8.8
5 [dB] ≤ SNNR < 10 [dB]	4.0	96.0	71.9.	72.5	70.2	79.5	75.6	74.5	22.4
0 [dB] ≤ SNNR < 5 [dB]	2.0	98.0	53.4	51.3	52.6	51.6	51.3	52.0	14.0
less than 0 [dB]	1.0	99.0	38.5	37.6	37.5	38.2	38.5	38.1	-

The weight decision processing for fission between modalities consists of three major steps: 1) the FUI calls an average speech recognition rate *(S)* depending on the defined SNNR, and fuzzy value *(G)* from the MMDS, then apply weights (W_S and W_G) in called-individual probability value, 2) and then calculate an expected value *(P_W)* via by Eq. (3), 3) return the fission result by calculated *P_W* to user. Where, the maximum fuzzy value for KSSL recognition is 3.5, and the minimum critical value is 3.2 (in programming). Accordingly, the normalized fuzzy value (*G*) of the embedded KSSL recognizer is defined Eq. (4). For example, 1) in case SNNR is more than 40 [dB], average speech recognition rate *(S)* is 97.2%, and then apply weights of $W_S = 98\%$ and $W_G = 2\%$ in Table 2, 2) if *Fuzzy Value_Current* in Eq. (4) is *3.2*, *P_W* is 0.971, 3) by the same principal, individual *P_W* values depending on SNNR and fuzzy value are shown in Table 3. (Because *KSSL probability* is changed according to *Fuzzy Value_Current*, *P_W* is changed justly.) As a result, if *P_W and SNNR* value are over than 0.934 and 20[dB], the FUI fissions and returns recognition result of speech recognizer based on Voice-XML, while the FUI fissions the embedded KSSL recognizer in case *P_W and SNNR* value are less than 0.909 and 15[dB].

$$P\_W = W_S \times S + W_G \times G \qquad (3)$$

- *P_W : an expected value after weight application*
- *W_S : Defined Weight for Speech recognition mode*
- *W_G : Defined Weight for KSSL recognition mode*
- *S : speech probability (an average speech recognition rate)*
- *G : KSSL probability (the critical value depending on normalized fuzzy value)*

$$G = \frac{\textit{Fuzzy Value\_Current}}{\textit{Fuzzy Value\_Max}} = \frac{\textit{Fuzzy Value\_Current}}{3.5} \tag{4}$$

- *Fuzzy Value_Current : Fuzzy value to recognize current gesture(KSSL)*
- *Fuzzy Value_Max = 3.5 : The maximum fuzzy value for KSSL recognition*

Table 3. In case *Fuzzy Value_Current* is 3.2, a system of measuring of *P_W* values

SNNR	Speech		KSSL		P_W
	W_S	S	W_G	G	
more than 40 [dB]	0.98	0.972	0.02	0.914	0.971
35 [dB] ≤ SNNR < 40 [dB]	0.95	0.963	0.05	0.914	0.961
30 [dB] ≤ SNNR < 35 [dB]	0.94	0.950	0.06	0.914	0.948
25 [Db] ≤ SNNR < 30 [dB]	0.92	0.948	0.08	0.914	0.945
20 [dB] ≤ SNNR < 25 [dB]	0.90	0.936	0.10	0.914	0.934
15 [dB] ≤ SNNR < 20 [dB]	Feed-Back				
10 [dB] ≤ SNNR < 15 [dB]	0.06	0.823	0.94	0.914	0.909
5 [dB] ≤ SNNR < 10 [dB]	0.05	0.755	0.95	0.914	0.906
0 [dB] ≤ SNNR < 5 [dB]	0.02	0.457	0.98	0.914	0.905
less than 0 [dB]	0.01	0.151	0.99	0.914	0.906

5 Experiments and Results

The experimental set-up is as follows. The distance between the KSL input module and the WPS with a built-in KSSL recognizer approximates radius 10M's ellipse form. In KSSL gesture and speech, we move the wireless data gloves and the motion

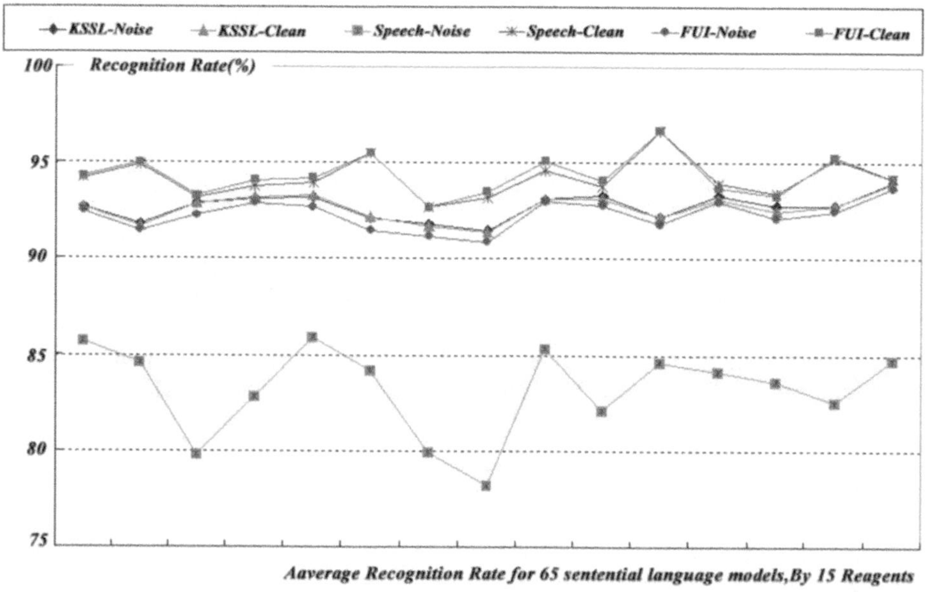

Fig. 5. The 65 sentence-based language recognition rates

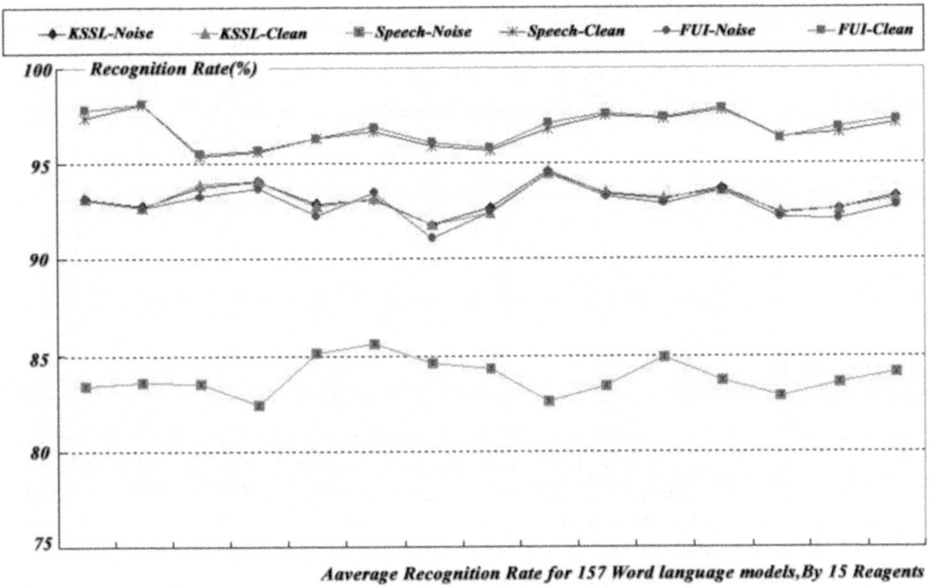

Fig. 6. The 157 word-based language recognition rates

tracker to the prescribed position. For every 15 reagents, we repeat this action 10 times in noisy and clean environments. While the user inputs KSSL using data gloves and a motion tracker, and speak using the blue-tooth headset in a telephone terminal. Experimental results, the uni-modal and the FUI's average recognition rate in noisy and clean environment for 65 sentential and 157 word language models, are shown in the comparison charts are given in Fig. 5, 6.

6 Conclusions

A wearable computing is an active topic of research, with areas of study including user interface design, augmented reality, pattern recognition, use of wearables for specific applications or disabilities, electronic textiles and fashion design. Many issues are common to the wearables, mobile computing, pervasive computing, ambient intelligence and ubiquitous computing research communities, including power management and heat dissipation, software architectures, wireless and personal area networks and sensor networks. This study fuses natural language and artificial intelligence techniques to allow human computer interaction with an intuitive mix of speech, gesture and sign language based on the WPS and Voice-XML. The FUI's average recognition rates for 65 sentential and 157 word language models were 94.31% and 96.81% in clean environments (e.g. office space), while 92.23% and 92.87% were shown in noisy environments. In addition, the FUI supports two major types of multi-modality for language recognition based on embedded and ubiquitous computing:

Finally, we clarify that this study is a fundamental study for implementation of an advanced multi modal recognizer integrating the human's five senses such as sight, hearing, touch, smell, and taste, to take the place of the traditional uni-modal recognizer for natural speech and sign language processing.

Acknowledgement

This research was supported by MIC, Korea under ITRC IITA-2006-(C1090-0603-0046).

References

1. Haniff, D.J., et al.: Human Factors of Multi-modal Ubiquitous Computing. In: Gellersen, H.-W. (ed.) HUC 1999. LNCS, vol. 1707, pp. 346–348. Springer, Heidelberg (1999)
2. Thorp, E.O.: The invention of the first wearable computer. In: Edward, O. (ed.) The Second International Symposium on Wearable Computers: Digest of Papers, IEEE Computer Society, Los Alamitos (1998)
3. McGlashan, S. et al.: Voice Extensible Markup Language (VoiceXML) Version 2.0. W3C Recommendation (1992), http://www.w3.org
4. Kim, J.-H., et al.: Hand Gesture Recognition System using Fuzzy Algorithm and RDBMS for Post PC. In: Wang, L., Jin, Y. (eds.) FSKD 2005. LNCS (LNAI), vol. 3614, pp. 170–175. Springer, Heidelberg (2005)
5. i.MX21 Processor Data-sheet.: http://www.freescale.com/
6. Duda, R.O., Hart, P.E., Stork, D.G.: Pattern Classification, 2nd edn. Wiley, New York (2001)
7. Paulus, D., Hornegger, J.: Applied Pattern Recognition, 2nd edn. Vieweg (1998)
8. Schuermann, J.: Pattern Classification: A Unified View of Statistical and Neural Approaches. Wiley&Sons (1996)
9. Kim, S.-G.: Korean Standard Sign Language Tutor. 1st, Osung Publishing Company, Seoul (2000)
10. Chen, C.H.: Fuzzy Logic and Neural Network Handbook, 1st edn. McGraw-Hill, New York (1992)
11. kandasamy, W.B.V.: Smaranda Fuzzy Algebra. American Research Press, Seattle (2003)

A Smart Space Architecture for Location-Based Spatial Audio Scenario Orchestration

Lila Kim[1], Doo-Hyun Kim[1,2,*], Hwasun Kwon[1], Dongwoon Jeon[1], and Keunsoo Lee[1]

[1] Embedded S/W and Sensor (Essens) Lab.
School of Internet and Multimedia Engineering
Konkuk University, Seoul, Korea
{otut,bebelo,birdybuddy,withholic}@konkuk.ac.kr
[2] New Millennium Hall 1203, School of Internet and Multimedia Engineering,
Konkuk University, Kwangjin-Gu, Seoul, 143-701, Korea
doohyun@konkuk.ac.kr

Abstract. Usual multimedia contents are represented as scenarios with markup language such as SMIL, and then delivered to be played back in terminal machines, e.g., PC or STB(Set-Top Box). However, these multimedia presentations are likely limited within single machine presentation where the speakers and display devices are attached together, so the spatial reality is degraded consequently. In order to enhance the spatial reality of an audio scenario presentation, each audio clip in the scenario should be assigned to the separate speaker node located close to the location where the author intended. In this paper, we propose a new architecture called L-DEAR (*Location-based Device Ensemble Architecture*) to organize a smart space using location information of each node in a local area network environment. The core of the L-DEAR is IBEE(*Immediate-But-Ephemeral device Ensemble*) which is a set of nodes picked out from the environment for playing assigned audio clips at a given time duration among the whole presentation. We will present the functional modules of L-DEAR and procedures for building IBEE, as well as functional requirements for L-DEAR such as extending the SMIL and using global clock, and show the results of our experimental implementations.

1 Introduction

In this paper, we propose architecture for a new flavor of distributed multimedia presentation enhanced with the spatial reality. The usual multimedia contents are represented as scenarios with markup language such as SMIL (Synchronized Multimedia Integration Language) [1], and then these scenarios are played back in terminal machines, e.g., PC or STB (Set-Top Box). However, these multimedia presentations are likely limited within single machine presentation where the speakers and display devices are attached together. Any visual component of a scenario can not be presented beyond the single display device, and similarly, all the audio components are mixed into one audio signal and then output through a single audio device, i.e.,

* Corresponding author.

J. Indulska et al. (Eds.): UIC 2007, LNCS 4611, pp. 123–132, 2007.

speaker. In such paradigm, the spatial information such as "*The audio clip A sounds at upper left of the audio clip B*" is ignored, and the spatial reality is necessarily degraded consequently. In order to enhance the spatial reality of an audio scenario presentation, each audio clip for each audio actor, dubbing artist or background music should be assigned a separate speaker close to the location where the author intended. This enhancement is not believed to be achieved within single machine presentation paradigm, but possibly within a networked multi-node computing environment. The goal of this paper is to derive necessary building-blocks and their integrated architecture, called L-DEAR (Location-based Device Ensemble Architecture), for achieving such spatial reality enhancement of the audio scenario presentation.

This paper is organized into the following sections. In section 2, we will discuss architectural requirements that should be considered for deriving the L-DEAR. In section 3, we propose a simplified approach for extending the SMIL to incorporate the ability to express spatial reality requirements in the scripts for multimedia presentations. In section 4, we break down the L-DEAR architecture into five modules along with the procedures for assigning devices in an IBEE for a give presentation script. Especially, for the device assignment procedure, we discuss using Voronoi Diagram. In section 5, we deal with implementation issues by mainly focusing on the global clock and the session initiation with capability negotiation, and explain results of our experimental implementation of L-DEAR. We conclude in section 6 with discussions on further research directions.

2 Architectural Requirements

A node is considered as a networked computing device with H/W and/or S/W for performing proper I/O operations such as decoding MP3 to its speaker. A *device ensemble* is defined as a set of nodes which are called out for playing back at least one assigned clip at a given time during the whole presentation. The device ensemble is definitely logical and ephemeral embodiment immediately brought into the execution of a presentation, thus, is called IBEE, *Immediate-But-Ephemeral device Ensemble,* which is actually a sort of Smart Space. The goal of this paper is to derive necessary building-blocks and their integrated architecture for achieving the spatial reality enhancement by embodying IBEE effectively. In order to achieve this goal, it is necessary to support key functional requirements covering diverse issues as follows:

- Extending mark-up language for spatial relationship representation: The single machine presentation paradigm seems to have affected the mark-up language, e.g., W3C SMIL (Synchronized Multimedia Integration Language) 2.0[1] not to consider representing spatial relationship among audio clips. It is required to extend this markup language so that authors can specify inter-location relationships in the phase of authoring.
- Acquiring location information of devices: There are many research results such as Cricket [2] for localization of mobile devices in indoor environment without using GPS. We may adopt these novel ideas for acquiring the location information of each device. Whichever location systems are used, L-DEAR should gather

relatively accurate location information from each device, and use it to form a proper IBEE immediately.

- Forming IBEE: The IBEE is actually to assign each clip to a specific node by seeking a match between the inter-clip spatial relationship specified in the authored script and the location information gathered from each node. This matching procedure is required to pursue an optimal matching between the authored spatial relationship requirement and physical locations of devices, and to produce a data structure.
- Facilitating global time within the IBEE: A device in an IBEE will eventually start playing an assigned audio clip. But if the device does no know the exact time planed to start or stop playing the specific clip, then the synchronized distributed presentation will be disordered. Therefore, we need to make the devices in an IBEE orchestrated on the basis of a global clock.

3 Mark-Up Language Extension

The SMIL [1] is a declarative markup language based on the XML (eXtensible Markup Language) for scripting presentations containing multimedia; audio, video, image, and text. The SMIL has unique features supporting the timing and synchronization among heterogeneous types of media. In order to enhance the spatial reality of multimedia presentation, it is necessary to extend the SMIL to embrace the capabilities to allow the authors to express their spatial requests intended for each element or clip.

Although the approaches for this extension can include the default rule approach, relative position approach, and test-and-switch approach as introduced in our previous works [6], we use a quite straight forward approach, so called, Absolute Position Approach, for simplifying our experiments. This approach allows SMIL script authors to use absolute 3-D or 2-D coordinates to specify locations where corresponding clips should sound. The author, as an example, can specify loc="7, 1", i.e. (70cm, 10cm), for audio3.mp3 clip, assuming that the speakers are arranged on a 2-D panel like a wall. Then, when the SMIL player executes the script, it constructs a *clip assignment map* (CAM), which is similar to the SRT(Spatial Relationship Tree) in [6], by seeking proper speakers of which physical locations are closest to the locations specified for each clip.

```
...
  <par>
        <audio src="audio2.mp3" begin="1" dur="7" end="8"
                                                        loc="-6,-6"/>
        <audio src="audio1.mp3" begin="8" dur="5" end="13"
                                                        loc="0,-4"/>
        <audio src="audio3.mp3" begin="13" dur="8" end="21"
                                                        loc="7,1"/>
  </par>
...
```

4 L-DEAR Architecture

The L-DEAR architecture as shown in Figure 1 consists of five major parts; 1) Extended SMIL Interpreter, 2) DIB(Device Information Base), 3) Orchestrator, 4) Global Time Base, and 5) Audio Decoding and Player. The Extended SMIL Interpreter reads and interprets a SMIL script and then produces both of a time schedule for presenting clips and an IBEE. For producing the IBEE, this interpreter refers location information contained in the DIB, and seeks a clip assignment map, i.e., CAM, by matching logical locations coded in SMIL script with physical locations of nearby devices.

Seeking the best CAM is one of keys for enhancing spatial reality. The way of seeking the best CAM is dependent on the representation scheme for denoting the logical locations in the SMIL script. If the author uses the Test-and-Switch or Relative Position Approaches, then we may need more flexible policies [6]. In this paper, however, we consider that the author uses only the Absolute Position Approach, hence, the procedure for seeking the best CAM becomes straight forward by using the well-known Voronoi Diagram [7], where the clips are assigned to the closest speakers in Euclidian distance measure.

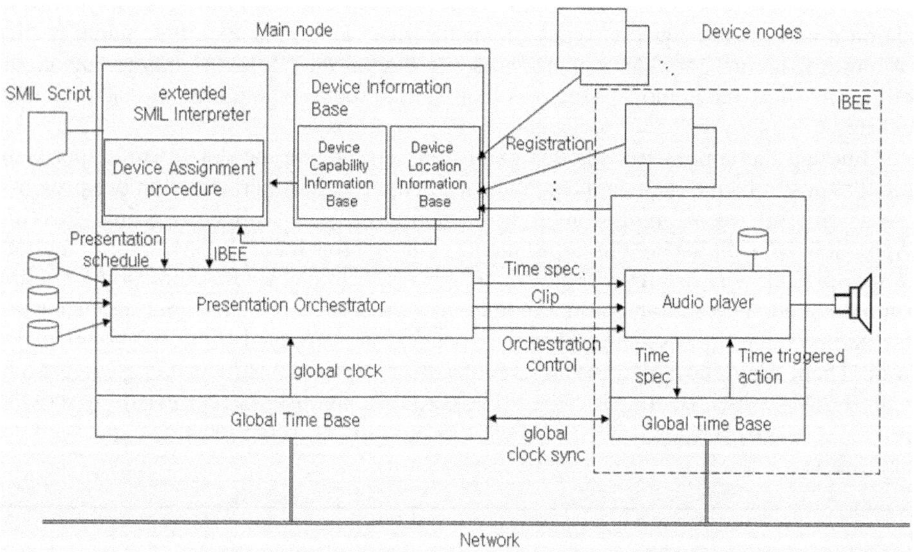

Fig. 1. Block diagram of L-DEAR

The Figure 2 shows a CAM produced as the result of a device assignment according to the rule following the Voronoi Diagram. The grid panel denotes a wall where the speakers can be attached in the unit of 10cm. The three small rectangles represent the three speaker systems located at (-8, -6), (-1, -3), and (7, 4) on the wall, and the small circles denote the audio clips in the SMIL script with absolute (x, y) locations.

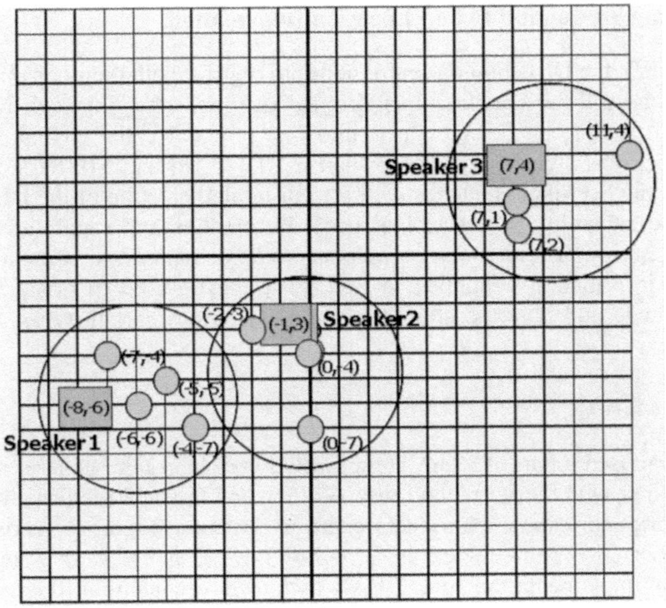

Fig. 2. Clip Assignment Map upon the speakers located at (-8,-6), (-1,-3) and (7,4)

The DIB in the Figure 1 is composed of the device capability information and location information. These two groups of information are acquired through a series of messages between the main node, i.e., Orchestrator node and device nodes. A device node initiates a session with the main node after the boot-up is finished, and then communicates with a series of messages to carry its physical location information and device capability information. The device capabilities may contain the list of audio formats that it supports. The Orchestrator executes presentation schedules over IBEE by feeding clip data files, e.g., audio.mp3, into each corresponding device in the IBEE along with start- and stop-time specifications for the clip. From this point, each node should play the given audio clips at the given time by using the global time base which is explained in the next chapter.

5 Implementation Issues and Experiments

5.1 Global Time Based Coordination of Distributed Multimedia Actions

First of all, the global clock mechanism should be a primary basis on which we should implement our L-DEAR. There are many excellent research results such as TMO (Time Triggered and Message Triggered Objects)[3,4] and NTP(Network Time Protocol)[5]. Among those, we propose to use TMO, since it supports a unified object oriented programming scheme for distributed and time-coordinated actions as well as global clock. TMO scheme provides a sound foundation for programming and executing distributed multimedia actions requiring global synchronization among the media units or among the nodes collectively engaged in a multimedia presentation performance. Once the device node in the IBEE receives time specifications, then the audio player in the node registers TMO with time-triggered action requests for executing start and stop functions on time.

5.2 Session Initiation with Capability and Location Information

In order to organize IBEE, the DIB should require nodes to register with their capability and physical locations. All those actions including connection, capability registration, and location registration can be integrated into one protocol called signaling protocol. Among the various signaling protocol such as H.323 [8] and SIP(Session Initiation Protocol)[9], the SIP likely matches well for our implementation of the DIB since its simplicity and capability of describing media information and capabilities. SIP supports session descriptions that allow participants to agree on a set of compatible media types. The information contained in SDP [10] can be used to organize an IBEE proper to decode and play the clip files compressed with certain types of algorithms.

5.3 Experimental Scenario

For our experiments, we used a part of <The Three Little Pigs> fairy tale scenario as shown in Table 1, together with the start, end time, location, and the mp3 file name of each clip. The SMIL script corresponding to the scenario is written as Figure 3. As the first experiment, we located the three speakers at (-8,-6),(-1,-3), and (7,4) over the wall, and executed our implementation of L-DEAR architecture containing the extended SMIL interpreter by feeding the pig.sml file, then a CAM was constructed by assigning the audio clips in the script to the nearest speakers as shown in Figure 4. The speaker located (-8,-6) was assigned wolf1.mp3, narration1.mp3, narration2.mp3,

Table 1. A part of <The Three Little Pigs> scenario

scenario		start time (sec)	end time (sec)	Logical loc. (10cm)	mp3 file
Wolf	Little pig, little pig, let me come in.	1	8	(-6,-6)	wolf1.mp3
1st pig	No, no, by the hair of my chiny chin chin.	8	13	(0,-4)	pig1a.mp3
Wolf	Then I'll huff, and I'll puff, and I'll blow your house in.	13	21	(7,1)	pig1b.mp3
Narration	He huffed, and he puffed, and he blew his house in, and ate up the little pig. The second little pig built his house with furze.	21	49	(-7,-4)	narration1.mp3
Wolf	Little pig, little pig, let me come in.	49	57	(0,-7)	wolf2.mp3
2nd pig	No, no, by the hair of my chiny chin chin.	57	62	(7,2)	pig2.mp3
Narration	He puffed, and he puffed, and he puffed, and he huffed, and at last he blew the house down, and he ate up the little pig.	62	86	(-4,-7)	narration2.mp3
3rd pig	I built my house with bricks.	86	91	(11,4)	pig3.mp3
Narration	The wolf came, as he did to the other little pigs, and said.	91	98	(-5,-5)	narration3.mp3
3rd pig	No, no, by the hair of my chiny chin chin.	98	108	(-2,-3)	pig4.mp3

```
<smil>
  <body>
    <par>
      <audio src="wolf1.mp3" begin="1" dur="7" end="8" loc="-6,-6"/>
      <audio src="pig1a.mp3" begin="8" dur="5" end="13" loc="0,-4"/>
      <audio src="pig1b.mp3" begin="13" dur="8" end="21" loc="7,1"/>
    </par>
    <par>
      <audio src="narration1.mp3" begin="21" dur="28" end="49" loc="-7,-4"/>
      <audio src="wolf2.mp3" begin="49" dur="8" end="57" loc="0,-7"/>
      <audio src="pig2.mp3" begin="57" dur="5" end="62" loc="7,2"/>
      <audio src="narration2.mp3" begin="62" dur="24" end="86" loc="-4,-7"/>
    </par>
    <par>
      <audio src="pig3.mp3" begin="86" dur="5" end="91" loc="11,4"/>
      <audio src="narration3.mp3" begin="91" dur="7" end="98" loc="-5,-5"/>
      <audio src="pig4.mp3" begin="98" dur="10" end="108" loc="-2,-3"/>
    </par>
  </body>
</smil>
```

Fig. 3. SMIL Script pig.sml for <The Three Little Pigs> scenario

and narration3.mp3. The speaker located (-1,-3) was assigned pi1a.mp3, wolf2.mp3, and pig4.mp3. And the speaker located (7,-4) was assigned pig1b.mp3, pig2.mp3, and pig3.mp3. This assignment is illustrated at Figure 2.

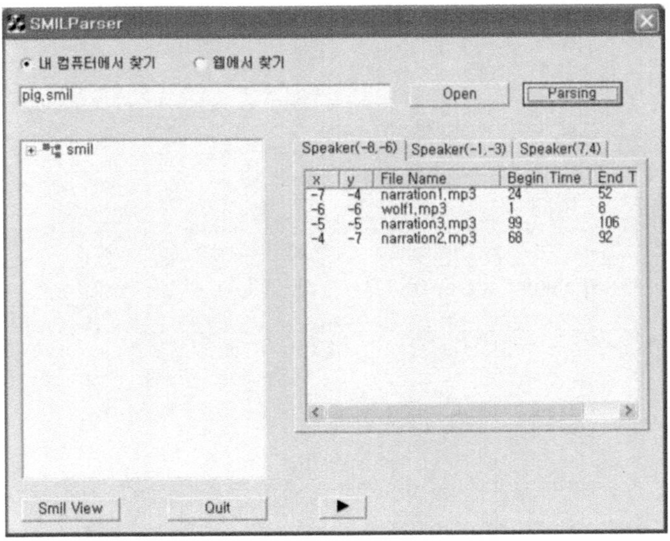

Fig. 4. A clip assignment to the speakers located (-8,-6)

As our second experiment, we changed the location of the speaker located at (-1,-3) to location (6, 2). Then, the assignment was changed accordingly, as shown at Figure 5. The speaker located (-8,-6) was assigned wolf1.mp3, pig1a.mp3, narration1.mp3, wolf2. mp3, narration2.mp3, narration3.mp3, and pig4.mp3, the speaker (6, 2) was assigned pig1b.mp3, pig2.mp3. The speaker located (7, 4) was assigned

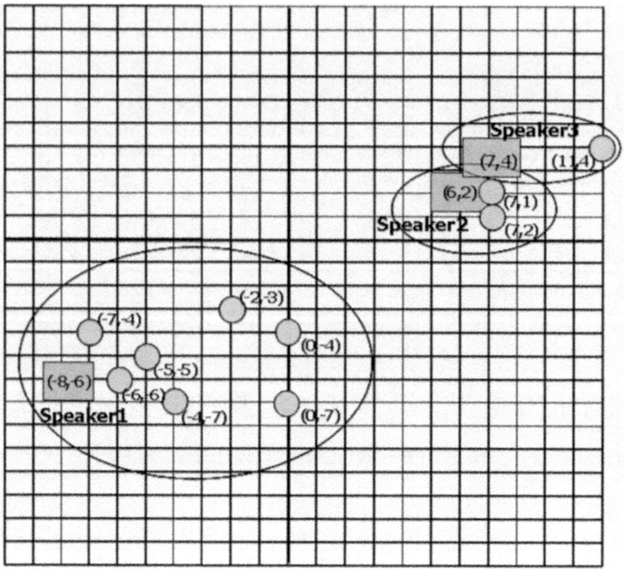

Fig. 5. Clip Assignment Map upon the speakers located at (-8,-6), (6,2) and (7,4)

pig3.mp3. Because of the location change of speaker2 from (-1,-3) to (6, 2), the audio clips pig1a.mp3, wolf2.mp3, and pig4.mp3 are moved to the speaker1 located at (-8,-6) which is nearest to them. In addition, audio clip pig1b.mp3 and pig2.mp3 were re-allocated to speaker2. As a result of the location change of the speaker2, the sequence of clip presentation at each speaker was changed as shown in Figure 6. Figure 6(a) shows the presentation sequence for the first experiment, and Figure 6(b) does for the second experiment.

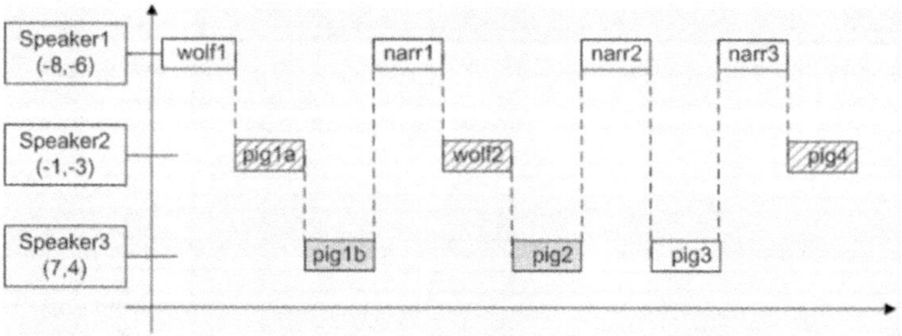

(a) Speakers at (-8,-6), (-1,-3) and (7,4)

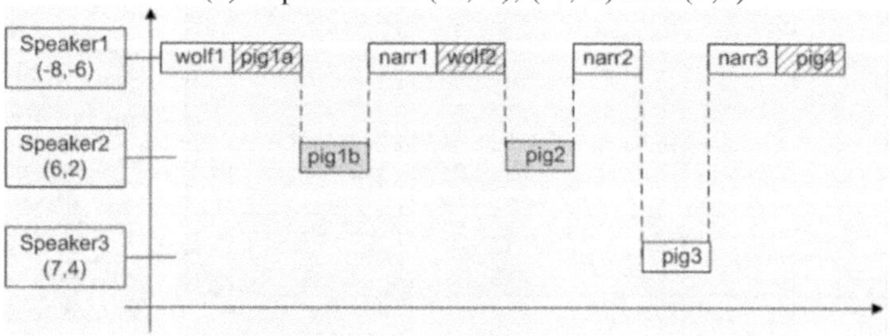

(b) (b) Speakers at (-8,-6), (6,2) and (7,4)

Fig. 6. Sequence of audio clip presentation at each speaker system

The Figure 7 shows our experimental facilities where each speaker was attached with an embedded system board with PXA270 microprocessor running embedded Linux. Each board was facilitated with WLAN USB stick and S/W MP3 player controlled by SIP user agent that actually communicates with the L-DEAR main node. The Cricket system [4] could be used for getting indoor location of each speaker, but, instead, we simulated it by programming each speaker to contain its designated location.

(a) Speakers at (-8,-6), (-1,-3) and (7,4)

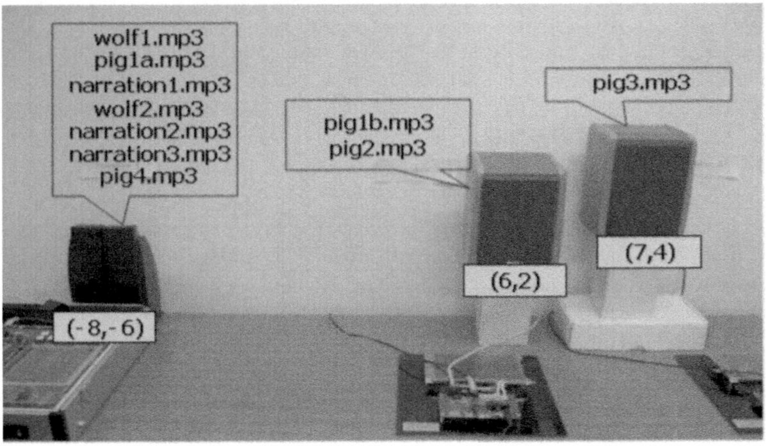

(b) Speakers at (-8,-6), (6,2) and (7,4)

Fig. 7. Experiment Facilities

7 Conclusions

We, in this paper, derived an architecture called L-DEAR (Location-base Device Ensemble ARchiteture) to embody the IBEE(Immediate But Ephemeral device

Ensemble) which is a smart space for location-based distributed audio scenario orchestration. We also raised the necessity to slightly extend the mark-up language, SMIL, for expressing spatial relationships among the clips, and proposed four approaches for extending SMIL including the default rule approach, relative position approach, test-and-switch, and absolute position approach.

In addition, we discussed important issues in implementing L-DEAR such as the global clock mechanism, session initiation, location and capability negotiation. Finally, we introduced our experiments with <The Three Little Pigs> fairy tale by writing its script with extended SMIL using the absolute position approach based on Voronoi diagram [7]. Our experiments showed that the IBEE for location-based audio scenario orchestration over WLAN was constructed as a smart space for the audio scenario orchestration dependent on device-situations. We, however, could not discuss about some advanced topics such as 3-D location information of the devices, or fine-grained synchronization. These topics will be considered later as further research issues.

Acknowledgement. This paper was partially supported by Seoul R&BD Program in 2007 and ITRC project from MIC, Korea.

References

1. W3C: Synchronized Multimedia Integration Language (SMIL 2.0), http://www.w3.org/TR/2005/REC-SMIL2-20050107 (2001)
2. Balakrishnan, H., R. Baliga, D. Curtis, M. Goraczko, A. Miu, N.B. Priyantha, A. Smith, K. Steele, S. Teller, K. Wang: Lessons from Developing and Deploying the Cricket Indoor Location System, http://nms.lcs.mit.edu/cricket (2003)
3. Kim, K.H., Ishida, M., and Liu, J.Q.: An Efficient Middleware Architecture Supporting Time-Triggered Message-Triggered Objects and an NT-based Implementation, Proc. ISORC '99 (The 2nd IEEE CS Int'l Symposium on Object-Oriented Real-time Distributed Computing), St. Malo, France (1999) 54-63
4. Kim, D.H., and K H (Kane) Kim: A TMO-based Software Architecture for Distributed Real-time Multimedia Processing, Proc, WORDS 2003(IEEE Workshop in Object-oriented Real-time Dependable Systems), Guadalajara, Mexico (2003)
5. http://www.ntp.org
6. Kim, D.H, L.L. Kim, H.S. Kwon, D.W. Jeon, and S.A. Chae: Location-based Device Ensemble Architecture for a Spatial Reality Enhancement of Distributed Multimedia Presentation, ICAT2006, Lecture Notes in Computer Science, Vol. 4282. Springer-Verlag, Berlin Heidelberg New York (2006) 372–383
7. Franz Aurenhammer: Voronoi Diagrams - A Survey of a Fundamental Geometric Data Structure, ACM Computing Surveys, 23(3) (1991) 345-405
8. ITU-T: Packet-based multimedia communications systems, Recommendation H.323
9. Handly, M., H. Schulzrinne, E. Schooler, and J. Rosenberg: SIP: session initiation protocol, RFC 2543, Internet Engineering Task Force (1999)
10. Handley, M. and V. Jacobson: SDP: session description protocol, RFC 2327 (1998)

CHASE: Context-Aware Heterogenous Adaptive Smart Environments Using Optimal Tracking for Resident's Comfort*

Navrati Saxena[1], Abhishek Roy[2], and Jitae Shin[1]

[1] School of Info. & Comm. Eng., Sungkyunkwan University, Suwon, South Korea
[2] WiBro System Lab, Samsung Electronics, Suwon, South Korea
{navrati,jtshin}@ece.skku.ac.kr, abhishek.roy@samsung.com

Abstract. An information-theoretic, optimal framework is developed for tracking the residents in a Context-aware Heterogenous Adaptive Smart Environments (CHASE). The framework envisions that each individual sensor-system operates fairly independently, and does not require public knowledge of individual topologies. The resident-tracking problem is formulated in terms of weighted entropy. The framework is truly universal and provides an optimal, online learning and prediction of inhabitants movement (location) profiles from the symbolic domain. Since the optimal tracking in heterogeneous smart homes is a NP-complete problem, a greedy heuristic for near-optimal tracking is proposed. The concept of Asymptotic Equipartition Property (AEP) is also explored to predict the inhabitants most likely path-segments (comprising of coverage areas of different sensor-systems) with very good accuracy. Successful prediction helps in on-demand operations of automated indoor devices along the inhabitants future paths and locations, thus providing the necessary comfort at a near-optimal cost. Simulation results on a typical smart home corroborate this high prediction success, thereby providing sufficient resident-comfort while reducing the daily energy consumption and manual operations.

1 Introduction

The concept of ubiquitous computing, as "Computing in the 21st century" [21] was initially germinated from the seminal work of Weiser and his group. Rapid growth in wireless technologies, proliferation of feature-enhanced, hand-held devices and advancement in the domain of smart sensor networks have significantly contributed to the actual realization of this concept. "Context-awareness" is perhaps, the key characteristic of the next generation of intelligent, ubiquitous networks and associated applications. It is expected that such pervasive environments will be filled up with wide range of computing technologies using different smart sensors and actuators. The most challenging problem in any such

* This work was supported by the Korea Research Foundation Grant funded by the Korean Government (MOEHRD) (KRF-2006-331-D00358).

J. Indulska et al. (Eds.): UIC 2007, LNCS 4611, pp. 133–142, 2007.

ubiquitous environment is to make system or environment sufficiently knowledgeable about the users' contexts. The proliferation of such different sensors (e.g. motes, RF-sensors etc.) with heterogenous sensing-technologies have made this challenge even more complex. The idea of a future smart environment, thus lies in encompassing multiple smart sensing technologies, with possibly significant differences in their individual characteristics, such as, coverage area (indoor/outdoor), transmission range, power and link bandwidth.

The problem of tracking an individual resident in a homogeneous smart environment has been extensively studied in literature. The heterogenous smart environment, however, offers a new set of challenges that has not yet been significantly addressed. The integrated heterogenous smart environment will be *loosely coupled, with no mandatory hierarchical or tiering relationship* among the component sensor-systems. Additionally, we also allow for multiple overlaps between arbitrarily-sized coverage-areas of different, heterogeneous sensor-networks. For example, the user can connect to different 802.11 WLAN or sensor networks, while at a smart-home, in the smart-office or at the smart-shopping-mall.

We have taken an information-theoretic approach to develop an indoor Context-aware Heterogeneous Adaptive Smart Environments (**CHASE**). The objective is to provide the residents of the environment with sufficient comfort at minimum possible cost. The mobility of the inhabitant inside the house always creates uncertainty of his/her locations and contexts. The concept of entropy in information theory [3] provides a key measure to evaluate and characterize this uncertainty. We have used the concept of *weighted entropy*, where the location uncertainty of the resident is weighed in proportion to the signaling costs associated with the particular sensor-network he/she is connected to. This indeed provides a more accurate model for measuring location uncertainty in heterogeneous smart environments, where different sensor systems or indoor networks have very different communication costs. Since the optimal tracking problem in heterogenous smart homes is *NP-complete* [19], [17], we have proposed a near-optimal greedy solution for this problem. An analysis of inhabitants daily routine reveals some possible patterns in his/her daily-life, which helps us to assume the inhabitants mobility as stochastic process. Although, in such a heterogenous smart environment, there exists a wide number of possible routes from one part to another, an inhabitant usually follows his/her most likely paths. Using information-theoretic concepts of *Asymptotic Equipartition Property* (AEP) [23], we can capture the inhabitants most frequent path-segments. We will show that reserving resources and activating the automated devices along the typical paths are two important steps behind the creation of an amicable, context-aware atmosphere in the heterogenous smart environment, yet attempting to minimize the overall energy consumption. The entire framework is designed on a *symbolic space*, which makes it *truly universal and capable of supporting all possible sensor-systems, without sharing the topological details of individual sensor-systems.*

The rest of the paper is organized as follows. In Section 2 we survey related work on smart environments and explain the motivation behind our approach. Section 3 presents the system description for CHASE-like smart heterogeneous environment. Section 4 presents a near-optimal greedy solution for the NP-complete user-tracking problem. Section 5 demonstrates the power of this predictive environment in providing the inhabitants comfort at a minimum possible cost. Simulations studies in Section 6 are used to evaluate the performance of our location management schemes. Finally, Section 7 concludes the paper.

2 Related Work on Smart Environments

Given the large body of work on resident tracking in a homogenous smart environment, we survey only the broad categories of these solutions. Applications like fleet management systems [22] and technologies like ad-hoc location sensing [4] and autonomous robots [5] are probably the first major step towards this ultimate goal of smart, ubiquitous computing paradigm.

The Active Badge [7] is perhaps the first infra-red based location tracking system developed for indoor offices. Active Bat [8] takes the help of ultrasonic time-of-flight lateration technique to improve the granularity of location-sensing offered by the badge system. On the other hand, MITs Cricket Location Support System [14] delegates the responsibility of location reporting to the mobile object itself. RADAR [2], another RF-based indoor location support system uses signal strength and signal-to-noise ratio to compute 2-D positioning. Microsofts Easy-living and Microsoft Home [9] projects use real-time 3D cameras to provide stereo-vision positioning capability in an indoor environment. Place Lab [20] is also providing low-cost, easy-to-use, device positioning for both indoor and outdoor location-aware computing applications. In the Georgia Techs Aware Home [13], the embedded pressure sensors capture inhabitants footfalls, and the system uses this data for position tracking and pedestrian recognition. The Neural Network House project [12] of the University of Colorado focuses on the development of an adaptive control of home environments (ACHE) to anticipate the needs of the inhabitants. The Intelligent Home Project [10] at the University of Massachusetts explores the application of multi-agent systems technology to develop and maintain a smart indoor environment. A location-aware resource management framework has also been developed in UTA's MAV Home [15].

Design and evaluation of smart interfaces and autonomy modes can be effectively performed by developing an information processing model of cognition [6] and human-like autonomous agents [11]. Experimental projects like, Berkley's 'The Center for the Built Environment (CBE)' and the 'Vital Signs Curriculum Materials Project' explores the effect of asymmetric distribution of building-components over human comfort [24]. Similarly, research of American Society of Heating, Refrigeration, and Air Conditioning Engineers (ASHRAE) concluded there is a range of combined temperatures and humidities that provides comfort to most people [1]. However none of these smart environments actually consider the heterogeneity of technologies deployed and their effects in the overall system. This motivates us to develop the framework for CHASE.

3 System Description and Location Uncertainty

Figure 1 shows the overview of a heterogeneous smart environment consisting of three different indoor sub-networks (sensors, WLANs and WPANs). Clearly, the coverage area of each individual sub-system can be discontinuous (e.g., a set of disconnected islands of IEEE 802.11-based hot-spots). Accordingly, the set of sub-networks that can be accessed concurrently by a mobile resident is not constant but a function of its current location. Let, the smart, ubiquitous environment network consists of N sub-networks or access technologies $\{A_1, A_2, \cdots, A_N\}$, where each sub-network is a collection of (either partitioned or overlapping) coverage-areas, such that X_i^j represents the jth coverage-area in the ith sub-network. Let $|A_i|$ represents the number of coverage-areas in A_i. Indeed, the overall network of a CHASE-like heterogenous smart-environment will often contain islands of indoor IEEE 802.11 LANs or motes-sensors, with which the resident is only intermittently connected. For notational convenience, let each sub-network have an additional coverage-area ϕ to capture this disconnected state. We can model the CHASE-like heterogenous smart-environment using the concept of weighted entropy [16]

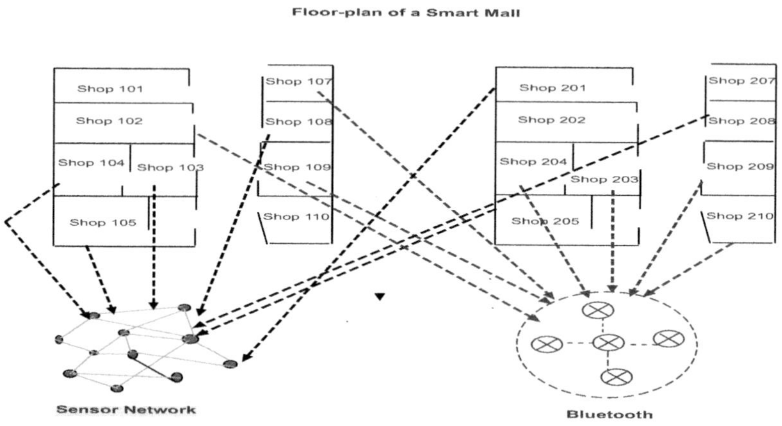

Fig. 1. Heterogeneous Smart Environment

Result 1. For a given stationary stochastic process ν, no location tracking scheme can predict the precise location of the Mobile Node (MN) (across all sub-networks) with a smaller average update cost, per change in state, than weighted entropy [16].

The weighted entropy of any user's movement and activity pattern thus provides a lower bound against which the performance of any practical location management scheme may be measured. In the next section, we will focus on feasible tracking strategies that employ on-line learning to asymptotically achieving this performance bound without knowing ahead of time what the exact bound is.

4 Optimal Tracking from Symbolic Domain

We have considered a heterogeneous smart environment, where a centralized location register is connected to each of the individual sensor-systems or indoor sub-networks. Any change in resident's location information is relayed by the corresponding sensor-system (or indoor sub-network) to the location register. The location register does not, however, need to know the topological layout of each sensor-system or sub-network. To determine the actual location of the resident, the tracking system consults the location register. The location strategy for resident's location information gathering is performed by extending the concept given in [18] into indoor environments. The problem of minimizing the associated expected tracking cost, of a user in CHASE-like heterogeneous smart environment is NP-complete as described in [19] and [17].

As the computation of an optimal tracking sequence is NP-complete, we focus on intelligent heuristics to derive a suitable searching sequence. Consider a user's movement in a heterogeneous smart home comprising two different sensor-networks A_1 and A_2, both with identical signalling cost normalized to 1. Let us assume that the coverage-areas of A_1 and A_2 are respectively represented by numbers and alphabets. A typical movement history of the MN may then consist of two-tuples $[(X_1^1, X_2^a), (X_1^1, X_2^e), (X_1^1, X_2^a), (X_1^2, X_2^a), (X_1^2, X_2^d), (X_1^1, X_2^d),$ (X_1^1, X_2^a) , $(X_1^1, X_2^f), (X_1^3, X_2^f), (X_1^5, X_2^f), (X_1^5, X_2^b)]$. From the movement history of the user, we notice that the user's residence in coverage-area X_2^a almost always occurs simultaneously with its residence in X_1^1. Hence, if the user is absent in coverage-area X_1^1, then with high probability it is also absent in coverage-area X_2^a. In other words, coverage-area X_1^1 and X_2^a are likely to have significant spatial overlap, and the probability of the user being in X_2^a but not in X_1^1 is ≈ 0.

Hence, after an unsuccessful searching attempt in coverage-area X_1^1, it is wise to eliminate the tuples containing X_1^1 in them before deciding the next coverage-area to be searched. Referring back to the original movement history, the removal of the tuples containing X_1^1 leaves us with the samples (X_1^2, X_2^a), (X_1^2, X_2^d), (X_1^3, X_2^f), (X_1^5, X_2^f), (X_1^5, X_2^b). Subsequently, the new first-order conditional probabilities is given by: $\rho(2|\widehat{1}) = 2/5$, $\rho(3|\widehat{1}) = 1/5$, $\rho(5|\widehat{1}) = 2/5$, $\rho(a|\widehat{1}) = 1/5$, $\rho(d|\widehat{1}) = 1/5$, $\rho(f|\widehat{1}) = 2/5$, $\rho(b|\widehat{1}) = 1/5$. The system can now select the coverage-area having the *highest conditional probability*, given that it is not in coverage-area 1, i.e., randomly any coverage-area from X_1^2, X_1^5, X_2^f. Suppose the coverage-area X_2^f is chosen. Now, if the user is not found even in X_2^f, then we can proceed in a similar iterative way to first eliminate the tuples having X_2^f, and then pick the next most likely coverage area. With this approach, we have the searching sequence $\{X_1^1, X_2^f, X_1^2\}$ which results in a lower expected tracking cost than $\{X_1^1, X_2^a, X_2^f, \ldots\}$.

This observation provides our greedy heuristic for defining the searching sequence. Intuitively, at each iteration of the algorithm, the greedy procedure selects the coverage-area where the user has the highest residence probability, given that it cannot simultaneously be in any of the coverage-areas already included in the sequence. For the heterogeneous multi-system environment, the conditional probability of each coverage-area should be normalized by the tracking cost associated with that coverage-area. It is shown that a particular inhabitant typically follows only a small subset of all the paths, which reflects his/her mobility profile in the long run [18]. The concept of *typical set* and *asymptotic equipartition property* (AEP) from information theory [3] helps in obtaining this *small set* of *highly probable* routes maintained by a particular inhabitant.

5 Inhabitant's Comfort with Energy Conservation

As discussed earlier the prime objective of smart home lies in providing the inhabitant with sufficient comfort at minimum possible energy consumption. However, the inhabitant's location uncertainty in an indoor environment leads to uncertainty in the inhabitant's activities and operation of smart indoor appliances. Once the location is managed properly, only then the house will be intelligent enough to make accurate predictions of inhabitant's activities and aid him/her with smart control of automated devices. This is one essential component to provide inhabitant's comfort at minimum possible cost.

5.1 Mobility Aware Energy Conservation

The energy consumption over the entire heterogenous smart home needs to be optimized for reducing the maintenance cost. At the same time we need to consider the inhabitant's comfort, by reducing the explicit manual operation and control of smart devices and appliances. We argue that predictive location and context awareness is the key behind such energy management framework. The automated lights and fans operate in a *pro-active mode* to conserve the energy during the inhabitant's prolonged absence in particular locations inside the home. The programmable devices (e.g. microwave etc.) work for the amount of time it has been programmed by the inhabitant.

Adaptive Temperature Control System. We have used a *distributed* temperature control system in various locations of the house, for energy conservation. The temperature control system is intelligent enough to bring the temperature of specific locations (inside the home) into an amicable one before the inhabitant enters those locations. The pro-active operation of temperature control is termed as *preconditioning*. The time needed for this preconditioning is *preconditioning period* and the *rate of energy* required during this period is known as *preconditioning load*. During this pre-conditioning period, the constant rate of energy at full capacity is supplied to bring down the temperature to the comfort level. The shorter the duration of pre-conditioning period, the larger is the preconditioning load. In order to get an estimate of this preconditioning load, it is required to know the characteristics of air temperature variation caused by constant unit rate of heat extraction from the specific locations. This is often termed as *room air temperature weighting factors for unit heat extraction*. In the cooling mode once the air conditioning is stopped when inhabitant's departure from specific location of the house, the temperature of that region increases rapidly. The same mechanism is repeated whenever the inhabitant is about to move into the specific locations inside the house.

5.2 Estimating Inhabitant's Comfort

While the prime goal behind the deployment of smart homes, lies in providing the inhabitants with sufficient comfort, this comfort is actually a subjective measure experienced by the inhabitants themselves. This experience of comfort varies from one person to another and involves complexity arising from a variety of factors, such as, temperature, humidity, light-intensity etc. Of these many factors, temperature and humidity are the most important in indoor environment. Hence, in our experiments on smart homes, we have investigated into the effects of temperature and humidity into inhabitant-comfort. There is no one temperature and humidity condition at which everyone is comfortable. Most People are generally comfortable at a range of temperatures and humidities. Researches from ASHRAE [1] and Berkley's CBE project [24] have pointed out that the human-comfort varies *exponentially* with temperature-variation. We support this conclusion and extend it to include the humidity factor into account. Thus, in our smart home the human-comfort varies jointly, with variation of both temperature and humidity, in an exponential fashion.

6 Performance Evaluation

We now present simulation results obtained using a discrete-event simulation framework that we developed for CHASE. A heterogeneous smart-environment, with different coverage-areas for each sensor-systems or sub-network, constitutes the heart of the simulation environment. Synthetic traces of user's activities are dynamically generated and feed in. The mobile resident is assumed to have a set of deterministic and statistical patterns reflecting his/her life-style. Before discussing the simulation results, we describe the parameters used in our study.

- In the weekdays a professor leaves from the house for university in morning at 8.00 AM and returns back in the evening at 5.30 PM. In the week-ends and holidays he stays more in the home performing house-hold activities with minimal mobility for pleasure.
- The location-aware energy and comfort management framework is compared with two different energy and comfort management platforms: (i) In the static energy management platform, a set of devices and lights are kept on for some amount of time. The temperature control system is used for the entire time to maintain the temperature of the entire house. (ii) In the optimal manual energy plan, the inhabitant manually operates all the devices whenever he enters and leaves the house. This is used to capture the minimum value (lower bound) of the energy consumed in a typical indoor environment.

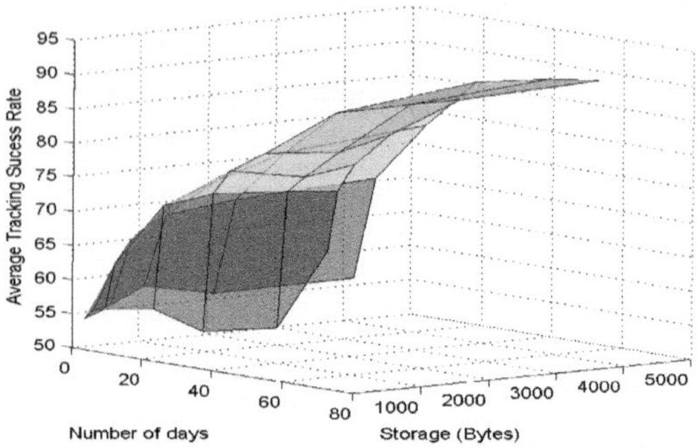

Fig. 2. Dynamics of Prediction-Accuracy with Storage

Success rate is the key factor for evaluation of any prediction scheme. Incorrect predictions results in erroneous system behavior, thereby incurring huge cost and performance overhead. Figure 2 corroborates this relationship between predictive accuracy and dictionary size over the entire period.

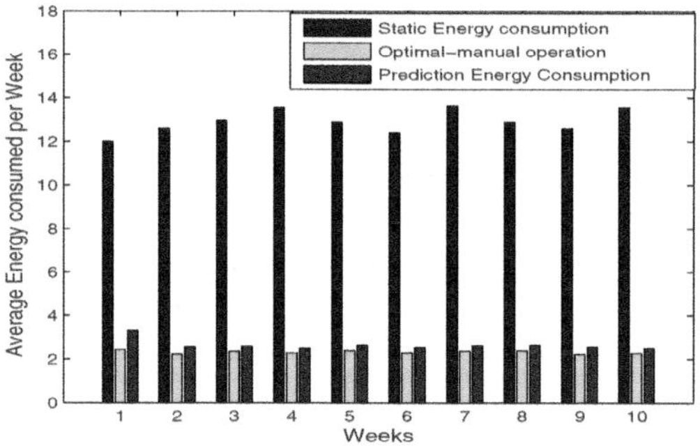

Fig. 3. Daily Energy Consumption

The main objective of this predictive framework at the context of Smart Home is to provide the inhabitant with necessary comfort at minimum possible cost. While moving from a particular zone to another, correct prediction of *typical routes* and next destination helps in triggering the actuators along those routes, thereby attempting to optimize the energy consumption. In Figure 3 we have compared this amount of energy consumption scheme resulting from our *predictive location-awareness* with the static and optimal energy plans and observed that our scheme closely follows the optimal energy consumption process. The minor deviation of this scheme from the optimal energy consumption process is a direct consequence of high prediction success rate. Figure 4 demonstrates the variation of inhabitant's average comfort with temperature and relative humidity. The highest possible (optimal) comfort value is assumed as 10. Our

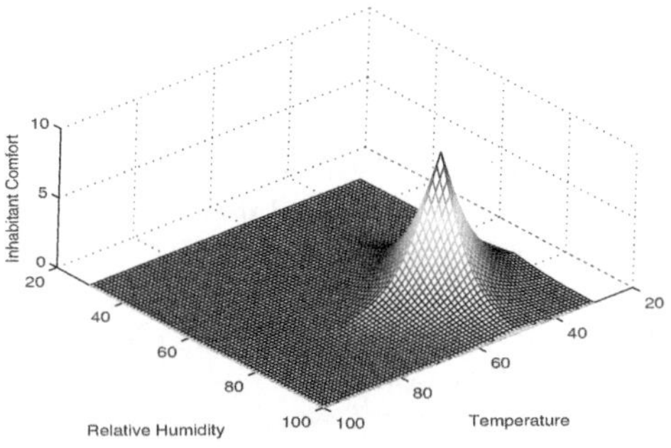

Fig. 4. Comfort Variation with Temperature and Humidity

experiments point out the maximum comfort (~ 9) is obtained in the temperature $\sim 75F$ and relative humidity $\sim 70\%$. However, comfort sharply decreases (exponentially) with changes in temperature and humidity.

7 Conclusions

In this paper we have proposed a near-optimal tracking and comfort management framework for context-aware, heterogeneous adaptive smart environments. It exploits the correlation in movement patterns between individual component sensor-networks, without assuming the existence of a centralized or publicly available topology database. Since the optimal tracking problem is NP-complete we have proposed a greedy solution for it. In order to minimize the uncertainty created by the inhabitants mobility, we have adopted the Bayesian Algorithm as the underlying technology for sensory data updates. The concept of typical set and asymptotic equipartition property helps in selecting the inhabitants most likely paths, which aids in minimizing the difference between the systems predicted paths and the inhabitants actual paths. Activation of smart temperature control system and automated devices along those typical paths assists in providing inhabitants necessary comfort at near optimal cost.

References

1. Thermal Environmental Conditions for Human Occupancy, American Society of Heating, Refrigerating, and Air-Conditioning (ANSI/ASHRAE), Standard No. 55-2004 (2004)
2. Bahl, P., Padmanabhan, V.: RADAR: An In-Building RF-based User Location and Tracking System. In: Proc. IEEE Infocom, IEEE CS Press, CA (2000)
3. Cover, T.M., et al.: Elements of Information Theory. John Wiley, Chichester (1991)
4. Doherty, L., et al.: Convex Position Estimation in Wireless Sensor Networks. In: Proceedings of Infocom 2001, IEEE CS Press, CA (2001)
5. Fox, D., et al.: A probabilistic Approach to Collaborative Multi-Robot Localization. Autonomous Robots (2000)

6. Goodrich, M.A.: Using Models of Cognition in HRI Evaluation and Design. AAAI (2004)
7. Harter, A., Hopper, A.: A distributed location system for the active office. IEEE Network 8(1) (1994)
8. Harter, A., Hopper, A., Steggles, P., Ward, A., Webster, P.: The anatomy of a context-aware application. In: Proc. 5th Int'l Conf. on Mobile Computing and Networking (1999)
9. Krumm, J., Harris, S., Meyers, B., Brumitt, B., Hale, M., Shafer, S.: Multi-Camera Multi-Person Tracking for Easy Living. In: Proceedings of 3rd IEEE International Workshop on Visual Surveillance (2000)
10. Lesser, et al.: The Intelligent Home Testbed, Autonomy Control Software Workshop (1999)
11. Marsella, S., Gratch, J.: Modeling Coping Behavior in Virtual Humans: Dont Worry, Be Happy. In: Proc. of. 2nd Intl. Joint Conf. on Autonomous Agents and Multiagent Systems (2003)
12. M. C. Mozer.: The Neural Network House: An Environment that Adapts to its Inhavitants. In: Proc. of the American Association for Artificial Intelligence Spring Symposium on Intelligent Environments (1998)
13. Orr, R.J., Abowd, G.D.: The Smart Floor: A Mechanism for Natural User Identification and Tracking. In: Proceedings of 2000 Conference on Human Factors in Computing Systems (CHI 2000), ACM Press, NY (2000)
14. Priyantha, N., Chakraborty, A., Balakrishnan, H.: The Cricket location support system. In: Proc. 6th Int'l Conference on Mobile Computing and Networking (2000)
15. Roy, A., DasBhaumik, S.K., Bhattacharya, A., Basu, K., Cook, D., Das, S.K.: Location-Aware Resource Management in Smart Homes. In: 1st IEEE Intl. Conf. on Pervasive Computing and Communications (PerCom) (2003)
16. Misra, A., Roy, A., Das, S.: An Information-Theoretic Framework for Optimal Location Tracking in Multi-System 4G Wireless Networks. In: INFOCOM (2004)
17. Roy, A., Misra, A., Das, S.: Minimum Cost Paging for Multi-System Wireless Networks. In: IEEE WiOpt, Modeling and Optimization in Mobile, Ad Hoc and Wireless Networks (2004)
18. Saxena, N., SHin, J., Roy, A.: CARP: Context-Aware Resource Provisioning for Multimedia over 4G Wireless Networks. In: ICCS, Beijing. LNCS, Springer, Heidelberg (2007)
19. Saxena, N., SHin, J., Roy, A.: The Minimum Cost Tracking Problem in Heterogeneous Smart Environments. In: The First International Conference on Ubiquitous Information Management and Communication, Korea (2007)
20. Schilit, B., LaMarca, A., Borriello, G., Griswold, W., McDonald, D., Lazowska, E., Balachandran, A., Hong, J., Iverson, V.: Challenge: Ubiquitous Location-Aware Computing and the Place Lab Initiative. In: Proc. of 1st ACM Intl. Workshop on Wireless Mobile Applications and Services on WLAN (WMASH 2003) (2003)
21. Weiser, M.: The computer for the 21st century. Scientific American 265(3) (1991)
22. Wolfson, O., Sistla, P., Xu, B., Zhou, J., Chamberlain, S.: DOMINO: Databases for moving objects tracking. In: ACM Int'l Conf. on Management of Data (1999)
23. Wyner, A., Ziv, Z.: Some Asymptotic Properties of the Entropy of a Stationary Ergodic Data Source with Applications to Data Compression. IEEE Transactions on Information Theory 35(6) (1989)
24. Zhang, H.: Human Thermal Sensation and Comfort in Transient and Non-Uniform Thermal Environments. Doctoral Dissertation, Architecture Dept., U.C. Berkley

A Methodology of Identifying Ubiquitous Smart Services for U-City Development

Ohbyung Kwon[1] and Jihoon Kim[2]

[1] School of International Management Kyunghee University
Seochun, Ghiheung, Yongin, Kyunggi-do, South Korea
obkwon@khu.ac.kr
[2] Research Center for Ubiquitous Business and Services, Kyunghee University
Seochun, Ghiheung, Yongin, Kyunggi-do, South Korea
hdlamb@khu.ac.kr

Abstract. Recently, developing a U-City as an integrated set of ubiquitous space services has been regarded as a promising field in realizing ubiquitous computing technology. However, researchers lack well-organized U-City requirement analyses to declare what specific kinds of ubiquitous space services are needed. Additionally, system developers also lack reliable strategies to determine which ubiquitous computing technologies to incorporate in order to meet the U-City users' needs. Hence, the dual goals of this paper are to propose a set of unique U-City construction philosophies, and to analyze which services should be offered in the U-Cities ubiquitous space services. To analyze U-City success factors, we used a CSF methodology to conduct a field survey of individuals who are potential end users of the ubiquitous space services. We then conducted focused group interviews with professionals in the ubiquitous computing technology field in Korea to identify the inter-relationships between ubiquitous space services and the associated critical success factors.

1 Introduction

U-City, a "ubiquitous city" is defined as a next generation urban space that includes a integrated set of ubiquitous services: a convergent form of both physical and online spaces. These services ultimately aim to enhance quality of life factors, such as convenience, safety and welfare. Recently, developing a U-City that aims to maximize residents' perceptions of these services' value has seen key advancements by fully optimizing ubiquitous computing technologies. The U-City space typically consists of traditional physical spaces—such as airport, campus, medical canter, home and car—and an augmented space that is a combination of both physical and virtual spaces. Representing a strategic use of ubiquitous computing technologies, the development of U-City goes beyond traditional urban engineering to embrace an inter-disciplinary effort between information systems developers and strategic management.

Including U-City development challenges as new information system and strategic management research issues stems from analyzing the differences between U-City

J. Indulska et al. (Eds.): UIC 2007, LNCS 4611, pp. 143–152, 2007.

and traditional or Internet-based cities. Features and development methodologies for fully-developed U-City-level ubiquitous services are still in nascent forms.

Legacy U-City development projects in Korea were originally (and continue to be) focused on accomplishing those services which meet residents' relatively lower needs such as convenience, cost effectiveness, and safety in terms of Maslow's Need Hierarchy Theory or Herzberg's Two-factor Theory [13, 10]. To increase the acceptance of residents who stay in U-City or Ubiquitous Space through the consideration of their satisfaction, more active services are requested the fulfillment of the higher needs such as relation, self-esteem, and growth. To date, though, service selection decision making seems to be not well-structured. Matching U-City residents' key needs to the appropriate ubiquitous services is a critical success factor to progress the U-City implementation projects.

Hence, this paper proposes a ubiquitous service selection methodology for U-City development. To do so, recent U-City projects world-wide are observed to identify the planned ubiquitous services. We suggest a requirement analysis method using approaches common to psychology and marketing to identify those services that residents most want. Finally, we propose an algorithm of service selection considering the resident's needs a U-City project size.

2 U-City

At present, U-City projects are undergoing development all over the world. In Finland, Helsinki's Virtual Village aims to accomplish a networked "information city" by grafting together public and personal spaces to provide innovative virtual community spaces. These virtual community spaces contain businesses and students who work together to design appliances, buildings, and spaces [24]. New York City's Lower Manhattan project aims to implement an environment that provides a variety of ubiquitous services for residents. The project uses communication technologies to eventually generate urban experiences and a public voice for the citizens [18]. In California, the Mission Bay project is constructing a gigabyte-level network that will, by 2010, allow citizens to benefit from various location-free information services such as weather service and distance learning [3]. In Singapore, the One-North project plans a future living space where the goal is to make possible a more efficient power system, a media-rich information environment, and increased network usage. Prototypes of One-North are slated to include a video conferencing center, a media square garden, or a People Mover System (PMS). In Korea, Seoul's Digital Media City (DMC) is developing a ubiquitous street where individuals can display and have hands-on experience with innovative digital media appliances [7]. Also in Seoul, the U-Seoul project is experimenting with several ubiquitous services to transform Seoul's traditional markets into digital, highly personalized spaces where visitors can enjoy ubiquitous blogging, social networking, shop recommendations, and traditional culture through various non-intrusive ubiquitous services.

However, it is not clear whether legacy U-City development projects are actually based on ubiquitous computing technology. A set of rules are required to clearly delineate traditional cities and U-Cities. Secondly, both potential citizens as well as experts in urban technology should be included in urban planning phase to select appropriate ubiquitous services. A structured method to reflect potential citizens' preferences should be considered. Next, even though there are many candidate services acceptable to the citizens, actual service selection is obviously subject to certain financial constraints. Therefore, a sort of prioritizing services rules needs to be prepared beforehand.

3 Ubiquitous Service Identification and Selection Methodology

3.1 Overall Methodology

Requirement analysis research for development of ubiquitous services—U-City projects' main elements—has been rare or unstructured. In this paper, we initially investigate conventional methods to collect citizens' opinions on ubiquitous services. Our methodology is based on Kleef's study, which categorizes 10 of the most common methods in this area in terms of what are their key features, strengths, weaknesses, and levels of appropriateness. The 10 categorizes can be categorized with some features such as 'Service Characteristic' and 'Purpose' [6, 8, 11, 12, 15, 20, 2, 5, 21, 16, 9, 25, 4]. The properties of service characteristics are conventional and new services. The properties of purpose are service development and marketing.

According to the methods' categorization, when the suggested ubiquitous services are improved from traditional information technology-based services, a focus group technique is adopted. On the other hand, when the requirement analysis of the new services is based on innovative ubiquitous computing technology, lead user technique will be used in this paper. Thus, we conjointly apply the following methods for ubiquitous space service selection and requirement analysis:

1. Collection of the characteristics and services proposed by the legacy U-City projects: literature survey method.
2. Observation what the potential citizens perceives on the success factors of ubiquitous space: Critical Success Factors (CSF).
3. Requirement analysis of ubiquitous space services using a focus group.

In this paper, we propose a requirement analysis methodology for ubiquitous space service as shown in Fig.1. First, based on the literature review about U-City building projects, we determine each project's building philosophy and also do the requisite analysis for each project. And then, based on the literature study for the selected city, we collect the city's requisites proposed by urban planning and construction experts. These requisites will be used for the survey items to inspect the city's success factor in terms of general users. Through a questionnaire analysis of general users who are expected to be potential U-City citizens, we deduce the likely critical success factors (CSFs). After that, we conduct a focus group interview (FGI) to derive the relationship between the CSFs and any ubiquitous space services that are now provided. By conducting the FGI, we select the critical ubiquitous space services that are related to CSFs. To conduct the requirement analysis for implementing the confirmed services more concretely, we determine the service architecture including both existing and new services. Then, we analyze the commercialization feasibility time using both functional and technical requirement analyses based on the service architecture. We then divide the commercialization feasibility time into short, middle, and long periods, and assign and classify the ubiquitous space services to each period. Based on each classified ubiquitous space service, we extract more subdivided service architecture and the smart objects that are needed in the architecture. Finally, with experts, we fully review the architecture and confirm the reports of service requirement analysis.

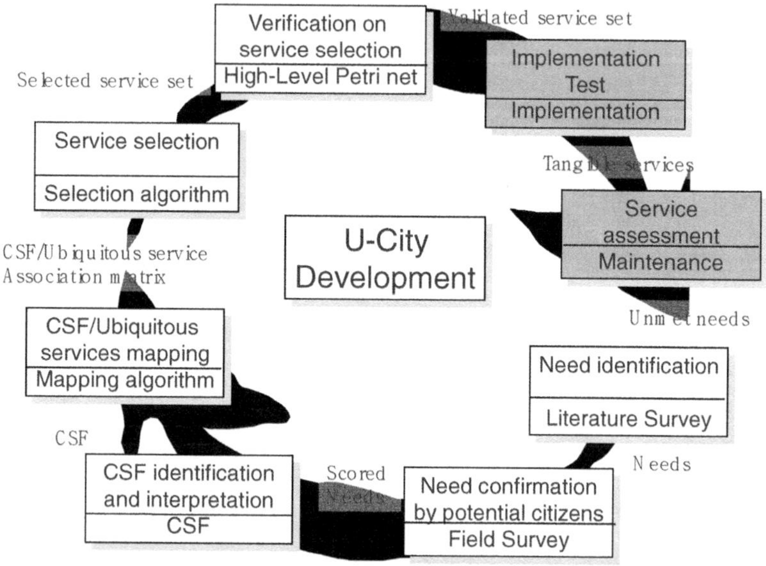

Fig. 1. Proposed Methodology

Among these methodologies, we will focus on the former six steps from need identification to validation on service selection in this paper.

3.2 Need Identification and Confirmation

To recognize the features of successful U-Cities, we collected experts' opinions on several items. First, we identified needs from the features of 'the good living city' at 'the special issue 2001: Good Living City' from Chosun Ilbo, the biggest newspaper in South Korea. Second, we also excerpted the pursued features by U-City projects from the literature which described the on-going U-City projects around the world including the cities in 2005. Based on the literature review, we discovered 145 'desirable city' needs to make a questionnaire for the potential citizens of U-City. From among the items in the questionnaire, we selected 93 questions after excluding the questions not related to the city. Finally, we surveyed the general users with a questionnaire including 93 questions and 11 service items and asked the users to evaluate it using a 7 point Likert-scale based on the users' subjectivity.

The survey was conducted from June 13th to 27th, 2005. We sent out 330 questionnaires and got back 264 questionnaires (return ratio = 80%). Among those returns, we chose 238 questionnaires excluding the 26 inappropriate answer sheets.

The respondents were all adults engaged in domestic finance, heavy industry, advertisement, etc. 47.1% of respondents were men. 39.9% of the respondents were in their 20s, 31.5% were in their 30s, with the balance being ≥ 40. The survey was conducted nationwide in South Korea.

Based on the responses, we first identify the relevant importance of the services in the general U-Cities. The respondents have selected public transportation, medical care, culture/art, information services, public services, education, public safety, leisure, entertainment and lodging services as more preferred services.

3.3 CSF Identification and Interpretation

Among the 93 items, we have selected the top 20 items (approx. 20%) according to the average score as the critical success factors. The result is shown in Table 1.

Table 1. Top 20% list among all questions (Selected)

Rank	Question	Average Score
1	I want to live in the city where I can breathe fresh air.	6.55
2	I want to live in the city where the crime rates are low.	6.51
3	I want to live in the city with many parks around the residential area.	6.50
4	I want to live in the city where I can drink fresh water.	6.48
5	I want to live in the city surrounded by clean nature nearby.	6.47
6	I want to live in the city with less pollution.	6.46
7	I want to live in the city helpful for educating my children's humanity.	6.45
8	I want to live in the city with lots of spaces to rest.	6.45
9	I want to live in the city respects the residents.	6.44
10	I want to live in the city where I can enjoy the cultural life.	6.42
11	I want to live in the safe city.	6.41
12	I want to live in the clean city.	6.40
...	...	...

According to the result of Table 1, the requirements about nature-friendly, health and safety have relatively higher scores as expected in the legacy U-City development projects. However, needs for citizens' pride and honor that were overlooked by the ongoing U-City projects were observed among the critical success factors. These overlooked needs tend to be higher in terms of need hierarchy originated by the traditional need theories. Hence, we made a comparative study between the needs considered by the on-going U-City projects and those expected the actual requirements by the potential citizens. To do this, we reconstructed the weighted average based on Alderfer's ERG(Existence-Relatedness-Growth) theory, which is one of the most referred theories as need hierarchy theory [1].

Fig. 2 shows the result of the relative importance between the needs considered by the developers who are in charge of the on-going U-City projects and those expected by potential citizens. As shown in Fig. 4, lower needs such as safety, convenience and economy are more emphasized by the U-City projects in comparison with social relationship, growth and humanism.

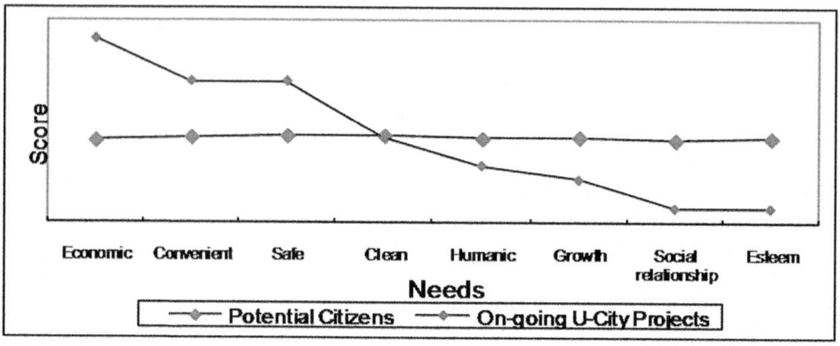

Fig. 2. The comparison of Needs

Based on the ERG theory, the needs in Fig.2 can be regrouped as the three needs as shown in Fig. 3. We could conclude that existence needs are overemphasized in U-Projects, while the relatedness and growth needs have less focus. Therefore, the construction of ubiquitous space in future U-City projects may want to emphasize higher needs such as social relationship, esteem, and growth in planning ubiquitous services.

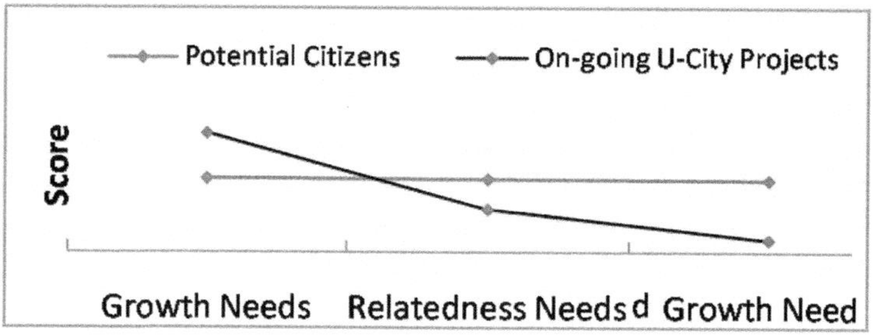

Fig. 3. The Score of Needs Based on ERG Theory

We also analyzed the result of survey on the point of Herzberg's two-factor theory [10]. The main point of Herzberg's theory is that the motivation factors are important to increase the individual motivation to perform a task, while the hygiene factors are irrelevant to task motivation. Motivation factors are related to the inside of human such as achievement, recognition for achievement, responsibility for task, interesting job, advancement to higher level tasks and growth. On the other hand, hygiene factors are related to the outside of human such as working conditions, quality of supervision, salary, status, safety, company, company policies and interpersonal relations. Current U-City projects seem to be more focused on hygiene factors such as safety and convenience. According to the two-factor theory, even though these factors are sufficiently provided to the residents, the residents of U-City might not explicitly be satisfied with the services. Therefore, when new ubiquitous space services are considered, the motivation factors such as honor, pride, honesty, justice, achievement and happiness should be considered importantly, too.

3.4 CSF/Ubiquitous Services Mapping and Service Selection

We conducted focus group interviews to determine which of the prototypes of existing ubiquitous services most satisfied general users' CSFs. To do this, we selected 147 ubiquitous computing experts: 74 doctoral researchers or project managers and 73 doctoral candidates involved in the ubiquitous computing projects sponsored by the Korean government. After individual contacts to ask them for interview with explaining the objectives and importance of this project, 72 researchers were selected (49%). 20 spaces, including a ubiquitous airport, were proposed in interviews, as well as 91 non-redundant services from existing U-City projects. The interviews were conducted during four weeks: from September 1st to September 28th 2005. According to the interview results, we could build ubiquitous services/CSF map as listed in Table 2. Based on the results, we have developed a service selection algorithm (Fig. 4) to choose the priority of U-City ubiquitous services.

Table 2. Ubiquitous services /CSF map

Ubiquitous Services	Freq	CSF1	CSF2	CSF3	CSF4	CSF5	….	CSF N
Ubiquitous Playground	43	2	1	3	1	10	…	7
Ubiquitous Immigration Service	41		8				…	1
Free Wireless Hotspot	40	1	1	1		1	…	3
E-Directory	39		2			1	…	2
Baggage Identity	37		6				…	1
U-Duty Free Comparative Shopping	35		2				…	
…	…	…	…	…	…	…	…	

Step 1: Let Υ be a set of ubiquitous space services υ_i. Then $\Upsilon = \{\upsilon_i, 0 \le i \le N\}$.
Step 2: Select the number of services (n) to be implemented from Υ.
Step 3: Prepare association matrix $M = \Sigma \times \Upsilon$, where Σ indicates a set of CSFs.
Step 4: Set threshold value, θ, which is the minimum requirement value of the total preferences of the service set.
Step 5: For all ${}_N C_n$ combinations, compute associative value of the set of services. For each loop, if the associative value is greater than θ, then add the set into candidate service set.
Step 6: Check out if the set of candidate service sets is empty. If empty, then proceed to Step 7. Else, go to Step 8.
Step 7: For all ${}_N C_n$ combinations, acquire a set of services, which associative value is maximal. Then go to Step 9.
Step 8: For all service sets in the candidate set, acquire a set of services, which associative value is maximal. Then go to Step 9.
Step 9: Determine the set as the optimal set.

Fig. 4. Ubiquitous service selection algorithm

To select ubiquitous space services following the process above, we developed a Java application. The program required four days to consider all possible combination in n=1~10. According to the selected ubiquitous space services based on the result, the associative value does not increase from n=6, with associative value of 1620.0.

This means that additional services do not contribute to an increased associative value, with the exceptions of {Airport, Traffic, Environment, Security, Ecology, Tourism}. Therefore, if other conditions are the same, the priority of ubiquitous space service development should be in order of Airport, Environment, Ecology, Tourism, Security, and Traffic.

3.5 Verification on Service Selection

Clearly, the selected set of ubiquitous services should be verified before system development begins. The questions for verification include the following:

- Is the service performed in either independent or combined manner?
- If the service is performed in a combined manner, is the service performed simultaneously?
- If the service is performed in a combined manner, is the service performed sequentially? If so, which services should precede and which services should follow?
- What would be happening if the arrival rate of service requests changes?
- What would be happening if the service composition changes?
- What would be the optimal service composition?

To address these questions, we applied a Timed Petri net to formulate the dynamic process of the selected services. A Timed Petri net has been proven to be optimal in terms of representation power and robustness of system verification in modeling dynamic systems–like a city-level ubiquitous service system. We developed a prototype system based on PIPE, an open source for Timed Petri net editor and simulator. Using Java 1.4.x, we customized PIPE as PIPE-USS, which can represent the general components of ubiquitous system: agents, ontology, sensors and web

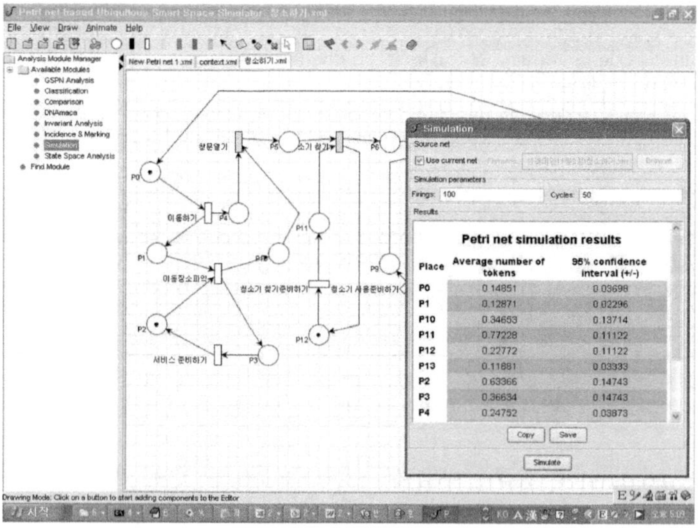

Fig. 5. PIPE-USS Screen Shot

services. Using PIPE-USS, we could model and analyze the sequence, composition and condition of the selected ubiquitous services as shown in Fig. 5.

4 Conclusion

U-City development provides an excellent opportunity to realize ubiquitous smart services based on ubiquitous computing technologies. U-City is more than just a set of online services grafted onto a physical space; it can be regarded as an integrated set of ubiquitous smart services. To do so, a U-City will be established that includes a sensory network and context-aware information management systems with a variety of distributed devices and autonomously working software.

One of the contributions of this paper is that we have proposed a structured and sophisticated identification methodology of ubiquitous service selections through evaluating the service priority for U-City development. We evaluate psychological requirement analysis methods; CSF, Target group interview, and Lead user technique are sequentially used to determine optimal service selection. This study's CSF method aims to determine which needs of the potential residents of the U-City and/or ubiquitous smart service users should be considered to select services, rather than asserting services based on the system developers' viewpoints. What and how to improve legacy services to determine ubiquitous features are identified through the target group interview method.

Moreover, we have observed that the gap between the actual potential users' desires and the philosophy of the legacy U-City development projects is considerable. In particular, regarding Maslow's Need Hierarchy Theory, users' higher needs—such as self-esteem and self-actualization—are priorities, not simply the users' physiological or safety needs.

Acknowledgments. This research is supported by the ubiquitous Computing and Network (UCN) Project, the Ministry of Information and Communication (MIC) 21st Century Frontier R&D Program in Korea.

References

1. Alderfer, C.P.: An Empirical Test of a New Theory of Human Needs. Organizational Behavior and Human Performance 4, 142–175 (1969)
2. Bruseberg, A., McDonagh-Philp, D.: Focus Groups to Support the Industrial/Product Designer: a Review Based on Current Literature and Designers' Feedback. Applied Ergonomics 33, 27–38 (2002)
3. CENIC: Can California Support a Ubiquitous Gigabyte Statewide Network by 2010?. Interact: A Networking Application Magazine 4 (2003)
4. Christensen, G.L., Olson, J.C.: Mapping Consumers' Mental Models with ZMET. Psychology & Marketing 19, 477–502 (2002)
5. Collins, A.M., Loftus, E.F.: A Spreading-Activation Theory of Semantic Processing. Psychological Review 82, 407–428 (1975)
6. Coombs, C.H.: A theory of data. Wiley, New York (1964)
7. DMC: (2005) http://dmc.seoul.go.kr/english/index.jsp

8. Green, P.E., Srinivasan, V.: Conjoint Analysis in Consumer Research: Issues and Outlook. Journal of Consumer Research 5, 103–152 (1978)
9. Gutman, J.: A menas-end chain model based on consumer categorization processes. Journal of Marketing 46, 60–72 (1982)
10. Herzberg, F.: Work and the Nature of Man, Chapter 6, pp. 71–91. World Publishing, New York (1966)
11. Krieger, B., Cappuccio, R., Katz, R., Moskowitz, H.: Next Generation Healthy Soup: An Exploration Using Conjoint Analysis. Journal of Sensory Studies 18, 249–268 (2003)
12. Leonard, D., Sensiper, S.: The Role of Tacit Knowledge in Group Innovation. California Management Review 40, 112–132 (1988)
13. Maslow, A.H.: A theory of human motivation. Psychological Review 50, 370–396 (1943)
14. Olson, E.L., Bakke, G.: Implementing the Lead User Method in a High Technology Firm: A Longitudinal Study of Intentions Versus Actions. Journal of Product Innovation Management 18, 388–395 (2001)
15. Polanyi, M.: The Tacit Dimension. Doubleday, New York (1966)
16. Sampson, P.: Using the Repertory Grid Test. Journal of Marketing Research 11, 78–81 (1972)
17. Sheth, J.N., Mittal, B., Newman, B.I.: Customer Behaviour: Consumer Behaviour and Beyond. Dryden Press, Orlando (1999)
18. Spectropolis: (2005) http://www.spectropolis.info
19. TagandScan: (2005) http://www.tagandscan.com/index.htm
20. Ulwick, A.W.: Turn Customer Input Into Innovation. Harvard Business Review, 92–97 (2002)
21. Urban, G.L., Hauser, J.R.: Design and Marketing of New Products. Prentice-Hall, Englewood Cliffs (1993)
22. Urban, G.L., Weinberg, B.D., Hauser, J.R.: Premarket Forecasting of Really-New Products. Journal of Marketing 60, 47–60 (1996)
23. van Kleef, E., van Trijp, H., Luning, P.: onsumer Research in the Early Stages of New Product Development: A Critical Review of Methods and Techniques. Food Quality and Preference 16, 181–201 (2005)
24. Virtual Village: (2005) http://www.helsinkivirtualvillage.fi
25. Von Hippel, E., Katz, R.: Shifting Innovation to Users via Toolkits. Management Science 48, 821–833 (2002)
26. Von Hippel, E.: Lead Users: A Source of Novel Product Concepts. Management Science 32, 791–805 (1986)
27. van Kleef, E., van Trijp, H.C.M., Luning, P.: Consumer research in the early stages of new product development: a critical review of methods and techniques. Food Quality and Preference 16, 181–201 (2005)

Simulated Intersection Environment and Learning of Collision and Traffic Data in the U&I Aware Framework

Flora Dilys Salim[1], Seng Wai Loke[2], Andry Rakotonirainy[3], and Shonali Krishnaswamy[1]

[1] Caulfield School of Information Technology, Monash University, Caulfield East, VIC 3145, Australia
{Flora.Salim,Shonali.Krishnaswamy}@infotech.monash.edu.au
[2] Computer Science and Computer Engineering, La Trobe University, Bundoora, Australia
s.loke@latrobe.edu.au
[3] Centre for Accident Research and Road Safety Queensland, Queensland University of Technology, Carseldine, QLD 4034, Australia
r.andry@qut.edu.au

Abstract. Road intersections have become the places of high road incidents and car collisions. Our hypothesis is that a system can be made aware of dangerous situations at road intersections and warn drivers accordingly. Moreover, over time, the system can learn (or re-learn) such "patterns" of danger for specific intersections given a history of rich collision data collected via sensors (that exist today). Based on the assumption that such a history of sensory data about colliding vehicles can be obtained, we show useful patterns that can be extracted. This paper presents our framework for intersection understanding, presenting simulated results suggesting that a fragment of the world (i.e. intersections) can be more deeply understood by mining appropriate sensor data. The simulated environment of the road intersections forming the basis of a real-world implementation and testing of the framework are discussed here. The recent results of mining traffic and collision data generated by the simulation are also included in this paper.

1 Introduction

The rate of fatalities of road intersection collisions has not significantly changed in more than two decades, regardless of improved intersection design, innovation of vehicles, and more sophisticated Intelligent Transportation System (ITS) technology [1]. Intersections are among the most hazardous sites on U.S. roads. The statistic of crashes in the year 2002 in the USA reported that 50 percents of all reported crashes, approximately 3.2 million crashes, were intersection-related [1]. 22 percents of the total fatalities on the road, which was 9,612 fatalities, and roughly 1.5 million injuries and 3 million collisions, happened at intersection surroundings [2]. The high accident and fatality rate in intersections is chiefly determined by the complexity at each intersection.

Currently, collision warning systems mostly only react to events that might cause collision [3]. However, intersection collision warning systems should also be able to

J. Indulska et al. (Eds.): UIC 2007, LNCS 4611, pp. 153–162, 2007.

analyse physical situations and proactively learn about the intersection from historical data and events, acquired via sensors. Indeed, since sensor technology in Intelligent Transportation Systems (ITS) has advanced in the past few years, a considerable amount of data from in-vehicles and roadside sensors can be feasibly collected and exploited through data analysis techniques that use the appropriate algorithms. Effective algorithms can facilitate better understanding of data, better ways to execute tasks, or improve performance [3]. Questions then arise: what kind of data should be considered, and what analysis can be done to such data to provide useful information about an intersection to help reduce intersection incidents? We address these questions, in part, in this paper. The broader question about smart worlds that we touch on here is: what situations of (a part of) the physical world should and can be automatically understood, and what data can be acquired, and how can such data be processed, in order to recognize, and subsequently react to, such situations?

In order to comprehend driver behaviors for uses in safety applications, simply relying on raw conventional sensor data, such as from ground loop sensors installed on the road, is insufficient, as data analysis techniques is necessary to extract significant traffic parameters [4]. For example, in implementing intersection safety solutions, monitoring the speed, location, and movement of each vehicle is essential. Two scenarios are analyzed in [4]: firstly, left turn across path subject vehicles versus other vehicles from opposite direction; secondly, red light running and dilemma zone.

Data mining is the development of methods and techniques for making sense of data by pattern discovery and extraction [5]. There have been a number of projects on data mining in the area of Intelligent Transportation Systems (ITS), such as for driver's behavior recognition, traffic optimization, and incident detection [3]. Pantheon Gateway Project mined real time highway data from traffic sensors which accumulates to 173,000 sensor readings every day being added to the database. The purpose of this research is to detect real time changes in traffic conditions (speed, volume, occupancy). Using a tree-based classifier, the condition change is further analyzed to detect the cause of it, which can either be weather related, accident, special events, or road construction [6]. Therefore, traffic condition changes can be detected in real-time based on the learnt traffic patterns. However, existing works of data mining for road safety in ITS are mainly done for highway safety [6], [7], [8], [9]. Although data mining has been effectively used for extracting useful knowledge from data storage, the advances in sensor technology have resulted in a large amount of sensor data to be understood. Therefore, it is not practical to store real-time sensor data for later processing. Preferably, data processing should be done on the streams of sensors data, not on sensors' data storage. Also, development of small devices encourages research of data mining on small devices rather than on huge superpower computer. Ubiquitous Data Mining (UDM) techniques can be used to analyse data streams to discover useful knowledge such as patterns and associations on mobile, embedded, and ubiquitous devices [5]. UDM has been used in ITS to monitor a vehicle's health and driver's characteristics and to identify drink driving behaviours [3]. We use UDM techniques in our framework.

By learning from historical data of collisions and near-collision events and traffic data, improved detection, automatic adaptations, and improved reactive behaviour can be achieved, since the learning results are incorporated into the knowledge base of the collision warning system. The system can then gain a better knowledge of the intersection over time for better crash prediction. We have proposed and implemented the Ubiquitous Intersection Awareness (U & I Aware) framework (Fig. 1) [3], which aims to achieve holistic situation recognition at road intersections. We have established the initial simulation scenarios, described our implementation of a mathematical based collision detection algorithm and initial data mining results [3]. This paper elaborates the simulation further and explains the late results of our data learning. Section 2 discusses the intersection simulation built for the purpose of generating a resembling real-world data. Section 3 discusses the results obtained so far from the learning of collision and traffic data. Section 4 concludes the paper.

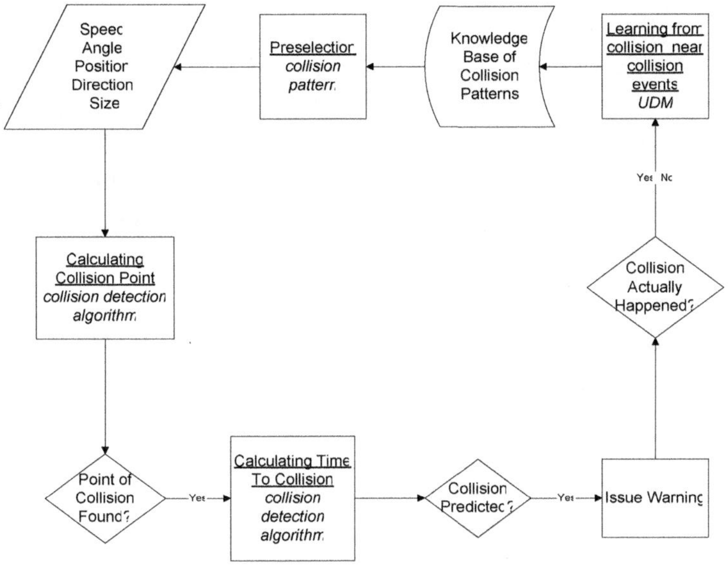

Fig. 1. U & I Aware Framework

2 Simulation

We use a computer based simulation of two different scenarios: intersection with traffic lights (Fig. 2) and without traffic lights [3]. At this stage, computer based simulation is an acceptable proof of concept, since the scenarios that we implement involve collisions that are difficult to be simulated in the real world due to the constraint of resources. The simulation attributes are as follows:

1. Intersection: intersection type, leg (size, count, angle, lane group), lane group (lanes, traffic control), lane (size, vehicle occupation), traffic control (signal time, period, timer)
2. vehicle: speed, acceleration, size, type, position, angle, maneuver
3. driver: profile, intended destination, choices of maneuver.

The simulation parameters have been instrumented to mirror real world situations so that prediction and learning may yield reasonable results. The length of each intersection leg is 30 meters. Each vehicle is should observe the traffic light signals. Traffic light colors periodically change based on the 15 seconds interval: each red period is 15 seconds, green period is 13 seconds, and yellow period is 2 seconds. The vehicles should follow a several traffic rules, such as safe following distance (3 seconds behind the vehicle ahead), safe stopping distance (2 seconds behind the vehicle ahead), and the speed limit.

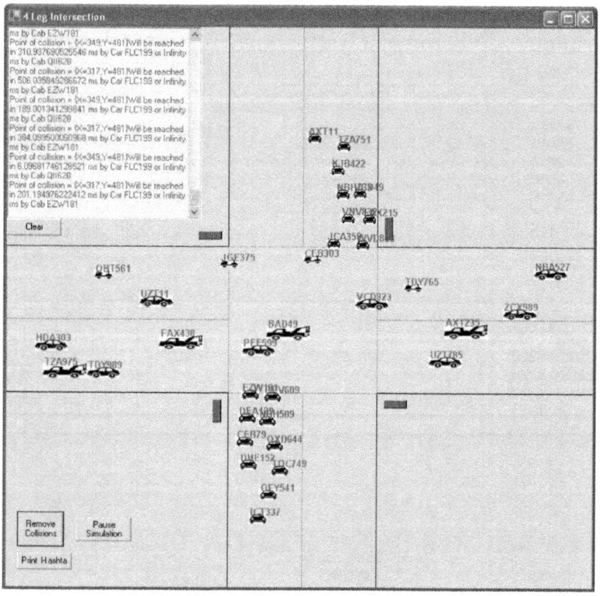

Fig. 2. Intersection Simulation

The vehicles are randomly generated in the intersection simulation with different speeds, maneuvers, position and trajectory at the end of each intersection leg. The density of vehicles generated in the simulation is based on four different time schemes: morning (6 a.m. to 12 noon), afternoon (12 noon to 6 p.m.), evening (6 p.m. to 12 midnight), and dawn (12 midnight to 6 a.m.) that are recorded in our intersection configuration file. There are four different vehicle types that are recorded in the vehicle configuration file: scooter, small sedan, large sedan, and truck. Each of the types has different sizes and range of speed that are scaled to real-world measurements. There is a random probability that one 1 out of 5 cars generated in the simulation is a "naughty car", which will have speed above the speed limit. Random "naughty" vehicles are generated in the simulation so that its impact on road safety can be analyzed. Human driving behaviors are also simulated in the intersection, such as attempts to beat the red light when vehicles are facing yellow light and located at the front line of leg and speeding when passing the intersection centre.

When the simulation is run (Fig. 2.), data from traffic and collision events are recorded in log files, one for each case of learning analysis. Different combinations of attributes are taken to feed the data mining algorithms. For example, to learn crash patterns, the input attributes are maneuver, conflicting paths, and angle between paths.

At this stage, we have up to six different scenarios where different sets of sensor data are simulated and collected every 5 milliseconds in our simulation, which produces up to 6.78 MB of data per minute. The frequency of the readings can be adjusted; however, we set 5 milliseconds for the purpose of measuring the scalability and performance of the system. Data generated from the simulation can also be retrieved in the real world using appropriate sensors that are capable to capture all the required information [3].

3 Current Experimental Learning Results

This section presents the latest results of our mining of collision data. We show that collision patterns are learned through classification and clustering. New events are matched with the existing classes in the patterns repository of the intersection's central (software) agent or the car's (software) agent, depending on where learning happens. For example, if a collision happens outside a known pattern, a learning process can detect a new collision pattern. Collision patterns in an intersection can be learnt when there is data about vehicle manoeuvres, direction, and angle. These data can be obtained from sensors. We have assumed these data in our traffic and collision simulation. The learning scenarios: (1) learning dangerous traffic and driving trends, and (2) learning collision patterns and trends, are described further below.

3.1 Learn Changes and Trends in Traffic Data

The main purpose of this learning is to determine whether the variation of speed and traffic volume may affect the number of collisions and different kinds of collisions in an intersection. The data is gathered periodically from our simulation, where different parameters of time of day (morning/afternoon/evening/dawn) and peak/off-peak hours are applied to produce different behaviours in speed and traffic volume. In each interval (which is 4 seconds in our simulation), a record is generated with the following attribute values: *average traffic volume, average speed, total number of collisions, total number of side collisions, and total number of rear-end collisions in the last interval* (Fig. 3). The Pantheon Gateway Project [8] uses a similar set of attributes of real world sensor data (speed, volume, occupancy) to learn changes in highway traffic.

Another set of data is used to identify dangerous driving trends and it consists of attributes that are collected from pairs of vehicles involved in a collision, which are *speed and distance to intersection of each vehicle, traffic light color faced by each vehicle, and the collision point* (Fig. 4). The purpose of this learning is to determine the boundaries of safe and dangerous driving behaviours. A new row is not recorded periodically, but only when a collision occurs. There are 20 – 30 records in the collision data. After applying Expectation-Maximization (EM) unsupervised clustering [10], the result shows that in this particular intersection, most of the collisions occur when one of the cars have speed over 49 – this is merely an indication of what can be learnt from such data. When we apply this knowledge to a collision warning system, an earlier prediction and extra precautions can be done to vehicle that speed above 49.

AvgTrafficVolume	AvgSpeed	Totalcollisions	TotalSideCollisions	TotalRearEndCollisions
17	46	0	0	0
19	48	7	1	6
11	48	0	0	0
18	47	0	0	0
19	53	5	0	5
13	52	0	0	0
17	53	1	1	0
17	51	0	0	0
20	47	10	0	10

Fig. 3. Periodic Traffic Data (in this sample, a row is recorded every 4 seconds)

SpeedCar1	DistanceTo IntersectionCar1	TLColor1	SpeedCar2	DistanceTo IntersectionCar2	TLColor2	CollisionPointX	CollisionPointY
99	-76	0	55	-104	0	463	369
51	-77	0	55	-104	0	437	369
55	-118	0	92	-94	0	354	406
57	-135	0	93	-103	0	455	400
50	-108	0	0	-9	1	305	392
50	-76	0	50	-108	0	309	424
94	-359	0	53	-392	0	456	657
55	-397	0	94	-364	0	356	136
52	-370	0	55	-397	0	337	130
50	-359	0	53	-392	0	424	657
48	30	3	0	1	3	359	530
28	34	3	0	4	3	445	261
53	-89	0	93	-70	0	369	377
50	-79	0	53	-98	0	378	372

Fig. 4. Collision Event Data with Attributes of Speed, Distance, Traffic Light Color, and Collision Point

The initial results of applying EM on the data generated from our simulation (with the size of 50 – 80 records per file) are as follows:

- The higher the traffic volume and speed, the higher is the risk of collision.
- The number of rear end collisions is heavily affected by traffic volume. The higher the traffic volume, the higher the possibility of rear end collision. Speed also contributes to rear end collisions.
- Side collision is not much correlated with traffic volume but with higher speeds, especially when the speed limit is violated.

Note that the above results are applicable only at the intersection where learning is performed. In another intersection, results may vary. This is why data mining can contribute to a generic model of intersection safety system that can self-adapt to different types of intersections – learning from the data specific to the intersection. Also, note that in some cases, there are a high number of collisions – this is due to simulated (simplified) vehicles, which when in the path of collision, as has been previously detected, will eventually collide. This is because our simulation is designed to focus on prediction and not avoidance at this stage. Our results suggest that there is value in mining such collision data (which current sensor technology can be used to acquire), of which our simulated data here is merely indicative. Note also that, in a real-world setting, it is not necessary for only data about actual collisions to be used for analysis, but even data about cars on the path to collision (even if an actual collision did not at the end happen due to some evasive action of the drivers) can be included in the analysis to provide indicative trends.

3.2 Learn Patterns in Collision Data

Secondly, to learn collision patterns and trends, the simulated sensor data has six attributes, three of which (i.e. *direction, manoeuvre, and angle*) are from colliding vehicle pairs. Whenever there is a collision or near-collision event in our intersection simulation, data from the colliding (or near-colliding) pair of vehicles are collected and mined. In the real world, such data can be collected with conventional sensors such as inductive loop detectors on the road, or speedometer in the vehicle. As described in [3], we include the following manoeuvres, which can be acquired via in-vehicle sensor implementation and Coupled Hidden Markov Model (CHMM) analysis: one car passing another, turning right, turning left, changing lane right, changing lane left, starting, and stopping, using our knowledge base of collision patterns. In the early experiments, we only included side collision data generated from the simulation, which has 10 – 20 side collision records. A side collision involves vehicles that travel in traversing paths. Hence, we exclude collisions that involve vehicles that travel in the same trajectory. We have successfully classified types of side collisions or perpendicular crashes in a cross intersection using data mining. We first implemented this with the C4.5 decision tree (using J48 classifier [10]) and the second vehicle direction (*Veh2_Direction*) attribute is nominated as the class. The implementation results also exhibit the most common crash patterns that exist within the particular intersection where the traffic data is acquired. For example, our results, using randomly seeded data, show that vehicles that travel with a straight manoeuvre from the left leg to the right leg of the intersection tend to collide with vehicles that travel with a straight manoeuvre from the lower leg to the upper leg (Fig. 5).

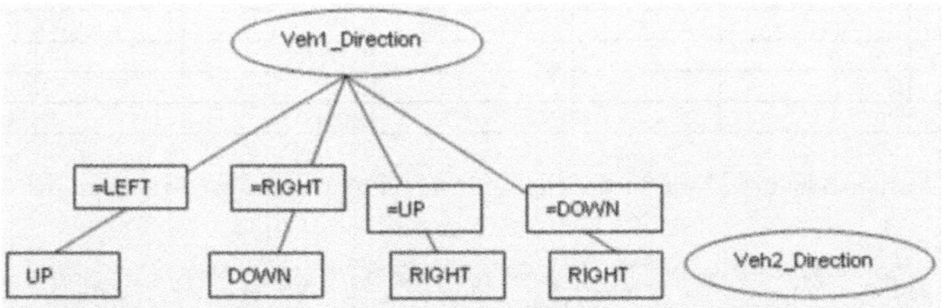

Fig. 5. Side Collision Patterns based on Vehicle Direction as classified by C4.5

Then, to realise all the possible crash patterns that involve straight driving manoeuvre in an intersection, a Bayesian Network classifier [10] is used to classify the same data. The crash patterns enumerate four possible straight driving directions in a four legs cross intersection, which are left, right, up, and down. The classification shows all the possible collision patterns that might happen with the probability rate of each crash pattern (See Fig. 6). The highest probability of a crash pattern in each direction is circled in red in Fig. 6. Out of all the collisions that occur to vehicles that travel from the right leg to the left leg (i.e. "LEFT" direction), 93.1% of the collisions occur with vehicles from the lower leg to the upper leg (i.e. "UP" direction). This result conforms to the result of classification with C4.5. Note that these results were obtained from our simulated data for one intersection. Applying the same technique to a different intersection (with different data) could lead to different likely situations for collisions – the point is that applying such learning techniques would enable such collision situations to be recognized automatically and identified as "dangerous" patterns.

Probability Distribution Table For Veh1_Direction

Veh2_Direction	UP	DOWN	RIGHT	LEFT
UP	0.014	0.014	0.042	0.931
DOWN	0.022	0.065	0.891	0.022
LEFT	0.583	0.25	0.083	0.083
RIGHT	0.611	0.278	0.056	0.056

Fig. 6. Side Collision Patterns based on Vehicle Direction as classified by Bayesian Network

Later, we also included data of rear collision events that occur in the simulation (Fig. 7). The test data now contain 7 attributes, i.e. *direction, manoeuvre, and angle* from each vehicle in a colliding pair, and *collision type* (side collision or rear end collision) and 20 – 30 rows in a file. In this particular intersection, when Bayesian Network classification is applied with *collision type* nominated as the class, the result shows that rear end collision occurs much more often than side collisions in this particular intersection (Fig. 8). Using the same set of data, when the EM is applied, it also exhibits the same highest probability of side collision patterns as in Fig. 6.

Veh1_Manouvre	Veh1_Direction	Veh1_angle	Veh2_Manouvre	Veh2_Direction	Veh2_angle	Coll_Type
STRAIGHT	RIGHT	0	STOPPED	DOWN	90	SideCollision
STRAIGHT	RIGHT	0	STRAIGHT	RIGHT	0	RearEndCollision
STRAIGHT	LEFT	0	STRAIGHT	LEFT	0	RearEndCollision
STRAIGHT	RIGHT	0	STRAIGHT	RIGHT	0	RearEndCollision
STRAIGHT	DOWN	90	STRAIGHT	DOWN	90	RearEndCollision
STRAIGHT	DOWN	90	STRAIGHT	DOWN	90	RearEndCollision
STRAIGHT	DOWN	90	STRAIGHT	DOWN	90	RearEndCollision
STRAIGHT	DOWN	90	STOPPED	LEFT	0	SideCollision
STRAIGHT	RIGHT	0	STRAIGHT	RIGHT	0	RearEndCollision

Fig. 7. Collision Event Data with Attributes of Maneuver, Direction, Angle, and Type

Probability Distribution Table For Coll_Type

Veh1_Direction	SideCollision	RearEndCollision
DOWN	0.411	0.589
UP	0.023	0.977
RIGHT	0.044	0.956
LEFT	0.145	0.855

Fig. 8. Collision Patterns based on Collision Types as classified by Bayesian Network

In order to find trends in manoeuvre involved in certain collisions, we use EM clustering and the C4.5 decision tree. Visualization of EM results shows clusters of side collision with stopped maneuver, rear end collision with straight maneuver, and rear end collision with stopping maneuver. This is confirmed by C4.5 result (Fig. 9). We conclude that in this particular intersection, most side collisions occur when one of the vehicle pair is stopped and rear end collisions happen mostly when both vehicles are on the move with straight manoeuvres and secondly when both vehicles are stopping.

When the same data is fed to Lightweight Clustering (LWC) [5], a ubiquitous data mining algorithm that works on a resource constrained devices (we use PDA in our implementation), the learning results show similar classification of side collision pattern, rear end collision patterns, and collision types. As LWC only accepts numerical values, we need to convert nominal values to numerical symbols and reinterpret the results. Although LWC is a one pass algorithm, compared with EM that uses 10-folds validation, the results are very similar with those yielded by data mining in the desktop environment. These results prove that mining traffic data can be done on resource constrained devices without losing its effectiveness. We have also fed the same data to Very Fast Machine Learning (VFML), a data mining tool that also include stream learning capability. When we apply Naïve Bayes algorithm in VFML to the same set of data fed to LWC, the result is the same. The main difference with LWC is that VFML algorithms cannot run on resource constrained devices.

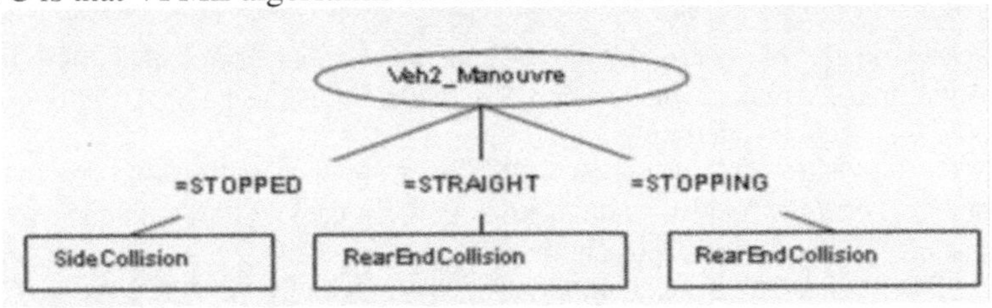

Fig. 9. Classification of Collision Types based on Vehicle Maneuvers

The results of the collision patterns learning are used to update the knowledge base of the collision detection in that particular intersection. Also, the highest possible collision pattern is placed on a higher priority for checking whenever there are situations that lead to such patterns. As a result, the intersection collision warning system can detect threats faster. Moreover, this knowledge can be submitted to the road traffic authority for further assessment and follow up.

4 Conclusion and Future Work

Data mining should be integrated into an intersection collision warning system to detect patterns to focus on when the system is to "look for" possible dangers or collisions. Our results use simulated data, but we contend that they hold in that such data can be feasibly collected via today's sensors. The simulation environment and the last learning results are elaborated here.

Our results, so far, are indicative that the combination of calculated collision points and learning high-risk collision patterns can help situation understanding at an intersection. The work shows that patterns can be found at intersections, and though we used a simulation which implies a simplification of the real world, it is easy to see how the results can be applicable to real world as sensors to acquire such information are already available. Learning from the history of events at an intersection in order to predict high risk incidents have been incorporated into our system through data mining on historical collision data generated from a four leg intersection simulation.

We still explore other issues in intersection safety through data mining, such as trends in collision points or areas, dangerous driving behaviors and anomalies in traffic conditions and driver behaviors that lead to crash. Once such dangerous situations at an intersection are understood, warnings can be suitably delivered. Future work also includes developing a communication model among the agents in the intersection to communicate predictions and warnings – such a model will help in predicting and estimating time to receive warnings, and how such warnings can be feasibly delivered. We are only at the tip of the iceberg. Such a model and our simulated results here which show what data can be used and what trends can be discovered, would then be part of a technical basis for future real-world smart intersections.

References

1. U.S. Department of Transportation – Federal Highway Administration, Institute of Transportation Engineers: Intersection Safety Briefing Sheet (2004), http://safety.fhwa.dot.gov/ intersections/interbriefing/index.htm
2. Frye, C.: International Cooperation to Prevent Collisions at Intersections. Public Roads Magazine, Federal Highway Administration, USA 65(1) (2001), http://www.tfhrc.gov/pubrds/julaug01/preventcollisions.htm
3. Salim, F.D., Loke, S.W., Rakotonirainy, A., Krishnaswamy, S.: U & I Aware (Ubiquitous Intersection Awareness): a Framework for Intersection Safety. In: Syukur, E., Yang, L., Loke, S.W. (eds.) Handbook on Mobile and Ubiquitous Computing: Innovations and Perspectives, American Scientific Publishers (2006)
4. Chan, C.-Y., Marco, D.: Traffic monitoring at signal-controlled intersections and data-mining for safety applications. In: Proc. of IEEE Intelligent Transportation System Conference, Washington D.C (2004)
5. Gaber, M.M., Krishnaswamy, S., Zaslavsky, A.: Resource-aware knowledge discovery in data streams. In: Proc. of First International Workshop on Knowledge Discovery in Data Streams, Italy (2004)
6. Grossman, R.L., Sabala, M., Alimohideen, J., Aanand, A., Chaves, J., Dillenburg, J., Eick, S., Leigh, J., Nelson, P., Papka, M., Rorem, D., Stevens, R., Vejcik, S., Wilkinson, L., Zhang, P.: Real Time Change Detection and Alerts from Highway Traffic Data. In: Proc. of ACM/IEEE Supercomputing, IEEE Computer Society Press, Los Alamitos (2005)
7. Abdel-Aty, M., Pemmanaboina, R.: Calibrating a real-time traffic accident prediction model using archived weather and ITS traffic data. IEEE Transactions on Intelligent Transportation Systems 7(2), 167–174 (2006)
8. Chong, M., Abraham, A., Paprzycki, M.: Traffic accident data mining using machine learning paradigms. In: Proc. of Fourth International Conference on Intelligent Systems Design and Applications (ISDA'04), Hungary, pp. 415–420 (2004)
9. Singh, S.: Identification of driver and vehicle characteristics through data mining the highway crash data. In: 2003 Conference Federal Committee on Statistical Methodology, Arlington, Virginia (2003) http://www.fcsm.gov/03papers/Singh8c.pdf
10. Witten, I.H., Frank, E.: Data Mining: Practical machine learning tools and techniques, 2nd edn. Morgan Kaufmann, San Francisco (2005)

Dynamic Scheduling Protocol for Highly-Reliable, Real-Time Information Aggregation for Telematics Intersection Safety System(TISS)

Wang Won Han, Hongjae Park, and Young Man Kim

Kookmin University, School of Computer Science, Seoul, 136-702, South Korea
{wwhan,hjpark0,ymkim}@kookmin.ac.kr
http://cclab.kookmin.ac.kr/

Abstract. Despite the fact that intersection collisions account for almost 30% of all crashes, intersection collision avoidance systems received less attention than the forward collision avoidance systems[1,2]. It is because the intersection collision problem is more complicated than rear-end crash and the limitations of the radar technology, the most widely used object sensing method in vehicle collision avoidance systems.

Recently, in [3,4], an intersection collision warning systems is reported and inter-vehicle data communication is done by direct broadcast based on 802.11[5] or DOLPHIN[6]. It is assumed that DGPS provides data to all the vehicles and all the 4-wheeled vehicles have the access to the navigation system. At a certain distance from the intersection, the vehicles begin to broadcast their locations, directions of travel and speeds. However, this approach has a shortcoming that broadcast is inherently unreliable without ACK messages from all the receiving peers, that is very difficult to be achieved in real-time environment.

In this paper, we evaluate a contention-free dynamic scheduling protocol, called *Telematics Scheduling Protocol(TSP)*, for WSN-based intersection safety system in terms of the real-time reliable information aggregation characteristics. In particular, we use ns-2[7] simulator to demonstrate the real-time data aggregation performance of TSP. The performance result of TSP shows very high throughput and short delivery time suitable for the real-time reliable Telematics Intersection Safety System(TISS).

1 Introduction

Despite the fact that intersection collisions account for almost 30% of all crashes, intersection collision avoidance systems received less attention than the forward collision avoidance systems[1,2]. It is because the intersection collision problem is more complicated than rear-end crash and the limitations of the radar technology, the most widely used object sensing method in vehicle collision avoidance systems. Most radar systems require Line-Of-Sight(LOS) for object detection. Yet in most intersection crash cases, the principle other vehicle (POV) is hidden

J. Indulska et al. (Eds.): UIC 2007, LNCS 4611, pp. 163–172, 2007.

from the line of sight of the subject vehicle (SV) until the last second before the collision. This renders ineffective most collision warning/avoidance systems that require LOS for threat detection.

The new communication systems that are prevalent in recent intersection collision warning and avoidance systems are mostly based on Cooperative Infrastructure Vehicle Communications technologies. These types of systems consist of vehicles continually relaying information to a beaconing base station located in the approaching intersection[8]. Another type of method to exchange these information is through Inter-Vehicle Communication in which no infrastructure is needed in intersections[9]. The system is based on vehicle-to-vehicle communication using ad hoc mobile networks. Crash threat detections are achieved by vehicles cooperatively sharing critical information for collision anticipation, i.e., location, velocity, acceleration, etc. By sharing the information between peers, each vehicle is able to predict potential hazards. However, this method inherently suffers from LOS problem like the above radar system.

Recently, in [3,4], an intersection collision warning systems is reported and inter-vehicle data communication is done by direct broadcast based on 802.11[5] or DOLPHIN[6]. It is assumed that DGPS provides data to all the vehicles and all the 4-wheeled vehicles have the access to the navigation system. At a certain distance from the intersection, the vehicles begin to broadcast their locations, directions of travel and speeds. However, this approach has a shortcoming that broadcast is inherently unreliable without ACK messages from all the receiving peers, that is very difficult to be achieved in real-time environment. Since many message transmission collisions occur in 802.11 and DOLPHIN due to hidden station problem and the inherent packet collision problem, the information delivery fails frequently so that the incomplete collision warning may invite a possible crash.

Formally, there are two *feasibility conditions*, for the above crash avoidance reaction to be just-in-time and comprehensive without neither *crash warning miss* nor *too late warning*, that the information aggregation network must satisfy: *bounded-delay condition*, restricting the information aggregation time no greater than a short upper-bound(e.g. 1 second), and *reliability condition*, guaranteeing the near-perfact crash warning information. These two feasibility conditions can be measured in the form of *total vehicle information aggregation delay* and *total throughput.*

In the companion paper[10], the feasibility of *Wireless Sensor Network*(WSN) employed as real-time reliable information aggregation network was studied. In particular, two popular WSN communication standards, IEEE 802.11 and 802.15.4[12], are selected and evaluated to reveal the performance level of its own real-time reliable traffic data transmission. However, both WSN protocols, IEEE 802.15.4 and 802.11, with common 250Kbps bandwidth for the fair comparison, are turned out to have an intolerably high packet loss rates. The critical performance defect of both protocols is due to the message contention in the data transmission. Therefore, in another companion paper[11], a highly-optimized, contention-free dynamic-scheduling protocol, called *Telematics Scheduling*

Protocol(TSP), was proposed to satisfy the real-time reliable data delivery requirements of WSN-based intersection safety system.

In this paper, TSP protocol is throughly evaluated in terms of the real-time reliable information aggregation characteristics. We use ns-2[7] simulator to demonstrate the real-time data aggregation performance of TSP. The performance result of TSP shows very high throughput and short delivery time enough to be used in the real-time reliable telematics intersection safety system.

The paper is organized as follows. Section I gives an introduction. Section II describes the WSN-based Telematics Intersection Safety System(TISS) employed in the paper. Then, a dynamic scheduling-based data delivery protocol, TSP, is summarized in Section III. Refer to [11] for the complete protocol description of TSP. The simulation configuration for the evaluation of TSP is described in Section IV. Section V discusses on the performance evaluation result of TSP. To make a firm analysis, two reference protocols, IEEE 802.11 and 802.15.4, are also employed in the simulation under the identical condition. Conclusions are drawn in Section VI.

2 Architecture of WSN-Based Telematics Intersection Safety System(TISS)

Telematics Intersection Safety System(TISS) for real-time crash warning announcement at intersection is depicted in Fig. 1. We employ each *branch WSN*, installed along the branch roads, as the information aggregation network that is routing the vehicle information from the vehicles to Base Station(BS), as shown in Fig. 2. In the figure, BS at the center of intersection broadcasts crash warning information periodically over all the approaching vehicles that, beforehand, should supply their own individual vehicle informations(location, ID, velocity, acceleration, etc.) to BS. In other words, WSN is responsible for the information delivery from vehicles up to BS in a just-in-time, reliable way. Since sensor node has a limited transmission range, WSN is configured as multi-hop ad hoc network. Each sensor node consisting of WSN is located along the lanes of the road,

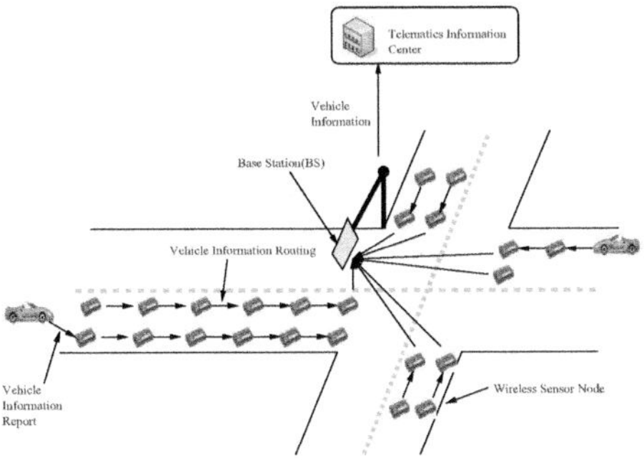

Fig. 1. Telematics Intersection Safety System(TISS) configuration

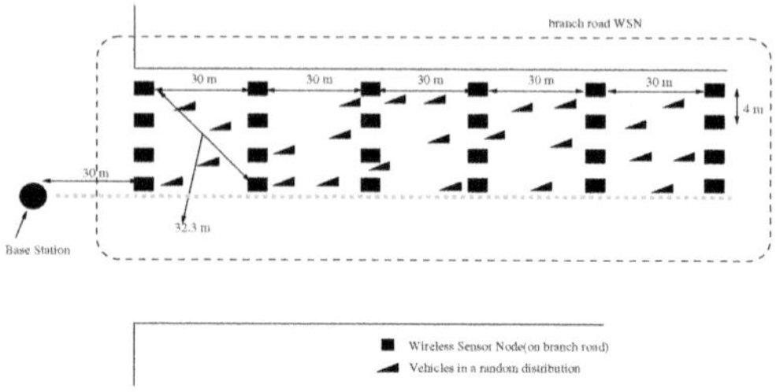

Fig. 2. WSN configuration allocated on a branch road segment

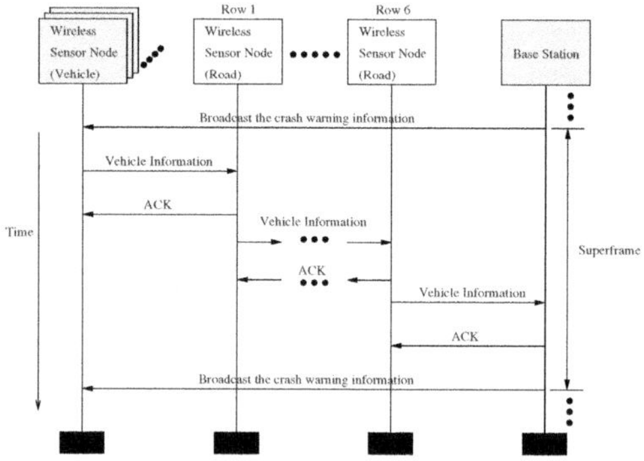

Fig. 3. TISS message exchange sequence diagram

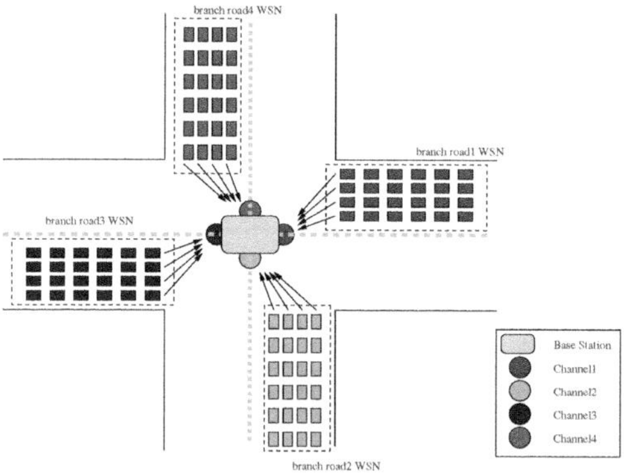

Fig. 4. Four different frequency channels allocated in each branch WSN

protected inside the cat's eye, and supposed to collect the vehicle information from the near-by passing vehicles and to route them up to BS.

Fig. 3 depicts the global message exchange sequence diagram. At the beginning of each superframe cycle, BS broadcasts the crash warning information to all approaching vehicles. After receiving it, each vehicle sends the local vehicle information to the fixed neighboring sensor node. Once the information is successfully received at the node, it is relayed in WSN until it arrives at BS. Fig. 2 shows the particular WSN configuration employed by the simulation executed in the following sections. For the simplicity of computation, we assume that each branch WSN uses a unique frequency channel so that any pair of branch WSNs experience no inter-branch transmission collision, as shown in Fig. 4. Likewise, it is assumed that a branch road consists of four lanes.

3 Telematics Scheduling Protocol(TSP)

Traffic information aggregation in TISS should meet two necessary conditions to guarantee the vehicle crash warning in a reliable and just-in-time fashion. First condition is *reliable information delivery* that the underlying network must aggregate all the driving information of each vehicle approaching the intersection so as not to miss any crash warning situation. Second condition is *real-time warning* that the aggregation of vehicle information and the crash analysis based on these data must be just-in-time to make some proper reaction to prevent the forcasted crash. In this paper, we assume that one second of aggregation-analysis-broadcast cycle, between the beginning of vehicle information aggregation and the crash warning broadcast, may satisfy real-time warning condition.

While Wireless Sensor Network(WSN) is one of the feasible information aggregation infrastructures employed in TISS, it is known that the popular protocols like IEEE 802.11 and 802.15.4 show a significant performance degradation due to transmission medium contention so that they don't meet the above conditions[10]. To resolve this performance degradation factor, we adopted the notion of contention-free, scheduling-based data aggregation into *TSP(Telematics Scheduling Protocol)* that is described in detail in [11]. In this paper, it is found that the data delivery of TSP is both very fast and reliable so that it satisfies these conditions, as the following sections will show the TSP performance.

4 Simulation Configurations

In this section, two performance simulation configurations, *error-free WSN* and *comprehensive TSP* configurations, are described. Error-free WSN configuration is prepared to evaluate the real-time reliable property of TSP protocol. To demonstrate the superiority of TSP, two popular wireless protocols, IEEE 802.15.4 and 802.11, are compared with TSP in the simulation. For the fair comparison between three protocols, the identical data transmission rate of 250Kbps is forced to be commonly used in the data transmission of all protocols. As the name of the configuration implies, no transmission error due to noise is assumed to clearly observe the defect of transmission collision inherent in IEEE 802.11 and 802.15.4. The physical sensor node deployment applied in the error-free WSN simulation is shown in Fig. 2. There are four lanes in each branch road. Along each lane, six nodes are allocated in a protected cat's eye, distributed uniformly with $30m$ of inter-node distance. In the next section, we will show that TSP is the only protocol to meet the real-time reliability condition feasible to TISS.

The second, comprehensive TSP configuration is prepared to exhaustively search the real-world performance of TSP protocol under various situations: the existance of transmission error due to noise, the distance between rows, and the number of the vehicles approaching the intersection.

In both simulation configurations, two performance metrics, *vehicle information delay* and *total throughput* are used to measure two feasibility conditions(real-time and reliability). In the following subsections, each configuration is explained in more detail. For both simulations, a static routing protocol is used to deliver the vehicle information from vehicles up to BS, since all the nodes in WSN are fixed along four lanes. Vehicle information size is fixed to 10 *bytes*. The simulation result and its analysis are presented in the next section.

Network Deployment Area	12m X 180m
MAC Protocol	TSP, IEEE 802.11, IEEE 802.15.4
Routing Protocol	Static Routing
Fixed Node Interval	30m
Radio Range	40m
Vehicle Information Size	10 bytes
Bandwidth	250 kbps
The Number of nodes	Wireless Sensor Node(Vehicle) : 30, 50, 70, 100 Wireless Sensor Node(Road) : 24 Base Station : 1
Statistical Processing	Average of 10 simulation results

(a) Error-free data transmission

Network Deployment Area	12m X 180m
MAC Protocol	TSP
Routing Protocol	Static Routing
Message error rate	0, 5, 10, 30, 50%
Vehicle Information Size	10 bytes
Bandwidth	250 kbps
The Number of nodes	Wireless Sensor Node(Vehicle) : 30, 50, 70, 100 Wireless Sensor Node(Road) : 20, 24, 36, 72, 144 Base Station : 1
Statistical Processing	Average of 10 simulation results

(b) Data transmission error

Fig. 5. Simulation parameters

4.1 Error-Free WSN Simulation Configuration

In error-free WSN configuration, the radio transmission range and bandwidth of the WSN nodes are set up to $40m$ and $250Kbps$, respectively. The vehicles are randomly distributed in the WSN range with four different populations: 30, 50, 70 and 100 vehicles. Since there are four lanes with $30m$ of row-to-row distance and six rows along the road, the number of sensor nodes deployed in this WSN configuration are 24. In addition, no transmission error due to noise is assumed to clearly observe the effect of transmission collision against real-time reliable performance. Fig. 5(a) enumerates the specific configuration parameter values used in error-free WSN simulation.

4.2 Comprehensive TSP Simulation Configuration

In comprehensive TSP configuration, the vehicles are also randomly distributed with four different populations: 30, 50, 70 and 100 vehicles. However, row-to-row distance is verying from 5m to 40m to examine the effect of row-to-row distance. Since the WSN coverage area is $12 \times 180m$, the number of nodes implemented on the road area is inversely proportional to row-to-row distance, from 144 to 20, respectively. Another important real-world factor is the message error rate due to air transmission noise, that is also considered in this simulation, varying from 0% to 50%. Fig. 5(b) enumerates the specific configuration parameter values used in comprehensive TSP simulation.

5 Performance Evaluation

5.1 Performance Evaluation of Error-Free WSN Configuration

Fig. 6(a) depicts total delivery delay from the vehicles up to BS. In the figure, total delay of IEEE 802.11 is too slow to be used in TISS. As the number of vehicles increases up to 100, even the delay rises over one second. On the other hand, 802.15.4 and TSP show reasonable delay of about 0.2*sec*. Fig. 6(b) shows total throughput, i.e., the aggregation rate of all vehicle information from each vehicle to base station. IEEE 802.15.4 shows the worst throughput of 28-50% among three protocols. Though IEEE 802.11 has much better throughput than 802.15.4, it still lose several messages that could cause critical crash warning miss. On the other hand, TSP shows the perfect throughput over all the number of vehicles.

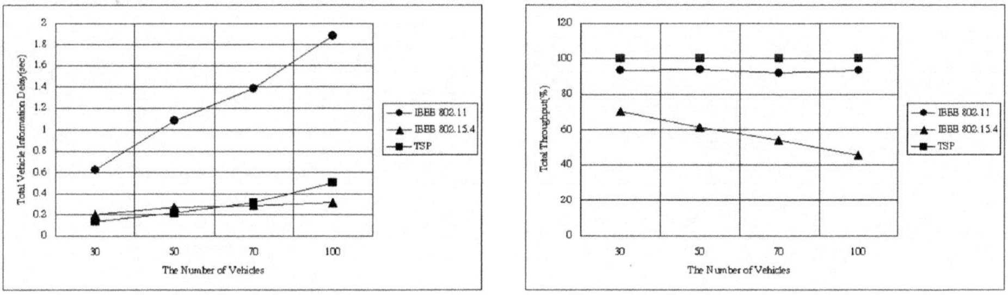

(a) Total delay

(b) Total throughput

Fig. 6. Total delay and throughput from the vehicles up to BS vs. the number of vehicles

The major reason of the performance degradation demonstrated in both 802.11 and 802.15.4 are the time slot contention mechanism inherent in two protocols. The simulteneous message transmission invites the transmission collision phenomenon and, thereby, message loss. On the other hand, TSP efficiently prevents such contention by dynamic time-slot scheduling.

The major reason of the delivery throughput difference between two channel-contention protocols, IEEE 802.11 and 802.15.4, is that 802.11 adopts maximum six retransmission trials before the packet in data link layer is dropped, instead of maximum three retransmissions in the case of 802.15.4. Another reason is that 802.11 uses RTS-CTS control message sequence to reduce the hidden station problem and, thus, the number of packet collisions is significantly reduced in the actual transmission period. However, in 802.15.4, RTS-CTS sequence is skipped and the information message is directly sent to the next node. In summary, although the packet loss rates of 802.11 and 802.15.4 with 30(100) vehicles are 93(92)% and 71(46)%, respectively, both 802.11 and 802.15.4 are not suitable as a reliable vehicle information aggregation network protocol.

5.2 Performance Evaluation of Comprehensive TSP Configuration

Fig. 7(a) depicts total delivery delay from the vehicles up to BS. In the figure, total delay of TSP is less than 1*sec* up to 30% of message transmission error except the extreme case of 50% message error, that represents too severe condition in the real world. Even 30% of error rate invokes the delay of more than one second as the number of vehicles increases to 100. Notice that the road area of $12m \times 180m$ crowded with 100 vehicles will inhibit the fast driving and invoke the attention from the other vehicle drivers so as not to preserve the fast driving speed. Anyway, this figure shows the upper-bound capacity of TSP, that is optimistically allowable in TISS based on WSN with bandwidth of 250kbps.

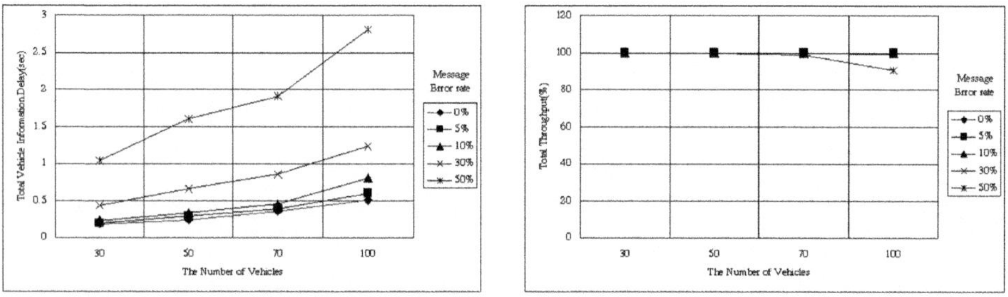

(a) Total delay (b) Total throughput

Fig. 7. Total delay and throughput from the vehicles up to BS vs. the number of vehicles under various errors

Fig. 7(b)shows total throughput, i.e., the aggregation rate of all vehicle information from each vehicle to base station. Except the hardest condition of 50% of error rate and crowded with 100 vehicles, TSP shows the perfect throughput over all span of the number of vehicles.

In the last simulation, the row-to-row distance varies from 5m to 40m and the number of vehicles are fixed to 50. Since the WSN area is fixed to $12m \times 180m$, the number of rows changes from 36 rows to 5 rows, respectively. Note that the larger the number of rows, the longer the number of hops up to base station and thus, the longer the total delay. Fig. 8(a) depicts total delivery delay from the vehicles up to BS. In the figure, as the row-to-row distance is no less than 10m, total delay of TSP is less than 1*sec* except the extreme case of 50% message transmission error.

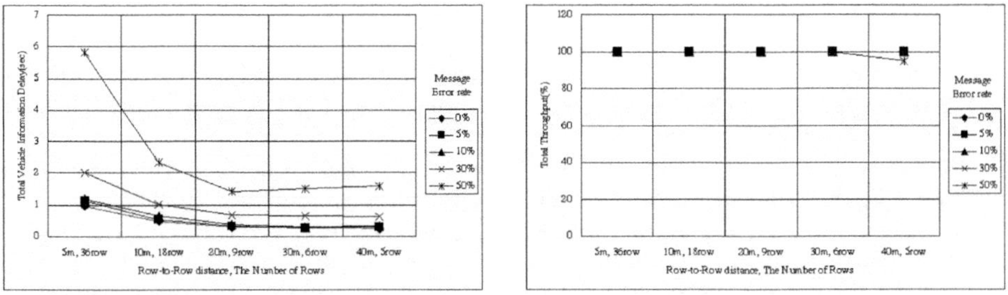

(a) Total delay (b) Total throughput

Fig. 8. Total delay and throughput from the vehicles up to BS vs. row-to-row distance under various errors

Fig. 8(b) shows total throughput, i.e., the aggregation rate of all vehicle information from each vehicle to base station. Moreover, except the hardest condition of 50% of error rate, TSP shows the perfect throughput over all span of the number of vehicles.

6 Conclusion

In this paper, we studied the feasibility of WSN as real-time reliable information aggregation network for the advanced vehicle crash warning system called TISS. In particular, by using ns-2 simulator to evaluate the real-time reliable performance of the data aggregation protocol called TSP, we showed that TSP guarantees the real-time reliable conditions necessary for TISS.

In the first, error-free WSN configuration, to prove the suprior performance of TSP, we compared TSP with two other popular communication standards, IEEE 802.11 and 802.15.4.

Though both WSN protocols, IEEE 802.15.4 and 802.11 with 250Kbps bandwidth, have an intolerably high packet loss rates and/or long delay, on contrary, TSP shows the excellent performance to satisfy the real-time reliable conditions. According to the in-depth simulation analysis, the fundamental reason for the high data loss occured in IEEE 802.11 and 802.15.4 is turned out to be the channel contention mechanism inherent in the class of CSMA-based protocols. Once the maximum number of retransmissions occurs due to a sequence of packet collisions, the corresponding information packets are removed from the sending data-link queue permanently.

In the second simulation configuration, we extensively examined the TSP performance under various dimensions: air transmission error, the number of rows in WSN and the number of vehicles in the WSN communication range. Except some extreme cases, TSP shows real-time reliable information delivery characteristics suitable for TISS.

References

1. Pierowicz, J., Jocoy, E., Lloyd, M., Bittner, A., Pirson, B.: Intersection Collision Avoidance Using ITS Countermeasures. Tech. Rep. DOT HS 809 171, NHTSA, U.S. DOT (2000)
2. Huang, Q., Miller, R., McNeille, P., Dimeo, D., Roman, G.-C.: Development of a peer-to-peer collision warning system. Ford Techincal Journal 5(2) (2002)
3. Ozguner, F., Ozguner, U., Redmill, K., Takeshita, O., Liu, Y., Korkmaz, G., Dogan, A., Tokuda, K., Nakabayashi, S., Shimizu, T.: A simulation study of an intersection collision warning. In: The 4th International Workshop on ITS Telecommunications, Singapore (2004)
4. Dogan, A., Korkmaz, G., Liu, Y., Ozguner, F., Ozguner, U., Redmill, K., Takeshita, O., Tokuda, O.: Evaluation of intersection collision warning system using inter-vehicle communication simulator. In: 2004 Proceedings of Intelligent Transportation Systems, Washington, D.C., USA, pp. 1103–1108 (2004)
5. IEEE 802.11, Wireless LAN Medium Access Control (MAC) and Physical Layer (PHY) Specifications, Standard. Technical report, IEEE (1999)
6. Tokuda, K., Akiyama, M., Fujii, H.: DOLPHIN for Inter-Vehicle Communication System. In: IEEE Intelligent Vehicles Symposium, pp. 504–509 (2000)
7. ns2 Simulation software tool, `http://www.isi.edu/nsnam/ns/`
8. Federal Highway Administration: Collision Countermeasures Systems Phase 1-2 Summary Report. Fhwa-rd-93-080, U. S. DOT (1994)
9. Miller, R., Huang, Q.: An Adaptive Peer-to-Peer Collision Warning System. In: Proceedings of IEEE Vehicle Technology Conference (Spring), Birmingham, Alabama (2002)
10. Park, H., Han, W.W., Kim, Y.M.: Feasibility of WSN as Vehicle Information Aggregation Network for Telematics Intersection Safety System. In: Proceedings of Int. Conf. on Ubiquitous Information Technology & Applications, Dubai, UAE (2007)
11. Han, W.W., Park, H., Kim, Y.M.: TSP: Highly-Reliable, Real-Time Multi-hop Ad Hoc Network Protocol for Telematics Intersection Safety System(TISS). In: Proceedings of Int. Conf. on Ubiquitous Information Technology & Applications, Dubai, UAE (2007)
12. The IEEE 802.15.4-2003 standard (2003) `http://standards.ieee.org/getieee802/download/802.15.4-2003.pdf`

Spontaneous Interaction Framework for Thin-Client Access to Services

Brian Y. Lim[1], Daqing Zhang[1], Manli Zhu[1], Song Zheng[1], and Mounir Mokhtari[2]

[1] Institute for Infocomm Research, Singapore
{yllim,daqing,mlzhu,szheng}@i2r.a-star.edu.sg
[2] GET/INT Institut National des Télécommunications, France
mounir.mokhtari@int-evry.fr

Abstract. Many physical spaces such as homes, museums, airports and shopping malls are being augmented with computers, sensors, wireless hotspots to provide digital content and services. However, often specialized hardware and software are needed to access the services available in a particular space. This paper proposes a lightweight service framework which can aggregate services offered by heterogeneous devices and sources in a smart space and allow the users of currently available mobile clients, such as, smart phones, PDAs and Ultra-Mobile PCs, to spontaneously discover and access services in heterogeneous spaces. By leveraging a captive and service portal mechanism, the desirable services can be discovered and presented automatically to the mobile client of the user, while the mobile devices do not need to install any additional software or hardware. In this paper, we present the system requirements for spontaneous interaction, the service framework design and implementation details.

1 Introduction

With the proliferation of mobile devices, such as smart phones, PDAs, and Ultra-Mobile PCs, and permeation of wireless connectivity in private and public spaces, we are a step closer to the vision of *ubiquitous computing*. Coupled with sensors and actuators in physical spaces such as homes, offices and shopping malls, these devices would allow for *spontaneous interaction* between users and services available in these *smart spaces*. Through the interfaces of their own mobile devices, users would be able to enter an *unfamiliar* space, discover more about the space, and what services are available.

Rukzio et. al. described Mobile Interaction Techniques as three forms: touching, pointing, and scanning [1]. While the former two are most appealing to users because they are more intuitive, they require more physical effort when the smart devices are out of reach. Scanning has the benefits of allowing for interaction with services that have no physical (device) counterpart, and for users to continue being mobile while invoking the services. Furthermore, in *unfamiliar* spaces, users would not know of existing services, and scanning can allow for a list of the services to be retrieved.

J. Indulska et al. (Eds.): UIC 2007, LNCS 4611, pp. 173–183, 2007.

However, the development of spontaneous interaction frameworks has been plagued by a few issues, such as:

- the need for augmented clients (RFID or Bluetooth enabled devices, or extra software to install) that are not pervasive in the market,
- universal aggregation of heterogeneous services, and
- uniform access of services across multiple spaces.

There have been many efforts to address service discovery and aggregation in heterogeneous spaces, leading to standards such as UPnP, Jini, and HAVi. However, as acknowledged by Helal [2], many of these platforms lack support on mobile devices.

Several projects exist to provide spontaneous interaction. Hodes and Katz [3] developed a framework that uses wireless beaconing to discover various services in a smart space. Their system is able to compose UIs for each of the services found. Another system, ICrafter [4], also can generate service UIs, while providing a robust framework to detect dynamically added services. The Universal Interaction framework [5] employs a Unit proxy to map input devices to output devices to mediate a heterogeneous space, and uses context awareness to facilitate the mapping and enable personalization. Building on that, the Personal Home Server [6] embeds software into mobile devices to allow coordination and control of home appliances. TinyMiddleware [7] utilizes mobile code to enable mobile devices to interact with smart spaces.

Many of these solutions require extra software to be embedded in the mobile clients, and do not allow readily available mobile devices to access services in smart spaces. We propose a framework to allow quick adoption for spontaneous access to services by requiring only a browser and Wi-Fi on the mobile clients. We have also focused on allowing access to multiple spaces, where each local service provider independently serves different services. Within each space, the local provider can also employ heterogeneous services that our system can aggregate.

2 Design Goals

We aim to build a system to provide rich services to mobile customers using currently ubiquitous technologies. Simply using web-enabled mobile devices, customers would be able to visit any smart space and invoke the services there.

2.1 Minimum Assumption for Client Devices

The high availability of web-enabled mobile devices, such as smart phones, PDAs, laptops, and Ultra-Mobile PCs, provides a convenient interface for services through network connectivity and web browsers. We propose that a spontaneous interaction framework should leverage on this existing minimal requirement to provide access to services rather than on technologies, such as proprietary beaconing that do are not as ubiquitous.

By relying on basic wireless capabilities and web browser functionality, our framework would allow services to be easily reachable to many customers who use currently available mobile devices. They would not need to buy specialized hardware or install any software, thus spurring rapid adoption of services.

2.2 Spontaneous Interaction Across Multiple Spaces

In the future, with smart spaces located in various places such as the home, office, shopping mall, and museum, people would like to access the services at each location in the same way, through their personal mobile devices. However, each service provider would have their own agendas and it may be difficult for a universal service provider to emerge.

We anticipate an ecosystem of distributed local service providers, where local spaces are controlled by individual entities, each providing their own set of services. Such apparent incongruity across multiple spaces can lead to unmanageable heterogeneity of services.

Adhering to the aforementioned minimal assumptions for mobile device, our spontaneous interaction framework can provide a common user interface (UI) for the various smart spaces a user would encounter.

2.3 Aggregation of Heterogeneous Devices and Services

Service aggregation in heterogeneous spaces is a heavily researched field, leading to many implementations and standards such as UPnP, OSGi, HAVi, and Jini. Each has their strengths and weaknesses, but none of them has yet to become the dominant standard used in industry. Furthermore, many proprietary services exist that do not follow any standards, causing the problem of devices and services that are incompatible. Customers would have to either accommodate multiple platforms or stick to one, constraining their options. We seek to develop a flexible framework that integrates many of these platforms, rather than creating a competing implementation or heavily subscribing to one. Our system would have adaptors that will allow these platforms to easily fit into the framework.

Other than just aggregating device-based services, the framework should also handle web-based services that are independent of devices and locality. For example, the del.icio.us and flickr websites aggregate web bookmarks, and online photos, respectively. Aggregators can be built over these web services to incorporate into the framework to offer more services.

While the aforementioned services provide for dynamic discovery of services, some services can be installed during configuration of the local server. These would be static and location dependent. With all these services available, our framework would be a hybrid system providing dynamically and statically available services. Furthermore, the user would interact with each service equally without the need to be aware of the aggregation that occurs.

3 Architecture

To satisfy the aforementioned design goals, we have developed a thin middleware that places no extra burden on client devices. The Spontaneous Interaction system consists of a two-tier client-server architecture, with a thin client, and most of the functionality contained in the middleware. Due to the heterogeneity of services and aggregations, the middleware has a thin core that can interface with services using a common programmatic interface. To connect services to users, we utilize the captive portal paradigm to pull mobile clients to service portals. This basic specification using portals and web interfaces allows for disparate local providers to easily publish their services through their own systems, so that customers can enjoy the same use of services across different spaces.

3.1 Client-Server Architecture

To allow rapid adoption of spontaneous access to services, our framework only requires the client to have wireless connectivity and a web browser, as depicted in Fig. 1. Users would need neither specialized devices nor software installations to discover and invoke the services. Similarly, the system running the Spontaneous Interaction middleware only needs a server, running the core to discover services, and a wireless access point running a captive portal to point clients to the server.

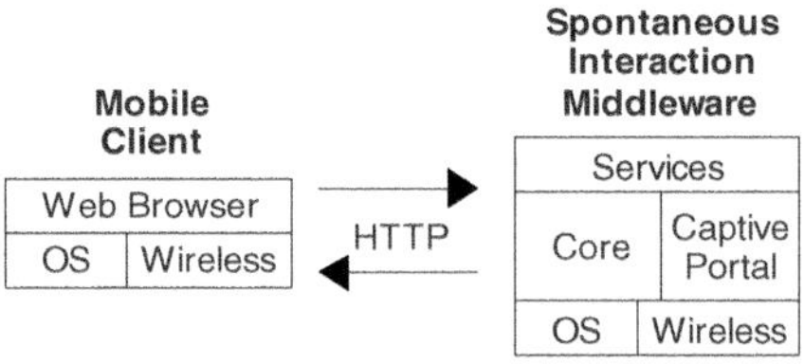

Fig. 1. The mobile client needs only wireless connectivity and a standard web browser to connect to any Spontaneous Interaction middleware. The middleware needs a server running the Spontaneous Interaction core, and a wireless access point, running a captive portal.

3.2 Centralized Infrastructure, Rich Services

The Spontaneous Interaction framework contains a core that has the basic functionality to install services as modules (see Fig. 2). The services installed can also be aggregators which point to other services. It is up to the providers to decide whether to provide generative UI functionality for the services they aggregate.

Overall, the framework would be service-centric, with the emphasis on the services provided to the user. For example, a service may control the lights in a room, or play tracks from a music album, and the user would focus on the task rather than the source device, such as the light or the media server.

However, there are countless unfathomable ways that services can be rendered, and it would be more appropriate to leave the design of the services and their interfaces to the service providers. Hence, we have chosen to design a thin middleware to discover and connect to proprietary service UIs rather than generate generic ones. Systems such as [1][2][3][4] do provide UI generative capabilities, but they would not be as aesthetically pleasing or as brand conscious as professionally designed UIs.

While this is similar to the Presentation URLs that UPnP services can provide [8] for the users to have a web interface to control the devices, our framework extends this to include non-device-based services (such as stocks tracking, and weather forecasting) and aggregators. Service providers can then write services for devices, aggregators, and non-device-based services. As the functionality is provided through HTML interfaces, users can use the common web paradigm to operate the services and would experience gentler learning curves.

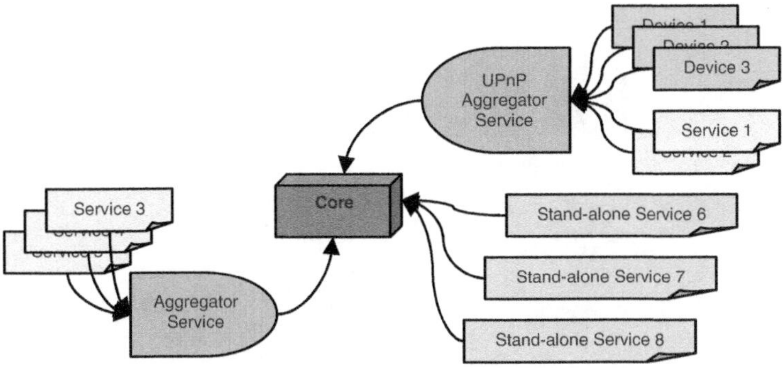

Fig. 2. The core of the Spontaneous Interaction framework is a thin middleware to provide a means to install services as modules. Services installed can be stand-alone, or aggregators for other services.

3.3 Captive and Service Portals

We have employed the portal paradigm for users to access services. Spontaneity of interaction is facilitated by the Captive Portal. When a user launches his browser in a smart space, he would immediately see the portal of services, without going through a series of buttons or links. The technical sequence of events is illustrated in Fig. 3.

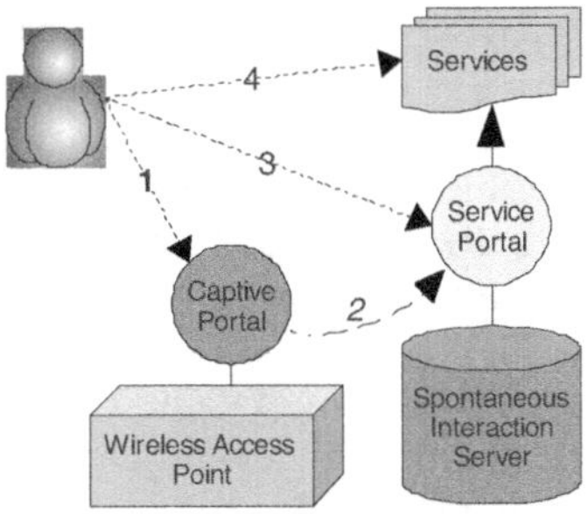

Fig. 3. When the user connects to a wireless hotspot, his browser is detected by the Captive Portal (1), and forwarded to the Service Portal (2). He can then browse the available services (3), and invoke a service through his mobile device (4).

3.4 Distributed Local Service Providers Employing the Same Framework

We anticipate that it would be difficult for a universal service provider to deliver services at various places and propose a framework for distributed local service providers that function independently. To provide users a seamless interface to services across multiple smart spaces, the Spontaneous Interaction system can be set up in each location (see Fig. 4). As the users' browsers connect to the wireless networks in each space, the resident captive portals would direct them to the respective service portals and users can equally able to access the available services.

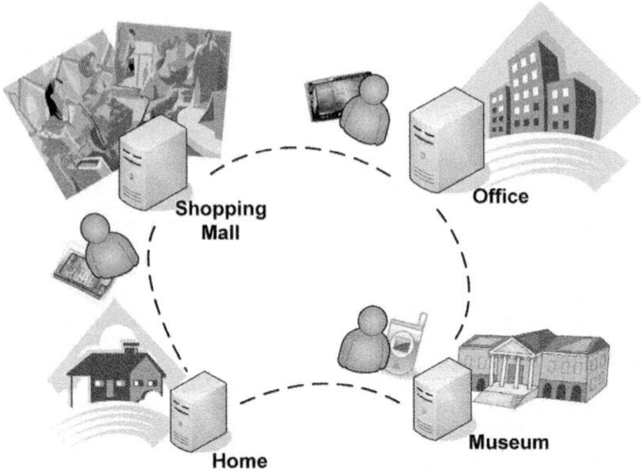

Fig. 4. Each smart space, such as the mall, office, museum, and home can have the Spontaneous Interaction framework installed to provide a seamless web-based interface to mobile clients across multiple spaces

4 Implementation

We have implemented a prototype of the Spontaneous Interaction framework using J2EE Servlets/JSP as the platform for the middleware, running off a dedicated desktop machine. The main presentation page for the framework is the Service Portal that displays installed and discovered services as icons. We have installed DD-WRT [9] as the Captive Portal on a Linksys WRT54GL router and directed it to forward browsers to the Service Portal server. See Fig. 5 for the architecture of the implemented framework, and Fig 6 for an example backend deployment.

Presently, the static services are hard-coded into the framework. Though they are location specific, since each smart space would have different services depending on what is programmed in them. To provide easier configuration, a plug-in infrastructure should be implemented. We propose using OSGi [10] where the core system would contain the OSGi framework, and the services would be contained as OSGi bundles which can be installed and run in the framework.

For aggregation of devices, we implemented a UPnP wrapper service built over the CyberLink for Java UPnP library [11], and added web access capabilities. Links generated in the Service Portal point to the Presentation URLs of the UPnP services. Web-based services, such as web bookmarks, are served by the del.icio.us service. Instead of storing web URL links in a local storage system, we utilize the popular del.icio.us social bookmarking web service [12] to store URLs which this service can retrieve and load onto the Service Portal.

To access media (pictures, music, and videos) in the smart space, we have developed a web-based Media Service, built over the Cidero UPnP Media Controller [13], to collate media across multiple UPnP Media Servers. For the office, we created the location-aware printing service to print documents at the nearest printer from the user. For video surveillance, we have also written an applet-based Video Surveillance service for users to monitor their surroundings.

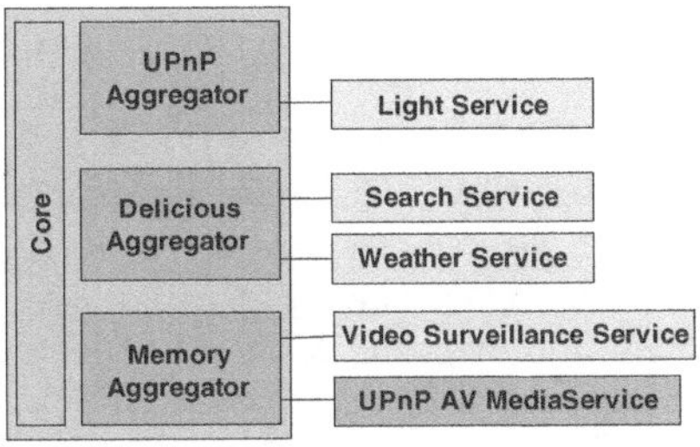

Fig. 5. Architecture of implemented aggregators and services. Note that while aggregators reside with the core in the Spontaneous Interaction Server, services can reside remotely. The UPnP AV Media Server is an example of an Aggregator Service.

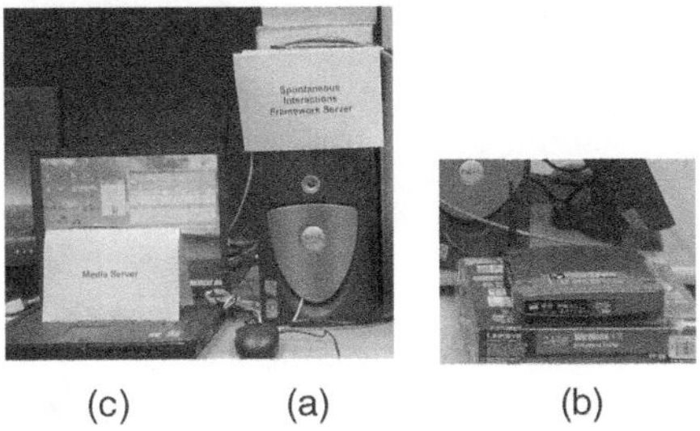

Fig. 6. The Spontaneous Interaction Server resides on a computer desktop (a) holding the core systems and basic aggregators, while the Media Service resides in the Media Server, a laptop (c). Captive Portal functionality resides in the firmware of the WRT54GL wireless router (b).

5 Walkthroughs

To demonstrate the functionality of our Spontaneous Interaction framework, we implemented a system for the office and another for the home.

5.1 Office

Fig. 7 shows the services a *new* user would see on entering his smart office and launching his browser after connecting to the wireless network. We have set up

Fig. 7. Accessing services in the office; service Portal for the office prototype showing office-specific services: location-aware printing, media access, search, and weather forecasting

hotspots at the entrance and several other areas in the building; each has been loaded with a different set of services.

Following the links to the search or weather services (see Fig. 8a) would bring the user to the respective web-based links. The links are maintained as bookmarks under the del.icio.us web service and retrieved by the del.icio.us Aggregator.

The Location-Aware Printing Service (see Fig. 8b) allows the user to print from the nearest printer. On following the Printing Service link, the user interacts with a web UI that allows him to upload his desired document to the print server. The application returns with the location of the printer shown in a map, informing the user where to find the document after it has been printed.

If he desires to listen to music, from his desktop, on his mobile device, he can invoke the UPnP AV Media Service (see Fig. 8c) to access media located on his Media Server. Once connected, he can move around the office and still listen to his favourite tunes, browse pictures, or watch videos.

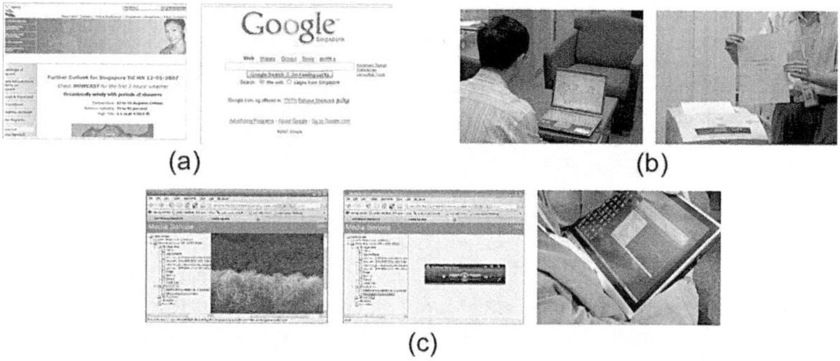

Fig. 8. Accessing services from the office set-up: (a) web-based search and weather services, (b) Location-Aware Printing: print anywhere in the office from the nearest printer, (c) Media Service: access media content (pictures, audio items, and videos) remotely

5.2 Home

When the user returns home, his browser would be directed to the home's Service Portal showing a different set of services. In the case of Fig. 9, he would still be able

Fig. 9. Accessing services at home; service Portal for the home prototype showing house-specific services: media access, video surveillance, search, and weather forecasting

to access his personal web-based services (see Fig. 10a), but would have some different services, such as the video surveillances of his gold fish and the house entrance (see Fig. 10c). Running through a web camera off a separate laptop, the Video Surveillance Service runs as a servlet serving a Java applet to clients. When the user follows the service link from the Service Portal, he can view the applet and track changes through the camera. The Media Service (see Fig. 10b) there also shows media from the home media servers.

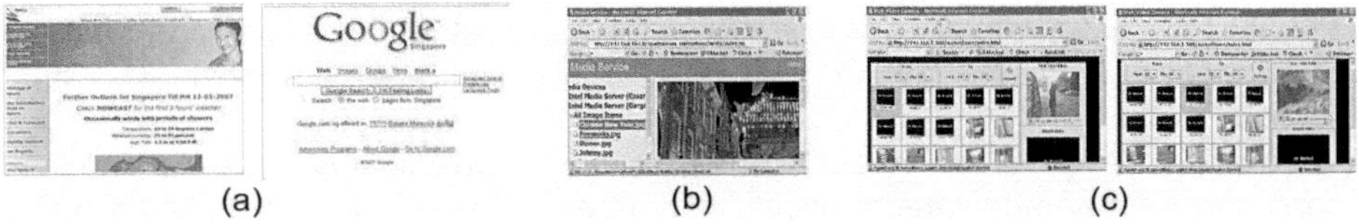

Fig. 10. Accessing services from the home set-up: (a) web-based search and weather services, (b) Media Service: access media content, (c) Video Surveillance: monitor the home entrance or the status of pet fish

6 Issues

We encountered some issues in designing our framework to support spontaneous access to services. While we derived our solutions, these concerns merit further consideration. Having implemented the framework in two scenarios, we have also gained insights into the difficulty of deploying such systems.

6.1 Design Concerns

To handle heterogeneous services, we have proposed using the HTML standards as interfaces to mobile clients, and off-loaded much complexity to the service providers. Each provider can provide their own services and aggregators, and our prototypes have demonstrated these on a small scale. However, problems of compatibility and programming interfaces may arise when numerous providers provide services and aggregators for single smart spaces. This issue of scalability in disparately controlled spaces can be investigated in the future.

Furthermore, the use of captive portals to direct browser activity to service portals can bring up usability issues. An alternative would be to provide an easy to remember URL for users to browse to when they desire to use our framework. However, this would require an extra step to discover the services. More work can be done to explore through some user studies.

Relying on users' personal details to enable certain services can pose threats to their privacy and security. Presently, our system does not deal with authentication measures to secure this. A possibility would be to house sensitive data on the personal mobile devices and provide an authentication mechanism on the client to validate the data locally on the device, rather than sending it over the network.

6.2 Experiences

By using Wi-Fi networks and hotspots, we found we could dissociate the location and cardinality of Spontaneous Interaction Servers to hotspots. Smart spaces would be associated with where the wireless routers are located. When the user comes into proximity with a wireless router, his browser would be redirected to the Service Portal associated with the space, but since it is referenced by a URL, the server hosting the portal may be anywhere on the Internet. Furthermore, multiple Service Portals can be hosted on the same server, and multiple spaces can even point to the same Service Portal. This can allow for savings in cost of hardware and maintenance, since the Spontaneous Interaction Servers can be centralized and administrated by a single service provider.

However, using WLAN or LAN to base services have also posed some problems, particularly for non-dynamic services, not based on frameworks of Service Discovery Protocols such as Bluetooth and UPnP. These services would not broadcast advertisements and would need to be pre-installed into the Spontaneous Interaction Servers, and be associated with a URL. The services may be located on a remote machine and their URLs may be dependent on IP address of that machine, which may change if the machine is mobile. As such the URLs may change with time and it is currently difficult to configure the Spontaneous Interaction Server to accommodate this.

6.3 Future Directions

Currently, our implementations deal with the office and home scenarios which are more familiar to users than public places such as shopping malls and museums. We hope to develop prototypes and services for the latter scenarios to test our framework, to verify that the scanning interaction is more useful for unfamiliar environments.

In the prototypes, we use only one wireless router with a captive portal installed to simulate one smart space. However, we are aware of problems that would arise in a space with multiple hotspots especially at the overlaps of the wireless zones where a client machine may connect to either network. This would lead to contentions of which Captive Portal and thus which Service Portal the user would connect to. To investigate this issue, we intend to acquire more wireless routers to set up an extended space with seamless multiple hotspots. This can also allow us to explore user interaction as they move around in this enlarged space.

Even though our framework only requires a web browser and Wi-Fi capabilities, and many laptops, PDAs and UMPCs have them, many mobile phones currently do not. These phones generally have cameras and Bluetooth chipsets instead. We could explore the interactions afforded by such different capabilities, in particular the *pointing* mobile interaction, and integrate a wider set of functionality into our framework. The resultant system would then be able to rely on more technologies to allow services to be accessed.

7 Conclusion

We have proposed a thin-client framework over which smart spaces can be built and designed a framework for spontaneous access to services. By relying only on the availability of wireless connectivity and a web browser on each client device, our framework allows many commonly available smart devices to spontaneously access services using a HTML interface. Using the captive and service portals paradigm, a common interface can be provided at multiple smart spaces even for heterogeneous services. Each hotspot needs only to provide a web-based portal to display discovered services, and each service needs only a URL to a HTML interface for the user to interact with. As services can be aggregators, existing frameworks such as UPnP can be encapsulated into aggregator services and integrated into our framework. While the current implementation shows encouraging results, we plan to investigate the scalability of this framework to more complex spaces with multiple service providers, multiple captive hotspots, and different scenarios.

References

1. Rukzio, E., et al.: An Experimental Comparison of Physical Mobile Interaction Techniques: Touching, Pointing and Scanning. In: International Conference on Ubiquitous Computing (Ubicomp) (2006)
2. Helal, S.: Standards for Service Discovery and Delivery. IEEE Pervasive Computing 1(3), 95–100 (2002)
3. Hodes, T.D., Katz, R.H.: Composable ad-hoc location-based services for heterogeneous mobile clients. Wireless Networks 5(5), 427–441 (1999)
4. Ponnekanti, S.R., Lee, B., Fox, A., Hanrahan, P., Winograd, T.: ICrafter: A Service Framework for Ubiquitous Computing Environments. In: Abowd, G.D., Brumitt, B., Shafer, S. (eds.) Ubicomp 2001: Ubiquitous Computing. LNCS, vol. 2201, pp. 56–75. Springer, Heidelberg (2001)
5. Nakajima, T., Kobayashi, N., Tokunaga, E.: Middleware Supporting Various Input/Output Devices for Networked Audio and Visual Home Appliances. In: Murakami, H., Nakashima, H., Tokuda, H., Yasumura, M. (eds.) UCS 2004. LNCS, vol. 3598, pp. 157–173. Springer, Heidelberg (2005)
6. Nakajima, T., Satoh, I.: A software infrastructure for supporting spontaneous and personalized interaction in home computing environments. Personal and Ubiquitous Computing, 379–391 (2006)
7. Zhang, D., Zhu, M., Cheng, H.S., Koh, Y.K., Mokhtari, M.: Handling Heterogeneous Device Interaction in Smart Spaces. In: Ma, J., Jin, H., Yang, L.T., Tsai, J.J.-P. (eds.) UIC 2006. LNCS, vol. 4159, pp. 250–259. Springer, Heidelberg (2006)
8. Universal Plug and Play (UPnP) (April 17, 2007), http://www.upnp.org
9. DD-WRT firmware for wireless routers (April 17, 2007), http://www.dd-wrt.com
10. Open Service Gateway Initiative (OSGi) (April 17, 2007), http://www.osgi.org
11. Konno, S.: CyberGarage Cyberlink for Java, Development package for UPnP devices (April 17, 2007), http://www.cybergarage.org/net/upnp/java/index.html
12. del.icio.us social bookmarking service (April 17, 2007), http://del.icio.us
13. Cidero UPnP Media Controller (April 17, 2007) http://www.cidero.com/

Towards a Model of Interaction for Mutual Aware Devices and Everyday Artifacts

Sea Ling[1], Seng Loke[2], and Maria Indrawan[1]

[1] Faculty of Information Technology, Monash University, Australia
{chris.ling,maria.indrawan}@infotech.monash.edu.au
[2] Department of Computer Science, La Trobe University, Australia
s.loke@latrobe.edu.au

Abstract. Devices like PDAs, mobile phones and Smartcards can communicate with each other and to exchange information and they should be made mutually aware of each other. For privacy reasons, it is essential for the devices to have different levels of awareness and concealment measures so that each device can control how much it wants to be aware of others and how much it wants to be concealed from others. Other works have modelled and implemented awareness among devices, but none, to our knowledge, has provided a formal grounding to their work. This paper proposes a formal model for mutual aware devices, deriving from previous work for virtual environment called spatial model of interactions. As proof of concept, two experimental prototypes based on our model are also described.

1 Introduction

There is a proliferation of devices of myriad forms today, and everyday objects from furniture, appliances to toys with some communication and computational abilities will continue to find applications and will potentially increase in number. A new generation of electronic appliances or the so-called "Smart Device" or "Information Appliances" were introduced to the market. What distinguishes these smart devices from the conventional appliances is that these smart devices are capable of processing information, animation, video, audio, or some other sensory data as well as establishing communication links with other smart devices. A scenario is one where artifacts within a living room (the furniture, the electronic appliances, the lights, the drapes, windows, etc) become aware of each other and can choose to interact for the purposes of the user. A new device brought home is instantly "noticed" by several other artifacts and assimilated into a distributed system. It might be useful for devices or artifacts to be aware of their surroundings and other interconnected devices and artifacts as services from one device can be provided to other devices and vice versa in an efficient manner. Software infrastructure technologies such as Jini and UPnP aim towards such interconnection among devices, facilitated by underlying technologies such as Bluetooth short-range wireless networking. Such infrastructures already exist

J. Indulska et al. (Eds.): UIC 2007, LNCS 4611, pp. 184–194, 2007.

in the real world but to the authors' knowledge, none has provided a formal definition for its behaviour.

Ideas on the transitive behaviour of awareness have been presented in [11]. This paper proposes a formal model for mutual awareness behaviour (rather than context awareness, in general) where artifacts can be made aware of each other and establish communication with one another. Given two devices A and B, when both device A and device B share the same physical space (up to a pre-specified limit), these two devices can be made aware of each other or be hidden from each other. The use of concealment and awareness rules in our model provides a mechanism to control a device's awareness towards other devices. By conforming to these rules, one device can be either made aware of another device, hide itself from other devices or be revealed to other devices. Our proposed model will not be restricted to two but cater for many devices. Our model also supports dissemination of a small amount of data about devices, inspired by presence technologies such as instant messaging systems [16]. Apart from the underlying networking and software infrastructure, there are at least two further issues involved. The first is how devices can be aware of one another in a controllable way, i.e. a device ought to have some way to determine how many (and which) other devices (or persons) it wants to be aware of and how many (or which) other devices (or persons) can be made aware of the device. The second issue is: if a device A is aware of another device B, then what is it about B that device A should be aware of? Devices might broadcast introductory information about themselves for other devices as well as receive such information from others. Some of these issues might be application specific but a more general model will be useful.

Our model is inspired by the *spatial model* of mutual awareness used in MASSIVE [5] for virtual environments, where entities in a virtual environment are made aware (or unaware) of one another via a spatial model involving notions such as *nimbus*, *focus*, and *aura* surrounding entities. We bring such concepts over to devices and everyday smart objects so that we can speak of the nimbus, focus and aura of artifacts. We also integrate into our model features of *presence* [16], typically used in instant messaging systems.

The goal is therefore to create a generic formal model of awareness by extending the spatial model of awareness [5] and presence [16]. In this paper, we first describe the background on context-aware models, providing an overview of the related concepts described in the literature. We then describe our model of mutual awareness and the rules of awareness and concealment. Using two prototype implementations, we then illustrate how our system is able to enhance and improve upon the existing models by comparison.

2 Modelling Device Awareness: An Overview

2.1 Context Aware Artifacts

Context-aware artifacts can communicate with other artifacts or human beings depending on the states of the artifacts, as reviewed in [10]. These artifacts could "reach out" towards other artifacts in order to perform other tasks or to inform human beings with certain messages. All of these complicated behaviors could be made possible with one or more sensors. For example, a potential buyer walks into a departmental store and touches a toaster; the toaster would then try to sell itself to that buyer. A more complex behavior would be when an authorized person walks toward a security door; the sensors automatically detect the identity of the person and authorize him by opening the door.

In mobile applications, the challenge of context-aware devices is the ability to connect hosts to exchange data in a dynamic manner as hosts arrive and leave (i.e., the network topology changes constantly). Thus, context-aware devices can be highly adaptive, opportunistic and relies on the resource availability [9]. With the possibility of context-aware behaviors from these devices, a whole new frontier of electronic devices in terms of functionalities that were impossible in the past are made possible.

In our project, we aim to create a system for context aware devices that are capable of entering and leaving the system, allowing devices to have control over what it can and cannot see, the use of metadata to store essential information to preserve privacy and the use of context information to perform more complex operations.

2.2 Spatial Model of Interaction and Presence

The *Spatial Model of Interaction* developed by [1] is used for managing and controlling the information flow in virtual environments. Its core concept is the space within which objects communicate. The way to achieve this is by allowing each object to have its own *aura*. As described by [3], aura is simply a subtle sensory stimulus of "attraction" that transmits "signals of attraction" governed by the "laws of attraction". Aura is also defined as a "sub-space which effectively bounds the presence of an object within a given medium which acts as an enabler of potential interaction" [1]. Each object has a territory of space that surrounds the object. Information exchange or establishment of connection between the two objects occurs when these territories crossover, making interaction between objects possible within the virtual space.

Objects are able to control the interaction by having *degrees* in the level of awareness between them. The level of awareness is realised by the concepts of *focus* and *nimbus* which define how one object's interaction can be redirected towards another object and how much aware it is of one object towards another [1,14]. Basically, the more an object is within your focus, the more aware you are of it and the more an object is within your nimbus, the more aware it is of you.

This means that objects can be made aware of other devices by manipulating the nimbus and focus within the shared space. By knowing the degrees of focus and nimbus between devices, awareness of devices can be determined. In our model, we make the degrees of focus and nimbus more concrete by assigning distinct numerical values to the focus and the nimbus of an object. Intuitively, an object A with a higher focus value over the nimbus value of another object B will be aware of object B. Alternatively, object A with a higher value of nimbus value over the focus value of B, will *not* allow B to be aware of A.

In recent years, instant messaging system has evolved using *presence* in the wireless and wired computing world. It models another type of awareness to other people based on the person's availability and whether he/she is currently online [16]. According to Nokia [12], presence is a dynamic user profile variable which represents itself towards others and others towards itself. It is also capable of sharing information and provides control services. Such information could be personal, location, contextual, device status and preferred contact method. It was agreed that this concept can be expanded from a simple online/offline description to a much richer presence [12].

Information on the availability, whereabouts, the conditions of user are continuously shared. By providing such knowledge on other users, presence allows users to have their own control on when and how they should be communicating with another user more effectively. However, security and privacy issues must be considered as the information sharing increases.

3 Formalisng Spatial Model with Presence for Mutual Aware Devices

The objective is to develop a formal model for electronic devices not only able to communicate with each other, but also able to understand and identify its surrounding devices. Thus, we propose a solution by combining the spatial model of interaction with presence from instant messaging system.

We use the principles of spatial model to control the availability of devices for communication and to facilitate the discovery of devices and establishing connections. The aura of each device is assumed to be the area within the range of the communication limit. The idea is that given the focus and nimbus of each device, the level of awareness is able to be controlled and devices can behave differently under different programmable conditions. We use the principle of presence to propose an identification mechanism which is capable of identifying the right devices as well as providing additional "condition" information. By incorporating presence, each device is provided with a metadata to uniquely identify itself and its current condition. The device would be able to change its metadata to inform its change to other devices.

The concepts described in Section 2 are now applied to our model. Nimbus is the level of concealment for each device. Focus is modelled by the level of awareness set for each device. Presence is the metadata containing device information. Every device possess different levels of awareness and concealment. For example, device X is aware of device Y (i.e., device Y is visible) if X's awareness level (focus) is higher than Y's concealment level (nimbus). Alternatively, X is not aware of Y (i.e., device Y is invisible) if Y's concealment level (nimbus) is higher than X's awareness level (focus).

We generalise the above for all devices.

Definition 1 (Awareness and Concealment). *For every device i, let a_i be its awareness level and c_i be its concealment level.*
Given any two devices x and y, the following holds:

- $a_x \geq c_y$ *if and only if x is aware of y.*
- $a_x < c_y$ *if and only if x is not aware of y.*

We have the following propositions:

Proposition 1 (Mutual Awareness). *Given any two devices x and y, x and y are aware of each other if and only if $a_x \geq c_y$ and $a_y \geq c_x$.*

Proof: By Definition 1.

Proposition 2 (Mutual Concealment). *Given any two devices x and y, x and y are not aware of each other if and only if $c_x > a_y$ and $c_y > a_x$.*

Proof: By Definition 1.

Proposition 3. *Given any two devices x and y, x is aware of y and y is not aware x if and only if $a_x \geq c_y$ and $c_x > a_y$.*

Proof: By Definition 1.

Proposition 4. *Given any three devices x, y and z, such that x is aware of y and y is aware of z, x is aware of z if $c_y \geq c_z$.*

Proof: Given $a_z \geq c_y$ and $a_y \geq c_z$, if $c_y \geq c_z$, then the result follows that $a_x \geq c_z$.

Theorem 1. *Given a set of devices $\{x^1, x^2, x^3, \cdots, x^k, \cdots, x^n\}$, for each $k(1 \leq k \leq n-1)$, if $a_{x^k} \geq c_{x^{k+1}}$ and $c_{x^k} \geq c_{x^{k+1}}$, x^k is aware of x^n.*

Proof: For each $k(1 \leq k \leq n-1)$, given $a_{x^k} \geq c_{x^{k+1}}, a_{x^{k+1}} \geq c_{x^{k+2}}, \cdots, a_{x^{n-1}} \geq c_{x^n}$, if $c_{x^{k+1}} \geq c_{x^{k+2}}, c_{x^{k+2}} \geq c_{x^{k+3}}, \cdots, c_{x^{n-1}} \geq c_{x^n}$, then from Proposition 4, $a_{x^k} \geq c_{x^{k+2}}, a_{x^{k+1}} \geq c_{x^{k+3}}, \cdots, a_{x^{n-2}} \geq c_{x^n}$. Since for all k and i where $i \geq k$, $c_{x^k} \geq c_{x^i}$ and $a_{x^k} \geq c_{x^i}$, $a_{x^k} \geq c_{x^n}$, i.e., all devices all aware of x^n.

Proposition 5. *Given any three devices x, y and z such that x is aware of y and y is aware of z, x is aware of z if $c_y \geq a_y$.*

Proof: Given $a_x \geq c_y$ and $a_y \geq c_z$, if $c_y \geq a_y$, the result follows that $a_z \geq c_z$.

Theorem 2. *Given a set of devices $\{x^1, x^2, x^3, \cdots, x^k, \cdots, x^n\}$, for each $k(1 \leq k \leq n-1)$, if $a_{x^k} \geq c_{x^{k+1}}$ and $c_{x^k} \geq a_{x^k}$, x^k is aware of x^n.*

Proof: If $c_{x^k} \geq a_{x^k}$ for all k, then given $a_{x^k} \geq c_{x^{k+1}}$, it follows that $c_{x^k} \geq c_{x^i}$ for all $i \geq k$. The result then follows from Theorem 1.

The implication of the above rules is that as long as each device maintains the condition in Theorem 1 or Theorem 2, the awareness relationship will be transitive, regardless of how many devices there are in the environment. Maintaining such a condition might be a "social-mile" imposed on each device in order to have a transitively aware society of devices. Hence, our model allows different situation of mutual (non-)awareness to be represented. Adjustments to the level of mutual (non-)awareness can be done by adjusting the levels of awareness and concealment for each device.

4 Experimental Prototypes

We describe briefly two experimental prototypes, i.e., proof-of-concept implementations of our model: one for artifacts without computational capabilities (using RFID tagging) and one for devices with computational capabilities (and Bluetooth enabled). While we describe them separately, combinations of the two technologies involves artifacts and computational devices are possible.

4.1 RFID

RFID technology uses tags and readers. The technology has an advantage of simulating a more complex device through programming techniques whilst keeping the focus on developing a model based on context awareness. Devices that use this technology are mostly keycards, key rings, or tags that normally do not possess processing and storage capability.

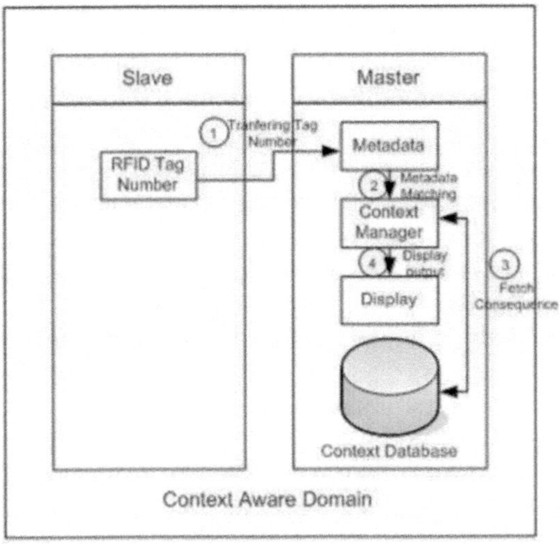

Fig. 1. RFID Implementation

Figure 1 illustrates the architecture consisting of a master and a slave. The figure uses multidirectional and bidirectional arrows to indicate the flow of information and actions throughout the simple system. There are four top level steps for this model. When the RFID tag of the slave is scanned and the master is able to "find" the slave device based on the rules of awareness and concealment, the tag number of the slave device is transferred to the master device (Step 1). Metadata contains information regarding the slave devices including their tag ids and the awareness and concealment levels. The information is stored in the master device.

Context Manager is the software component that deals with the discovery of new slave devices entering and leaving the boundaries of the master device. It also deals with generating context actions based on the information fetched from the Context Database which is data repository containing information about slave devices and the consequences or actions that corresponds to the context information. A list of consequences is stored in the database and the retrieval of these consequences is based on the matching of context information provided by the slave devices.

In Step 2 and Step 3, the Context Manager detects any incoming slave devices based on the rules of Awareness and Concealment. The slave device's metadata (Presence information) is then collected and processed. The processed data is then used as query to the Context Database to retrieve any relevant information regarding the slave device and provide a list of possible actions to be taken. The forth and final step is the display of what actions both the master device and slave device take.

4.2 Bluetooth

Another way to implement the model of mutual aware artifacts is to use Bluetooth[1] technology as the communication medium for devices with processing and storage capability. The nature of this technology enables the discovery of devices easily, and we have considered how this can be exploited in our model. Bluetooth devices are capable of discovering other Bluetooth devices when they are within range of each other. In the context aware manner, the discovery of these devices is not necessarily part of the system. The only way the device can be recognized by the system is through the recognition of device IDs provided in the metadata and only if it passes the rules of Awareness and Concealment as given in Section 3.

The metadata here consists of the essential information of a particular Bluetooth device which includes information such as device ID, awareness and concealment levels, device owner, contextual information, etc. The previous implementation using RFID technology can be converted to Bluetooth platform without much modification. The architecture is therefore similar to the RFID implementation as shown in Figure 1. There is however one key difference. The slave store its own metadata. The metadata stored on slave devices eliminates the need for the master device to have a metadata collection as in the RFID technology example. With RFID technology, the tagged slaves might not have computational/storage capabilities. Thus, it might not be able to store metadata, thereby requiring the master device to store such metadata. With the Bluetooth technology, the slaves are assumed to have computational/storage capabilities to store metadata describing themselves. The processing of metadata and the fetching of consequences is the same as in the RFID technology except the actions are sent back to the slaves.

---

[1] More information on Bluetooth can be found in Bluetooth Special Interest Group at www.bluetooth.com

5 Related Work

Context-aware devices were initially researched by Schilit et al. [15] whose intention is to make devices aware of other devices, the surrounding environment and to allow communication to take place. In subsequent years, several similar projects on context awareness such as MASSIVE [5], AROMA [13], Context Unity [9] and SOCAM [7] have evolved. Each model is targeted at different application domains such as location tracking, virtual worlds and mobility.

Table 1. Explanation of the criteria used in the comparison

Criteria	Explanation
Concept	The key concept that has been adopted for the model.
Year	The year that the model is being developed and published.
Application Domain	The domain in which the model is being applied.
Awareness	Can be of one of two types: dynamic or static. The former being the object is able to discover and interact with other objects dynamically. The latter being the object is able to interact with predefined objects only.
Perception of Space	Either yes or no. If yes, the object is able to determine itself and the space/domain where it belongs to. Its abilities also include how it visualise other objects and whether it can use the interfaces of these objects [5].
Engagement	Whether the objects are bonded together for communication. It could link two objects together and establish a connection link between them.
Navigation	The constant movement of objects within the environment and the ability to pick the right objects for communication [5].
Scalable	The ability of the model to cope with the growing number of objects.
Sensors	The ability to use physical sensors such as temperature detection, infrared, etc.
Reasoning	The ability to interpret contextual information and derive useful information and answers to queries [7].
Context Definition	The ability to represent and express context information using this model.
Context Capturing	The ability to record and process context information to produce useful information for other objects.

MASSIVE (Model, Architecture and System for Spatial Interaction in Virtual Environments) [1] is a prototype implementation based on the Spatial Model of Interaction in virtual context aware environment. Context UNITY is a model of mutual awareness theory with the presence of mobility extending the work on Mobile UNITY [9]. Mobile UNITY is based on the UNITY model [2] with additional notations for mobility and proof logic. It provides a formal representation for mobility to the context-aware environment to allow reasoning mechanism and behaviour manipulation according to the change of context. The SOCAM (Service Oriented Context-Aware Middleware) project [7] is an architecture for developing context-aware services. The aim of this project is to offer an efficient infrastructure support for context-aware services. AROMA is a model of

Table 2. Comparison of existing models based on the criteria specified in Table 1

	MASSIVE	AROMA	Context UNITY	SOCAM	Our Model
Concept	Spatial Model of Interaction	Pure Abstraction	Context Representation	Ontology-based Context Model	Spatial Model of Interaction
Technology	non-specific	non-specific	Mobile UNITY	Java and OWL	non-specific
Year	1994	1997	2004	2004	2006
Application Domain	Virtual Environment	Generic	Mobile Environment	Middleware Support	Generic
Awareness	Dynamic	Static	non-specific	Dynamic	Dynamic
Perception of Space	Yes	Yes	non-specific	Yes	Yes
Engagement	Yes	non-specific	non-specific	Yes	Yes
Navigation	Yes	No	non-specific	non-specific	Yes
Scalable	Yes	No	non-specific	non-specific	Yes
Sensors	not applicable	Yes	not applicable	Yes	Yes
Reasoning	None	None	Yes	Yes	Yes
Context Definition	No	Yes	Yes	Yes	Yes
Context Capturing	Yes	Yes	Yes	Yes	Yes

mutual awareness developed by Pedersen and Skoler [13]. This model uses a different approach to MASSIVE. It uses a pure abstract representation for objects, re-mapping on media signals and extending the application domain to include social interactions.

To compare existing work mentioned above with our work, we focus on the comparison criteria shown in Table 1. Based on these criteria, a comparison of these models has been made and is shown in Table 2.

6 Conclusion

We have proposed a model for mutual aware artifacts by combining a Spatial Model of Awareness [1] with Presence [16]. The model includes the mechanism to control the awareness levels of devices using the Rules of Awareness and Concealment. We have also adapted ideas from Instant Messaging Systems by storing presence data in metadata form. The model can be used as the fundamental layer for context aware systems where devices are made aware of one another. By only exposing essential information of a device to other devices, the model preserves the devices' privacy and enables the levels of awareness and concealment to be changeable (e.g. at runtime). Two prototypes are also presented based on RFID tags and Bluetooth technology. They serve to check the validity of the proposed model to handle mutual awareness between multiple devices.

It is possible in the model for some device to set its awareness and concealment values such that it is invisible to others but aware of as many devices as possible. But depending on the intention, the idea is that the device may want itself to be aware of by others in a controllable fashion (note that a device can tune its awareness and concealment levels to suit its intentions, e.g., start at some level and adjust that till a required number of devices is within scope) in order that others might initiate communication with it or be utilized by others (offering, perhaps even chargeable, services).

Other possible extensions of the proposed model of awareness are:

1. Intelligent Mobile Agents
   The integration with intelligent mobile agents will enable the mutual awareness capability to further enhance agents' capabilities.
2. Context Systems with Artificial Intelligence
   The implementation of large scale context aware system with the assistance of intelligent searching would greatly enhance the output choices.

For a more realistic application, we are currently extending this model to enable location tracking. The system implementation utilises the Ekahau positioning engine. While tracking the locations of devices, we are investigating what it means to have different mobile device auras to collide in the spatial model. Initial results suggest that the model can be further enhanced to reflect different levels of granularity in representing interaction and services.

Location technologies tend to have inaccuracies so that an object is represented as being within a (perhaps distorted) circle of a particular radius (from several centimetres to a few metres depending on the technology). One can interpret this "circle" as the aura of the object and exploited for mutual object pre-interaction (e.g., preparations on the objects before actual message exchanges once overlapping of aura (or "circles") is detected).

We are also working on extending the model to consider finer grained boundaries for awareness and concealment, i.e., not only based on the pre-set levels but also richer context of the devices themselves.

References

1. Benford, S., Bowers, J., Fahlen, L.E., Greenhalgh, C.: Managing Mutual Awareness in Collaborative Virtual Environments. In: Proceedings of Virtual Reality Software Technology Conference '94, ACM Press, Singapore (1994)
2. Chandy, K.M., Misra, J.: Parallel Program Design: A Foundation. Addison-Wesley, NY, USA (1988)
3. Ferscha, A., Hechinger, M., Mayrhofer, R., Rocha, D.S., Franz, M., Oberhauser, R.: Digital Aura. Pervasive Computing. In: Second International Conference, Pervasive 2004, Vienna (2004)
4. Fontana, J.: Presence applications poised for takeoff. (Accessed: 18th September 2006) [WWW] Available: `http://www.nwfusion.com/news/2004/090604specialfocus.html`

5. Greenhalgh, C., Benford, S.: MASSIVE: A Collaborative Virtual Environment for Teleconferencing. ACM Transactions on Computer-Human Interaction 2(3), 239–261 (1995)
6. Greene, D., O'Mahony, D.: Instant Messaging and Presence Management in Mobile Ad-Hoc Networks. In: 2nd IEEE Conference on Pervasive Computing and Communications Workshops, PerCom 2004 Workshops, pp. 55–59 (2004)
7. Gu, T., Pung, H.K., Zhang, D.Q.: Toward an OSGi-based infrastructure for context-aware applications. IEEE Pervasive Computing 3(4), 66–74 (2004)
8. Herrero, P., Antonio, D.A.: A Human Based Perception Model For Cooperative Intelligent Virtual Agents. CoopIS/DOA/ODBASE, pp. 195–212 (2002)
9. Julien, C., Payton, J., Roman, G.C.: Reasoning About Context-Awareness in the Presence of Mobility. Electronic Notes in Theoretical Computer Science 97, 259–276 (2004)
10. Loke, S.: Context-Aware Artifacts: Two Development Approaches. IEEE Pervasive Computing 5(2), 48–53 (2006)
11. Loke, S.: Context-Aware Pervasive Systems: Architectures for a New Breed of Applications. Auerbach Publications (Taylor and Francis, CRC Press), Abington (2007)
12. Nokia: Staying in touch with presence, white paper (Accessed: 18th September 2006). [WWW] Available: http://www.nokia.com/BaseProject/Sites/NOKIA_MAIN_18022/CDA/Categories/Networks/Technologies/MessagingandPresence/PresenceandInstantMessaging/_Content/_Static_Files/presence_a4_0711.pdf
13. Pedersen, E.R., Sokoler, T.: AROMA: Abstract Representation of Presence Supporting Mutual Awareness. In: Conference on Human Factors in Computing Systems, Proceedings of the Special Interest Group on Computer-Human Interaction (SIGCHI) conference on Human factors in computing systems (1997)
14. Rodden, T.: Populating the Application: A Model of Awareness for Cooperative Applications. In: Proceedings 1996 ACM Conference on Computer Supported Cooperative Work (CSCW'96), pp. 87–96. ACM Press, New York (1996)
15. Schilit, B.N., Adams, N., Want, R.: Context-Aware Computing Application. In: Proceedings of the Workshop on Mobile Computing Systems and Applications, Santa Cruz, CA, pp. 85–90. IEEE Computer Society, Los Alamitos (1994)
16. Vogiazou, Y.: Wireless Presence and Instant Messaging (Accessed: 18 September 2006). [WWW] Available: http://www.jisc.ac.uk/index.cfm?name=techwatch_report_0207

A Peer-to-Peer Semantic-Based Service Discovery Method for Pervasive Computing Environment

Baopeng Zhang, Yuanchun Shi, and Xin Xiao

Key Laboratory of Pervasive Computing, Ministry of Education
Department of CS, Tsinghua University, Beijing, P.R. China
{zbp02,xiaoxin00}@mails.tsinghua.edu.cn, shiyc@tsinghua.edu.cn

Abstract. The paper proposes a novel distributed service discovery method for the pervasive computing environment. The method is based on the concept of small world, policy-based advertisement and semantic-based intelligent forwarding of service request. We utilize the policy-based proactive advertisement method to establish the service community of every node, which fully consider the node capability of computation and communication. For service beyond service community, each node maintains a few distant nodes called contacts to create a small world network for increasing the semantic coverage view. Based on the hierarchical service attribute model, we integrate three-level topology character (node level, location level and service level) in contact selection mechanism. Utilizing semantic-covered network, we realize the semantic-based service discovery. Simulation result shows that our method has better search efficiency for service with different popularity than broadcast-based method.

1 Introduction

In the past few year peer-to-peer applications become popular, such as file sharing, media streaming. The service-oriented mode is more and more recognized. The common driving force behind the two kinds of model is to strive for better search mechanisms.

There are two classes of solutions currently proposed for decentralized peer-to-peer search, unstructured and structured. The former relies on the flooding queries to all peers, and many works use smarter search or data replication algorithms to improve the search performance. The latter address the scalability through Distributed Hash Table (DHT) abstract. Content-based Index is a common measure for both them to conduct the searching process. Content-based communication is a kind of communication service transferring the messages according to message content, rather than explicit addresses assigned by senders, and service provider can publish the service information, and service consumer can declare their search interests by means of selection predicates.

Service discovery play an important role in pervasive computation environment. As pervasive computing environment, the mobile ad hoc network (MANET) consists of a set of wireless mobile nodes dynamically forming infrastructure-less network. Even though developed independently of each other, P2P overlay network in the

J. Indulska et al. (Eds.): UIC 2007, LNCS 4611, pp. 195–204, 2007.

internet and mobile wireless ad hoc networks share many key characteristic such as self-organization, decentralization, hop-by-hop connection and frequently changing topology. Just due to the peer-to-peer nature of MANETs, all protocols designed for it are inherently peer-to-peer. So application and middleware design should take account of the characters of network level.

In this paper, we propose the semantic-based service discovery scheme. Instead of indexing all service attributes owned by each service in a peer node, only a portion of service attributes are registered with the index. Those service attributes are hierarchically organized to express the attributes significance, and peers are organized based on their service attribute relation and their interests in a similar way as proposed in [1], [2]. In the same time, fully considering the node, location and service level characters, we introduce small world network idea and establish service information index network which efficiently ease the semantic-based service discovery in the pervasive computing environment.

2 Related Work

The related work lies in the areas of routing and service discovery in ad hoc networks and peer to peer computing environment. Service discovery architectures like jini, UPnP, and Service Location Protocol have been developed over the past few years to discover infrastructure-based service. It is inappropriate in pervasive computing environment/ad hoc network. There are some discovery protocols, such as Konark[9], and GSD[5], designed for infrastructure-less networks. Konark use gossips method to complement information knowledge among nodes. GSD utilize service group to advertise service information and index discovery. Similar to GSD, our method take account of intelligent forward mechanism rather than broadcast in blind searching process.

The routing protocol can be broadly classified as: proactive (table-driven), reactive (on-demand) and hybrid. Proactive protocol such as OLSR, FSR, etc, periodically broadcast the update, which is resource consuming for a large scale network. Reactive protocol DSR, AODV, reduce the communication overhead at expense of delay due to route search. For combining proactive and reactive method advantages, some hybrid routing protocols were proposed, such as ZRP[6], SHARP[7], CARD[4] and so on, based on the zone idea. We have a viewpoint the service discovery method should consider cross-level design to improve the discovery efficiency.

Most peer-to-peer search systems [1][8] are proposed to establish intelligent search mechanism according to the node characters. Our semantic-based service discovery method utilizes the service function class and location information, not the ip addresses or word character, to establish the relation between nodes for partially context-aware service discovery.

3 Multi-level Structure of Service Discovery Network

We assume every node has one or multiple service. Service description was implemented by ontology-based approach having advantage which describes function and capability, as well as the further constraints and relationships among services.

3.1 Hierarchical Service Attribute Tree

Service description provides the elaborate expression about service semantic characters. In view of our method requirement, we category the service attributes as hierarchical tree corresponding with service discovery semantic logic which expresses the thinking habit of human being. As Fig.1 shown, the service attribute category tree includes: Function Class (SD_f): the service function can be classified in the light of service execution effect. Such as print class, display device class and so on. Location Information (SD_l): physical space location information is expressed by coordinate system model and symbol space model [10]. Invoking interface (SD_i): similar to the OWL service description mechanism, invoking interface describes the input/output compatibility, i.e. how to use the service. Regulation Parameter (SD_p): this part describe service operation parameter such as printer resolution, display device size, transcoder service frame rate, and some statistical information of service execution quality, availability, reputation and so on. This hierarchical tree structure implies the ordered relation of priority, $SD_f \succeq SD_l \succ SD_i \succ SD_p$, in discovery process.

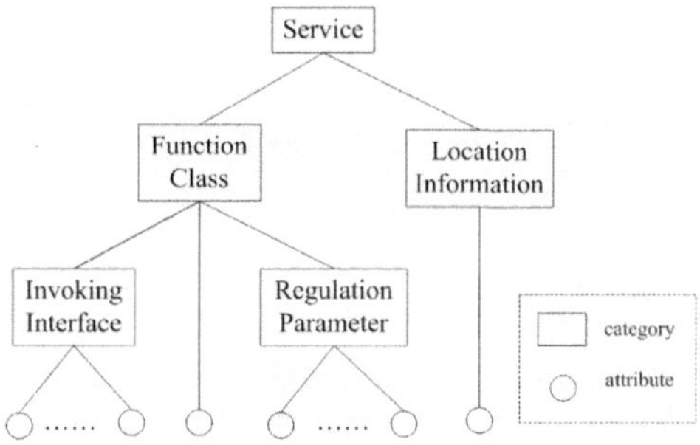

Fig. 1. Hierarchical Service Attribute Tree

3.2 Service Discovery Network

From bottom to top, three levels of topology are defined as node level topology, location level topology and service level topology Every node has the information on physical link of the nodes in the vicinity. Node level topology provides the physical communication relation among the nodes. The location level topology defines location information about the physical space — zone and space. The location information includes the two-dimension zone-based coordinate information which can divide the flat space into non-overlapped zone, and the space-based symbol information which expresses social domain location knowledge, such as the room ID in a building. The service level topology is relation expression of service function class information. It includes same class relation and dependence relation. The same group relation defines that every service node knows their neighbor service node belonging to same service class. The dependence relation expresses the association between the different service function. In this paper, we emphasize the same service class relation. Three kind of topology can efficiently enhance the semantic connection degree of node and reduce the search space in order for lesser discovery time and lesser node disturbance.

4 Service Discovery Algorithm Overview

Intuitively, our method works as follows: we regard the service function class as service key of node. The service keys of every node include primary key and secondary key. According to service information of every node, the local service function class is consider as the primary key K_p, and non-local ones is designate as secondary key K_s. Every node has two node sets, primary set and secondary set, based on the service key criterion. The primary sets are consisted of neighbor nodes with same service function class.

When a query happens in a node, the query for specified service class Q_s needs to be forwarded only to nodes with same K_p in the network. If the query node has same K_p, it will perform the service matching and forward request to neighbor node with same K_p for partial search. Otherwise, it will select nodes with same K_p to Q_s in its secondary sets and forward query to them. When the secondary set does not have same K_p to Q_s, the query node on-demand selects extended contact to resolve the discovery request.

4.1 Hybrid Peer-to-Peer Cache Method

This idea is based on the concept of *small worlds* where characterized by two properties: (1) Local contact with small average path length. (2) A small numbers of long range contacts with large clustering coefficient [3].We adopt the hybrid method to establish the service discovery network.

4.2 Establishing and Maintain Community Information

Our peer-to-peer cache method employs a hybrid of proactive and reactive approaches for information collection. Every node periodically advertises a list of its services to all the nodes within limited distance. Every node has service class information within a limited radius community.

Many nodes of pervasive computing environment have different memory, computation and communication capability. In view of heterogeneity, we adopt policy-based adaptive advertisement and forward method.

- Every node can advertise service information in own-controlled advertisement diameter. The advertisement diameter can be determined by node capability and mobility possibility. Lower capability nodes have a smaller information coverage area, and the fixed node can advertise service information to much many nodes within larger diameter area. This mechanism efficiently guarantees the published information stability, energy-based and mobility-based adaptability.

- When receiving the advertisement message, a node can modify advertisement hop counts according to the own capability. If the forwarding node has low capability, low energy, low communication bandwidth or high mobility possibility, it should reduce the hop counts or stop to forward advertisement information. This lends itself to guarantee the stability and the availability of the routing path.
- We also utilize the semantic-supported advertisement mechanism to establish service level topology. Node can specify the predicate of advertisement and forward. Some nodes advertise their service information to special physical location, for example, the same room, under the observation of similarity between network proximity and physical space proximity.

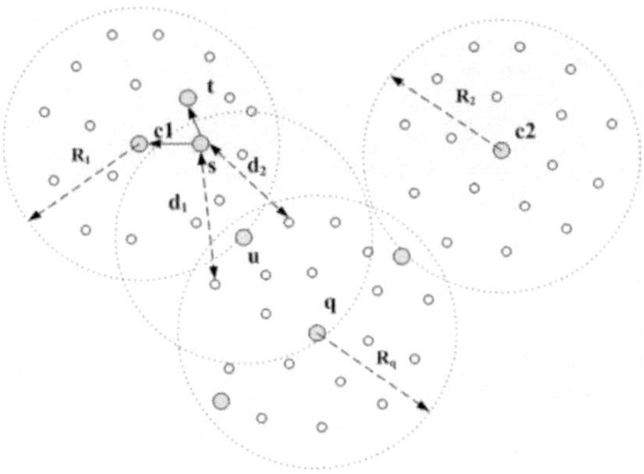

Fig. 2. Long Contact Node Selection

4.3 Contact Selection Mechanism

Our contact-selection mechanism takes two characters, network proximity and semantic proximity in consideration. When a node did not discovery the requisite service class information within its community, it can select semantic-related contact to improve the search view instead of broadcasting service discovery message. The design requirements of our contact selection mechanism include minimizing service community overlapping degree, maximizing semantic coverage of long contact node, and maximizing connectivity among kindred nodes.

4.3.1 Kindred-Based Contact Selection

Kindred-based contact selection has two considerations. One is to find the long contact node containing more service function class information and overlapping fewer dominant community of service request node. The other is to find a long contact for establishing the kindred node topology to guarantee the higher reachability among the kindred nodes. Hence, it is important for a contact to have a proximity that does not overlap significantly with that of the query node or other contacts of the query node. So, the long contact node selection criteria include three processes.

Frontier Node Selection

As Fig.2 shown, the node q can obtain the node information of its service community without requiring extra overhead. The frontier nodes set of node q is important because their next hop node information is not known to the node q. According to the theory of triangle, we define selection criterion as the distance between selected frontier nodes is $R+1$. Then, we regard the frontier node of frontier node as jumping-off point of contact node selection. The target is to select the nodes whose service community does not include any other frontier nodes of q or have similar long distance d from any other frontier nodes of node q. In Fig.2, u is the frontier node of q, and the frontier node of u is s. Frontier node selection algorithm is shown as follow:

```
FN _ selection(q):
// choose FN of query node
choose a random FN u with false from FN _ set of q
while the tag of any frontier node is false
  FN _ result = FN _ result.add(u);
  for each node v in FN _ set of q
   if (u.SC include v) & (v.tag == false)
    {    v.tag = true;
         u.SC _ FN = u.SC _ FN.add(v);
         if v is the frontier node of u
           u = v's 1-hop neighbor with false;
    }
end while;
for every FN u of FN _ result do
   if (FN s of u not belong to q.SC)
     if (( s.SC not include any nodes wi of u.SC _ FN )or
      (d(s, w_i) > constant value))
         EFN _ result = EFN _ result.add(s);
 end for
end
```

Contact Discover Direction

After selecting valid frontier node for forwarding contact discovery message, how to control the forward direction is efficiently mechanism for reducing false discovery direction. Considering the policy-based advertisement effect, some resource-constrain or mobility-prone nodes become the community edge. So due to the autonomic of node advertisement policy, we adopt probabilistic method to dynamic select long contact discover direction for avoiding the unstable path. From Fig.2, s is selected frontier node. Node s selects its exterior neighbor node $c1$ and t which does not belong to the service community of the node u to forward contact discover message. We define the number Num_i of advertisement message delivering from the exterior neighbor node EN_i, every message delivering hop number $Hop[j]$, every message advertisement diameter $D_{\max}[j]$. So the probabilistic forward function is expressed as

$P_{Forward}\left[EN_i\right]=\prod_{j=1}^{Num_i}(1-Hop[j]/D_{\max}[j])$. This method can make contact selection capacity-aware, and better deal with node heterogeneity.

Contact Node Selection
The long contact node selection is completed in a serial fashion. The selection criterion is non-overlapping or minimum overlapping between SC of contact nodes. The optional contact can use a communication-efficient manner, bloom filters technique to judge the membership of the long contact set of SQ .

In constructing service discovery network, we adopt kindred-priority mechanism to take consider of the primary kindred contact selection in the first place. If the node SQ already has many kindred neighbor node, the secondary kindred contact selection is emphasized instead.

We assume the node has Num_srv kinds of services function class information and maintenance list $\langle S\_id, N\_num\rangle$, where S_id expresses service function class, N_num is the number of node containing S_id service. If long contact node is kindred node of the query node, we directly select this node to be long contact node. It can be optimized with service function class information density through comparing the selected node with other nodes of its SC . We define the service function class information density as $p(i)=N\_num[i]\Big/\sum_{j=1}^{Num\_srv}N\_num[j]$

If long contact node is not kindred node of the query node, how to semantically enhance the query node view is our aim. We propose the concept of relative semantic information value of node — RSI which quantitatively expresses the similarity between two nodes. Supposed the number of same service function class contained by the node c and q is SS_num , the RSI value of node c for q is defined as $RSI(q,c)$. We utilize the idea on information content of semantic concept [18], and simply set: $RSI(q,c)=-\log p(sc)$, where $p(sc)$ is ratio of the number of same service function class and total number in contact node c , i.e. $p(sc)=\sum_{i=1}^{SS\_num}N\_num[i]\Big/\sum_{j=1}^{Num\_srv}N\_num[j]$.

4.3.2 Location-Aware Contact Selection

Location information is important to service discovery in pervasive computing environment. Proximity-based and space-based service selection has been getting more attention for user end application. According to our proposed policy-advertisement mechanism above, the location level topology is established. So, we can see every node have the service information of location-proximity nodes. The main idea behind of location-aware contact selection mechanism is choose the node with different location information from service community of query node. This contact-selection algorithm enhances the location semantic consideration on the basis of node distance relation with reference to communication range, and efficiently lends itself to high-level semantic query. The algorithm aims to achieve optimal average hop in querying the service with specified location requirement. We utilize the space-based symbol information to express social domain location knowledge. According a hierarchical location symbol model, the node location information loc_id can be denoted by string expression. For example: FIT/Floor.2/Sect.1/502. We assume $Q_{SQ}\{loc\_id\}$ as the set of different loc_id information known by the SQ node, our location-aware contact selection mechanism can be expressed as expectation: $\{loc\_id(c)\} \cap Q_{SQ}\{loc\_id\} = \varnothing$.

The proposed service discovery method supports partial search and location-aware discovery. The requirement for service of limited number or specified attribute range is regarded as partial search.

5 Performance Evaluation

It has been observed that the popularity keyword search strings in both traditional web searches and Gnutella P2P network follows a zipf-like distribution. In the pervasive computing environment, service distribution is also likely to be skewed as some services are common or significantly more popular than others. We use Zipf distribution to generate node numbers of every service function class in our simulation scenario.

As known to all, the success of search is closely related to data or service popularity. We define a new metric, *balance capacity of discovery efficiency* that quantitatively expresses difference of average overhead in discovering different popularity service. The value of balance capacity of discovery efficiency should predict the overhead proportion relation of service discovery method to discover a service with different popularity in pervasive computing environment. According to our observation, when the service advertisement diameter is increased the service information will be cached in more nodes, it means the service discovery overhead is directly proportional to service advertisement diameter. The further the requested service is away form query source, the lesser is the chance of service discovery and the higher is the service discovery overhead. So the success rate of service discover is inversely proportional to the distance between the source and request destination. The distance implicitly is proportional to the number of requested service function class. So we mainly focus on the condition with long distance between query source and destination for better embodying our performance metric. Taking these factors into consideration, we can define *balance capacity of discovery efficiency* as:

$$Balance\ capacity = \underset{i=1}{\overset{Num\_srv}{SIM}} \left(\frac{Query\_Cost_i}{Num_i(discovery\ result)}\right)$$

Here, the $Query\_Cost_i$ is message overhead of service discovery. Due to supporting partial search in our proposed method, so we average effect of discovery result number $Num_i(discovery\ result)$ discovered in the specified simulation time range or

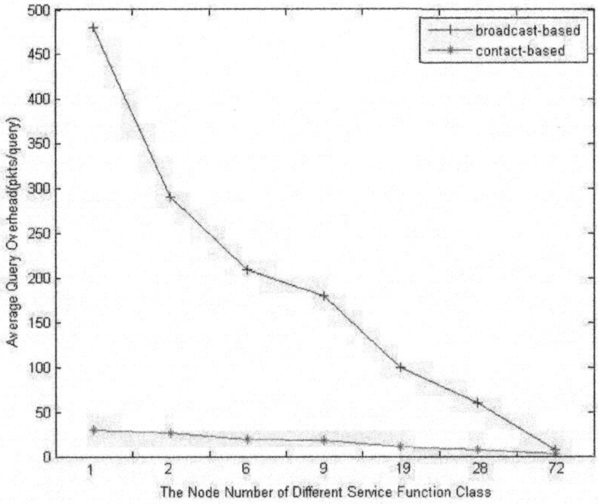

Fig. 3. Balance Capacity of Broadcast-based vs Contact-based Method

specified constraints C. SIM function is to repress the similarity between different service function class discovery.

For the purpose of the simulation, we used representative service $SF0$ to $SF10$ to represent actual service function class. The service advertisement diameter is set to 3. We use J-Sim [11] simulation tools to carry out experiments to evaluate the proposed method with respect to standard broadcast-based method in the relative stable condition. As Fig.3 shown, we can see the more popular is the service function class, the lesser is the average overhead. For the unpopular service function class, the broadcast-based method has worse query performance. Broadcast-based method has lesser balance capacity than our proposed method.

6 Conclusion and Future Work

In this paper, we propose a new P2P-based semantic service discovery method, which utilizing the contact-based small world idea, to facilitate efficient semantic-based service discovery. In view of service advertisement information, Peer node self-organize into a small world network which has efficient search performance with low maintenance overhead. In small world network construction, we fully consider the node, location and service level characters to integrate the semantic into service discovery mechanism. The proposed method can adapts to node heterogeneity, physical space constrains, and node autonomy. We will further tune the performance of the method, exploit other relative quality of performance with other methods and take account of dependency-based service discovery mechanism.

Acknowledgements

This is supported by the National 973 Plan, No.2006CB303106.

References

1. Zhang, R.M., Hu, Y.C.: Assisted Peer-To-Peer Search With Partial Indexing. In: The 24th Annual Joint Conference of the IEEE Computer and Communications Societies. Proceedings IEEE Infocom, pp. 1514–1525 (2005)
2. Kunwadee, S., Bruce, M., Zhang, H.: Efficient Content Location Using Interest-Based Locality in Peer-To-Peer Systems. In: Twenty-Second Annual Joint Conference of the IEEE Computer and Communications Societies. IEEE Infocom, pp. 2166–2176 (2003)
3. Kleinberg, J.: The Small-world Phenomenon: An Algorithm Perspective. In: Proceedings of ACM Symposium on Theory of Computing, pp. 163–170. ACM Press, New York (2000)
4. Ahmed, H., Saurabh, G.: CARD: A Contact-based Architecture for Resource Discovery in Wireless Ad Hoc Networks. Mobile Networks and Applications Journal 10, 99–113 (2005)
5. Chakraborty, D., Joshi, A.: Toward Distributed Service Discovery in Pervasive Computing Environments. IEEE Transactions on Mobile Computing 5, 97–112 (2006)
6. Haas, Z., Pearlman, M.: The Zone Routing Protocol (ZRP) for Ad Hoc Networks. IETF Internet draft for the Manet group (1999)
7. Ramasubramanian, V., Haas, Z., Sirer, E.G.: SHARP: A Hybrid Adaptive Routing Protocol for Mobile Ad Hoc Networks. In: MOBIHOC Conference, pp. 303–314 (2003)
8. Prasanna, G., Sun, Q.X., Hector, G.M.: Yappers: A Peer-To-Peer Lookup Service over Arbitrary Topology. In: Twenty-Second Annual Joint Conference of the IEEE Computer and Communications Societies. IEEE Infocom, pp. 1250–1260 (2003)
9. Choonhwa, L., Abdelsalam, H., Nitin, D., Varun, V., Bekir, A.: Konark: A System and Protocols for Device Independent, Peer-To-Peer Discovery and Delivery of Mobile Services. IEEE Transactions on Systems, Man and Cybernetics 33(6), 682–696 (2003)
10. Jiang, C.H., Steenkiste, P.: A Hybrid Location Model with Computable Location Identifier for Ubiquitous Computing. In: UbiComp02, pp. 246–263 (2002)
11. J-Sim, http://www.j-sim.org/

Ubiquitous Healthcare Architecture Using SmartBidet and HomeServer with Embedded Urinalysis Agent

SungHo Ahn[1], Kyunghee Lee[1], Doo-Hyun Kim[2,*], and Vinod Cherian Joseph[3]

[1] Convergence Interaction Research Team, ETRI, Korea
{ahnsh,kyunghee}@etri.re.kr
[2] School of Internet and Multimedia Engineering, Konkuk University, Seoul, Korea
doohyun@konkuk.ac.kr
[3] Wireless Terminals Division, Samsung Electronics Corp., India
vinod.j@samsung.com

Abstract. In this paper, we propose architecture with SmartBidet and Agent embedded in videophone-based HomeServer for a ubiquitous and intelligent healthcare service. SmartBidet is a toilet stool with a urine measurement sensor that is connected to the videophone HomeServer. The SmartBidet serves as an ambient intelligent device to the users in the digital home and performs urinalysis of the user. The basic urinalysis is performed by an agent resided in the HomeServer and the result is displayed on the videophone screen and announced to the user in the restroom using the text-to-speech module. The detailed urinalysis and other medical diagnosis are performed by the hospital computing facilities over the healthcare information network. We illustrate three use cases that are categorized according to the criticality of the urinalysis.

1 Introduction

Recently, with the invention of ubiquitous computing paradigm, ubiquitous healthcare is regarded as one of the practical services providing people better quality of life. In order to implement this promising and socially meaningful service, it is likely required that human-oriented devices be converged upon the digital home network. Besides, the mass adoption of these services requires healthcare information systems to facilitate users with ambient intelligence with limited interaction.

In this paper, we focus on personal healthcare based on urinalysis, and propose a system model with SmartBidet, HomeServer, and an agent embedded in the HomeServer. The HomeServer acts as a central entity to integrate Home Networking and Consumer Electronic Devices in the digital home [1, 2, 3]. The SmartBidet accepts urine from users with human-oriented interface, performs urine measurement, and provides the result to the HomeServer over RS-232/USB. The agent in HomeServer immediately performs urine analysis with a rule-based primitive intelligence and delivers the result with TTS(Text-To-Speech)[4] to the user. This result is presented

* Corresponding Author: New Millennium Hall 1203, School of Internet and Multimedia Engineering, Konkuk University, Kwangjin-Gu, Seoul, 143-701, Korea.

J. Indulska et al. (Eds.): UIC 2007, LNCS 4611, pp. 205–213, 2007.

to the user when the obtained measurement is within the actual threshold or within a variance of 10% of the threshold.

The system model is derived from our understanding on the levels of intelligence for providing wide range of healthcare actions. We understand that the urine healthcare system need to have three levels of intelligence; acquisition by sensors, screening by threshold rules, and action by knowledge-based reasoning. This model is convinced by the use case analysis on the three cases; normal, careful and critical use cases. The three-tired intelligence and system model are described in section 2, and then, the use case analysis of the normal mode, careful mode and the critical mode are described in section 3. We also present the case study of the advantage of SmartBidet considering the effects and diagnosis for a patient suffering from Jaundice.

In section 4, we illustrate the basic system architecture and building blocks of our SmartBidet and videophone-based HomeServer with agent in the digital home. In section 5, we show our prototype implementation, and then conclude the paper with pointers to future works.

2 Three-Tired Intelligence and System Model

2.1 Three-Tired Intelligence

We understand that the urine input can be processed in three steps. The first step is to accept the urine and elicit meaningful values by converting analog to digital measurements. This step is realized by sensors attached in the Bidet. The second step is to preliminarily compute the meaning of the measurements by applying simple rule-based screening procedure. This step can be followed by immediate actions such as alerting to user if necessary. The third step is to reason about the gathered measurements with stored knowledge, and plan for reacting according to the result of the knowledge-based reasoning. This step can involve computing in a healthcare server and/or experts like doctors, and medical domain specialists. In case of using the computer system, it is likely difficult to build a qualified expert system. In this paper, therefore, we assume that the third step is performed by human experts. Table 1 summarizes our understanding on the levels of intelligence and proper devices corresponding to each level.

Table 1. Levels of intelligence and related systems

	First Level	Second Level	Third Level
Level of Intelligence	Bio-Sensing	Screening	Action
Methodology	Data Acquisition (A/D conversion)	Rule(threshold) Matching	Knowledge Processing(Reasoning)
Device or system	Sensors	Home Server	Human Expert
Communication	RS232 / Wireless Sensor Network		Internet
Information Networking Infra	Healthcare Information Network		

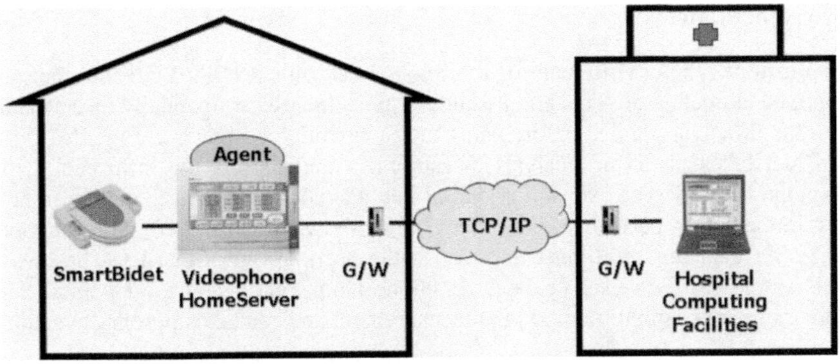

Fig. 1. System Model with SmartBidet, HomeServer, Agent and Hospital

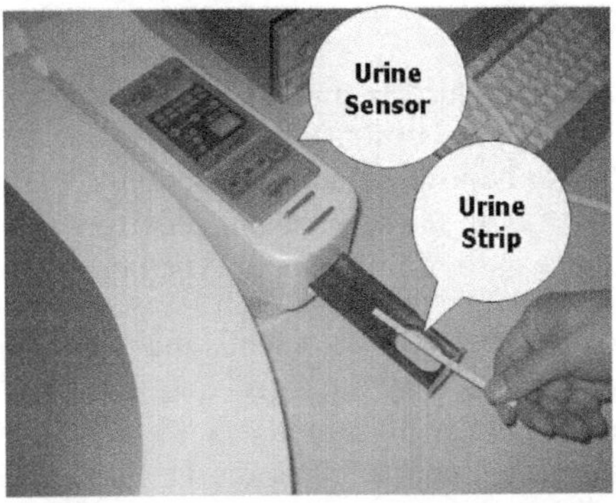

(a) Inserting Urine Strip into Urinalysis Device of SmartBidet

(b) HomeServer Screen Shot of Urine Analysis Result

Fig. 2. SmartBidet and HomeServer

2.2 System Model

Fig. 1 illustrates the environment of the SmartBidet with RS-232/USB interface to the videophone HomeServer. This architecture requires the user to manually insert the urine strip in the urinalysis device before using the SmartBidet as shown in Fig. 2(a) [5]. The SmartBidet takes the urine analysis measurement and reports the information to the videophone HomeServer over the digital Home Network, and then the agent in HomeServer immediately performs urine analysis as shown in Fig. 2(b). The videophone HomeServer also sends the measurement to the hospital over Ethernet. The measurement is stored for each user in the videophone HomeServer and the Hospital Server. The doctor in the hospital monitors the measurement and can take appropriate actions.

3 Use Case Analysis

3.1 Normal Use Case

The SmartBidet performs urine measurement of such compounds as Blood, Bilirubin, Urobilonogen, Ketones, Protein, Nitrite, Glucose, pH, Specific Gravity, Leucocytes. The several compounds can be used to compute the physical condition of the human body. The normal use case is to do nothing but reporting the data of measurements. Fig. 3 shows the normal use case of SmartBidet. The operation is as follows:

(1) SmartBidet checks the user's urine. It sends the result to the videophone HomeServer. The result is analyzed by the Agent and saved for later use.
(2) Fortunately, the urinalysis result is good.
(3) Hence, the Agent reports the result to the user's doctor. This data is also stored in the hospital database.

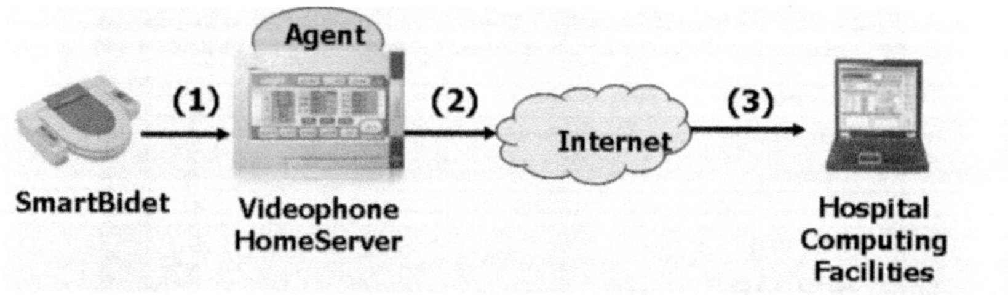

Fig. 3. Normal Use Case of SmartBidet

3.2 Careful Use Case

The urinalysis result is assumed to have exceeded the threshold variance for the particular urine portion. However, the variance is not above the critical threshold and thereby requires the user to be cautious and monitor his health constantly. The videophone HomeServer notifies the user to be cautious about the disease corresponding to the compound with the audio output from the TTS module. This data is stored in the videophone HomeServer and also notified to the doctor for next consultation. The user may choose to immediately consult his family doctor and initiate the V2oIP (Voice and Video over IP) communication to the doctor.

Consider the case of Bilirubin and Urobilinogen exceeding the sensitivity variance but below the critical threshold for the user. The normal value for Bilirubin is either negative or may vary up to +1mg/dL. The normal value for Urobilinogen is either negative or may vary up to 2mg/dL. However, a variance above this threshold is indicative of some disorder in the human liver. Such variance may cause Jaundice (yellow fever), Hepatitis or other liver disease. Our HomeServer Agent enables early detection of these critical diseases and facilitates user's to take additional care of their health before deterioration to critical level. This helps them recover in a week compared to the month's time required to cure Jaundice or Hepatitis.

The Agent is based on a rule-based urinalysis engine that computes the occurrence of disease based on the threshold level of the compound. Let us consider the case where the patient has normal Bilirubin levels but Urobilinogen exceeds the threshold variance significantly. This symptom is an indication towards the occurrence of Hemolytic Jaundice. Now, let us consider that the user has significant variance of both compounds. This denotes the occurrence of Hepatocellular Jaundice. However, the variation of Bilirubin with normal values for Urobilinogen indicates the occurrence of Obstructive Jaundice. The timely detection and cure of these diseases with the help of our SmartBidet based videophone HomeServer prevents the occurrence of cancer and/or advanced liver syndrome.

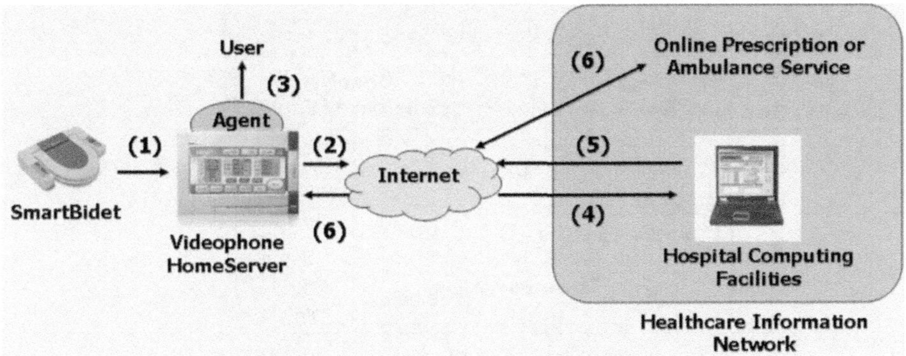

Fig. 4. Critical Use Case of SmartBidet

3.3 Critical Use Case

Fig. 4 shows the critical use case of SmartBidet over the environment of healthcare information network. The operation is as follows:

(1) SmartBidet checks the user's urine. It sends the result to the videophone HomeServer. The result is analyzed by the Agent and saved for later use.
(2) Unfortunately, the urinalysis result is not good. Let us assume the result exceeds the variance threshold.
(3) The HomeServer Agent immediately alerts the user that he may have occurrence of the disease.

(4) Hence, the HomeServer Agent immediately sets up a V2oIP communication with the user's family doctor for consultation.
(5) The doctor accepts the consultation request and takes appropriate action.
(6) Until user is admitted to the hospital, the doctor may provide immediate prescription, ambulance service and/or other services as required for this particular patient based on his medical condition.

4 System Architecture

4.1 SmartBidet

The basic SmartBidet has an embedded urine analysis device. The user manually inserts the urine strip and obtains the measurement. The measurement is sent over the USB/RS-232 interface to the videophone HomeServer. The enhanced SmartBidet may have a built-in sensor measurement device that seamlessly provides measurement parameters over the Sensor Network to the videophone HomeServer. The sensor node may run NanoQplus OS [7] and is a node in the Ubiquitous Sensor Network. For the prototype implementation of our architecture, we used a commercialized bidet, CC 2103 Plus A [5], attached with urine analysis sensor as a SmartBidet.

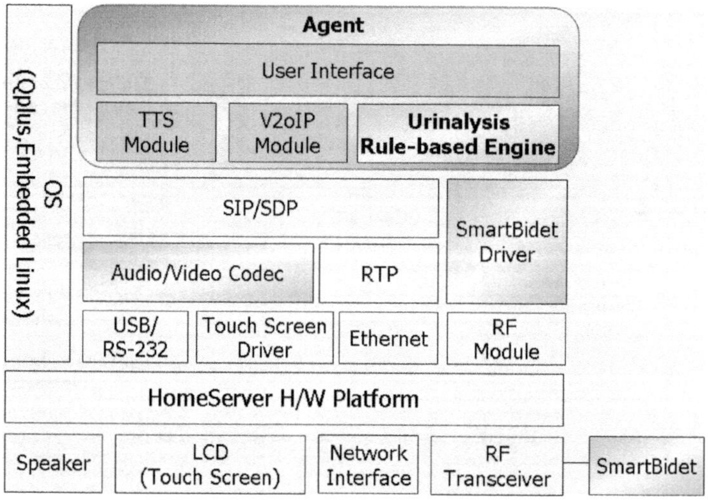

Fig. 5. Block Diagram of HomeServer with SmartBidet and Agent

4.2 HomeServer

The videophone HomeServer is built on top of Intel Xscale core based on PXA255 processor [6] with built-in interfaces to serial and USB 1.1. It has a VIA AC97 Stereo Codec that outputs the sound to the built-in Stereo Speaker. The System uses SIP (Session Initiation Protocol) [8] for signaling and RTP (Real-time Transport Protocol)

[9] for V2oIP. Healthcare data is sent over TCP/Ethernet. The input to the videophone is obtained over the touchscreen 7" display or a built-in hardware keyboard with 6-keys. The output is displayed on the 800x460(SVGA) resolution screen. The system runs QplusCE based on embedded linux [7].

4.3 Agent

The TTS module in the HomeServer Agent was developed from FreeTTS [4], and enables the urinalysis module to provide normal speech feedback to the user based on the threshold/criticality of the obtained measurement.

The several compounds measured by the SmartBidet can be used to compute the physical condition of the human body. The Table 2 denotes the color blocks associated with the variance in measurement portions. The colors range through various shades of pink to violet for Bilirubin and from beige to dark pink for Urobilinogen. We used the Table 2 for making rules for the careful use case [5, 10].

Table 2. Urinalysis Test Portions Sensitivity & Unit, their Variances, and Related Diseases

Test Portion	Related Disease	Sensitivity &Unit	Test Result						
			Normal	Range	Color Block & Value				
Blood	Cystitis, Hematuria, Hemolytic Anemia	5RBC/μℓ 0.015mg Hemoglobin/dL	Neg	Neg-300 RBC/μℓ	± 5	+1 10	+2 50	+3 250	
Bilirubin	Jaundice, Hepatitis	0.5mg/dL	Neg	Neg-4 mg/dL	+1 1	+2 2	+3 3		
Urobilonogen	Hepatitis, Jaundice	0.1 unit/dL	Norm	Norm-12 mg/dL	+1 1	+2 2	+3 4	+4 8	
Ketones	Diabetes, Pyrexia	5 mg/dL Acetoacetic Acid	Neg	Neg-100 mg/dL	± 5	+1 15	+2 40	+3 100	
Protein	Nephritis, Cystitis, Hypertension	10mg/dL	Neg	Neg-500 mg/dL	± 15	+1 30	+2 100	+3 300	+4 500
Nitrite	Urinary Tract Infection	0.05mg/dL	Neg	Neg, Pos	+1 Pos				
Glucose	Diabetes, Pancreatitis	50mg/dL (2.8mM/L)	Norm	Norm-500 mg/dL	+1 100	+2 250	+3 500		
pH	Urinary Tract Infection, Alkalosis	±1 pH unit	7	5-9	5	6	7	8	9
Specific Gravity	Chronic Bright's Disease	±0.005 g/ml	1020-1030 g/ml	1000-1040g/ml	1000	1005	1015	1020	1030
Leucocytes	Bright's Disease, Pyelitis	10 WBC/μℓ	Neg	Neg-500 WBC/μℓ	+1 25	+2 75	+3 500		

5 Prototype Implementation

Fig. 6 illustrates a demonstration snapshot of our basic videophone HomeServer with SmartBidet. The urinalysis measurement is displayed on the videophone LCD. The laptop denotes the doctor terminal in the hospital with detailed analysis of the urine measurement.

Fig. 6. Home Miniature and Demonstration of SmartBidet

6 Conclusions

We proposed architecture with SmartBidet and videophone-based HomeServer Agent for an ubiquitous and intelligent healthcare service. SmartBidet as a human-oriented user interface with ambient intelligence to facilitate users at home with early detection of urine related diseases and prevention of critical diseases by early detection and cure. The basic urinalysis is performed by an agent resided in the HomeServer and the result is displayed on the videophone screen and announced to the user in the restroom using the text-to-speech module.

The HomeServer has a broadband interface. As one of future works, by utilizing this broadband access to the healthcare information network, we will study enabling seamlessly connectivity to the Ambulance Service, relevant doctors concerned with the disease reported, online-pharmacy for Smart Medicine and complex analysis using advanced bio-informatics schemes at specialist analysis centers.

References

1. Lee, K.H., Kim, D.-H., Kim, J., Sul, D., Ahn, S.H.: Requirements and Referential Software Architecture for Home Server based Inter-Home Multimedia Collaboration Services. IEEE Transactions on Consumer Electronics 50(1), 145–150 (2004)
2. Ho, A.S., Joseph, V.C., Hyun, K.D.: Embedded Healthcare System for Senior Residents using Internet Multimedia HomeServer and Telephone. In: Baik, D.-K. (ed.) Systems Modeling and Simulation: Theory and Applications. LNCS (LNAI), vol. 3398, pp. 177–186. Springer, Heidelberg (2005)
3. Joseph, V.C.: Integrated IP Multimedia Architecture for Intelligent Healthcare Solutions. In: World Wireless Congress, San Francisco, USA (2005)
4. http://freetts.sourceforge.net/docs/index.php
5. http://www.soltap.com/keeper1.htm
6. http://www.intel.com/design/intelxscale/
7. http://www.qplus.or.kr/
8. Internet Engineering Task Force: SIP: Session Initiation Protocol, RFC 2543 (1999)
9. Schulzrine, Casner, Frederick, Jacobson.: RTP: A Transport Protocol for Real-Time Applications, RFC 1889, Internet Engineering Task Force (1996)
10. http://www.webmd.com/hw/health_guide_atoz/hw6580.asp

Proactive Agriculture: An Integrated Framework for Developing Distributed Hybrid Systems

Christos Goumopoulos[1], Achilles Kameas[1,2], and Brendan O'Flynn[3]

[1] Research Academic Computer Technology Institute,
Distributed Ambient Information Systems Group, N. Kazantzaki, 26500 Rio Patras, Hellas
{goumop,kameas}@cti.gr
[2] Hellenic Open University, 23, Sahtouri Str, Patras, Hellas
kameas@eap.gr
[3] Tyndall National Institute, Lee Maltings, Prospect Row, Cork, Ireland
boflynn@tyndall.ie

Abstract. In this paper we discuss research work that enables the development of hybrid systems consisting of communicating plants and artefacts and we investigate methods of creating "interfaces" between artefacts and plants in order to enable people to form mixed, interacting communities. Our research objective is to develop hardware and software components that enable a seamless interaction between plants and artefacts in scenarios ranging from domestic plant care to precision agriculture. This paper deals with the approach that we follow for the development of such hybrid systems and discusses both hardware and software architectural aspects, with a special focus on describing the modular platform for wireless sensor network implemented and the distributed context management process followed. The latter imposes a proactive computing model by looping sensor data with actuators through a decision-making layer. The deployment of the system in a precision agriculture application is also presented.

1 Introduction

Currently, there are few discussions on the integration of biological elements of the real (natural) environment into pervasive computing applications [1, 2, 3]. In this paper, we present our research efforts to create digital interfaces to nature, in particular to selected species of plants. Our approach goes beyond the use of sensor networks for environmental monitoring [4] by emphasizing the development of a system architecture that incorporates the plants and associated computation as an integral part of the system, and allows the interaction of plants and artefacts in the form of synergistic and scaleable mixed societies. The ambient intelligence technology is used to encompass plant requirements, by establishing a three-way interaction between plants, people and objects. This approach enables the development of hybrid systems consisting of communicating plants and artefacts in scenarios ranging from domestic plant care to precision agriculture.

Precision agriculture is an agricultural concept relying on the existence of in-field variability across an array of cropping systems [5]. Thanks to developments in the field of wireless sensor networks as well as miniaturization of sensor systems, new

J. Indulska et al. (Eds.): UIC 2007, LNCS 4611, pp. 214–224, 2007.

trends have emerged in the area of precision agriculture. Wireless networks allow the deployment of sensing systems and actuation mechanisms at a much finer level of granularity, and in a more automated implementation than has been possible before.

At present the information gathered by sensor networks deployed in a field are mainly used for monitoring and reporting on the status of the crops [1, 6, 7]. However, agricultural environments make a good candidate for using proactive-computing approaches for applications which require a faster than human response time or which requires precise, time-consuming optimization.

In this paper we describe an integrated framework for developing hybrid systems. A hybrid system consists of various entities including software components, hardware components (sensors, actuators and controllers), datastores (knowledge base, raw data), biological elements (plants) and environmental context. By positioning sensors around particular plants (proximal remote sensing) the delivered technology is capable of reacting (via actuators) to stimuli (perceived via sensor networks), aiming to maintain a coherent plant state and support efficient plant growth. Our research has focused on the provision for proactive applications by deploying sensor networks and connecting sensor data with actuators through a decision-making layer which attempts also to resolve aspects of data uncertainty.

The remainder of the paper is organized as follows. Section 2 presents the rationale behind mixed societies of communicating plants and artefacts and describes its basic elements. The pillars of the integrated framework defined for developing hybrid systems are discussed in the next section. A layered modular architecture of the system is proposed to enable system flexibility and extensibility, while the need to cope with uncertainty of the data is also explored. A detailed example application from the precision agriculture domain is given in section 4. Related work is discussed in section 5 and finally the conclusions of our work are presented.

2 Mixed Societies of Communicating Plants and Artefacts

The communicating plant concept [8] fits well within the vision of Ambient Intelligence where the virtual (computing) space will be seamlessly integrated with our physical environment. By regarding plants as virtual "components", which can communicate with other artefacts in the digital space we can shape mixed societies of them. From an engineering perspective, a mixed society of communicating plants and artefacts can be regarded as a multi-layered, hierarchical distributed system, which will globally manage the resources of the society, its function(s) and its interaction with the environment.

An ePlant component, in particular, may represent the digital self either of a specific plant or a group of plants (a group may be defined in terms of a specific plant species or in terms of plant vicinity, a number of plants in a geographical region) and is responsible for the back-end computation with respect to the sensor network computing. Through a software layer (middleware), ePlant communicates with the sensor network, implements a decision-making scheme for assessing plant states and alarms and handles the interaction with other eEntities.

eEntities that represent domain-specific objects with the capabilities of information processing and exchange are also called artefacts. These artefacts have the capability of communicating with other artefacts based on local networks, as well as accessing or exchanging information at a distance via global networks. In our case artefacts may represent expressive devices (speakers, displays, etc.), resource-providing devices (e.g. lamps, irrigation/fertilization/shading system) or any other everyday object (e.g., cell phone, camera).

Sensor systems range from standalone sensor devices to wireless sensor networks monitoring micro-climates in a crop field. Standalone sensor devices may be shared among a number of ePlants so that the context needs to be determined. On the other hand, the actuator systems will allow the plant to influence the environment that it resides in.

3 Integrated Framework for Developing Hybrid Systems

3.1 Wireless Sensor/Actuator Network Hardware Platform

The hardware platform used is the 25mm mote developed at Tyndall [9, 10]. The Tyndall25 mote is a miniaturised wireless sensor platform that addresses the issues of reconfigurability, power-efficiency and size which are desirable and necessary characteristics for a wireless sensor network platform (Figure 1).

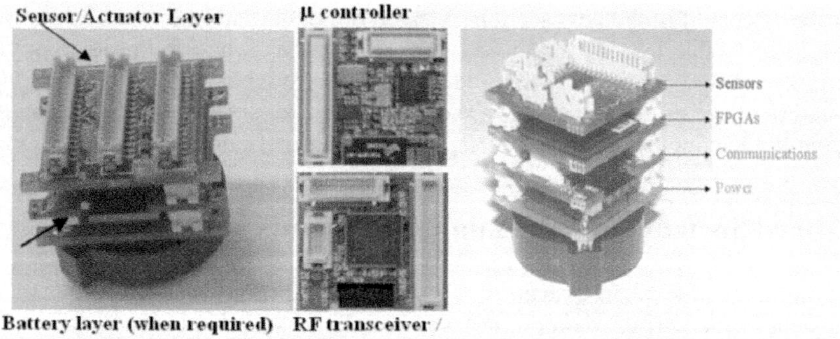

Fig. 1. Tyndall25 modular platform

The hardware platform is analogous to a Lego™-like 25mm x 25mm stackable system. Layers can be combined in an innovative plug and play fashion and include communication, processing, sensing and power supply layers. The communication layer is comprised of a microcontroller, RF transceiver and integrated antenna [11]. The module contains an Atmel ATMega128L microcontroller and a Nordic VLSI 2401 RF transceiver both of which are combined on a single layer. The microcontroller is equipped with 128KB in-system flash memory and can be programmed to handle analogue to digital conversion of sensor data and the communication networking protocols necessary for interfacing with the RF transceiver to achieve communication with other motes. Stacked upon this RF microcontroller layer is the custom sensor/actuator interface layer. On the software side, the microcontroller runs a tailored version of TinyOS [12], an optimised operating system that allows fast configuration of the sensor nodes implementing active message protocol (AMP) [13]. The power layer may include batteries or other energy supply or power harvesting mechanisms. Finally, an optional FPGA layer can be integrated into the system whenever high-speed Digital Signal Processing is required.

The sensor/actuator interface layer allows any combination of eight different sensors or actuators to be connected to the 25mm module. In the agricultural application domain, the sensor interface portion allows soil moisture probes, thermistors and ethylene sensors to be interrogated by the controlling software running on the mote.

3.2 Software System Architecture

Figure 2 illustrates a general overview of the system architecture. In the lower layer various sensors/actuators that can form collectively sensor networks, provide the raw data. In the drivers' layer, a specific driver is designed and implemented for each sensor device/network implementing the communication protocol with the hardware.

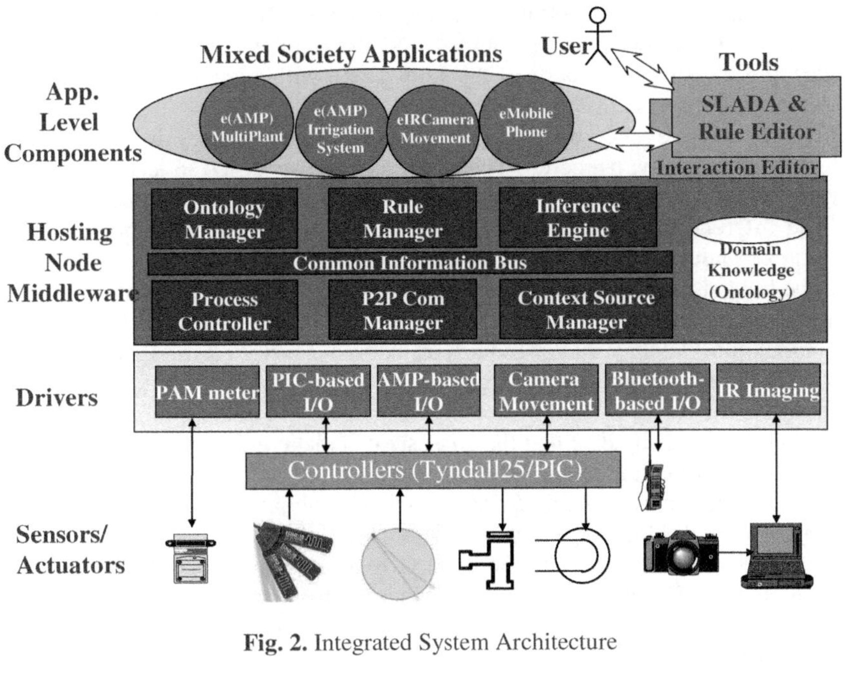

Fig. 2. Integrated System Architecture

The role of a hosting node in the distributed management system reflected by mixed societies is mainly to act as a gateway between the wireless sensor network and domain-specific applications. In that sense the hosting node software represents a middleware layer that supports interaction with other nodes, back-end monitoring and performing of control/management services. In particular, the *P2P Communication Module* is responsible for application-level communication and interaction between the various hosting nodes. The *Process Controller* is the coordinator module and the main function of this module is to monitor and execute the reaction rules defined by the supported applications. These rules define how and when the infrastructure should react to changes in the environment. The *Context Source Manager* is responsible for dealing with contextual information and in particular with context gathering, inference, aggregation, history and monitoring. It handles the runtime storage of node's context values, reflecting both the hardware environment (sensors/actuators) at each particular moment (primitive context), and properties that are evaluated based on sensory data and P2P communicated data (composite context). The *Inference Engine* is responsible for the evaluation of composite properties (e.g., state assessment) according to a set of rules, which are obtained from plant science research; its implementation is currently based on the Jess (Java Expert System Shell) environment [14]. The rule management can be separated from the evaluation logic by using a high-level rule language and a translator that translates high-level rule specifications to XML that can be exploited then by the evaluation logic. This management is the responsibility of the *Rule Manager* module. To support the development of applications we have defined an *Ontology* that encodes domain knowledge (description of eEntities, sensors, actuators, parameters, states; and application logic as aggregation, inferring and action rules). Thus an *Ontology Manager* module has been defined for the manipulation of the knowledge represented into the ontology and to provide the other modules of the system with parts of this knowledge with a level of abstraction. Details on the organisation of the ontology can be found in [15, 16].

The application level components hold the logic that specifies the conditions under which actions are to be triggered. The conditions are specified in terms of correlation of events. Events are specified up front and types of events are defined in the ontology. The Inference Engine subscribes to events (specified in applications logic) and the Context Manager generates events and notifies the Inference Engine when the subscribed events occur. When the conditions hold, the Process Controller performs the specified actions, which could consist of, e.g., sending messages through the P2P Communication Manager and/or request an external service (e.g., toggling irrigation).

When building context-aware applications in pervasive computing environments one faces the difficult problem of dealing with uncertain context information. Quality indicators can be specified so that the end-user can make judgements on the confidence level that the information entails. We model uncertainty in our environment by enhancing the rules with *certainty/confidence factors* (*CF*) about how certain the conclusions drawn from the rules may be. Certainty factors are guesses by an expert about the relevance of evidence. We are using the scale -1 to 1 and we assume the following interpretation: as the CF approaches 1 the evidence is stronger for a hypothesis; as the CF approaches -1 the confidence against the hypothesis gets stronger; a CF around 0 indicates that there is little evidence either for or against the hypothesis.

Certainty factors may apply both to facts and to rules, or rather to the conclusion(s) of rules. Conditions for rules are formed by the logical "*and*" and "*or*" of a number of facts. The certainty factors associated with each condition are combined to produce a certainty factor for the whole condition. For two conditions *P1* and *P2* it holds that: $CF(P1\ and\ P2) = min(CF(P1), CF(P2))$ and $CF(P1\ or\ P2) = max(CF(P1), CF(P2))$. The combined CF of the condition is then multiplied by the CF of the rule to get the CF of the conclusion. The CF scheme has been implemented through FuzzyJ ToolKit [17], a library that can be integrated with JESS for the provision of fuzzy reasoning.

3.3 Rule Editor

The *Rule Editor* works in cooperation with the *Supervisor Logic and Data Acquisition Tool* (*SLADA*); the former manages dynamically the rules taking part in the decision-making process while the later can be used to view knowledge represented into the Ontology and monitor plant/environmental parameters. The Editor provides a Graphical Design Interface for managing rules, based on a user friendly node connection model. The advantage of this approach is that rules will be changed dynamically in a high-level manner without disturbing the operation of the rest of the system.

Figure 3 shows the design of the Heat stress calculation rule for the ePlant. The rule consists of three conditions combined with a logical AND gate. The first condition checks the applicability of a specific area (Right Center) of the field layout for which we need to evaluate the heat stress state. The second condition checks whether the absolute difference between environmental and average temperature, in that area, is below 0.9° C. The third condition checks whether the average moisture in the specific area is over 60%. The rule, as designed, states that when all three conditions are met then the heat stress state of the RC area must be set to active.

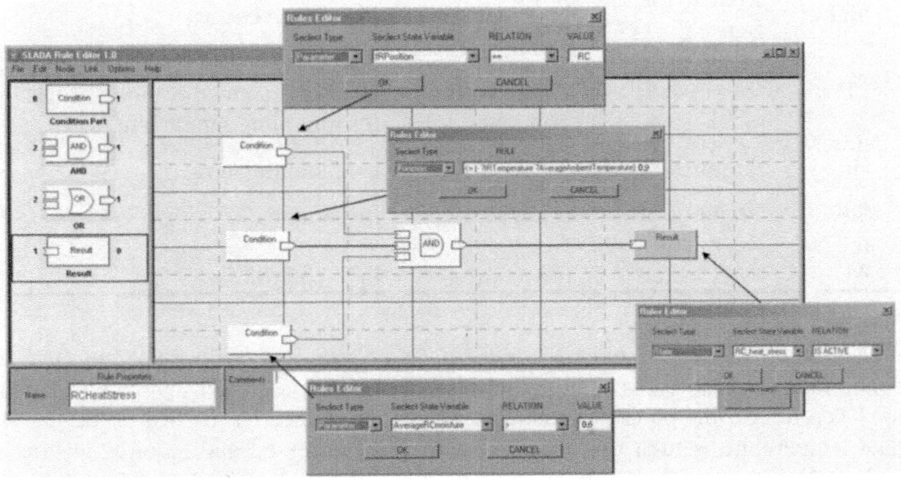

Fig. 3. Editing the Heat Stress rule of the ePlant

Using a rule editor for defining application business rules emphasizes system flexibility and run-time adaptability. In that sense, our system architecture can be regarded as a reflective architecture that can be adapted dynamically to new requirements. The decision-making rules can be configured by domain experts external to the execution of the system. End-users may change the rules without writing new code. This can reduce time-to-production of new ideas and domain-specific research results to a few minutes. Therefore, the power to customize the system is placed in the hands of those who have the knowledge to do it effectively.

4 Precision Agriculture Example Application

The example application described in this section is composed of a strawberry plant where the plant is controlling irrigation and supplementary light. Irrigation is applied according to the specific requirements of the plants in different parts of the crop array, thus illustrating the precision delivery of agricultural inputs.

4.1 Plant/Environmental Signals

The plant/environmental signals explored for the application development are: Plants' leaf Temperature (PT), Chlorophyll Fluorescence (CF), Ambient Temperature (AT), Ambient Light (AL) and Soil Moisture (SM). For each signal a different type of sensor is required. Table 1 summarizes the signals and the corresponding sensors used as well as the associated knowledge that will be stored in the ontology for supporting the monitoring and decision-making process.

Table 1. Plant/Environmental Signals and Sensors

Signal	Measuring Sensor	State Assessment	Possible Actions
CF	PAM meter[1]	photo-stress; photosynthetic efficiency	light control; estimate/adapt threshold values for providing input resources
PT	thermistor	drought stress; heat stress	irrigation/misting
SM	Probe EC-10[2]	drought stress	irrigation
AT	thermistor		
AL	PAR meter[3]	photo-stress	light control

Heat stress can occur independently of water stress when the ambient environmental temperature gets very high and plant transpiration cannot maintain leaf cooling. Therefore, if the plant has adequate water (determined by the SM probe) but the plant temperature is high this means that it is heat stressed and requires misting to cool it. However, if the temperature is high and the moisture content low, then pot irrigation is required. The CF and AL parameters are used to determine photo-oxidative stress and adjust supplementary light.

4.2 Prototype Setup and Evaluation

The prototype setup consists of an array of 96 plants placed in a glasshouse, arranged in an array of 12 by 8. The setup consists of 4 different zones: Left-Edge (LE), Right-Edge (RE), Left-Center (LC), Right-Center (RC) and also one zone specified for misting which coincides with the RC zone. The setup integrates the thermistors and

[1] Junior PAM, Gademann Instruments: http://www.gademann.com/
[2] ECHO probe model EC-10: http://www.ech2o.com/specs.html
[3] Skye SKP215 Quantum Sensor: http://www.alliance-technologies.net

soil moisture probes into one system that can irrigate when required and also determine when to stop the irrigation. This deployment takes into account differences in the location of the plants in the overall area and will allow for independent irrigation of edge or centre zone plants as required. Each zone can be controlled using individual solenoids. Misting can be applied only to the RC due to infrastructure limitations.

A total of 10 Tyndall25 motes are required to implement the above prototype: 8 modules are used for connecting the various sensors, each one 'supervising' the sensors in the neighbourhood of an array of 3 by 4 plants; 1 module is sensorless and is used as a communication relay with the hosting node; and 1 module is used for controlling the irrigation system. The nodes are housed tightly in IP-67 rated water-proof packaging to withstand the harsh conditions of the field. The sensor nodes are manually placed however the mapping to the zones is administered at a higher level in the hosting node (ePlant), as part of its description. For energy-efficiency and power consumption considerations, the sensor nodes are reporting data once per five minutes. The data collected by the sensor nodes is gathered by the hosting node, for local processing and logging. Interaction then is possible between the hosting node and other devices for managing the delivery of agricultural input according to an adaptable decision-making scheme.

The application business logic is expressed upon a set of plant parameters, plant states and actions to be performed. Table 2 illustrates such variables defined in the ontology of the application.

Table 2. Application business logic variables

Parameters	States	Action Requests
`AmbientAvgTemp`	`"Z"DroughtStress`	`"Z"NeedIrrigation`
`"Z"AvgTemp`	`"Z"HeatStress`	`"Z"NeedMisting`
`"Z"AvgMoisture`		

The "Z" prefix in the name of a variable is substituted by one of the possible zone names of the crop array (LE, RE, LC, RC). For the NeedMisting variable the prefix can be omitted since there is only one zone specified for misting. Two additional parameters must be defined for the prototype to be properly working; the duration of irrigation/misting and an idle time which specifies the amount of time the rules should be disabled, after the action is performed. This is to allow the ecosystem to absorb the changes. The values used for the application were 1 min and 4 hours respectively.

The actual logic of the prototype is captured in a set of rules. Table 3 contains the applicable rules for the RC zone. Rules for evaluating the plant states and actions to be performed are shown. Confidence Factor values are also included. CF values in square brackets are defined by the domain-expert, while in curly brackets by the system Inference Engine. The user for example can specify a policy where actions with confidence below 50% shouldn't be triggered but the user should be notified.

Table 3. Application rules with Confidence Factors shown

Rule	Body
RCDrought Stress *[CF=0.8]*	IF RCAvgTemp-AmbientAvgTemp>0.75°C *[CF=0.9]* THEN RCDroughtStress ← TRUE ELSE RCDroughtStress ← FALSE *{CF=0.72}*
RCHeat Stress *[CF=0.9]*	IF RCDroughtStress *{CF=0.72}* AND RCAvgMoisture>60% *[CF=0.9]* *{CF=min(0.72, 0.9)=0.72}* THEN RCHeatStress ← TRUE ELSE RCHeatStress ← FALSE *{CF=0.65}*
RCNeed Irrigation *[CF=1]*	IF RCDroughtStress *{CF=0.72 }* AND NOT RCHeatStress *{CF=0.65 }* *{CF=min(0.72, 0.65)=0.65}* THEN RCNeedIrrigation ← TRUE ELSE RCNeedIrrigation ← FALSE *{CF=0.65}*
Need Misting *[CF=1]*	IF RCDroughtStress *{CF=0.72 }* AND RCHeatStress *{CF=0.65}* *{CF=min(0.72, 0.65)=0.65}* THEN NeedMisting ← TRUE ELSE NeedMisting ← FALSE *{CF=0.65}*

The reliability of the wireless sensor network is of great importance as lost of data may hinder the decision support layer of the system and thus the correct delivery of inputs. There are several measures that have been taken to alleviate this risk. First each sensor node will store each measurement in its local memory and will overwrite it when an acknowledgement is received. In addition the use of sequence numbers in the packets allows the hosting node to detect easily lost packets, if the MAC-layer fails to deliver them after attempting a number of retransmissions.

On the agronomic part of the experiment the instrumentation of the strawberry field with the wireless sensor network and the plant-driven irrigation leads to a notable reduction in water consumption (15-20%) with respect to traditional agricultural practices involving user defined timed irrigation based on rules of thumb. The later was applied in a parallel setup for the same growing period (early development stage) of the crop. The deployment of smart water management on a large farming scale is extremely important given the irrigation needs of the agricultural sector (irrigation uses up to 80% of total water in some regions) and the decreasing availability of water for irrigation.

5 Related Work

Attempts to use environmental sensor networks in order to improve crop cultivation by monitoring and reporting on the status of the field are reported in [1, 7]. These approaches provide decision-support to the user who responds by providing the required treatment. In the same way the approach discussed in [6] uses a centralized architecture to gather data followed by an analysis phase so that a grower becomes able to examine crop conditions in trial-and-error scheme. This is in contrast to our plant-driven distributed management system that imposes a proactive computing model for the crop treatment.

A UbiComp application called PlantCare that takes care of houseplants using a sensor network and a mobile robot are investigated in [18]. The proposed framework in this paper supports both ambient and agricultural applications where in the later case the integration of a large number of sensors and the complexity of the communication and the decision-making processes are the focal points.

MoteWorks™ is a general-purpose software platform for the development of wireless sensor network systems [19]. MoteWorks, utilizes comparable solutions to our framework at the mote network tier level. However, at the middleware tier, the objectives differ and are not comparable, as our approach views applications in the form of cooperating objects in our natural environment with context management and adaptive decision-making requirements. Instead, MoteWorks in order to be generic provides a simple API from the Intra/Internet to the wireless sensor network.

On the hardware platform side comparisons with other similar sensing nodes in this class, namely the Mica2, Mica2Dot and Intel motes, revealed advantages and disadvantages of each [10]. The modular nature and robust connectivity mechanism of the Tyndall mote made it ideal for use in the application domain explored.

6 Conclusions and Future Directions

We have been involved with a facet of precision agriculture that concentrates on plant-driven crop management. By monitoring soil, crop and climate in a field and providing a decision support system, it is possible to deliver treatments, such as irrigation, fertilizer and pesticide application, for specific parts of a field in real time and proactively. We have presented in this paper an integrated framework consisting of hardware, software components and a rule editor that support efficiently the development of distributed hybrid systems.

Moving our research towards to a more autonomous system with self-adaptation and self-learning characteristics, we have been exploring ways of incorporating learning capabilities in the system. Machine-learning algorithms can be used for inducing new rules by analysing logged datasets to determine accurately significant thresholds of plant-based parameters. Finally, regarding the sensor network platform work is underway to implement a version of the current 25mm square form factor transceiver node in a 10mm and 5mm cube form factor.

Acknowledgement

This paper describes research carried in the PLANTS (IST-38900) and ASTRA (IST-29266) projects; the authors wish to thank their fellow researchers in the consortiums.

References

1. Burrell, J., Brooke, T., Beckwith, R.: Vineyard Computing: Sensor Networks in Agricultural Production. IEEE Pervasive Computing 3(1), 38–45 (2004)
2. Bohlen, M., Tan, N.: Garden Variety Pervasive Computing. IEEE Pervasive Computing 3(1), 29–34 (2004)
3. Mainwaring, A., Polastre, J., Szewczyk, R., Culler, D.: Wireless Sensor Networks for Habitat Monitoring. In: Proceedings of the 1st ACM International Workshop on Wireless Sensor Networks and Applications, pp. 88–97. ACM Press, New York (2002)
4. Martinez, K., Hart, J., Ong, R.: Environmental Sensor Networks. IEEE Computer 37(8), 50–56 (2004)
5. Koch, B., Khosla, R.: The Role of Precision Agriculture in Cropping Systems. Crop Production 8, 361–381 (2003)
6. PhyTech, Phytomonitoring^{TM}. http://www.phytech.co.il/ introduction.html
7. Zhang, W., Kantor, G., Singh, S.: Integrated Wireless Sensor/Actuator Networks in an Agricultural Application. In: Proceedings of the 2nd ACM International Conference on Embedded Networked Sensor Systems (SenSys), p. 317. ACM Press, New York (2004)
8. Calemis, I., Goumopoulos, C., Kameas, A.: Talking Plant: Integrating Plants Behavior with Ambient Intelligence. In: Proceedings of the 2nd IET International Conference on Intelligent Environments, pp. 335–343. IET Press (2006)
9. O'Flynn, B., et al.: The Development of a Novel Miniaturized Modular Platform for Wireless Sensor Networks. In: Proceedings of the 4th International Conference on Information Processing in Sensor Networks (IPSN'05), Article 49, IEEE Computer Society Press, Los Alamitos (2005)
10. Bellis, S.J., et al.: Development of Field Programmable Modular Wireless Sensor Network Nodes for Ambient Systems. Computer Communications J. 28(13), 1531–1544 (2005)
11. O'Flynn, B., et al.: A 3-D Miniaturised Programmable Transceiver. Microelectronics international J. 22(2), 8–12 (2005)
12. TinyOS Community Forum http://www.tinyos.net
13. Buonadonna, P., Hill, J., Culler, D.: Active Message Communication for Tiny Network Sensors. UC Berkeley Technical Report (2001), http://www.tinyos.net/papers/ammote.pdf
14. Jess - the Rule Engine for the Java Platform, http://herzberg.ca.sandia.gov/jess/
15. Goumopoulos, C., et al.: The PLANTS System: Enabling Mixed Societies of Communicating Plants and Artefacts. In: Markopoulos, P., Eggen, B., Aarts, E., Crowley, J.L. (eds.) EUSAI 2004. LNCS, vol. 3295, pp. 184–195. Springer, Heidelberg (2004)
16. Christopoulou, E., Goumopoulos, C., Kameas, A.: An ontology-based context management and reasoning process for UbiComp applications. In: Proceedings of Joint sOc-EUSAI'2005 conference, pp. 265–270. ACM Press, New York (2005)
17. FuzzyJ ToolKit: http://www.iit.nrc.ca/IR_public/fuzzy/fuzzyJToolkit2.html
18. LaMarca, A., et al.: PlantCare: An Investigation in Practical Ubiquitous Systems. In: Borriello, G., Holmquist, L.E. (eds.) UbiComp 2002. LNCS, vol. 2498, pp. 316–332. Springer, Heidelberg (2002)
19. Crossbow Technology Inc.: MoteWorks. http://www.xbow.com/Products/Product_pdf_files/Wireless_pdf/ MoteWorks_OEM_ Edition.pdf

Integrating RFID Services and Ubiquitous Smart Systems for Enabling Organizations to Automatically Monitor, Decide, and Take Actions

Thierry Bodhuin, Rosa Preziosi, and Maria Tortorella

RCOST - Research Centre On Software Technology
Department of Engineering, University of Sannio
Via Traiano, Palazzo ex-Poste – 82100, Benevento, Italy
{bodhuin,preziosi,tortorella}@unisannio.it

Abstract. Various organizations use the RFID technology for linking, tracking and identifying objects in their operative context. Nevertheless, the RFID components cannot yet be considered as mobile, intelligent and communicating elements of the organization's information infrastructure. They are not always used for accomplishing the linkage between the physical world and the adopted Information Technologies (IT) solutions. Therefore, they are not used for enabling organizations to automatically monitor, decide, and take actions. Heterogeneous networked devices and services installed within the organizations, often work independently instead of collaborating for offering a better quality of the daily activities to the end-user. This paper discusses the adoption of a Smart Ubiquitous Platform (SUP) for monitoring and managing the documents circulation by using the RFID technology. Advantages of the adoption of RFID are discussed too.

1 Introduction

Following the technological evolution, organizations have extended and changed the way they conduct their business and interact with their partners and customers [12]. In fact, Client/server solutions favoured business process automation, the Internet helped organizations to gain a global visibility, and ubiquitous computing allowed all organizations' resources (physical, human and informational assets) acquiring a more widespread mobility. This mobility is stimulating the search of solutions for linking, tracking and identifying objects in the organizations' context.

Radio Frequency Identification (RFID) technology offers a possible solution to the cited exigency [1, 7]. Within certain technical constraints, it can offer the opportunity of acquiring and storing in a database a vast ammount of data coming in real time. RFID technology was applied in heterogeneous organizations working in different areas.

The Wal-Mart Stores were among the first practitioners to engage a real RFID experience to supply chain management [14]. After their positive experience, many other organizations (e.g., HP, Sun, IBM, Windows, Intel, Ford Motor Co., ...) have adopted RFID in supply chain management. Medical organizations use RFID for tracking medical instruments, as well as patients and hospital personnel [4, 15]. NEC

J. Indulska et al. (Eds.): UIC 2007, LNCS 4611, pp. 225–234, 2007.

Corp obtained a contract for a project with a Japanese bank for an RFID-based document management system. In this project, antennas are attached to bookshelves and filing cabinets. They communicate data from RFID tags embedded in documents are monitored by antennas and events are sent toward software systems. In this way, real-time document tracking is attained. Moreover, as the RFID system can be combined with the employees' identification systems (e.g., cards, fingerprint sensors or tags) [11], real-time recording of the employees that are removing or replacing a given document can be enabled.

Even if currently different projects using RFID technology exist, many organizations have still doubts regarding its real benefits. RFID is not for everyone and obstacles to be overcome still exist. Its introduction may affect applications, infrastructures, business processes and personnel. RFID should be a part of the Information Technology (IT) infrastructure and not only another application [15]. It is not a single, simple piece of technology, but it requires millions of tags, containing data with standardized encoding, and thousands of tags readers. In turn, these tags transmit relevant data to multiple software applications, including middleware, databases, legacy systems and new applications [13]. The authors believe that the diffidence towards RFID can be reduced if RFID solutions are integrated within an ubiquitous platform endowed with intelligence, or Smart Ubiquitous Platform (SUP). Such a platform can allow RFID to meet possible expectation. It can concretely: (a) make the tagged entities become mobile, intelligent and communicating components of the organization's overall information infrastructure [10]; and (b) realize the linkage between the physical world and the IT for enabling computers and organizations to automatically monitor, decide, and take actions [2].

With this in mind and supported by previous experiences made in the ubiquitous computing area, advantages coming from the adoption of the RFID technology are analysed and the support coming from the integration of RFID services in a SUP is discussed. The presented analysis regards the RFID adoption within organizations where document circulation has an important role in business processes. This choice was encouraged from: (a) the interest of the National Centre for Computing inside the Public Administration (CNIPA) in Italy towards the RFID adoption in the Public Administration [3]; and (b) the opportunity to offer a new RFID-based administrative service by re-using a developed smart ubiquitous and extensible software platform. This platform was designed and developed for facilitating the interoperability of different heterogeneous networked electronic devices and offering a middleware supporting different levels of intelligence in different living environments [8, 9].

In the following, Section 2 presents the advantages of using the RFID technology within the organization's offices. Section 3 introduces the adopted SUP. Section 4 describes an RFID administrative service integrated in the proposed SUP in order to explain how existing and new technologies can be put together in an innovative way for supporting organizations' business processes. Conclusions are given in the last section.

2 RFID Technology Within Organizations

Organizations consume and produce information contained in paper documents, even if they automated their business processes. Paper documents represent the central business entities of an organization and the activity flow of a business process very often depends on the moving of specific documents from an office to another one. These documents are out of the control of the used automated document management system and/or they are not included within an electronic mail system. The RFID-based administrative service that authors have in mind aims at offering functionalities that are not available in a Traditional Document Management System (TDMS). In particular, a TDMS does not support the tracking of paper documents nor is enabled to automatically monitor, decide and take actions. In this paper, the enhancement of a TDMS by including this functionality is discussed. The following scenarios explains the authors' vision:

a) an accounting office is obliged to keep payment receipts, faxes, invoices and other paper documents for a given number of years, in accordance with the current body of legislation. So, *valuable staff* time is spent for identifying them and activating the procedures for eliminating those documents that the office is not beyond legally obliged to keep;
b) staff's private information (e.g., curriculum, contracts) are stored in folders. They are often kept on shelves and *guarantees for their secure access* is required;
c) legal offices often move their dossiers outside the organization and can lose them. A mechanism for *rapidly finding* them is needed;
d) some administrative procedures have to follow a given bureaucratic course to be closed. A sequence of written and signed orders often have to cross a given number of desks and managers, and a given user could need to know the state of these procedures before *taking his/her decisions*.

The following organization's needs emerge with reference to the management of paper documents:

- reduction of labour time;
- increase of guarantees for security accesses;
- increase of capability to quickly locate documents;
- increase of project managers awareness and users satisfaction;

The listed needs can be just partially satisfied by using a traditional bar code system. This technology is used for supporting recording and inventorying tasks, but it is not useful for tracking the movements of paper documents or taking decisions. The RFID technology offers the concrete opportunity for linking, tracking and identifying various objects from the real world. Nevertheless, RFID technology cannot alone automatically manage information coming from the real world.

Multiple RFID tags can be read at the same time and they can be detected without passing each document on a scanner as with bar code-based system. In addition, an RFID tag can keep useful information in its on-board memory. It can be generic information useful for detecting and tracking the documents. In particular, the service described in this paper considers RFID passive tags. Unlike an active tag, a passive tag can be attached to a document and remains attached to it. Antennas placed inside the organization's strategic points, generate the magnetic field activating the RFID tags. When a tag is activated, it can send information to or receive information from a reader. Passive tags have memory on board and are univocally identifiable by means of an Unique Identifier (UID). This identifier allows reading simultaneously multiple tags that are within the operating range of a specialized reader.

Above all, the RFID available memory can store information such as the name of the organization managing the document and email address and number phone of the office responsible of attaching the RFID tag on the document. In this way, whoever outside or inside the organization finds a lost tagged document can contact its responsible if he/she can access an RFID antenna for reading the information stored in the tag. This qualifies a document as recognizable independently from the availability of accessing the database of the organization that produced it.

A document can also be linked to a variety of other informative parameters beyond those on board an RFID tag. For example, interesting parameters may be: document description; destination office; office responsible for its storage; beneficiary of the burocratic procedure; production date; expiration date; priority; access authorization; tags' UIDs referencing other documents; an optional start and/or stop label that represents an indication of start or stop of the business process to which the selected document is connected. These parameters can be kept into a database and can be accessed through the UID of the tag of the managed paper document. In this way, the database is a useful mine of information and allows the construction of the workflow history of a tagged document. The information that is possible to extract from it could be linked to business intelligence tools, with the purpose of supporting the enterprise users to take better business decisions, and/or to a SUP with the aim of improving enterprise performances. In this paper authors are interesting to the integration between RFID and an existing SUP.

3 A Smart Ubiquitous Platform

The use of a SUP supporting the RFID technology, integrated with the organization's TDMS, can favorite the gathering of additional data regarding the document management. The analysis of this data helps an organization to improve its knowledge regarding the operative flow of the business activities. As a result, some advantages could be obtained: tagged documents may become mobile, intelligent, communicating components, facilitating the interaction between business activities and IT solutions; less time for performing a business process may be consumed; capability of planning and taking decisions may increase; evaluation errors may decrease; and economic advantages may be obtained.

Afterward the adopted SUP for verifying authors' hypothesis is introduced. It has been developed within a research projects as a general ubiquitous computing common execution environment [8,9]. It allows the access of available information from heterogeneous types of terminals (e.g. WAP or UMTS cellular phones, laptops, PDAs, common PCs or with reception system via satellite) and can be used in the described context for improving the quality of the work condition of the employees. Figure 1 shows the logical architecture of the used system. It is characterized of two main coarse-grained levels: *User Services* and *Environment Support*. This environment is thought as a layered software infrastructure accepting basic services. One of these services is named RFID and is used for identifying and localizing the tags. The following additional basic services are useful to automatically support business processes:

- RMI provides the remote interfaces for the available services and offers the opportunity of using different protocols (e.g., SSL, TCP, HTTP, HTTPS, SOAP) through JERI abstraction;
- INTELLIGENCE allows the execution of rules from a rule engine named Jess [5]. The rules describe the relations between events and actions and may be created by system users or be automatically generated by a learning system that is developed on the basis of the WEKA (Waikato Environment for Knowledge Analysis) tool [6];
- LOCALIZATION allows the determination of the topografical position of devices, persons and other objects that are moving inside the space of a given environment and for the calculus of the distance between entities with RFID tags.

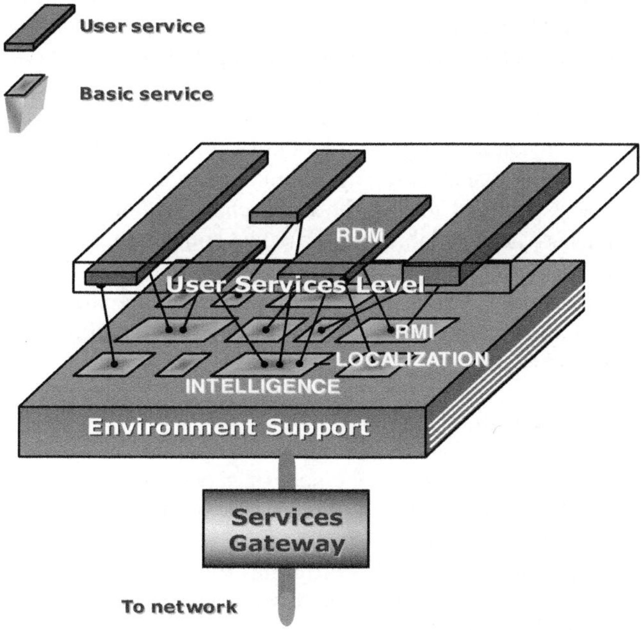

Fig. 1. Extensible and ubiquitous architecture endowed with intelligence

Each basic services has its own concern and coordinates suitable software objects and heterogeneous networked devices for providing basic functionalites and making possible the realization of a general ubiquitous computing common execution environment. Thus, the Support Environment occurs as an off-the shelf contribution that is customizable from software developers at the level of User Services. The components of this level are accessible from multiple types of user interfaces (e.g. Java/Java Web Start Application, Web browser, Wap browser, Jini browser) and they aggregate the functionalities that are provided by the basic and/or other user services with those exported from single networked devices. The obtained aggregated functionalities aim at providing services for end-users. It is at this level that the RFID-based administrative services are introduced. In the following, an example of RFID Document Management service (RDM) is introduced.

4 The RFID Document Management Service

If work time is wasted before a document is moved from the desk of a staff member to another one, the activities that depend on this movement can suffer a delay. This waste of time frequently happens and depends on different common reasons, e.g., a document can remain under an incorrect or long stack of other documents and can be forgotten or lost. The produced delay can be a foreseen management delay and result harmless, or the cause of the rescheduling of the planning of the organization and can be source of an economic damage. For example, if a team leader is waiting for the reception of the needed resources before starting the research activities of his/her group, and those resources do not arrive because their *purchase order* is lost or forgotten, and did not reach the desk of the *Director*, *Administrative secretary* or the responsible of the *Accounting office*, for being signed, the team leader research can suffer a delay. In the worse case, the team leader can even suffer of economic damages if (a) he is obliged to pay the researchers without they work because the required resources are not available, and/or (b) he could even loose the reserved funds because the purchase procedure has not been completed within the time limit. Similar problems can be avoided with a major control regarding the circulation of paper documents within an organization. Afterward a possible solution is proposed and its deployment is introduced.

4.1 The Proposed Solution

Automating the monitoring and management of paper documents circulation, permits to obtain useful information regarding the documents involved in a business process, such as: who took which document; if a document is outside fixed boundaries; if a document moves through a path that is different from the defined or authorized one; if the movement of a document through a path suffers of an interruption or delay. Using this information, who manages, carries out and uses a business process improve its knowledge regarding the activity flows that are executed within the organization. Therefore, less time is needed for performing a business process, the capability for planning and taking decisions increases, the evaluation errors decrease and economic advantages are obtained [7].

The designed RDM service aims at addressing these needs. It acts transversally to the existent enterprise solutions without changing them, but only their methodical behaviours. In particular, this service is designed for:

a) communicating with the readers of the antennas attached to the desks of the organization and in other strategic points for knowing if a tagged document referring another tagged document exists within an open business process.

b) controlling that all the used RFID tags are within the range of reading of an available antennas. This condition is violated when an RFID tag is registered how activated but it is not within the range of reading of any antennas. In this case, an alert event can be launched and a timer activated. It the condition is again violated after a fixed interval of time, an alarm can be launched to the responsible of examining the tagged document within the related business process, if this one is open, or to the office responsible for its storage, if the related business process is closed. In this way the accidental lost of documents can be avoided;
c) controlling if there are tagged documents that have assigned an urgent priority. When this condition is verified, a message is sent to who has to receive the tagged document. In this way, the procedure that has to manage an urgent document can be more promptly executed;
d) communicating with the antennas attached to bookshelves and drawers for knowing the existence of expired stored and tagged documents that can be eliminated. Each time the designed service verifies this condition, a message can be sent to the person that is responsible for managing and inventorying the document. Notifications continue to be sent till when the tag is not removed from the expired document and all the documents it refers, and/or a label of expiration is not written in the database with reference to the UID of the disarmed tag;
e) communicating with the antennas attached near the entry/exit to/from the organization and its offices for knowing if tagged documents are brought outside the authorized boundaries. Each time the designed service verifies this condition, an alarm sending a vocal message can be launched, the luminosity of the area of entry/exit is increased and a camera is turned on. This camera can be the nearest one to the alarm point that is able to film the person that moves the document in an unauthorized area.

The introduction of RDM services brings some benefits for document management. For example, it is possible to require the list of all the business processes that are in execution and use documents. For each process in execution, it is possible to build virtual dynamic chains of the managed documents for tracking and monitoring their movements and correlations. The documents chains represent a virtual track that thanks to the LOCALIZATION basic service permits to show at runtime, the state of the business process in execution. Using the engine of the RDM service, a manager or business process responsible can gain a global vision of the way the employees work and he can revise the business process schedule, if needed. In particular, it is possible to understand if a business process is open, closing, or, simply, its execution point. The information collected through this mechanism can in future help formulating a more accurate estimation of the time needed for executing the analysed business process. In addition, a manager can be supported by the INTELLIGENCE basic service of the platform and used by the RDM service. For example, when a tagged document is not referred from any other document, an event can be launched from the RDM service and a timer activated. If after a fixed interval of time, the service does not find another tagged document referring the tagged document in examination, an alarm can be launched to the office to which the document is destined. In this way, the office responsible can be pressed for understanding the cause of the interruption of the procedure and resolving it.

The introduction of the RDM service does not want to substitute the current technique of document management. Actually, most current document management systems can be easily improved and integrated with other systems. This paper proposes a solution to manage a document management system integrated with a paper archive integrated in the first one. Different reasons make useful to consider the double recording of documents. A first reason is that, in both public and private organizations, the paper recoding is compulsory, even if the electronic recording is useful. On one hand, the electronic recording is safer for both protection of the information confidentiality and disastrous events. On the other hand, the traditional archives are less secure of the electronic ones in case of intruder events, fire, or inundations. In fact, electronic archives adopting advanced technologies are inaccessible to whoever does not own the right to access, and, as they have reduced dimensions, they can be easily kept in a secure manner. Moreover, the data can be rapidly transferred to remote sites through Internet. Finally, the proposed approach offers a solution for keeping paper documents long-term and being able to recover them in the future. In the authors' knowledge, nowadays technologies addressing this problem do not exist.

4.2 The Deployment

The RFID technology is not plug and play and RFID readers have to be part of a network. So, technological support is needed for introducing RFID within an organization and integrating it into its business processes. Organization's offices and paper documents circulating through them have to be suitably equipped. In particular, the following actions are required:

- installation of the available SUP environment on a PC connected to a network and connection of the RDM service to a suitable database;
- attachment of passive RFID tags onboard the documents that are produced during a specific business process;
- antennas and readers installation in each office where tagged paper documents are stored and on each entry/exit to/from offices where the organization's staff works.

In this way, by using existent RFID basic services, the RDM service has the potentiality of showing real time views regarding documents circulation for a considered business process. These views can be obtained thanks to (a) the UID of the tags attached on the produced documents and (b) SUP support. A view can be useful for decreasing evaluation errors, improving planning capability and taking more careful decisions. In addition, the RDM service may also help for inventorying documents and managing the elimination of those documents that were stored and are not any more needed.

5 Conclusions

This paper has presented an investigation for analysing the effect of the adoption of the RFID technology for supporting the management of business processes of an organization. With this in mind, the integration of an RDM service within a SUP has been analyzed. The proposed service is integrated in a SUP endowed with intelligence and can:

(a) detect and trace the movement of documents produced and managed in a business process;
(b) inform the employees when a document is expired, it is not any more needed to store it and can be eliminated;
(c) control that the time for filling a request is bounded. When this time is expiring the system can inform the employees responsible with an email or sms and, if the number of requests to be filled is greater than a given threshold, the system can inform its beneficiary that there is a delay for completing its request.

Such facilities are designed for improving performances of organizations' offices and consequently customer satisfaction level.

Future directions will regard the completion of the implementation of the designed RDM service. As well as, its experimentation in various real contexts is needed for obtaining an evaluation of its real performances and the Return On Investment improvement with the RFID introduction in an organization.

References

1. Guide to Understanding and Evaluating RFID: An Application White Paper (September 2005) Ryzex Group (April 22, 2007) www.ryzex.com/pdf/RFID_Whitepaper.pdf
2. IBM RFID solutions - RFID and the Electronic Product Code Perspectives on a Business Driven Roadmap. June 2004. In: CCGD & FCPMC RFID Conference (April 22, 2007) http://www.fcpmc.com/Member/resources/events/presentations/IBM.pdf
3. Osservatorio RFID (April 22, 2007) http://www.cnipa.gov.it/site/it-IT/Attivit%c3%a0/Tecnologie_ innovative_per_la_PA/RFID/Osservatorio_Rfid/
4. RFID in the hospital. July 2004. RFID Gazette (April 22, 2007) www.rfidgazette.org/2004/07/rfid_in_the_hos.html
5. Sandia National Laboratories: Java Expert System Shell (April 22, 2007) http://146.246.238.73/ jess/
6. Waikato Environment for Knowledge Analysis Project (April 22, 2007) http://www.cs.waikato.ac.nz/ ml/
7. Bodhuin, T., Preziosi, R., Tortorella, M.: Building an RFID Document Management Service. In: Proceedings of Innovations in Information Technology, International Conference, Dubai, November 19-21, 2006. IIT'06 (2006)
8. Bodhuin, T., Canfora, G., Preziosi, R., Tortorella, M.: An Extensible Ubiquitous Architecture for Networked Devices in Smart Living Environments. In: Enokido, T., Yan, L., Xiao, B., Kim, D., Dai, Y., Yang, L.T. (eds.) Embedded and Ubiquitous Computing – EUC 2005 Workshops. LNCS, vol. 3823, pp. 21–30. Springer, Heidelberg (2005)
9. Bodhuin, T., Canfora, G., Preziosi, R., Tortorella, M.: Hiding complexity and heterogeneity of the physical world in smart living environments. In: Proceedings of the 2006 ACM Symposium on Applied Computing. SAC '06, Dijon, France, April 23 - 27, 2006, pp. 1921–1927. ACM Press, New York (2006)
10. Curtin, J., Kauffman, R.J., Riggins, F.J.: Making the most out of RFID technology: A research agenda for the study of the adoption, usage and impact of RFID. 2005. Minneapolis, 11. Carlson School of Management, University of Minnesota (October 30, 2005) (April 22, 2007) http://www.misrc.umn.edu/workingpapers/fullpapers/2005/0522_103005.pdf

11. Kallender, P.: Japanese bank taps RFID for document security. 2004. InfoWorld, (August 18, 2004) (April 22, 2007) http://www.infoworld.com/ article/04/08/18/ HNjapanrfid_1.html
12. Hammer, M., Champy, J.: Reengineering the Corporation: a Manifesto for Business Revolution. HarperCollins, NY (1993)
13. Quaadgras, A.: Who Joins the Platform? The Case of the RFID Business Ecosystem. In: Proceedings of the Proceedings of the 38th Annual Hawaii international Conference on System Sciences (Hicss'05) - Track 8. HICSS, January 03 - 06, 2005, vol. 08, p. 269.2. IEEE Computer Society, Washington, DC (2005)
14. Songini, M.: Wal-Mart details its RFID journey (March 2006) Computerworld (April 22, 2007) http://www.computerworld.com/industrytopics/retail/
15. Wang, S., Chen, W., Ong, C., Liu, L., Chuang, Y.: RFID Application in Hospitals: A Case Study on a Demonstration RFID Project in a Taiwan Hospital. In: Proceedings of the 39th Annual Hawaii international Conference on System Sciences. HICSS, January 04 - 07, 2006, vol. 08, p. 184.1. IEEE Computer Society, Washington, DC (2006)

Towards an RFID-Oriented Service Discovery System*

Beihong Jin, Lanlan Cong, Liang Zhang, Ying Zhang, and Yuanfeng Wen

Technology Center of Software Engineering, Institute of Software,
Chinese Academy of Sciences, Beijing, China
beihong@iscas.ac.cn, lacong@microsoft.com,
{zhangliang1216,zhangying,wenyuanfeng}@otcaix.iscas.ac.cn

Abstract. Service discovery and resource location have become the fundamental for information sharing, access and integration in distributed and mobile systems including RFID applications. The paper describes Service CatalogNet, an RFID-oriented service discovery system, which can support particular semantic description requirements for RFID-related services by a concise service model and offer scalability with respect to service information by multi-proxy collaboration, dynamic service storage splitting and history-based service information replication. Moreover, it provides service adaptation for changing contexts. Experiment results also show Service CatalogNet outperforms two existing solutions, namely, LDAP solution and XPath-based solution.

1 Introduction

Service discovery and resource location are prerequisites for information sharing, access and integration in distributed and mobile systems including RFID applications. Services concerned here are network-enabled applications which perform certain computation or management tasks and are usually accessed by access points such as IP addresses/URLs or particular client software called service stubs. Scenarios are often found in RFID applications about querying product information services according to RFID electrical codes and other product attributes, for instance, querying the nearest maintenance service from the current position of an RFID-labeled product. The three specific technical challenges for discovering an RFID-oriented service are to (1) provide the enough expressiveness for users to describe the appropriate services in terms of a single RFID tag code or a range of codes, user's context information (e.g., location) and other attributes, (2) be scalable to large amounts of services and concurrent users and responsive even if RFID-related services may suffer from frequent updates, which implies that we have to trade off between expressiveness of service model and performance of service discovery while tackling (1) and (2) simultaneously. (3) provide location-aware services for mobile clients holding PDAs embedded with RFID-readers.

In a response, we developed Service CatalogNet, an RFID-oriented service discovery system whose model for service description and query adopts hierarchy structure and supports some useful semantic representations which are required by

* This work was supported by the National Hi-Tech Research and Development 863 Program of China under Grant No. 2006AA01Z231.

J. Indulska et al. (Eds.): UIC 2007, LNCS 4611, pp. 235–245, 2007.

RFID applications. This system provides efficient service management including effective service tree storage, dynamic splitting strategy and soft-state service maintenance mechanism. Depending on collaboration query on proxies' overlay, this system provides exact matching, partial matching and semantic operator matching that excel the companion solutions in query performance. The system also shows dynamic adaptation to varying service requirements imposed by mobile service requestors when this system's client software is deployed on handheld devices.

The rest of this paper is organized as follows. Section 2 overviews related work. Section 3 outlines the system including the service model and the system architecture, and introduces a particular RFID application demonstrating the usage of Service CatalogNet. Section 4 presents the storage and splitting strategy of service information. Section 5 describes collaboration service query and evaluates its performance by examining the query execution time for different matching strategies. The final section concludes the paper.

2 Related Work

Conventional directory services [1] such as LDAP [2] may be the candidate solutions but they are not rightly suitable for RFID applications innately because their models are short of describing a range of attribute values, which kind of requirement is demanded frequently in RFID environment, and query performance will decline while interleaving with update operations due to the implied maintenance cost of indexes. What's more, since service access goes beyond the scope of directory services, RFID applications have to develop this functionality if a directory service is adopted directly. On the other hand, XPath query can be served for RFID scenarios in an intuitional sense if the service descriptions are based on XML. But it suffers from lower system performances due to inefficient DOM processing of XML documents.

The above solutions can not work under the mobile environments where RFID applications are apt to be deployed in the long term. However, existing service discovery systems can support either infrastructure-based wireless environment (e.g. UPnP [3]-compatible systems, INS [4, 5] and SDS [6]) or mobile ad hoc network (e.g. GSD [7], [8] and Konark [9]). The main weakness of various service discovery systems lies in the lack of query for the content of the RFID tags, although some recent systems have provided more flexible service descriptions beyond the service templates adopted by the earlier protocols such as SLP[10] and Bluetooth SDP[11]. For improving the scalability, INS logically partitions all name resolvers within the system to a number of virtual spaces, each of which maintains only a certain type of services. Moreover, INS can automatically spawn for a heavy-loaded name resolver a peer resolver, which will offload a portion of the service queries on it. To realize the same goal, SDS organizes its servers into multiple shared hierarchies based on different policies such as administrative domain or network topology. Although the strategies of server partition, replication and hierarchical categorization do enhance the system scalability to some extent, they do not offer how to deal with the bottleneck caused by the rapid increasing of services and the frequent concurrent service queries in a single server. As for context-aware support, Splendor [12] supports nomadic users and mobile services in service discovery by using the tag's information to determine their locations, but here locating user is confined to the existence of tag. As the extension of INS, Solar system framework [13] designs “context-processing operators” to calculate the desired context aggregation and can notify users immediately as contexts update under the assumption that service names are permitted to be adjusted while contexts change. But that assumption is not true for RFID scenarios.

In addition, existing service discovery protocols (e.g. UPnP and Bluetooth SDP) mainly aim for services provided by hardware, lack of extensibility for soft services. So far, there is no proper service discovery system for RFID applications which has addressed the issues mentioned in Section 1.

3 System Overview

3.1 Service Model

SDMDH (Service Description Model supporting Diversity and Heterogeneity of services), the service model in Service CatalogNet, adopts hierarchy structure embedded with attribute-value pairs, in which an attribute-value pair (av-pair in short) with the form [attr. = val.] or a single attribute with [attr.] represents a basic unit of service description, similar to XML. Table 1 gives the grammar of SDMDH, where operators “Range”, “<”,”>”, “<=” and “>=” are used for defining the range of attributes and boolean relations between attribute values can be expressed by “NOT”, “AND” and “OR”. Oper-1, oper-2 and oper-3 are generally called semantic operators in our system.

In SDMDH, some attribute tags, such as Identifier, Expiration, Classification, Context, Type and Access, are predefined as template elements, so that the instance of the model can describe the following information: (1) service basic information, including the service identifier, the service provider information, and the service lifecycle; (2)

Table 1. The grammar complied by SDMDH

<table>
<tr><td>attr.</td><td>::= a string</td></tr>
<tr><td>oper-1</td><td>::= “Range”</td></tr>
<tr><td>oper-2</td><td>::= ‘<’|‘>’| “<=”| “>=” | “NOT”</td></tr>
<tr><td>oper-3</td><td>::= “AND” | “OR”</td></tr>
<tr><td>val.</td><td>::= a string|‘*’, oper-1, “*(”, a string, ‘,’, a string, ‘)’ | ‘*’, oper-2, ‘*’, a string,|‘*’, oper-3, ‘*’, ‘(‘, a string, ‘,’, a string, {‘,’, a string}, ‘)’</td></tr>
<tr><td>av-pair</td><td>::= ‘[‘, attr., ‘=’, val., ’]’</td></tr>
<tr><td>servicedescription</td><td>::= av-pair | ‘[‘, attr., ‘=’, val., servicedescription*, ’]’|‘[‘, attr., servicedescription*, ’]’</td></tr>
</table>

Table 2. An example of service description

[Service [Service-Specifier
[Classification = Regional Product Quality Report]
[EPCCode-Range = *Range*(6A7969CBD1000000, 6A7969CBD1FFFFFF)]
[Context [Location = Beijing] [Device = PDA [Resolution = 240*320] [Processing = High]]
[Bandwidth = High]]]
[Service-Record [Identifier = 0000000001] [Description = Beijing Second Quarter Dairy Product Quality Report][Version = 1]
[Proxy-Node = 2] [Copy-Record = 1, 3][Provider = Beijing Quality Supervision Bureau] [Type = Document]
[File = Report_PDA.doc] [Expiration = 2007-09-01] [Access = Public]]]

service content information, including the classification of the services and the content-related attributes such as a range of RFID codes; (3) service context information, including geographic region, device type and network status; (4) service access mode, including the invocation mode, the path to the service stub/information of the access point, the service access rights, and etc. The root tag of SDMDH is "Service" whose subordinates contain predefined "Service-Specifier" and "Service-Record". Meanwhile, SDMDH's built-in extensibility allows user-defined tags tailored to a specific service as well as to express the nested or orthogonal relations among defined tags.

SDMDH can express both service descriptions provided by service providers and query conditions presented by service requestors. Table 2 describes an example of service that reports regional product quality.

3.2 System Architecture

Service CatalogNet is organized into client/multi-server structure. Figure 1 shows the key components and deployment of Service CatalogNet. Servers called proxies are fully connected in wired network and comprise the overlay network in the application layer. By storing in every proxy the topology of the whole overlay, proxies can communicate with each other through HTTP and collaborate in implementing service information management, query and access. Thus, a service provider, as the entity providing service resources in distributed environment, can register the services and provide service stubs if necessary with the aid of browser after obtaining the well-known entry of proxy (i.e., a URL). Furthermore, after installing client software, service requestors can interact with proxies through wired or wireless network, soliciting information of services and accessing the resultant services. Service requestors can get access to services with client/server model by invoking the downloaded service stubs from proxies, paying no attention to heterogeneous services invocation modes and complexity of various communication mechanisms. Taking advantage of service stubs, service requestors also work well in case service is located behind firewall or client needs to interact with services through a private or unsupported protocol such as FTP which is normally not supported by mobile devices.

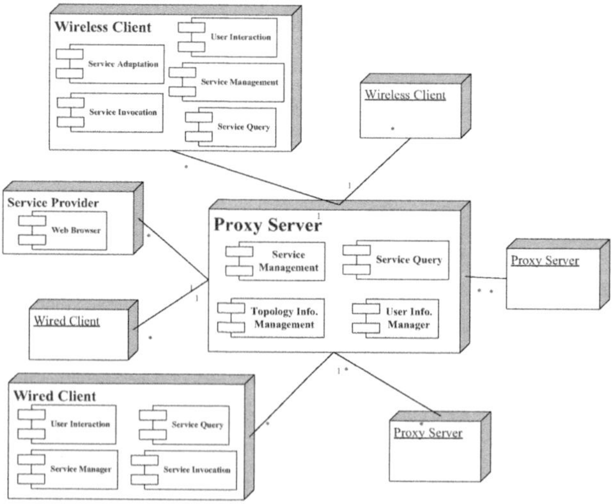

Fig. 1. The key components and deployment for Service CatalogNet

The presence of an RFID tag, as well as the requestor's location, is detected by the service adaptation module in client software. After observing the change of RFID tags or location deviation is larger than a specific threshold, the service adaptation module will trigger the validation inspection and the subsequent updating for the invalid services: transparently assemble corresponding service query in terms of the current context and submit query to overlay network for alternative services to replace the invalid ones. The whole procedure is carried out without interfering with the requestors.

Service information maintenance in proxies adopts soft-state message dissemination [14] which can efficiently avoid the existence of useless or invalid services. Aiming at this goal, service expiration time is required to provide at service registration and proxies periodically check whether services have timed out and then delete those out-of-date services.

3.3 Example for Locating RFID-Related Services

Service CatalogNet can be deployed in a shopping mall. While equipped with a smart phone or PDA which supports GPRS or WiFi connection and has either an SDIO or a CF Type II extension slot available for an RFID reader card, user can install client software of Service CatalogNet and obtain the product's tag code through the RFID reader card, and then find the service pertaining to the product. For example, users can find the try-out service for a certain Internet game product, and download a pilot edition as a service stub and try it out. If the device supports a GPS receiver, device mobility can be achieved fully in Service CatalogNet. For example, Dell Axim X51 connecting Dongyuan Smart SDIO-RFID Reader in SD Slot and Eagletec ET-CF2GPRS card in CF Slot is the target PDA satisfying the above requirements. Holding this mobile device in hand, the user can find the service for a certain product e.g. about local quality report and then run this service's stub in mobile environment.

4 Storage and Splitting of Service Information

Service information and service provider data are stored in overlay in a decentralized way. The *source proxy* storing above information is decided by hashing the service provider's login information and looking up the mapping from hash value to proxy node. Service infor- mation will be replicated in the overlay according to historical statistical data of query.

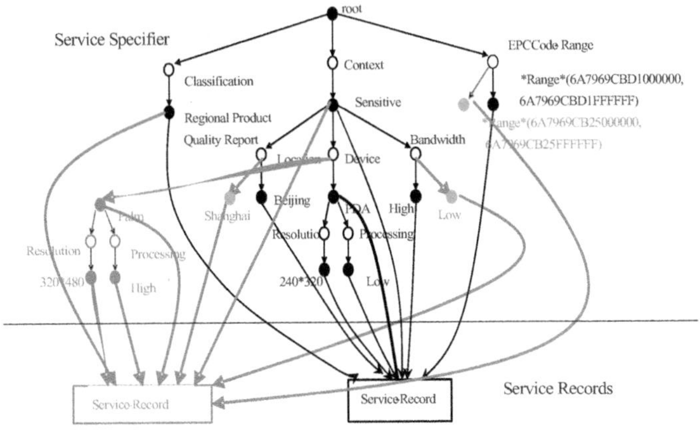

Fig. 2. An example of service tree

In a proxy, all of the service information desc- ribed by SDMDH is stored in a service tree [4], which consists of upper "service specifier" and lower "service records". In service specifier, there are two kinds of nodes: attribute nodes (marked with hollow circle) and value nodes (marked with filled circle). Nodes along with the same path are aggregated together in the service tree. Figure 2 gives an example of service tree, in which the part corresponding to the example shown in Table 2 is in bold.

With the increasing of sharing service information in overlay network, a single service tree will be subjected to a great deal of query and management operations (i.e., add/update/delete operations for service information) and become the system bottleneck. Therefore, we design and implement a dynamic splitting algorithm. According to the splitting algorithm, a service tree will be split into two service trees while the service scale or the number of concurrency operations is larger than a specified threshold. Gradually, the service information in a proxy will spread around a collection of service trees, i.e., a service forest. The algorithm also keeps the consistency between the service information in memory and the serialization version in stable storage during splitting. Figure 3 gives the main procedure for setting splitting boundary and splitting the service tree.

```
//Split Service-Tree T from attribute node Ta
Split (Service-Tree T, AttrituteNode Ta)

//Initialize Set1 as a set of service records in T
Set1 ← Service-Record-Set of T
Set2 ← a new, empty Service-Record-Set
K := boundary for split, initialized as null
//Get the number of service records in T
totalNum ← Set1.size()
//Get all value nodes in Ta
List(Tv) = getList(Ta.children)
//Sort by certain rule
SortedList(Tv) = Sort(List(Tv))
foreach Tv in SortedList(Tv)
    num ← Tv's Service-Record-Set.size();
    if Set2.size()+num<=totalNum/2
       Append Tv's Service-Record-Set to Set2
       Delete Tv's Service-Record-Set from Set1
       K ← Tv
   else
     break

//Reserve 2-bit mark for every node
foreach Service-record in Set1
    //Mark as 1 first bit of all upper nodes
    //connecting to this service record
    Mark(Service-record, 1);
foreach Service-record in Set2
    //Mark as 1 second bit of all upper nodes
    //connecting to this service record
    Mark(Service-record, 2);
splittedTree ← a new, empty Service-Tree
foreach node Tn in T
    if Tn.mark.Equals("11")
         //for common nodes used by two sets
       deep copy Tn out to splittedTree

    if Tn.mark.Equals("01")
         //for nodes used only in Set2
       deep copy SubTree(Tn) out to splittedTree;
       delete subTree(Tn) from T
return   splittedTree
```

Fig. 3. The dynamic splitting algorithm

The splitting operations can be executed together with reading and updating for service description. The concurrency control strategy here is as follows: before reading or writing the service-tree or its serialization version, check first whether the splitting procedure is running and identify the current status by the variable *IsSplitting*. If *IsSplitting* equals true, the read or write operations will wait until the splitting finishes. After notified, the read or write operations will re-invoke themselves to locate the appropriate target tree and continue their operations.

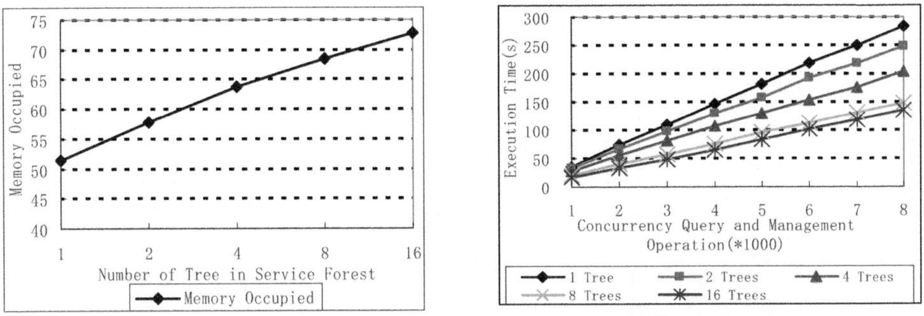

(a) Memory occupied (b) Execution time

Fig. 4. The splitting effect comparisons

We compare the memory occupied and the time required by executing the same management and query operations on 20000 service description before and after the splitting, i.e., in the form of 1, 2, 4, 8 and 16 trees. Figure 4 shows the experiment results.

We can observe from Figure 4 that dynamic splitting algorithm can apparently increase the performance of concurrency operations at the expense of a relatively slow growth of memory consumption. For example, when splitting from 4 trees to 8 trees, the memory used by the service forest increases by 7.11% from 63.84MB to 68.38MB, but the time spent on concurrency query and management operations decreases by 28.18% from 106.52s to 76.60s.

In addition, the moderate splitting shows stable enhancements on the performance of operation execution. As shown in Figure 4, the execution time for concurrency operations decreases by 11.08%, 17.63% and 27.21% respectively while splitting from 1 tree to 2 trees, 2 trees to 4 trees, and 4 trees to 8 trees. But the gain drops below the average and reaches only by 13.54% when further splitting to 16 trees, which indicates the inclination of excessive splitting that we would like to avoid.

5 Service Query

5.1 Collaboration Service Query

After receiving the client's query request, the proxy first matches the query locally, and then forwards it to other peers directed by the "nearest-position from client first" rule until finding the service meeting the conditions and returning it to the client. If the client does not satisfy with the results, he can send a "continue querying" message to the original proxy and this proxy will continue the search along the forwarding path in overlay until finding the satisfied service resource or traversing all the proxies.

The query forward strategy respecting location-first will enable to locate the nearest service resources, enhancing the client's satisfaction, the way of returning the matched resource immediately and waiting for client's confirmation will also accelerate query's responses. Figure 5 illustrates the primitives between a client and proxies. The arrows point out interaction directions.

To support a potentially large number of client queries, proxies employ history-based service information replication. Every proxy in overlay network

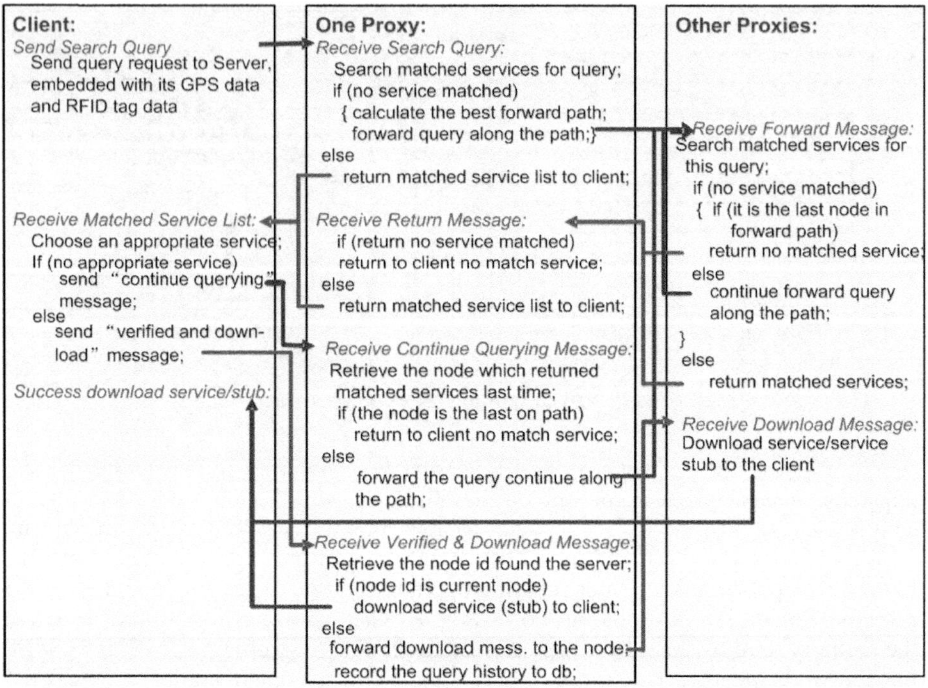

Fig. 5. The interaction procedure for collaboration querying

periodically polls the client query histories, keeping track of the access counts for service resources not stored locally. When the access count of a remote resource is larger than a predefined threshold *rep_value*, the proxy will copy all the data respecting that resource from the source proxy. On the other hand, when the total access count of remote resource drops below the predefined threshold *del_value*, the proxy will delete this replica.

To guarantee the consistency of service information, the proxy records service replication location in service's Service-Record. Following the Copy-Record attribute in Service-Record of source proxy, we can find the service replication tree rooted from the source node of this service. As such, when service information is updated, the updating information will propagate along the replication tree to keep all the replicas up-to-date.

5.2 Query Performance

We evaluate the query performance for Service CatalogNet, comparing with XPath-based solution and LDAP solution in the form of three queries, i.e., XPath query for XML-fashion services in .NET framework, and two LDAP queries for Netscape LDAP server v6.2 and IBM Tivoli LDAP server v5.2. Our experiments are conducted in a Pentium4 2.8GHz PC with 512MB of RAM, running Windows XP.

We take into account query involving the RANGE operator as mentioned in Section 3.1, and use the following substitute strategy to enable range query for the XML and LDAP models. For XML, two tags are presented in the service description with one for the minimum range boundary and another for the maximum, and then the XPath filter is expressed by restricting the specific value greater than the minimum and smaller than the maximum. The LDAP model achieves range query in a similar way. We record the time required for the above four systems by executing semantic-equivalence queries.

As shown in Figure 6, 3.01s for every 500 concurrency query operations on a tree of 10000 services is required by Service CatalogNet. However, Netscape LDAP server, IBM LDAP server, and .NET XPath engine take 8.37s, 10.80s and 49.16s respectively for fulfilling the same functionality. When keeping the concurrency query number at 2000, query time in Service CatalogNet varies with tree's size by 5s as starting point and average 2s/1000services as growth rate, but average growth rates for query time are 5, 7 and 20s/1000services for Netscape LDAP server, IBM LDAP server, and .NET XPath engine.

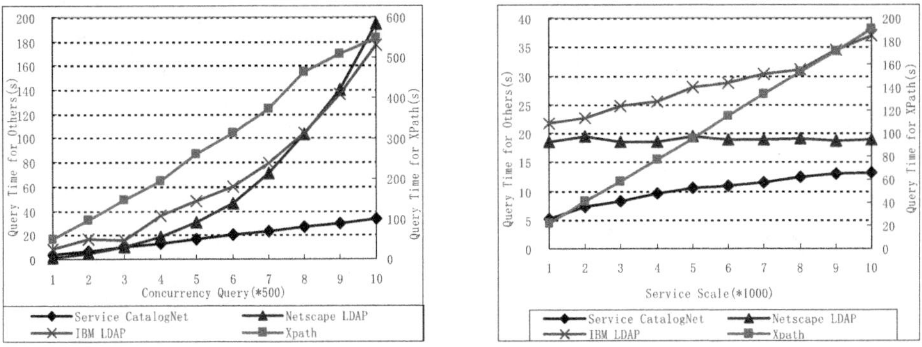

(a) Under a fixed service's scale (10000 services)

(b) Under a fixed concurrency query number (2000)

Fig. 6. The performance comparisons for semantic query

Considering the frequent updating for service information, we compare the time of accomplishing equivalent partial matching operations as well as equivalent hybrid operations which consist of 80% partial matching operations and 20% management operations.

Figure 7(a) and 7(b) plot the execution time required by the four systems handling partial matching operations, where we vary concurrency operations from 500 to 5000 and service size from 1000 to 10000. As shown in Figure 7(a), the query time of Service CatalogNet increases linearly with a step of 0.33s per 500 operations on average, so does .NET XPath engine's performance with a step of 47.39s per 500 operations. It should be noted in Figure 7(b) that the query time in Service CatalogNet has fewer bearing on the scale of the service tree, what ascribes to the hash table adopted in node matching for every layer in the service tree. Both Netscape LDAP server and IBM LDAP server present the similar trends in Figure 7(a) and 7(b), always faster than .NET XPath engine but slower than Service CatalogNet. Figure 7(c) and 7(d) examine the execution time for hybrid operations. We vary the number of concurrency operations and the number of services. In Figure 7(d), fluctuations are observed in Netscape LDAP server and IBM LDAP server as the service size varies. In contrast with Figure7(b), the execution time for

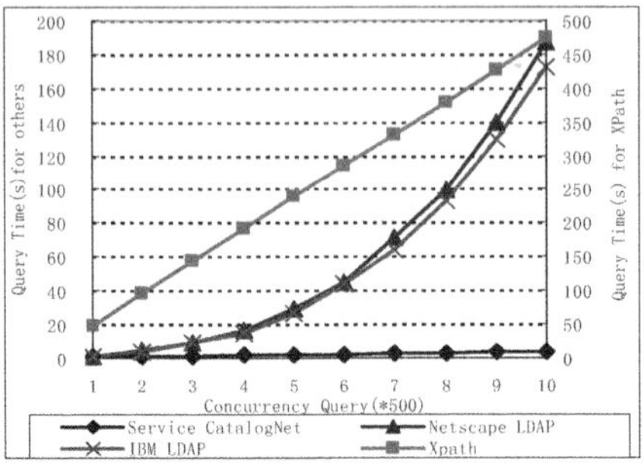

(a)Execute partial matching under a fixed service scale (10000 services)

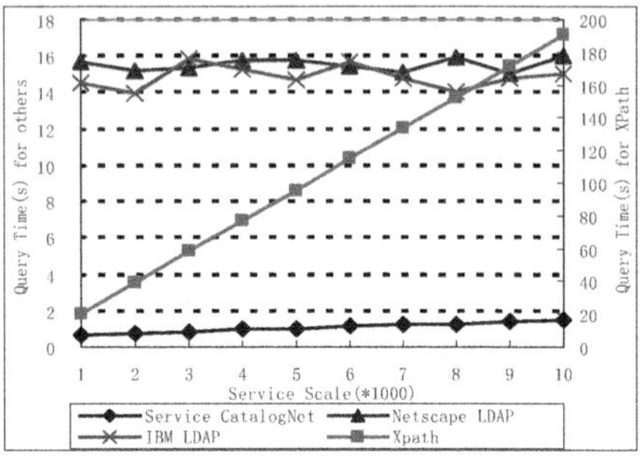

(b)Execute partial matching under a fixed concurrency query number (2000)

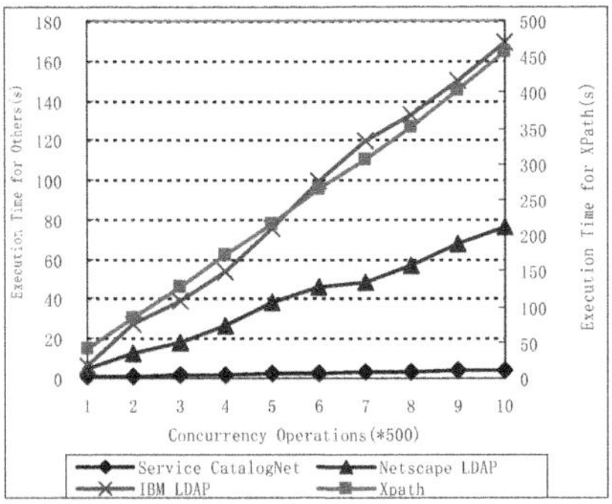

(c)Execute hybrid operations under a fixed service scale (10000 services)

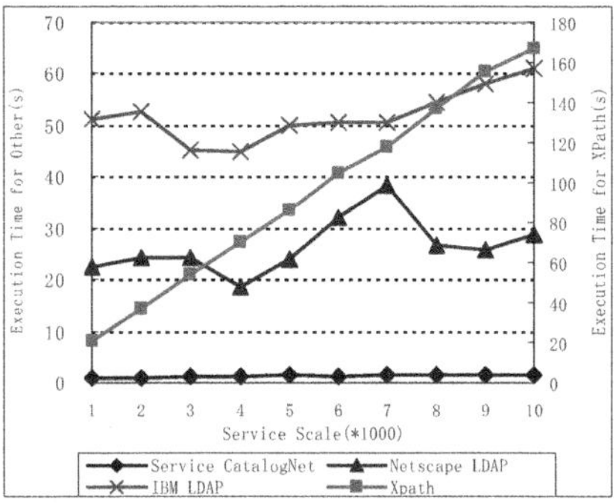

(d) Execute hybrid operations under a fixed concurrency query number (2000)

Fig. 7. The performance comparisons for partial matching

Netscape LDAP server and IBM LDAP server increases by 10.95s and 37s on average, which proves management operations cause performance declining and unstable probably due to the index adjustments and affords the negative evidences of locating services by using directory services. As to Service CatalogNet, the performance remains stable regardless of pure queries or hybrid operations.

6 Conclusion

Handheld devices with wireless connection and RFID reader create new opportunities for RFID applications. Discovering and locating RFID-related services can simplify the development of RFID applications. This paper describes an RFID-oriented service discovery system Service CatalogNet. Service CatalogNet can support particular semantic description requirements for RFID-related services by a concise service model. Based on its multi-proxy architecture, the system provides scalability with respect to service information with the aid of dynamic service storage splitting and history-based service information replication. Moreover, Service CatalogNet offers excellent performance with regard to RFID-related operations such as queries involved RFID-code range, partial matches and hybrid operations, compared with XPath-based solution and LDAP solution. It can react to the change of environment including the presence of RFID and the user's location, providing context-aware service adaptation. Our further work on Service CatalogNet includes enhancing discovery mechanism to satisfy qualities of services users specified, and combining access control and fault tolerant component into the system.

References

1. Coulouris, G., et al.: Distributed Systems Concepts and Design, 4th edn. Addison-Wesley, Reading (2005)
2. Wahl, M., Conlbeck, A., Howes, T., Kille, S.: Lightweight Directory Access Protocol (v3), RFC 2252 (1997)
3. Microsoft Corporation, Universal Plug and Play Device Architecture Version 1.0 (2000), http://www.upnp.org/download/UPnPDA10_20000613.htm
4. Adjie-Winoto, W., Schwartz, E., Balakrishnan, H., Lilley, J.: The Design and Implementation of an Intentional Naming System. In: 17th ACM Symposium on Operating System Principles, pp. 186–201 (1999)
5. Balazinska, M., Balakrishnan, H., Karger, D.: INS/Twine: A Scalable Peer-to-Peer Architecture for Intentional Resource Discovery. In: 1st International Conference on Pervasive Computing, pp. 195–210 (2002)
6. Czerwinski, S.E., et al.: An Architecture for a Secure Service Discovery Service. In: 5th Annual International Conference on Mobile Computing and Networks, pp. 24–35 (1999)
7. Chakraborty, D., Joshi, A., Yesha, Y., Finin, T.: Toward Distributed Service Discovery in Pervasive Computing Environments. IEEE Transactions on Mobile Computing 5(2), 97–112 (2006)
8. Sailhan, F., Issarny, V.: Scalable Service Discovery for MANET. In: the 3rd IEEE International Conference on Pervasive Computing and Communications, pp. 235–244 (2005)
9. Helal, S., Desai, N., Verma, V., Lee, C.: Konark: A service discovery and delivery protocol for ad hoc networks. IEEE Wireless Communications and Networking 3, 2107–2113 (2003)
10. Guttman, E.: Service Location Protocol: Automatic Discovery of IP Network Services. IEEE Internet Computing 3(4), 71–80 (1999)
11. Bluetooth SIG, Specification of the Bluetooth System (2003)
12. Zhu, F., Mutkal, M., Ni, L.: Splendor: A Secure, Private, and Location-aware Service Discovery Protocol Supporting Mobile Services. In: 1st IEEE International Conference on Pervasive Computing and Communications, pp. 235–242 (2003)
13. Chen, G., Kotz, D.: Context-Sensitive Resource Discovery. In: 1st IEEE International Conference on Pervasive Computing and Communications, pp. 243–252 (2003)
14. Raman, S., McCanne, S.: A Model Analysis, and Protocol Framework for Soft State-based Communication. In: the ACM conference on Applications, Technologies, Architectures, and Protocols for Computer Communication, pp. 15–25 (1999)

Activity Recognition Using an Egocentric Perspective of Everyday Objects

Dipak Surie[1], Thomas Pederson[1], Fabien Lagriffoul[1], Lars-Erik Janlert[1], and Daniel Sjölie[2]

[1] Department of Computing Science, Umeå University, SE-901 87 Umeå, Sweden
{dipak,top,fabien,lej}@cs.umu.se
[2] VRlab / HPC2N, Umeå University, SE-901 87 Umeå, Sweden
deepone@hpc2n.umu.se

Abstract. This paper presents an activity recognition approach based on the tracking of a specific human actor's current object manipulation actions, complemented by two kinds of situational information: 1) the set of objects that are visually observable (inside the "observable space") and 2) technically graspable (inside the "manipulable space"). This "egocentric" model is inspired by situated action theory and offers the advantage of not depending on technology for absolute positioning of neither the human nor the objects. Applied in an immersive Virtual Reality environment, the proposed activity recognition approach shows a recognition precision of 89% on the activity-level and 76% on the action-level among 10 everyday home activities.

1 Introduction

Inspired by "digital assistant" design research efforts such as [1], our vision is to design computer systems intended to facilitate personal, practical and user-defined everyday activities. Such systems should have awareness about the actor's current activity, situation and intention before the activity is actually completed to provide appropriate support. Capturing actor's intention implicitly is a very hard challenge, but could be simplified by capturing his/her situative information. This calls for an understanding of the actor's situative information while performing the activities from his/her perspective. Such systems can be used in providing assistance to people suffering early stages of dementia disease in completing their activities of daily living (ADL). Typical problems include the forgetting of performing an activity or an action within an activity; not being able to get started in the first place; not being able to continue after having been interrupted; or missing some operations that are mandatory for the completion of an activity. A system that could help overcome the above mentioned problems would enable patients to stay in their home for a longer period of time, have a normal independent life, and also reduce the burden on family members and caregivers.

Activity recognition based on user's body movements using accelerometers is described in [3], [4], and [5]. Such approaches are restricted to recognizing a subset of

J. Indulska et al. (Eds.): UIC 2007, LNCS 4611, pp. 246–257, 2007.

everyday human activities involving body movements like walking, running, brushing teeth, etc. Activity recognition based on audio is described in [6], but such approaches once again are restricted to a subset of sound-related activities. Recognizing activities using single but complex sensors like a camera is described in [7]. Such approaches are severely hampered by the complexity in extracting valuable features, even though human beings use the sense of vision effectively. Many activity recognition systems are heavily driven by currently available sensor technology. However, we believe that starting out from a perspective more centred around how humans literally perceive the world, based on the weight that current cognitive science give to this source of information as an activity-driving factor, could offer a valuable complement. In particular, it could offer a conceptual design platform robust enough to survive and handle generations of changes in the field of sensor technology.

Recognizing activities based on object manipulation is becoming an important research approach [10], [11]. We consider such an approach but extend it by also considering the changes to the set of objects seen and to the set of objects touchable by an actor in recognizing activities. According to situated action theory [12], the situation of an actor is a very important factor in determining what action the actor will perform. In performing various everyday activities, objects enter and leave the actor's observable space and manipulable space in a dynamic fashion. We recognize activities based on a simplified model of human perception limitations and considering Janlert's "proximity principle" [13], things that matter are close, and things that are close matter. Recognizing activities by attaching simple state change sensors to relevant objects (cf. [14]) is another interesting approach that we would consider in the future. Everyday human activities are modelled using a 3-level abstraction of activity, action and operation inspired from activity theory [2].

2 An Egocentric Perspective of Everyday Objects

The term 'egocentric' has been chosen to signal that it is the body and mind of a specific human actor that (sometimes literally, as will be shown later) serve as centre of reference to all his/her interaction with everyday objects.

2.1 A Situative Space Model: Bridging the Intent-Action Gap

A *situative space model* is developed on the basis of what a specific human actor can see and not see, touch and not touch at any given moment in time (Fig. 1). Human actors situate themselves closer to the objects relevant for their current activity. Such explicit situatedness gives an indication of the actor's intent (the needs and wants of the actor to satisfy some goal). By capturing the changes to the actor's observable space and manipulable space, we are indirectly capturing the actor's intentions.

The situative space model serves as a conceptual tool for determining what situative aspects of human activities need to be captured and in what detail. For our current prototype we consider only *the presence* of objects within the actor's observable space and manipulable space. In the future we intend to include *states* within individual objects to capture additional situative information. We also intend to include information about any other human actors present in the monitored spaces.

2.2 Applying the Egocentric Perspective

We have chosen to operationalize the situated space model (Fig. 1) as follows:

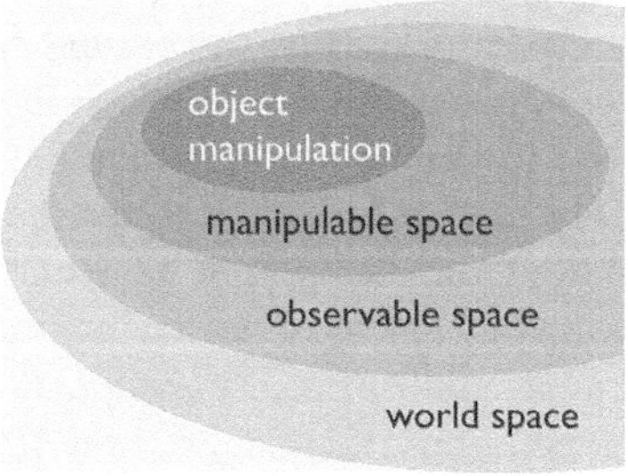

Fig. 1. A situative space model adapted from [15]

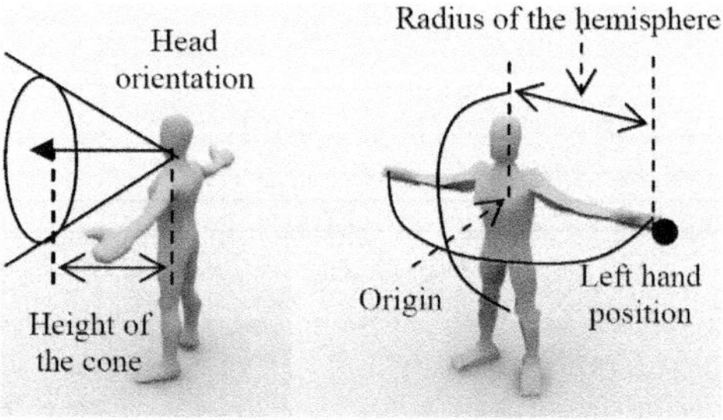

Fig. 2. **(a)** Observable space, **(b)** manipulable space

- The *world space* contains the set of all objects known to the system. In a real-world setting it might be determined by all objects carrying an RFID tag. In the Virtual Reality (VR) setting used for our evaluation purposes, it is the set of all objects included in the VR model simulating a kitchen environment.
- The *observable space* (OS) is the set of objects within a cone in front of the human actor's eyes with this cone following the head movements as shown in Fig. 2(a). The height of the cone is limited by the walls in an indoor environment and visual occlusion further affects the number of objects within this space.
- The *manipulable space* (MS) is the set of objects within a hemisphere in front of the human actor's chest (Fig. 2(b)). Such a shape is motivated by the fact that humans have two hands and the assumption that they manipulate objects within reach of their hands. The hemisphere follows the human actor's chest movements and its radius is equal to the maximum distance between the chest and a hand.
- *Object manipulation* (OM). When objects are manipulated by an actor, two events can be generated: *objectID_grabbed* and *objectID_released*. Although the actor can manipulate objects with both hands, we do at the moment not make any distinction between right and left. A similar approach is described in [16], [10] and [11]. Object manipulations represent the operations performed by an actor during the accomplishment of an action (and activity).

3 Activity Recognition System

Virtual Reality is used as a test-bed in order to speed up the design (and re-design) process and to compensate for the limitations with the currently available sensing technologies. A VR model, developed using the Colosseum3D real-time physics platform [17] is used to simulate a physical home environment with wearable sensors and sensors on everyday objects to capture an actor's object manipulation (OM), observable space (OS) and manipulable space (MS). Fig. 3 shows a snap-shot of the VR environment. OS and MS are captured at 1 Hz, while OM is captured when a grab/release event occurs. Refer to Fig. 4 for our system architecture. We have experimented with 70 object types. Object types include mobile object types like *fork*, *knife*, *plate* etc. and stationary object types like *microwave oven*, *sink*, *stove*, etc. We only consider the *type* of object in recognizing activities, not the identiy (e.g. *fork_1* and *fork_2* are both considered as *fork* type).

Fig. 3. Virtual Reality home environment

There are many objects that overlap for several activities. For instance, *fork*, *knife*, *plate*, etc. are used for several activities like *preparing breakfast*, *preparing the table*, *having breakfast*, *doing the dishes*, etc. This makes the classification problem harder compared to taking an approach where the recognition system is strongly characterised by one or two objects that are unique to the activity. We do have some activities like for instance *preparing_rice*, where the *rice_bag* is a unique object for this activity. But this does not simplify the classification problem for the following reasons: 1) we are not only recognizing the actor's current activity, but also the actor's current action. The *rice_bag* is not manipulated by an actor while performing all the actions within this activity, but only while performing a few actions within this activity; 2) the *rice_bag* manipulation might be a noise created by the actor while performing another activity, and 3) the recognition system should recognize the activity and action before they are actually completed to provide appropriate assistance to the actor. Hence the system cannot wait until the unique object is manipulated to recognize the activity and action.

3.1 Feature Extraction

OS and MS both consist of sets of objects that need to be quantified. Our quantification scheme builds $\vec{S}_A$ and $\vec{S}_B$ as shown in Fig. 4, where the vectors represent the list of distinct object types with their corresponding number of occurrences. A log function is applied on $\vec{S}_A$ and $\vec{S}_B$ to give more importance to the type of objects present within those spaces compared to the number of their occurrences. One limitation of our quantification scheme may be its scalability to a large number of object types, since the dimension of the quantification vector depends on the total number of object types. We have experimented with 70 types of objects and have obtained good results.

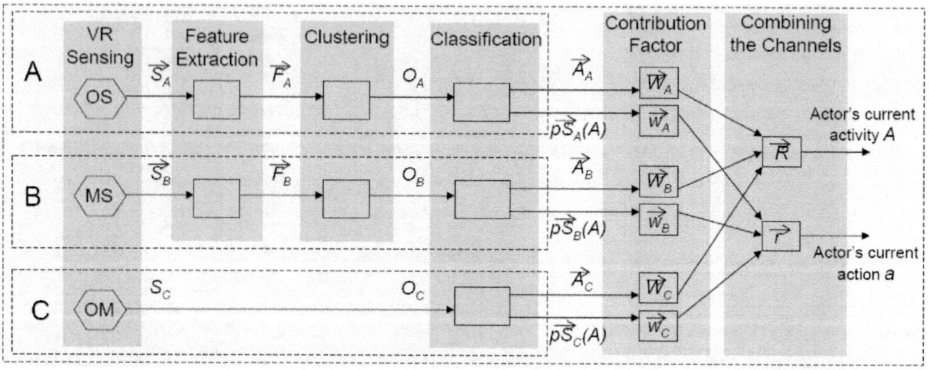

Fig. 4. The proposed activity recognition system architecture (D) combining three information channels (A, B and C) corresponding to the Observable Space, Manipulable Space, and Object Manipulation components pictured in Fig. 1 earlier

3.2 Clustering

$\vec{F}_A$ and $\vec{F}_B$ are fed into two distinct clustering algorithms to retain the features provided within their respective information channels. We obtain the cluster centre for observable space (O_A) and manipulable space (O_B) which is used for further classification as shown in Fig. 4. Growing neural gas (GNG) clustering algorithm [18] offers the possibility for online learning, maintaining steady learning rate and creating new clusters with additional training data compared to classical clustering techniques like K-Means or Kohonen SOM. Our goal is to not force the end-user to be involved in fine-tuning our system when new clusters are added. However, for our current implementation, we use GNG algorithm in the batch learning mode with fixed number of clusters. We intend to include online learning in the future.

3.3 Classification

The probabilistic generative framework of hidden-markov model (HMM) [19] is used because of its clear bayesian semantics, its ability to handle time-varying signals and the availability of efficient algorithms for state and parameter estimation. HMMs reduce the system's configuration space into a number of finite discrete states together with the probabilities for transition between the states. One limitation of HMMs is that the model structure has to be user-defined, which includes the number of states and the connections between the states. The model structure cannot be determined by standard learning methods. This should not pose a major problem since the activities recognized are user-defined. The actor provides ground truth for both activities and actions. Each activity is modelled using a separate HMM with the number of states corresponding to the number of actions within that activity. Similarly, the transitions between states correspond to the transitions between different actions within that activity. HMMs have shown good results in many activity recognition systems including [6], [8], [9] and [11].

The activity recognition system uses three information channels (refer to Fig. 4). Each information channel produces a sequence of observations that are fed into ten HMMs (one for each activity). For each information channel, the outputs from the ten HMMs are used to build an activity probability vector ($\vec{A}_A$, $\vec{A}_B$ and $\vec{A}_C$) containing the probabilities for each possible activity. The element of the activity probability vector with the highest value gives the actor's current activity and its most probable state gives the actor's current action.

3.4 Combining the Information Channels

The three information channels are combined using activity contribution factors ($\vec{W}_A$, $\vec{W}_B$ and $\vec{W}_C$) and action contribution factors ($\vec{w}_A$, $\vec{w}_B$ and $\vec{w}_C$). $\vec{W}_A$, $\vec{W}_B$ and $\vec{W}_C$ consist of the recognition precision values for each activity while $\vec{w}_A$, $\vec{w}_B$ and $\vec{w}_C$ consist of the recognition precision values for each action. These factors are automatically generated from the training data. We first determine the actor's current activity by computing $\vec{R}$, the weighted sum of all the three information channels:

$$\vec{R} = \vec{W}_A * \vec{A}_A + \vec{W}_B * \vec{A}_B + \vec{W}_C * \vec{A}_C \quad (1)$$

Where * represents element-by-element multiplication. The element of $\vec{R}$ with the highest value gives the actor's current activity *A*. Once the activity is known, we determine the actor's current action by calculating $\vec{r}$ using the following formula:

$$\vec{r} = \vec{w}_A * p\vec{S}_A(A) + \vec{w}_B * p\vec{S}_B(A) + \vec{w}_C * p\vec{S}_C(A) \quad (2)$$

Where $p\vec{S}_A(A)$, $p\vec{S}_B(A)$ and $p\vec{S}_C(A)$ are the vectors of state probabilities of the HMM representing the actor's current activity *A* for observable space, manipulable space and object manipulation respectively. $\vec{w}_A$, $\vec{w}_B$ or $\vec{w}_C$ is equal to zero if their respective channel is not supportive to the activity determined previously. The element of $\vec{r}$ with the highest value gives the actor's current action. We have not combined the three information channels before classification since we want to evaluate them independently, allowing us to include additional channels without affecting the overall infrastructure of our activity recognition system.

4 Evaluation

The experiments were performed by 4 subjects in a virtual reality home environment[1]. 10 activities were included as shown in Table 1. The activities were performed 20 times as part of various scenarios. A scenario comprises of a few related activities performed in some sequence. For example, we used *breakfast scenario*, *lunch*

[1] The subjects were initially taught how to perform activities in a virtual reality environment and then given a time period to practice in this environment. Only when the subjects were comfortable with the environment, they were allowed to perform the activities.

Table 1. List of actions and activities based on the AMPS framework [20]

	Activity # and name	Actions within individual activities
List of 10 activities	1 - Preparing rice	Get the rice bag, Pour rice into the cooker, Pour water into the cooker, Add salt, Put back the rice bag
	2 - Preparing fried vegetables	Get some vegetables, Cut those vegetables, Fry those vegetables, Add spices, Place the chopper in the sink
	3 - Preparing cake	Get the baking plate, Add some eggs, Add some milk, Add some sugar, Add some cake powder, Place the baking plate in the oven
	4 - Preparing coffee	Take some coffee powder, Pour water into the coffee machine, Get some cups, Pour some coffee into the cups
	5 - Preparing breakfast	Toast some bread slices, Boil some eggs, Prepare some juice, Prepare the cereals
	6 - Doing the dishes	Clean the dishes, Dry the dishes on the rack, Wash the hands
	7 - Having lunch	Have the main meal, Have the dessert, Drink coffee, Place the used dishes in the sink
	8 - Having breakfast	Have the main meal, Place the used dishes in the sink
	9 - Preparing the table	Place the table mats, Get some cutlery, Get some plates, Get some glasses, Get the food, Place some napkins
	10 - Cleaning the kitchen	Clean the table, Clean the stove, Clean the rack, Clean the floor

scenario, *free-time scenario*, etc. Some activities were common for several scenarios like the activity of *doing the dishes* which is common to both the *lunch scenario* and the *breakfast scenario*. The subjects were allowed to perform the activities in their own style (often in many different ways).

When a subject begins performing his/her activity, each object is in the location where it was last placed in the subject's previous activities. This makes our experiments realistic compared to having a fixed initial location for each objects. Cases when the subjects dropped an object on the floor or grabbed the wrong object were also included in our dataset. A real chair was used for the subjects to perform the activities of *having breakfast* and *having lunch.* Subjects' body postures and locomotion within the VR environment were realistic. For instance, the subjects were not allowed to pass through a table, even though it is possible in a VR environment.

The *number of clusters* and the *observation sequence length* were empirically determined for individual information channels based on the recognition accuracy. We have trained and tested the system on recorded data, using various combinations of these parameters. The optimal parameters are not sharply defined, allowing a variation of around 10% without altering the results significantly. Refer to Table 2.

Table 2. Optimal parameters for "A", "B" and "C"

	Observable Space ("A")	Manipulable Space ("B")	Object Manipulation ("C")
Number of clusters	55	70	No clusters
Sequence length	15	15	7

4.1 Precision, Recall and Confusion Matrix

We used the "Leave-One-Out Cross-Validation" (LOOCV) scheme to obtain the precision and recall figures (see Table 3). We define precision and recall as follows:

$$precision = \frac{TruePositives}{TruePositives + FalsePositives} \qquad recall = \frac{TruePositives}{TruePositives + FalseNegatives}$$

Table 3. Precision (P) and recall (R) in percentage (%) for each activity (Act) and action (An) using the three information channels (A, B, and C). The last column represents the precision (P) and the recall (R) obtained by combining the three information channels. The last row represents global values (G) in percentage (%).

Act #	Observable space				Manipulable space				Object manipulation				Combination			
	Activity		Action		Activity		Action		Activity		Action		Activity		Action	
	P	R	P	R	P	R	P	R	P	R	P	R	P	R	P	R
1	85	100	70	100	80	100	62	100	100	100	70	100	100	100	83	99
2	80	100	61	100	63	100	40	100	91	99	55	98	93	100	76	99
3	79	99	43	99	69	100	34	99	94	88	73	84	89	98	72	95
4	72	100	60	100	69	100	58	100	73	92	49	86	76	96	67	92
5	80	98	69	98	76	99	59	99	87	94	78	94	92	98	84	98
6	84	94	67	92	79	93	44	88	76	89	51	84	93	99	74	97
7	86	99	49	96	90	100	50	99	65	94	49	93	90	100	67	91
8	81	97	68	95	83	98	77	97	56	94	38	92	81	98	74	98
9	85	98	80	97	83	99	67	98	80	100	73	100	91	96	87	96
10	82	99	76	99	78	97	68	96	65	97	52	95	83	97	76	96
G	**81**	**98**	**64**	**98**	**77**	**99**	**56**	**98**	**79**	**95**	**59**	**92**	**89**	**98**	**76**	**96**

Considering the information channels independently, observable space (OS) shows the best results, both at the activity-level and action-level. A deeper analysis of the clusters formed within OS shows that it contains more than simple situative information. For the same OS (e.g. *"Around the stove"*), several clusters are formed for different activities (e.g. *"Stove + objects for cooking"*, *"Stove + ingredients for preparing cake"*). The clusters actually contain information about both the situation (location) and the activity, considering the objects brought by the user while performing the activity. So the clusters formed in OS are not only snapshots of patterns in the environment, they also represent the dynamic changes done by the user when he/she performs the activities. This also explains why the optimum number of clusters is high for both OS and MS. MS works in a similar manner, though within a smaller space.

From Table 3 it is also clear that the set of objects in close vicinity to the user (MS) is an important clue to the user's activitiy. Recognition using this information produces results at the activity-level as well as at the action-level similar to object manipulation (OM), which has been a dominant approach in recognizing human activities [10], [11]. For certain activities (1, 2, 3, 5, 9), the actions are recognized better using OM while there is another subset of activities for which the actions are recognized better using MS. This is not just a coincidence since activities 1, 2, 3, 5 and 9 are precisely the "prepare" activities, like for instance *preparing cake* or *preparing the table*, wherein a set of objects has to be picked up from different places and brought to a particular place. On the other hand, manipulable space is more efficient for activities like *having lunch* or *having breakfast*, in which a set of objects is already present at the beginning of the activity and remain present until the end of the activity. The principle of closeness discussed earlier is applicable here where for

Table 4. Confusion matrix

	Recognized Activities									
Actual Activities	1	2	3	4	5	6	7	8	9	10
1	684	0	0	0	0	0	0	0	0	0
2	241	3174	0	0	0	0	0	0	0	0
3	6	119	1187	0	11	0	0	0	0	0
4	0	18	231	1128	0	0	0	0	0	33
5	20	6	1	133	2715	0	0	0	0	30
6	0	0	6	0	171	2430	0	8	0	0
7	0	0	0	60	0	137	3967	0	298	0
8	0	0	0	0	0	0	83	2068	344	48
9	0	0	0	0	4	0	26	166	2529	50
10	0	0	4	0	142	13	23	1	352	2643

instance during the action *have the dessert*, the user pushes away the main meal and brings the fruit bowl closer, then pushes the fruit bowl away and brings the coffee jar and cups closer. Refer to Table 4 for confusion matrix.

4.2 Information Channels Complement Each Other

By combining all three information channels, we obtain a recognition precision of 89% at activity level and 76% at action level. Such a high precision with fine granularity at the action level is possible due to the combination of the information channels that represent different and complementary aspects of the user activities. In Fig. 5, for the activity of *doing the dishes*, action 1 (*clean the dishes*) and 2 (*dry the dishes on the rack*) share similar object manipulation data. However, the separation is improved by using observable space, which includes the *sink* for action 1 and the *rack* for action 2.

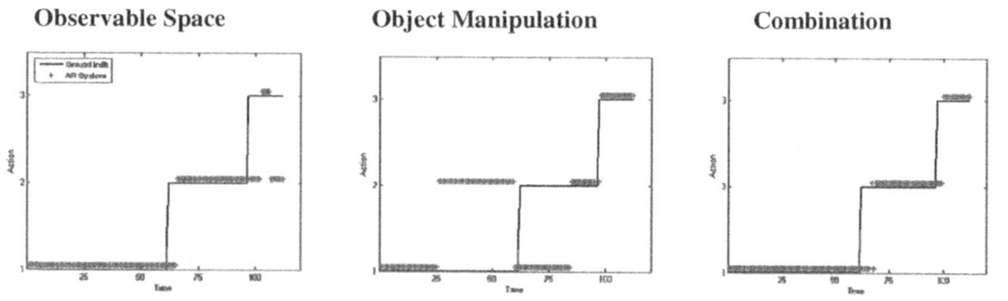

Activity - Doing the dishes: (1) Clean the dishes - (2) Dry the dishes on the rack - (3) Wash the hands

Fig. 5. Observable space as the dominant information channel for activity recognition

In some activities, like for instance *preparing fried vegetables*, the actions take place in a fixed location, and the set of objects remains the same because all the objects needed for this activity are already around the user. In such cases, observable space data produces less discriminating information compared to object manipulation at the action-level (see Fig. 6).

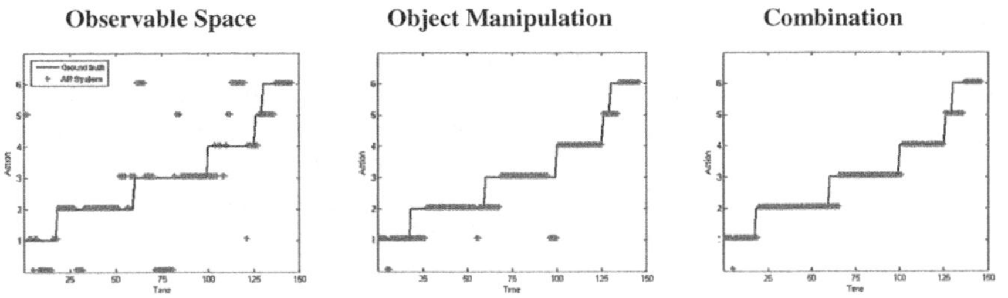

Activity - Preparing fried vegetables: (1) Get some vegetables – (2) Cut those vegetables – (3) Fry those vegetables – (4) Add spices – (5) Put the chopper in the sink – (6) Put back the spices (extra action performed sometimes).

Fig. 6. Object manipulation as the dominant information channel for activity recognition

Activity recognition approaches like [10] and [11] that focus only on object-manipulation patterns encounter difficulties in classifying activities that involve similar sets of objects. For example, [11] keeps track of the number of times an object was touched to differentiate between the activity of *preparing the table* and the activity of *having breakfast* that uses a similar set of objects. Such an approach requires many parameters that need to be fine-tuned for individual cases, thereby limiting its scalability to a variety of activities.

5 Discussion and Future Work

Transferability to Real-World Applications. VR simulations offer "clean" sensing with little noise and uncertainty in the collected signals, as opposed to real-world sensing. OM and MS require the identification of objects close to the actor's body which can be reliably obtained using RFID technology [21] as shown in many applications including [16], [10] and [11]. MS would require an RFID reader with higher power compared to OM due to the larger reading range necessary. Sensing OS is instead more complicated than OM and MS due to limitations in currently available sensing technologies. However, our VR experiment shows a limited contribution of that space (approximately 4%) to the overall activity recognition precision and we have therefore chosen to ignore OS in our current hardware development activities.

Scalability to Number of Activities. Human actors may require assistance for a potentially large number of activities. Since we use individual models for each activity, our approach should be able cope.. But by increasing the number of activities, the recognition accuracy might decrease. The 10 activities used for evaluating our system all took place in a kitchen environment. We estimate that the total number of activities of the same kind, in the same kind of environment, and at the same level of granularity, is less than 10 times as many. We think our approach will be able to handle such a scaling factor. Furthermore, we believe that although the total repertoire of everyday activities for a person may be large, they may be fairly well distributed over different environments. This would mean a moderate number of possible activities for each environment that need to be distinguished between.

Adaptation to Variations in Activity Patterns. Human actors may perform the same activity in several different ways. We have addressed this issue to some extent by including those variations in the training data. However with time, the actors may change the underlying structure of some activities. Thus, a modelling approach capable of dynamically changing its internal model with time would be desirable, but represents a major challenge. We are currently investigating possible techniques to enhance the capabilities of our HMMs modelling activities to be adaptive with time.

Handling Interrupted and Interleaved Activities. Human activities may be interrupted or interleaved with another activity, which is to some extent addressed in [11]. By introducing states within individual objects to keep track of "key" object state changes, we hope to be able to improve our approach in recognizing the end of an action/activity and thus, the handling of interrupted/interleaved activities.

6 Conclusions

In this paper we have presented a prototype activity recognition system developed on the basis of an "egocentric" view of how an actor interacts with objects to perform everyday activities. When evaluated in a VR-simulated home environment 1) activity and action recognition accuracies using OS and MS has shown promising results comparable to OM-based approaches [10], [11]; 2) fine-grained activity recognition at the action-level has also been demonstrated using the combination of all three information channels (OS, MS, OM). Our work provides an activity-aware platform for further investigations into the development of personal and user-defined activity-assistive systems. We have also demonstrated the utility of a VR-based development methodology when developing ubiquitous and wearable computing systems.

Acknowledgements

We would like to thank Gösta Bucht, Björn Sondell, Kenneth Bodin, Anders Backman and Marcus Maxhall from Umeå University, Sweden. This work is partially funded by the EC Target 1 structural fund program for Northern Norrland, Sweden.

References

1. Starner, T.: The Challenges of Wearable Computing: Part 1 & 2. IEEE Micro 21(4), 44-52, 54–67 (2001)
2. Nardi, B. (ed.): Context and Consciousness: Activity Theory and Human-Computer Interaction. MIT Press, Cambridge (1995)
3. Bao, L., Intille, S.: ctivity Recognition from User-Annotated Acceleration Data. In: Ferscha, A., Mattern, F. (eds.) PERVASIVE 2004. LNCS, vol. 3001, pp. 1–17. Springer, Heidelberg (2004)
4. Lee, S.W., Mase, K.: Activity and location recognition using wearable sensors. IEEE Pervasive Computing 1(3), 24–32 (2002)

5. Kern, N., Schiele, B., Schmidt, A.: Multi-Sensor Activity Context Detection for Wearable Computing, European Symposium on Ambient Intelligence (2003)
6. Chen, J., Kam, A., Zhang, J., Liu, N., Shue, L.: Bathroom Activity Monitoring Based on Sound. In: Gellersen, H.-W., Want, R., Schmidt, A. (eds.) PERVASIVE 2005. LNCS, vol. 3468, pp. 47–61. Springer, Heidelberg (2005)
7. Haritaoglu, I., Harwood, D., Davis, L.: W4: Real-Time Surveillance of People and Their Activities. IEEE Transactions on Pattern Analysis and Machine Intelligence 22(8) (2000)
8. Lukowicz, P., Ward, J., Junker, H., Stäger, M., Tröster, G., Atrash, A., Starner, T.: Recognizing Workshop Activity Using Body Worn Microphones and Accelerometers. In: Ferscha, A., Mattern, F. (eds.) PERVASIVE 2004. LNCS, vol. 3001, pp. 18–32. Springer, Heidelberg (2004)
9. Lester, J., Choudhury, T., Kern, N., Borriello, G., Hannaford, B.: A Hybrid Discriminative/Generative Approach for Modeling Human Activities. 19th International Joint Conference on Artificial Intelligence (2005)
10. Philipose, M., Fishkin, K., Perkowitz, M., Patterson, D., Fox, D., Kautz, H., Hähnel, D.: Inferring Activities from Interactions with Objects. IEEE Pervasive Computing, 50–57 (2004)
11. Patterson, D., Fox, D., Kautz, H., Philipose, M.: Fine-Grained Activity Recognition by Aggregating Abstract Object Usage. In: Ninth IEEE International Symposium on Wearable Computers (2005)
12. Suchman, L.: Plans and situated actions: the problem of human machine interaction. Cambridge University Press, Cambridge (1987)
13. Janlert, L.-E.: Putting Pictures in Context. In: Proceedings of AVI2006, pp. 463–466. ACM Press, New York (2006)
14. Tapia, E., Intille, S., Larson, K.: Activity Recognition in the Home Using Simple and Ubiquitous Sensors. In: Ferscha, A., Mattern, F. (eds.) PERVASIVE 2004. LNCS, vol. 3001, pp. 158–175. Springer, Heidelberg (2004)
15. Pederson, T.: From Conceptual Links to Causal Relations — Physical-Virtual Artefacts in Mixed-Reality Space. PhD thesis, Dept. of Computing Science, Umeå university, report UMINF-03.14 (2003) ISBN 91-7305-556-5
16. Pederson, T.: Magic Touch: A Simple Object Location Tracking System Enabling the Development of Physical-Virtual Artefacts in Office Environments. Journal of Personal and Ubiquitous Computing 5, 54–57 (2001)
17. Backman, A.: Colosseum3D – Authoring Framework for Virtual Environments. In: Proceedings of EUROGRAPHICS Workshop IPT & EGVE Workshop, pp. 225–226 (2005)
18. Fritzke, B.: A growing neural gas network learns topologies. In: Tesauro, G., Touretzky, D.S., Leen, T.K. (eds.) Advances in Neural Information Processing Systems 7, pp. 625–632. MIT Press, Cambridge, MA (1995)
19. Rabiner, L.: A Tutorial on Hidden Markov Models and Selected Applications in Speech Recognition. Proceedings of the IEEE 77(2) (1989)
20. AMPS. (2nd January, 2007) http://www.ampsintl.com/
21. Finkenzeller, K.: RFID Handbook, 2nd edn. John Wiley and Sons, New York, USA (2003)

A Novel Price Prediction Scheme of Grid Resources Based on Time Series Analysis*

Yu Hua and Dan Feng

School of Computer Science and Technology
Huazhong University of Science and Technology, Wuhan, China
csyhua@hust.edu.cn

Abstract. Grid computing generally allows heterogeneous resources to achieve resources sharing and service-oriented scheduling. Grid economy-based management has been viewed as a feasible approach to carrying out fair, efficient and reliable scheduling. One key issue in grid economy-based strategy is to contain accurate and predictable prices of heterogeneous resources. In this paper, we present a novel price prediction scheme of grid resources for achieving accurate prices for resource management in the context of grid economy. Our proposed scheme utilizes Time Series Analysis (TSA) tool to predict and generate resources prices. We examine the practical performance by presenting simulation-based results, which demonstrate that proposed scheme is feasible and efficient in the grid economy.

1 Introduction

Grid computing aims to efficiently manage and utilize distributed and heterogeneous resources to achieve resources sharing and cooperation. Grid economy, one of main proposed schemes, has displayed its significant advantages in terms of grid resource management. However, one key issue is to accurately determine the future resource price based on the precious and current actual prices. Resource prices potentially have dependency within different time stages and the trends of price increments and decrements can efficiently indicate future prices with the aid of time series analysis (TSA) tool.

1.1 Grid Economy

Grid economy utilizes the strategy and approaches based on market economy to manage heterogeneous grid resources and carry out resources sharing and efficient scheduling. Since grid resources significantly show their distributed and dynamic characteristics, the economy-based schemes can efficiently be applied into related

* This work was supported by National Basic Research 973 Program under Grant No. 2004CB318201, New Century Excellent Talents Program of Ministry of Education under Grant.NCET-04-0693 and Scientific Program of Wuhan City under Grant.20061002031 and 200750730307.

J. Indulska et al. (Eds.): UIC 2007, LNCS 4611, pp. 258–266, 2007.

problems, such as resource management, tasks allocation and adaptable scheduling, accompanied with cost and deadline limitations to achieve time and cost optimization [1, 12, 13].

Resource prices are tightly associated with the actual performance of resource allocation and task scheduling in the context of grid economy, utilizing different prices of grid resources and auction models [6]. Existing frameworks and implementations in [1, 4, 5, 8] have presented and designed the basic components and constructed general platform for developing new emerging strategies and algorithms. General economy-driven resource management system, with related frameworks, components and function of grid resource broker, algorithms for optimizing the time and cost constraints of economical elements, can provide the agent-based architecture to combine many middleware, tools and software components to carry out heterogeneous resource management.

1.2 Grid Resource Price

Grid computing system needs to allocate and schedule all kinds of heterogeneous resources based on their available attributes, which usually are described as different time intervals. Since there are cost and time constraints in grid economy, we need to utilize the rule of maximized return and minimized risks to manage heterogeneous resources, especially for critical resources. Meanwhile, one selection process in the context of grid economy is potentially similar to portfolio optimization in real market environments, which may use the asset-liability models in the classical economy theory [13]. One fundamental problem is to carry out optimal schedule strategies to satisfy system-based performance model and concrete application requirements.

Resource price displays the attributes of grid resources and can be utilized comprehensively to represent the availability and capacity of grid resources. Grid resource price has become an important index to describe economical activities and provide one consistent label, describing the capacities, cost and risks of heterogeneous grid resources.

1.3 Portfolio Optimization

Portfolio optimization is one basic context of applying resource price in grid economy. We simply present some basic conception and ideas of portfolio optimization in economical fields.

One market is generally a decentralized and dynamic self-organized system, in which there are many price-based transactions for competitive resources [7]. The problem of portfolio optimization in a market environment aims to provide one efficient solution to allocate existing wealth among various expenditures and investment opportunities over time, typically representing the investor's expected lifetime, to maximize the achievements.

Markowitz's mean-variance (M-V) portfolio selection model [3] in a single period is a classical model, which aims to maximize the final wealth with the mean time to minimize the risk. The risk was represented as the variance to enable investors to seek highest return with the acceptable risk level. Some further literature display the improvements on the classical model and take into accounts new emerging economical models and data [5, 6].

The classical portfolio model is:

$$Max\ (1-w)\times \sum_{i=1}^{n} R_i x_i - w\times \sum_{i=1}^{n}\sum_{j=1}^{n} \delta_{ij} x_i x_j \tag{1}$$

where n is the number of securities, x_i is the proportion of investment in security i, R_i is the expected returns in security i, δ_{ij} is the co-variance of expected returns between security i and j, w is used to describe the aversion degree to risks, $0 \le w \le 1$. When $w=1$, the investor is conservative extremely and he only focuses on the risk, not the returns. On the contrary, when $w=0$, the investor pursues the returns regardless of the risks.

1.4 Grid Resource-Based Model

We present basic grid resource-based model to exhibit the following resource prediction scheme using time series analysis. Generally, resource ability can vary with time series, represented as a random variable. The return and risk are respectively the mean of resource abilities and covariance between them. Concretely speaking, the return of resource i at time t is $E(r_{i,t})$ for resource i at time t. The covariance between resource i and j at time t can be presented as $\delta_{i,j,t}$. As the definition in classical economy [3], grid environments could be a market with friction. The transaction charge ratio is defined in each unit at time t for resource i, $k_{i,t}$. At the same time, adjustment and re-scheduling are assumed to happen at time $t+1$. Furthermore, we assume that the transaction cost at time $t+1$ is function of V type (i.e., it is the difference between known portfolio at time t and new one at time $t+1$). Then, transaction Cost for resource i at time $t+1$ may be $k_{i,t+1}\left|x_{i,t+1}-x_{i,t}\right|$. The total transaction cost at time $t+1$ is $\sum_{i=1}^{n} k_{i,t+1}\left|x_{i,t+1}-x_{i,t}\right|$. Therefore, the portfolio model in grid economy can be described as:

$$(1-w)\times\left[\sum_{i=1}^{n} E(r_{i,t})x_{i,t} - \sum_{i=1}^{n} k_{i,t+1}\left|x_{i,t+1}-x_{i,t}\right|\right] - w\times\sum_{i=1}^{n}\sum_{j=1}^{n}\delta_{i,j,t}x_{i,t}x_{j,t} \tag{2}$$

1.5 Roadmap

In this paper, we present efficient price prediction method for grid resources by utilizing time series analysis tool. In section 2, we present the resource prediction scheme based on time series analysis tool and furthermore, in section 3, we examine our proposed scheme by utilizing the simulation-based performance evaluation. Section 4, we conclude our paper.

2 Price Prediction Based on Time Series Analysis

In this section, we present the price prediction scheme based on time series analysis tool and associated theoretical analysis.

2.1 Time Series Analysis Approach

Price prediction aims to provide accurate and efficient price information of resources to allow efficient resource management. Its function is pivotal to achieve reliable decision support. Here, we can utilize the prediction methods of time series analysis, [9], [10] and [11], to carry out price prediction of grid resources in the context of grid economy.

The time series $\{x_t\}$ with historical data $x_t, x_{t-1}, \cdots, x_{t-n}$ can be used to predict the price values in $t+\tau$ $(\tau \in N)$. $\hat{x}_t(\tau)$ is the predicted value after τ steps. The difference between predicted and real values $x_{t+\tau}$ can be $\tilde{x}_{t+\tau} = x_{t+\tau} - \hat{x}_t(\tau)$. Furthermore, the feasible methods can allow the difference value to get smaller. Based on the attributes of the random variables, $x_{t+\tau}$ and $\hat{x}_t(\tau)$, the criterion of Expected Values can be used to evaluate the performance, i.e., $\min_{\hat{x}_{t+\tau}} E\{x_{t+\tau} - \hat{x}_t(\tau)\}^2$ and $\hat{x}_t(\tau) = E(x_{t+\tau} | x_t, x_{t-1}, \cdots, x_{t-n})$.

Thus, the linear space based on series $\{x_t\}$ and $\{z_t\}$ may be :

$$\varsigma_t = \left\{ \sum_{j=0}^{\infty} b_j x_{t-j}, \sum_{j=0}^{\infty} |b_j| < \infty \right\} \text{ and } \zeta_t = \left\{ \sum_{j=0}^{\infty} a_j z_{-j}, \sum_{j=0}^{\infty} |a_j| < \infty \right\} \tag{3}$$

2.2 Time-Based Predication

According to the definitions above, we further have:

$$x_t = b_1 x_{t-1} + \cdots + b_p x_{t-p} + z_t - a_1 z_{t-1} - \cdots - a_q z_{t-q} \tag{4}$$

$$\hat{x}_t(\tau) = \hat{E}\left(\sum_{j=1}^{p} b_j x_{t+\tau-j} | \varsigma_t \right) + \hat{E}(z_{t+\tau} | \zeta_t) - \hat{E}\left(\sum_{j=1}^{q} a_j z_{t+\tau-j} | \varsigma_t \right) \tag{5}$$

Based on the projection rule, we can achieve the following results:

When $\tau > 0$, we have

$$\begin{gathered} \hat{E}(x_{t+\tau} | \varsigma_t) = \hat{E}(x_{t+\tau} | \zeta_t) = \hat{x}_t(\tau) \\ \hat{E}(z_{t+\tau} | \varsigma_t) = \hat{E}(z_{t+\tau} | \zeta_t) = 0 \end{gathered} \tag{6}$$

Input: Data series: $\{x_t, x_{t-1}, \cdots x_{t-p+1}\}$ with p historical data; τ value for the prediction steps;

Output: The prediction values $\hat{x}_t(\tau)$ for the prices of grid resources;

Algorithm Description:

Create the array to temporarily store historical data: $price_t = \{x_t, x_{t-1}, \cdots x_{t-p+1}\}$;

While ($0 < t \leq T$) do

Switch τ

Case $\{\tau\} < \{p, q\}$; RP_1;

Case $\{\tau\} > \{p, q\}$: RP_2;

Case $p < \tau < q : RP_3$;

Case $q < \tau < p : RP_4$;

Default: send error message;

Compute confidential interval;

Send the values, $\hat{x}_t(\tau)$, and confidential interval to the requestor;

$t := t + 1$

Collect the new price information and update the vector $price_t$;

End While.

Fig. 1. Price prediction algorithm using TSA

When $\tau \leq 0$, we have

$$\begin{aligned} \hat{E}(x_{t+\tau}|\varsigma_t) &= \hat{E}(x_{t+\tau}|\zeta_t) = x_{t+\tau} \\ \hat{E}(z_{t+\tau}|\varsigma_t) &= \hat{E}(z_{t+\tau}|\zeta_t) = z_{t+\tau} \end{aligned} \tag{7}$$

When $0 < \tau \le p$, we have

$$\hat{x}_t(\tau)=b_1\hat{x}_t(\tau-1)+b_2\hat{x}_t(\tau-2)+\cdots+b_{\tau-1}\hat{x}_t(1)+b_\tau x_t+\cdots+b_p x_{t+\tau-p} \tag{8}$$

When $\tau > p$, we have

$$\hat{x}_t(\tau)=b_1\hat{x}_t(\tau-1)+b_2\hat{x}_t(\tau-2)+\cdots+b_p\hat{x}_t(\tau-p) \tag{9}$$

2.3 Predicted Resource Price

Thus, we can further conjecture the predicted prices of grid resources according to different conditions. The following procedure shows the time-series-based algorithm to efficiently and accurately predict grid resources prices. We define that the price vector is $\{price_t, t=1,2,\cdots\}$ and set $price_t > 0$ to explicitly represent the prediction process.

We show some description to simplify the descriptions of price prediction based on TSA by representing

$$RP_1=\sum_{j=1}^{\tau-1} b_j\hat{x}_t(\tau-j)+\sum_{j=\tau}^{p} b_\tau x_{t+\tau-j}-\sum_{j=\tau}^{q} a_j z_{t+\tau-j}$$

$$RP_2=\sum_{j=1}^{p} b_j\hat{x}_t(\tau-j)$$

$$RP_3=\sum_{j=1}^{p} b_j\hat{x}_t(\tau-j)-\sum_{j=\tau}^{q} a_j z_{t+\tau-j}$$

$$RP_4=\sum_{j=1}^{\tau-1} b_j\hat{x}_t(\tau-j)+\sum_{j=\tau}^{p} b_\tau x_{t+\tau-j}$$

3 Performance Evaluations

In this section, we present the simulation-based performance evaluation to examine our proposed grid resource price prediction scheme using time series analysis tool.

3.1 Preliminary

In order to verify the methods and price prediction algorithm, we conduct the comparisons between the cubic interpolation and time-series-based prediction approaches. We generate the initial values by utilizing the integration of different data that are associated with the Normal Distribution. The basic value of resource price is 25 and the whole process can last for 15 time units. In addition, we define $p = 2$ and $q = 2$.

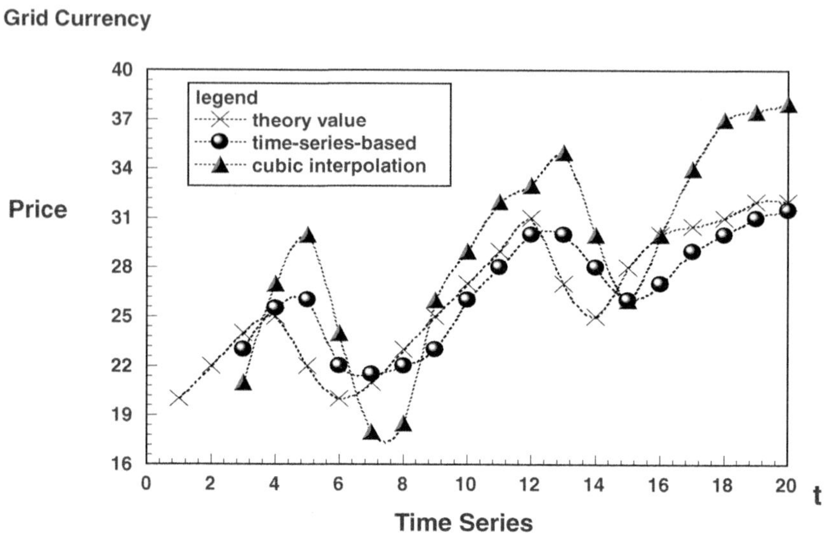

Fig. 2. The performance analysis of resource price ($\tau = 1$)

We represent $S(x)$ as the function of the cubic interpolation and further the quadratic derivative of $S(x)$ is the value of $M_i = S''(x_i)$. Therefore, $S_i(x)$ can be expressed as:

$$S_i(x) = M_{i-1}\frac{(x_i - x)^3}{6h_i} + M_i\frac{(x - x_{i-1})^3}{6h_i} + \left(y_{i-1} - \frac{M_{i-1}}{6}h_i^2\right)\frac{x_i - x}{h_i} + \left(y_i - \frac{M_i}{6}h_i^2\right)\frac{x - x_{i-1}}{h_i}$$

3.2 Results Analysis

The whole process is carried out under $\tau = 1$ and $\tau = 3$ conditions. The corresponding results can be presented in Fig.2.

When $\tau = 1$ and $p = 2$, the prediction process starts at $t = 3$ and the theory values display the added curves with fluctuation. The interval from $t = 4$ to $t = 8$ further presents the price trends of the whole process. At $t = 6$, the price vector can achieve the smallest value. The time-series-based methods can control the average error around 4.6% less than 18.7% of the cubic interpolation.

In another interval from $t = 12$ to $t = 16$, the average errors of time-series-based methods and the cubic interpolation are 3.5% and 24.3, respectively. Obviously, the time-series-based methods are more accurate.

Fig.3 exhibits the prediction accuracy when $\tau = 1$ and $p = 2$. The prediction process begins from $t = 2$ and shows the prices after $\tau = 3$. It has been seen that the overall prediction accuracy of time-series-based and cubic interpolation methods is decreased due to the larger value of τ. However, the average errors are 21.4% and 34.7% respectively for time-series-based methods and the cubic interpolation between $t = 4$ and $t = 8$.

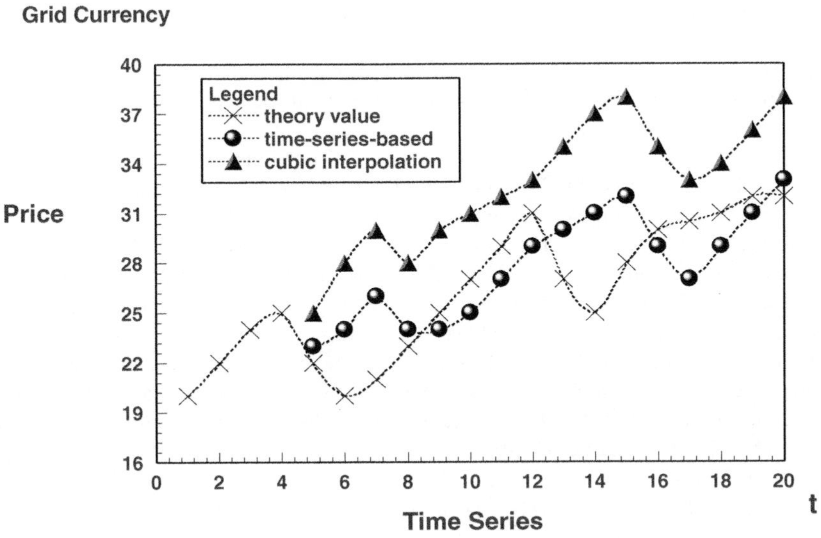

Fig. 3. The performance analysis of resource price($\tau = 3$)

At the same time, the smooth process from $t = 9$ to $t = 11$ shows 10.7% and 14.9% respectively for the time-series-based methods and the cubic interpolation. We can conclude that the time-series-based methods are more feasible and accurate than cubic interpolation.

4 Conclusions

Price prediction for grid resources is one key problem to efficiently manage heterogeneous and distributed resources in the context of grid economy. In this paper, we present efficient price prediction scheme of grid resources based on time series analysis. We introduce the definitions, models and existing solution to solve the portfolio optimization and implement resource management using price prediction approach. Grid economy exists in a dynamic and distributed environment, in which price prediction of grid resources allows to be pivotal to carry out the optimal selection and allocation of resources. We demonstrate the efficiency of time-series-based scheme through theoretical analysis and simulation results. The time-series-based scheme for price prediction can be efficiently applied to achieve resource management and task scheduling in the grid economy.

References

1. Buyya, R., Abramson, D., Venugopal, S.: The Grid Economy (Special Issue on Grid Computing). Proceedings of the IEEE 93(3), 698–714 (2005)
2. Michael, Z.S., Warren, B.P.: The Dynamic Assignment Problem. Transportation Science 38(4), 399–419 (2004)

3. Markowitz, H.M.: Portfolio Selection Efficient Diversification of Investment. Wiley, New York (1959)
4. Chris, K., Giorgos, C.: Architecture Requirements for Commercializing Grid Resources. In: Proceedings of the 11th IEEE International Symposium on High Performance Distributed Computing, pp. 215–224 (2002)
5. Buyya, R., Abramson, D., Giddy, J.: A case for economy grid architecture for service-oriented grid computing. In: The 10th IEEE International Heterogeneous Computing Workshop, IEEE Computer Society Press, Los Alamitos (2001)
6. Wellman, M.P., Walsh, W.E., Wurman, P.R., MacKie-Mason, J.K.: Auction Protocols for Decentralized Scheduling. Games and Economic Behavior 35, 271–303 (2001)
7. Simaan, Y.: Estimation risk in portfolio selection The mean variance model versus the mean absolute deviation model. Management Science 43(10), 1437–1446 (1997)
8. Kenyon, C., Cheliotis, G.: Grid Resource Commercialization Economic Engineering and Delivery Scenarios. In: Grid resource management: state of the art and future trends table of contents, pp. 465–478. Kluwer Academic Publishers, Norwell, MA, USA (2004)
9. Durbin, J.J.: Time Series Analysis by State Space Methods. Oxford University Press, Oxford (2001)
10. Shumway, R.H., Stoffer, D.S.: Time Series Analysis and Its Applications. Springer, Heidelberg (2000)
11. Box, G.E.P., Jenkins, G.: Time Series Analysis, Forecasting and Control. Holden-Day, Incorporated (1990)
12. Yu, H., Dan, F., Chanle, W.: Scalable Resources Portfolio Selection with Fairness based on Economical Methods. In: Ma, J., Jin, H., Yang, L.T., Tsai, J.J.-P. (eds.) UIC 2006. LNCS, vol. 4159, pp. 1019–1027. Springer, Heidelberg (2006)
13. Yu, H., Chanle, W.: Dynamic Multi-Stage Resource Selection with Preference Factors in Grid Economy. In: Zhuge, H., Fox, G.C. (eds.) GCC 2005. LNCS, vol. 3795, pp. 668–677. Springer, Heidelberg (2005)
14. Kantz, H., Schreiber, T.: Nonlinear Time Series Analysis. Cambridge University Press, Cambridge (2004)
15. Brillinger, D.R.: Time series data analysis and theory. Society for Industrial and Applied Mathematics Philadelphia, PA, USA (2001)
16. Reinsel, G.C.: Elements of Multivariate Time Series Analysis. Springer, Heidelberg (2003)
17. Hanssens, D.M., Parsons, L.J.: Market Response Models Econometric and Time Series Analysis. Springer, Heidelberg (2001)
18. Yu, J., Venugopal, S., Buyya, R.: A Market-Oriented Grid Directory Service for Publication and Discovery of Grid Service Providers and their Services. The Journal of Supercomputing 36(1), 17–31 (2006)

Adaptive Multicast Trees on Static Ad Hoc Networks: Tradeoffs Between Delay and Energy Consumption

Sangman Moh

School of Computer Eng., Chosun University
375 Seoseok-dong, Dong-gu, Gwangju 501-759, South Korea
smmoh@chosun.ac.kr

Abstract. This paper proposes *adaptive multicast trees* (*AMTs*) on static ad hoc networks. The proposed function *f*: $(\alpha, \beta) \rightarrow \text{AMT}(\alpha, \beta)$ provides a wide range of tradeoffs between the most energy efficient AMT and the fastest AMT by adjusting two parameters α and β, where nonnegative integers α and β are correlated with each other such that if $\alpha > 0$ and $\beta > 0$, $\alpha\beta$ is α or β; otherwise, $\alpha + \beta = 1$. AMT(α, β) is a breadth-first spanning tree (BT) with $\min_{i\in[1,k]} E_i^{\alpha} T_i^{\beta}$ among k BTs for a multicast group with k members, where E_i and T_i are the normalized energy consumption and delay for a multicast in BT_i, respectively. The simulation study shows that AMT(0, 1) reveals about 60 percent shorter delay than AMT(1, 0) while AMT(1, 0) consumes up to 45 percent less energy than AMT(0, 1). Therefore, if delay is the most important factor, AMT(0, 1) should be the choice while AMT(1, 0) is most efficient when energy consumption is the primary concern. One of various AMTs can be appropriately chosen in accordance with the operation requirement.

1 Introduction

Recently, infrastructure-free *wireless ad hoc networks* [1, 2] attract a lot of attention with the advent of inexpensive wireless network solutions [3, 4]. Wireless ad hoc networks can be categorized into *mobile* and *static* networks according to whether nodes are mobile or not. *Static ad hoc networks* can be extensively employed in many *sensor networks* [5].

However, wireless ad hoc networks pose many challenging problems. With limited bandwidth and restricted battery capability, *delay* and *energy efficiency* may be the most important design criteria because the communication delay can be a bottleneck of collaborative tasks and the remaining energy determines the system lifetime. The (end-to-end) delay is a primary performance metric in many applications. On the other hand, the energy efficient network protocols are important since the energy consumption due to wireless communication may represent more than half of total system energy consumption [6]. As an extreme approach, minimum connected dominating set can be considered [7] to save energy, but it may result in impractically poor delay. As a result, the engineering tradeoff or optimization between delay and energy consumption is necessarily required in practical applications.

This paper exploits the tradeoff of delay and energy consumption in multicasting on static ad hoc networks. *Multicasting* has been extensively studied for wireless

J. Indulska et al. (Eds.): UIC 2007, LNCS 4611, pp. 267–275, 2007.

ad hoc networks [8, 9, 10, 11, 12]. A multicast packet is delivered to multiple receivers through a network structure such as *multicast tree* or *mesh*. In the static ad hoc networks, the link redundancy to ensure alternative paths against the mobility is not required any more. So, the *mesh-based multicast* protocols have no benefit of many redundant links but still consume much energy because of broadcast-style communication and overhearing [13]. That is, in the static ad hoc networks, *tree-based multicast* protocols are faster than mesh-based ones because they have much less overhead of broadcast redundancy. Furthermore, tree-based protocols are much more energy efficient. A wireless *network interface card* (*NIC*) typically accepts only two kinds of packets: unicast and broadcast packets. For unicast transmission along the multicast tree, only the designated receivers need to receive the transmitted data. Thus, a node in tree-based protocols can safely put itself into a *low-power sleep-mode* [14] to conserve energy if it is not a designated receiver.

In this paper, *adaptive multicast trees* (*AMTs*) on static ad hoc networks are proposed. The proposed function f: $(\alpha, \beta) \rightarrow \text{AMT}(\alpha, \beta)$ provides a wide range of tradeoffs between the most energy efficient AMT (*i.e.*, AMT(1, 0)) and the fastest AMT (*i.e.*, AMT(0, 1)) by adjusting two parameters α and β, where nonnegative integers α and β are correlated with each other such that if $\alpha > 0$ and $\beta > 0$, $\alpha\beta$ is α or β; otherwise, $\alpha + \beta = 1$. AMT(α, β) is a breadth-first spanning tree (BT) [1] with $\min_{i\in[1,k]} E_i^{\alpha} T_i^{\beta}$ among k BTs for a multicast group with k members, where E_i and T_i are the normalized energy consumption and delay for a multicast in BT_i, respectively. The proposed *AMT construction algorithm* makes every member of a multicast group construct the same multicast tree in a distributed manner and, thus, no dissemination of the multicast tree is necessary. The performance study shows that AMT(0, 1) reveals about 60 percent shorter delay than AMT(1, 0) while AMT(1, 0) consumes up to 45 percent less energy than AMT(0, 1). It is also shown that AMT(1, 1) is a performance tradeoff of AMT(0, 1) and AMT(1, 0). More sophisticated tradeoffs are possible by adjusting the two parameters α and β.

The rest of the paper is organized as follows: Tree-based multicast, power saving mechanism and energy model for static ad hoc networks are briefly described in Section 2. In Section 3, the function for tradeoffs is derived and the AMT construction algorithm is presented. The performance evaluation using simulation is discussed in Section 4. Finally, the conclusions are covered in Section 5.

2 Preliminaries

This section briefly describes the fundamental overview of tree-based multicast, power saving mechanism, and basic energy model for static ad hoc networks.

2.1 Tree-Based Multicast

As presented in Introduction, in the static ad hoc networks, the tree-based multicast protocols are preferable compared to mesh-based ones. The tree-based multicast

---

[1] A depth-first spanning tree on the other hand is not taken into consideration because it requires more number of transmissions resulting in longer delay and more energy consumption.

protocols basically construct a tree structure to deliver multicast messages. In the mobile ad hoc networks, a common approach to maintain the tree structure is for multicast group members to periodically exchange control packets (*e.g.*, join messages [8]) to refresh the structure. In the static ad hoc networks, however, every member node can determine a multicast tree at the group creation time and agree on the same multicast tree for the same root node since there is no node mobility and the network topology does not change. Note here that any node failure during network operation is not taken into account throughout the paper.

Tree-based multicast can be further classified as either *per-source tree multicast* or *shared tree multicast* [15]. In the per-source tree approach, each source has to construct a separate multicast tree rooted at itself. Therefore, there will be as many trees as the number of sources and a significant amount of control overhead is required to maintain them. On the other hand, shared tree multicast has lower control overhead because it maintains only a single tree shared by all sources [16]. A multicast packet is (unicast) delivered to the root node first and then (multicast) delivered to all group members along the tree structure. However, the path is not necessarily optimal, and the root node is easily overloaded due to the sharing of the single tree. The proposed AMTs are based on the shared tree structure.

2.2 Power Saving Mechanism and Energy Model

Recent wireless LAN specifications usually provide power saving mechanisms for energy-constrained applications. For example, Bluetooth network interface operates in time-division multiplexing (TDM), where a master node controls up to seven neighboring slaves. Each slave node has a designated time slot for communication and can sleep in other time slots to conserve energy [17]. In IEEE 802.11 standard, a master node, or called an *access point (AP)*, periodically sends a beacon packet followed by *TIM (Traffic Indication Map)* that indicates the desired receivers. Each slave wakes up when beacons are sent and checks whether it is the intended receiver. If it is not, it sleeps again; otherwise, it stays awake to receive data [4].

IEEE 802.11 ad hoc power saving mechanism operates in a similar fashion but without APs. Any node requiring communication sends beacons to synchronize with nodes in its vicinity. A beacon period starts with *ATIM (ad hoc TIM)*, during which all nodes listen, and the pending traffic is advertised. Each node turns itself on or off depending on the advertised traffic [4]. Unlike the AP-based mechanism, packets are buffered at the sender and are directly transmitted to the receiver. This power saving mechanism reduces the available channel capacity because useful traffic cannot be transmitted during the ATIM window. It also suffers from longer packet delay because each intermediate node needs to buffer the packet until the next beacon period.

The abovementioned power saving mechanisms favor unicast over broadcast communication. For unicast, all other neighbors do not need to wake up and thus can save energy. However, if a sender has more than one receiver, it must resort to broadcast that results in many unnecessary receptions as well as wasted energy.

Let the total energy consumption per unit multicast packet be denoted as E, which includes the transmission energy (E_{TX}) as well as the energy required to receive the transmission (E_{RX}). This paper only considers data packets for simplicity. According to the *first-order radio model* [18], $E = E_{TX} + E_{RX} = N_{TX} \cdot e_{TX} + N_{RX} \cdot e_{RX}$, where N_{TX} and N_{RX} are the number of transmissions and the number of receives, respectively, and

e_{TX} and e_{RX} are the energy consumed to transmit and receive a unit multicast message via a wireless link, respectively[2].

Let Γ_+, Γ_1, and Γ_0 be the set of tree nodes with more than one receiver, with exactly one receiver, and with no receiver, respectively. Thus, the set of all tree nodes is $\Gamma = \Gamma_+ + \Gamma_1 + \Gamma_0$. It is straightforward to show that, in a multicast tree, N_{TX} is the number of tree nodes except the leaf receiver nodes (*i.e.*, root and intermediate nodes) and N_{RX} is $\sum_{i \in \Gamma_+} f_i + |\Gamma_1|$, where f_i is the number of neighbors of node *i*.

3 Adaptive Multicast Trees

This section presents the proposed *adaptive multicast trees* (*AMTs*) for static ad hoc networks as tradeoffs between delay and energy consumption. The function for tradeoffs is presented first and the *AMT construction algorithm* is then discussed with examples.

3.1 Function for Tradeoffs

Given a multicast group with *k* members, *k* breadth-first spanning trees (BTs) can be generated rooted at every member node in a distributed manner and labeled as BT_1, BT_2, ..., BT_k. For providing tradeoffs between the most energy efficient tree and the fastest tree, given tradeoff parameters α and β, a *adaptive multicast tree* (*AMT*) called AMT(α, β) is defined as follows:

Definition 1. The AMT(α, β) is a BT with $\min_{i \in [1,k]} E_i^{\alpha} T_i^{\beta}$ among *k* BTs for a multicast group with *k* members, where E_i and T_i are the normalized energy consumption and delay for a multicast in BT_i, respectively, and nonnegative integers α and β are correlated with each other such that if $\alpha > 0$ and $\beta > 0$, $\alpha\beta$ is α or β; otherwise, $\alpha + \beta = 1$.

The following Theorem 1 with proof shows that *f*: (α, β) → AMT(α, β) is a function providing tradeoffs between the most energy efficient AMT and the fastest AMT.

Theorem 1. *f*: (α, β) → AMT(α, β) is a function providing tradeoffs between the most energy efficient AMT (*i.e.*, AMT(1, 0)) and the fastest AMT (*i.e.*, AMT(0, 1)), where nonnegative integers α and β are correlated with each other such that if $\alpha > 0$ and $\beta > 0$, $\alpha\beta$ is α or β; otherwise, $\alpha + \beta = 1$.

Proof. According to the correlation between two tradeoff parameters α and β shown in Table 1, the most energy efficient AMT, AMT(1, 0), does not consider delay but energy consumption while the fastest AMT, AMT(0, 1), does vice versa. On the other hand, AMT(1, 1) considers both energy consumption and delay equally and, thus, it is a tradeoff between AMT(1, 0) and AMT(0, 1). If $\alpha \geq 2$, then $\beta = 1$ by Definition 1

[2] In reality, e_{TX} and e_{RX} are slightly different. For example, e_{TX} = 300mA and e_{RX} = 250mA for WaveLAN-II from Lucent [3].

and possible AMTs are AMT(2, 1), AMT(3, 1), …, which pay more attention to energy consumption with larger α and are tradeoffs between AMT(1, 1) and the most energy efficient AMT, AMT(1, 0). On the contrary, if $\beta \geq 2$, then $\alpha = 1$ by Definition 1 and possible AMTs are AMT(1, 2), AMT(1, 3), …, which pay more attention to delay with larger β and are tradeoffs between AMT(1, 1) and the fastest AMT, AMT(0, 1). Therefore, f: $(\alpha, \beta) \rightarrow$ AMT(α, β) is a function providing tradeoffs between AMT(1, 0) and AMT(0, 1). **Q.E.D.**

3.2 Tree Construction Algorithm

Given the parameters α and β defined by Definition 1, the primary goal of our study is to construct an adaptive multicast tree, AMT(α, β), with $\min_{i \in [1,k]} E_i^{\alpha} T_i^{\beta}$ among k BTs for a multicast group with k members in a static ad hoc network. A static ad hoc network can be represented with a graph $G = (V, E)$ in which each vertex in $V(G)$ is a node and each edge in $E(G)$ is a wireless link between nodes. Under the assumption that all the nodes have the same capability such as transmission power and bandwidth over the network, multicast delay and energy consumption can be normalized by the height of the multicast tree and the value of $N_{TX} \cdot e_{TX} + N_{RX} \cdot e_{RX}$ for a multicast, respectively, without other traffic congestion. Given a multicast group with k members, k BTs can be constructed at every member node in a distributed manner. Of them, a tree with $\min_{i \in [1,k]} E_i^{\alpha} T_i^{\beta}$ is selected as the multicast tree.

Fig. 1 shows the AMT construction algorithm. The proposed algorithm makes every member node of a multicast group construct the same multicast tree in a distributed manner and, thus, no dissemination of the multicast tree is necessary. Note here that every member node runs the algorithm at the group creation time and agrees on the same multicast tree for the same root node. The tradeoff parameters α and β can be appropriately chosen in accordance with the operation requirement. For example, when delay is more important than energy consumption, $\alpha = 0$ and $\beta = 1$ can be employed. On the other hand, if energy performance is a critical factor, $\alpha = 1$ and $\beta = 0$ can be used. As a tradeoff between delay and energy consumption, $\alpha = 1$ and $\beta = 1$ can be taken into consideration when both delay and energy consumption are

Algorithm 1. Construct_AMT(G, M, α, β)
1. Let $G = (V, E)$ be a static ad hoc network represented as a graph of node set $V(G)$ a nd link set $E(G)$, $M = \{m_0, m_1, \ldots, m_{k-1}\}$ be the set of k member nodes, and α and β be tradeoff parameter constrained by Definition 1.
2. Generate k BTs (*i.e.*, BT_1, BT_2, …, BT_k) rooted at every member node.
3. Select a BT with $\min_{i \in [1,k]} E_i^{\alpha} T_i^{\beta}$ (*i.e.*, AMT(α, β)), where E_i and T_i are the normal ized energy consumption ($N_{TX} \cdot e_{TX} + N_{RX} \cdot e_{RX}$) and delay (tree height) for a multic ast in BT_i, respectively, and nonnegative integers α and β are correlated with each other such that if $\alpha > 0$ and $\beta > 0$, $\alpha\beta$ is α or β; otherwise, $\alpha + \beta = 1$.
4. In case of tie, select the BT with the root node of the lowest identifier.

Fig. 1. The AMT construction algorithm

equally important. Note that more sophisticated tradeoffs are possible by adjusting the two parameters α and β appropriately.

4 Performance Evaluation

In this section, the performance of the proposed AMT(α, β) is evaluated and compared. The network environment, communication model, multicast traffic model, and simulation parameters are described first, and then simulation results are discussed in Section 4.2.

4.1 Simulation Environment

Our performance study simulates and compares the proposed AMT(α, β) in terms of *average multicast delay* (*i.e.*, average end-to-end delay for multicast packets) and *total energy consumption*.

Our simulation is based on the simulation of static nodes spread over a square area of 1200×1200 m^2 for 15 minutes of simulation time. The radio transmission range is assumed to be 250 *m* and a free space propagation channel is assumed with a data rate of 2 Mbps. Note that omni-directional antennas and symmetric radio links are assumed in conjunction with the same transmission power. That is, all the nodes have the same capability over the network. Note here that, given network area A and radio transmission range R, the radio coverage C is $\pi R^2/A$ and the average node connectivity[3] γ is given by $nC = \pi n R^2/A$, where n is the total number of nodes. For example, if $n = 20$ and $R = 250$ meters in the above network environment, $\gamma = \pi \times 20 \times 250^2/1200^2 = 2.7$.

In our simulation, a constant bit rate (CBR) source and its multiple destinations are randomly selected among the nodes. A CBR source sends a 512-byte multicast packet every 100 *msec* during the simulation. For simplicity, we assume a multicast message consists of one data packet. The hop propagation delay including node processing time is assumed to be 2 *msec* on average in the condition where no congestion is encountered. Packet queueing delay is added as well.

For measuring the two performance metrics of average multicast delay and total energy consumption, two simulation factors of *average node connectivity* and *group size* (*i.e.*, the number of member nodes in a multicast group) are varied in a meaningful range; *i.e.*, the average node connectivity from 5.5 (40 nodes) to 27.3 (200 nodes) and the group size from 20 to 200 are applied. The default values for the group size and the total number of nodes are 20 and 200, respectively.

4.2 Simulation Results and Discussion

The following four graphs show the performance impact of the proposed algorithm on the node connectivity and the group size of multicast. Comparative discussion based on the simulation results is given in this subsection.

---

[3] Node density, defined as the number of nodes per unit area, does not indicate the connectivity between wireless nodes. Node connectivity is a relative measure of the node density compared to the radio transmission range of underlying wireless network interface; *i.e.*, it is the number of neighboring nodes a node can communicate.

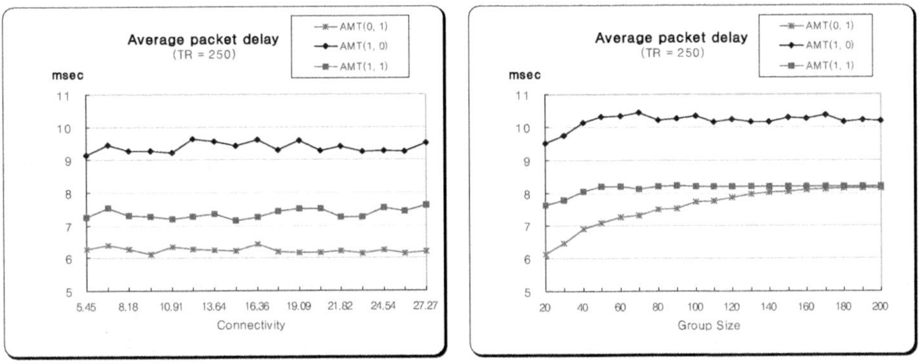

(a) Varying node connectivity (b) Varying group size

Fig. 2. Average multicast delay

Fig. 2 shows *average multicast delay* for various node connectivity and group size. Note that the multicast delay is end-to-end delay for multicast packets. Varying node connectivity, AMT(0, 1) reveals about 60 percent shorter delay than AMT(1, 0). AMT(1, 1) does about 25 percent longer delay than AMT(0, 1). The multicast delay is almost constant and out of influence on the increased node connectivity since the member nodes in a multicast group are randomly spread over the whole network. It is shown that AMT(1, 1) is a tradeoff of AMT(0, 1) and AMT(1, 0) in terms of multicast delay. Varying group size, the multicast delay is increased with relatively small groups but it is almost saturated with large groups. In addition, the multicast delay of AMT(1, 1) is almost the same as that of AMT(0, 1) after saturation in Fig. 2(b). This effect is mainly due to the fact that, for large groups, the number of BTs to be constructed is inherently limited and, as a result, AMT(1, 1) is similar to AMT(0, 1).

Fig. 3 shows the network-wide *total energy consumption* for different node connectivity and group size. AMT(1, 0) consumes up to 45 percent less energy than AMT(0, 1). It is also shown that AMT(1, 1) is also a tradeoff of AMT(0, 1) and

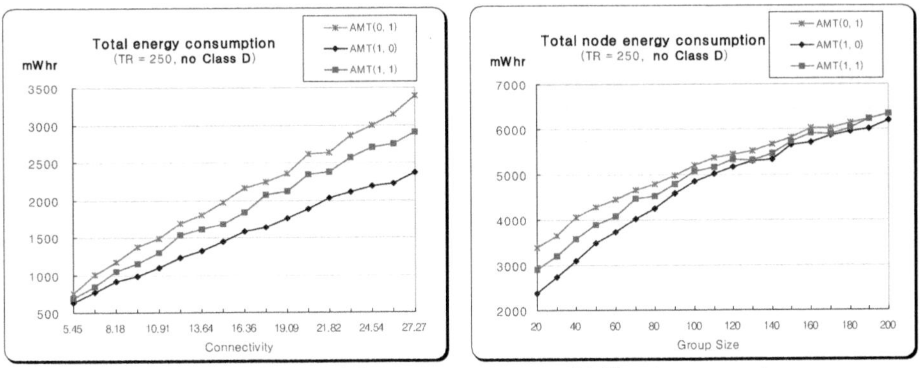

(a) Varying node connectivity (b) Varying group size

Fig. 3. Total energy consumption

AMT(1, 0) in terms of energy consumption. The total energy consumption is almost linearly proportional to group size as well as node connectivity since more nodes are involved directly or indirectly in a multicast. As group size increases, the energy difference of the three AMTs becomes smaller and smaller. This is due to the fact that more and more nodes are involved in multicast operation; *e.g.,* in an extreme case, all the nodes are the member nodes of a multicast group and little difference is shown as expected.

From the simulation results, it is easily inferred that the multicast tree can be constructed in accordance with what the primary concern of multicast operation is. That is, if the multicast delay is the most important factor, AMT(0, 1) should be the choice while AMT(1, 0) is most efficient when energy consumption is the primary concern. Since AMT(1, 1) is a performance tradeoff between AMT(0, 1) and AMT(1, 0), it is preferable when both multicast delay and energy consumption are moderately taken into consideration. Note that adjusting the two parameters α and β allows more sophisticated tradeoffs between AMT(0, 1) and AMT(1, 0).

5 Conclusions

In this paper, *adaptive multicast trees* (*AMTs*) on static ad hoc networks have been proposed as tradeoffs between delay and energy consumption. The proposed function f: $(\alpha, \beta) \rightarrow$ AMT(α, β) provides tradeoffs between the most energy efficient AMT and the fastest AMT by adjusting two parameters α and β. The AMT construction algorithm makes every member node of a multicast group construct the same multicast tree in a distributed manner and, thus, no dissemination of the multicast tree is necessary. According to the performance evaluation results, AMT(0, 1) reveals about 60 percent shorter delay than AMT(1, 0) while AMT(1, 0) consumes up to 45 percent less energy than AMT(0, 1). As a future work, we are investigating a network environment in which static and mobile nodes exist together and a multicast source may be either static or mobile.

References

1. Perkins, C.E.: Ad Hoc Networking. Addison-Wesley Pub. Co., Upper Saddle River, NJ (2001)
2. Siva Ram Murthy, C., Manoj, B.S.: Ad Hoc Wireless Networks. Prentice Hall, Upper Saddle River, NJ (2004)
3. Kamerman, A., Monteban, L.: WaveLAN-II: A High-Performance Wireless LAN for the Unlicensed Band. Bell Labs Technical Journal, pp. 118–133 (1997)
4. Woesner, H., Ebert, J., Schlager, M., Wolisz, A.: Power-Saving Mechanisms in Emerging Standards for Wireless LANs: The MAC Level Perspective. IEEE Personal Communications 5, 40–48 (1998)
5. Hac, A.: Wireless Sensor Network Designs. John Wiley & Sons, West Sussex, England (2003)
6. Kravets, R., Krishnan, P.: Power Management Techniques for Mobile Communication. In: Proc. of Int. Conf. on Mobile Computing and Networking (MobiCom), pp. 157–168 (1998)

7. Acharya, T., Roy, R.: Distributed Algorithm for Power Aware Minimum Connected Dominating Set for Routing in Wireless Ad Hoc Network. In: Proc. of ICPP 2005 Workshop on Wireless and Sensor Networks, pp. 387–394 (2005)
8. Lee, S.-J., Su, W., Hsu, J., Gerla, M., Bagrodia, R.: A Performance Comparison Study of Ad Hoc Wireless Multicast Protocols. In: Proc. of IEEE Infocom 2000, vol. 2, pp. 565–574 (2000)
9. Wang, B., Gupta, S.K.S.: On Maximizing Lifetime of Multicast Trees in Wireless Ad Hoc Networks. In: Proc. of 2003 Int. Conf. on Parallel Processing (ICPP) (2003)
10. Wei, W., Zakhor, A.: Connectivity for Multiple Multicast Trees Schemes in Ad Hoc Networks. In: Proc. of Int. Workshop on Wireless Ad Hoc Networks (IWWAN) (2004)
11. Wan, P.-J., Calinescu, G., Yi, C.-W.: Minimum-Power Multicast Routing in Static Ad Hoc Wireless Networks. IEEE/ACM Trans. on Networking 12, 507–514 (2004)
12. Floreen, P., Kaski, P., Kohonen, J., Orponen, P.: Lifetime Maximization for Multicasting in Energy-Constrained Wireless Networks. IEEE Journal on Selected Areas in Communications 23, 117–126 (2005)
13. Youn, H.Y., Yu, C., Lee, B., Moh, S.: Energy Efficient Multicast in Ad Hoc Networks. In: Ilyas, M. (ed.) The Handbook of Ad Hoc Wireless Networks, pp. 23.1–23.12. CRC Press, Boca Raton, Florida (2003)
14. IEEE Std 802.11-1999, Local and Metropolitan Area Network, Specific Requirements, Part 11: Wireless LAN Medium Access Control (MAC) and Physical Layer (PHY) Specifications (1999)
15. Xylomenos, G., Polyzos, G.C.: IP Multicast for Mobile Hosts. IEEE Communications Magazine, pp. 54–58 (1997)
16. Chiang, C.-C., Gerla, M., Zhang, L.: Adaptive Shared Tree Multicast in Mobile Wireless Networks. In: Proc. of IEEE Global Telecomm. Conf (GlobeCom), vol. 3, pp. 1817–1822 (1998)
17. Frodigh, M., Johansson, P., Larsson, P.: Wireless Ad Hoc Networking – The Art of Networking without a Network. Ericsson Review, pp. 248–263 (2000)
18. Heinzelman, W.R., Chandrakasan, A., Balakrishnan, H.: Energy-Efficient Communication Protocols for Wireless Microsensor Networks. In: Proc. of Hawaii Int. Conf. on System Sciences, pp. 3005–3014 (2000)

Reliable Multicast MAC Protocol for Wireless Ad Hoc Networks

Sung Won Kim[1] and Byung-Seo Kim[2]

[1] School of Electrical Engineering and Computer Science, Yeungnam University, Gyeongsangbuk-do, 712-749, Korea
ksw@ieee.org

[2] Motorola Inc., 1301 Algonquin Rd. Schaumburg, IL, 60196 USA
Byungseo.Kim@motorola.com

Abstract. Reliable multicast in wireless ad hoc networks is important for the applications such as distributed computing, chat, and whiteboard. Due to the wireless channel characteristics, obtaining the reliability in multicast packet transmission is a difficult and challenging task. Even though IEEE 802.11 is widely adopted medium access control (MAC) protocol in wireless ad hoc networks, it does not support reliable multicast. Thus, several MAC layer protocols have been proposed that can provide reliable multicast. In this paper, we propose the reliable multicast MAC protocol which is based on the orthogonal frequency division multiple access (OFDMA) systems. The proposed method reduces the overhead required for control packets. Analysis results validate the reliability and efficiency of our multicast MAC protocol.

1 Introduction

Multicast or broadcast in the medium access control (MAC) layer refers to the process of sending data packets to some or all of the neighbors of a node. Thus, broadcast can be seen as a special case of multicast. Multicast communications are necessary for delivering acceptable quality of service in many applications of wireless communications such as distributed computing, chat, whiteboard, emergency report, and video conference. Several higher layer protocols rely heavily on reliable and efficient MAC layer multicast.

When data has to be sent to multiple recipients, multicast incurs less network cost compared to unicast. Multicast limits the transmission of redundant data and saves the bandwidth as well as energy. However, most research on wireless ad hoc networks have focused on reliable unicast. Reliable multicast has been studied relatively little compared to reliable unicast. In the IEEE 802.11 specification [1], the multicast sender simply listens to the channel and then transmits its data packet when the channel becomes idle for a period of time. There is no MAC-level recovery on multicast packet. As a result, the reliability of multicast is reduced as the probability of packet loss resulting from interference or collisions increases.

J. Indulska et al. (Eds.): UIC 2007, LNCS 4611, pp. 276–284, 2007.

Recently, a few multicast MAC protocols have been proposed to enhance the reliability and the efficiency of the IEEE 802.11 multicast protocol. Reliable multicast at the MAC layer proposed for IEEE 802.11 in the literature can be categorized into two basic types : multiple ACKs and leader-based ACK. In the multiple ACKs scheme, the sender collects the information of multicast packet reception from all of the multicast group member nodes. However, multiple ACK transmissions degrade the channel efficiency and reduce the overall network performance. The degradation is exaggerated as the number of member nodes increases. On the other hand, leader-based ACK scheme reduces the overhead caused by multiple ACK packet transmissions by allowing only a leader to send an ACK. Thus, the overhead of a leader-based ACK scheme is just the same as that of the unicast. If a node other than the leader experiences a failure of a data packet reception, it transmits a negative ACK (NACK) to make a collision of ACK from the leader. By using the NACK, this scheme guarantees some degree of the reliability. However, when one of the member nodes fails to receive a data packet because of hidden node problems, it can not send a NACK packet since it can not recognize that the received packet is multicast and it is the destination of the packet. Since the node does not send a NACK, no collision of ACK is experienced at the sender. Therefore, leader-based ACK scheme may not be reliable in terms of the detection of the failed reception.

In this paper, we propose a reliable multicast MAC protocol. The proposed method adopts the RTS/CTS handshaking to mitigate the hidden node problem. To reduce the overhead caused by control packets, we introduce the Orthogonal Frequency Division Multiple Access (OFDMA) method. The remainder of this paper is organized as follows. The next section presents the related work. In Section 3, the proposed method is described. In Section 4, we investigate the enhancement of the proposed method with some numerical results. Finally, the paper is concluded in Section 5.

2 Related Work

The paper in [2] proposes Broadcast Medium Window (BMW). In BMW, a sender exchanges RTS, CTS, DATA, and ACK packets with one of the member nodes, and then RTS and ACK packets are exchanged with all of the member nodes. These RTS and ACK packets are transmitted through contention based channel access. As an enhanced version of BMW, Batch Mode Multicast MAC (BMMM) protocol is proposed in [3]. The transaction of BMMM between the sender and member nodes is a sequence of multiple RTS/CTS exchanges, data packet transmission, and multiple Request ACK (RAK)/ACK exchanges. During this sequence, there is no contention-based channel access. Therefore, compared to BMW, BMMM reduces the overhead due to multiple contention periods of the access channel for transmitting RTS/ACK. However, there is still overhead of multiple control packets of RTS, CTS, RAK, and ACK. This overhead increases as the number of nodes increases.

In [4], the authors propose Leader-Based Protocol (LBP) for multicast to reduce the overhead caused by multiple CTSs and ACKs. A sender in LBP selects one node among the multicast group member nodes, called a leader. Then, only the leader responses with a CTS and an ACK corresponding to the RTS and the data packet. If a member node fails to receive a data packet, it sends a NACK packet at the end of the data packet and this NACK causes a collision with the ACK from the leader. If there is a collision after the data packet transmission, the sender recognizes that at least one node fails to receive the data packet. In that case, it sends the data packet again. Even though LBP reduces the overhead, it suffers from the hidden node problems. If there is a hidden node to one of multicast group member nodes, the receiver may not detect the transmission and may not respond with NACK. Thus, the leader cannot detect the failure of the packet reception.

Multicast aware MAC Protocol (MMP) is proposed in [5]. Unlike the aforementioned protocols, MMP does not use RTS and CTS handshaking, but uses data and ACK. After a data packet is transmitted, all of the member nodes transmit their ACK packets to the sender following the pre-assigned sequential order. If a receiver fails to receive a data packet, it sends a NACK packet in its pre-assigned location. In that case, the sender retransmits the data packet. Thus, the ACK period of MMP increases as the number of group member increases. Because MMP does not use RTS and CTS, it suffers from the hidden node problem.

In the previous work, the control packets are the tradeoff between the reliability and the bandwidth efficiency. For example, if we use RTS/CTS control packets, we can reduce the failure such as hidden node problems. However, this also reduces the system throughput.

3 Proposed Multicast MAC Protocol

3.1 OFDMA-Based Reliable Multicast

We propose new types of CTS and ACK packets, called OFDMA-based CTS (OCTS) and OFDMA-based ACK (OACK). We also propose a new multicast method that utilizes the OCTS and the OACK, called OFDMA-based Reliable Multicast (ORM). Fig. 1 shows an example of the OFDMA frequency band. Sub-channel data carriers are orthogonal with each other and they are used to transmit OFDM symbols. OCTS and OACK are control packets consisting of a preamble and OFDM symbols with a cyclic prefix [6]–[8].

Each member node has a unique pre-assigned sub-carrier location. The process of assigning a unique sub-carrier location is described in the following subsection. When a member node receives a RTS packet from the sender, it allocates an OFDM symbol into the pre-assigned sub-carrier of the CTS packet. The allocated symbol is one of the two BPSK symbols, 1 or -1. A successful reception of the RTS packet is indicated by a BPSK symbol 1 on the sub-carrier. On the contrary, a BPSK symbol -1 indicates a failed reception of the RTS packet. If a member node can not demodulate even the MAC header of the RTS packet, it will not

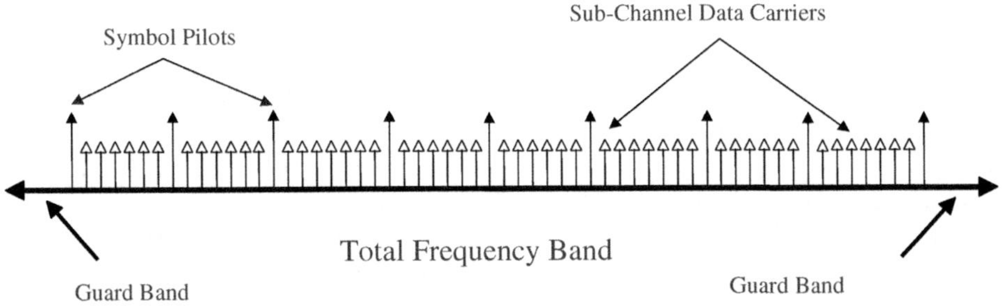

Fig. 1. An example of OFDMA sub-channel allocation

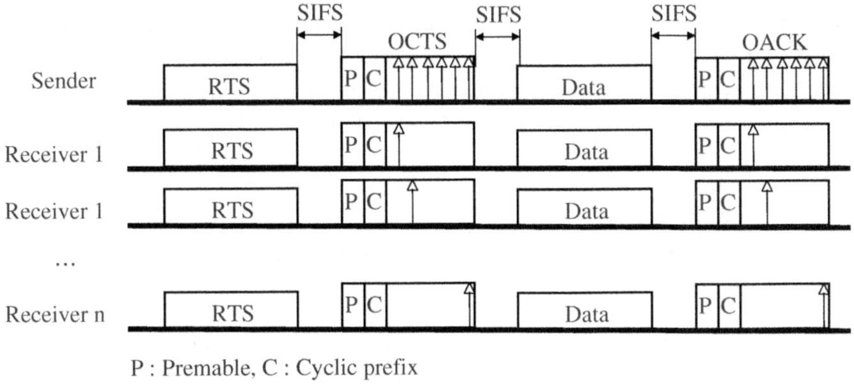

Fig. 2. An example of a data packet transmission cycle

generate an OFDMA symbol. An OFDM symbol generated by each member node for the acknowledgement has only one sub-carrier with a data symbol and the other sub-carriers are empty. The collection of these OFDMA symbols constitutes the payload of the OCTS packet. After being attached with the preamble, these OFDM symbols are sent to the multicast sender. It is assumed that all of the member nodes send their OFDMA symbols at the same time after SIFS idle period. At the multicast sender, the sub-carriers in the received OCTS are loaded by BPSK symbols to indicate each member's reception status.

An example scenario of the proposed method is shown in Fig. 2. A sender multicasts a RTS packet to the member nodes which are from Receiver 1 to Receiver n. All of the receivers response with an OFDMA symbol to the pre-assigned sub-carrier and these symbols are merged at the sender as an OCTS packet. Note that the payload part in OCTS packet is illustrated by frequency domain and the overall transmission sequence is illustrated by time scale in the figure. If Receiver n does not receive the RTS packet, it will not send an OFDMA symbol to the sender. After receiving OCTS, the sender checks the sub-carriers, which are assigned to member nodes. If any one of the member node sub-carriers is not allocated with any symbol or is allocated with the BPSK symbol -1, the sender prepares to retransmit the RTS packet.

When an OCTS is received correctly, the sender transmits a multicast packet to member nodes. When a member node receives a multicast packet from the sender, it allocates a symbol on the pre-assigned sub-carrier as an acknowledgement for the packet. The generation of OACK is the same as that of OCTS. An example scenario of OACK is illustrated in Fig 2.

For the time offset problem due to imperfect time-synchronization and different propagation delays from all of the member nodes, it is solved by using a longer cyclic prefix shown in [6]–[8] which is longer than a delay spread profiles.

3.2 Sub-channel Assignment

The sub-channel assignment is managed by a multicast leader (ML). Each multicast group has an ML. When a node wants to join a multicast group, it broadcasts a multicast join request (MJREQ) packet. When the ML receives the MJREQ, it assigns an empty sub-channel to the requesting node. Then, the ML responds with a multicast join acknowledgement (MJACK) packet that has the information of the allocated sub-channel. The assigned sub-carrier has to be unique for each node within the same multicast group address.

If there is no ML, MJACK is not responded. In that case, i.e., if there is no response within some time threshold, the requesting node becomes a new ML for that multicast group address.

When an ML wants to leave a multicast group, it unicasts a multicast leader request (MLREQ) packet to one of the multicast group members. If the node responds with a multicast leader acknowledgement (MLACK), the responding node becomes a new ML. If there is no MLACK within some time threshold, ML selects another node and transmits the MLREQ packet until the new ML is selected.

4 Packet Delay Analysis

4.1 Average Packet Delay

To compare the performance of the proposed method with that of MMP, we adopt the analytical model used in [9]–[13]. The channel conditions are assumed ideal, i.e., no hidden terminals, no channel error, and no capture effect. We consider a system consisting of N nodes. Each node always has a packet available for transmission. In other words, we operate in saturation conditions where the transmission queue of each node is assumed to be always nonempty. We consider a multicast group which has R member nodes. All the nodes are located in the transmission range of the sender.

The duration of the backoff is determined by the contention window (W) size which is initially set to W_{min}. The W value is used to randomly choose the number of slot time (σ) in the range of $[0, W-1]$, which is used for backoff duration. In case of an unsuccessful transmission, the W value is updated to $2 \times W$ while it does not exceed W_{max}. Let us adopt the notation $W_i = 2 \times W_{i-1}$ where $i \in \{1, \ldots, m\}$ is called the backoff stage and m is the maximum backoff stage such that $W_{max} = 2^m W_{min}$.

We assume that all the nodes operate synchronously. A discrete and integer time scale is adopted: t and $t+1$ correspond to the beginnings of two consecutive changes of backoff time counter. We call the time interval between t and $t+1$ as "counter time slot". Note that the counter time slot (variable duration) is different with the slot time (constant duration). Since the decrement of backoff time counter is stopped when the channel is sensed busy, the time interval between the beginnings of two consecutive backoff time counter instants may be much longer than the constant slot time size .

Let us denote the event that a node transmits a packet into a counter time slot as X. We are interested in the *unconditional probability* $\tau = \text{Prob}(X)$ that a node transmits a packet into a counter time slot. Let p_c be the *conditional probability* that a transmitted packet sees a collision on the channel. Once the independence is assumed and p_c is supposed to be a constant value, it is possible to solve τ and p_c using numerical techniques. The numerical method for finding τ and p_c is illustrated in [10][13].

Let M be the number of counter time slots required for multicast receivers to receive the multicast packet successfully. Let $E[c_i]$ be the average value of the backoff counter extracted by a node entering stage i. $E[c_i]$ is equal to $W_i/2$ in the assumption of the uniform distribution in the range of (0, $W_i - 1$). The average value of M is given as

$$E[M] = \sum_{i=0}^{m} \Big\{1 + E[c_i]\Big\}\pi_i, \tag{1}$$

where π_i is the steady state probability of backoff stage i [13].

Let T_{RTS}, T_{CTS}, T_{DAT}, T_{ACK}, T_{SIFS}, and T_{DIFS} be the transmission durations of RTS packet, CTS packet, data packet, ACK packet, SIFS, and DIFS, respectively. Let T_{tx} be the time duration of a data packet transmission cycle. T_{tx} includes all time durations required for a data packet transmission such as control packets, data packet, and IFS (refer to Fig. 2). In our proposed method, the average value of T_{tx} is given as

$$E[T_{tx}^{ORM}] = T_{RTS} + T_{CTS} + T_{DAT} + T_{ACK} + 3T_{SIFS} + T_{DIFS}, \tag{2}$$

because the new packet transmission starts after the DIFS duration. On the contrary, the average value of T_{tx} in MMP is given as

$$\begin{aligned} E[T_{tx}^{MMP}] = T_{RTS} + T_{CTS} + T_{DAT} + R \times (T_{ACK} + T_{SIFS}) \\ +2T_{SIFS} + T_{DIFS}, \end{aligned} \tag{3}$$

because MMP requires R ACK packets.

The mean value of counter time slot T_{ct} is calculated as follows. The probability that a sender sees an idle channel during a counter time slot is Prob[idle] = $(1-\tau)^N$, which takes time σ. The probability of successful transmission during a counter time slot is Prob[success] = $N\tau(1-\tau)^{N-1}$, which takes time T_{tx}. The probability of unsuccessful transmission during a counter time slot is Prob[fail] = 1 - Prob[idle]- Prob[success], which takes time T_{tx}. In ORM, the mean value of counter time slot, $E[T_{ct}^{ORM}]$, is given as

$$\begin{aligned} E[T_{ct}^{ORM}] &= \text{Prob[idle]}\sigma + \text{Prob[success]}E[T_{tx}^{ORM}] + \text{Prob[fail]}E[T_{tx}^{ORM}] \\ &= (1-\tau)^N\sigma + N\tau(1-\tau)^{N-1}E[T_{tx}^{ORM}] \\ &\quad +[1-(1-\tau)^N - N\tau(1-\tau)^{N-1}]E[T_{tx}^{ORM}] \\ &= (1-\tau)^N\sigma + [1-(1-\tau)^N]E[T_{tx}^{ORM}]. \end{aligned} \tag{4}$$

Similarly, the mean value of counter time slot of MMP is given as

$$\begin{aligned} E[T_{ct}^{MMP}] &= \text{Prob[idle]}\sigma + \text{Prob[success]}E[T_{tx}^{MMP}] + \text{Prob[fail]}E[T_{tx}^{MMP}] \\ &= (1-\tau)^N\sigma + N\tau(1-\tau)^{N-1}E[T_{tx}^{MMP}] \\ &\quad +[1-(1-\tau)^N - N\tau(1-\tau)^{N-1}]E[T_{tx}^{MMP}] \\ &= (1-\tau)^N\sigma + [1-(1-\tau)^N]E[T_{tx}^{MMP}]. \end{aligned} \tag{5}$$

The packet delay is defined as the time period from the start of a packet becoming a head-of-line (HOL) in the queue to the end of the packet removal from the queue [14]. The packet removal is caused by a successful reception by all the members. The sender must process every ACK received for the packet. Whenever the sender has not received ACKs from all the receivers for the packet, the packet must be re-multicasted, the backoff stage is increased, and the backoff timer is restarted. Let us denote the packet delay of ORM by D^{ORM}. Considering that the sender contends the channel for M counter time slots before the packet removal from the queue, average packet delay of ORM is

$$E[D^{ORM}] = E[M]E[T_{ct}^{ORM}]. \tag{6}$$

Similarly, the average packet delay of MMP is

$$E[D^{MMP}] = E[M]E[T_{ct}^{MMP}]. \tag{7}$$

From the second term of (5), it is noted that the effect of $E[T_{tx}^{MMP}]$ on $E[T_{ct}^{MMP}]$ increases as the number of nodes N increases. Also note in (3), (5), and (7) that the packet delay increases as the number of receivers R increases. Thus, the packet delay of MMP largely depends on the number of nodes. These trends will be shown in the next subsection.

4.2 Numerical Results

The values shown in the following figure have been obtained by using the system parameters in Table 1 and are based on the orthogonal frequency division multiplexing (OFDM) physical layer used in IEEE 802.11a standard [15].

Table 1. Parameter values

Parameter	Value
m	6
W_{min}	16
W_{max}	1024
SIFS time	16 μs
DIFS time	34 μs
slot time	9 μs
MAC header	272 bits
PHY header	46 bits
Preamble	16 μs
ACK time	44 μs
RTS time	52 μs
CTS time	44 μs
packet payload	8192 bits
channel bit rate	6 Mbps

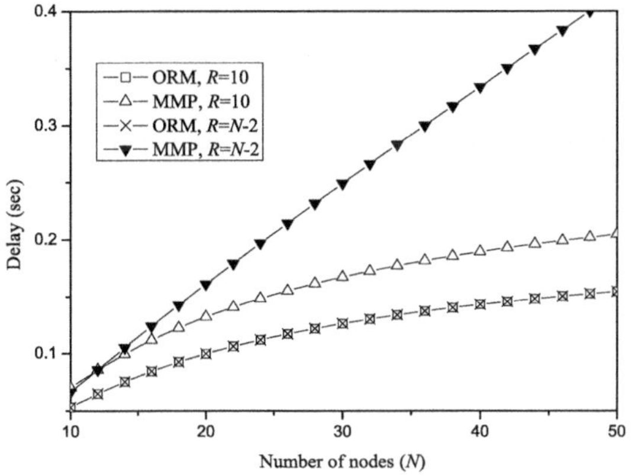

Fig. 3. Packet delay of ORM and MMP

Fig. 3 shows the packet delay of ORM and MMP. The number of receivers R is set to constant 10 and variable $N-2$. As the number of nodes increases, the delay also increases. This is because the average number of counter time slots $E[M]$ in (1) and the average value of counter time slot $E[T_{ct}]$ in (4) and (5) increases which affects the average packet delay $E[D]$ in (6) and (7), respectively. For MMP, the delay of variable R is larger than that of constant R. This is because the number of ACK packets increases according to the number of receivers. On the contrary, the delay of ORM is the same for the two cases of R. This is because ORM requires only one ACK packet irrespective of R. Thus the proposed method can show better performance than MMP when there are many multicast receivers.

5 Conclusion

We proposed a reliable multicast MAC protocol for wireless ad hoc networks. The proposed method adopts the RTS/CTS handshaking to mitigate the hidden node problem. The proposed method uses the OFDMA method in order to combine the multiple CTS and ACK packets. By reducing the time used for the CTS and ACK packets, the proposed method can reduce the packet transmission delay, significantly. The proposed method is robust to the increase of the number of receivers because the CTS and ACT time durations are irrespective of the number of receivers.

References

1. IEEE Std 802.11: 1999(E): Wireless LAN Medium Access Control (MAC) and Physical Layer (PHY) Specifications (1999)
2. Tang, K., Garcia, M.: MAC reliable broadcast in ad hoc networks. In: Proc. IEEE MILCOM 2001, pp. 1008–1013 (2001)
3. Sum, M.T., Huang, L., Arora, A., lai, T.H.: Reliable MAC layer multicast in IEEE 802.11 wireless networks. Wireless Communication and Mobile Computing 3, 439–453 (2003)
4. Kuri, J., Kasera, S.K.: Reliable multicast in multi-access wireless LANs. ACM Wireless Networks 7, 359–369 (2001)
5. Gossain, H., Nandiraju, N., Anand, K., Agrawal, D.P.: Supporting MAC layer multicast in IEEE 802.11 based MANETs: Issues and solutions. In: Proc. IEEE LCN 2004, pp. 172–179. IEEE Computer Society Press, Los Alamitos (2004)
6. Cao, Z., Tureli, U., Yao, Y.D.: Deterministic multiuser carrier-frequency offset estimation for interleaved ofdma uplink. IEEE Trans. Commun. 52, 1585–1594 (2004)
7. Kaiser, S., Krzymien, W.A.: Performance effects of the uplink asynchronism in a spread spectrum multicarrier multiple access system. Eur. Trans. Commun. 10, 399–406 (1999)
8. Kapoor, S., Marchok, D.J., Huang, Y.F.: Adaptive interference suppression in multiuser wireless ofdm system using antenna arrays. IEEE Trans. Signal Processing 47, 3381–3391 (1999)
9. Bao, C.W., Liao, W.: Performance analysis of reliable MAC-layer multicast for IEEE 802.11 wireless LANs. In: Proc. IEEE ICC 2005, pp. 1378–1382 (2005)
10. Bianchi, G.: Performance analysis of the IEEE 802.11 distributed coordination function. IEEE J. Select. Areas Commun. 18, 535–547 (2000)
11. Vitsas, V.: Throughput analysis of linear backoff scheme in wireless LANs. IEE Elect. Lett. 39, 99–100 (2003)
12. Hui, J., Devetsikiotis, M.: Designing improved MAC packet schedulers for 802.11e WLAN. In: Proc. IEEE Globecom 2003, San Francisco, CA, USA, IEEE Computer Society Press, Los Alamitos (2003)
13. Kim, S.W., Kim, B., Fang, Y.: Downlink and uplink resource allocation in IEEE 802.11 wireless LANs. IEEE Trans. Veh. Technol 54, 320–327 (2005)
14. Towsley, D., kurose, J., Pingali, S.: A comparison of sender-initiated and receiver-initiated reliable multicast protocols. IEEE J. Select. Areas Commun. 15, 398–406 (1997)
15. IEEE Std 802.11a-1999: Wireless LAN Medium Access Control (MAC) and Physical Layer (PHY) Specifications: Higher-speed Physical Layer in the 5 GHz Band (1999)

Mobility Tracking for Mobile Ad Hoc Networks

Hui Xu, Min Meng, Jinsung Cho*, Brian J. d'Auriol, and Sungyung Lee

Department of Computer Engineering
Kyung Hee University, Yongin 449-701, Korea
xuhui@oslab.khu.ac.kr

Abstract. In mobile ad hoc networks (MANETs), nodes mobility cause network topologies to change dynamically over time, which complicates important tasks such as broadcasting and routing. Mobility tracking is the task to determine a trajectory of the mobile node in time which can facilitate the forwarding decision in network protocols' design. In this paper, we investigate the regularity of mobility patterns and propose comprehensive mobility predication models, that is, not only piecewise linear but also nonlinear models which are based on nodes' historical location/speed information. As for historical information, we consider not only periodical update but also conditional update networks. Simulation results validate the accuracy of our proposed tracking schemes. We also compare the performance of those schemes and observe their relationship with parameters of update protocols.

1 Introduction

Mobile ad hoc networks (MANETs) are composed of possibly mobile devices such as sensors, laptops, or PDAs. The absence of a fixed infrastructure in MANETs makes them suitable for applications such as military battlefields, disaster relief and emergency situations. However, the mobility of nodes leads to dynamic network topology changes which complicates important network tasks such as efficient broadcasting and routing.

In most existing localized protocols for MANETs, each node emits "Hello" messages to advertise its presence and update its information. The update protocol can be classified into two kinds: periodical update and conditional update when there is considerable direction change. In periodical update, "Hello" intervals at different nodes can be asynchronous to reduce message collision. Each node extracts neighborhood information from received "Hello" messages to construct its local view for network topology and make decisions based on this view. However, when consider a general case where broadcasting or routing occurs within "Hello" message intervals, while nodes move during this interval, forward decisions will be based on outdated network topology.

Forward decisions based on outdated network topology view may be inaccurate and hence cause delivery failure which can induce poor coverage of broadcast task or route failures. The left part of Fig.1 represents the view of node i, and

* Corresponding author.

J. Indulska et al. (Eds.): UIC 2007, LNCS 4611, pp. 285–294, 2007.

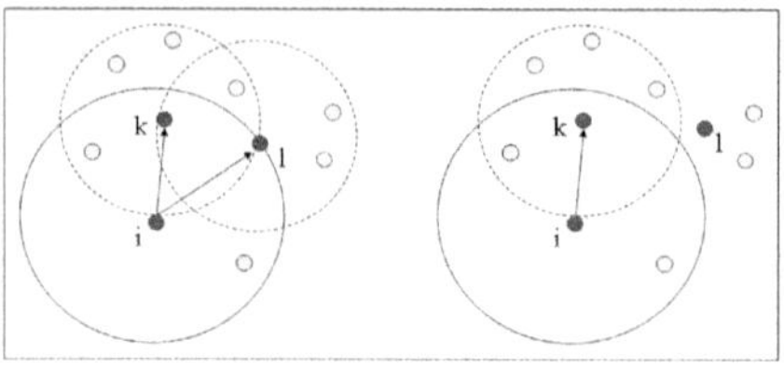

Fig. 1. Impact of outdated topology view on delivery

right part is the real physical topology. Based on an inaccurate local view, node i selects forward nodes k and l and assigns forward nodes' transmission radiuses. However, in real physical topology, node l moves out of the transmission range of i and can't receive the message and forward it. If the dynamics of the network topology could be predicted in advance, appropriate forward decision can be made in order to avoid or reduce delivery failures. In ad hoc networks, the network topology dynamics can be inferred from the mobility of the nodes. Mobility tracking is the task to determine a trajectory of the mobile nodes position in time. Therefore, it could be of significant benefit to the design of network protocols.

We employ here proactive mobility management solutions, mobility prediction, to address the above outdated view problems. We propose both piecewise linear and nonlinear prediction models which make use of node's historical information to predict a trajectory of the mobile nodes position.

The main contributions of this paper are as follows:

- Propose piecewise linear and nonlinear mobility tracking schemes.
- Conduct a simulation study to verify the accuracy of our proposed schemes.
- Compare the performance of these mobility tracking schemes and observe the relationship between the tracking accuracy and update protocols parameters.

The remainder of this paper is organized as follows: Section 2 presents related work and the motivation of our work. In Section 3, we propose the mobility tracking methods based on historical information. Section 4 shows simulation work and results. In Section 5, we conclude this paper.

2 Related Work

The node's mobility has a great impact on the performance and capacity of mobile ad hoc networks as discussed in [1].

Much work on mobility management has been done for the design of routing protocols. In the work of Su et al. [2], location information is used to estimate the expiration time of the link between two adjacent hosts which determines the selection of route path. In [3] an overview of existing mobility prediction schemes is given. However, those predictions are also for link availability and path reliability estimation.

Very little work has been tried to maintain an accurate topology view to assist the route path selection. There are two existing works: one is [4], where a stable zone and a caution zone of each node have been defined based on a node's position, speed, and direction information obtained from GPS. Specifically, a stable zone is the area in which a mobile node can maintain a relatively stable link with its neighbor nodes. A caution zone is the area in which a node can maintain an unstable link with its neighbor nodes. Another is that Wu and Dai ([5]) proposed a conservative "two transmission radius" method to compensate the outdated topology local view. However, all of above approaches are passive since they just try to compensate the inaccuracy of the network topology view rather than to predict mobile nodes' positions (mobility tracking) to construct a network topology view in time.

Few mobility tracking for MANETs has been done. One existing work is Zaidi et al. [6]. A first-order autoregressive (AR-1) model is used as mobility model. Each node uses an extended Kalman filter to estimate its own mobility state by incorporating network-based signal measurements, such as received signal strength indicators (RSSI) and time-of-arrival (TOA), and the position estimates of the neighbor nodes. The problem of their work is based on special AR-1 model rather than widely used mobility models, which is not suitable to assist the design of network protocols.

3 Proposed Method

In this section we first present two update protocols and then propose mobility tracking schemes based on historical information extracted from updates.

3.1 Update Protocols

In MANETs the update protocol [7] can be classified into periodical update with fixed time interval and conditional update when there is considerable direction change in a node's motion velocity or direction.

Conditional Update. Suppose that the periodic check for a particular node occurs at time t_c with actual location at (x_c, y_c, z_c). Further suppose that its own most recent update was generated at time t_h with location (x_h, y_h, z_h), speed v and direction (d_x, d_y, d_z). Then expected location (x_e, y_e, z_e) at t_c can be calculated as

$$\begin{cases} x_e = x_h + (t_c - t_h) \cdot v \cdot d_x \\ y_e = y_h + (t_c - t_h) \cdot v \cdot d_y \\ z_e = z_h + (t_c - t_h) \cdot v \cdot d_z . \end{cases} \quad (1)$$

Now the node should check whether the deviated distance D is larger than δ, that is, if $\sqrt{(x_e - x_c)^2 + (y_e - y_c)^2 + (z_e - z_c)^2} > \delta$ update will be generated. This situation is illustrated in Fig. 2 (a).

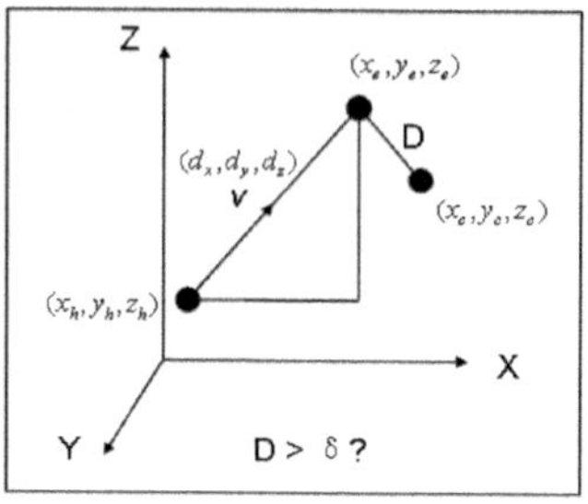

(a) Conditional update

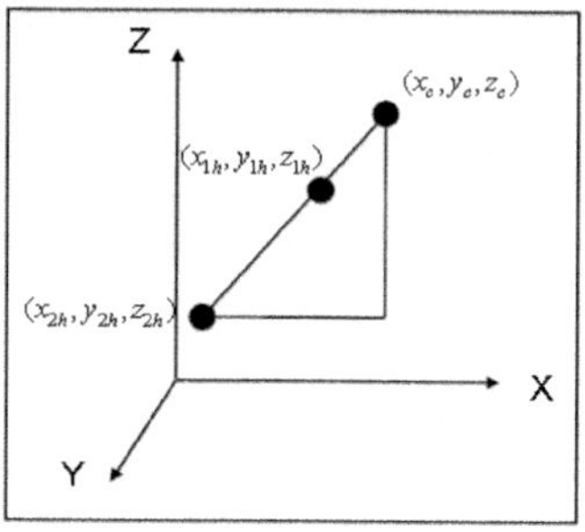

(b) Location-based prediction model

Fig. 2. Update and prediction models sketch

3.2 Mobility Tracking

Camp et al.[8] gave a comprehensive survey on mobility models for MANETs, from which we can find that in some models before changing direction nodes move linearly. The other models are not precisely linearly movement, while in a segment view, nodes also move linearly. Therefore we propose two **piecewise linear** models: location-based and velocity-aided predictions. We also propose one **nonlinear** model which bases on the principle that in high speed mobility networks we can assume the force acting on the node moving is constant, that is, nodes move with constant acceleration.

Location-based Prediction: Suppose that there are two latest updates records for a particular node respectively at time t_{2h} and t_{1h} ($t_{2h} < t_{1h}$) with location information of (x_{2h}, y_{2h}, z_{2h}) and (x_{1h}, y_{1h}, z_{1h}). Assume at least within two successive update periods the node moves in a straight line with fixed speed (depicted in Fig. 2 (b)), we get

$$\begin{cases} \frac{x_{2h}-x_{1h}}{t_{2h}-t_{1h}} = \frac{x_c-x_{1h}}{t_c-t_{1h}} \\ \frac{y_{2h}-y_{1h}}{t_{2h}-t_{1h}} = \frac{y_c-y_{1h}}{t_c-t_{1h}} \\ \frac{z_{2h}-z_{1h}}{t_{2h}-t_{1h}} = \frac{z_c-z_{1h}}{t_c-t_{1h}}, \end{cases} \tag{2}$$

then the location (x_c, y_c, z_c) at a future time t_c can be calculated as

$$\begin{cases} x_c = x_{1h} + \frac{x_{2h}-x_{1h}}{t_{2h}-t_{1h}} \times (t_c - t_{1h}) \\ y_c = y_{1h} + \frac{y_{2h}-y_{1h}}{t_{2h}-t_{1h}} \times (t_c - t_{1h}) \\ z_c = z_{1h} + \frac{z_{2h}-z_{1h}}{t_{2h}-t_{1h}} \times (t_c - t_{1h}). \end{cases} \tag{3}$$

However in conditional update networks since the latest update represents considerable changes compared to previous update, this model cannot be used.

Velocity-aided Prediction: Let (x_{1h}, y_{1h}, z_{1h}) and (v'_x, v'_y, v'_z) respectively be the location and velocity of its latest update for a particular node. Assume the

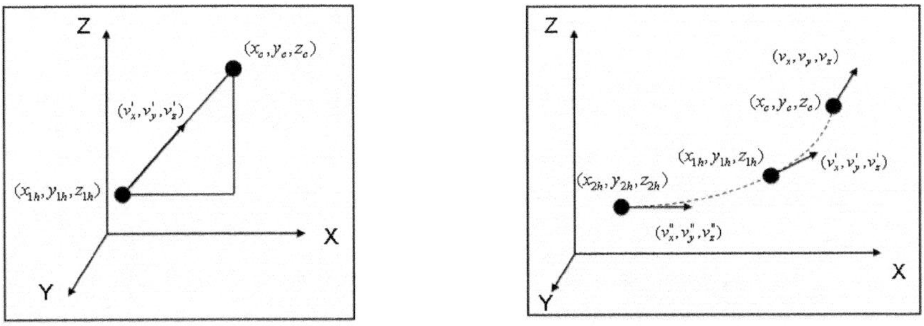

(a) Velocity-aided prediction model (b) Constant acceleration prediction model

Fig. 3. Prediction models sketch

node moves with that speed within one update period (depicted in Fig. 3 (a)), the location (x_c, y_c, z_c) at a future time t_c can be calculated as

$$\begin{cases} x_c = x_{1h} + v'_x \cdot (t_c - t_{1h}) \\ y_c = y_{1h} + v'_y \cdot (t_c - t_{1h}) \\ z_c = z_{1h} + v'_z \cdot (t_c - t_{1h}). \end{cases} \tag{4}$$

Constant Acceleration Prediction: Let (x_{1h}, y_{1h}, z_{1h}) and (x_{2h}, y_{2h}, z_{2h}) be the latest two updates for a particular node at t_{1h} and t_{2h} $(t_{2h} < t_{1h})$. Let (v'_x, v'_y, v'_z) and (v''_x, v''_y, v''_z) respectively be the velocity of those two update for a particular node. Now assume to predict the location (x_c, y_c, z_c) of the node at a future time t_c before new update time comes(depicted in Fig. 3 (b)). As all know the principle motion law

$$V = v + at \tag{5}$$

and

$$S = vt + \frac{1}{2}at^2 = \bar{v}t = \frac{v+V}{2}t, \tag{6}$$

here S is the displacement, v is the initial velocity and a is acceleration during period t. We employ V denoting the final velocity after period t.

Assume the fixed acceleration is (a_x, a_y, a_z) and apply above principle to X-dimension, we can get

$$\begin{cases} v'_x = v''_x + a_x(t_{2h} - t_{1h}) \\ v_x = v'_x + a_x(t_c - t_{1h}) \\ x_c - x_{1h} = \frac{(v'_x + v_x)}{2}(t_c - t_{1h}). \end{cases} \tag{7}$$

Then we can get expected location x_c as

$$x_c = x_{1h} + \frac{2v'_x + (v'_x - v''_x)\frac{t_c - t_{1h}}{t_{2h} - t_{1h}}}{2}(t_c - t_{1h}). \tag{8}$$

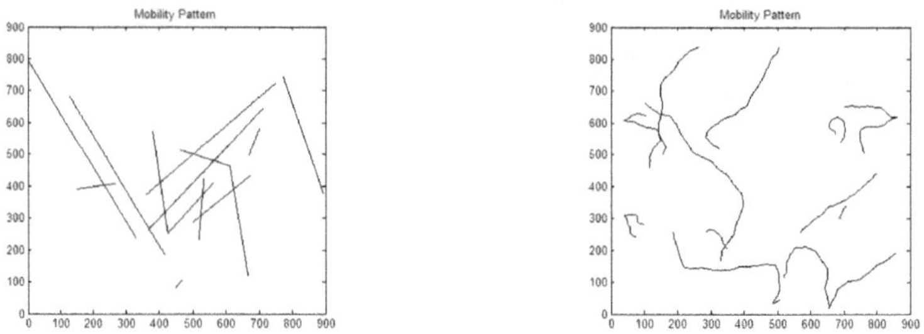

(a)under Random Waypoint model (b) under Gauss-Markov model

Fig. 4. Traveling pattern of MNs

Since Y and Z dimensions are the same with X-dimension, finally we have

$$\begin{cases} x_c = x_{1h} + \frac{2v'_x + (v'_x - v''_x)\frac{t_c - t_{1h}}{t_{2h} - t_{1h}}}{2}(t_c - t_{1h}) \\ y_c = y_{1h} + \frac{2v'_y + (v'_y - v''_y)\frac{t_c - t_{1h}}{t_{2h} - t_{1h}}}{2}(t_c - t_{1h}) \\ z_c = z_{1h} + \frac{2v'_z + (v'_z - v''_z)\frac{t_c - t_{1h}}{t_{2h} - t_{1h}}}{2}(t_c - t_{1h}). \end{cases} \quad (9)$$

Above we proposed mobility tracking schemes to predict nodes' trajectories. However, there exist several possible **imprecision factors:** GPS reading obtained may not always be accurate due to various reasons (e.g., multi-path fading, indoor conditions, etc.); node suddenly changes its direction before future prediction time; the movement speed of node can accelerate or decelerate; node moves nonlinearly (only for piecewise linear models). In the real world, these factors cause predicted trajectories inaccurate .

4 Performance Evaluation

In this section, we evaluate the performance of our mobility tracking schemes and the effect of update protocols on them.

4.1 Simulation Environment

We use ns-2.28 [9] and its CMU wireless extension as the simulation tool. To demonstrate the comprehensive effectiveness of our prediction proposals, we do experiments in both linear (Random Waypoint) and nonlinear (Gauss-Markov) mobility models [8] which are widely used in simulating protocols designed for MANETs. Fig. 4 shows the traveling pattern of MNs using those two mobility models. Table 1 displays our mobility tracking simulation parameters.

Table 1. Simulation parameters for mobility tracking

Parameters	Value
Simulation network size and nodes number	$900 \times 900\ m^2$ and 12
Mobile nodes speed range	$[0, 15]\ m/s$
Simulation time	$150\ s$
Location record/check interval	$2\ s$
Prediction interval	$20\ ms$
Reference distance for conditional update	$5\ m$

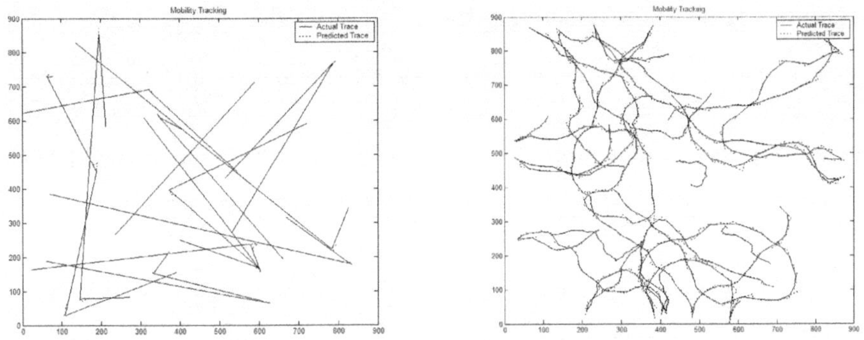

(a)under Random Waypoint model (b) under Gauss-Markov model

Fig. 5. Example of mobility tracking in periodical update case

4.2 Evaluation of Mobility Tracking

A sample simulation result with location-based prediction under periodical update is illustrated in Fig. 5. We can see that our mobility tracking scheme performs well, especially under Random Waypoint Mobility Model.

We use *root mean square prediction error (RMSE)* as a metric to evaluate the accuracy of mobility prediction models. Suppose there are N nodes in simulation networks and for any node j, assume there are K prediction points for it and let x_i, y_i, z_i represent the actual location for the ith point and x'_i, y'_i, z'_i be the predicted location with a certain prediction model, then the RMSE for the node (E_j) can be calculated as

$$\sqrt{\frac{1}{K}\sum_{i=1}^{K}[(x'_i - x_i)_2 + (y'_i - y_i)^2 + (z'_i - z_i)^2]}. \quad (10)$$

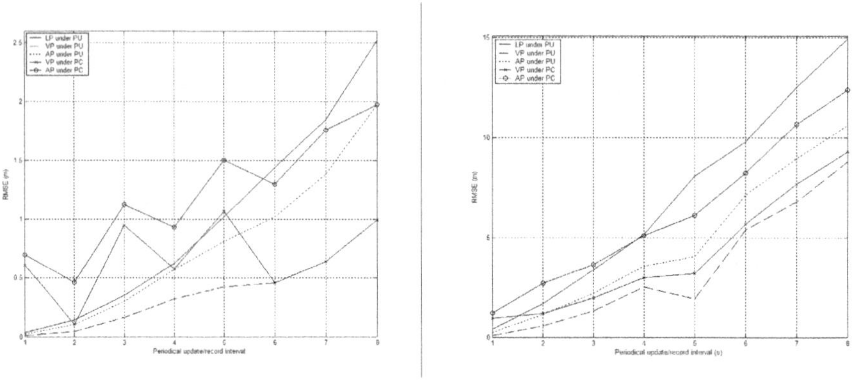

(a)under Random Waypoint model (b) under Gauss-Markov model

Fig. 6. The accuracy of prediction models with various record/check intervals

Table 2. RMSE of mobility prediction schemes under Random Waypoint Model

Records Type	Prediction Scheme	RMSE Value
Periodical Record	Location-based	0.144803
	Velocity-aided	0.0448978
	Constant Acceleration	0.103663
Periodical Check	Velocity-aided	0.104336
	Constant Acceleration	0.460686

And the RMSE for a prediction model (E_p) will be the mean value

$$E_p = \frac{1}{N}\sum_{j=1}^{N} E_j. \tag{11}$$

The smaller the RMSE, the more accurate the prediction model is.

Table 2 shows the RMSE results of our proposed schemes under the Random Way Point Model. Table 3 shows the RMSE results of our proposed schemes under the Gauss-Markov Model. These tables indicate again that our mobility tracking scheme performs better in Linear Mobility Models than in Nonlinear Mobility Model. Under periodical update protocols, the RMSE of our velocity-aided mobility tracking is smallest and that of location-based tracking is largest, that is, velocity-aided tracking is most accurate and nonlinear tracking is more accurate than location-based scheme. Under conditional update protocols, velocity-aided tracking is yet more accurate than constant acceleration tracking scheme.

To observe the effect of periodical record interval on the tracking performance, Fig. 6 shows the accuracy (RMSE) of prediction models obtained under various periodical record/check intervals. In Fig. 6 LP represents location-based

Table 3. RMSE of mobility prediction schemes under Gauss-Markov model

Records Type	Prediction Scheme	RMSE Value
Periodical Record	Location-based	1.67795
	Velocity-aided	0.564541
	Constant Acceleration	1.14196
Periodical Check	Velocity-aided	1.19953
	Constant Acceleration	2.68946

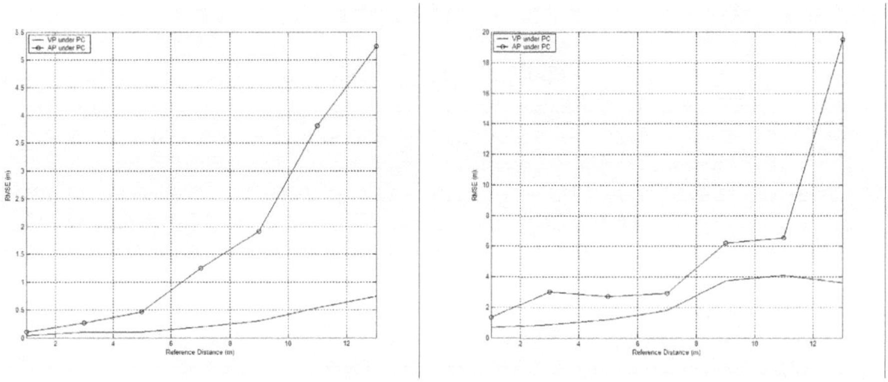

(a)under Random Waypoint model (b) under Gauss-Markov model

Fig. 7. The accuracy of prediction models with various reference distances

prediction; VP represents velocity-aided prediction; AP represents constant acceleration prediction; PU represents periodical update; PC represents periodical check (conditional update). As expected, when the update frequency decreases, the accuracy of the mobility tracking also decreases. Therefore we should choose small enough update interval to guarantee the tracking accuracy.

To observe the effect of reference distance for periodical check on the prediction accuracy, Fig. 7 shows the accuracy (RMSE) of prediction models obtained with various reference distances. Increasing the update reference distance tends to greatly degrade the tracking performance of velocity-based scheme, and under the nonlinear mobility model, the effect is more obvious. But the tracking performance of constant acceleration scheme remains fairly stable.

5 Conclusions

In this paper, we proposed both piece-wise linear and constant acceleration mobility tracking schemes to predict nodes' trajectory. Our prediction schemes are based on historical information achieved through periodic or conditional updates. In simulation work, we focus on evaluating the accuracy (RMSE) of our schemes and observe the trend of RMSE under varied update/check interval and varied reference distance in conditional update protocols. From the comparison of those schemes, we can see that the velocity-based scheme is best.

Acknowledgment

This work was supported by grant No. R01-2005-000-10267-0 from Korea Science and Engineering Foundation in Ministry of Science and Technology.

References

1. Grossglauser, M., Tse, D.: Mobility Increases the Capacity of Ad-Hoc Wireless Networks. IEEE Infocom, Alaska, USA (2001)
2. Su, W., Lee, S.-J., Gerla, M.: Mobility Prediction and Routing in Ad Hoc Wireless Networks. International J. Network Management 11(1), 3–30 (2001)
3. Chellappa Doss, R., Jennings, A., Shenoy, N.: A Review of Current Mobility Prediction Techniques for Ad Hoc Networks. In: The 4th IASTED International Multi-Conference Wireless And Optical Communications, Banff, Canada, pp. 536–542 (2004)
4. Kim, W.-I., Kwon, D.H., Suh, Y.-J.: A reliable route selection algorithm using local positioning systems in mobile ad hoc networks. In: The IEEE International Conference on Communications, Amsterdam, USA (2001)
5. Wu, J., Dai, F.: Mobility Control and Its Applications in Mobile Ad Hoc Networks. In: Handbook of Algorithms for Wireless Networking and Mobile Computing, 22-501-22-518 (2006)
6. Zaidi, Z.R., Mark, B.L.: A Distributed Mobility Tracking Scheme for Ad Hoc Networks Based on an Autoregressive Model. In: The 6th International Workshop of Distributed Computing, Kolkata, India, pp. 447–458 (2004)
7. Shah, S.H., Nahrstedt, K.: Predictive location-based QoS routing in mobile ad hoc networks. In: IEEE International Conference on Communications, New York, USA (2002)
8. Camp, T. (ed.): A Survey of Mobility Models for Ad Hoc Network Research. Wireless Comm. and Mobile Computing, special issue on mobile ad hoc networking: research, trends and applications 2(5), 483–502 (2002)
9. Fall, K., Varadhan, K.: The ns Manual. The VINT Project, UCB, LBL, USC/ISI and Xerox PARC (2002)

Handover Cost Optimization in Traffic Management for Multi-homed Mobile Networks

Shupeng Wang[1], Jianping Wang[2], Mei Yang[3], Xiaochun Yun[1], and Yingtao Jiang[3]

[1] Institute of Computing Technology, Chinese Academy of Engineering, Beijing, 100080, China
{wshp,yxc}@hit.edu.cn
[2] Department of Computer Science, City University of Hong Kong, Kowloon, Hong Kong
jianwang@cityu.edu.hk
[3] Department of Electrical and Computer Engineering
University of Nevada, Las Vegas, NV 89154, U.S.A.
{meiyang,yingtao}@egr.unlv.edu

Abstract. In this paper, we study the traffic management problem for multi-homed mobile networks with the objective of minimizing the overall handover cost. Two different traffic distribution modes are considered in our study: the Fractional Flow Assignment (FFA) mode which assumes the bandwidth demand from one connection is infinitely splittable and can be assigned to different wireless access networks, and the Integral Flow Assignment (IFA) mode which assumes that at any time the bandwidth demand from each connection can only be assigned to a single wireless network. We show that the general FFA problem and the IFA problem are both NP-hard and propose optimal solutions to the four special cases of the FFA problem and heuristic solutions to the general FFA problem and the IFA problem. Extensive simulations are conducted to verify the impact of the capacity-demand ratio on the performance of the proposed solutions.

1 Introduction

Providing Internet connectivity in a vehicle such as ships, aircrafts, and trains that contain mobile networks is desirable for passengers and also commercially attractive to the transportation systems [13][15]. In the next few years, mobile network communication is expected to grow rapidly [15]. In a typical vehicular communication scenario, the communication devices in large vehicles (e.g. buses or trains) form a local area network and connect to the mobile router (MR) which is installed on the vehicle and connected to the Internet. By employing an MR as the gateway, all devices within the mobile network can achieve Internet connectivity [10][13].

The mobile network may be multi-homed, which means that the MR has several interfaces each connected to a different base station or there exist multiple

J. Indulska et al. (Eds.): UIC 2007, LNCS 4611, pp. 295–308, 2007.

MRs in the mobile network [13]. Multi-homing provides fault-tolerance and load sharing capabilities to the mobile networks. Potential multi-homed configurations for mobile networks and the solutions that support such configurations are discussed in [12].

When a wireless access network is not available in an area, the traffic carried on that wireless access network has to be switched to other wireless access network(s) available in that area, which incurs a handover process associated with certain cost. For a multi-homed mobile network moving on a predefined route, the wireless access networks available in different geographic areas are known to the mobile network. Such a pre-knowledge makes it feasible for the mobile router to seamlessly switch to the available wireless access networks when moving into a new area. It also provides information for traffic management which aims to assign the traffic demands from the mobile network to different available wireless access networks along the journey with minimum handover cost.

Traffic management in multi-homed mobile networks is important and challenging. In the literature, Montavont *et al.* investigated the multi-homing issue in nested mobile networks and proposed an optimal method for the hosts to discover the hierarchy of mobile routers [10]. However, it does not consider the problem of optimizing handover cost between different wireless access networks. In [6], Goldenberg *et al.* studied the problem of how to assign traffic dynamically such that cost and performance are optimized assuming that the user is already multi-homed to a set of ISPs. Nevertheless, the smart routing algorithm proposed in [6] is not applicable to mobile networks where the available wireless access networks are dynamically changing along the journey. In [4], the authors studied the traffic distribution scheme to maximize the total profit for the mobile hotspot given the service classes provided in a mobile vehicular network. Two traffic distribution schemes are considered in their study, *in-transit* which computes the optimum traffic distribution on-the-fly and *pre-transit* which computes the traffic distribution before the journey starts. However, no handover cost has been considered in their study.

In this paper, we investigate the traffic management problem for multi-homed mobile networks which is to distribute the traffic to different available wireless access networks with the objective of minimizing the total handover cost. In the rest of the paper, we first present the problem description in Section II. In Section III, we study the fractional flow assignment problem. The study of the integral flow assignment problem is presented in Section IV. Section V presents the simulation results of the proposed algorithms for the two problems. Section VI concludes the paper.

2 Problem Description

Without loss of generality, we assume that the entire journey contains S geographic stages and N different wireless networks. For each stage s, $1 \leq s \leq S$, the availability of each wireless access network i is known in advance, where $1 \leq i \leq N$. Specifically, we use $a_{si} = 1$ to denote that wireless access network i

is available for stage s, and $a_{si} = 0$ for otherwise. Assume that the bandwidth capacity of wireless access network i is B_i, then $a_{si}B_i$ gives the available bandwidth from wireless access network i at stage s, and the total available bandwidth at stage s is given by $\sum_{i=1}^{N} a_{si}B_i$. We also define the duration of a wireless network i at stage s, denoted by L_{si} and $L_{si} = min\{s^{'}|s^{'} \geq s|a_{s^{'}i} = 0 \; or \; s^{'} = S\} - s + 1$, as the number of stages for which the wireless access network will be continuously available from stage s.

Assume there are M different connections. Each connection $m, (1 \leq m \leq M)$ has a bandwidth demand d_m that has to be guaranteed during the lifetime of the connection. We use $D = \sum_{i=1}^{M} d_m$ to denote the total bandwidth demand from all connections. Let S_m^S and S_m^E denote the starting stage and the ending stage of connection m during the journey, respectively. The duration of a connection m (in the number of stages) can be represented as: $I_m = S_m^E - S_m^S + 1$.

At the beginning of a stage s, because the network availability changes, some connections may need to be switched from one wireless network i to another wireless network j, which is referred to as a *handover*. In [11], it defines the handover cost as a function of the bandwidth demand, charging rate, and power consumption. For ease of understanding, we assume that the handover cost from wireless access network (shortened as network) i to network j is determined by $C_{ij}x$ for a connection with bandwidth demand x, where C_{ij} is referred to as the handover cost coefficient between network i to network j. C_{ij} can be determined according to the detailed requirements of a specific application. The *traffic management problem* is to assign the connections to different wireless networks with the objective to minimize the total handover cost for all connections during the entire journey subject to that the bandwidth requirement for each connection is satisfied in any stage.

Similar to [6], we consider two traffic distribution modes: the Fractional Flow Assignment (FFA) mode and the Integral Flow Assignment (IFA) mode. Under the FFA mode, it is assumed that flows are infinitely splittable and the traffic demand from one connection can be assigned to multiple wireless networks simultaneously. For the FFA mode, the resource can be utilized efficiently with the cost of extra management complexity due to synchronization overhead. On the other hand, the IFA mode assumes that at any time the bandwidth demand from each connection can only be assigned to a single wireless network, though multiple connections can share one wireless network subject to the bandwidth constraint. For ease of presentation, we refer the traffic management problem under the FFA mode as the FFA problem, and the traffic management problem under the IFA mode as the IFA problem.

3 Fractional Flow Assignment Problem

In real applications, the starting and ending stages of each connection may be varied. According to the situations of the staring and ending stages, we classify the FFA problem into five cases, as shown in Tab. 1. Case I is the general case, in which each connection starts from a random stage and ends at a random

Table 1. Five cases of the FFA problem

	Starting Stages	Ending Stages	Handover Coefficient
Case I	Random	Random	Different
Case II	Identical	Identical	Different
Case III	Random	Identical	Different
Case IV	Identical	Random	Different
Case V	Random	Random	Identical

stage. In Case II, all connections start from the same stage and end at the same stage. In Case III, all connections start from random stages and end at the same stage. In Case IV, all connections start from the same stage and end at random stages. We also consider a special case, Case V, which assumes the handover cost coefficient is identical between any two networks and there is no constraint for the starting/ending stage of the connections. In Cases I, II, III and IV, the handover coefficient is assumed to be different for different pairs of networks.

In this section, we study the five cases of the FFA problem as follows. We first show that Case I of the FFA problem (i.e., the general FFA problem) is NP-hard. Then we provide optimal solutions to Cases II, III, and IV of the FFA problem based on the network flow model. Next we show the optimal solution to Case V. Finally, we propose two heuristic algorithms to solve Case I of the FFA problem.

Theorem 1. The decision version of the general *FFA* problem is NP-complete. The theorem is proved by the reduction from the set-packing problem, a known strongly NP-complete problem [5], to the decision version of the general FFA problem. Due to space limit, the proof is omitted here.

For the general FFA problem, we will propose two heuristic algorithms to solve it. As these two algorithms will use part of the solutions to Cases II-IV, we will first present the solutions to these three cases.

3.1 Solutions to Cases II, III, and IV of the FFA Problem

The solutions to Cases II, III, and IV of the FFA problem all base on the minimum cost network flow algorithm. But the network flow models constructed for each case are slightly different. Hence, we describe the construction of the network flow model for each case first.

The network flow model for Case II is constructed as follows.

Step 1. For each stage s and network i, if $a_{si} = 1$, we define two nodes, denoted by V_{si} and V'_{si}, and add an edge from V_{si} to V'_{si} with its capacity set as B_i and its cost set as 0.

Step 2. For any two nodes at adjacent stages s and $s+1$, i.e., V'_{si} and $V_{s+1,j}$, we add an edge from V'_{si} to $V_{s+1,j}$ with its capacity set as infinity (∞) and its cost set as C_{ij} if $i \neq j$ or 0 if $i = j$.

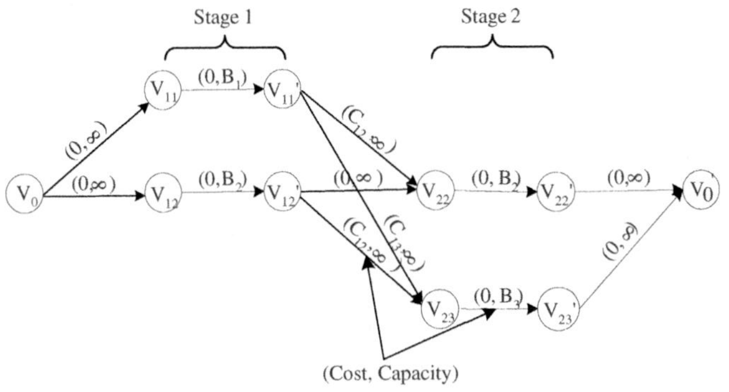

Fig. 1. Network flow model of Case II of the FFA problem

Step 3. Define a single sink node V_0', and add an edge from each node V_{Si}' to V_0' for $i = 1, \cdots, N$ with its capacity set as ∞ and its cost set as 0. Here S represents the ending stage.

Step 4. Define a single source node V_0, and add an edge from V_0 to each node V_{1i} for $i = 1, \cdots, N$ with its capacity set as ∞ and its cost set as 0.

Fig. 1 shows the network flow model of Case II for an example with two stages and three networks where networks 1 and 2 are available in stage 1 and networks 2 and 3 are available in stage 2.

We can construct the network flow model for Case III by modifying the model for Case II as follows. All connections can be partitioned into sets, each including connections starting from the same stage. We denote these sets as $E_1, E_2, \cdots, E_S$, where E_s represents the set with connections starting from stage s ($1 \leq s \leq S$). Then we construct the network flow model following the first three steps for case II and adding the following steps.

Step 4. Define a single source node V_0.

Step 5. For each nonempty connection set E_s, $1 \leq s \leq S$, do the following steps:
- If there are more than one node in stage s, then define one node V_s and add an edge from V_s to each node in stage s with its capacity set as ∞ and its cost set as 0.
- Add an edge from V_0 to V_s (or to the single node in the stage) with its capacity set as $\sum_{m \in E_s} d_m$ and its cost set as 0.

Similarly we can construct the network flow model for Case IV by modifying the model for Case II. Firstly, we partition the connections into different sets, each including connections ending at the same stage. We denote these sets as $E_1, E_2, \cdots, E_S$, where E_s represents the set with connections ending at stage s. Then we construct the network flow model following the first two steps for case II and adding the following steps.

Step 3. Define a single source node V_0, and add an edge from V_0 to each node V_{1i} for $i = 1, \cdots, N$ with its capacity set as ∞ and its cost set as 0.
Step 4. Define a single sink node V_0'.
Step 5. For each nonempty connection set E_s, $1 \leq s \leq S$, do the following steps:
- If there are more than one node in stage s, then define one node V_s' and add an edge from each node in stage s to V_s' with its capacity set as ∞ and its cost set as 0.
- Add an edge from V_s' (or from the single node in the stage) to V_0' with its capacity set as $\sum_{m \in E_s} d_m$ and its cost set as 0.

Then on the network flow model constructed for each case of the FFA problem, we need solve the Minimum Cost Network Flow (MCNF) problem which sends D units of flow from V_0 to V_0'. The MCNF problem is a classic optimization problem and can be solved readily using algorithms presented in [1]. From the network construction, we see that there is a one to one mapping between a feasible solution to the MCNF problem and a feasible solution to the corresponding case of the FFA problem, and the flow cost of a solution to the MCNF problem exactly reflects the handover cost of a solution to the FFA problem. Therefore, we have the following theorem.

Theorem 2. Cases II, III, and IV of the FFA problem can be solved in polynomial time by a minimum cost network flow algorithm.

3.2 Solution to Case V of the FFA Problem

We then consider Case V of the FFA problem which assumes identical handover cost coefficient between any two networks, i.e., $C_{ij} = C$ for all $i \neq j$. We propose a more efficient greedy algorithm for this special case. When all handover cost coefficients are equal, the key factor to the total handover cost is the number of handovers. The ideas of the greedy algorithm are 1) to postpone a handover as late as possible, and 2) to choose a network that has the longest duration when a handover is needed. We first formally state these two properties as follows.

Greedy Algorithm
Begin
  Initialization: Let $x_{in} = 0$ for $i = 1, \cdots, N$
  For stage $s = 1, \cdots, S$, **do**
    1. Keep the bandwidth assignment in the previous stage if possible:
      For $i = 1, \cdots, N$, **do**
        If $x_{s-1,i} > 0$ **and** $a_{si} = 1$, **then**
          let $x_{si} = x_{s-1,i}$.
          let $B'_{si} = a_{si} B_{si} - x_{si}$ be the left available bandwidth.
    2. Calculate the total bandwidth that needs to be switched as $D_s = D - \sum_{i=1}^{N} x_{si}$.
      Sort available networks in the nonincreasing order of their current available duration.
    3. Let the networks after sorting be $\pi(1), \pi(2), \ldots, \pi(N)$, i.e.,
      $L_{s,\pi(1)} \geq L_{s,\pi(2)} \geq \cdots \geq L_{s,\pi(N)}$.
      Find a minimum k such that $\sum_{i=1}^{k} L_{s,\pi(i)} \geq D_s$.
      Assign D_s to the first $k-1$ networks, each with the remaining bandwidth capacity of the network and assign D_s to $\pi(k)$ with $D_s - \sum_{i=1}^{k-1} L_{s,\pi(i)}$.
End

Theorem 3. For the FFA problem with identical handover cost coefficient, there exists an optimal solution in which 1) no traffic will be switched if its current network is still available at the next stage; and 2) when some traffic is switched, it must be switched to an available network with the longest duration.

The proof is omitted due to space limit. Theorem 3 leads to the following greedy algorithm, where we use x_{si} to denote the bandwidth usage of network i at stage s.

3.3 Two Heuristic Algorithms for the General FFA Problem

As shown in Section 3, the general case (Case I) of the FFA problem is NP-hard. In the following, we propose two heuristic algorithms for this case.

The first heuristic algorithm is based on the idea of grouping the connections with the same ending stage in one group and assigning the connections in such a group at one time. Similarly, we can group the connections with the same starting stage in one group and assign the connections following the group order. Here, we just use the first grouping method to elaborate the algorithm as the grouping method has not much impact to the algorithm performance. As one may see, the solution to Case III of the FFA problem can be directly applied to solve the assignment of the connections in each group. We hence name this heuristic algorithm as the Minimizing Group Connection Cost (MGCC) algorithm. The assignment order of these groups follows the order of the ending stage of these groups in such a way that the later the ending stage, the earlier the group is assigned. The MGCC algorithm works as follows.

MGCC Algorithm
Begin

1. Divide the connections into different groups such that the connections in a group have the same ending stage. Sort them in the decreasing order of their connections' ending stage. Let the sorted groups be $g(1), g(2), \cdots, g(S)$, i.e., $e_{g(1)} > e_{g(2)} > \cdots > e_{g(S)}$, where $e_{g(i)}$ denotes the ending stage of the $g(i)$ for $i = 1, \cdots, S$.
2. Select one unassigned group $g(i)$ following the sorted order. Construct the network flow model for the group following the steps for Case III (refer to Section 3.1), except only defining nodes of connections from the first stage to the ending stage.
3. Solve the FFA problem on the constructed network flow model using the MCNF algorithm.
4. Update the available bandwidth capacity of each network in each stage by subtracting it by the bandwidth allocated to all connections in group $g(i)$.
5. Repeat Steps 2 to 4 until all groups are assigned.

End

The second heuristic algorithm is based on the idea of assigning one connection at one time. Hence, we name the second heuristic algorithm as the Minimizing Single Connection Cost algorithm of FFA (MSCC-FFA). The assignment order of the connections follows the order of the duration of these connections, i.e., the longer the duration, the earlier the connection is allocated. The MSCC-FFA algorithm works as follows.

MSCC-FFA Algorithm
Begin
1. Sort the connections in the nonincreasing order of their duration (in the number of stages), and sort the connections with identical duration in the nonincreasing order of their bandwidth demand. Let the sorted connections be $\pi(1), \pi(2), \cdots, \pi(M)$, i.e., $I_{\pi(1)} \geq I_{\pi(2)} \geq \cdots \geq I_{\pi(M)}$, where $I_{\pi(m)}$ denotes the duration of connection m.
2. Select an unassigned connection $\pi(m)$ following the sorted order. Construct the network flow model for the connection according to the steps used for Case II (refer to Section 3.1).
3. Solve the FFA problem on the constructed network flow model using the MCNF algorithm.
4. Update the available bandwidth capacity of each network in every stage by subtracting it by the bandwidth allocated to connection $\pi(m)$.
5. Repeat Steps 2 to 4 until that all connections are assigned.

End

For each connection, the MSCC-FFA algorithm allocates its bandwidth demand using the MCNF algorithm. Hence, it will run the MCNF algorithm M times to allocate all the M connections. The complexity is larger than that of the MGCC algorithm, which only needs to run the number of groups times of the MNCF algorithm.

4 Integral Flow Assignment Problem

4.1 Problem Formulation

The IFA problem can be described by an integer linear programming. The following variables are defined.

y_{sim}: binary variable, $y_{sim} = 1$ if connection m is assigned to network i at stage s.

Z_{sm}: handover cost for connection m at stage s.

Then the objective of the IFA problem is to minimize the total handover cost:

$$\sum_{m=1}^{M} \sum_{s=2}^{S} Z_{sm}$$

subject to

$$\sum_{i=1}^{N} y_{sim} = 1, \text{ for } s = 1, \cdots, S; m = 1, \cdots, M. \tag{1}$$

$$\sum_{m=1}^{M} y_{sim} d_m \leq B_i, \text{ for } s = 1, \cdots, S; i = 1, \cdots, N. \tag{2}$$

$$Z_{sm} \geq (y_{s-1,im} + y_{sjm} - 1) C_{ij}, \text{ for } s = 1, \cdots, S; i, j = 1, \cdots, N; m = 1, \cdots, M. \tag{3}$$

$$y_{sim} \in (0, 1), \text{ for } s = 1, \cdots, S; i = 1, \cdots, N; m = 1, \cdots, M. \tag{4}$$

In the formulation, constraint (1) guarantees that any connection will be assigned to a single network at any time; constraint (2) states that all bandwidth allocated is bounded by the bandwidth capacity of each network; and constraint (3) is used to measure the handover cost of each connection at each stage.

The following theorem shows that the IFA problem is computational intractable [5].

Theorem 4. The decision version of the IFA problem is NP-complete.
The theorem is proved by by the reduction from the 3-Partition problem, a known strongly NP-complete problem [5], to the decision version of the IFA problem. The proof is omitted here due to space limit.

Although the IFA problem can also be classified into different cases as for the FFA problem, any case of the IFA problem is NP-hard. Hence, we do not differentiate the different cases of the IFA problem.

4.2 Heuristic Algorithm

We instead propose a heuristic algorithm for the IFA problem. Similar to the MSCC-FFA, the heuristic algorithm is based on the idea of assigning one connection at one time. The IFA problem with one connection can be solved using the MCNF algorithm.

For the IFA problem with one connection starting from the first stage and ending at the last stage, the network flow model can be constructed as follows, which is different from the steps described in Section 3.1.

Step 1. For each stage s and network i, if $a_{si} = 1$, we define one node V_{si} with bandwidth capacity B_i.

Step 2. For any two nodes at adjacent stages s and $s+1$, i.e., V_{si} and $V_{s+1,j}$, we define an edge from V_{si} to $V_{s+1,j}$. The capacity of the edge is set as 1 if V_{si} has enough bandwidth to satisfy the bandwidth requirement of the connection or 0 otherwise. And the cost of the edge is set as C_{ij} if $i \neq j$, or 0 if $i = j$.

Step 3. Define a single source node V_0 and an edge from V_0 to each node V_{1i} for $i = 1, \cdots, N$ with its capacity set as 1 and its cost set as 0.

Step 4. Define a single sink node $V_0^{'}$ and an edge from each node V_{Si} to $V_0^{'}$ with its capacity set as 1 and its cost set as 0.

For the IFA problem with one connection starting from a random stage and ending at a random stage, we can apply the above steps to construct the network flow model except only defining nodes from the starting stage to the ending stage.

On the constructed flow network, we then solve the MCNF problem which sends 1 unit of flow from V_0 to $V_0^{'}$ with the minimum cost using the MCNF algorithms [1]. The solution to the IFA problem with one connection can be obtained from the solution to the MCNF problem by taking the nodes (networks) with its incoming or its outgoing edge having 1 unit of flow.

We name the heuristic algorithm as the Minimizing Single Connection Cost algorithm of IFA (MSCC-IFA). As shown below, the steps in the MSCC-IFA algorithm are similar to the steps in the MSCC-FFA algorithm.

MSCC-IFA Algorithm
Begin

1. Sort the connections in the nonincreasing order of their duration, and sort the connections with identical duration in the nonincreasing order of their bandwidth demand. Suppose that the connections after sorting are $\pi(1), \pi(2), \cdots, \pi(M)$, i.e., $I_{\pi(1)} \geq I_{\pi(2)} \geq \cdots \geq I_{\pi(M)}$.
2. Select an unassigned connection $\pi(m)$ following the above order. Construct the network flow model for the connection according to the steps described above.
3. Solve the IFA problem on the constructed network flow model using the MCNF algorithm.
4. Update the available bandwidth capacity of each network in every stage by subtracting it by the bandwidth allocated to connection $\pi(m)$.
5. Repeat Steps 2 to 4 until that all connections are assigned.

End

The complexity of the MSCC-IFA algorithm is similar to the complexity of the MSCC-FFA algorithm.

5 Performance Evaluation

To evaluate the performance of the proposed solutions to the FFA and IFA problems in Sections III and IV, simulations have been conducted for different scenarios. For the FFA problem, the MGCC and MSCC-FFA for the general case (Case I) are simulated as the solutions to other cases are optimal. For the IFA problem, the MSCC-IFA for Case I is simulated.

5.1 Simulation Settings

For all the simulations, we assume that the bandwidth capacity of each network and the bandwidth demand of each connection follow uniform distribution. The following notations are used in describing simulation settings.

B_A: the average bandwidth capacity of the networks.
B_T: the expectation of the total bandwidth capacity of the networks.
P: the probability of the networks being available.
D_T: the expectation of the total bandwidth demand of the connections.
D_A: the average bandwidth demand of the connections.
M_A: the average number of connections in one stage.

Hence the expectation of the total bandwidth capacity provided by the N networks can be calculated as: $B_T = B_A * P * N$. The expectation of the total bandwidth demand required by the M connections can be calculated as: $D_T = D_A * M_A$. In addition, we define the ratio of the total bandwidth capacity to the total bandwidth demand (referred as the *capacity-demand ratio*) as:

$$R_T = \frac{B_T}{D_T} \tag{5}$$

In order to satisfy all the bandwidth demand, we should have $R_T \geq 1$.

Table 2. Basic simulation settings

Parameter	Value
Range of bandwidth demand of connections	Uniform distribution in $[50, 512]Kbps$
Range of bandwidth capability of networks	Uniform distribution in $[5, 10]Mbps$
Handover cost coefficient	Uniform distribution in [5,10]
Network availability probability (P)	80%

In the following, we will present the simulation results of the total handover cost with three varying parameters: the number of connections (M), the number of networks (N), and the number of stages (S). For all experiments, 1000 instances are simulated and the results shown are the average of successful cases (i.e., the cases that have all bandwidth demand satisfied). By default, the number of successful cases is over 50% of the 1000 instances.

The basic simulation settings for the experiments are shown in Tab. 2. Then we have $B_A = 7.5Mbps$. Note that for different cases, the calculation of M_A is different, which leads to the different R_T values even with the same setting.

5.2 Simulation Results

In the following, we present the results of MGCC, MSCC-FFA, and MSCC-IFA for the general case. In the simulations, we assume that each connection may start at a random stage and end at a random stage and the starting and ending stages of the connections follow uniform distribution. Three experiments are conducted. For all experiments, we use the R_T value to analyze the results.

In order to calculate R_T, we need calculate D_T. Hence we need find out M_A, which can be calculated in the following way. According to the assumption, the probability that one connection starts from the k_{th} stage is $1/S$ and the probability that the connection ends at the $l_{th}(l \geq k)$ stage is $1/(S-k+1)$. The expectation of the duration of a connection m can be computed as: $I_m = \sum_{k=1}^{S}(\frac{1}{S} * \sum_{l=k}^{S} \frac{l-k+1}{S-k+1})$, and the total duration of all the connections is $I_{sum} = M * I_m$. Then we can get $M_A = I_{sum}/S$. Then, we have $D_T = D_A * M_A$.

Experiment 1. In the first experiment, we vary the number of connections and fix the number of stages and the number of networks at 5 and 5, respectively. The number of connections is chosen from the range of 20 to 100 in the step of 20. The upper bound of 100 connections is chosen because the minimum value of the maximum number of connections that can be supported by the networks is set by $B_T/D_A = 109.3$.

The average total handover costs of MSCC-FFA, MGCC, and MSCC-IFA are shown in Tab. 3. As shown in the table, the total handover costs of MSCC-IFA are larger than the results of MSCC-FFA and MGCC except for M=20, which is due to the natures of the IFA problem and the FFA problem. And the results of all three algorithms increase with the number of connections increasing while R_T's value decreasing. This is consistent with our intuition that when R_T's value

Table 3. The total handover cost results vs. number of connections for Case I

M	20	40	60	80	100
MSCC-FFA	642.327	915.08	1646.02	2949.96	3513.59
MGCC (FFA)	641.683	912.173	1569.94	2695.47	3130.92
MSCC-IFA	641.683	919.268	1659.46	3041.22	3490.19
R_T	13.64	6.82	4.55	3.41	2.73

is decreased, limited bandwidth is shared by more number of connections, which causes more number of handovers.

Experiment 2. In the second experiment, we vary the number of networks and fix the number of stages and the number of connections at 5 and 50, respectively. The maximum value of the minimum number of networks that are needed to support all the connections is given by $D_T/(P * B_A) = 1.8$. Hence we choose the number of networks from 2 to 10 in step of 2.

The results of the second experiment are shown in Tab. 4. According to Tab. 4, the handover costs of MSCC-FFA, MGCC, and MSCC-IFA all decrease with the number of networks increasing while R_T's value increasing. This is also consistent with our intuition that when R_T's value is increased, more bandwidth is available for fixed number of connections, which leads to less number of handovers.

Table 4. The total handover cost results vs. number of networks for Case I

N	2	4	6	8	10
MSCC-FFA	3745.86	2427.79	752.405	246.314	125.015
MGCC (FFA)	4331.13	2354.01	747.493	244.584	124.75
MSCC-IFA	5124.92	2441.07	763.149	250.933	125.63
R_T	2.17	4.35	6.52	8.7	10.9

Table 5. The total handover cost results vs. number of stages for Case I

S	5	10	15	20	25
MSCC-FFA	68.235	1776.91	5468.02	11326.9	17887.3
MGCC (FFA)	68.97	1786.13	5478.71	11330	17894.1
MSCC-IFA	67.22	1775.19	5460.08	11314.8	17868.7
R_T	10.9	13.4	14.6	15.2	15.6

Experiment 3. In the third experiment, we vary the number of stages from 5 to 25 and fix the number of networks and the number of connections at 10 and 50, respectively. The results of this experiment are shown in Tab. 5. According to Tab. 5, the handover costs of the MSCC-FFA, MGCC and MSCC-FFA algorithm increase with the number of stages increasing while R_T's value increasing.

This is due to the fact that the increasing of the number of stages causes dramatic increase of the total handover cost, which overweighs the decrease of the handover cost due to the increasing of R_T's value.

In summary, as shown in Tabs. 3-5, both the capacity-bandwidth ratio R_T and the average duration per connection have significant impacts on the total handover costs of all algorithms for all cases. In general, the total handover cost decreases with R_T's value increasing. And longer average duration per connection leads to larger total handover cost.

6 Conclusion

In this paper, we investigated the traffic management problem with the objective of minimizing the total handover cost for multi-homed mobile networks on a journey base. We studied the problem under two different modes, the FFA mode and the IFA mode. We showed that the general FFA problem is NP-hard and proposed two heuristic algorithms for the FFA problem. For the four special cases of the FFA problem, we proposed optimal solutions based on the MCNF algorithm on the network flow models. We proved the IFA problem is NP-hard and proposed the MSCC-IFA algorithm to solve it. Extensive simulations have been conducted to study the impacts of capacity-demand ratio and other factors on the proposed algorithms.

Our results will make the mobility transparency in multi-homed mobile networks a reality and help in maximizing the revenue of the transportation system by providing seamless Internet connectivity to different users in the mobile environment.

References

1. Ahuja, R.K., Magnanti, T.L., Orlin, J.B.: Network Flows: Theory, Algorithms, and Applications. Prentice Hall, Upper Saddle River, New Jersey (1993)
2. Bechler, M., Storz, O., Franz, W., Wolf, L.: Efficient Discovery of Internet Gateways in Future Vehicular Communication Systems. In: Proc. 57th IEEE Vehicular Tech. Conf (VTC), pp. 965–969. IEEE Computer Society Press, Los Alamitos (2003)
3. Ben-Othman, J., Valois, F.: Multiservice Allocation in Hierarchical Cellular Networks. In: Proc. 4th IEEE Symp. Computers and Communications, pp. 80–86. IEEE Computer Society Press, Los Alamitos (1999)
4. Chung, A., Hassan, M.: Traffic Distribution Schemes for Multihomed Mobile Hotspots. In: Proc. IEEE VTC, pp. 2127–2131. IEEE Computer Society Press, Los Alamitos (2005)
5. Garey, M., Johnson, D.: Computers and Intractability: A Guide to the Theory of NP-Completeness. Freeman, San Francisco, CA (1979)
6. Goldenberg, D.K., Qiu, L., Xie, H., Yang, Y.R., Zhang, Y.: Optimizing Cost and Performance for Multihoming. In: Proc. SIGCOMM, pp. 79–92 (2004)
7. Kellerer, W., Bettstetter, C., Schwingenschl, C., et al.: (Auto) mobile Communication in a Heterogeneous and Converged World. IEEE Personal Communications 8(6), 41–47 (2001)

8. Li, L., Li, B., Li, B., Cao, X.: Performance Analysis of Bandwidth Allocations for Multi-Services Mobile Wireless Cellular Networks. In: Proc. IEEE WCNC, pp. 1072–1077. IEEE Computer Society Press, Los Alamitos (2003)
9. Mani, M., Crespi, N.: Handover Criteria Considerations in Future Convergent Networks. In: Proc. Globecom, pp. 1–5 (2006)
10. Manner, J., Kojo, M.: Mobility Related Terminology. Internet Draft, IETF (2004)
11. Montavont, N., Noel, T., Ernst, T.: Multihoming in Nested Mobile Networking. In: Proc. Int. Symp. Applications and the Internet-Workshops (SAINT), pp. 184–189 (2004)
12. Ng, C., Paik, E., Ernst, T., Bagnulo, M.: Analysis of Multihoming in Network Mobility Support. Internet Draft, IETF (2006)
13. Perera, E., Sivaraman, V., Seneviratne, A.: Survey on Network Mobility Support. Mobile Computing and Communications Review 8(2), 7–19 (2004)
14. Randhawa, T.S., Hardy, R.H.S.: Performance Analysis of Multi-Service Cellular Networks with Mobile Users. In: Proc. IEEE WCNC, pp. 1390–1397. IEEE Computer Society Press, Los Alamitos (2000)
15. Ronai, M., Petrescu, A., Tnjes, R., Wolf, M.: Mobility Issues in OverDRiVE Mobile Networks. In: Proc. IST Mobile Summit, pp. 16–18 (2003)

2-Level Hierarchical Cluster-Based Address Auto-configuration Technique in Mobile Ad-Hoc Networks*

Uhjin Joung and Dongkyun Kim**

Department of Computer Engineering, Kyungpook National University, Korea
ujjoung@monet.knu.ac.kr, dongkyun@knu.ac.kr

Abstract. In a mobile ad-hoc network (MANET), in order to route a packet between any two nodes, nodes should have their own unique IP address in the network. We introduce an address auto-configuration mechanism that utilizes a clustering technique, called CBA (Cluster-Based Address auto-configuration). Until now, most of existing clustering techniques have been applied to routing protocols. This paper, however, is the first trial that allows address auto-configuration to take advantage of the clustering technique. We propose a novel 2-level hierarchy cluster construction mechanism and present how to utilize clusters for the purpose of efficient address auto-configuration. We evaluate our proposed CBA through NS-2 simulations and prove that CBA is more suitable for a network with a large number of nodes which are joining/leaving at the same time.

1 Introduction

A mobile ad-hoc network (MANET) is a wireless network that consists of mobile nodes without any infrastructure. In a MANET, as its network topology is so dynamic due to node mobility, routing packets in the network is very important and difficult, as compared to the fixed Internet.

In order to route a packet between any two nodes, they should be able to be identified uniquely within the network. Hence, for the purpose of this identification, a node is assigned its unique IP address by considering future smooth integration with the fixed Internet. Obviously, we don't need to confine a unique address to the IP address. In particular, an effort to standardize so-called address auto-configuration protocol has been made for the purpose in IETF Autoconf Working Group [1]. In the address auto-configuration technique, two main processes are considered. First, an efficient protocol should be proposed that allows a new joining node to acquire its unique ID address in its joining network. Second, a MANET can be easily partitioned into several sub-networks and they

* This work was supported by the Korea Research Foundation Grant funded by the Korean Government (MOEHRD) (KRF-2005-003-D00295).

** The corresponding author.

J. Indulska et al. (Eds.): UIC 2007, LNCS 4611, pp. 309–320, 2007.

can be merged into one MANET due to node mobility. In addition, several independent MANETs can be merged into one MANET. As an address assignment can be performed independently of the different networks, the duplicate address detection and resolution mechanisms in the merged should be also devised.

To perform auto-configuration, a gateway node positioned between a MANET and the fixed network makes the solution so simple. However, a MANET can be easily detached from the fixed network. Therefore, two nodes in a detached MANET should be able to communicate with each other and a new joining node should obtain its unique IP address in the network. In addition, a centralized address assignment approach, where one selected server in the network is responsible for assigning unique addresses to all joining nodes, is not desirable due to the overhead such as server election, in case that the server moves out of the network. Hence, distributed IP address assignment mechanisms have been proposed.

In this paper, we exploit the concept of clustering to efficiently manage IP addresses in a MANET. Nodes are clustered according to our novel 2-level cluster management technique. A node with the highest-connectivity in the network (i.e. the largest number of neighbor nodes) is selected as a cluster head. The cluster head also selects the high-connectivity nodes as subcluster heads using its neighbor information. Each subcluster is assigned its address prefix by the cluster head. Each subcluster head assigns a unique address to a joining node with this assigned prefix. In particular, since many MANET routing protocols utilize the clustering concept, our proposed auto-configuration can be easily applied to these routing protocols. Through the clustering technique, our scheme can efficiently handle the network partitioning and merging.

The rest of our paper is organized as follows. In Section 2, we introduce some related works. Our cluster-based addressing technique is described in Section 3. We discuss the scalability issue in Section 4, which is followed by a simulation study using NS-2 in Section 5. Finally, some concluding remarks are given in Section 6.

2 Related Work

Recently, IETF Autoconf Working Group [1] has performed standardization efforts for the auto-configuration framework of stand-alone ad-hoc networks [2]. Based on the framework, GAP [3] and AMG [4] were suggested to assign a global address using the Internet gateways. As mentioned above, however, the schemes using gateways are not suitable for MANETs formed independently.

In addition, most research regarding address auto-configuration can be categorized in two classes according to the address space management: stateful and stateless techniques. Stateful auto-configuration techniques assign a priori unique address to a node by maintaining common address pool, thus resulting in address assignment without duplicate address. Dynamic Address Configuration Protocol (DACP) [5] utilizes an elected Address Authority (AA) to maintain state information of the network, such as node addresses, as well as their lease lifetime and a unique network identifier.

In stateless auto-configuration techniques, nodes construct addresses by themselves, usually based on hardware ID or random number. Duplicate Address Detection (DAD) mechanisms are used to ensure the uniqueness of the address. In MANETconf [6], each node maintains a list of all IP addresses in use in the network. A new node obtains an IP address through an existing node in the network. This approach has the overhead to maintain the address list and to receive ACKs from all other nodes in the network. Perkins [7] suggested strong duplicated address detection (SDAD). Simply, the scheme used address request (AREQ) and address reply (AREP) messages. A new joining node sets its address and examines it in a MANET using a temporary address. It, however, did not mention the collision of temporary addresses. The DAD process is repeated until the node requesting an address gets a unique address. This means that the address allocation time is in proportion to the number of failures. In addition, it did not introduce the solution of network merging and partitioning. The challenge in stateless approaches is to detect the potential address duplication fast and with low overhead. The advantage of stateless techniques is their relative simplicity, as compared to stateful ones.

3 Our Scheme: Cluster-Based Address Auto-configuration (CBA)

Clustering schemes proposed for ad-hoc networks have aimed to efficiently manage a number of mobile nodes by utilizing a hierarchical structure of the networks. By distributed clustering mechanisms [8,9,10,11], the cluster heads act as local coordinators to provide important features such as channel access, routing, power control and bandwidth allocation in the networks. Based on these clustering schemes, many hierarchical routing protocols for ad-hoc networks have been proposed [12,13].

In this paper, however, we attempt to exploit clustering schemes as an address auto-configuration technique in order to efficiently manage the addresses. For the purpose of address auto-configuration, the cluster head should have information used for cluster maintenance, as well as information for address management. We, therefore, propose a cluster-based address auto-configuration (CBA) for a MANET. In CBA, as shown in Figure 1, an entire network is regarded as one cluster. The cluster consists of several subclusters. Hence, 2-level hierarchy clusters are created. The cluster head manages the subcluster heads and assigns a prefix of address space to each subcluster. Using the prefix, each subcluster head performs address allocations/collections to/from its members. In this section, we explain our 2-level hierarchical cluster construction mechanism and the address assignment mechanism.

3.1 Assumption and Notations

We assume that every node has a unique identifier, and these identifiers are uniformly assigned throughout the network. For a description of our CBA, we use the following notations.

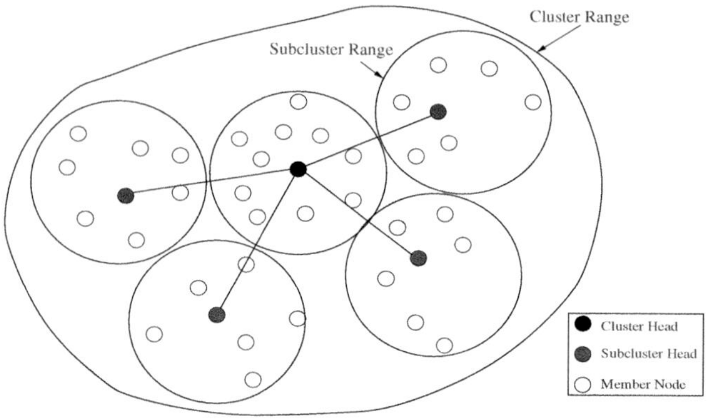

Fig. 1. The Example of the Clustered Network

- N_{ID} = node ID (predetermined value).
- NEI_{MAX} = a node with the highest connectivity (i.e. the largest number of neighbor nodes).
- N_{CH} = cluster head.
- N_{SCH} = subcluster head.
- N_{MGCH} = a merged network's N_{CH}.
- $AINF$ = when more than two networks are merged, a cluster head sends an AINF message to other cluster heads. The message contains all prefixes of its subclusters.
- CH_TIMER = timer set by N_{CH}. It is an interval of N_{CH}'s broadcasting a new CLUSTMAKE message to subcluster heads.
- SCH_TIMER = timer set by N_{SCH}. It is an interval of N_{SCH}'s broadcasting a new SCH message to its member nodes.

3.2 Cluster Construction

Figure 2 shows the process of the cluster head selection and the cluster construction mechanism. When a node joins a network, it enters the start state, and when its address is acquired, it enters the end state. More detailed descriptions of Figure 2 are as follows:

1. Each node broadcasts ND (Neighbor Discovery) messages continuously during the predefined time (ND_DURATION), in order to obtain its neighbor information. ND messages include a neighbor table and the information on a node with the highest connectivity (NEI_{MAX}). The neighbor table contains 3 fields: Node ID, the number of neighbor nodes, and nextHop. The nextHop field is used to avoid a propagation loop of the neighbor information.

2. A node with the highest connectivity (NEI_{MAX}) is selected as a cluster head (N_{CH}). N_{CH} selects subcluster heads by using its neighbor information. N_{CH} also broadcasts CLUSTMAKE messages periodically (the period is CH_TIMER.).

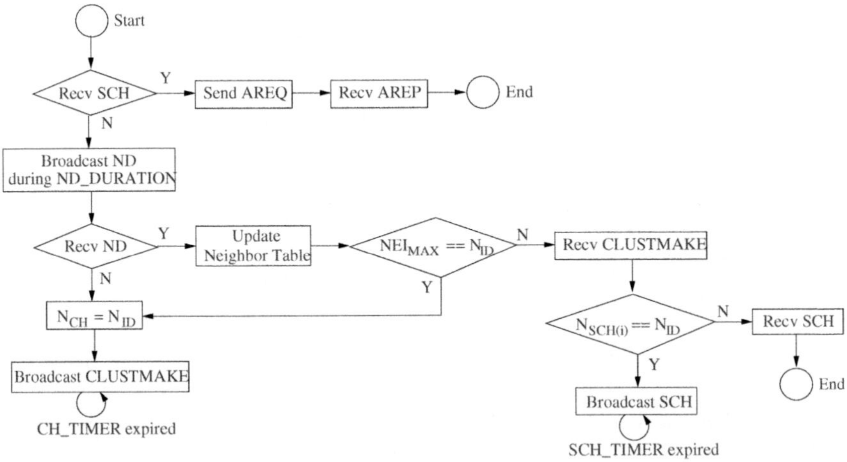

Fig. 2. Cluster Construction in CBA

3. If a node receives a CLUSTMAKE message and the node's ID appears in the CLUSTMAKE message, the node is selected as a N_{SCH}. Otherwise, it is a member node of N_{CH} or N_{SCH}. The CLUSTMAKE message format conforms to the generalized message format, as specified in [14]. In the message, cluster IDs are filled with the N_{CH}'s neighbor information.

4. If a node is N_{SCH}, it allocates addresses to its member nodes and collects unused addresses for its member nodes. Each N_{SCH} allocates addresses to joining nodes within its subcluster and periodically (every SCH_TIMER) broadcasts an SCH message to manage them (the SCH message is scope-broadcasted only within the subcluster). Considering the overhead for cluster head and subcluster heads to manage the address of the nodes, each subcluster consists of nodes which are reachable within 3 hops of each other in our CBA scheme. In addition, each subcluster head broadcasts SCH messages to manage its subcluster members address allocations and collections. As the broadcasting is unreliable, a successful transmission of SCH messages in the multi-hop transmission cannot be guaranteed.

3.3 Assigning an Address to a New Joining Node

Each N_{SCH} node floods the SCH message containing an address prefix within its subcluster. Therefore, when a new node joins a clustered network, the node can receive SCH messages periodically from one of the subcluster heads. A new joining node randomly picks a temporary address for its temporary purpose of routing request and reply messages. Using the address prefix from the SCH message and its own node ID, the node creates a candidate address. An AREQ message containing the candidate address will be transmitted to N_{SCH} over the reverse path of the received SCH message. (If the timer for an AREQ message

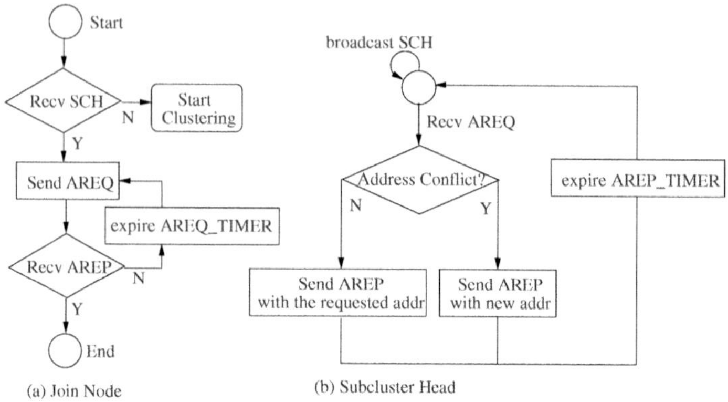

Fig. 3. The Address Allocation Process of a Joining Node

expires, the new joining node retransmits the AREQ message.) When N_{SCH} receives an AREQ message, it checks the availability of the candidate address. If the candidate address is a duplicate address, an available address is selected by N_{SCH}, which will be transmitted to the joining node. Once the address request process is finished, the temporary IP address is released. Figure 3 shows an address allocation process of a joining node.

3.4 Managing the Cluster Head and Node Mobility

To manage the cluster, N_{CH} periodically broadcasts a CLUSTMAKE message. If N_{SCH} does not receive the message during the predetermined time, N_{SCH} negotiates with other subcluster heads to elect a new N_{CH}. Each N_{SCH} also periodically broadcasts an SCH message. If N_{SCH} disappears, its subcluster members negotiate and elect a node with the highest-connectivity in the subcluster to be a new N_{SCH}. Afterward, the new N_{SCH} informs N_{CH} that it has been selected as the new subcluster head.

In addition, auto-routing mechanisms using address prefix information could be employed without dependence on any routing algorithms. In such a case, in order to manage the addresses efficiently and to extend our scheme to be applied to the selected routing technique, nodes in the same subcluster should have the same prefix information. Since nodes are mobile in a MANET, however, a node can move to other subclusters. An immediate change of its address is impossible and frequent changes of the address degrade the performance. In CBA, therefore, when a node moves to other subclusters, a new subcluster head informs the previous subcluster of the movement. After a predetermined time, the node will finally change its address.

3.5 Network Merging and Partitioning

Algorithm 1 shows the network merging process in CBA. Initially, the edge nodes of each network receive messages including different network IDs from other clusters and their prefix information, which will be also forwarded to their N_{SCH}s. N_{SCH} broadcasts an AINF message into the merged network and it also forwards the received network ID and address prefix to N_{CH}. An AINF message contains all of the subcluster address prefix information. Using the prefix information in the AINF message, N_{SCH} with a duplicated prefix can change its address prefix. The AINF message uses the same format as the CLUSTMAKE message.

Algorithm 1. Network Merging Algorithm

```
if the message received by an edge node contains the unknown address prefix then
    Edge node sends the received message to N_CH.
    N_CH sends an AINF message with all prefixes of its subclusters to N_MGCH.
    if one of N_MGCH's subclusters is the subcluster using the same prefix as the
    prefix included in the AINF message then
        N_MGCH changes the address prefix of its subcluster head. The subcluster head
        also changes its members' addresses.
        N_MGCH sends an AINF message with all prefixes of its subclusters to N_CH.
        N_MGCH becomes an N_CH's subcluster.
    end if
end if
```

4 Discussion

Since CBA considers an entire network as one cluster whereby all nodes are reachable within 7 hops, our CBA scheme should accommodate larger networks. In order to address the scalability issue, our 2-level hierarchy clustering approach can be extended to the n-level hierarchy clustering approach, where n is > 2. As an example shown in Figure 4, an entire network is regarded as a few clusters, where a supercluster head can be selected from the cluster heads. Therefore, the

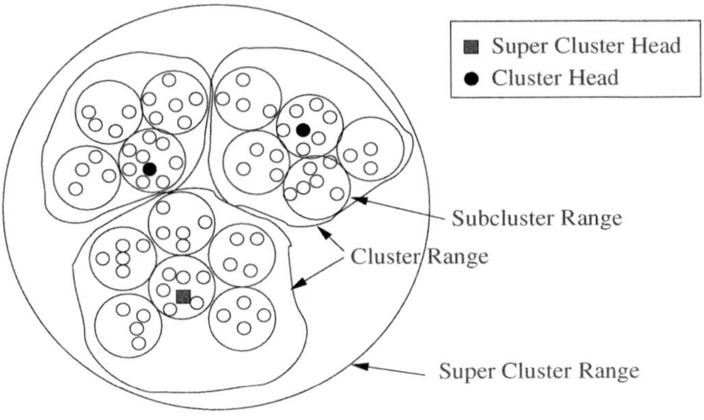

Fig. 4. The Extension of Our Clustering Scheme

supercluster head assigns address prefixes to cluster heads, and the cluster heads assigns longer prefixes to their subcluster heads. More detail research work for the extension is one of our future works.

5 Performance Evaluation

In order to evaluate our proposed CBA scheme, we compared it with the existing efficient address auto-configuration schemes without clustering techniques, namely LiA and LiACR [15]. LiA (Linear Allocation) assigns addresses to new nodes in a linear fashion. If several nodes request their addresses during a beacon interval, a node with the smallest identifier will win the contention and select the current maximum address in the network + 1 as its address. The others have to re-attempt the address requisition process.

In LiACR (LiA with Collision Resolution), which is an enhanced version of LiA, all contenders for the current maximum address + 1 wait for a predetermined period, listen to other requests for the same address and then pick up their addresses according to a precedence value based on the identifiers of all requesting nodes. It results in reducing the number of attempts needed to acquire addresses. Refer to [15] for details.

5.1 Simulation Environments

We implemented LiA, LiACR and CBA by using the NS-2 simulator [16]. In this simulation, we measured three performance metrics: (a) address allocation time (denoted by AAT); (b) the number of address conflicts; and (c) the number of control messages exchanged. AAT is the average time that a joining node takes to obtain its address successfully.

Fifty nodes were initially positioned randomly over an area of 670 m x 670 m. Each node had a transmission range of 250 m and the propagation delay was assumed to be 200 ms. We tested two scenarios: (a) a scenario where a large number of nodes join the network simultaneously during a beacon interval time (called many-in-B scenario) and (b) a scenario with network merging events.

Other simulation parameters are summarized in Table 1.

5.2 The Many-in-B Scenario

Figure 5(a) shows the average number of address conflicts for LiA, LiACR and CBA, with various number of nodes that join simultaneously. Accordingly, as more nodes request the same address at the same time, LiACR has more address conflicts because of the unreliable broadcasting of control messages. If joining nodes do not receive the other nodes' address request messages, the number of address conflicts increases because they can assign the same address. In CBA, however, after the cluster construction, each member is allocated a unique address without an address conflict. Figure 5(a) shows that our CBA has up to 100 % improvement, regarding address conflict.

Table 1. Simulation Parameters

Parameter	Value
Total Number of Nodes	50 nodes
Simulation Area	670 m x 670 m
Simulation Time	500 seconds
Simulation Topology	RANDOM Topology
Propagation Delay	200 ms
CH_TIMER	2 x Propagation Delay
SCH_TIMER	CH_TIMER
ND_DURATION	6 x Propagation Delay

Figure 5(b) shows how the AAT is affected. LiA and LiACR allocate addresses sequentially during a beacon interval. Hence, if several nodes request IP addresses during such an interval, collisions occur, which causes AAT values to increase. A larger number of address requests need larger AAT values. Nodes which did not receive the current maximum address information due to unreliable broadcasting, select their own address randomly, and they even flood its information into the network using the unreliable broadcasting. In addition, LiACR has another problem in that some nodes cannot hear the address requests from other nodes, which creates more address conflicts and may cause some nodes to get the same address. In LiACR, although collisions among joining nodes are avoided, it has the similar AATs to LiA because the time for all contenders to request and obtain their unique addresses is almost the same in either of LiA or LiACR. In CBA, however, the AAT value is determined according to the times needed to perform neighbor discovery, the subcluster head selection and the broadcasting of an SCH message. Hence, as more nodes request the same address at the same time, CBA can reduce AAT more than LiA and LiACR.

Figure 5(c) investigates the overhead of control messages exchanged. In LiACR, the messages to request addresses from other joining nodes are gathered during a predetermined time and a node with the smallest identifier sets the requested address to its address. As mentioned before, however, some nodes may not receive the messages to request addresses from other nodes in LiACR. They increase the number of contending nodes, thus producing collisions. In CBA, however, the overhead of control messages is not in proportion to the number of contention nodes. This is because only a few messages are needed except for ND messages, in order to construct a cluster. Hence, CBA reduces the control message overhead.

5.3 Network Merging Scenario

Figure 6(a) shows the average number of address conflicts. In LiA, as the merging message has a range of address conflicts, all nodes experiencing an address conflict must receive the merging message. In CBA, however, AINF messages can be reliably sent to subcluster members with the duplicated prefix. There are only a few

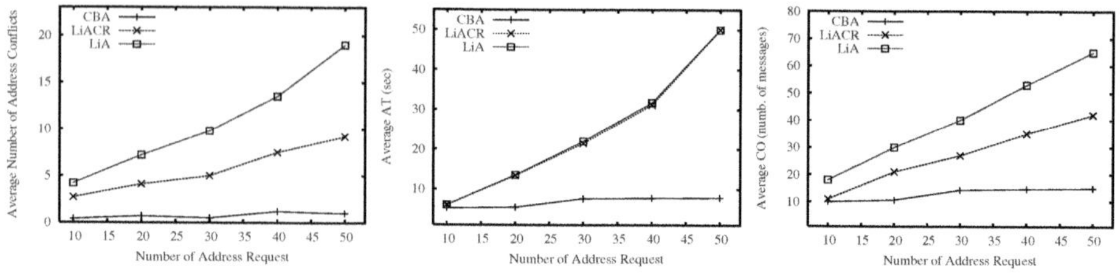

(a) The Number of Address Conflicts.

(b) AAT.

(c) Control Message Overhead.

Fig. 5. Many-in-B Scenario

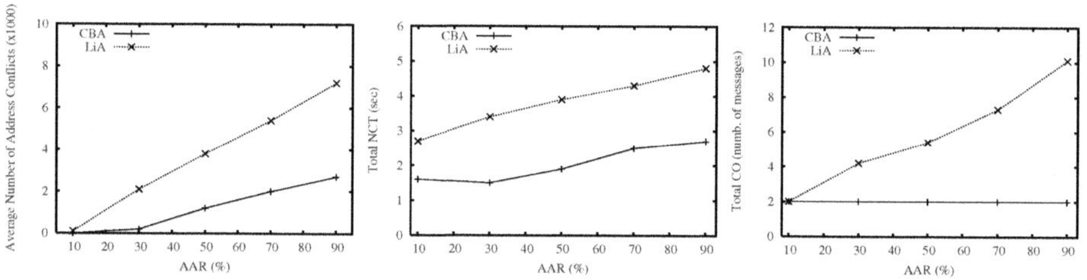

(a) The Number of Address Conflicts.

(b) NCT.

(c) Control Message Overhead.

Fig. 6. Network Merging Scenario

address conflicts when the address allocation ratio (denoted by AAR) is below 50 % because nodes use the same address prefix as their subcluster head. AAR is defined as the number of addresses in use versus the total number of usable/available addresses. It is unlikely that there is a duplicated prefix in CBA.

Figure 6(b) shows how NCT (Network Convergence Time) is affected by the address allocation ratio in the merging scenario. NCT is defined as the total amount of time between when a network merging event has occurred and when all address conflicts are resolved. In LiA, since a merging message can be lost, NCT also increases according to the increased number of address allocation ratio. As mentioned before, it is unlikely that a duplicated prefix occurs in CBA. Hence, CBA reduces NCT than LiA.

Figure 6(c) shows the number of total control messages in the network merging scenario. In LiA, a merging message can change all duplicated addresses if a broadcasting scheme is reliable. Nevertheless, in LiA, the unusable address range exists and the merging messages broadcasted include the same range when the network merging and partitioning occur frequently. In CBA, the unique control message needed for merging is an AINF message with the subcluster prefix information. Hence, CBA can reduce the control overhead than LiA. Additionally, we can avoid the existence of the unusable address range in CBA because subcluster heads can allocate addresses in a sequential manner.

6 Conclusions

In this paper, we attempt to exploit clustering schemes as an address autoconfiguration technique in order to efficiently manage the addresses. Nodes are clustered according to our proposed 2-level cluster management technique. A node with the highest-connectivity in the network (i.e. the largest number of neighbor nodes) is selected as a cluster head. The cluster head also selects the high-connectivity nodes as subcluster heads using its neighbor information. Each subcluster is assigned its address prefix by the cluster head. Each subcluster head assigns a unique address to a joining node with this assigned prefix. Through NS-2 simulations, we proved that regardless of the number of nodes that join a network simultaneously, our CBA performed better than other techniques without clustering. CBA enables the number of address conflicts to be reduced because it is able to reduce the number of retransmission of control messages. Hence, CBA required lower address allocation time and less overhead to complete address allocation. Finally, investigating scalability issues with larger networks is one of our future works.

References

1. IETF Ad-hoc Network Autoconfiguration (autoconf) Working Group: `http://www.ietf.org/html.charters/autoconf-charter.html`
2. Mase, K., Adjih, C.: A Common Framework for Autoconfiguration of Stand-Alone Ad Hoc Networks (draft-mase-autoconf-framework-02) (2006)
3. Mase, K., Owada, Y.: Gateway Aggregation Protocol (GAP) for Mobile Ad Hoc Networks (New I-D) (draft-mase-autoconf-gap-00) (2006)
4. Ruffino, S., Stupar, P.: Automatic Configuration of IPv6 Addresses for MANET with Multiple Gateways (AMG) (draft-ruffino-manet-autoconf-multigw-03.txt) (2006)
5. Sun, Y., Belding-Royer, E.M.: Dynamic Address Configuration in Mobile Ad hoc Networks. UCSB Technical Report 2003-11 (2003)
6. Mesargi, S., Prakash, R.: MANETconf: Configuration of Hosts in a Mobile Ad Hoc Network. In: Proceedings of the IEEE Conference on Computer Communications (INFOCOM) New York (2002)
7. Perkins, C., Malinen, J., Wakikawa, R., Belding-Royer, E., Sun, Y.: IP Address Autoconfiguration for Ad Hoc Networks, Internet draft, draft-ietf-manet-autoconf-01.txt (2001)
8. Kwon, T.J.: Mario Gerla: Clustering with Power Control. In: Proceedings of IEEE MILCOM99, Atlantic City, NJ (1999)
9. Kwon, T.J., Gerla, M., Pei, G.: On Demand Routing in Large Ad hoc Wireless Networks with Passive Clustering. In: Proceedings of IEEE WCNC 2000, Chicago, IL (2000)
10. Ohta, T.: An Adaptive Multihop Clustering Scheme for Highly Mobile Ad Hoc Networks, IEEE Autonomous Decentralized Systems (2003)
11. Yu, J.Y., Chong, P.H.H.: 3hBAC(3-hop between adjacent clusterheads): A Novel Non-overlapping Clustering Algorithm for Mobile Ad Hoc Networks. In: IEEE Pacrim'03, pp. 318–321 (2003)

12. Chiang, C., Wu, H., Liu, W., Gerla, M.: Routing in Clustered Multihop, Mobile Wireless Networks with Fading Channel. In: Proc. of the IEEE Singapore Int'l Conf. on Networks, pp. 197–211 (1997)
13. Basagni, S.: Distributed clustering for ad hoc networks. In: Proc.99' Int'l Symp. on Parallel Architetures, Algorithms, and Networks, pp. 310–315 (1999)
14. Clausen, T., Dearlove, C., Dean, J., Adjih, C.: Generalized MANET Packet/Message Format (draft-ietf-manet-packetbb-02.txt) (2006)
15. Choi, N., Toh, C.-K., Seok, Y., Kim, D., Choi, Y.: Random and Linear Address Allocation for Mobile Ad Hoc Netwokrs. In: IEEE Wireless Communications and Networking Conference (WCNC) 2005, New Orleans, USA (2005)
16. VINT Group: UCB/LBNL/VINT Network Simulator ns (version 2), http://www.isi.edu/nsnam/ns

Replication in Intermittently Connected Mobile Ad Hoc Networks

Ke Shi

Service Computing Technology and System lab, Cluster and Grid Computing lab, School of Computer Science and Technology, Huazhong University of Science and Technology, Wuhan 430074, China
keshi@mail.hust.edu.cn

Abstract. Data replication is a widely used redundancy scheme for improving data availability and performance in distributed systems. However, currently existing replication schemes do not take into account that the mobile ad hoc network is often partitioned in smaller portions, enjoying only intermittent connectivity thanks to mobile nodes traveling across partitions. A novel replication scheme, RICMAN (Replication in Intermittently Connected Mobile Ad Hoc Networks), is proposed to address this problem. Desired data items are replicated to the nodes with rather stable neighboring topology and with enough resources such as energy and storage space. A semi-probabilistic data disseminating protocol is employed to distribute the replicas and propagate the updates, which can identify the potential mobile nodes traveling across partitions to maximize data delivery despite network partitions and intermittent connectivity. Simulation results demonstrate that RICMAN scheme leads to good successful data access ratios and latencies with small overheads.

1 Introduction

In a wireless and mobile ad hoc network (MANET), when nodes are in motion, links can be obstructed by intervening objects. When nodes must conserve power, links are shut down periodically. These events result in intermittent connectivity. At any given time, when no path exists between source and destination, network partition is said to occur.

Accessing remote data has been a fundamental application in both fixed and mobile networks. However, distributed data access in such intermittently connected MANETs (ICMAN) has proved to be a much more difficult problem than in the full-connected networks. Network partitions prevent access to data objects residing in a network partition by nodes which are currently placed outside this partition. Thus, data accessibility and availability in ICMAN can be significantly lower than in full-connected networks. In this work, we define data accessibility as the ability to obtain information about the data from other nodes and to access those data when needed.

A possible solution to the low accessibility of data in ICMANs is to replicate data items on several mobile nodes. As depicted in the example in Fig. 1, replicas of data items D_1 and D_2, which are replicated on nodes in the two network partitions before network partitioning caused by the movement of node Q happened, allows every mobile node in the network to access the data objects, in spite of the network partitioning.

J. Indulska et al. (Eds.): UIC 2007, LNCS 4611, pp. 321–330, 2007.

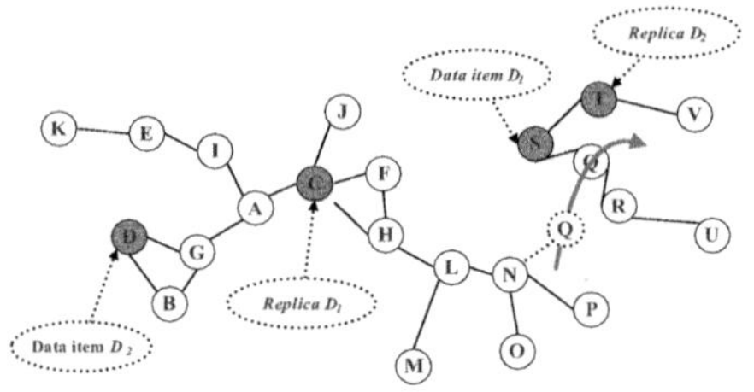

Fig. 1. Data replication can improve data accessibility

However, the replication schemes developed for wired network needs to be reexamined for the ICMAN case. Considering the example in Fig. 1, if data item D_1 is updated, this update needs to be propagated to its replicas in the other partition as soon as possible; otherwise the nodes in the other partition may get stale data. In this example, whether node Q or other nodes will move into the previous locating area of Q to connect two separate partitions again in a finite delay has a significant influence on the performance of replication-based data access.

In this paper, we present a novel replication scheme, RICMAN (Replication in Intermittently Connected Mobile Ad Hoc Networks), to address this issue. In RICMAN, desired data items are replicated to the nodes with rather stable neighboring topology and with enough resources such as energy and storage space. A semi-probabilistic data disseminating protocol is employed to distribute the replicas and propagate the updates, which can identify the potential mobile nodes traveling across partitions to maximize data delivery despite network partitions and intermittent connectivity. The rest of the paper is organized as follows:

The detail of RICMAN, including semi-probabilistic data disseminating protocol, is given in Section 2. Sections 3 present the results of performance evaluation. Conclusions and future work are considered in section 4.

2 RICMAN Scheme

RICMAN focuses on the application scenarios where the mobile devices such as laptops, PDAs and smart phones carried by humans construct MANETs by the needs of humans to socialize or cooperate, e.g., disaster relief teams in the emergency, platoons of soldiers in the battlefield, and groups of people in a party. RICMAN must enable forms of disconnected communication where data may be carried by a mobile node and forwarded opportunistically across partitions, therefore allowing communication between areas of the network that are never connected by an end-to-end path. Fortunately, the movement based on human decisions and socialization behaviors in the application scenarios improve connecting opportunities between the pair of nodes in the intermittently connected network [1].

In RICMAN, we assume that the nodes present in the system cooperate to share the data with each other, including hosting the replicas and delivering the data. In other words, we do not consider the case of nodes that may refuse to store a replica or deliver a data item.

2.1 Semi-probabilistic Data Dissemination Protocol

In the semi-probabilistic data dissemination protocol, a mobile node maintains a disseminating zone of h hops from itself. If the receiving node is present in the disseminating zone of the sending node, data is delivered synchronously based on local zone information. If data cannot be delivered synchronously, data are forwarded towards a subset of nodes in the disseminating zone that have the higher chance of successful delivery. The chances of successful delivery are synthesized from locally available zone information such as the rate of change of connectivity of a node (the likelihood of it connecting other nodes) and its current energy level (the likelihood of it remaining alive to deliver the message). Therefore, this approach performs data disseminating by combining probabilistic and deterministic decisions: the former is resilient to change and therefore addresses dynamicity, while the latter reduces indiscriminate propagation by guiding messages towards the receivers.

We define profile as the set of attributes that describe the aspects of the system that can be used to optimize the process of data dissemination. Every node periodically exchanges both the information related to the deterministic data dissemination and probabilistic data dissemination. For deterministic data dissemination, every node maintains a routing table to all the nodes in its disseminating zone (We use DSDV [2]). For probabilistic data dissemination, every node maintains a list containing its delivery probabilities for the data receivers. The propagation of such profile information only within a neighborhood of h hops provides reasonable accuracy while keeping the overhead under control, since h is can be adjusted according to the network operation conditions.

Each node periodically calculates its delivery probabilities based on locally available profile information. The delivery probability of a node i for disseminating data j can be computed as:

$$P_{ij} = \begin{cases} 1 & \text{if node } i \text{ is the receiver of data } j \\ P_{ij}^{d} & \text{otherwise} \end{cases} \quad (1)$$

If node i is a receiver for data j, its delivery probability is the highest possible, equal to 1. If node i is not a receiver, it can still act as intermediate forwarder or carrier in the disseminating process, with P_{ij}^{d} representing its effectiveness either as a forwarder or a *carrier* of disseminating data j to its corresponding receivers.

Many parameters affect the ability of a node to be a good forwarder or a carrier in the data disseminating process. In our work, the profile only includes two attributes, i.e., the change degree of connectivity and the probability of receiver co-location. These are indeed the most important attributes for our purposes, and by limiting ourselves to their description we keep our solution simpler. However, the profile is general and open to inclusion of any other attribute. Formally, we define P_{ij}^{d}, as:

$$P_{ij}^{d} = w_{cdc} U_{cdc,i} + w_{col} U_{col,ij} \quad (2)$$

$U_{cdc,i}$ represents the estimated value of the change degree of connectivity of node i, i.e., the number of connections and disconnections that the node has experienced over the last T seconds. A high value of this estimate means that node i is likely to be in reach of a large number of different nodes. Instead, $U_{col,ij}$ summarizes the history of co-location of i with receivers of data j (in the i's disseminating zone). A high value of $U_{col^{c}ij}$ means that i is likely to become co-located with one or more receivers of j ▷

Let $n(t)$ be the set of the neighbors of i at time t. $U_{cdc,i}$ at time t is computed by comparing the members of $n(t)$ against those at the beginning of the previous period,

$$U_{cdc,i} = \frac{|n(t-T) \cup n(t)| - |n(t-T) \cap n(t)|}{|n(t-T) \cup n(t)|} \quad (3)$$

Intuitively, the formula above yields the number of nodes who became neighbors or disappeared in the time interval $[t - T^c t]$, normalized by the total number of nodes met in the same time interval. The computation of $U_{col^{c}ij}$ is much simpler: $U_{col^{c}ij} = 1$ if *a j's receiver* is in the i's disseminating zone, and $U_{col^{c}ij} = 0$, otherwise. The computation of delivery probability implies the assumption that the only information a node has about its position is logical connectivity information. In particular, we assume that a node is not aware of its absolute geographical location nor of the location of those to whom it might deliver the data. Although this information could potentially be useful, it is currently unreasonable to assume the existence of GPS for all potential application domains for this technology.

The data disseminating process is as follows:

1) Deterministic information is exploited, if available. Upon receiving data j, node i always sends the received data to all the receivers of data j in its disseminating zone by utilizing the underlying synchronous routing mechanism.

2) Probabilistic data disseminating is divided into two parts: forwarding and carrying. Forwarding process make the data spread to all the receivers in the same network partition quickly. The data j is sent to the nodes in the disseminating zone of node i whose delivery probabilities are larger than or equal to forwarding threshold σ. The value of σ indicates the tradeoff among resource consumption, coverage and delay under certain network conditions. This forwarding process is complemented by a store-and-forward approach to deliver data across different network partitions by utilizing the intermittent connectivity. After forwarding of data j has occurred at node i, j is also stored in i's buffer if the delivery probability P_{ij} is larger than or equal to carrying threshold τ. If the carrier, while moving, meets a receiver, the data is transfer to the receiver. The optional rule is that when the carrier meets a node with a higher delivery probability, the data is transferred to the node with the higher delivery probability. With a proper τ value, data can be delivered to the nodes in the different network partitions in a bounded delay with reasonable overhead (i.e., buffer space, number of transmissions) with high probability.

To avoid duplicated data transferring, a forwarding node forwards the same data only once and discards the data already received. If the node has relayed the data to one destination using the deterministic information, the probabilistic forwarding to the same destination will be cancelled. The node never forwards the data into the node it came from. For the carrying nodes, the carried data is transferred only once to the same receivers or the same nodes with higher delivery probability. A First Come First Served (FCFS) buffer management scheme is utilized to manage the buffer space on the carrying nodes.

2.2 Replicating Nodes Election and Replica Distribution

In RICMAN, a distributed replicating nodes election scheme is employed to find the nodes with rather stable neighboring topology and with enough resources such as energy and storage space acting as replicating nodes.

This is an initial setup stage for replicating nodes election when the network is constructed. A node may become a replicating node if it is found to be the most stable and powerful node among its neighborhood of h_r hops. Otherwise, it is in client state. Every node calculates a hosting fitness value to indicate the potentials of this node to be a replicating node. The hosting fitness is computed as:

$$f = \frac{C}{M} = \frac{w_s S + w_p P + w_e E}{U_{cdc}} \tag{4}$$

where C is the capacity of node defined as the weighted sum of normalize storage space, energy and process power, and M is the mobility of node defined as the change degree of connectivity of node. The node with larger capacity and less mobility has higher f value.

All nodes broadcast their hosting fitness among its neighborhood of h_r hops. After an election period, T_A, each node compares its own hosting fitness value with those of its neighbors of h_r hops. If a node has the highest value, it enters into the status of a replicating node. All nodes maintain a list containing the information of elected replicating nodes and periodically exchange the information about this list. Therefore, every node can find all elected replicating nodes with a bounded delay with high probability. In RICMAN, semi-probabilistic data disseminating protocol regard the replicating nodes in this list as the receivers for replicas or updates.

After election, Replica distribution disseminates replicas onto the elected replicating nodes. The owner of the data initiates the replica distributing process to disseminate the data to all the nodes in its replicating nodes list by employing the semi-probabilistic data disseminating protocol discussed in subsection A. Small σ and τ values are preferred in this process to make the data been spread to all the replicating nodes quickly.

In RICMAN, the data owner does not try to maintain the status of its replicas through some kind of data structures such as tables because maintaining the state information may cause too much overhead that is unacceptable in ICMANs and because these information may not be accurate due to frequent partitions.

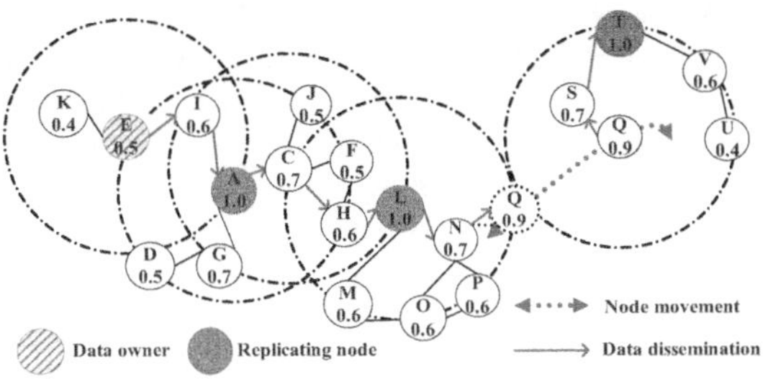

Fig. 2. An example of partitioned MANET where semi-probabilistic data dissemination protocol is exploited to distribute replicas

Fig.2 illustrates an example of partitioned MANET where semi-probabilistic dissemination protocol is exploited to distribute replicas. Node A, L and T are replicating nodes, whose delivery probabilities are 1.0. Node E is the owner of data. The delivery probabilities are calculated using the formula described in the subsection A and the results are marked in the figure. The disseminating zone is two hops. The value of σ is set to 0.65 and τ is 0.8. Since A is in the E's disseminating zone, the data can be delivered to A through T using the deterministic information. A becomes the disseminating node and forwards data to C since C's delivery probability 0.7 is larger than σ. C forwards data to L through H since I is the replicating nodes in the C's disseminating zone. L forwards data to N and Q since their delivery probabilities are larger than σ. Since N only forward the same data once, N does not forward the data to Q anymore. Since Q's delivery probability is larger than τ, Q carries the data. When Q moves into the other partitions, it transfers the data to T through S.

2.3 Update Propagation and Consistency

There is a consistency issue in our replicating scheme. Due to impairments of wireless transmission and frequent network partitions, it is not practical to maintain strong consistency among replicas. In our scheme, a weak consistency model called eventual consistency model is adopted, which stipulates that all replicas eventually converge to the same state.

From an implementation point of view, the issues to solve in order to guarantee eventual consistency are: (1) update propagation: each update must eventually reach all replicas, and (2) update ordering: all updates must be eventually applied in the same order at each replica to ensure that the last update is the same at all replicas.

In RICMAN scheme, we assume that only the owner of original copy could update the data items. The owner of original copy propagates the updates to all the replicating nodes in its replicating nodes list by utilizing semi-probabilistic data disseminating protocol. The σ and τ values can be adjusted according to the urgent degree of updates and the network operational conditions. Since the semi-probabilistic data disseminating protocol is a best-effort protocol, the updates may reach the replicating nodes in different orders.

To solve this issue, the owner of original copy timestamps the updates by an incremental version number, whose original value is zero and will add one for every update. The replicating nodes apply the received updates in the ascending order of their version numbers. Since the updates with small version number may be delayed in the disseminating process and arrive later than the updates with large version numbers, the replicating nodes manage a small buffer where out-of-sequence updates are held temporarily awaiting the filling in of gaps in the sequence when delayed updates turns up.

The node requesting the data saves the version number of the data got in the last successful data access. If the version number of the data got in current data access is smaller than the saved value, the node knows it gets stale data.

3 Performance Evaluation of RICMAN

In this section, we compare our approach against others, and assess the impact of protocol parameters through simulation. A community based mobility model [3] is utilized to describe the moving behaviors of mobile nodes. Our simulated network consists of 160 mobile nodes in a non-wrapping 1000[m] × 1000[m] square area. The simulation area is divided into a grid—4 × 4 in our experiments. There are 8 nodes in each square and the rest 32 nodes act as traveler nodes (2 travelers in each square) moving across different grids. The node's speed v is selected uniformly from the range of 0.5-3 [m/s]. The pause time is 30 [s]. The speed of traveler nodes is elected uniformly from the range of 2-4 [m/s] to differentiate their roles in the simulation. The pause time is 5 [s]. The radio communication range of each mobile node is a circle with the radius of r, 100 [m]. The MAC protocol is 802.11b.

A 10% of the nodes are chosen randomly to be the owners of original data items. The size of data item is 10 [KB]. We assume the replicating nodes have enough capacity to store all these data items. The updating interval follows exponential distribution with mean value, 120[s]. Each node generates a single stream of data requests following a Poisson point process. The rate of request generating is 20[s]. The interval T, which determines the frequency of the nodes exchanging the profile information and computing delivery probability, is inversely proportional to the node speed, so networks with different mobility experience the same acceptable accuracy level of information. Here T is set to 6 [s]. Considering communicating range and nodes' speed, this value is small enough to achieve accuracy zone information with very high probability.

The weights for computing delivery probability are $w_{cdc} = w_{col} = 0.5$. The default values for semi-probabilistic data dissemination protocol are $\sigma = 0.4$, $\tau = 0.6$, $h = 2$ and $h_r = 4$. The simulation time is set to 600 s. No data was collected for the first 200s of the simulations while the initial replicating nodes election process finished.

We mainly concentrate our analysis on the ratio of successful data access (the ratio of successful access requests to the number of all access requests issued by all the nodes in the network) and network traffic. The network traffic includes the traffic caused by maintaining the information of disseminating zone, electing replicating nodes, distributing replicas, propagating updates, and retrieving replicas in the network, which is measured by the total number of transmissions made by all the nodes in the network.

We compare the performance of our scheme against the replication methods using the synchronous routing and pure probabilistic routing to disseminate replicas and updates. The replicating nodes election policy used in these two schemes is the same as the policy used in our scheme.

Synchronous routing (we use AODV[1]) does not have the ability to bypass partitions, and therefore leads to low successful data access ratio, 0.39, according to our simulation. The network traffic is 291,020[2]. As illustrated in Fig.3, with $\sigma = 0.4$ and $\tau = 0.6$, the successful data access ratio of RICMAN reaches 0.79, an almost 100% improvement, with only 20% extra network traffic, from 291,020 to 351,078. When using synchronous routing, AODV wastes a lot of traffic trying to find an end-to-end path between the pairs of nodes. The traffic caused by successful data transferring is

[1] We utilize reactive routing protocol because it performs better than proactive protocol in our case. Do not confuse it with the DSDV protocol used in our scheme, which aims for maintaining the information of disseminating zone.

[2] When using synchronous routing, these two values are fixed and do not change with the value σ and τ. Thus, we do not plot them in the figure.

lower than the corresponding traffic in our scheme. The extra network traffic in our scheme mainly results from successful data transferring, in our case, 212,123 transmissions are used to transferring data from the replicating nodes to the requesting nodes. If the size of data item is larger, this trend will become more obvious. If the size of data item is quite large, the network capacity must be considered to avoid network congestion that will degrade the performance of data access.

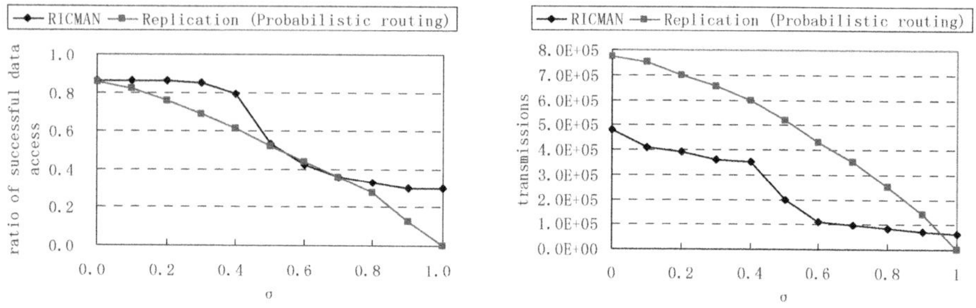

(a) Successful data access (b) The number of transmissions

Fig. 3. Successful data access ratio and network traffic vs. forwarding threshold σ (τ= 0.6)

Fig.3 and Fig.4 also show the performance results of the replicating method using probabilistic routing, in which each node forwards and stores the data at a certain probability (1-σ or 1-τ for the convenience of comparing), re-forwards the data when meeting new neighbors. As illustrated in Fig.3 and Fig.4, RICMAN outperforms this method in most cases. This method may achieve high successful data access ratio at the cost of very heavy network traffic. Compared with RICMAN, this method causes twice the network traffic to get the same successful data access ratio.

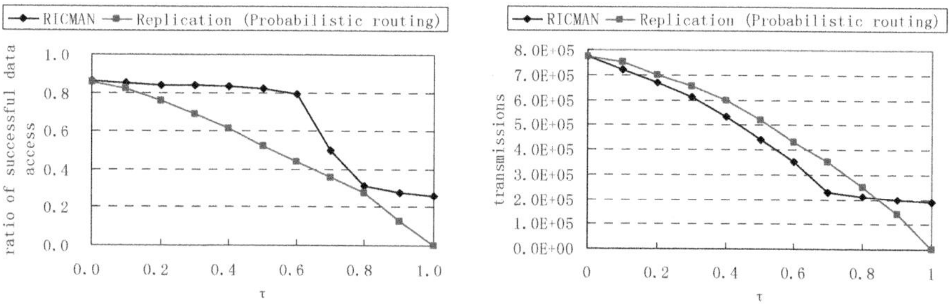

(a) Successful data access (b) The number of transmissions

Fig. 4. Successful data access ratio and network traffic vs. carrying threshold τ (σ= 0.4)

The reason is that probabilistic routing is actually a controlled flooding. The selection of forwarding nodes and carrying nodes are totally random, which do not consider the local topological information and historical contacting information. Thus, extra traffic is caused by the blinding carrying and forwarding.

As shown in Fig.3, if σ is too large, our scheme fails to find appropriate subset of nodes to forward data, successful data access ratio is low and network traffic is also low. If σ is too small, each node forwards the data, which cause unnecessary network traffic helpless to improve successful data access ratio. In our simulation, the value of σ which leads to good tradeoff between success data access ratio and network traffic is around 0.4.

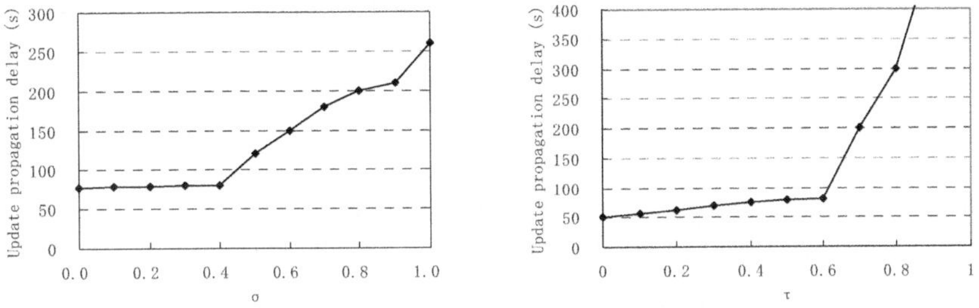

(a) vs. forwarding threshold σ (b) vs. carrying threshold τ

Fig. 5. Update propagating delay

We can observe the same phenomena in Fig.4. τ should be set to a proper value to ensure our scheme can find the appropriate subset of nodes to carry data across different network partitions. Small τ causes a lot of nodes carrying and re-forwarding data, which leads to too much network traffic. The nodes also need more buffer space to store these data. Large τ leads to low successful data access ratio because only few nodes can carry and re-forward the data. Under the simulated network conditions, τ should be around 0.6. Based on the simulation results, the values of σ and τ may have significant effects on the performance of our method.

As shown in Fig.5, update propagating delay is more sensible to parameters τ. If τ is too large, our scheme fails to find appropriate subset of nodes to carry the data across different partitions, update propagating delay will be very large since forwarding process can only spread the data in the same partitions no matter what σ is. On the contrary, with appropriate τ, our scheme always can find some suitable nodes carrying the data and disseminating the data to the replicating nodes. Of course, large σ makes the data spread to the carrying nodes fast.

4 Conclusion and Future Direction

In this paper, a novel replication scheme, RICMAN is proposed to improve the performance of data access in intermittently connected MANETs, which employs a semi-probabilistic data disseminating protocol to distribute the replicas and propagate the updates despite network partitions and intermittent connectivity. Simulation results demonstrate that RICMAN scheme leads to good successful data access ratios and latencies with small overheads.

Future work will address the inclusion of additional profile information and corresponding analyzing techniques in identifying potential carriers, for example, including residual energy in the profile, using some kind of prediction technique to predict the co-location. How to decide optimal σ, τ and h value according to network conditions and application requirements is an interesting problem needing further research.

Acknowledgments

This work is supported by SRF for ROCS, SEM and the Program of Key International Science and Technology Cooperation Projects, Hubei.

References

1. Chaintreau, A., Hui, P., Crowcroft, J., Diot, C., Gass, R., Scott, J.: Impact of human mobility on the design of opportunistic forwarding algorithms. In: Proc. of IEEE INFOCOM'06, pp. 1–13 (2006)
2. Perkins, C.E., Bhagwat, P.: Highly dynamic Destination-Sequenced Distance-Vector routing (DSDV) for mobile computers. In: Proc. of ACM SIGCOMM'94, pp. 234–244 (1994)
3. Musolesi, M., Mascolo, C.: A Community Based Mobility Model for Ad Hoc Network Research. In: Proc. of ACM REALMAN'06, pp. 31–38 (2006)

Rate-Adaption Channel Assignment and Routing Algorithm for Multi-channel WirelessMAN Mesh Networks

Eric Hsiao-Kuang Wu[1], Wei-Li Chang[2], and Hsuan-Hao Chan[3]

Department of Computer Science and Information Engineering
National Central University, Chung-Li, Taiwan, R.O.C.
hsiao@csie.ncu.edu.tw[1], ali@wmlab.csie.ncu.edu.tw[2],
chuck@wmlab.csie.ncu.edu.tw[3]

Abstract. Wireless mesh networks provide an easy deployed and extensible solution to access Internet or communicate with each other for both enterprises and individuals. With the help of multi-channel and multi-radio, wireless mesh network can support more traffic load to meet higher and higher bandwidth requirement in this modern time. There have been researches that focus on channel assignment and routing algorithm for IEEE 802.11 multi-channel environment to achieve better network throughout. However, the data rate and transmission range of 802.11 is limited and is not suitable for a large area metropolitan mesh network deployment. This paper presents a rate-adaption channel assignment and routing algorithm for IEEE 802.16 multi-channel multi-radio network in mesh mode which is expected as the last-mile wireless broadband connectivity. We takes 802.16 TDMA characteristic and modulation/rate adaption into consideration. The Simulation results show that our channel assignment procedure uses fewer channels and better channel utilization than the migrated 802.11 greedy approach. Among the three comparing routing protocols, our protocol performs better in multi-rate 802.16 mesh network and results in higher aggregate throughput.

Keywords: IEEE 802.16, Wireless Mesh Network, Channel Assignment, Routing, Rate-Adaption.

1 Introduction

1.1 Multi-channel Wireless Networks

With the rapid growth of bandwidth request, multi-channel wireless network has been intensely researched and widely implemented. Multi-channel solution gives a way to increase concurrent transmissions by using orthogonal physical channels to transmit, which reduces the interference from adjacent links and therefore improves performance. However, the number of channel is limited, the links which use the same channel still interfere with each other especially in multi-hop or large-topology scenario [1]. So there are many researches investigate how to make good use of available channels and radios for each station. [10] [11] [12] [13] [14] mainly address multi-channel hidden terminal problem either with

J. Indulska et al. (Eds.): UIC 2007, LNCS 4611, pp. 331–339, 2007.

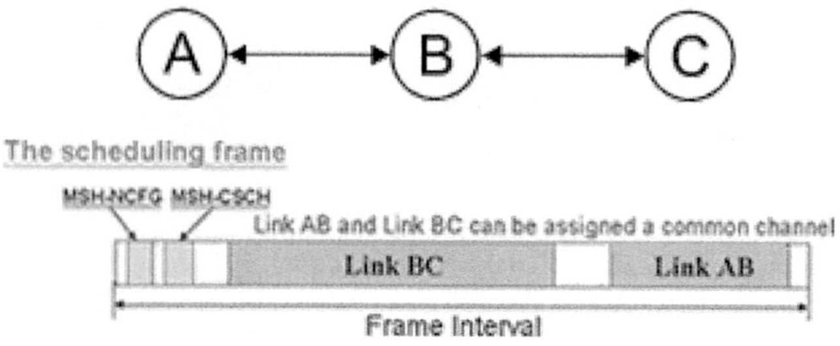

Fig. 1. Link AB and link BC can be assigned with the same channel if the bandwidth requirement is allowed

single transceiver or with multiple transceivers in ad-hoc networks. Their network environment is on a fast time scale such as on a packet-by-packet basis and put little attention to how channels, radios and links should be bounded, which greatly effects the interference between adjacent links. And several research efforts like [2] [3] [4] [5] [6] [8] [9] that aim to exploit multi-channel multi-radio in a 802.11 network, while [7] focuses on capturing the key practical aspects of such systems and characterize the constraints binding their behavior.

In this paper, we extend channel assignment and routing algorithm of multi-channel wireless network to IEEE 802.16 WirelessMAN. Differ from its wireless brethren 802.11, 802.16 allows the adjacent links to transmit in the same channel in one frame without any contention. Figure 7 shows the concept of the control messages exchange procedure and channel assignment for the links. When the bandwidth requirement of link AB and link BC does not exceed the capacity of the channel, both of them can be assigned with this channel and transmit data in turn in one frame. Also, IEEE 802.16 supports different modulation level over different links, which makes 802.16 has higher flexibility for channel assignment and routing algorithm. In this paper, we propose a Rate-Adaption Channel Assignment and Routing Algorithm to tie in 802.16 TDMA and multi-rate characteristics.

1.2 Goal of the Paper

In this paper, a Rate-Adaption Channel Assignment and Routing Algorithm for IEEE 802.16 wireless mesh network are proposed. The channel assignment should use fewer channels and achieve better channel utilization. The routing algorithm is supposed to be adapted to the link capability and ease the bottleneck.

1.3 Paper Organization

The remaining of this paper is organized as follows. The proposed Rate-Adaption Channel Assignment and Routing Algorithm will be described in Chapter 2. In Chapter 3, we show the ns-2 simulation results for the proposed scheme. At the end of the paper, we summarize our solution and results, and point out what can be done in the future in Chapter 4.

2 Proposed Scheme

2.1 IEEE 802.16 Control Messages

In IEEE 802.16 mesh mode, there are several important control messages:

Control Messages \ Attributes	Sender	Important Parameters
MSH-NCFG	broadcast by BS and SS	• Time stamp and Synchronization hop count • Number of logical channels
MSH-NENT	by BS and SS	• Network entry information
MSH-DSHE	by each Station	• Distributed scheduling information
MSH-CSCH	by BS and SS	• Centralized scheduling information
MSH-CSCF	broadcast by BS and re-broadcast by SS	• Centralized scheduling configuration

Fig. 2. IEEE 802.16 mesh network control messages

MSH-NCFG messages provide a basic level of communication between nodes in different nearby networks whether from the same or different equipment venders or wireless operators. All the nodes in the Mesh network shall transmit this message. MSH-NENT messages provide the means of a new node to gain synchronization and initial network entry into a Mesh network. MSH-DSCH messages shall be transmitted in Mesh mode when using distributed scheduling. A MSH-CSCH message shall be created by a Mesh BS when using centralized scheduling: The Mesh BS shall broadcast the MSH-CSCH message to all its neighbors, and all the nodes with hop count fewer then threshold shall forward the message to their neighbors that have higher hop count. Nodes can use MSH-CSCH messages to request bandwidth from Mesh BS setting the Grant/Request Flag = 1. The parameter Configuration Sequence Number indicates which configuration shall be used to interpret this packet. A MSH-CSCF message shall be broadcast in Mesh mode when using centralized scheduling. The Mesh BS shall broadcast the MSH-CSCF message to its neighbors, and all nodes shall forward the message according to its index number specified in the message. In our proposed scheme, Mesh BS uses MSH-CSCF message to tell all the stations the configuration that contains the channel-radio pair for each station. And Mesh BS can adjust the channel assignment either by broadcasting a new MSH-CSCF or indicating which MSH-CSCF shall be used by MSH-CSCH.

2.2 Proposed Channel Assignment

In order to provide reliability, our channel assignment should not alter network topology which might lead to cost from node failure. Figure 3 points out the condition of inferior channel assignment.

In our Rate-Adaption Channel Assignment (RA-CA) procedure, Link Criticality (LC) is introduced to accommodate the TDMA nature of 802.16 networks:

$$LinkCriticality_i = \frac{L_i}{C_i} \tag{1}$$

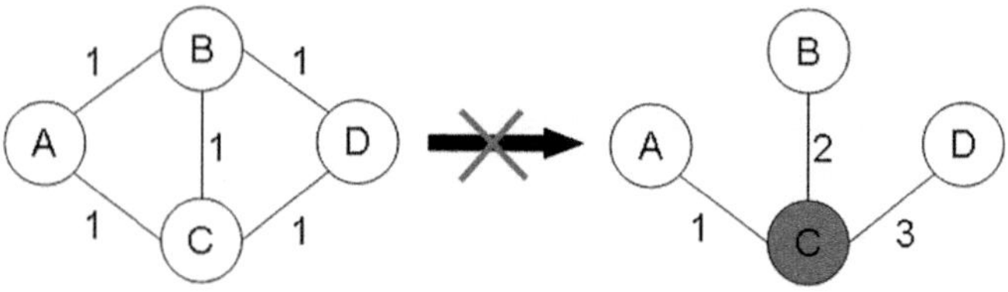

Fig. 3. Channel assignment procedure should not alter network topology

In equation 1, L_i is the link load and C_i is the capacity for the channel. Link Criticality has two characteristics in our scheme. First, it intuitively presents the priority of the links that needed to be assigned channel. The higher the LC is, the higher the priority. Secondly, it can be viewed as the slot number that should be scheduled in one Frame. For example, if link X has a 30Mbps traffic load on it and the capacity of the channel is 60Mbps, the Mesh BS may assign 50% time slots of the Frame for channel to link X. Moreover, we define a sufficient condition that link i can be assigned with channel k:

$$K_i = \sum I_{kj} + \frac{L_i}{C_i} + M \tag{2}$$

$$\sum I_{kj} + \frac{L_i}{C_i} + M < 1 \tag{3}$$

In equation 3, $\sum I_{kj}$ denotes the Link Criticality of link j that interferes with i in channel k. M is the 802.16 MAC overhead for a frame. This equation makes sure the ongoing channel assignment will not exceed the capacity of the channel by considering the interference from nearby links.

In the scheduling phase, Mesh BS stores the requests from the Mesh SSs and sort the Link Criticality in a decreasing order. After the bandwidth request, Mesh BS starts to assign the channels to links according to the decreasing order of Link Criticality. When scheduling channel for links, the assigned channel should be checked first by equation 3. Otherwise, the channel with the least result of K_i in equation 2 will be assigned.

When traffic load is above link capacity, Mesh BS can ask SS to transmit with a more stable modulation because there might be more links can be used. Takes figure 4 for example, there are only four links with 16-QAM modulation. Link BS-A may become the bottleneck when the traffic load is getting higher. In this scenario, Mesh BS can ask D to turn on its second radio to channel 3 with QPSK modulation and as does the Mesh BS. Station D can now directly communication with Mesh BS without relaying packets from station A and thus ease the bottleneck.

Channel assignment can be viewed as graph-coloring problems. However, because there are limited radios at each node and the number of channel is also a constraint, channel assignment problem brings special specification for multi-channel environment. In node-multi-coloring formulation, it ignores the fact that

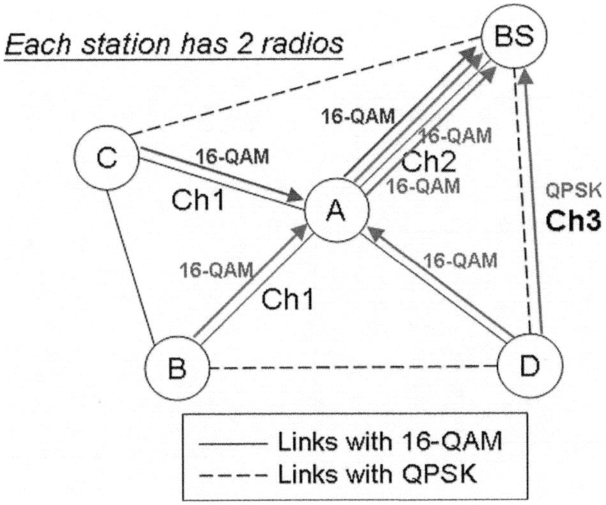

Fig. 4. Different modulation level brings different network topology

the transmission pairs should be painted with the same color in order to communicate with each other. An edge-coloring formulation faces the problem that the radios on a node are limited. And both of the coloring formulations didn't apply TDMA concept that the close-by links could be painted with the same color if the bandwidth requirement is allowed. In order words, the graph-coloring problem in multi-channel 802.16 CA should take the following factors into consideration: (1) The number of radios on a node is limited. We cannot assign channels for a node more than the number of radios. (2) The transmission pair should be bound to a common channel with one radio of each node. (3) Interference from adjacent links cannot be ignored. (4) TDMA characteristic should be added to the coloring principle.

We categorize the channel assignment into three cases, we are going to assign channel to link AB. First, each of A and B uses a number of radios fewer than available number of channel. In this case we first check if there is one channel used by A or B that satisfies equation 3. If not any assigned channel is qualified, the Mesh BS will assign a new channel for the link. Secondly, A has all of its radios assigned and B uses a number of radio fewer than available numbers of channel. We only check if there is one channel used by A that satisfies equation 3. If not any assigned channel is qualified, the Mesh BS will assign a channel with least K value of equation 2 for the link. Finally, both A and B have all of their radios assigned. We check if there is one channel used by A or B that satisfies equation 3 in turn when merging channels of A or B into a common channel for link AB.

Figure 5 shows how RA-CA should be performed. Mesh BS (station D) gather bandwidth requests from all the stations and stores LC of each link in a decreasing order. Each channel assignment is needed to be checked by equation 3 to

Degree of Link Criticality

Ch1	0.875
Ch2	0.781
Ch3	0.75 + 0.125
Ch4	0

Link Criticality

$L_{DE} : C_{DE}$	84 : 96
$L_{AB} : C_{AB}$	50 : 64
$L_{BD} : C_{BD}$	72 : 96
$L_{EF} : C_{EF}$	32 : 64
$L_{EG} : C_{EG}$	8 : 32
$L_{BC} : C_{BC}$	8 : 64

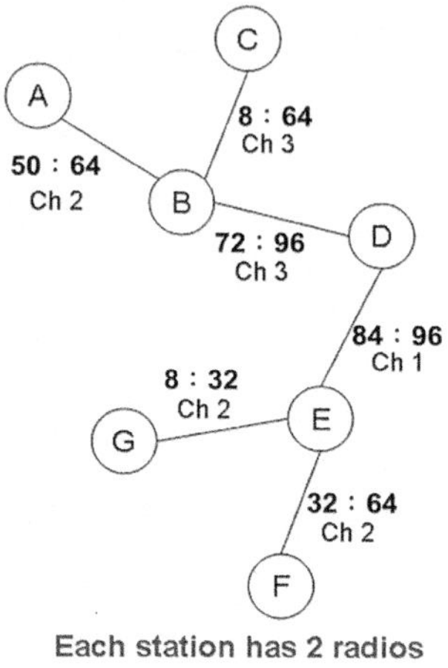

Fig. 5. Rate-Adaption Channel Assignment

ensure the sufficient capacity of the channel for the link. Degree of Link Criticality denotes the summation of LC that will interfere with the assigning link. It also represents how many time slots of the channel are used. The upper-left table shows the Degree of Link Criticality for link BC. By equation 3 in which we assume the MAC overhead is 0.1, therefore channel 3 is the resulting channel to be assigned.

2.3 Proposed Routing Algorithm

The RA-CA is not tied to any specific routing algorithm. For our ns-2 simulation, we inherit the two routing algorithm from hyacinth: (1) Shortest Path Routing (SPR) and (2) Randomized Multi-Path Routing (RMR). We also proposed a (3) Rate-Adaption Randomized Multi-Path Routing (RA-Routing for brief) to accommodate the multi-rate 802.16 network environment. RA-Routing takes link capacity into routing consideration. The more aggregate link capacity a route has, the higher possibility the packet will be transmitted through the path. For different hop-count routes, the aggregate link capacity of each route can be divided by hop-count to give a more objective view.

3 Simulation

In this chapter, we evaluate our proposed channel assignment and routing algorithm for multi-channel IEEE 802.16 Mesh Networks by ns-2 simulation. In our scenarios each station is equipped with two radios with either 16-QAM modulation or QPSK modulation. For a 20Mhz channel size, the peak data rate is 32Mbps and 64Mbps for QPSK and 16-QAM, respectively. The network is supposed to be error-free, and all the traffic flows are using constant-bit-rate. We first examine our RA-CA performance by channel usage and channel utilization. Because of

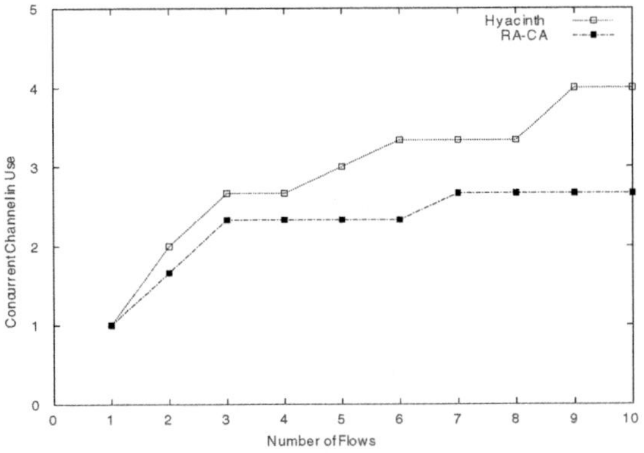

Fig. 6. Channel usage comparison between RA-CA and migrated-Hyacinth

the limitation of wireless channels, we are going to show RA-CA needs a lower requirement for number of channel. Next part we represent the benefits from IEEE 802.16 multi-rate environment. Each station can change their radios to different modulation levels and may gain extra available links for transmitting data. RA-Routing is proposed to ease the bottleneck while not make the weaker link to be a new one. We will compare Shortest-Path-Routing, Randomized-Multipath-Routing and proposed Rate-Adaption Randomized-Multipath-Routing for several different scenarios.

3.1 Channel Usage and Utilization

We first show that RA-CA is more suitable for multi-channel IEEE 802.16 Mesh networks. Figure 6 represents the channel usage for migrated Hyacinth and RA-CA. Each point is the average number of channel usage for three different network topologies. Obvious, RA-CA uses fewer numbers of channels than migrated-Hyacinth. This is because RA-CA takes an approach that assigned channel should be checked first if there is available bandwidth for the link while Hyacinth will assign the least interfered channel that usually be an empty channel for the link. That is, migrated-Hyacinth will not assign used channel to links until there is no radios can be assigned or runs out of channels. Therefore, RA-CA has lower requirement for number of channels.

In order to take a deeper view of how channel is being used, we investigate the aggregate channel utilization for one of the topology used. The figure shows load per channel over different number of traffic flow. The line drop means a new channel is assigned for a certain link. Consider the difference when the number of flow equals to 2, in which RA-CA gets a burst while migrated-Hyacinth gets a line-drop. The reason is that RA-CA assigned the link with the same channel as flow 1 does, and migrated-Hyacinth will assign channel 2 for flow 2. In this scenario, RA-CA uses only two channels and migrated-Hyacinth uses four channels. RA-CA uses a new channel at the second flows, migrated-Hyacinth assigns

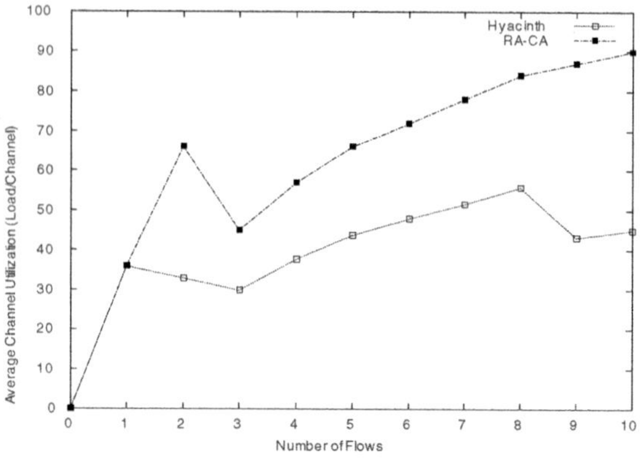

Fig. 7. The figure shows load/channel over different number of traffic flow. The line drop means a new channel is assigned for a certain link.

new channels at 2nd, 3rd, 9th flows. Notice that the network topology contains links which is far from interfering with each other in the same channel, that's why the load per channel can exceed the physical constraints.

4 Conclusion

In this paper, we proposed a Rate-Adaption Channel Assignment and Rate-Adaption Randomized Multi-path Routing algorithm for multi-channel IEEE 802.16 wireless Mesh networks. We show that Rate-Adaption Channel Assignment can reduce the concurrent number of channel in use while get better channel utilization across the whole network by taking advantages of TDMA nature of 802.16. And Multi-Rate is another interesting characteristic worthy to be investigated. Without rate-adaption, there are no particular ways to improve the performance except adding stations into the network to meet the requirement. RA-CA and RA-Routing exploit the links with different modulation level. We proved that RA-CA eases the bottleneck when the traffic load is high. RA-Routing proportionally separates traffic load into different routes according to route capacity. Unlike Randomized-Multipath-Routing, RA-Routing takes weak links into consideration and will not turn the bottleneck to weaker links. Generally speaking, our proposed scheme performs better than no rate-adaption solution up to 75%, and up to 25% when comparing to SPR and RMR with rate-adaption.

In the future, we want to expand the scenario into a larger topology. More traffic loads should be generated to give a more general view for the performance improvement. Finally, we consider migrating the RA-CA and RA-Routing protocol into Distributed Multi-channel IEEE 802.16 wireless Mesh network, more complex CA scheduling between different local networks will introduce another challenge.

Acknowlegements. This research is supported by the Mobile Media Technology Center Networks and Multimedia, Taiwan, under Instituteby Institute for Information Industry (III) and the projet number is (A6K01221).

References

1. Jain, K., Padhye, J., Padmanabhan, V.N., Qiu, L.: Impact of interference on multi-hop wireless network performance. In: Proc. ACM MobiCom, pp. 66–80. ACM Press, New York (2003)
2. Raniwala, A., Gopalan, K., Chiueh, T.: Centralized Channel Assignment and Routing Algorithms for Multi-Channel Wireless Mesh Networks. ACM Mobile Computing and Communication review 8, 50–65 (2004)
3. Raniwala, A., Gopalan, K., Chiueh, T.: Architecture and Algorithms for an IEEE 802.11-Based Multi-Channel Wireless Network. In: INFOCOM, vol. 3, pp. 2223–2234 (2005)
4. Alicherry, M., Bhatia, R., Li (Erran) Li.: Joint Channel Assignment and Routing for Throughput Optimization in Multi-Radio Wireless Mesh Networks. MobiCom, 58–72 (2005)
5. Yuan, S., Vannat, S., Juex, J.P.: Minimum-Color Path Problems for Reliability in Mesh Networks. In: INFOCOM, vol. 4, pp. 2658–2669 (2005)
6. Ramachandran, K., Belding, E., Almeroh, K., Buddhikot, M.: Interference-Aware Channel Assignment in Multi-Radio Wireless Mesh Networks. In: INFOCOM (to appear, 2006)
7. Kodialam, M., Nandagopal, T.: Characterizing the Capacity Region in Multi-Radio Multi-Channel Wireless Mesh Networks. MobiCom, 73–87 (2005)
8. Bahl, V., Adya, A., Padhye, J., Wolman, A.: Reconsidering wireless systems with multiple radios. ACM SIGCOMM Computer Communication Review 34, 39–46 (2004)
9. Hsiao, P.H., Hwang, A., Kung, H.T., Vlah, D.: Load-Balancing Routing for Wireless Access Networks. In: INFOCOM, vol.2, pp. 986–995 (2001)
10. So, J., Vaidya, N.: Multi-Channel MAC for Ad Hoc Networks: Handling Multi-Channel Hidden Terminals Using A Single Transceiver. MobiHoc, 222–233 (2004)
11. Wu, S., Lin, C., Tseng, Y., Sheu, J.: A New Multi-Channel MAC Protocol with On-Demand Channel Assignment for Multi-Hop Mobile Ad Hoc Networks. In: I-SPAN, 2000, p. 232 (2000)
12. Jain, N., Das, S.R., Nasipuri, A.: A Multichannel CSMA MAC Protocol with Receiver-Based Channel Selection for Multihop Wireless Networks. In: IC3N, 2001, pp. 432–439 (2001)
13. Tang, Z., Garcia-Luna-Aceves, J.J.: Hop-Reservation Multiple Access (HRMA) for Ad-Hoc Networks. In: INFOCOM, vol. 1, pp. 194–201 (1999)
14. Tzamaloukas., A., Garcia-Luna-Aceves, J.J.: A Receiver-Initiated Collision-Avoidance Protocol for Multi-channel Networks. INFOCOM 1, 189–198 (2001)

Neighbor-Aware Optimizing Routing for Wireless Ad Hoc Networks

Xianlong Jiao, Xiaodong Wang, and Xingming Zhou

National Laboratory for Parallel and Distributed Processing, National University of Defense Technology, Changsha, China 410073
jiaoxianlong1982@gmail.com, {xdwang,xmzhou}@nudt.edu.cn

Abstract. Wireless ad hoc networks are consisted of mobile nodes with limited bandwidth, computing ability and energy, which is different from the traditional wired networks. On demand routing protocols are proposed for this type of network, and they scale well with the topology of ad hoc network. But due to lack of knowledge of global topology and the mobility of nodes, they may be not optimal. We propose a Neighbor-Aware Optimizing Routing algorithm (called NAOR) based on SHORT [1] which uses hop comparison array to optimize the routing protocol. Our NAOR algorithm solves those special cases which SHORT fails to handle. Finally, we use ns-2 simulator to evaluate the performance of AODV, AODV using SHORT and AODV using NAOR. The results show that NAOR gets better improvement on performance such as delivery rate and latency than SHORT.

1 Introduction

Wireless ad hoc networks are consisted of mobile nodes with limited bandwidth, computing ability and energy, which is different from the traditional wired networks. Ad hoc networks do not have any fixed infrastructure, while traditional wireless mobile networks are supported by a wired fixed infrastructure, such as the cellular networks. Therefore, ad hoc networks can be applied to many situations, such as battle, disaster recovery, and so on.

If some node in the ad hoc networks wants to communicate with another node far away from it, the packet it sends usually has to be transmitted in a multi-hop path. The packet may not be sent to the destination because of the dynamic changing topology, interference, exhausted energy and some other reasons. Therefore, much work has been done on routing issues on ad hoc networks in recent years. Table driven protocols (such as DSDV [2], OLSR [3], TBRPF [4] and FSR [5]), which are efficient protocols in wired networks, are exploited for the ad hoc networks. These protocols, however, have to exchange information periodically, which will bring high routing overhead and will not be efficient due to the limited bandwidth of the ad hoc networks. So, on demand protocols (such as TORA [6], AODV [7] and DSR [8]) are then proposed to solve this problem. These protocols exchange information only when it's needed. Each node tries to reduce routing overhead as it sends packets only when needed.

J. Indulska et al. (Eds.): UIC 2007, LNCS 4611, pp. 340–349, 2007.

Large effort has been made on the routing protocol for ad hoc networks (such as [9], [10], and [11]). In this paper, we focus on further optimizing the existing routing protocol (AODV), and we have presented a Neighbor-Aware and Optimizing Routing algorithm (called NAOR) for ad hoc networks. It's based on Self-Healing and Optimizing Routing Technique (called SHORT), and tries its best to optimize the routing path by finding the short-cut path which is discussed in SHORT. NAOR gives solution to some special cases which is discussed in SHORT. We have implemented the NAOR algorithm in ns-2 simulator and have shown the advantage in terms of performance (such as packet delivery rate) compared with AODV and SHORT. The results show that our NAOR exceeds SHORT in both static and mobile situations.

The rest of the paper is organized as follows. In Section 2, we give an overview of the related work concerning optimizing routing technique. Neighbor-aware optimizing routing algorithm called NAOR is described in Section 3. In Section 4, we evaluate the NAOR algorithm and give the detailed results. Finally, we present the conclusion in Section 5.

2 Related Work

In [1], a framework of self-healing and optimizing routing techniques for mobile ad hoc networks is proposed. SHORT improves routing optimality by monitoring routing paths continuously, and gradually redirecting path towards a currently more optimal one. The basic idea is to let neighbors of a routing path, together with the on-route nodes, monitor the route, so that up-to-date information about relative local topology and link quality is exploited. The (n, 1) short-cut path and (n, 2) short-cut path are exploited to improve route performance. We will talk about the short-cut path in detail later in Section 3.

Marcelo Spohn et al. present the neighborhood aware source routing protocol (NSR) in [12]. They derive the protocol from the performance improvements observed in DSR when link caches were used, and nodes can easily inform their neighbors of their own neighbors. The key feature of NSR is that nodes reduce the effort required to fix source routes due to node mobility by using alternate links available in their two-hop neighborhood.

In [13], a reliable on-demand Node-Disjoint Multipath Routing Protocol (NDMR) is proposed to overcome the shortcomings of on-demand unipath routing protocols. NDMR has two novel aspects in that it reduces routing overhead dramatically by recording the shortest number hops of loop-free paths in the reverse route table entry and achieves multiple node-disjoint routing paths. They modify AODV to include path accumulation in RREQ packets and to use the path accumulation information to decrease routing overhead. We also incorporate path accumulation characteristic in our algorithm, but there is some difference that the intermediate nodes on the route path also need to record the path accumulation information.

Sudarshan Vasudevan et al. [14] consider the problem of neighbor discovery in wireless networks with directional antennas. They propose two class of probabilistic neighbor discovery algorithms, viz. Direct-Discovery Algorithms in which nodes discover their neighbors only when they hear transmissions from their neighbors and Gossip-Based Algorithms in which nodes gossip about location information about their neighbors. In AODV, hello message is exploited to discover the neighbors, and we directly exploit the neighbor information in our algorithm.

In DSR routing protocol, nodes have the knowledge of the information of the entire route, so it's very easy to find the (n, 1) short-cuts with the help the neighbor list, but can't find the (n, 2) short-cuts. AODV and DSDV, however, don't have the information of the entire route, and it's not easy for these protocols to find (n, 1) short-cuts or (n, 2) short-cuts.

3 Neighbor-Aware Optimizing Routing

3.1 Problem Description of AODV and SHORT

As AODV does not record the route path, it will incur the following problem as shown in Figure 1(a). If A has the route to I through D, and A wants to communicate with D, and as it only has the next hop and destination node address in its route table, it has no route to D, then it has to perform a route discovery process to find D. As discussed above, AODV exploits broadcasting to discover the route, and it will consume the limited bandwidth and result in packet collision. So, we propose a new method to solve this problem which is discussed in section 3.2.

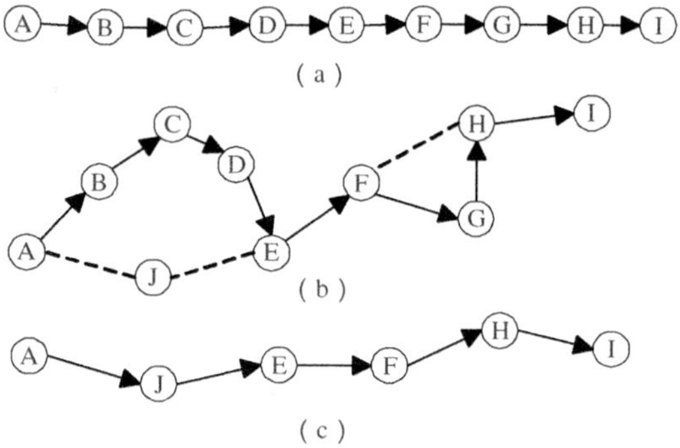

Fig. 1. An example in SHORT

SHORT considers the following problem as shown in Figure 1. Figure 1(a) is the initial path which is discovered by the path discovery process. Node A routed its packet to node I through eight hops. And as a result of the node's movement, the routing path while maintaining the connectivity is shown in Figure 1(b). A new node J is in the transmission range of A, and E is in the transmission range of J. Similarly H is in the transmission range of F. SHORT optimizes this path to the one shown in Figure 1(c) by inducing a hop comparison array. However, SHORT has to incur additional overhead to store the hop comparison array, and adapts the dynamic topology change not fast to optimize the path between the source and the destination. We induce path accumulation characteristic and neighbor information to improve the algorithm. We will discuss our algorithm detailedly in section 3.2.

3.2 NAOR: Detailed Algorithms

As discussed in [1], due to lack of precise global information and distributed operation manner, the ad hoc routing protocol cannot make globally optimal decision at the routing setup time. Similarly, NAOR will monitor the valid path as long as the path is set up and packets begin to flow along it. In this paper, we detailed the NAOR algorithm.

3.2.1 NAOR

First, we modify AODV to include the path accumulating characteristic in order to solve the problem of AODV discussed above. The method is like the one discussed in [14], but there is some difference that every intermediate node needs to record the path to the source node by analyzing RREQ packet and the path to destination by analyzing RREP packet, as shown in Figure 2.

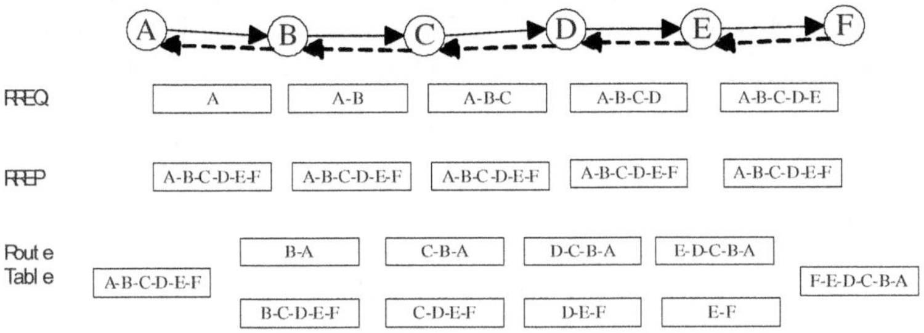

Fig. 2. An example for path accumulation

As can be seen from Figure 2, we modify the RREQ packet and the RREP packet to include the path information. After finding the route to node F, node A will find the whole path A-B-C-D-E-F in its route table, and if A wants to communicate with node D, node A doesn't have to perform the discovery process which will consume the limited bandwidth and result in packet collision. This can improve the performance of the routing protocol.

To support the proposed NAOR algorithm, each data packet needs to carry the "Path" field in its header. The Path field is filled at the source node with the valid path in the route table. NA, which is the neighbor's address from which the packet is broadcasted, is also needed in NAOR algorithm. The process of NAOR is shown in Figure 3.

Take an example to show the correctness of the algorithm. For convenience of comparison, we consider the routing path in Figure 4(a) (It's a little different from Figure 1(b)). Let node A as the source and node I as the destination. We will track the routing path step by step.

The process is shown in the following steps:

1) When A starts to send a packet to the destination node I, it finds that, although node B is common in the neighbor list and in the Path, the hop distance between node A and node B in the Path is not more than 1, so node A continues to send the packet to node B without doing anything.

NAOR Algorithm

When node i is the source node or node i receives or overhears a packet P,

BEGIN

1. IF node i is the final destination address, consumes the packet. GOTO END;
2. Compare the Path with all the neighbors in the neighbor list in order to find the common node;
3. (Assume that some node j is common in both the Path and the neighbor list. As there may be more than one common node, we only consider the last common one in the path to achieve better optimality.)

   IF node i is in the Path, and the hop distance between node i and node j in the Path is more than 1, then node i can optimizes this Path by deleting the middle nodes between node i and node j, and modifying the next hop to the address of node j. In addition, node i records the modified path in its routing table. Here, node i finds a (n, 1) short-cut path.

   IF node i is not in the Path, and IF the hop distance between node NA (it can be achieved from the packet) and node j is more than 2, and node j is after node NA in the Path, then node i finds a (n, 2) short-cut path and does the following:

   3.1. Send a message to NA to update the routing table such that the next hop address for destination node DA is modified to the address of node i;

   3.2. Modify its routing table by making the next-hop address for destination DA as the address of node j, and record the modified path in its routing table;
4. IF the packet is destined to i as the next-hop node, then i processes the packet for forwarding further. GOTO END;

END

Fig. 3. NAOR Algorithm

2) When receiving the packet, node B finds that, node A and node C are both in its neighbor list and in the Path, and their hop distances to node B don't match the condition, so node B further forwards the packet to node C.
3) Node J while overhearing the packet from A, however, finds that, node E is the common node in the Path and the neighbor list, and the hop distance between node E and node A (which is the NA node of node J) is more than 2, so node J sends a message to node A to update its routing table to point to J for destination I. J modifies its own routing table to make the next-hop node for destination I as E. Thus the (n, 2) short-cut path A-J-E is found for the earlier route A-B-C-D-E.
4) Similarly node C further forwards the packet to node D, as the hop distances to its neighbors (node B and node D) do not match the optimizing condition.

5) Node D and node E do the same thing as node C, since the hop distances to their neighbor nodes don't match the optimizing condition.
6) When F starts to send the packet, it finds that, node I is common in its neighbor list and the path, and the hop distance between F and I in the path is more than 2, so it deletes the node G and the node H from the path, and modifies the next hop to node I. Here, the (n, 1) short-cut path F-I is found.
7) Finally node I consumes the packet as it is the destination node.
8) The final path is shown in Figure 4(b).

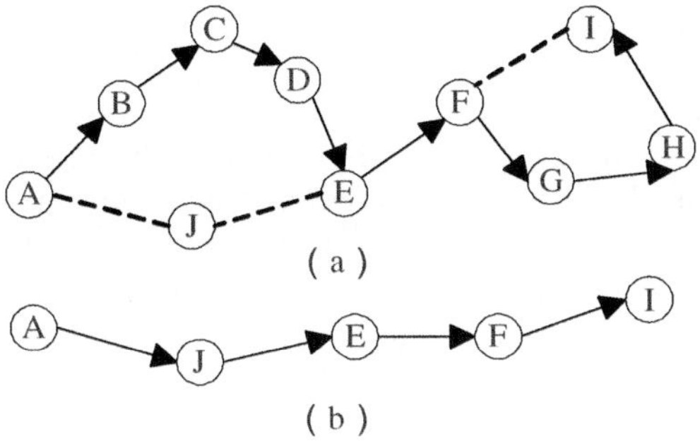

Fig. 4. An example for describing NAOR

3.3.2 Solution to Special Cases in SHORT

There are some special cases in the topologies of ad hoc network which is not solved by the basic SHORT algorithm. These cases are shown in Figure 5.

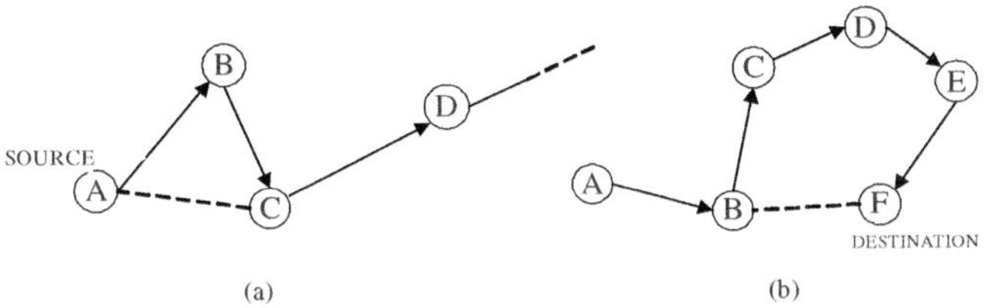

Fig. 5. Special cases in SHORT

In Figure 5(a), when node A sends the packet to node B with HC=0, since SHORT exploits hop distance array to find the short-cut path, A, B and C all record 0 in hop comparison array when receiving or overhearing the packet. B continues to send the packet to C with HC=1. While receiving the packet from B, C forwards the packet to D with HC=2, and A finds that the HC difference is not more than 2 when overhearing the packet. So the short-cut path A-C is not detected by SHORT algorithm. Also, in Figure 5(b), as the destination node F will not forward the packet further, B can't find the short-cut path B-F. NAOR, however, exploits the information in the path and the neighbor list, and will find the short-cut path A-C (or B-F) as soon as A (or B) starts to send the packet, since C (or F) is common in the neighbor list and in the path, and the hop distance between A and C (or B and F) is more than 1 in the path.

4 Simulation and Results

We use ns-2 simulator which is downloaded from the web site to evaluate our algorithm. VINT project develops ns-2 simulator, and then Monarch extends the simulator for wireless network. We exploit Lucent's WaveLAN with a nominal bit rate of 2Mb/sec and a nominal range of 250 meters as the radio model. Two-ray ground model is used as the radio propagation model. Motion follows the random way point model.

4.1 Analysis for Static Networks

We first test our algorithm in static scenarios. 100 static nodes are located within a rectangular field of 2000m×600m in size which is the same to what is used in SHORT. Therefore, the hop difference between source node and destination node can be large enough. The simulation lasts for 1000 seconds. For the traffic model, our application traffic is CBR (constant bit rate). We randomly choose the source node and the destination node, and use 16 simultaneous flows with different packet sending rate as 4, 6, 8, 10, 12, 14 and 16, and all the application packets are 256 bytes long. Therefore data transfer rate can be computed as 8, 12, 16, 20, 24, 28, 32 kbps for each simultaneous flow. We implement our algorithm on AODV, and compare the performance with SHORT and AODV. These protocols are referred to as AODV-NAOR, AODV-SHORT and AODV respectively.

In our simulation, we study the following four metrics:

1) Average Path Length: average number of hops a packet takes to successfully reach its destination.
2) Packet Delivery Rate: the ratio of the number of data packets successfully delivered to the number of data packets generated by the CBR sources.
3) Normalized Routing Overhead: the number of routing packets transmitted per data packet delivered at the destination. Each hop-wise packet transmission is counted as one transmission.
4) Average End-to-End Delay: all possible delays caused by buffering during routing discovery, queuing at the interface queue, retransmission at the MAC layer, propagation, and transfer time.

Figure 6 shows the average path length, packet delivery rate, normalized routing overhead and average end-to-end delay as a function with respect to the data transfer rate. From Figure 6, we can see that the performance of AODV and AODV-SHORT decreases with the increase of data transfer rate and is very close, and AODV-NAOR achieves better performance than the other protocols. When data transfer rate increases, collision among the packets increases and the probability of successfully sending the packets to the destination becomes smaller, so the performance will decrease. Note that average path length will decrease with the increase of the data transfer rate, this is because if the hop distance between source and destination node is smaller, the packets will be sent more successfully, and only the successfully sent packets are considered to compute average path length. AODV-NAOR uses path

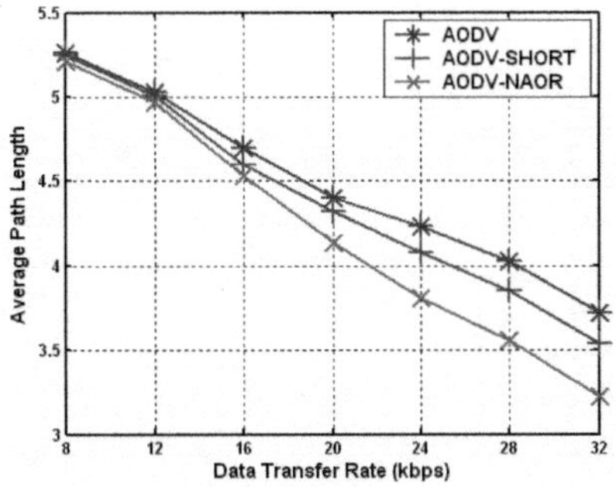

(a) Average Path Length

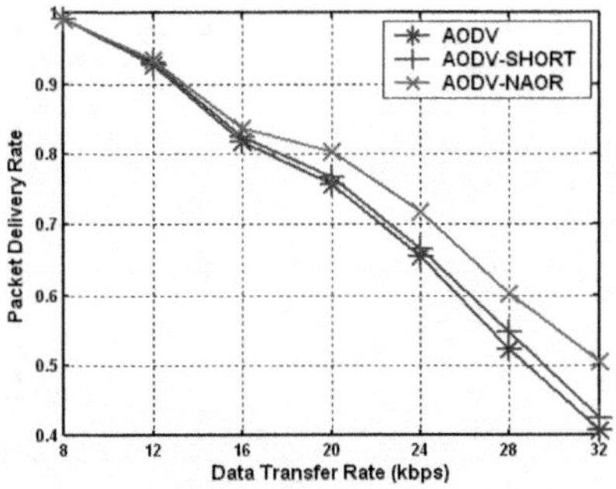

(b) Packet Delivery Rate

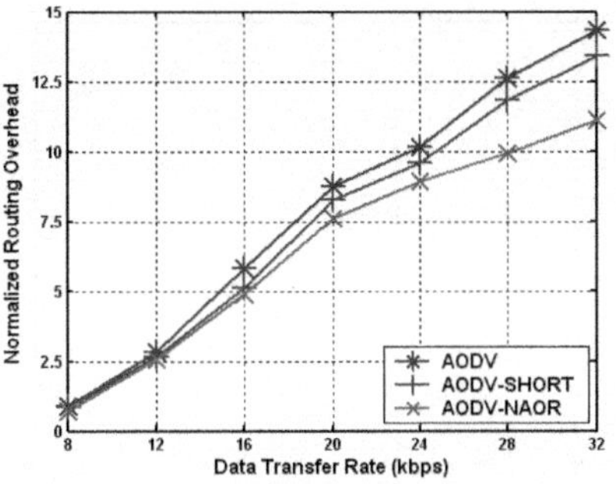

(c) Normalized Routing Overhead

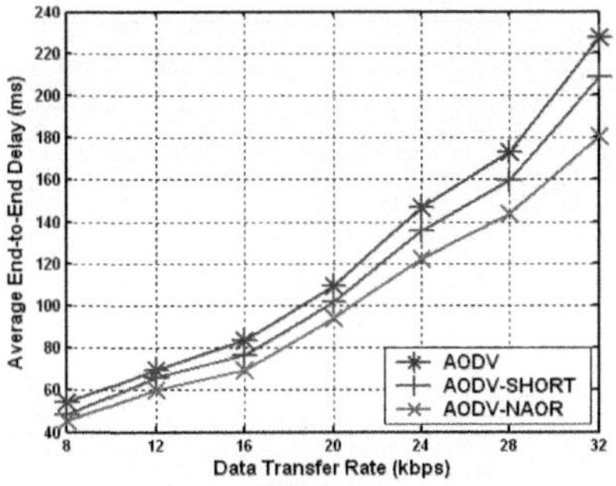

(d) Average End-to-End Delay

Fig. 6. Network Performance in Static Scenarios

accumulation characteristics to avoid invoking some route discovery processes, and more packets can successfully reach the destination nodes, so it achieves better performance than the other protocols.

4.2 Effect of Mobility

In the mobile traffic model, we test 16 simultaneous flows with different source-destination pairs, and data transfer rate is 8 kbps, that is sending 4 CBR packets per second. In order to analyze the effect of mobility, different values of pause time (such as 90, 180, 270, 360, 450 simulation seconds) are used in our simulation. Nodes move with maximum speed as 20 m/s.

Figure 7 shows the average path length, packet delivery rate, normalized routing overhead, and average end-to-end delay as a function with respect to pause time. When nodes don't move, the performance of three protocols is very close. AODV's routing performance drops significantly with the decrease of the pause time. AODV-SHORT and AODV-NAOR shows better routing optimality than AODV as a result of the short-cut path. As when nodes move frequently, the path a packet takes will be longer, and it will result in larger probability of packet collision. Furthermore, with

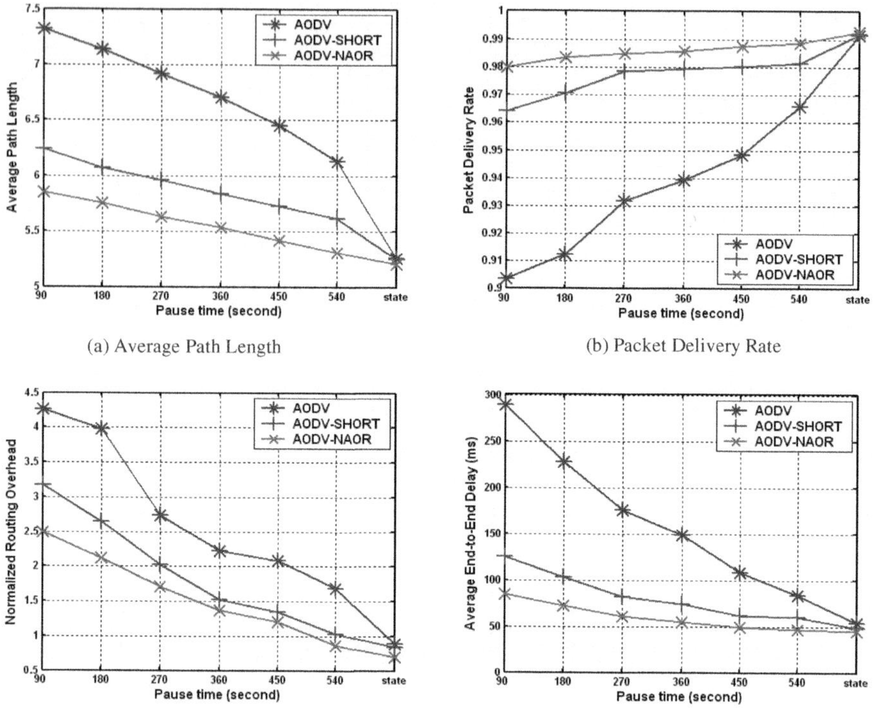

(a) Average Path Length

(b) Packet Delivery Rate

(c) Normalized Routing Overhead

(d) Average End-to-End Delay

Fig. 7. Network Performance in Mobile Scenarios

the help of path accumulation characteristic, AODV-NAOR avoids many route discovery processes and solves the special cases which are not solved by SHORT, so it exceeds AODV-SHORT in route optimality in the mobile scenarios.

5 Conclusion and Future Work

In this paper, we present a Neighbor-Aware Optimizing Routing algorithm based on SHORT which uses hop comparison array to optimize the routing protocol. NAOR exploits path accumulation characteristic to record valid route information, and try to find the (n, 1) short-cut path and (n, 2) short-cut path with the help of neighbor information. In static scenarios, route discovery process is avoided in some extent due to path accumulation characteristic, so better routing performance can be achieved by NAOR than AODV and SHORT. In mobile scenarios, with the help of path accumulation characteristic and short-cut paths, NAOR also exceeds AODV and SHORT in routing performance such as average path length, packet delivery rate and so on. In future, we will test other metrics such as energy efficiency of NAOR in both static scenarios and mobile scenarios. Furthermore, we will incorporate our algorithm into other on-demand routing protocols, such as DSR.

References

1. Gui, C., Mohapatra, P.: SHORT: Self-Healing and Optimizing Routing Techniques for Mobile Ad Hoc Networks. In: Proceedings of ACM International Conference on Mobile Computing and Networking (MOBIHOC) (2003)
2. Perkins, C.E., Bhagwat, P.: Highly Dynamic Destination-Sequenced Distance-Vector Routing (DSDV) for Mobile Computers. In: Proceedings of ACM SIGCOMM, pp. 234–244 (1994)
3. Clausen, T., et al.: Optimized Link State Routing Protocol. IETF Internet Draft (2003), http://www.ietf.org/internet-drafts/draft-ietf-manet-olsr-11.txt
4. Ogier, R., Lewis, M., Templin, F.: Topology Dissemination Based on Reverse-Path Forwarding (TBRPF). IETF Internet Draft (2003), http://www.ietf.org/internetdrafts/draft-ietf-manet-tbrpf-09.txt
5. Pei, G., Gerla, M.: Fisheye State Routing: A Routing Scheme For Ad Hoc Wireless Networks. In: Proc. IEEE ICC'00, New Orleans, LA (2000)
6. Park, V.D., Corson, M.S.: A Highly Adaptive Distributed Routing Algorithm for Mobile Wireless Networks. In: Proceedings of IEEE INFOCOM (1997)
7. Perkins, C.E., Belding-Royer, E., Das, S.R.: Ad hoc On-Demand Distance Vector (AODV) Routing, RFC 3561 (2003), http://www.ietf.org/rfc/rfc3561.txt
8. Johnson, D.B., Maltz, D.A., Hu, Y., Jetcheva, J.G.: The Dynamic Source Routing Protocol for Mobile Ad Hoc Networks (DSR). IETF Internet Draft (2002), http://www.ietf.org/internet-drafts/draft-ietf-manet-dsr-07.txt.
9. Biswas, S., Morris, R.: ExOR: Opportunistic Multi-Hop Routing for Wireless Networks. In: Proceedings of ACM SIGCOMM (2005)
10. Yu, X., Kedem, Z.: A Distributed Adaptive Cache Update Algorithm for the Dynamic Source Routing Protocol. In: Proceedings of IEEE INFOCOM (2005)
11. Frey, H., Stojmenovic, I.: On delivery guarantees of face and combined greedy-face routing in ad hoc and sensor networks. In: Proceedings of MOBICOM (2006)
12. Spohn, M., Garcia-Luna-Aceves, J.J.: Neighborhood Aware Source Routing. In: Proc. ACM International Symposium on Mobile Ad Hoc Networking & Computing (MOBIHOC), ACM Press, New York (2001)
13. Li, X., Cuthbert, L.: A Reliable Node-Disjoint Multipath Routing with Low Overhead in Wireless Ad hoc Networks. In: Proceedings of the 7th ACM international symposium on Modeling, analysis and simulation of wireless and mobile systems (MSWiM) (2004)
14. Vasudevan, S., Kurose, J., Towsley, D.: On Neighbor Discovery in Wireless Networks With Directional Antennas. In: Proceedings of IEEE INFOCOM (2005)

Gateway Zone Multi-path Routing in Wireless Mesh Networks

Eric Hsiao-Kuang Wu[1], Wei-Li Chang[1], Chun-Wei Chen[1], and Kevin Chihcheng Hsu[2]

[1] Department of Computer Science and Information Engineering
National Central University, Chung-Li, Taiwan, R.O.C.
hsiao@csie.ncu.edu.tw, {ali,weiwei}@wmlab.csie.ncu.edu.tw
http://wmlab.csie.ncu.edu.tw/wmlab/teacher/teacher.htm
[2] Department of Information Management
National Central University, Chung-Li, Taiwan, R.O.C.
khsu@mgt.ncu.edu.tw

Abstract. Internet and multimedia services are widely-provided in All-IP based networks. There has been growing demand for mobile users to get those services. The Wireless Mesh Network (WMN) extends communication range and provides Internet connectivity to mobile users with low upfront investment. In WMN, the traffic usually passes through the gateway and makes it become the common destination of the traffic. Conventional multipath routing protocols in the ad hoc networks do not allow intermediate nodes to reply the route request messages, so the flooding messages make the area near the gateway become congested and degrade the performance. In this paper, we proposed Gateway Zone Multi-path Routing (GZMR) protocol. GZMR uses node around the gateway to form a Gateway Cooperative Zone and ceases the routing control messages flooding from outside the zone. Border nodes in the zone can help replying gateway information to reduce route discovery delay. Our simulation results show that by lowering routing overheads and utilizing multiple paths from source to gateway, GZMR can shorten average end-to-end delay and improve the packet delivery in WMNs.

1 Introduction

In recent years, the rapid growing of the Internet services and on-demand multimedia services in the All-IP networks increase mobile users' demand for acquiring Internet services. The integration between Wireless Networks and the Internet becomes an important issue. Gateways may be put into Wireless Ad Hoc Networks for mobile users connecting to the Internet or other networks. This kind of wireless network is called Wireless Mesh Network (WMN).

General WMNs consist of mesh routers and mesh clients, where mesh routers have minimal mobility and form the backbone of WMNs ([1,2]). Mesh clients can be either stationary or mobile devices, and can form a client mesh network among themselves and with mesh routers. WMNs can be classified into three

J. Indulska et al. (Eds.): UIC 2007, LNCS 4611, pp. 350–359, 2007.

groups: Infrastructure/Backbone WMNs, Client WMNs and Hybrid WMNs. Hybrid WMNs is the most applicable because mesh clients can not only directly communicate with other mesh clients, but also access the Internet service through mesh routers. Many studies ([3], [4]) in the WMNs focus on Infrastructure/ Backbone WMNs. In this paper, we focus on Hybrid WMNs, especially on mesh clients (e.g. Mobile Ad Hoc Network (MANET)) accessing Internet service through gateway supported mesh routers.

In this paper, we present Gateway Zone Multi-path Routing (GZMR) protocol that nodes around the gateway form a Gateway Cooperative Zone to cease the routing control messages flooding from outside the zone and solve *routing control messages flooding problem.* And Border Nodes in the zone can help replying gateway information to nodes outside the zone to solve *gateway congested problem.* The reducing routing overheads and multiple paths from source to the gateway can help reducing average end-to-end delay and improving the packet delivery in wireless mesh networks.

The rest of the paper is organized as follows.We propose our GZMR protocol in Section II. In Section III, the performance evaluation is presented through ns2 simulation and we concluded this paper in Section IV.

2 Gateway Zone Multi-path Routing

2.1 Overview

Our objective in this section is to design an efficient multipath routing mechanism, Gateway Zone Multi-path Routing (GZMR), to help reducing routing overheads around the gateway and improving packet delivery in the wireless mesh network.

2.2 System Model

System Architecture. First of all, we introduce the system architecture of our scheme in Fig. 1. It is a hybrid wireless mesh network thats mesh clients connect to a mesh router with gateways support (or Internet Gateway) to access Internet service. We define a Gateway Cooperative Zone (GCZ), which is formed by two or three hops neighbors of the Internet Gateway (IGW). Border Nodes (BNs) are in the rim of GCZ. Mobile Nodes (MNs) and BNs can move in the rang of IGW and communicate to Fixed Nodes (FNs) in the Internet. BNs act as guard nodes, which restrain Route Request (RREQ) messages flooding into GCZ. Fig 2: Protocol stacks of mobile nodes, Internet gateways and fixed nodes. The network layer is coordinated by GZMR (Fig 3), composed by zone formation, gateway/route discovery, neighbor history record (NHR) and data forwarding.

Message Formats. According to [6] and [7], we use RREQ_I and RREP_I, which are Route Request(RREQ) message with Internet-Global Address Resolution Flag (I-flag) and Route Reply (RREP) with I-flag in brief to support gateway discovery operations. The purpose of RREQ_I message is to reactively

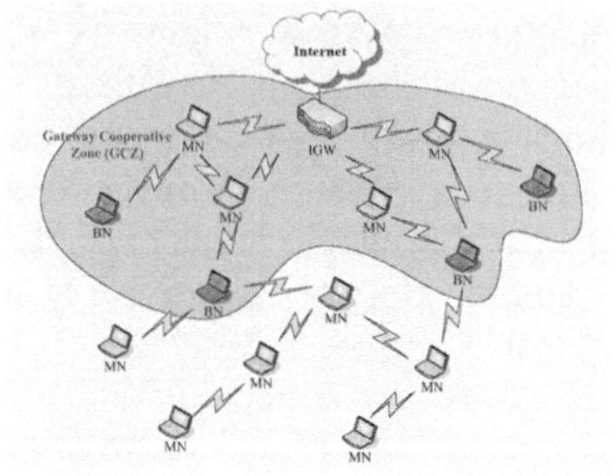

Fig. 1. System Architecture of GZMR

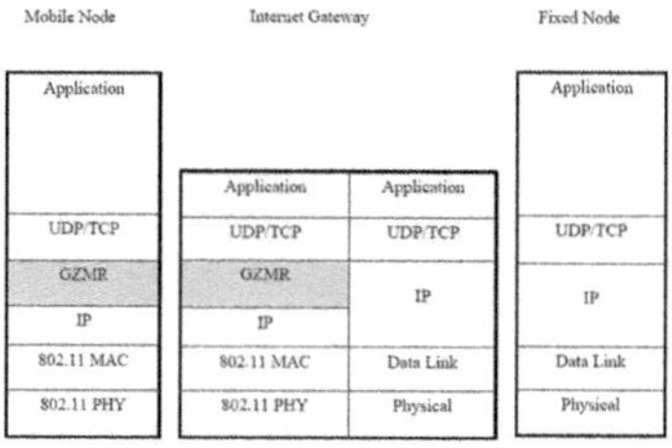

Fig. 2. Protocol stacks of mobile nodes, Internet gateways and fixed nodes

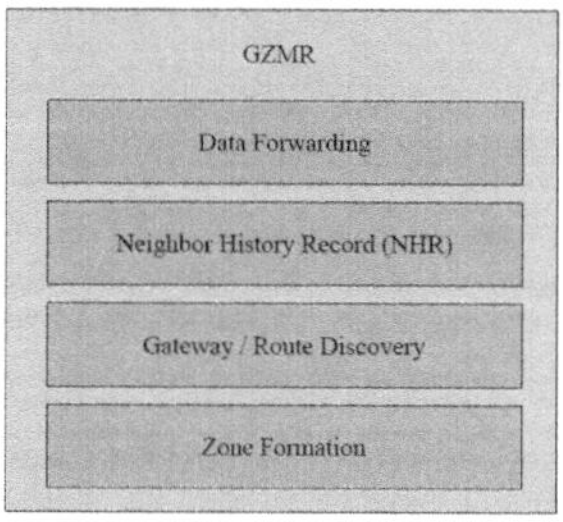

Fig. 3. Protocol stacks of GZMR

discovery a gateway. The message formats of RREQ_I and RREP_I can refer to [6] and [7].

There are various types of nodes defined in GZMR. They are GW_NODE, GCZ_NODE, BN_NODE and USUAL_NODE. We further design routing mesages, such as Route Request with B-flag(RREQ_B), Route Reply with B-flag(RREP_B) and Route Reply with BI-flag(RREP_BI), to process route discovery from different types of nodes. The purpose of RREQ_B is for nodes in the GCZ to request for a route to unknown destinations, and RREP_B is for GW_NODE and GCZ_NODE to build reverse paths to the mobile sources. RREP_BI is a combined message of RREP_B and RREP_I sent by BN_NODE when receiving RREQ from

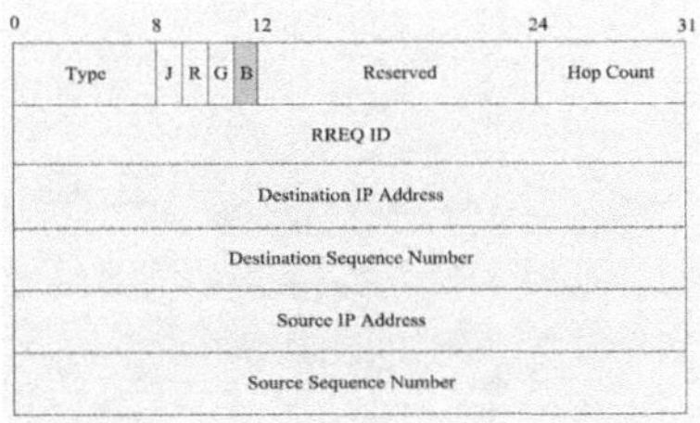

Fig. 4. RREQ_B Message Format

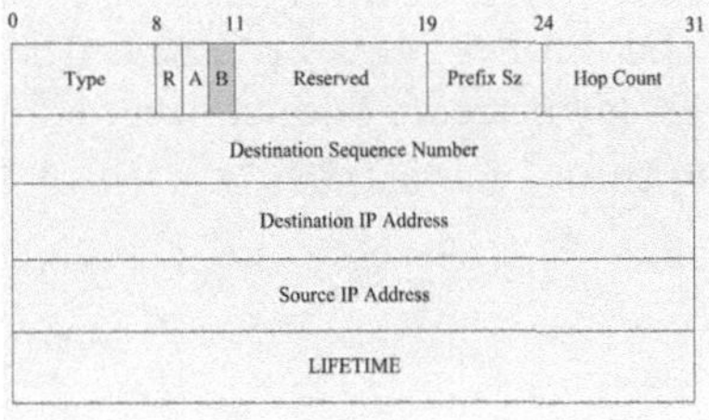

Fig. 5. RREP_B Message Format

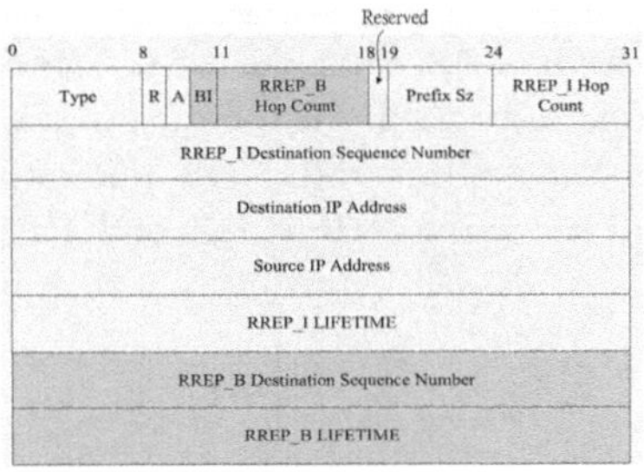

Fig. 6. RREP_BI Message Format

USUAL_NODE and having no route information to destination. See the message formats in Fig. 4, Fig. 5, and Fig. 6.

Fig. 7 shows the message format of Gateway Advertisement(GWADV) broadcasteing by IGW, and the Neighbor Cache in the GWADV is used for BNs (or BN_NODEs) to keep tracks of GCZ_NODEs.

Routing Table and Neighbor History Record. The routing table used in GZMR is similar to AOMDV. Each entry in the routing table includes the destination's address, sequence number, multiple paths to the destination and the max hop-count of all the paths. We create a timer to periodically purge expired paths to avoid using stale paths.

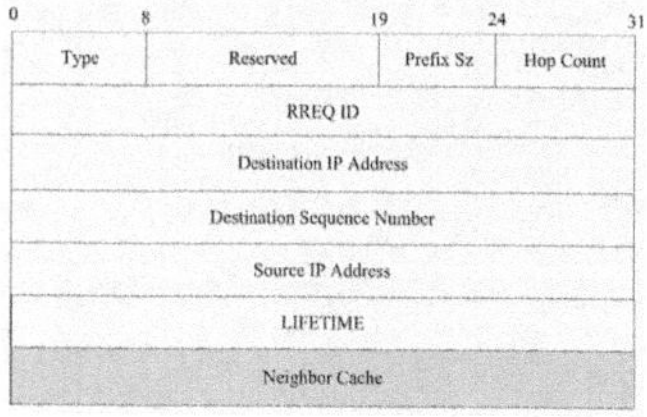

Fig. 7. Gateway Advertisement(GWADV) Message Format

Neighbor History Record (NHR) is designed for GCZ_NODE to keep tracks of the directions where the data packets are came from. The purpose of using NHR is to quickly recover downstream connection and avoid RREQ_B flooding. GCZ_NODE who has the record in its NHR will unicast RREQ_B to find paths to the mobile nodes.

2.3 Gateway Discovery

In GZMR, We apply hybrid gateway discovery mechanism that IGW periodically broadcasts the Gateway Advertisement(GWADV) messages. Nodes inside GCZ (GCZ_NODEs) can obtain IGW information and establish multiple paths to default IGW from receiving GWADs . BNs will record the *Neighbor Cache* in each received GWADV into its routing table. Nodes outside the Gateway Cooperative Zone have two approaches to acquire IGW information: (1) Broadcasting RREQ_Is to find the gateway and get RREP_Is from BN_NODEs. (2) Broadcasting RREQs and receiving RREP_BIs or RREP_Is from BN_NODEs or USUAL_NODEs.

2.4 Route Discovery

The mechanisms of discovering routing paths are different from the nodes in GCZ and those outside GCZ. The nodes in GCZ will be fully-meshed connected. The others outside GCZ will have routing paths which are link-disjointed.

Mobile Nodes Communicate to Fixed Nodes

Mobile nodes outside GCZ. In order to make an on-demand connection with Fixed Nodes (FN) in the wired network, the mobile node outside the GCZ (USUAL_NODE) will broadcast the Route Request (RREQ) message when it doesn't know where the destination is. When the RREQs are flooded to BNs (BN_NODEs), each BN firstly checks its routing table and broadcasts RREP_BI if it has no information about the destination. When GCZ_NODE receives RREP_BI, it establishes multiple fully meshed paths to source, converts RREP_BI to RREP_B and rebroadcasts it to IGW. The USUAL_NODE who receives a RREP_BI converts

RREP_BI to RREP_I and establishes forward paths to IGW. The way of broadcasting RREP_BI is to build the reverse paths to the sources for the IGW in advance, because we know most of the connections related to accessing the Internet services are interactive.

After receiving RREP_I, the source establishes multiple link-disjoint forward paths to BNs. After the timeout event of a RREQ occurs but no RREPs are received, the source will then determine that the destination is a FN in the wired network and forward data packets to IGW.

Mobile nodes inside GCZ. We use B-flag to distinguish the route request sent by nodes inside GCZ from that sent by nodes outside GCZ. When making an on-demand connection with FN, the node in the GCZ (e.g. BN_NODE, GW_NODE and GCZ_NODE) will send the Route Request with B flag (RREQ_B) messages when it doesn't know where the destination is. While receiving the RREQ_B, GW_NODE can reply to it if it has route to the requested destination; GCZ_NODE and BN_NODE can also reply to it if they have routes and the requested destination is not a FN. If the source gets no reply from the requested destination after the timeout event of the RREQ_B occurs, it then determines that the destination is a FN in the wired network.

Mobile Nodes Communicate to Mobile Modes. We take the situation when USUAL_NODE communicates to GCZ_NODE into consideration. The entries in the BNs' routing table established when receiving GWADV are helpful. BNs can quickly reply to USUAL_NODE and build paths to GCZ_NODE.

However, when GCZ_NODE communicates to USUAL_NODE, the route discovery procedure is similar to the first time GCZ_NODE communicate to FN by broadcasting RREQ_B. When USUAL_NODE destination receives the RREQ_Bs, it sends RREPs back to the GCZ_NODE.

Down-Stream Route Discovery. When the traffic is from FN to MN, downloading data from the Internet for example, the IGW becomes a bottle-neck. The paths broke easily most of the time because of the collision rather than node mobility. Here we design a NHR Module to handle this situation.

Original GZMR: IGW Broadcast RREQ_B in GCZ. The original way is the same as AODV and AOMDV. In order to find a route, IGW broadcasts RREQ_B in GCZ. And any node which has routes to the destination can reply the RREQ_B, or the RREQ_B will be rebroadcasted to the requested destination. See Fig. 8.

GZMR with NHR Module: Use Node History Record(NHR). The Neighbor History Record (NHR) is used to help reducing the broadcasting RREQ_B messages in GCZ. GCZ_NODEs keep tracks of the directions where the data packets are coming from. According to NHR, downstream connections can be quickly recovered by GCZ_NODE unicasting RREQ_B to find routes to MN source. If there is no other replies back to IGW, IGW will set the through-flag to 1 and broadcast the RREQ_B again. The rest of steps are the same as Original GZMR. See Fig. 9.

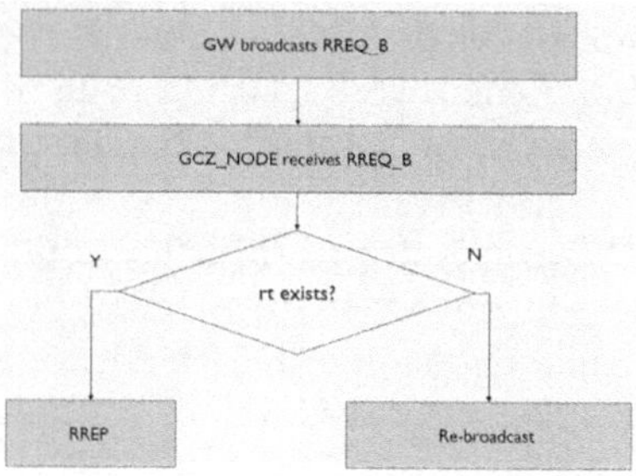

Fig. 8. Original GZMR

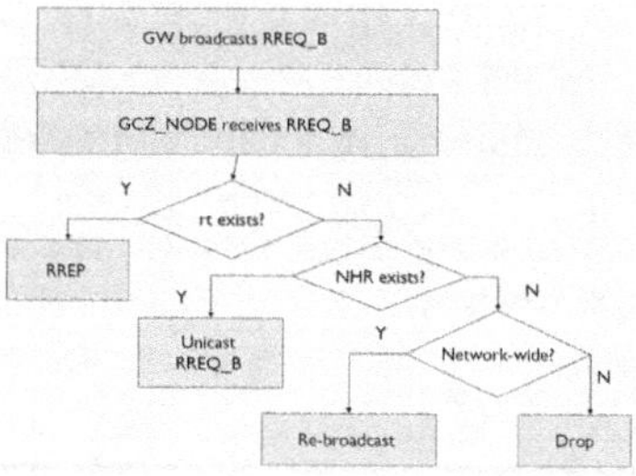

Fig. 9. GZMR with NHR Module

2.5 Data Forwarding

In GZMR, a node always chooses the lest hop-count path when forwarding data packets. If there are same hop-count paths, the node will choose the fresher one. This a little bit different form AOMDV, which uses paths according to the path built sequence. When a node detects the using path is broken, it then switches to another path to salvage packets.

2.6 Route Maintenance

When forwarding a data packet, the node uses data packet acknowledgment to judge the status of the link. The link is "DOWN" when there is no data packet acknowledgments back. If there is no other paths exist, the node will re-discovery the route if it is the source of the traffic, and if it is a intermediate node, it will simply drop the data packet and broadcast the Route Error (RERR) message to its neighbors.

3 Performance Evaluation

3.1 Simulation Environment

The simulation environment was created in the famous network simulator NS-2[8] to develop and analyze the proposed protocol GZMR. There are total 60

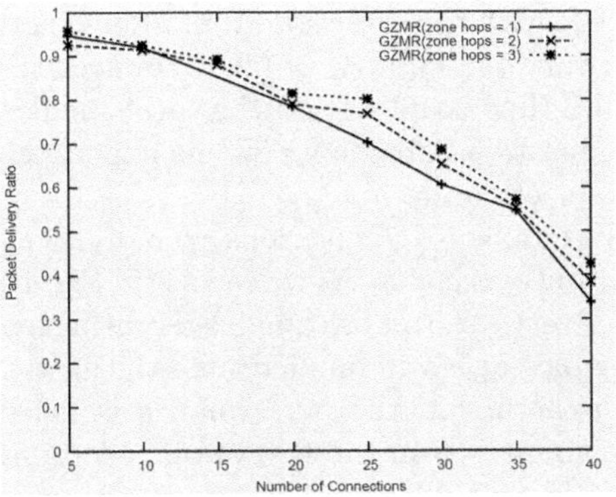

Fig. 10. Packet Delivery Ratio vs. Connections

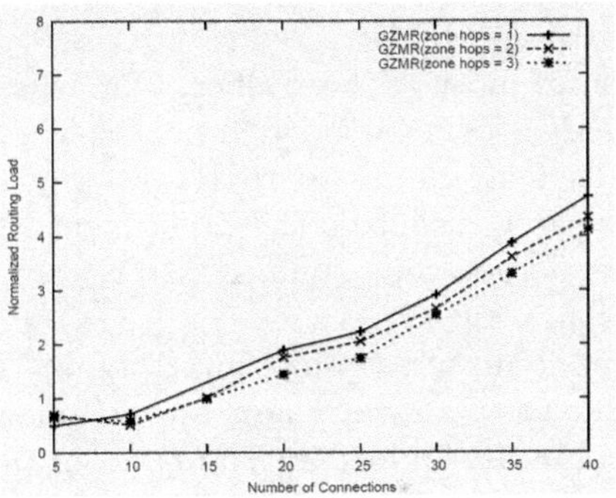

Fig. 11. Normalized Routing Load vs. Connections

mobile nodes, one Gateway and 10 fixed nodes in a 1500m x 750m topology with Gateway placed at (1450,380). We use traffic generator to develop the simulated TCP and CBR traffic sources, and use Random way-point model as the mobility model. The channel capacity is 11 Mbps and we use the IEEE 802.11[9] Distributed Coordination Function(DCF) as the medium access control protocol. We use AOMDV+ as samples for comparison. We modified AOMDV[5] to AOMDV+ with the ability to have gateway support according to AODV+[7], which is developed by Ali Hamidian to extend AODV to have gateway support. In the following simulations we evaluate CBR and TCP traffics by varying the node mobility and the number of connections.

3.2 Simulation Results

Performance of varying GCZ size in GZMR. In order to analyze the impact of GCZ size, we first set up a simulation environment and vary the size of GCZ to see the effect on the packet delivery ratio, normalized routing load, average end-to-end delay,and route discovery duration. The traffics we generate in this scenario are CBR with the direction from mobile nodes to the fixed nodes through gateway. We vary the number of CBR connections with the maximum speed 5 m/s. The pause time is 100s , and the total simulation time is 300s. We vary the GCZ size from 1 to 3 hop counts in this experiment due to the average hop counts of each connection are 6 or 7.

The increasing of the number of connections cause much more link breaking and also produce more routing overheads. As we can see in Fig. 10. When the GCZ size is larger, the Packet delivery ratio and Normalized routing load (Fig. 11) are better because of less routing messages will flood around the gateway.

According to this experiment, the performance is better when GCZ size is larger, we choose hop count = 3 in the rest of our experiments.

4 Conclusions and Future Work

We proposed the Gateway Zone Multi-path Routing(GZMR) in Wireless Mesh Networks. The concept of GZMR is to reduce routing overheads around IGW, which is the destination of most of the traffics. Our scheme uses Border Nodes to effectively cease RREQs being flooded from outside Gateway Cooperative Zone (GCZ) and act as relay nodes to reply gateway information to mobile nodes outside GCZ. As can be see from the experiment results, GZMR provides lower latency and higher performance than AOMDV when accessing the Internet services in Wireless Mesh Network.

As a future work, we intend to use more metrics (e.g. Node stability, residual power, etc.) to determine the Gateway Cooperative Zone and Border Node, and now we only use hop-count as the metric. To make our proposed protocol more adaptive to real situations, we plan to simulate various kinds of applications (e.g. E-mail, Video on-demand,etc.) to evaluate the performance of our protocol. Finally, the further research to apply our protocol in different networks is needed. We intend to implement it not only in 802.11 but also in 802.16.

Acknowlegements. This research is supported by the Mobile Media Technology Center Networks and Multimedia, Taiwan, under Instituteby Institute for Information Industry (III) and the projet number is (A6K01221).

References

1. Akyildiz, W.X., I.F., Wang, W.: Wireless mesh networks: A survey. Computer Networks Journal (2005)
2. Whitehead, P.: Mesh networks: a new architecture for broadband wireless access systems. In: Proc. of IEEE Conference on Radio and Wireless (RAWCON), 2000, pp. 43–46 (2000)
3. Draves, R., Padhye, J., Zill, B.: Comparisons of routing metrics for static multi-hop wireless networks. In: ACM Annual Conference of the Special Interest Group on Data Communication (SIGCOMM) 2004, pp. 133–144 (2004)
4. Draves, R., Padhye, J., Zill, B.: Routing in multi-radio, multi-hop wireless mesh networks. In: ACM Annual International Conference on Mobile Computing and Networking (MOBICOM), 2004, pp. 114–128 (2004)

5. Marina, M.K., Das, S.R.: On-demand multipath distance vector routing in ad hoc networks. In: Proc. of IEEE International Conference on Network Protocols (ICNP), 2001, pp. 14–23 (2001)
6. Wikikawa, R., Malinen, J.T., Perkins, C.E., Nilsson, A., Tuominen, A.J.: Global connectivity for ipv6 mobile ad hoc networks. IETF Internet Draft, draft-wakikawa-manet-globalv6-00.txt, Working-progress (2001)
7. Hamidian, A.: A study of internet connectivity for mobile ad hoc networks in ns 2. Masters thesis. Department of Communication Systems, Lund Institute of Technology, Lund University (2003)
8. ns-2 simulator, `http://www.isi.edu/nsnam/ns`
9. IEEE Standards. Department Wireless LAN medium access control (MAC) and physical layer (PHY) specifications. IEEE standard 802.11 (1997)

On Estimating Path Capacity in Wireless Mesh Networks

Qinqi Wang[1], Ming Xu[1], and Xingui He[2]

[1] School of Computer, National University of Defense Technology, Changsha 410073, China
wangqinqi@nudt.edu.cn, xuming64@public.cs.hn.cn
[2] School of Electronics Engineering and Computer Science, Beijing University, Beijing 100084, China
hexg@cae.cn

Abstract. Accurate capacity measures for a path in wireless mesh network can be useful to many applications, including routing protocol design, QoS guarantees, congestion control and other related areas. In this paper, we propose the local virtual probing analytical model. A linear programming problem of both channel assignment and packet scheduling is formulated to determine the capacity of any given path, and hence we propose a path capacity evaluating algorithm based on greedy strategy (PCEAGS) to solve it. Finally, we discuss the impact of several factors, such as hop count of path, amount of packets and numbers of available channels and radios per node, on the accuracy of PCEAGS in detail. The result shows that our algorithm can estimate path capacity accurately in lower average time complexity and also has better expansibility.

1 Introduction

Recently, wireless mesh networks (WMN) have attracted a lot of attention. WMN represent a good solution to providing wireless Internet connectivity in large scale area with lower deployment cost than any other kinds of wireless networks. Comparing with traditional ad hoc network, there are several significant characteristics of WMN [1], such as multi-radio and multi-channel, dedicated routing infrastructures and backbone between mesh routers, etc.

It is a fundamental issue to measure the maximum end-to-end throughput, named as *path capacity* later in this paper, of a given path in WMN. The information of path capacity can be used in routing protocol to find path with maximum capacity or to evaluating the performance of different routing protocol. Path capacity estimation problem in WMN is much more complicated due to the multi-channel and multi-radio properties of WMN, i.e., the channel assignment problem, which had already been proved as a NP-complete problem[6], need to be carefully concerned.

In this paper, we propose a local virtual probing analysis model for WMN, which means local nodes know about global topology and simulate the packets probing procedure itself without affect normal traffics and occupy bandwidth.

The rest of this paper is organized as follows. We discuss the related work in Section 2. In Section 3, we propose the network model and some assumptions. Detailed discussion

J. Indulska et al. (Eds.): UIC 2007, LNCS 4611, pp. 360–369, 2007.

of both necessary and sufficient conditions for interference-free transmission in WMN and problem statement is presented in Section 4. In Section 5, we put forward the greedy strategy and hence design a path capacity evaluating algorithm based on greedy strategy(PCEAGS). Simulation results and related discussion are shown in Section 6. Finally Section 7 concludes this paper.

2 Related Work

The path capacity problem in wired networks such as Internet has been extensively studied[7], however, the end-to-end path capacity estimation in traditional wireless networks is still challenging, because wireless path capacity estimation depends not only on the narrow link along the path (as in a wired network), but also on the topology, interference between nodes and several other environmental factors.

Most of the existing researches on wireless network capacity are under saturation case[3]-[5],[9]. However, the saturation assumption makes them not suitable to analyze the path capacity. Because in a saturated wireless network, each node always have packets to send, that will cause frequent data collision and significantly degrade the performance of whole network. But that is not true in real network environment because most of the actual networks are unsaturated or not always saturated.

While there have few works on estimate throughput without saturation assumption[2][8]. However, all those studies are based on single channel or single radio wireless networks and are difficult to extend to WMN environment. Some other researchers are using packet probing techniques to estimate the path capacity along network path[10][11]. This method produces very realistic results, but is not very practical since the probing packet stream may heavily impact the existing traffic and introduce extra transmission overhead into network.

On the basis of above discussion, in this paper, we also focus on packet probing techniques to estimate the path capacity in WMN. In order to avoid affecting normal traffic along the path, we propose a virtual probing model and greedy channel assignment and packet scheduling algorithm, which can be used on local nodes to estimate capacity for a given path with polynomial time complexity.

3 Network Model and Some Assumptions

3.1 Network Model

We represent the network with a directed graph $G=(V,E,E^I)$ where V represents the set of nodes in the network, E denotes the set of directed links that can carry data (data links), and E^I the set of directed links that indicate interference (interference links) but cannot carry data. We assume that both data links and interference links are bi-directional. There are K orthogonal channels in the network, denoted by $CH=\{1,2,\ldots,K\}$. Let each node v has $k(v)$ radios. Obviously we have $k(v)\leq K$ in actual network environment because of channel overlapping.

Table 1. Definition and Explanation of Variables Used in Network Model

n	Node number of WMN	c_i	Rate of channel i
$\sigma(e)$	Set of available channels of e	$\Vert \sigma(e) \Vert$	Number of channels of e
$N(v)$	Data link neighbors of v	$E(v)$	Data links incident with v
$N^I(v)$	Interference link of v	$E^I(v)$	Interference links incident with v
p	Single packet	$\Vert p \Vert$	Size of packet p
$path$	Sequential set of nodes from s to d	$f(s,d)$	Data flow that from s to d
$\Vert path \Vert$	Path hop	$\Vert f \Vert$	Size of flow f

3.2 Assumptions

For the sake of simplicity, in generally we assume that our network model satisfies the following conditions:

1. Communication is perfect and network topology is stable, which means to ignore the environment noise and packet loss, etc.
2. Using perfect four-way handshake MAC protocol to transmit data flow, this implies that hidden terminals effect will not degrade the network performance.
3. Data flow only generated from the given source node, i.e., all the other nodes along to same path only need to forward packets.

Noted that we only consider the capacity of single path, the issue about multi-path end-to-end throughput is beyond the scope of this paper.

4 Constrains and Problem Statement

4.1 Constrains

Let t denote time. For any given data link $e \in E$ and channel $i \in \sigma(e)$, we have:

$$g_e^i(t) = \begin{cases} c_i & \text{If link } e \text{ is active on channel } i \text{ in time } t \\ 0 & \text{Otherwise} \end{cases} \tag{1}$$

The physical characteristic of wireless channel determines that there would be interference and collides when two or more channel working on same spectrum simultaneously, which degrade the performance of network significantly. In order to guarantee interference-free transmission, Kodialam[3] propose the necessary and sufficient conditions of interference-free transmission in wireless networks. We extend those conditions to WMN environment. Definition and detailed explanation of these constrains are as follows.

Radio number constrain: For any given node $v \in V$, in any time t, there are no more than $k(v)$ channels can be activated simultaneously on node v, as follows.

$$\sum_{\forall e \in E(v)} \sum_{\forall i \in \sigma(e)} \frac{g_e^i(t)}{c_i} \le k(v), \forall v \in V, \forall t \tag{2}$$

Interference Constrain: In order to guarantee interference-free transmission, for any given node $v \in V$, if node v is using channel i belonged to data link e to transmit packets in any time t, then all the data link neighbors and interference neighbors of node v would not use channel i at the same time t.

$$\sum_{\forall e \in (E(v) \cup E^{I}(v))} \frac{g_e^i(t)}{c_i} \leq 1, \forall i \in CH, \forall v \in V, \forall t \qquad (3)$$

Channel Number Constrain: For any given data link $e \in E$, in any time t, there are no more than $\| \sigma(e) \|$ transmitting procedures simultaneously on data link e, as follows.

$$\sum_{\forall i \in \sigma(e)} \frac{g_e^i(t)}{c_i} \leq \|\sigma(e)\|, \forall e \in E, \forall t \qquad (4)$$

4.2 Problem Statement

Let $p(t)$ denote the value of data link that packet p activated in time t. That means, in any given time t, if packet p is transmitting through any data link e using any channel $i \in e$, then $p(t)=c_i$, otherwise $p(t)=0$. According to the definition of $p(t)$,

$$f(t) = \sum_{\forall p \in f} p(t) \qquad (5)$$

Let $S(p)$ denote the accumulative value of data links that packet p activated in its whole lifetime, then we have

$$S(p) = \int_0^{\infty} p(t)dt \qquad (6)$$

Likewise, let $S(f)$ denote the accumulative value of data links that activated by network flow f in its entire lifetime, as follows.

$$S(f) = \int_0^{\infty} f(t)dt \qquad (7)$$

Lemma 1. For any given packet p and routing path $path$, $S(p)=\|path\|*\|p\|$.

Proof: Suppose $path=\{v_1,v_2,\ldots,v_l\}$. Let $s_k=(t_k,i_k)$ denote that packet p is begin to be sending in time t_k using channel i_k from node $v_k \in path$, then we have $schedule=\{s_1,s_2,\ldots,s_{l-1}\}$, which represent a schedule solution when packet p transmitting through path $path$. In this paper, we ignore the packet processing time of both transmitting node and receiving node. Therefore we can calculate the arrival time of packet p for each s_k as follows:

$$arrival_{k+1} = t_k + \|p\| / c_{i_k} \qquad (8)$$

Similarly, according to the definition of $p(t)$ we know that $p(t)$ would not equal to zero only when packet p was transmitting through any data link in given time t. That means $p(t) \neq 0$ if and only if $t \in [t_k, arrival_{k+1}]$, $1 \leq k \leq l-1$. So we can rewrite equation (6) as follows:

$$S(p) = \int_0^{t_1} 0dt + \sum_{1\le k\le l-1} \int_{t_k}^{arrival_{k+1}} p(t)dt + \sum_{1\le k\le l-1} \int_{arrival_{k+1}}^{t_{k+1}} 0dt + \int_{arrival_l}^{\infty} 0dt \tag{9}$$
$$= \sum_{1\le k\le l-1} \int_{t_k}^{t_k + \|p\|/c_{i_k}} p(t)dt$$

According to the definition of $p(t)$, if packet p is transmitting by using channel i_k in given time t, then $p(t)=c_{i_k}$. Substitute it into the equation (9):

$$\begin{aligned} S(p) &= \sum_{1\le k\le l-1} \int_{t_k}^{t_k + \|p\|/c_{i_k}} c_{i_k} dt \\ &= \sum_{1\le k\le l-1} \|p\| \\ &= \|p\| * \|path\| \end{aligned} \tag{10}$$

Apparently, the value of $S(p)$ is independent with respect to both the survival time of packet p and the schedule schema when p transmitting along the path. That means no matter how long it spend and how to assign channels when transmitting p through the path, the value of $S(p)$ is a constant.

Therefore, we derive Theory 1 as follows based on Lemma 1.

Theory 1. For any given network data flow f and routing path *path*, $S(f) = \| f \| * \| path \|$.

Proof: According to the definitions of $S(f)$ and $f(t)$, substitute equation (10) into (7), then we have following equation

$$\begin{aligned} S(f) &= \sum_{\forall p\in f} \int_0^{\infty} p(t)dt \\ &= \sum_{\forall p\in f} \|p\| * \|path\| \\ &= \|f\| * \|path\| \end{aligned} \tag{11}$$

The goal of this paper is to estimate the capacity of a given path, i.e., as discussed in Section 2, to find the maximum traffic rate in given path. Also we know that the value of $S(f)$ is independent with the survival time of data flow f based on Theory 1. So in this paper, the path capacity problem can be regard as to find a minimal time T^* that satisfy the following equation

$$\begin{aligned} S'(f) &= \int_0^{T^*} f(t)dt \\ &= \|f\| * \|path\| \end{aligned} \tag{12}$$

That means to find a minimal time T^* so that the data flow f can be transmitted along this path under constrains (2)-(4) within time T^*, thus, the traffic rate of data flow f can be regard as the capacity of the path.

Furthermore, for given network $G=(V,E,E^I)$, routing path *path* in G and data flow f that transmitting along *path*, we formulate the path capacity problem as follows:

$$\min T^*$$
$$subject\ to$$
$$\int_0^{T^*} f(t)dt = \|f\| * \|path\|$$
$$\sum_{\forall e \in E(v)} \sum_{\forall i \in \sigma(e)} \frac{g_e^i(t)}{c_i} \le k(v), \forall v \in V, \forall t$$
$$\sum_{e \in (E(v) \cup E^I(v))} \frac{g_e^i(t)}{c_i} \le 1, \forall i \in CH, \forall v \in V, \forall t$$
$$\sum_{\forall i \in \sigma(e)} \frac{g_e^i(t)}{c_i} \le \|\sigma(e)\|, \forall e \in E, \forall t \qquad (13)$$

5 Algorithm Design and Analysis

As shown in equation (13), the path capacity problem in WMN is formulated as channel assignment and packet scheduling problem. It is well known that the channel assignment problem in multi-channel multi-radio networks is NP-hard, and thereby, in this paper, we focus on finding a polynomial algorithm to solve the problem with acceptable cost.

According to Theory 1 we notice that when data flow f is transmitted, no matter how long it takes, the value of $S'(f)$ is permanently equal to $\| f \| * \| path \|$. Moreover, as proved in Lemma 1, when packet p stepped hop by hop along the path, the decrease value of $S(p)$ was always equal to $\| p \|$. Therefore, in this paper, we propose an algorithm based on greedy strategy to solve the path capacity problem. Our goal is to finish transmitting data flow f along the given path within time T^* as soon as possible, and hence we can calculate the capacity of given path:

$$capacity = \| f \| / T^* \qquad (14)$$

Since we aim to finish transmitting packets as soon as possible, there are two key issues need to be concerned when designing greedy algorithm:

- To deliver more packets within given time. That means, in the case of estimating path capacity, we should first schedule the packet that can be transmitted in the earliest time.
- Spatial reuse of channel spectrum among path. Apparently spatial reuse will highly improve the capacity of given path because of the increase of concurrent transmission among path. In order to fully explore the potential ability of concurrent transmission, we need to spread the packets to entire spatial domain of the given path as soon as possible. Let *interval* denote the number of nodes among the path that one node can affect within its interference range. For a given path, it is clearly that the bigger the interval, the smaller the ability of spatial reuse. It is also a useful parameter for our greedy algorithm. As shown in Fig.1, the circles with dash line represent the interference range, and *interval*=2. There are two packets needed to be transmitted: *p1* on node ***a*** and *p2* on node ***c***. Suppose *p1* will arrive at node ***b*** in 1 second if delivered

first, *p2* will arrive at node ***d*** in 1.5 second if delivered first. If we only take into account of the issue mentioned before, we should schedule *p1* because it can be done in earliest time. But actually we need to schedule *p2* first, since after *p2* arrive at node ***d***, we can simultaneously schedule both *p1* and *p2* next round to improve the capacity.

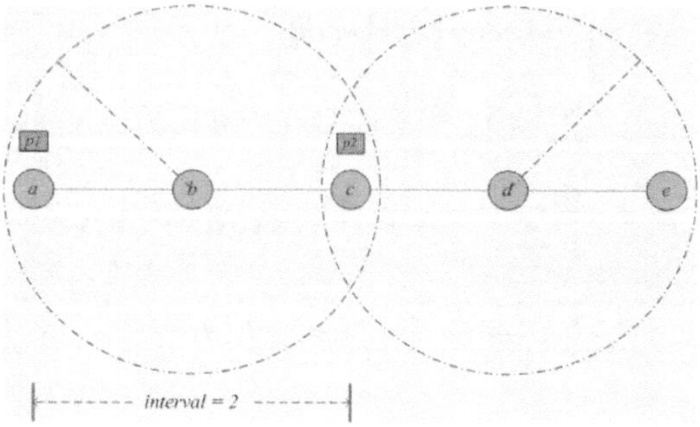

Fig. 1. Effects of *interval*

Based on above discussion, we design the PCEAGS(Path Capacity Evaluating Algorithm based on Greedy Strategy), which aims to improve the spatial reuse and efficient channel usage, to estimate capacity of given path. Detailed algorithm in pseudo codes are as follows.

Algorithm: Path Capacity Evaluating Algorithm based on Greedy Strategy

Input:	Network *G*, Network flow *f*, Routing Path *path* and *interval*
Output:	Path capacity *C* and schedule solution *schedule* for each packet *p*

```
△ = ‖f‖ * ‖path‖ ;T* = 0;C = 0;
while △ > 0 do
    min_n = null; min_ch = null; min_intf = null; min_time = ∞;
    for each node v∈path-{dst} in reverse order do
        if node v has packets to deliver then
            for each intf∈k(v) do
                if intf.freetime < min_intf.freetime then
                    min_intf = intf;
            for each i∈ σ(e(v,v.next) do
                t=max(i.freetime, min_intf.freetime);
                if t < min_time - interval* ‖p‖ /c_i then
                    min_ch = i; min_n = v; min_time = t + ‖p‖ /c_i;
    pkt = min_n.queue.pop();
    pkt.schedule(min_n,min_n.next, min_ch, min_intf, min_time);
    for each node v∈N(min_n) do
        for each v'∈N(v)-{min_n} do
            v'.min_ch.freetime = min_time;
    TP* = min_time; △ = △ - ‖p‖ ;
end while
C = ‖f‖ / T*;
```

Correctness Analysis: Based on the discussion in Section 4.2, algorithm PCEAGS is correct if satisfies all the (2)-(4) constrain conditions. In pseudo codes of the algorithm, sentences 8-13 guarantees the radio number constrain and channel number constrain, respectively. 15-17 guarantee the interference constrain.

Above all, algorithm satisfies all the (2)-(5) constrain and is correct.

Time Complexity Analysis: Suppose there are M packets in data flow f. Each node among path has $N_{neighbor}$ neighbors and R_{if} interfaces and L_{ch} orthogonal channels.

It is shown in the pseudo codes that the time complexity of sentence 1 and 20 is $O(1)$. The time complexity of sentences 3,13 and 14 is $O(1)$.

As mentioned above, each node has R_{if} interfaces and L_{ch} channels, so the time complexity of sentences 6-8 and 9-12 is $O(R_{if})$ and $O(L_{ch})$, respectively. It is known that the hop count of path is $\| path \|$, i.e., sentence 4 will execute $\| path \|$ -1 times, so the time complexity of the entire loop 4-12 is $O(\| path \| *(R_{if}+L_{ch}))$. Time complexity of sentences 15-17 is $O(N_{neighbor}^2)$. Since $\triangle$ decrease $\| p \|$ every time, sentence 4 will execute $\| path \| * \| f \| / \| p \|$ =M* $\| path \|$ times. Therefore, the time complexity is $O(M* \| path \| *(\| path \| *(R_{if}+L_{ch})+N_{neighbor}^2))$.

In the worst case, i.e., $R_{if}=L_{ch}$=K, $N_{neighbor}=n$ and $\|path\|=n$-1, the time complexity of algorithm is $O(M*n*(2K*n+n^2))$. Generally $2K<n$, so the time complexity of algorithm can be represented as $O(M*n^3)$.

However, in realistic situation, especially when focus on one given path, $\| path \|$, R_{if}, L_{ch} and $N_{neighbor}$ are of the same order of magnitude and usually less than 10. Therefore, the average time complexity can be represented as $O(M* \| path \|^3)$.

Actually when estimating path capacity, M can be a smaller number. That is, we only need the packets to be spread to entire path and transmitted continuously for a while. Thus make its cost more acceptable.

6 Performance Evaluation

In this section, we study the impacts of several factors, such as hop count or the number of channel and radio per node, on the capacity of a given path. Moreover, as discussed in Section 5, the value of M(packet number) can be different when using PCEAGS to estimate the path capacity. We verify the accuracy of resulted path capacity estimated by PCEAGS using different M.

We set the data rate of each channel to 2 MByte/s. Packet size is set to 1024 bytes. We use a centralized implementation of PCEAGS that developed by ourselves to estimate path capacity.

We investigate a 9-hop optimal path topology with *interval*=2. We use PCEAGS to estimate path capacity with 50-950 packets, represented as $PC_{evaluate}$ respectively. For the simplicity of discussion, let PC_{upper} denote the achievable upper bound of path capacity that estimated with 10000 packets. In order to describe the accuracy gap between $PC_{evaluate}$ and PC_{upper}, we derive the following equation:

$$Gap = (1 - \frac{PC_{evaluate}}{PC_{upper}}) * 100\% \qquad (15)$$

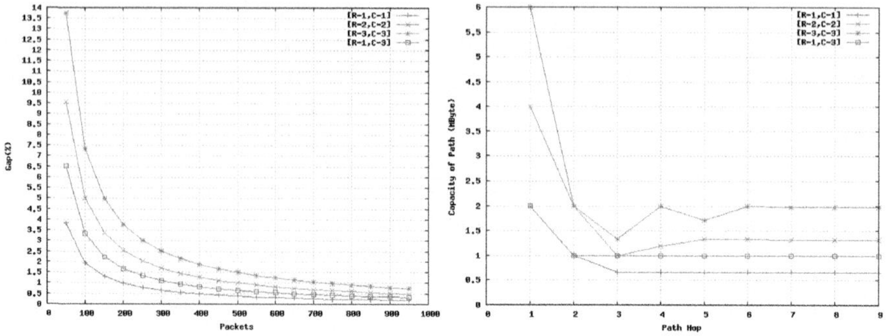

(a) Influence of packet number (b) Impacts of hop on path capacity

Fig. 2.

As shown in Fig.2 (a), [R=1,C=1] means 1 radio and 1 channel per node, and so on. We can see that in a single channel and single radio wireless networks, the accuracy gap between $PC_{evaluate}$ and PC_{upper} can not exceed 2% by using 100 packets. But for a 3 radios and 3 channels wireless network, we need 400 packets to achieve the same goal. The reason is, when estimating path capacity by using PCEAGS, we need to spread the packets to entire path and transmit it continuously for a while. However, comparing with single channel and single radio path, it is well known that multi-channel and multi-radio path has higher bandwidth and can accommodate more packets in given time. So we need more packets to fill in the path links.

Fig.2 (b) shows the impact of hop count in the optimal path topology on path capacity. In order to keep the accuracy gap within 1%, we use 950 packets to estimate the path capacity. From Fig.2 (b) we can see that in a single channel and single radio optimal path topology, path capacity will decrease along with the increasing of hop count when hop<2**interval*, after that, the capacity of the path will be stable. However, for a multi-channel and multi-radio optimal path topology, path capacity will decrease along with the increasing of path hop when hop<2**interval*, as same as in single channel and single radio path, but after that, capacity of path increase because FCEAGS can find the existence of spatial reuse and schedule packets simultaneously.

In summary, our local virtual probing analytical model and algorithm can estimate approximate path capacity in acceptable time, and is also suitable for different path topology.

7 Conclusion

The information of path capacity can be used in routing protocol to find path with maximum capacity or to evaluating the performance of different routing protocol, it also can be used in congestion control algorithm to reject excessive traffic to avoid collision, even can be used as a effective routing metric.

In this paper, we focus on estimating the capacity of a given path. Benefiting from packet probing techniques, we propose the local virtual probing analytical model to estimate the path capacity. By state the necessary and sufficient conditions for interference-free transmission in WMN, we formulate the path capacity problem to a linear programming problem of joint channel assignment and packet scheduling, and hence construct a path capacity evaluating algorithm based on greedy strategy (PCEAGS), which can solve the problem in polynomial time complexity $O(M^* \| path \|^3)$. Finally, we discuss the impact of several factors, such as hop count of path, amount of packets and numbers of available channels and radios per node, on the accuracy of PCEAGS in detail. The result shows that our algorithm can find approximate path capacity in lower average time complexity and also has better expansibility.

An important extension of this work would be to study the multi-path end-to-end throughput in future. Another interesting extension would be to study the end-to-end available bandwidth for QoS guarantee.

References

1. Akyildiz, I.F., Wang, X., Wang, W.: Wireless mesh networks: A survey. Computer Networks Journal 47(4), 445–487 (2005)
2. Fang, Y., McDonald, A.B.: Theoretical network capacity of multi-hop wireless ad hoc networks. In: Proc. of the 6th IEEE Int'l Conf. on Mobile and Wireless Communications Networks, pp. 181–186. IEEE Press, Paris (2004)
3. Kodialam, M., Nandagopal, T.: Characterizing the capacity region in multi-radio and multi-channel mesh networks. In: Proc. of ACM MOBICOM, 2005, pp. 73–87. ACM Press, New York (2005)
4. Gupta, P., Kumar, P.R.: The capacity of wireless networks. IEEE Trans. on Information Theory 46(2), 388–404 (2000)
5. Kyasanur, P., Vaidya, N.: Capacity of multi-channel wireless networks: Impact of number of channels and interfaces. In: Proc. of ACM MOBICOM, pp. 43–57. ACM Press, New York (2005)
6. Raniwala, A., Gopalan, K., Chiueh, T.: Centralized Algorithms for Multi-channel Wireless Mesh Networks. ACM Mobile Computing and Communications Review 8(2), 50–65 (2004)
7. Kapoor, R., Chen, L.-J., Lao, L., Gerla, M., Sanadidi, M.Y.: CapProbe: A Simple and Accurate Capacity Estimation Technique. In: Proc. of ACM SIGCOMM, pp. 280–291. ACM Press, New York (2004)
8. Wang, K., Yang, F., Zhang, Q., Xu, Y.: Modeling Path Capacity in Multi-hop IEEE 802.11 Networks for QoS Services. In: IEEE International Conference on Mobile Ad hoc and Sensor Systems, pp. 771–776 (2006)
9. Cali, F., Conti, M., Gregori, E.: Dynamic tuning of the IEEE 802.11 protocol to achieve a theoretical throughput limit. IEEE/ACM Trans. on Networking 8(6), 785–799 (2000)
10. Lakshminarayanan, K., Padmanabhan, V., Padhye, J.: Bandwidth Estimation in Broadband Access Networks. In: Proc. of ACM SIGCOMM Conference on Internet Measurement (IMC), pp. 314–321 (2004)
11. Sun, T., Yang, G., Chen, L.-J., Sanadidi, M.Y., Gerla, M.: A Measurement Study of Path Capacity in 802.11b based Wireless Networks. In: Proc. of International Workshop on Wireless Traffic Measurements and Modeling(WitMeMo), pp. 31–37 (2005)

A Meta Service Description Assisted Service Discovery Protocol for MANETs

Zhenguo Gao[1,⋆], Ling Wang[2], Mei Yang[3], and Jianping Wang[4]

[1] Department of Automation, Harbin Engineering University
Harbin, 150001, P.R. China
gag@ftcl.hit.edu.cn
[2] Department of Computer Science and Technology, Harbin Institute of Technology
Harbin, 150001, P.R. China
lwang@ftcl.hit.edu.cn
[3] Department of Electrical and Computer Engineering
University of Nevada, Las Vegas, NV 89154, U.S.A.
meiyang@egr.unlv.edu
[4] Department of Computer Science, City University of Hong Kong
Kowloon, Hong Kong
jianwang@cityu.edu.hk

Abstract. The ability to discover services offered in Mobile Ad-Hoc Networks (MANETs) is the major prerequisite for effectively utilizing these services. Caching service advertisements is an essential component in service discovery protocols for MANETs. To fully utilize the advantage of the cached service advertisements, the cached service description can be advertised with the local service description in a vicinity, which however will increase packet size. To reduce packet size, a better solution is to representing the cached service advertisements with a meta service description. In this paper, we introduce a fine-grained group-based meta service description scheme and propose an efficient service discovery protocol: Meta Service Description Assisted Service Discovery Protocol (MSDASDP) for MANETs, where the number of forwarding nodes of request packets is minimized with the help of the fine-grained meta service description. Simulation results both show that MSDASDP is an effective, efficient, and prompt service discovery protocol for MANETs.[1]

1 Introduction

Mobile Ad-Hoc Networks (MANETs) [1] are temporary infrastructure-less multi-hop wireless networks that consist of many autonomous wireless mobile nodes.

⋆ Corresponding author.

[1] This work is supported by National Postdoctoral Research Program (No.060234), Postdoctoral Research Program of HeiLongJiang (No.060234), Natural Science Foundation of HeiLongJiang(No.F2004-17), Fundamental Research Foundation of Harbin Engineering University (No.HEUFT06009), Foundation of Experimentation Technology Reformation of Harbin Engineering University (No.SJY06018).

J. Indulska et al. (Eds.): UIC 2007, LNCS 4611, pp. 370–381, 2007.

Effective exploitation of networked services provided in MANETs requires discovering the services that best match the application's requirements and invoking such services for the application. Service discovery protocol (SDP) which aims to advertise and discover the services available in the current environment plays an important role in service-oriented MANETs.

Service discovery protocols were originally studied in the context of wired networks where the service providers register their services to the service repositories and the clients can send the query to the service repositories for the required services. SDPs for wired networks include IETF's Service Location Protocol (SLP) , Sun's Jini, Microsoft's Universal Plug and Play (UPnP), Salutation consortium's Salutation, etc. With the development of MANETs, a number of service discovery protocols are proposed. Some of them [2,3,4] are adapted from service discovery protocols of wired networks, and some others are designed specially for MANETs [5]-[9]. In current various approaches, to facilitate service discovery operation, nodes are organized into different structures. According to these structures constructed, application layer approaches are classified into three classes: one-layer approaches, two-layer approaches, and multi-layer approaches. A more detailed survey can be found in [10].

The general common components of these service discovery protocols include *caching service advertisements, managing service descriptions, requesting services, replying to the requests*, and *applying policies* (e.g., caching refreshment rate, cache size, advertisement frequency, and vicinity diameter) [9].

In general, the SDPs for MANETs work as follows. The service request packet is flooded from the source to the neighbors. When receiving a service request packet, if either its local services or the cached services match the service request, a node will respond with a service reply packet to the corresponding source, otherwise, each node will flood the service request packet to its neighbors.

A general technique to reduce the overhead of the flooding-based service discovery is caching service advertisements, where cached information are regarded as a valid source for service matching. Different caching policies are studied in the literature, e.g., decentralized caching policy where each node caches the service advertisements it hears in the vicinity [5,6] or centralized caching policy where a central directory is elected to cache the service advertisements heard in a vicinity on behalf of all nodes in that vicinity [8]. Some service discovery protocols also consider the cache replacement and refreshment policies.

Service advertisements caching can reduce the service discovery delay. However, if both the local services and the cached services are advertised, it will increase packet size and thus waste more network bandwidth. A better solution is to replace the cached service information with smaller meta service description.

In the Group-based Service Discovery (GSD) protocols [5], the meta service description is defined as the service group information. Each node's advertisement packets contain the service descriptions of the local services and the group information of the cached services. The group information can partially solve the broadcast storm problem in flooding-based protocols since the source will only approach the nodes which potentially have the information for the required service and each intermediate node will only forward the service request packet to candidates which with potential matchment.

In this paper, we introduce a fine-grained group-based meta service description based on the service group information used in GSD and propose an efficient service discovery protocol which exhaustively utilize the meta information to minimize the number of so called forwarding nodes. The proposed protocol is called as Meta Service Description Assisted Service Discovery Protocol (MSDASDP). In MSDASDP, a service request packet is broadcasted out with the tentative recipient list which is determined by the meta service description for the cached service advertisements. Additionally, using a greedy algorithm, the number of forwarding nodes of a service request packet is minimized. Therefore, the number of successive request packets sent by the forwarding nodes is reduced. The proposed meta service description and the scheme of forwarding service request packets can be readily integrated with other components of the service discovery protocols existing in the literature to enhance their performance.

The rest of the paper is organized as follows. In Section 2, an overview of GSD is given. Section 3 presents the notations and definitions used in the paper. In Section 4, operations of MSDASDP are described in details. In Section 5, simulation results and comparison of MSDASDP and several other service discovery protocols are presented and discussed. Section 6 concludes the paper.

2 Overview of GSD

GSD is a service discovery protocol that adopts the meta service description approach. The three basic operations of GSD are: service advertisement packet spreading, service request packet forwarding, and service reply packet routing.

2.1 Service Advertisement Packet Spreading

In GSD, each server will periodically generate service advertisement packets which can be cached in the Service Information Cache (SIC) of the receiving nodes and forwarded by these nodes. To reduce the size of the service advertisement packet, a group-based meta service description approach is used in GSD, where the service advertisement packet contains the group information of the cached services instead of the detailed descriptions. The group information will then be used in forwarding request packets towards so-called candidate nodes which has some services belonging to the same group as the requested service.

2.2 Service Request Packet Forwarding

When a node needs services and there is no matched service in its SIC, the node constructs a service request packet and sends one copy of the packet towards each elaborately selected nodes in unicast mode. These nodes are selected with the criterion that they have seen some services belonging to the same group as the requested service. Clearly, this service request will get matched at these selected nodes with high probability. When receiving the packet sent by the current node, each selected node should forward the packet further, unless the packet has reached or exceeds its hop limit.

2.3 Service Reply Packet Routing

If the node that receives a new request packet finds matched services, it unicasts a service reply packet to the sender of the service request packet. The service reply packet will be relayed to the sender (client) of the corresponding SDP session along the reverse path.

2.4 Improvements Can Be Made

Although GSD's group-based meta service description is simple and interesting, its utilization of the meta service description is far from efficient.

- Large packet redundancy is caused by too many unicast request packets. It may be very often that many nodes are selected for forwarding request packets where redundant unicast request packets will be sent.
- When forwarding request packets, number of nodes in the search space is not minimized and the method to select valid receivers is inefficient.

3 Preliminaries

In MSDASDP, a fine-grained group-based meta service description is introduced and more effective utilization of the meta service description when guiding request packet forwarding is achieved. To facilitate the description of MSDASDP in the following sections, some notations and definitions are given in the section.

3.1 Notations and Definitions

Def. 1 (Candidate Node): A *candidate node* of node u is a node in $C(u, g)$.

Def. 2 (Forwarding node): A *forwarding node* of node u is a node indicated by $f(u, s)$.

$F(u, g) = \{f(u, s)|s \in C(u, g)\}$ represents the set of all forwarding nodes. $C_f(u, f_0, g) = \{s|s \in C(u, g), f(u, s) = f_0\}$. represents the set of candidate nodes that share the same forwarding node f_0.

Def. 3 (Remote Candidate Node): A *remote candidate node* is a candidate node unreachable by the current request packet because of hop limit.

$C_R(u, g) = \{s|s \in C(u, g), e(u, s).\textit{hop-distance} > V_{\textit{remain-hop}}\}$ represents the set of all remote candidate nodes where $V_{\textit{remain-hop}}$ is the value of the request packet's *remain-hop* field.

Def. 4 (Hidden Server): A *hidden server* of a candidate node s is a node in $H_c(u, s, g)$. The set of all hidden servers seen by the current node u, denoted as $H_{ALL}(u, g)$, can be expressed as $H_{ALL}(u, g) = \cup_{s \in C(u,g)} H_c(u, s, g)$.The set of all

Table 1. Notations used in the paper

Notation	Description
c:	the client that generates the request.
u:	the current node.
t:	the sender of the service request packet received by u.
d:	the maximum number of hops that advertisement packets can travel.
g:	the group that the requested service belongs to.
$R(t)$:	the set of nodes selected by the sender t. They should forward service request packet. At the service request packet's client u, $t = u$, $R(t) = \{u\}$.
$N_x(u)$:	the set of nodes that are at most x-hop away from node u. It is node u's x-hop neighbor set (excluding node u).
$e(u, s)$:	the entry that corresponds to node s in node u's SIC(Service Info Cache).
$E(u)$:	the set of entries in node u's SIC.
$H_c(u, s, g)$:	the set of nodes in $N_d(s)$ that provide services belonging to group g. node s is a server in $N_d(u)$.
$S(u)$:	the set of servers in $N_d(u)$.
$C(u, g)$:	$C(u, g) = \{s \mid H_c(u, s, g) \neq \emptyset\}$.
$f(u, s)$:	the next-hop node on the path from node u to s.

hidden servers of some candidate nodes that share the same forwarding node f_0 can be expressed as:$H_f(u, f_0, g) = \cup_{s \in C_f(u, f_0, g)} H_c(u, s, g)$.

Def. 5 (Extended Coverage): If node u receives a request packet of an SDP session, then each server s in $N_d(u)$ is in the *extended coverage* of the SDP session. Then s is said to be extendedly-covered by the SDP session, or s is extendedly-covered by node u.

Def. 6 (Virtual Coverage): If node u sends a request packet for a service belonging to group g towards a candidate node s, then all hidden servers in $H_c(u, s, g)$ are in the *virtual coverage* of the current node u. We also say that they are virtually-covered by node u.

Def. 7 (Coverage-Needed Hidden Server): A *coverage-needed hidden server* of a node u is a hidden server that should be virtually-covered by node u. The set of coverage-needed hidden servers of the current node u is denoted as $H_{TC}(u, g)$. Since some hidden servers may have already been extendedly-covered by some other nodes, not all hidden servers seen in $H_{ALL}(u, g)$ should be virtually-covered by node u. Hence, $H_{TC}(u, g) \subseteq H_{ALL}(u, g)$.

Def. 8 (Dominating Forwarding Node Set (DFNS)): When forwarding request packets, a *DFNS* of the current node u is a set of forwarding nodes guaranteeing that all hidden servers seen by the current node u could be extendedly-covered by the current SDP session. A DFNS of the current node u is denoted as $F_{DFNS}(u, g)$.

3.2 Finding Minimum Dominating Forwarding Node Set

Each forwarding node should forward the service request packet, unless that it has found matched services or the hop-limit is reached. Hence, in order to reduce request packet overhead, the size of DFNS should be minimized. For ease of presentation, we use H to represent the set of coverage-needed hidden servers $H_{TC}(u,g)$, C to represent the family of sets $\{H_f(u, f_0, g) | f_0 \in F(u,g)\}$, and F to represent the set of all forwarding nodes $F(u,g)$. Then we define the DFNS problem as follows:

DFNS problem: Given H, C, and F, find a dominating forwarding node set $F_{DFNS}(u,g) \subseteq F$ with minimum size.

Since $\cup H_f(u, f_0, g) = H_{ALL}(u,g) \supseteq H$ and there is a 1-to-1 correspondence between C and F, the decision version DFNS Problem can be defined formally as: Given a positive integer k, $H = \{h_1, \cdots, h_n\}$, $C = \{C_1, \cdots, C_m\}$, and $\cup C_i \supseteq H$, decides whether there is subset $C' \subseteq C$ with size k such that $\cup_{C_i \in C'} C_i \supseteq H$.

Theorem 1: The decision version of the DFNS problem is NP-complete.

The proof is omitted due to space limit.

Since the DFNS problem is NP-complete, a greedy algorithm is proposed to select a dominating forwarding node set $F_{DFNS}(u,g)$ from H, C, and F.

Greedy Algorithm for Finding Minimum DFNS

Begin

1. Let $F_{DFNS}(u,g) = \emptyset$ (empty set), $H_{RC}(u,g) = \emptyset$.
2. Find node f_0 among $F(u,g)$ with maximum $|(H_f(u, f_0, g) \cap H_{TC}(u,g)) \backslash H_{RC}(u,g)|$. In case of a tie, select f_0 with maximum $|H_f(u, f_0, g) \cap H_{TC}(u,g)|$.In case of a new tie, select f_0 with smallest ID.
3. Set $F_{DFNS}(u,g) = F_{DFNS}(u,g) \cup \{f_0\}, F(u,g) = F(u,g) - \{f_0\}$
4. Set $H_{RC}(u,g) = H_{RC}(u,g) \cup H_f(u, f_0, g)$.
5. If $(H_{RC}(u,g) \subset H_{TC}(u,g)) \cap F(u,g) \neq \emptyset$, go to Step 2; otherwise, exit.

End

---

4 MSDASDP

The three basic operations of GSD are retained in MSDASDP. The service reply packet routing operation in MSDASDP is the same as that in GSD, hence only the other two operations are described in the section.

4.1 Meta Service Description in Service Advertisement Packet Spreading

In MSDASDP, when generating new service advertisement packets, a server should construct the meta service description based on its cached services and enclose it into the packet. Here the meta description is the list of service groups in the vicinity and each group (e.g., group "a")appended with the list of corresponding servers(e.g., servers that provide services belonging to group"a"). To implement this, a new compound filed named *other-group* is inserted which contains a list of sub-field named *group-item*. Each *group-item* field corresponds to one service group. The *other-group* field is constructed as follows:

$G_{other}(u,g) = \{e.\textit{server-id} | e \in E(u), e.\textit{local-group} = g\}$.
$G_{other}(u) = \{e.\textit{local-group} | e \in E(u)\}$.

Fig. 1 shows an example of service advertisement packet spreading operation in MSDASDP which illustrates the implementation of the fine-grained group-based meta service description. In Fig. 1, circles represent mobile nodes; the string in circles indicates the identity of the node and the services it provides. For example, string $\{A, a_1\}$ indicates that the node is A and it provides service a_1, which belongs to service group a. No service is provided by nodes D, E, and I, indicated by "_" in the figure. Double-headed arrows between two nodes indicate that these two nodes can communicate with each other directly. The white table adjacent to a node represents its SIC (not all fields are shown). For example, the third item in node A's SIC, $\{H, C, 2, b_4, (a(A, J), b(C))\}$ indicates that 1) this entry corresponds to node H, 2) the next hop node from A to H is C), 3)the distance between A and H is 2, 4) H provides service b_4, 5) In $N_x(u)$, nodes A and J provide group a services, and node C provides group b services. Arcs around a node indicate the transmission of a service advertisement packet. After several cycles of advertisement spreading operations, each node has created its own SIC. Then when generating new advertisement packets, meta service descriptions are also enclosed. The grey table over the arcs represents the content of the service advertisement packet being transmitted (not all fields are shown). For example, a service advertisement packet sent by node A, $\{A, a_1, b(B, C, H), 1\}$, shows that 1) the server that generates the packet is node A, 2) node A provides service a_1, which belongs to group a, 3) In $N_x(u)$, nodes B, C, and H provide some group b services, and 4) this service advertisement packet can still travel 1 hop. In Fig. 1, advertisement packets are restricted to 2 hops.

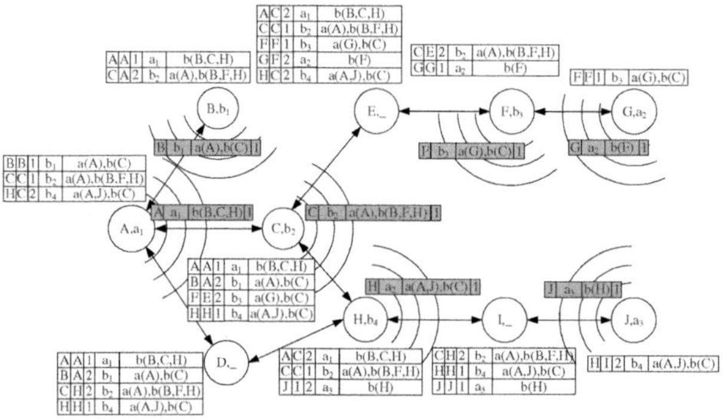

Fig. 1. Example of service advertisement packet spreading in MSDASDP

4.2 Meta Service Description Guided Request Packet Forwarding

When receiving a new service request packet, each node knowing about some matched services should respond with a service reply packet. Otherwise, the node forwards the request packet if either of the following two conditions is matched.

- The *receiver-number* field of the packet's *receiver-list* field is set to 0.
- The *receiver-number* field of the packet's *receiver-list* field is greater than 0 and the current node is in the *receiver-list* field.

If the current node determines to forward the service request packet, it will perform the following algorithm to forward the packet.

Algorithm for Service Request Packet Forwarding
Begin

1. Determine the set of coverage-needed hidden servers as follows:
$H_{TC}(u,g) = \cup_{s \in (C(u,g)-C_R(u,g))} H_c(u,s,g) - R(t) \cup \{c,t,u\} \cup C(u,g) - \cup_{s \in (R(t) \cup \{c,t,u\}) \cap C(u,g)} H_c(u,s,g)$.
2. Call the DFNS greedy algorithm to obtain a dominating forwarding node set $F_{DFNS}(u,g)$ from $H_{TC}(u,g)$, $F(u,g)$, and $\{H_f(u,f_0,g) | f_0 \in F(u,g)\}$.
3. Enclose nodes in $F_{DFNS}(u,g)$ into the service request packet's *receiver-list* compound field, and set the *receiver-number* field of the *receiver-list* field to the number of nodes in $F_{DFNS}(u,g)$.
4. Decrease the *remain-hop* field by 1.
5. Send the service request packet in broadcast mode.

The correctness of excluding $\cup_{s \in (R(t) \cup \{t,u\}) \cap C(u,g)} H_c(u,s,g)$ and $R(t) \cup \{t,u\} \cup C(u,g)$ is shown in the following Lemmas and Theorem 2, which are based on the following assumption.

Assumption: Packet transmissions are error-free.

Lemma 1: $R(t) \cup \{c,t,u\} \cup C(u,g)$ can be removed from $H_{TC}(u,g)$.

Lemma 2: $\cup_{s \in (R(t) \cup \{t,u\}) \cap C(u,g)} H_c(u,s,g)$ can be removed from $H_{TC}(u,g)$.

Theorem 2: The set of coverage-needed hidden servers of current node u can be expressed as

$$H_{TC}(u,g) = \cup_{s \in (C(u,g)-C_R(u,g))} H_c(u,s,g) - R(t) \cup \{c,t,u\} \cup C(u,g) - \cup_{s \in (R(t) \cup \{c,t,u\}) \cap C(u,g)} H_c(u,s,g).$$

The proofs of Lemma 1, Lemma 2, Theorem 2 are omitted due to space limit.

The above lemmas and theorem show that in MSDASDP the meta service description is exhaustively used to reduce the number of service request packets by minimizing the number of coverage-needed hidden servers and the size of dominating forwarding node set.

Compared with GSD, MSDASDP is more computation intensive. But considering that in most cases bandwidth is more precious for network nodes, MSDASDP is more preferable than GSD.

5 Performance Evaluation

In our simulations, we implemented MSDASDP and GSD as well as flooding and the Flexible Forward Probability based Service Discovery Protocol (FFPSDP) [6] for comparison purpose. Let P denote the probability of a node without matched services deciding to forward the packet. Flooding which has P=1 is selected as the baseline (referred as BASIC in the following text). In FFPSDP, P varies with the travel of service request packets as $P = P_{F,min} + (P_{F,max} - P_{F,min}) \times (H_{remain}/H_{max})$, where $P_{F,max}$ is the maximum value of the probability that a node will forward an unmatched request packet, $P_{F,min}$ is the corresponding minimum value, H_{remain} is the value of the *remain-hop* field of the request packet to be forwarded, and H_{max} is the maximum number of hops that request packets can travel.

5.1 Performance Metrics

Four performance metrics are considered in our simulations.

- *Request-Packet-Number:* It measures the number of service request packets sent in one simulation. It can exhibit the direct effect of BSU and forwarding node minimization (FNM).
- *Succeeded-SDP-Number:* It is the number of SDP sessions in which the client has received at least one reply packet. It reflects the effectiveness (service discoverability) of service discovery protocols.
- *First-Response-Time:* It is the interval between the arrival of the first reply packet and the generation of the corresponding request packet. This metric is averaged over all succeeded SDP sessions. It measures the promptness of service discovery protocols. It can also reflect the average distance between clients and the corresponding first repliers.
- *Succeeded-SDP-Number/Total-SDP-packet-number (Suc2Total):* This metric is the ratio of Succeeded-SDP-number to the number of all service request packets and reply packets. It reflects the protocol's efficiency. To make a more discriminative comparison between GSD and MSDASDP, effect of service advertisement packets is omitted.

5.2 Simulation Settings

Simulations are performed using Glomosim. Random waypoint model is used as the mobility model. In this model, nodes move towards their destinations with a randomly selected constant speed V. When reaching its destination, a node keeps static for a random period T_P. When the period expires, the node randomly selects a new destination and moves to the new destination with new speed. The process will repeat permanently. In our simulations, T_P is fixed at 0. Some basic parameters used in all the simulations are shown in Table 2. At the beginning of each simulation, 100 nodes are randomly distributed in the scenario area, and a predetermined number of nodes are randomly selected as servers. These selected servers provide randomly selected services. During each simulation, 200 SDP sessions are started at randomly selected time by randomly selected nodes.

5.3 Simulation Results

Node speed is a major factor that affects the performance of service discovery protocols. To inspect the effect of node speed on protocol performance, we run

Table 2. Basic parameters used in simulations

Parameters	Value	Parameters	Value
Network area	$1000m \times 1000m$	Service advertisement interval	20
Node number	100	Valid time of SIC item	30
Simulation time	$1000s$	Number of service group	1
Wireless bandwidth	$1Mbps$	Number of service info in each group	20
SDP session number	200	Maximum hop of request packets	3
$P_{F,max}(FFPSDP)$	1	Maximum hop of advertisement packets	1
$P_{F,min}(FFPSDP)$	0.4		

four sets of simulations that use the four selected service discovery protocols, respectively. In these simulations, the radio range is set as $150m$ and the number of servers is set as 100. Each set includes 6 subsets of simulations, where node speed is set as $0m/s$, $1m/s$, $5m/s$, $10m/s$, $15m/s$ and $20m/s$, respectively. Each subset consists of 100 similar simulations except for different random seeds. Fig. 2 shows the four performance metrics under different node speeds. All results shown are averaged over 100 simulations.

Fig. 2(a) shows that MSDASDP has the lowest service request packet overhead under different node speeds. For example, when node speed is $20m/s$, the *request-packet-number* metric of MSDASDP is only about 24.3% of GSD, 15.2% of FFPSDP, and 6.2% of BASIC. This effect is due to the following facts. First, the BSU scheme uses a broadcast request packet to substitute several unicast request packets so that the number of service request packets is significantly reduced. Second, using a greedy heuristic, the FNM scheme minimizes the number of forwarding nodes, which leads to fewer service request packets sent by the selected forwarding nodes. As node speed increases, this metric of MSDASDP and GSD decreases gradually. The reason is that node's movement expands the spreading range of the service advertisement packets.

Fig. 2(b) shows the effect of node speed on the *succeeded-SDP-number* metric. As shown in the figure, MSDASDP is generally the most effective protocol under different node speeds. Noticeably, the superiority of MSDASDP becomes more significant as node speed increases. This is due to more effective packet transmissions resulted from fewer request packets in MSDASDP, which is more significant with higher speed.

Fig. 2(c) shows the effect of node speed on the *first-response-time* metric. MSDASDP is the most prompt protocol under different node speeds. MSDASDP and GSD are much superior to BASIC and FFPSDP in this metric. This is due to the service advertisement packet spreading operation, through which all nodes in a server's d-hop neighbor set can see the services provided by the server. Thus, a service request will be matched in fewer hops. MSDASDP outperforms GSD in this metric because of fewer packet collisions resulted from fewer packets.

Fig. 2(d) shows the effect of node speed on the *Suc2Total* metric. The superiority of MSDASDP in this metric is more significant with higher node speed.

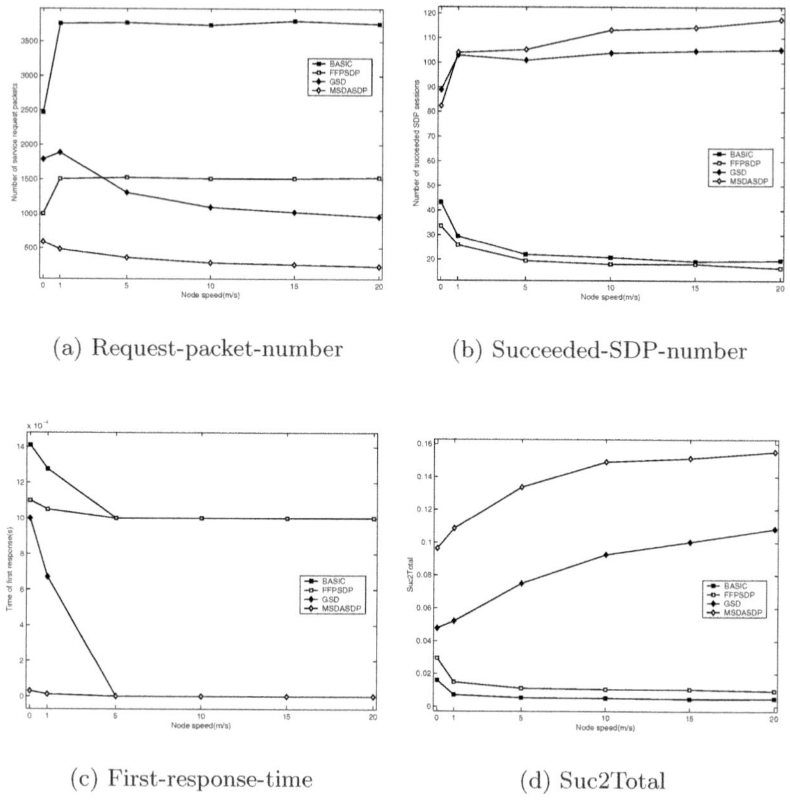

(a) Request-packet-number (b) Succeeded-SDP-number

(c) First-response-time (d) Suc2Total

Fig. 2. Simulation results under different node speed

When node speed is $20m/s$, the efficiency of MSDASDP is about 1.4 times of GSD, 16.5 times of FFPSDP, and 32.6 times of BASIC.

In summary, from the above simulation results, we can see that MSDASDP is generally the most effective, efficient, and prompt one among all tested service discover protocols. Generally, the superiority of MSDASDP over other tested protocols is generally more significant with higher node speed. Although MSDASDP is more computation intensive, but considering that in most cases bandwidth is more precious for network nodes, MSDASDP is more preferable.

6 Conclusion

In this paper, an efficient meta service description assisted service discovery protocol for MANETs is proposed. Meta service description in MSDASDP helps providing useful information for service request packet forwarding, thus effectively reduce the service discovery overhead. Simulations shew that MSDASDP outperforms other existing service discovery protocols in terms of the number of request packets, the number of succeeded SDP sessions, and the first response time. The proposed meta service description and the service request packet forwarding scheme can be readily integrated with other components proposed in existing service discovery protocols to improve their performance.

Future work includes extension of MSDASDP to reduce packet overhead when the number of forwarding nodes is 0 (in such cases request packets will be broadcasted to all neighbors) and investigation of new service discovery protocols making use of the information in service reply packets.

References

1. IETF, Mobile ad-hoc network (MANET) working group. Mobile ad-hoc networks (MANET) `http://www.ietf.org/html.charters/manet-charter.html`
2. Engelstad, E., Zheng, Y.: Evaluation of Service Discovery Architectures for Mobile Ad hoc Networks. In: Proc. 2nd Wireless On-demand Networks and Services (WONS), pp. 2–15. 2005, St. Moritz, Switzerland (2005)
3. Motegi, S., Yoshihara, K., Horiuchi, H.: Service Discovery for Wireless Ad hoc Networks. In: Proc. 5th Wireless Personal Multimedia Communications (WPMC). 2002, Honolulu, Hawai, USA, pp. 232–236 (2002)
4. Penz, S.: SLP-based Service Management for Dynamic Ad-hoc Networks. In: Proc. 3rd Middleware for Pervasive and Ad-hoc Computing. Grenoble, 2005, France, pp. 1–8 (2005)
5. Chakraborty, D., Joshi, A., Yesha, Y., Finin, T.: GSD: a Novel Group-based Service Discovery Protocol for MANETs. In: Proc. 4th IEEE Mobile and Wireless Communications Networks. 2002, Stockholm, Sweden, pp. 140–144 (2002)
6. Gao, Z.G., Yang, X.Z., Ma, T.Y., Cai, S.B.: RICFFP: an Efficient Service Discovery Protocol for MANETs. In: Proc. 1st Embedded and Ubiquitous Computing. Aizu-Wakamatsu City, 2004, Japan, pp. 786–795 (2004)
7. Ratsimor, O., Chakarborty, D., Joshi, A.: Allia: Alliance-based Service Discovery for Ad-hoc Environments. In: Proc. 2nd ACM Mobile Commerce, Georgia. USA, 2002, pp. 1–9. ACM Press, New York (2002)
8. Sailhan, F., Issarny, V.: Scalable Service Discovery for MANET. In: Proc. 3rd IEEE Pervasive Computing and Communications, 2005, Kauai, Hawaii, USA, pp. 235–244 (2005)
9. Cortes, C., Blair, G., Grace, P.: A Multi-protocol Framework for Ad-hoc Service Discovery. In: Proc. 4th Middleware for Pervasive and Adhoc Computing, 2006, Melbourne, Australia (2006)
10. Gao, Z., Yang, Y., Zhao, J.: Service Discovery Protocols for MANETs: a Survey. In: Proc. 2nd Mobile Ad Hoc and Sensor Networks, 2000, Hong Kong, China, pp. 232–243 (2006)

On Characterizing Economic-Based Incentive-Compatible Mechanisms to Solving Hidden Information and Hidden Action in Ad Hoc Network

Yufeng Wang[1], Yoshiaki Hori[2], and Kouichi Sakurai[2]

[1] College of Telecommunications and Information Engineering, Nanjing University of Posts and Telecommunications, Nanjing 210003, China
[2] Department of Computer Science and Communication Engineering, Kyushu University, Fukuoka 812-0053, Japan
wfwang@njupt.edu.cn

Abstract. This paper attempts to comprehensively characterize economic-based incentive compatible routing and forwarding mechanisms in ad hoc network, including hidden information in routing phase, and hidden action in forwarding phase. By incentive compatibility it means that system designer should respect rationality of nodes, and design proper incentive mechanisms to encourage nodes to conduct something beneficial to the whole system, while nodes pursued their own utility. Firstly, based on analysis of extensive game form, we argue that, for each participant, truth-telling is the expected dominant strategy equilibrium in VCG-like routing mechanism, even under the situation of mutually dependent link cost. Then, Individual rationality (IR) and Incentive Compatibility (IC) constraints are formally offered, which should be satisfied by any game theoretical routing and forwarding scheme. And different solution concepts are investigated to characterize the economic meanings of two kind forwarding approaches, that is, Nash equilibrium with no per-hop monitoring and dominant strategy equilibrium with per-hop monitoring. Finally, we discuss frugality problem in VCG-like mechanism.

1 Introduction

Traditional system design assumes that participants behave according to the intentions of the system architects. But wireless ad hoc network is composed by autonomous nodes determining their behaviors independently and shared by rational (selfish) users with different and competing interests. Naturally, in ad hoc network, system designer should respect rationality of nodes, and design proper incentive mechanisms to encourage nodes to conduct something beneficial to the whole system, while nodes pursued their own utility, that is incentive-compatibility. Specifically, there exist hidden information and hidden action attacks in ad hoc networks. Hidden information means that nodes possess private information (e.g., costs for forwarding packet)

* Research supported by the NSFC Grants 60472067, JiangSu education bureau (5KJB510091) and State Key Laboratory of Networking and Switching Technology, Beijing University of Posts and Telecommunications (BUPT).

J. Indulska et al. (Eds.): UIC 2007, LNCS 4611, pp. 382–391, 2007.

which is not known to all of the parties involved. For example, in traditional routing protocol which selects low-cost routing path, there is no guarantee that any wireless node will reveal its cost truthfully unless it is convinced that is cannot do better by declaring a different cost. Hidden actions represent what made attractive by a lack of observation. For example, in the forwarding phase, without proper incentive mechanism, each participant in the low-cost path has inventive to drop packet. In brief, selfish wireless nodes may hinder the functioning of the network completely, thus a stimulation mechanism is required to encourage the users to provide service to other nodes. A great deal of research efforts focused on incentive mechanisms in Ad hoc network, which can be classified into the following types: Reputation-based schemes [1-3], and payment-based schemes [4-6]. In this paper, we focus on the payment-based mechanisms. There are several papers similar to our work. Ref. [7] adopts Mechanism Design (MD) to design Ad hoc-VCG routing scheme. But this paper ignores the challenge in wireless ad hoc networks that link cost is determined by two neighboring nodes together, namely mutually dependent link cost. Ref. [8] investigates incentive-compatible routing and forwarding protocols, Corsac, in wireless ad hoc network, which integrates VCG with a novel cryptographic technique to address the challenge of mutual-dependent link cost in wireless ad-hoc networks, but their work offers weak theorems. Based on principal-agent model, Ref. [4] shows how the hidden-action problem can be overcome through appropriate design of contracts, and generalizes existing mechanisms that deal with hidden-information to handle scenarios involving both hidden-information and hidden-action, but they neither provide the formal definition of Incentive Rationality (IR) and Incentive Compatibility (IC) constraints, which should be satisfied by any game theoretical routing and forwarding scheme, nor analyze the integrated incentive mechanisms in routing and forwarding.

The paper's contributions lie in the following aspects: Firstly, for mutually dependent link cost, based on analysis of extensive game form, we argue that truth-telling is the expected dominant strategy equilibrium, and repeated game can be used to achieve this equilibrium; Then, this paper formally describes the constraints of individual IR and IC in ad hoc routing and forwarding game, and uses different solution concepts to characterize the features of ad hoc network game with per-hop monitoring and without per-hop monitoring; finally, we investigate the frugality of VCG-payment.

The paper is organized as follows. In section 2, system models used in this paper were described, including the cost model of ad hoc nodes, and related constraints and equilibrium solutions in game theory and mechanism design. In section 3, based on extensive game analysis, we argue that truth-telling is the expected best choice of each participant in VCG-like routing mechanisms even facing the problem of mutual-dependent link cost. In section 4, the formal definitions of IR and IC in the loss link are offered, and different solution concepts are used to characterize the economic meanings of forwarding games with per-hop monitoring and without per-hop monitoring. Section 5 illustrates the source node's preference for relative short-hop path, and provides the modified social selection function to achieve the tradeoff between shortest-cost path and shortest-hop path. Finally, we briefly conclude the paper in section 6.

2 System Model

2.1 Cost Model

We assume ad hoc network to be an arbitrary, connected graph, $G=\{V,E,\omega\}$, of selfish ad hoc nodes $V=\{1,\ldots,N\}$ that represents mobile devices, a set $E \subseteq V * V$ of directed edges (i,j) that connect two nodes, and a weight function $c: E \rightarrow R$ for each edge (i,j) that indicates the cost of transmitting a data packet from node i to node j. Each node i has an individual parameter α_i indicating its cost-of-energy. If node i send a message using emission power P^{emit}, then it must receive at least remuneration amount $\alpha_i * P^{emit}$ to compensate for its energy cost.

An energy-efficient routing protocol ensures that a packet from a source to a destination gets routed along the most cost-efficient path possible via intermediate nodes. The total cost of a routing path is the sum on the energy cost incurred at the source and at each intermediate node. If a sender appends its emission power into the packet header, then the receiver can infer the required minimal power, and forward the value to the sender. That is:

$$P_{i,j}^{\min} = \frac{P_i^{emit}}{P_{i,j}^{rec}} P_{\min}^{rec} \tag{1}$$

P_i^{emit} denotes peer i's emission power; $P_{i,j}^{rec}$ is the received power level by peer j; P_{min}^{rec} is the required power level to guarantee certain QoS level. Thus, the cost of transmitting packet from i to j is given as follows:

$$c(i,j) = \alpha_i P_{i,j}^{\min} \tag{2}$$

For the given path, we omit subscript j, let

$$c(i,j)=c_i. \tag{3}$$

It is easily seen that a node alone cannot determine transmission power level because it needs feedbacks from its neighbors, which is the unique challenge of mutually dependent link cost in ad hoc network. The above feature may allow one node to cheat its neighbors in order to raise its own welfare. In next section, based on analysis of extensive game, we argue that truth-telling is the expected dominant strategy for each node in Ad hoc network.

2.2 Concepts in Mechanism Design

The goal of MD (also called "inverse game") is to define the strategic situation, or "rules of the game", so that the system as a whole exhibits good behavior in equilibrium when self-interested nodes pursue self-interested strategies [10]. The standard setting of mechanism design is described as follows:

- There exist a set of agents $i \in I$ (with N agents altogether), and each agent i has private type $\theta_i \in \Theta_i$;

- A mechanism $m=(o,p)$ is composed two elements, outcome specification $o \in O$ which maps the set of private type to an allowed outcome based on the optimization of social selection function $f(\hat{\theta})$. $\hat{\theta} \in \Theta = (\Theta_1 \times \cdots \times \Theta_N)$ is vector of reported types by agents. We write $\hat{\theta}$ to emphasize that agents can misreport their true types. Mechanism also calculates N-tuple of payment $p = (p_1, \cdots, p_N)$ by (or to) each agent.
- Each agent i has utility $u_i(o;\theta_i)$, agent i's utility for report $\hat{\theta}_i$, given others' reports $\hat{\theta}_{-i} = \{\hat{\theta}_1, \cdots, \hat{\theta}_{i-1}, \hat{\theta}_{i+1}, \hat{\theta}_N\}$, is $u_i(o(\hat{\theta}_i, \hat{\theta}_{-i});\theta_i)$. Generally, utility is quasi-linear in value and payments, defined as $u_i(o;\theta_i) = p_i - c_i(o;\theta_i)$.

Note that, in routing phase, each node's private type can represent its transmission cost (hidden information); in forwarding phase, each node's private type can represent the hidden action conducted by peer (like forwarding packet or not). There are two types of constraint on the designer in building ad hoc routing and forwarding mechanism: individual rationality and incentive compatibility.

Individual rationality (IR) constraints

The first type of constraint is the following. The utility of each agent has to be at least as great as the utility that the agent would receive if it did not participate in the mechanism, so-called fallback utility. Otherwise, agent would not participate in the mechanism. This type of constraint is called an IR (also called participation constraint). Without loss of generality, we assume that each agent's fallback utility is zero.

Definition 1. A mechanism is IR if for any agent i and any type of $\theta_i \in \Theta_i$, we have $E_{(\theta_1,\ldots,\theta_{i-1},\theta_{i+1},\ldots,\theta_N)|\theta_i}(p_i(\theta_1,\ldots,\theta_N) - c_i(\theta_i, o(\theta_1,\ldots,\theta_N))) \geq 0$, which states that the utility to an agent, given prior beliefs about the preferences of other agents, is at least the utility gained from not participating to the mechanism.

Incentive compatibility (IC) constraints

The second type of constraint states that the agents should never have an incentive to misreport their type. For this type of constraint, two most common variants (or solution concepts) are implementation in Nash equilibrium, and implementation in dominant strategies.

Definition 2. A mechanism is said to implement its outcome and payment function in Nash equilibrium, If, given the truth-telling strategy in equilibrium, $(\theta_1^*, \ldots, \theta_i^*, \ldots, \theta_N^*)$, no agent has an incentive to deviate unilaterally from the strategy profile. Formally, for any agent i, any type $(\hat{\theta}_1, \ldots, \hat{\theta}_i, \ldots, \hat{\theta}_N) \in \Theta_1 \times \cdots \times \Theta_i \times \cdots \times \Theta_N$, any alternative type report $\hat{\theta}_i \in \Theta_i$ we have $p_i(\theta_1^*, \ldots, \theta_i^*, \ldots, \theta_N^*) - c_i(\theta_i, o(\theta_1^*, \ldots, \theta_i^*, \ldots, \theta_N^*)) \geq p_i(\theta_1^*, \ldots, \hat{\theta}_i, \ldots, \theta_N^*) - c_i(\theta_i, o(\theta_1^*, \ldots, \hat{\theta}_i, \ldots, \theta_N^*))$.

Definition 3. A mechanism is said to implement its outcome and payment function in dominant strategies if truth-telling is always optimal even when the types reported by the other agent are already known. Formally, we have $p_i(\hat{\theta}_1,\ldots,\theta_i^*,\ldots,\hat{\theta}_N)-c_i(\theta_i,o(\hat{\theta}_1,\ldots,\theta_i^*,\ldots,\hat{\theta}_N))\geq p_i(\hat{\theta}_1,\ldots,\hat{\theta}_i,\ldots,\hat{\theta}_N)-c_i(\theta_i,o(\hat{\theta}_1,\ldots,\hat{\theta}_i,\ldots,\hat{\theta}_N))$.

3 Hidden Information and Routing Mechanisms

Ad hoc-VCG mechanism works as follows [7]: based on each node's declaration of forwarding cost, assume $S,1,\ldots,i,j,\ldots,D$ denote the chosen cost-effective path. According to VCG mechanism, the remuneration amount received by node i is:

$$p_i := \left|SP^{-i}\right| - \left|SP \setminus (i,j)\right| = \left|SP^{-i}\right| - \left|SP\right| + c(i,j) \tag{4}$$

where $\left|SP^{-i}\right|$ represents the minimal path cost without node i; $\left|SP \setminus (i,j)\right|$ represents the minimal path cost, when the cost of link (i, j) equals zero.

Although the VCG mechanism has been applied to many networking problems in general and to routing protocols in particular, wireless ad-hoc networks poses unique challenges, that is, mutually dependent link cost. Ref.[8] adopts cryptography to solve the mutual-dependent link cost. We argue that, based on analysis of extensive game, it needs not to use considerable cryptography-based effort to guarantee the truth-telling property in VCG routing mechanism, even though there exist the mutually dependent link cost problem. We consider an extensive game model of ad hoc routing game. The basic component of the extensive form is the game tree which is a directed graph. The variable T is used to denote the game tree and the variables V and E are used to denote the collections of vertices and edges of the graph, i.e. $T = (V, E)$, the set of players is denoted by N and individual players are indexed using the variable i. The vertices are further divided into sets of terminal and non-terminal vertices. Terminal vertices have no successors, i.e. child vertices, and they define an outcome for the game, which can be associated with a payoff. Thus the path fully defines the outcome of the game. Each non-terminal vertex $v \in V$ is labeled using one of the players of the game and V_i is defined to be the collection of vertices that are labeled with i. At each non-terminal vertex $v \in V_i$, player i needs to perform an action.

For limited space, the detail analysis process to prove the truth-telling property in challenge of mutually dependent link cost is given in [11]. Our result is interesting because the cryptographic approach taken in [8] represents considerable engineering effort to align the incentives. In fact, it is not necessary and worthwhile to spend the considerable cryptography-based effort at aligning the incentives in ad hoc routing game.

4 Hidden Actions in Message Forwarding

Mechanism in the above section for the ad hoc routing game assumes that once the transit cost have been obtained, and the shortest cost path (SP) has been determined, the nodes on the SP obediently forward all packets, and that there is no lost in the network, i.e, k=0, k is the per-hop loss rate. In fact, the wireless link faces relatively high loss rate. So, intuitively, each intermediate node should get higher remuneration to bear the threat of loss link than in lossless environment. Furthermore, actually, nodes' actions may be unobservable by entities that buy the routing and forwarding service from Ad hoc network, so-called principal. Principal may be the source node, destination node or the authorized third party. In this section, we investigate the equilibrium properties of forwarding game in ad hoc network, under the condition of per-hop monitoring and no per-hop monitoring.

The simplified model is given as follows: multiple agents perform sequential hidden action, that is, each agent can choose to drop or forward packet; Principal can observe: the final outcome only (without per-hop monitoring); the per-hop outcome (with per-hop monitoring). Action $a_i \in \{0,1\}$, $a_i = 0$ means that node i drops packet, otherwise, $a_i = 1$; Outcomes: $R(a) = r \in \{r^G, r^B\}$, r^G means that packet reaches destination; r^B means that packet doesn't reaches destination; Utility of node i: $u_i(m_i, c_i, a_i) = m_i - a_i c_i$. Note that, in order to persuade node i to face the threat of loss link, obviously, m_i should large than p_i obtained in equation (4).
Given a per-hop loss rate of k, we can express the probability that a packet is successfully delivered from node i to its successor i+1 as: $Pr(r^G_{i \to i+1} | a_i) = (1-k)a_i$, where $r^G_{i \to i+1}$ denotes a successful transmission from node i to j.

Ref. [8] uses the scenario of no per-hop monitoring scheme to illustrate the Theorem 1 proposed in their paper, "There does not exist a forwarding-dominant protocol for ad hoc games". But, their proof procedure violates the basic constraint, IR, that is, in their situation, no node will join the game (Refer to [11] for detailed description).

Base on different solution concepts, this paper attempts to characterize the economic meanings of forwarding game with per-hop monitoring and without per-hop monitoring.

Theorem 1. In ad hoc forwarding game, let the payment scheme be:

$$0 \le m_i^B < \min_{j \in SP}\{p_j - c_j\};\ m_i^G = \frac{p_i}{(1-k)^{n-i+1}}$$

where m_i^G and m_i^B denote the payment to node i under the outcome of r^G and r^B.
Then, forwarding game without per-hop monitoring can achieve Nash equilibrium.
Let the payment scheme be

$$0 \le m_i^B < \min_{j \in SP}\{p_j - c_j\};\ m_i^G = \frac{p_i}{(1-k)}$$

That is, payment to node i is m_i^G, if the packet has reached node i+1, and m_i^B otherwise. Then, per-hop monitoring mechanism provides the dominant strategy equilibrium.

Proof: ① **Nash equilibrium in no per-hop monitoring**

The IR and IC in Nash equilibrium can be formally described as follows:

IR:

$$Pr(r^G_{S\to i}|a_{j<i}=1)\left(Pr(r^G|a_{j\geq i}=1)m_i^G+Pr(r^B|a_{j\geq i}=1)m_i^B-c_i\right)+Pr(r^B_{S\to i}|a_{j<i}=1)m_i^B\geq 0$$

This constraint says that the expected utility from participating is greater than or equal to zero (reservation utility), if all other nodes forward.

IC:

$$Pr(r^G_{S\to i}|a_{j<i}=1)\left(Pr(r^G|a_{j\geq i}=1)m_i^G+Pr(r^B|a_{j\geq i}=1)m_i^B-c_i\right)+Pr(r^B_{S\to i}|a_{j<i}=1)m_i^B$$
$$\geq Pr(r^G_{S\to i}|a_{j<i}=1)\left(Pr(r^G|a_i=0,a_{j>i}=1)m_i^G+Pr(r^B|a_i=0,a_{j>i}=1)m_i^B\right)+Pr(r^B_{S\to i}|a_{j<i}=1)m_i^B$$

The constraint says that the expected utility from forwarding is greater than or equals to its expected utility from dropping, if all nodes forward as well.

Based on the loss link model, the above general equations can be represented as:

IC:

$$(1-k)^i\left((1-k)^{n-i+1}m_i^G+\left(1-(1-k)^{n-i+1}\right)m_i^B-c_i\right)+\left(1-(1-k)^i\right)m_i^B\geq 0$$

IR:

$$(1-k)^i\left((1-k)^{n-i+1}m_i^G+\left(1-(1-k)^{n-i+1}\right)m_i^B-c_i\right)+\left(1-(1-k)^i\right)m_i^B\geq$$
$$(1-k)^i m_i^B+\left(1-(1-k)^i\right)m_i^B$$

Base on the proposed payment scheme, it is easy to verify that IR and IC conditions can be satisfied, which implies that there exist Nash equilibrium.

② **Dominant strategy equilibrium in per-hop monitoring**

In this approach, the principal make the payment schedule contingent on whether the packet has reached the next hop or not. Under monitoring mechanism, the principal has to satisfy the following constraints:

IR: $Pr(r^G_{S\to i}|a_{j<i}=1)\left(Pr(r^G_{i\to i+1}|a_i=1)m_i^G+Pr(r^B_{i\to i+1}|a_i=1)m_i^B-c_i\right)\geq 0$

IC:

$$Pr(r^G_{S\to i}|a_{j<i}=1)\left(Pr(r^G_{i\to i+1}|a_i=1)m_i^G+Pr(r^B_{i\to i+1}|a_i=1)m_i^B-c_i\right)\geq$$
$$Pr(r^G_{S\to i}|a_{j<i}=1)\left(Pr(r^G_{i\to i+1}|a_i=0)m_i^G+Pr(r^B_{i\to i+1}|a_i=0)m_i^B\right)$$

The above two conditions can also be represented as:

IR: $(1-k)^i\left((1-k)m_i^G+km_i^B-c_i\right)\geq 0$

IC: $(1-k)^i\left((1-k)m_i^G+km_i^B-c_i\right)\geq(1-k)^i m_i^B$

So, obviously, IR and IC conditions can be satisfied.

As shown in Ref. [4], it is also easy to verify that the expected payment is identical in those two approaches, per-hop monitoring and no per hop monitoring. But the fundamental difference between two scenarios is the solution concepts used. If no per-hop monitoring is used, the strategy profile is Nash equilibrium, which means that no agent has an incentive to deviate unilaterally from the strategy profile. In contrast, per-hop monitoring implies that the best action chosen by each node is always to forward packet, irrespective of other nodes' behaviors. Therefore, per-hop monitoring provides us with dominant strategy equilibrium, so an argument for designing mechanism with dominant strategies is that it makes the game much easier for the agent to play (that is, participants need not worry about doing any research into how the agents are likely to play). Ref. [6] designs payment schemes, Sprite, to prevent several types of selfish behaviors, in which receipt is used as per-hop monitoring mechanism. But unfortunately, the procedure has weak points. That is, decision that peer *i* whether forward packet will depend on not only the actual forwarding behavior of peer *i*, but the behavior of the next-hop peer *i*+1 to report receipt, which is another kind of mutual decision scenarios. For this receipt-based per-hop monitoring, we also investigate peers' incentive to provide receipt [11], for limited space in this paper, we omit this part.

5 Frugality in Forwarding Game

Usually, mechanism design views the payment only as an inducement to the agents to bid truthfully, while the mechanism really care about optimizing some unrelated objective function, such as finding the shortest path in a graph. When the mechanism is applied to perform a task (for example, source node pays each intermediate nodes for forwarding packets), it makes sense to try to keep the total payment low. One drawback to the VCG mechanism when applied to the shortest path problem is that it can be forced to pay a huge amount, compared to the actual cost of the path.

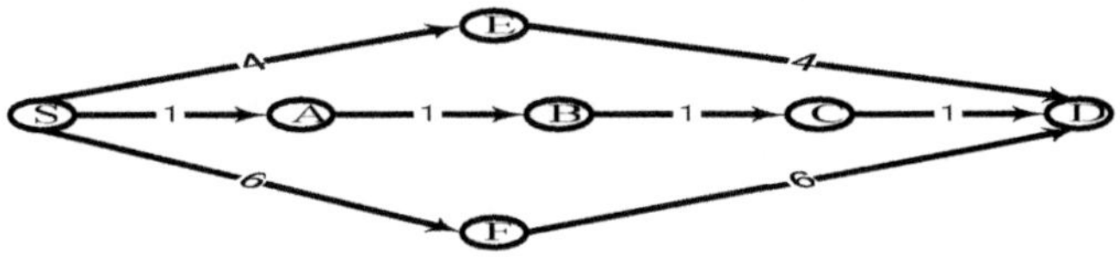

Fig. 1. Illustration: Incentive of source node to lie about the network topology

We use Fig.1 to illustrate that source node has incentive to lie about the network topology. For clarity of description, we assume lossless link. If the total payment by source *S* equals the sum of remuneration of each node, then this choice will leave space for a strategic behavior of the source node *S*. for example, just illustrated in Fig.1, if source node *S* truthfully reveals its neighborhood relationship, the shortest cost path is $S \to A \to B \to C \to D$, then the total payment in VCG mechanism is 1+5+5+5=16; if source node *S* lies that it is not a neighbor of *A*, then its shortest path becomes $S \to E \to D$. Now the total payment is 8+4=12 to send a packet. Thus, source node *S* benefits by lying about its neighborhood connection information. This problem rises from the fact that the least cost path is not necessarily the path that source node pays the least. One reason of this phenomenon is that source node should pay premium for each intermediate node in the shortest cost path. So, source node may give preference to paths with fewer nodes (hops). Furthermore, the relative short-hop path also implies improved performance experienced by source node, like relative low delay. If we restrict ourselves to selecting the shortest path, then VCG is the only truthful mechanism. However, it is conceivable that choosing an almost-shortest path might yield a better payment. Specifically, we attempt to achieve a tradeoff between the shortest-hop path and shortest-cost path to accommodate source node's preference for relative shorter-hop path. Inspired by [12], for each path, we evaluate some function of the bids on its edges, and select the path with the minimum function value. Specifically, We set the social selection function as: $f_P(b_P) = ln(1+|P|)\sum_{e\in P} b_e$, where $|P|$ is the number of intermediate nodes in a path. Notice that the VCG shortest path mechanism is a special case, where the function f_P simply sums the bids along the path P. Then, we show that mechanism based on the above social selection function is truth-telling mechanism. Recall that, in ad hoc routing and forwarding game, each node has its valuation on participating in the routing and forwarding game, which is given by $v_i = -q_i c_i$. The binary quantity q_i represents whether peer i is in the selected routing path.

Definition 4. Threshold mechanism. Suppose that the quantities q_i are binary, and $v_i = -q_i c_i$. For each b_{-i}, suppose there is some threshold bid $T_i(b_{-i})$ such that if $b_i < T_i(b_{-i})$ then i "wins" (i.e., q_i=1), while if $b_i > T_i(b_{-i})$ then i loses (i.e., q_i=0). If $b_i = T_i(b_{-i})$, then we do not care whether i wins or loses. If i loses, it is paid zero. If she wins, it is paid $T_i(b_{-i})$. Such mechanism was called threshold mechanism.

Theorem 2. A mechanisms with binary allocations is truthful if and only if it is a threshold mechanism. The detailed proof can be found in Ref. [11].

Ref. [9] proposes alternative way to address the cheating behavior of source node, which sets the total payment by source S equal the cost of the minimum cost path that does not contain any of the nodes in SP, so-called the global replacement path. So, it is obvious to see that with the above definition, any false declaration of the node S have not effect on the benefit of node S, Thus, the truthfulness of the mechanism is not impaired. But the common assumption of bi-connected communication graph doesn't imply that a global replacement path always exists.

6 Conclusion

Recently, cross-disciplinary efforts involving economics and computer security have proliferated. One main reason is that open network architecture already made computing infrastructure possess characteristics of an economy-society entity as well as those of computer system. Specifically, wireless ad-hoc networks are often formed by rational and autonomous nodes determining their behaviors independently. Intuitively, those nodes do not cooperate unless they have incentive to do so. Thus, both routing and packet forwarding become games. Generally, in ad hoc networks, there exist hidden information in routing game and hidden action in forwarding game. Furthermore, there exists unique feature in Ad hoc routing game, that is, mutually dependent cost link, which means that one link cost is determined by two neighboring nodes together. In this paper, based on economic models, we re-examine several proposals in related papers, and firstly argue that, based on analysis of extensive game, the VCG-like routing mechanism is expected dominant strategy equilibrium in the mutually dependent link cost environment. Then, we formally describe the Individual Rationality (IR) and Incentive Compatibility (IC) constraint which should be satisfied by any routing and forwarding game in Ad hoc network, and investigate the economic meanings of per-hop monitoring scheme and no per-hop monitoring scheme using different solution concepts. That is, with proper payment structure, no per-hop monitoring scheme provides Nash equilibrium, and per-hop monitoring scheme provides dominant strategy equilibrium. Finally, we illustrate the incentive of source node's preference for short-hop path, and adopt the proper social selection function to achieve the tradeoff between the shortest-cost path and the shortest-hop path, and formally prove the truth-telling property of this special kind of social selection function.

References

1. Michiardi, P., Molva, R.: Core: a COllaborative REputation mechanism to enforce node cooperation in mobile Ad Hoc networks. In: Proc. of IFIP Conference on Communications and Multimedia Security (2002)
2. Buchegger, S., Boudec, J.Y.L.: Performance analysis of the CONFIDANT protocol: cooperation of nodes-fairness in distributed Ad-hoc networks. In: Proc. of IEEE/ACM Workshop on Mobile Ad Hoc Networking and Computing, 2002, ACM Press, New York (2002)
3. Yu, W., Liu, K.J.R.: Attack-resistant cooperation stimulation in autonomous Ad Hoc networks. IEEE Journal on Selected Areas in Communications: Autonomic Communication Systems (2005)
4. Feldman, M., Chuang, J., Stoica, I., Shenker, S.: Hidden-action in multi-hop routing. In: Proc. of the 6th ACM Conference on Electronic Commerce (2005)
5. Buttyan, L., Hubaux, J.: Stimulating cooperation in self-organizing mobile ad hoc network. ACM/Kluwer Mobile Networks and Applications 8 (2003)
6. Zhong, S., Chen, J., Yang, Y.R.: Sprite: A simple, cheat-proof, credit-based system for mobile Ad-Hoc Networks. In: Proc. of IEEE INFOCOM, IEEE Computer Society Press, Los Alamitos (2003)
7. Anderegg, L., Eidenbenz, S.: Ad hoc-VCG: a truthful and cost-efficient routing protocol for mobile Ad hoc networks with selfish agents. In: Proc. of ACM Mobi. Com., ACM Press, New York (2003)
8. Zhong, S., Li, L.E., Liu, Y.G., Yang, R.Y.: On designing incentive-compatible routing and forwarding protocols in wireless Ad-Hoc networks-an integrated approach using game theoretical and cryptographic techniques. In: Proc. of ACM Mobi. Com., ACM Press, New York (2005)
9. Eidenbenz, S., Resta, G., Santi, P.: COMMIT: A sender-centric truthful and energy-efficient routing protocol for Ad Hoc networks with selfish nodes. In: Proc. IEEE Workshop on Algorithms for Wireless, Mobile, Ad Hoc and Sensor Networks (2005)
10. Nisan, N., Ronen, A.: Algorithmic mechanism design. Games and Economic Behavior 11 (2001)
11. Wang, Y.F., Hori, Y., Sakurai, K.: On studying incentive-compatible mechanism in open networks. Technical Report, Kyushu University (2006)
12. Archer, A.F.: Mechanisms for discrete optimization with rational agents. Available online: http://www.research.att.com/ aarcher/Research/thesis-final.ps

A Study on USN Technologies for Ships

Seong-Rak Cho, Dong-Kon Lee, Bu-Geun Paik, Jae-Hoon Yoo, Young-Ha Park, and Beom-Jin Park

Maritime & Ocean Engineering Research Institute, 104 Shinseong st., Yuseong-gu, Daejeon 305-343, Korea
scho@moeri.re.kr

Abstract. This paper describes the ubiquitous computing technologies for ship, which is produced and assembled by many steel blocks. It particularly describes the testing of a 2.4 GHz wireless communications platform, especially zigbee, on a number of intelligent devices, with the blocks disturbing the wireless communication. The power line communication that is established in a ship already is also experimented for some data transfer. At last, the RFID technology is applied at the test bed that is composed of three steel containers. In this paper, we implemented some USN technologies in the test bed simulating a ship environment and investigated the basic characteristics of ubiquitous computing technologies. Possible applications of such ubiquitous computing technologies to ships are also introduced here in.

1 Introduction

A ship is a kind of vehicle that moves on water for various purposes. Compared with other vehicles, a ship moves slowly and is thus tiring for people. Despite some shortcomings, however, ships can convey many persons and loads at a low cost, due to which ship technologies have continuously been developed.

The dominant points of ship technologies are the ship's hull form for their purpose and devices for propulsion and sailing. These points have been studied for a long time according to the standards of International Maritime Organization. However, the technique for enhancing the convenience and safety of passengers and crew, and especially cargo is relatively still insufficient. As most ships should stay on the sea, their efficiency and safety do not depend only on their hull form and sailing devices. Enhancing people's convenience and collecting some data for securing safety could be more important than the ship's hull form and sailing technique.

In this paper, the u-tech on land was not merely relocated into the ship. The ship was made of steel, which disturbs radio communications such as RFID, USN and UWB even on land. The minimum steel thickness of the common wall on the ship was 3~10 mm, and the steel thickness of the ship frame was more than 100 mm. The ship's inner space was also blocked by steel in most areas. In the case of the small glass, a window was prescribed so that the cover hatch would have a steel cover on the glass window.

Therefore, a ubiquitous special technology must be applied to most ships, and must be tested and analyzed in advance. This ubiquitous technique can also be used for special purposes in a ship. There are very few studies on applying ubiquitous

J. Indulska et al. (Eds.): UIC 2007, LNCS 4611, pp. 392–401, 2007.

technologies to ships. In this paper, the ubiquitous technologies that were tested in a steel container similar to a ship are explained, and their possible areas of application in a ship are introduced. These are expected to contribute significantly to the application of the ubiquitous technique for the advancement of ships.

2 USN Technologies for Ship

Several communications methods for transporting data from one device to another have been developed all over the world. These methods are generally classified into wired and wireless communications. They include power line communications, Home PNA, Ethernet, IEEE1394, and USB for wired communications, and RFID, zigbee, Home RF, Bluetooth, IEEE 801.11, and UWB for wireless communications.

Among these communications technologies, power line communications and 2.4GHz zigbee were chosen for this study so that ship data can be gathered everywhere. RFID was also chosen for information on materials, devices and people. The acquired data were sent to the middleware and used for the convenience of the ship passengers and crew.

2.1 Zigbee

Zigbee, which has low power consumption, was developed only recently. It is composed of many sensor nodes, which can send sensor data to the router; a router, which gets the data from the sensor node and passes it on to the coordinator; and a coordinator, which connects it to Internet service or middleware. The zigbee system can connect with many sensors such as for temperature, humidity, light, vibration, etc., so it can be a small network with a maximum of 255 nodes per coordinator. Because of this advantage, it can communicate more with other devices than can Bluetooth and home RF, and is a low-cost yet effective network. It is also small because it was developed with only one chip including the CPU, the RF module. Moreover, the user can set the communications cycle as he wants. Consequently, it spends little on battery, as its battery can last for six months or even a year. Its data rate is normally 500 kbps, slightly lower than that of Bluetooth and home RF, but enough for application to a ship if the appropriate sensor data are selected.

Zigbee has several problems for ship application, though. It cannot penetrate thick hulls and its communications capability depends sensitively on the antenna of each device. Its battery will not last long if the sensor used consumes much power. It can also conflict with other radio communications technologies, especially wireless LAN and Bluetooth.

2.2 RFID

RFID is a data collection technology that uses electronic tags to store data. The tag, also known as a transponder, is made up of an RFID chip attached to an antenna. Transmitting in the kHz, MHz and GHz ranges, tags should be battery-powered or driven by the RF waves from the reader. Whereas bar codes must be in close proximity and at the line of sight of the scanner for reading, RFID tags do not require alignment with such line of sight and can be embedded within packages. Depending on the type of tag and its application, it can be read at various distances. In addition, RFID-tagged cartons rolling on a conveyor belt can be read many times faster than bar-coded boxes.

2.3 PLC

PLC (power line communications) is a wired data communications technology that uses the power line in a house, company, factory or anywhere else where it is available. Technologies such as coupling between the powerline and a signal, signal decoding, and noise filtering have been developed. It may be easy to set up and cheaper than other wired communications technologies. The speed of its data transfer has increased only recently to 200 Mbps. While other wired communications technologies such as Ethernet must be installed separately, PLC could be tested directly, since the power line already exists in the ship.

However, it is difficult to send data far away with PLC because the power line is made for high power capacity. There are three dominant noises in the PLC system: impulse noise, harmonic noise and white noise. These can conflict with other PLC data due to the use of only one power line in a ship

3 Applications to Ships

3.1 Monitoring for Equipment Failure or Abnormal Operation

A ship has many types of equipment on board. Since the pumps or motors in the main engine room are closely related to the supply or discharge of cooling water, their failure or abnormal operation can cause serious troubles in the ship's operation. If they are not properly maintained or replaced in advance, they may cause significant problems with other equipment or the main engine system itself. Some ships monitor the equipment that is related to essential parts of their propulsion or maneuvering system in real time. Although there are basic sensors in the equipment that are arranged for the deck house, they merely let workers know if the equipment is out of order or not. The more important thing is that workers should check and monitor the sensors themselves with their own common sense.

This paper proposes the concept of a ubiquitous technology that enables one to monitor more sensing data in the main engine room. The sensors detecting current, temperature and pressure are attached to equipment. These equipments have several operation modes according to the operating conditions. The reference data obtained for each mode under normal operating conditions are stored in the middle server, after which real-time data are compared to reference data to detect equipment failure.

3.2 Monitoring for Fire Prevention in Dangerous Regions

It is not easy to ask for external help for putting out a fire in a ship because a ship spends most of its time on the sea, and much time is needed for rescue ships to reach it. Therefore, preventing a fire in advance by assessing its possibility during operation is very important. IMO requires the installation of a fire detection sensor in each cabin and major zone in a ship. The current practice when a fire is detected on a ship based on the ship's temperature or the presence of smoke is to notify its passengers and crew and to sound an alarm, after which fire suppression systems are operated either automatically or manually.

The operation of fire suppression systems after a fire breakout may result in unavoidable damages, however, no matter how fast the fire is extinguished. Sometimes, the environmental conditions of a specific fire zone hinder the proper suppression of fire and result in a large-scale fire. It is much better to prevent a fire by assessing its possibility before it actually occurs. This was very difficult to do, however, with the previous technology.

Therefore, this study proposes a new system for the advance detection of the possibility of a fire. It uses the USN technique and the fire engineering method. The suggested system will be able to monitor and analyze the environmental factors that may cause a fire, such as temperature, smoke, and CO_2 and oil mist concentrations. The data from each sensor is analyzed to assess the possibility of a fire. This assessment program, which is based on experimental, theoretical and empirical data, can estimate the possibility of a fire and provide users with the estimated results.

3.3 Tracking and Safety Management of Passengers and Crew

Ship passengers have to be extra-attentive because they are many and must stay inside a small deck house, compared with other accommodation spaces on-shore. Passenger management is most important, and it is necessary to install a proper system for counting passengers while they are boarding or leaving a ship, and for ensuring their

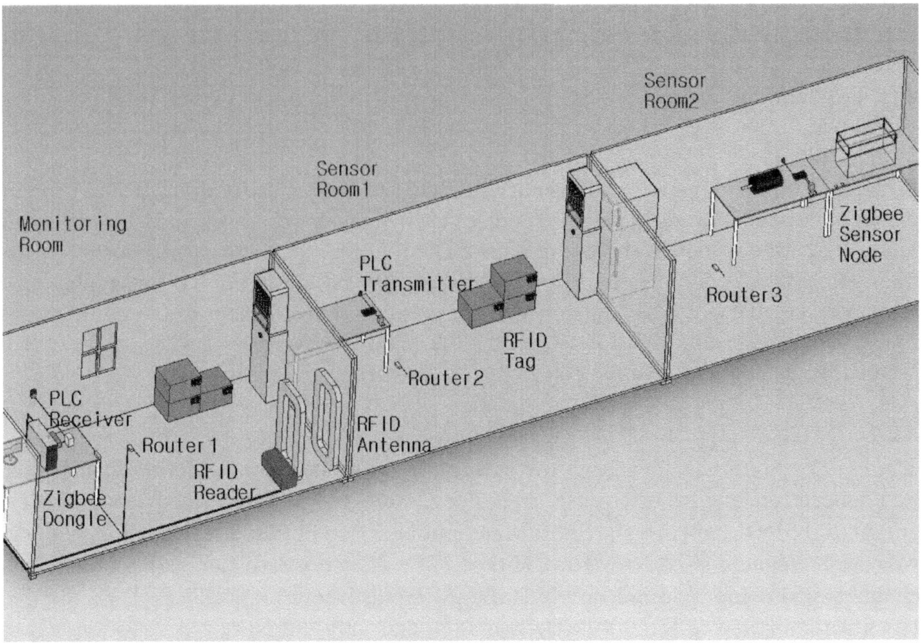

Fig. 1. The sketch of the total system

safety or security after they have boarded the ship. An emergency call should be sent to nearby crew when passengers are close to a dangerous zone. A higher safety level can be achieved if passengers are tracked. Such tracking system will also be useful in a military ship, which has relatively many crew members. Military ships undergo many training missions, but the training is not evaluated properly since few objective references are available. Therefore, a tracking system that adopts a ubiquitous technology enables efficient use of a management or training system in military ships.

4 The USN Test Bed

4.1 System Description

In this study, the ship condition was simulated with three containers to test the ubiquitous technologies, as shown in Fig. 1. In the test bed, the zigbee system, RFID devices, and PLC were located and operated. There was also an air conditioner, a small motor, a small aquarium, a refrigerator, etc. to simulate a real cabin or facility inside a ship. The size of each of the three containers was 3 x 6 x 2.6m^3, and the steel thickness of the container was about 1.6mm. In the monitoring room, there were three windows, a server, and dongles of each communications technology, such as a zigbee coordinator, a PLC receiver, and an RFID reader. There were also a router for transmitting the zigbee data to the coordinator and the entire RFID system. The sensor rooms 1 and 2 were fully closed and had no windows. They had only a steel gate and a 10mm hole for the antenna of the zigbee module in the room. Many sensor nodes and routers for zigbee communications, temperature sensors and a PLC transmitter for PLC communications were arranged in the test bed.

4.2 Experiment Setup

4.2.1 Zigbee

In the test bed, a temperature, humidity, light, CO_2, O_2, CO, vibration, IR, and supersonic wave sensor were installed to detect each sensing value. Each of the data was relayed by each router to the coordinator. The topology of the total network was the tree type, which is composed of four depths and five children. Each of the routers had two antennas that got the data from the sensors and relayed them to the coordinator. There were 15 sensors in all powered by AA batteries. Wireless LAN and Bluetooth laptops were set to confirm the conflict to the 2.4GHz radio frequency.

4.2.2 RFID

The RFID system was located in the monitoring room because the RFID reader must be connected to the server by RS-232. There were not just two fixed readers, Mercury's 900 MHz and Intsys's 13.56 MHz, but also two portable readers, Intsys's 900 MHz and Gigatek's 13.56 MHz CF type. The Mercury's reader had four antenna channels and could read not only metal tags but also liquid tags. The inlay and label types were applied to the 900 MHz and ISO, and only the inlay type was applied to the 13.56 MHz.

4.2.3 PLC

The temperature sensor connected to the PLC transmitter was installed in sensor rooms 1 and 2, as shown in Fig. 1. The transmitter sent the sensing data from the sensor to the PLC receiver using the power line. The PLC receiver was connected to a server using an RS-232 cable. The speed of PLC communications was 9.6 kbps. There were 8 nodes in all in the PLC system.

A communications test with distance variations was prepared using a 500m portable wire reel. There was also a 3 kW motor, a 4 kW air-conditioner, etc. to prove some noise problems such as impulse noise, harmonic noise and white noise. To perform the conflict test, a high-speed PLC modem that sends 85Mbps data was used.

4.3 Experiment Results

Basic tests for zigbee, RFID and PLC were performed, as mentioned in section 4.2. The zigbee system was designed and implemented in the test bed as a priority because zigbee communications is the core technique of this project.

4.3.1 Zigbee

At first, a test without any barrier on land was accomplished. A light sensor node sent data and the coordinator detected it simply. The distance was changed from a 5m interval to a 100m interval between a node and a coordinator. Also, the heights from the node to the ground were 0.2 m and 1.5 m.

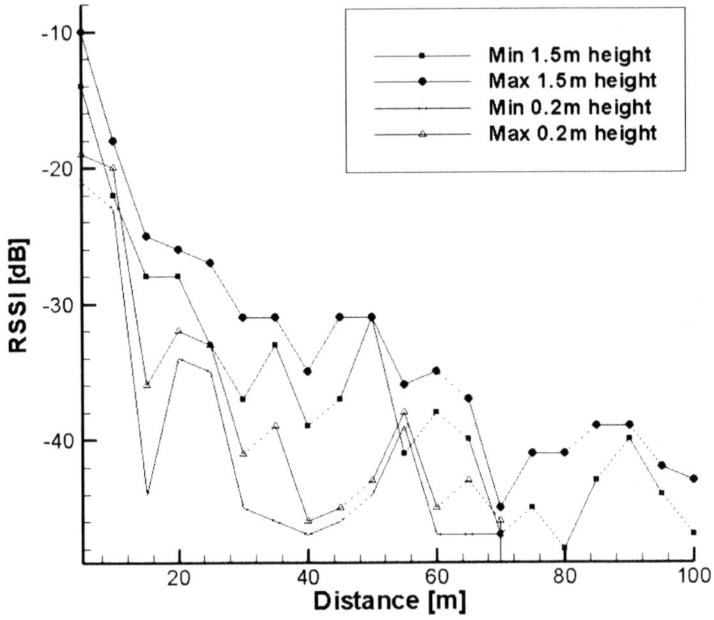

Fig. 2. Result of the RSSI of the distance test on land

As shown in Fig. 2, the RSSI value of the proximity was higher than the far node. Generally, the RSSI of the 1.5m altitude was stronger than that of the 0.2m altitude because the RSSI of the 0.2m altitude was communicated up to 70 m. The fluctuation of the RSSI at the 1.5m altitude was slightly significant, however, and its communication showed a good result. This data can be a dominant reference to apply zigbee to ship.

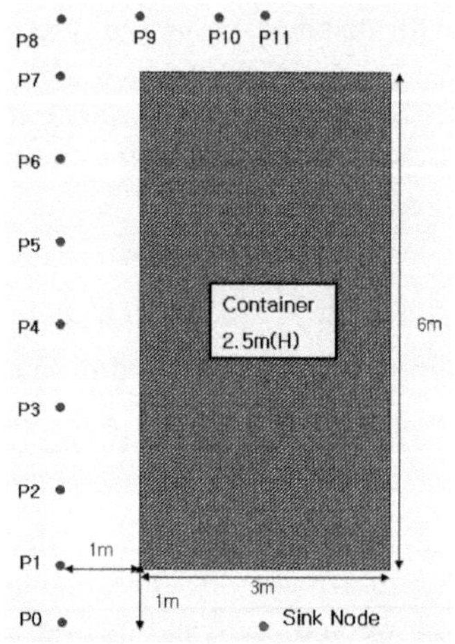

Fig. 3. Arrangement of a sink node and sensor node in diffraction test

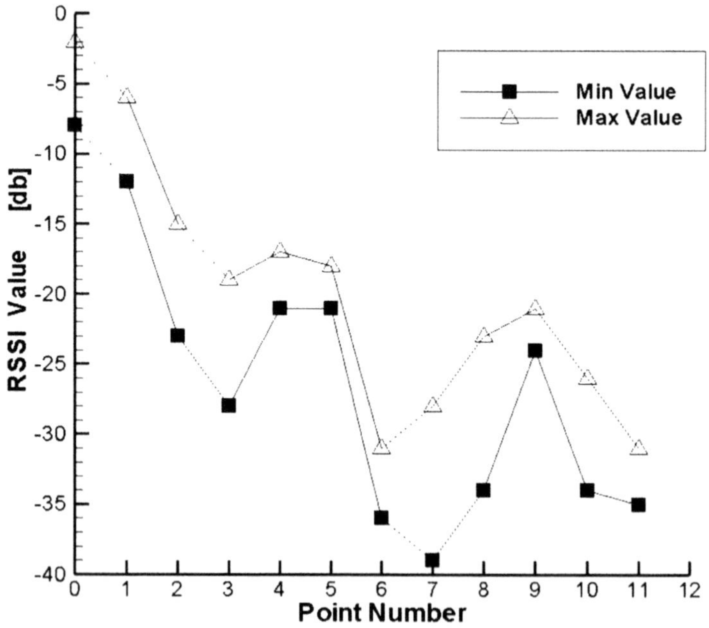

Fig. 4. Result of the RSSI of the diffraction test with container

Performed next was a diffraction test using a container. Fig. 3 shows the placement of both the sensor node and the coordinator in a common container. The coordinator was fixed and the sensor node was moved along the point indicated in Fig. 3. The altitude of 1 m was reached in this case. Fig. 4 shows the strength and fluctuation of the RSSI in the diffraction test, which indicate that the level of communication was higher than expected. The diffraction test was also examined at the distance of 0.3 m between the container and the sensor node or coordinator.

Finally, the simulations in which the zigbee system was applied to the test bed were designed and tested. The system was composed of a coordinator, three routers and two light sensors, as shown in Fig. 1 and Fig. 5. The test condition was the elimination of an antenna for each router; that is, the test situation was similar to the ship surroundings. The altitude of the router was 2.2 m, and was expected to be installed in the ship later. As mentioned, the antenna of the routers consisted of an inner and outer antenna.

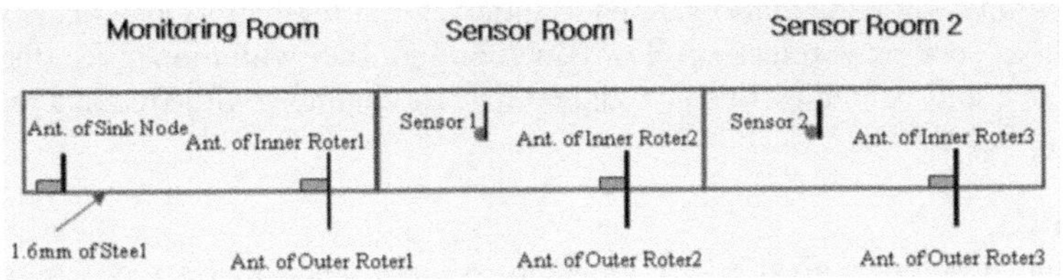

Fig. 5. Arrangement of the zigbee in antenna test(top view)

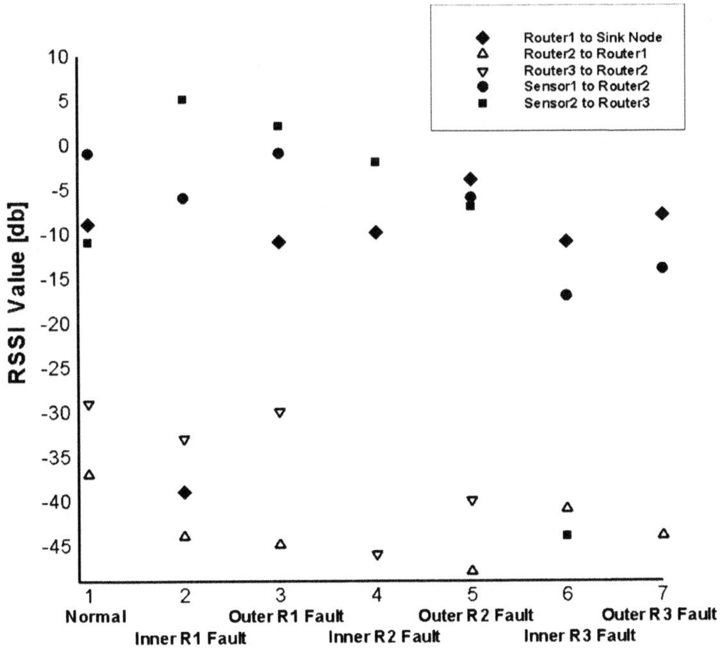

Fig. 6. Result of the RSSI of antenna test in test bed

Figure 6 indicates that communication in a container is better than between containers. If an inner antenna is eliminated, except for router 1, the status of the communication will be bad. Even if router 1 is defective, routers 2 and 3 can cope with communication using windows of container 1. Eliminating an outer antenna shows better communication than eliminating an inner antenna. However, router 3 will not be able to operate well if the outer antenna of router 3 is defective, because of multi-hopping.

Therefore, if the antenna is located properly, the zigbee can be used satisfactorily in a ship. Even if there is no hole for an antenna in a ship, the zigbee can still be used because it is available with either a window or a ventilating hole. Consequently, the zigbee can diffract around a container and fully penetrate a steel plate.

The consumption rate of each battery will be tested to select the best sensor in future. A power adaptor can be used if the specific sensor is really needed. Because the zigbee also sends battery information with sensor data, the battery can be replaced with a new one when the alarm sounds to indicate that the battery is already empty. If other devices such as wireless LAN or Bluetooth conflict with the zigbee, the channel of the zigbee can be changed, since zigbee has 16 channels with frequencies ranging from 2.4 to 2.4835 GHz.

4.3.2 RFID

There is no problem with the RFID system in land, since RFID is a common technique today. The RFID system in the container was not normal, however, because its tag could be read by the reader at any location in the container. An airtight container yields the best conditions in the RFID system. Thus, it can be applied with tracking and safety management.

4.3.3 PLC

PLC gets sensor data fully. It was experimented on without disconnection until 350 m, on time. It did not conflict with other PLC nodes and with a high-speed PLC modem. However, a harmonic noise was detected with the inverter-type lights. This noise was eliminated using a noise filter. It had to be tested on several electric home appliances such as a TV, an audio player, a telephone, etc. for a long time.

The power in a ship is unstable because it is from a generator. Thus, it will be tested in a real ship later. The power line in a ship is composed of three lines, R, S and T. A three-phase interfacer can help each PLC communicate with others.

5 Conclusion

This paper presented the authors' experience in designing and applying ubiquitous technologies to ships. The technologies selected were zigbee, RFID and PLC, the basic characteristics of which were tested. Possible areas of application of these ubiquitous technologies to ships were also introduced. The test bed used consisted of three steel containers, and the zigbee was especially able to diffract around a container and penetrate through a gap or a break between steel plate. The RFID system and the PLC method are currently being tested under various conditions. If appropriate services using ubiquitous technologies that satisfy a ship's purpose are provided, the convergence of ubiquitous technologies and ship technologies will be successfully realized.

Acknowledgement

This research was supported by the research project entitled "Development of Smart Operation Technologies for Exploration Fleets based on the Ubiquitous Concept."

References

1. Nguyen, T.V., Nelson, H.W.: A Systematic Approach to Machinery Condition Monitoring and Diagnosis. In: Proceedings of the 4th Annual Systems Engineering Conference (2001)
2. Hakem, N., Misson, M.: Study on the Throughput of the Wireless Home Automation Network Using the Encapsulation of Two Medium-access Methods. In: Proceedings of Communication Systems and Networks (2002)
3. Yaoxue, Z., Yuezhi, Z.: Transparent Computing: A New Paradigm for Pervasive Computing. In: Proceedings of the 3rd international conference on Ubiquitous Intelligence and Computing (2006)

A New Modeling and Delay Analysis of IEEE 802.11 Distributed Coordination Function

Fan Zhang, Lai Tu, Jian Zhang, and Benxiong Huang

Department of Electronics & Information Engineering
Huazhong University of Science & Technology
Wuhan 430074, P.R. China
zhangview@yahoo.com.cn

Abstract. This paper attempts to make a summary of current models used to evaluate the performance of IEEE 802.11 DCF and develops a new modeling to analyze the packet delay. The main contribution of this paper is that we found the backoff process of DCF can be considered as a Bernoulli Trials process. The new modeling based on the Bernoulli Trials can be a standard to analyze and validate other analytical methods. It can avoid confusion and conflicting produced by different simulation and calculating methods. In contrast to traditional work in the literature, we use our modeling to calculate the average backoff windows and average packet delay. At the same time, verify the analytical results by Monte Carlo and OPNET. The conclusion shows that the new modeling and analysis are comprehensible, simple and accurate.

1 Introduction

IEEE 802.11 based wirelesses LAN technology has now being widely accepted and deployed. The IEEE 802.11 standard specifies two different medium access control (MAC) mechanisms for WLANs. The distributed coordination function (DCF) is the basis method of IEEE 802.11. In the DCF, a set of wireless stations communicate directly with each other using a contention-based channel access method, namely, Carrier Sense Multiple Access with Collision Avoidance (CSMA/CA) [1]. Many distributed mechanisms that derived from DCF are widely used in a variety of wireless networks, such as 802.15.4 in WPAN and SMAC in sensor networks, etc. So the CSMA based MAC schemes have been attract much research work.

Many research efforts have been conducted on modeling the performance of DCF since the standardization of IEEE 802.11 MAC. Most of the Performance evaluation focuses on the throughput and the average packet delay of DCF. The bi-dimensional Markov chain modeling and its derived models are the mainly methods to compute the saturated or unsaturated throughput of 802.11. And in delay computing, some queuing models are developed to being complementary.

This paper focuses on the delay analysis of IEEE 802.11DCF. Nowadays, to the best of the authors' knowledge, most of the delay analysis has two problems. The one is that most analytical results were given but not compared with other person's research works. Many papers, which have given the analytical formula, are not coincident. Different expressions are proposed on average packet delay, but their

J. Indulska et al. (Eds.): UIC 2007, LNCS 4611, pp. 402–411, 2007.

correctness and relationship are not easily to distinguish. So need a practicable standard to avoid confusion and conflicting produced by different simulation and calculating methods. The other problem is many models are very costly computationally. They are not practical and not comprehensible.

According to above two problems, our paper wants to give some improvement. There are three major contributions of this paper. First we attempt to make a summary of current models used to compute the packet delay and compare our analytical results with some of them. Second, we point out that the backoff process of IEEE 802.11 DCF can be considered as a Bernoulli Trials process. And we use Monte Carlo method to simulate the backoff process. Finally, In contrast to traditional work in the literature, we use our modeling to calculate the average backoff windows and packet delay. At the same time, we use Monte Carlo and OPNET to verify the analytical results. The conclusion shows that the expressions are simple and validity.

The remainder of the paper is organized as follows. Section 2, discussed the related works. Section 3 describes the basic technique of IEEE 802.11. The new modeling is presented in Section 4. Simulation study is carried out in Section 5. Section 6 concludes this paper.

2 Related Works

Extensive research has been raised on the performance of 802.11 DCF, including approximate mathematical models and simulation validation. Generally speaking, the mathematical models are about two types. One is using Markov chain modeling; the other is a similarity of queuing model. The bi-dimensional Markov chain modeling and its derived models are the mainly methods to compute the throughput of 802.11. And some queuing models are developed in delay computing.

The bi-dimensional Markov chain modeling, first introduced by Bianchi in [2], has become the most common method for calculating the saturated throughput performance of the IEEE 802.11 protocol. Bianchi assumes that packet retransmissions are unlimited and that a packet is being transmitted continuously until its successful reception. Wu et al. [11] and Chatzimisios et al. [12] extend Bianchi's analysis to take the maximum retry limit into account.

Ziouva in [5] develops a Markov chain model that introduces an additional transition state to the Bianchi's model and actually allows stations to transmit consecutive packets without activating the backoff process. This feature is not specified in any IEEE 802.11 standard. In [3], Chatzimisios et al. provide the calculation of the packet delay, the packet drop probability, and the packet drop time. The mathematical analysis is validated by using OPNET 802.11 simulation results and compare with the analysis of Wu's and Ziouva's model. Vukovic [13] improves models by reducing Bianchi's model from two-dimensional to one-dimensional Markov chains. The one-dimensional models are elegant and make simple computations. In [10], P. Raptis compares analytical results of their model to the models of Vukovic and Chatzimisios. Yun Li in [8] presents new expressions to analyze the channel access delay of 802.11 DCF. Generally speaking, literatures [3, 5, 8, 10, 13] are all using the similarity of model styles to compute the average packet delay. In this paper, we compare analytical results of all this models.

The analyses of [6, 14, 15] are based on the two basic equations of Bianchi's model and add the computation of the probability distribution function of delay. [6] presents an original method to compute the delay distribution of 802.11 DCF. [14] carries out an original fairness analysis based on the probability distribution of the delay. [15] presents an analytical model to compute the average service time and jitter experience by a packet when transmitted in a saturated single-hop IEEE 802.11 ad hoc network.

Several other papers in the literature [4, 9, 16, 17, 18] have attempted to analyze the performance of 802.11 by using queue model. Winands et al. in [16] develop a finite-source feedback queuing model for 802.11 DCF. [17] proposes an M/MMGI/1/K queuing model of IEEE 802.11 DCF using RTS/CTS. K. Medepalli in [18] builds upon the average cycle time derivation to obtain individual queue delays using a G/G/1 queuing model. [9] presents a Markovian state dependent single server queue to model the 802.11 protocol. Tickoo in [4] model each node as a discrete time G/G/1 queue and derive the service time distribution. However computing the probability distribution function values is very costly computationally and hence the approaches of [4] are of little practical use to perform e.g. admission control functionality [6].

Through a comprehensive review of analytical models of 802.11 DCF, this paper will evaluate some representative models and present them in a figure. We develop a new modeling to analyze the average backoff windows, average packet delay and the packet inter-arrival time.

3 Brief Review of the IEEE 802.11 DCF

The 802.11 DCF can be approximated as p-persistent CSMA protocol [1], and the packet sending probability can be derived according to different contention window size. The backoff timer value for each station is uniformly chosen in the interval [0, $W_i - 1$] where W_i is the current CW size and i is the backoff stage. The backoff timer is decremented when the medium is idle, is frozen when the medium is sensed busy, and resumes only after the medium has been idle for longer than DIFS. A station initiates a packet transmission when the backoff timer reaches zero. The value of W_i depends on the number of failed transmissions of a packet; at the first transmission attempt, $W_0 = CW_{min} = W$. After each retransmission due to a packet collision, W_i is doubled up to a maximum value, $W_{m'} = CW_{max} = 2^{m'}W$, where m' is the number of backoff stages. Once W_i reaches CW_{max}, it will remain at this value until it is reset to CW_{min} in the following cases: (a) after the successful transmission of a data packet or (b) when SSRC reaches the short retry limit. When the short retry limit is reached, retry attempts will cease and the packet will be discarded. The SSRC is reset to 0 whenever an ACK is received in response to a data packet.

4 Mathematical Modeling

4.1 Modeling Binary Exponential Backoff

In the analysis, several popular assumptions have been made: (1) There are a finite number of stations (say N) in the network, and all the stations can hear each other (i.e., single-hop network); (2) Stations are always backlogged, meaning that a station always has packets waiting to be transmitted; (3) Ideal channel conditions (i.e., no transmission error or capture); (4) collision probability of a data packet transmission is constant and independent of the number of collisions the packet has suffered in the past. (5) The data packets have a fixed length.

Let τ be the probability that a station transmits in a slot time in a WLAN with N stations under saturation conditions. Following the analysis of [11], the relationship betweenτ and p is as following two equations:

$$p = 1-(1-\tau)^{N-1} \tag{1}$$

And

$$\tau = \frac{2(1-2p)\ (1-p^{m+1})}{W(1-(2p)^{m'+1})(1-p)+(1-2p)[(1-p^{m+1})+W2^{m'}p^{m'+1}(1-p^{m-m'})]} \tag{2}$$

Where m is the Retry Limit, $W = CW_{min}$, m' is such that $CW_{max} = 2^{m'}CW_{min}$ and p is the probability that a transmission attempt collides. Equations (1) and (2) represent a nonlinear system with two unknowns$\tau$and p, which can be solved using numerical techniques and only has a unique solution [2]. If we assume that m and m' are constant, we can see that p is only dependent on N in saturated environment. When N changes in $[1, \infty]$, p has different value in the range of [0, 1].

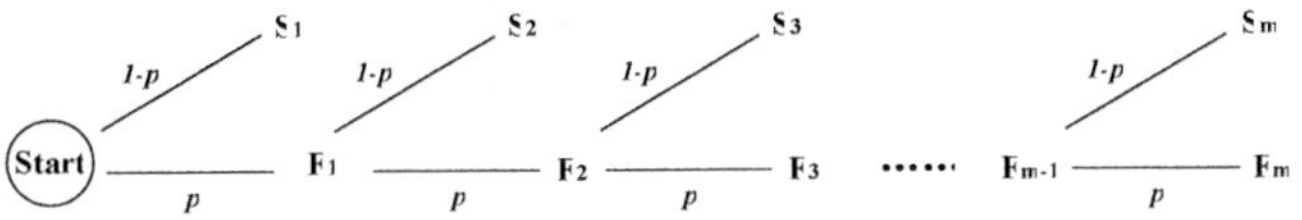

Fig. 1. Backoff process of DCF

4.2 Motivation of Our Work

To make things simpler, and to bester understand the effect of backoff mechanism, we take no account of each different backoff windows in each backoff stage temporarily. Then the result of each backoff stage is either success or failure. When successful, the transmission begins without contention. And a new backoff stage starts if failed to access the channel. So we can describe the backoff process in Fig. 1. Let S_i represent a node access the channel successfully through ith backoff stage and F_i refer to failure of the ith backoff. Where $i \leq m$, m is the Retry Limit, p is the probability that a transmission attempt collides. If we think that each backoff process is an independent experiment, then we get the definition 1.

Definition 1. The backoff process can be considered as a *Bernoulli Trials process.*

- Each backoff process has two possible outcomes, which we may call success and failure.
- When N is invariable, the probability p of failure on each experiment is the same for each experiment, and the probability is not affected by any knowledge of previous outcomes.
- The experiment is end when successful or retry limit is reached.

The *i*th experiment has different backoff timer. Let us adopt the notation W_i to be the backoff windows in *i*th backoff stage. The backoff timer value for each experiment is uniformly chosen in the interval $[0, W_i]$. If $i \leq m'$, $CW_{max} = 2^{m'} CW_{min}$, $W_i = 2^i W - 1$. Else $W_i = CW_{max} - 1$.

4.3 Analysis of Backoff Windows

The average backoff windows *E[W]* is the average number of slot times required for a successful packet transmission. If a packet is dropped because it has reached the specified retry limit, the backoff windows for this packet will not be included in the calculation of the average backoff windows since this packet is not successfully transmitted.

The total backoff windows *T[W]* is the average number of slot times spent by a packet transmission, including successfully transmitted and dropped.

Then we give the expression of *E[W]* and *T[W]*. We shall be particularly interested in the probability that in *n* Bernoulli trials there is one success. We denote this probability by $b(n;p)$. $b(n;p) = p^{n-1}(1-p)$, $(n \leq m+1)$. Then average backoff windows can be calculated by two modes.

Mode 1: According to succeed to access the channel, with probability $b(1;p)/(1-p^{m+1})$ the transmission is successful and the average backoff window of such a packet is $CW_{min}/2$. With probability $b(2;p)/(1-p^{m+1})$ the first transmission fails and the packet is successfully transmitted in the second attempt which experienced two times backoff and the average backoff window changed to $(CW_{min}/2+2CW_{min}/2)$. Continuing along these lines for cases with large number of losses, the average backoff window in the saturate case is given by

$$E[W] = \sum_{i=0}^{m} \left(\frac{p^i(1-p)}{1-p^{m+1}} \sum_{j=0}^{i} \frac{W_i}{2} \right) \tag{3}$$

Mode 2: The second mode to computer average backoff windows is classified by backoff stage. Except the packet that is dropped by trying *m* times, the other packets that are not discarded all experience the first backoff stage with probability 1 and the average backoff window is $CW_{min}/2$. With probability $(p - p^{m+1})/(1 - p^{m+1})$ the packets all undergo the second backoff stage, which are successful transmission at last. Continuing along these lines for cases with large number of losses, the average backoff window in the saturate case is given by

$$E[W] = \sum_{i=0}^{m} \left(\frac{W_i}{2} \cdot \frac{p^i - p^{m+1}}{1 - p^{m+1}} \right) \tag{4}$$

It can be proved that Equations (3) and (4) are the same. According the expression, we can drew the relationship between *p* and *E[W]*.

Because *T[W]* includes the total backoff windows of successful and dropped packets. Consequently, *E[W]* can be calculated as

$$T[W] = E[W] \cdot (1 - p^{m+1}) + \left(\sum_{i=0}^{m} \frac{W_i}{2} \right) \cdot p^{m+1}. \tag{5}$$

4.4 Delay Analysis

The delay *E[D]* for a successfully transmitted packet is defined to be the time interval from the time the packet is at the head of its MAC queue ready for transmission, until an acknowledgement for this packet is received. If a packet is dropped because it has reached the specified retry limit, the time delay for this packet will not be included in the calculation of the average packet since this packet is not successfully received.

And the packet inter-arrival time, denoted as $E[D_{inter}]$, is defined as the time interval between two successful packet receptions at the receiver [3].

The average packet delay *E[D]* is given by

$$E[D] = E[W] \cdot E[slot] \tag{6}$$

Let E[*slot*] be the average length of a slot time. *E[slot]* is given by

$$E[slot] = (P_S \cdot T_S \ + \ P_N \cdot \sigma \ + \ P_C \cdot T_C) \tag{7}$$

Where considering that a random slot is empty with probability P_N. P_S is the probability that an occurring packet transmission is successful and a collision with probability P_C. For a wireless LAN of N contending stations, the probabilities P_N, P_S and P_C are given by

$$P_S = N\tau(1-\tau)^{N-1} \tag{8}$$

$$P_N = (1-\tau)^N \tag{9}$$

$$P_C = 1 - P_S - P_N \tag{10}$$

σ is the duration of an empty slot, T_S and T_C are the average durations the medium is sensed busy due to a successful transmission and a collision, respectively [1].

$$\begin{cases} T_S = DIFS + H + E[P] + \delta + SIFS + ACK + \delta \\ T_C = DIFS + H + E[P] + \delta \end{cases} \tag{11}$$

Where H is the packet header (equal to the sum of MAC and physical header) and δ is the propagation delay. *E[P]* is the length of the transmitted packet.

$$H = PHY_{herder} + MAC_{header} \tag{12}$$

We can calculate *E[D]* from Equation (6) to Equation (12). To calculate the average packet inter-arrival time $E[D_{inter}]$, we can use

$$E[D_{inter}] = T[W] \cdot E[slot] \tag{13}$$

E[D] and $E[D_{inter}]$ can be derived from *E[W]* and *T[W]* respectively. The expression of $E[D_{inter}]$ has been presented in [3] and [19]. It can be simply obtained from throughput. Figure 3 includes the analytical results of Equation (14).

$$E[D_{inter}] = \frac{N \cdot E[P]}{S}. \tag{14}$$

5 Simulation Study

5.1 Model Validation

Monte Carlo simulation can be used either to estimate the performance of systems that are too complex to be analyzed, or to verify the results obtained analytically.

Now we will use Monte Carlo experiments to simulate the Bernoulli Trials of backoff process, and the simulation outcomes will be compared with that obtained analytical result through the above section.

The modeling and analysis presented in the previous sections is independent of physical layer parameters and can be applied to all IEEE 802.11 PHY standards. The parameters used in both the analytical model and our simulations follow the parameters in [2] and are summarized in Table 1. The system values are those specified for the frequency hopping spread spectrum (FHSS) PHY layer utilized in IEEE 802.11b [1].

Table 1. Parameter of Simulation and Analysis

Parameter	Value	Parameter	Value
CW_{min}	16	Slot time, σ	50μs
CW_{max}	1024	MAC header,	272 bits
m'	6	PHY header,	128 bits
Retry Limit (m)	7	ACK packet,	112 bits
Channel bit rate, C	1Mbps	DIFS	128μs
Packet payload, $E[P]$	8192 bits	SIFS	28μs
Propagation delay, δ	1μs	ACK_Timeout	300μs

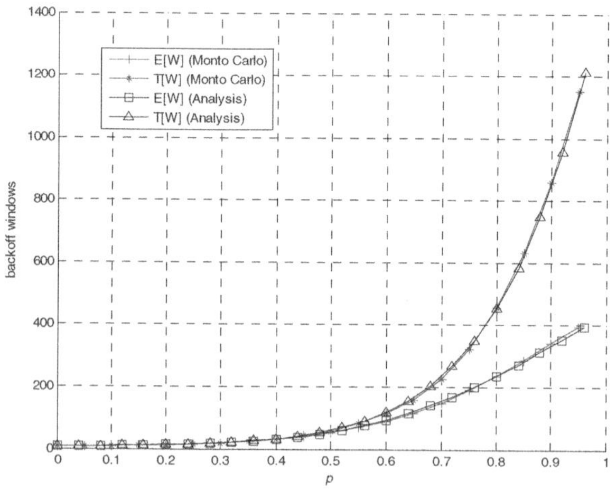

Fig. 2. $E[W]$ and $T[W]$: analysis versus Monte Carlo simulation

Using Monte Carlo experiments to simulate the Bernoulli Trials of backoff process is not complex. According to the Definition 1, the statistic outcomes are given by

$$E[W] = \frac{\text{Sum[number of slot times for each successful packet transmission]}}{\text{Sum[number of successful transmission packets]}} \tag{15}$$

$$T[W] = \frac{\text{Sum[number of slot times for each packet transmission]}}{\text{Sum[number of packets]}} \tag{16}$$

We draw the statistic results from 10000 times Monte Carlo experiments. Figure 2 plots *E[W]* and *T[W]* versus collision probability p. p changes in the range of (0, 1). Figure 2 shows that the analytical results are accurate comparing with the Monte Carlo experiments outcomes. When p is less than 0.8, the analytical results are larger than Monte Carlo simulation results, while they are less than the simulation results when p is beyond 0.8.

5.2 Simulation Analysis

In this subsection, we compare the modeling and analysis proposed by this paper with some current methods. The new modeling of using the Monte Carlo and analysis based on Bernoulli Trials are all supposed that each packet collides with constant and independent probability p. Based on this presupposition, Considering the backoff process of IEEE 802.11 DCF as a Bernoulli Trials process is valuable.

Markov chain modeling introduced by Bianchi gives us a mapping relationship between p and N under saturation conditions. So using the relation, we can calculate the throughput, delay and other important performance.

Our modeling can be a standard when supposed that each packet collides with constant and independent probability p, because the Bernoulli Trials is an explicit description and easy to analyze. The new modeling can avoid confusion and conflicting produced by estimating other different simulation and calculating

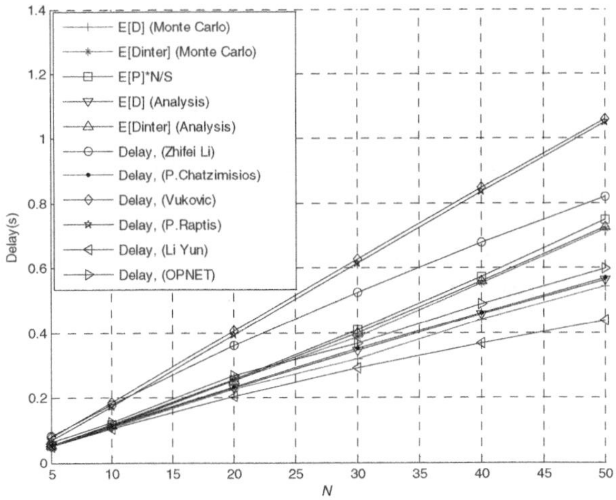

Fig. 3. Delay: analysis versus simulation

methods. In this paper, we use the Monte Carlo method to simulate the Bernoulli Trials and their statistic results are creditable.

Figure 3 plots the packet delay calculated using our methods as well as some current methods and OPNET simulation results. By comparing with Monte Carlo simulation, the differences between different methods could be seen. Because the result in [5] is much larger than other curves, it is not shown in Figure 3. The performance comparison shows that our packet delay analysis gives results in high agreement with OPNET simulations. We can observe that the model in [10, 13, 14], cause a high overestimation of the packet delay and [8] is lower than other models.

It could be seen that Equation (6) has the same pattern with the expression 9 in [3]. But they are based on different models. Equation (6) is a formula generated from Bernoulli Trials. According to the simulation results of Monte Carlo and OPNET, the analysis of this paper is the most precise of the several methods mentioned. And it is also the most understandable and convictive.

6 Conclusion

In this paper, we develop a new modeling to analyze the packet delay of IEEE 802.11 DCF. And we point out that the backoff process of DCF can be considered as a Bernoulli Trials process. This is the main contribution of this paper. The new modeling can be a standard to analyze and validate other methods. It can avoid confusion and conflicting produced by estimating other different simulation and calculating methods.

We use the analysis based on the Bernoulli Trials to calculate the average backoff windows, average packet delay and the packet inter-arrival time, and verify the results by Monte Carlo simulation. The analytical results that are in high agreement with OPNET simulations are the most precise of the several methods mentioned. The new modeling and analysis are comprehensible, simple and accurate.

References

1. IEEE: Wireless LAN Medium Access Control (MAC) and Physical Layer (PHY) Specifications. IEEE Std. 802.11, 1999 edn. (1999)
2. Bianchi, G.: Performance analysis of the IEEE 802.11 Distributed Coordination Function. IEEE Journal On Selected Areas in Communications, pp. 535–547 (2000)
3. Chatzimisios, P., Boucouvalas, A.C., Vitsas, V.: IEEE 802.11 wireless LANs: performance analysis and protocol refinement. EURASIP Journal on Wireless Communications and Networking, pp. 67–78 (2005)
4. Tickoo, O., Sikdar, B.: Queueing Analysis and Delay Mitigation in IEEE 802.11 Random Access MAC based Wireless Networks. In: Proceedings of INFOCOM 2004. vol. 2, pp. 1404–1413 (2004)
5. Ziouva, E., Antonakopoulos, T.: CSMA/CA performance under high traffic conditions: throughput and delay analysis. Computer Communications. 25, 313–321 (2002)
6. Banchs, A.: Analysis of the distribution of the backoff delay in 802.11 DCF: a step towards end-to-end delay guarantees in WLANs. In: Proceeding of QoFIS (2002)

7. Li, B., Battiti, R.: Performance Analysis of An Enhanced IEEE 802.11 Distributed Coordination Function Supporting Service Differentiation. In: Proceedings of International Workshop on Quality of Future Internet Service (2003)
8. Li, Y., Long, K., Zhao, W., Wang, C.: Analyzing the channel access delay of IEEE 802.11 DCF. In: Proceedings of IEEE GLOBECOM (2005)
9. Foh, C.H., Zukerman, M.: Performance Analysis of the IEEE 802.11 MAC Protocol. In: Proceeding of European Wireless (2002)
10. Raptis, P., Vitsas, V., et al.: Packet delay modeling of IEEE 802.11 Wireless LANs. In: Proceedings of the International Conference on Cybernetics and Information Technologies, Systems and Applications (2005)
11. Wu, H., Peng, Y., Long, K., Cheng, S., Ma, J.: Performance of Reliable Transport Protocol over IEEE 802.11 Wireless LAN: Analysis and Enhancement. In: Proceedings of IEEE INFOCOM (2002)
12. Chatzimisios, P., Boucouvalas, A.C., Vitsas, V.: IEEE 802.11 packet delay – a finite retry limit analysis. In: Proceeding of GLOBECOM. vol. 2, pp. 950–954 (2003)
13. Vukovic, I., Smavatkul, N.: Delay Analysis of Different Backoff Algorithms in IEEE 802.11. In: Proceeding of IEEE Vehicular Technology Conference (2004)
14. Li Z., Das A., Gupta K.A., Nandi S.: Performance Analysis of IEEE 802.11 DCF: Throughput, Delay, and Fairness. Appeared in http://www.cs.jhu.edu/ zfli/Publications.htm
15. Carvalho, M., Garcia-Luna-Aceves, J.: Delay Analysis of IEEE 802.11 in Single-Hop Networks. In: Proceedings of IEEE International Conference on Network Protocols (2003)
16. Winands, E.M.M., Denteneer, T.J., et al.: A Finite-Source Queueing Model for the IEEE 802.11 DCF. European Transactions on Telecommunications 16, 77–89 (2005)
17. Ozdemir, M., McDonald, A.B.: An M/MMGI/1/K Queuing Model for IEEE 802.11 Ad Hoc Networks. In: Proceedings of the 1st ACM international workshop on Performance evaluation of wireless ad hoc, sensor, and ubiquitous networks, 107–111 (2004)
18. Medepalli, K., Tobagi, F.A.: Throughput Analysis of IEEE 802.11 Wireless LANs using an Average Cycle Time Approach. In: Proceeding of IEEE Global Telecommunications Conference (2005)
19. Bianchi, G., Tinnirello, I.: Remarks on IEEE 802.11 DCF Performance Analysis. IEEE Communications Letters 9, 765–767 (2005)

Proactive Data Delivery Scheme with Optimal Path for Dynamic Sensor Networks

Kwang-il Hwang[1], Tea-young Kim[2], and Doo-seop Eom[2]

[1] Department of Computer Control, Incheon City College
Do-hwa 2 Dong, Nam-gu, Incheon 402-750, Korea
brightday@icc.ac.kr

[2] Department of Electronics and Computer Engineering, Korea University
5-1ga, Anam-dong, Sungbuk-gu, Seoul, Korea
tykim@final.korea.ac.kr

Abstract. In sensor networks, it is crucial to reliably and energy-efficiently deliver sensed information from each source to a sink node. Specifically, in mobile sink (user) applications, due to the sink mobility, a stationary dissemination path may no longer be effective. The path will have to be continuously reconfigured according to the current location of the sink. Moreover, the dynamic optimal path from each source to the sink is required in order to reduce end-to-end delay and additional energy wastage. In this paper, an *Adaptive Reversal Optimal path Tree* (AROT) protocol is proposed. Information delivery from each source to a mobile sink can be easily achieved along the AROT without additional control overhead, because the AROT proactively performs adaptive sink mobility management. In addition, the dynamic path is optimal in terms of hop counts and the AROT can maintain a robust tree structure by quickly recovering the partitioned tree with minimum packet transmission. Finally, the simulation results demonstrate that the AROT is a considerably energy-efficient and robust protocol.

1 Introduction

Recently sensor networks have led to tremendously incremental utilization in many military and civil applications such as battlefield surveillance, environmental control, and security management. In such applications, it is crucial to reliably and energy-efficiently deliver sensed information from each source to a sink node. However, if a sink moves to the other place, the dissemination path may no longer be effective. The path will have to be continuously reconfigured according to sink movement. The continuous reconfigurations can bring about tremendous traffic and energy wastage in the network. In particular, energy is considered as one of the most expensive resources in sensor networks. In addition, path optimality from each source to a dynamic sink is regarded as another important design factor in sensor network protocol design space, since the optimal path reduces the end-to-end delay and additional energy wastage.

In order to efficiently manage the dissemination path in sensor networks with a mobile sink, several schemes are proposed [1,2,3,4,5]. Directed Diffusion [2],

J. Indulska et al. (Eds.): UIC 2007, LNCS 4611, pp. 412–421, 2007.

SAFE [3], and DST [5] concentrate on managing the dissemination path initiated from a sink, whereas source initiated dissemination protocols, such as TTDD [1] and SEAD [4], use a method that mobile sinks access on the dissemination path constructed on the basis of each source. Although these methods aim to solve the problem using different techniques, high maintenance overhead is still required to continuously update the dissemination path.

In this paper, to address these several challenges on the mobile sink problems, an *Adaptive Reversal Optimal path Tree* (AROT) protocol is proposed. The AROT is able to maintain the dynamic tree with optimal path by adaptively reversing links with minimum communication overhead in the network.

The remainder of this paper is organized as follows. Section 2 introduces the proposed AROT including sink mobility management, data dissemination, and error recovery. Section 3 evaluates the optimality of AROT. In section 4, performance evaluation through simulation is presented. Section 5 concludes this paper.

2 Adaptive Reversal Optimal-Path Tree (AROT)

In this section, the detailed operation of *Adaptive Reversal Optimal-path Tree (AROT)*is presented. Since the AROT proactively performs adaptive sink mobility management, data dissemination from each source to a mobile sink can be easily achieved along the AROT, without additional control overhead. In addition, the AROT can maintain a robust tree structure by quickly recovering the partitioned tree with minimum packet transmission.

2.1 Sink Mobility Management

At the initial stage, a sink node enters the sensor field, with broadcasting the Sink_Update. The update message is used to notice the current sink's location to the network and thereby a temporary root node is changed to a new node that is currently near the sink. In general, the Sink_Update message is periodically broadcasted by the update rates, which represents the time interval for a user to obtain information sensed from the sensor field. However, it is also allowed that the update request of the sink is broadcasted asynchronously (Non-periodically) only when the sink wants.

All nodes that received the Sink_Update message transmit the Root_Request message to the sink node. The sink appoints a new sink as a new root node and replies with the Root_Reply to the node. However, if one of these nodes is the previous root, the sink does not change the root, because this means the sink has not moved far away from the root since the last update. If the *tree construction field* in the Root_Reply message is set, (i.e. the sink requests a new dissemination tree), the root node initiates construction of an initial spanning tree by flooding the entire network. The tree is directed to the current root node.

Figure 1 illustrates an example when managing the sink mobility of the AROT. As the sink moves to a new location, a new root node is appointed

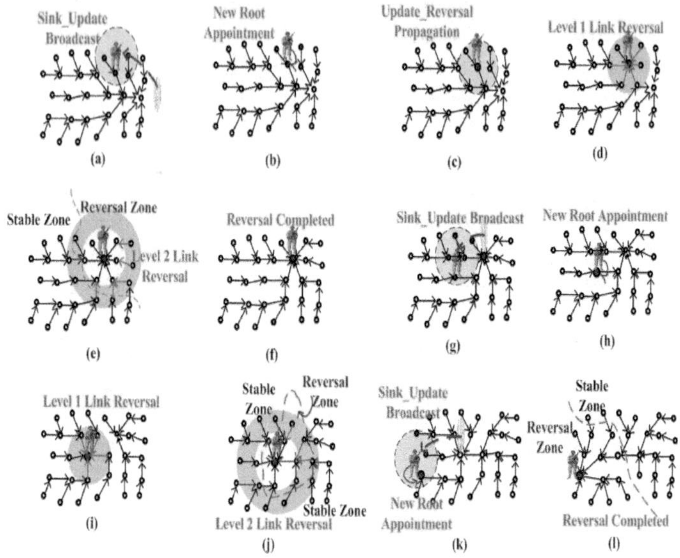

Fig. 1. Example of adaptive sink mobility management via the AROT

and the adaptive reversal process is triggered from the node. In the AROT, the *stable zone* and the *reversal zone* are defined as the area where update activity does not occur, and as the area where reversal of each node is updated, respectively. The update reversal process for each update request proceeds until update propagation meets the stable zone. It is important to note that in spite of sink movement, update reversal is only required in a partial area (reversal zone), not the entire network. The size of stable zone and update rate interval represents a trade off. The stable zone presents the set of nodes which are already correctly directed to the new root node. On the other hand, the reversal zone stretches out from an area, where the last update was invoked, to that adjacent to the current root node. Accordingly, in the case of a long update interval, a sink may move further away from the old root, so that it leads the extension of the reversal zone. In section 4, the working node rates are investigated, revealing the ratio of reversal zone over the entire field, with respect to the variation of sink speed.

2.2 Proactive Data Dissemination Via AROT

Since the AROT manages sink mobility proactively, data of each source is simply disseminated upwardly along the tree as other tree-based dissemination protocols are. The two types of data model can be applied in AROT: *one-time event* and *periodic reporting* of detection node. In particular, the latter model is useful for applications such as mobile target tracking. In this model, the node that detects target should disseminate event to the sink with specific update rate during the time when a target residues there. By collecting the data from each event source,

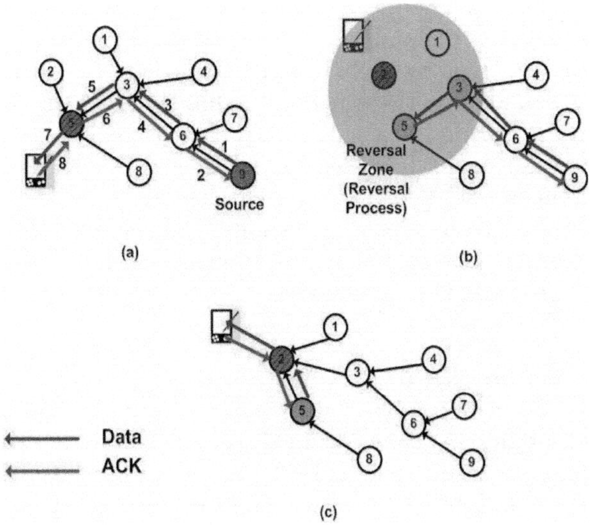

Fig. 2. Data dissemination along the AROT: each node on the path utilizes ACK

the sink can identify current location and trajectory history of the target. Event update rate is given by the sink when an interest (query) is flooded. Remember that the AROT utilizes *reversal update* by sink periodically for the path freshness of the tree. In the periodic reporting data model, if the reversal update rate is longer than update rate of sources, freshness of the data will be deteriorated as well as delay will be increased . Thus, the reversal update rate should be taken by smaller value than event update rate. This can enables the data dissemination with low delay along the tree.

Figure 2 illustrates data dissemination process from a source to the sink. Every node on the path from the source to the sink has the responsibility to reliably deliver the data to the sink. Therefore, Data and ACK mechanism between each link is used as shown in fig. 2 (a). If a node meets reversal process on the way to deliver, the node in the reversal zone waits until the reversal process is completed (new path is reconstructed). Then, the data dissemination process is restarted from that node to sink as shown in fig. 2 (c).

As a result, the data dissemination cost from each source to mobile sink can be accomplished with the $O(n\sqrt{N})$ along the tree, where n is the number of source nodes and N is the number of deployed sensor nodes. In the case of many sources, the cost will be reduced greater by use of in-network processing.

2.3 Error Recovery to Failures

A link on the tree can be broken by various reasons, such as node failures, obstacles, and so on. Such link breakages result in partitioned trees. However, it is important that the tree should always maintain robust connectivity from all sensor nodes to sinks. Therefore, in order to keep the robust tree, the AROT exploits simple but fast, robust error-recovery. As mentioned in the pervious subsection, each data sent by a child is acknowledged by each parent. By this acknowledge, we can identify the status of the link whether the tree is partitioned or not. As soon as the root of a partitioned tree comes to realize the breakage of its uplink, it broadcasts a Join_Request message to its neighbors. Only nodes, where their parent is not the sender, reply with the Join_Reply to the root of the partitioned tree. The node completes joining the active tree by selecting one of them as its parent. The selection condition is the node having the smallest height to current root node of active tree.

3 Optimal Path Analysis

Due to the sink mobility, the shape of the dissemination path is transformed from original one. Some protocols such as DST only focus on the energy efficiency in energy efficiently maintaining the dissemination path in dynamic mobile sink. Therefore, the optimal path is not guaranteed at any instance. In addition, the path tends to get worse as far as the sink moves continuously.

In particular, we mainly focus on the hop count cost for the optimal path since the hop distance can reflect each physical distance between sources and sink under the assumption that sensor nodes are densely deployed. This means the shorter path, the lower is delay. In addition to this, this shortest path can provide the physical shortest path to the target. Therefore, the optimality of dissemination path is one of the most important performance factors. In this Section, we analyze a path optimality of AROT.

It is assumed that a square sensor field of area A in which N sensor nodes are uniformly distributed as shown in fig. 3(a), so that on each side there are approximately $\sqrt{N}$ sensor nodes. We denotes each source and sink i and s, where $\forall i \in N$. It is also assumed that all nodes have the same radio range and the range is limited in the distance including only each node's neighbors (left, right, up, and down). This means a neighbor located at diagonal direction is not included.

Theorem 1. All of the sources, $i \in N$, in the AROT constructed by initial flooding have optimal path to the sink.

Proof. By assumptions mentioned above, the network plane can be coordinated to (x, y) and we also assume that the sink is located at the left corner as shown in fig. 3 (a). As validated in that figure, route from an arbitrary node with (x, y) on the tree to the sink along the tree is the shortest path. This means that all the routes on the tree present the minimum hop count value in all the routes that are reachable from a arbitrary point (x, y) to the sink (0, 0). In addition, the minimum hop count for (x, y) is x + y. For example, there is no route from node (3, 3) to the sink (0, 0) with less than 6 and the minimum hop count for node (7, 7) is 14.

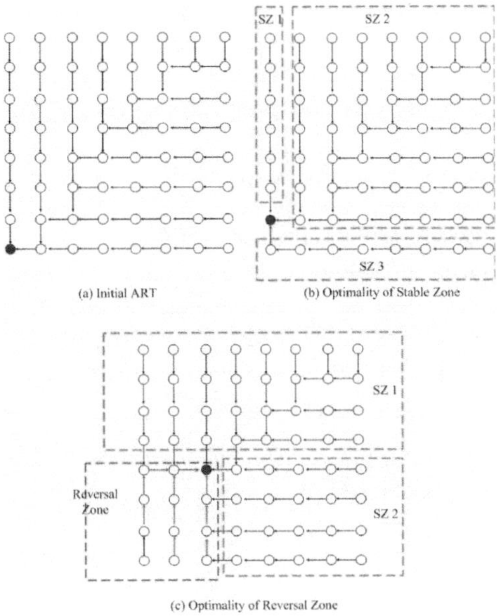

Fig. 3. Path optimality of AROT

Lemma 1. Let N be a full stable AROT. If F is a sub-tree of N rooted at a node$f$, i.e., $F \subset N$, all the routes along the tree from each source, $i \in F$ to the root $f$have optimal path.

Proof. Suppose a tree in which each node has only one child, respectively. The tree L can be represented by the following set, $L = \{l_1, l_2, l_3, l_4, ..l_k\}$. By assumption, each pair consisting of a parent and a child is one hop. So that all sources in F, a sub-tree of L, rooted at l_i, for example $F_3 = \{l_3, l_4, ..l_k\}$, have optimal path to the l_i.

Theorem 2. All of the routes along the AROT from each source to sink are optimal after reversal process is completed.

Proof. If a sink node moves to (0, 1) and requests adaptive reversal, all neighbors around the sink changes their parent direction to the sink node. Then, they propagate the reversal request. However, as shown in fig. 3 (b), the reversal is not propagated any more from their current neighbors. This is because the rest nodes are already directed to its parent. As mentioned in the previous section, the area where reversal process regarding current reversal request does not occur is called stable zone. As shown in figure 3 (b), the stable zone with respect to current reversal request can be divided into the three sub zone, SZ1, SZ2, and SZ3. Let be t current request time. If the tree was optimal regarding all the sources at the last request time t-1 as in fig. (a), each stable zone at current request time t is a sub-tree of (a). Accordingly, by lemma 1, all the stable zones, SZ1, SZ2, and SZ3, are optimal tree. In addition, since all the sub-trees are connected to the sink with one-hop distance, all of the routes along the AROT from each source to sink are optimal even after reversal process is completed as shown in fig 3 (b).

Now suppose that the sink moves to (2, 4). By algorithm, the reversal process at request time $t+1$ creates two partial stable zone, SZ1 and SZ2, and one reversal zone as shown in fig. 3 (c). Reversal process finds shorter path from its own to current sink by comparing distance in the reversal request message received from its neighbors. In the end, the after completing the current reversal process, all the sources in the reversal zone have optimal path to current sink. Consequently, the whole tree consisting of stable zone and reversal zone is optimal as shown in fig. 3 (c).

4 Performance Evaluations

In this section, the performance of the presented AROT is evaluated in terms of various metrics, including success ratio, average end-to-end delay, communication overhead and dissipated energy.

The presented AROT is implemented as an independent routing agent module in ns-2.27. In the basic simulation setting, the same energy model is used, which is a two-ray ground model and omni-directional antenna, as adopted in Directed Diffusion, and TTDD implementation in ns. 802.11 DCF is used as the underlying MAC protocol. A sensor node's transmitting, receiving, and idling power consumption rate is set to 0.66W, 0.395W and0.035W, respectively. The network in the simulation consists of 400 sensor nodes randomly distributed in 1000m x 1000m. Each simulation run lasts for 500 seconds. Each query packet is 36 bytes and each data packet is 64 bytes in length, in order to facilitate comparisons with other protocols.

4.1 Robustness of AROT

In this subsection, we evaluate the robustness of the proposed AROT. We observed success ratio with respect to increase of sink speeds (5 – 30) at different failure node rates (5% - 20%). Randomly selected nodes send data to its uplink (parent).

In the end, each source data is delivered to the sink along the AROT. Ideally, the success ratio for end-to-end success ratio of AROT is almost 100%. However, some links on the tree will be broken by various reasons, such as node failures, obstacles, and so on. To cope well with these failures, AROT utilizes simple but robust self-recovery. Figure 4 illustrates the success ratio of AROT in various percentages of node failure. As shown in fig. 4, self recovery function of AROT can perform more than 85 % success rate even in 20% of failure nodes. This is because all the links maintain the fresh connectivity to the sink. So, the partitioned tree by failures can be fast recovered in local area.

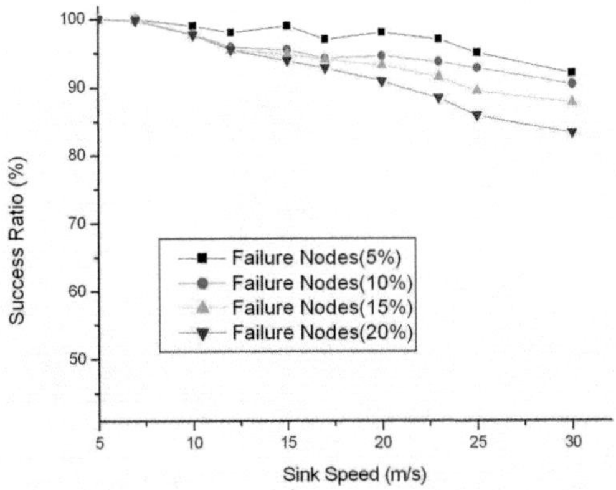

Fig. 4. Success ratio vs. Sink speed

4.2 Communication Overhead

In this subsection, the communication overhead (CO) in the network with respect to sink mobility is evaluated. Communication overhead rate is defined as the ratio of the number of working nodes, participating in the update reversal, over the total number of nodes.

First, the CO at each update rate from 5 seconds to 20 seconds with respect to sink movement (to each specific moving distance) is observed. In the second experiment, the Average CO at different sink speeds, from 5m/s to 30m/s, is examined respectively. As presented in fig.5, the simulation results illustrate that the presented AROT enables to maintain the dissemination path only with the number of working nodes less than approximately 14% of all nodes in the network, even in highly mobile sink environments.

4.3 Evaluation of End-to-End Delay

In this subsection, end-to-end delay is evaluated. We observed the end-to-end delay (from source to sink) with respect to increase of sink speeds (5 – 20) at different update reversal rates (5 – 20 seconds). Randomly selected nodes send data to its uplink (parent).

We measured the total time spent in delivering data to sink and averaged the delay. In addition, each source generates event data with data update rate smaller than reversal rate. Data is generally disseminated upwardly along the tree. However, during the time when link is not stable, some nodes must wait until the next reversal process by sink is completed. Figure 6 shows the variation of average end-to-end delay with respect to increase of sink speed at different reversal rate. It is demonstrated that even if delay is more increased at less frequent reversal rate, since the tree keeps the optimal path, overall end-to-end delay with respect to the sink speed is gradually increased.

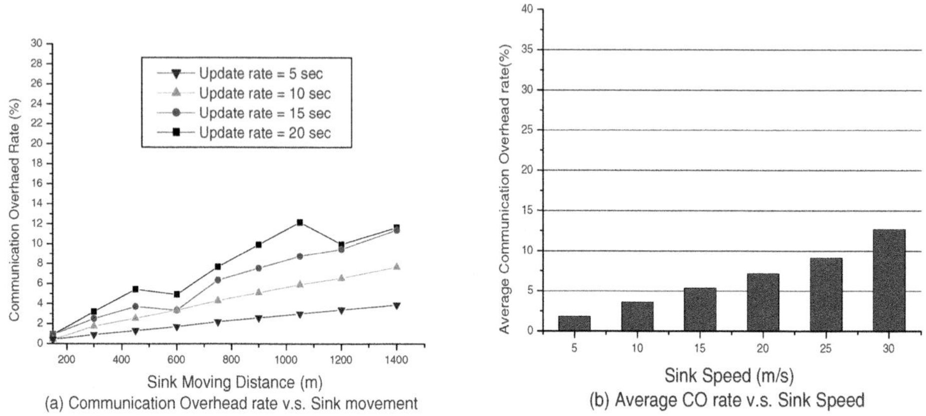

Fig. 5. Evaluations of communication overhead

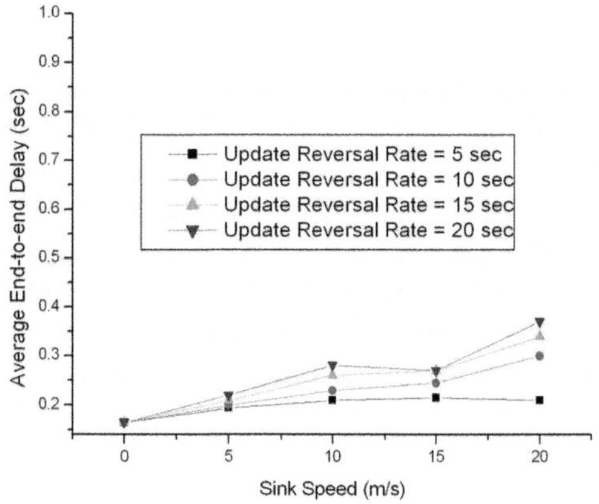

Fig. 6. Average End-to-end delay vs. Sink speed

5 Conclusions

In this paper, in order to cope with mobile sink environments, an *Adaptive Reversal with Optimal Path Tree* (AROT) protocol is proposed. The AROT is able to maintain the dynamic tree by adaptively reversing links with minimum communication overheads in the network, in spite of a highly mobile sink environment. Since the AROT proactively performs adaptive sink mobility management, data dissemination from each source to a mobile sink can be easily achieved along the AROT, without additional control overhead. In addition, the dynamic path is optimal in terms of hop counts and the AROT can maintain a robust tree structure by quickly recovering the partitioned tree with minimum packet transmission. Finally, the simulation results demonstrate that the AROT is a considerably robust protocol with optimal path.

References

1. Luo, H., Ye, F., Cheng, J., Lu, S., Zhang, L.: TTDD: Two-tier Data Dissemination in Large-scale Wireless Sensor Networks. In: ACM/Kluwer Mobile Networks and Applications, Special Issue on ACM MOBICOM (2002)
2. Intanagonwiwat, C., Govindan, R., Estrin, D.: Directed diffusion for Wireless Sensor Networking. IEEE/ACM Transaction on Networking 11 (2003)
3. Kim, S., Son, S.H., Stankovic, J.A., Li, S., Choi, Y.: SAFE: A Data Dissemination Protocol for Periodic Updates in Sensor Networks. In: Proceedings of the 23 rd International Conference on Distributed Computing Systems Workshops (ICDCSW'03) (2003)
4. Kim, H.S., Abdelzaher, T.F., Kwon, W.H.: Minimum-energy asynchronous dissemination to mobile sinks in wireless sensor networks. In: Proceeding of Embedded Networked Sensor Systems (SenSys03), Los Angeles, California, USA (2003)
5. Hwang, K.-i., In, J., Eom, D.-s.: Dynamic Shared Tree for Minimum Energy Data Aggregation of Multiple Mobile Sinks in Wireless Sensor Networks. In: Römer, K., Karl, H., Mattern, F. (eds.) EWSN 2006. LNCS, vol. 3868, Springer, Heidelberg (2006)

Low-Latency Routing for Energy-Harvesting Sensor Networks

Hyuntaek Kwon, Donggeon Noh, Junu Kim, Joonho Lee, Dongeun Lee, and Heonshik Shin

School of Computer Science and Engineering, Seoul National University, Sillim-dong, Gwanak-gu, Seoul 151-744, Korea
{htkwon,dgnoh,kesker,jlee108,eundong}@mobisys.snu.ac.kr, shinhs@snu.ac.kr
http://mobisys.snu.ac.kr

Abstract. This paper presents low-latency routing strategies that take account of energy-harvesting sensor nodes in wireless sensor networks. Currently, in the case of tree-based network connectivity, 'lazy' nodes with a long interval between computational activities may slow down communication if deployed along a routing path. To cope with this problem, we suggest a random graph in which a node may have multiple parent nodes, thus allowing a choice of path to the sink node. We also propose three path selection schemes for the network topology on the basis of (a) the cost of a single hop from the current node, (b) the cost of two hops, and (c) the cost of a single hop plus a cost estimate for the remainder of the path to the sink, respectively. The proposed strategies are shown to outperform the existing routing algorithm for a tree-structured energy-harvesting sensor network.

1 Introduction

As the term 'ubiquitous' has made frequent appearances in recent years, diverse applications for wireless sensor networks (WSNs) are now receiving significant attention, including home networks, monitoring systems, and intrusion alarms [1]. Due to constraints on the size and cost of hardware, a sensor node in a WSN is usually powered by a small and inexpensive battery. The life of the battery at each sensor node determines how long the entire network can remain active. A lot of previous research has therefore focused on reducing energy consumption [2,3]. But even after optimization, batteries alone cannot provide enough running time for most applications. Finding more durable energy sources remains as a challenging problem.

Energy harvesting, or scavenging, is a technology that has recently been introduced to overcome the short lifetime of a traditional battery. By generating electricity from environmental energy, such as solar energy, temperature variation, kinetic energy, and vibration, this technology offers reduced dependency on batteries, or even their elimination [4,5,6]. However, little work has yet been devoted to routing for sensor nodes running on environmental energy and their effect on the overall network.

J. Indulska et al. (Eds.): UIC 2007, LNCS 4611, pp. 422–433, 2007.

Once a sensor has been deployed, maintaining it is not a trivial problem, so sensors should operate autonomously as far as possible. Thus, each sensor node in an energy-harvesting WSN should be aware that the amount of environmental energy it can gather will depend on the time, the location, and the node's surroundings; and this awareness needs to be reflected in its pattern of operation.

In this paper we will consider how a node in an energy-harvesting WSN can be kept in perpetual operation, and we will also consider how this affects the network topology. We will go on to propose new data routing schemes with reduced latency.

The rest of this paper is organized as follows. The next section contains an analysis of existing routing schemes for energy-harvesting nodes. Section 3 and 4 describes the characteristics of our low-latency routing schemes in terms of duty cycle and network topology. We then give an overview of our simulation environment and evaluate our strategies in Section 5. Finally, conclusions are drawn in Section 6.

2 Related Work

The size and power requirement of the elements of WSN nodes, such as sensors, signal conditioners, controllers and RF transceivers, are becoming smaller, while the level of integration is increasing. These changes motivate research on obtaining power from the environment [7,8,9,10]. Fig. 1 [8] shows power density versus service life for batteries and environmental energy sources. The operating time of a node can be extended indefinitely using energy-harvesting techniques, due to the reusable nature of environmental energy. However, most research has focused on hardware design or on prototype energy-harvesting nodes, rather than on topologies and routing protocols suitable for energy-harvesting networks, because the application of energy-harvesting techniques to wireless networks and intelligent sensors is in its infancy.

An energy-harvesting sensor node can be expected to require a harvester, an ultra capacitor and a rechargeable battery, in addition to more general

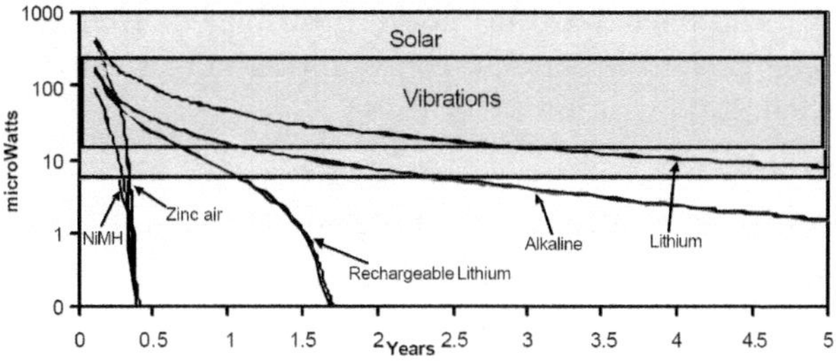

Fig. 1. Power density vs. lifetime of different power sources

components, such as a micro controller, an RF transceiver and memory. The harvester must be adapted to the source of energy, which may be solar, vibration, piezoelectric, thermoelectric and so on. Solar cells are very popular due to their low cost and high efficiency. An ultra capacitor allows low level of harvested power to be used to recharge the battery.

Many researchers have proposed prototypes with this sort of composition. As shown in Fig. 2, the Heliomote [10], Prometheus [11] and Solar Biscuit [12] are representative nodes.

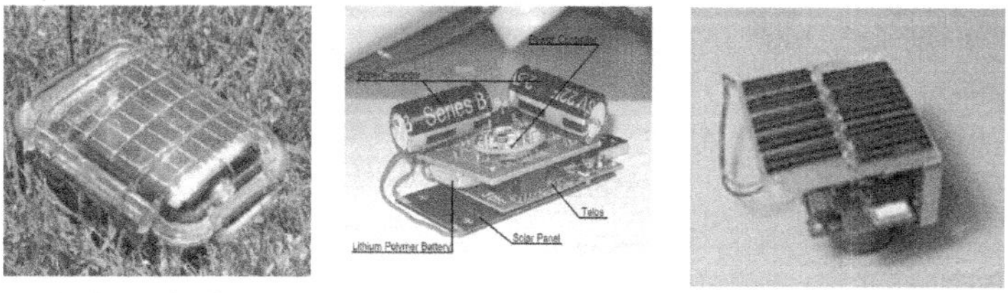

Heliomote @ UCLA   Prometheus @ Berkeley   Solar Biscuit @ Tokyo Univ.

Fig. 2. Some energy-harvesting nodes

While a lot of works have been put into the design and development of sensor nodes, only makeshift topologies and routing protocols have been implemented, for test purposes.

At a time when energy-harvesting techniques were less attractive, there was some research [13,14] on integrating a small number of solar-powered nodes into existing routing protocols. A small number of harvesting nodes were added to an otherwise battery-powered sensor network. The well-known routing protocols, LEACH [15] and Directed Diffusion [16] were modified to prolong network activity by placing heavier workloads on to energy-harvesting nodes. But such a network cannot, of course, keep operating indefinitely, because most of the nodes in the network are battery-powered.

In the Heliomote [10] project, perpetuity of operation was considered in the context of task management, network topology and the routing protocol. The UCLA team's prototype harvesting node, itself called 'Heliomote', suggested ways to model energy harvesting and consumption numerically, and resulted in a scheme for indefinite operation.

3 Duty Cycle of a Node in Energy-Harvesting Sensor Networks

As shown in Fig. 3, a node in a WSN periodically wakes up and briefly activates a transmitter-receiver module; but it stays in idle mode for most of the time in order to maximize the sustainability of the network. The proportion of time

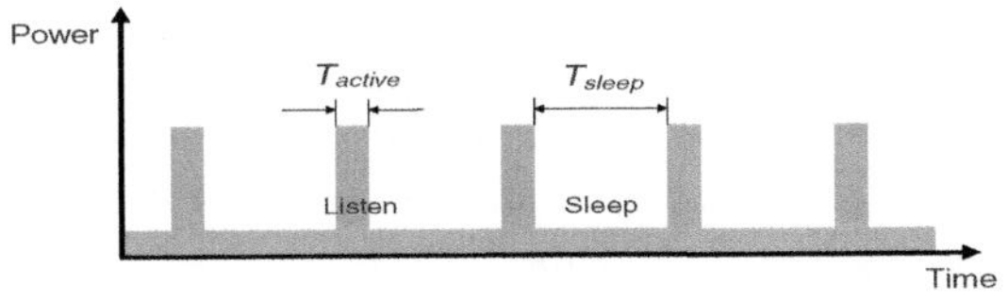

Fig. 3. Periodic activation of a node

for which a node is active is referred to its duty cycle d, which can be calculated as follows:

$$d = \frac{T_{active}}{T_{active} + T_{sleep}}$$

In WSNs, generally, the duty cycle is around 0.1%∼2.0%.

In a rather simplistic node of operation, all the nodes have the same duty cycle. But this means that heavily-loaded nodes use up their energy too quickly. When more than the half the nodes in a WSN can no longer operate, the workload of each remaining node increases dramatically and the network soon shuts down completely.

Each node in an energy-harvesting sensor network uses its environmental power source as much as possible, while surplus electricity, stored in the rechargeable battery, is treated as a secondary power source. If each node has a sensible duty cycle, it can operate perpetually except external problems such as hardware defects.

3.1 Duty Cycle for Perpetual Operation

The quantity of energy harvested from the environment can be very different from node to node due to the diversity of harvesters, the locations of the nodes, the deployment policy, the rate of harvesting, and so on. Fig. 4 shows the daily pattern of power generation by a solar cell over two months, collected by a Mica2 mote [17].

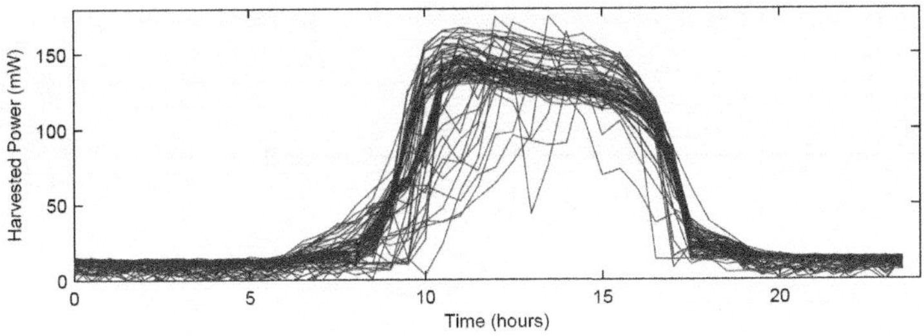

Fig. 4. Daily power generation by a solar cell

Kansal et al. [17] suggested a mathematical condition which would express the conditions under which a sensor node can operate perpetually, through an analysis of the relationship between harvested and consumed energy.

Suppose $E(t)$ is the power output of any energy source at time t, then the energy harvested during any finite time T can be estimated as follows:

$$\rho T - \sigma_1 \leq \int_T E(t)dt \leq \rho T + \sigma_2$$

Therefore, if there is enough historical data, we can make a good estimate of the energy that will be supplied to a node during a given period.

$E_c(t)$ is the power consumption of a node at time t and satisfies the following constraint for any value of T:

$$\int_T E_c(t)dt \leq \rho' T + \sigma$$

Each node in an energy-harvesting network must have a sensible plan to control the energy that it consumes by means of an energy budget based on adequate historical data. That means that a node must have an energy storage capacity of more than $\sigma + \sigma_1 + \sigma_2$ and satisfy $\rho' < \rho$ in order to operate perpetually. Since the energy consumption of each active mode is fixed, the duty cycle d of a perpetually operating node completely depends on the calculated value of ρ' [17].

3.2 Latency Between Nodes in an Asynchronous Network

In self-sustaining energy-harvesting sensor networks, each node wakes up at a different time due to the different values of the duty cycle d. Therefore, the sender must know the duty cycle of the receiver in advance, and can then wait for the receiver to be ready to receive the packet.

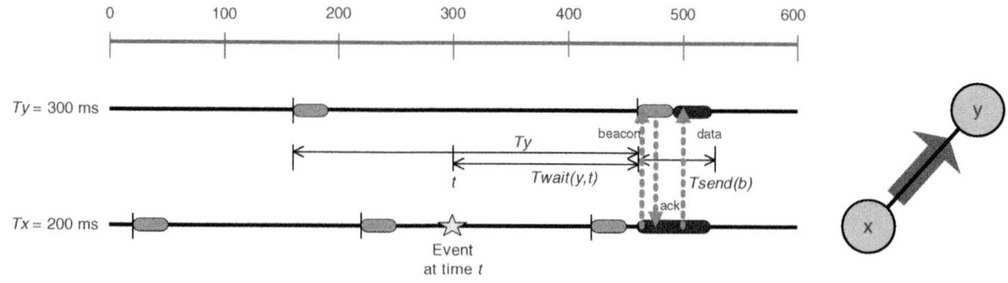

Fig. 5. Latency between two nodes which have different duty cycles

As shown in Fig. 5, for a node x to send b bits of data to node y at time t involves a waiting time $T_{wait}(y,t)$ and a transmission time $T_{send}(b)$, assuming that node x already knows that the duty cycle of node y has a period T_y. The transmission time is composed of two parts: T_{beacon} for two-phase handshaking using a beacon, and T_{data} for link-layer transmission. Assuming that R is the data bandwidth of the channel between the nodes, the expected latency between node x and node y at time t can be calculated as follows:

$$\begin{aligned} L(x, y, t) &= T_{wait}(y, t) + T_{send}(b) \\ &= \{T_y - (t - t_{setup})\,\%T_y\} + \left(T_{beacon} + \frac{b}{R}\right) \end{aligned}$$

If a node has many neighbors within its transmission range, it must choose one candidate from among them. Determining to which neighbor to transmit data is critical because it determines the delay which the data experiences in reaching its destination. As shown in Fig. 6, node x can transmit data with various latencies depending on the receiving node. In Fig. 6, node x can get the data to its destination faster if it chooses node y instead of node z as the recipient. Therefore, in perpetually operating WSNs in which each node has its own duty cycle, a routing algorithm which considers those duty cycles is necessary if the delay in data reaching the sink is to be reduced.

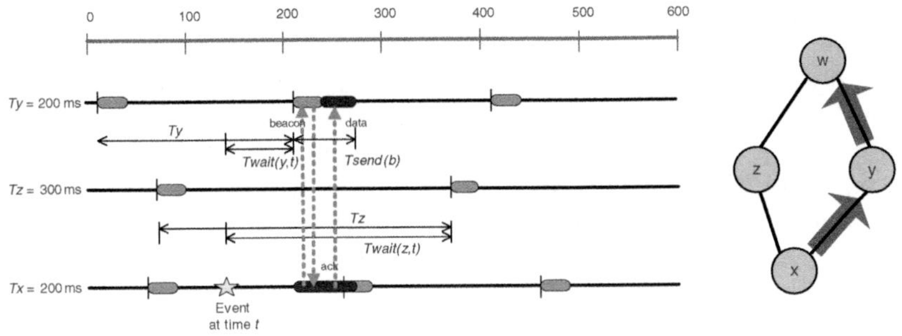

Fig. 6. Path selection for low latency

4 Network Topology and Routing Scheme

4.1 Topology Considerations

A hierarchical topology causes a cluster head to use more energy than other nodes due to its longer transmission range and higher workload. Therefore of this, the duty cycle of the cluster head may be shortened to conserve energy. On the contrary, a flat topology distributes energy consumption more fairly across all nodes. A random tree is the simplest flat topology, and has been used in the energy-harvesting sensor network [17]. To initialize the random tree topology, the sink node broadcasts an INIT message which contains its duty cycle and waits for ACKs from neighbor nodes, for a certain period of time. The nodes within the transmission range of the sink node receive the INIT message and set

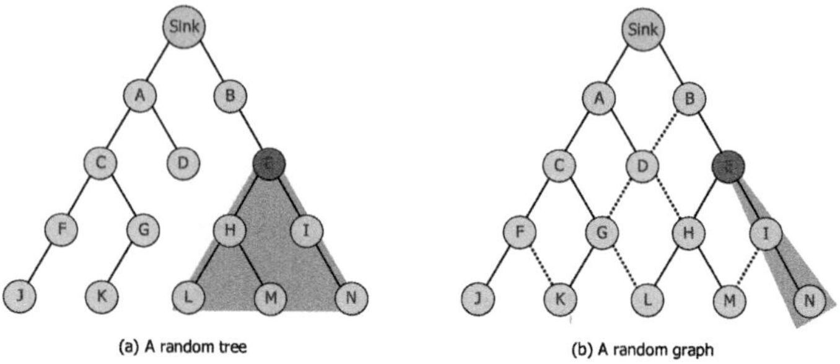

Fig. 7. The effect of a lazy node

the sink node as their parent. After a random backoff time, each node returns an ACK message to the sink node, which adds these nodes to its child set. This procedure is then repeated recursively at each node. Nodes which receive no ACK messages become leaf nodes.

The random tree topology is easy to configure however it can take a long time for messages from leaf nodes to reach the sink. Also, if a node fails for any reason, its descendants cannot transmit to the sink node until the topology has been re-initialized. In Fig. 7(a), the node E has a relatively low duty cycle, and may be called a lazy node such a node can increase the latency of communication with its descendants (i.e. nodes H, I, L, M and N in Fig. 7(a)).

Using a random graph reduces the latency caused by a lazy node. The random graph topology allows a node to have multiple parents so that it can choose a faster path which avoids lazy nodes. The dotted lines in Fig. 7(b) show additional paths, which allow paths to be chosen which avoid the lazy node. For example, laze node E affects only node I and node N. If the nodes are sufficiently sparse, the random graph will approximate a tree.

4.2 Low-Latency Routing Schemes

We will use the random graph topology because of the advantages itemized above. Now we consider path selection schemes for the random graph topology.

Single-Hop Selection. In single-hop selection, a message is transmitted to the parent with the lowest latency. In the example of Fig. 8(a), node x, whose parents are nodes y_1, y_2 and y_3, needs to transmit a message towards the sink. Since each parent has a different duty cycle, their values of T_{wait} also differ. The node x will transmit to the parent with the lowest T_{wait}, which is the one which will wake up earlier than the other parents.

If node x is sending a message to its parent y at time t, we will write the latency as $L(x, y, t)$, and we will say that the parent node set of node x is P_x. Then we can express the minimum latency $P(x, t)$ as follows:

$$P(x, t) = \min_{y \in P_x} \{L(x, y, t)\}$$

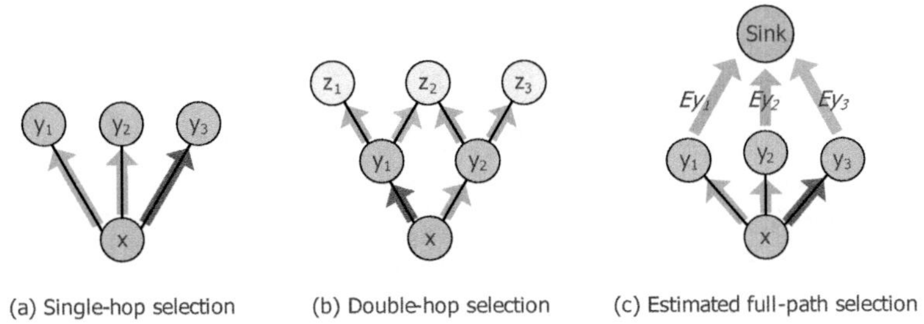

Fig. 8. Proposed low-latency routing schemes

This scheme is simple and does not involve a significant overhead. However, it cannot consider lazy nodes.

Double-Hop Selection. Double-hop selection chooses the parent which allows a message to reach a grandparent with the lowest latency. In the example of Fig. 8(b), node x has parents y_1 and y_2 and grandparents z_1, z_2 and z_3. Node x needs to know the duty cycle of its grandparents as well as those of its parents.

If node x is sending a message to its parent y at time t, we will call the latency $L(x, y, t)$ and we will say that its parent node set is P_x. Then, the latency to reach the grandparent $PP(x, t)$ is the sum of the latency from the node to parent y and the latency from parent y to grand parent z. This can be calculated as follows:

$$\begin{aligned} PP(x,t) &= \min_{y \in P_x} \{L(x,y,t) + P(y, t + L(x,y,t))\} \\ &= \min_{y \in P_x} \left[L(x,y,t) + \min_{z \in P_y} \{L(y,z,t+L(x,y,t))\} \right] \end{aligned}$$

This scheme is better at reducing latency than the single-hop selection. However, since it requires additional information about grandparents, it will increase additional traffic and computational overheads. Double-hop selection can avoid a single lazy node, but not a 'lazy zone', made up of several contiguous lazy nodes.

Estimated Full-Path Latency Selection. Estimated full-path latency selection is based on the single-hop selection and it also considers the estimated latencies over the whole path to the sink node from parent nodes. In Fig. 8(c), node x has three parents, y_1, y_2 and y_3. Because node x knows the duty cycle of each parent and an estimate of the latency from each parent to the sink node, it can estimate the total latency.

If node x is sending a message to its parent y at time t, we will call the latency $L(x, y, t)$, the parent set P_x, and the estimated latency from the node y to the sink node E_y. We can then estimate the total latency to the sink node, $S(x, t)$, as follows:

$$S(x,t) = \min_{y \in P_x} \{L(x,y,t) + E_y\}$$

E_y is calculated from the sink node to the leaf nodes, and if T is the least common multiple of the duty cycles of the parents of node y, E_y can be found as follows:

$$\begin{aligned} E_y &= \frac{1}{T} \int_T S(y,t)dt \\ &= \frac{1}{T} \int_T \min_{z \in P_z} \{L(y,z,t) + E_z\} dt \end{aligned}$$

This scheme is an estimate and cannot generally find globally optimal paths. However it does not involve any extra data transfer, because the estimated average latency E_y can be transmitted with the INIT messages. Also, since lazy nodes and lazy zones are considered in calculating E_y, this scheme has a chance to avoid them.

5 Performance Evaluation

We designed a simulation to evaluate the performance of our scheme. Visual C++ was used to develop our simulator which is based on NS2.

We simulated WSNs containing 50∼400 sensor nodes, spread randomly over 50m×50m and 100m×100m. The maximum radio range of each node is 10m and its data bandwidth is 3MB/s. The value of T_{beacon} for two-phase handshaking is set to 250ms and the size of a data packet is 32KB. The wake-up periods of the nodes follow a normal distribution, with an average of 2000ms and a standard deviation of 500ms. We observed the path latency from the source node to the sink while varying the time of the sensing event.

Fig. 9 shows the average latency of packets during 1 minute which have the same hop count to the sink node, when the 100 sensor nodes are spread over 50m×50m field. Our three schemes based on a graph topology all work much better than the previous scheme based on a tree topology in terms of end-to-end latency. Among our schemes, double-hop selection shows the best performance.

To look at a larger network at the same node density, we simulated 400 nodes randomly located in a 100m×100m field. As shown in Fig. 10, the greater distance to the sink node classifies the difference in performance between schemes. In addition, estimated full-path latency selection achieves faster end-to-end transmission than double-hop selection when the length of a path exceeds 14 hops. This crossover is to be expected as double-hop selection examines a shrinking proportion of the total path.

To compare the performance at a different node density, we simulated 400 nodes in a 50m×50m area. Fig. 11 also shows that the random graph topology is still advantageous, and the difference in performance between double-hop selection and estimated full-path latency selection becomes very small when the node density is high.

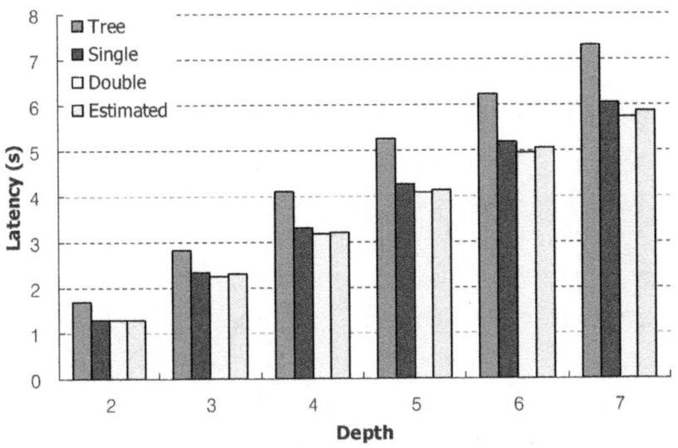

Fig. 9. Average latency of 100 nodes in a 50m×50m field

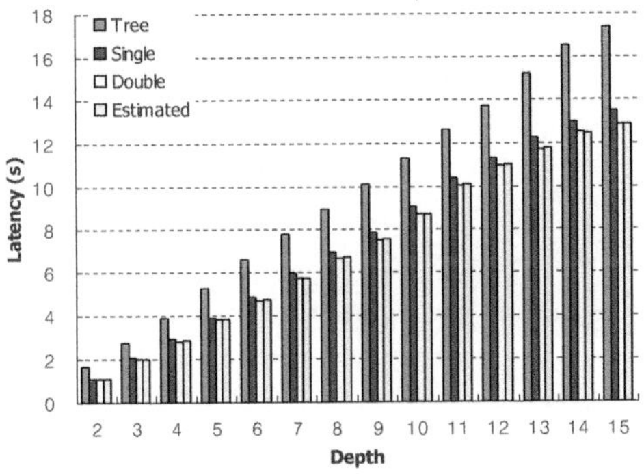

Fig. 10. Average latency of 400 nodes in a 100m×100m field

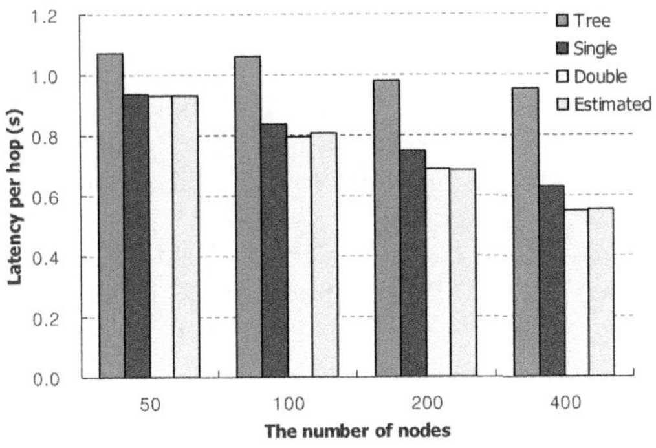

Fig. 11. Average Latency per hop at different node densities

6 Conclusion

We have presented a graph topology for an energy-harvesting sensor network and proposed low-latency routing schemes. These schemes perform better when the duty cycle is lower and the node density is higher. We also expect that their performance will increase with growth in the number of transmission errors. Among our three schemes, estimated full-path latency selection is the most suitable for practical energy-harvesting sensor networks because it involves no extra overhead and shows a good performance in the aspect of end-to-end delay.

In the future, we plan to formulate the end-to-end delay from a leaf node to the sink node by extending current inter-node cost formulation. We also intend to compare the performance of our schemes with that of optimal path selection. Before too long, we hope to be able to explore our schemes in a real WSN.

Acknowledgement

This work was supported by BK21 Research Fellowship from the Ministry of Education and Human Resources Development in Korea.

References

1. Akyildiz, I.F., Su, W., Sankarasubramaniam, Y., Cayirci, E.: A survey on sensor networks. IEEE Communication Magazine 40(8), 102–114 (2002)
2. Min, R., Bhardwaj, M., Cho, S., Shih, E., Sinba, A., Wang, A., Chandrakasan, A.: Low-power wireless sensor networks. In: Proceedings of the Fourteenth International Conference on VLSI Design (January 2001)
3. Shah, R.C., Rabaey, J.: Rabaey: Energy aware routing for low energy ad hoc sensor networks. In: Proceedings of the IEEE Wireless Communications and Networking Conference, March 2002, IEEE Computer Society Press, Los Alamitos (2002)
4. Mahlknecht, S., Roetzer, M.: Energy supply considerations for self-sustaining wireless sensor networks. In: Proceedings of the Second European Workshop on Wireless Sensor Networks (February 2005)
5. Raghunathan, V., Kansal, A., Hsu, J., Friedman, J., Srivastava, M.: Design considerations for solar energy harvesting wireless embedded systems. In: Proceedings of the Fourth International Symposium on Information Processing in Sensor Networks (April 2005)
6. Torregoza, J.P.M., Kong, I., Hwang, W., Kim, J.: Battery model for wireless networks using photovoltaic cells. In: Proceedings of the Eighth International Conference on Advanced Communication Technology (February 2006)
7. Warneke, B.A., Scott, M.D., Leibowitz, B.S., Zhou, L., Bellew, C.L., Chediak, J.A., Kahn, J.M., Boser, B., Pister, K.S.J.: An autonomous 16mm^3 solar-powered node for distributed wireless sensor networks. In: Proceedings of the First IEEE International Conference on Sensors, June 2002, IEEE Computer Society Press, Los Alamitos (2002)
8. Roundy, S., Otis, B., Chee, Y.H., Rabaey, J., Wright, P.: A 1.9ghz RF transmit beacon using environmentally scavenged energy. In: Proceedings of the International Symposium on Low Power Electronics and Design (August 2003)

9. Rahimi, M., Shah, H., Sukhatme, G., Heidemann, J., Estrin, D.: Studying the feasibility of energy harvesting in a mobile sensor network. In: Proceedings of the IEEE International Conference on Robotics and Automation, September 2003, IEEE Computer Society Press, Los Alamitos (2003)
10. Kansal, A., Hsu, J., Zahedi, S., Srivastava, M.B.: Power management in energy harvesting sensor networks. ACM Transactions on Embedded Computing Systems (to appear)
11. Jiang, X., Polastre, J., Culler, D.: Perpetual environmentally powered sensor networks. In: Proceedings of the Fourth International Symposium on Information Processing in Sensor Networks (April 2005)
12. Minami, M., Morito, T., Morikawa, H., Aoyama, T.: Solar Biscuit: a battery-less wireless sensor network system for environmental monitoring applications. In: Proceedings of the Second International Workshop on Networked Sensing Systems (June 2005)
13. Voigt, T., Dunkels, A., Alonso, J., Ritter, H., Schiller, J.: Solar-aware clustering in wireless sensor networks. In: Proceedings of the Ninth IEEE Symposium on Computers and Communications (June 2004)
14. Voigt, T., Ritter, H., Schiller, J.: Utilizing solar power in wireless sensor networks. In: Proceedings of the IEEE Conference on Local Computer Networks (October 2003)
15. Heinzelman, W., Chandrakasan, A., Balakrishnan, H.: Energy-efficient communication protocol for wireless microsensor networks. In: Proceedings of the 33rd Hawaii International Conference on System Sciences (January 2000)
16. Intanagonwiwat, C., Govindan, R., Estrin, D.: Directed diffusion: a scalable and robust communication paradigm for sensor networks. In: Proceedings of the Sixth ACM International Conference on Mobile Computing and Networking, August 2000, ACM Press, New York (2000)
17. Kansal, A., Potter, D., Srivastava, M.B.: Performance-aware tasking for environmentally powered sensor networks. In: Proceedings of the ACM Conference of Special Interest Group for the Computer/Communication System Performance Community, June 2004, ACM Press, New York (2004)

A Localized Link Quality-Aware Optimization Mechanism for Routing Protocols in Wireless Sensor Networks

Zhen Fu[1], Yuan Yang[2], Wen-Cheng Yang[1], Jung-Hwan Kim[1], and Myong-Soon Park[1,*]

[1] Internet Computing Lab, Computing Science and Engineering Department
Korea University, Seoul, Republic of Korea
{fuzhen,wencheng,glorifiedjx,myongsp}@ilab.korea.ac.kr
http://ilab.korea.ac.kr
[2] Research Laboratory Control & Solution Group,
LG Digital Appliance Company, Republic of Korea
yangyuan@lge.com

Abstract. Many routing protocols have been proposed for wireless sensor networks. However, few of the existing routing protocols have considered the link quality, such as the different communication rate, different Packet Loss Ratio (PLR). As a result, the routes tend to have the shortest hop count may contain weak links, which may lead to low performance and are susceptible to breaks in the presence of mobility. In this paper, we analyze the impact of link quality in data transmission and propose a Link Quality-Aware Optimization Mechanism for routing protocols. Specifically, the link quality is measured by PLR and each sensor node upon the routes will maintain a Link Quality Table (LQ-Table) which records link quality information of its neighboring nodes. By computing to select alternative sensor nodes for data transmission, the mechanism can assist the routing protocol to avoid transmitting data through bad link and efficiently prevent intolerable delay or unnecessary energy consumption due to the bad link's packet loss. Simulation and experiment results show that our design can efficiently improve the performance of routing protocols in energy efficiency and transmission latency.

1 Introduction

Recent fast development of wireless communication, sensor technique and micro-electro-mechanical systems (MEMS) enable the fast development of inexpensive, low-power and multifunctional micro-sensors. A mass of these micro-sensors coordinate by wireless communication to compose a wireless sensor network [1] [2]. Such networks can be deployed in military or citizen fields to collect data and monitor environments [3]. Nodes in network could be homogeneous (all nodes are same) or heterogeneous (nodes are different in function, energy-level, etc). They collect sound, temperature, light etc, and communicate via radio to finish data collection tasks

* Corresponding author.

J. Indulska et al. (Eds.): UIC 2007, LNCS 4611, pp. 434–443, 2007.

coordinately. For the difficulty of the battery renewal and the long period demand of application, such as battle field monitoring and wild animal tracking, energy becomes one of the most precious resources in wireless sensor network.

Recent years have seen extensive interest in wireless sensor networks for which many routing protocols have been proposed [4][5] which provides the means of discovering routes for data transmission in wireless sensor networks. Usually, a route is consisted of data links. However, because of different distances and various propagation paths, the data links in wireless sensor networks may have different quality. Despite the massive research on the routing protocols, most of them adopt hop count as the metric, neglecting the quality differences among the links. In consequence, a route may have a short hop count and contains weak links, which provide low communication rate and high Packet loss rate (PLR). Because of the low rate, weak links become the bottleneck of the routes; high PLR causes retransmissions, wasting much bandwidth [6]; and the throughput of the whole network is affected [7]. The complex wireless environment often makes things worse.

To address this problem, in this paper, we propose a localized link quality-aware optimization mechanism for routing protocols in wireless sensor networks. Our design tends to improve routing protocols' performance by utilizing link quality information. If a routing protocol doesn't consider link quality, then the original route from node A to node B discovered by the protocol may be a bad link. Then it will become a bottleneck of the route. With our design, by computing to select alternative sensor nodes for data transmission, it can assist the routing protocol to avoid transmitting data through bad links from node A to node B which may cause intolerable delay or unnecessary energy consumption. Thus our design isn't trying to intervene in the routing discovery phase of routing protocols to discover new routes, but assist the original routing protocol to improve the data transmission performance between two neighboring router nodes. Here "router node" represents the nodes upon the route.

The rest of paper is organized as follows: Section 2 introduces the related work. Section 3 proposes our design. Section 4 presents the simulation results and gives a performance analysis. Finally section 5 concludes the paper.

2 Related Works

In the on-demand routing protocols, when the source node tries to communicate with the destination node and there is no route available, a new route is discovered. Ad-hoc On-demand Distance Vector Routing (AODV) is proposed by [8], which is a routing protocol designed for ad hoc mobile networks. AODV is capable of both unicast and multicast routing. It is loop-free, self-starting, and scales to large numbers of mobile nodes.

Some works are dedicated to investigating the influence of bad links on wireless sensor networks' performance. Gang Zhou et al. studied impact of radio irregularity on wireless sensor networks in [9]. The results showed that radio irregularity has a significant impact on routing protocols, but a relatively small impact on MAC protocols. Jerry Zhao et al. briefly described architecture for sensor network monitoring in [10]. Their research showed that packet loss brought by bad links can significant impact the computation of some classes of digests.

A few routing protocols have considered the link quality. Suhua Tang et al. proposed LHAOR [11], where the link quality and mobility are considered. By utilizing the local update and received signal strength indicator information, the routes adapt to the topology variation and link quality changes, and reach the local optimum quickly, which contains strong links and has a small metric. Srihari et al. proposed BAF [12]. It took advantage of the fact that the nodes and therefore their adjacencies are relatively static, for scalable packet carries a *blacklist*, a minimal set of degraded-quality links encountered along its path, and the next hop was determined based on both its destination and blacklist.

However, all of these researches are tending to propose new routing protocols to discover new routes based on link quality. And none of them proposed any localized optimization mechanism based on link quality evaluation for existing routing protocols without any intervene in route discovery.

3 Our Proposed Schema: Link Quality-Aware Optimization Mechanism

Our design is composed of four steps. The first step is the link quality evaluation. Link quality is evaluated by packet loss rate. The second step is white list formation. In this step, router nodes depend on neighboring router nodes' white list information to select alternative links with good link quality. The third step is white list exchanging. Some control messages such as WL_Update message and Update_Reply message are introduced for white list exchanging and guaranteeing successful exchange communication. The final step is white node selection. In this step, an algorithm is designed to select the most efficient link for the routing optimization. Our design will be described in details step by step.

3.1 Link Quality Evaluation

To evaluate a link's quality, according to [10], we use packet loss rate to be the criterion for link quality evaluation. Here packet loss rate means in a certain period, the rate of failed packet transmission in all the packet transmission attempts.

To facilitate the white list formation that will be introduced in the next section, we form a Link Quality Table for each router node. The Link Quality Table is as table 1 shows, R_{LOSS} field denotes Packet Loss Rate, d denotes the estimated communication distance to the neighboring node. According to [10], packet loss rate can be obtained by periodical measure of beaconing messages on neighbor-to-neighbor communication. Many proposed sensor network protocols for medium access [17] and for topology control [18], [19] include periodic beaconing. This design is to guarantee the timely update of link quality information for router nodes.

Data in Link Quality Table is from periodical measure. According to [13], d can be estimated by signal strength. Considering wireless network's unstable wireless connection, the signal strength detected may be different in each time, thus we use average value of detected signals' strength.

Table 1. LQ-Table

Neighboring Node ID	R_{LOSS}	d
1	23%	1m
2	21%	1.2m
..	..	..

Quantity of failed packet transmissions and quantity of packet transmission attempts are used to compute packet loss rate in the following way. Assume the quantity of packet transmission attempts is P, and the quantity of failed packet transmissions is P_{err}, then $R_{LOSS}= P_{err} /P*100\%$. However, when the quantity of all the packet transmission attempts on a link is already very large and the link suddenly disrupts, for example when a sensor node dies or wireless communication interference occurs, the subsequent consecutive failure of packet transmission won't make the packet loss rate increase conspicuously. In this case, the packet loss rate statistic isn't able to reflect the actual quality of the disrupted link. To solve this problem, when consecutive failure of packet sending occurs, a weight value λ will be introduced in the computation of R_{LOS}. The pseudo code is as the following shows.

Pseudo code of Algorithm to compute packet loss rate

```
FUNCTION ComputePacketLossRate:
  Perr = Quantity of failed packet transmissions;
  P = Quantity of packet transmission attempts
  Consecutive_Fail_Limit = 5;
  IF (Transmission_Fail <= Consecutive_Fail_Limit)
    RLOSS= (Perr /P)*100%
  ELSE IF (Transmission_Fail > Consecutive_Fail_Limit)
    RLOSS=(((Perr-                          (Transmission_Fail-
    Consecutive_Fail_Limit))      +λ+λ^2+λ^3...+λ^(Transmission_Fail-
    Consecutive_Fail_Limit))/ P)*100%
  END IF
RETURN RLOSS
```

3.2 White List Formation

After setting up the Link Quality table, router nodes will begin to exchange link quality information with each other. As for data transmission, only the information of links with good links is requisite. The router node's neighboring nodes with good links will be collected in a list called "white list". We designed an algorithm to decide which links are good links.

Assume all the neighboring nodes are not far away from each other. Thus, according to [13] the energy spent for transmission of an l-bit packet over distance d is

$$E_{tx}(l,d)=lE_{elec}+l\epsilon_{fs}d^2 \quad (1)$$

According to equation 1, $E_{tx}(l,d)$ is proportional with communication distance d. As packet loss rate stands for the rate of failed packet transmission, rate of successful transmission is $1\text{-}R_{loss}$. Thus nergy required to successfully send l-bit packet is:

$$E_{succ} = E_{tx}(l,d)/\,(1\text{-}R_{loss}) \tag{2}$$

According to equation 1 and 2, thus we define

$$Cf = E_{succ}\,/\,l = (E_{elec} + \epsilon_{fs} d^2)/\,(1\text{-}R_{loss}) \tag{3}$$

as the unit energy cost of the link. The bigger the Cf is, the more energy will be consumed in the relay process on this link.

Because we have already known d and R_{loss} for each node in the LQ-Table, we can caculate each node's Cf value. Moreover, we define a threshold value $Cf_{threshold}$, only the nodes whose Cf values are smaller than this threshold value can be added into white list. With this design, unqualified nodes can be filtered before the white list forming, so the size of white list can be reduced.

To calculate this threshold value, we need some estimation at the deployment phase of the network. Assume the number of nodes is N, and the area to deploy is A, The sensors in the wireless sensor network are distributed randomly in 2-dimensional space. Assume node i's coordination in area A is $(x_i,\ y_i)$, then the average distance between two arbitrary nodes is

$$d_{avg} = \frac{1}{(N-1)+(N-2)+..+1} \sum_{\substack{0\le i\le N-1 \\ 0\le j\le N-1 \\ i\ne j}} \sqrt{(x_i - x_j)^2 + (y_i - y_j)^2} \tag{4}$$

According to equation 3 and 4, the threshold value $Cf_{threshold}$ can be defined as

$$Cf_{threshold} = (E_{elec} + \epsilon_{fs} d_{avg}{}^2)/\,(1\text{-}R_{threshold}) \tag{5}$$

$R_{threshold}$ is a value from 0 to 1. According to specific requirements of the application, it can be adjusted to achieve the best performance.

3.3 White List Exchanging

White list exchanging is for router nodes to exchange link quality information with each other. This exchanging is between two neighboring router nodes.

SRC_ID	WL1_ID	WL1_Cf	WL2_ID	WL2_Cf	WL3_ID	WL3_Cf	....

Fig. 1. WL_Update Messag

With the algorithm stated in section 3.2, each router node builds a white list containing its neighboring nodes with good links. This white list will be capsulated in a WL_Update message which contains source router node's ID and attributes of the nodes in its white list. The structure of WL_Update message is as the Figure 1 shows, SRC_ID means the unique ID of the source node in white list exchanging and WL*_ID means unique ID of the source node's white list node and WL*_Cf means the Cf value of the node with the WL*_ID.

WL_Update will be sent to the neighboring router nodes according to the direction of data routes. To reduce WL_Update message's size and transmission frequency in order to save energy, we designed an incremental update mechanism. Assume node A needs to send white list information to node B:

1) At the first time to exchange white list, node A capsulates the white list formed according to section 3.2 in WL_Update message and send it to node B. Obtaining the WL_Update message, the receiver will store it temporarily for further processing and send back an Update_Reply message for acknowledgement.
2) In the following white list updates, node A only records the incremental data in the white list. Only when a white list node's packet loss rate's change exceeds a packet loss rate threshold value α , this node's link quality will be updated. This latest link quality information needed to be updated is recorded in WL_Update message, thus node B that received WL_Update message will replace old data with the new data. Different from the first WL_Update message, now WL_Update message only contains *ID* and *Cf* value of the white list nodes which need to be updated. Similar with step 1, after receiving WL_Update message, node B needs to send back an Update_Reply message for acknowledgement.
3) If node A doesn't receive any Update_Reply message from node B for a certain time, it will be regarded as a time-out transmission. Step 1) and Step 2) will be repeated to retransmit the WL_Update message.

3.4 White Node Selection

White node stands for the candidate node with the best link quality to route data between two neighboring router nodes.

With both of node A and node B's white lists, node A will compute out a candidate node list containing the candidate nodes that can be used to forward data to node B.

Assume WL_A is A node's white list, and WL_B is B node's white list. Then A node's candidate list $CL_A = WL_A \cap WL_B$, which means any node in CL_A is in A node's white list and also in B node's white list, thus the node's links with A node and B node are both in good quality. Therefore, the white node must be in $CL_{A.}$

To select white node from $CL_{A,}$ it needs following definitions:

C_i: unit energy cost to forward *1-bit* data from node A to node B through i_{th} candidate node.
Cf_A: unit energy cost to forward *1-bit* data from A to i_{th} candidate node.
Cf_B: unit energy cost to forward *1-bit* data from i_{th} candidate node to node B.

Assume node i's candidate list is CL_i, in which there are n candidate nodes $\{CN_{1..}CN_n\}$. For each CN_j, $j \in [1, n]$,

$$C_j = Cf_A + Cf_B \tag{6}$$

According to equation 3,

$$C_j = (E_{elec} + \epsilon_{fs} d_A^2) / (1 - R_{A\text{-}loss}) + (E_{elec} + \epsilon_{fs} d_B^2) / (1 - R_{B\text{-}loss}) \tag{7}$$

By computing all the candidate nodes' unit energy cost according to equation 7, we can get candidate list node's unit energy cost list $Cost = \{C_1, C_2 ... Cn\}$. The smaller C_j is, the smaller the unit energy cost to transmit *1-bit* data from node A to node B is. Thus we select the smallest one in *Cost* list as the white node.

4 Simulation and Performance

In this section we evaluate our design. It is implemented on the basis of AODV-UU [16], which is suitable for both simulation and testbed evaluation.

In order to evaluate the performance of our design in a sensor network environment, we port our Localized Link Quality-Aware Optimization Mechanism into ADOV-UU ns2 source code and simulate AODV with our design and original AODV for comparison with ns2 tool [14] which can simulate a layered network protocol stack and wireless channel. IEEE 802.11 [15] distributed coordination function (DCF) is used as the medium access control protocol. The simulations are conducted within a square network topology of fixed size. The sensor nodes are placed randomly within the simulation area and remain stationary throughout the duration of the simulation. Network traffic events are generated using an exponential random traffic model. GOOD Link Rate is defined as 30%, Weight value λ is defined as 2 and $R_{threshold}$ is set to 35%.

We compare original AODV and AODV with our design in two aspects: Route lifetime and End to end delay / packet delivery ratio. Route lifetime's comparison can provide the evaluation of our design's performance in saving router nodes' energy. End to end delay / packet delivery ratio provides evaluation of our design's performance of assisting routing protocol to reduce transmission latency.

4.1 Route Lifetime

To measure route lifetime, we use the approach of constantly adjusting the rate of bad links in all the data links of the network. Randomly selected nodes will keep on sending data along the routes discovered by AODV routing protocol to the base station and the traces are recorded down for analysis. Route lifetime denotes the duration between the time a route is discovered and the time the route corrupted. And average lifetime of all the routes will be calculated for the performance comparison of the 2 routing schemas.

Figure 2 shows the average route lifetime under the 2 routing schemas. As the Figure 2 shows, as rate of bad links increases, the average route lifetime decreases for both of the two schemas. But AODV with our design is constantly longer than

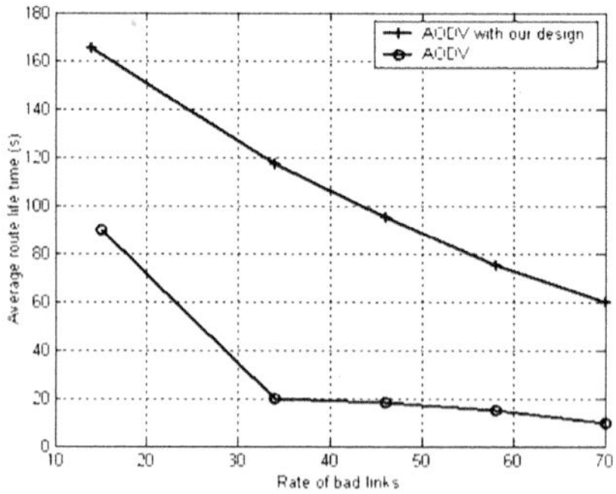

Fig. 2. Average route lifetime

original AODV. This is because of the frequent route breaks caused by bad links in AODV, but AODV of our design can effectively reduce unnecessary retransmission attempts by selecting white node for data forwarding and thus save the sensor energy to prolong route lifetime.

4.2 End to End Delay and Packet Delivery Ratio

To measure the end to end delay and packet delivery ratio, we use the similar approach with section 4.1 by constantly adjusting the rate of bad links of the network and look into the average end to end delay and average packet delivery ratio of all the routes set up by the AODV routing protocol.

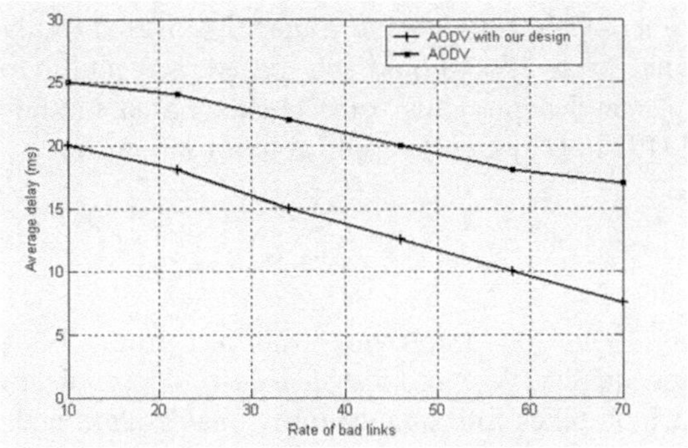

Fig. 3. Average end to end delay

Figure 3 shows the measured average end to end delay under different rate of bad links. From Figure 3, we can find out that AODV with our design's average delay is conspicuously and constantly less than original AODV. This means our design successfully avoids selecting links with bad quality to forward data and can reduce the transmission delay apparently comparing to the original AODV routing protocol.

Figure 4 shows the packet delivery ratio. AODV's packet delivery ratio is constantly lower than AODV with our design. And as the rate of bad links increases,

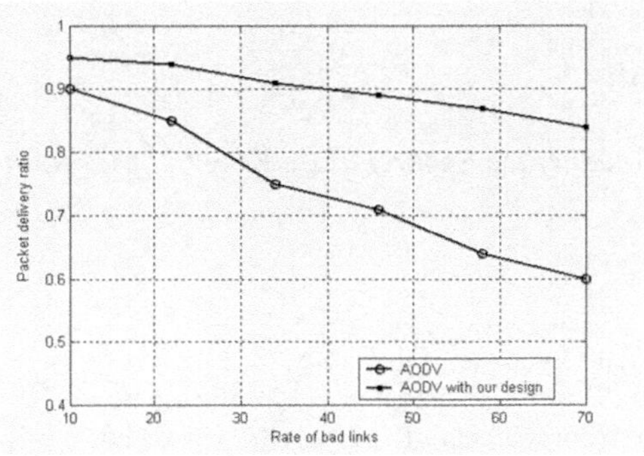

Fig. 4. Packet delivery ratio

AODV's packet delivery ratio obviously decreases because of increasing transmission collision due to the increasing rate of bad links. However, with our design, AODV's performance in packet delivery ratio can be improved significantly. Even when the rate of bad links is very high, up to 50%, it can still maintain a relatively good performance that its packet delivery ratio can be still higher than 80%. This is because by always selecting good links to forward data, AODV with our design can effectively reduce unnecessary re-transmission of data due to the packet loss.

The simulation results show our design can significantly improve performance of AODV routing protocol. Because our design is a localized mechanism for routing protocols in wireless sensor networks, the design can also be adapted to some of other routing protocols. However, not all the routing protocols can adopt this mechanism to improve their performance because our design is concentrating on reducing the negative effects of the bad links upon the routes discovered by the routing protocol. The eligible routing protocols should be based on multihop route discovery mechanism to adopt our design. Thus some cluster based routing protocols such as LEACH and LEACH-C in [13] are not applicable for our design.

5 Conclusion

In this paper, we focus on improving routing protocols' performance with consideration of link quality. We propose a localized optimization mechanism for routing protocols, which takes link quality into consideration and assists the routing protocols against the negative influence brought by bad links.

Specifically, we evaluate the link quality by packet loss rate and design several algorithms for computing packet loss rate, white list forming and white node selection. By link quality evaluation, a candidate list of sensor nodes for forwarding data is formed to white list and the best node for data transmission (white node) will be selected for the packet forwarding. This design can effectively avoid high packet loss because of the corrupted links along the route.

Our simulation results have shown that our design achieves both energy savings and low latency. Our proposed scheme is useful in various applications and scenarios, which desire to improve the performance of routing protocols, reduce end to end delay, increase packet delivery ratio and prolong route lifetime.

Acknowledgement

This work was supported by the Second Brain Korea 21 Project.

References

1. Clare, P., Agre.: Self-Organizing Distributed Sensor Networks. In: SPIE Conference on Unattended Ground Sensor Technologies and Applications, pp. 229–237 (1999)
2. Chandrakasan, A., Amirtharajah, R., Cho, S., Goodman, J., Konduri, G., Kulik, J., Rabiner, W., Wang, A.: Design considerations for distributed microsensor systems. Tech. Rep, Massachusetts Institute of Technology (2000)

3. Simic, S.N., Sastry, S.: Distributed environmental monitoring using random sensor networks. In: Zhao, F., Guibas, L.J. (eds.) IPSN 2003. LNCS, vol. 2634, pp. 582–592. Springer, Heidelberg (2003)
4. Clausen, T., Jacquet, P.: Optimized link state routing protocol. RFC 3626 (2003)
5. Johnson, D.B., Maltz, D.A., Hu, Y.C.: The dynamic source routing protocol for mobile ad hoc networks. draft-ietf-manet-dsr-09.txt (2003)
6. De Couto, D.S.J., Aguayo, D., Chambers, B.A., Morris, R.: Performance of multihop wireless networks: Shortest path is not enough. ACM SIGCOMM Computer Communication Review 33(1), 83–88 (2003)
7. Heusse, M., Rousseau, F., Berger-Sabbatel, G., Duda, A.: Performance anomaly of 802.11b. In: IEEE INFORCOM 2003, vol. 2, pp. 836–843 (2003)
8. Perkins, C.E., Belding-Royer, E., Das, S.: Ad Hoc on-demand distance vector (AODV) routing. RFC3561 (2003)
9. Gang, Z., Tian, H., Sudha, K., John, A,S.: Impact of Radio Irregularity on Wireless Sensor Networks. In: MobiSYS'04 (2004)
10. Jerry, Z., Ramesh, G., Deborah, E.: Computing Aggregates for Monitoring Wireless Sensor Networks. IEEE, Los Alamitos (2003)
11. Suhua, T., et al.: A link heterogeneity-aware on-demand routing protocol utilizing local update and RSSI information. IEICE Trans. Commun. E88-B(9) (2005)
12. Srihari, N., Sanghwan, L., et al.: Blacklist-Aided Forwarding in Static Multihop Wireless Networks. In: IEEE SECON (2005)
13. Wendi, B.H., Anantha, P.C., Hari, B.: An Application-Specific Protocol Architecture for Wireless Microsensor Networks. IEEE Transactions on wireless communications 1(4) (2002)
14. A network simulation tool, http://www.isi.edu/nsnam/ns/
15. IEEE Computer Society LAN MAN Standards Committee: Wireless LAN Medium Access Protocol (MAC) and Physical Layer (PHY) Specification. IEEE Std 802.11-1997, IEEE, Los Alamitos (1997)
16. http://www.docs.uu.se/docs/research/projects/scanet/aodv/aodvuu.shtml
17. Ye, W., Heidemwin, J., Estrin, D.: An energy-efficient mac protocol for wireless sensor networks. In: Proceedings of the IEEE INFOCOM, IEEE Computer Society Press, Los Alamitos (2002)
18. Xu, Y., Heideman, J., Estrin, D.: Geography-informed energy conservation for ad hoc muting. In: Proceedings of the ACM/EEEE International Conference on Mobile Computing and Networking, Rome, Italy, pp. 70–84 (2001)
19. Cerpa, A., Estrin, D.: ASCENT: Adaptive self-configuring sensor networks topologies. In: Proceedings of the IEEE Infocom, New York. USA, IEEE Computer Society Press, Los Alamitos (2002)

Minimum Energy and Latency MAC Protocol for Wireless Sensor Networks*

Muhammad Ali Malik, Byoung-Hoon Lee, Young-Bae Ko, and Jai-Hoon Kim

Graduate School of Information and Communication
Ajou University, Republic of Korea
{ali,componer,youngko,jaikim}@ajou.ac.kr

Abstract. Wireless sensor network consists of sensor nodes having limited resources. Energy saving is very important to increase the life time of these networks. In this paper, we propose Minimum Energy and Latency MAC (MELM) protocol for wireless sensor networks. MELM uses dual frequency radio setup inspired by STEM and LEEM to minimize the energy consumption and the latency in a multi-hop environment. Both LEEM and STEM protocols squander energy and increase latency because of overhearing, over-transmission and packet collisions. MELM eliminates these problems by maintaining a scheduling table in all nodes having logical 2-hop distance from the receiver node and by using advance channel reservation mechanism. MELM eradicates the hidden terminal and the exposed terminal problems, which is a key advantage, by maintaining a 2-hop receiver centric scheduling table.

1 Introduction

Wireless sensor networking has many applications including environmental monitoring, smart spaces, medical systems and robotic explorations but few characteristics can be assumed about the sensor network. First, the sensors are static. Second, energy is limited and it is inconvenient or impossible to replenish the energy source frequently [1] [2] [3].

Energy is very limited in sensor nodes and should be saved at each layer of the protocol stack. In this paper we address the MAC layer to minimize the energy consumption. We propose the MELM protocol which not only saves the energy but also minimizes the latency in a multi-hop environment. MELM is based on LEEM and STEM protocols and the main focus of MELM is to minimize the packet collisions during the data transmission. LEEM and STEM protocols have some deficiencies which causes packet collisions and throughput degradation during the data transmission. These packet collisions increase the energy consumption and the latency in sensor networks.

---

* This research was supported by the Ubiquitous Computing and Network (UCN) Project, the Ministry of Information and Communication (MIC) 21st Century Frontier R&D Program in Korea and the MIC(Ministry of Information and Communication), Korea, under the ITFSIP(IT Foreign Specialist Inviting Program) supervised by the IITA(Institute of Information Technology Assessment).

J. Indulska et al. (Eds.): UIC 2007, LNCS 4611, pp. 444–453, 2007.

There are three major sources of unnecessary energy consumption. The first one is packet collision. When packet collides at the destination node, it has to be discarded and follow on retransmissions of that packet increases energy consumption and latency. The second source is overhearing, meaning that the node may receive packets which are not destined for it. The third source is over transmission, meaning that the node may transmit packets when the destination node is busy or in a sleeping state. A considerable amount of energy can be saved by eliminating these problems.

In our proposed protocol, we try to minimize overhearing, over transmission and packet collisions by maintaining a 2-hop receiver centric scheduling table. MELM uses a dual channel radio setup, a Control Channel and a Data Channel inspired by STEM and LEEM protocols. The control channel wakes up periodically to check if there is any data for transmission. The control channel is used to reserve time slots for upcoming data transmissions. The data channel activates only at a specific time when there is any data for transmission. MELM minimizes packet collisions by using a scheduling table and minimizes the delay by using advance channel reservation mechanism. The node reserves channel for imminent data which minimizes the delay in a multi-hop environment.

2 Related Work

The Sparse Topology and Energy Management (STEM) [5] scheme improves the network life time by using a dual channel radio setup, namely Wakeup Channel and Data Channel. Both channels work on different frequencies. The data channel always remains in a sleeping mode. If any node has some data to transmit to its neighboring node, it sends a wakeup signal with receiver ID to the wakeup channel. The destination node sends acknowledgement after receiving the wakeup signal and both nodes activate their data channel for actual data transmission. We found three main problems in STEM protocol. The first problem is a packet collision due to a hidden terminal problem. Any node out of the data range and within the sensing range of the sender node may cause packet collision at the receiver node. The second problem is throughput degradation due to an exposed terminal problem. Any node within the sensing range of the receiver node does not start its transmission even though its transmission does not cause any collision at the receiver node. The third problem is latency added with the number of hops. Each time the node has to wait for its wakeup channel to get activate before sending packets to the next hop node.

Latency Minimized Energy Efficient MAC (LEEM) [8] protocol also uses a dual channel mechanism. LEEM uses a control channel to maintain the wakeup schedule for the data channel radio. It uses a scheduling mechanism to minimize the delay in a multi-hop environment. LEEM uses one-hop and N-hop reservation scheme depending on the data packet size. We found four problems in the LEEM protocol. The first problem is latency. LEEM increases latency if the next hop node is busy. LEEM sends negative acknowledgment packet if the next hop data channel is busy. The source node has to wait for a next wakeup period to transmit the REQ packet again. This increases latency and energy consumption. The second problem is packet collision. LEEM uses low power for its control channel and high power for its data channel which causes collision at the data channel. Energy consumption and latency is increased due to the collision at the data channel. The third problem is packet collisions due to the hidden terminal problem. LEEM maintains a scheduling table within a 1-hop distance which causes the packet collision at the data channel due to a hidden terminal problem. The fourth problem is throughput degradation. LEEM maintains the scheduling table within a 1-hop distance which causes an exposed terminal problem.

In this paper we proposed MELM (minimum energy and latency MAC) protocol to minimize energy consumption and latency in a multi-hop environment. MELM uses a scheduling table mechanism to improve the idea of LEEM. MELM maintains a scheduling table within a 2-hop distance from the receiver node to eliminate the hidden terminal and the exposed terminal problems.

3 Proposed Scheme

MELM uses a dual channel namely Control channel and Data channel. The control channel is used for the control data transmission and the data channel is used for the actual data transmission. MELM uses a periodic sleep and wakeup mechanism for the control channel inspired by LEEM and STEM. The time ratio between sleep and wakeup depends on the application. The data channel remains in the sleeping mode and only gets activated when there is some data to transfer.

MELM uses a scheduling mechanism to control data transmission. A scheduling table decides the time when data transmission starts between the nodes. MELM uses a distributed scheduling table and each node maintains a scheduling table to control the data transmission. The control channel is used to maintain the scheduling table and the data channel uses that scheduling table to make wakeup and sleep decision. MELM maintains a scheduling table within a 2-hop distance from the receiver node to perform a collision free data transmission. MELM eliminates hidden terminal and exposed terminal problems by using 2-hop scheduling table. MELM does not require CSMA/CA mechanism for its data channel.

Nodes perform reservations after control channel activation. The sender node initiates reservation request by sending the REQ packet. The receiver node replies with the REQ-ACK packet containing slot numbers. For example, node A has some data to transfer to its neighboring node B. Node A sends the REQ packet to get a slot reservation for data transmission. The receiver node B sends the REQ-ACK packet containing slot numbers. The REQ packet must have a starting slot number and a required number of slots fields. The default value of a starting slot number and a required number of slots fields are zero and one respectively. If a sender node sends the REQ packet with a default value of the starting slot number then the receiver node issues slot numbers depending on its scheduling table. For example, if the receiver node is busy for 4 time slots then it issues slot number 5 for data transmission to the sender node. Due to the distributed nature of the scheduling table, each node may have different scheduling table. The sender node may issue a REQ packet by mentioning the starting slot number which indicates that the sender node is busy until that slot. If the value of the starting slot number is not default then the receiver node issues slot numbers after the mentioned starting slot number. Both the receiver and the sender nodes activate their data channel for data transmission at an agreed slot number.

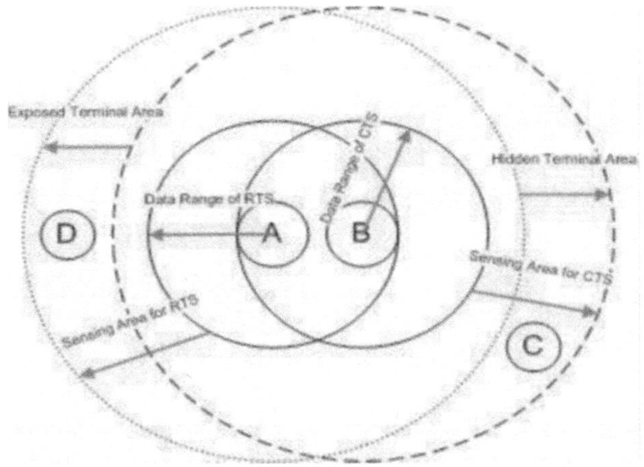

Fig. 1. Logical partitioning of transmission area, nodes in the hidden terminal area create hidden terminal problem and nodes in the exposed terminal Area create exposed terminal problem

MELM uses a receiver centric 2-hop reservation mechanism. Each node within logical 2-hop distance from the receiver node updates its scheduling table. MELM eliminates the hidden and the exposed terminal problems by using a receiver centric 2-hop reservation mechanism. Fig.1 shows the logical partitioning of the transmission area. Any node from a hidden terminal area starts transmission during the current transmission in the RTS data range causes the collision at the receiver node. For example, a packet collision occurs at the receiving node B if node C and node A start transmission at the same time. All nodes in the hidden terminal area have a maximum logical 2-hop distance from the receiver node B. All nodes in the hidden terminal area should be updated about the current data transmission between node A and node B. MELM updates all nodes having a logical 2-hop distance from the receiver node which includes all nodes in the hidden terminal area. Any node from the hidden terminal area does not start transmission as its scheduling table is updated. MELM eliminates exposed terminal problems by updating the scheduling table only in those nodes having a logical 2-hop distance from the receiver node. Fig.1 shows that exposed terminal area is out of the CTS sensing range, which indicates that all nodes in the exposed terminal area are out of 2-hop distance from the receiver node. The schedule table of all nodes in the exposed terminal area will not be updated. All nodes in the exposed terminal area can start transmission during the current transmission between node A and node B. For example, node D may start transmission while node A is transmitting data to node B. Node D's data transmission does not cause any collision at the receiver node B as node B is out of the sensing range of the node D. The exposed terminal problem does not occur in MELM.

Data transmission and slot reservation can be performed parallel because of dual channel radio mechanism. The parallel slot reservation minimizes the delay in a multi-hop environment. Nodes may reserve slots for an upcoming data transmission.

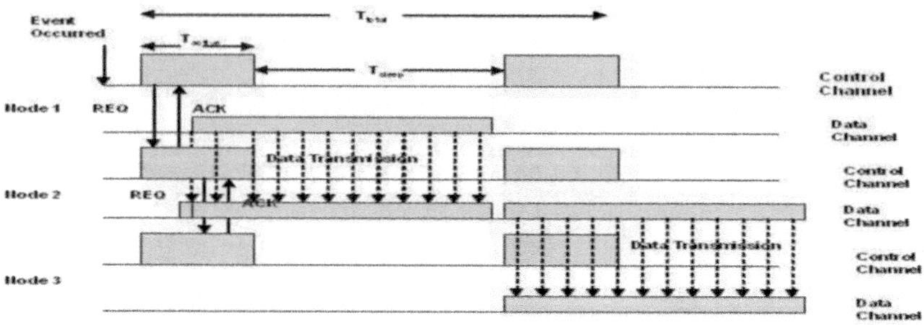

Fig. 2. Basic mechanism of MELM

MELM also uses advance channel reservation mechanism to minimize the delay in a multi-hop environment. In a multi-hop environment, the receiver node may be a sender node for the next hop node. So the receiver node may intimate reservation request as a sender node after transmitting REQ-ACK packet. In this way the channel can be reserved in a multi-hop environment to minimize the delay.

4 Theoretical Analysis

In this section we compare STEM and LEEM protocol with MELM. To make the analysis simple we are not considering the probability of collision at the data channel which is high in case of LEEM and STEM.

4.1 Energy Estimation

In this section we present energy consumption estimation of STEM, LEEM and MELM. The total energy consumption of any of these MAC protocols is the sum of the energy consumption of the control channel and the data channel.

$$E_{total} = E_{control\_channel} + E_{data\_channel} \tag{1}$$

4.1.1 STEM

The total energy consumption at the control channel in STEM can be calculated by using eq.2

$$E_{control\_channel} = E_{idle} + E_T + E_R \tag{2}$$

Energy consumption of the control channel in an idle state can be calculated as

$$E_{total\_idle} = T_{idle} \times E_{idle} \tag{3}$$

Energy consumption in a transmitting state and receiving state can be calculated as

$$E_{total\_Transmission} = T_T \times E_T \tag{4}$$

$$E_{total\_Receiving} = T_R \times E_R \tag{5}$$

$\lceil T_{bz} / T_{sleep} \rceil$ is the total activation time of the control channel while the data channel of the next hop node is busy. Energy consumption at the control channel, while next hope node is busy, can be calculated by using eq.6

$$E_{bz\_Transmission} = (\lceil T_{bz} / T_{sleep} \rceil) \times T_T \times E_T \tag{6}$$

Energy consumption at the control channel, while next hope is busy, can be calculated by using eq.7

$$E_{bz\_receiving} = (\lceil T_{bz} / T_{sleep} \rceil) \times T_R \times E_R \tag{7}$$

If the destination node is N hop away from the source node and the K number of events occurs and M is the number of nodes hear extra signal due to the broadcast nature of the wireless media.

$$E_{control\_channel} = (T_{idle} \times E_{idle}) + ((P_{bz} \times ((\lceil T_{bz} / T_{sleep} \rceil) \times T_T \times E_T) + (T_T \times E_T)) \times (K \times N)) + ((P_{bz} \times ((\lceil T_{bz} / T_{sleep} \rceil) \times T_R \times E_R) + (T_R \times E_R)) \times ((K \times N) + (K \times M))) \tag{8}$$

The energy consumption at the data channel can be calculated as

$$E_{data\_channel} = (T_{Data} \times K \times N) \times (E_T + E_R) \tag{9}$$

Total energy consumption can be calculated by substituting the values of equation 8 and 9 in equation 1.

4.1.2 LEEM

Energy consumption at the control channel in LEEM can be calculated by using eq.8

$$E_{control\_channel} = (T_{idle} \times E_{idle}) + ((P_{bz} \times ((\lceil T_{bz} / T_{sleep} \rceil) \times T_T \times E_T) + (T_T \times E_T)) \times (K \times N)) + ((P_{bz} \times ((\lceil T_{bz} / T_{sleep} \rceil) \times T_R \times E_R) + (T_R \times E_R)) \times ((K \times N) + (K \times M))) \tag{10}$$

The energy consumption at the data channel in LEEM can be calculated as

$$E_{data\_channel} = (T_{Data} \times K \times N) \times (E_T + E_R) \tag{11}$$

4.1.3 MELM

Energy consumption at the control channel in MELM

$$E_{control\_channel} = (T_{idle} \times E_{idle}) + (T_T \times E_T) \times (K \times N \times M) + ((T_R \times E_R) \times ((K \times N) + (K \times M \times (M + M)))) \tag{12}$$

Energy consumption at the data channel in MELM

$$E_{data\_channel} = (T_{Data} \times K \times N) \times (E_T + E_R) \tag{13}$$

Equation 12 shows that MELM uses more energy than STEM and LEEM. This energy is being used to maintain the scheduling table within a 2-hop distance. The collision at the data channel causes more energy consumption than maintaining the scheduling table.

4.1.4 Simulation Result

We use the GlomoSim [13] simulation environment and customized C++ program to perform the energy consumption comparison between STEM, LEEM and MELM in a multi-hop environment. Parameters during simulation are as following

Terrain Dimension 120 * 120 meter, Number of neighbors of each node 5, Transmission range 20 meters, Active time 100ms, Sleep time 500ms, Simulation Time 50 sec, Data and Control channel Bandwidth 2.4 kbps, Network Protocol flooding and Mobility none.

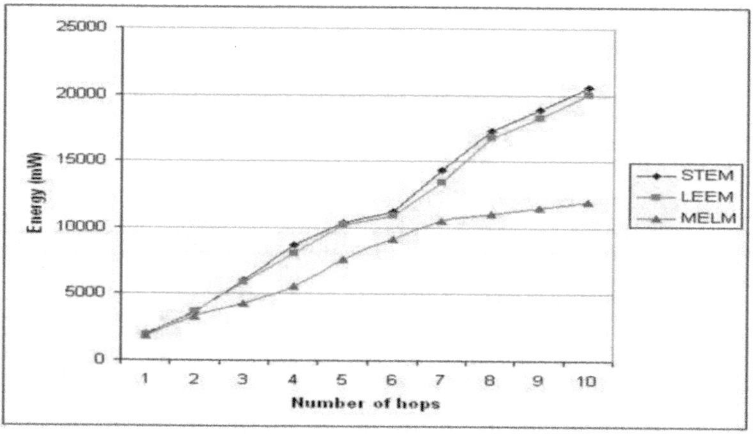

Fig. 3. Energy Consumption between STEM, LEEM and MELM in multi-hop environment

Simulation result shows that the energy consumption increase with the number of hops and MELM uses less energy as compare to LEEM and STEM due to its collision avoidance mechanism.

4.2 End to End Latency Estimation

In this section we perform end to end latency comparison between LEEM, STEM and MELM.

4.2.1 STEM

Setup time is the sum of average waiting time for control channel to get activated and the time required to transmit the REQ and the ACK packets.

$$T_{setup} = (T_{sleep}/2) + T_{Req} + T_{Ack} \tag{14}$$

If P_{bz} is the probability of any node to be busy then node has to wait T_{wait} time

$$T_{wait} = P_{bz}(T_{bz} + T_{sleep}/2 + T_{Req} + T_{Ack}) \tag{15}$$

The data transmission time from the source node to the next hop node can be calculated as

$$L_{source} = T_{setup} + T_{wait} + T_{Data} \tag{16}$$

By substituting the values in equation (3) we get

$$L_{source} = (T_{sleep}/2 + T_{Req} + T_{Ack}) + P_{bz} \times (T_{bz} + (T_{sleep}/2) + T_{Req} + T_{Ack}) + T_{Data} \tag{17}$$

For an average case we assume that any node has to wait ($T_{sleep}/2$) time before transmitting REQ packet. Latency at ith node can be calculated by using eq.18

$$L_i = ((T_{sleep}/2) + T_{Req} + T_{Ack}) + P_{bz} \times (T_{bz} + (T_{sleep}/2) + T_{Req} + T_{Ack}) + T_{Data} \tag{18}$$

Total latency in multi-hop environment can be calculated by using eq.19

$$L_{total} = L_{source} + \sum_{i=2}^{n} L_i \tag{19}$$

4.2.2 LEEM

Setup time in LEEM is same as in STEM.

$$\text{Setup Time} = (T_{sleep}/2) + T_{Req} + T_{Ack} \tag{20}$$

If P_{bz} is the probability of any node to be busy then node has to wait T_{wait} time

$$T_{wait} = P_{bz}(T_{bz} + T_{sleep}/2 + T_{Req} + T_{Ack}) \tag{21}$$

The delay at the source node in LEEM can be calculated by using eq.22

$$L_{source} = (T_{sleep}/2 + T_{Req} + T_{Ack}) + P_{bz} \times (T_{bz} + (T_{sleep}/2) + T_{Req} + T_{Ack}) + T_{Data} \tag{22}$$

If the data transmission time is less than the sleeping time of the control channel then the latency can be calculated as

$$L_i = (T_{sleep} - T_{Data}) + (T_{Req} + T_{Ack}) + P_{bz} \times (T_{bz} + (T_{sleep}/2) + T_{Req} + T_{Ack}) + T_{Data} \tag{23}$$

When the data transmission time is greater than the sleeping time of the control channel then the latency can be calculated by using eq.24

$$L_i = P_{bz} \times (T_{bz} + (T_{sleep}/2) + T_{Req} + T_{Ack}) + T_{Data} \tag{24}$$

Total latency in multi-hop environment can be calculated by using eq.25

$$L_{total} = L_{source} + \sum_{i=2}^{n} L_i \tag{25}$$

4.2.3 MELM

Setup time in MELM is same as in STEM and LEEM

$$\text{Setup Time} = (T_{sleep}/2) + T_{Req} + T_{Ack} \tag{26}$$

If the next hop data channel is busy then MELM perform reservation by using the advance channel reservation mechanism. Latency at the source node can be calculated as

$$L_{source} = (T_{sleep} / 2 + T_{Req} + T_{Ack}) + P_{bz}(T_{bz}) + T_{Data} \tag{27}$$

Latency at any intermediate node can be calculated by using eq.28

$$L_i = P_{bz} \times (T_{bz}) + T_{Data} \tag{28}$$

Total latency in multi-hop environment can be calculated by using eq.29

$$L_{total} = L_{source} + \sum_{i=2}^{n} L_i \tag{29}$$

4.2.4 Simulation Result

Simulation environment is same as section 4.1.4.

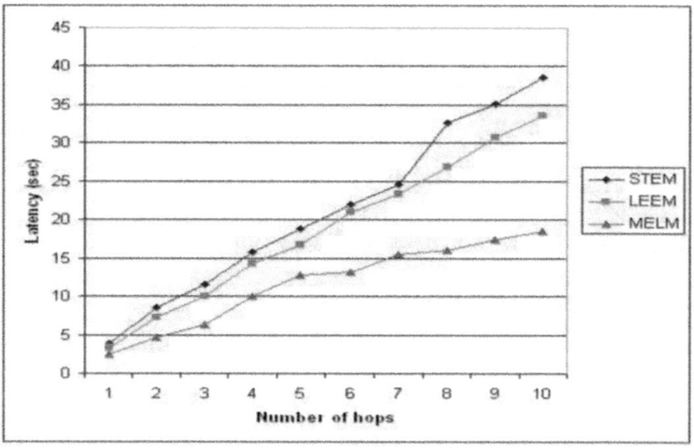

Fig. 4. End to end latency in multi hop environment

Simulation result shows that delay in MELM is less than LEEM and STEM because of its collision avoidance scheduling algorithm and sue to its advance channel reservation mechanism.

5 Conclusion

In this paper, we present Minimum Energy and Latency MAC protocol (MELM). MELM uses dual frequency radio setup. MELM minimizes the delay in multi hop environment by using efficient reservation mechanism. The LEEM and the STEM protocols spend unnecessary energy and increase latency because of overhearing, over-transmission and packet collisions. MELM eliminates these problems by maintaining a 2-hop receiver centric scheduling table. MELM eliminates the hidden terminal and the exposed terminal problems by maintaining distributed scheduling table. CSMA/CA mechanism is not required in MELM during data transmission which not only saves energy but also minimizes the delay. Our simulation results show that MELM saves energy and minimizes latency in multi-hop environment.

References

1. Estrin, D., Govindan, R.: Next century challenges: scalable coordination in sensor networks. In: Mobicom (1999)
2. Ye, W., Heideman, J., Estrin, D.: An energy efficient MAC protocol for wireless sensor networks. In: IEEE INFOCOM (2002)
3. Miller, M.J, Vaidya, N.H.: Minimum energy consumption in sensor networks using wakeup radio. In: IEEE WCNC (2004)
4. Ye, W., Hidemann, J., Estrin, D.: An energy efficient MAC protocol for wireless sensor networks. In: INFOCOM (2002)
5. Schurgers, C., Tsiatsis, V., Srivastava, M.B.: STEM: Topology Management for Energy Efficient Sensor Networks. In: IEEE Aerospace Conference (2002)
6. Raghavendra, C.S., Singh, S.: PAMAS-Power Aware-Access protocol with Signaling for Ad Hoc Networks. ACM, New York (2000)
7. Yang, X., Vaidya, N.: A Wakeup Scheme for Sensor Networks: Achieving Balance between Energy Saving and End-to-end Delay. IEEE Real-Time and Embedded Technology and Application Symposium (2004)
8. Dhanaraj, M., Manoj, B.S., Murthy, C.S.R.: A New Energy Efficient Protocol for Minimizing Multi-Hop Latency in Wireless Sensor Networks. IEEE Pervasive Computing and Communications (2005)
9. Pursley, M.B., Russell, H.B., Wysocarski, J.S.: Energy-efficient transmission and routing protocols for wireless multiple-hop networks and spread-spectrum radios. In: EUROCOMM (2000)
10. Monks, J.P., Bharghavan, V., Hwu, W.M.W.: A power controlled multiple access protocol for wireless packet networks. In: INFORCOM (2001)
11. Suh, C., Ko, Y.-B., Kim, J.-H.: Enhanced Power Saving for IEEE 802.11 WLAN with Dynamic Slot Allocation. MSN (2005)
12. Karn, P.: MACA- a New Channel Access for Packet Radio. In: ARRL/CRRL Armature Radio 9th Computer Networking Conference (1990)
13. http://pcl.cs.ucla.edu/projects/glomosim

An Efficient Bi-Directional Flooding in Wireless Sensor Networks

Woosuk Cha[1], Eun-Mi Kim[2], Bae-Ho Lee[3], and Gihwan Cho[4]

[1] Research Center for Ubiquitous Information Appliances, Chonnam National University, Gwangju, South Korea
wscha@chonbuk.ac.kr
[2] Dept. of Computer Engineering Chonnam National University, Gwangju, South Korea
Koreaeunmi@yahoo.com
[3] Dept. of Electronics and Computer Engineering, Chonnam National University, Gwangju, South Korea
bhlee@chonnam.ac.kr
[4] Division of Electronic & Information Engineering, Chonbuk National University, Chonju, South Korea
ghcho@chonbuk.ac.kr

Abstract. Broadcast has been widely used in wireless sensor networks to disseminate information to all reachable nodes. The simplest way of realizing broadcast is via omnidirectional flooding. However, it generates an excessive amount of redundant traffic and exaggerates interference in the shared medium among the neighboring nodes. In order to mitigate these problems, this paper proposes an efficient flooding scheme with directional antennas, called BDF (Bi-Directional Flooding). The BDF scheme limits the propagation range of the packet forwarding to two directions over four, in order to minimize an overlapped area due to omnidirectional flooding. To analyze its performance, BDF has been compared with omnidirectional flooding and NEDF schemes.

1 Introduction

Wireless sensor networks typically refer to large ensembles of interconnected nodes that have processing and communication capabilities, and one or more sensing devices. The deployment of such networks is usually done in an ad hoc manner which implies that nodes need to be self-organized into a multi-hop wireless networks.

Broadcast has been widely used in wireless networks as a communication mean to disseminate information to all reachable nodes [1]. Especially, it is used to transfer control message in order to establish a basic path from source node to destination node in mobile ad hoc networks. The simplest way of realizing broadcast is via flooding. Upon receipt of a broadcast packet, a node simply sends it out in all directions.

Mobile nodes in mobile ad hoc networks or sensor networks usually share a single common channel. In these networks, synchronization among the nodes is very difficult, and global network topology information is usually unavailable to facilitate the scheduling of a broadcast. So, flooding is used for broadcasting in network layer.

J. Indulska et al. (Eds.): UIC 2007, LNCS 4611, pp. 454–463, 2007.

However, [2] shown that a great redundancy, contention and collision could be identified if the flooding is done blindly. These problems associated with flooding are referred as broadcast storm problem.

Directional antennas scheme may provide fewer links in wireless networks. Then, utilizing directional antennas includes the potential benefits such as range extension, better spatial reuse, multi-path diversity, interference suppression, capacity increase [11]. The use of directional antennas has not been widely explored in wireless networks. Recently, some works to mitigate MAC level contention and interference and to improve the performance of routing protocols has been reported, respectively, in [3–8] and in [9–11].

This paper proposes an efficient directional flooding scheme based on directional antennas, named Bi-Directional Flooding (BDF). In the proposed BDF scheme, the propagation range of the packet forwarded is limited to the maximum two directions over four, in order to minimize an overlapped area when the packet is transmitted omni-directionally. As a result, it is possible to reduce an amount of redundant traffic and collision. To analyze its performance, BDF has been compared with Omnidirectional Flooding (OF) [1] and NEDF schemes [13]. The simulation results indicate that BDF provides excellent performance in terms of redundancy and collision.

The paper consists as follows. Section 2 describes the existing works with directional antennas in wireless networks. Section 3 represents a model for directional antennas and BDF scheme in detail. Section 4 analyzes the result of simulation. Finally section 5 concludes of our work.

2 Related Work

An excellent taxonomy and comparison of existing broadcast schemes with an omni-directional antenna is discussed in [1]. Our paper makes mention of simple flooding only among the several protocols, because it does not require additional information such as the network topology, transmission distance, and neighbor knowledge. Simple flooding starts with a source node broadcasting a packet to all neighbors. Each of those neighbors in turn rebroadcast the packet exactly one time and this continues until all reachable network nodes have received the packet. It is referred as Omnidirectional Flooding (OF).

The directional flooding methods using directional antennas for broadcast is described in [12-13]. In on/off directional broadcast [12], similar to the omnidirectional broadcast scheme, when a node receives a broadcast packet that it has not seen before, it forwards it after a uniformly distributed Random Delay Time (RDT). If the same packet is received again for RDT, the node makes a note of all the beams where that packet arrived at, and marks them. Upon expiration of the delay timer, the node will forward the packet in only those directions other than those in which the packet arrived. Because it assumes that several directional antennas are available to transmit signals simultaneously, it does not suffer from a sweeping delay. At the same time, it does not offer any increase in the coverage area as well.

Similar to on/off directional broadcast, New Enhanced Directional Flooding (NEDF) [13] does not rebroadcast in the antenna beams where it received the broadcast packet. The difference between NEDF and on/off directional broadcast is that NEDF defines an order in which the transmission will be carried out. In NEDF, a node selects the beams which are vertically opposite to the beams where the node received the broadcast packet. And then, the beams which are adjacent to these vertically opposite beams are chosen. This continues till all the selected beams are covered. In on/off directional broadcast and NEDF, the basic idea is that a node forwards the packet in other all directions except direction where the packet is received. Therefore, these protocols still cause an excessive amount of redundant traffic and collisions.

Relay-node-based directional broadcast [12] assumes the one hop neighbor awareness. In relay-node-based directional broadcast, each node designates only one relay node in each direction on the basis of the received signal strength of *hello* packets in this particular direction. For the purpose of maintaining one-hop neighbor information, every node periodically transmits *hello* packets. The node whose *hello* packet is received with the weakest signal is selected to be the relay in that direction. Before forwarding, a node waits for a random delay and does not designate any relay node in directions where the packet arrives. Although relay-node-based directional broadcast using a single relay node cause very few packet transmissions, it may also lead to a partition in the network.

To overcome the drawbacks found in relay-node-based directional broadcast, the Probabilistic Relay Broadcasting (PRB) is proposed [13]. In PRB, each node records the received power of the hello packet from the farthest node in each beam, denoted as P_f. Whenever a node receives the packet, it retrieves its received power, say P_r, and calculates the ratio of P_f/P_r. It is the probability with which it will rebroadcast. In addition, the order of rebroadcast in PRB will be similar to the one proposed in NEDF. Both relay-node-based directional broadcast and PRR require additional means to measure signal strength. They still have the network partition problem.

3 Bi-Directional Flooding (BDF) Scheme

The BDF aims to mitigate broadcast storm problem [2] and supports directional flooding using directional antennas and Directional Broadcast Packet (DBP) table.

3.1 Antenna Model

To begin with, it is assumed that each node has a transceiver and shares a common wireless channel. As shown in Fig. 1(a), the directional antennas consist of four

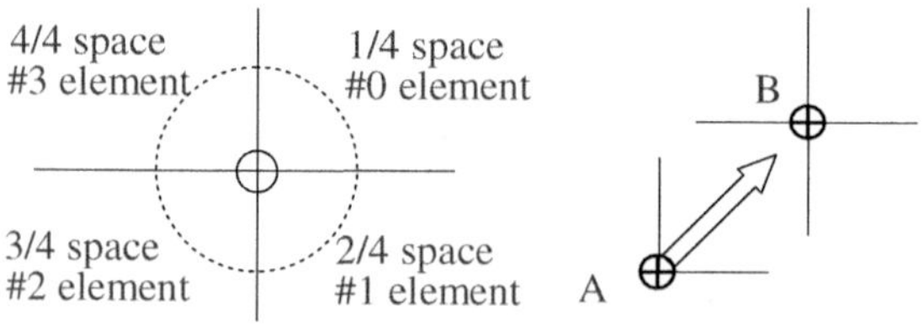

(a) antenna modeling (b) directional flooding

Fig. 1. Antenna model

antennas and each antenna is numbered to indicate the direction in which the signal is received and transmitted. Each antenna has 90 degrees beam width and conical radiation pattern and does not overlapped with the other ones. Consequently four antennas cover for full angle of 360 degrees. In the Fig. 1(b), an example of directional flooding is presented, that is, node *A* communicates with node *B* through #0 and #2 antennas respectively.

3.2 Single Directional Flooding (SDF) Scheme

Using only one direction may be the best efficient directional flooding method to mitigate the broadcast storm problem. Let's call it as Single Directional Flooding (SDF). Fig. 2(a) shows the basic SDF operation. For example, in Fig. 2(a), if node *S* sends a broadcast packet in #0 direction, node *R* will receive it in #2 direction. In SDF, node *R* forwards it in only #0 direction which opposite to the one where the packet was received. In case of on/off directional broadcast in [12]. Node *R* forwards it in three directions except #2 direction in which was received the packet.

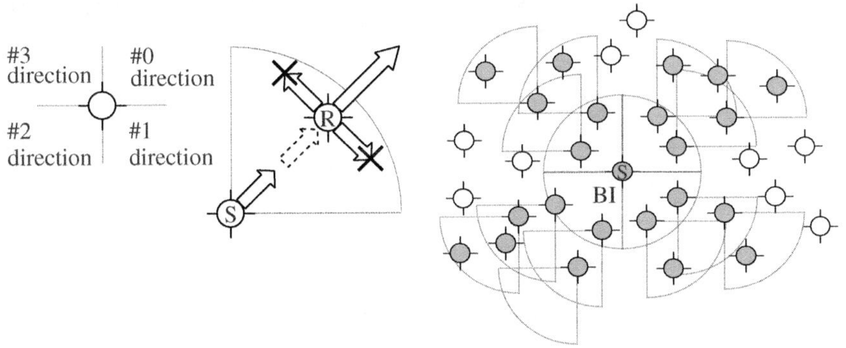

(a) the basic operation (b) the broadcast example

Fig. 2. The SDF operation

However, SDF has a critical problem to lead a partition in the network as depicted in Fig. 2(b). Node *S* (BI: Broadcast Initiator) transmits it in #0, #1, #2, and #3 directions in turn. The intermediated nodes forward it in the direction which opposite to the one where it was received. As a result of the flooding in SDF, the partition of the networks may be caused. In Fig. 2(b), a shadow circles indicate the nodes to receive the packet, but on the other hand, a white circles present the nodes not to receive it.

3.3 BDF Scheme

The basic idea of BDF is that the propagation range of packet forwarding is limited to the maximum two directions over four, in order to reduce the overlapped area due to omni-directional broadcasting. One is the direction which is opposite to the one where the packet was received, and the other is its left side direction. This may solves the network partition problem occurred in SDF.

Fig. 3(a) shows the basic operation of BDF. In Fig. 3 (a), node *S* forwards the broadcast packet in #0 direction. And then, node *R* receives the packet in #2 direction and forwards it in #0 (the opposite direction) and #3 (the left side direction) direction in turn. This process will continue till all nodes in the networks receive it repeatedly. Similar to OF scheme [1], whenever a node receives a broadcast packet that it has not seen before, it forwards the packet after updating DBP table. Fig. 3(b) depicts the broadcast example in BDF. It is possible for node *S* to send the broadcast packet in #0, #1, #2, and #3 directions in turn. However, for simplicity, it is assumed that node *S* sends the broadcast packet only in #0 direction. In Fig. 3(b), a bold dotted line indicates the direction which is opposite to the one where the packet was received. A bold solid line depicts its left side direction.

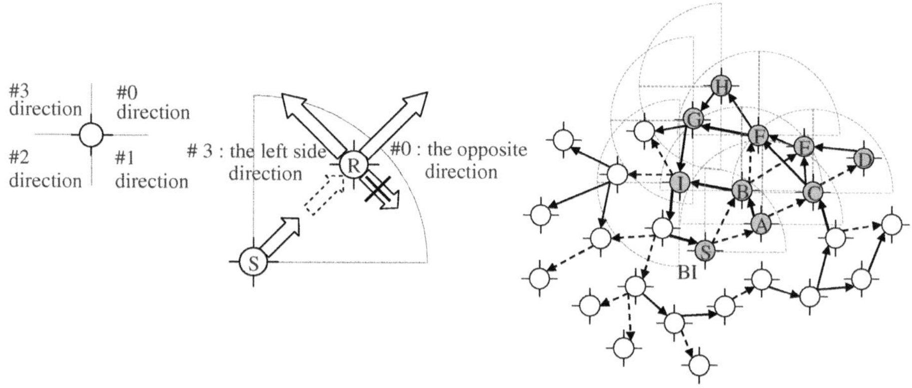

(a) the basic operation (b) the broadcast example

Fig. 3. The BDF operation

BDF makes use of DBP table to avoid forwarding of the same packet which was received before repeatedly. DBP table maintains the information of the packets which have forwarded for a period. Table 1 shows the DBP table structure of node *B* in Fig. 3(b).

Table 1. DBP table

PID	*RD*	*FD*
PID(S)	{#1, #2}	{#0, #3}
:	:	:

- *PID* (Packet ID): the ID of packet which a node receives and forwards
- *RD* (Receiving Direction): the direction where a node receives the packet of the same PID (e.g., *PID(S)*)
- *FD* (Forwarding Direction): the direction where a node forwards the packet of the same PID (e.g., *PID(S)*).

Before forwarding the received packet according to BDF, a node has to confirm the redundancy of packet by using DBP table. To do so, the below algorithm is performed. The following symbols are used.

- *C(RD_DBP):* the contents of RD field in DBP table
- *C(FD_DBP)*: the contents of FD field in DBP table
- *C(PID_DBP):* the contents of PID field in DBP table
- *P(PID(S))*: the packet which node S (broadcast initiator) broadcasts
- *fd*: the direction where a node forwards the packet
- *rd*: the direction where a node receives the packet

```
Procedure DIRECTIONAL_FLOODING()
input: P(PID(S))
BEGIN
 IF C(PID_DBP) ∋ PID(S) THEN
  IF C(RD__DBP) ∋ rd THEN
    Discard P(PID(S))
  ELSE
    add rd to C(RD__DBP)
    FD1 := (rd + 2) %4
    FD2 := FD1 -1
    IF FD2 < 0 THEN
      FD2 := 3
    ENDIF
    IF (C(FD__DBP) ∋ FD1) and (C(FD__DBP) ∋ FD2) THEN
      Discard P(PID(S))
    ELSE IF (C(FD__DBP) ∋ FD1) THEN
           forward P(PID(S)) in FD2
           add FD2 to C(FD__DBP)
         ELSE IF C(FD__DBP) ∋ FD2 THEN
                forward P(PID(S)) in FD1
                add FD1 to C(FD__DBP)
              ELSE
                forward P(PID(S)) in both FD1 and FD2
                add both FD1 and FD2 to C(FD__DBP)
              ENDIF
         ENDIF
```

```
        ENDIF
      ENDIF
    ELSE
      FD1 := (rd + 2) %4
      FD2 := FD1 -1
      IF FD2 < 0 THEN
        FD2 := 3
      ENDIF
      add PID(S) to C(PID__DBP)
      add rd to C(RD__DBP)
      add both FD1and FD2 to C(FD__DBP)
      forward P(PID(S)) in both FD1 and FD2
    ENDIF
  END
```

4 Performance Analysis

The simulation has been implemented in NS-2 (version 2.28) [14]. The proposed BDF scheme has been analyzed for its performance with OF [1] and NEDF [13].

4.1 Simulation Model

The same parameters presented in table 2 are utilized to evaluate the performance of OF, NEDF, and BDF. Transmission range of both an omnidirectional antenna and

Table 2. Simulation parameters for analyzing the efficiency

Parameters	Values
Simulation area	1000 × 1000 m
Simulation time	50 seconds
Transmission range	Omnidirectional antenna : 150 m Directional antennas : 200 m
Density (the number of nodes)	50 ~ 140
Antennas model	4 beam directional antennas
MAC Protocol	IEEE 802.11
Packet size	512 bytes
Bandwidth	1 Mbps
RDT (Random Delay Time)	10 ms

directional antennas are 150m and 200m respectively. The nodes have placed in random locations in a square area of size 1000m × 1000m. If the 40 and less nodes are deployed in the network of the simulation, some nodes may be out of transmission range among nodes. Therefore, the nodes from 50 to 140 are randomly deployed over the networks.

4.2 Performance Evaluation

The simulation results have been analyzed in terms of following three performance criteria:

- The rate of packet redundancy: the frequency rate that a node receives the same packets repeatedly
- Collision rate: the rate that the collision occurs in the link layer
- Broadcast completion delay: the delay time between the initial simulation time when the broadcast originator generates the broadcast packet and the final simulation time when all of the nodes in the networks receive it

Fig. 4 indicates the redundancy rate according to the network topology respectively. It is measured as dividing the number of the whole redundant packets by the number of the whole receiving packet except the packets discarded due to collision. From Fig. 5, we could have confirmed how many packets are unnecessarily flooded. In addition, we have confirmed that the redundancy rate of OF, NEDF, and BDF has slightly increased in proportion to increasing of nodes.

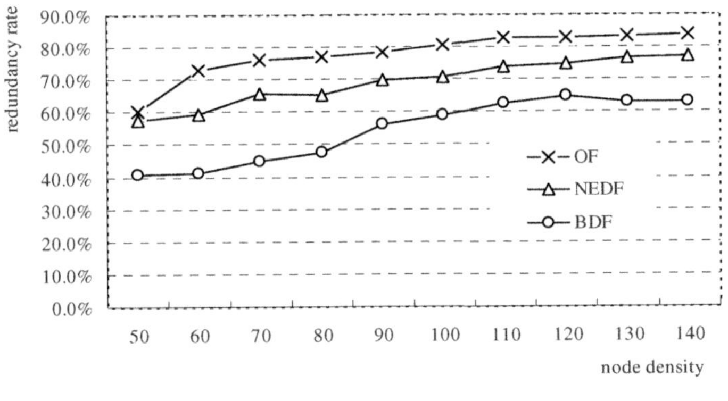

Fig. 4. Redundancy rate in each node

Fig. 5 indicates the collision rate according to the increase of nodes respectively. It is measured as dividing the number of collided packets by the sum of packets transmitted in the link. OF scheme is based on an omni-directional antenna, but on the other hand, other schemes are based on directional antennas. Therefore, it is natural that the collision number of OF scheme is more than those of other schemes. In additional, the simulation result shows that the collision rate is proportional to the increase of nodes.

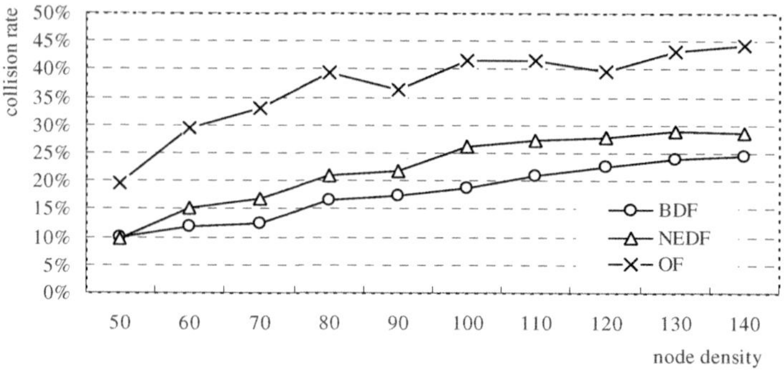

Fig. 5. Collision rate

Fig. 6 shows the broadcast completion delay time which is needed for the broadcast packet initiated from broadcast initiator to be flooded to all of nodes deployed in the networks successfully. The hop count means the number of nodes which the broadcast packet has passed when every node in the networks has received it successfully. It is affected by the transmission range of packet. As described in table 2, the simulation applies 150m and 200m to the transmission range of an omni-directional antenna and that of directional antennas respectively. Therefore, it is possible to infer that the hop count of BDF is less than that OF. The simulation result shows that the average of broadcast completion delay in OF and BDF are about 47.5ms and 21.3ms respectively, and that of NEDF is 88.2ms.

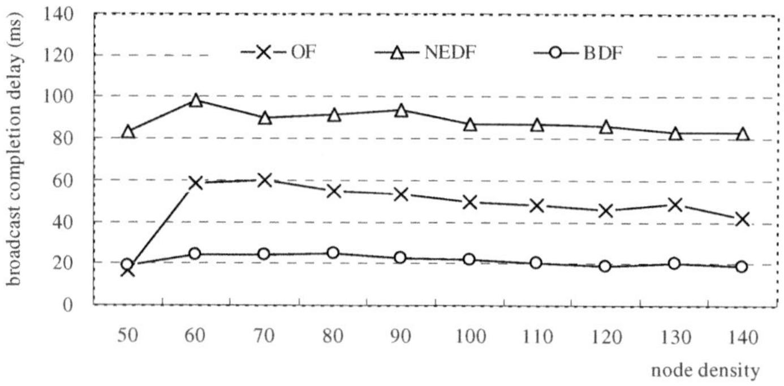

Fig. 6. Broadcast completion delay time

5 Conclusion

The main problems with broadcast include a large amount of traffic redundancy, contention, and collision as called the broadcast storm problem, which typically cause unproductive bandwidth congestion as well as inefficient use of node resources.

This paper has proposed the BDF scheme with directional antennas to mitigate the broadcast storm problem. The basic idea of BDF is limiting the propagation range of packet forwarding to two directions over four, in order to reduce an overlapped area due to omnidirectional flooding. To analyze its performance, BDF is compared with OF and NEDF schemes. The results indicate that BDF provides excellent performance in terms of redundancy, collision, and broadcast completion delay.

References

1. Williams, B., Camp, T.: Comparison of Broadcasting Techniques for Mobile Ad Hoc Networks. In: Proc. of ACM Mobile Ad Hoc Networking and Computing, pp. 194–205 (2002)
2. Tseng, Y., NI, S., Chen, Y., Sheu, J.: The Broadcast Storm Problem in a Mobile Ad Hoc Networks. Wireless Networks 8, 153–167 (2002)
3. Nasipuri, A., Ye, S., You, J., Hiromoto, R.E.: A MAC Protocol for Mobile Ad Hoc Networks Using Directional Antennas. In: Proc. of WCNC 2000, pp. 1214–1219 (2000)
4. Takai, M., Martin, J., Bagrodia, R., Ren, A.: Directional Virtual Carrier Sensing for Directional Antennas in Mobile Ad Hoc Networks. In: Proc. of ACM MobiHoc, pp. 183–193. ACM Press, New York (2002)
5. Ramanathan, R.: On the Performance of Ad Hoc Networks with Beamforming Antennas. In: Proc. of MobiHoc, pp. 95–105 (2001)
6. Choudhury, R.R., Yang, X., Ramanathan, R., Vaidya, N.H.: Using Directional Antennas for Medium Access Control in Ad Hoc Networks. In: Proc. of Mobicom, pp. 59–70 (2002)
7. Bandyopadhyay, S., Hausike, K., Horisawa, S., Tawara, S.: An Adaptive MAC and Directional Routing Protocol for Ad Hoc Wireless Networks Using ESPAR Antenna. In: Proc. of ACM MobiHoc, ACM Press, New York (2001)
8. Ko, Y.B., Shankarkumar, V., Vaidya, N.H.: Medium Access Control Protocols Using Directional Antennas in Ad Hoc Networks. In: Proc. of IEEE INFOCOM, pp. 13–21 (2000)
9. Nasipuri, A., Mandava, J., Manchala, H., Hiromoto, R.E.: On-Demand Routing Using Directional Antennas in Mobile Ad Hoc Networks. In: Proc. of ICCCN, pp. 535–541 (2000)
10. Choudhury, R.R., Vaidya, N.H.: On Ad Hoc Routing Using Directional Antennas. In: Proc. of ICSS (2002)
11. Nandyopadhyay, S., Hausike, K., Horisawa, S., Tawara, S.: An Adaptive MAC and Directional Routing Protocol for Ad Hoc Wireless Networks Using ESPAR Antenna. In: Proc. of ACM MobiHoc, ACM Press, New York (2001)
12. Hu, C., Hong, Y., Hou, J.: On Mitigating the Broadcast Storm Problem with Directional Antennas. In: Proc. of ICC, pp. 104–110 (2003)
13. Joshi, T., Cordeiro, C., Vogety, S., Yin, J., Gossain, H., Agrawal, D.P.: Broadcasting over switched single beam antennas. In: Proc. of IEEE ICON (2004)
14. NS-2 Network Simulator.: http://www.isi,edu/nsnam/ns

Maximizing Network Lifetime Under Reliability Constraints Using a Cross–Layer Design in Dense Wireless Sensor Networks

Shan Guo Quan and Young Yong Kim

Department of Electrical and Electronic Engineering, Yonsei University, 134 Shinchon-dong, Seodaemun-gu, Seoul 120-749, Korea
{sgquan,y2k}@yonsei.ac.kr

Abstract. Recent experimental studies have shown that radio links between low-power devices are extremely unreliable. In particular, the instability and unpredictability of low-power radio links in dense wireless sensor networks(WSNs) makes it extremely challenging to improve energy efficiency for reliable communication. In this paper, we propose a novel energy efficient cross-layer based scheme for WSNs. We consider the joint design of the physical(PHY)layer and the medium access control(MAC) to maximize network lifetime under reliability constraints. Our approach consists of opportunistic transmission power control and cell-based efficient time slot assignment. Our approach can support more reliable and energy-efficient data transmission in dense cluster-based WSNs. Performance evaluation results show that our cross–layer based approach outperforms traditional layered protocols. Furthermore, our approach is more energy efficient and can maximize the network lifetime. The network lifetime in our approach has more than doubled compared with the current scheme.

1 Introduction

Many specific applications which are composed of a large number of energy-limited sensor devices continue to appear in diverse areas, such as monitoring or controlling some environment. These applications require an efficient way to conserve the energy of the sensor nodes. Improving energy efficiency can maximize the network lifetime. Designing an energy-efficient way to maximize network lifetime requires consideration of the following major causes of energy dissipation in WSNs[1].

1. Idle listening wastes considerable energy. The node must keep the radio turned on at all times because it does not know when it will receive incoming packets.
2. Collisions occur because some nodes transmit packets simultaneously in the interference range. When that happens, packets are destroyed and require retransmission, which consumes more energy.

J. Indulska et al. (Eds.): UIC 2007, LNCS 4611, pp. 464–474, 2007.

3. The control packet overheads consume energy for transmitting, receiving and listening to the control packets.
4. Overhearing refers to a condition in which a node may receive packets destined for other nodes.
5. Unnecessarily high transmitting power not only results in high power consumption but may also induce more interference at other nodes.

In this respect, TDMA-based schemes can be viewed as a natural choice to conserve energy for WSNs because sensor nodes can be turned off during idle listening times. They can also prevent overhearing problems and collisions under high contention. They are particularly useful to protect the high transmission power within a specified slot from interference with other nodes. TDMA normally requires nodes to form clusters analogous to the cellular communication systems[2,3,4,5,6,7]. One node within a cluster is selected as the cluster-head(CH) and acts as the base station. Even though this contention-free scheme in intra-cluster communication (e.g., LEACH[3]) can reduce energy consumption, it is not very adaptable in dense WSNs because they have too many sensor nodes. By intuition, the CH consumes more energy to receive data from a large number of member nodes in the cluster. Therefore, if some active sensors are within a single coverage area, an excessive amount of energy will be wasted because of redundant active sensors. Then, excessive packet collisions may occur as a result of sensors sending packets simultaneously in the presence of certain triggering events. Hence, it is neither necessary nor desirable for all nodes to be in the active mode simultaneously[8]. To support more reliable data transmission, it is important to minimize the number of nodes participating in data transmission while conserving network coverage.

On a different note, recent empirical studies have demonstrated that the radio links between low-power devices are extremely unreliable. To improve energy efficiency for reliable communication using unreliable radio links, *D.Son et al.* experimentally investigated the impact of variable transmission power on link quality and introduced a variable power link quality control technique with blacklisting for reliable communication over WSNs[9]. Nonetheless, that technique can't guarantee coverage because of unconditional weak link removal. In [10], the authors demonstrated that dynamic transmission power control consumes less energy than fixed transmission power control. However, that incurs high complexity for power control in dense networks. In [11], the authors used a closed-loop transmission power control, but it is rather hopeless in dense cluster-based WSNs because the CH will transmit or receive huge numbers of power control signals, which critically damage the CH. However, a cross-layer interaction can improve system performance by enabling adaptation of the networking protocol[12]. In this paper, we present a novel energy-efficient cross-layer based approach for dense cluster-based WSNs. Due to unreliable links in dense WSNs, one of the most important factors for providing high performance and energy efficiency is radio link quality. We propose a novel link quality aware protocol. Our approach maximizes cluster lifetime though the use of redundant sensors that are periodically sent to sleep. Hence, it can improve energy efficiency and prolong the overall network lifetime as well.

The remainder of this paper is organized as follows: In section II, we introduce our energy efficient cross-layer based approach. In section III, we provide performance evaluations and analysis. Finally, we conclude in section IV.

2 Proposed Approach

2.1 System Model

We assume that a large number of homogeneous, stationary, and power-constrained sensor nodes spread randomly(with a uniform distribution) in a two-dimensional square sensing field. The network coverage is divided into a virtual grid[13], and the entire network coverage is divided into non-overlapping same-sized cluster structures, as shown in Fig.1.

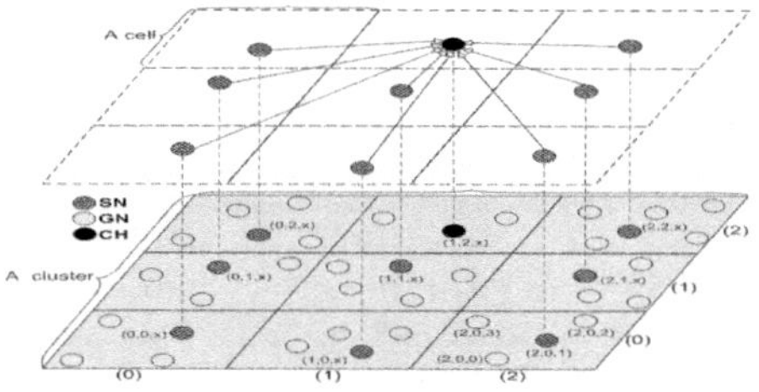

Fig. 1. Network coverage divide into clusters and cells by a virtual grid

There is one CH per cluster. Each CH must be rotated within each cluster. The CH gathers and aggregates the sensed data from its member nodes. Often voronoi diagrams are used to describe most of the clusters, but that is impractical in the real world. Instead, we use square shapes, which are simple to construct in the real world. To simplify the analysis, we assume that each cluster divides into the nine cells shown in Fig.1; each cell has at least one node, and each cell can be covered by a sensor node. Our approach rotates the CH to distribute energy consumption by using the remaining power level. Deployed sensor nodes have to guarantee that every point of the area is covered by at least one sensor node. Only selected one node(SN)in each cell is active while the non-selected nodes(GNs) stay in sleep mode to reduce the number of redundant active nodes in each cell. In particular, only one CH is active in the cell in which it is included. Each sensor in the cell is distinguished using its cell address(x, y, n)[14], where x and y are the coordinates of the cell and n is the nth node in the cell. Nodes belong to only one cell, even if they are the boundary of two cells or the point of intersection of several cells. The deployed sensor nodes have identical transmission ranges and identical sensing ranges, R_t and R_s, respectively. Furthermore, the relationship between the two parameters is $R_t \geq 2R_s$[8]. We define R_t as equal to the diagonal line of a cluster and R_s as equal to the diagonal line of a cell. We define the network lifetime as the time interval from the point that the sensor network starts its operation until the point that all nodes within a cell lose the necessary connectivity and sensing coverage because of exhausted energy. The basic idea of our approach is cross-layer interaction. That is, if the MAC layer receives the information about link quality from the PHY layer, then the cell-based time slot assignment implements on the MAC layer. A few selected nodes also do opportunistic transmission power control at the PHY layer. We will discuss this in more detail in subsection 2.3.

2.2 Wireless Radio Channel

Most of the channel path loss models in the literature are isotropic, which means that path loss is same in different directions if the distance from transmitter to receiver is same. However, empirical studies have shown a common and non-negligible phenomenon of radio irregularity in WSNs[15]. The radio signal from transmitter to receiver has different path losses in different directions even if receivers are the same distance from the transmitter. The variance in received signal strength continues with incremental changes in the propagation direction from a transmitter. The radio irregularity model(RIM)[15] approximates the real radio signals. Our approach refers to the RIM model as Eq.1.

$$\begin{aligned} RxPower &= TxPower - DOI_{pathloss} + Fading \\ &\quad where\ DOI_{pathloss} = pathloss \times k_i \end{aligned} \tag{1}$$

where k_i is a coefficient representing the difference in path loss in different directions. The degree of irregularity(DOI)is the maximum path-loss percentage variation per unit degree change in the direction of radio propagation. The coefficient k_i is the ith degree coefficient, which is calculated by Eq.2. It can generate $360k_i$ values for different directions.

$$k_i = \begin{cases} k_{i-1} \pm R \times DOI & \text{if } \ 0 < i < 360, i \in N \\ & \text{where} \quad k_0 - k_{359} \le DOI \\ 1 & \text{if } \ i = 0 \end{cases} \tag{2}$$

In the equation, R is a Weibull distribution, it has a probability density function defined by the Eq.3.

$$f_x = \begin{cases} (a/b)^a \times x^{a-1} \times e^{-(\frac{x}{b})^a} & \text{if } \ x \ge 0 \\ 0 & \text{if } \ x < 0 \end{cases} \tag{3}$$

We used the set of parameters with the highest likelihood value[15], where the shape parameter is $a = 0.58$ and the scale parameter is $b = 0.17$. For the direction that has an actual number of angles from the starting direction, the k_i value is based on the values of the two adjacent directions, which have integer angles from the starting direction.

$$\begin{aligned} k_i &= k_s + (i - s) \times (k_t - k_s) \\ &\quad where\ s = \lfloor i \rfloor, \lceil i \rceil\ mod\ 360, 0 < i < 360, i \notin N \end{aligned} \tag{4}$$

The RIM model demonstrates that the CH is dynamically changed with rotation, which means that path-loss from a member node to the CH will change because the direction changes when the CH changes every round. In addition, other studies have revealed the existence of distinct reception regions in wireless links: connection, transition, and disconnection[16]. The transitional region is often quite significant in size and is generally characterized by high variance in reception rates and asymmetric connectivity. Particularly in dense WSNs, a large number of links in the network(even higher than 50%) can be unreliable due to the transitional region[16]. We carried out an experiment to observe the relationship between transmission power level and packet reception rate(PRR), the transition region when changing the transmission power levels($0dBm - 10dBm$), and the distance from the transmitter to the receiver($0 - 50m$).

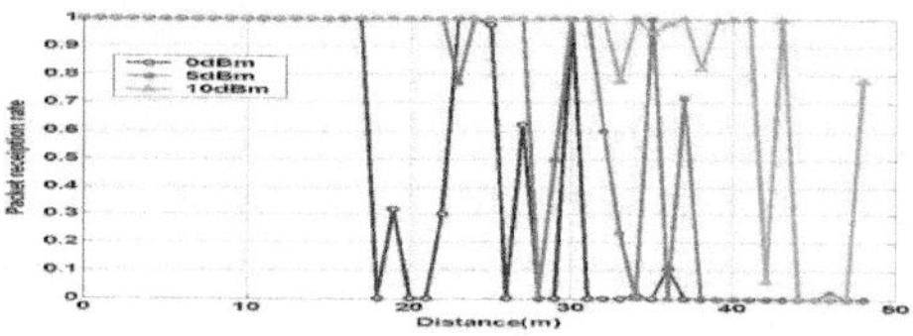

Fig. 2. Transition region variance with different power levels

Fig.2 shows plots of the packet reception rate and transition region at the different transmission power levels for comparison. We found the starting point of the transition region moves toward long distances when the transmission power level is high. Based on both of the radio channel characteristics, we propose a new radio channel model made by combining forms of radio irregularity and the transition region because they can coexist at a specific transmission power level.

2.3 Energy Efficient Cross-Layer Protocol

Most research work does not consider time slot allocation, which can also be used to improve energy efficiency in WSNs. We propose an efficient time slot allocation to more effectively support intra-cluster communication, but traditional TDMA has some disadvantages that limit its use in WSNs[17]. In particular, member nodes send data to the CH at most once per frame during their allocated transmission time slot when clustering and TDMA are combined. The duration of each slot in which a node transmits data is constant; that is, every time slot is uniform size. In addition, TDMA protocols have limited scalability and adaptivity to changes in the numbers of sensor nodes. Developing an efficient schedule with frequent topology changes is very hard. Furthermore, these problems can be more serious in dense WSNs because of the large number of member nodes. To overcome these weaknesses, our approach uses a link quality parameter, that is, PRR values to classify and select links because the different links have considerably different packet reception properties[18]. We refer to the link layer model derived in [16] to estimate the PRR value for each link, as in Eq.5 where D is the transmitter-receiver distance, $\gamma(D)$ is signal to noise ratio calculated using the wireless radio model described in subsection 2.2, ψ is the encoding ratio, and f is the frame length.

$$PRR(D) = \left(1 - \frac{1}{2}\exp^{-\frac{\gamma(D)}{2}\frac{1}{0.64}}\right)^{\psi 8 f} \tag{5}$$

We use the PRR value in the CH setup phase. The CH broadcasts an advertisement message, and each member node transmits feedback to it. The feedback includes the node cell address and the CH's cell address. Then, the CH can collect overall PRR values from the feedback information and classify them according to cell address. Based on the collected information, the CH selects the maximum PRR value as in Eq.6 for each cell except its own because only the CH turns on to reduce redundant active nodes in the cell.

$$\underset{i,j=0, i \notin C}{\arg\max^{N_i}} (\mathrm{PRR}_{\mathrm{i,j}}) \tag{6}$$

Where i is i^{th} cell in a cluster and j is j^{th} node in a cell and N_i is the total number of nodes in i^{th} cell. C expresses a cell that contains a CH. If a node has the highest PRR(PRR_{max}) and satisfies the requirement $PRR_{max} \geq PRR_{threshold}$ where $PRR_{threshold}$ is larger than zero, then the CH records the node's cell address. If more than one node has the same PRR_{max} value, the CH randomly selects one of them to distribute energy dissipation and records its cell address. On the contrary, when $PRR_{max} < PRR_{threshold}$, we use a heuristic scheme. That is, the candidate node with the second highest PRR in the same cell(PRR_{next}) to get a multipath diversity gain[19]. In other words, if $PRR = 1 - (1 - PRR_{max})(1 - PRR_{next}) > PRR_{threshold}$, the CH also records their cell addresses. In the opposite case, the PRR value obtained through the multipath is less than $PRR_{threshold}$, the CH chooses only the node with PRR_{max} and records its cell address even if several nodes have the same PRR_{max} value. The reason for choosing only two PRR values in the scheme is to prevent energy consumption because of too many nodes in the multipath. Using the information about the selected nodes, the CH creates a TDMA schedule, and the schedule is multicast to the group of nodes that record their cell addresses in the CH. The SNs will be in active mode, and the GNs in each cell turn off until the start of the next round. In that way, our scheme not only reduces redundancy among the active nodes in each cell but also improve energy efficiency and prolongs WSN lifetime. Moreover, the scheme of time slot allocation depends only on the number of cells in each cluster. Therefore it can conquer the limited scalability and adaptivity of TDMA caused by changes in the number of nodes. The number of nodes given time slots is quite smaller than the total number of nodes in dense WSNs. According to time-slot assignment, the selected member nodes begin to transmit their sensed data to the CH. Since the energy consumption of each path to CH depends on the transmission power, our approach implements opportunistic transmission power control during allocated time slots without any influence on neighbor nodes because of separated time slots, as described in Fig.3.

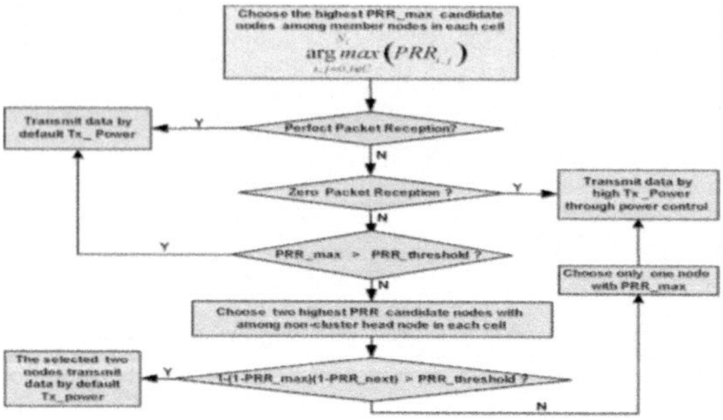

Fig. 3. The procedure of opportunistic transmission power control scheme

3 Performance Evaluation

We have developed a simulator to evaluate the performance of our proposed algorithm. Our simulation was conducted with discrete event simulation using C++. We compare the performance of our scheme with the conventional TDMA-based intra-cluster communication schemes. For the performance comparison, there are several protocols[2][4,5,6,7], which have same TDMA-based intra-cluster communication scheme as LEACH[3]. Therefore, our study concentrates on intra-cluster communication because the network coverage divides into same-sized clusters and runs the same operations simultaneously. For a fair comparison, we assume that CHs and member nodes are in the same position for both schemes except the different intra-cluster communication schemes. In other words, our proposed scheme is cross-layer based, but other protocols follow the traditional layer based scheme. Hereinafter, we describe the intra-communication scheme of LEACH as *old scheme*. We assume that every member node always has a constant packet to send, and our simulation time is the same as the network lifetime, as mentioned above. The simulation setup is summarized in Table.1.

Data aggregation in the CH refers to [20] and is defined as a simple data aggregation formulation in Eq.7, where m_{child} is the constant packet length

Table 1. Simulation setup

Simulation parameter	Value
Cluster size	45×45
Battery power	3.00(J)
Default transmission power	0dBm
Cell side	15m
Cluster side	45m
Time slot	20ms
Data aggregation ratio	0.5
Packet size	50 bytes
$PRR_{threshold}$	0.6

transmitted to the CH from each member, p is the probability that the messages are aggregated, and c is the number of members for each CH.

$$m_{agg} = m_{child}(c - \lceil pc \rceil + 1) \tag{7}$$

In our simulation, we verified two factors that represent energy efficiency and network lifetime. One is the number of dead nodes; the other is the value of average energy consumption per node, as in Eq.8. Where $\overline{E}_c$ is the average energy consumption per node,

$$\overline{E}_c = \frac{\sum\limits_{i,j=0,i \neq C}^{N_i} (E^c_{i,j})}{N} \tag{8}$$

if the value of $\overline{E}_c$ is low, the network lifetime will be extended. N is the total number of nodes deployed in a cluster, and $E^c_{i,j}$ is the energy consumption of the jth node in the ith cell. $E^c_{i,j}$ separates two types of values. That is, one value is based on default transmission power without power control during the specified time slot; the other value is based on the transmission power control scheme in [3]. We first simulated a scenario in which a cluster has 100 nodes in its coverage area. Fig.4(a) shows that our approach consumes much less energy than the old scheme. In this paper, average energy consumption per node equals the sum of the total of energy consumption divided by the total number of nodes in a cluster. The old scheme's network lifetime is 60 rounds, but our approach can prolong it to 130 rounds. That means that our approach has more than double the old scheme's network lifetime in the same high-density WSNs. Therefore, Fig.4(b) shows the number of dead nodes during the network lifetime. Our approach has fewer nodes dead than the old scheme.

In Fig.5(a) and Fig.5(b), node density d is the number of nodes divided by the square area. For example, if the number of nodes is 100, then $d = 100/(45 \times 45)$. We compared the results when the number of nodes was 100, 200 and 400. Fig.5(a) shows that the proposed scheme can obtain better energy efficiency than the old scheme. The old scheme tends to have similar energy efficiency regardless of the

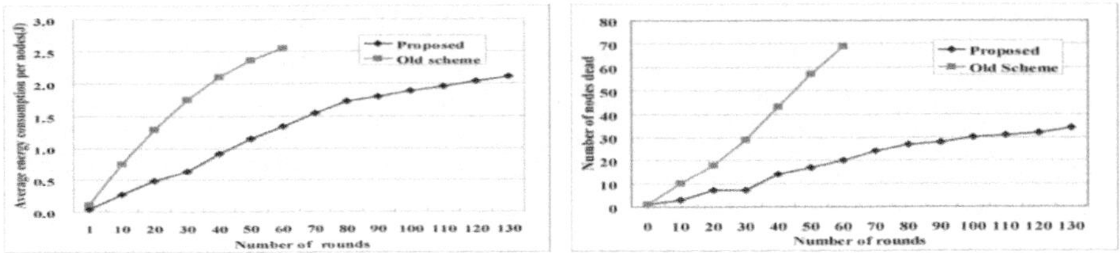

(a) The avg. energy consumption per node (b) The number of dead nodes

Fig. 4. The comparison of the average energy consumption per node and the number of dead nodes between the old scheme and the proposed scheme when a cluster has 100 nodes

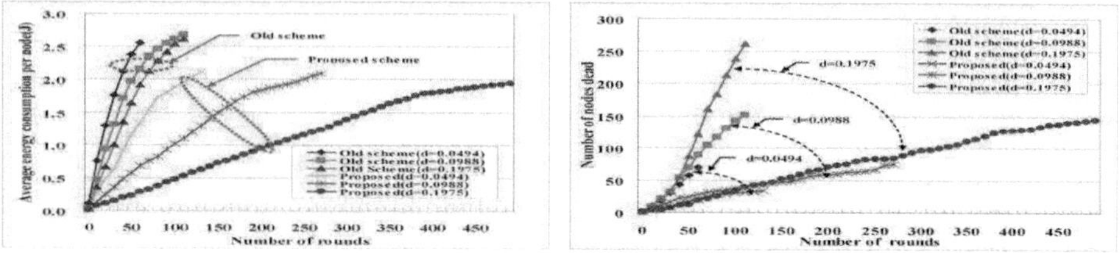

(a) Average energy consumption per node (b) Number of dead nodes

Fig. 5. A comparison of the average energy consumption per node and the number of dead nodes at different node densities

incremental changes of node density. However, our scheme can obtain high energy efficiency in a high density environment. That implies that our scheme does will work well in the high-density WSNs because they provide more opportunities to select CHs from high remaining power nodes during CH rotation.

Fig.5(b) shows that our scheme can reduce the number of dead nodes. Fig.5(b) also shows that the performance gap between the old scheme and our approach can be large as node density increases. As density increases, too many sensor nodes try to connect to the CH. When that happens, energy consumption increases, and then many nodes are exhausted their own energy. However, our scheme gets more chances to rotate with high energy levels for a long time using redundant nodes. Our approach also needs to satisfy the PRR requirements. For the old scheme, we define the average PRR value as expressed in Eq.9. Because all member nodes transmit data to the CH, we then calculate the average value to compare it with our approach.

$$\overline{PRR_i} = \frac{\sum_{i,j=0, i \neq C}^{N_i} PRR_{i,j}}{N_i} \quad (9)$$

Where $\overline{PRR_i}$ is the average PRR value for the ith cell, except the cell including the CH; $PRR_{i,j}$ is the instant value of PRR for the jth nodes in the ith cell, and N_i is the total number of nodes in the ith cell. In Fig.6(a) and Fig.6(b), OCH is expressed as the 'Cell address including the CH for old scheme' and NCH is expressed as the 'Cell address including CH for the proposed scheme'. R expresses the number of rounds. For the simulation, we only selected two sets of arbitrary number of rounds because of the limited space: R=10,30,50 and R=20,40,60, respectively.

Fig.6(a) and Fig.6(b) show that both schemes can obtain larger the PRR values than $PRR_{threshold}$. Furthermore, the old scheme has some PRR variance according to the increment of the number of rounds because the PRR values of the old scheme uses an average value, whereas our scheme only use the maximum value. The average PRR value fluctuations in old scheme imply that some nodes

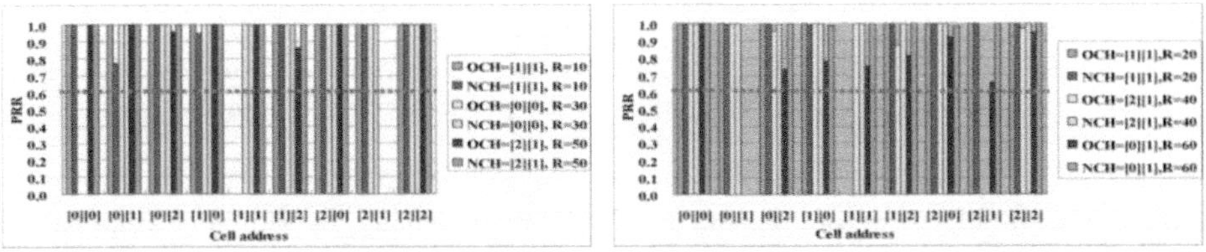

(a) The number of rounds=10,30,50 (b) The number of rounds=20,40,60

Fig. 6. The comparison of PRR values between old scheme and proposed scheme

possibly have less the PRR values than $PRR_{threshold}$ if $PRR_{threshold}$ is very high. The results mean that our approach is more reliable and stable than the old scheme.

4 Conclusion

In this paper, we proposed an energy-efficient cross-layer approach for dense WSNs. Our scheme considers the joint design of opportunistic power controls in the PHY layer and efficient time slot allocation in the MAC layer. Simulation results show that our design leads to a more energy-efficient model and provides better system performance than the existing protocol. Moreover, we found that the proposed approach is very suitable to dense WSNs. Our approach reduces the number of nodes with high transmission power control and the number of redundant active nodes in each cell. If our approach is applied to heterogeneous CH node based WSNs, performance will be better than with the current homogeneous status because the CH will have has enough resources to perform its functions. However, the proposed approach can not guarantee fault-tolerance because there are more centralized heterogeneous functions. In future work, we will calculate optimal transmission power levels correlated to node density.

Acknowledgement

This research was supported by the MIC(Ministry of Information and Communication), Korea, under the ITRC(Information Technology Research Center) support program supervised by the IITA(Institute of Information Technology Assessment)(IITA-2006-C1090-0603-0038).

References

1. Sinchitiu, M.L.: Cross-layer scheduling for power effciency in wireless sensor networks. In: IEEE INFOCOMM'04, IEEE Computer Society Press, Los Alamitos (2004)

2. Li, J., Lazarou, G.Y.: A bit-map-assisted energy-efficient mac scheme for wireless sensor networks. In: ACM IPSN'04, ACM Press, New York (2004)
3. Heinzelman, W., Chandrakasan, A.P., Balakrishnan, H.: An application-specific protocol architecture for wireless microsensor netowrks. IEEE Transaction on Wireless Communications 1, 660–670 (2002)
4. Younis, O., Fahmy, S.: Heed:a hybrid, energy efficient, distributed clustering approach for ad-hoc sensor networks. IEEE Transactions on Mobile Computing 3, 366–379 (2004)
5. Pei, G., Chien, C.: Low power tdma in large wireless sensor networks. In: IEEE MILCOM'01, pp. 347–351. IEEE Computer Society Press, Los Alamitos (2001)
6. Chen, X., Niu, Z.: A randomly delayed clustering method for wireless sensor networks. In: IEEE ICC'06, IEEE Computer Society Press, Los Alamitos (2006)
7. Cho, S., Kanuri, Cho, K.W., Lee, J.Y., June, S.: Dynamic energy efficient tdma-based mac protocol forwireless sensor networks. In: IEEE ICAS-ICNS'05 (2005)
8. Zhang, H., C.-Hou, J.: Maintaining sensing coverage and connectivity in large sensor networks. Ad hoc and sensor wireless networks 1, 89–124 (2005)
9. Son, D., Krishnamachari, B., Heidemann, J.: Experimental study of the effects of transmission power control and blacklisting in wireless sensor networks. In: IEEE SECON'04, IEEE Computer Society Press, Los Alamitos (2004)
10. Jeong, J., Culler, D.E., Oh, J.H.: Empirical analysis of transmission power control algorithms for wireless sensor networks. Technical Report NO.UCB/EECS-2005-16, UC Berkery (2005)
11. Lin, S., Zhang, J., GangZhou, Gu, L., He, T., Stankovic, J.A.: Atpc: Adaptive transmission power control for wireless sensor networks. In: ACM SENSYS'06 (2006)
12. Goldsmith, A., Wicker, s.: Design challenges for energy constrainted ad-hoc wireless networks. IEEE Wireless Communication 9, 8–27 (2002)
13. Xu, Y., Heidemann, J., Estrin, D.: Geogrpahic-informed energy conservation for ad-hoc routing. In: ACM MobiCom'01, ACM Press, New York (2001)
14. Choi, J., Kim, H., Baek, i., Kwon, W.: Cell based energy density aware routing: A new protocol for improving the lifetime for wireless sensor networks. Elsevier Computer Communication 28, 1293–1302 (2005)
15. Zhou, G., He, T., Krishnamurthy, S., Stankovic, J.A.: Model and solutions for radio irregularity in wireless sensor networks. ACM Trans. on Sensor Networks 2, 221–262 (2006)
16. Zunjiga, M., Krishnamachari, B.: Analyzing the transitional region in low power wireless links. In: IEEE SECON'04, IEEE Computer Society Press, Los Alamitos (2004)
17. Ye, W., J.H., Estrin, D.: Medium access control with coordinated adaptive sleeping for wireless sensor networks. IEEE/ACM Transaction on Networking 12, 493–506 (2004)
18. Zhao, J., Govindan, R.: Understanding packet delivery performance in dense wireless sensor networks. In: ACM Sensys'03, ACM Press, New York (2003)
19. Felemban, E., Lee, C.G., Ekici, E., Boder, R., Vural, S.: Probabilistic qos guarantee in reliablity and timeliness domain in wireless sensor networks. In: IEEE INFOCOMM'05, IEEE Computer Society Press, Los Alamitos (2005)
20. Hu, F., Cao, X.J., May, C.: Optimized scheduling for data aggregation in wireless sensor networks. In: IEEE ITCC'05, IEEE Computer Society Press, Los Alamitos (2005)

Adaptive Data Aggregation for Clustered Wireless Sensor Networks

Huifang Chen[1,2], Hiroshi Mineno[2], Yoshitsugu Obashi[3], Tomohiro Kokogawa[3], and Tadanori Mizuno[2]

[1] Dept. of Information Science and Electronic Engineering, Zhejiang University
No. 38, Zheda Road, Hangzhou 310027, P.R. China
chenhf@zju.edu.cn
[2] Dept. of Computer Science, Shizuoka University
3-5-1 Johoku, Hamamatsu, Shizuoka 432-8011, Japan
{mineno,mizuno}@inf.shizuoka.ac.jp
[3] NTT Service Integration Lab., NTT Corporation
3-9-11 Midori, Musashino, Tokyo 180-8585, Japan
{obashi.yoshitsugu,tomohiro.kokogawa}@lab.ntt.co.jp

Abstract. Wireless sensor network (WSN) has emerged as an event-driven paradigm based on the collective effort of numerous sensing nodes. Due to the dynamic topology and random deployment, incorporating adaptive behavior into protocols in WSNs is important. Hence, we propose an adaptive data aggregation (ADA) scheme for the clustered WSNs. In ADA scheme, the temporal aggregation degree controlled by the reporting frequency at sensor nodes and the spatial aggregation degree controlled by the aggregation degree at Cluster Heads (CHs) are determined by the current scheme state according to the observed reliability. Furthermore, the ADA scheme is mainly performed at the sink node, with a few functions at CHs and sensor nodes. Performance results show that the scheme state converges to the desired reliability starting from any initial state.

1 Introduction

Wireless Sensor Networks (WSNs) have emerged as a new information-gathering paradigm relying on the collective effort of numerous sensor nodes. The ultimate goal of a WSN is to detect the specified interest event in a sensor field. Since the detection range of the sensor nodes often overlaps, the same event is usually reported by numerous sensor nodes, which leads to the data redundancy. In-network data aggregation has been proposed as an essential paradigm for routing in WSNs [1].

WSNs are severely energy-constrained. And replacing batteries on up to thousands of sensor nodes in possibly harsh terrain is infeasible. These necessitate devising the energy conserving solutions for some traditional wireless problems [2]. To ensure the scalability and increase the efficiency of network operations, clustering approaches have become an emerging technology for building scalable, robust, energy-efficient WSN applications [3]. Efficient data aggregation scheme is also an essential candidate for the clustered WSNs, where data aggregation is executed parallel at the Cluster Heads (CHs).

J. Indulska et al. (Eds.): UIC 2007, LNCS 4611, pp. 475–484, 2007.

Almost all of the clustering and data aggregation protocols presented in the literature aim to prolong the network lifetime. WSNs exhibit complex distributed behavior rendering the static pre-configuration useless. Therefore, it is important to incorporate adaptive behavior into the protocols in such dynamic networks. On the other hand, WSNs are envisioned to consist of many inexpensive sensor nodes, each with limited sensing, computing and wireless communicating capabilities. It is necessary to minimize the functions of the data aggregation required at sensor nodes and shift the burden to the resource-rich sink node. With these motivations, we proposed an Adaptive Data Aggregation (ADA) scheme for the clustered WSNs. In the proposed scheme, the reporting frequency at sensor nodes and the aggregation degree at CHs are configured by the current scheme state relying on the observed reliability. In addition, most functions of ADA scheme are performed at the sink node, which a little part is implemented at CHs and sensor nodes.

2 Related Work

In the last few years, many clustering and hierarchical structure schemes aiming to improve energy efficiency, such as LEACH [5], HEED [6], and so on, have been proposed for ad hoc and sensor networks. Our work does not address the clustering protocol, just utilizes the clustering architecture. Our ADA scheme can be combined with any proposed clustering protocol.

Because of its well-known energy efficiency properties, data aggregation techniques have been extensively investigated, and many data aggregation algorithms targeting different sensor network scenarios have been proposed. Directed diffusion is a data-centric architecture where sink node broadcasts interests for the relevant data [1]. Sensor nodes producing relevant information respond and data paths back to the sink node are formed. Data is aggregated when a node is part of various data paths. SPIN does not really use an explicit aggregation mechanism [7]. In [8], Xue et al. addressed the problem of maximizing lifetime routing for data aggregation in WSNs and presented a tree-based approximation algorithm. In [9], we presented a novel data aggregation scheme in clustered WSNs, which used the meta-data negotiation to improve the energy efficiency. Many other data aggregation schemes exist. Our ADA scheme, distinguishes itself from existing solutions in that the spatial and temporal aggregation degree is adaptive to the dynamic state of WSNs via the interaction between the sink node and the CHs.

Several WSN papers addressed the need for incorporating adaptive behavior into the protocols. SPIN makes adaptive decisions to participate in data dissemination based on current energy levels and the communication cost. SPEED utilizes neighborhood information to make more informed routing decisions in response to network congestion and changing traffic patterns [10]. ESRT adjusts the reporting frequency of source nodes in order to reach the target reliability level and conserve energy [11]. While many more examples of adaptive protocols exist, these solutions provide relevant example of how adaptation is beneficial in the unpredictable and dynamic WSNs. Our work is elicited by [11] and [4]. Many of these examples are orthogonal and can coexist with our work.

3 Problem Definition

In this paper, we consider a single-hop clustered WSN application involving the detection of event features based on the collective information of numerous sensor nodes. Assume an event happen at some place in the detected area, the sensor nodes in the sensing range of the event S, referred as *source nodes*, can sense it and generate the sensing information, and try to transmit the information to their corresponding CHs. On receiving the collected data from its Cluster Members (CMs), CH performs the data aggregation and sends the aggregated data to the sink node. The data aggregation process is illustrated in the Fig. 1.

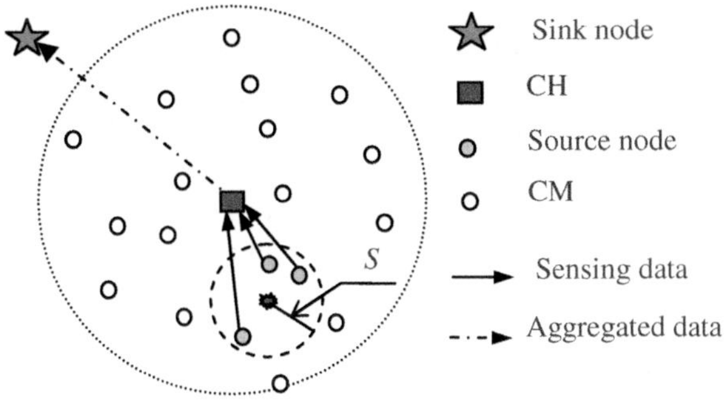

Fig. 1. Data aggregation process in single-hop clustered WSN

As mentioned above, since the detection range of the sensor nodes often overlaps, there are several source nodes for a happened event. That is the data redundancy problem. For each source node, it periodically reports the collected data, which is called as the *temporal redundancy* and can be aggregated at node-level by controlling the reporting frequency, f. For each cluster, the sensing data of the same event received by CH will be same or analogical, which is called as the *spatial redundancy* and can be aggregated at cluster-level by controlling the aggregation degree, d.

Assume the sink node make a decision on the event features every τ time units, where τ denotes the duration of a decision interval and depends on the application. At the end of each decision interval, the sink node makes a decision on reliability r based on the data received from the sensor field during that interval. Assume that r_i be calculated only using the available information at the sink node during the ith decision interval, which is extracted from the received data. Therefore, the reliability of the event features is related with the number of the received data of the sink node. Fig. 2 shows the hypothetic relationship between the reliability of the event features r and the number of the received data N according to the spatial and temporal correlation model in [4]. In Fig. 2, when $N < N_1$, r increases exponentially with N; when $N_1 \leq N \leq N_2$, r increases linearly with N; and when $N > N_2$, r increases logarithmically with N.

There are two kinds of reliability, the observed one and desired one. From Fig. 2, the observed reliability r_i can be defined as the number of received data during the ith decision interval at the sink node. And the desired reliability R is the number of data

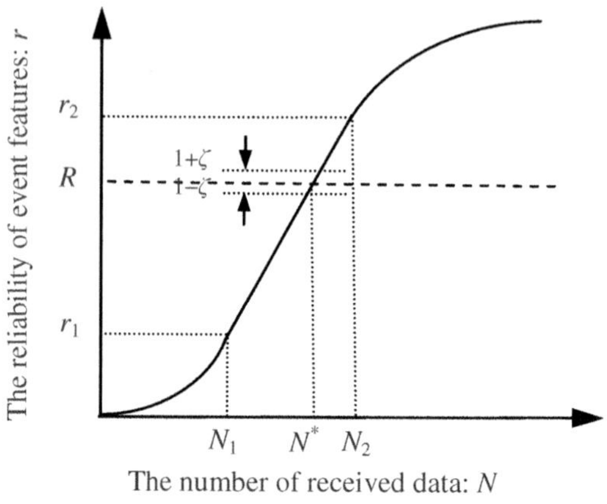

Fig. 2. Hypothetic relationship between r and N

needed for reliable event detection, which is determined by the application. If r_i is greater than R, the event can be detected reliably. Otherwise, appropriate action needs to be taken to improve the reliability until R is achieved.

When an event happens in the detected field, there are n sensor nodes in the sensing range of the event. For the sensing data are received by the sink node with the temporal redundancy and the spatial redundancy removed at node level and cluster level, the total number of received data by sink node in each decision interval is

$$N = n\tau f / d \tag{1}$$

The adaptive data aggregation problem for the clustered WSNs is to configure f of sensor nodes and d of CHs so as to achieve the desired reliability of detected event, R, at the sink node with the energy efficiency. Due to the dynamic characteristics of WSNs, it is necessary for the ADA scheme to keep track of the observed reliability in the sink node and accordingly adjust the aggregation parameters, f and d.

4 An Adaptive Data Aggregation Scheme

Without loss the generality, R can be represented as the spatial reliability R_s and the temporal reliability R_t, which are controlled by d and f, respectively. When CH receives the data from the source nodes in its cluster, it does not forward all of these data to sink node, but select a part of them. When d is configured, R_s is determined by the data from the selected source nodes. Similarly, when f is configured, R_t is determined by the data from one of the selected source nodes.

4.1 State and Region

The normalized reliability is defined as $\vec{\eta}_i = (\eta_{s,i}, \eta_{t,i})$, where $\eta_{s,i} = r_{s,i}/R_s$ $\eta_{t,i} = r_{t,i}/R_t$. $r_{s,i}$ and $r_{t,i}$ are the observed spatial reliability and the observed temporal reliability in the ith decision internal, respectively. R_s and R_t are the desired spatial reliability and the desired temporal reliability. The goal of our ADA scheme is to operate with $\vec{\eta}=(1, 1)$ as close as possible. When $\vec{\eta}=(1, 1)$, the number of received data is the optimal value N^*. For practical propose, a tolerance zone with width 2ζ around $r=R$ is shown in Fig. 2, which means a tolerance zone with width $2\vec{\theta}$ around $\vec{\eta}=(1, 1)$, and $\vec{\theta}=(\theta_s,\theta_t)=(\zeta/R_s,\ \zeta/R_t)$.

We define nine characteristic regions using the following decision boundaries.

- **LSR/LTR** (Low Spatial Reliability, Low Temporal Reliability Region): $\eta_s<1-\theta_s$ and $\eta_t<1-\theta_t$
- **LSR/OTR** (Low Spatial Reliability, Optimal Temporal Reliability Region): $\eta_s<1-\theta_s$ and $1-\theta_t\le\eta_t\le1+\theta_t$
- **LSR/HTR** (Low Spatial Reliability, High Temporal Reliability Region): $\eta_s<1-\theta_s$ and $\eta_t>1+\theta_t$
- **OSR/LTR** (Optimal Spatial Reliability, Low Temporal Reliability Region): $1-\theta_s\le\eta$ $\le1+\theta_s$ and $\eta_t<1-\theta_t$
- **OOR (OSR/OTR)** (Optimal Operation Region): $1-\theta_s\le\eta_s\le1+\theta_s$ and $1-\theta_t\le\eta_t\le1+\theta_t$
- **OSR/HTR** (Optimal Spatial Reliability, High Temporal Reliability Region): $1-\theta_s\le\eta_s\le1+\theta_s$ and $\eta_t>1+\theta_t$
- **HSR/LTR** (High Spatial Reliability, Low Temporal Reliability Region): $\eta_s>1+\theta_s$ and $\eta_t<1-\theta_t$
- **HSR/OTR** (High Spatial Reliability, Optimal Temporal Reliability Region): $\eta_s>1+\theta_s$ and $1-\theta_t\le\eta_t\le1+\theta_t$
- **HSR/HTR** (High Spatial Reliability, High Temporal Reliability Region): $\eta_s>1+\theta_s$ and $\eta_t>1+\theta_t$

Let $\mathbf{S}_i$ denote the data aggregation state variable at the end of the ith decision interval. The sink node decides $\vec{\eta}_i$ at the end of the ith decision interval. Then, $\mathbf{S}_i\in$ {**LSR/LTR**, **LSR/OTR**, **LSR/HTR**, **OSR/LTR**, **OSR/HTR**, **HSR/LTR**, **HSR/OTR**, **HSR/HTR**, **OOR**}. The primary motivation of our ADA scheme is to achieve and maintain operation in state **OOR**.

For r_s and r_t is controlled by d at CHs and f at source nodes respectively, the simplified ADA scheme state model and transitions are shown in Fig. 3, where the symbol x denotes the spatial dimension or the temporal dimension. Generally, the data aggregation state resides in one of nine states {**LSR/LTR**, **LSR/OTR**, **LSR/HTR**, **OSR/LTR**, **OSR/HTR**, **HSR/LTR**, **HSR/OTR**, **HSR/HTR**, **OOR**}. According to the current state $\mathbf{S}_i$, the sink node calculates f_{i+1} and/or d_{i+1} and broadcasts to CHs, and CHs broadcast f_{i+1} to the corresponding CMs.

4.2 Scheme Operation

The ADA scheme determines the current state $\mathbf{S}_i$ from $\vec{\eta}_i$ at the ith decision interval. According to $\mathbf{S}_i$, d_i, f_i and $\vec{\eta}_i$, the scheme computes d_{i+1} at CHs and f_{i+1} at sensor nodes. Subsequently, at the end of the $(i+1)^{th}$ decision interval, the sink node calculates $\vec{\eta}_{i+1}$ using the data received during the $(i+1)^{th}$ decision interval using d_{i+1} at CHs and f_{i+1} at sensor nodes, and then identifies $\mathbf{S}_{i+1}$ again. Therefore, the task of our ADA scheme is mainly performed on the sink node, with a little function at the CHs and sensor nodes. This process is performed repeatedly until the scheme state is

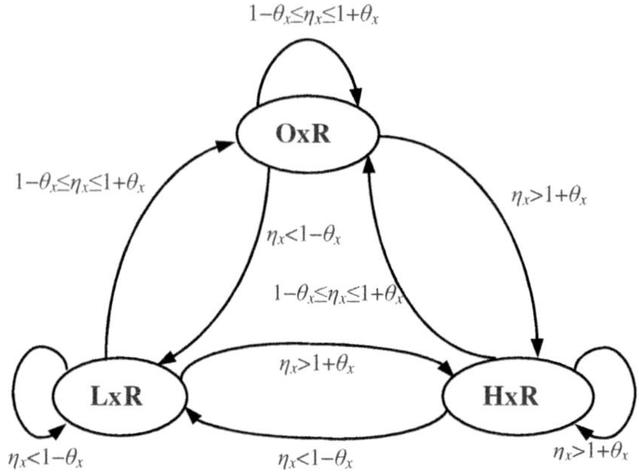

Fig. 3. Simplified state model and transitions

OOR. Because of the dynamic characteristics of WSN, the ADA scheme needs to continuously observe the state even if **OOR** is reached.

Adjusting policy of spatial aggregation degree. The detailed policies for adjusting d are related to the current state.

When the current state is **LSR**, $\eta_{s,i}<1-\theta_s$, that means d_i is so large that the received data cannot provide enough information and the observed spatial reliability is lower than the required one. In order to reach the desired spatial reliability of event features, it is necessary to decrease d. Thus, d_{i+1} can be calculated as

$$d_{i+1} = \frac{d_i}{2}(1+\eta_{s,i}) \tag{2}$$

When the current state is **HSR**, $\eta_{s,i}>1+\theta_s$, that means d_i is so small that the received data provide excessive information, and the observed spatial reliability is higher than the required one. Excessive transmitted data consume the excessive energy. In order to conserve energy, it is necessary to increase d. Thus, d_{i+1} can be calculated as

$$d_{i+1} = d_i \eta_{s,i} \tag{3}$$

When the current state is **OSR**, $1-\theta_s\leq\eta_{s,i}\leq1+\theta_s$, that means the required spatial reliability is reached. Therefore, d keeps current value for the next decision interval.

$$d_{i+1} = d_i \tag{4}$$

Adjusting policy of temporal aggregation degree. When the current state is LTR, ηt,i<1−θt, that means fi is so small that the received data from a source node cannot provide enough information and the observed temporal reliability is lower than the required one. In order to reach the desired temporal reliability of event features, it is necessary to increase f. Thus, fi+1 can be calculated as

$$f_{i+1} = f_i / \eta_{t,i} \tag{5}$$

When the current state is **HTR**, $\eta_{t,i}>1+\theta_t$, that means f_i is so large that the received data from a source node provide excessive information, and the observed temporal reliability is higher than the required one. In order to conserve energy, it is necessary to decrease f. Thus, f_{i+1} can be calculated as

$$f_{i+1}=\frac{f_i(1+\eta_{t,i})}{2\eta_{t,i}} \tag{6}$$

When the current state is **OTR**, $1-\theta_t\leq\eta_{t,i}\leq 1+\theta_t$, that means the required temporal reliability is achieved. Then, f maintains current value for the next decision interval.

$$f_{i+1}=f_i \tag{7}$$

If the deployed clustered WSN supports tracking different types of events, our ADA scheme is applicable in the same way. If different events have different desired reliabilities, different modules at the sink node are set up to perform the ADA scheme corresponding to the different events.

5 Performance Analysis

For an effective scheme, the data aggregation state must converge to state **OOR** stating from any initial state $\mathbf{S}_0$, where $\mathbf{S}_0\in${**LSR/LTR, LSR/OTR, LSR/HTR, OSR/LTR, OSR/HTR, HSR/LTR, HSR/OTR, HSR/HTR, OOR**}. Starting from **OOR**, the scheme state converges. Here, we analyze that the scheme state converges to state **OOR** starting from any of other eight initial states.

5.1 Analytical Results

LEMMA 1. Starting from $\mathbf{S}_{s,0}$=**LSR**, with the linear reliability behavior when the number of received data is greater than N_1, the scheme state remains unchanged until it converges to state **OSR**.

PROOF: The linear reliability behavior for $N_s>N_{s,1}$ can be described as $N_s=\alpha\eta_s$, where α denotes the slope. On the other hand, N_s is reversely proportional to d, that can be expressed as $N_s=\beta/d$, where β denotes the proportion coefficient. Therefore, the relationship between d and η_s is $d=\beta/\alpha\eta_s$.

When the current state is $\mathbf{S}_{s,i}$=**LSR**, d_{i+1} is calculated as (2). Then,

$$\eta_{s,i+1}=\frac{2\eta_{s,i}}{1+\eta_{s,i}} \tag{8}$$

Since $d_{i+1}<d_i$ from (2), it follows that $\mathbf{S}_{s,i+1}\in${**LSR**, **HSR**, **OSR**}, $\forall i\geq 0$, until the scheme state converges. If possible, let $\mathbf{S}_{s,i+1}$=**HSR** when $\mathbf{S}_{s,i}$=**LSR** for some $i\geq 0$ before the scheme state converges. Then,

$$\eta_{s,i+1}=\frac{2\eta_{s,i}}{1+\eta_{s,i}}>1+\theta_s \tag{9}$$

It means that $\eta_{s,i} > \frac{1+\theta_s}{1-\theta_s}$, but $\eta_{s,i} < 1-\theta_s$ since $\mathbf{S}_{s,i}$ =**LSR**. Therefore, $\mathbf{S}_{s,i+1} \neq$ **HSR** for any $i \geq 0$ until the scheme state converges. Consequently, it can be concluded that $\mathbf{S}_{s,i+1}$=**LSR** $\forall i \geq 0$, until the scheme state converges to state **OSR**. ■

LEMMA 2. Starting from $\mathbf{S}_{s,0}$=**LSR**, with the linear reliability behavior when the number of received data is greater than N_1, the scheme state converges to state **OSR** in $\tau\left\lceil \log_2\left(\frac{1-\eta_{s,0}}{(1+\eta_{s,0})\theta_s}\right)+1\right\rceil$ time units, where τ is the duration of the decision interval.

PROOF: Let the ith decision interval be the first one where $\mathbf{S}_{s,i}$=**OSR**. It follows from *LAMMA 1* that i is the least suffix such that $\eta_{s,i}>1-\theta_s$. Using (8),

$$\begin{aligned} \eta_{s,i} &= \frac{2\eta_{s,i-1}}{1+\eta_{s,i-1}} > 1-\theta_s \\ \eta_{s,i-1} &= \frac{2\eta_{s,i-2}}{1+\eta_{s,i-2}} > 1-2^1\theta_s \\ &\vdots \\ \eta_{s,1} &= \frac{2\eta_{s,0}}{1+\eta_{s,0}} > 1-2^{i-1}\theta_s \end{aligned} \tag{10}$$

Therefore, $i > \log_2\left(\frac{1-\eta_{s,0}}{(1+\eta_{s,0})\theta_s}\right)+1$ and the result follows. ■

LEMMA 3. Starting from $\mathbf{S}_{s,0}$=**HSR**, with the linear reliability behavior when the number of received data is smaller than N_2, the scheme state converges to state **OSR** aggressively.

PROOF: The linear reliability behavior for $N_s<N_{s,2}$ can be described as $N_s=\alpha\eta_s$, where α denotes the slope. On the other hand, N_s is reversely proportional to d, that can be expressed as $N_s=\beta/d$, where β denotes the proportion coefficient. Therefore, the relationship between d and η_s is $d=\beta/\alpha\eta_s$.

When the current state is $\mathbf{S}_i$=**HSR**, d_{i+1} is calculated as (3). Thus $\eta_{s,i+1}=1$, and the scheme state aggressively converges to the state **OSR**. ■

LEMMA 4. Starting from $\mathbf{S}_{t,0}$=**LTR**, with the linear reliability behavior when the number of received data is greater than N_1, the scheme state converges to state **OTR** aggressively.

LEMMA 5. Starting from $\mathbf{S}_{t,0}$=**HTR**, with the linear reliability behavior when the number of received data is smaller than N_2, the scheme state remains unchanged until it converges to state **OTR**.

LEMMA 6. Starting from $\mathbf{S}_{t,0}$=**HTR**, with the linear reliability behavior when the number of received data is smaller than N_2, the scheme state converges to state **OTR** in $\tau\left\lceil \log_2\left(\frac{\eta_{t,0}-1}{\theta_t}\right)\right\rceil$ time units, where τ is the duration of the decision interval.

The proof of the LAMMA 4, 5 ,6 is similar to that of the LAMMA 1, 2 ,3.

In order to calculate the convergence times of ADA scheme starting from $\mathbf{S}_{x,0}$=**LxR** with $N<N_1$, and $\mathbf{S}_{x,0}$=**HxR** with $N>N_2$, the nonlinear reliability behavior needs to tracked analytically. Due to the limited space, we are not including these two case.

5.2 Simulation Results

In order to validate the analytic results in section 5.1, we developed an evaluation environment using MATLAB 7.1. The cluster protocol used in simulation is LEACH, the first cluster protocol proposed for WSNs [5]. Assume that 100 sensor nodes are randomly deployed in the detected area with a size of 100m×100m. The sink node locates at outside of the detected area. The percentage of the CHs is 4, and the sensing range of an event is 40m.

The convergence results is shown in Table 1 for the initial scheme state $\mathbf{S}_0$=**LSR/LTR**, **HSR/LTR, LSR/HTR,** and **HSR/HTR**, where tolerance $\theta_s=\theta_t=5\%$.

Table 1. The corresponding (d_i, $\eta_{s,i}$, f_i, $\eta_{t,i}$) and scheme states

	i	0	1	2	3	4
1	$\mathbf{S}_i$	**LSR/LTR**	**LSR/OTR**	**LSR/OTR**	**LSR/OTR**	**OOR**
	d_i	5.4	4.3546	3.8318	3.5705	3.4345
	$\eta_{s,i}$	0.6128	0.7599	0.8636	0.9283	0.9635
	f_i	0.8	4.9261	4.9261	4.9261	4.9261
	$\eta_{t,i}$	0.1624	1.0073	1.0073	1.0073	1.0073
2	$\mathbf{S}_i$	**LSR/HTR**	**LSR/HTR**	**LSR/HTR**	**LSR/HTR**	**OOR**
	d_i	5.4	4.3546	3.8318	3.5705	3.4345
	$\eta_{s,i}$	0.6128	0.7599	0.8636	0.9283	0.9635
	f_i	7.8	6.3631	5.6446	5.2855	5.1059
	$\eta_{t,i}$	1.5834	1.2917	1.1458	1.0729	1.0423
3	$\mathbf{S}_i$	**HSR/LTR**	**OOR**			
	d_i	2.16	3.3048			
	$\eta_{s,i}$	1.532	1.0013			
	f_i	0.8	4.9261			
	$\eta_{t,i}$	0.1624	1.0073			
4	$\mathbf{S}_i$	**HSR/HTR**	**OSR/HTR**	**OSR/HTR**	**OSR/HTR**	**OOR**
	d_i	2.16	3.3048	3.3048	3.3048	3.3048
	$\eta_{s,i}$	1.532	1.0013	1.0013	1.0013	1.0013
	f_i	7.8	6.3631	5.6446	5.2855	5.1059
	$\eta_{t,i}$	1.5834	1.2917	1.1458	1.0729	1.0423

From this table, we observe that the ADA scheme for $\mathbf{S}_0$=**HSR/LTR** converges in a total of two decision intervals and the ADA scheme for $\mathbf{S}_0$=**LSR/LTR**, **LSR/HTR,** and **HSR/HTR** converges in a total of five decision intervals.

6 Conclusions

Due to the dynamic topology and random deployment, it is important to corporate the adaptive characteristic into the protocols for WSNs. Furthermore, since sensor nodes are resource-constrained, it is necessary to minimize the responsibilities required at sensor nodes and shift the burden to the resource-rich sink node. In this paper, we proposed an ADA scheme for the clustered WSNs. In this scheme, the reporting frequency at sensor nodes and the aggregation degree at CHs are determined by the current scheme state based on the observed reliability. The task of the ADA scheme is mainly performed on the sink node, with a little function at the CHs and sensor nodes. Analytical and simulation results show that the scheme state converges to the desired reliability starting from any initial state.

References

1. Intanagonwiwat, C.R., Govindan, C.R., Estrin, D.: Directed Diffusion: a Scalable and Robust Communication Paradigm for Sensor Networks. In: Proc. of MobiCom, pp. 56–67 (2000)
2. Akyildiz, I.F., Su, W., Sankarasubramaniam, Y., Cayirci, E.: Wireless Sensor Networks: A Survey. Computer Networks 38, 393–422 (2002)
3. Gober, P., Ziviani, A., Todorova, P., Amorim, M.D., Hunerberg, P., Fdida, S.: Topology Control and Localization in Wireless Ad Hoc and Sensor Networks. Ad Hoc & Sensor Networks 1, 301–322 (2005)
4. Vuran, M.C., Akyildiz, I.F.: Spatial Correlation-Based Collaborative Medium Access Control in Wireless Sensor Networks. IEEE/ACM Trans. on Networking 14(2), 316–329 (2006)
5. Heinzelman, W.R., Chandrakasan, A., Balakrishnan, H.: An Application-Specific Protocol Architecture for Wireless Microsensor Networks. IEEE Trans. on Wireless Communications. 1(4), 660–667 (2002)
6. Younis, O., Fahmy, S.: HEED A Hybrid, Energy-Efficient, Distributed Clustering Approach for Ad-hoc Sensor Networks. IEEE Trans. on Mobile Computing. 3(4), 660–669 (2004)
7. Heinzelman, W., Kulik, J., Balakrishnan, H.: Adaptive Protocols for Information Dissemination in Wireless Sensor Networks. In: Proc. of MobiCom, pp. 174–185 (1999)
8. Xue, Y., Cui, Y., Nahrstedt, K.: Maximizing Lifetime for Data Aggregation in Wireless Sensor Networks. Mobile Networks and Applications (2005)
9. Chen, H., Mineno, H., Mizuno, T.: A Meta-Data-Based Data Aggregation Scheme in Clustering Wireless Sensor Networks. In: MDM 2006 Workshop MLASN, pp. 43–49 (2006)
10. He, T., Stankovic, J., Lu, C., Abdelzaher, T.F.: SPEED: A Stateless Protocol for Real-Time Communication in Sensor Networks. In: Proc. of ICDCS (2003)
11. Sankarasubramaniam, Y., Akan, O.B., Akyildiz, I.F.: ESRT: Event-to-Sink Reliable Transport in Wireless Sensor Networks. In: Proc. of MobiHoc, pp. 177–188 (2003)

Directed Diffusion Based on Link-Stabilizing Clustering for Wireless Sensor Networks

Zude Zhou, Wenjun Xu, Fangmin Li, and Xuehong Wu

School of Information Engineering, Wuhan University of Technology,
Wuhan, Hubei Province, China
{xuwenjun,zudezhou,lifangmin}@whut.edu.cn

Abstract. Reducing power consumption to extend network lifetime with limited energy resource is one of the most important challenges in wireless sensor networks. In addition, the issue of real-time communication is also very important in some practical applications. A directed diffusion algorithm based on link-stabilizing clustering (DDLSC), which is a delay-energy aware routing protocol for wireless sensor networks is proposed in this paper. DDLSC enable a wide range of tradeoffs between delay and energy consumption. The two major components of DDLSC are: a novel stable clustering scheme that forms a wireless sensor network into two layers and the cluster heads construct a virtual backbone for multi-hop communications, and a directed diffusion routing protocol based on the clustering scheme. It is simple, fast to converge, fully distributed and dynamic, and be scalable to the change in network size, density and topology. The performance of DDLSC remains very good even in large-scale sensor networks, and it scales with density. Through analysis and simulation evaluations, we show that DDLSC improves the packet delay and system energy consumption compared to other current data-centric routing protocols.

1 Introduction

Wireless sensor networks have got increasing attention in recent years. There is a multiplicity of scenarios in which such networks might find uses, such as military command and surveillance system, environmental control in office buildings, robot control and guidance in automatic manufacturing environments, and some other commercial applications include managing inventory, monitoring disaster areas [1,2].

It is critically important to save energy in wireless sensor networks, so many current researches on routing [3-7] in wireless sensor networks mostly focused on protocols that are energy aware to maximize the lifetime of the network, are scalable to accommodate a large number of sensor nodes, and are tolerant to sensor damage and battery exhaustion. Nowadays, many routing protocols [3,4] for wireless sensor networks are designed for flat networks. But research [8-10] shows that when the network scale becomes very large, which is usually the feature of sensor networks, those protocols designed for flat networks will generate significant routing overhead and finally make the network performance unacceptable. Cluster networks can

J. Indulska et al. (Eds.): UIC 2007, LNCS 4611, pp. 485–494, 2007.

performance well in that situations, therefore routing protocol based on clustering is considered to be a better solution for the large-scale wireless networks.

In this paper we present a Link-Stabilizing Clustering (LSC) algorithm which could be applied to the practical applications of wireless sensor networks, and enable all nodes in network clustering stably. For the reason that some practical applications, for example, consider a sensor/actuator network of accelerometers and dampers installed in a building to detect and react to unusual/strong building vibration. Accelerometer data indicating an earthquake or a strong windstorm requires an immediate response by the dampers that react to this data. Those applications mentioned above need a rapid response to sensor information, in order to meet the real-time requirement of the applications, directed diffusion algorithm which is a classical and data-central routing protocol for sensor networks has be combined with LSC algorithm that we proposed to improve network latency versus energy efficiency tradeoffs in this paper, and we denote it as "Directed Diffusion based on Link-Stabilizing Clustering (DDLSC)".

The remainder of this paper is organized as follows: Section 2 reviews the related work. Section 3 gives our network model. Section 4 presents LSC algorithm for wireless sensor networks. Section 5 explains directed diffusion based on LSC (DDLSC) in detail. Section 6 provides an in-depth analysis and evaluation of the network stability, average delay and energy consumption of DDLSC compared to some current important routing protocols for sensor networks. Section 7 concludes the paper.

2 Related Work

LEACH [5] is the basic research of cluster-based energy-efficient communication protocol, and many other improved protocols such as TEEN [6] and HEED [11] had been proposed in recent years. Each group of sensors has a cluster head that is a specified node being less energy-constrained in LEACH, and the cluster heads aggregate the received data and send them to the sink. LEACH is a cluster forming method that can minimize network energy consumption and communication latency. But it still has some disadvantages [12]:

(i) The cluster head transmit the information to a sink node by one-hop, and the higher transmit power will cause more energy consumption;
(ii) The cluster head is elected based on a round-robin strategy, and this strategy will change the topology of clusters frequently because the selected cluster head may has less energy;
(iii) In addition, LEACH has too many assumptions on sensor nodes. For example, nodes must have the same initial energy level, and be static. These assumptions are not practical in reality, so it could not suit to dynamic network environments, and be hard for people to apply it into practical applications.

IEEE 802.15.4 [13] is a standard addressing the needs of Low-Rate Wireless Personal Area Networks (LRWPAN) with a focus on enabling various pervasive and ubiquitous applications that require interactions with our surrounding environments.

And it is extensible to form multi-hop wireless sensor networks. The specification of IEEE 802.15.4 proposes a cluster-tree topology, however, the cluster-tree topology is not always efficient in sensor networks cases [10]. For example, as shown in Figure1, the traffic has to be relayed by the root cluster head if the communicating nodes are located at different branches although a more efficient route exists.

The Link State Clustering Algorithm presented in reference [10] is a cluster forming protocol without the assumptions that are not practical in reality. But the protocol even exists unclustered node after clustering stage, furthermore the routing through an overlay among cluster heads is still a normal flat routing protocol and not suitable for many applications of large-scale sensor networks.

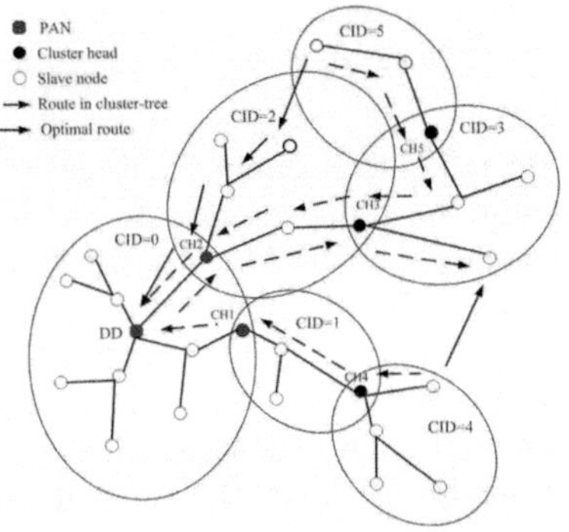

Fig. 1. IEEE 802.15.4 route in cluster-tree mo

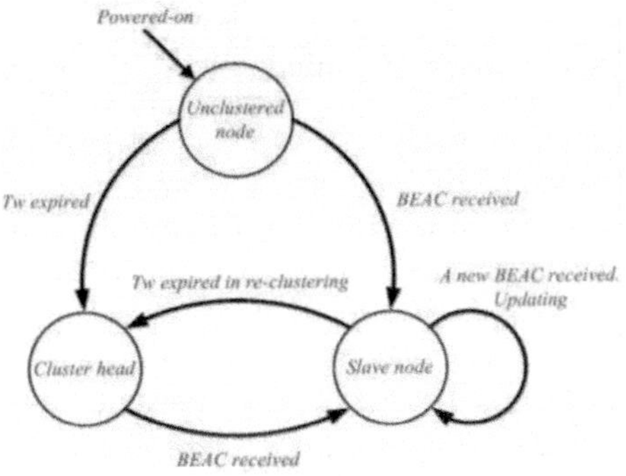

Fig. 2. Node state transition

3 Network Module

We model the wireless sensor networks consisting of a set of nodes N = (n1, n2,..., ni,...) that are uniformly distributed in a square area. Nodes share a common wireless channel by using omni-directional antennas.

We make the following assumptions [14]: (i) The nodes N are quasi-stationary. This is typical for several types of wireless sensor networks; (ii) All nodes have similar capabilities and equal significance; (iii) Each node has a fixed number of transmission power levels; (iv) The routing protocol computes routing tables at each power level; (v) The node's transmission radius is linear to its energy and the sink node is located in a remote place from the network. Note that in our model, no assumptions are made about any of the following: (i) Homogeneity of node dispersion in the field; (ii) Location-awareness, i.e., being equipped with GPS-capable antennae; (iii) Network density or diameter; and (iv) Distribution of energy consumption among nodes.

For the reason that reducing power consumption to extend network lifetime with limited energy resource is one of the most important challenges in wireless sensor networks, so we study the performance measures of network energy consumption firstly. In addition, the issue of real-time communication is also important in many practical applications, hence, the performance measures of average end-to-end latency also be studied in this paper.

4 Link-Stabilizing Clustering for Wireless Sensor Networks

The work introduced in this section is based on the algorithms recently introduced in reference [10]. New clustering algorithms are proposed for practical applications of wireless sensor networks to enable the clusters form stably and improve the network topology while avoiding situations such as having holes in the network or even having unclustered nodes.

Link-stabilizing clustering for wireless sensor networks is illustrated as follows:

4.1 Cluster Forming

When a node in the network is powered-on, it marks itself unclustered and sets up a random waiting timer T_{wI} and starts to monitor the radio channel if were there a control frame (Beacon, BEAC) from another node. If no BEAC is heard within T_{wI}, the node marks itself as a cluster head and sends a BEAC immediately. The nodes receive the BEAC frame will send back a Beacon_Reply (BEAC_R) control frame to the corresponding cluster head, and the cluster head will add this node to its Slave_Table. Slave node transmits information to the corresponding cluster head by one-hop. Figure 2 present the node state transition during the cluster forming stage.

Since the cluster heads coordinate their slaves all the time, the energy drains faster than other nodes. In order to increase the overall network lifetime, the cluster heads are re-elected by an energy-efficient algorithm described in Part 4.3 below.

4.2 Cluster Updating

If a node has received a new BEAC from another node, it will compare the link state information with the previous one and choose the node which need less transmit power to communicate with to be its own cluster head. Here we define P_m to be the minimum transmission power level at the source node, and the value can be calculated as:

$$P_m = \frac{P_t R_t}{P_r} \tag{1}$$

Where P_t is the transmitted power, R_t is the minimum necessary RSSI for the reception of a frame, and P_r is the power received by the destination node.

Every node can obtain the minimum transmit power value by Equation (1). If $P_{m\_new} > P_{m\_old}$, the node that received the new BEAC will update its cluster head and send two control frames: a BEAC_R to inform the new cluster head, and a Beacon_Cancel (BEAC_C) to inform the old cluster to remove it from its Slave Table.

If a cluster head hears a BEAC, it will set itself as a slave of that cluster head and sends a information to its slaves by BEAC_R, then the slaves come into a re-clustering state.

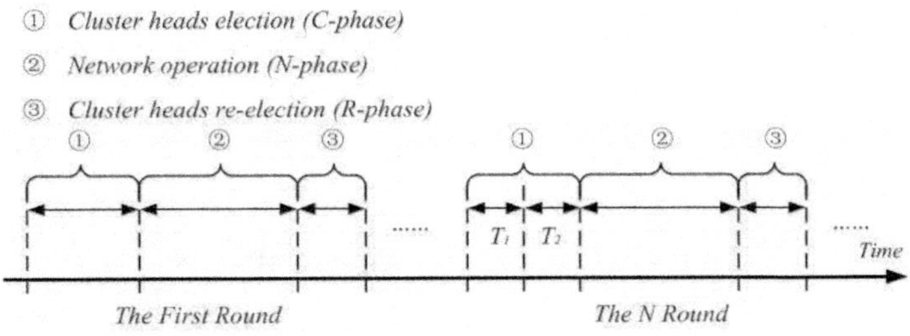

Fig. 3. Network timing

4.3 Cluster Heads Re-electing

The network runs periodically in rounds and each round consists of three phases: i) Cluster heads election (C-phase), ii) Network operation (N-phase), and iii) Cluster heads re-election (R-phase). We denote them as T_c, T_n and T_r respectively, as shown in Figure 3.

In R-phase time, LSC invoke a node budget to perform the cluster heads re-election, and the node budget is battery residual E_{new} given by:

$$E_{new} = E_{old} - E_{expend} \tag{2}$$

Where E_{expend} is the energy consumption in the current round.

Firstly the cluster head broadcasts a BEAC_RE to its slaves in R-phase time, and notify them return their E_{new}. Then the slave node embeds its E_{new} in BEAC_RER packet and sends back to its cluster head. The node that has the highest E_{new} will be a cluster head in next C-phase.

In the first C-phase time, it clusterizes a network by random competition clustering. In other C-phases there exist two time phases T_1 and T_2. The re-elected cluster heads complete their clustering work in T_1, and the uncluster nodes will form clusters according to the algorithms described in Part 4.1 in T_2.

4.4 Power Control Scheme in LSC

Transmit power control is a highly effective technique for minimizing interference and energy consumption in wireless networks. In [15], the effects of using different power levels on the average energy consumption and network throughput are investigated. For the power control scheme advantages and to guarantee global connectivity, all the nodes are able to have two transmission power levels in LSC, the lower one P_{t_sl} is for intra-cluster communications, and the higher one P_{t_sh} is for inter-cluster communications.

As shown in Figure 4, R_b and R_c are defined to be the intra-cluster and inter-cluster communications ranges. If the node density is large enough so that at any position x, there exists at least one node to be potential cluster head, the cluster head after clustering can be connected if $R_c \geq 2\cos15R_b \approx 2R_b$ [10].

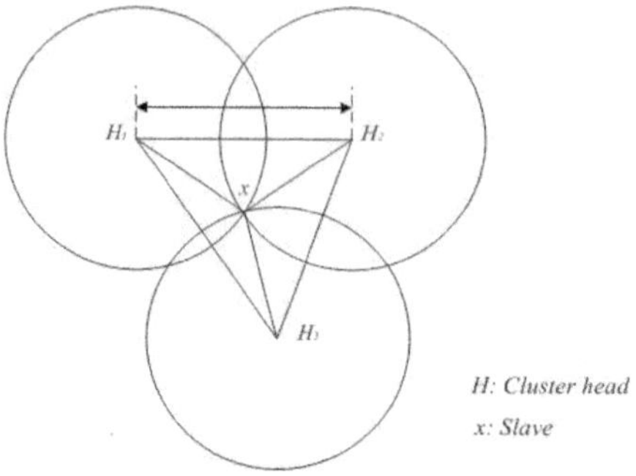

Fig. 4. Communication range for connectivity

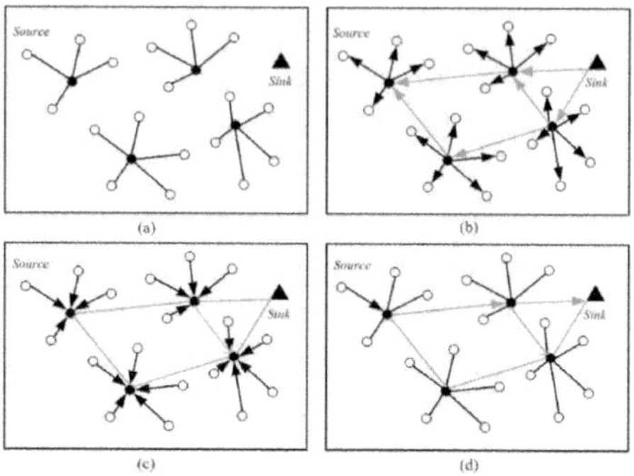

Fig. 5. Network operation in DDLSC

5 Directed Diffusion Based on LSC

In many applications of sensor networks, it is not feasible to assign global identifiers to each node due to the sheer number of nodes deployed. So the traditional address-based routing is not suitable for large-scale sensor networks. This consideration has led to data-centric routing be managed [16].

Directed diffusion [4] is an important milestone in the data-centric routing research of sensor networks. The idea aims at diffusing data through sensor nodes by using a naming scheme for the data. The main reason behind using such a scheme is to get rid of unnecessary operations of network layer routing in order to save energy. But it is still a flat routing mainly depend on flooding and may generate significant routing overhead in large-scale networks. An energy-efficiency directed diffusion routing protocol that depends on reducing network topology by clustering has been proposed in reference [17]. With the contributions of reference [17], in order to reduce the significant overload cause by the flat scheme, and be able to cover a large area of interest without degrading the service for sensor networks, a new routing protocol which combine directed diffusion with LSC algorithm has been proposed in this paper, we denote it as "Directed Diffusion based on Link-Stabilizing Clustering (DDLSC)".

Once the network is clustered, it runs into N-phase. The interests are broadcasted by the sink node through the cluster heads, then the cluster heads broadcast the sink interest to their slave nodes (as shown in Figure 5b). Each node receiving the interest can do caching for later use, and the cluster heads also have the ability to do in-network data aggregation. The nodes that have the data with the values in the interests should be the source.

The flooding routing is only among the cluster heads, and the interests in the cluster heads caches are used to compare the received data. The interest entry also contains several gradient fields. Hence, by utilizing interest and gradients, paths are established between sink and sources, as shown in Figure 5d.

To increase the overall network lifetime, the cluster heads re-election should be deployed in R-phase. In cluster heads re-election phase, cluster head select the node that has highest battery residual as the next cluster head and sends it a control packet to notify it. The new cluster heads also have the interest information, furthermore, the sink node will broadcast the interest periodically to ensure the robust of the networks.

6 Performance Evaluation

We have developed a simulator using NS2, a discrete event simulation framework, to evaluate the DDLSC protocol, and compare the performance of the protocol with 2 other data-centric routings. We implement and compare DDLSC with flooding and directed diffusion. In addition, Matlab is used to evaluate the topology of DDLSC networks.

We generate a variety of sensors fields of different sizes ranging from 100 to 350 nodes in increments of 50 nodes. The intra-cluster communications range (R_b) is 100m, and the inter-cluster communications range (R_c) is 200m. The sensors field with fixed nodes was generated by randomly placing nodes in a square area of S=600×600m^2. Other simulation environment settings are as shown in Table 1.

Table 1. Other simulation eviroment settings

Tx Power (transmit range is 200m)	800w
Tx Power (transmit range is 100m)	200w
Rx Power in all cases	400w
Media Access Control	IEEE 802.11

6.1 Network Stability

The first observation of simulation is the stability of the network in DDLSC. As shown in Figure 6, the sensors field with 300 nodes was generated by randomly placing nodes in a 600m by 600m square. Once the network is deployed, the cluster heads are elected and all the slave nodes are covered by them in cluster heads election phase. When R_c is 200m, all the clusters are connected, and there is no uncluster node exist in the networks, as present in Figure 7.

As shown in Figure 8, cluster heads and slaves keep rather stable during the simulation. And actually, cluster heads converges as the total number of nodes increases when the R_b is fixed, as shown in Figure 9. This makes the network scalable and very useful in large-scale wireless sensor networks.

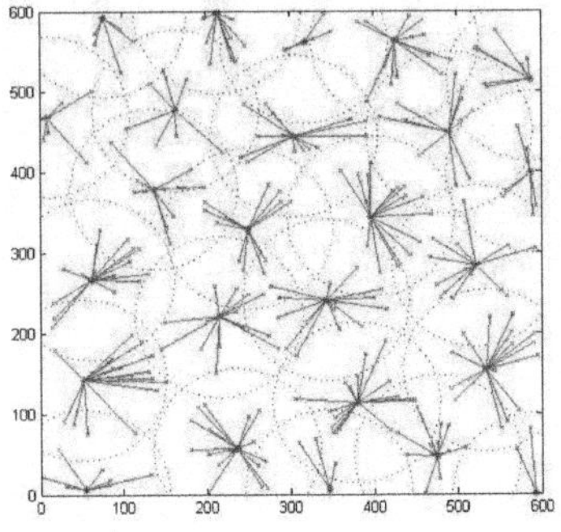

Fig. 6. Network topology

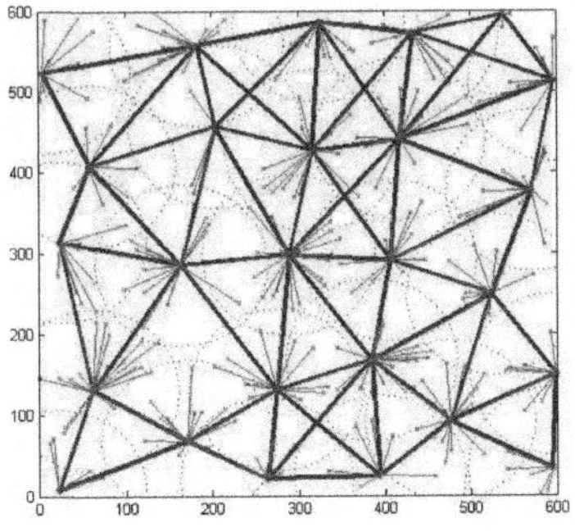

Fig. 7. All the clusters are connected

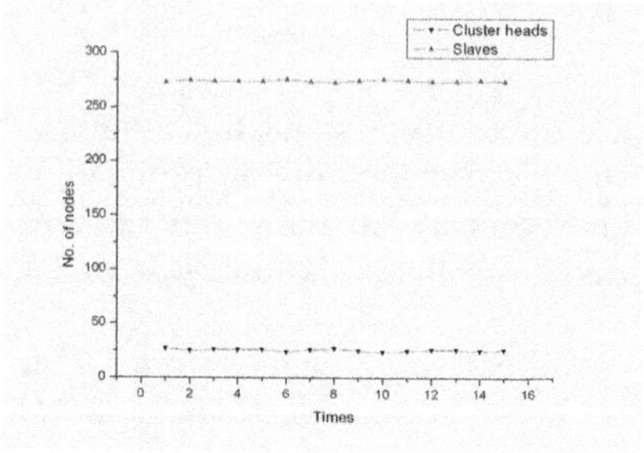

Fig. 8. Number of cluster heads and slaves

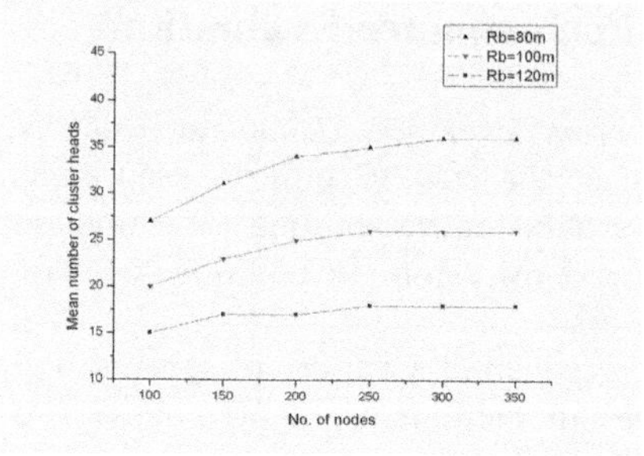

Fig. 9. Mean number of cluster heads

6.2 Average Delay

In our setup, 3 nodes were made to generate traffic to sink node, and we measure the average latency from sending out a data at the sensor to receiving it at the sink.

We present the flat flooding and directed diffusion results with node radio range of 100m, respectively. Figure 10 shows that the average delay for flooding is highest and when the network size increases, it also increases quickly. Comparing the delay of flooding, direct diffusion and DDLSC both has large improvement, furthermore, DDLSC has the minimum average latency. There are two reasons: one is that the data flow toward the sensor along the smallest hop-count routing instead of randomly broadcasting to neighbors in directed diffusion and DDLSC. The other is that DDLSC is based on a clustering scheme, the network topology is improved, and the interest flooding routing is only among the cluster heads by the higher transmission power. The network size has little effect on the delay of DDLSC.

6.3 Energy Consumption

We evaluate the average energy consumption of the 3 different protocols based on the metric joules/node/sec in networks.

Figure 11 shows the average energy cost of flooding, directed diffusion and DDLSC in different network size. It can be seen that as the network scale grows, directed diffusion shows no significant energy drain increment, but the energy consumption in flooding are increased, and it increases dramatically. DDLSC nearly

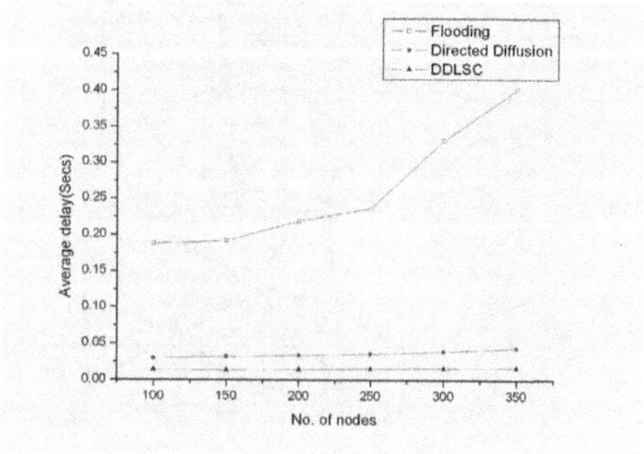

Fig. 10. Average delay

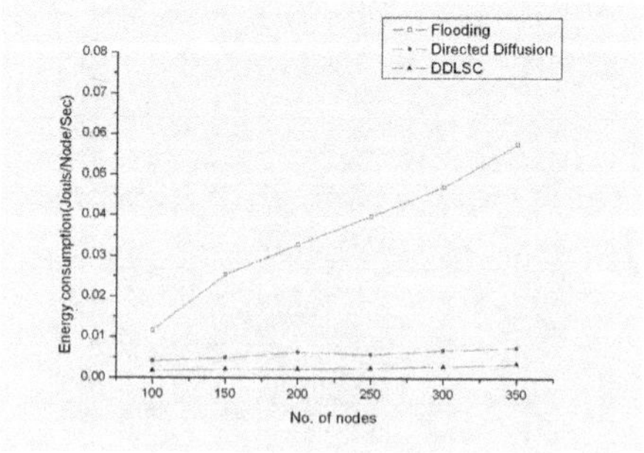

Fig. 11. Energy consumption

performs as well as directed diffusion, but consumes less power as compared to it. Since the results that presented in the figure, we can assert that in a large-scale wireless sensor network, DDLSC that proposed in this paper gives much better and stable energy performance than those data-centric routing protocols, such as flooding and directed diffusion.

7 Conclusion

In this paper we presented a directed diffusion algorithm based on link-stabilizing clustering (DDLSC), which is a delay-energy aware routing protocol for wireless sensor networks. The algorithm has two main components: a novel stable clustering scheme that forms a wireless sensor network into two layers and the cluster heads construct a virtual backbone for multi-hop communications, and a directed diffusion routing protocol based on the clustering scheme. DDLSC is simple, fast to converge, fully distributed and dynamic. It supports a good performance by enabling flexible tradeoffs between the packet delay and the energy consumption, and be scalable to the change in network size, node type, node density and topology.

Our approach can be applied to the practical applications designed of several types of sensor network protocols that require stability, prolonged network lifetime, shorten end-to-end latency, and fault tolerance.

Acknowledgment

This work is supported by the Major International (Regional) Joint Research Program of the National Science Foundation of China (No.50620130441), the Program for New Century Excellent Talents in University of China (No. NCET-05-0657)□Hubei Province Young Talent Foundation Item (No.2006ABB028) and the Key (Key grant) Project of Chinese Ministry of Education (No. 107130).

References

1. Akyildiz, I., Su, W., Sankarasubramaniam, Y., Cayirici, E.: A Survey on Sensor Networks. IEEE Transactions on Communications Magazine 40(8), 102–114 (2002)
2. Marín, I., Arceredillo, E., Zuloaga, A., Arias, J.: Wireless Sensor Networks: A Survey on Ultra-Low Power-Aware Design. Transactions on Engineering, Computing and Technology 8, 44–49 (2005)
3. Kulik, J., Heinzelman, W.R., Balakrishnan, H.: Negotiation-Based Protocols for Disseminating Information in Wireless Sensor Networks. ACM Transactions on Wireless Networks 8(2/3), 169–185 (2002)
4. Intanagoniwiwat, C., Govindan, R., Estrin, D.: Directed Diffusion: A Scalable and Robust Communication Paradigm for Sensor Networks. In: Proceedings of ACM MobiCom'00, pp. 56–67 (2000)
5. Heinzelman, W., Chandrakasan, A.: An Application-Specific Protocol Architecture for Wireless Microsensor Networks. IEEE Transactions on Wireless Communication 1(4), 660–670 (2002)

6. Manjeshwar, A., Agrawal, D.: TEEN: A Routing Protocol for Enhanced Efficiency in Wireless Sensor Networks. In: Proceedings of the 15th Int'l Parallel and Distributed Processing Symp (IPDPS), pp. 2009–2015 (2001)
7. Younis, M., Youssef, M., Arisha, K.: Energy-Aware Routing in Cluster-Based Sensor Networks. In: Proceedings of the 10th Int'l Symp. on Modeling, Analysis and Simulation of Computer and Telecommunication Systems (MASCCTS) (2002)
8. Cano, J.-C, Manzoni, P.: A Performance Comparison of Energy Consumption for Mobile Ad Hoc Network Routing Protocols. In: Proceedings of the 8th Int'l Symp. on Modeling, Analysis and Simulation of Computer and Telecommunication Systems (MASCCTS) (2000)
9. Bandyopadhyay, S., Coyle, E.J.: An Energy-Efficient Hierarchical Clustering Algorithm for Wireless Sensor Networks. In: Proceedings of IEEE INFOCOM (2003)
10. Gao, C., Jantti. R.: Link-State Clustering Based on IEEE 802.15.4 MAC for Wireless Ad-hoc/Sensor Networks. In: Proceedings of IEEE WCNC (2006)
11. Younis, O., Fahmy, S.R.: Heed: A Hybrid, Energy-Efficient, Distributed Clustering Approach for Ad Hoc Sensor Networks. IEEE Transactions on Mobile Computing 3(4), 660–669 (2004)
12. Wei-Dong, W., Qing-Xin, Z.: A Hierarchical Clustering Algorithm and Cooperation Analysis for Wireless Sensor Networks. Journal of Software 17(5), 1157–1167 (2006)
13. IEEE Wireless Medium Access Control (mac) and Physical Layer (phy) Specifications for Low-Rate Wireless Personal Area Networks. IEEE 802.15.4 WorkGroup (2003)
14. Fouad, M.R., Fahmy, S., Pandurangan, G.: Latency-Sensitive Power Control for Wireless Ad-Hoc Networks. In: Proceedings of MSWiM (2005)
15. ElBatt, T.A, Krishnamurthy, S.V, Connors, D., Dao, S.: Power Management for Throughput Enhancement in Wireless Ad-Hoc Networks. In: Proceedings of IEEE ICC (2000)
16. Akkaya, K., Younis, M.: A Survey of Routing Protocols in Wireless Sensor Networks. Transactions on Ad Hoc Networks 3, 325–349 (2002)
17. Liu, X., Li, F., Kuang, H., Wu, X.: The Study of Directed Diffusion Routing Protocol Based on Clustering for Wireless Sensor Network. In: Proceedings of IEEE WCICA (2006)

Voronoi Tessellation Based Rapid Coverage Decision Algorithm for Wireless Sensor Networks

Lei Wang, Haowei Shen, Zhe Chen, and Yaping Lin

Software School, Hunan University, 410082 Changsha, P.R. China
wanglei@hnu.cn

Abstract. The coverage problem is a fundamental issue in the research of sensor network. A novel Voronoi tessellation based rapid coverage decision algorithm is proposed, in which the region of interest is partitioned into some square grids firstly, and then the complex area coverage problem is transformed into simple vertices coverage problem, on the basis of the good characteristics of Voronoi tessellation such as being able to divide the planner area into a set of simple geometric simplexes. Theoretical analysis and simulation results show that, the new algorithm can decrease the computation complexity of networks, especially for sensor networks with *n* different sensors, it can solve the coverage problem correctly for any given region of interest with time costs of $O(nlogn)$ only.

1 Introduction

For the numerous monitoring applications of sensor networks, every single sensor in the network is responsible for collecting the local information and transmitting it to the Sink node. By aggregating all the local information, a complete picture of interest region p is depicted at Sink. To ensure the completeness of the whole information, the Sink has to determine whether the inertest region is covered by a set of specified sensor nodes sufficiently. The importance of coverage research in sensor networks is therefore self-evident. In a fire accident, for instance, early detection of the critical area can probably prevent harmless fires from turning into monstrous infernos. In general, the coverage can be seen as a measure of quality of service in sensor networks.

On account of the great characteristic in converting a planner area into a set of simple geometric simplexes, the Voronoi grid is widely used in solving the coverage problem of sensor networks. Motivated by the Voronoi grid, in 2001, Meguerdichian[1] proposed an algorithm of At Least or At Best coverage path in sensor networks, which determines how a sensor node covers the surrounding in the case of maximal breach path or maximal support path. In 2003, Li[2] improved the algorithm of Meguerdichian in the perspective of energy consumption, and based on which, reference [3-4] further investigated coverage problems like telling whether an inertest region is covered by some nodes in the network. Reference[5] gives a general description of the coverage problem, namely k-coverage problem, it studies on determining whether or not a random node in P is covered by a subset with k nodes in the sensor network. Also motivated by k-coverage problem, Huang[6-7] depicted two algorithms

J. Indulska et al. (Eds.): UIC 2007, LNCS 4611, pp. 495–502, 2007.

to solve the coverage problem in two and three dimensions in 2003 and 2004 respectively, in the worse case, the two algorithms' complexity is O(n^2log$n$) and O(n^3log$n$). Subsequently, in 2005, So&Ye[8] proposed an algorithm for solving the coverage problem in two dimensios with O($n$log$n$) complexities, however, due to the centralized property, more extra computations are required to find out the corners of P, especially for those complex region P.

In this article, we propose a Voronoi tessellation based rapid coverage decision algorithm for wireless sensor networks on the basis of the great characteristic of voronoi tessellation in converting a planner area into a set of simple geometric simplexes. Firstly, in our algorithm, the Sink partitions the interest region into square grids, by utilizing the information collected, the region R^2 is then partitioned into Voronoi grids, thus transforming a complicated coverage problem to a simple vertices coverage problem. Theoretical analysis and simulation results demonstrate that, compared to the algorithm proposed by So&Ye, for a sensor network with n nodes, the new algorithm can also solve the coverage problem in region P with $O(nlogn)$ complexities, but our algorithm is more competitive since it efficiently reduces the computation complexity of the network and requires less computation consumptions in total.

2 Preliminaries

In a sensor network, suppose that n sensor nodes$\{s_1,s_2,\ldots,s_n\}$ are deployed in a two dimensional region R^2. If Sink wants to collect the information of region $P \subseteq R^2$ at any moment t, it has to determine that whether all the nodes of sub-region $P \subseteq R^2$ are sufficiently covered.

The above-mentioned problem can be formulated as follows:

Let P be the region of interest and $\{s_1,s_2,\ldots,s_n\}$ are n sensor nodes randomly deployed in a region R^2 ($P \subseteq R^2$), for an arbitrary location i in P, if there exists at least one sensor node $s_j \in \{s_1,s_2,\ldots,s_n\}$ covering location i within its sensing radius, then we say $\{s_1,s_2,\ldots,s_n\}$ covers sub region P.

To be precise, a_i is denoted as the position of sensor node s_i, all the nodes have identical sensing radius r, and $A_{s_i}=\{x| \; dist(a_i, x) \leq r, \forall x \in P\}$ is defined as the coverage area of sensor node s_i . Apparently, the coverage area of s_i is a disk centered at a_i with radius r.

Hence, we formally state the definition as:

Definition 1 (Coverage disk). Let a denote the position of sensor node s, which is deployed in a two dimensional space R^2 with sensing radius r, then $A_s=\{x| \; dist(a, x) \leq r, \forall x \in R^2\}$ is the coverage disk of sensor s.

On the basis of the above-mentioned statement, the coverage problem can be simplified into the definition as:

Definition 2 (The Coverage Problem). Let p denote the region of interest, and $\{s_1,s_2,\ldots,s_n\}$ are defined as n sensor nodes in a two dimensional space R^2 ($P \subseteq R^2$), all the nodes have identical sensing radius r. For any node i in region p, if there exists at least one sensor node $s_j \in \{s_1,s_2,\ldots,s_n\}$ to make $i \in A_j=\{x| \; dist(a_j, x) \leq r,$

$\forall x \in R^2\}$,where a_j denotes the location of sensor s_j, then $\{s_1,s_2,\ldots,s_n\}$ covers sub region P.

Definition 3 (Voronoi cell). Let $S=\{s_1,s_2,\ldots,s_n\}$ denote n sensor nodes in region R^2 and a_j be the location of sensor s_j, then $Cell(s_i)$ = $\bigcap_{j=1,j\neq i}^{n} \{x \mid dist(a_i,x) \leq dist(a_j,x), \forall x \in R^2\}$ is said to be the Voronoi cell of s_i, where $dist(p, q)$ represents the *Euclidean* distance between p and q.

Evidently, for a two dimensional space R^2 ($P \subseteq R^2$) with n sensor nodes $\{s_1,s_2,\ldots,s_n\}$, definition 3 partitions R^2 into $Cell(s_1),Cell(s_2),\ldots,Cell(s_n)$

Definition 4 (Voronoi grid). Let $S=\{s_1,s_2,\ldots,s_n\}$ denote n sensor nodes in region R^2 ,then R^2's partition, which consisting of $Cell(s_1),Cell(s_2),\ldots,Cell(s_n)$, is called the Voronoi grids generated by S.

Definition 5 (Voronoi neighbor). Let $S=\{s_1,s_2,\ldots,s_n\}$ denote n sensor nodes in region R^2 , $Cell(s_1),Cell(s_2),\ldots,Cell(s_n)$ are defined the Voronoi cells in the Voronoi grids generated by S, s_i, s_j are then said to be Voronoi neighbors if there is a common edge between $Cell(s_i)$ and $Cell(s_j)$.

The lemma 3.1 in reference [9] proves that:

Lemma 1. For an arbitrary sensor node $s \in S$, if $s_{i_1}, s_{i_2}, \ldots, s_{i_k}$ ($s_{i_t} \in S$, t=1,2,…,k) are the neighbors of s, then any sensor node has $A_s \bigcap A_{s'} \subseteq \bigcup_{t=1}^{k} A_{s_{i_t}}$,where $S=\{s_1,s_2,\ldots,s_n\}$ denotes as n sensor nodes in region R^2 , A_s, $A_{s'}$, $A_{s_{i_t}}$ (t=1,2,…,k) is denoted as the coverage disk of s, s' and s_{i_t} (t=1,2,…,k) respectively.

On the basis of Lemma 1, consider that $S=\{s_1, s_2,\ldots, s_n\}$ denotes n sensor nodes in region R^2. For an arbitrary sensor node s, s'$\in S$, if the coverage disk of s' intersects with the one of s, then that intersection is covered by the coverage disk of s 's Voronoi neighbor.

Definition 6 (*r*-square grid). For a given region P, the area portioned by the following method is called an r-square grids.

1) Calculate the the maximal length l and width w in region P;
2) Calculate $[l/\sqrt{2}r]$ and $[w/\sqrt{2}r]$, where $[x]$ represents the minimal integer more than or equal to x;
3) Partition the sub region P into $[l/\sqrt{2}r] * [w/\sqrt{2}r]$ squares;
4) Remove the squares which do not cover any node in region P.

Definition 7 (*r*-square coverage). For an arbitrary given node v in a two dimensional space R^2, suppose that C_v is the circle centered at v with radius r, then the inscribed square R_v of C_v is said to be r-square coverage of v.

Lemma 2. For an arbitrary given node v in a two dimensional space R^2, let R_v represent the r-square coverage of v and s be the position of any arbitrary sensor node in R^2, A_s denotes the coverage disk of s, $A_s \bigcap R_v = \phi$ (Void) if $dist(s, v) > 2r$.

Definition 8 (Voronoi coverage nodes set). Let v denote an arbitrary given node in a two dimensional space R^2, $S=\{s_1,s_2,\ldots,s_n\}$ is defined as the location of n sensor nodes in R^2, $v \notin S$, and $v=s_{n+1}$, $S'=S+\{v\}=\{s_1,s_2,\ldots,s_n, s_{n+1}\}$, then in the Voronoi grids generated by S', $S_v=\{ s_{v1}, s_{v2}, \cdots, s_{vk} \}$ is the Voronoi coverage nodes set of v if all the Voronoi neighbors of v are $\{ s_{v1}, s_{v2}, \cdots, s_{vk} \} \subseteq S$.

Lemma 3. For an arbitrary given node v in a two dimensional space R^2, suppose that R_v is the r-square coverage of v, $S=\{s_1,s_2,\ldots,s_n\}$ denotes the location of n sensor nodes in R^2, and $v \notin S$, $S_v=\{ s_{v1}, s_{v2}, \cdots, s_{vk} \}$ denotes the Voronoi coverage nodes set of v, then $R_v \subseteq \bigcup_{i=1}^{n} A_{s_i} \Leftrightarrow R_v \subseteq \bigcup_{i=1}^{k} A_{v_i}$,where A_s represents the coverage disk of sensor node s.

Definition 9 (Quadratic Voronoi Grid). For an arbitrary given node v in a two dimensional space R^2, $S=\{s_1,s_2,\ldots,s_n\}$ defines the location of n sensor nodes in R^2, $v \notin S$,and $S_v=\{ s_{v1}, s_{v2}, \cdots, s_{vk} \}$ is the Voronoi coverage nodes set of v, then the Voronoi grids generated by S_v is said to be the quadratic Voronoi grids of v.

Definition 10 (Vertices and Intersections of Quadratic Voronoi). For an arbitrary given node v in a two dimensional space R^2, suppose that R_v is the r-square coverage of v , then all the vertices of the Voronoi cell in the quadratic Voronoi grid generated by v are said to be the quadratic Voronoi vertices, at the same time, all the intersections between the Voronoi cell' edge and R_v in the Voronoi grid generated by v are said to be the quadratic Voronoi intersections.

On the basis of above depictions, it is feasible to prove the validity of lemma 4.

Lemma 4. For an arbitrary given node v in a two dimensional space R^2, R_v is defined as the r-square coverage of v , $S=\{s_1,s_2,\ldots,s_n\}$ are n sensor nodes in R^2 , and all the nodes have identical sensing radius r. R_v is covered by $s_1,s_2,\ldots,s_n$ if all the quadratic Voronoi vertices and the quadratic Voronoi intersections of v, and the four vertices of R_v, are covered by the coverage disk of s_{v1} , s_{v2} ,$\cdots$, s_{vk} ,where $S_v=\{ s_{v1}, s_{v2}, \cdots, s_{vk} \}$ is the Voronoi coverage nodes set of v.

Based on lemma 4, the judgement theorem of coverage problem in definition 2 is described as follows:

Theorem 1 (Judgement theorem of coverage problem). Consider the interest region P of *Sink*, $\{s_1,s_2,\ldots,s_n\}$ are n sensor nodes arbitrarily deployed in a two dimensional space R^2 ($P \subseteq R^2$), and all the nodes have identical sensing radius r $\Psi=\{R_1,R_2,\cdots,R_m\}$ is defined as the r-square grid of P, in which $R_1,R_2,\cdots,R_m$ are all the squares in the r-square grids of P, v_i denotes the barycenter of R_i (i=1,2,…,m), { v_{i1}, v_{i2}, v_{i3}, v_{i4} } denotes the set consists of four vertices in R_i (i=1,2,…,m),and S_i={ s_{i_1}, s_{i_2},⋯, s_{i_k} } denotes the Voronoi coverage nodes set of v_i. P is covered by s_1,s_2,…,s_n if all the quadratic Voronoi vertices{V_1,V_2,…,V_x} and the quadratic Voronoi intersections{I_1,I_2,…,I_y} of v_i and the four vertices { v_{i_1}, v_{i_2}, v_{i_3}, v_{i_4} }of R_v, are covered by the coverage disk of s_{i_1}, s_{i_2},⋯, s_{i_k}, where v_i (i=1,2,…,m) is randomly selected.

3 Voronoi Tessellation Based Rapid Coverage Decision Algorithm

Let P denote the interest sub region of *Sink*, {s_1,s_2,…,s_n} are n sensor nodes arbitrarily deployed in a two dimensional space R^2 ($P \subseteq R^2$), all the nodes have identical sensing radius r. The Voronoi tessellation based rappid coverage decision algorithm can be described as follows:

Algorithm VT-RCDA (*Voronoi Tessellation based Rapid Coverage Decision Algorithm*):

***Step* 1:** Firstly, r-square grids Ψ ={R_1,R_2,…,R_m} of region P are constructed by *Sink*, where R_1,R_2,…,R_m are all the squares in r-square grids of P. Secondly, *Sink* calculates the barycenter v_i for every R_i (i=1,2,…,m) and the position of four vertices { v_{i_1}, v_{i_2}, v_{i_3}, v_{i_4} }; Furthermore, *Sink* broadcasts the positions of the barycenter{v_1,v_2,…,v_m} in all the squares to every sensor node .

***Step* 2:** For an arbitrary sensor node A, the distance {d_1,d_2,…,d_m} between itself a and {v_1,v_2,…,v_m} will be calculated when it receives the information broadcasted by *Sink*, the sensor node will send the feedback $\bigcup_{i=1}^{k}\{v_i, a\}$ to *Sink* if there exist { d'_1, d'_2,…, d'_k } $\subseteq$ {d_1,d_2,…,d_m} satisfy $Max\{d'_1, d'_2, \ldots, d'_k\} \le 2r$.

***Step* 3:** For every $v_i \in$ {v_1,v_2,…,v_m}, if all the sensor nodes with distance less than $2r$ from v_i collected by *Sink* gather as { s_{i_1}, s_{i_2},…, s_{i_t} }, then the Voronoi coverage nodes set is revealed at *Sink* through calculating the Voronoi grids generated by {v_i, s_{i_1}, s_{i_2},…, s_{i_t} }. Subsequently,the Voronoi vertices and the Voronoi intersections of v_i are obtained.

***Step* 4:** For every $v_i \in$ {v_1,v_2,…,v_m}, on the basis of the Voronoi vertices and the Voronoi intersections of v_i along with the four vertices position of R_i, by utilizing theorem 1 *Sink* determines whether all the Voronoi vertices and the Voronoi intersections of v_i and the four vertices of R_v are covered by the coverage disk of the nodes in the Voronoi coverage nodes set.

4 Algorithm Analyses and Simulation

Theorem 2: For an arbitrary given region P with n sensor nodes, the complexity of VT-RCDA is $O(nlogn)$ at most .

Proof: Reference[10] has already shown that, for n arbitrary nodes in a two dimensional space R^2, the complexity of constructing the Voronoi grids of R^2 is $O(nlogn)$, based on which , we subsequently list the estimated complexity of every single step in algorithm VT-RCDA.

***Step*1:** For the given interest region P, constructing the r-square grids $\Psi = \{R_1,R_2,\cdots,R_m\}$of P and calculating all the barycenter$\{v_1,v_2,\cdots,v_m\}$ as well as the vertices of them respectively has $O(1)$ complexity.

***Step*2:** Given interest region P, calculating the distance $\{d_1,d_2,\cdots,d_m\}$ between the position a of any sensor node and $\{v_1,v_2,\cdots,v_m\}$ has $O(1)$ complexity, where m denotes a constant.

***Step*3:**

1) Due to the complexity of calculating the Voronoi grid of every $\{v_i, s_{i_1}, s_{i_2},\ldots, s_{i_t}\}$ is +1)$log(t+1)$)= $O(tlogt)$, suppose that the Voronoi coverage nodes set of v_i (i=1,2,...,m) includes t_i (i=1,2,...,m,) nodes, clearly, $t_i \leq n$. Thus, calculating the Voronoi grids generated by $\{v_i, s_{i_1}, s_{i_2},\ldots, s_{i_t}\}$, i=1,2,...,m at Sink owns complexity of $O(t_1 log\ t_1)$+ $O(t_2 log\ t_2)$+...+ $O(t_m log\ t_m) \leq O(nlogn)$.

2) Since the number required to be considered when Sink obtaining the Voronoi coverage nodes set from the Voronoi grids generated by $\{v_i, s_{i_1}, s_{i_2},\ldots, s_{i_t}\}$ is t $\{s_{i_1}, s_{i_2},\ldots, s_{i_t}\}$, during which $O(t)$ complexities are needed, then the *Sink* obtaining Voronoi coverage nodes set generated by $\{v_1,v_2,\cdots,v_m\}$ has $O(t_1)$+ $O(t_2)$+...+ $O(t_m \leq O(n)$ complexities.

3) By following the analysis in Step 2.1) , it is evident that the complexity of *Sink* obtaining the quadratic Voronoi grids of $\{v_1,v_2,\cdots,v_m\}$ will not exceed $O(nlogn)$.

4) Finally, the complexity of *Sink* obtaining the quadratic Voronoi vertices and intersections of $\{v_1,v_2,\cdots,v_m\}$ will apparently not exceed $O(n)$.

***Step* 4:** By utilizing the theorem 1, the complexity of *Sink* determining whether all the Voronoi vertices and intersections along with four vertices of R_v are covered by the coverage disk of the coverage nodes set is at most $O(n)$.

To conclude, algorithm VT-RCDA has no more than $O(1)$+$O(1)$+$O(nlogn)$+$O(n)$+$O(nlogn)$+$O(n)$=$O(nlogn)$ complexities in total. [End]

Based on the above theorems, we did a simulation experiment in a 800*1000 area, in which 500-4000 sensor nodes with sensing radius 50 randomly distributed. By showing the percentage of sensor nodes used in the whole network, Fig.1 demonstrates the comparison between algorithm VT-RCDA and the So&Ye's algorithm mentioned in reference[8].

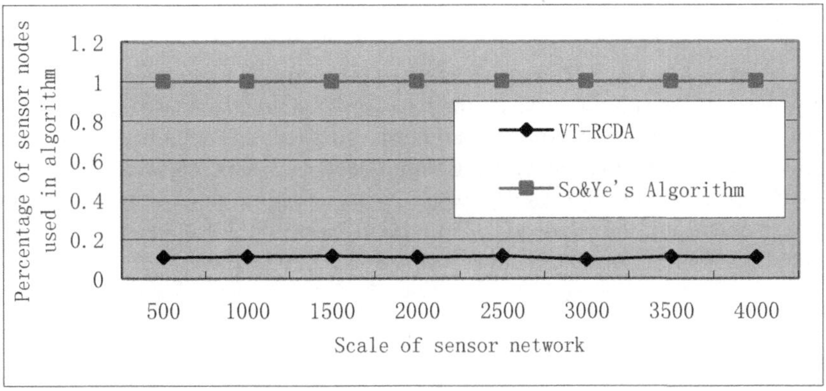

Fig. 1. Comparison between algorithm VT-RCDA and So&Ye in percentage of sensor nodes used in the whole network

From what is revealed in Fig.1, it is known that algorithm So&Ye has to take the advantage of all the sensor nodes to determinate the coverage situation, in contrast, approximately 10% sensor nodes are required in algorithm VT-RCDA. Without a doubt , the new algorithm reduces the complexity dramatically.

To further demonstrate the superiority of algorithm VT-RCDA, Fig.2 depicts a comparison with So&Ye's Algorithm in computation time consumption

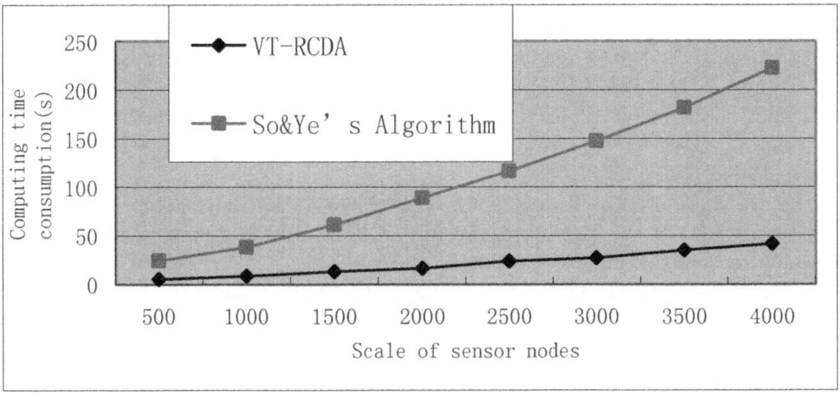

Fig. 2. Comparison between VT-RCDA and So&Ye in computation time consumption

Fig.2 shows the result that computation time consumption of algorithm VT-RCDA is much lower than that of So&Ye 's algorithm, which from another aspect verifies what is shown in FIGURE 9: algorithm VT-RCDA utilizes only parts of the sensor nodes rather than all the nodes.

4 Conclusion

In this paper, we propose a Voronoi Tessellation based rapid coverage decision algorithm for wireless sensor networks on the basis of its great characteristic in converting a planner area into a set of simple geometric simplexes. Theoretical analysis and simulation results show that the new algorithm decreases the computation complexity of the network efficiently. However, when it comes to the three dimensional space coverage problem and k-coverage(k>2) problem based on Voronoi grids model and the method proposed in our paper, there is much work to be done.

References

1. Meguerdichian, S., et al.: Coverage Problems in Wireless Ad Hoc Sensor Networks. IEEE INFORCOM 3, 1380–1387 (2001)
2. Li, X., Wan, P., Frieder, O.: Coverage in Wireless Ad Hoc Sensor Networks. IEEE Transactions on Computers 6, 753–763 (2003)
3. Tian, D., Georganas, N.D.: A coverage-preserving Node Scheduling Scheme for Large Wireless Sensor Networks. In: Proceedings of 1st ACM International Conference on Wireless Sensor Networks and Applications, pp. 32–41. ACM Press, New York (2002)
4. Ye, F., Zhong, G., Cheng, J., et al.: PEAS: A Robust Energy Conserving Protocol for Long-lived Sensor Networks. In: Proceedings of the 23rd International Conference on Distributed Computing Systems, pp. 28–37 (2003)
5. Zhou, Z., Das, S., Gupta, H.: Connected K-Coverage Problem in Sensor Networks. In: Proceedings of the 13th International Conference on Computer Communications and Networks, pp. 373–378 (2004)
6. Huang, C.F., Tseng, Y.C.: The Coverage Problem in a Wireless Sensor Net-work. In: Proceedings of the 2nd ACM International Conference on Wireless Sensor Networks and Applications, pp. 115–121. ACM Press, New York (2003)
7. Huang, C.F., Tseng, Y.C., Lo, L.C.: The Coverage Problem in Three Dimensional Wireless Sensor Networks. In: Shah, R. (ed.) Proc. of the GLOBECOM, pp. 3182–3186. IEEE Press, Dallas (2004)
8. So, A.M.-C., Ye, Y.: On Sloving Coverage Problems in a Wireless Sensor Network Using Voronoi Diagrams. In: Proceedings of the 1st Workshop on Internet and Network Economics, pp. 584–593 (2005)
9. Bogdan, C., Ananth, G.: Jan Vitek: Coverage Preserving Redundancy Elimination in Sensor Networks. In: Proceedings of the 1st IEEE International Conference on Sensor and Ad Hoc Communications and Networks, pp. 377–386. IEEE Computer Society Press, Los Alamitos (2004)
10. Aggarwal, A., Leonidas, J., et al.: A Linear Time Algorithm for Computing the Voronoi Diagram of a Convex Polygon. Discreate and Computational Geometry 6, 591–604 (1989)

A Clustering-Based Approximation Scheme for In-Network Aggregation over Sensor Networks

Lei Xie, Lijun Chen, Daoxu Chen, and Li Xie

State Key Laboratory of Novel Software Technology
NJU-POLYU Cooperative Laboratory for Wireless Sensor Network
Nanjing University, Nanjing, China
xielei@dislab.nju.edu.cn
{chenlj,cdx,xieli}@nju.edu.cn

Abstract. Recently in-network aggregation has gained much attention for effectively reducing energy consumption over sensor networks. In this paper, we present CASA, a clustering-based approximation scheme for in-network aggregation, which significantly reduces the overall energy consumption while maintaining user-specified data quality. We explore two ideas to support the approximation scheme. First, we propose a clustering-based framework to effectively utilize temporal coherency tolerance (*tct*) in conjunction with in-network aggregation to save communication cost over sensor network. Secondly, we propose an adaptive *tct*-reallocating technique to further reduce communication cost and maintain load balance. Our experiment results indicate that significant benefits can be achieved by using our CASA approximation scheme.

1 Introduction

Advances in MEMS and wireless communication technology have enabled deployment of large scale wireless sensor networks. A major constraint for effective wide-scale deployment of such sensor networks is the limited battery power. So developing energy-efficient strategies for wireless sensor network applications is of utmost importance. Recently a database approach [1] has been introduced into sensor networks, mainly utilizing the in-network aggregation scheme to effectively extract useful information through user queries. With in-network aggregation [2][3], a part of the computation work for aggregation is performed within the sensor nodes before they send the results out to the base station. Some approximation methods [4][5][6] have been proposed to further reduce energy consumption for in-network aggregation. While playing with the accuracy/energy tradeoff, a large amount of energy can be saved and the final aggregate results still can be controlled within specified tolerance bound.

In this paper, we try to leverage the hierarchical caching scheme to approximate sensor readings within users' tolerance, avoiding unnecessary data transmission at best effort. The goal of our paper is to devise an effective approximation scheme for processing continuous aggregate queries over sensor networks so as to (a)satisfy

J. Indulska et al. (Eds.): UIC 2007, LNCS 4611, pp. 503–513, 2007.

monitoring quality constraint (b)minimize communication cost (c)maximize network lifetime by load balance. The rest of the paper is organized as follows. In Section 2 we discuss in-network aggregation scheme. Section 3 outlines the approximation problem in WSNs. Section 4 exhibits our clustering based approximation architecture in detail. Section 5 presents our adaptive tolerance reallocating technique. The experiment results can be found in Section 6. Section 7 introduces related works, we conclude in Section 8.

2 In-Network Aggregation Model

In-network aggregation [2][3] has been considered as an energy-efficient approach to answer users' aggregate queries. After a routing tree is built, all raw sensor readings and partial aggregate records are combined in-network, each intermediate node only forwards a data copy in aggregate form, and what the base station receives is actually the final aggregate result. Huge amounts of communication cost can be reduced in contrast to the conventional approach which aggregates all the raw sensor readings at base station. In this paper we investigate into approximation scheme for continuous aggregate queries, for which new results are generated periodically. Such queries can be expressed using an extended SQL select statement:

SELECT AggregationFunction(attributes)
FROM sensors s
WHERE s.loc in Range R
EPOCH DURATION i
VALUES WITHIN tct

The first three clauses are the same as in standard SQL. The new clause *EPOCH DURATION i* was introduced by TAG [3], parameter i specifies arrival rate of new results. The clause *VALUES WITHIN tct* was first proposed by TiNA [4] to express the temporal coherency tolerance, this clause raises precision constraint for approximated aggregate result V' to ensure that the exact aggregate result V is within the specified tolerance bound $[V' \cdot (1 - tct), V' \cdot (1 + tct)]$.

3 The Approximation Problem

During the continuous monitoring for aggregate queries, periodically transmitting all sensor data up the network requires a lot of energy. To keep the aggregate results within user-specified quality, it is possible to partially transmit sensor data up the network, leveraging the approximation scheme. We observe that by maintaining a synchronized prediction model [4][7] between local node and parent node, it is unnecessary for each node to report every new value to its parent node when the new value is very close to the predicted value that its parent is aware of. To be more specific, every parent node keeps a prediction value v' and a corresponding tolerance tct for each child node, both the parent and child nodes agree on the prediction model, so each child node has to report a new value to the parent node only when the tolerance bound is violated by the new value v ($|v - v^{'}| > v^{'} \cdot tct$). When the parent node doesn't hear from a child node, it assumes that the new value is within the bound $[v^{'} \cdot (1 - tct), v^{'} \cdot (1 + tct)]$. With such an approximation approach much communication cost can be reduced compared with the conventional approach. Recently several prediction methods have been proposed[4][6][7]. The cache scheme [8] which utilizes previously reported value as the predicted value for future readings is an appropriate choice for its simplicity and scalability. With support from the cache-based prediction model, how to construct an energy-efficient routing architecture and effectively deploy relative tolerances for different nodes to sufficiently extend the network lifetime remains a problem for us to investigate into.

4 Clustering-Based Approximation Architecture for In-Network Aggregation

4.1 Problem of Tree-Based Approximation Architecture

Conventional approximation approaches for in-network aggregation generally utilizes the tree-based aggregation architecture to implement the approximation scheme. TiNA [4] is the first work that exploits temporal correlation to support approximation for in-network aggregation, leveraging the tree-based aggregation architecture. As user specifies in query the temporal coherency tolerance (tct), TiNA applies the tolerance bound tct to all leaf nodes which generate raw sensor readings in the aggregation tree, for internal nodes which generate the partial aggregate values, TiNA applies tct=0 at the partial aggregate level so as to fulfill quality requirement of the final aggregate result. As we investigate further into the tree-based approximation scheme, as Fig. 1 shows, we note that only data for leaf nodes can be effectively approximated by caching method within tolerance bound tct, while intermediate nodes applied with tct=0. A considerable amount of intermediate nodes cannot well utilize the approximation scheme because they have tight tct constraints (tct=0).

4.2 Properties of Hierarchical Caching Method

We propose our hierarchical caching method with a 2-level cluster architecture, which is similar to LEACH-based cluster structure [9]. As Fig. 2 shows, with the same sensor network deployment as the tree-based architecture depicted in Fig. 1, we construct 3 clusters with cluster heads (CH) tagged with black color. The CH nodes along with the base station form backbone paths to transmit the partial aggregate values, in terms of that, only 3 CH nodes in the network operate as intermediate nodes to send partial state record (PSR), all the other nodes operate as leaf nodes. This clustering-based architecture allows the approximation scheme to take advantage of the temporal coherency tolerance at best effort

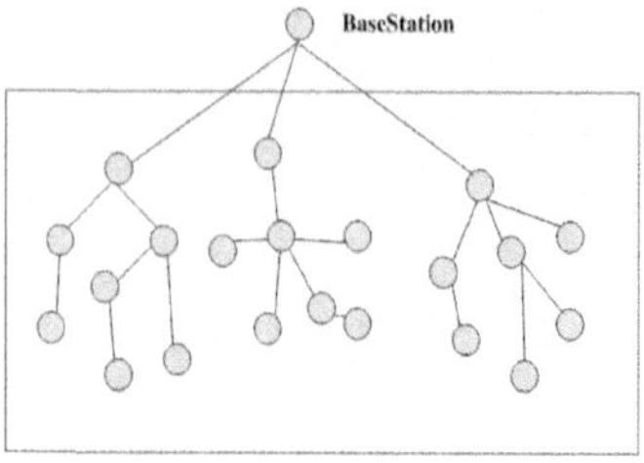

Fig. 1. Tree-based Architecture

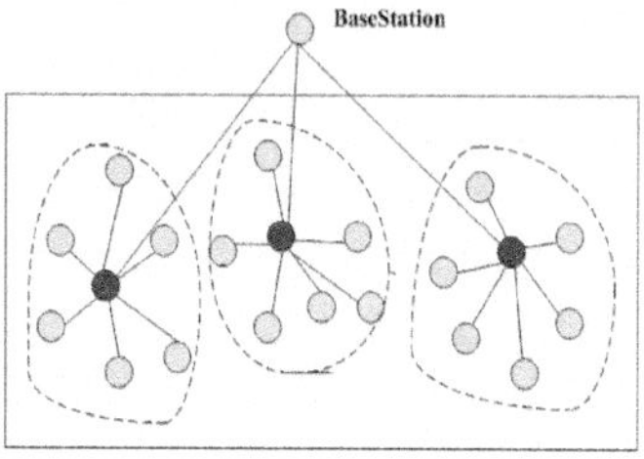

Fig. 2. Cluster-based Architecture

to reduce communication cost. We describe our hierarchical caching method as follows: As a cluster structure is properly formed, each CH node keeps copies of the last reported data for leaf nodes within its cluster, and each leaf node keeps that last reported copy locally. The base station keeps copies of the last reported *PSRs* from each CH node, and each CH node keeps last reported *PSR* copy locally. We apply tolerance *tct* to all leaf nodes and set the tolerance to zero for CH nodes. We formally depict properties of our hierarchical caching method through formula 1-3, assume all raw sensor readings are set to be positive:

$$AggValue = \sum_{j=1}^{N_c} PSR_j \tag{1}$$

$$AggValue \cdot tct = \sum_{j=1}^{N_c} (PSR_j \cdot tct) \tag{2}$$

$$PSR_j^{'} \cdot tct = \sum_{i \in Cluster_j} (v_i^{'} \cdot tct) \tag{3}$$

Formula 1 denotes that the final aggregate result is composed of partial aggregate values (*PSR*) from N_c clusters (N_c is the total number of clusters). So the overall tolerance specified by user (*AggValue·tct*) can be effectively divided into partial error tolerances (*PSR·tct*) contributed by each cluster, while each cluster has the same relative tolerance *tct*, just as formula 2 denotes. The *PSR'* is the cached copy of partial aggregate value *PSR*, and is always coherent with *PSR* because the tolerance for partial aggregate values is set to zero. Formula 3 shows that the tolerance of *PSR* can be further divided into error tolerances ($v^{'} \cdot tct$) contributed by each single non-CH node within corresponding cluster. Therefore utilizing this hierarchical caching method, we can ensure the final aggregate result within user-specified *tct*.

4.3 Optimum Number of Clusters

A key issue of the clustering-based approximation architecture is how to control the size of clusters so as to efficiently minimize overall energy consumption over senor networks. Because when there is only one cluster, although the number of leaf nodes is maximized, the non-CH nodes often have to transmit data over quite long distances to reach the CH node, draining their energy. So it makes sense to find the optimum number of clusters to efficiently maximize lifetime of sensor network.

Assume that there are N nodes distributed uniformly in an M*M region. If there exist k clusters, there are on average N/k nodes per cluster. Each cluster head dissipates energy by receiving data from non-CH nodes, doing data aggregation and sending the aggregate data to base station. We utilize an energy model proposed in LEACH [9] for the radio hardware energy dissipation. To transmit an l-bit message to a distance d, the radio expends:

$$E_{Tx}(l,d) = E_{Tx-elec} + E_{Tx-amp}(l,d) = \begin{cases} lE_{elec} + l\varepsilon_{fs}d^2 & d < d_{crossover} \\ lE_{elec} + l\varepsilon_{mp}d^4 & d \geq d_{crossover} \end{cases} \quad (4)$$

To receive this message, the radio expends:

$$E_{Rx}(l) = E_{Rx-elec}(l) = lE_{elec} \quad (5)$$

We denote the probability that each round a non-CH node will send a message to cluster head as P_{Ts}, we call one transmission over several rounds as an update event, therefore the energy dissipated in the CH node during one round is:

$$E_{CH} = lE_{elec}(\frac{N}{k} - 1)P_{Ts} + lE_{DA}\frac{N}{k} + lE_{elec} + l\varepsilon_{mp}d^4_{toBS} \quad (6)$$

The energy used in each non-CH nodes is:

$$E_{non-CH} = (lE_{elec} + l\varepsilon_{fs}d^2_{toCH})P_{Ts} \quad (7)$$

As we have learned from LEACH, there exists:

$$E[d^2_{toCH}] = \frac{1}{2\pi}\frac{M^2}{k} \quad (8)$$

Therefore for non-CH nodes the energy consumption is:

$$E_{non-CH} = (lE_{elec} + l\varepsilon_{fs}\frac{1}{2\pi}\frac{M^2}{k})P_{Ts} \quad (9)$$

The energy dissipated within a cluster in one round is :

$$E_{cluster} = E_{CH} + (\frac{N}{k} - 1)E_{non-CH} \approx E_{CH} + (\frac{N}{k})E_{non-CH} \quad (10)$$

And the total energy consumption over all k clusters is:

$$E_{total} = kE_{cluster} = l(E_{elec}[(N-k)P_{Ts} + k] + k\varepsilon_{mp}d^4_{toBS} + E_{DA}N + E_{elec}NP_{Ts} + \varepsilon_{fs}\frac{1}{2\pi}\frac{M^2}{k}NP_{Ts}) \quad (11)$$

Therefore from this expression we can find the optimum number of clusters by setting the derivative of E_{total} with respect to k to zero:

$$k_{opt} = \frac{M\sqrt{N}}{\sqrt{2\pi}}\sqrt{\frac{\varepsilon_{fs}P_{Ts}}{E_{elec}(1-P_{Ts})+\varepsilon_{mp}d_{toBS}^{4}}} \tag{12}$$

The above expression shows the k_{opt} value with the parameter P_{Ts}, which denotes the probability for a non-CH node to send a message to cluster head under our approximation scheme. So by appropriately approximating the transmission probability P_{Ts}, we can calculate the optimum number of clusters. Assuming the series of update events over sensor network accords with Poisson Process with parameter λ, which denotes the constant rate of arrivals (update-counts/round). So according to property of Poisson Process, the probability of one arrival per round P_{Ts}, is equal to the expectation of arrival rates λ, there exists $\mathrm{EX}(\lambda)=P_{Ts}$, in terms of this in order to get the transmission probability P_{Ts} we only have to approximate the value of λ through a learning phase before the clusters are constructed over sensor network.

5 Adaptive Tolerance Reallocating Scheme

So far we have proposed a hierarchical cache-based approximation scheme with each non-CH node having a uniform relative tolerance *tct* that conforms to formula 3. That means the overall tolerance of the partial aggregate values (*PSR*) for each cluster is equally divided for each non-CH node in relative formulation, therefore each non-CH node has an equal relative tolerance *tct* coherent with the overall *PSR* tolerance. But this approach may not be cost efficient, since different sensor sources may have different changing rates. For those sensors whose values do not change much, it is beneficial to assign them smaller error tolerances and assign the slack tolerance to those more active sensors. So based on the above idea, we can assign different tolerances to different nodes according to their changing rates, so as to further reduce update transmissions and enhance load balance. Formula 13 shows the formalization of constraint for variable tolerance assignment:

$$PSR_j^{'} \cdot tct = \sum_{i \in Cluster_j} (v_i^{'} \cdot tct_i) \tag{13}$$

Describing exactly activities of different sensor sources can be difficult, especially over the resource constrained sensor networks. Previous work [6] proposed to maintain a statistical model for sensor network at base station, but still this strategy may be too complex to implement well through an energy-efficient approach. We propose a simple strategy for estimating sensor nodes activities based on update frequencies. During the steady transmission phase, a reallocating process is always initiated by the cluster heads. Each cluster head counts the update frequencies f_i for each child node i within its cluster for a fixed number of rounds n. Then f_i is the number of updates a child node i makes during n rounds, and $0 \leq f_i \leq n$. After every n rounds each CH nodes gets the update frequency f_1,

$f_2, \cdots, f_m$ for child nodes within its cluster, where m denotes the number of non-CH nodes in the cluster. For each cluster the CH node will reallocate relative tolerances tct_i for each child node i based on the series of update frequencies. We utilize the following criterion to initiate the tolerance reallocation:

$$\frac{1}{n}\sqrt{\frac{1}{m}\sum_{i=1}^{m}(f_i - \bar{f})^2} \geq r_{th} \tag{14}$$

The left part of formula 14 denotes the ratio of $\sigma(f)$ against n, where $\sigma(f)$ is the standard deviation of update frequencies. So the above formula means that if the deviation of the update frequencies is beyond threshold r_{th}, then the tolerance reallocation process should be initiated.

During the tolerance reallocation process the cluster head leverages the cached update frequencies as weights to support allocating the relative tolerances, which is denoted as follows:

$$\frac{tct_1}{f_1} = \frac{tct_2}{f_2} = \cdots = \frac{tct_i}{f_i} = \cdots = \frac{tct_m}{f_m} = C \tag{15}$$

In order to satisfy the equivalence constraint for variable tolerance assignment denoted in formula 13, finally the CH nodes can calculate:

$$tct_i = C \cdot f_i = \frac{\sum_{i=1}^{m}(v_i' \cdot tct)}{\sum_{i=1}^{m}(v_i' \cdot f_i)} \cdot f_i \tag{16}$$

For each cluster after the cluster head has successfully calculated the new relative tolerance tct_i for each child node i, it just sends the new reallocated tolerance to each child node to locally implement the new tolerance tct_i over new generated sensor readings.The tolerance reallocation process periodically executes after every n rounds when the tolerance reallocation criterion is satisfied.

6 Experiments and Results

To study the effects of our proposed approximation scheme, we created a simulation environment. Simulation parameters are summarized in Table 1.

Energy Cost Model. As mentioned before, for the 2-level cluster-based structure we utilize the energy dissipation model denoted by formula 4 and 5, and for the tree-based structure we utilize the same dissipation model, where we assume that the communication distance is always within the threshold $d_{crossover}$, therefore the free space model is used.

Random Walk Model. Sensor readings for our environment are generated following a random walk model[4]. The domain of values is between 20 and 100. A sensor reading is generated once each round. A new generated sample is supposed to be the same as before with a probability known as *randomness degree (RD)*, otherwise a different new value is generated. We used the *Random Step Size Limit* to restrict how much the new value may deviate from its previous value, it is expressed as a percentage over the domain of values.

Table 1. Parameters of Simmulations

Parameter	Value	Default
Area	100*100	
Number of Nodes	100	
Location of BS	(50,50),(50,150),(50,200)	(50,50)
Packet Size	4000 bits	
Number of Rounds	1000	
tct	0%-30%	10%
Random Degree	0.0-1.0	0.5
Random Step Size	0.5	
r_{th}	0.1	

6.1 Effect of Routing Structure with tct Support

Sensitivity to the temporal coherency tolerance. In the first experiment we test the sensitivity to *tct* for four different strategies: Tree/Cluster based routing structure with/without *tct* support. Over the specified monitoring area with BS set to the center, we respectively constructed tree-based routing structure and cluster-based routing structure. From Fig. 3(a) we note that both tree and cluster based routing scheme without *tct* support have much higher energy consumption than their approximation scheme with *tct* support. When tct=0.2 the tree-based approximate scheme can reduce 52% of total energy consumption compared to conventional tree-based approach, and our cluster-based approximation scheme can further reduce overall energy consumption by 48% than the tree-based approximate scheme. This can be explained by the increasing number of leaf nodes over sensor network.

Sensitivity to the number of clusters. In the next experiment we test how the actual number of clusters affects the overall energy consumption for sensor networks. As Fig. 3(b) shows, we varied the number of clusters from 1 to 50. We find that the overall energy consumption reaches its lowest point when the number of clusters is between 6 and 10, and we get the optimum number of clusters k_{opt} =8 calculated by formula 12, which right falls into the actual optimal range 6-10. The reason is that when there're only a few clusters, the non-CH nodes often have to transmit data very far to reach their cluster heads, draining their energy, and when there're more than 10 clusters, the number of intermediate nodes grows and they all have to transmit data directly to the Base Station, which costs a large amount of energy.

6.2 Evaluating the Adaptive tct Reallocating Scheme

In this experiment, we measure the performance of our adaptive adjusted *tct* scheme. In order to simulate various changing ratios among sensor nodes' readings, we randomly divide those sensor nodes into two parts, one part with RD=0.1 and the other part with RD=0.9, we set the tolerance *tct* to 0.2. As

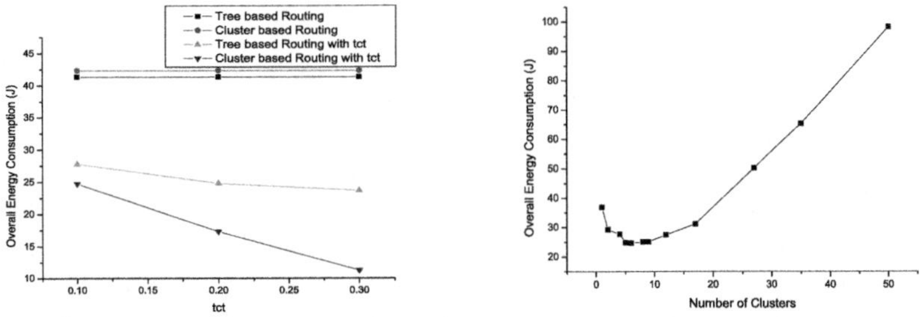

(a) Energy Consumption vs *tct* (b) Energy Consumption vs Number of Clusters

Fig. 3. Effect of Routing Structure with *tct* Support

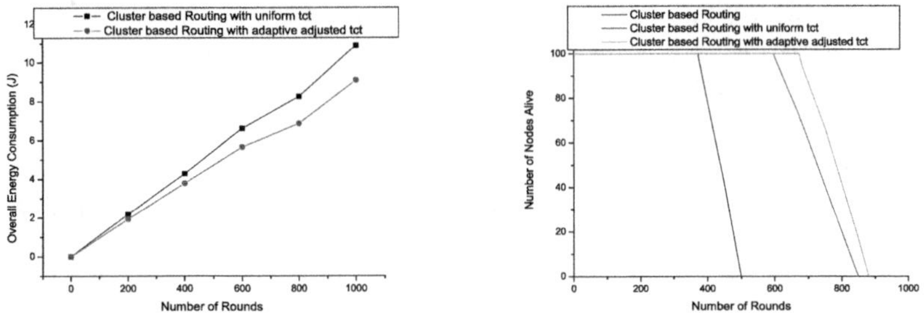

(a) Energy Comparison for Different *tct* Strategies (b) Measurement of Network Lifetime

Fig. 4. Evaluating the Adaptive *tct* Reallocating Scheme

Fig. 4(a) shows, we make the energy comparison between two approximation schemes with different *tct* strategies. We can see that our approximation scheme with adaptive reallocated *tct* can further reduce the energy consumption compared to the approximation scheme with uniform *tct*. After 1000 rounds, our adaptive tolerance relocating scheme can achieve 16% energy savings than uniform tolerance allocating scheme. This means that by adaptively reallocating *tct* according to different changing ratios we can avoid unnecessary data updates at best effort. We further compare their network lifetime, Fig. 4(b) depicts network lifetime of three cluster-based processing strategies, for the cluster-based approach without *tct* support, the first node dies at round 372, for the approximation scheme with uniform *tct*, the first node dies at round 596, and for the approximation scheme with adaptive reallocated *tct*, the first node dies at round 674, further extend the lifetime by 13% than the former approximation scheme.

7 Related Work

Research works on quality-aware sensor data collection address the relations between quality requirement and energy consumption. Sharaf et al. have successfully proposed TiNA [4]: a tree-based approximation scheme for temporal coherency-aware in-network aggregation. Deshpande et al. have introduced interactive approximate querying over sensor networks with statistical modeling techniques [6]. Tulone et al. have presented PAQ [7]: a method for approximating the values of sensors based on time series forecasting, relying on local autoregressive models. Hellerstein et al. have proposed a wavelet-based compression approach to approximate aggregate values over sensor network [5].

8 Conclusion

In this paper we explored two ideas to reduce energy consumption in the context of in-network aggregation: (1) proposing a clustering-based approximation framework with hierarchical caching method (2) imposing an adaptive *tct*-reallocating technique with goal of further reducing overall energy consumption and keeping load balance. Our approximation scheme provides a balance between energy efficiency and accuracy of aggregate data over sensor network. We have shown by experiment that our approximation scheme results in large energy savings for in-network aggregation without significant loss in quality of data.

Acknowledgments

This work is supported by the China NSF grant (60573132), the Jiangsu Provincial High-Tech Research Program (2006029), the China 973 project (2006CB303000) and the China 863 project (2006AA01Z199). I would like to express my thanks to Mao Ye, for his helpful comments and for assistance with literature.

References

1. Yao, Y., Gehrke, J.: Query processing in sensor networks. In: Proceedings of the First Biennial Conference on Innovative Data Systems Research (CIDR) (2003)
2. Krishnamachari, B., Estrin, D., Wicker, S.B.: The impact of data aggregation in wireless sensor networks. In: ICDCS Workshops (2002)
3. Madden, S., Franklin, M.J., Hellerstein, J.M., Hong, W.: Tag: A tiny aggregation service for ad-hoc sensor networks. In: Proceedings of OSDI (2002)
4. Sharaf, M.A., Beaver, J., Labrinidis, A., Chrysanthis, P.K.: A scheme for temporal coherency-aware in-network aggregation. In: Proceedings of MobiDE (2003)
5. Hellerstein, J.M., Hong, W., Madden, S., Stanek, K.: Beyond Average: Toward Sophisticated Sensing with Queries. In: Proceedings of IPSN (2003)
6. Deshpande, A., Guestrin, C., Madden, S., Hellerstein, J.M., Hong, W.: Model-based approximate querying in sensor networks. VLDB J. 14(4), 417–443 (2005)

7. Tulone, D., Madden, S.: PAQ: Time Series Forecasting for Approximate Query Answering in Sensor Networks. In: Römer, K., Karl, H., Mattern, F. (eds.) EWSN 2006. LNCS, vol. 3868, Springer, Heidelberg (2006)
8. Olston, C., Widom, J.: Best-effort cache synchronization with source cooperation. In: SIGMOD Conference (2002)
9. Heinzelman, W.B., Chandrakasan, A.P., Balakrishnan, H.: An application-specific protocol architecture for wireless microsensor networks. IEEE Transactions on Wireless Communications 1(4) (2002)

Real-Time Data Delivery in Wireless Sensor Networks: A Data-Aggregated, Cluster-Based Adaptive Approach

Shao-liang Peng, Shan-shan Li, Yu-xing Peng, Wen-sheng Tang, and Nong Xiao

School of Computer, National University of Defense Technology, Changsha, China
{pengshaoliang,ssli,pyx,tws,xn}@nudt.edu.cn

Abstract. Since sensor networks deal with real world, real-time data delivery is often necessary for communication. The cluster-based data aggregation has emerged as a basic technique in sensor networks. However, there is a trade-off issue between aggregation waiting delay and aggregation accuracy. Therefore, we propose a Delay Sensitive Feedback Control (DSFC) model to solve the trade-off issue. More, we present a new inter-cluster congestion avoidance mechanism: Emergent Packet Channel Reservation (EPCR) to accelerate the transmission of emergent packets in inter-cluster routing. Our goal is to build an end-to-end fast path for emergent packets when emergent event occurs. Simulation results verify the performance of DSFC and EPCR, and demonstrate their attraction.

1 Introduction

There are many mission-critical applications in wireless sensor networks (WSN), such as target tracking in battlefields, nuclear leak alert, habitat temperature monitoring in forests and hazardous environment exploration [1]. Although these applications for sensor network remain diverse, one commonality they all share is the need for a timely delivery of sensory data. Without a real-time communication service, applications cannot react to the changes of the environment quickly enough to be effective. Therefore, in this paper we propose a comprehensive mechanism to meet real-time constraint of packets generated in crisis states.

Data aggregation has emerged as a basic tenet in sensor networks. The key idea is to combine the data coming from different sensors – eliminating redundancy, minimizing the number of transmissions and thus saving energy. Data aggregation can also provide a rich, multi–dimensional view of the environment being monitored [2]. However, nowadays many works on data aggregation are based on cluster topology [3]. All vicinal clustering members aggregate data at cluster head. Clustering–based aggregation has high energy efficiency due to intra-cluster data redundancy.

Although clustering benefits from data aggregation, which may not be the only reason for using clusters. Clustering makes the system scalable. Instead of having a centralized control over thousands of nodes, or having a distributed protocol that operates over thousands of nodes, it is better to organize nodes into smaller clusters, and assign the responsibility of MAC and routing in each cluster to a single cluster head node. So we propose a bursty real-time mechanism which is cluster-based.

J. Indulska et al. (Eds.): UIC 2007, LNCS 4611, pp. 514–523, 2007.

However, there are problems for cluster-based data aggregation: higher latency and less accuracy, especially when a lot of emergent packets are generated within a short period. We try to find the optimal point for the trade-off between aggregation delay and accuracy. That is to decrease delay as much as possible within the accuracy bound. In this paper, a distinguished feedback control model is proposed to adaptively aggregate data in a delay sensitive manner while not damage the gathering accuracy. In addition, high data rate leads to a high probability of packet collision and the worst case, congestion. The situation is further exacerbated by the fact that many packets from different clusters are delivered and convergent on inter-cluster routing. Therefore, a protection mechanism is also proposed in inter-clustering routing to differentiate packets with different priority and guarantee the real-time constraints. Our goal is to build an end-to-end (E2E) fast path for packets of emergent events.

The paper is organized as follows. Section 2 describes some related work. In Section 3, we discuss the issues of delay/accuracy trade-off and propose a Delay Sensitive Feedback Control (DSFC) model to solve it. In Section 4, we present an inter-cluster congestion avoidance mechanism: Channel Reservation (CR) to accelerate the transmission of emergent packets. Several simulations described in Section 5 verify the obtained theoretical results. The paper ends with conclusion.

2 Related Work

Interactions between sensor networks and the physical world require real-time services to play an important role. Several real-time methods have been proposed for sensor and ad hoc networks. SPEED [4] protocol is designed to provide soft end-to-end deadline guarantees for real-time packets in sensor networks. MM-SPEED [5] extends SPEED to support different delivery velocities and levels of reliability.

However, previous approaches are efficient only when most traffic requires low reporting rates, which is not the case for many sensor networks especially with bursty events. Also, it is not adaptive to dynamics of data collection. Besides the real-time protocol design, several researches approaches focus on the delay analysis for data aggregation. In [6], Athanassios et al. only focus on data aggregation: an energy–accuracy trade-off, but they can not mention aggregation delay. However, all the prior work has been mainly concerned with the benefits of aggregation and has only superficially acknowledged the delay/accuracy trade-off present.

A hierarchical network organization will not only facilitate data aggregation, but will facilitate the formation of uniform, robust backbones, and give an opportunity for nodes to sleep while not sensing or transmitting. Many clustering protocols have been investigated [7]. However, prior work has rarely been concerned with the delay of aggregation. In order to build an E2E quick path for packets of emergent events, we will put forward a bursty real-time mechanism which is ground on clustering.

The E2E delay of emergent packet is crucial when bursty events happen. The delay is mainly composed of (i) intra-cluster data aggregation (ii) inter-cluster routing. We will take into account the delay issue from these two segments.

3 Delay Sensitive Feedback Control in Intra-cluster Data Aggregation

In this Section, we first briefly describe priority based packets classification and scheduling method because latter some mechanisms are based on it. Then, in Section 3.2, we analyze the delay due to data aggregation. Finally, in Section 3.3 we discuss the issues of delay/accuracy trade-off and propose a DSFC model to solve it.

3.1 Priority Based Packets Classification and Scheduling

We will borrow the idea of QoS from Internet which has been proposed using two different methods –the Differentiated services (DiffServ) and the Integrated services (IntServ). We can classify the packets into two classes: emergent packet and regular packet, according to the semantic characteristics of packets. Packets classification is implemented by setting a bit in the TOS field. Cluster head assigns the TDMA slots for each node in the region according to the application of every source node, creates a TDMA schedule for its nodes and broadcasts it every round aggregation. TDMA also can be modified to allocated more and earlier slots to emergent packets.

3.2 Delay Due to Data Aggregation

There is a tradeoff - potentially greater delay because data from different sources may have to be held back at a cluster head in order to be aggregated with data coming from other sources. Fewer transmissions should be achieved at the cost of delay, especially when bursty events happen and many emergent packets appear.

Generally there are three factors affecting the delay of intra-cluster data aggregation: **(i)Aggregation Routing (AR)**, (ii) **Aggregation Function (AF),** (iii) **Aggregation Waiting (AW)**. Earlier data from different sources may have to wait at a cluster head in order to be aggregated with subsequent data coming from other sources. The problem of AW delay will be aggravated especially when emergent events occur. The delay of AW is the most important bottleneck of data aggregation.

3.3 Trade-Off Between AW Delay and Aggregation Accuracy

3.3.1 Problem Statement

In order to addressing the delay bottleneck of aggregation waiting, we must take into account the loss of aggregation accuracy. However, many nodes in the same cluster are located at the close geographical area, their gatherings are correlated and accordingly some accuracy loss is acceptable. We can consider to aggregate partial data to reduce the AW delay on the condition of meeting the desired aggregation accuracy. Therefore, there is a trade-off issue between AW delay and aggregation accuracy.

The trade-off issue can be regarded as a problem of Multiobjective Optimization. AW delay and aggregation accuracy are two main objects but they come into conflict with each other. Consequently, we use Optimization Method to solve this trade-off problem. The AW delay of emergent packet is crucial when bursty events happen, so we will aim at the goal of reducing AW delay.

3.3.2 Delay Sensitive Feedback Control Model

We present a Delay Sensitive Feedback Control (DSFC) model to solve the problems on delay/accuracy trade-off. We can use the model to adaptively aggregate partial data to reduce the AW delay on the condition of meeting the desired aggregation accuracy.

Definition1. Aggregation Scale (AS): The ratio of emergent packets arrived at cluster head to total produced emergent packets in a round of data aggregation. The calculation of AS is as followed:

$$AS(i) = \frac{N_{arrived}(i)}{N_{total}(i)}, \quad \text{i is round number, i=1,2,3,4....} \tag{1}$$

$N_{total}(i)$ is the total number of produced emergent packets in the ith round aggregation. $N_{arrived}(i)$ is the factual number of emergent packets that arrive at cluster head and need to be aggregated in the ith round. Obviously, $AS \le 1$. $N_{total}(i)$ can be calculated by cluster head because all source nodes must request to send packets at a certain reporting rate when the source nodes sense an emergent event. Cluster head can execute a centric control every round according to the request of every source node. $AS(i)$ is used to control the aggregation accuracy and AW delay. Figure 1 shows the feedback controller, and it can control the parameter of **Aggregation Function (AF)**. The concrete definition of AF is specific to the application of WSN, and can be expressed as $AF(i, AS(i))$. For example, $AF(i, 1)$ means that cluster head carry out full data aggregation until all data of source node reach cluster head. The aggregation accuracy of full data aggregation is the highest but the AW delay is the longest.

Definition2. Error (E): The error of partial data aggregation. It can be calculated as followed:

$$E(i) = |AF(i,1) - AF(i, AS(i))| \tag{2}$$

E(i) is the difference between partial and full aggregation which means of data aggregation accuracy at i round. It can be used to adjust the AS (i+1) at (i+1) round aggregation. The Closed-loop Feedback Control model is illustrated as equation (3):

$$AS(i+1) = AS(i) + \alpha(E(i) - E_0) \tag{3}$$

α is the controller coefficient and can be well approached by some off-line experiments. E_0 is the minimal error that is related to specific applications of WSN.

The DSFC architecture is shown in figure 1:

Our goal is transmit the emergent packets as fast as possible when emergent events occur. Emergent packets are partially aggregated in the proportion of $AS(i+1)$. The DSFC can adaptively decrease the AW delay at the cost of accuracy. We can continuously reduce the AS, namely $AS(i+1)$, as long as the aggregation accuracy meets the

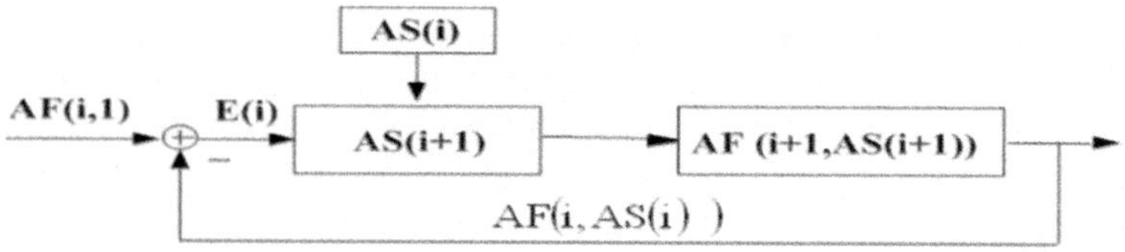

Fig. 1. The Architecture of DSFC Model

requirement of applications. The DSFC system tends to be steady until E(i) is close to E_0.

The total time of the i(th) round data aggregation AT(i) is composed of three parts, which is illustrated as equation (4):

$$AT(i) = S + C + \sum_{j=1}^{N_{arrived}} T_j \tag{4}$$

S: The synchronization time of intra-cluster nodes

C: The intercommunion time that cluster head executes a centric control and harmonization before the source data arrive at cluster head. The course includes source node requesting phase and cluster head assigning time slots phase.

T_j: The time slot of packet j. T_j is assigned by cluster head.

4 Inter-cluster Congestion Avoidance: Channel Reservation

Network may suffer from severe congestion when emergent events occur due to the generation of many emergent packets. During congestion, emergent packets may be dropped with regular packet differentially, which will nullify the purpose of sensor networks. The main cause of congestion is the wireless channel contention. Data flows from different sources may convergecast to one point, which will result in much interference, collision, and channel contention. Many traditional methods always take measures only when the congestions are about to occur or have occurred. The transmission of emergent packets has already been affected seriously by congestions when the measures taking effect. [11]

We adopt an inter-cluster congestion avoidance mechanism: Emergent Packets Channel Reservation (EPCR) to accelerate the transmission of emergent packets using the method of channel reservation. In detail, we assume only cluster head nodes take part in inter-cluster routing. These emergent packets will appear and be aggregated at cluster head when some emergent events happen in some clusters. When any intermediate node receives an emergent packet, it will inform upstream nodes that regular packets can be decelerated or transmitted along other paths. The appearance of the first emergent packet in inter-cluster means large numbers of emergent packets will be followed. Furthermore, severe congestion may arise. In this way, EPCR can effectively alleviate channel contention and accelerate the transmission of emergent packets to BS at the cost of the delay of transmission of regular packets. However, delay of regular packets is not so crucial and the moderate delay and loss of regular packets can be tolerated in many applications of WSN. Altogether, EPCR can efficiently increase the speed of transmission of emergent packets through alleviating channel contention which regular packets incur and improve wireless channel utilization.

As described above, we illustrate the work process of DSFC model and EPCR mechanism in detail at figure 2. Data flows from different sources may convergecast to node D. We build a "green" E2E fast path for emergent packets when emergent event occurs in the region A. Node A aggregates partial emergent packets according to the DSFC model and uses the green channel reservation to transmit the emergent packets. In contrast, regular packets from node B and C can be decelerated or transmitted along other paths when node D notifies node B and C.

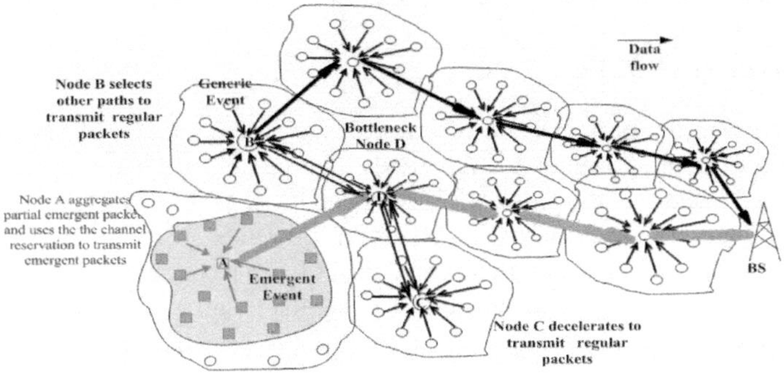

Fig. 2. Working Process of DSFC and EPCR

5 Performance Evaluation

5.1 Simulation Settings

We simulate DSFC and EPCR using GloMoSim [9], a scalable discrete-event simulator developed by UCLA. This software provides a high fidelity simulation for wireless communication with detailed propagation, radio and MAC layers. Table 1

Table 1. Simulation settings

Routing	Shortest Path
MAC Layer	TSMA (Intra-Cluster), 802.11 (Inter-Cluster)
Radio Layer	RADIO-ACCNOISE
Propagation Model	TWO-RAY
Bandwidth	200Kb/s
Payload Size	32 Byte
TERRAIN	(300m, 300m)
Node Number	300
Radio Range	30~50m
Clustering Method	HEED [3]
Cluster Radius	25 m

illustrates the detailed configuration for our simulation. The communication parameters are chosen in reference to the Berkeley mote specification.

We use a simulation model based on GlomoSim and conduct extensive experiments to evaluate its performance. To make dense network with a strong connectivity and have more choice to construct cluster and paths, we deploy 300 nodes with a radio range of 30m to 50m. A channel error rate of 10% is uniformly distributed around the network (With max ARQ of 802.11).Our works is not based on a certain routing protocol, so we select the Shortest Path routing protocol and long-hop standpoint. In our evaluation, we present the following set of results: (1) DSFC model to adaptively control Aggregation Scale, (2) AW delay and error under different scenarios, (3) aggregation communication energy consumption. All experiments are repeated 16 times with different random seeds.

5.2 Performance of DSFC

First, we examine the performance of intra-cluster DSFC model. In figure 3 we present the DSFC control model to adaptively aggregate partial emergent packets to reduce the AW delay at the three different scenarios. DSFC can effectively and directly control the AF to converge at a certain value according to E(i) and the data correlation. Figure 4 illustrates the AW delay of different scenarios. The emergent packets data aggregation based clustering generally aggregate all intra-cluster data.

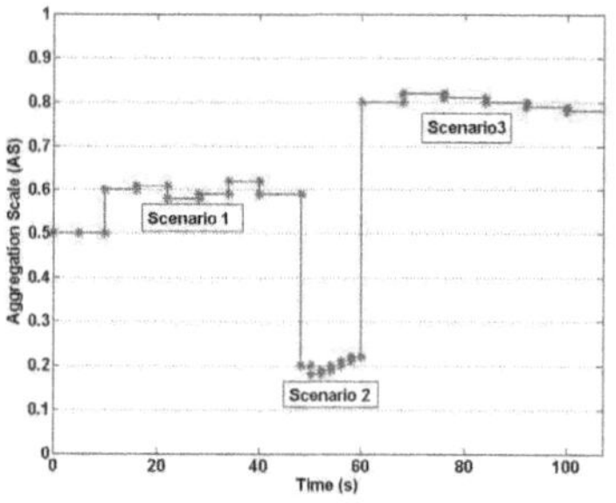

Fig. 3. Control process of DSFC model

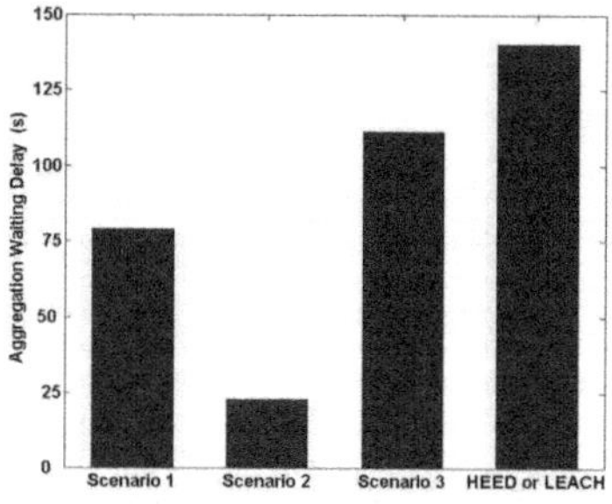

Fig. 4. AW delay of Different Scenarios

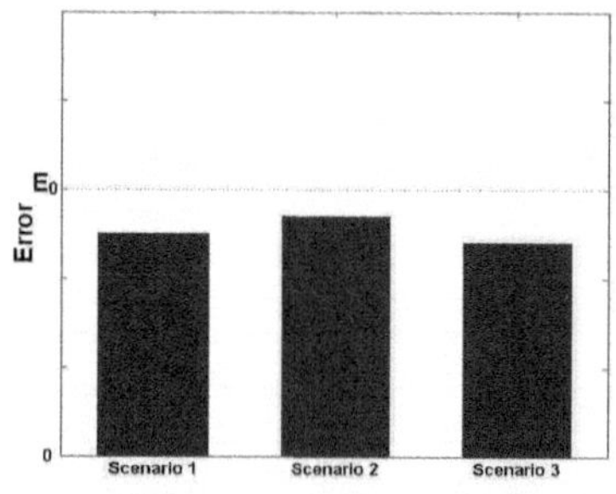

Fig. 5. Error of Different Scenarios

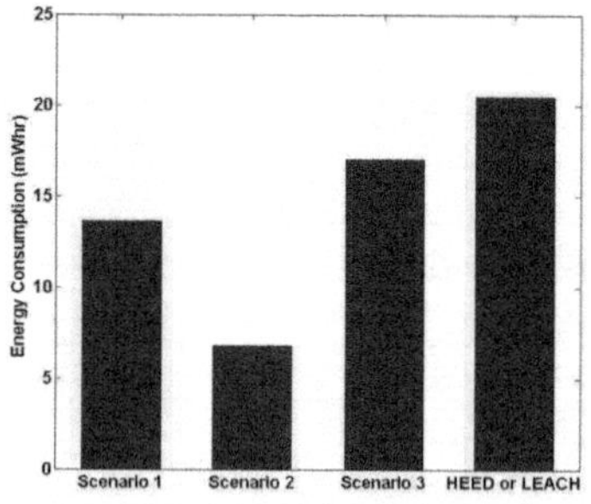

Fig. 6. Intra-cluster Energy Consumption

So, cluster head has to wait for a long time in order to be aggregated all data coming from other sources. We can see clearly in Figure 4 the AF delay of HEED and LEACH [3] is longer than that in scenario1, 2, and 3.

Figure 5 shows the error of partial data aggregation under different scenarios. All the errors of 3 scenarios are all less than the minimal error, E_0. Figure 4 and Figure 5 illuminate DSFC can effectively reduce the AW delay on the condition of meeting the desired aggregation accuracy.

Under energy constraints, it is vital for sensor nodes to minimize energy consumption in radio communication to extend the lifetime of sensor networks. From the results shown in Figure 6, we argue that partial aggregation based DSFC tends to reduce the transmission of emergent packets in cluster, thus saving energy. Figure 6 shows fewer intra-cluster transmissions in scenario1, 2, and 3 consume less energy than HEED and LEACH [3], which always carry out the traditional full aggregation.

5.3 Performance of Combination of DSFC with EPCR

End-to-end delay of data packets includes all possible delays during data dissemination from source to sink, which is composed of two parts in our works: intra-cluster aggregation delay and inter-cluster transmission delay. We can decrease the intra-cluster aggregation delay by using DSFC model, as is showed in section 5.2. However, the inter-cluster transmission delay of emergent packets has already been affected seriously by congestions. To solve this problem, we adopt an inter-cluster congestion avoidance mechanism: EPCR to accelerate the transmission of emergent packets using the method of channel reservation.

As is shown in figure 7, we present the average E2E delay comparison between EPCR and non-EPCR. The average E2E delay comparison includes emergent packets and regular packets. For simplicity, we choose the Shortest Path routing protocol in our experiment. As shown in figure 7, the average E2E delay of emergent packets under EPCR is far less than non- EPCR because EPCR can effectively alleviate channel contention by using channel reservation for emergent packets. As is analyzed in section 4, EPCR accelerate the transmission of emergent packets to BS at the cost of the delay of transmission of regular packets.

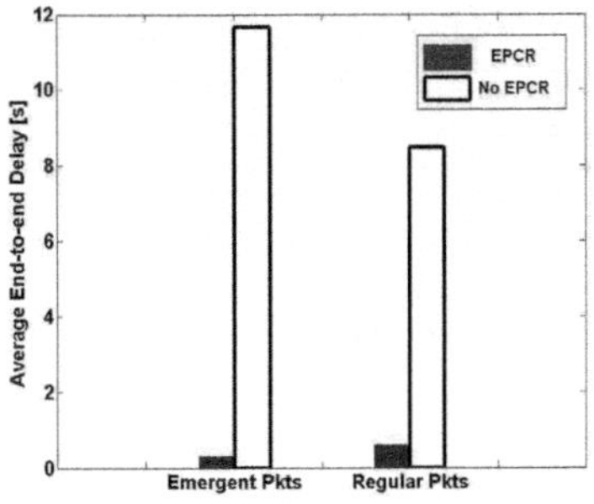

Fig. 7. Average E2E delay Comparison

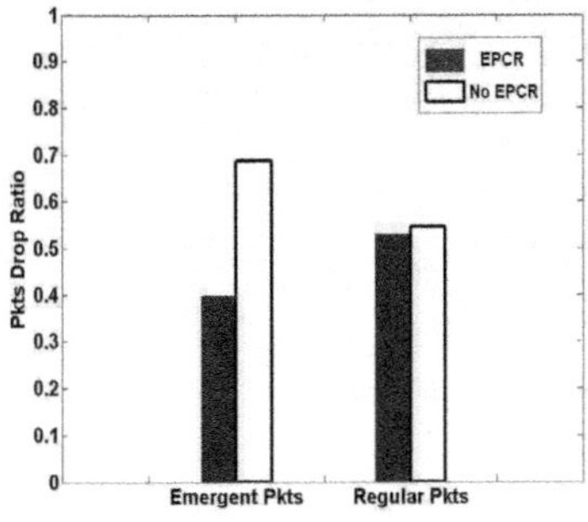

Fig. 8. Packets Drop Ratio Comparison

However, we can see the average E2E delay of regular packets under EPCR is also less than non- EPCR. This is mainly because EPCR can alleviate channel contention by making regular packets to be decelerated or transmitted along other paths.

The packet delivery ratio is defined as the ratio of the number of data packets delivered to the sink to the number of packets generated by the source node. It is also an important metric in wireless sensor networks because the wireless channel is vulnerable. So we lay out the packets drop ratio in figure 8. We can see clearly the packets drop ratio is lower under EPCR than Non-EPCR whatever the packets are emergent or regular packets. Furthermore, the emergent packets drop ratio is especially much lower than regular packets under EPCR. This point accords with the characteristics of WSN because delay of regular packets is not so crucial. The moderate delay and loss of regular packets can be tolerated in many applications of WSN.

In addition, DSFC and EPCR use a relatively low number of control packets. The only control packet used in DSFC is periodic synchronization beacon, which is always used in nearly all clustering protocol. DSFC may not use more other control packets besides the synchronization beacons. EPCR uses one type of on-demand beacons to notify neighbors of the emergent packets' coming. This control cost is also very low. In conclusion, DSFC and EPCR may not bring additional control cost.

6 Conclusion

Unlike most existing literature on real-time transport in sensor networks that focuses on periodic traffic, we have focused on bursty events and cluster-based data aggregation where the key challenges are intra-cluster speedy aggregation and inter-cluster fast transmission of emergent packets. To address the unique challenges, we have proposed a DSFC model to solve the trade-off issue between AW delay and aggregation accuracy, we have also designed a new inter-cluster congestion avoidance mechanism, EPCR to accelerate the transmission of emergent packets in inter-cluster routing. Our goal is to build a end-to-end fast path for emergent packets when emergent event occurs. Our simulations on GloMoSim demonstrate DSFC model can adaptively aggregate partial data to reduce the AW delay on the condition of meeting the desired aggregation accuracy, and EPCR can accelerate the transmission of emergent packets using the method of channel reservation. The costs of energy consumption and control packets in DSFC and EPCR are also very low. In a certain sense, this combination of DSFC and EPCR improves the end-to-end delay and decreases the packets drop ratio for not only emergent packets but also regular packets.

References

1. Lewis, F.L.: Wireless Sensor Networks, Smart Environments: Technologies, Protocol and Applications (2004)
2. Enachescu, M., Goel, A., Govindan, R., Motwani, R.: Scale-Free Aggregation in Sensor Networks. Theoretical Computer Science: Special Issue on Algorithmic Aspects of Wireless Sensor Networks 344(1), 15–29 (2005)
3. Younis, O., Fahmy, S.: Distributed Clustering in Ad-hoc Sensor Networks: A Hybrid, Energy-Efficient Approach. In: Proceedings of IEEE INFOCOM (2004)

4. He, T., Stankovic, J.A., Lu, C., Abdelzaher, T.: SPEED: A stateless protocol for real-time communication in sensor networks. In: Proc. of the 23rd International Conference on Distributed Computing Systems ICDCS-23 (2003)
5. Felemban, E., Lee, C.-G., Ekici, E., Boder, R., Vural, S.: Probabilistic QoS guarantee in reliability and timeliness domains in wireless sensor networks. In: Proceedings of 24th Annual Joint Conference of the IEEE Computer and Communications INFOCOM, pp. 2646–2657. IEEE Computer Society Press, Los Alamitos (2005)
6. Boulis, A., Ganeriwal, S., Srivastava, M.: Aggregation in Sensor Networks: An Energy-Accuracy Trade-off. In: Proc. of IEEE SANPA, pp. 11–17 (2003)
7. Heinzelman, W.B., et al.: An Application-Specific Protocol Architecture for Wireless Microsensor Networks. IEEE Transactions on Wireless Communications 1(4) (2002)
8. Shao-Liang, P., Shan-Shan, L., Xiang-Ke, L., Yu-Xing, P., et al.: Feedback Control with Prediction for Thread Allocation in Pipeline Architecture Web Server. In: ICDCN (2006)
9. Zeng, X., Bagrodia, R., Gerla, M.: GloMoSim: a Library for Parallel Simulation of Large-scale Wireless Networks. In: Proceedings of the 12th Workshop on Parallel and Distributed Simulations – PADS '98, pp. 26–29 (1998)
10. Hongwei, Z., Anish, A., Young-ri, C.: Reliable Bursty Convergecast in Wireless Sensor Networks. MobiHoc, 266–276 (2005)

A Location-Unaware Connected Coverage Protocol in Wireless Sensor Networks

Yingchi Mao[1,2], Lijun Chen[2], and Daoxu Chen[2]

[1] College of Computer and Information Engineering, Hohai University,
210098 Nanjing, China
yingchimao@hhu.edu.cn
[2] Department of Computer Science, Nanjing University
210093 Nanjing, China
{chenlj,cdx}@nju.edu.cn

Abstract. Sensor networks consist of autonomous nodes with battery powered. Nodes can be sleep to extend the lifetime of network without compromising area coverage and network connectivity. Most existing approaches to connected coverage require knowledge of accurate location information. However, the energy cost and system complexity involved in obtaining the accurate location information may compromise the effectiveness of proposed solution as a whole. This paper addresses the problem of maximizing network lifetime while providing coverage and connectivity without accurate location information of sensor nodes. Our solution is based on the theoretical analysis of the sensing area coverage property of minimal dominating set. We establish the relationship between point coverage and area coverage in random geometric graphs. Based on the analytical results and Rule K algorithms constructing the connected dominating set, a Location-Unaware Connected Coverage Protocol (LUCCP) is proposed. Simulation studies show that the proposed LUCCP can effectively maintain both high quality sensing coverage and connectivity for a long time.

1 Introduction

In wireless sensor networks (WSNs) that consist of a large number of low-power, short-lived, unreliable sensors, one of the main design challenges is to obtain long network lifetime without sacrificing sensing quality and network connectivity. The connected coverage is one of the most important problems in WSNs. The existing algorithms in maintaining connected coverage usually rely on the availability of accurate location information such as that obtained with the GPS systems and the directional antenna technology. However, the energy cost and system complexity involved in obtaining the accurate location information may compromise the effectiveness of proposed solution as a whole. Furthermore, it is still a very difficult issue to estimate sensors' locations, since GPS and other complicated hardware devices consume too much energy and the costs are too high for tiny sensors [1]. Therefore, we solve a challenging problem: without accurate location information, how to energy-efficiently schedule sensor nodes to meet both constraints of sensing area coverage and network connectivity.

J. Indulska et al. (Eds.): UIC 2007, LNCS 4611, pp. 524–534, 2007.

Our work is based on the (connected) dominating set (CDS), which has extensively been investigated sparse structure in ad hoc wireless networks. Much work has been done to derive distributed algorithms [2-5] to construct minimal (connected) dominating set (MDS) with different objective functions. It is obvious that MDS provide coverage of points in an area (termed point coverage) when the sensing range (Rs) equals the transmission range (Rt). Although it is considered that point coverage is equivalent to area sensing area coverage in the high density of deployed sensors [6]. However, point coverage is in general not equivalent to area coverage. In this paper, we analyze the relationship between them, and derive the upper and lower bound that the point coverage of MDS is equivalent to area coverage in random geometric graphs. Based on the theoretical results, we propose a Location-Unaware connected coverage protocol (LUCCP) that incorporates existing CDS selection algorithms to determine the set of active nodes. In LUCCP, every sensor node can adjust its own transmission range based on local nodes density, and schedule its own status to construct CDS without accurate location information. The active nodes can maintain both high quality of sensing coverage and network connectivity.

The remainder of the paper is organized as follows. Section 2 presents a review of related work in connected coverage. The next section introduces some necessary notations. Section 4 establishes the analytical results on relationship between the point coverage and sensing are coverage. LUCCP is proposed and evaluated in Section 5 and Section 6, respectively. Finally, we conclude the paper.

2 Related Work

Recently, researches have considered connectivity and coverage in an integrated platform. In [7], the authors consider an unreliable sensor network and sensor nodes are deployed strictly in grids. The necessary and sufficient conditions for the area coverage and network connectivity with high probability are provided. In [8], it is proved that to ensure that the full sensing area coverage of a convex area also guarantee the connectivity of the active nodes, if $Rt \geq 2Rs$. Therefore, the connected coverage problem is simplified to maintain a complete coverage. Based on the analytical results, Zhang et al. proposed OGDC protocol [8]. Wang et al. draw the same conclusion in [9], and presented a unified framework to study both coverage and connectivity problems. They used the SPAN [10] protocol to maintain coverage, and a separate CCP protocol to maintain coverage. Gupta et al defined the connected sensor cover, and demonstrated that the calculation of the smallest connected sensor cover is NP-hard and they proposed both centralized and distributed approximate algorithms to solve it and provide the performance bounds as well [11]. Zou et al considered the variable radii k1-connected k2-cover problem by adjusting the sensing range and transmission range [12]. The authors proposed a distributed and local Voronoi–based and relative neighborhood graph (RNG)-based algorithm to preserve k1 connectivity and k2 coverage. However, unlike our approach, the above algorithms all require each sensor node to be aware of its precise location in order to check its local coverage redundancy.

3 Preliminary

A dominating set (DS) of an undirected graph G(V, E) is a subset V' of the vertex set V such that every vertex in V-V' is adjacent to a vertex in V'. A minimal dominating set (MDS) is a dominating set which ceases to be a dominating set if any vertex is removed from it. A dominating set V' is connected if for any two vertices u and v $\in$ V', a path from u to v in E exists. Some notations are as follows.

(1) $B_i(r_i)$: let $B_i(r_i)$ be a disk centered at a point $z_i \in \mathbf{R}^2$ with radius r_i, B_i for short.
(2) $\pi_i(x)$: the power distance of a point $x \in \mathbf{R}^2$ from B_i, defined as $\pi_i(x)=\|x-z_i\|^2-r_i^2$.
(3) B_i^j: $B_i^j=\{x\in\mathbf{R}^2 | \pi_j(x)\le\pi_i(x)\le 0\}$, B_i^j is the portion of B_i on B_j's side of the bisector.
(4) P_i, P_i^j, P_j^{ik}: let P_i, P_i^j, P_j^{ik} be length of the circle arcs in the boundaries of B_i, B_i^j and $B_j^i \cap B_j^k$.
(5) A_i^j, A_j^{ik}: let A_i^j, A_j^{ik} be area of B_i^j and $B_j^i \cap B_j^k$, that is $A_i^j = Area(B_i^j)$ and A_j^{ik}=Area($B_j^i \cap B_j^k$).
(6) $\mathbf{r}=[r_1,r_2,\ldots,r_n]$, $\mathbf{z}=[z_1,z_2,\ldots,z_n]$: let $\mathbf{r}$ and $\mathbf{z}$ denote vectors of disk radii and positions of centers, respectively.
(7) $A\mathbf{r}$: $A\mathbf{r}$ is a function of the position of the disks as well as their radii, that is $A\mathbf{r}=f(\mathbf{r},\mathbf{z})$. $A\mathbf{r}$ denotes the numeric area of the union of n disks.

4 Problem Analysis

According to the definition of MDS, MDS set can control the non-MDS set. When $Rt=Rs$, MDS can provide coverage of points in the region M (termed point coverage). In addition, MDS$\subseteq$CDS, CDS not only meet the requirement of point coverage, but can ensure the network connectivity. However, point coverage is in general not equivalent to area coverage. In this section, we analyze the relationship between the point coverage and sensing area coverage, and derive the upper and lower bound that point coverage is equivalent to area coverage in random geometric graphs.

Theorem 1. *Given sensing range Rs and transmission range Rt, let Area(V) be the geometric area covered by all nodes in the network and Area(MDS) be the geometric area covered by the MDS. We have* $\frac{Rs^2}{(Rs+Rt)^2} \le \frac{Area(MDS)}{Area(V)}$.

The main idea is from the work on the area and perimeter derivatives of a union of disks [13]. Before delving to the proof, we first introduce some lemmas.

Lemma 1. Assume A be the geometric area covered by n disks deployed in a plane $\mathbf{R}^2$. The derivative of the numeric area $A\mathbf{r}$ of a union of n disks with radius vector $\mathbf{r}$ is $\mathrm{D}A\mathbf{r} = \frac{\partial f(\mathbf{r},\mathbf{z})}{\partial \mathbf{r}} = 2\pi\sum_{i=1}^{n} r_i\sigma_i$, where $\sigma_i = 1-(\sum_j P_i^j - \sum_{j,k} P_i^{jk})/2\pi r_i, i=1,2,\ldots,n$.

In lemma 1, σ_i denotes the contribution of disk B_i's boundary to the perimeter of A. In particular, if a disk is fully contained inside A, the disk does not share boundary with A, and σ_i=0.The proof of lemma 1 refers to [13].

Lemma 2. *Let $A(r)$ be the numeric area of the union of n disks with the same radius r on a plane. Its derivative with respect to r is given by* $\frac{\mathrm{d}A(r)}{\mathrm{d}r}=\sum_{i=1}^{n}2\pi r\sigma_i$, *where* $\sigma_i = 1-(\sum_j P_i^j - \sum_{j,k} P_i^{jk})/2\pi r, (i=1,2,...,n)$.

Lemma 3. *For a differentiable function* $g: R^+ \to R^+$, *if* $\forall x \in R^+$, $g'(x) \le \frac{2g(x)}{x}$, *then* $\frac{g(x_1)}{g(x_2)} \le \frac{x_1^2}{x_2^2}$, $0 < x_2 \le x_1 \in R^+$.

Lemma 4. *Assume two disks B_i and B_j of radius r_i and r_j centered as z_i and z_j respectively. Let S_i (S_j) be the sector defined by the arc P_i-P_i^j (P_j-P_j^i) and the line segments that join the two end points of P_i-P_i^j (P_j-P_j^i) and its center z_i (z_j).Then Area($S_i \cap S_j$)=0.*

Due to the limit of the length of paper, we omit the proof of Lemma 2, 3 and 4.

Now we are in the position to prove Theorem 1.

Proof. (Theorem 1) Consider a dominator node u. Define D_u be the set of nodes that are dominated by u including u itself, $D_u=\{v\in V|d(u,v)\le Rt\}$. A point p is covered by nodes in D_u only if p is within ($Rs+Rt$) from node u. Therefore, the maximum possible geometric area covered by D_u is Area(D_u)=$\pi(Rs+Rt)^2$. The numeric area covered by node u is $Area(u)=\pi Rs^2$. Therefore, the ratio between the numeric areas covered by u and D_u is $\frac{Area(u)}{Area(D_u)} \ge \frac{Rs^2}{(Rs+Rt)^2}$. By definition of the DS, we have $\bigcup_{i=1}^{i=m} D_i = V$, where m=|MDS|. There are two cases.

(1) None of the coverage area of the nodes in MDS overlap. Summing up coverage area of all the nodes in MDS, we have $Area(MDS) = Area(\bigcup_{i=1}^{i=m} B_i(Rs)) = m\cdot \pi Rs^2$. On the other hand, the coverage area of some nodes in $D_i (i=1,2,...,m)$ may overlap. We get $Area(V) \le Area(\bigcup_{i=1}^{i=m} B_i(Rs+Rt)) = m\pi(Rs+Rt)^2$ .Therefore $\frac{Area(MDS)}{Area(V)} \ge \frac{Rs^2}{(Rs+Rt)^2}$.

(2) The coverage area of some nodes in MDS overlap. The area function of $A(r)$ is $A(r) = \left|\bigcup_{i=1}^{i=n} B_i(r)\right|$. Let $A(Rs) = Area(MDS(Rs))$ and $A(Rs+Rt) = Area(MDS(Rs+Rt))$.

While $Area(V) \le Area(\bigcup_{i=1}^{i=m} B_i(Rs+Rt))$, we have $\frac{Area(MDS)}{Area(V)} \ge \frac{A(Rs)}{A(Rs+Rt)}$ .Therefore, to prove $\frac{Area(MDS)}{Area(V)} \ge \frac{Rs^2}{(Rs+Rt)^2}$, it is sufficient to prove $\frac{A(Rs)}{A(Rs+Rt)} \ge \frac{Rs^2}{(Rs+Rt)^2}$, that is to say, we need to prove that $\forall 0 < r_2 \le r_1 \in R^+$, $\frac{A(r_1)}{A(r_2)} \ge \frac{r_1^2}{r_2^2}$ .By Lemma 3, it is sufficient to show that the derivative $A'(r) \le \frac{2A(r)}{r}, \forall r > 0$.

From Lemma 2, we have

$$\frac{dA(r)}{dr} = \sum_{i=1}^{n} 2\pi r \sigma_i = 2\pi r \sum_{i=1}^{n} (1 - (\sum_j P_i^j - \sum_{j,k} P_i^{jk}) / 2\pi r) \tag{1}$$

The term $\sigma_i = 1 - (\sum_j P_i^j - \sum_{j,k} P_i^{jk}) / 2\pi r, (i = 1, 2, ..., n)$ gives the portion of the perimeter of B_i that is at the boundary of $A(r)$.

Let $S_{i,mi}$ be the set of sectors defined by the arc segment of P_i at the boundary of $A(r)$ and the line segments that join the end points of the arc segments and its center z_i, where m_i is the number of disks which intersect with disk B_i. Therefore,

$$\pi r^2 \sigma_i = Area(\bigcap_{l=1}^{m_i} S_{i,l}) = Area(S_{i,m_i}) \tag{2}$$

As the same way, $\pi r^2 \sigma_j$ =Area($S_{j,mj}$), where m_j is the number of disks which intersect with disk B_j. Since $S_{i,mi} \subseteq S_i$ and $S_{j,mj} \subseteq S_j$, From Lemma 4,$\forall$i,j, $Area(S_i \cap S_j)$=0. Therefore, $Area(S_{i,mi})+Area(S_{j,mj})=Area(S_{i,mi} \cup S_{j,mj})$.

Since $S_{i,mi} \subseteq S_i \subseteq B_i$, combining Equation (1) and (2), we get

$$A'(r) \times r/2 = (2\pi r \sum_{i=1}^{n} \sigma_i) \times r/2 = \sum_{i=1}^{n} \pi r^2 \sigma_i = \sum_{i=1}^{n} Area(S_{i,m_i}) = Area(\bigcup_{i=1}^{n} S_{i,m_i}) \le Area(\bigcup_{i=1}^{n} S_i) \le Area(\bigcup_{i=1}^{n} B_i) = A(r)$$

Thus, $\forall r > 0, A'(r) \le \frac{2A(r)}{r}$. Therefore, $\frac{Area(MDS)}{Area(V)} \ge \frac{A(Rs)}{A(Rs+Rt)} \ge \frac{Rs^2}{(Rs+Rt)^2}$. □

Obviously, if the nodes are densely deployed, MDS can coverage almost of the monitored region when *Rt=Rs*. That is to say, the denser the deployment of sensors is, the better sensing coverage the MDS can provide. On the other hand, we can see as long as *Rt* is significantly small, MDS can provide comparable sensing coverage as that of all sensor nodes. However, as *Rt* goes smaller, the number of nodes in MDS becomes larger, which results in the more energy consumption. Therefore, it is necessary to adjust the appropriate *Rt* for each sensor node to ensure MDS can provide the high quality of sensing coverage.

Theorem 2. *Suppose sensor nodes follow Poisson point process of density* λ *in the plane* $\mathbf{R}^2$*. For* $\forall\varepsilon>0$ *and* $\forall p\in \mathbf{R}^2$*, then there* $\exists r$ *s.t.* $P(\exists u\in MDS\ d(u,p)\le r+Rt)\ge 1-\varepsilon$.

Proof. Consider an arbitrary point $p \in \mathbf{R}^2$. A sufficient condition that point p is within $(r+Rt)$ distance from any one dominator node v is that there exists a node u within r distance from point p.

Since there is a node u within r distance from point p, i.e., $d(u,p) \le r$, there are two cases. Case one: If $u \in$ MDS, point p must lie within $(r+Rt)$ distance from the node u, that is $d(u,p) \le r+Rt$. Case two: If $u \notin$ MDS, there must exist one dominator node v which can dominate node u by the definition of MDS. That is to say, node u lies within Rt distance from dominator v, $d(u,v) \le Rt$. Combining two cases, we get $d(v,p) \le d(u,v)+d(v,p) \le Rt+r$, namely, point p is within $(r+Rt)$ distance from any one dominator node v (as illustrated in Fig 1).

From the above, we have $P(\exists v\in MDS,\ \text{s.t.}\ d(v,p)\le r+Rt) \ge P(\exists u\in V,\ \text{s.t.}\ d(u,p)<r)$. Since $\forall p\in \mathbf{R}^2$, there $\exists u\in V$, s.t. $d(u,p)\le Rs$, where V is the set of all sensor nodes. Thus, we have $P(\exists u\in V,\ \text{s.t.}\ d(u,p)<r)=1$ when $r\ge Rs$. On the other hand, since nodes follow a

Poisson point process at density λ, the sensing coverage of such a sensor network is $f_a = 1 - e^{-\pi\lambda Rs^2}$, we have $P(\exists u \in V,$ s.t. $d(u,p)<r) = \frac{1-e^{-\pi\lambda r^2}}{1-e^{-\pi\lambda Rs^2}}$ when $d(u,p)<r<Rs$. Therefore, the following equality holds,

$$P(\exists v \in MDS, \text{ s.t. } d(v,p) \le r+Rt) \ge P(\exists u \in V, \text{ s.t. } d(u,p)<r) = \begin{cases} 1, r \ge Rs \\ \frac{1-e^{-\pi\lambda r^2}}{1-e^{-\pi\lambda Rs^2}}, r < Rs \end{cases}.$$

Let $\frac{1-e^{-\pi\lambda r^2}}{1-e^{-\pi\lambda Rs^2}} \ge 1-\varepsilon$, we get $r \le \sqrt{\frac{-\ln(\varepsilon+(1-\varepsilon)e^{-\pi\lambda Rs^2})}{\pi\lambda}}$. Therefore, $\forall \varepsilon>0$ *and* $\forall p \in \mathbf{R}^2$,

$\exists r = \min(Rs, \sqrt{\frac{-ln(\varepsilon+(1-\varepsilon)e^{-\pi\lambda Rs^2})}{\pi\lambda}})$, s.t. $P(\exists u \in MDS \wedge d(u,p) \le r+Rt) \ge 1-\varepsilon$. □

From Theorem 2, we have the following result:

$$Rt = Rs - r = Rs - \min(Rs, \sqrt{\frac{-ln(\varepsilon+(1-\varepsilon)e^{-\pi\lambda Rs^2})}{\pi\lambda}}) \quad (3)$$

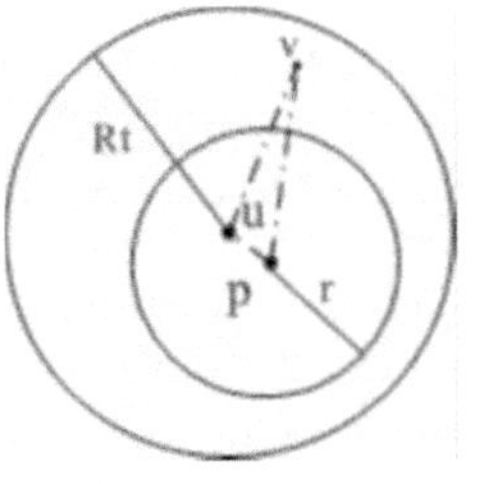

Fig. 1. Illustration of Theorem 2

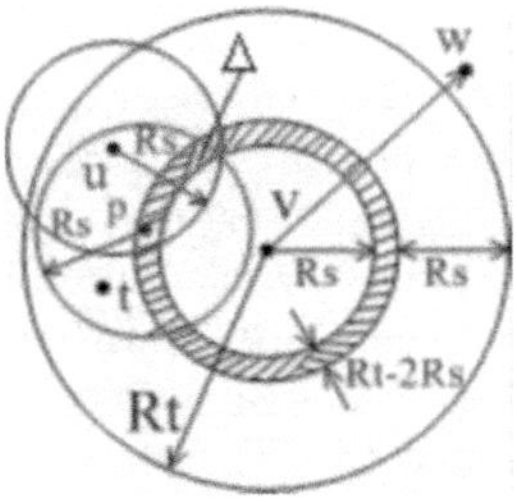

Fig. 2. Illustration of Theorem 3

Theorem 3. *Given sensing range Rs, if all points in the monitored region are covered by sensor nodes, then there exists a point p not covered by MDS for Rt>2Rs.*

Proof. We use a proof by contradiction. Suppose every point in the region is covered by MDS for $Rt>2Rs$. Without loss of generality, consider an arbitrary dominator $v \in$ MDS. Let S_v be the set of nodes in MDS that are on the boundary or inside of disk B_v excluding node v, that is $S_v = \{u | d(u,v) \le Rt \wedge u \in \text{MDS}\} - \{v\}$. Thus, $S_v \ne \emptyset$ for $Rt>2Rs$. This is because if $S_v = \emptyset$, the points with distance between Rs and $Rt/2$ from node v (the region is $B_v(Rt/2)$-$B_v(Rs)$, as illustrated in shadow part of Fig 2) are not covered by either node v (since $Rt/2>Rs$) or other nodes excluding node v in MDS (since these points are at least $Rt/2$ away from nodes in MDS-$\{v\}$). Hence these points are not covered by the MDS, which contradicts every point is covered by the MDS.

Since $S_v \ne \emptyset$, S_v can dominate the node v. These are two cases about the relationship between S_v and D_v, Define $D_v = \{w | d(w,v) \le Rt, w \in V\}$.

(1) *Case 1*: $D_v - \{v\} \subseteq S_v$, i.e., $(V - S_v \cup \{v\}) \cap D_v = \emptyset$. If node v is removed from MDS, the nodes in S_v still dominate the nodes in D_v. In another word, the resulting set MDS-$\{v\}$ is still a dominating set. This contradicts with the definition of MDS.

(2) *Case 2*: D_v-$\{v\}\not\subset S_v$, i.e., there exists a node $u\in(V\text{-}S_v\square\{v\})\cap D_v$. Define δ=Rt-$2Rs$. Let $\triangle$ be the area, where the sensing area of node u intersects with the two concentric circles centered at node v with radius Rs and Rs+δ, equivalently, $\triangle$= $B_u(Rs)\cap(B_v(Rs+\delta)\text{-}B_v(Rs))$ (shown in the red-marked part of Fig 2). Clearly, $\triangle\neq\varnothing$.

Since $d(v,p)>Rs$, for $\forall p\in\triangle$, point p is not covered by the dominator v. Second, for $\forall w\in$ MDS-S_v, since $d(w,v)>Rt$ and $Rs<d(v,p)<Rs+(Rt\text{-}2Rs)=Rt\text{-}Rs$, we have $d(w,p)>d(w,v)\text{-}d(v,p)>Rt\text{-}(Rt\text{-}Rs)=R$s. Thus, the point p is not covered by node w. Based on the assumption that every point is covered by MDS, the point p must be covered by at least one node $\forall w\in S_v$, or equivalently, $\exists t\in S_v$ s.t. $d(t,p)\leq Rs$. Otherwise, point p is not covered by MDS.

Now, we have $d(u,t)\leq d(u,p)+d(p,t)\leq Rs+Rs<Rt$, in another word, dominator t can dominate node u. This implies $\forall u\in D_v$, $\exists t\in S_v$ s.t. $d(u,t)\leq Rt$. Therefore, if dominator v can be removed from MDS, the nodes in S_v still dominate the nodes in D_v. Equivalently, the resulting set MDS-$\{v\}$ is still a dominating set. This contradicts with the definition of MDS. By case 1 and case 2, Theorem 3 holds. □

5 LUCCP Protocol

Theorem 2 and 3 give the upper and lower bound that transmission range of sensors respectively. We propose a Connected Coverage Protocol (LUCCP) that provides good sensing coverage and ensures the network connectivity. LUCCP protocol consists of two parts. First, nodes adjust the appropriate transmission range. Second, construct CDS using Rule K algorithm [5] to meet the requirement of connected coverage. It is proved that the resulting dominating set from the Rule K algorithm must be connected [5]. Therefore, LUCCP protocol can provide the good sensing coverage and ensure the network connectivity. LUCCP like other coverage algorithm also involves round-operation for energy-consumption balance. In every round, each sensor node adjusts the appropriate Rt and executes the Rule K algorithm to construct the CDS. The nodes in CDS become the working nodes to execute the monitoring task and transfer the sensed data.

5.1 Adjust the Transmission Range

By the Equation (3), we have Rt=Rs-min (Rs, $\sqrt{\frac{-\ln(\varepsilon+(1-\varepsilon)e^{-\pi\lambda Rs^2})}{\pi\lambda}}$), where λ is the density of sensors. With the execution of the WSN, sensors are prone to failure, the value of λ is changing. For a single node, it is very difficult to know the change of λ. Therefore, each sensor determines a local node density λ_{local} by counting the number of nodes in its k -hop neighborhood using the maximum transmission range $Rt_{\max}$. The local node density λ_{local} can be approximated as the network density λ and can reflect the variations of node density. λ_{local} can be computed as follows:

$$\lambda_{local}=\frac{|c|+1}{\pi(Rt_{\max})^2k^2} \tag{4}$$

where |c| is the number of k-hop neighbors. The larger the value of k is, the more accurate the approximation of λ_{local} is.

However, the increase of the number of messages will results in the more energy consumption. LUCCP estimates the local density λ_{local} by counting the number of nodes in its 1-hop neighborhood. Let $\varepsilon_0 = \varepsilon + (1-\varepsilon)e^{-\pi\lambda Rs^2}$. Clearly, $\varepsilon_0 \in (0,1)$. Combing the Equation (3) and (4), we have

$$Rt = Rs - \min(Rs, \sqrt{\frac{-\ln \varepsilon_0}{\pi\lambda}}) = Rs - \min(Rs, Rt_{\max}\sqrt{\frac{-\ln \varepsilon_0}{|c|+1}}) \tag{5}$$

Therefore, each sensor can adjust the appropriate the transmission range by the number of nodes in its 1-hop neighbors and Equation (5).

6 Simulation Results

In this section, we evaluate LUCCP's performance by conducting simulations in terms of evaluating the number of working nodes, coverage ratio, the network lifetime and control overhead. In the simulation, 400-800 sensor nodes are randomly deployed in a 100×100 (m^2) region, and each sensor has a sensing range of 10 meter and the maximum transmission range of 20 meter.

6.1 Effectiveness of LUCCP

In the experiment, we vary ε_0 in the LUCCP from 0.1 to 0.9 and investigate its impact on the sensing area coverage of the resulting working nodes and the number of working nodes. Two scenarios are considered with sensor nodes 400 and 800 randomly distributed in the monitored area respectively.

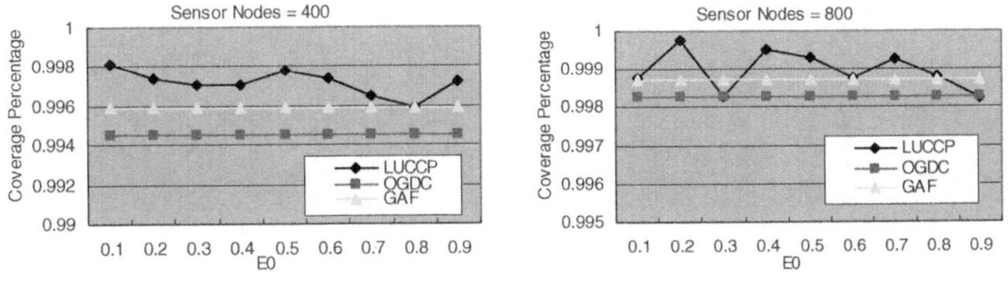

(a) sensor nodes = 400 (b) sensor nodes = 800

Fig. 3. coverage percentage vs.ε_0 in the different density

From Fig. 3 and 4, we observe that the value of ε_0 has no much impact on the sensing coverage and the number working nodes for LUCCP. In general, when ε_0=0.5, LUCCP can provide the best sensing coverage in the different node density. Therefore, we choose ε_0=0.5 when investigating the network lifetime. Compared to LUCCP, OGDC and GAF is not relevant to the parameter ε_0=0.5. Thus, for OGDC and GAF, the curves of the number of working nodes and sensing coverage are parallel to X axis.

On the other hand, in the most situations, LUCCP can provide above 99.5% sensing coverage for the different node density. LUCCP requires 2-hop neighboring information to provide the connected coverage without the location information of sensors; therefore the number of working nodes by LUCCP is greater 13%~30% and 7%~26% than that of OGDC and GAF respectively. However, compared with the number of all deployed sensor nodes, the number of working nodes by LUCCP is reasonable. In addition, the number of working nodes under LUCCP does not greatly increases with the number of deployed nodes.

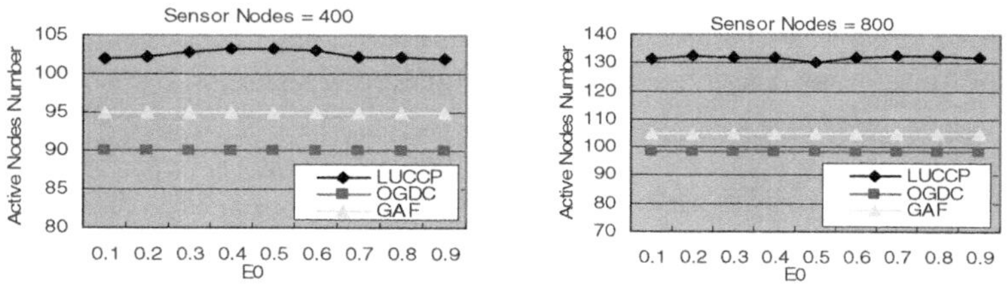

(a) sensor nodes = 400 (b) sensor nodes = 800

Fig. 4. the number of active nodes vs.ε0 in the different density

6.2 Network Lifetime

If the sensing coverage is lower than the threshold or if the network is disconnected, WSNs could not perform the monitoring task. Thus, we consider the lifetime of network is over in such a situation. In the simulation, if the sensing coverage is lower than 70 % or the network is not connectivity, we think the network lifetime is over.

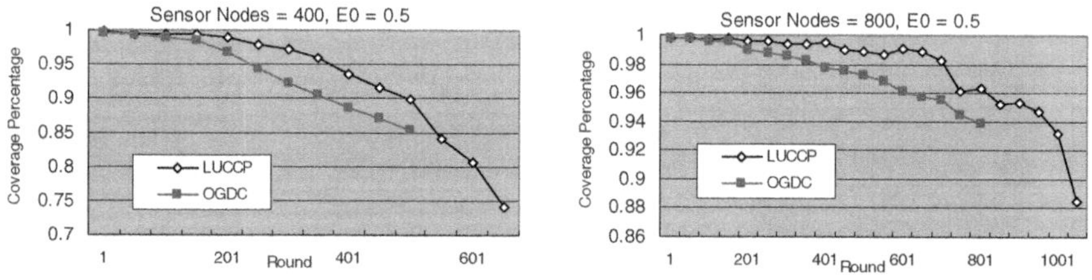

(a) sensor nodes = 400 (b) sensor nodes = 800

Fig. 5. network lifetime vs. time in the different density

Fig. 5 shows the curves of lifetime for LUCCP and OGDC with the different density of sensors. From Fig. 5, in the given network configuration, the sensor network is disconnected before the obtained sensing coverage drop to 70%. In addition, the coverage ratio drop more slowly in LUCCP than that in OGDC, and the lifetime of LUCCP is 35% longer than that of OGDC. This is due to the fact that every node can adjust its own transmission range to make its decision based on Rule K algorithm in LUCCP, which consumes less energy than OGDC protocol.

7 Discussion

This paper studied the area coverage property of minimal dominating set, and established the relationship between point coverage and area coverage, and derived the upper and lower bound that point coverage is equivalent to area coverage in random geometric graphs. Based on the analytical results and Rule K algorithm, LUCCP protocol is proposed. The experiment studies show that the proposed LUCCP protocol can effectively maintain both high quality sensing coverage and connectivity for a long time.

Acknowledgments. This research is partially supported by the NSF of China under Grant No. 60573132, 60573106.

References

1. Stojmenovic, I.: Position Based Routing in Ad Hoc Networks. IEEE Communications Magazine 40(7), 128–134 (2002)
2. Wan, P.J., Alzoubi, K.M., Frieder, O.: Distributed Construction of Connected Dominating Set in Wireless Ad Hoc Networks. In: Proceedings of the 21st IEEE Conference on Computer Communications (INFOCOM), New York, USA, IEEE Press, Los Alamitos (2002)
3. Alzoubi, K.M., Wan, P.J., Frieder, O.: Message-optimal Connected Dominating Sets in Mobile Ad Hoc Networks. In: Proceedings of the 3rd ACM International Symposium on Mobile Ad Hoc Networking and Computing(MobiHoc), Lausanne, Switzerland, pp. 157–164. ACM, New York (2002)
4. Wu, J., Dai, F.: Broadcasting in Ad Hhoc Networks Based on Self-pruning. In: Proceedings of the 22nd IEEE Conference on Computer Communications (INFOCOM), San Francisco, USA, 2003, pp. 2240–2250. IEEE, Los Alamitos (2003)
5. Dai, F., Wu, J.: An Extended Localized Algorithm for Connected Dominating Set Formation in Ad Hoc Wireless Networks. IEEE Transaction on Parallel and Distributed Systems 15(10), 908–920 (2004)
6. Cardei, M., Wu, J.: Energy-Efficient Coverage Problems in Wireless Ad-hoc Sensor Networks. Computer communication 29, 413–420 (2006)
7. Shakkottai, S., Srikant, R., Shroff, N.: Unreliable Sensor Grids: Coverage, Connectivity and Diameter. In: Proceedings of the 22nd IEEE Conference on Computer Communications (INFOCOM), San Francisco, USA, 2003, pp. 2240–2250. IEEE, Los Alamitos (2003)
8. Zhang, H., Hou, J.C.: Maintaining Sensing Coverage and Connectivity in Large Sensor Networks. Ad Hoc & Wireless Networks 1(1), 89–124 (2005)
9. Wang, X., Xing, G., Zhang, Y., Lu, C., Pless, R.: Integrated Coverage and Connectivity Configuration in Wireless Sensor Networks. In: Proceedings of the 2003 International Conference on Embedded Networked Sensor Systems (SenSys), Los Angeles, CA, pp. 28–39. ACM, New York (2003)
10. Chen, B., Jamieson, K., Balakrishnan, H., Morris, R.: SPAN: An Energy-Efficient Coordination Algorithm for Topology Maintenance in Ad Hoc Wireless Networks. In: Proceedings of the 7th International Conference on Mobile Computing and Networking (MobiCom), Rome, Italy, pp. 85–96. ACM Press, New York (2001)

11. Gupta, H., Das, S.R., Gu, Q.: Connected Sensor Cover: Self-Organization of Sensor Networks for Efficient Query Execution. In: Proceedings of the 4th ACM International Symposium on Mobile Ad Hoc Networking and Computing (MobiHoc), Annapolis, Maryland, USA, pp. 189–200. ACM, New York (2003)
12. Zhou, Z., Das, S.R., Gupta, H.: Fault Tolerant Connected Sensor Cover with Variable Sensing and Transmission Ranges. In: Proceedings of 2nd Annual IEEE Conference on Sensor, Mesh and Ad Hoc Communications and Networks (SECON), Santa Clara, CA, pp. 594–604. IEEE, Los Alamitos (2005)
13. Cheng, H.L., Edelsbrunner, H.: Area and Perimeter Derivatives of a Union of Disks. In: Klein, R., Six, H.-W., Wegner, L. (eds.) Computer Science in Perspective. LNCS, vol. 2598, pp. 88–97. Springer, Heidelberg (2003)

Fuzzy-Based Reliable Data Delivery for Countering Selective Forwarding in Sensor Networks*

Hae Young Lee and Tae Ho Cho

School of Information and Communication Engineering, Sungkyunkwan University
300 Cheoncheon-dong, Jangan-gu, Suwon 440-746, Korea
{sofware,taecho}@ece.skku.ac.kr

Abstract. In wireless sensor networks, an adversary can use compromised nodes or outside jammer to launch selective forwarding attacks in which malicious nodes may refuse to forward certain messages and simply drop them, ensuring that they are not propagated any more. Multipath routing can be used to counter selective forwarding attacks. However, communication overheads in multipath routing increase dramatically as the number of paths increases. In this paper, we propose a fuzzy-based reliable data delivery method to counter selective forwarding attacks. The number of paths for data delivery is determined by a fuzzy logic with consideration of the energy level of the network and the number of malicious nodes. The proposed method uses the propagation limiting method as a means for routing if multipath routing is insufficient for reliable data delivery.

1 Introduction

Recent advances in micro-electro-mechanical systems and low power highly integrated digital electronics have enabled the development of low-cost sensor networks [1,2]. Sensor networks consist of a large number of sensor nodes that monitor the environment, and a few base stations that collect the sensor readings [3]. Sensor networks are expected to interact with the physical world at an unprecedented level to enable various new applications [4]. In many applications, prompt detection and reporting of each relevant event in the field are important [5]. However, as shown in Fig. 1, an adversary can use compromised nodes or outside jammer to launch *selective forwarding attacks* in which malicious nodes may refuse to forward certain messages and simply drop them, ensuring that they are not propagated any further [6].

Selective forwarding attacks are typically most effective when the attacking nodes are explicitly included on the path of a data flow. They can corrupt a

* This research was supported by the MIC (Ministry of Information and Communication), Korea, under the ITRC (Information Technology Research Center) support program supervised by the IITA (Institute of Information Technology Advancement). (IITA-2006-C1090-0603-0028).

J. Indulska et al. (Eds.): UIC 2007, LNCS 4611, pp. 535–544, 2007.

number of existing routing protocols such as TinyOS beaconing, Directed Diffusion, GPSR, GEAR, and clustered-based protocols, especially when they are used in combination with other attacks such as wormhole and sinkhole attacks [5]. *Multipath routing* can be used to counter selective forwarding attacks [6]. Multipath routing allows the establishment of multiple paths between source and destination, which provides an easy mechanism to increase the likelihood of reliable data delivery by sending multiple copies of data along difference paths [7]. Messages over n paths whose nodes are completely disjoint are completely protected against selective forwarding attacks involving at most n compromised nodes and still offer some probabilistic protection over n nodes are compromised [6]. However, communication overheads in multipath routing increase dramatically as the number of paths increases [6].

Generally, sensor nodes are limited in power and irreplaceable since these nodes have limited capacity and are unattended [8]. Nodes in sensor networks can fail due to the depletion of their batteries. If a region of the network goes silent, then the network may be unable to complete its intended function [9].

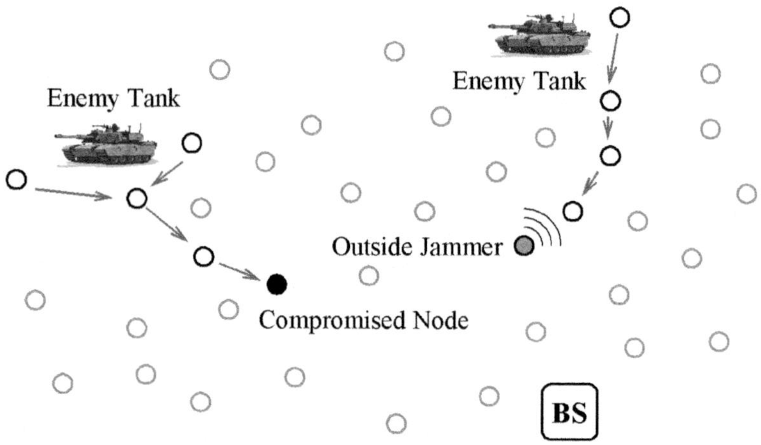

Fig. 1. In *selective forwarding attacks*, malicious nodes may refuse to forward certain messages and simply drop them, ensuring that they are not propagated any further

In this paper, we propose a fuzzy-based reliable data delivery method to counter selective forwarding attacks. The number of path for data delivery is determined by a fuzzy logic with consideration of the energy level of the network and the number of malicious nodes. If multipath routing is insufficient to deliver data within the network, the propose method uses the propagation limiting method proposed by Chi and Cho [8] as a means for routing since flooding is a robust means against selective forwarding attacks [6]. The reliable data delivering capability of the proposed method is particularly effective for mission-critical applications.

The remainder of the paper is organized as follows: Section 2 briefly describes the propagation limiting method as background knowledge. Section 3 shows the details of the proposed method. Section 4 reviews the simulation result. Finally, conclusion is discussed in Section 5.

2 Propagation Limiting Method Overview

In [8], Chi and Cho proposed the propagation limiting method (PLM) in which the data transmission area is limited according to a threshold value for reducing the energy consumption in the network (Fig. 2). A fuzzy rule-based system is exploited to determine the threshold value by considering the energy and density of all the deployed nodes. Compare to the classical flooding, PLM consumes the limited energy more efficiently since only part of the nodes participates in the propagation process. Thus, the nodes that do not participate in the propagation can save their energy, which results in the prolong network lifetime.

When information on a specific region is requested, the base station can strategically select a subset of the network to sense the environment at a specific time. The base station determines a target region based on location information of deployed nodes, and it adds the length of the optimal path to an interest message with the threshold value obtained by the fuzzy logic. The interest messages created within the base station are forwarded toward the neighbor nodes. After an intermediate node receives the message and stores it in its interest entry, the node calculates distance using location information of the base station, itself, and a source point within the target region. If the node is an interior node then it continues the propagation toward the target point, otherwise the propagation is terminated.

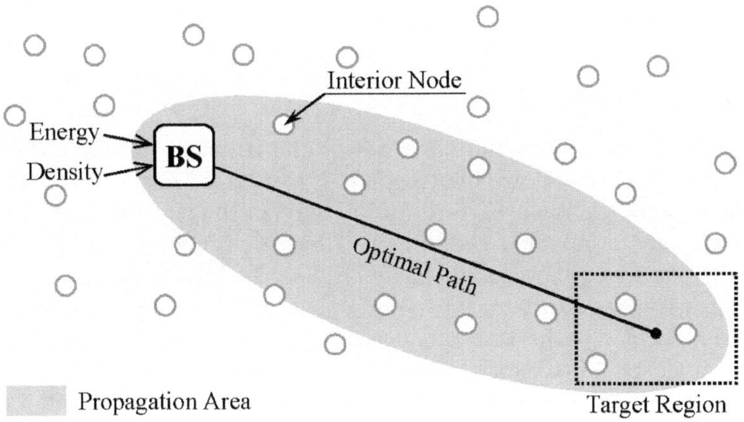

Fig. 2. PLM limits the flooding area according to a threshold value, which is determined by a fuzzy logic system with the consideration of energy and density, for reducing the energy consumption

3 Reliable Data Delivery Method

In this section, we describe the proposed method in detail.

3.1 Assumptions

The proposed method uses the energy level of the network and the number of malicious nodes to determine the number of paths for data delivery. PLM uses the energy level and the density of the network to determine a threshold value [8]. Thus, we assume that the base station can know or estimate the information about them approximately. To detect malicious nodes, we can use the selective forwarding detecting scheme proposed by Yu and Xiao [5]. PLM assumes that all nodes need to know their locations [8]. The location of nodes may be available directly by communicating with a satellite using low power GPS and GPS cards [10,11,12]. In this paper, we only consider the disjoint multipath routing, because the braided multipath [13] can easily be transformed into disjoint multipath [7].

3.2 Overview

In the proposed method, the base station determines the number of paths for data delivery, n_{path}, periodically or on demand with a fuzzy rule-based system. The fuzzy rule-based system uses the energy level of the network and the number of malicious nodes to determine n_{path}. Thus, the base station needs to store the information about them. If the new n_{path} is differs from the current, the base station broadcasts the new n_{path} to all nodes within the network (Fig. 3(a)). After flooding, source nodes send their sensing data to the base station along n_{path} disjoint paths (Fig. 3(b) or (c)). There may be less than n_{path} disjoint paths from a source to the base station since completely disjoint paths may be difficult to create [6]. The source sends its data by using PLM (Fig. 3(d)) if n_{path} exceeds the number of existing disjoint paths.

3.3 Input Parameters

Generally, sensor nodes are limited in power and irreplaceable since these nodes have limited capacity and are unattended [8]. Nodes in sensor networks can fail due to the depletion of their batteries. If a region of the network goes silent, then the network may be unable to complete its intended function [9]. Therefore, we have to determine n_{path} based on the energy level of the network.

Multipath routing can be used to counter selective forwarding attacks. Messages routed over n paths whose nodes are completely disjoint are completely protected against selective forwarding attacks involving at most n compromised nodes and still offer some probabilistic protection when over n nodes are compromised [6]. However, communication overheads in multipath routing increase dramatically as the number of paths increases [5]. Thus, we have to adaptively determine n_{path} based on the number of malicious nodes.

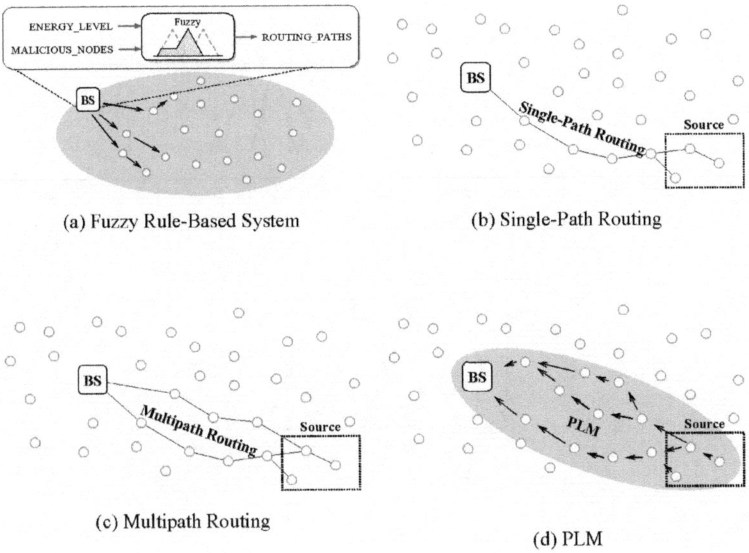

Fig. 3. In the proposed method, the number of paths for data delivery is determined by a fuzzy logic with consideration of the energy level and the number of malicious nodes (a). The data can be delivered along a single path (b) or multiple paths (c). If multipath routing is insufficient for reliable data delivery, the proposed method uses PLM as a means for routing.

3.4 Fuzzy Logic Design

Fig. 4 illustrates the membership functions of the input/output parameters of the fuzzy logic. The labels in the fuzzy variables are presented as follows:

- MALICIOUS_NODES = {MN_VS, MN_S, MN_M, MN_L, MN_VL}
- ENERGY_LEVEL = {EL_E, EL_L, EL_F}
- ROUTING_PATHS = {RP_VS, RP_S, RP_M, RP_L, RP_VL}

If all nodes in the network have sufficient energy for data delivery and no malicious node exists, n_{path} can be very small (e.g., 1).

Rule1: IF ENERGY_LEVEL IS EL_F
AND MALICIOUS_NODES IS MN_VS
THEN ROUTING_PATHS IS RP_VS

If all nodes have enough energy for data delivery and a few malicious nodes exist, n_{path} should be greater than the number of malicious nodes.

Rule 3: IF ENERGY_LEVEL IS EL_F
AND MALICIOUS_NODES IS MN_M
THEN ROUTING_PATHS IS RP_M

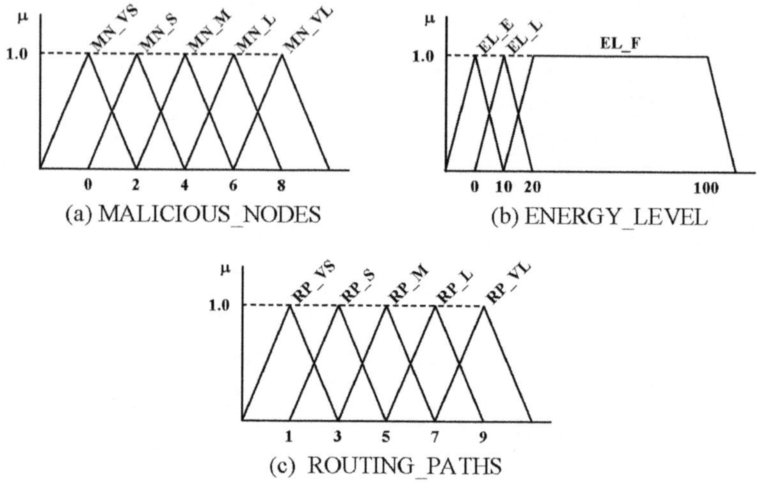

Fig. 4. The membership functions of the input/output parameters of the fuzzy logic are shown

Rule 4: IF ENERGY_LEVEL IS EL_F
AND MALICIOUS_NODES IS MN_L
THEN ROUTING_PATHS IS RP_L

If the energy level of the network is not enough for reliable data delivery, we may as well use PLM as a means for routing, i.e., set n_{path} to the maximum value.

Rule 12: IF ENERGY_LEVEL IS EL_E
AND MALICIOUS_NODES IS MN_S
THEN ROUTING_PATHS IS RP_VL

Rule 13: IF ENERGY_LEVEL IS EL_E
AND MALICIOUS_NODES IS MN_M
THEN ROUTING_PATHS IS RP_VL

Fig. 5 shows the output surface determined by the fuzzy logic. Basically, the number of paths is determined based on the number of malicious nodes when the network has enough energy. If the energy level of the network is low, the fuzzy logic chooses a more number of paths.

3.5 Data Delivery

After the broadcast of n_{path}, source nodes send their sensing data along n_{path} disjoint paths to the base station. There may be less than n_{path} disjoint paths from a source to the base station since completely disjoint paths may be difficult to create [6]. The source sends its data by using PLM if n_{path} exceeds the

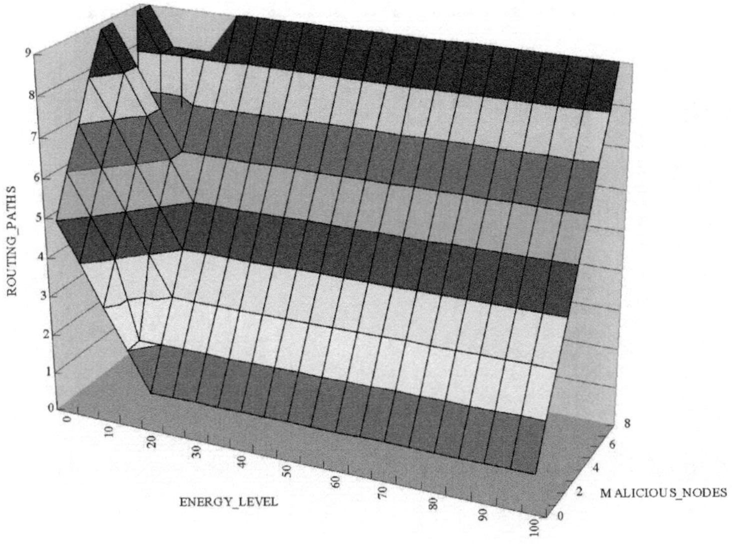

Fig. 5. The output surface determined by the fuzzy logic is shown

number of existing disjoint paths. PLM uses the energy and density of sensor nodes to determine transmission area. A threshold value is needed to limit the transmission area. The threshold value is determined by a fuzzy logic system with the consideration of the energy and density. To archive a threshold value, every node needs to store the information about the energy and density approximately. However, it is almost impossible to do. Moreover, the fuzzy logic system is too heavy to run on every node. Thus, n_{path} and a threshold value for PLM should be broadcasted *simultaneously* by the base station. Then, each node can use PLM as a means for data delivery.

4 Simulation Result

In this section, we evaluate the performance of the proposed method through simulations. The proposed method has been compared with a single-, dual-, and tripartite-path routing-based networks. We use a field size of $1,000 \times 1,000\text{m}^2$, where 4,000 nodes are uniformly distributed. Each node takes $390/300\mu$J to transmit/receive a report [4]. The routing protocol of the network is Directed Diffusion [11].

Fig. 6 shows the ratio of delivered data when the number of malicious nodes is between 0 and 8, and the energy level of the network is full. As shown in the figure, the proposed method (filled rectangles) achieves 100% convergence since a means for data delivery is determined by the number of malicious nodes within the method. On the other hand, the others cannot deliver over 40 percent of the

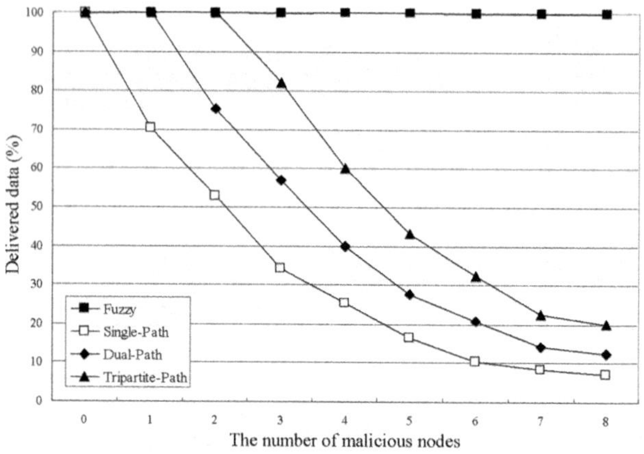

Fig. 6. This figure shows the ratio of delivered data when the number of malicious nodes is between 0 and 8

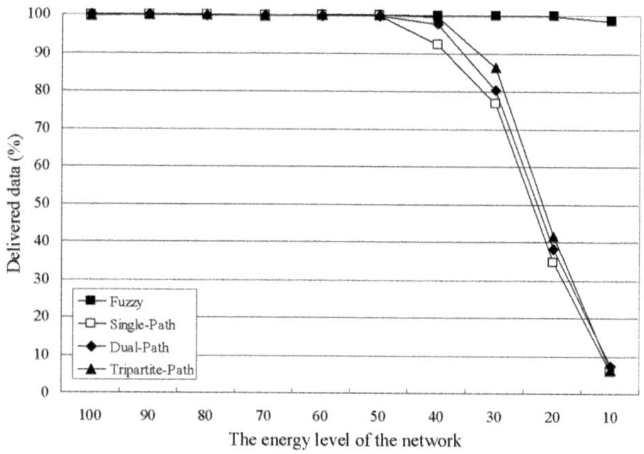

Fig. 7. This figure shows the ratio of delivered data when the energy level of the network is between 100% and 10%

total traffic to the base station if the number of malicious nodes exceeds the number of routing paths.

Fig. 7 shows the ratio of delivered data when the energy level of the network is between 100% and 10%, and no malicious node exists. As shown in the figure, the proposed method achieves 100% convergence since PLM may be chosen within the method if the energy level of the network is low. On the other hand, the others can not provide reliable data delivery if the energy level of the network falls to under 40%.

Fig. 8 shows the average energy consumption per report forwarding when the number of malicious nodes is between 0 and 8, and the energy level of the network

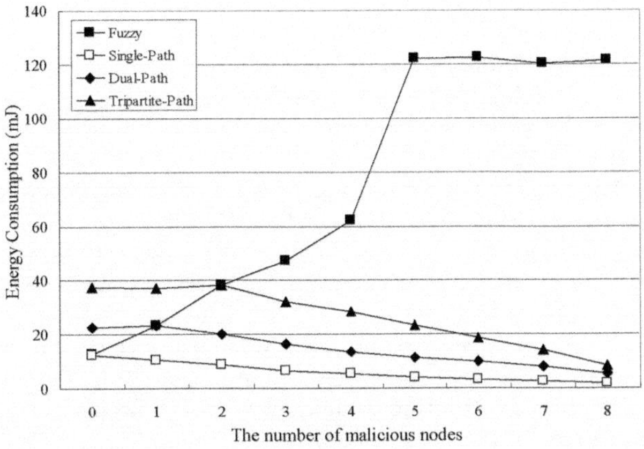

Fig. 8. This figure shows the average energy consumption per report forwarding when the number of malicious nodes is between 0 and 8. Each node has four disjoint paths.

is full. Each node has four disjoint paths for data delivery to the base station. As shown in the figure, the proposed method consumes more energy than the others since the method chooses PLM as a means for data delivery if the number of malicious nodes exceeds the number of disjoint paths, 4. However, it provides reliable data delivery. On the other hand, the others can conserve energy but cannot guarantee reliable data delivery.

5 Conclusion and Future Work

In this paper, we proposed a fuzzy-based reliable data delivery method to counter selective forwarding attacks. The number of path for data delivery is determined by a fuzzy logic with consideration of the energy level of the network and the number of malicious nodes. If multipath routing is insufficient to deliver data within the network, the propose method chooses PLM for routing since flooding is a robust means against selective forwarding attacks. The reliable data delivery capability of the proposed method is particularly effective for mission-critical applications.

Currently the proposed method consumes too much energy when PLM is chosen as a means for routing. Thus, we plan to integrate the selective attacks detecting techniques (e.g., [5]) with the proposed method. Then, we can design more efficient data delivery method that can evade silent areas.

References

1. Akyildiz, I., Su, W., Sankarasubramaniam, Y., Cayirci, E.: A survey on sensor networks. IEEE Commun. Mag. 40(8), 102–114 (2002)
2. Akkaya, K., Younis, M.: A survey on routing protocols for wireless sensor networks. Ad hoc Netw. 3(3), 325–349 (2004)

3. Buttyan, L., Dora, L., Vajda, I.: Statistical wormhole detection in sensor networks. Lect. Notes Comput. Sc. 3813, 128–141 (2005)
4. Ye, F., Luo, H., Lu, S.: Statistical en-route filtering of injected false data in sensor networks. IEEE J. Sel. Area Comm. 23(4), 839–850 (2005)
5. Yu, B., Xiao, B.: Detecting selective forwarding attacks in wireless sensor networks. In: Proc. of IPDPS (2006)
6. Karlof, C., Wagner, D.: Secure routing in wireless sensor networks: Attacks and countermeasures. Ad Hoc Netw. 1(2-3), 293–315 (2005)
7. Dulman, S., Nieberg, T., Wu, J., Havinga, P.: Trade-off between traffic overhead and reliability in multipath routing for wireless sensor networks. In: Proc. of WCNC, pp. 1918–1922 (2003)
8. Chi, S., Cho, T.: Fuzzy logic based propagation limiting method for message routing in wireless sensor networks. Lect. Notes Comput. Sc. 3983, 58–67 (2006)
9. Al-Karaki, J.N., K.A.E.: Routing techniques in wireless sensor networks: A survey. IEEE Wirel. Comm. 11(6), 6–28 (2004)
10. Intanagonwiwat, C., Govindan, R., Estrin, D., Heidemann, J., Silva, F.: Directed diffusion for wireless sensor networking. IEEE ACM T. Network 11(1), 2–16 (2003)
11. Xu, Y., Heidemann, J., Estrin, D.: Geography-informed energy conservation for ad-hoc routing. In: Proc. of MobiCom, pp. 70–84 (2001)
12. Ganesan, D., Govindan, R., Shenker, S., Estrin, D.: Highly-resilient, energy-efficient multipath routing in wireless sensor networks. Mobile Comput. Comm. Rev. 5(4), 11–25 (2004)
13. Staddon, J., Balfanz, D., Durfee, G.: Efficient tracing of failed nodes in sensor networks. In: Proc. of WSNA, 122–130 (2002)

An Efficient Grid-Based Data Gathering Scheme in Wireless Sensor Networks*

Shiow-Fen Hwang, Kun-Hsien Lu, Hsiao-Nung Chang, and Chyi-Ren Dow

Department of Information Engineering and Computer Science
Feng Chia University, Taichung, Taiwan 40724
{sfhwang,p9217988,m9201472,crdow}@fcu.edu.tw

Abstract. Data gathering is an important operation in wireless sensor networks. Due to the limited battery power, sensor nodes consume significant energy and drain out of it quickly if each node transmits its sensed data directly to a distant base station, even though the delay time is minimized in a round of communication. Hence, there is a trade-off between minimizing both of the energy consumed by sensor nodes and the delay time, then the overall cost is defined as the energy $\times$ delay cost. In this paper, we propose an Efficient Grid-based Data Gathering (EGDG) scheme which adopts a hierarchical grid structure and constructs cycles by connecting heads in each order of the hierarchy. Data transmissions move toward a leader from two starter nodes simultaneously in each cycle. The objective of EGDG is to achieve a better result for the energy $\times$ delay cost comparing to other schemes, and also to accomplish significant coverage-preserving at the same time. Simulation results show that EGDG outperforms than LEACH and PEGASIS in terms of rounds, the energy $\times$ delay cost and coverage-preserving.

1 Introduction

With advances in micro-electro-mechanical systems (MEMS) technology, wireless communications and digital electronics have enabled the development of wireless sensor with low cost processor and low power consumption [1]. Wireless sensor networks (WSNs) usually consist of numerous sensor nodes that are able to monitor a variety of environments or track objects. Data gathering is an important operation for sensor applications. The simple method that can accomplish a data gathering task is direct transmission. Each sensor node collects the interesting information and transmits its sensed data to the base station (BS) directly in a round of communication. However, the nodes will consume significant energy and drain out of it quickly, even though the delay time is minimized per round. Therefore, two techniques have been proposed to save energy for data gathering. One technique is data fusion [2] that combines two or more data packets into a single same-size packet so that the number of data packets

* This research is supported by the National Science Council of Republic of China under grant number NSC-94-2213-E-035-027.

J. Indulska et al. (Eds.): UIC 2007, LNCS 4611, pp. 545–556, 2007.

transmitted in the sensor network is reduced. Another proposed technique is multi-hop transmission that utilizes cooperation among nodes, and then only some designated nodes (e.g. cluster heads) take turns transmitting data packets to the BS. Hence, the energy dissipation among nodes is reduced and the network lifetime is extended.

Many data gathering schemes have been proposed and they employed both of two techniques to reduce the energy dissipation and prolong the network lifetime. These schemes usually organize all nodes into different architectures such as clusters [3][4], a chain [5][6], and a tree [7][8]. LEACH [3] is a well-known cluster-based scheme which employs randomization in cluster head selection and then forms a small number of clusters. Each cluster head collects the data from nodes in its cluster, fuses and transmits the gathered data to the BS for processing. LEACH achieves better performance than direct transmission in terms of energy dissipation. In chain-based schemes such as PEGASIS [5], all nodes are formed by chain. Each node only communicates with its close neighbor, and takes turns serving as a leader. The leader is responsible for transmitting the fused data of the chain to the BS. PEGASIS achieves longer network lifetime than LEACH. In [7], H. O. Tan et. al proposed a minimum spanning tree-based scheme called PEDAP. PEDAP considers that the weight of edges is the ratio of the transmission cost between two connected nodes to the residual energy of the sending node. The goal of PEDAP is to minimize the total energy expended in a round of data gathering and balance the energy consumption among nodes. However, the routing information used in PEDAP has to be re-computed excluding dead nodes after some certain of rounds.

In this paper, we propose an Efficient Grid-based Data Gathering (EGDG) scheme which adopts a hierarchical grid structure and constructs cycles by connecting heads in each order of the hierarchy. Data transmissions move toward a leader from two starter nodes simultaneously in each cycle. The main objective of EGDG is to reduce both of the total energy consumption and the delay time incurred in gathering the sensed data. Hence, the lower energy $\times$ delay cost comparing to other existing schemes can be achieved, then significant coverage-preserving is also accomplished at the same time. This paper is organized as follows. In Section 2 we introduce network model including grid construction. In Section 3 the proposed efficient grid-based data gathering scheme is presented. Section 4 is performance evaluation. Section 5 concludes the paper.

2 Network Model

2.1 Assumptions

Some basic assumptions of the sensor network in EGDG are declared as follows. First, sensor nodes are uniformly deployed, stationary, and energy-constrained. When sensor nodes are deployed in the sensor network, they have global time synchronization. Second, each sensor node is aware of its location, e.g. through receiving location information from the BS. Finally, sensor nodes have the ability

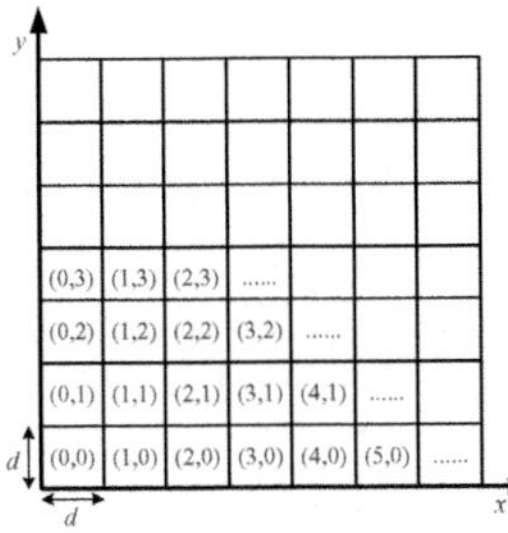

Fig. 1. Logical grids to partition physical sensor field

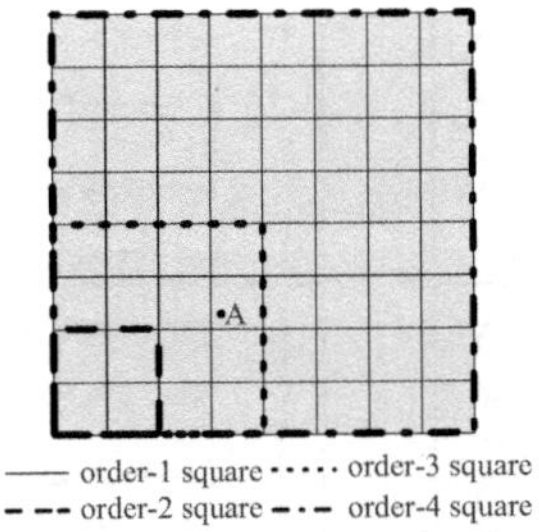

Fig. 2. An example of the hierarchical grid structure in EGDG

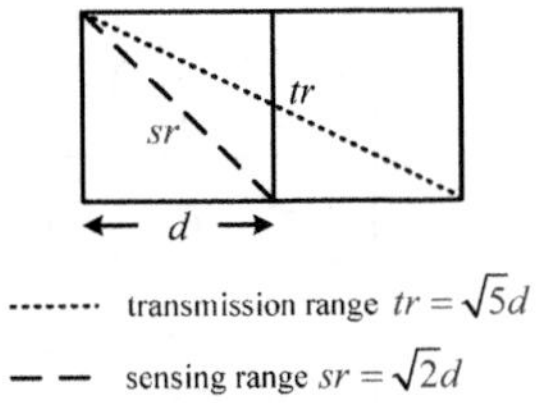

Fig. 3. The relationships between grid length d, sensing range sr and transmission range tr

to adjust their transmission range according to the distance of transmission in order to communicate with another node such as the BS located at a fixed location.

2.2 Grid Construction

The sensor field is partitioned into several 2D logical grids. Each grid is a square of $d \times d$, denoted by (x, y) as shown in Fig. 1. Therefore, each node located in an order-1 square can map its location into a grid coordinate (x, y). EGDG adopts a hierarchy of grids with squares of increasing size. Figure 2 illustrates an example of the hierarchical grid structure. After the hierarchical grid structure is constructed, each node can obtain a relative grid coordinate $(x, y)_i$ if it locates in an order-$(i-1)$ square with respect to the order-i square where it resides in. For example, in Fig. 2, the grid coordinate of node A is (3,2) and its relative grid coordinates are $(1, 0)_2$, $(1, 1)_3$ as well as $(0, 0)_4$.

Let sr and tr be sensing range and normal transmission range of a node, respectively. In order to provide sufficient coverage-preserving, the relationships between three values, sr, tr and d are defined as $sr = \sqrt{2}d$ and $tr = \sqrt{5}d$ as shown in Fig. 3. Hence, a node located in arbitrary location of a grid can cover and gather the information of that grid, then the sensed data can be transmitted to any node located in a neighboring grid.

For each grid, one node is designated to be a *head*, i.e. an active node. The head is responsible for sensing, receiving and forwarding data. In the network initialization phase, each node broadcasts a HELLO packet to build a neighbor table consisting of the number of nodes and each node's ID in the grid. The node with the smallest ID in the grid will first serve as the head. Other nodes in the grid enter to sleeping mode for conserving energy. When the residual energy of the head is below a threshold value, this indicates that the head can not operate for transmitting and receiving data packets and is considered as a dead node. Therefore, the head will wake up the node with the second smallest ID to be the new head. Finally, when the head with the largest ID in the grid is dead, the grid becomes empty.

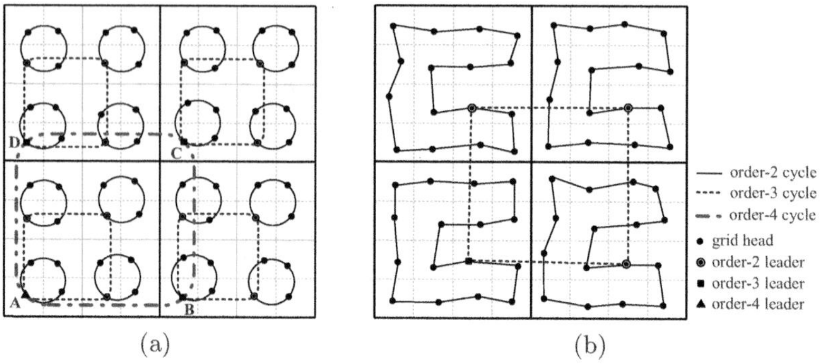

Fig. 4. Two examples of the data gathering process in EGDG

3 The Proposed Efficient Grid-Based Data Gathering (EGDG) Scheme

3.1 Overview

In EGDG, the sensor field is divided into a hierarchical grid structure (e.g. order-n, $n \geq 1$), then only one node in an order-1 square serves as a head. All heads in the same order-i square form the order-i cycle. In the order-i cycle, the heads take turns serving as the order-i leader. The order-i leader is responsible for collecting the fused data, where receiving from other heads in the same order-i cycle. Then, all order-i leaders in the same order-$(i+1)$ square continue to form the order-$(i+1)$ cycle. Finally, a head serving as the top order-n leader of the order-n cycle in the order-n square collects the fused data of the sensor field and transmits it to the BS.

Figure 4(a) shows two examples of the data gathering process in EGDG. In Fig. 4(a), the number of heads in an order-2 square is 4, and then 16 order-2 cycles are formed. A head is designated as the order-2 leader in each order-2 cycle, and then four order-2 leaders form an order-3 cycle in an order-3 square. Finally, four order-3 leaders (i.e. head A, B, C, and D) form an order-4 cycle in the order-4 square and head A serves as the order-4 leader. In EGDG, the number of an order-$(i-1)$ squares in an order-i square can be adjusted according to different sensing requirements. Figure 4(b) shows an example that an order-2 square is composed of 16 order-1 squares while an order-3 square comprises four order-2 squares.

3.2 Cycle Construction

As mentioned in Section 2.2, each node can calculate its relative grid coordinates $(x, y)_i$ for different order-i squares, where $i \geq 2$. A position mapping function is proposed to map a relative grid coordinate $(x, y)_i$ into a position $p(x, y)_i$. Therefore, each head can know its position on an order-i cycle. The position mapping function is presented as the following equation (1).

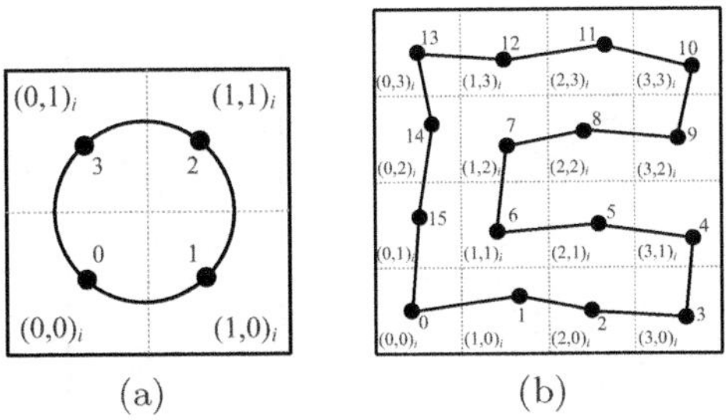

Fig. 5. Two examples of cycle construction: (a) 4 heads form a cycle, (b) 16 heads form a cycle. The number represents the position of a head on a cycle, and $(x, y)_i$ indicates the relative grid coordinate of a head in an order-i square.

$$p(x,y)_i = \begin{cases} (m_i - y) \bmod m_i & if\ x = 0 \\ (\sqrt{m_i} - 1)y + (-1)^y x + \frac{[1-(-1)^y]}{2}\sqrt{m_i} & if\ x \neq 0 \end{cases} \tag{1}$$

where m_i is the number of order-$(i-1)$ squares in an order-i square and $i \geq 2$. For example, assume that an order-2 square consists of 4 or 16 order-1 squares as shown in Fig. 5 when $i = 2$. In Fig. 5(a), four heads form an order-2 cycle and $m_2 = 4$. Therefore, if the relative grid coordinate of a head is $(0,0)_2$, then its position calculated by equation (1) is 0. When the relative grid coordinate of a head is $(1,0)_2$, then its position is 1, and so on. After each head maps its relative grid coordinate to a fixed position, an order-2 cycle is formed and the position number is from 0 to 3. Figure 5(b) is also similar to Fig. 5(a) when $m_2 = 16$. The position information of a head on an order-i cycle will be used for data transmissions during data gathering process.

3.3 Data Gathering in EGDG

For data gathering in an order-1 square, a head gathers the interesting data of that grid and transmits it to another head in one of neighboring order-1 squares. Assume that current data gathering round is number j. A head on position $((j-1) \bmod m_i)$ serves as the order-i leader of the order-i cycle in the order-i square. The position of a head on an order-i cycle with regard to round j can be presented as the equation (2).

$$pos(j, m_i, \alpha) = \left(j + \frac{m_i}{2} + \alpha\right) \bmod m_i \tag{2}$$

where α is an integer and $(-\frac{m}{2} - 1) \leq \alpha \leq (\frac{m}{2} - 1)$. By using the equation (2), it can determine whether a head is a starter node or not and the position of a head that need to receive the fused data. Then, two heads except the leader are designated as the starter nodes. In each round of data collection, data transmissions move toward an order-i leader from two starter nodes in an order-i cycle. The data transmission rules in EGDG are as follows. In an order-i cycle, the grid head on position $pos(j, m_i, 0)$ becomes a starter node and transmits its

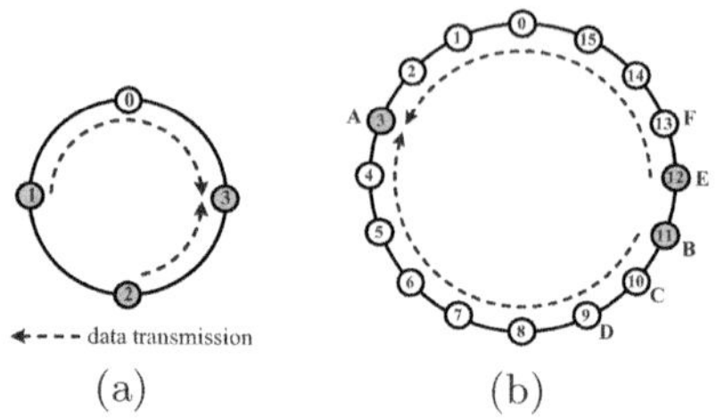

Fig. 6. Two examples of data gathering in different sizes of order-2 cycles : (a) $m_2 = 4$, (b) $m_2 = 16$

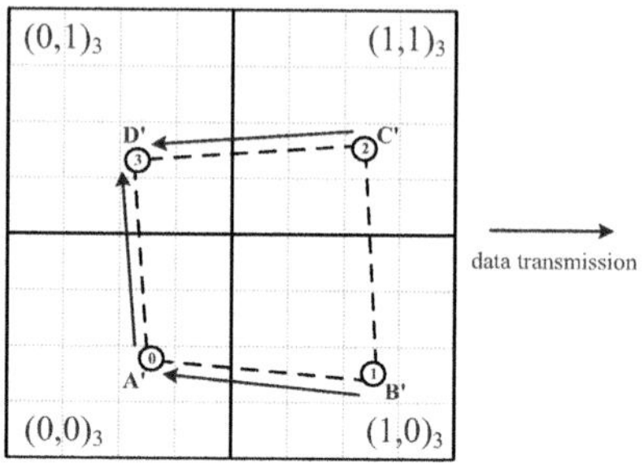

Fig. 7. An example of data gathering in an order-3 cycle

sensed data to the head on position $pos(j, m_i, 1)$. That is, the head on position $pos(j, m_i, \alpha)$ receiving the fused data from the head on position $pos(j, m_i, \alpha - 1)$ fuses the received data and its own to a single data packet, and then transmits it to the head on position $pos(j, m_i, \alpha + 1)$ with increasing α value.

Similarly, the head on position $pos(j, m_i, -1)$ also becomes a starter node and transmits its sensed data to the head on position $pos(j, m_i, -2)$. Hence, the head on position $pos(j, m_i, \alpha)$ receiving the fused data from the head on position $pos(j, m_i, \alpha + 1)$ fuses the received data and its own to a single packet, and then transmits it to the head on position $pos(j, m_i, \alpha - 1)$ with decreasing α value. With data transmissions from two starter nodes toward the leader, the delay time in an order-i cycle can be significantly reduced. Moreover, data fusion is performed at every head except two starter nodes in an order-i cycle and can reduce the amount of data transmitted to save energy.

Figure 6 illustrates two examples of data gathering in different sizes of order-2 cycles when $m_2 = 4$ or 16. Assume that the data gathering round is $j = 4$. In Fig. 6(b), a head A on position $((4 - 1) \bmod 16) = 3$ serves as the order-2 leader and is responsible for collecting the fused data of this order-2 cycle. The head B on position $pos(4, 16, -1) = 11$ becomes a starter node and transmits its sensed data to head C on position $pos(4, 16, -2) = 10$. When head C receives the sensed data from head B, it will fuse the received data and its own to a single data packet, then transmits the fused data to head D on position $pos(4, 16, -3) = 9$. Finally, the fused data of half order-2 cycle will be transmitted along $11 \rightarrow 10 \rightarrow 9 \rightarrow 8 \rightarrow 7 \rightarrow \cdots \rightarrow 3$ clockwise direction until the leader, head A, is reached. Similarly, the fused data of remainder half order-2 cycle is also transmitted to head A along $12 \rightarrow 13 \rightarrow 14 \rightarrow 15 \rightarrow 0 \rightarrow \cdots \rightarrow 3$ counterclockwise direction. The data gathering process in Fig. 6(a) is similar to Fig. 6(b) when $m_2 = 4$.

When all order-i leaders in the same order-$(i + 1)$ square have collected the fused data of all order-i squares, these order-i leaders continue to form the order-$(i + 1)$ cycle in this order-$(i + 1)$ square. In the order-$(i + 1)$ cycle, an order-i

leader also serves as the order-$(i+1)$ leader and two order-i leaders except the order-$(i+1)$ leader are designated as the starter nodes in each round of data gathering. The rules of choosing the order-$(i+1)$ leader and two starter nodes are the same as the rules for an order-i cycle as mentioned above. Two order-i leaders serving as the starter nodes in the order-$(i+1)$ cycle also use the same data transmission rules and the fused data of all order-i squares are transmitted to the order–$(i+1)$ leader. Note that an order-i leader needs to appropriately adjust its transmission range in order to reach another neighboring order-i leader and the fused data can be received by the neighboring order-i leader.

Figure 7 shows an example of data gathering in an order-3 cycle. As mentioned above, the data gathering round is $j = 4$ and the number of order-2 squares in an order-3 square is $m_3 = 4$. The head D' on position $((4-1) \bmod 4) = 3$ serves as the order-3 leader. Then, head C' on position $pos(4, 4, 0) = 2$ and head B' on position $pos(4, 4, -1) = 1$ are the starter nodes and begin to transmit their gathered data toward head D' along counterclockwise and clockwise direction, respectively. This data gathering process is repeated until the top order-n leader has collected the fused data of whole sensor field. Finally, the order-n leader transmits the fused data to the BS and round j is completed.

During data transmissions in an order-i cycle, when a grid head G_1 transmits the fused data to another head G_2, head G_1 has to receive an ACK packet from head G_2 to ensure that head G_2 has received the fused data. The operation of transmitting ACK packet is to increase the reliability of data gathering and useful for cycle maintenance. The size and cost of ACK packet are very small such as a control token used in [5]. If head G_1 do not receive the response from head G_2 after a period of time, it considers that all sensor nodes in the grid of head G_2 are dead and the grid of head G_2 is empty now. Then, cycle maintenance described in the next subsection will be incurred.

For next data gathering round $(j+1)$, the order-i leader on position $((j-1) \bmod m_i)$ informs the head on position $(j \bmod m_i)$ to be the new leader by sending a confirm_leader packet. Moreover, the starter node on position $pos(j, m_i, 0)$ informs the head on position $pos(j+1, m_i, 0)$ to be a new starter node for next round by sending a confirm_starter packet. The confirm_starter packet contains the information about data transmission direction (i.e. increasing or decreasing α value) for next round. The size and cost of a confirm_leader and a confirm_starter packet are very small as an ACK packet. Similarly, the head on position $pos(j+1, m_i, -1)$ also becomes a new starter node. Then, data transmissions will begin from two new starter nodes to the new order-i leader again.

3.4 Cycle Maintenance

When all sensor nodes in a grid are dead, the grid becomes empty. The cycle maintenance is incurred and is simply classified into three cases as follows.

In the case 1, support for an order-i cycle, if a head G_1 do not receive an ACK packet from another head G_2, it will directly transmit the fused data to next head G_3 by increasing or decreasing α value described in the equation (2).

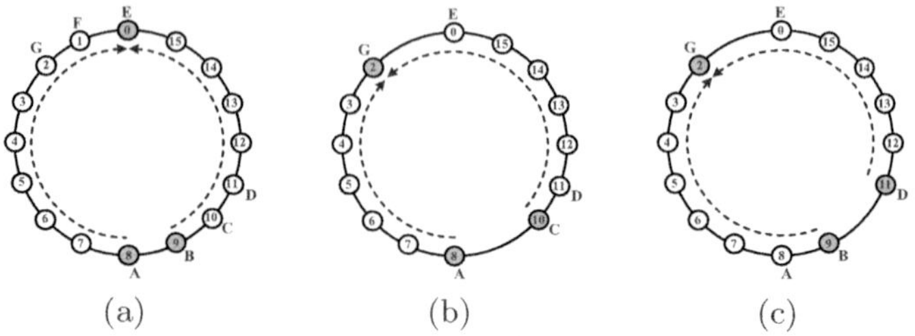

Fig. 8. Three examples of cycle maintenance : (a) round $= j$, (b) the grids of head B and head F are empty when round $= j+1$, (c) the grids of head C and head F are empty when round $= j+1$

Then, head G_1 stores the position information about the grid of head G_2 since the grid of head G_2 is empty. Therefore, head G_1 can bypass empty grids when transmitting data packets to head G_3 in next round. In addition, if head G_1 is a starter node, it also piggybacks the position information about the grid of head G_2 when transmitting a confirm_starter packet to the new starter node, so that the new starter node can bypass empty grids in coming round.

In the case 2, when a head G_1 sends a confirm_starter packet to another head G_2 in round j, but head G_1 do not receive the response after a period of time. The head G_1 will be responsible for being the new starter node temporarily in next round $(j+1)$. For example, in Fig. 8(a), assume that two heads, A and B, are the starter nodes in round j. After round j is completed, head A and head B will inform head B and head C to be the new starter nodes, respectively. Head A and head B have to receive the responses from head B and head C, respectively. If the grid of head B only remain one node (i.e. head B) and its energy is below the threshold value, then head B does not transmit the response to head A. After a period of time, head A will designate itself as the new starter node temporarily in round $(j+1)$ as shown in Fig. 8(b). When round $(j+1)$ is finished, head A and head C will inform head C and head D to be the new starter nodes for round $(j+2)$, respectively. However, when head B informs head C to be the new starter node, but the energy of head C is below the threshold value. In this condition, head B will not replace head C to be the new starter node temporarily because head B receives a confirm_starter packet form head A and is designated as the new starter node by head A. Therefore, head B will inform head D to be the starter node for round $(j+1)$ as shown in Fig. 8(c).

Figure 8 also illustrates the case 3. The head E is responsible for being the leader in round j, then head E has to send a confirm_leader packet to head F for next round $(j+1)$. If head E does not receive the response form head F, thus it considers that the grid of head F is empty now. Therefore, head E will sends a confirm_leader packet to head G to be the new leader node. Note that head E also stores the position information about the grid of head F in order to bypass empty grids when transmitting data packets to head G in coming round.

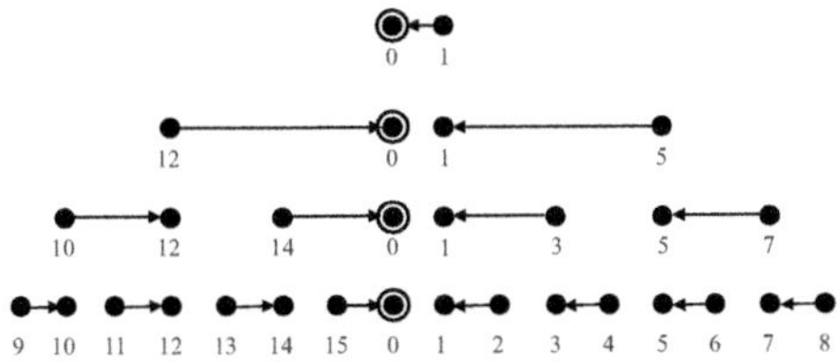

Fig. 9. The improvement of EGDG using parallel communications

3.5 The Improvement of EGDG

In [5], the chain-based binary scheme has been proposed to future reduce the delay cost comparing to PEGASIS by using parallel communications between pairs of nodes. With CDMA capable sensor nodes, the binary scheme performs energy $\times$ delay well. Hence, we also apply parallel communications to EGDG when an order-i square is composed of 16 order-$(i-1)$ squares. For example, in non-CDMA sensor environment, the units of delay for an order-i cycle can be considered as 8 units at most when $m_i = 16$. However, by applying parallel communications, EGDG can reduce the delay time to be $\lceil \log_2 m_i \rceil$ units. Figure 9 shows that parallel communications are applied to an order-i cycle consisting of 16 heads and the number represents the position of a head. Obviously, the units of delay can be reduced from 8 units to 4 units.

4 Performance Evaluation

This section presents simulation results of different schemes. The sensor field is $100m \times 100m$ and divided into 8×8 grids. The number of nodes is 400, and all nodes are uniformly deployed. Each node has 0.25J initial energy. The first radio model described in [3] is used to calculate the energy consumption of each node. The size of a data packet is 2,000 bits and 5 nJ/bit energy is consumed when using data fusion. The BS is located at (50,200) or (50,50). We represent EGDG as $m$order-n, where m is the number of order-1 squares in an order-2 square and order-n is the top cycle in the hierarchy. Therefore, when the BS is located at (50,200), 4order-4 and 16order-3 are evaluated as shown in Fig. 4(a) and Fig. 4(b), respectively. However, if the BS is located at (50,50), 4order-3 and 16order-2 are evaluated. We compare EGDG with LEACH, PEGASIS and the chain-based binary scheme. Three evaluated metrics are the number of rounds, coverage ratio and energy $\times$ delay cost.

4.1 The Number of Rounds and Coverage Ratio

Figure 10 illustrates the number of rounds and coverage ratio until first, 20%, 50%, 70%, 80%, 90% and 100% of nodes die when the BS is located at (50,200),

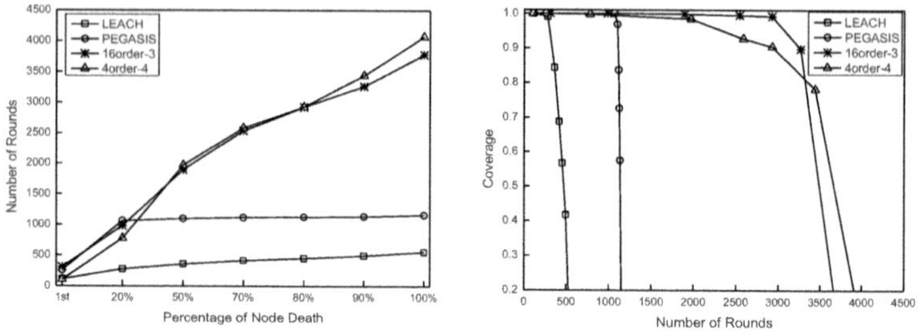

(a) (b)

Fig. 10. Simulation results for BS location at (50,200), 400 nodes

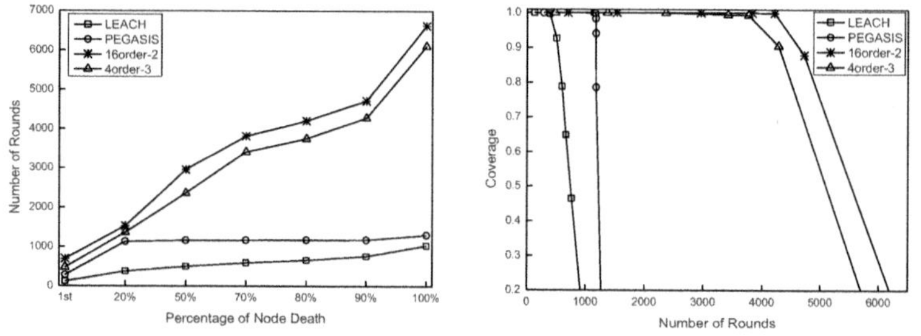

(a) (b)

Fig. 11. Simulation results for BS location at (50,50), 400 nodes

while Fig. 11 shows the results but the BS is located at (50,50). The simulation results in Fig. 10 and Fig. 11 show that:

- EGDG outperforms than LEACH and PEGASIS in terms of the number of rounds because the number of active nodes and total energy consumed per round are minimized.
- EGDG provides significant coverage-preserving than LEACH and PEGASIS because the total energy consumed is distributed over all grids and energy-balanced is also achieved between all grids.
- 4order-4 has slightly more number of rounds than 16order-3 because the distance of data transmission between a pair of nodes in 4order-4 is smaller than that in 16order-3 when 90% and 100% of nodes die. On the contrary, 16order-2 has more number of rounds than 4order-3 because the BS is located at the center of the sensor field and an order-2 leader can directly transmits the fused data to the BS in 16order-2.
- 16order-3 and 16order-2 achieve better coverage-preserving than 4order-4 and 4order-3, respectively, because 16order-3 and 16order-2 are more balanced energy consumption among all grids.

Table 1. 400 Nodes, BS location at (50,200)

Scheme	Energy (J)	Delay	Energy × Delay
PEGASIS	0.093392	400	37.3568
Chain-based binary	0.105771	10	1.05771
16order-3	0.027749	11	0.30524
Improved 16order-3	0.030905	7	0.21634
4order-4	0.029327	7	0.20529

4.2 Energy × Delay Cost

Table 1 gives the results for the energy cost, the delay cost, and the energy × delay cost for EGDG, PEGASIS, and the chain-based binary scheme. The improved 16order-3 indicates that parallel communication is applied to reduce the delay time. The results show that all versions of EGDG, especially 4order-4, have lower energy × delay cost than PEGASIS and the binary scheme, even though the binary scheme employs parallel communications to reduce the energy × delay cost than PEGASIS. We also can observe that the improved 16order-3 has lower energy × delay cost than 16order-3 because the delay time is reduced. However, it has slightly higher energy cost than 16order-3 since the average distance of data transmission between a pair of nodes increases.

5 Conclusions and Future Work

In this paper, we proposed an efficient grid-based data gathering scheme, called EGDG, for partitioning the sensor field into a hierarchical grid structure and constructing cycles by connecting heads in each order of the hierarchy. EGDG allows the nodes except heads entering to sleeping mode and thus reduces the total energy consumed per round. Moreover, EGDG also reduces the delay time per round so that the energy × delay cost can be minimized. Simulation results show that EGDG outperforms LEACH, PEGASIS, the chain-based binary scheme in terms of the number of rounds, the energy × delay cost, and coverage-preserving under different number of nodes and BS locations. In the future, we plan to devise an efficient node scheduling approach to improve EGDG and simulate EGDG for various sensor environments.

References

1. Akyildiz, I.F., Su, W., Sankarasubramaniam, Y., Cayirci, E.: Wireless sensor networks: a survey. Computer Networks 38(4), 393–422 (2002)
2. Hall, D.L.: Mathematical Techniques in Multisensor Data Fusion. Artech House, Boston, MA (1992)
3. Heinzelman, W., Chandrakasan, A., Balakrishnan, H.: Energy-Efficient Communication Protocol for Wireless Microsensor Networks. In: Proc. of the 33rd Hawaii International Conference on System Sciences (2000)

4. Manjeshwar, A., Agrawal, D.P.: TEEN: A Routing Protocol for Enhanced Efficiency in Wireless Sensor Networks. In: Proc. of the 15th IPDPS (2001)
5. Lindsey, S., Raghavendra, C., Sivalingam, K.M.: Data Gathering Algorithms in Sensor Networks Using Energy Metrics. IEEE Trans. on Parallel and Distributed Systems 13(9), 924–935 (2002)
6. Du, K., Wu, J., Zhou, D.: Chain-Based Protocols for Data Broadcasting and Gathering in the Sensor Networks. In: Proc. of the 17th IPDPS (2003)
7. Tan, H.O., Korpeoglu, I.: Power Efficient Data Gathering and Aggregation in Wireless Sensor Networks. ACM SIGMOD Record 32(4), 66–71 (2003)
8. Kim, H.-S., Han, K.-J.: A Power Efficient Routing Protocol Based on Balanced Tree in Wireless Sensor Networks. In: Proc. of the First International Conference on Distributed Frameworks for Multimedia Applications, pp. 138–143 (2005)

Grid-Based Sense Schedule for Event Detection in Wireless Sensor Networks

Xianghua Hu and Xuejun Yang

School of Computer Science, the National University of Defense Technology, PRC
{huxianghua,xjyang}@nudt.edu.cn

Abstract. In this paper, we propose a efficient grid-based sense schedule scheme for event detection in Wireless Sensor Networks. The target environment is partitioned into grids and the sensors within each grid elect one representative to carry out the sense task in turn, with low communication overhead, balanced energy consumption and good scalability. It is demonstrated by analysis and simulation that the grid-based sense schedule can achieve energy saving proportional to the node density and guaranty better detection quality than random schedule. The scheme also provides means to balance network lifetime and detection quality by adjusting size of grid and duty time of node.

1 Introduction

As a new means for collecting information, Wireless Sensor Networks[1] has become a hot subject of research and has broad prospect in various domains[2,3] like military surveillance and environment monitoring. Event detection is one kind of its main applications. For example, sensors are dispatched in battlefields by planes to surveil enemy movements, such as airdropped solders and passing-by tanks. Once thoses targets emerge, Wireless Sensor Networks must detect the targets, report to the commander or activate weapons like landmines or missiles. The following requirements must be satisfied for event detection: 1) the whole network must survive as long as detection tasks demand, 2) the occurrence can not be predicted, which means the events will not occur most of the time and have to be detected immediately once they arise.

Due to the limited power capacity[4,5] used by sensors and inconvenient replacement of run-out battery, energy becomes a bottleneck that affects the service time of Wireless Sensor Networks. Node schedule is an effective solution by scheduling some nodes to execute sense and communication tasks, and meanwhile rest of the nodes to sleep. It optimizes the data flow in Wireless Sensor Networks, reduces energy consumption in sense and communication, and prolongs network lifetime. Since most nodes are inactive for the most of time in event detection applications, there are few communications among nodes. Energy consumption in sense task accounts for the major part. Then our work will focus on the research of sense schedule scheme.

Recently, the research in sense schedule is mainly on sense coverage[6], i.e. how to minimize the number of nodes participating in sense tasks on condition

J. Indulska et al. (Eds.): UIC 2007, LNCS 4611, pp. 557–566, 2007.

that target environment is fully covered at any time. In regard to event detection applications, full coverage enables nodes to detect event at once. However, this nonstop strategy definitely consumes more energy and reduces the lifetime of network. As a solution, partial coverage strategy [7,8] compromises between the demand for longer lifetime and for instant detection, in which target environment is only partially covered by active nodes at a particular time and meanwhile every location within the target environment can be sensed by nodes within limited period. In other words, it is partial coverage in spatial dimension and full coverage in temporal dimension. This paper presents a sense schedule method based on partial-coverage strategy and verifies by analysis and simulation that the method can effectively prolong network lifetime and provide timely respond.

The rest of the paper is organized as follows. Chapter 2 describes a system model for event detection. Chapter 3 elaborates grid-based sense schedule as well as the algorithm of electing grid representative. Chapter 4 analyzes and justifies the method in theory and with experiments. Conclusion comes in the end.

2 System Model

Node. The communication and sense range of every node is a round areas with the node as its center and with the same communication radius R and sense radius r and $R > r$. To be simplified, the circle with radius R and node as center is referred to as the Communication Range of node. And the circle with radius r and node as center is referred to as the Sense Range of node. In contrast with the Sense Range of node is the Exposure Range of target, which is the circle with target as center and radius r. All nodes can figure out their own position through GPS device and time for neighbouring nodes can be loosely synchronized.

Deployment. Target environment is an $L \times L$ two-dimensional square, within which N sensors are evenly and randomly distributed. Area of target environment is $A = L^2$. Node density $d = N/A$ is enough to guaranty fully coverage of target environment when all nodes active, which means each position is within the Sense Range of at least one sensor.

Application Mode. Assume that the node invalidation is only resulted from battery depletion. Any target within the node Sense Range is definitely to be detected, otherwise not. Take the target emerged within the target environment as point regardless of the physical size and shape and this point target move in straight line with the rate of v.

Energy Model. The sense unit and radio unit of a node consume in its work status an amount of $\varepsilon_s$and ε_c of energy per unit time respectively and both can be individually turned off.

Based on the above assumptions, the theorem on the characteristics of node distributionis is deduced as follows.

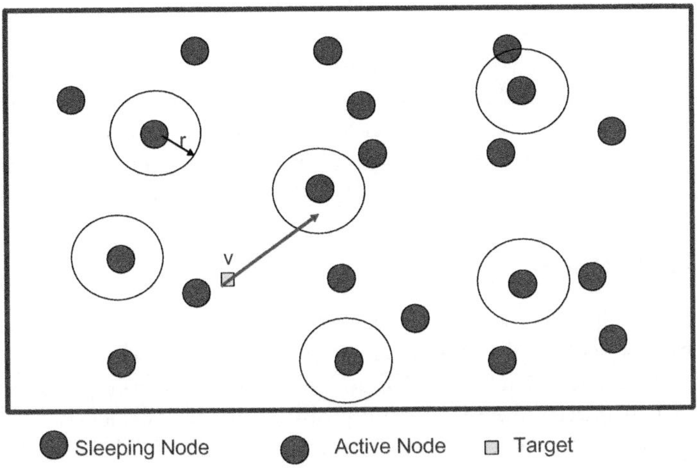

Fig. 1. Event detection model

Theorem 1. *Assuming an amount N of sensors are distributed evenly within the target environment of area A and the sense radius of each node is r, then an amount n of nodes exists within the Sense Range of radius r has a probability of*

$$\frac{(\pi r^2 \frac{N}{A})^n}{n!} e^{-(\pi r^2 \frac{N}{A})}, n = 0, 1, 2, \ldots, N \tag{1}$$

Obviously the physical meaning of N/A is the average density d in node distribution, hereinafter referred to

$$\alpha = \pi r^2 N/A = \pi r^2 d$$

And the physical meaning of α is the average number of nodes within the Sense Range. The above theorem can also be understood as that the probability of any physical location being covered by an amount n of nodes is $\frac{\alpha^n}{n!} e^{-\alpha}$, where $n = 0, 1, 2, \ldots, N$.

In general, detection delay is defined to measure the event detection quality, which includes the delay in both detecting event occurence and transferring information from nodes to base station. This paper mainly focuses on the delay of nodes' detecting in event occurence and gives the following definition.

Definition 1. *Event detection delay is the interval between the event occurrence and the earliest event detection of the nodes.*

In fact due to the uncertainty of the event occurrence and the randomicity of node distribution within the target environment, the major concern is the maximum value and probability distribution of event detection delay. The former is the upper limit of interval and the latter describes the probability characteristics of detection delay.

3 Grid-Based Sense Schedule

The grid-based sense schedule is divided into initialization phase and detection phase. During the initialization phase, target environment is partitioned into grids. And the detection phase is divided into rounds, during each of which the elected representative of nodes within the grid executes detection tasks on behalf of the others. The two phases are presented as follows in details.

3.1 Grid Partition

GAF protocol [9] is a communication-schedule method for purpose of assuring network connectivity. It partitions target environment into nonoverlapping equal-size grids, within each of which nodes take turns to route. Our work adopts the similar grid-partition method to guaranty network connectivity. Grid partition method has to meet the following two requirements: (1)Any nodes within one grid can communicate directly to each other. (2)Any nodes located in two adjacent grids can communicate directly to each other. Here "adjacent" means horizontally, vertically or diagonally adjacent.

Figure 2 sets the side of each grid to be g and the distance between any two nodes must be less than the communication radius of nodes in order to meet the above requirements, i.e.$(2g)^2 + (2g)^2 \leq R^2 \Rightarrow g \leq R/\sqrt{8}$.

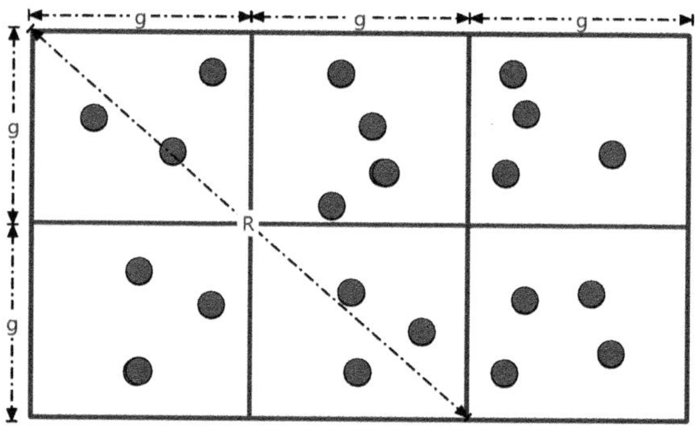

Fig. 2. Grid Partition

Similar to the previous section, it can be proved that the number of nodes inside each grid obeys the Poisson distribution with the parameter $\beta = g^2N/A = g^2d$, i.e. the probability of the existence of an amount n_g of nodes in each grid is $\frac{\beta^{n_g}}{n_g!}e^{-\beta}, n_g = 0, 1, 2, \ldots, N$.

During the initialization phase, every node obtains its own location information through GPS supporting. Based on the predetermined location of target environment and size of grid, every node figures out the grid number g_j which it belongs to and the total amount n_g^j of nodes inside the same grid. Assume that

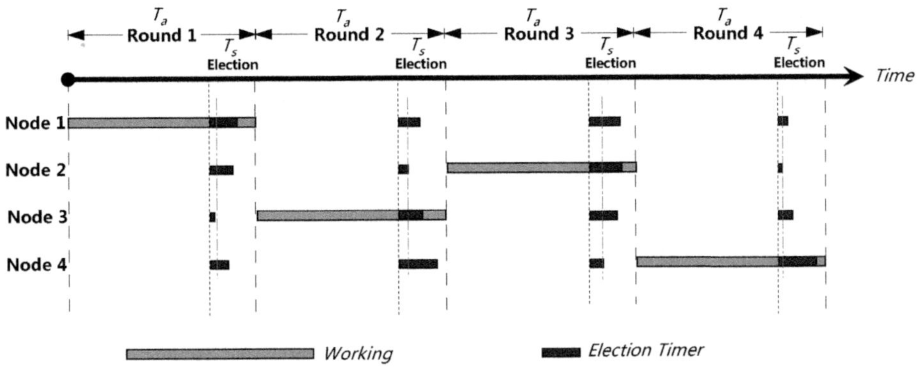

Fig. 3. Example of Representative Election (4 nodes)

adjacent nodes can get loose synchronization with the help of GPS. Comparing with the lifetime of the network, the initialization phase only accounts for a very small portion, so that its energy consumption can be reasonably neglected.

3.2 Election of Representative

The detection phase is divided into rounds, during which only one node is working in each grid and the rest of nodes are sleeping. With the rotation of working nodes, it can be ensured that any location is covered by nodes within limited period and consumption of energy is balanced among nodes.

Figure 3 gives an example to demonstrate the basic idea of the representative-election algorithm. During the initialization phase, nodes will elect the representative node for the first round of detection by executing the algorithm. Then, before the end of each round the algorithm will be executed to elect the representative for the next round. As illustrated by Figure 3, the time length of each round is set to be T_a and the algorithm is to be executed within the time T_s before the end of each round. The probability of being elected as the representative depends on the remaining energy and the times of not being elected for each node. The more the remaining energy is and the more the times of not being elected consecutively are, the greater the chance of node to be elected as the representative of next round. The above election rules ensures an balanced energy consumption among nodes and guranties election finished within the limited interval. Meanwhile, the algorithm effectively reduces the overhead of communication and calculation.

In the algorithm the voting timer of node n_i is as long as $t_i^k T_s$ during round k, where t_i^k is a random value within the range of $(0 - (1 - T_i^k))$ generated by node n_i. The following is the formula of getting T_i^k

$$T_i^k = \frac{1}{n_g^j} \left[\frac{E_{current}}{E_{init}} + \left(\frac{r}{n_g^j} \right) \left(1 - \frac{E_{current}}{E_{init}} \right) \right] \tag{2}$$

Algorithm 1. Election of representative node (Grid g_j, Node n_i, Round$k = 1, 2, 3, \ldots$)

Require: Grid n_iNode g_jRound k
Ensure: Determine if node n_i becomes the representative for the next round
if Remaining energy $E_{current}$ is lower than expectation threshold value$E_{predict}$ **then**
    $PREDICT = True$
else
    $PREDICT = False$
end if
Construct election message $[k, g_j, n_i, PREDICT]$
Calculate the voting timer$t_i^k T_s$
Activate timer t_i^k and wait for timer to trigger or receive the election messages from other nodes inside the same grid
if The election messages are received from other nodes inside the same grid **then**
    if $PREDICT == True$ **then**
        Set the total number of nodes in grid g_j to be $n_g^j = n_g^j - 1$
    end if
    Cancel timer, give up election and go to sleep
else
    Broadcast election messages of being elected as the representative for round $k+1$
end if

In the above formula, n_g^j is the total number of nodes in grid g_j; r is the times of not being elected consecutively, which will be reset to 0 once the node being elected; $E_{current}$ is the remaining energy of the node and E_{init} is the initial battery energy. It can be seen that the bigger $E_{current}/E_{init}$, the bigger T_i^k and that the smaller the range where t_i^k is located, the smaller $t_i^k T_s$ is, the earlier nodes broadcast election messages and the more chances of being elected. In other words, nodes with the least consumed energy shall be elected as the representative by the introduction of $E_{current}$ and E_{init}. And the nodes which are not elected as representative consecutively for long time have the biggest chance of being elected, for that when r approaches n_g^j, T_i^k increases to $1/n_g^j$ leading to the smallest value of $t_i^k T_s$.

4 Performance Analysis

4.1 Network Lifetime

For naive method, all nodes open sense unit and communication unit, leading to a total energy consumption of $E_{naive} = n_g^j(\varepsilon_s + \varepsilon_c)T_a$. While for grid-based schedule, only the representative executes sense and communication tasks on behalf of the others, who only open their communication units during the election period as long as T_s to vote for the representative of next round. The representative consumes an amount $(\varepsilon_s + \varepsilon_c)T_a$ of energy and the other nodes in the same grid consume a total amount $(n_g^j - 1)\varepsilon_c T_s$ of energy, which results in an energy consumption ratio of

$$\frac{E_{grid}}{E_{naive}} = \frac{(\varepsilon_s + \varepsilon_c)T_a + (n_g^j - 1)\varepsilon_c T_s}{n_g^j(\varepsilon_s + \varepsilon_c)T_a} \tag{3}$$

When the setting of T_a/T_s gets bigger, the above ratio approaches n_g^j, i.e. the lifetime of grid-based network is n_g^j times that of the naive one.

Here is a further analysis on communication overhead during the election. When the first node broadcasts election message, the rest of the nodes who have received the message will cancel their own election broadcast messages. Therefore, there is only one sending operation, but $n_g^j - 1$ receiving operation during the election, which totals n_g^j communication operations. However, there are $(3n_g^j - 2)$ communication operations based on FULL algorithm and en_g^j based on RANDOM algorithm of literature [8]. It is concluded through comparison that the communication overhead based on the representative-election algorithm is nearly 30% of that based on FULL or RANDOM algorithm.

4.2 Detection Delay

It is previously assumed that each location inside the target environment is covered by at least one node. Grid-based sense schedule guaranties each node become representative within the period of $\max\{n_g^j\}T_a$. Hence, as far as immobile target are concerned, the maximum detection delay is $\max\{n_g^j\}T_a$. While for mobile target, the detection delay would be infinite, i.e. inability to detect the target, if the node covering the moving track of target events happens to be sleeping when target passes. However, the uncertainty of an event occurrence makes the probability of detection more meaningful in practice. The probability analysis model proposed by literature [7] can prove that the above assumption of the worst case is a rarely event and the actual detection delay can still meet the demand of applications.

Followed are the basic idea in analyzing the probability feature of detection delay.

1. Firstly assume only one node exists within the exposure coverage of the target and calculate the probability of target-detection delay t;
2. Based on Theorem 1 that the node number within the exposure range of the target obeys Poisson distribution, using following Theorem 2 to calculate the probability of detection delay t of the target covered by at least one node.

Theorem 2. *Assuming that the probability of event D occurrence in one type of experiment is p and that the number of experiments done complies with Poisson distribution of parameter α, the probability of event D occurring at least once during all experiments is*

$$P = 1 - e^{-p\alpha} \tag{4}$$

So we get that the detection delay of immobile targets being less than t has a probability of

$$\begin{aligned} DP_{static} &= 1 - e^{-\alpha P(t_d \leq t)} \\ &= 1 - e^{-\alpha((1+\frac{t}{T_a})\delta)} \end{aligned} \tag{5}$$

where, $\delta = e^{-\beta} \int_0^\beta \frac{e^x - 1}{x} dx$, $0 \leq t \leq (\frac{1}{\delta} - 1)T_a \alpha = \pi r^2 d, \beta = g^2 d.$

Similarly, we get probability distribution of detection delay for fast moving target as follows:

$$\begin{aligned} DP_{static} &= 1 - e^{-\gamma P(t_d \leq t)} \\ &= 1 - e^{-\gamma(\delta(1+\frac{\pi r t}{v T_a(2vt + \pi r)}))} \end{aligned} \tag{6}$$

where, $\delta = e^{-\beta} \int_0^\beta \frac{e^x - 1}{x} dx$, $v \geq \frac{2r}{(1/\delta - 1)T_a}$, $\gamma = (\pi r^2 + 2rvt) \times d.$

4.3 Simulation

In order to further verify the result, a serious of experiments are done with Matlab tool based on the settings listed in Table 1. Comparison with the random schedule method of literature [7] is also done. To simulate event detection of immobile target, set $T_a = 1$ and take $g = 20, 30, 40, 50$ respectively. The target location is generated randomly within the target environment and the detection delay is recorded for each experiment. The number of cases where the delay is less than $1, 2, 3, \ldots, 10$ during the 10,000 experiments is caculated as delay probability. Secondly, set $g = 40$ and take $T_a = 0.5, 1, 2, 4$ respectively. The experiments on mobile targets are basically the same as those on immobile targets except that the target moving direction needs to be randomly selected. For the sake of simplification, the track is completely within the target environment.

Table 1. Simulation parameters

Parameters	Setting
Target environment($L \times L$)	600×600
Quantity of nodes(N)	1800
Average density(d)	1/200
Sense radius(r)	20
Target velocity(v)	40
Round time(T_a)	$0.5, 1, 2, 4$
Size of grid(g)	$20, 30, 40, 50$

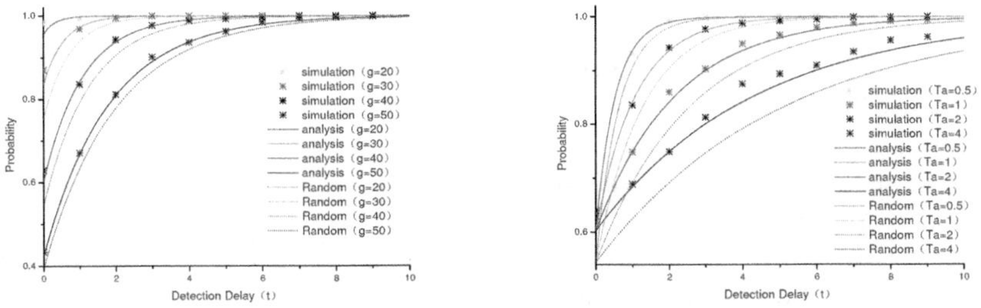

Fig. 4. Probability of Detection Delay for immobile target

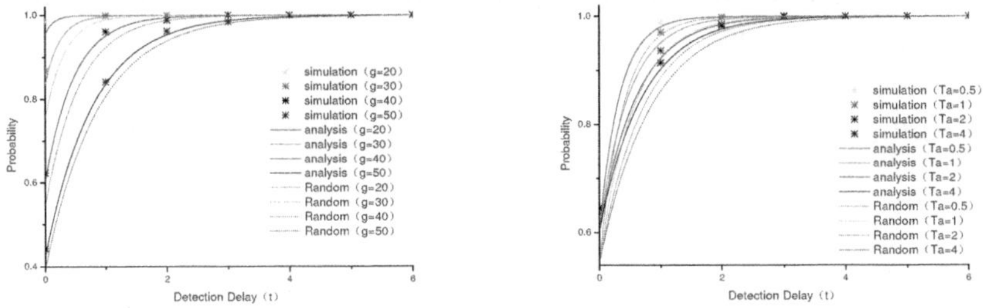

Fig. 5. Probability of Detection Delay for mobile target

It can be concluded as follows from the results illustrated in Figure 4 and 5. Firstly the simulation data matches the theoretical curve, testifying the validity of the previous analysis. Secondly, on condition of $T_a = 1$ where T_a means the duration of each round, the bigger the grid is, the lower the probability of target detection during the time t. For example, in case of $t = 0$, the probability when $g = 20, 30, 40, 50$ is $0.96, 0.77, 0.56, 0.41$ respectively, because the bigger the grid is, the more nodes there are in the grid and the less frequently each node is activated. Meanwhile, in case of fixed grid side $g = 40$, the bigger T_a, the less probability of target detection during t. For example, in case of $t = 1$ for immobile targets, the probability where $T_a = 0.5, 1, 2, 4$ is $0.91, 0.78, 0.68, 0.61$ respectively due to the same season as above mentioned. Thirdly, a limited detection delay t exists for both immobile and mobile targets with the probability close to 1. Moreover, the maximum detection delay for mobile target is smaller than that for immobile one. The reason is that target movement enables more nodes to detect it. In other words, it enhances the frequency of each node being activated. Fourthly, by setting the same working duration and duty cycle, the grid-based sense schedule is superior to the random schedule in the ability of event detection, because grid partition brings an even distribution of active nodes and avoids the problem of too many active nodes crowding, which can not avoid by random schedule.

5 Conclusion

An effective grid-based sense schedule scheme is proposed in this paper to prolong network lifetime and shorten detection delay to meet the demand of event detection applications. Grid partition is a method of clustering based on location information with less overhead and good scalability. Besides guarantying communication connectivity, it realizes an even partition among nodes and a balanced distribution of workload and energy consumption. The representative election is a distributive algorithm with consideration on energy effeciency and election times, which enables an balanced energy consumption as well as limited detection delay. Comparing with the existing election algorithms, our work effectively cut down the overhead of communication and computation. Moreover, the simulation verify that the grid-based sense schedule is superior to the random schedule for event detection.

References

1. Akyildiz, I.F., Weilian, S., Sankarasubramaniam, Y., Cayirci, E.: A survey on sensor networks. Communications Magazine, IEEE 40(8), 102 (2002)
2. Alan, M., David, C., Joseph, P., Robert, S., John, A.: Wireless sensor networks for habitat monitoring (2002)
3. Ning, X., Sumit, R., Krishna Kant, C., Deepak, G., Alan, B., Ramesh, G., Deborah, E.: A wireless sensor network for structural monitoring (2004)
4. Crossbow: Power management and batteries (October 2004), `http://www.xbow.com/Support/appnotes.htm`
5. Powers, R.: Batteries for low power electronics. Proceedings of the IEEE 83, 687–693 (1995)
6. Hongke, Z., Ren Yan, Z.S.: Theories and algorithms of coverage control for wireless sensor networks. Journal of Software(Chinese) 17(2), 10 (2006)
7. Cao, Q., Yan, T., Stankovic, J., Abdelzaher, T.: Analysis of target detection performance for wireless sensor networks (3560). In: Prasanna, V.K., Iyengar, S., Spirakis, P.G., Welsh, M. (eds.) DCOSS 2005. LNCS, vol. 3560, p. 276. Springer, Heidelberg (2005)
8. Paolo, S., Janos, S.: Silence is golden with high probability: Maintaining a connected backbone in wireless sensor networks. In: Wireless Sensor Networks. LNCS, p. 17. Springer, Heidelberg (2004)
9. Ya, X., John, H., Deborah, E.: Geography-informed energy conservation for ad hoc routing (2001)

GPSR Compliance

The European Union's (EU) General Product Safety Regulation (GPSR) is a set of rules that requires consumer products to be safe and our obligations to ensure this.

If you have any concerns about our products, you can contact us on ProductSafety@springernature.com

In case Publisher is established outside the EU, the EU authorized representative is:

Springer Nature Customer Service Center GmbH
Europaplatz 3
69115 Heidelberg, Germany

Batch number: 10844669

Printed by Printforce, the Netherlands

Lecture Notes in Computer Science 4611

Commenced Publication in 1973
Founding and Former Series Editors:
Gerhard Goos, Juris Hartmanis, and Jan van Leeuwen

Jadwiga Indulska Jianhua Ma
Laurence T. Yang Theo Ungerer
Jiannong Cao (Eds.)

Ubiquitous Intelligence and Computing

4th International Conference, UIC 2007
Hong Kong, China, July 11-13, 2007
Proceedings

Springer

Volume Editors

Jadwiga Indulska
The University of Queensland, St. Lucia, QLD 4072, Australia
E-mail: jaga@itee.uq.edu.au

Jianhua Ma
Hosei University, Tokyo 184-8584, Japan
E-mail: jianhuamah@gmail.com

Laurence T. Yang
St. Francis Xavier University, Antigonish, NS, B2G 2W5, Canada
E-mail: lyang@stfx.ca

Theo Ungerer
University of Augsburg, 86135 Augsburg, Germany
E-mail: ungerer@informatik.uni-augsburg.de

Jiannong Cao
Hong Kong Polytechnic University, Kowloon, Hong Kong, China
E-mail: csjcao@comp.polyu.edu.hk

Library of Congress Control Number: 2007930224

CR Subject Classification (1998): H.4, C.2, D.4.6, H.5, I.2, K.4

LNCS Sublibrary: SL 3 – Information Systems and Application, incl. Internet/Web and HCI

ISSN 0302-9743
ISBN-10 3-540-73548-8 Springer Berlin Heidelberg New York
ISBN-13 978-3-540-73548-9 Springer Berlin Heidelberg New York

Springer is a part of Springer Science+Business Media

springer.com

Printed in Germany

Typesetting: Camera-ready by author, data conversion by Scientific Publishing Services, Chennai, India
Printed on acid-free paper SPIN: 12088690 06/3180 5 4 3 2 1 0

Preface

This volume contains the proceedings of UIC 2007, the 4th International Conference on Ubiquitous Intelligence and Computing: Building Smart Worlds in Real and Cyber Spaces. The conference was held in Hong Kong, July 11-13, 2007. The event was the fourth meeting of this conference series. USW 2005 (1st International Workshop on Ubiquitous Smart World), held in March 2005 in Taiwan, was the first event in the series. This event was followed by UISW 2005 (2nd International Symposium on Ubiquitous Intelligence and Smart Worlds) held in December 2005 in Japan, and by UIC 2006 (3rd International Conference on Ubiquitous Intelligence and Computing: Building Smart Worlds in Real and Cyber Spaces) held in September 2006 in Wuhan and Three Gorges, China.

Ubiquitous computers, networks and information are paving the road towards a smart world in which computational intelligence is distributed throughout the physical environment to provide trustworthy and relevant services to people. This ubiquitous intelligence will change the computing landscape because it will enable new breeds of applications and systems to be developed; the realm of computing possibilities will be significantly extended. By embedding digital intelligence in everyday objects, our workplaces, our homes and even ourselves, many tasks and processes could be simplified, made more efficient, safer and more enjoyable. Ubiquitous computing, or pervasive computing, composes these many "smart things/u-things" to create the environments that underpin the smart world. A smart thing can be endowed with different levels of intelligence and may be context-aware, active, interactive, reactive, proactive, assistive, adaptive, automated, sentient, perceptual, cognitive, autonomic and/or thinking. The field of intelligent/smart things is an emerging research field that covers many disciplines. A series of grand challenges exist to move from the world of ubiquitous computing with universal services of any means/place/time to the smart world of trustworthy services with the right means/place/time.

The UIC 2007 conference offered a forum for researchers to exchange ideas and experiences in developing intelligent/smart objects, environments, and systems. This year, the technical program of UIC drew from a very large number of submissions: 463 papers submitted from 26 countries representing four regions — Asia Pacific, Europe, North and South America. Each accepted paper was reviewed (as a full paper) by at least three reviewers, coordinated by the international Program Committee. The Program Committee accepted 119 papers out of 463 submissions, resulting in an acceptance rate of 25.7%.

The accepted papers cover a wide range of research topics that were grouped into nine conference tracks: smart objects and embedded systems, smart spaces/environments/services, ad-hoc and intelligent networks, sensor networks, pervasive communication and mobile systems, context-aware applications and systems, service-oriented middleware and applications, models and services for intelligent computing, and security/safety/privacy. In addition to the refereed papers, the proceedings include Tosiyasu L. Kunii's keynote address on "Autonomic and Trusted Computing for Ubiquitous Intelligence," and an invited paper from Norio Shiratori on "Symbiotic Computing: Concept, Architecture and Its Applications." We believe that the conference not only presented novel and interesting ideas but also will stimulate future research in the area of ubiquitous intelligence and computing.

Organization of conferences with a large number of submissions requires a lot of hard work and dedication from many people. We would like to take this opportunity to thank the numerous people whose work made this conference possible and ensured its high quality. We wish to thank the authors of submitted papers, as they contributed to the conference technical program. We wish to express our deepest gratitude to the Program Vice Chairs, Antonio Maña Gomez, Marius Portmann, Zhijun Wang, and Daqing Zhang, for their hard work and commitment to quality when helping with paper selection. We would also like to thank all Program Committee members and external reviewers for their excellent job in the paper review process, the Advisory Committee for their continuous advice, and Stephen S. Yau for organizing a panel on "Future Trends of Autonomic and Ubiquitous Computing." We are also in debt to Bin Xiao for the conference local arrangements, to the Publicity Chairs for advertising the conference, to Lin Chen and other people from the Local Organizing Committee for managing registration and other conference organization-related tasks, and to Hong Kong Polytechnic University for hosting the conference. We are also grateful to Tony Li Xu and Liu Yang for their hard work on managing both the conference Web site and the conference management system, and for their help with editing the UIC proceedings.

July 2007

Jadwiga Indulska
Jianhua Ma
Laurence T. Yang
Theo Ungerer
Jiannong Cao

Organization

Executive Committee

General Chairs	Jiannong Cao, Hong Kong Polytechnic University, Hong Kong
	Emile Aarts, Philips, The Netherlands
Program Chairs	Jadwiga Indulska, University of Queensland, Australia
	Antonio Puliafito, University of Messina, Italy
	Laurence T. Yang, St. Francis Xavier University, Canada
Program Vice Chairs	Antonio Maña Gomez, University of Malaga, Spain
	Marius Portmann, University of Queensland, Australia
	Zhijun Wang, Hong Kong Polytechnic University, Hong Kong
	Daqing Zhang, National Institute of Telecommunication, France
Steering Committee	Jianhua Ma (Chair), Hosei University, Japan
	Laurence T. Yang (Chair), St. Francis Xavier University, Canada
	Hai Jin, Huazhong University of Science and Technology, China
	Jeffrey J.P. Tsai, University of Illinois at Chicago, USA
	Theo Ungerer, University of Augsburg, Germany
International Advisory Committee	Makoto Amamiya, Kyushu University, Japan
	Leonard Barolli, Fukuoka Institute of Technology, Japan
	Keith Chan, Hong Kong Polytechnic University, Hong Kong
	Yookun Cho, Seoul National University, Korea
	Sumi Helal, University of Florida, USA
	Ali R. Hurson, Pennsylvania State University, USA
	Qun Jin, Waseda University, Japan
	Janusz Kacprzyk, Polish Academy of Science, Poland
	Moon Hae Kim, Konkuk University, Korea
	Beniamino Di Martino, Second University of Naples, Italy
	Christian Müller-Schloer, University of Hannover, Germany

	Timothy K. Shih, Tamkang University, Taiwan
	Norio Shiratori, Tohoku University, Japan
	Ivan Stojmenovic, Ottawa University, Canada
	Makoto Takizawa, Tokyo Denki University, Japan
	David Taniar, Monash University, Australia
	Jhing-Fa Wang, National Cheng Kung University, Taiwan
	Stephen S. Yau, Arizona State University, USA
	Yaoxue Zhang, Tsinghua University, China
	Albert Zomaya, University of Sydney, Australia
	Xingshe Zhou, Northwestern Polytechnic University, China
Publicity Chairs	Jiang (Linda) Xie, University of North Carolina at Charlotte, USA
	Yan Zhang, Simula Research Laboratory, Norway
	Evi Syukur, Monash University, Australia
	Wenbin Jiang, Huazhong University of Science and Technology, China
	Stephen Yang, National Central University, Taiwan
International Liaison Chairs	Giuseppe Anastasi, University of Pisa, Italy
	Mieso Denko, University of Guelph, Canada
	Jong Hyuk Park, Hanwha S & C, Korea
	Akira Namatame, National Defense Academy, Japan
Publication Chairs	Yu Hua, Huazhong University of Science and Technology, China
	Agustinus Borgy Waluyo, Institute for Infocomm Research, Singapore
Award Chairs	Vipin Chaudhary, University at Buffalo, SUNY, USA
	David Simplot-Ryl, University Lille 1, France
	Thanos Vasilakos, University of Western Macedonia, Greece
Panel Chairs	Stephen S. Yau, Arizona State University, USA
	Victor Callaghan, University of Essex, UK
Financial Chair	Lin Chen, Hong Kong Polytechnic University, Hong Kong
Web Chairs	Tony Li Xu, St. Francis Xavier University, Canada
	Liu Yang, St. Francis Xavier University, Canada
Local Organizing Chairs	Bin Xiao, Hong Kong Polytechnic University, Hong Kong
	Wei Lou, Hong Kong Polytechnic University, Hong Kong
	Kang Ying Allan Wong, Hong Kong Polytechnic University, Hong Kong

Program Committee

Waleed Abdulla	University of Auckland, New Zealand
Bessam AbdulRazak	University of Florida, USA
Bernady Apduhan	Kyushu Sangyo University, Japan
Sebastien Ardon	NICTA, Australia
Juan Carlos Augusto	University of Ulster at Jordanstown, UK
Sasitharan Balasubramaniam	Waterford Institute of Technology, Ireland
Christian Becker	University of Mannheim, Germany
Paolo Bellavista	University of Bologna, Italy
Neil Bergmann	University of Queensland, Australia
Claudio Bettini	University of Milan, Italy
Han-Chieh Chao	National Dong Hwa University, Taiwan
Hao Che	University of Texas at Arlington, USA
Guanling Chen	University of Massachusetts, USA
Yuh-Shyan Chen	National Taipei University, Taiwan
Zixue Cheng	The University of Aizu, Japan
Michele Colajanni	University of Modena and Reggio Emilia, Italy
Paul Davidsson	Blekinge Institute of Technology, Sweden
Michael Ditze	University of Paderborn, Germany
Monica Divitini	Norwegian University of Science Technology, Norway
Hakan Duman	British Telecom, UK
Elgar Fleisch	University of St. Gallen, Switzerland
Michael Gardener	Chimera, UK
Paolo Giorgini	University of Trento, Italy
Frank Golatowski	University of Rostock, Germany
Tao Gu	Institute for Infocomm Research, Singapore
Jinhua Guo	University of Michigan at Dearborn, USA
Hirohide Haga	Doshisha University, Japan
Sunyoung Han	Konkuk University, Korea
Günter Haring	University of Vienna, Austria
Karen Henricksen	NICTA, Australia
Ching-Hsien Hsu	Chung-Hua University, Taiwan
Hui-Huang Hsu	Tamkang University, Taiwan
Chung-Ming Huang	National Cheng Kung University, Taiwan
Runhe Huang	Hosei University, Japan
Brendan Jennings	Waterford Institute of Technology, Ireland
Dongwon Jeong	Kunsan National University, Korea
Young-sik Jeong	Wonkwang University, Korea
Weijia Jia	City University of Hong Kong, Hong Kong
Tao Jiang	University of Michigan, USA
Achilles Kameas	Hellenic Open University, Greece
Judy Kay	University of Sydney, Australia
Tetsuo Kinoshita	Tohoku University, Japan
Mohan Kumar	University of Texas at Arlington, USA

Stan Kurkovsky	Connecticut State University, USA
Choonhwa Lee	Hanyang University, Korea
Deok-Gyu Lee	Electronics and Telecommunications Research Institute, Korea
Jae Yeol Lee	Chonnam National University, Korea
Wonjun Lee	Korea University, Korea
Vincent Lenders	Swiss Federal Institute of Technology (ETH), Zurich
Hong-Va Leong	HongKong Polytechnic University, Hong Kong
Jiandong Li	Xidian University, China
Jiang (Leo) Li	Howard University, USA
Kuan-Ching Li	Providence University, Taiwan
Weifa Liang	The Australian National University, Australia
Yinsheng Li	Fudan University, China
Shih-Wei (Steve) Liao	INTEL, USA
Seng Loke	La Trobe University, Australia
Antonio López	University of Oviedo, Spain
Philip Machanick	University of Queensland, Australia
Mary Lou Maher	University of Sydney, Australia
Francesco Marcelloni	University of Pisa, Italy
Pedro Jose Marron	University of Stuttgart, Germany
Andreas Meissner	Fraunhofer IPSI, Germany
Geyong Min	University of Bradford, UK
Tim Moors	NICTA, Australia
Soraya Kouadri Mostefaoui	Open University, UK
Max Mühlhäuser	Darmstadt University of Technology, Germany
Maurice Mulvenna	University of Ulster, UK
Amiya Nayak	University of Ottawa, Canada
Wolfgang Nejdl	University of Hannover, Germany
Daniela Nicklas	University of Stuttgart, Germany
Thomas Noel	Louis Pasteur University of Strasbourg, France
Symeon Papavassiliou	Technical University of Athens, Greece
Tom Pfeifer	Waterford Institute of Technology, Ireland
Asad Pirzada	NICTA, Australia
Rosa Preziosi	University of Sannio, Italy
Aaron J. Quigley	University College Dublin, Ireland
Andry Rakotonirainy	Queensland University of Technology, Australia
Carlos Ramos	Polytechnic of Porto, Portugal
Anand Ranganathan	IBM T.J. Watson Research Center, USA
Marc Rennhard	Zurich University of Applied Sciences, Switzerland

Ricky Robinson	NICTA, Australia
Corrado Santoro	University of Catania, Italy
Elhadi Shakshuki	Acadia University, Canada
Yuanchun Shi	Tsinghua University, China
Behrooz Shirazi	Washington State University, USA
Carsten Sorensen	London School of Economics, UK
George Spanoudakis	City University London, UK
Bala (Srini) Srinivasan	Monash University, Australia
Tsutomu Terada	Osaka University, Japan
Bruce Thomas	University of South Australia, Australia
Anand Tripathi	University of Minnesota, USA
Klaus Turowski	University of Augsburg, Germany
Javier Garcia Villalba	Complutense University of Madrid, Spain
Cho-li Wang	Hong Kong University, Hong Kong
Guojun Wang	Central South University, China
Sheng-De Wang	National Taiwan University, Taiwan
Ying-Hong Wang	Tamkang University, Taiwan
Ryan Wishart	NICTA, Australia
Hongyi Wu	University of Louisiana at Lafayette, USA
Lu Yan	Turku Centre for Computer Science, Finland
George Yee	National Research Council, Canada
Masao Yokota	Fukuoka Institute of Technology, Japan
Zhiwen Yu	Nagoya University, Japan
Arkady Zaslavsky	Monash University, Australia
Manli Zhu	Institute for Infocomm Research, Singapore
Jingyuan (Alex) Zhang	University of Alabama, USA
Krzysztof Zieliński	AGH University of Science and Technology, Poland

Additional Reviewers

Chong Wang	Jose M. Enguita	Guohua Bai
Ha Dang	Venet Osmani	Dario Maggiorini
Xiaojuan Xie	Indradip Ghosh	Neil Bergmann
Florian Michahelles	Li Gao	Shinyoung Lim
Silvia Elaluf-Calderwood	Yingxiao Xu	Dario Bottazzi
Volker Derballa	Shui Yu	Bessam Abdulrazak
Derek Corbett	Haiming Huang	Jakob Salzmann
Majid Iqbal Khan	Arno Wagner	Daniele Riboni
Kofi Boateng	Branko Celler	Mirco Marchetti
Ken C.K. Tsang	Georgios Androulidakis	Emmanuel Lochin
Henrik Petander	Nigel Lovell	Harald Widiger
Huaiguo Fu	Benoit Gaudin	Liping Shen
Alessandra Toninelli	Voker Derballa	Michelle Liang
Wilfried Gansterer	Devdatta Kulkarni	Mario G.C.A. Cimino

Mario Di Francesco
Stefano Chessa
Carlos Ramos
Stella Kafetzoglou
Jack Tsai
Yoshihiro Kawahara
Hun Jung
Vasileios Karyotis
Lei Pan
Rajesh Prasad
Zhenghao Shi
Fiona Mahon
Raghu Srinivasan
Vassilis Chatzigiannakis
Jaime Serrano-Orozco
Linda Pareschi
Riccardo Lancellotti
Su Xia
Ralf Behnke
Dominik Lieckfeldt
Haining Chen
Jan Blumenthal
Miao Ju
Alan Davy
Keara Barrett
Adrian Frei
Gianluca Dini
Borgy Waluyo
Gamel Wiredu
Mark C.M. Tsang
Yu Wang
Zhipeng Yang
Jan Kietzmann
Anil Kumar Kapu
Guillaume Jourjon
Robert Mullins
John Ronan
Yu Zhou
Claire Fahy
Peter Danielis
Hendrik Bohn
Theo Koulouris
Yasue Kishino
Aaron Harwood
Gajaruban Kandavanam
Hui Cheng
Weigang Wu
Hailun Tan
Timotheos Kastrinogiannis

An Integrated and Flexible Scheduler for Sensor Grids

Hock Beng Lim[1] and Danny Lee[2]

[1] Intelligent Systems Center, Nanyang Technological University
limhb@ntu.edu.sg
[2] School of Computing, National University of Singapore

Abstract. The integration of wireless sensor networks and grid computing is an emerging and promising area of research. Sensor grids extend the grid computing paradigm to the sharing of sensor resources in wireless sensor networks. By combining the complementary strengths of sensor networks and grid computing, sensor grids can support applications that require real-time information from the physical environment and vast amount of computational and storage resources.

One of the major challenges in the design of sensor grids is how to efficiently schedule sensor jobs across the collection of sensor resources in a sensor grid. In this paper, we design an integrated and flexible scheduler for a sensor grid testbed. The scheduler makes use of several scheduling and load balancing algorithms to suit the characteristics of sensor jobs. We performed extensive evaluations to characterize the behaviour and performance of these scheduling and load balancing algorithms. Our performance results indicate that the sensor grid scheduler can provide a good tradeoff betweeen performance objectives such as sensor resource utilization, sensor job throughput, and sensor grid lifetime.

1 Introduction

Wireless Sensor Networks (WSNs) consist of groups of small, inexpensive, low-power, and self-contained sensor nodes with sensing, data processing, and wireless communication capabilities [1,2]. They enable the direct monitoring of the physical environment, and the seamless coupling of real-time sensor data with the digital world. The sensor nodes are resource-constrained since they have limited sensing capability, processing power, and communication bandwidth. However, with the aggregation of a large number of such nodes over a wide area, a wireless sensor network has substantial data acquisition and processing capabilities. Thus, wireless sensor networks can be regarded as distributed computing resources that can be shared by multiple users and applications.

Grid computing is based on the concept of the coordinated sharing of distributed and heterogeneous resources to solve large-scale problems in dynamic virtual organizations [3]. The types of shared resources can be computational servers, storage, or even sensors. They are owned by institutions or individuals in *virtual organizations (VOs)*. Rules exist to ensure fairness and quality of service for users of grid resources, and to maximize the utility of these resources. In fact, the grid computing paradigm can be extended to include the sharing of sensor resources in WSNs. A *sensor grid* [4] is formed by the integration of WSNs with the conventional wired grid fabric.

J. Indulska et al. (Eds.): UIC 2007, LNCS 4611, pp. 567–578, 2007.

A sensor grid processes multiple sensor job requests from different users. In a typical workflow, sensor jobs arriving at a sensor grid should be handled automatically by the system. This raises the issues of how the sensor grid efficiently schedules incoming jobs to be executed, and how it allocates sensor resources to these jobs. The scheduling of jobs in distributed, parallel, and grid computing systems has been extensively studied in the past. However, these previous works deal with the scheduling of computational jobs. There are some important differences between sensor jobs and computational jobs. Thus, existing scheduling algorithms and schedulers for traditional distributed and parallel systems may not work well in the context of sensor grids.

Previously, we proposed a sensor grid architecture called the *Scalable Proxy-based aRchItecture for seNsor Grid (SPRING)* [4]. In this paper, we design an integrated and flexible scheduler for a sensor grid testbed based on the SPRING framework. Several scheduling and load balancing algorithms were implemented within this scheduler to suit the unique characteristics of sensor jobs. The scheduler can use an appropriate scheduling or load balancing algorithm to suit the requirements of the resource owner and users. We performed extensive evaluations to measure the impact of these scheduling and load balancing algorithms using several performance metrics. Our performance results indicate the suitability of the scheduling and load balancing algorithms to satisfy performance objectives such as sensor resource utilization, sensor job throughput, and sensor grid lifetime. With these algorithms, our scheduler can provide a good tradeoff between the performance objectives of a sensor grid.

The rest of this paper is organized as follows. Section 2 provides an outline of our SPRING architecture and the sensor grid testbed system implemented. We discuss the design of our sensor grid scheduler in Section 3, including the scheduling and load balancing algorithms used. Sections 4 and 5 present the evaluation of the scheduling and the load balancing algorithms respectively, and also discuss the significance of the results. Finally, Section 6 concludes this paper.

2 Sensor Grid Architecture and Testbed

The key idea of the SPRING framework [4] is to use proxy systems as interfaces between WSNs and the grid fabric. This enables the functionality of the sensor nodes to be exposed to the grid although they are resource-constrained. As shown in Figure 1, SPRING is based on a layered-architecture approach. The layers represent the main middleware components that connect different type of systems to the grid network. Each layer defines services that are accessible via Application Programming Interfaces (APIs) for the application or other layers.

The WSN Proxy comprises of various *Proxy components*, which are shown in Figure 2. Please refer to [4] for a detailed description of the SPRING framework and the WSN Proxy components. We have developed a sensor grid testbed prototype to implement the SPRING framework [4]. For this testbed, the WSN is based on the Crossbow motes platform.

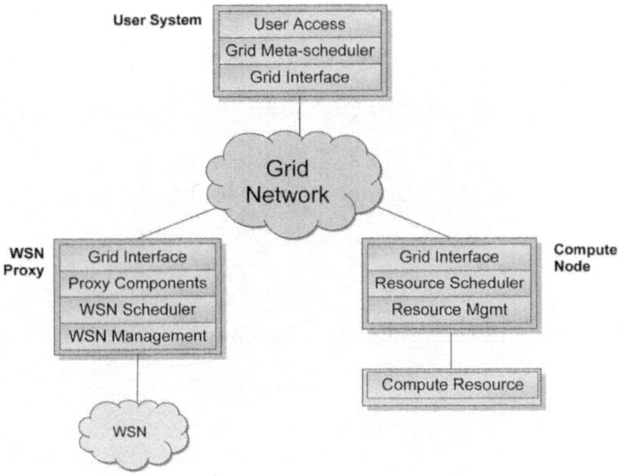

Fig. 1. The SPRING Framework

3 Sensor Grid Scheduler Design

3.1 Characteristics of Sensor Jobs

The design of a sensor grid scheduler is influenced by some important differences between sensor jobs and computational jobs. Unlike computational jobs, sensor jobs are not multitasking in nature. A sensor node can execute only one sensor job at a time, and it cannot execute multiple sensor jobs via multitasking. Thus, sensor jobs are not preempt-able. While computational jobs automatically terminate upon completion, the durations of sensor jobs have to be explicitly specified in advance. Sensor jobs are also likely to require specific time slots for execution compared to general computational jobs.

In addition, sensor jobs are not only time-sensitive, but may also be location and resource-sensitive in some cases. Certain jobs can only run on certain sensor nodes in the correct location. Another aspect of resource sensitivity is that a single sensor job can run on more than 1 sensor node simultaneously, which makes the load balancer more significant in allocating these jobs.

3.2 Sensor Job Scheduling Algorithms

In this work, we adapted four existing multiprocessor scheduling algorithms to suit the sensor grid scenario. The scheduling algorithms we have chosen to implement are relatively simple and deterministic, in line with the consideration that the scheduler should be lightweight and provide reliable performance. One common modification that we made was such that none of the scheduling algorithms support preemptive scheduling.

1. **Earliest Deadline First (EDF):** EDF is a scheduling algorithm that allocates higher priorities to jobs closer to their deadline. Created as a alternative to the static priority schedulers, it guarantees schedulability when node utilization is full [5]. In

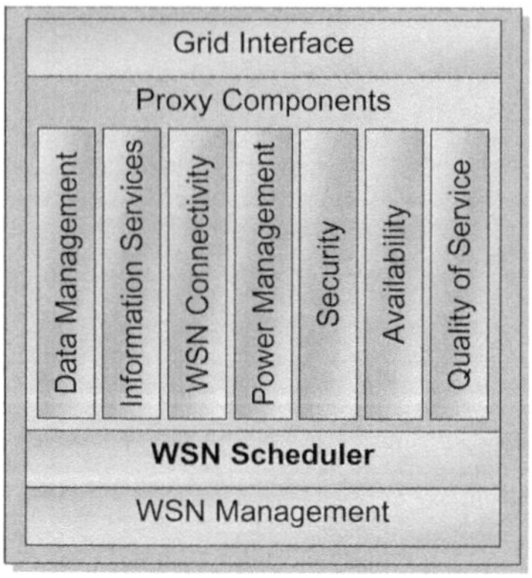

Fig. 2. The Proxy Component Architecture

the case where deadlines are equal, we modified the algorithm to use the duration of the job as a tie breaker, with shorter duration jobs given a higher priority.

2. **First Come First Served (FCFS):** FCFS or First In First Out (FIFO) is the simplest of the four scheduling algorithms. Using a queue structure, this algorithm simply adds new jobs to the end of the queue as they arrive, picking jobs for execution only from the front of the queue.
3. **Least Laxity First (LLF):** A derivative of EDF, LLF is a scheduling algorithm that allocates priorities on the amount of laxity a job has: the lower the laxity, the higher the priority. The laxity, or slack time, is the time left until its deadline after the job is completed, assuming that the job could be executed immediately [6]. In the case when laxity is equal for two jobs, the algorithm was modified to allocate a higher priority to the job with the nearer deadline.
4. **Shortest Job Next (SJN) :** SJN allocates priorities statically depending on the duration of jobs. Shorter jobs are favoured, and are given higher priorities. Similar to LLF, the modification made to the algorithm was to allocate a higher priority to the job with the nearer deadline when durations are equal.

3.3 Load Balancing Algorithms

Load balancing algorithms are important for resource owners to manage their sensor resources. By spreading out the allocation of jobs to sensor nodes according to different criteria, resource constraints of WSNs such as sensor node battery life and wireless network bandwidth can be taken into account. For example, resource owners may want to spread out sensor jobs to different sensor nodes in a WSN to even out the power consumption across nodes and prolong the WSN lifetime, provided the jobs do not have affinity to specific nodes.

Our scheduler provides the flexibility for the user to select whether he wants specific resource allocation, such as in the case when the job is location sensitive. Alternatively, the user may want automatic resource allocation, in which all nodes in a WSN are eligible to run the job, and thus he simply needs to specify how many nodes he wishes to execute the job on.

1. **No Priority (Earliest Slot First):** If there is no criteria for load balancing, we choose to let the job finish as soon as possible, without any specific priority consideration. This form of load balancing will consider the combination of nodes required with the earliest available time in which the sensor job can fit into, which gives it the alternate name of *Earliest Slot First*. In the case of tied earliest times, the algorithm will randomly select a combination of nodes to execute the job.
2. **Battery Priority:** In our testbed, we assume that we have the facility to query the amount of battery life remaining in the sensor nodes (motes). When a job arrives at the load balancer, the battery levels of the motes will be queried. Depending on the number of motes specified by the user, the system will examine the average instantaneous battery levels for all combinations of motes, then consider the battery threshold level. The threshold, varying from 0.0 to 1.0, indicates the percentage of highest battery levels that the load balancer will consider. That is, a threshold of 0.5 will cause the combinations with the top 50% average battery levels to be considered. Out of this subset of combinations, the load balancer will then choose the combination with the earliest time. Theoretically, a threshold of 1.0 should be no different from the load balancing algorithm of "No Priority". However in the case of a tie between average battery and time, the choice of which combination to choose will be random.
3. **Load Time Priority:** One property of sensor jobs is that job durations are clearly specified before execution, which we leverage here to provide a more balanced indicator of load. The load balancer maintains a table of mote information internally, including the number of minutes of jobs scheduled to be executed, i.e. the Load Time for each mote. Similar to Battery Priority load balancing, when a job arrives to be allocated to the motes, the load balancer will check the Load Times and generate a list of average load times for all possible combinations of motes. Like Battery Priority load balancing, it will consider the threshold when selecting a combination of motes for allocation, selecting the combination with the earliest timeslot within the threshold level.

3.4 Dropping Jobs

After the phases of job scheduling and load balancing, there are 2 simple criteria that can dictate whether jobs will be executed or not: (1) whether a job will exceed its specified deadline if it is a "hard" deadline, and (2) whether the motes allocated to the job have run out of battery.

3.5 Implementation of the Scheduler

The scheduler was implemented in Java, which is a language compatible with the Globus API. We developed a grid service that runs in the Globus container that accepts job details and interfaces with the scheduler to schedule the job.

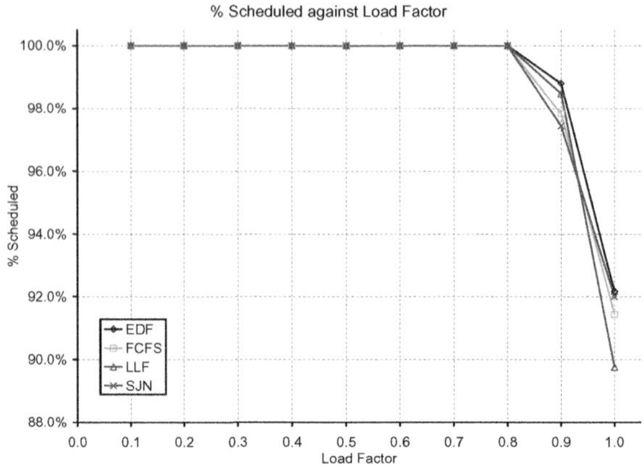

Fig. 3. % Scheduled vs Load Factor

As mentioned earlier, ideally we should be able to query the battery life of the motes dynamically. However, due to the limitations of the Crossbow motes platform, we cannot obtain actual data on battery usage in the motes. Thus, we simulate the level of battery usage in our scheduler. We add an extra field in the job parameters called *Battery Usage*, which indicates the percentage of the total battery life that the job will consume per minute of execution. This is to simulate the different rates of battery consumption that different jobs have. Studies have shown that it is possible to predict the power usage of a given mote executable via simulation, and thus we can obtain a predicted rate of battery consumption [7].

4 Evaluation of Scheduling Algorithms

In the evaluation of scheduling algorithms, we show how the different execution orders of jobs affect the job turnaround time, the number of jobs that meet their deadlines, and the effective utilization of the motes. We also study how the scheduling algorithms behave as the job load increases, i.e. when timing constraints become tighter.

4.1 Experimental Methodology

To achieve this, we primarily aimed to vary the type of scheduling algorithm, while we do not use any load balancing. In addition, we also choose to vary the *Load Factor*, which is defined as:

$$\text{Load Factor}\ , F = \frac{\text{sum of all generated job durations}}{\text{total execution time period}} \tag{1}$$

We used the soft deadline type here as we wanted to prevent jobs being dropped due to timing constraints from affecting the overall times.

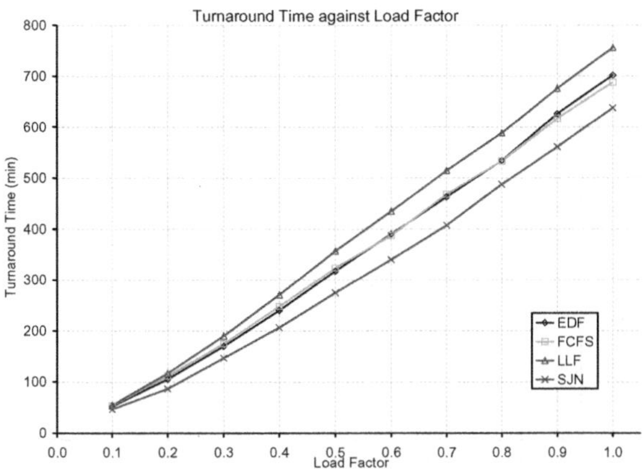

Fig. 4. Turnaround Time vs Load Factor

We developed a workload generator to create 25 batches of 50 jobs each to simulate user input for each of the 10 Load Factor levels. We used this same set of input jobs to test each scheduling algorithm to ensure that the results are comparable against each other. Each batch consists of jobs that have start times that follow a Poisson distribution over the first hour, and have deadlines 24 hours after the start time. Job durations were randomly specified, to simulate the unpredictable nature of user requirements. We use a sensor grid testbed with a WSN consisting of 5 motes. To minimize the case of uneven resource allocation, we let the system fully decide the way motes are allocated by using an automatic allocation type. A uniform random distribution was used for the number of motes required per job.

We chose the parameters such that jobs were not constrained by resources, i.e. no jobs will be dropped due to lack of battery due to the nominal battery usage values, and that load balancing have as little impact as possible on time allocation. This would mean that the best possible situation would be created in terms of turnaround and utilization due to the closer packing of jobs.

4.2 Performance Metrics

i. **% Scheduled**
This is the ratio of the number of jobs that successfully finish before their deadlines over the total number of jobs. The resource owner would prefer a value that is as high as possible for this metric.

ii. **Turnaround Time**
This is the average time that a job will take from submission until completion. Users would like this to be as low as possible, as it means that they can get their data back sooner.

iii. **% Unutilized Time**
This is the percentage of time left unused after the jobs are scheduled. A lower value is desired as it indicates better utilization of the resource.

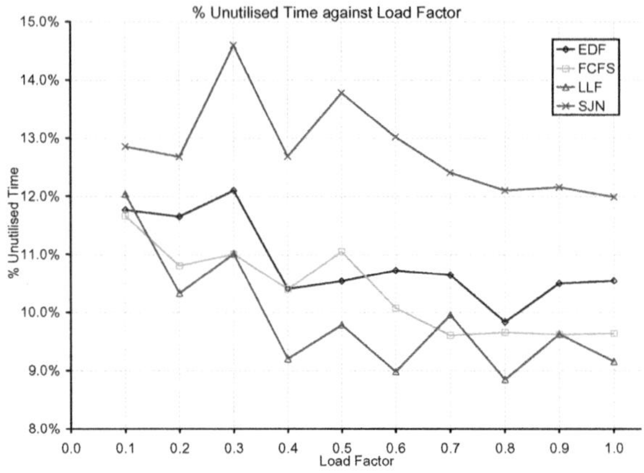

Fig. 5. % Unutilized Time vs Load Factor

4.3 Results and Discussion

The graphs shown on Figure 3 to Figure 5 are based on the averaged values of each set of 25 trials. From this experiment, we can see that users would prefer the SJN scheduling algorithm, since it provides the shortest turnaround times amongst all the scheduling algorithms. However, SJN performs poorly for utilization and missed time, which resource owners would be concerned about. SJN will execute short jobs first, which means that long jobs will constantly be delayed, up until the point where they begin to miss their deadlines.

The most suitable choice for resource owners is EDF, which also satisfies users with a reasonable turnaround time. It drops the fewest number of jobs, has a consistent amount of % Unutilized Time of about 12% and misses the lowest number of jobs by a relatively short amount. EDF in this case cannot ensure full schedulability when the Load Factor is less than or equal to 1 due to the resource requirements of the jobs. This is a major differences between computational and sensor jobs that has been demonstrated in this experiment.

LLF provides the least amount of gaps between jobs, but otherwise performs poorly. We noticed that this algorithm tended to schedule long jobs first, since given the same deadline as a short job, the laxity of a long job is lower. As a result, short jobs wait long times before executing, affecting turnaround time. An additional side effect is that given the same data set, more short jobs will tend to miss their deadlines than algorithms like SJN, so the % scheduled is lower.

It is interesting to note that FCFS is average in all metrics, which was unexpected, given its unpredictable nature. Upon examining the individual trial results, we found that there were many large variations, but were evened out by the averaging function. This is the benefit of taking a comparatively larger set of samples, suggesting that FCFS may be a "good enough" algorithm as the number of trials gets large.

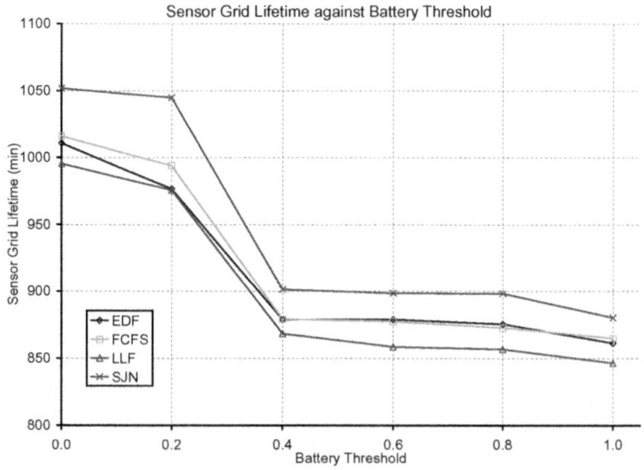

Fig. 6. Sensor Grid Lifetime vs Battery Threshold

5 Evaluation of Load Balancing Algorithms

The evaluation of load balancing algorithms aims to show the effect of load balancing in combination with the different scheduling algorithms on the resource lifetimes and the number of schedulable jobs. We also wanted to explore the effect of increasing the threshold on the respective load balancing algorithms, to find the optimum value of threshold that has the highest utilization and at the same time the longest resource lifetime. Lastly, we want to compare the two load balancing algorithms to find out which one produces a more consistent output.

5.1 Experimental Methodology

We vary the threshold values over 6 steps from 0.0 to 1.0 for each of the scheduling algorithms, and will repeat the experiment for each of the load balancing types. We picked the Load Factor of 0.5 to ensure that the jobs are guaranteed to meet their deadline regardless of scheduling algorithm, and not to use an extremal value that has been observed to cause the scheduling algorithms to behave erratically.

For each batch of 50 jobs, the job parameters are generally the same as the ones from the previous section with the same rationale, except for the amount of battery use. As mentioned in section 3.5, we had to simulate the battery usage in our program. In order to test the minimum network lifetime, we had to get the situation when the batteries would be exhausted. Therefore when the battery usage was generated, it was generated with the goal of depleting all the battery life of all the motes.

5.2 Performance Metrics

i. **Sensor Grid Lifetime**
This metric refers to the minimum time until a mote becomes inactive due to lack of battery. When this happens, the sensor grid is unable to service all possible jobs,

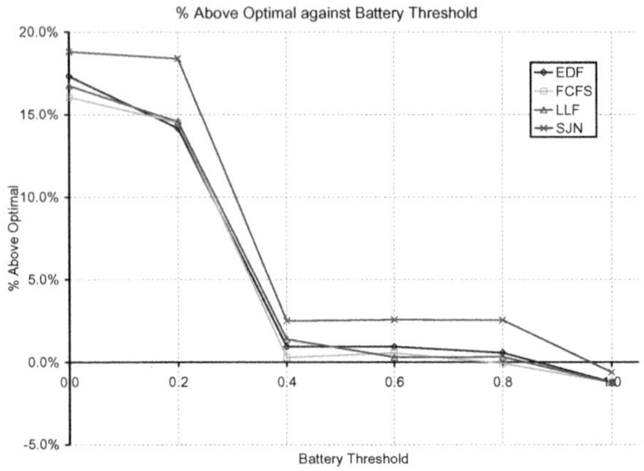

Fig. 7. % Above Optimal vs Battery Threshold

reducing its usefulness. The resource owner would want to keep this value as high as possible.

ii. **% Above Optimal**

For this experiment, we are assuming that the case of no load balancing will produce the optimal time. By defining the "completion time" as the time from the start of the first job to the end of the last job, we can define this metric as the completion time for the trial with the given load balancing scheme over the completion time for no load balancing. Therefore for the best utilization, the resource owner would want this value to be as close to zero as possible.

5.3 Results and Discussion

Comparing the two load balancing algorithms from the results shown in Figure 6 to Figure 9, we can see that in general, the Load Time Priority scheme produces more consistent results as the threshold increases for all scheduling algorithms. Battery Priority on the other hand experiences a drastic change in all metrics as the threshold goes from 0.2 to 0.4. Generally, we can conclude that when the rate of battery usage is not known, Load Time Priority can provide an adequate approximation of balanced battery load that prolongs sensor grid lifetime.

Comparing the difference between scheduling algorithms, it seems that the scheduling algorithm SJN in conjunction with the Load Time Priority load balancer produces the best and most consistent results for both users and resource owners in this experiment, that is, when the battery usage is high. SJN provides the longest sensor grid lifetimes, up to 80 minutes more than LLF when threshold is 1.0, and is able to schedule the largest percentage of jobs. However it does have the drawback that it consistently extends the completion time for a set of jobs by the largest amount. This is mitigated when the chosen threshold value is about, such that the sensor grid lifetime is balanced by the corresponding increase in completion time.

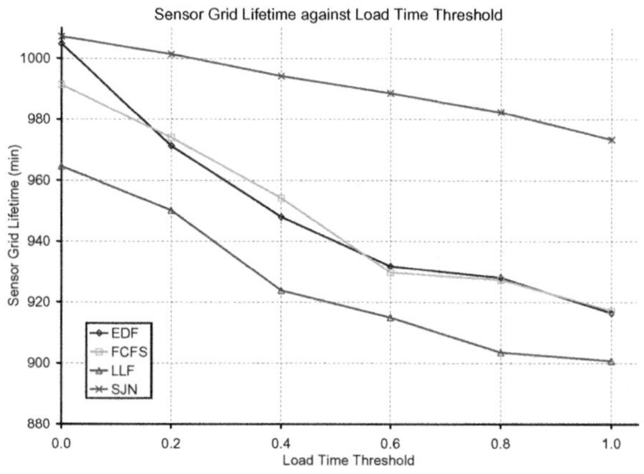

Fig. 8. Sensor Grid Lifetime vs Load Time Threshold

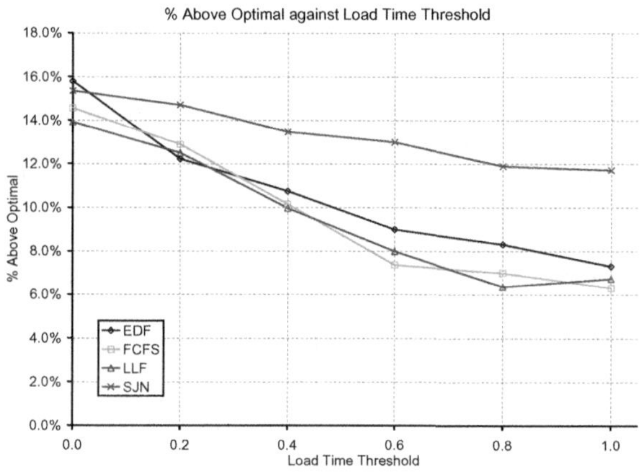

Fig. 9. % Above Optimal vs Load Time Threshold

EDF is an average performer when load balancing is introduced, but continues to produce consistent results. LLF would probably not be the choice of anyone but the resource owner most concerned with maximizing his utilization. FCFS again produces average values for both load balancing algorithms, suggesting again that it may be "good enough" for general cases.

6 Conclusion

Sensor grids are a new and emerging field of research, with many important unresolved issues, one of which is the scheduling of sensor jobs. In this paper, we addressed the design of an integrated and flexible sensor grid scheduler. We adapted scheduling algorithms to suit the characteristics of sensor jobs, and these modified algorithms perform differently from their conventional counterparts. We also incorporated a load balancing scheme that caters to the limitations of sensor grids, and found that it has an impact on the sensor grid utilization and useful lifetime.

In conclusion, we have design a flexible and tunable sensor grid scheduler and implemented it on a testbed that we have created. The various scheduling and load balancing algorithms were also characterized such that the scheduler can readily select one that suits the performance objectives such as sensor resource utilization, sensor job throughput, and sensor grid lifetime. We plan to develop a dynamic scheduler that can adaptively select the appropriate scheduling and load balancing algorithms according to the sensor job requirements and the sensor grid's resource status.

References

1. Akyildiz, I.F., Su, W., Sankarasubramaniam, Y., Cayirci, E.: Wireless sensor networks: A survey. Computer Networks 38(4), 393–422 (2002)
2. Culler, D., Estrin, D., Srivastava, M.: Overview of sensor networks. IEEE Computer , 41–49 (2004)
3. Foster, I., Kesselman, C., Tuecke, S.: The anatomy of the Grid: Enabling scalable virtual organizations. Intl. Journal of Supercomputer Applications 15(3), 200–222 (2001)
4. Lim, H., Teo, Y., Mukherjee, P., Lam, V., Wong, W., See, S.: Sensor grid: Integration of wireless sensor networks and the grid. In: Proc. of the IEEE Conf on Local Computer Networks (LCN 2005), Sydney, Australia, pp. 91–99. IEEE Computer Society Press, Los Alamitos (2005)
5. Liu, C., Layland, J.: Scheduling algorithms for multiprogramming in a hard-real-time environment. Journal of the ACM (JACM) 20(1), 46–61 (1973)
6. Oh, S.-H., Yang, S.-M.: A modified least-laxity-first scheduling algorithm for real-time tasks. In: The Fifth International Conference on Real-Time Computing Systems and Applications, Hiroshima, Japan, pp. 31–36 (1998)
7. Shnayder, V., Hempstead, M., Chen, B.R., Allen, G.W., Welsh, M.: Simulating the power consumption of large-scale sensor network applications. In: 2nd International Conference on Embedded Networked Sensor Systems, Baltimore, MD, USA, pp. 188 – 200 (2004)

A Lightweight Scheme for Node Scheduling in Wireless Sensor Networks

Ming Liu[1], Yuan Zheng[2], Jiannong Cao[2], Wei Lou[2], Guihai Chen[3], and Haigang Gong[1]

[1] School of Computer Science & Engineering, University of Electronic Science and Technology of China, Chengdu 610054, P.R. China
wing.lm@gmail.com
[2] Internet and Mobile Computing Lab, Department of Computing, Hong Kong Polytechnic University, Hung Hom, Kowloon, Hong Kong, P.R. China
[3] State Key Laboratory for Novel Software Technology, Nanjing University, Nanjing 210093, China

Abstract. The coverage problem in wireless sensor networks (WSNs) is to determine the number of active sensor nodes needed to cover the sensing area. The purpose is to extend the lifetime of the WSN by turning off redundant nodes. In this paper, we propose a mathematical method for calculating the coverage fraction in WSNs. According to the method, each active node can evaluate its sensing area whether covered by its active neighbors. We assume that the network is sufficiently dense and the deployed nodes can cover the whole monitored area. In this scenario, if a node's sensing area is covered by its active neighbor nodes, it can be treated as a redundant node. Based on this idea, we propose a lightweight node scheduling (LNS) algorithm that prolongs the network lifetime of the sensor network by turning off redundant nodes without using location information. Simulation study shows that LNS scheme can save considerable energy for data gathering while meeting the desired coverage fraction imposed by application.

1 Introduction

Technology advances in sensors, embedded systems, and low power-consumption wireless communications have made it possible to manufacture tiny wireless sensor nodes with sensing, processing, and wireless communication capabilities. The low-cost and low power-consumption sensor nodes can be deployed to work together to form a wireless sensor network. The sensor nodes in a sensor network are able to sense surrounding environment, carry out simple processing tasks, and communicate with the neighboring nodes within its transmission range. By means of the collaborating among sensor nodes, the sensed and monitored environment information (e.g. temperature, humidity) is transmitted to the base station for future processing. A large-scale wireless sensor network can consist of tens of thousands of tiny sensor nodes, with high density of sensors (up to 20 nodes/ m^3 [1]). The high density of sensors may result in comparatively large energy consumption due to conflicting in

J. Indulska et al. (Eds.): UIC 2007, LNCS 4611, pp. 579–588, 2007.

accessing the communication channels, maintaining information about neighboring nodes, and other factors. A widely-used strategy for reducing energy consumption while at the same time meeting the coverage requirement is to turn off redundant sensors by scheduling sensor nodes to work alternatively [2-6]. The coverage problem in wireless sensor networks (WSNs) is to determine the number of active sensor nodes needed to cover the sensing area.

A widely used strategy [7-11] is to determine the active nodes by using the location information about the sensor nodes and their neighborhood. However, relying on complicated hardware equipments such as the GPS (Global Positioning System) or the directional antenna will greatly increase the hardware cost of sensor nodes and energy consumption. At the same time, the message transmission and calculation of the locations and directions will also consume the energy of a node. Therefore, it is desirable for a solution to the coverage problem that independs on location information.

Most applications may not require the full area coverage and can tolerance a small part of uncovered area at certain intervals. If the active nodes in a sensor network can maintain reasonable area coverage, the requirements of most applications can be met. Coverage can be regarded as one metric of the quality of service of a sensor network that evaluates its monitoring capability [12]. If the coverage fraction is below a certain threshold, the sensor network cannot work normally. propose a simple method that can, in a statistical sense, evaluate the coverage fraction which meets the coverage requirement of the application without location information. In this paper, we propose a mathematical method for calculating coverage fraction in WSNs without the use of location information and then propose a lightweight node scheduling algorithm. Unlike most existed solutions [2, 9-11] which focus on providing full coverage, the proposed scheme gives a solution for fractional coverage. As achieving full coverage can be very costly and energy consuming, fractional coverage is an energy efficient approach which meets the requirements of many applications such as the ones in [5] [13]. Moreover, our work is more general when comparing to those ones using theoretical methods for coverage analysis without using location information, which is a special case of our work.

The rest of the paper is organized as follows. In section 2, we present sensor network models and preliminary definitions. In section 3, we propose a mathematical model for calculating the coverage fraction in a random deployed network. In section 4, a lightweight node scheduling algorithm is proposed based on the above mathematical model. Simulation results are provided and discussed in section 5. Section 6 concludes the paper.

2 Preliminary

In this paper, we use $p(x, y)$ to represent the location of node v_i, and use $v_i(x, y)$ to represent an arbitrary point in v_i's communication range. The communication range of v_i is denoted by $C(v_i)$, and the sensing range of v_i is denoted by $S(v_i)$. To facilitate the discussion, we introduce following definitions:

Definition 1. Neighboring area $\aleph(v_i(x, y))$. For an arbitrary point in node v_i's communication range, its neighboring area is defined as

$$\aleph(v_i(x, y)) = \{\forall(x, y) \in C(v_i) | ((x - v_i(x))^2 + (y - v_i(y))^2 \leq r^2)\} \tag{1}$$

Definition 2. Centre area $C'(v_i)$. The centre area of node v_i is defined as

$$C'(v_i) = \{\forall(x, y) | ((x - p(x))^2 + (y - p(y))^2) \leq (R - r)^2\} \tag{2}$$

According to the above definition, we use $C(v_i) - C'(v_i)$ to indicate non-centre area.

Definition 3. Desired coverage fraction Q. The desired coverage fraction indicates the ratio of the area covered by all active nodes to the entire monitored area. It can be defined as

$$Q = \frac{|\bigcup S(v_i) \cap A|}{|A|} \tag{3}$$

Intuitively, for a sensor node v_i, if the fraction of $C(v_i)$ covered by its active neighbor nodes equal to the desired coverage fraction Q imposed by the application, node v_i can be regarded as a redundant node; otherwise, node v_i should keep working until it has enough active neighbor nodes. Therefore, the goal of our proposed mathematical method is to achieve the desired coverage fraction with a minimum number of active nodes. As this method indicates the relationship between the desired coverage fraction and the minimum number of active nodes, each active node can calculate the number of active neighbor nodes needed for the desired coverage fraction, and then determine its working or sleep status.

3 Fractional Coverage Analyses for Dense Wireless Sensor Networks

For an arbitrary point $v_i(x, y)$ within the communication range of node v_i, it is covered if there exists at least one sensor node deployed in its neighboring area $\aleph(v_i(x, y))$. We assume that all sensor nodes are randomly deployed in the entire monitored area with the uniform distribution. As a result, for a sensor node v_i, the distribution of its neighbor nodes in the communication range of v_i can also approximate to the uniform distribution. Therefore, the probability that a neighbor sensor node of v_i is deployed in the neighboring area of point $v_i(x, y)$, say q, equals to $\frac{|\aleph(v_i(x, y))|}{|C(v_i)|}$. The neighboring area of node v_i may have two cases. If the point $v_i(x, y)$ locates in $C'(v_i)$, the size of neighboring area $|\aleph(v_i(x, y))|$ equals to πr^2 ; otherwise, if the point $v_i(x, y)$ lies in $C(v_i) - C'(v_i)$, the size $|\aleph(v_i(x, y))| \leq \pi r^2$.

Since the distribution of nodes can be regarded as a Poisson process in the region $C(v_i)$, the probability that an arbitrary point $v_i(x, y)$ is covered equals to the probability that at least one sensor falls in its neighboring area, we can easily obtain the probability of $v_i(x, y)$ being covered as follows:

$$\begin{aligned} p_c(v_i(x, y)) &= C_n^1 q(1-q)^{n-1} + C_n^2 q^2 (1-q)^{n-2} + \cdots\cdots + C_n^n q^n \\ &= 1 - (1-q)^n \end{aligned} \tag{4}$$

According to Eq. (4), for any two points in $C(v_i)$, if the sizes of their neighboring area are equal, the probabilities of being covered are also equal. Obviously, for each point within the communication range of node v_i, if the distance between this point and the node v_i is identical, the size of its neighboring area is also identical, i.e., the probability of being covered is identical. For each point that lies within the marginal region $C(v_i) - C'(v_i)$, the size of its neighboring area is less than πr^2 . Especially, when the point lies on the edge of C, its neighboring area is the smallest one, and thus its probability of being covered is also the smallest one. For $\forall v_i(x, y) \in C'(v_i)$, the neighboring area of node v_i is equal to πr^2 . Therefore, the probability of an arbitrary node deployed in the neighboring area of $v_i(x, y)$ $(v_i(x, y) \in C'(v_i))$ equals to $\frac{r^2}{R^2}$. If $R >> r$, the average size of the neighboring areas of all points within the communication range of node v_i can approximate to πr^2 . According to [13], the desired coverage fraction can be calculated by the following equation:

$$E_{cf} = 1 - e^{-\lambda \pi r^2} \tag{5}$$

According to Eq. (4), a designer can use Eq. (5) to approximately calculate at which node density a large-scale sensor network can meet the desired coverage fraction. If the sensing range r is long enough compared to the communication rang R, the border effect cannot be ignored. In such a case, using Eq. (5) to calculate the desired coverage fraction will lead to a deviation beyond tolerance. In order to have an accurate estimation on the relationship between the minimum number of active nodes and the desired coverage fraction, we have to calculate the average size of the neighboring areas of all points within the communication range of node v_i .As shown in Fig.1, the point $v_i(x, y)$ lies in $C(v_i) - C'(v_i)$, and we use l to denote the distance between the point $v_i(x, y)$ and location of node v_i. Obviously, $l > R - r$. According to the Definition 1, the point $v_i(x, y)$'s neighboring area is the shadowed region shown in Fig.1. We can easily obtain the value $|\aleph(v_i(x, y))|$ by the equation as follows:

$$\left|\aleph\left(\forall v_i(x, y)\middle|\{(x, y) \in (C(v_i) - C'(v_i))\}\right)\right| = 2\left(\int_{l-r}^{\frac{R^2-r^2+l^2}{2l}} \sqrt{r^2 - (y-l)^2}\,dy + \int_{\frac{R^2-r^2+l^2}{2l}}^{R} \sqrt{R^2 - \right.$$

$$= \frac{1}{2}\pi(r^2 + R^2) + r^2 \arcsin\frac{R^2 - r^2 - l^2}{2l}\sqrt{r^2 - \frac{(R^2 - r^2 - l^2)^2}{4l^2}}$$

$$- R^2 \arcsin\frac{R^2 - r^2 + l^2}{2lR} - \frac{R^2 - r^2 + l^2}{2l}\sqrt{R^2 - \frac{(R^2 - r^2 + l^2)^2}{4l^2}} \qquad (6)$$

Eq. (6) is a general expression for calculating the neighboring area of an arbitrary point lied in $C(v_i) - C'(v_i)$. According to Eq. (6), for an arbitrary point lied in $C(v_i) - C'(v_i)$, the size of neighboring area is only determined by l. Observing $Eq.6$, for the average size of neighboring area of all points in $C(v_i) - C'(v_i)$, we have

$$\left|\aleph(v_i(x, y))^{C(v_i)-C'(v_i)}\right| = \frac{\iint_{C(v_i)-C'(v_i)} \aleph(v_i(x, y))d\sigma}{|C(v_i) - C'(v_i)|}, \qquad (7)$$

where we use $\aleph(v_i(x, y))^{C(v_i)-C'(v_i)}$ to denote the average size of neighboring area of all points in $C(v_i) - C'(v_i)$.

Hence, the average size of neighboring area of all points in $C(v_i)$ can be calculated by the following equation:

$$\left|\aleph(v_i(x, y))^{C(v_i)}\right| = \frac{\left|\aleph(v_i(x, y))^{C(v_i)-C'(v_i)}\right|\left(R^2 - (R-r)^2\right) + r^2(R-r)^2}{R^2} \qquad (8)$$

Observing Eq. (4) and Eq. (8), despite that the border effect cannot be ignored, it is reasonable to consider that the probability of each point in $C(v_i)$ being covered is equal to $1 - (1 - \frac{\left|\aleph(v_i(x, y))^{C(v_i)}\right|}{|C(v_i)|})^n$, where n denotes the number of selected active neighbor sensor nodes of v_i . Therefore, the expectation of the covered region of $C(v_i)$ is given by

$$E_{the\ size\ of\ covered\ region\ of\ C(v_i)} = \iint_{C(v_i)} \left(1 - \left(1 - \frac{\left|\aleph(v_i(x,y))^{C(v_i)}\right|}{C(v_i)}\right)^n\right) d\sigma$$
$$= \pi R^2 \left(1 - (1 - \frac{\left|\aleph(v_i(x,y))^{C(v_i)}\right|}{|C(v_i)|})^n\right) \tag{9}$$

Obviously, the expectation of coverage fraction is given by

$$E_{the\ fraction\ of C(v_i)\ being\ covered} = 1 - (1 - \frac{\left|\aleph(v_i(x,y))^{C(v_i)}\right|}{|C(v_i)|})^n \tag{10}$$

Given the desired coverage fraction, we can derive from Eq. (10) the minimum number of active neighbor sensor nodes that ensures the desired coverage fraction even when node v_i itself turns off. Assume that the number of active neighbor nodes is K . For any node v_i , if there are more than K neighbor sensor nodes within $C(v_i)$, the desired coverage fraction of the entire monitored area can be guaranteed. Based on this idea, we propose a lightweight node scheduling scheme (LNS) in the next section.

4 Lightweight Node Scheduling Scheme (LNS)

We have known from the previous section that given a desired coverage fraction, the required number of active neighbor nodes can also be calculated. This information can be pre-set in each node before deployment if the desired coverage fraction is fixed in the entire lifetime of the network, or it can be broadcasted by a base station.

LNS is a local distributed algorithm, in which each sensor node periodically broadcasts the $Working\_Msg$ to its active neighbor nodes with a static interval time WT . If the number of its active nodes is larger than the analytical result K , it broadcasts the $Sleep\_Msg$ to all its neighbor nodes. Before a sensor turning off itself, it will back-off a random time $RT(RT_{\min} < RT < RT_{\max})$. Using the back-off strategy, the big sensing hole can be avoided by reducing the probability that several neighbor nodes sleep simultaneously [2]. However, if the node perceives that the number of its active nodes is smaller than the threshold K in the duration of back-off time, it will keep working until it has enough active neighbor nodes. Hence, we have $WT < RT_{\min}$.

Here we set $RT_{\min} = 2WT$ to guarantee the $Working\_Msg$ of all active neighbor nodes can be received in duration RT .In order to perform well, each node needs to maintain a neighborhood table to store the information about its neighbors such as node's ID and residual energy. The ID indicates the unique identification of the neighbor nodes. Without losing generality, we use an integer value to label a node's identification like TinyOS [14]. After a node v has received the

```
// Each node executes this process after deployment
while state = working
  if have enough neighbors
    state ← back-off
    break
  endif
  if ((current time – starting time) mod WT) =0
    broadcast Working_Msg
  endif
  if received Msg from neighbor NT[i]
    update NT[i] according to the content of Msg
  endif
endwhile
while state = back-off
  if Timer of RT has not expired
    if received Msg from neighbor NT[i]
      update NT[i] according to the content of Msg
    endif
  else
    if have enough neighbors then
      state ← sleeping
      broadcasting Sleeping_Msg
    else
      state ← working
    endif
  endif
endwhile
while state = sleeping
  if timer of sleeping time expired
    state ← working
    broadcast Working_Msg
  endif
endwhile
```

Fig. 1. Pseudo code of node scheduling

$Working\_Msg$ or $Sleep\_Msg$, v will update its neighborhood table according to the content of message. For example, if v receives the $Working\_Msg$ from its neighbor node which is labeled with sleeping state in its neighborhood table, v will update the neighbor node's state as working state and record the start working time of this neighbor in v's neighborhood table. For another example, if v receives the $Sleep\_Msg$ from a neighbor, according to the content of the $Sleep\_Msg$, v will record the starting time for back-off and the duration of back-off time RT of this neighbor in its neighborhood table, and change the state of this neighbor as back-off. After $RT + WT$ time, if v does not receive the $Working\_Msg$ from this neighbor, it will update the state of this neighbor as sleeping; otherwise, it will update the state as working. Before falling asleep, v will reset its neighborhood table. After falling asleep for a period of time ST (sleeping time), v will wakeup and update its neighborhood table as mentioned above. In order to prolong the network lifetime, we use the residual energy as a prime parameter for computing the random back-off time RT. Therefore, the more residual energy a node has the higher chance the node will work longer. The pseudo code of LNS is shown in Fig.1.

5 Simulation Study

5.1 Simulation Parameters

In the simulation experiments, we mainly focus on evaluating the effectiveness of LNS, and the relationship between the number of active nodes and the desired coverage fraction. The evaluation of other aspects of LNS will be conducted in future work. The simulation parameters are identical with [15]. Unless otherwise specified, every simulation result shown below is the average of 200 independent experiments where each experiment uses a random seed to generate a uniform topology of the sensor network. For simplicity, we assume that the wireless channel is ideal that the probability of signal collision and interference in the channel is ignorable. We also assume that the radio transmitter and radio amplifier are the main energy consumers of a sensor node. Furthermore, we assume that sleeping energy consumption is zero. In the simulation, we use the same radio model shown in [15, 16] for the radio hardware energy dissipation. We argue that such assumptions can not drastically impact the simulation results, although are not always true in a real system.

5.2 Simulation Results

a. Effectiveness of LNS

In this subsection, we have evaluated the effectiveness of LNS. As shown in Fig.2, LNS can effectively meet the desired coverage fraction required by applications. However, LNS cannot provide a perfect matching between the real coverage fraction and the desired coverage fraction, because LNS is an algorithm that schedules nodes in a statistical way. Note that providing the perfect desired coverage fraction is very difficult or even unrealistic in a real application.

b. Relationship between the number of active nodes and the desired coverage fraction

As shown in Fig.3, no matter what the density of network is, the actual number of active nodes is only determined by the desired coverage fraction after executing LNS. This feature is similar to other scheduling algorithms [8-10], but LNS can achieve the

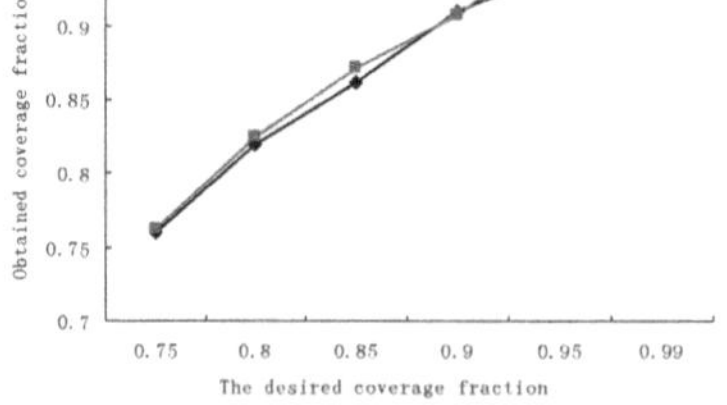

Fig. 2. Effectiveness of LNS

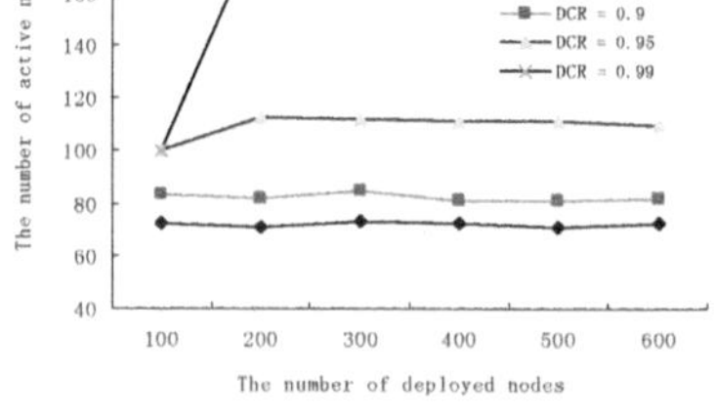

Fig. 3. The relationship between the number of active nodes and desired coverage fraction

desired coverage fraction without using any location information. However, if the number of deployed nodes cannot provide the desired coverage fraction even when all nodes are in active, LNS plays no roles. Fig.3 shows that LNS cannot provide 95% coverage fraction, when the number of deployed nodes equals to 100. Fig.3 also demonstrates that higher desired coverage fraction requirements need more active nodes, and thus more energy will be consumed. For example, if the 99% coverage fraction is required, the number of active nodes should be more than 180 after executing LNS. Therefore, it is a very important issue in node scheduling algorithms that how to achieve a better tradeoff between the desired coverage fraction and the lifetime of network according to the application requirements.

6 Conclusion

In this paper, we propose a lightweight node scheduling algorithm that has several nice features. LNS is very simple and totally localized and distributed, so it can apply in a large scale sensor network. The performance of LNS is independent of the location information of the sensor node. As a result, it can not only save considerably energy for obtaining and maintaining the location information, but also reduce the cost of sensor node. According to the desired coverage fraction required by application, LNS can dynamically adjust the density of active sensor nodes so that it will significant prolong the network lifetime. Furthermore, LNS neither requires the synchronization of sensor nodes, nor does it require the operation in a round-by-round fashion. Therefore, LNS can easily apply to a real application.

Acknowledgement

The work is partly supported by the Hong Kong Polytechnic University under the ICRG grant A-PF77, China NSF grants (60573131, 60673154) Jiangsu Provincial NSF grant (BK2005208), and China 973 projects (2006CB303004, 2002CB312002). The Conference Participation is supported by Nokia Bridging the World Program.

References

1. Shih, E., Cho, S., Ickes, N., Min, R., Sinha, A., Wang, A., Chandrakasan, A.: Physical layer driven protocol and algorithm design for energy-efficient wireless sensor networks. In: proceedings of the seventh annual international conference on Mobile computing and networking (MobiCom 01), Italy, pp. 272–287 (2001)
2. Tian, D., Georganas, N.D.: A Coverage-preserved Node Scheduling scheme for Large Wireless Sensor Networks. In: Proceedings of First International Workshop on Wireless Sensor Networks and Applications (WSNA'02), Atlanta, USA, pp. 32–41 (2002)
3. Liu, C., Wu, K., Xiao, Y., Sun, B.: Random Coverage with Guaranteed Connectivity: Joint Scheduling for Wireless Sensor Networks. IEEE Transactions on Parallel and Distributed Systems (TPDS) (to appear)

4. Ye, F., Zhong, G., Lu, S., Zhang, L.: PEAS: A robust energy conserving protocol for long-lived sensor networks. In: Proceedings of the 23nd International Conference on Distributed Computing Systems (2003)
5. Wu, K., Gao, Y., Li, F., Xiao, Y.: Lightweight Deployment-Aware Scheduling for Wireless Sensor Networks. ACM/Kluwer MONET Journal, Special Issue on Energy Constraints and Lifetime Performance in Wireless Sensor Networks 10(6), 837–852 (2005)
6. Hsin, C., Liu, M.: Network coverage using low duty-cycled sensors: Random & coordinated sleep algorithm. In: Proceedings of the Third International Symposium On Information Processin In Sensor Networks (IPSN 2004) (2004)
7. Slijepcevic, S., Potkonjak, M.: Power efficient organization of wireless sensor networks. In: Glisic, S. (ed.) Proc. of the IEEE Conf. on Communications, pp. 472–476. IEEE Press, Helsinki (2001)
8. Cardei, M., MarCallum, D., Cheng, X., Min, M., Jia, X., Li, D., Du, D.: Wireless sensor networks with energy efficient organization. Journal of Interconnection Networks 213–229 (2002)
9. Xu, Y., Heidemann, J., Estrin, D.: Geography-Informed energy conservation for ad hoc routing. In: Proc. of the 7th Annual ACM/IEEE Int'l Conf. on Mobile Computing and Networking, pp. 70–84. ACM Press, New York (2001)
10. Zhang, H., Hou, J.C.: Maintaining scheme coverage and connectivity in large sensor networks. Wireless Ad Hoc and Sensor Networks: An International Journal 89–123 (2005)
11. Wang, X., Xing, G., Zhang, Y., Lu, C., Pless, R., Gill, C.D.: Integrated coverage and connectivity configuration in wireless sensor networks. In: Proc. of the 1st Int'l Conf. on Embedded Networked Sensor Systems, pp. 28–39. ACM Press, New York (2003)
12. Meguerdichian, S., Koushanfar, F., Potkonjak, M., Srivastava, M.: Coverage problems in wireless ad-hoc sensor networks. In: Proc of the IEEE INFOCOM. Anchorage, pp. 1380–1387. IEEE Press, Anchorage (2001)
13. Liu, B., Towsley, D.A.: study on the coverage of large-scale sensor networks. In: Proc. of the 1st IEEE Int'l Conf. on Mobile Ad-Hoc and Sensor Systems, IEEE Press, Los Alamitos (2004)
14. Culler, D.E., Hill, J., Buonadonna, P., Szewczyk, R., Woo, A.: A Network-Centric Approach to Embedded Software for Tiny Devices. In: Henzinger, T.A., Kirsch, C.M. (eds.) EMSOFT 2001. LNCS, vol. 2211, pp. 114–130. Springer, Heidelberg (2001)
15. Heinzelman, W.R.: An application-specific protocol architecture for wireless microsensor networks. IEEE Trans. on Wireless Communications 1(4), 660–670 (2002)
16. Younis, O., Fahmy, S.: Distributed clustering in Ad-hoc sensor networks: A hybrid, energy-efficient approach. In: Proc. of the IEEE INFOCOM, IEEE Computer Society Press, Los Alamitos (2004)

A Multi-tier, Multimodal Wireless Sensor Network for Environmental Monitoring

Carlos Eduardo R. Lopes, Fernando D. Linhares,
Michele M. Santos, and Linnyer B. Ruiz

Universidade Federal de Minas Gerais (UFMG)
Belo Horizonte – MG – Brazil
{dlopes,linnyer}@cpdee.ufmg.br, {fernandoduli,mimes}@ufmg.br

Abstract. WSNs are distributed sensing tools with monitoring capabilities unavailable until now. Network elements (sensor nodes) are frequently pointed out as a new computer systems class due to its ubiquitous an analytical features. Wireless Sensor Networks have evolved quickly in recent years. Such evolution lead to specializations such as Wireless Visual Sensor Networks and Multi-tier, Multimodal Wireless Sensor Networks (M^2 WSN). The desing, modeling and implementation development of a WSN M^2 for environment monitoring is treated in this work. Simulations with such network shows that they present better usage of components and energy resources with little sacrifice to the application performance.

1 Introduction

Wireless Sensor Networks (WSNs) applications development traditionally are based on a single-tier architecture with homogeneous sensor nodes. One may expect however, a positive behavior from a WSN that makes use of heterogeneous elements organized into different groups or tiers. This work deals with such challenge: the design, modeling and implementation of a Multi-tier, Multimodal Wireless Sensor Network (M^2 WSN) for environmental monitoring of wild life in remote areas. The development of a M^2 WSN will act as proof of concepts for this WSN specialization.

In a WSN M^2, *multi-tier* relates to the way the network elements are organized: into hierarchical levels according to their functionalities and capabilities. By *multimodal* it is meant that different sensing modalities are employed to achieve a common goal [1]. For these networks, from the lower hierarchy tiers till the top ones, an increase on sensor node capabilities (computational power and communication range for example) is expected along with the complexity of the tasks to be performed. Hence, in network deployment constrained elements are densely distributed over the sensing area performing simple tasks, while more capable elements with sparse deployment execute more complex tasks.

The M^2 WSNs can present advantages over single tier, unimodal WSNs: lower monetary costs, higher coverage, functionality and reliability. It is not difficult to find a WSN that presents better performance than a M^2 WSN in one of the

J. Indulska et al. (Eds.): UIC 2007, LNCS 4611, pp. 589–598, 2007.

network requirements just mentioned. A WSN using simple and cheaper sensor nodes can present low monetary costs and high coverage but functionality is comprised since the nodes can note deal with more complex tasks such as image or audio processing. Network reliability can also be sacrificed due to the known WSNs energy constraints. A sensor network with high functionality, on the other hand, can be developed using high performance nodes but with a high monetary cost. This also compromises network coverage. As seen, optimizing only the network costs, coverage, functionality or reliability leads to a network where one or more of these requirements are forgotten [1]. By using heterogeneous sensor nodes to execute tasks with different needs, a M^2 WSN can promote a better balance among costs, coverage, functionality and reliability requirements.

Tsiatsis *et al.* [2] relates the M^2 WSNs to cache memories found in computer architectures. Cache are small, fast and expensive memories that use temporal and spatial locality properties to efficiently access main memory. A computer memory architecture based on cache appears to be as fast as cache memories and as big as the main memory. In an analogous way, a M^2 WSN presents energy consumption and network coverage similar to a homogeneous flat network using simple nodes, showing the high functionality and reliability common in flat networks employing high performance sensor nodes.

As a case study, the paper presents the design, modeling and implementation of a M^2 WSN for environmental monitoring of wild life in remote areas. The network employs two sensing modalities, passive infrared sensing and visual sensing (video cameras) and has its sensor nodes distributed over three distinct tiers. In orther to validate the M^2 WSN design, simulated evaluations are realized.

The document is organized in the following way. Section 2 presents a review concerning WSNs. Section 3 describes the M^2 WSN for environmental monitoring design and modeling, Section 4 details the network simulation. Results concerning simulations are present in Section 5 and Section 6 concludes the text.

2 Sensor Networks - Concepts and Characteristics

A Wireless Sensor Network (WSN) is a special kind of an ad-hoc network composed by hundreds, even thousands, of sensor nodes witch have computational and sensing capabilities, wireless communication and power resource autonomy. It is a distributed tool for sensing, processing and disseminating collected data from environment phenomena to one or more observers.

Wireless Sensor Networks are self-users, that is, they produce, process and disseminate their own information. The main services provided by a WSN are sensing, processing and dissemination. Its sensing quality is related to sensor calibration, environment interferences over sensing device and exposure. Processing quality depends on its processor, memory capacity and robustness of the algorithms used. Dissemination quality is characterized by latency, throughput/delay rate and lost messages.

Advances in wireless communications, integrated circuits and microelectronics technologies provided the development of several sensing devices and sensor node platforms [3,4]. Such advances also made possible the appearance of the Visual Sensor Networks (VSNs), that is, networks of visual sensors that are equipped with enough processing power to support image analysis functionality [5]. There are many situations where the use of a VSN is advantageous. For example, *environmental monitoring* where visual sensor nodes are used for the observation of wild animals behavior in their habitat with minimum human intervention and *Surveillance* where visual sensor nodes are used to detect, identify and alert about intruders in restricted or large areas such as airports, stadiums and factories.

The standard approach used to deploy a VSN application consists in choosing a convenient sensor modality, a convenient node platform and programming the motes to execute the tasks of the application. This approach leads to a flat homogeneous network. Tsiatsis *et al.* [2] claims that the use of just one node platform is not scalable enough to enclose all complexity and dynamic range of applications foreseen to the WSN technology, specially the multimedia ones.

Another challenge concerning VSNs relates to dissemination of the sensed data. Besides the great amount of gathered data, other dissemination constraints deserves attention as pointed out by Gürses and Akan [6]. An event-based or query-driven dissemination model should be used instead of the expensive continuous one. In-network aggregation should be avoided once simple aggregation functions such as mean, max and threshold do not fit multimedia data. Local inter-sensor communication, specially for aggregation purposes, are not suitable for WSN once it introduces extra costs related to data compression besides the energy spent exchanging this data. Finally, direct communication between any sensor and the network sink node using a low bandwidth, error prone channel should be avoided. Multi-hop communication over short distances using high bandwidth and low error rate channels adjust better to network's quality-of-service (QoS) requirements.

3 A M^2 WSN for Environment Monitoring

This section presents the design and modeling of a M^2 WSN for environmental monitoring of wild life employing visual tracking. The sensor network is self-organized into three tiers of distinct sensor nodes. The first one interacts preferably with the second, the second interact preferably with the third obeying a scalable hierarchy (interaction that breaks such hierarchy are allowed but uncommon). Two sensor modalities are used to accomplish the sensing service, passive infrared and visual sensing. Figure 1 shows a schematical representation of the proposed M^2 WSN architecture.

During a tracking application, network elements follows the movement of objects over the sensing field like, for example, wild animals in jungles and intruders in restrict areas. Interesting events for this application however, occurs very infrequently leading to long periods of inactivity. In such scenario, it is expected that sensor nodes remain idle most of the time and in the presence of an interest event they work without any restrictions.

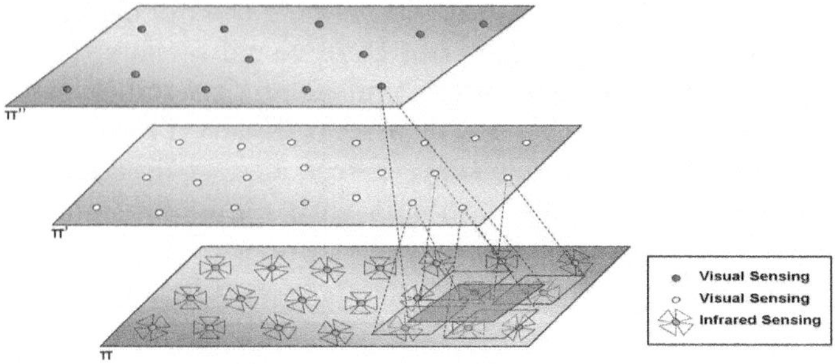

Fig. 1. Schematic representation of the proposed M^2 WSN to environmental monitoring. The sensor network is composed by three tiers of distinct sensor nodes and employs two sensor modalities, infrared sensing and visual sensing.

Energy resources conservation and sensing quality are conflicting requirements for most tracking sensor networks, specially when tracking employs visual sensor nodes. Without energy restrictions, a sensing field could be completely monitored just turning on all the network cameras. Due to the inherently power constraints over WSNs, sensing quality becomes inversely proportional to the network lifetime if no management strategies are adopted. With moving targets, full coverage is not necessary since a network with small uncovered areas is still capable to detect the presence of intruders with little delay. Traditional sensors like magnetometers and accelerometers, with low energy costs, might be used in target detection and later activation of visual sensors.

3.1 Network Organization

Splinting an application into several tasks and posterior distribution of this tasks within the network tiers represents two of the most important design choices in a WSN ^{2} application design. A typical tracking application presents three key tasks: *i)* object detection, *ii)* object identification and *iii)* target tracking. These tasks are related, one cannot start until its predecessor is finished. An object can only be identified when it has been detected, for example.

The M^2 WSN for environmental monitoring is organized into three tiers of sensor nodes. The first one (plane Π on Figure 1) makes use of sensor nodes equipped with passive infrared sensors (PIR) capable of detecting objects over the sensing field that emit heat (animals, human beings). PIR sensors presents low power consumption, low costs and size, low processing requirements and reliable results [7]. The PIR nodes continuously sense the environment looking for rough variations on collected radiation (a strong indication to the presence of intruders). Since these sensors can not identify detected objects, they disseminate activation messages their visual sensor neighbors.

The second tier (plane Π' on Figure 1) is equipped with smart visual nodes that can identify objects under its field of view. This process allows the sensor node to determine if the detected object attempts application's need and if its tracking is necessary. The M^2 WSN for environmental monitoring identify objects by their predominant color.

To the third tier (plane Π' on Figure 1) is left the task of tracking targets as they move through the environment. The set of sensor nodes that composes this tier must compute target's current position and path. Tracking responsibility hand-off between the elements of the tier (an intra-node interaction) can also be used but, in the context of this work, this approach is not necessary since the lower tiers keep alerting the higher ones. Further details about network implementation are discussed in Section 4.

3.2 Network Operation

Efficiently network resource usage demands that expensive elements to be activated only during opportunist moments. So the developed W^2 WSN presents a event-driven behavior concerning visual sensing. The sensor nodes behavior for each tier was modeled as states and transitions were due to specific events.

The first tier has three operational states as seen in the state transition diagram shown in Figure 2(a). During ***State 1*** the sensor node stays monitoring the environment looking after rough variations, beyond a pre-established value, in the observed infrared radiation levels. A sudden change characterizes the presence of a possible target and causes the transition to ***State 2***. In this state the sensor nodes create a wake up message to alert second tier nodes about intruders in the neighborhood. The broadcast of this message to the network leads to ***State 3***. Sensor node ***State 3*** is characterized by the absence of any activity. This period is necessary since the object may remain in the sensing range of the node even after its detection causing a network flood. At the end of this interval the node returns to ***State 1***.

Diagram from Figure 2(b) presents the four operational states and possible transitions for the sensor nodes of the second tier. After network boot up, visual nodes turn off all their components except for the transceiver witch remains active waiting for wake up messages from infrared nodes (diagram ***State 1***). Upon the receive of a wake up message, the node starts operating under ***State 2***, where the visual sensor is activated and, during a predefined time interval the camera capture images from the environment searching for moving objects. This interval has the same duration of the period where infrared nodes are idle. If a moving object is seen within ***State 2***, a transition to ***State 3*** takes place otherwise, transition is back to ***State 1***. On ***State 3*** the object is identified by its predominant color. A set of digital image processing techniques are used to this end. Being an interest target the operational cycle advances to ***State 4*** where the sensor node disseminates another wake up message, but now targeting a third layer node. Being an invalid target the cycle returns the first state.

The third tier behavior is similar to the one just presented. The only difference is that there is no need to broadcasts wake up messages since there are no higher tiers. Then these sensor nodes have just three operational states. In ***State 1*** the sensor nodes radio remains waiting for a wake up message from the second tier with other devices powered off. A transition to ***State 2*** occurs when such

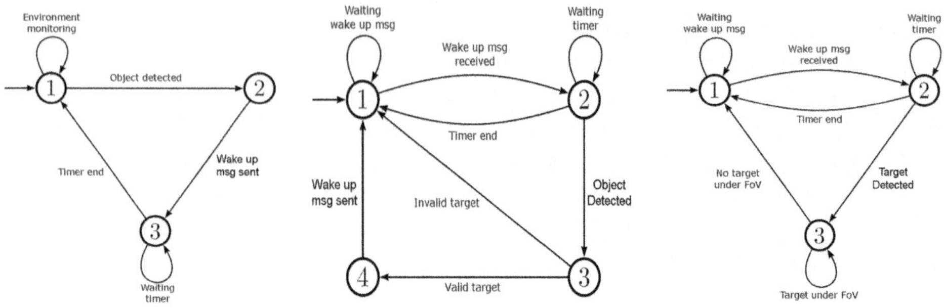

(a) First Tier (b) Second Tier (c) Third Tier

Fig. 2. State transition diagram showing the operational cycles from the first and second tiers of an environmental monitoring application

message arrives activating the visual sensor. Node permanence in ***State 2*** is controlled by a timer during witch the visual sensor monitors the environment. At timer end, if no target has been seen, the node returns to ***State 1*** otherwise it goes to ***State 3*** where target tracking takes place. The visual node keeps tracking the target until it leaves camera's FoV. Figure 2(c) shows the transition state diagram that summarizes the behavior just described.

An important detail should be mentioned about ***State 2*** in second and third tiers. If a wake up message is received within the node sensing interval, the interval is restarted.

3.3 Network Communication

The presence of smart visual sensor capable of extracting high level information from collected data propitiates a reduction on the amount of data disseminated thought the network. Hengstler and Aghajan [8] claims that as the network level of intelligence increases, bandwidth requirements on the underlying data transmission network decrease accordingly. The multi-tier nature of the M^2 WSN, on the other side, implies on extra exchange of control and wake up messages.

In order to alert the neighborhood about intruders on the monitoring field PIR sensor nodes from the first tier disseminate broadcast wake up messages to the network elements of the second tier. To avoid that visual nodes away from the events get unnecessarily wakened, the transmission power of the PIR nodes is adjusted to reach only surrounding elements (with greater interest in the event). There are no restriction to the number of second tier neighbors to be awaken, only the distance restriction is considered.

In a similar way, smart visual nodes from the second tier send wake up messages to third tier elements. In such case however, stronger then the idea of neighborhood is the concept of overlapping fields of view. The development of the M^2 WSN assumed that all visual sensor nodes had their cameras calibrated. Thus, during network boot up, elements from the third tier disseminate (in broadcast) hierarchy messages with the coordinates of their FoV (relative to the sensing field) besides its own network identifiers. With this information second tier nodes check if a FoV overlapping has occurred and in a positive case they set that node as their third tier covering node.

The above data dissemination schemes manage great part of the network communication. The GEAR routing protocol is used in order to disseminate tracking information (mainly made by the third and in smaller scale by the second tier). This protocol is able to handle the routing service since the information disseminated consists basically of text data describing the target path and current position.

4 Experimental Evaluation

In this work, simulations are used in a comparative analysis between the M^2 WSN described on Section 3 and two other approaches: a Multi-tier Visual Sensor Network composed by heterogeneous sensors and a Single-tier Visual Sensor Network. Simulations were conducted using the NS-2 [9] simulation software. Originally, NS-2 does not provide support to WSNs simulation. To overcome this limitation, the MannaSim Framework [10] is used together with NS-2. MannaSim Framework is a set of classes that extends NS-2 introducing new modules that make easier WSNs design, development and analysis.

In order to simulate all three networks and explore the hardware heterogeneity faced by M^2 WSNs designers, three sensor node profiles were considered. MicaZ Mote [11] equipped with four PIR sensors providing the node with a 360° sensing range. MicaZ Mote equipped with the CMUcam2 visual system [12] providing the node with a overheard view of the monitoring area. And the Stargate [11] high performance platform equipped with a webcam. Concerning the sensor nodes communications, a 250 Kbps bandwidth and a 20 m transmission range was adopted for the MicaZ Motes. Stargate was configured with a 11 Mbps bandwidth and 40 m transmission range. Table 1 lists power dissipation for common operations executed during the simulation. The energy budget of the profiles MicaZ/PIR, MicaZ/CMUcam2 and Stargate/WebCam was set to 2.000, 2.000 and 4.000 joules, respectively.

M^2 WSN simulation employed the MicaZ/PIR profile in object detection tier, MicaZ/CMUcam2 profile in object identification tier and the Stargate/Webcam profile in target tracking tier. The behavior of these nodes is the one described in Sections 3.1 and 3.2: continuous infrared sensing, reactive visual sensing and

Table 1. Node profiles power dissipation (in watts) for common operations executed during during simulations

	trans.	**recep.**	**idle**	**proc.**	**sens.**	**wake up**
MicaZ/PIR	0.042	0.059	0,001	0.024	0.015	–
MicaZ/CMUcam2	0.042	0.059	0.001	0.099	1.165	–
Stargate/Webcam	1.425	0.925	0.045	1.374	1.653	1.348

state based modeling. Sensor nodes were uniformly distributed over a square area in groups composed by one MicaZ/PIR sensor, four MicaZ/CMUcam2 nodes and one Stargate/Webcam node. These groups were organized in a 2×2 grid covering a 20×20 m^2 area. Second tier sensing interval upon the receive of a wake up message was set to 5 s.

Multi-tier VSN is characterized by heterogeneous sensor nodes organized in two tiers. This network was inspired on SensEye as described by Kulkarni *et al.* [1]. Sensor nodes of the MicaZ/CMUcam2 profile were used for target detection and identification. This tier presented a continuous sensing behavior and keeping the nodes awake all time was not practical. The strategy taken was the usage of duty cycle (periodically CMUcam2s are activated, execute their tasks and return to an idle state). Stargate/Webcam nodes were used in the tracking tier. Such elements remain waiting for a wake up message to activate their visual sensors. Network topology consisted of groups of sensor nodes uniformly distributed over a square area. Each group had four MicaZ/CMUcam2 and one Stargate/Webcam nodes forming a 2×2 grid that covers a 20×20 m^2 area. The duty cycle for first tier elements was set to 60 s (5 s sensing time and 55 s idle time). Stargate/Webcam nodes were configured with a 5 s sensing tolerance upon the receive of a wake up message.

Sing-tier VSN represented an homogeneous network of high performance nodes equipped with visual sensors. Stargate/Webcam sensor nodes were considered during simulations. The behavior presented by such nodes was according to a duty cycle regimen executing all the application tasks. Sensor nodes were uniformly distributed in a square area. The duty cycle was set to 61.3 s (1.3 s for visual sensor activation time as pointed out by Margi *et al.* [13], 5 s of sensing time and 55 s of idle time). If a wake up message was received during the idle time, the visual sensor was activated and kept monitoring the environment while there was a target under its FoV or until its sensing time have ended.

Simulated targets described a series of little uniform linear displacements with a constant speed equals to 2.5 m/s. These objects presented also uniform color distribution and their movement occurred in the bidimensional plane. All experiments were limited to 3000 seconds simulation time due to hardware restrictions. Each scenario was simulated 33 times and the results presented in Section 5 correspond to an average mean of these simulations and have a confidence interval of 95%.

5 Experimental Results

Besides putting side-by-side the performance of three sensor networks according to energy expenses, visual sensors effective usage and first time seen delay, experimental evaluation intended to compare network scalability. Four different area sizes were considered: 100×100, 120×120, 140×140 e 160×160 m^2.

Figure3(a) presents the average energy consumption of the WSNs according to the size of monitored area. Energy resources expenses observed for the M^2 WSN were, at least, 2.2 times smaller than the expenses of the Multi-tier VSN

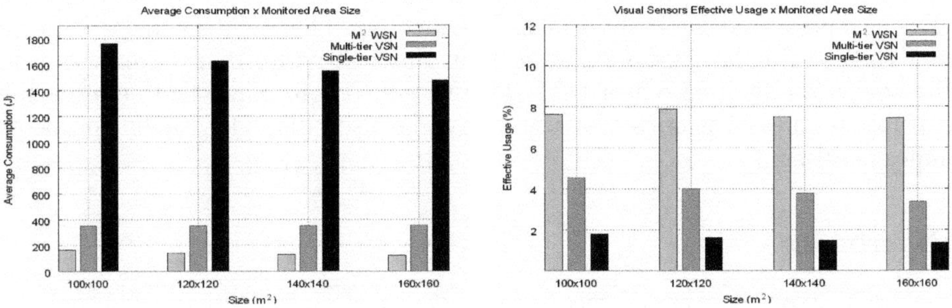

(a) Mean Energy Expenses (b) Camera Effective Usage

Fig. 3. Simulation results for the considered WSNs over different sized monitoring areas

and, at least, 11 times smaller than the expenses faced by the Single-tier VSN. This significant difference shows that the event-based behavior is superior to the duty cycle one whenever an environmental monitoring application using visual tracking is considered. Concerning network scalability, as the monitored area grows energy resources usage decreased 27% for the M^2 WSN and 16% for the Single-tier VSN.

The effective usage rate performance for the three simulated networks is shown on Figure 3(b). The M^2 WSN approach was the most scalable maintaining the visual sensors usage rate close to 7.5% throught all monitoring areas. M^2 WSN performance was superior to all other networks, specially the Single-tier VSN (4.94 times superior on average). Both the Multi-tier and Single-tier VSNs faced a performance drop of 25% with the growing of the monitoring area.

The interval until a target was seen for the first time by a tracking node was also considered. The Single-tier VSN presented the smallest average delay (17 s). The M^2 WSN faced a 25 s average delay but, it is worth ti say that this network had to use two other sensor tiers before. Multi-tier VSN failed this analysis presenting delays greater than 100 seconds. The usage of duty cycle and event-based operations was the main reason for such a significant delay.

6 Conclusion

This work presented the design, modeling and implementation of a M^2 WSN for environmental monitoring. The network consisted of three tiers of distinct sensor nodes in two sensing modalities (infrared and visual sensing). PIR nodes used a continuous sensing while visual nodes presented event-based operation. M^2 WSN sensor nodes behavior was modeled into states and network events characterized transitions between them.

A comparative simulation was realized with the M^2 WSN and two other approaches, a Multi-tier VSN and a Single-tier VSN. Experimental results have shown that the M^2 WSN energy expenses were at least 2.2 and 11 times smaller than the Multi-tier VSN and a Single-tier VSN. The network described in this work also presented the best visual sensor effective. The architecture faced target first time seen delay just 8 s greater than the best performance even requiring the activation of three sensor tiers. These results confirms that M^2 approach is superior to the other ones that use just one sensing modality or homogeneous nodes network.

References

1. Kulkarni, P., Ganesan, D., Shenoy, P., Lu, Q.: Senseye: A multi–tier camera sensor network. In: Proceedings of the ACM Multimedia, Singapore, pp. 229–238. ACM Press, New York (2005)
2. Tsiatsis, V., Kumar, R., Srivastava, M.B.: Computation hierarchy for in-network processing. ACM Mobile Networks and Applications 10, 505–518 (2005)
3. Lymberopoulos, D., Savvides, A.: Xyz: a motion-enabled, power aware sensor node platform for distributed sensor network applications. In: The 4th International Symposium on Information Processing in Sensor Networks, California (2005)
4. Dutta, P., Grimmer, M., Arora, A., Bibyk, S., Culler, D.: Design of a wireless sensor network platform for detecting rare, random, and ephemeral events. In: Proceedings of the 4th international symposium on Information processing in sensor networks, Los Angeles, California (2005)
5. Obraczka, K., Manduchi, R., Garcia–Luna–Aveces, J.: Managing the information flow in visual sensor networks. In: 5th International Symposium Wireless Personal Multimedia Communicationson, vol. 3, pp. 1177–1181 (2002)
6. Gürses, E., Akan, Ö.: Multimedia communication in wireless sensor networks. Annals of Telecommunications 60, 799–827 (2005)
7. de Vlaam, S.: Object tracking in a multi sensor network. Master's thesis, Computer Engineering, Parallel and Distibuted Systems, Delft University of Technology, Delft, The Netherlands (2004)
8. Hengstler, S., Aghajan, H.: A smart camera mote architecture for distributed intelligent surveillance. In: ACM Workshop on Distributed Smart Cameras, ACM Press, New York (2006)
9. Vint, P.: The network simulator (ns–2) (Acessed: Outubro de 2006) Available on the WWW: `http://nsnam.isi.edu/nsnam/`
10. Lopes, C.E.R., e Melo, J.C., de Assunção, H.P., Aguiar, F.S., Braga, T.R.M., Ruiz, L.B., Loureiro, A.A., Nogueira, J.M.S.: Mannasim: Simulando redes sensores sem fio. In: Salão de Ferramentas of XXIV Simpósio Brasileiro de Redes de Computadores (SBRC2006), Curitiba, Brazil (2006)
11. Crossbow, T.: Wireless sensor networks (Acessed: Setembro de 2005) Available on the WWW: `http://www.xbow.com`
12. Rowe, A., Rosemberg, C., Nourbakhsh, I.: A second generation low cost embedded color vision system. In: Embedded Computer Vision Workshop (CVPR), San Diego, USA (2005)
13. Margi, C.B., Manduchi, R., Obraczka, K.: Energy consumption tradeoffs in visual sensor netowrks. In: XXIV Simpósio Brasileiro de Redes de Computadores (SBRC2006), Curitiba, Brazil (2006)

Wireless Sensor Networks, Making a Difference Tomorrow

Mohamed Khalil Watfa

Computer Science Department, American University of Beirut, Lebanon, 1107-2020
Mohamed.Watfa@aub.edu.lb
http://www.cs.aub.edu.lb/mw11

Abstract. Embedding smart sensors in humans has been a research challenge due to the limitations imposed by these sensors from computational capabilities to limited power. In this paper, a practical WSN application that will enable blind people to see what their neighboring partners can see is proposed. The challenge is that the actual mapping between the input images to brain pattern is too complex and not well understood. We also study the connectivity problem in 3D/2D wireless sensor networks and propose distributed efficient algorithms to accomplish the required connectivity of the system. A novel connectivity algorithm *CDCA* to connect disconnected parts of a network using cooperative diversity is introduced. Through simulations, the connectivity gains and energy savings provided by this novel form of cooperative diversity in WSNs are analyzed.

1 Introduction and Related Work

Two major causes of blindness, age-related macular degeneration (AMD) and retinitis pigmentosa (RP), damage the photoreceptor cells in the light-sensitive membrane in the eye (retina) but leave the nerve connections to the brain intact. Patients eventually lose their vision. Scientists funded by the U.S. Department of Energy (DOE) Biological and Environmental Research (BER) program are developing a prototype artificial retina that could help provide a solution for this growing challenge. Ultimately, the goal is to restore useful vision for patients blinded by AMD and RP. This work builds upon a first-generation device containing a 16-electrode array on a miniature disc that can be implanted in the back of the eye to replace a damaged retina. After years of research and laboratory prototypes, artificial vision is being tested in humans for the first time. Artificial vision researchers take inspiration for another device, the cochlear implant, which has successfully restored hearing to thousands of deaf people. But the human vision system is far more complicated that the hearing system. The eye perceives millions of distinct points of light. Light entering through the pupil, is converted to electrical signals anatomical rods and cons, the light sensitive cells in the retina. Those electrical pulses are carried through the optic nerve to the brain, where they yield images to the world.

In this paper, we consider another approach to artificial eye vision using wireless sensor networks. To the best of our knowledge, our proposed idea of using wireless sensor networks for improving sight has never been approached yet. Because the

J. Indulska et al. (Eds.): UIC 2007, LNCS 4611, pp. 599–609, 2007.

sensor devices are placed in the human body, the research problems differ from traditional wireless sensor networks. Most work concerning artificial vision has included a digital camera transmitting wireless data to a micro-chip in the eye [1]. The challenge is that the actual mapping between the input images to brain pattern is too complex and not well understood. Since the sensors are irreplaceable and incase of emergency, we need to report to the central computer, we require that our network to be connected at all time if some sensor nodes were deployed on near by objects to form a connected network. Some of the health applications for sensor networks are providing interfaces for the disabled; integrated patient monitoring; diagnostics; drug administration in hospitals; monitoring the movements and internal processes of insects or other small animals; monitoring of human physiological data; and tracking and monitoring doctors and patients inside a hospital [2]. As technology advances, smart sensor nodes and actuators can be buried in appliances, such as vacuum cleaners, micro-wave ovens, refrigerators, and VCRs [3]. They allow end users to manage home devices locally and remotely more easily. Although the technology of biomedical sensors is relatively new, a number of interesting applications are already out there. A glucose level monitor is one application that had emerged recently. Another application is cancer detectors. Wireless sensors have also been proposed for use as implanted general health monitors. Swallowing a pill containing smart sensors enables wireless transmission of information about contractions of intestinal muscles or intestinal acidity that will help doctors diagnose the disease.

We also provide algorithms for achieving connectivity of a system in a three dimensional space. In wireless networks, signal fading arising from multipath propagation is a particularly severe channel impairment that can be mitigated through the use of diversity [5-8]. Space, or multi-antenna, diversity techniques are particularly attractive as they can be readily combined with other forms of diversity, *e.g.*, time and frequency diversity, and still offer dramatic performance gains when other forms of diversity are unavailable. In contrast to the more conventional forms of space diversity with physical arrays, our work examines the problem of creating and exploiting space diversity using a collection of distributed sensor nodes cooperating in order to achieve maximum connectivity with minimum energy consumption. The work in [4] introduces coverage configuration protocol (CCP) that can dynamically configure the network to provide different coverage degrees requested by applications. Our connectivity technique is based on some other interested works in the field of cooperative diversity. Cooperative diversity utilizes intermediate transmitters as repeaters to extend the range of transmission of a source. The advantage of cooperation is the accumulation of power from all relays, which is a source of diversity, and also of signal to noise ratio improvement. In [9] the authors understand cooperative transmission in the sense that several sensor nodes transmit symbols simultaneously to achieve a power gain. The broadcast-coverage of a system using cooperative transmission is analyzed. Their results simplify the modeling and leads to closed-form solutions and formulations.

The rest of the paper is organized as follows. In section 2, we propose the new approach to artificial eye vision using wireless sensor networks and the challenges that will arise. In section 3, we provide algorithms for achieving connectivity of the sensor network when the initial deployment resulted in a disconnected network. Simulation results that validate out proposed algorithms are presented in section 4. The paper is concluded in section 5.

2 Novel Application

Before we present our approach, let us identify some of the challenges of using wireless sensor networks for this particular kind of application:

1- *Limited Power and Computation*: Small physical size of the sensor and also the absence of wires make them have very limited power supply and thus limited computational capabilities.
2- *Shape, Size and Material*: Since the sensors will be implanted inside the human body, restrictions are made on the shape, size and the material used for the sensors.
3- *Energy Constraints*: Once a sensor is implanted in the human body, it is required to operate for years without interruption.
4- *Distributed Network*: A failure of one node should not affect the entire network of sensors.
5- *Fault tolerance*: Device redundancy and consequently information redundancy can be utilized to ensure a level of fault tolerance in individual sensors.
6- *Dynamic sensor scheduling*: Dynamic reaction to network conditions and the optimization of network performance through sensor scheduling.
7- *Moral issues*: People suffering from the disease under experiment are likely to volunteer to advance science in this area. Safe tests that are harmless to patients should be the only kind of tests that are performed.

In its simplest form, vision is produced when light entering the eye is turned into electrical signals that are carried by the optic nerve to the brains visual cortex. When the circuit is broken, blindness results. The idea is to replace the broken circuit with electronics. The goal of this proposed approach is to allow people with no vision or with low vision to see what their neighboring partners can see. Unlike some other artificial vision proposals, this approach is applicable to virtually all causes of blindness. Our device may also help some legally blind low vision patients because the cortex of sighted people responds to stimulation similarly to the cortex of blind people. A lot of work has been done to try to imitate the functionality of the human eye and artificial vision techniques have been proposed. ***The challenge is that the***

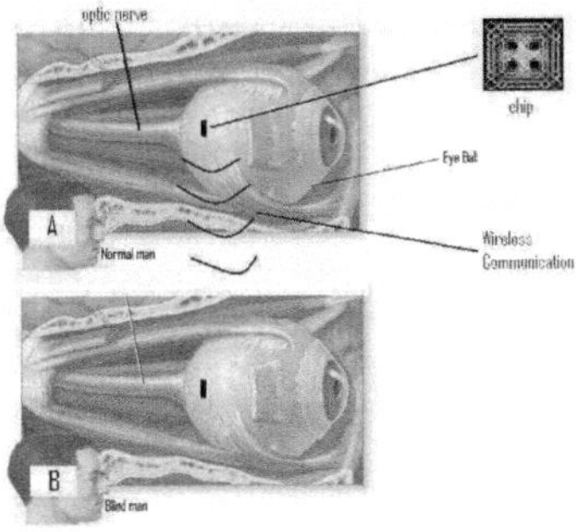

Fig. 1. The proposed approach for eye vision

actual mapping between the input images to brain pattern is too complex and not well understood. In our case, we do not need to understand that complex mapping pattern since human brains function in a similar way and the input to one brain (sent from another human with normal vision) could well be analyzed in the same way as if it was originated from the blind man's brain.

The sensor implants are inside both the eye of the blind man's eye and a normal man's eye (Fig 1.).Vision is established using the following steps:

A. Light entering through the pupil, is converted to electrical signals. Those electrical pulses are converted to data and are stored in the retinal implant of the normal eye.
B. The data is then transmitted using the wireless transceiver to the blind mans eye.
C. The signal travels along a tiny wire to the retinal implant.
D. The back side of the retina is stimulated electrically by the sensors on the chip.
E. These electrical signals are converted to chemical signals by tissue structures and the response is carried via the optic nerve to the brain.

The unique difference between our approach and any other is that by using the data from one man's eye we do not need to understand the complex mapping of an image from the retina to the brain via the optic nerve. This application might be very useful in scenarios where the blind person and his partner are focusing their attention on a static phenomenon (e.g. watching a movie, attending a lecture...).

3 Connectivity Algorithms in WSNs

In some other envisioned scenarios where a sensor network would be deployed on near by objects and will fuse the data and send them to the sensor node on the blind man's eye we provide a greedy solution to establish a connected network between the sensor nodes and a given sink. In a typical WSN deployment, it is usually assumed that the entire sensor network is connected. This may not always be true, especially when sensors have limited communication range, and are distributed randomly. The main problem is that, while individual sensors over a large area can be queried directly the sensors can only respond and hence, be detected by the user through the network. In case of an emergency the bio sensors need to report to a central computer. To do that the network need to be connected at all time.

3.1 Problem Formulation

Consider a sensor network comprising of n sensors: S_1, S_2....S_n each with a sensing radius R_s and communication radius R_c respectively. Let A_{is} and A_{ic} be the sensing and communication regions of sensor S_i respectively. Let $\overline{C} = \bigcup_{i=1}^{i=m} A_{is}$ and $\overline{\overline{C}} = \bigcup_{i=1}^{i=m} A_{ic}$ be the sensing space and communication space of a set of sensor nodes $C = \{S_1, S_2, ...S_m\}$ respectively.

Definition 1: A set of sensors $C_i = \{S_{a1}, S_{a2}, \ldots S_{am}\}$ is said to **cover** the region R if and only if $R \subseteq \overline{C_i}$.

Definition 2: A set of sensors $C_i = \{S_{a1}, S_{a2}, \ldots S_{am}\}$ is **connected** if $\forall$ a, b $\in \overline{\overline{C_i}}$, $\exists$ a continuous function f : [0,1] → $\overline{\overline{C_i}}$ such that : $f(0) = a$, $f(1) = b$, $a \leq t \leq b, f(t) \in \overline{\overline{C_i}}$ C_i is **connected** if $\forall S_a, S_b \in C_i$ $\Leftrightarrow \exists$ $a\ path\ 'P'\ from\ S_a\ to\ S_b$.

So the connectivity problem is simply checking if a path exists between any two nodes in the network leading to the whole network being connected.

3.2 Simple Connectivity Algorithm (*SCA*)

When we don't have complete coverage, we provide an algorithm that will always form a connected path between the origin sensor (e.g. eye sensor) and the sink (e.g. emergency center). This can be established if there is at least one path between the source and the destination i.e. the network is connected. However if the network is disconnected then we provide in the next section a unique approach to form a connected network from a disconnected one using cooperation between the sensor nodes. We designed a greedy algorithm *SCA* to select a Connected Sensor Set CSS of optimal size. In short, the greedy algorithm works by selecting, at each stage, a communication path of sensors that connects an already selected sensor to the origin sensor S_0. The selected path is then added to the already selected sensors at that stage. We classify the messages sent into 2 types:

1. Downstream messages originated from the sink.
2. Upstream messages originated from the origin.

The algorithm terminates when the selected set of sensors is connected to the designated sink S_{sink} i.e. when the upstream path meets the downstream path. A subset of the network of sensors between them will be selected to form a connected path. Let us assume that CSS_0 is the set of sensors already selected for inclusion in the Connected Sensor Set of S_0. Initially, CSS_0 contains only S_0 (origin sensor). At each stage, the greedy algorithm selects a sensor S_1 from the set of neighbors who has a downstream path to the sink otherwise just form an upstream path to the sink. CSS_0 is updated to $CSS_0 = CSS_0 \cup CSS_1$. Thus, at any stage of the algorithm, the communication graph induced by CSS_0 is connected. The algorithm terminates when S_{sink} is a subset of CSS_0.The computational complexity of the algorithm developed in this section is O(N) where $N = \left(\max_{i=1}^{n} |N(i)| \right)$ is the maximum number of nodes in the neighbor set of any sensor in the network.

3.3 Cooperative Diversity Connectivity Algorithm (*CDCA*)

A problem with *SCA* is that the loss of connectivity of the deployed sensor nodes in the path between the source sensor node and the destination node may lead to partitioning the network. This scenario might happen when the density of deployed sensor nodes is not large enough or due to some environmental conditions leading to higher noise in the channel and thus preventing two neighboring nodes from communicating with each other. Also, a disconnected network might be formed after the some sensor nodes have ran out of energy. The communication range of the nodes is limited and therefore leading to isolated partitions in the network as depicted in Fig 2. Initially, we had one connected network (one big cluster) but the failure of two nodes F1 and F2 lead to dividing the network into four small clusters and preventing the source from establishing a connected path to the destination.

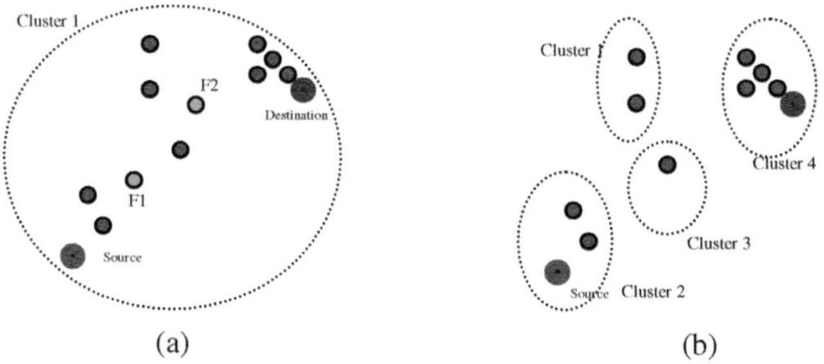

Fig. 2. (a) A connected sensor network with one cluster. (b) A disconnected network with four clusters.

Cooperative transmission is suggested where transmission redundancy is used. A group of nodes can combine their transmission powers and thus achieve a virtual wider range of communication with their neighbors. The idea is that the nodes working as a group can transmit identical signals synchronously to superimpose the emitted waves on the physical medium. The destination receives a sum of waves and thus a total higher power. Cooperative diversity is a recent breakthrough at the physical layer, which exploits the broadcast nature of the wireless channel to emulate a Multi Input Single Output system. Nodes participating in a cooperative diversity scheme, broadcast the same packet simultaneously. By providing the receiver with multiple replicas of the same signal, one can achieve the same benefits of an antenna system mounted on a single node. The research at the physical layer has proved the significant potential of cooperative diversity. To the best of out knowledge, the techniques introduced in this paper to establish connectivity in a WSN have never been addressed yet.

A technique is proposed in which the network is initially classified into different connected clusters and then cooperative diversity techniques are used to connect neighboring clusters together. Within a cluster, we can use SCA since the nodes within a cluster are connected so we can establish a connected path between any two. To divide the network into clusters of connected nodes, each node will exchange HELLO packets with its neighbors in a distributed fashion. Each HELLO packet will contain an Identification of the sender node and a cluster number. Each receiving node will set their cluster number to the same cluster number as its neighbors until no more updates are needed i.e. $\forall S_i \in N(S_j), CN(S_i) = CN(S_j)$ where $N(S_j)$ is the set of neighboring sensor nodes within the communication range of S_j and $CN(S_i)$ is the cluster number for which S_i belongs to. An initiator (source) starts a transmission session to a destination. If the destination is within the same cluster then we use a simple multi-hop communication strategy to connect to the destination. However, if the network is not connected i.e. the destination belongs to a different cluster then the nodes who hear the packet within the same cluster decode and retransmit. The retransmissions are done simultaneously, even though they may not be synchronized. The retransmissions continue until every node who can hear the others retransmits once. Due to simultaneous transmissions, the reception power is enhanced, and packets can reach farther distances. The nodes decode and retransmit if and only if their received signal-to-noise ratio (SNR) exceeds a certain threshold η. The network performance crucially depends on the threshold. One would like to make it as low as possible to maximize the number of nodes who participate in transmission. On the other hand, a low threshold means decreased communication rate, or higher probability of error. Inherently, there exists a trade-off between the transmission rate and the number of participants in each transmission. Let $P_{t,i}$ be the transmission power of a sensor node S_i, $P_{r,i}$ be the receiving power of a sensor node S_i, $d_{i,j}$ be the Euclidean distance between two sensor nodes S_i and S_j and η be SNR threshold.

Suppose a source S_0 initiates the transmission. Every node S_i will check if $P_{r,i} = \frac{P_{t,0}}{d_{i,0}^{\;2}} > \eta$. If that is true, it will decode and retransmit the same packet right after reception. The nth node will hear the transmission with power $P_{r,n} = \sum_{i=1}^{n} \frac{P_{t,0}}{d_{i,n}^{\;2}}$.

We assumed squared distance path attenuation, but our results could easily be generalized to any path loss model. The noise is assumed to be of unit power. We also assume every node knows its received SNR and if the SNR is high enough, it will decode the packet without any errors.

The performance of the connectivity algorithm over time will also be studied through simulations to determine the benefits of using our algorithm over traditional flooding or simply making all the sensor nodes send the message using cooperative diversity techniques. This is done by assuming that each sensor node has a limited energy supply of 300 Joules and is deactivated when the available energy is used up. The performance is evaluated in terms of *connectivity lifetime.* The *connectivity lifetime* is the continuous operational time of the system before the connectivity drops below a specified threshold.

4 Simulation Results and Analysis

The theoretical developments in section 3 are validated through numerical examples in this section. By combining the transmitting power with neighboring nodes, nodes can increase their radio range and thus increase the connectivity of the network. In addition to that, our connectivity algorithm uses SCA to achieve connectivity between nodes belonging to the same cluster.

Sensor nodes are uniformly deployed over a 2D region of size 1000 units by 1000 units (or a 3D region of size 1000x1000x1000). The communication radius of each sensor node is 20 meters. We compare between four different connectivity strategies: Simple flooding, *SCA*, *CDCA* and Cooperative Communication where each node transmits to its 1-hop neighbors and each neighbor will retransmit along with the initiator until the destination is reached. When nodes use the cooperative transmission, each node will repeat a received message several times. It will do this together with all other nodes who at the same time received the same message. The number of times a sensor node resends the message is a simulation parameter and we vary it from 1, 2 or n where n is the maximum number of times needed to rebroadcast the message until the destination is reached. We conducted a series of experimental simulations to analyze and validate some of our results.

In the first experiment, we are concerned about the connectivity level achieved using different algorithms under different random deployment scenarios. A number of trials were conducted and the resulting connectivity average was calculated. Fig. 3a and Fig. 3b show, as we vary the number of sensor nodes deployed from 100 to 1000, the resulting connectivity measure for six connectivity algorithms: Flooding, *SCA*, *CDCA*, CC1, CC2, CCn where CC1, CC2 and CCn are when each sensor node cooperatively resends the message simultaneously along with its neighbors one time, two times and n times (until the destination is reached). The best results are achieved by the CCn. This behavior is as expected as CCn forces each sensor node to retransmit the message multiple times until the destination is reached. This behavior will however lead to a great increase in the energy usage as will be depicted in the next experiment. As for *CDCA*, it outperforms all the other connectivity algorithms as it maximizes the connectivity of the nodes with the destination while minimizing the energy consumption over time (or multiple queries). In Fig. 3b, the advantages that *CDCA* can contribute are highlighted as it increases the connectivity gain in sparse settings. When approximately 700 nodes are present using simple flooding (or *SCA*), the connectivity measure is 0.5 i.e. only 50% of the nodes are connected to the sink; However, using SDCA, the connectivity measure is 0.83 which means 33% more nodes are connected to the sink.

The performance of the system over time was also studied to determine the benefits of using a reduced cover. This is done by assuming that each sensor node has a limited energy supply of 300 Joules and is deactivated when the available energy is used up. The performance is evaluated in terms of energy usage or *connectivity lifetime.* Fig. 4 show the overall connectivity obtained over time as the WSN processes a series of queries. An initial deployment of 1000 sensor nodes is simulated. It can be seen that the overall connectivity drops over time as the available energy is used in processing the queries and establishing a connection to the sink. Using *CDCA*, it is seen that the resultant connectivity over time is significantly better that all the others since it maximizes the connectivity while minimizing the energy usage. When the system is all connected the connectivity using SCA or simple flooding will be better but as soon as the network would be portioned then some nodes away from the destination will lose connectivity and the overall connectivity measure will drop significantly. CDCA performs better since each node in the network uses multi-hop connectivity *SCA* when possible and when there is no other choice it will use cooperative diversity to establish a connection to neighboring nodes resulting in more efficient communications and less energy expenditure per query. This improvement in the connectivity lifetime comes at a cost. *CDCA* requires the communication between a node and its neighbors and as a result, a portion of energy is used up during the initialization stage of the network which justifies *SCA* performing better at starting stages but over time when the nodes start wasting their energy and deactivating the resulting network will be disconnected and all the nodes away from the sink won't be able to reply to a query resulting in a big drop in the connectivity measure using *SCA* (or flooding). Using Multi-Level cooperative communication where each node sends a message and together with its neighbors sends it again and so on until the destination is reached has the worst connectivity lifetime since a lot of energy is wasted due to unnecessary communications.

In our previous work [10 and 11], the coverage problems in both 2D and 3D regions were rigorously analyzed. In this experiment (Fig. 4b), we analyze the minimum number of nodes needed to guarantee connectivity. The maximum line connectivity (the 1st bisector) is shown in the figure in order to visualize where the total number of deployed nodes would be enough to guarantee connectivity. When the

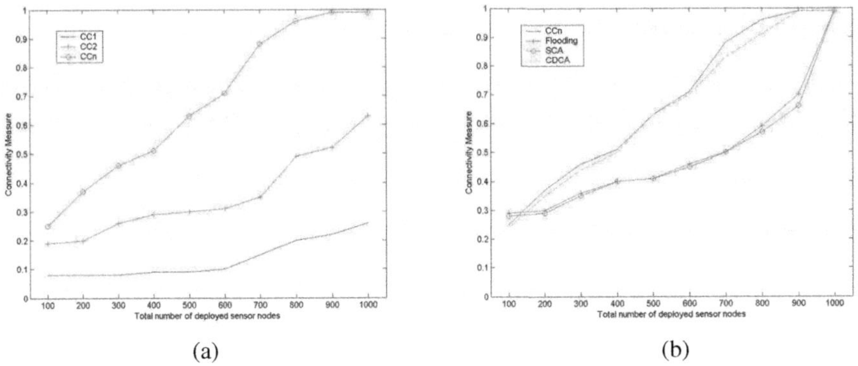

Fig. 3. (a) The connectivity measure of 3 algorithms CC1, CC2, and CCn as the number of deployed nodes vary. (b) The connectivity measure of 4 algorithms CCn, Flooding, SCA and CDCA as the number of deployed nodes vary.

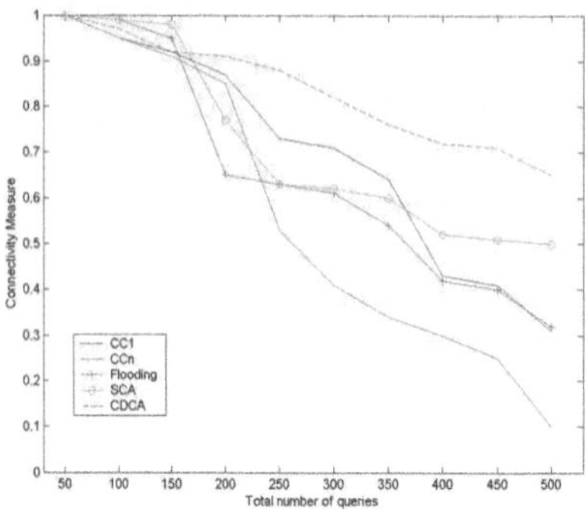

(a)

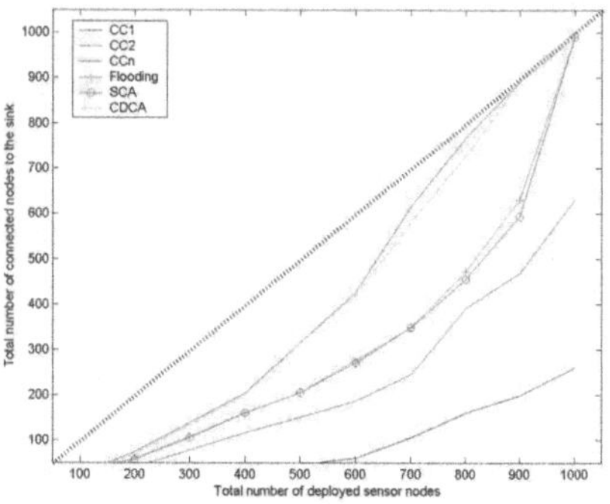

(b)

Fig. 4. (a) The connectivity lifetime (*Energy Usage*) of the network as the number of queries is increased. (b) The total number of deployed sensor nodes that are connected to the sink as we vary the number of deployed sensor nodes.

total number of deployed nodes is about 800 nodes then CDCA and CCn will result in almost 100% connectivity. This puts a lower bound on the number of nodes needed to be deployed in a region of interest to guarantee connectivity.

5 Conclusions

Billions of dollars are being committed to the research and development of sensor networks in order to address the many technical challenges and wide range of immediate applications. In the first part of this paper, we have described our initial approach to a wireless sensor network implant in a human eye, which will be refined further as testing and developments continue. In the second part of this paper, we provided algorithms to achieve connectivity in a sensor network when the network is not completely connected.

Acknowledgements

The authors gratefully acknowledge the assistance of the University Research Board (URB) at the American University of Beirut in supporting this work through grant # DDF-11135-788146.

References

1. Veraart, C., Duret, F., Brelen, M., Delbeke, J.: Vision Rehabilitation with the Optic Nerve Visual Prosthesis. In: Proceedings of the 26th annual international conference of the IEEE EMBS, San Francisco, CA, USA, pp. 4163–4165. IEEE Computer Society Press, Los Alamitos (2004)
2. Nam, Y.H., et al.: Development of remote diagnosis system integrating digital telemetry for medicine. In: Proceedings of International Conference IEEE-EMBS, Hong Kong, pp. 1170–1173. IEEE Computer Society Press, Los Alamitos (1998)

3. Petriu, E.M., Georganas, N.D., Petriu, D.C., Makrakis, D., Groza, V.Z.: Sensor-based information appliances. IEEE Instrumentation and Measurement Magazine 31–35 (2000)
4. Zhang, H., Hou, J.C.: Maintaining sensing coverage and connectivity in large sensor networks. International Journal of Wireless Ad Hoc and Sensor Networks 1(2), 89–124 (2005)
5. Maric, I., Yates, R.: Efficient multihop broadcast for wideband systems. In: Proceedings of DIMACS Workshop on Signal Processing for Wireless Transmission, Piscataway, pp. 285–299 (2002)
6. Sendonaris, A., Erkip, E., Aazhang, B.: Increasing uplink capacity via user cooperation diversity. In: Proceedings of IEEE International Symposium on Information Theory p. 156 (1998)
7. Sendonaris, A., Erkip, E., Aazhang, B.: User cooperation - Part I: System description, and User cooperation - Part II: Implementation aspects and performance analysis. IEEE Transactions on Communications 51(11), 1927–1938 (2003)
8. Laneman, J., Tse, D., Wornell, G.: Cooperative diversity in wireless networks: Efficient protocols and outage behavior. IEEE Transactions on Information Theory 50(12), 3062–3080 (2004)
9. Sirkeci-Mergen, B., Scaglione, A.: Coverage analysis of cooperative broadcast in wireless networks. In: Proceedings of the Fifth IEEE Workshop on Signal Processing Advances in Wireless Communications (SPAWC), Lisbon, Portugal, pp. 16–20 (2004)
10. Watfa, M., Commuri, S.: Coverage strategies in 3D wireless sensor networks. International Journal of Distributed Sensor Networks 2(4), 333–353 (2006)
11. Watfa, M., Commuri, S.: The three dimensional coverage problem. Journal of Networks, JNW 1(4), 10–20 (2006)

Enabling Distributed Messaging with Wireless Sensor Nodes Using TinySIP

Sudha Krishnamurthy[1] and Lajos Lange[2,*]

[1] Deutsche Telekom Laboratories, Berlin, Germany
sudha.krishnamurthy@telekom.de
[2] University of Wismar, Wismar, Germany
lajoslange@googlemail.com

Abstract. Smart sensor nodes have the potential to bridge the gap between the physical and digital world. To realize this potential, we need to integrate a network of sensors within a larger context-aware network, so that we can seamlessly interact with everyday objects embedded with sensor nodes. However, sensor networks currently lack high-level messaging abstractions that support convenient user-level interactions. In this paper, we present TinySIP, which is a messaging library that has been designed with the goal of enabling a client on a traditional network to seamlessly interact with the sensor nodes through diverse communication abstractions and familiar devices. TinySIP leverages the communication abstractions provided by the Session Initiation Protocol (SIP). The clients interact with the sensor nodes by sending SIP messages that provide publish-subscribe, instant messaging, and session-based semantics. A gateway maps the SIP messages to a more energy-efficient TinySIP message format, and forwards them to the sensor nodes, which then parse and react to the incoming TinySIP messages. We present the challenges in adapting SIP for resource constrained nodes and report the performance of our TinySIP implementation on Zigbee motes running TinyOS.

1 Introduction

Emerging technological trends are making the sensor nodes smarter, thereby making it increasingly feasible to view a wireless sensor network as a large-scale, decentralized information system that is capable of providing data services and event services. By embedding everyday objects with sensor nodes, it is possible to communicate with these innate objects and extract information about them in real-time. Thus, wireless sensor networks have the potential to change the way people interact with the physical world, because of their ability to gather information about the physical world in real-time. Our view is that the true potential of sensor services can be realized only if they become an integral part of a larger context-aware distributed system. In order to integrate the sensor

[*] Work done as an intern at Deutsche Telekom Labs.

J. Indulska et al. (Eds.): UIC 2007, LNCS 4611, pp. 610–621, 2007.

nodes as part of a larger distributed system, we need a remote messaging mechanism that supports diverse user-level communication abstractions and allows the sensor services to be seamlessly accessible to remote users through devices that they are already familiar with. In addition, the application-layer messaging protocol should enable sensor nodes across different networks to communicate with each other, as in any other distributed system.

Instead of developing a new messaging mechanism to interact with the real-time services provided by a sensor network, our approach is based on the premise that key protocols that work well in fixed networks will have to be adapted to access services provided by ad-hoc sensor networks. The advantage of such an approach is that it allows users to communicate with the sensor nodes using abstractions that they are already familiar with. We studied some well-known sensor network applications, such as smart home, smart hospital, and emergency response services, in order to identify the different interactions we need to support in a user-level messaging protocol for sensor networks. We concluded that it would be useful to support different messaging semantics, including publish-subscribe for event notification, instant messaging for short queries and control, and session-based semantics for continuous data streams. We also need the ability to send a request in parallel to multiple sensor end-points and forward messages to other sensor nodes, when the resources of the current nodes are depleted. Both the sensor nodes as well as the users that interact with the sensor nodes may be mobile. Hence, we need to support context-based delivery of messages. Furthermore, users should be able to use the messaging protocol with both static and mobile devices. To support these diverse interactions for a broad spectrum of sensor-based services, we proposed a messaging protocol called TinySIP [7], which makes use of the communication abstractions provided by the Session Initiation Protocol (SIP) [13], as a basis for interacting with sensor nodes.

In Section 2, we provide an overview of SIP and discuss how it serves as a basis for TinySIP. In Section 3, we describe the implementation of the TinySIP messaging library using the TinyOS platform [5]. We currently use a gateway for mapping SIP messages to a more compact TinySIP message format and then disseminating them to the MicaZ sensor nodes. In Section 4, we briefly illustrate the use of TinySIP methods for interactions in a hospital environment. In Section 5, we evaluate the performance of the TinySIP implementation. In Section 6, we briefly describe related work and in Section 7, we present our conclusions.

2 Overview of TinySIP

TinySIP is a messaging library that enables users to communicate with sensor nodes through diverse communication abstractions using static and mobile devices, such as mobile phones, PDAs, and laptops. In addition, TinySIP can be used as a high-level messaging protocol that allows sensor nodes within and across networks to communicate with each other. Thus, the goal of TinySIP is to seamlessly integrate the sensor nodes within a larger distributed system and allow them to be easily accessible through convenient application-level interactions. TinySIP makes use of the communication abstractions provided by SIP. In this section, we briefly discuss the SIP communication methods [13] and summarize how it serves as a basis for TinySIP. [7] provides more details about the justification for choosing SIP-based methods as a basis for a messaging library for sensor nodes.

2.1 Summary of SIP

SIP is an application-layer protocol that allows multiple end-points to establish media sessions with each other. As part of this, it performs end-point discovery, session establishment, and session termination. A SIP infrastructure consists of user agents and network servers. A user agent is an entity that acts on behalf of someone who wants to participate in message exchanges. A SIP user agent is identified by its SIP URI, which is essentially a combination of attributes. SIP user agents register their current contact information by sending a REGISTER request and update that information when their location or context changes. In addition to user agents, there are two types of network servers: *proxy* and *redirect server*. Usually SIP user agents are associated with a proxy server through which all outgoing requests are sent and incoming responses are received. A proxy receives a request, contacts the location service to obtain the current contact information for the end-point, and forwards the message to the next hop server. The attribute-based addressing feature, combined with the ability of the SIP network servers to discover the current contact information of the end-points while routing the messages, makes SIP a useful messaging mechanism for accessing sensor-based services.

SIP defines an extensible set of communication abstractions that can be used to provide session semantics, publish-subscribe semantics, and instant messaging. These abstractions are useful in the context of many sensor network applications. Session setup allows two end-points to interact continuously over a period of time. One of the end-points initiates the session by sending an INVITE message to the remote end-point. SIP allows invitations to be sent point-to-point, or to a group of end-points. SIP provides a general framework for event notifications [11,12]. A SIP end-point requests asynchronous notifications about an event of interest by sending a SUBSCRIBE request to the entity monitoring the event (known as *event publisher*). The event publisher informs its event state compositor (ESC) about any changes in the state of an event by sending a PUBLISH message. The ESC then notifies the subscribers about the event through the NOTIFY method. The SIP protocol allows participants to exchange short messages in near real-time using the MESSAGE method [1,2]. SIP also has a provision for exchanging instant messages within an active session [10]. In addition, SIP allows requests to be handled in different ways. A proxy server can fork a request, sending it in parallel to multiple next-hop servers. SIP has rules for merging and returning multiple responses to the client. This feature is useful in the case of sensor queries, when the final destination of the request is not concretely specified and therefore, the proxy servers need to try different possibilities. SIP also provides the REFER method [14] that allows an end-point to transfer or redirect the session that it is currently participating in, to another end-point and this is useful when the energy resources of the nodes that are currently participating in a session get depleted.

SIP users can publish their current context, which includes current location, available communication devices, and other resources in the neighborhood. The SIP network servers can use the information that is published, for delivering messages based on the current context of the user. Thus, SIP inherently provides a good framework for user mobility. SIP interoperates well with different kinds of media. Several enterprises have invested considerably in the SIP infrastructure. Many mobile devices already support SIP and this trend is likely to continue in future mobile devices. Hence, the familiarity of the SIP interface further strengthens the case for choosing a SIP-based approach for providing seamless access to sensor-based services.

2.2 Design Choices for TinySIP

The SIP communication methods described above provide many of the messaging semantics that are useful for interacting with the sensor-based services that are of interest to us. Hence, we have chosen those methods as a basis for the TinySIP messaging protocol, with the goal of enabling distributed interactions with sensor nodes. However, there are some challenges in using the current SIP infrastructure to connect to ad-hoc sensor environments and we considered two different design options for TinySIP, in order to overcome these challenges.

One option is to deploy a lightweight SIP infrastructure within a sensor network. SIP assumes an underlying IP-based infrastructure for routing messages. However, on account of the ad-hoc nature of the sensor networks, a fixed infrastructure of proxies, registrars, and location databases that a regular SIP infrastructure depends on, is not readily available in sensor networks. Sensor networks typically consist of resource-constrained nodes that do not support a sophisticated IP stack. Sensor nodes primarily communicate with peer nodes that are within their radio range and use routing schemes based on geographic routing or attribute-based routing (e.g. [6]), which are currently not supported in the Internet infrastructure. There have been efforts to port a lightweight TCP/IP stack on embedded sensors [4]. These trends are promising and may serve as a basis for deploying a lightweight SIP infrastructure within a sensor network in the future.

In this paper, we do not address the issue of deploying a lightweight SIP infrastructure on the sensor nodes. The alternative we have adopted does not depend on the sensor nodes to have an IP address, and this allows us to easily add or remove the sensor nodes deployed as part of a larger network in environments, such as a smart hospital or a smart home. Our design uses a gateway at the edge of a sensor network to interface between the SIP clients and TinySIP-enabled sensor nodes. We have implemented the TinySIP messaging library to run on the sensor nodes, so that it takes into account the resource constraints of the sensor nodes, while at the same time conforming to the messaging semantics of SIP. The role of the gateway is twofold. First, it performs a mapping between the standard SIP messages and the more compact, energy-efficient TinySIP message format designed for sensor nodes. This involves mapping addresses and field names represented by ASCII strings to numeric codes and performing the reverse translation for messages that are sent from the sensor nodes to the external SIP clients. The use of a gateway allows us to use a more energy-efficient version of SIP for sensor nodes, without changing the abstractions that standard SIP clients are already familiar with, and this in turn, enables easier integration. Second, the SIP address of the gateway serves as a contact address for the sensor network. Thus, the use of a gateway enables us to forward TinySIP messages to the sensor nodes using routing protocols that are more appropriate for a sensor network, without depending on either the sensor nodes to support an IP stack or the mobile devices to support a Zigbee interface.

3 Implementation of TinySIP

We have implemented the TinySIP library using TinyOS and tested it on MicaZ motes. The motes are equipped with temperature, humidity, light, accelerometer, and magnetic sensors. Each sensor node in the network has an identifier that uniquely identifies the node within the network. The end-point of a TinySIP message may be an individual sensor node or a group of nodes. We assume that the sensor network is within the communication range of one or mo re gateways that map SIP methods to TinySIP methods. However, to simplify the explanation in the following subsections, we limit ourselves to a single gateway. Sensor nodes discover their gateway by pre-configuration or by sending discovery requests. Each gateway has a SIP URI and is associated with only one sensor network. The individual sensor nodes do not have a SIP URI. Instead, the SIP URI of a sensor gateway serves as the contact address of the sensor network it is associated with. We now explain the TinySIP message format and the library components.

3.1 TinySIP Message Format

SIP is a text-based protocol. SIP messages use ASCII strings and allocate one byte for each character and this results in long messages. On the other hand, a normal TinyOS message allows a 29-byte payload. Although it is possible to increase this payload length, it is important to minimize the communication overhead in sensor networks, because transmitting a byte of data consumes 0.8μJ, while receiving a byte of data consumes about 1.9μJ [3]. Hence, one of the challenges we faced in implementing TinySIP was to design an energy-efficient message format for the SIP protocol which would allow a SIP message to be accommodated in a 29-byte payload, while at the same time conform to the SIP messaging semantics. In addition, the message format should allow a mote to parse the TinySIP messages in an energy-efficient manner. We now describe the TinySIP message format, which is shown in Figure 1.

A TinySIP message is transmitted as a payload within a TinyOS message. The TinySIP message format has 3 parts: a **start-line**, a **header**, and a **body**

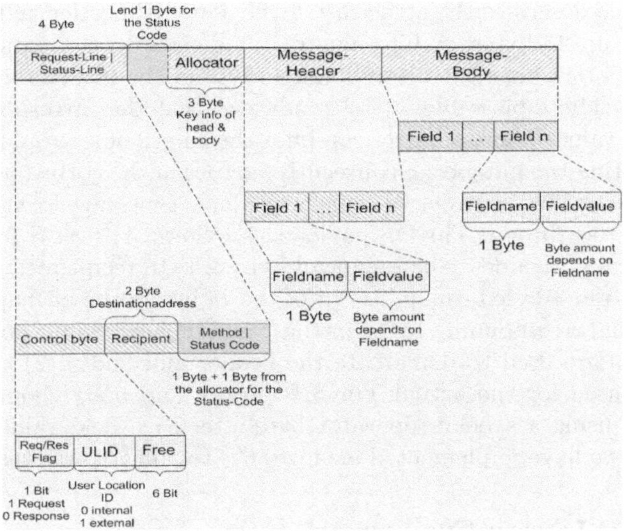

Fig. 1. TinySIP message format

segment. The start-line begins with the control-byte which consists of a request/response flag and the User-Location-Identifier (ULID) flag. If the request/response flag is set to 1, the message is a TinySIP request, otherwise it is a response message. TinySIP has been designed to serve as a messaging mechanism not only between external users and the sensor nodes in a WSN, but also as a distributed messaging mechanism between sensor nodes within and across different sensor networks. However, when the end-points are not within the same sensor network, then we need the mediation of the TinySIP gateway. If the ULID flag is set to 1, then it indicates to the sensor node that the TinySIP message was forwarded by the TinySIP gateway on behalf of an external sender and hence, the response has to be sent through the TinySIP gateway. The control byte is followed by the recipient address. When the TinySIP gateway receives a message, it extracts the TinySIP payload and uses the recipient address to route the message to the final recipient. The recipient address field is followed by the communication method. While a SIP message uses ASCII strings to denote method names (like REGISTER, INVITE etc.), we tokenize the method names and map them to numeric codes to achieve a more compact message format.

The TinySIP header and message body consist of a series of 1-byte field name followed by a field value of variable length. We use variable length field values, because it results in more efficient use of space. However, we restrict the maximum length of the field value in the current TinySIP version to 4 bytes. The main issue to address when parsing variable length field values is how to efficiently separate consecutive fields. Using a special separator byte to signal the end of a field value would consume 1 extra byte for each field. Instead, we use a bitmap allocator, which results in a more compact solution. The 3-byte bitmap in the start line describes the structure of the TinySIP header and body, which together take up 21 bytes. A bit value of 1 indicates to the parser module in the TinySIP library that the corresponding byte in the header/body is part of a field name, while a bit value set to 0 indicates that the corresponding byte is part of a field value. Thus, a parser can infer the length of a variable-length field value by counting the number of consecutive zeroes in the corresponding bitmap positions. In summary, in order to achieve a compact message format, a TinySIP message uses the 29-byte TinyOS payload as follows: 1) first 8 bytes are used for the start-line (includes 1-byte control byte, 2-byte recipient address, 2-byte method code, and 3-byte bitmap. 21 out of the 24 bits in the bitmap point to the contents of the corresponding bytes in the TinySIP header and body, while the remaining bits are used to demarcate the header and body); 2) the remaining 21 bytes are used for the actual TinySIP header and body. Compared to the alternative of using a special separator byte after each field value, the bitmap solution that we have implemented achieves 6% to 19.5% (best case) efficiency.

3.2 TinySIP Library Components

The key components of the TinySIP messaging library are the Event Handler, Message Handler, and Communication Center. The event handler element is responsible for registering and publishing events. The event handler associates appropriate sensors with the events of interest and monitors the information reported by the sensors, in order to publish events. The event handler is also responsible for periodically sending HELLO packets to signal the presence of the sensor nodes at their locations. Currently, the location is determined by the nearest gateway in the neighborhood of the sensor node. However, in the future, we plan to use more fine-grained location tracking algorithms that will enable a client to query the location of an object tagged with the sensor node more accurately. The message handler element is responsible for parsing and handling incoming TinySIP messages, sending provisional responses in accordance with the SIP method semantics, and handling errors. The TinySIP methods that are currently handled by the message handler component include ACK, BYE, INVITE, MESSAGE, NOTIFY, OPTION, PUBLISH, and SUBSCRIBE. The communication center element provides the messaging interface to send and receive TinySIP messages and is built on top of the TinyOS GenericComm interface. TinySIP messages use the Active Message channel number 0xAC (channel is equivalent to port), because 0xAC in binary view is 101'0'110'0 and this can be interpreted as 5'0'6'0 (5060 is the port used by standard SIP messages).

4 Application of TinySIP Communication Abstractions

Sensor nodes can be used to provide proactive healthcare as well as to monitor and track a variety of clinical resources in real-time in a hospital environment. The use of sensor nodes also helps automate many mundane tasks and alleviates the loss of revenue in hospitals. We have developed a prototype application that demonstrates the use of TinySIP in a smart hospital environment. In our prototype, we use MicaZ motes with different sensors to monitor different phenomena, and communicate the information using TinySIP. We have developed a GUI client to interact with the deployed sensors in a smart hospital environment. Users install the GUI on a programmable mobile device, such as a T-Mobile MDA, that has a Windows Mobile environment and use the mobile device to interact with the sensor nodes using TinySIP. Before users can interact with a sensor node, the node needs to register its services. An individual node offering a service, or a manager that represents a group of nodes offering the service, can register the service by sending a TINYSIP-REGISTER request to the gateway. The registration message includes the validity period of the registration, attributes of the service (e.g. instantaneous temperature of blood samples), and the identity of the node that is registering (e.g. mote-id, group-id, or a location identifier). When the TinySIP gateway receives a TINYSIP-REGISTER request from a sensor node, it records the information in a local database and uses that information to route a message to the appropriate sensor node.

After the services are registered, a user can use TinySIP to interact with the sensor nodes with the help of the GUI client on the mobile device. For example, using our prototype, a hospital staff member, such as a nurse, can use the SUBSCRIBE method in order to be notified when the temperature of the blood samples in a blood bank exceeds a certain threshold. This is useful to detect bacterial growth and prevent transfusion errors. When temperature sensors detect the event, they PUBLISH the event to the TINYSIP gateway, which then uses the NOTIFY method to deliver the notification as a text message on the mobile device of the subscribers. The MESSAGE method can be used to send an instant message to query the vital statistics of a patient or to control smart devices deployed in the hospital facility. Session semantics allows a phenomenon to be continuously monitored over a period of time and the corresponding data to be streamed from the sensor end point to the user. In the smart hospital scenario, this abstraction is useful for remotely monitoring the temperature of blood samples or of a patient, as shown in Figure 2. A nurse or administrator uses the GUI client on the mobile phone (shown in Figure 2(a)) to initiate a session with the temperature sensors that monitor the temperature of a patient, who is performing a treadmill test and to request the temperature data to be streamed to her for the duration of the test period. The exchange of messages that follows is shown in Figure 2(b). The request from the GUI client is first translated into a SIP INVITE request by the GUI application and sent to the contact URI for the sensors. When the sensor gateway receives the INVITE, it maps the request to a TINYSIP-INVITE message and routes the request to the appropriate sensor nodes. According to the standard SIP semantics [13], clients that initiated a session receive provisional responses before the session is finally established. These provisional responses are typically identified by a code. In the normal case, the sensor node that is responsible for providing the requested information accepts the invitation by returning an affirmative response (200 OK). The gateway node forwards the response from the sensor network to the client. In turn, the client acknowledges the response from the sensor nodes by sending an ACK. After this handshake, the sensor nodes begin the media transfer according

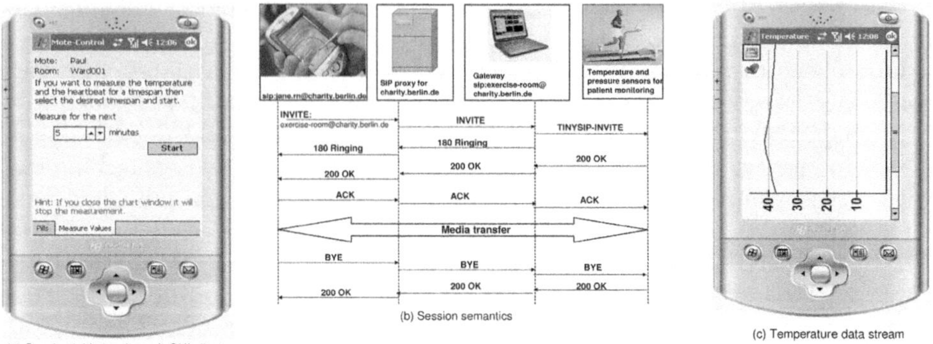

(a) Session initiation through GUI client (b) Session semantics (c) Temperature data stream

Fig. 2. Session semantics using TinySIP

to the parameters agreed upon during the session establishment. In the example shown, the data stream from the sensor node consists of raw temperature values. As and when the GUI application receives the temperature stream, it displays the variation of the temperature values graphically, as shown in Figure 2(c). Finally, the session is terminated by the client by sending a BYE request.

5 Performance Evaluation

We evaluated the performance of TinySIP using our testbed, which consists of Zigbee motes and a small number of PDAs. We measured the communication and processing time for different types of TinySIP interactions, both at the gateway and at a sensor node. In this section, we report a few of our experimental results. In our first experiment, we measured the time for transmitting and processing a short query using the instant message abstraction (MESSAGE). Each query was initiated by the GUI client on the mobile phone-cum-PDA device and was intercepted by the TinySIP gateway, which ran on a Linux laptop. Each time the TinySIP gateway received a MESSAGE request, we started the timer. The gateway looked up a local database to determine the destination sensor address and then mapped the SIP message to a TinySIP message. Based on our measurements, the processing of the short MESSAGE at the gateway consumed on an average 11.31 ms. The gateway then forwarded the TinySIP message to the sensor node, which took around 1.75 ms. When the sensor node received the message, it used the TinySIP library to parse the message and return a 200 OK response. The processing of the message on the mote took around 1.34 ms. The gateway received the TINYSIP 200 OK message, mapped it to a SIP message, and forwarded it to the client. This final processing at the gateway took on an average 16.36 ms. This completed the timing experiment for a single MESSAGE request. Based on our experiments, the average round-trip time for an instant message interaction using TinySIP was 35 milliseconds, and the processing on the gateway contributed to 77% of the overhead, while the processing on the sensor node contributed to only about 2% of the overhead. Compared to the

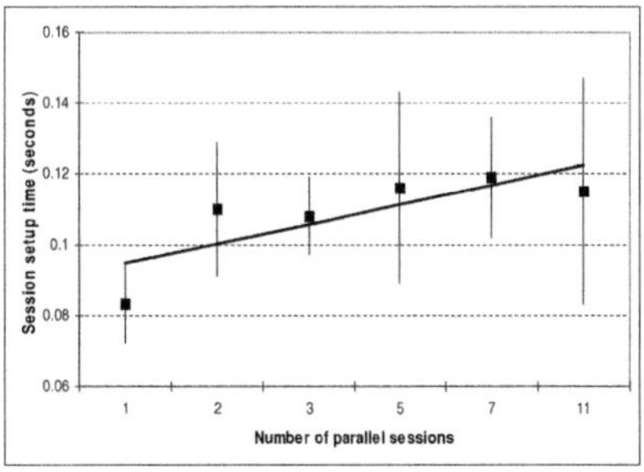

(a) Session setup

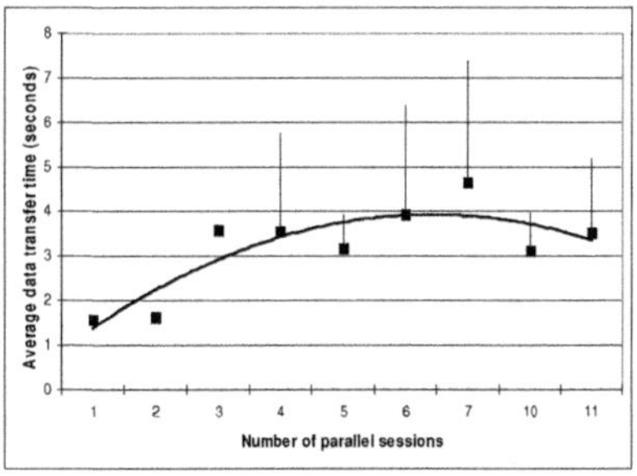

(b) Data transfer during a session

Fig. 3. Scalability of session-based interactions using TinySIP

HTTP-based TinyREST protocol which results in an average round-trip time of 40-50 ms for a simple query [8], TinySIP has a lower round-trip time.

TinySIP is designed to handle multiple clients in parallel. We conducted experiments to evaluate how the performance of TinySIP scales with the number of clients. Since we had only a limited number of PDAs, we ran our clients from a laptop. We started our experiment with a single SIP client and added a client in each subsequent experiment. Multiple sessions were setup in parallel through a single TinySIP gateway. Each client initiated a session by sending an INVITE message to a group of motes monitoring the temperature and each session was set up with one of the motes in this group, using the process described in Section 4. After the session was set up, each mote transmitted 9 TinyOS messages in each session, effectively transferring close to 260 bytes of temperature data to the client (each TinyOS message allows a payload of 29 bytes). Figure 3(a) shows the average time for setting up parallel TinySIP sessions, while Figure 3(b) shows the average time to transfer 260 bytes of data in each session, as the number of parallel TinySIP sessions is increased from 1 to 11. All of the results are plotted at 95% confidence interval. For a single client, the average session setup time was 0.083 seconds and the data transfer time was 1.6 seconds. As the number of parallel sessions increases, we see from the graphs that there is a sub-linear increase in both the setup time and data transfer time. While the performance of TinySIP does not significantly degrade for the number of parallel sessions that we used, larger number of parallel sessions can be more effectively handled by using multiple TinySIP gateways as well as by taking advantage of the redundancy in a sensor network.

6 Related Work

There have been other related work on bridging the communication gap between traditional networks and sensor networks using Internet protocols. For example, the HTTP-based TinyREST [8] protocol also uses a gateway to mediate interactions between the Internet and a sensor network. TinyREST uses the POST and

GET method for short interactions and the REST extensions to HTTP for event subscriptions. While an HTTP-based approach provides a simple and viable option for remotely accessing a sensor network, it does not support some of the rich semantics and request-handling features for providing ubiquitous access to sensor services. For example, while HTTP provides methods for sending short, instant messages, it does not offer abstractions to support continuous session semantics. HTTP is useful for point-to-point messaging, but unlike SIP, does not inherently support parallel transmission of a request to multiple end-points. An HTTP-based approach primarily delivers responses to the end-point that originated the request, but does not offer a convenient mechanism to forward and redirect messages based on the current context of the message recipient. Moreover, HTTP uses TCP as the underlying transport, while SIP can work over any underlying transport protocol. Our remote messaging approach is related but orthogonal to sensor network query mechanisms, such as TinyDB [9]. TinyDB employs a database approach using SQL-like operators to provide a limited, but useful interface for users to access raw data from the sensors. Unlike our SIP-based approach, TinyDB does not address the issue of providing ubiquitous access to in-network sensor services from remote networks and devices. However, TinySIP can be used for transporting queries composed in the TinyDB language to the sensor nodes.

7 Conclusions

In the next few years, we expect that common entities that we are already familiar with, will become increasingly embedded with smart sensor nodes. In order to interact with these sensor nodes and integrate them as part of a larger, context-aware, distributed network, we need a distributed messaging protocol that supports diverse, high-level, communication abstractions. In addition, such a protocol has to be aware of the resource constraints of the sensor nodes. However, sensor networks currently lack a standard set of high-level messaging abstractions for interacting not only among themselves, but also with users and devices on traditional networks. In this paper, we have described the design and implementation of the TinySIP messaging protocol, with the goal of enabling distributed, application-level interactions with sensor nodes in the context of typical sensor network applications, such as emergency response, surveillance, smart home, and other smart environments. While we have tested our implementation using MicaZ motes attached to different sensors, the TinySIP messaging library can also be used on other embedded nodes that are compatible with the TinyOS platform.

One of the advantages of TinySIP is that it allows users to interact with the sensor nodes using abstractions and devices that they are already familiar with, because SIP is a well-known standard supported by many communication devices. However, adapting a standard protocol that has been designed for traditional networks also introduces challenges, because these protocols have not been designed for resource-constrained nodes. One of the challenges we had to address was to design the TinySIP message format and message exchange, so that the communication overhead and parsing overhead on the sensor nodes can be minimized, while at the same time conforming to the SIP semantics.

As part of future extensions, it would be useful to couple TinySIP with a service lookup mechanism that allows messages to sensor services to be addressed based on attributes that are relevant to sensor nodes. While we have currently chosen the gateway-based approach to mediate between the SIP users and the sensor nodes, in the future, we are interested in looking at the challenges involved in deploying a lightweight SIP infrastructure within a sensor network. Finally, while we have primarily used TinySIP for interactions between a user on a traditional network and the sensor nodes, we are also looking at extending TinySIP to serve as a basis for a group communication protocol for interactions among sensor nodes, both within and across different sensor networks. This can then serve as a basis for developing distributed sensor network applications.

References

1. SIP for Instant Messaging and Presence Leveraging Extensions (SIMPLE). IETF Working Group
2. Campbell, B., Rosenberg, J., Schulzrinne, H., Huitema, C., Gurle, D.: Session Initiation Protocol Extension for Instant Messaging. RFC 3428 (December 2002)
3. Desnoyers, P., Ganesan, D., Shenoy, P.: TSAR: A Two Tier Storage Architecture Using Interval Skip Graphs. In: Proc. of Sensys (2005)
4. Dunkels, A., Alonso, J., Voigt, T.: Making TCP/IP Viable for Wireless Sensor Networks. In: Proc. of EWSN (2004)
5. Hill, J., Szewczyk, R., Woo, A., Hollar, S., Culler, D.E., Pister, K.S.J.: System Architecture Directions for Networked Sensors. In: Proc. of Architectural Support for Programming Languages and Operating Systems (ASPLOS), pp. 93–104 (2000)
6. Intanagonwiwat, C., Govindan, R., Estrin, D.: Directed Diffusion: A Scalable and Robust Communication Paradigm for Sensor Networks. In: Proc. of Mobile Computing and Networking (MOBICOM), August 2000, pp. 56–67 (2000)
7. Krishnamurthy, S.: TinySIP: Providing Seamless Access to Sensor-based Services. In: Proc. of Mobiquitous, Workshop on Advances in Sensor Networks (July 2006)
8. Luckenbach, T., Gober, P., Arbanowski, S., Kotsopoulos, A., Kim, K.: TinyREST: A Protocol for Integrating Sensor Networks into the Internet. In: Proc. of REAL-WSN (2005)
9. Madden, S., Franklin, M., Hellerstein, J., Hong, W.: TinyDB: An Acquisitional Query Processing System for Sensor Networks. ACM Transactions on Database Systems 30(1), 122–173 (2005)
10. Manner, M., Toikkanen, T.: Session Initiation Protocol and Instant Messaging. Seminar on Instant Messaging and Presence Architectures (2005)
11. Niemi, A.: Session Initiation Protocol Extension for Event State Publication. RFC 3903 (October 2004)
12. Roach, A.B.: Session Initiation Protocol Specific Event Notification. RFC 3265 (June 2002)
13. Rosenberg, J., Schulzrinne, H., Camarillo, G., Johnston, A., Peterson, J., Sparks, R., Handley, M., Schooler, E.: Session Initiation Protocol. IETF RFC 3261 (June 2002)
14. Sparks, R.: The Session Initiation Protocol (SIP) Refer Method. RFC 3515. (April 2003)

Localization and Synchronization for 3D Underwater Acoustic Sensor Networks

Chen Tian, Wenyu Liu, Jiang Jin, Yi Wang, and Yijun Mo

Dept. of Electronics and Information Engineering, Huazhong University of Sci & Tech, 430074 Wuhan, Hubei, China
tianchen@mail.hust.edu.cn

Abstract. Three-dimensional Under-Water Acoustic Sensor Networks (UWASN) are supposed to be deployed for many applications. However, a protocol for sensors' self-localization and time-synchronization in UWASN remains a challenge problem. In this paper, we developed a multilateration algorithm which could reliably localize and synchronize underwater sensor networks by acoustic ranging. To our best knowledge, this is the first scheme which could achieve both them for 3D UWASN simultaneously. Simulation results are also given to illustrate its effectiveness.

1 Introduction

Three-dimensional Under-Water Acoustic Sensor Networks [1, 2] could enable a broad range of applications including but not limit to: Ocean Sampling, Environmental Monitoring, Undersea Explorations, Disaster Prevention, Assisted Navigation, Distributed Tactical Surveillance and Mine Reconnaissance [2]. Different from existing small-scale Underwater Acoustic Network [21, 22, 23], UW-ASNs rely on localized monitoring and coordinated networking amongst a large number of underwater sensors. An example large-scale real-time 3D UW-ASN for military purpose is illustrated in [4].

Compared with ground-based sensor networks, some challenges are fundamentally different in underwater research. Among all those open issues for 3D UW-ASNs, distributed underwater GPS-free localization and time synchronization service is the most critical one. As the basis of self-organization, sensors' self-localization and time-synchronization are key requirements for every sensor network [19]. Most ground sensor networks rely on GPS or anchor nodes with GPS receivers for localization and synchronization. The problem is: in underwater environment, GPS is unavailable, and anchor nodes could only be placed on the water surface. What's more, underwater signal propagation delay and physical water properties have profound implications on most existing localization and time synchronization algorithms [5, 6, 7, 20]. Further more, most researches discuss 2-D scenarios and only a few concerns with 3-D underwater scenarios. No existing protocols could meet the demands to implement a localized, relatively accurate e networking technology in a 3D aquatic environment [7].

In this paper, we developed a multilateration algorithm for reliably localizing and synchronizing underwater sensor networks by acoustic ranging. To our best

J. Indulska et al. (Eds.): UIC 2007, LNCS 4611, pp. 622–631, 2007.

knowledge, this is the first scheme which could achieve them for 3D UWASN simultaneously. Our contributions can be summarized as follows:

- Identify the assumptions and goals of localization and time synchronization for military purpose Large-scale Real-time 3D Underwater Acoustic Sensor Networks.
- Present the basic idea of achieving localization and synchronization for large scale 3D underwater sensor network in a short latency. Through atomic multilateration and iterative multilateration, we provide a simple but effective scheme for self localization and time synchronization
- Error propagations introduced in iterative multilateration process are successfully controlled.

The paper is organized as follows. Section 2 presents some background and related works. Section 3 formally introduces the problem and the assumptions used. In section 4 we present our effective but simple method. Simulation results and discussions are provided in Section 5. The paper is concluded in Section 6.

2 Background and Related Works

2.1 Localization and Time Synchronization in Terrestrial Sensor Networks

GPS- based localization and synchronization is the most important 3D localization system today. For terrestrial sensor networks, the task of localization and time synchronization could be easy by simply embedding a GPS receiver into each node. Or, anchor nodes (i.e. nodes whose locations and times are already known by GPS receivers) could be used to help the organization of passive nodes (i.e. nodes whose locations and time are yet unknown).

For time synchronization, anchors could broadcast the synchronization packets in the speed of light to passive nodes. Localization is a litter more complex, and a number of distributed localization schemes have been proposed to date. These schemes can be broadly classified into two categories: range-based schemes, and range-free schemes [7]. Distributed range-based positioning algorithms use range or bearing information obtained by range technologies like ToA (Time of Arrival), RSSI (Receiver Signal Strength Indicator), TDoA (Time Difference of Arrival) and AoA (Angel of Arrival). They generally have three positioning phases: (i) the distance estimation phase, where nodes use one or combinations of those range technologies to estimate distances to nearby nodes; (ii) the position estimation phase, where a system of linear equations is generally solved using a least squares approach to estimate the position of the node, and finally (iii) a refinement phase, where the accuracy of the algorithm is improved by using an iterative algorithm. The N-Hop Multilateration Scheme [8], the Hop-TERRAIN and Refinement Scheme [10], Ad Hoc Localization System (AHLoS) [9] and Ad Hoc Positioning System (APS) "Distance Propagation" and "Euclidian Propagation" Schemes [11] all fall into this category.

Distributed range-free localization schemes are schemes that do not uses range or bearing information, they can be further classified into hop count based schemes and area-based schemes. The centroid scheme [12], DV-Hop [13] and Density aware Hop-count Localization (DHL) [14] fall into this category. The advantage of these schemes lies in their simplicity, as sensors do not need to make any ToA, RSSI, TDoA or AoA measurements. However, range free schemes only provide a coarse estimation of a node's location. It's clear that rang-free algorithms are not suitable for military purpose sensor networks due to their inaccuracy.

2.2 Localization and Time Synchronization for UW-ASNs

Underwater localization can be achieved by utilizing the low speed of sound in water, which permits relatively accurate timing of signals. These node distance data can later be used to perform localization calculation, similar to that of terrestrial localization. The performance of different range-based positioning schemes in underwater sensor networks is simulated and compared in [6]. The problem is: first, under these schemes, not all the nodes in the system can be localized, even though the network might be fully connected. For example, the nodes which do not satisfy the position uniqueness conditions described in [8] might not be able to calculate their locations. Second, their refinement phase requires a relatively long time which is inappropriate for many task. What's more, few of they concerns 3D scenarios.

A dedicated time synchronization protocol: Time Synchronization for High Latency Acoustic Networks (TSHL) is proposed in [15], which well manages the errors induced by the large propagation latency. Localization is not provided in this algorithm. A distributed 3D space coverage scheme and a detection/classification scheme are studied for tactical underwater surveillance systems in [3]. Localization and time synchronization are not needed for this system due to its unusual deployment method.

2.3 3D Space Partition and Localization

In 3D applications, the shape of the cell must be a polyhedron that tessellates a 3D space. According to [16, 17], the truncated octahedron is the best choice. For a given cell radius Rs, truncated octahedron could tessellate the space with the minimum cell number. Figure 1 is taken from 3D NET software [18] to illustrate its tessellation.

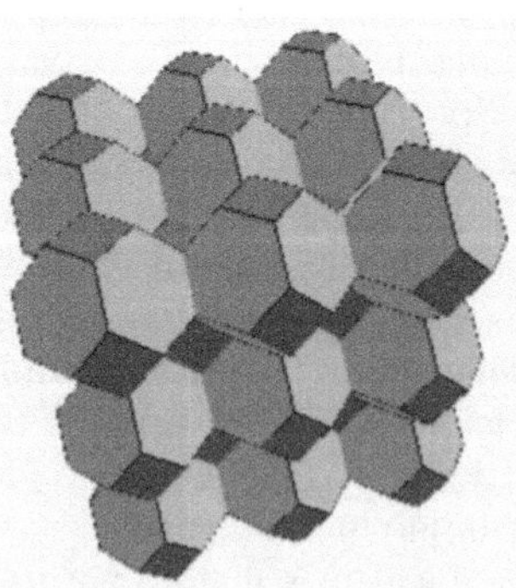

Fig. 1. Truncated octahedron tessellation

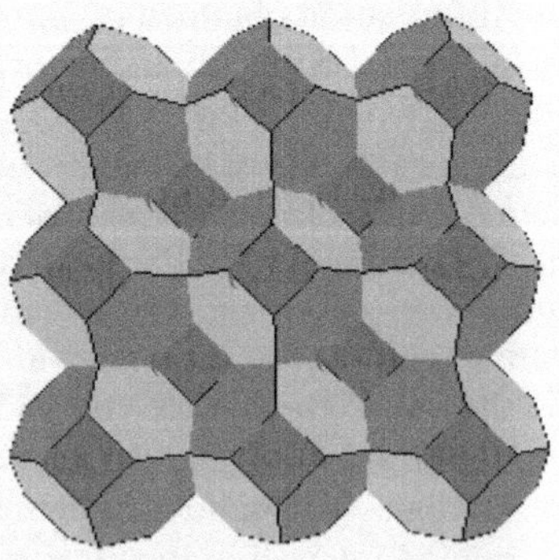

Fig. 2. Surface arrange

3 Problem Statement

A dedicated self organization method which could achieve both localization and time synchronization for large scale 3D underwater sensor networks is needed. The main assumptions and the goals of this work are defined as follows:

Assumptions

- The sensors are densely distributed over a 3D underwater space. The 3D space should be partitioned into equal sized non-overlapping cells. In order to maintain connectivity, the distance between one a node and any other active node in its first-tier neighboring cell can not exceed the transmission range.
- All underwater sensor nodes are identical and initially unknown about its location and time. They have identical transmission/sensing range and the transmission/ sensing region of each node can be represented by a sphere of radius R_t / R_s which having the sensor at its center.
- The anchor nodes are buoys on the surface of the ocean which already known their locations and time without errors.
- Unlike radio speed used in GPS, underwater sound speed is variable. For simplicity, we assume that in one node's transmission range the speed is constant.

Goals

- Find an algorithm to achieve both localization and time synchronization for large-scale real-time 3D underwater sensor networks in a short latency.
- Identify the best way to partition the network into cells in three-dimension such that the cell number is minimized. Given a sensor range R_s, deduced the minimum transmission range R_t to maintaining full connectivity. And given the calculated coordinates, a sensor should determine its belonging cell.
- Control error propagation hence improves localization and time synchronization accuracy.

4 Our Methods

A. Basic Idea

A sensor need to obtain only two coordinates (x, y) in 2D sensor networks. While in 3D scenarios, (z) coordinates are also needed. First we illustrate the relations between anchor nodes and passive nodes. A anchor node could transmit a synchronize packet to a passive node which is try to calculate its (x, y, z) . The packet contains anchor node's coordinates $(x0, y0, z0)$ and the transmit time $t0'$. Let v be the speed of sound, and t be the receive time of the packet which is still unknown. If a passive node receive from at least 5 anchor nodes, its location and local time could be presented as shown in (1), $(xi, yi, zi, ti'), i \in [0,1,2,3,4]$ are the locations and transmit times of 5 synchronize packets. Here we assume the first packet is from $(x0, y0, z0, t0')$, and let $(\Delta t1', \Delta t2', \Delta t3', \Delta t4')$ denotes the arrival time shift of packet 1, 2, 3 and 4. Linear least square solutions are given in (2)-(5).

$$\begin{cases} \sqrt{(x0-x)^2+(y0-y)^2+(z0-z)^2} = v*(t-t0') \\ \sqrt{(x1-x)^2+(y1-y)^2+(z1-z)^2} = v*(t+\Delta t1'-t1') \\ \sqrt{(x2-x)^2+(y2-y)^2+(z2-z)^2} = v*(t+\Delta t2'-t2') \\ \sqrt{(x3-x)^2+(y3-y)^2+(z3-z)^2} = v*(t+\Delta t3'-t3') \\ \sqrt{(x4-x)^2+(y4-y)^2+(z4-z)^2} = v*(t+\Delta t4'-t4') \end{cases} \quad \begin{cases} t0 = t0' \\ t1 = t1'-\Delta t1' \\ t2 = t2'-\Delta t2' \\ t3 = t3'-\Delta t3' \\ t4 = t4'-\Delta t4' \end{cases}$$

$$\begin{cases} \sqrt{(x0-x)^2+(y0-y)^2+(z0-z)^2} = v*(t-t0) \\ \sqrt{(x1-x)^2+(y1-y)^2+(z1-z)^2} = v*(t-t1) \\ \sqrt{(x2-x)^2+(y2-y)^2+(z2-z)^2} = v*(t-t2) \\ \sqrt{(x3-x)^2+(y3-y)^2+(z3-z)^2} = v*(t-t3) \\ \sqrt{(x4-x)^2+(y4-y)^2+(z4-z)^2} = v*(t-t4) \end{cases} \tag{1}$$

$$A=\begin{bmatrix} 2(x0-x1) & 2(y0-y1) & 2(z0-z1) & (t0^2-t1^2) & 2(t1-t0) \\ 2(x0-x2) & 2(y0-y2) & 2(z0-z2) & (t0^2-t2^2) & 2(t2-t0) \\ 2(x0-x3) & 2(y0-y3) & 2(z0-z3) & (t0^2-t3^2) & 2(t3-t0) \\ 2(x0-x4) & 2(y0-y4) & 2(z0-z4) & (t0^2-t4^2) & 2(t4-t0) \end{bmatrix} \in C^{4x5}, \quad M=\begin{bmatrix} x \\ y \\ z \\ v^2 \\ v^2 t \end{bmatrix} \in C^{5x1}, \tag{2}$$

$$B=\begin{bmatrix} (x0^2-x1^2)+(y0^2-y1^2)+(z0^2-z1^2) \\ (x0^2-x2^2)+(y0^2-y2^2)+(z0^2-z2^2) \\ (x0^2-x3^2)+(y0^2-y3^2)+(z0^2-z3^2) \\ (x0^2-x4^2)+(y0^2-y4^2)+(z0^2-z4^2) \end{bmatrix} \in C^{4x1}, \qquad A*M=B, \qquad M=A^{-1}*B$$

Our basic idea is simple: Multilateration. First, we put a set of anchors somewhere on the surface, and a group of nearby passive nodes can be located and synchronized; these nodes became new anchor nodes and thereafter broadcast new synchronize packets to a larger range; one by one, tier by tier, the whole network are expected to be totally organized in a short latency. However, a minimum density of sensors is required to guarantee the multilateration. Despite an anchor node's location and transmit time, a special field "Tier number" is added to synchronize packet content. Tier number refers to the tier of the transmitted nodes in the multilateration. We defined anchor nodes in tier 0; a node record all tier numbers of the packets which used in its calculation; after localization , new anchor node would use the largest tier number plus 1 as its own tier for broadcasting. First in part B, we determine the best cell partition method and cell numbering rule. Given a sensor range, we also Other details are given in part C.

B. Cell Partition and Numbering

Using the approach in [16] and [17], we partition the 3D space to the shape of truncated octahedrons. After partitioning the 3D space into shaped cells, the transmission range Rt of the nodes should be at least equal to the distance between the furthest points of two first-tier neighbor cells. Thus in topology control, we could keeping only one node active at a time inside each cell hence minimizes the number of active nodes and maximizes network lifetime while maintaining full connectivity [17]. Suppose a sensor's sensing range is Rs, then the radius of the cell $R = \frac{1}{2} Rs$ could ensure full coverage for any active sensor in a cell. Let the side length of hexagons as a, we can get $Rt = \frac{\sqrt{85}}{5} Rs$.

Suppose we are tessellating a cuboid, we can arrange the area as shown in Figure 3(look from up): let square faces of truncated octahedrons align with the border of the target volume. Let $d = \sqrt{2}a$. After normalize all length and coordinates to d, we can numbering cells ID by their centre coordinates as that shown in Figure 3. If the transmission range Rt is set to be $\sqrt{34}a = \sqrt{17}d$, we could evaluate the broadcasting range for each sensor. The number of neighbors totally depends on sensor density and would greatly affect the multilateration process.

C. Atomic and Iterative Multilateration

In atomic phase, anchors are put in the surface centre of the target area. Passive nodes heard enough anchors are called tier 1 node, they could calculate their coordinates and clock times. After atomic multilateration phase, tier 1 nodes became new anchor nodes and thereafter broadcast new synchronize packets to a larger range. The iterative multilateration begins. As stated in part A, every passive node could deduce its location and time by received enough synchronization packets.

Calculations of nodes could simple follow (2). But due to precision limit, each calculated value has rounding errors. These errors would cause bigger errors in the subsequent calculations of other nodes, which are known as error propagation. What's more, some coefficient matrix of simultaneous linear equations (SLR) maybe "sick": litter error of input floating-point numbers may greatly change the solutions of system. These errors would iteratively amplify themselves in the iteration of tiers, which are proved by the simulations.

There are two solutions. First, we could alleviate the harm of error propagation in advance by limit some new anchor sensors from broadcasting which has a high probability to cause harm. A coefficient matrix's sick extent could be expressed as

$$cond(A)_v = \|A^{-1}\|_v \|A\|_v \quad (v = 1, 2, \infty) \tag{3}$$

So SLR with big $cond(A)_v$ could be regard as a "pollution candidate", and we can forbid such a sensor to propagates its information, but a proper boundary value for method 1 is hard to find and maybe related to scenario setting. Or, we can explore the diversity of received packets. By using super-coupled equations, a least-squares solution can be obtained as in (4). The second approach is adopted. A simple method for determining a sensor's respective cell number is also developed. The node's cell centre must be within a cubic, which has the node as the centre and has $2d$ as the length. Then a node could simply calculate all possible centers in this range and chooses the one has the minimum distance with it.

$$A=\begin{bmatrix} 2(x0-x1) & 2(y0-y1) & 2(z0-z1) & (t0^2-t1^2) & 2(t1-t0) \\ 2(x0-x2) & 2(y0-y2) & 2(z0-z2) & (t0^2-t2^2) & 2(t2-t0) \\ \cdots\cdots & & & & \\ 2(x0-xi) & 2(y0-yi) & 2(z0-zi) & (t0^2-ti^2) & 2(ti-t0) \\ \cdots\cdots & & & & \\ 2(x0-xn) & 2(y0-yn) & 2(z0-zn) & (t0^2-tn^2) & 2(tn-t0) \end{bmatrix} \in C^{nx5}, \quad M=\begin{bmatrix} x \\ y \\ z \\ v^2 \\ v^2 t \end{bmatrix} \in C^{5x1},$$

$$B=\begin{bmatrix} (x0^2-x1^2)+(y0^2-y1^2)+(z0^2-z1^2) \\ (x0^2-x2^2)+(y0^2-y2^2)+(z0^2-z2^2) \\ \cdots\cdots \\ (x0^2-xi^2)+(y0^2-yi^2)+(z0^2-zi^2) \\ \cdots\cdots \\ (x0^2-xn^2)+(y0^2-yn^2)+(z0^2-zn^2) \end{bmatrix} \in C^{nx1}, \quad i\in[1,n] \qquad \begin{cases} A^T A * M = A^T * B, \\ M=(A^T A)^{-1} * (A^T * B) \end{cases} \tag{4}$$

5 Results and Analysis

5.1 Evaluation Methodology

We have implemented the algorithm in a dedicated simulator. The target area is 30x20 km with 6 km depth, and almost 900 nodes are deployed in the volume. Sensors are uniformly distributed in the 3D space as an ideal deployment scenario. Each cell has only 1 sensor and it is placed near the centre of the cell. N is the number of required synchronize packets, and N-1 is the number of acquired equations. Thus N should not less than 7; because a cell has 14 neighbors, we set 14 as the upper boundary of N. The bigger is N, the more synchronized neighbors needed by an unsynchronized sensor. The evaluation metrics used in our experiments include: (i) localize right ratio: the localize right ratio is defined as the nodes which successful get its cell id versus the total nodes number; (ii) average distance error: the distance between a node's calculated position and its real position; (iii) average time error: the time difference between a node's calculated time and its real time; (iv) maximum tier number and (v) process complete time to evaluate the whole network performance.

5.2 Results

In this part, localization and synchronization characteristics with different N are given in Figure 3-5.

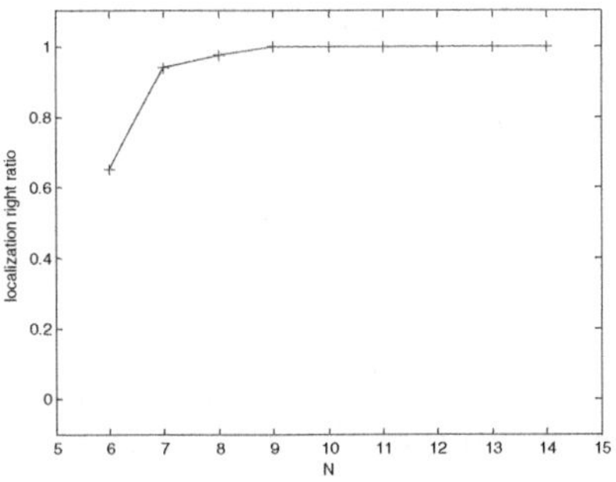

Fig. 3. Localization right ratio

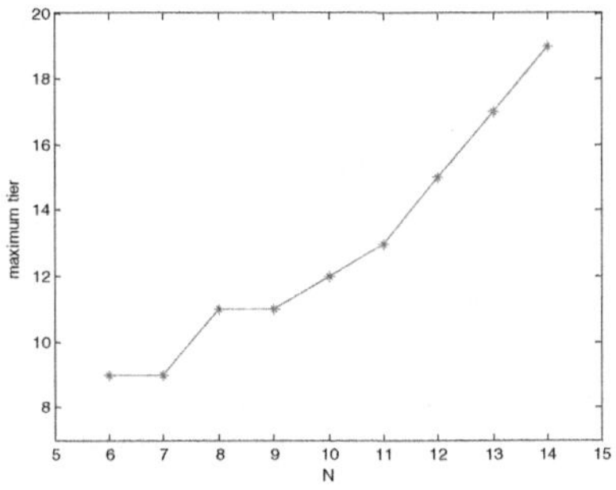

Fig. 4. Maximum tier number

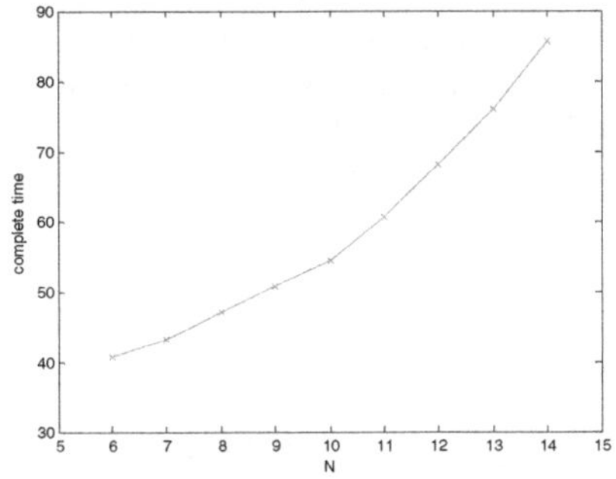

Fig. 5. Process complete time

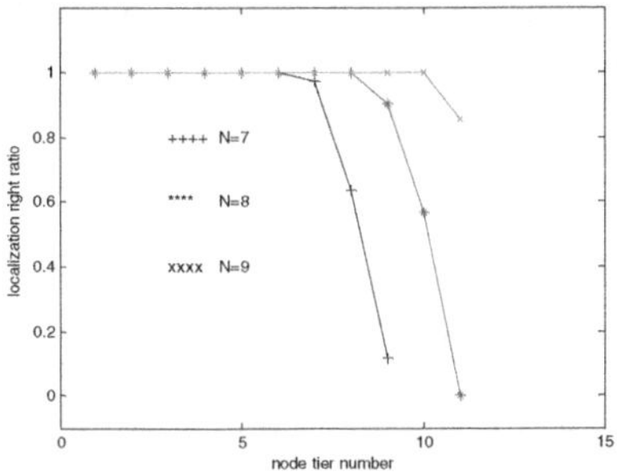

Fig. 6. Localization right ratio

As we can see, the total localization right ratio increases when N increases, while the maximum number of required tier and process complete time increase too. In Figure 6-8, localization and synchronization characteristics in different tiers are shown when N equals 6,7 and 8. With the tier number increases, localization right ratio drops and average distance/time error increase sharply. It is clear that more methods should be taken to control error propagation than least square equations. We

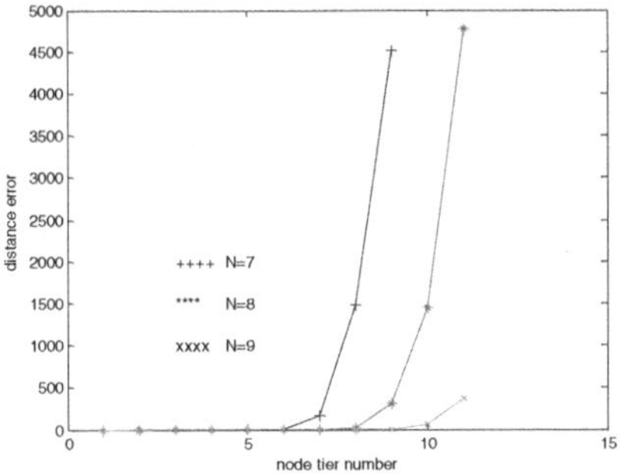

Fig. 7. Average distance error

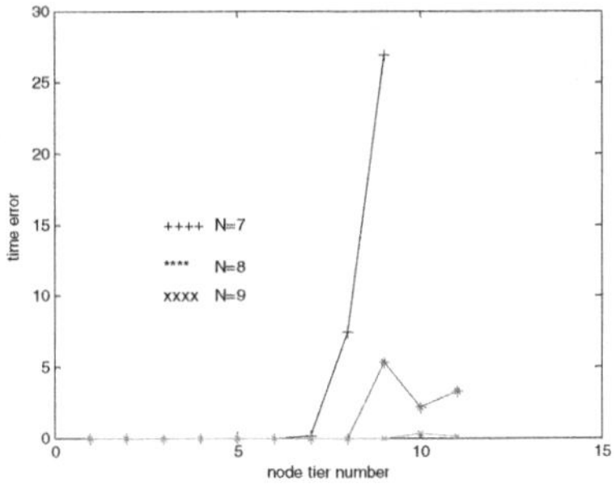

Fig. 8. Average time error

are currently consider: (i) neighbors selection, combine error estimation information in the multilateration to enable a node to select only "good" neighbors; (ii) weighted least square, adjust the impact of neighbors by their tier number; (iii) refinement, add a incremental refinement phase after initial estimation.

6 Conclusions

Under-Water Acoustic Sensor Networks (UW-ASN) are novel networking paradigms and some applications call for 3D space deployment for special military or civilian purpose. In such a network, sensor localization and synchronization remains a challenge problem. In this paper, we developed a service for reliably localizing and synchronizing underwater sensor networks by acoustic ranging. To our best knowledge, this is the first scheme which achieves localization and time synchronization simultaneously for 3D UW-ASN. We are currently working in three directions. First we will consider the influence to ranging by speed variance in underwater environment. Second, more methods should be taken to control error propagation than least square equations. Third, a separated synchronization phase and localization phase may greatly improve the performance.

Acknowledgment

The project is supported by The National Natural Science Foundation of China (No.60572063) and Specialized Research Fund for the Doctoral Program of Higher Education (Granted No. 20040487009).

References

[1] Heidemann, J., Ye, W., Wills, J., Syed, A., Li, Y.: Research Challenges and Applications for Underwater Sensor Networking. In: IEEE , Las Vegas, Nevada, USA (2006)
[2] Akyildiz, I.F., Pompili, D., Melodia, T.: State-of-the-Art in Protocol Research for Underwater Acoustic Sensor Networks. In: Proc. of ACM International Workshop on UnderWater Networks, ACM Press, New York (2006)
[3] Cayirci, E., Tezcan, H., Dogan, Y., Coskun, V.: Wireless sensor networks for underwater surveillance systems. Ad Hoc Networks 4, 431–446 (2006)
[4] Kong, J., Cui, J.-h., Wu, D., Gerla, M.: Building Underwater Ad-hoc Networks and Sensor Networks for Large Scale Real-time Aquatic Applications. In: IEEE Military Communications Conference, Atlantic City, New Jersey, USA (2005)
[5] Stojanovic, M.: Acoustic (underwater) Communications. In: Proakis, J.G. (ed.) Encyclopedia of Telecommunications, John Wiley and Sons, Chichester (2003)
[6] Garcia, J.: Positioning of sensors in Underwater Acoustic Networks. In: Proceedings of the MTS/IEEE OCEANS Conference, Washington DC, USA, IEEE Computer Society Press, Los Alamitos (2005)
[7] Chandrasekhar, V., Seah, W.K., Choo, Y.S., Ee, H.V.: Localization in Underwater Sensor Networks — Survey and Challenges. In: ACM WUWNet'06 (2006)

[8] Savvides, A., Park, H., Srivastava, M.: The bits and flops of the N-hop multilateration primitive for node localization problems. In: Proceedings of First ACM International Workshop on Wireless Sensor Networks and Applications, Atlanta, Georgia, USA, ACM Press, New York (2002)

[9] Savvides, A., Han, C.C., Srivastava, M.B.: Dynamic finegrained localization in ad-hoc networks of sensors. In: Proceedings of the 7th ACM International Conference on Mobile Computing and Networking, Rome, Italy (2001)

[10] Savarese, C., Rabay, J., Langendoen, K.: Robust Positioning Algorithms for Distributed Ad-Hoc Wireless Sensor Networks. In: Proceedings of the USENIX Technical Annual Conference, Monterey, CA, USA (2002)

[11] Nicolescu, D., Nath, B.: Ad-Hoc Positioning System. In: Proceedings of IEEE Global Communications Conference, San Antonio, Texas, USA, IEEE Computer Society Press, Los Alamitos (2001)

[12] Bulusu, N., Heidemann, J., Estrin, D.: GPS-less Low Cost Outdoor Localization for Very Small Devices. IEEE Personal Communications Magazine 7(5), 28–34 (2000)

[13] Niculescu, D., Nath, B.: DV Based Positioning in Ad Hoc Networks. Telecommunication Systems 22(1-4), 267–280 (2003)

[14] Wong, S.Y., Lim, J.G., Rao, S.V., Seah, W.K.G.: Multihop Localization with Density and Path Length Awareness in Non-Uniform Wireless Sensor Networks. In: Proceedings of the 61st IEEE Vehicular Technology Conference, Stockholm, Sweden (2005)

[15] Syed, A., Heidemann, J.: Time synchronization for high latency acoustic networks. In; IEEE INFOCOM 2006 (2006)

[16] Alam, S.M.N., Haas, Z.J.: Coverage and Connectivity in Three-Dimensional Networks. In: Proceedings of the Twelfth Annual International Conference on Mobile Computing and Networking, Los Angeles, CA, USA (2006)

[17] Alam, S.M.N., Haas, Z.J.: Topology Control and Network Lifetime in Three-Dimensional Wireless Sensor Networks, (Submitted for publication) http://www.cs.cornell.edu/ smna/

[18] 3DNET, http://www.cs.cornell.edu/ smna/3DNet/

[19] Xu, C Y, Heidemann, J.: Geography-informed Energy Conservation for Ad Hoc Routing. In: MOBICOM 2001 (2001)

[20] Garcia, J.E.: Accurate positioning in underwater acoustic networks. IEEE OCEANS 2005 Europe, Brest, France (2005)

[21] Urick, R.J.: Principles of Underwater Sound. McGraw-Hill, New York (1983)

[22] Sozer, E.M., Stojanovic, M., Proakis, J.G.: Undersea Acoustic Networks. IEEE Journal of Oceanic Engineering 72–83 (2000)

[23] Proakis, J.G., Sozer, E.M., Rice, J.A., Stojanovic, M.: Shallow Water Acoustic Networks. IEEE Communications Magazine, 114–111 (2001)

An Energy-Efficient Framework for Wireless Sensor Networks with Multiple Gateways

Jinglun Shi[1,2], Taekyoung Kwon[2], Yanghee Choi[2], Junkai Huang[1], and Weiping Liu[1]

[1] Department of Electronic Engineering, Jinan University, Guangzhou, 510632, China
{jlshi,jkhuang,wpl}jnu.edu.cn
[2] School of Computer Engineering, Seoul National University, Seoul, Korea
{jlshi,yhchoi,tkkwon}@mmlab.snu.ac.kr

Abstract. Wireless sensor networks are expected to be widely deployed in the future. Due to their unique features, energy-efficient data dissemination from source is getting more and more attention. In this paper, an energy-efficient dissemination framework with multiple gateways (EDF), which can significantly reduce communication costs resulting in prolonged network lifetime and improve the data source management efficiency by integrated with Internet, is proposed. In our scheme, 3-level architecture with a load-balancing node is proposed, and an efficient algorithm to find a nearest gateway among the multiple gateways for detected information is provided. In the algorithm, it mostly consists of several elements: (i) interest, gradients from source to multiple gateways, and exploratory data message, (ii) scheme for deciding nearest gateway, and (iii) reinforcement and aggregation. By EDF, detected information can be sent to the nearest gateway. Our analysis and simulation results reveal that EDF performs better than the existing algorithm in terms of the average dissipated energy.The abstract should summarize the contents of the paper and should contain at least 70 and at most 150 words. It should be set in 9-point font size and should be inset 1.0 cm from the right and left margins. There should be two blank (10-point) lines before and after the abstract.

1 Introduction

A wireless sensor network (WSN) consists of a large number of densely deployed sensor nodes with limited resources: battery, computation power, communication range, and memory size. It can be widely used in the areas of medical care, military, and disaster recovery. Now it brings us significant impact on those areas with its advantages such as reliability, accuracy, flexibility, cost-effectiveness and ease of deployment.

Earlier works have explored the design of mechanisms for the above issues in WSNs [4-6].In the project IrisNet (Internet-scale resource-intensive sensor network services) [15], an architecture and a system are designed to enable easy deployment of a wide-area sensing services. Its aim is to provide the missing software components for realizing a worldwide sensor web, and broaden the traditional notion of sensor networks to include wide-area "sensor webs", such as those comprising Internet connected, widely-dispersed PC-class nodes with powerful CPUs. It provides a software infrastructure for a platform that lets users query globally distributed collections of high-bit-rate sensors powerfully and efficiently.

J. Indulska et al. (Eds.): UIC 2007, LNCS 4611, pp. 632–640, 2007.

Motivated by reliability and energy efficiency, this paper proposes an energy-efficient dissemination framework with multiple gateways (EDF) for WSNs. In our scheme, we mainly pay attention to the following issues:

1. Energy-efficient: In order to get energy-efficient, we try to provide a solution with multiple gateways and an efficient routing algorithm to decrease the energy consume in data transmission and routing.
2. Energy self-organization: As the time goes, the energy distribution will change. And some nodes become invalid, and the related routing information gets outdated. In this case, in our algorithm, the sources can adapt such dynamic, change the route and find the nearest gateway quickly.
3. Flexible to integrate Internet with WSNs: It is widely accepted for the integration Internet with WSNs to improve the management for the reason the internet has flexibility, facility of development, and convenience of access. In our scheme, a 3-level architecture with a load-balancing node and multiple gateways is designed to integrate Internet and WSNs flexibly.

In our design, an integrated solution EDF with Internet, load-balancing node, multiple gateways, and sensor nodes is designed. It provides a multiple gateways solution to solve the bottleneck in a single gateway or proxy in the integrated networks. At the same time, it can separate the complicated management such as authenticating users, managing and analyzing queries from gateway. By the routing algorithm, the source can reach the nearest gateway and adapt to the dynamic environments. It consists of several elements: (i) interest, gradients from source to multiple gateways, and exploratory data message, (ii) scheme for deciding nearest gateway, and (iii) reinforcement and aggregation.

2 Related Work

Directed Diffusion (DD) proposes a new data dissemination paradigm in [4], where the sink node requests data by broadcasting interests. Fig. 1 shows the detail of DD.

The interest diffuses through the network hop by hop, and is broadcast by each node to its neighbors. As the interest is propagated throughout the network, gradients are set up to draw data satisfying the query toward the sink. Each sensor that receives the interest sets up a gradient toward the sensor nodes from which it receives the interest. This process continues until gradients are set up from the sources back to the sink node. After the source node receives the interest, it sends an exploratory data message to each neighbor for whom it has a gradient. After the sink node starts receiving the exploratory data, it reinforces one or multiple neighbors by sending a positive reinforcement message. Similarly, a negative reinforcement message is used to remove a link form a path. In [3], original DD is extended to a DD protocol family, which includes: (1) two-phase pull diffusion (2) push diffusion, (3) one-phase pull diffusion.

In DD, multiple paths may be reinforced, but it is different from the multiple paths routing we focus on in this paper. Firstly, there are no guarantees provided that the multiple paths are disjoint. Secondly, when the exploratory data message is forwarding to sink node, there are a lot of exploratory data message in the high density network, which results in higher overhead and more energy consumption.

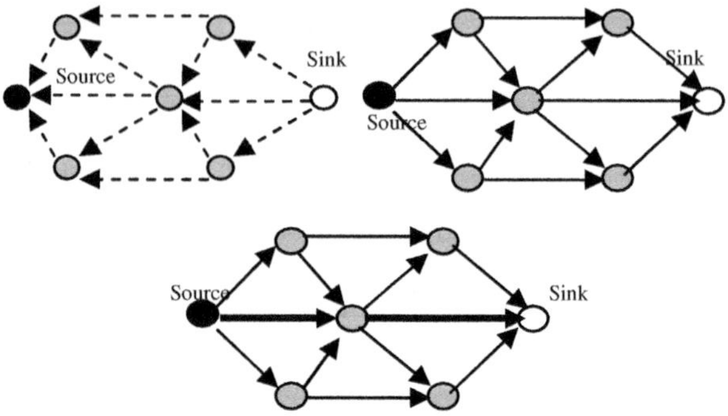

Fig. 1. An example of Directed Diffusion

Based on the previous researches and other application scenarios, some major challenges are identified in the energy-efficient routing algorithm design for WSNs: (i) flexible and efficient system architecture. Well-designed system architecture can integrate the components together easily, and make them cooperate well. At the same time, the architecture should support different applications. The architecture is important to enable the integrated system to take advantage of salient features of different protocols targeting different application scenarios. In other words, a flexible architecture will be helpful for the system's compatibility, extensibility, and performance; (ii) reliable communication protocols. It includes the effective task dissemination and the robust data collection under severe conditions. For WSNs' inherent characteristics, energy conservation issue still plays an important role in the communication protocols. It is also difficult to make those communication protocols interact seamlessly across the integrated networks; (iii) effective processing method for the data collected from WSNs. The integrated networks will include a lot of WSNs for different application, and a lot of users with different queries. How to process data collected from WSNs and answer the users in a limited time is a crucial issue; (iv) how to solve the bottleneck in the gateway or proxy connecting WSN and Internet. As we state in section II, current solutions not only creates a single point of failure but also puts all the complicated operations such as aggregating the sensor data, managing and analyzing queries to the single gateway or proxy. As we know, the data include the queries in the integrated networks will be very enormous. It is a challenge for a single gateway or proxy.

3 Energy-Efficient Dissemination Framework with Multiple Gateways (EDF)

WSNs typically consist of a large number of nodes that work at a very low data rate. For the data-centric routing, a unique node identifier may not be required. Similar to DD[3], EDF is based on data-centric and uses the localized information (gradients) to find target(s) for different applications. It consists of several elements. A sensing task initiates from the user in the Internet, and is randomly allocated to one gateway by load-balancing node. This task is disseminated throughout the sensor network as an interest for named data. This dissemination sets up gradients from target(s) to multiple gateways to "draw" data matching the interest, which is different with DD just for one sink node. Data starts flowing towards the nearest gateway from each target according to our framework. Reinforcement is used to choose path and local data aggregation is executed in the nearest gateway. Following are the details about our framework.

3.1 System Model

The system architecture for the wireless sensor networks and Internet is shown in Fig. 4. It consists of a 3-level hierarchy (Fig. 2); Internet, load-balancing node and multiple gateways (between Internet and wireless sensor network), sensor nodes. In the Internet, only a load-balancing node is known to users. As a user in Internet wants to query some data, it will send a request to the load-balancing node with a list of attribute-value pairs. And load-balancing node will distribute those requests to multi-gateways, and find a nearest gateway from the source which can provide the requested data. As the gateway gets request from the load-balancing node, it will flood the request in the wireless sensor network. In the wireless sensor network, the request normally is called as interest. As the interest flooding in the wireless sensor network, the gradient is set up from the source to multiple gateways. When the interest reaches the source node, the source node will send exploratory data messages to its neighbors. When a gateway gets exploratory data messages, it will aggregate them and send an exploratory-result message (ERM), which includes the hop counts to source, to load-balancing node. After the load-balancing node gets such messages, it will compare the message, and choose the nearest gateway for the source.

EDF consists of several elements: (i) scheme for choosing gateway, (ii) interest and gradients from source to multiple gateways, (iii) exploratory data message, (iv) scheme for deciding nearest gateway, and (v) reinforcement and aggregation. In this section, we detailed describe these elements of EDF.

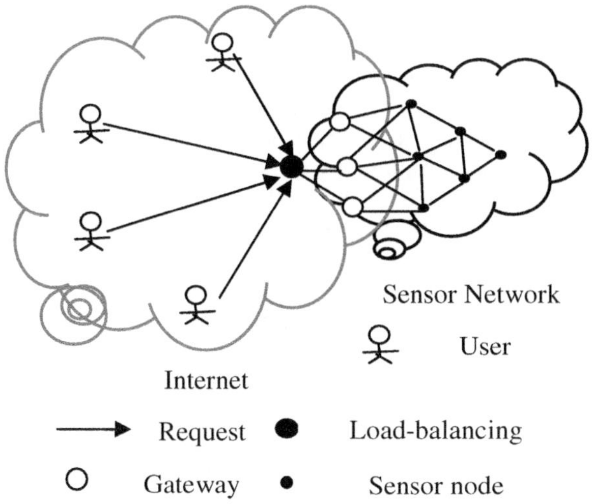

Fig. 2. System architecture

Firstly, as requests concentrate on the load-balancing node, it will use a simple scheme to choose gateway.

i. If there are no similar records with the request, the load-balancing node will choose a gateway from the multi-gateway randomly.
ii. If there are similar records with the request, the load-balancing node will choose the gateway according to the records, the gateway visited with latest time will be chosen.

3.2 Energy-Efficient Scheme with Multiple Gateways

According to the scheme for choosing gateway, the request can reach the nearest gateway by the cache in load-balancing node. If the cache gets invalid or expired, a new interest flooding will initiate.

Interest is constituted by the description of request. Request will be analyzed in the load-balance node, then scheme for choosing a gateway starts, a gateway from the multiple gateways will be appointed as the original to flood the interest.

As a gateway A gets the interest from the load-balancing node, the gateway floods the interest. As the intermediate node gets the interest, it will forward it to all of its neighbors. As the interest reaches the source, the gradients from source to multi-gateways are set up. This phase is introduced in Fig. 3.

If the source receives the interest, it sends the exploratory data message to each neighbor. When the intermediate nodes get the exploratory data message, they will obey the rules in EDF to forward it:

i. Each intermediate node (not including gateway) will forward the exploratory data message to its neighbors according to its gradients.
ii. As a gateway gets exploratory data messages, it will not forward the exploratory data messages, and just aggregate them and send the exploratory-result message (ERM) to load-balancing node, which includes the hop counts to source, source ID, etc., to load-balance node.

Fig. 4 illustrates how exploratory data message are flooded. As the load-balance node gets ERMs, it will use different schemes according to the number of source. If the number of source is one, load-balance node will choose the gateway which is nearest to the source (which can judge by the hop counts or delay time) as the working gateway, and a reply message is sent to this gateway. If the number of source is multiple, load-balance node will choose a nearest gateway for each source. At the same time, reply message is sent to related gateway. Fig.5 illustrates this case. According to the hop counts, B_1 will choose gateway A_1 as its working gateway, B_2 will choose gateway A_2 as its working gateway, and so on.

If the gateway gets a reply message from load-balancing node, it will reinforce one of its neighbors in order to reach the source node. To reinforce this neighbor, the gateway re-sends the original interest message but with a small interval (higher data rate).The neighbor is chosen according to the reach time of the exploratory data message. And as the neighbor node receives this reinforcement, it will use its data cache to choose one neighbor to reinforce, and the same local rule applies. Then the reinforcement message is forwarding reversely hop by hop to the source node. As the source node gets the reinforce messages, it can get the path to route the detected information.

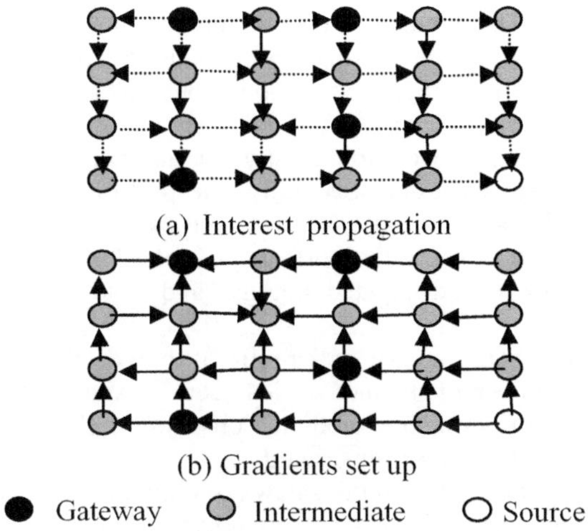

Fig. 3. Interest and Gradients

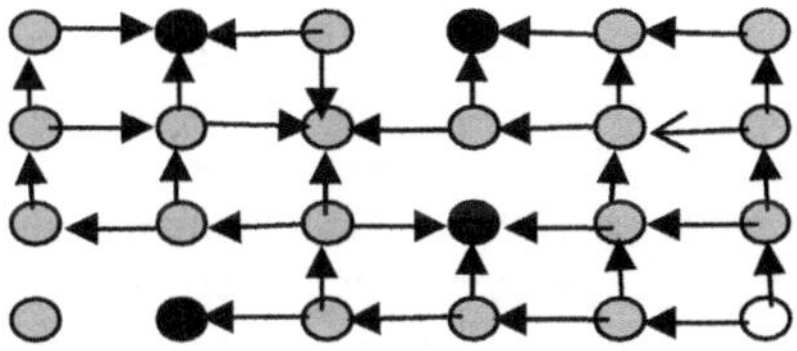

Fig. 4. An example of exploratory data message

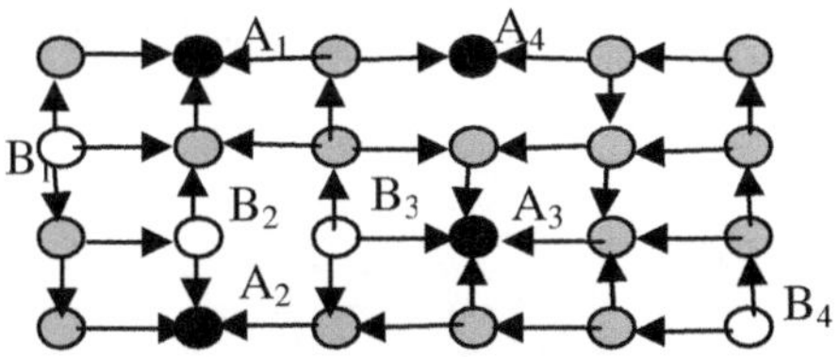

Fig. 5. Choosing the nearest gateway for each source

4 Performance Evaluation

In this section, we use Qualnet to evaluate EDF. The distributed coordination function (DCF) of IEEE 802.11(b) for wireless LANs is used as the MAC layer, and the radio range is set as 30 meters. In order to study the effects of the network density, networks with different number of nodes are analyzed. In our experiments, we use 50 to 500 static nodes to study the density effects and nodes are uniformly distributed within a 200m×200m area. Following assumptions are similar with DD: each source generates two events per second, events are modeled as 64 byte packets, interests as 32 byte packets, interests are periodically generated every 5 seconds, and the interest duration is 15 seconds. The parameters of radio energy model are also the same as the ones in DD: the idle time power dissipation is about 35mW, which is 10% of its receiving power dissipation (395mW), and about 5% of its transmitting power dissipation (660mW).

Our evaluation consists of two parts. Firstly, the number of multiple gateways with different network density is tested. Secondly, the performances between EDF, and DD with multiple sink nodes (MDD) in different cases are evaluated.
Two metrics are chosen to show the performance of EDF with different number of multiple gateways: average dissipated energy, and load distribution between the multi-gateways.

Average dissipated energy measures the ratio of total dissipated energy per node in the network to the number of distinct events seen by sinks. This metric is used to quantity the average work done by a node in delivering each sensory data to the sink. It also hints the overall lifetime of sensor nodes.

Load distribution between the multi-gateways shows the number of requests dealt by each gateway. It hints the system's self-organization capacity.

In the experiment, the number of multi-gateways is set 3 and 4 respectively. In the first case, the multiple gateways are respectively deployed in (33, 100), (99, 100), and (165, 100). In the second case, the multiple gateways are respectively employed in (50, 50), (150, 50), (50, 150), and (150, 150), respectively named G_A, G_B, G_C and G_D. The requests from users is uniformly distributed in the 200m×200m area, we can get this by adjusting the interest's Rect area and its distribution. The effect of the number of multi-gateways on EDF's performance is shown in Fig. 11. It tells us that the average dissipated energy per event decreases as the network density increases. And it also shows that the average dissipated energy gets lower as the number of multiple gateway increases.

To show EDF's performance clearly, we compare it with other algorithm: DD with multiple sink nodes (MDD). In this case, we assume that the number of multiple gateways is 4. The sink nodes of MDD are deployed at the same place with the multiple gateways in EDF.

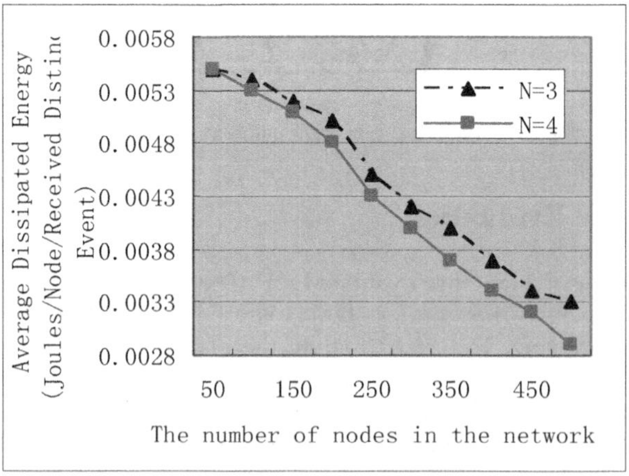

Fig. 6. Average Dissipated Energy with different network density

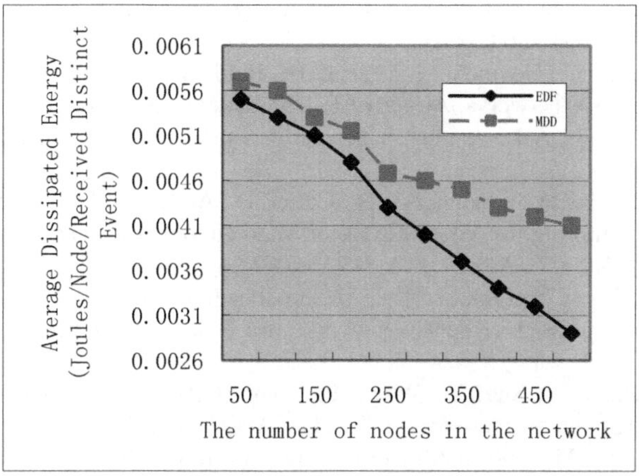

Fig. 7. Average Dissipated Energy with different network density

In the Fig. 7, MDD costs more energy than EDF, and as the network's density gets higher, the difference are clearer.

5 Conclusions and Future Work

In this paper, an energy-efficient dissemination framework with multiple gateways, which can significantly reduce communication costs resulting in prolonged network lifetime and improve the data source management efficiency by integrated with Internet, is proposed. In our scheme, 3-level architecture with a load-balancing node is proposed, and an efficient algorithm to find a nearest gateway among the multiple gateways for detected information is provided. In the algorithm, it mostly consists of several elements: (i) interest, gradients from source to multiple gateways, and exploratory data message, (ii) scheme for deciding nearest gateway, and (iii) reinforcement and aggregation. By EDF, detected information can be sent to the nearest gateway. Our analysis and simulation results reveal that EDF performs better than the existing algorithm in terms of the average dissipated energy. In our future work, how can our scheme self-organize to adapt to such change quickly, and adjust the load distribution among the multiple gateways? The simulation as energy or network topology changes will be tested.

References

1. Al-Karaki, J.N., Kamal, A.E.: Routing techniques in wireless sensor networks: a survey. IEEE Wireless Communications (2004)
2. Ganesan, D., Govindan, R., Shenker, S., Estrin, D.: Highly-resilient, energy-efficient multipath routing in wireless sensor networks. ACM Mobile Computing and Communications Review, 5(4) (2001)

3. Silva, F., Heidemann, J., Govindan, R., Estrin, D.: Directed diffusion. USC/ISI Technical Report ISI-TR-2004-586 (2004)
4. Intanagonwiwat, C., Govindan, R., Estrin, D., Heidemann, J., Silva, F.: Directed diffusion for wireless sensor networks. ACM/IEEE Transactions on Networking 11(1), 2–16 (2003)
5. Akyildiz, I., et al.: A survey on sensor networks. IEEE Commun. Mag. 40(8), 102–114 (2002)
6. Mainwaring, Polastre, J., Szewczyk, R., Culler, D., Anderson, J.: Wireless sensor networks for habitat monitoring. In: First ACM Workshop on Wireless Sensor Networks and Applications (WSNA 2002), Atlanta, GA, USA (2002)
7. Heinzelman, W., Chandrakasan, A., Balakrishnan, H.: Energy-efficient communication protocol for wireless microsensor networks. In: Proc. 33rd Hawaii Int'l. Conf. Sys. Sci. (2000)
8. Zhang, L., Zhao, Z., Shu, Y., Wang, L., Yang, O.W.W.: Load balancing of multipath source routing in ad hoc networks. IEEE, Los Alamitos (2002)
9. Lee, S.-J., Gerla, M.: Split multipath routing with maximally disjoint paths in ad hoc networks. IEEE, Los Alamitos (2001)
10. Shi, J., Ling, Z., Dong, S., Jie, Z.: A stability-based multipath algorithm for ad hoc networks. In: IEEE PIMRC, Beijing, China (2003)
11. Pearlman, M., Haas, Z., Sholander, P., Tabrizi, S.S.: On the impact of alternate path routing for load balancing in mobile ad-hoc networks. In: MobiHoc'2000, Boston, USA (2000)
12. Chen, J., Druschel, P., Subramanian, D.: An efficient multipath forwarding method. In: Proceedings of IEEE INFOCOM'98, San Francisco, CA, pp. 1418–1425 (1998)
13. Dulman, S., Nieberg, T., Wu, J., Havinga, P.: Trade-off between traffic overhead and reliability in multipath routing for wireless sensor networks. IEEE, Los Alamitos (2003)
14. QualNet. Network simulator (2003), Available at http://www.qualnet.com
15. Gibbons, P.B., Karp, B., Yank e, Nath, S., Seshan, S.: IrisNet: an architecture of worldwide sensor web. IEEE Pervasive Computing (2003)
16. Dai, H., Han, R.: Unifying micro sensor networks with the Internet via overlay networking. In: Proceeding of the 29th Annual IEEE International Conference on Local Computer Networks (LCN'04), IEEE Computer Society Press, Los Alamitos (2004)
17. Cheng, L., Zhang, Y., Lin, T., Ye, Q.: Integration of wireless sensor networks, wireless local area networks and the Internet. In: Proceeding of the 2004 IEEE International Conference on Networking, Sensing & Control, Taipei, Taiwan (2004)
18. Dunkels, A., Voigt, T., Alonso, J., Ritter, H., Schiller, J.: Connecting wireless sensornets with TCP/IP networks. In: WWIC2004 (2004)
19. Hwang, K.-i., In, J., Park, N., Eom, D.-s.: A design and implementation of wireless sensor gateway for efficient querying and managing through World Wide Web. IEEE Transactions on Consumer Electronics 49(4) (2003)
20. Dai, H., Han, R.: Unifying micro sensor networks with the Internet via overlay networking. In: Proceeding of the 29th Annual IEEE International Conference on Local Computer Networks (LCN'04) (2004)
21. Jinglun, S.: A energy-efficient multipath routing algorithm for wireless sensor networks. In: Ma, J., Jin, H., Yang, L.T., Tsai, J.J.-P. (eds.) UIC 2006. LNCS, vol. 4159, pp. 438–446. Springer, Heidelberg (2006)
22. Jinglun, S., Liu, W.P.: A service-oriented model for wireless sensor networks with Internet. In: The 5th International Conference on Computer and Information Technology, pp. 1045–1049 (2005)

Self-configurable Structure for Tracking Moving Objects in Wireless Sensor Networks

Sang-Sik Kim and Ae-Soon Park

Electronics and Telecommunications Research Institute
{pstring,aspark}@etri.re.kr

Abstract. Wireless sensor networks generally have three objects: sensors generating data, sinks gathering the data, and users that send queries and receive data via the sinks. In addition, the user and the sinks are mostly connected to each other by infrastructure networks. The users, however, should receive the data from the sinks through multi-hop communications between disseminated sensor nodes if such users move into the sensor networks without infrastructure networks. To support mobile users in wireless sensor network, previous work has studied various user mobility models. Nevertheless, such approaches are not compatible with the existing data-centric routing algorithms, and it is difficult for the mobile users to efficiently gather data from sensors due to their mobility. To improve the shortcomings, we propose a view of mobility for wireless sensor networks and propose a model to support a user mobility that is independent of sinks. The model is flexible regarding the number of sinks. Furthermore, it considers a situation in which there is no sink and user. The proposed model, finally, is evaluated by simulation of delivery ratio, latency, and network lifetime.

Keywords: User Mobility Support, Wireless Sensor Networks.

1 Introduction

Wireless sensor networks typically consist of three objects, as shown in Fig. 1: user, sink, and sensor node [1].

Firstly, a user is an object that disseminates an interest in the sensor field and collects data about the interest from sensor nodes. Secondly, a sink is an object that collects data. The sink receives an interest from a user and disseminates the interest inside sensor fields. The sink receives sensing data from sensor nodes and forwards the sensing data to the user. Lastly, a sensor node is an object that generates data about the interest and delivers the data to a sink.

As shown in Fig. 1, the user and the sinks are mostly connected to each other by infrastructure networks. The users, however, should receive the data from the sinks through multi-hop communications between sensor nodes if such users move into the sensor networks without infrastructure networks. Recently, applications transmitting data to moving users inside sensor fields, such as rescue in a disaster area or maneuvers in a war zone, have been on the rise in large-scale sensor networks [5]. (Firefighters and soldiers are users gathering data from sensors.)

J. Indulska et al. (Eds.): UIC 2007, LNCS 4611, pp. 641–652, 2007.

To support mobile users in wireless sensor network, previous work has studied various user mobility models. But, until now, only three models supported the mobility of users for these applications: the direct user-network communication model, the GPS-based user-network communication model, and the topology-control-based user-network communication model.

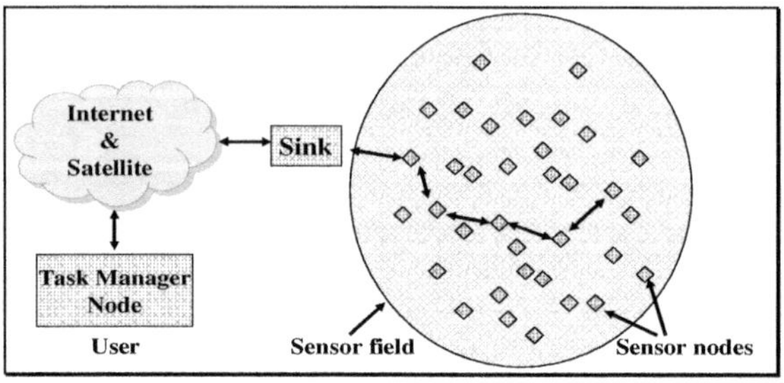

Fig. 1. Traditional Wireless Sensor Networks Model

The **direct user-network communication model (D-COM)** is shown in Fig. 2. It supports the mobility of a user on the assumption that the user communicates directly with sinks through infrastructure networks, namely, the Internet, such as communication systems in traditional sensor networks [1]. And, users can communicate directly with the networks via the sinks. But, in applications such as rescues in a disaster area or maneuvers in a war zone, circumstances without infrastructure networks, except sensor networks, are more prevalent. Hence, the assumption that a user and a sink can communicate directly through the Internet is not entirely accurate.

The **GPS-based user-network communication model (G-COM)** is seen in Fig. 3. G-COM is source-based topology [5], [6], [7]. In G-COM, sensors proactively construct a GRID system with GPS receivers. G-COM assumes that all sensors have their own GPS receivers and an ability that constructs a GRID when a stimulus is detected. A sensor (source) with a stimulus is going to make a GRID in a sensor field. Once a GRID is set up, mobile user floods its interests within a cell only where the user is located. When a sensor on a GRID receives interests, it sends interests to the source along a GRID path and data from the source are forwarded to the user along the reverse path.

Table 1. Taxonomy of Mobility Type

Mobility Type	Compatibility with Existing Static Sink Routing Protocols	Feasibility	GPS receivers for sensors	Control Overheads according to user mobility	Control Overheads to support multiple users	Help of infrastructure networks
D-COM	High	Low	Needless	Low	Low	Mandatory
G-COM	Low	Middle	Mandatory	Middle	Low	Needless
T-COM	Low	High	Needless	High	High	Needless
A-COM	High	High	Needless	Low	Low	Needless

The **topology-control-based user-network communication model (T-COM)** is seen in Fig. 4. It also identifies a user with a sink. This model supports the mobility of the user by reflecting the movement of the user [8], [9]. In T-COM, the user and sensors construct a tree that is rooted at the user. The user always maintains the tree and gathers data from sensors.

Intuitively, G-COM and T-COM seem to be suitable for the aforementioned applications. But, these models also have various problems. First of all, they cannot use existing effective data collection algorithms [2], [3], [4] between a sink and sensor nodes based on the data in static sink sensor networks because of low protocol compatibility. Accordingly, such algorithms can hardly be exploited if users in sensor networks have mobility.

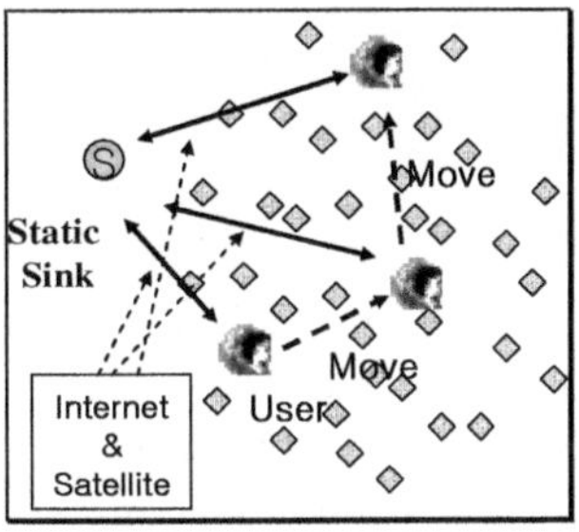

Fig. 2. Direct user-network communication model

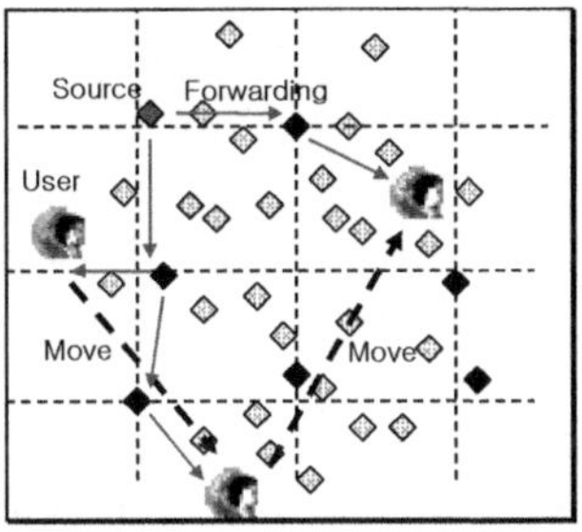

Fig. 3. GPS based user-network communication model

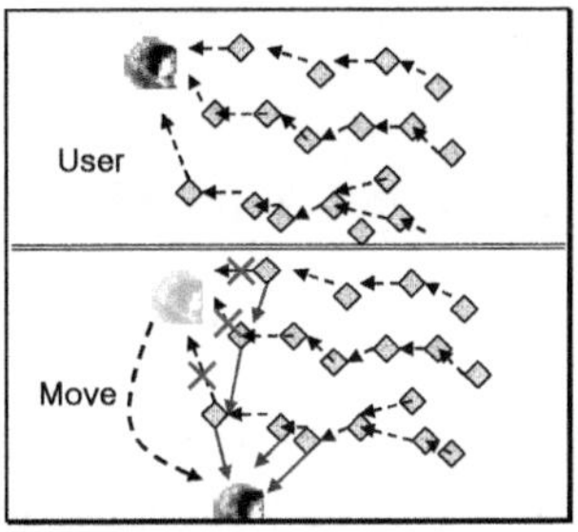

Fig. 4. Topology control based user-network communication model

The other problem is that the cost of the overhead to reorganize the network topology and reconstruct dissemination paths from sensor nodes to the mobile user is expensive. In G-COM, all sensors make the topology based on location information. Accordingly, each sensor must have its own GPS receiver. The cost of GPS receivers is decreasing, but the overall cost is still high. In T-COM, similarly, user mobility causes topology reconstruction. Users in T-COM have a tree that is rooted at each mobile user. If users move into a new location, then the root of trees must be changed, as seen in fig. 4. This leads to enormous overhead to sensor nodes with constrained energy.

Hence, this paper proposes a novel **agent-based user-network communication model (A-COM)**. A-COM collects data through a temporary agent and delivers the data to mobile users. In A-COM, if a user intends to obtain data while moving, the user appoints a sensor to act as an agent, and the agent forwards interests to the sink via a sensor network. The sink, having received interests from the user, collects data from sensor nodes using the existing data collection algorithm in static sink sensor networks [2], [3], [4]. The collected data are finally forwarded to the user. (If there is no sink, the agent directly disseminates interests to the whole networks and collects data.)

A-COM has various advantages, as can be seen in Table 1. First of all, A-COM has the compatibility of existing static sink routing protocols without infrastructure networks. In addition, the users in A-COM do not make a topology (tree or GRID) and communicate only with agents. So, the users, while moving, are free from topology control. The user's freedom saves much energy, and enables more users to participate in the proposed model even if the sensors have no GPS receivers.

We verified through simulation that the lifetime of sensor networks is prolonged because the user's freedom decreases the energy consumption of the sensor nodes. Also, we verified that the performance of the data delivery ratio and the delay never decreases. Nevertheless, the movement of the user is supported by only sensor nodes without infrastructure networks.

The rest of this paper is organized as follows. Section 2 describes the proposed model. Simulation results are presented in Section 3 to evaluate the effectiveness of our design and to analyze the impact of important parameters. Section 4 concludes the paper.

2 Model Analysis

In our model, if a user intends to obtain data while moving, the user appoints a sensor to act as an agent and forwards an interest to the agent. If there is one or more sinks, the agent forwards interests to sensor networks via sinks. The number of sinks, however, depends on the network policy. A network administrator might want to set a single or more sinks in the sensor field, or alternatively the sensor field may be hazardous as he cannot reach the field. Hence, we consider three scenarios according to the number of sinks and describe the scenarios based on following assumptions.

This paper makes the following assumptions:

- A user can communicate with static sinks only through sensors because networks within sensor fields are infrastructure-less networks.
- It is possible that multiple sinks are deployed in sensor networks and are connected to each other via the Internet. How to connect a sink with other sinks is out of the range of this paper, but this helps maximize the efficiency of gathering data.
- Multiple static sinks are located in the outskirts of sensor fields.

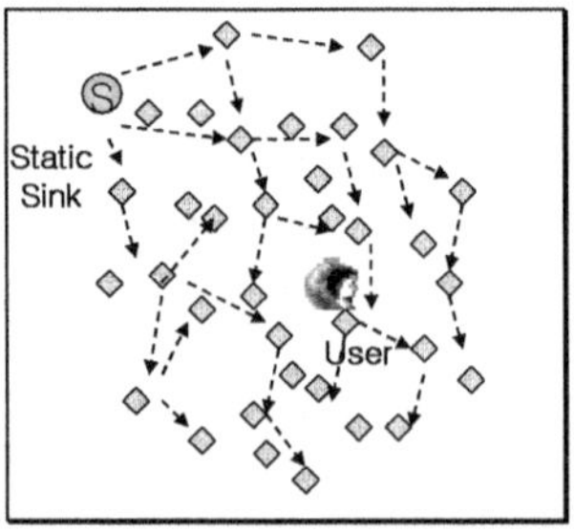

Fig. 5. Dissemination of Sink Announcement Message

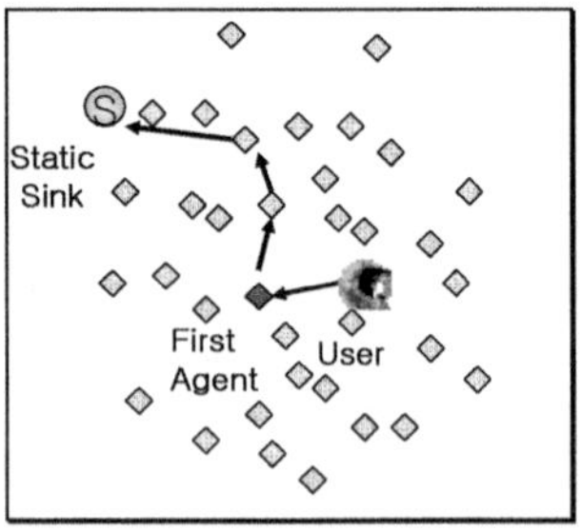

Fig. 6. Interest Dissemination of the user

- The data which one sink collects is aggregated by the sink. The aggregated data is shared by every multiple static sink through the infrastructure network, namely, the Internet.
- The interest from a user describes how many times the sink forwards a gathered data set to a user.

2.1 Scenario 1: Sensor Fields with Only One Sink

Dissemination of sink announcement message. In the initial stage of the sensor network, the network administrator sets a sink in a suitable position: center, outskirt, or a special position according to his or her policy. If a sink is located in an arbitrary position in sensor fields, it floods a sink announcement message to announce itself as inside the whole sensor field (Fig. 5). As a result of the flooding announcement message, every sensor node knows the hop counts and next hop neighbor sensor node to the sink.

Interest dissemination of the user. While moving inside the sensor fields, if a user wants to collect data, the user selects the nearest node as the first agent, as shown in Fig. 6. The user delivers an interest to the first agent. The first agent, to which the user has delivered an interest, forwards the interest to the next hop neighbor node toward the sink. The next hop sensor node, which has had the interest delivered to it, also forwards the interest to the next hop neighbor node toward the sink. This process continues until the sink receives the interest of the user. Also, a route for the interest from the sink to the user has been established through this process. Based on our assumptions, the established route vanishes from the networks when the described period in the interest is over.

Data collection of sink. A sensor network with a static sink is a network where sensing data from sensor nodes should be transmitted to the static sink through multi-hop communication. So, existing routing algorithms for a static sink can be used (e.g., routing algorithms collecting data by periods, routing algorithms collecting a minority event, or routing algorithms detecting a moving object.) Hence, the network administrator can support a suitable routing protocol for users, and besides, a user can select and use the most appropriate routing algorithm with a static sink according to the policy of the networks. Such research has already been advanced [2], [3], [4]. So we will not mention it further in this paper. Rather, we use one of the existing routing algorithms to collect data in this paper. In Fig. 7, the static sink can forward interests from users to sensors and gather data from sensor networks according to the existing routing protocols. If all data are gathered by routing protocols, the static sink aggregates all data and forwards an aggregated data to the first agent.

Mobility support of the user. A user may move to another place after sending an interest to the first agent. In this case, the user selects another agent that can communicate with the first agent. Also, the user makes a new connection between the newly selected agent and the original agent. (While moving inside the sensor fields, the user can make more agents and connections.) These agents and connections are used for forwarding the aggregated data from the sink.

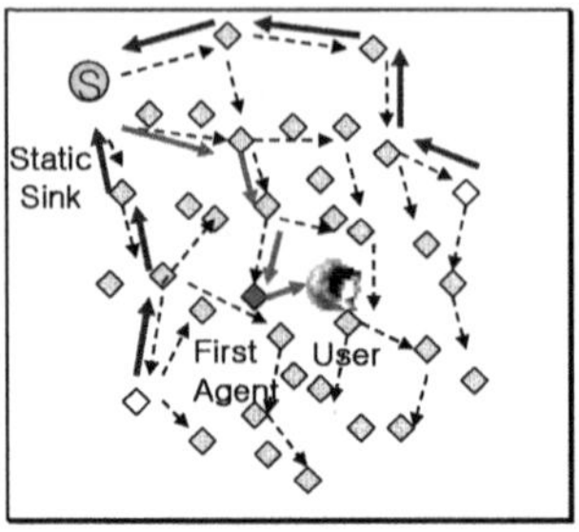

Fig. 7. Data Propagation to the user

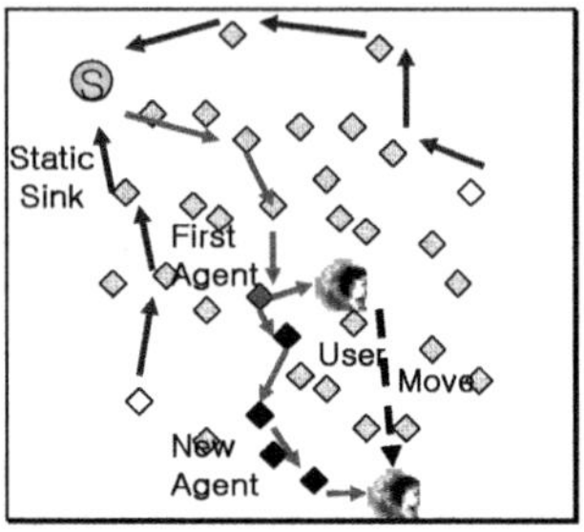

Fig. 8. Mobility support of the user

Data propagation of the sink. A sink delivers the aggregated data to the first agent through the reverse path of interest forwarding. The first agent delivers the aggregated data to the last agent through the connection of agents. The last agent delivers the aggregated data to the user. As shown in Fig. 8, the user can surely receive the aggregated data from the sink.

2.2 Scenario 2: Sensor Fields with Multiple Sinks

Separation of the sensor fields. Basically, the difference between Scenario 1 and Scenario 2 is only the number of sinks. If there are more sinks in the sensor field, this means a separation of the sensor fields. As a result of sink announcement message dissemination in this case, all sensor nodes know the nearest sink according to the hop counts. Accordingly, Interest dissemination of the user targets the nearest sink from the agent, as shown Fig 9. The targeted sinks can be changed whenever the user wants to send its interests (see Fig. 10). Nevertheless, Mobility support of the user and data propagation of the sink is still the same as with Scenario 1. In addition, users may not be able to recognize how many static sinks are in the sensor fields. This means that the proposed model is independent of the number of sinks.

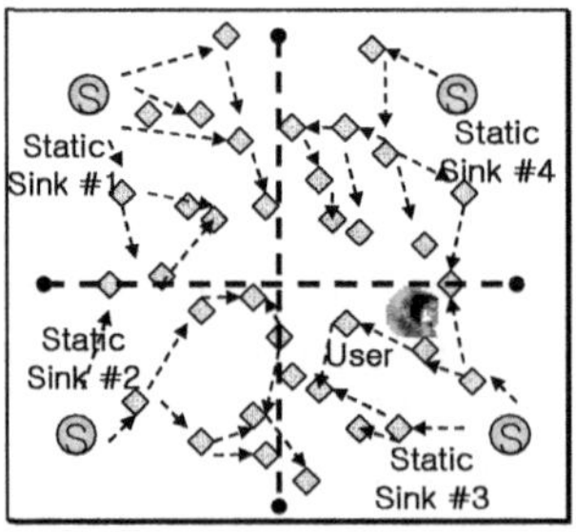

Fig. 9. Seperation of the Sensor Fields

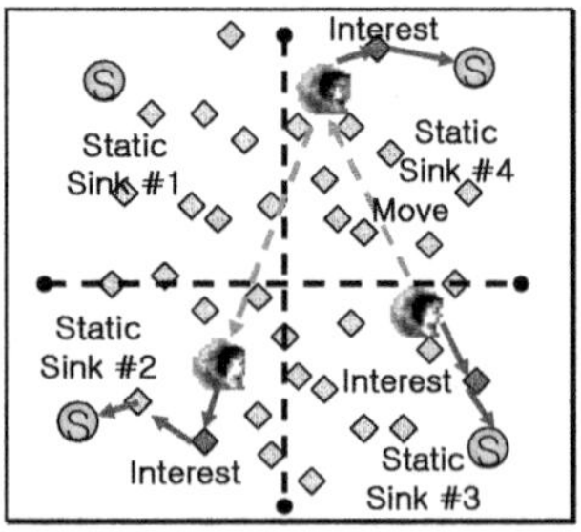

Fig. 10. Interest Dissemination of the user with multiple sinks

Data sharing of multiple static sinks. As shown in Fig. 1, a sink in typical sensor networks takes charge of the function as gateways for the connection with infrastructure networks [1]. And various papers in relation to multiple static sinks also indicate the connection between a sink and an infrastructure network and the connection between all sinks as an assumption [10], [11].

Therefore, in this paper, it is assumed that each sink placed in the edge of a sensor field can communicate with the other sinks via the infrastructure networks. Hence, the proposed model of this paper collects data by one sink through sensor fields. And the aggregated data of the collected data will be shared by multiple static sinks through the infrastructure network.

Advantages with multiple static sinks. A proposed model can obtain various advantages with multiple static sinks. First of all, a user can receive the data from the nearest sink to its position. Therefore short hops communications between a user and a sink are possible. This saves energy, enhances the data delivery ratio, and reduces delay. Also, because a user requires a dissemination of interests through multiple static sinks, locations of data collection are diverse. It relieves a hot spot problem which has carried a disproportionate amount of traffic to sensor nodes near the sink [13]. As a result, the lifetime of the sensor networks will be able to increase because a balance of energy consumption of the sensor nodes is made possible.

2.3 Scenario 3: Sensor Fields with No Sink

Hazardous sensor fields. The sensor fields without a sink are a special type of the sensor networks. If the sensor field is hazardous as network administrator cannot reach the field (ex. Battlefield), it may not have any sinks. In a battle field, users (or soldiers) may move into the sensor field which has no sink and gather data from sensors. In this case, users must gather data for themselves.

Dissemination of sink announcement message. Because there is no sink in the sensor field, the sensor network cannot practice sink announcement message dissemination process for itself. In this case, users must appoint the nearest sensor node as first agent, and the first agent disseminates sink announcement message. As shown Fig 11 and 12, users which want to gather data from sensors examine nearby sensor nodes whether there is a sink in the sensor field or not. If not, users appoint the nearest sensor node to first agent. Once a sensor node becomes first agent, it acts like the sink of Scenario 1. Hence, other processes such as sink announcement message

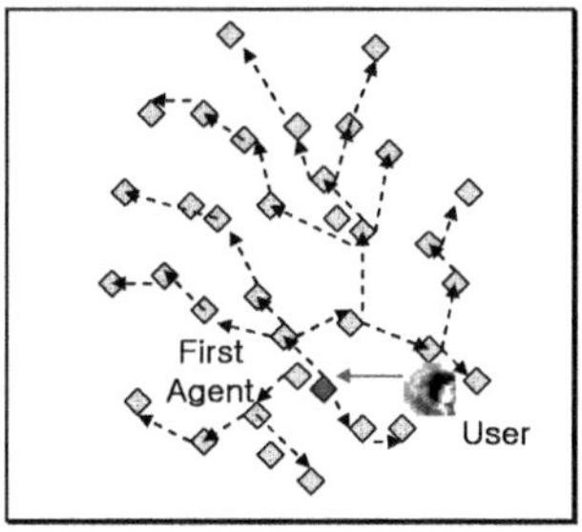

Fig. 11. First Agent Selection and Announcement

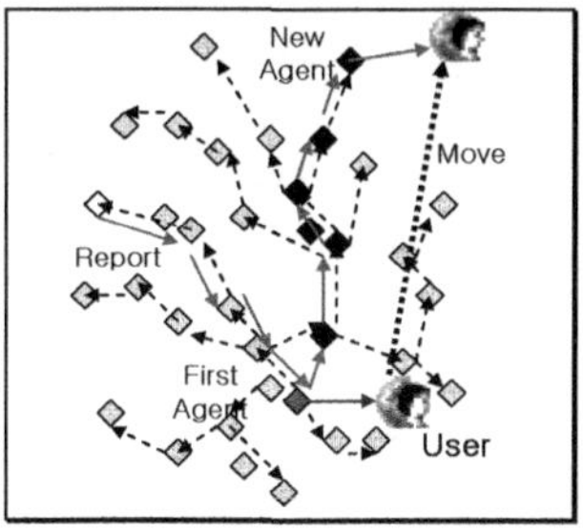

Fig. 12. Mobility support of the user

dissemination, interest dissemination of the user, Mobility support of the user, data propagation of the sink are the same as Scenario 1.

Advantages with idle sensor network. Based on our assumptions, the proposed model in this scenario may create many first agents periodically. The first agents must return to the original state after the described period. This means that the first agents are appointed whenever users want to send its interest. Then, the first agents are reactively selected and practice all process for user mobility. In the whole network, therefore, the sensor network can remain in an idle state in case there is no user in the sensor field. From the standpoint of whole network, this is a positive effect because there is no control of messages and interests in the idle state sensor network.

3 Performance Evaluation

In this section, we evaluate the performance of a proposed model through simulations. We first describe our simulation model and simulation metrics. We next evaluate how environmental factors and control parameters affect the performance of a proposed algorithm.

3.1 Simulation Model and Metric

We evaluate the proposed model in Qualnet, a network simulator [12]. A sensor node's transmitting and receiving power consumption rate are 0.66W and 0.39W. The transceiver in the simulation has a 50m radio range in an outdoor area. Each interest packet is 40 bytes long and the data packet has 64 bytes. The sensor network consists of 100 sensor nodes, which are randomly deployed in a 300m x 300m field.

We consider three scenarios for the proposed model according to the number of sinks. Hence, the number of sinks and users is changed for this evaluation. The multiple static sinks are located in the outskirts of sensor fields. And the user which follows a random waypoint model of 10m/s speed and 10 second pause time moves into the sensor field. The user disseminates an interest at an interval of every 10 seconds. Every sensor node receives the interest and generates only one sensing data

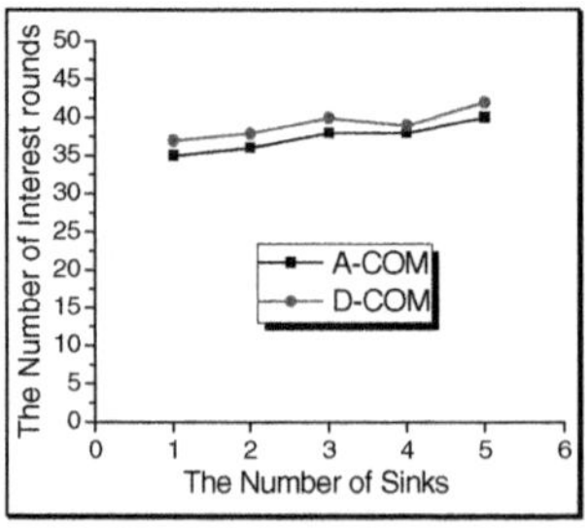

Fig. 13. Network lifetime for the Number of Sinks

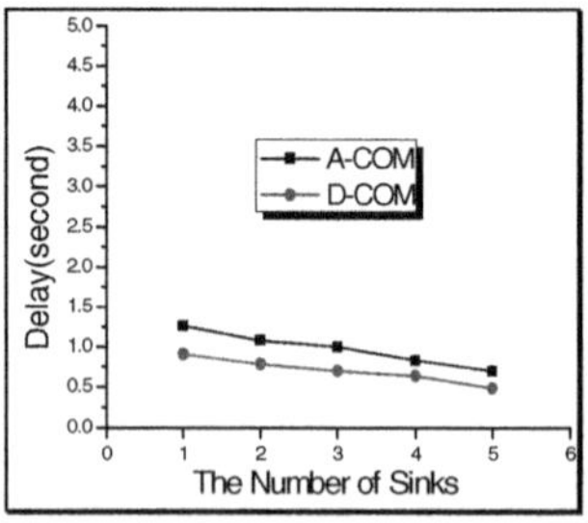

Fig. 14. Delay for the Number of Sinks

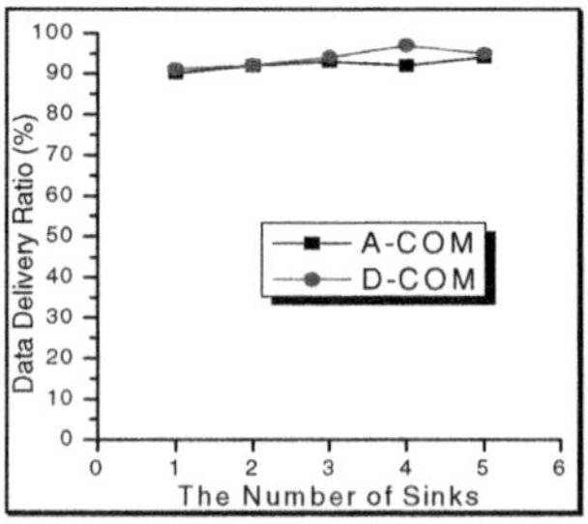

Fig. 15. Data Delivery Ratio for the Number of Sinks

for the interest. This is defined as one interest round. Namely, one interest round is 10 seconds. The simulation lasts for 500 seconds.

We use metrics to evaluate the performance of the proposed algorithm. **The network lifetime** is defined as the number of the interest round when the first sensor node dies. **The data delivery ratio** is the ratio of the number of successfully received reports at a user to the total number of reports generated by every sensor node. **The delay** is defined as the average time between the time a user transmits an interest and the time the user receives the report. We compare three mobility types (D-COM, G-COM, T-COM) in table 1 with the proposed model in the simulation.

3.2 Impact of the Number of Multiple Static Sinks

Scenarios 1 and 2 of A-COM can be compared with the D-COM because G-COM and T-COM have no static sink. We first study the impact of the number of sinks on A-COM's performance. The number of sinks varies from 1, 2, 3, 4 to 5. And there is only one user in the sensor field. In this part, we compare Scenarios 1 and 2 to D-COM regarding lifetime, delay, and delivery ratio.

A difference between A-COM and the D-COM is how to communicate between a user and a sink. Fig. 13 shows the number of interest rounds, namely, network lifetime. As shown in Fig. 13, the number of interest rounds shows little difference between A-COM and D-COM. This means that A-COM can manage sensor fields as well as D-COM without infrastructure that connects users with sinks. In addition, the lifetime is increased according to the number of sinks. This is a side effect of multiple sinks. Multiple sinks separate the sensor field, and besides, users only use the nearest sink to send interests and receive replies. Users can use the shortest path to communicate with multiple sinks. As a result of the shortest communication, the lifetime in A-COM is enhanced according to the number of sinks.

The delay is also enhanced by this side effect of multiple sinks. A-COM basically has some delay due to multi-hop communication between users and sinks. However, the delay is diminished according to the number of sinks, as shown in Fig. 14. Nevertheless, the data delivery ratio of A-COM is comparable with D-COM, as shown in Fig. 15. This also proves that the proposed model can manage sensor fields as well as D-COM without infrastructure.

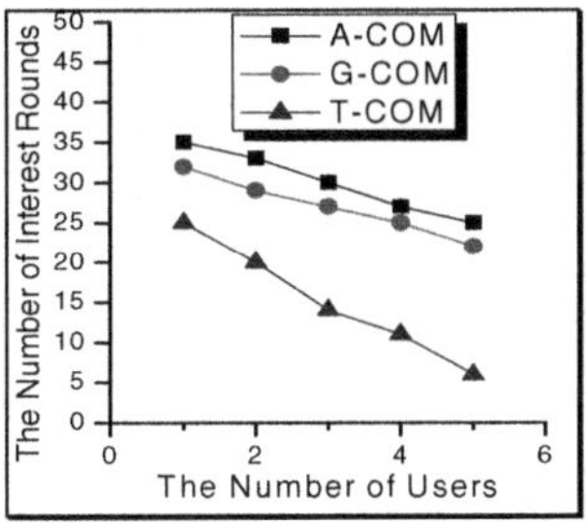

Fig. 16. Network Lifetime for the Number of Users

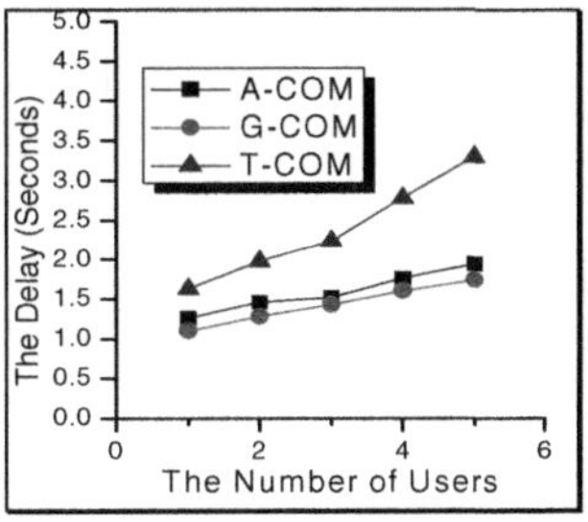

Fig. 17. Delay for the number of Users

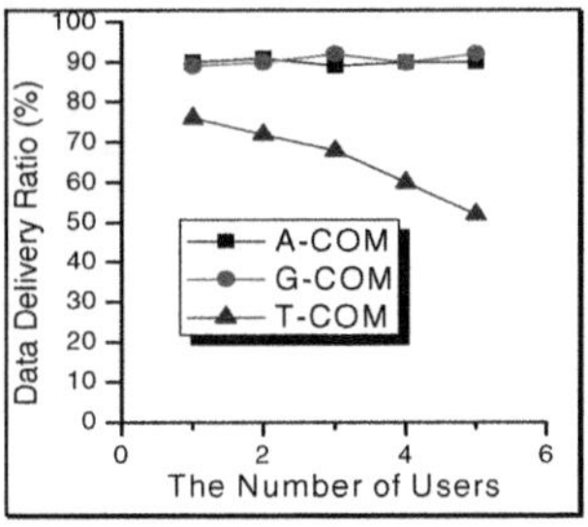

Fig. 18. Data Delivery Ratio for the Number of Users

3.3 Impact of the Number of Multiple Users

The number of users only results in the path increase between users and sinks. D-COM uses direct communication between users and sinks, and A-COM uses multi-hop communication. A-COM has more paths and consumes more energy. (e.g., five users in A-COM consumes five times of the energy that is consumed by one user.) However, it is a tradeoff between energy and infrastructure. Although A-COM has more energy consumption and delays than D-COM, the merit of A-COM is infrastructure-less communication systems.

Scenario 3 of A-COM can be compared with G-COM and T-COM because Scenario 3 of A-COM, G-COM, and T-COM have no static sinks. There are no sinks, and the number of users varies from 1, 2, 3, 4 to 5. In this part, we compare Scenario 3 of A-COM to G-COM and T-COM regarding lifetime, delay, and delivery ratio.

G-COM and T-COM make and change the topology proactively, but Scenario 3 of A-COM reactively makes and shares it among users. Generally, users move about the sensor field only and generate its interest occasionally. Hence, sensors in Scenario 3 can save considerable energy. Alternatively, sensors in G-COM and T-COM maintain a topology continuously. Fig. 16 shows each lifetime of these sensor networks. As shown in Fig. 16, the lifetime of T-COM is considerably low due to frequent topology change and the one of G-COM is relatively low due to GRID maintenance.

In Fig. 17, G-COM has little delay due to proactive GRID topology by the GPS receiver. T-COM proactively creates the topology, but frequent topology changes of T-COM delay data delivery considerably. The delay of Scenario 3, as shown in Fig. 17, however, is only a little high due to the reactive first agent selection and topology construction. In the case of the data delivery ratio, A-COM and G-COM in Fig. 18 are similar except for T-COM. The reason is frequent topology change. Topology change messages disturb the data delivery ratio.

3.4 Impact of the Number of Sensor Nodes

Evaluating A-COM with other models according to the number of sensors is of no real consequence. It is closely related to the performance of routing protocols which is used in the network. Hence, we do not evaluate the proposed model with this factor.

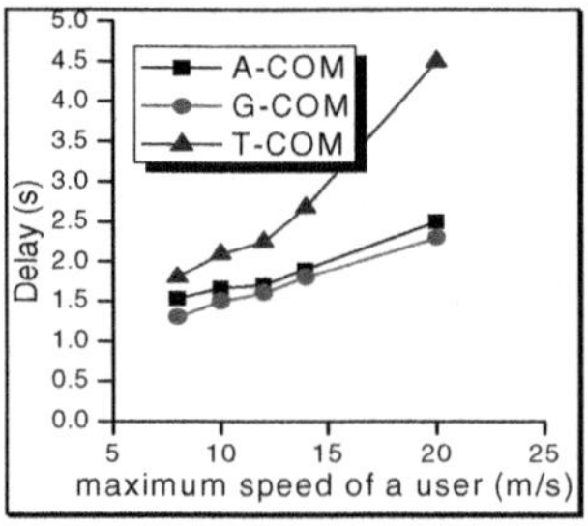

Fig. 19. Delay for User Speed

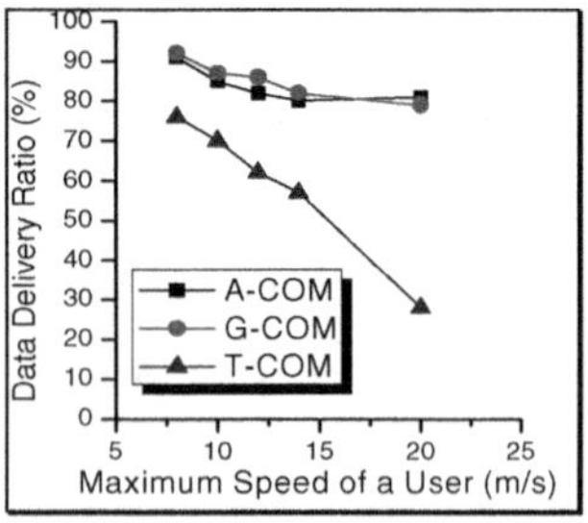

Fig. 20. Data Delivery Ratio for User Speed

3.5 Impact of the User Mobility

We last evaluate the impact of user speed on A-COM. We vary the maximum speed of a user from 8, 10, 12, 14 to 20m/s. And we assume that there is one user in the sensor field. In this part, we compare Scenario 3 to G-COM and T-COM because D-COM is independent of user speed. Fig. 19 shows the delay in data delivery, which slightly increases as the user moves faster. The delay depends on a movement operation that is processed by the user. The faster a user moves, the more the user needs time to establish a connection between the user and the network. Nevertheless, the delay of A-COM is comparable with G-COM because A-COM creates only one communication path between a user and its first agent. The delay of T-COM, on the other hand, is relatively higher than the others due to frequent topology changes.

And, Fig. 20 shows the data delivery ratio when the user's moving speed changes. The data delivery ratio of A-COM is slightly decreased according to the delay. But the data delivery ratio remains around 0.8 - 0.9; nevertheless, the user moves faster. Besides, the data delivery ratio of G-COM remains high because the GPS receiver may help the user with geographical routing. On the other hand, the data delivery ratio of T-COM is relatively lower than the others because it has too many topology changes when moving. The results in Fig. 19 and Fig 20 mean that A-COM is fast and stable without GPS receiver.

4 Conclusion and Further Work

In this paper, we propose a novel agent-based user-network communication model to support the mobility of users in wireless sensor networks. In the proposed network model, the user can receive the data with a higher data delivery ratio and in a faster time without infrastructure.

We verified that the lifetime of sensor networks is prolonged because the reactive path construction decreases the energy consumption of sensor nodes. Also, we verified that performance of the data delivery ratio and the delay never falls; nevertheless, communication between the user and the network for guaranteeing movement of the user is supported by only sensor nodes without infrastructure networks.

There is further work that is related to this research. In a mobile environment, many sensor nodes can shift from one place to another frequently. The mobile sensor node environment makes more dynamic sensor networks. The issue of node mobility requires further study.

References

1. Akyildiz, I.F., et al.: A survey on sensor networks. IEEE Communications Magazine 40, 102–114 (2002)
2. Intanagonwiwat, C., et al.: Directed diffusion: A scalable and robust communication paradigm for sensor networks. In: ACM Mobicom (2000)

3. Schurgers, C., Srivastava, M.B.: Energy efficient routing in wireless sensor networks. In: IEEE MILCOM (2001)
4. Heinzelman, W.R., et al.: Adaptive Protocols for Information Dissemination in Wireless Sensor Networks. In: ACM Mobicom (1999)
5. Ye, F., et al.: A Two-Tier Data Dissemination Model for Large-scale Wireless Sensor Networks. In: ACM MobiCOM (September 2002)
6. Kim, S., et al.: SAFE: A Data Dissemination Protocol for Periodic Updates in Sensor Networks. In: Distributed Computing Systems Workshops (2003)
7. Xuan, H.L., Lee, S.: A Coordination-based Data Dissemination Protocol for Wireless Sensor Networks. In: IEEE ISSNIP (December 2004)
8. Hwang, K., et al.: Dynamic sink oriented tree algorithm for efficient target tracking of multiple mobile sink users in wide sensor field. In: IEEE VTC (September 2004)
9. Gandham, S.R., et al.: Energy Efficient Schemes for Wireless Sensor Networks with Multiple Mobile Base Stations. In: IEEE GLOBECOM (December 2003)
10. Ferriere, H., et al.: Efficient and Practical Query Scoping in Sensor Networks. In: IEEE International Conference on Mobile Ad-hoc and Sensor Systems (October 2004)
11. Oyman, E.I., Erso, C.: Multiple Sink Network Design Problem in Large Scale Wireless Sensor Networks. In: IEEE ICC (June 2004)
12. Scalable Network Technologies, Qualnet, [online] available: http://www.scalable-networks.com
13. Dai, H., Han, R.: A node-centric load balancing algorithm for wireless sensor networks. In: IEEE GLOBECOM (December 2003)

Secure Dynamic Network Reprogramming Using Supplementary Hash in Wireless Sensor Networks*

Kwangkyu Park[1], JongHyup Lee[1], Taekyoung Kwon[2], and Jooseok Song[1]

[1] Dept. of Computer Science, Yonsei University, Seoul, 120-749, Korea
{scheme,jhlee,jssong}@emerald.yonsei.ac.kr

[2] Dept. of Computer Engineering, Sejong University, Seoul, 143-747, Korea
tkwon@sejong.ac.kr

Abstract. Wireless Sensor Networks (WSNs) consist of highly resource constrained sensor nodes. A large number of sensor nodes are deployed over a wide geographical area and operate in unattended fashions. These features of WSNs make difficult the manual intervention through physical access. Thus, secure network reprogramming is a critical requirement for WSNs. So far, the previous studies have focused only on the authenticity and integrity of program images. However, the delayed authentication problem caused by the packet loss should be considered. In this paper, we propose two schemes in the way of providing the recovery method for verification processes at packet loss, using supplementary hashing: *Redundant Hash* scheme and *Page Digest* scheme. Our schemes show improved performance than previous studies.

1 Introduction

Wireless Sensor Networks (hereafter WSNs) consist of a large number of highly resource constrained small size sensor nodes. Since a large number of sensor nodes are deployed over a wide geographical area and operate in unattended fashions, when it is required to change nodes' operational behavior or maintain the buggy code, the update via physical access to node is usually impractical. Therefore, a number of schemes [1,2,3,4] have been proposed to support such updates. Unfortunately, none of them considered security aspects. To resolve this security problem, several approaches [5,6,7] have been proposed. Though these studies guarantee the integrity of update data, they still have a *delayed authentication* problem. Therefore, we propose two new schemes for providing the integrity of update data and to handle the delayed authentication problem.

The rest of this paper is organized as follows. In Section 2, review of related works and problem definition is provided. In Section 3, we present our schemes

* This research was supported by the MIC(Ministry of Information and Communication), Korea, under the ITRC(Information Technology Research Center) support program supervised by the IITA(Institute of Information Technology Advancement) (IITA-2006-C1090-0603-0028).

J. Indulska et al. (Eds.): UIC 2007, LNCS 4611, pp. 653–662, 2007.

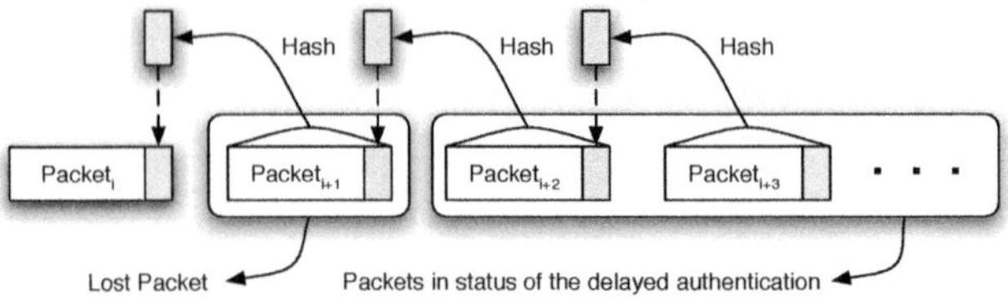

Fig. 1. Delayed authentication problem due to the packet loss

in detail. Section 4 provides analysis and performance evaluations with regard to storage overhead, communication overhead and security aspect. This paper is concluded in Section 5.

2 Related Works and Problem Definition

2.1 Secure Dynamic Network Reprogramming

Recently, several studies have been done in the area of secure dynamic network reprogramming. All of these studies use digital signatures and cryptographic hashing as cryptographic primitives. Sluice [6] forms a hash chain at page levels. this requires little spatial and temporal overheads but the coarse granularity of hash chains gives a chance of attacking with leverage effects to adversaries. Hence, in [7], the hash chain is constructed at packet levels. It has the advantage that the individual malicious packet can be detected earlier at a cost of more per-packet overheads than Sluice. J. Deng *et al.* [5] proposed a hybrid scheme, the combination of hash chain based and hash tree based schemes. At the page level, the hash chain based scheme is used but the hash tree is applied at the packet level in order to tolerate the out-of-order arrival of packets.

2.2 Delayed Authentication Problem

In WSNs, transmitted packets can not reach the receiver due to various reasons. When a packet is lost, though secure dynamic network reprogramming schemes have retransmission mechanisms of lost packet, the subsequent packets of the lost packet, cannot be authenticated before the lost packet is recovered. Fig. 1 depicts this situation. The hash tree based scheme [5] also has similar problems.

Because it is an energy intensive operation to write into the flash memory, the *unverified packets*[1] have to remain in the internal memory of the sensor nodes and wait for the recovery of the lost packet. However, when the *buffer*, which is assigned memory area for containing the unverified packets, overflows, later packets should be dropped or written into the flash memory without verifying. In case of the lossy wireless channel or active DoS attack, this problem causes severe performance degradation of the whole system.

[1] The packet in the status of the delayed authentication is represented as an *unverified packet* hereafter.

Table 1. Notations

Symbol	Meaning
pkt_n	$(n+1)$-th packet of the update data packet stream
D_n	Payload data of pkt_n
$H(X)$	A cryptographic hash of X
H_n	$H(pkt_n)$
SK	A secret key in a public key system
$[X]_{SK}$	X is signed with SK
$X\|Y$	Concatenation of X and Y
K	A number of pages in the entire update data
N	A number of packets in each page (except possibly the last page)
M	A number of packets in the entire update data
p	A packet loss rate

3 Proposed Schemes

In this section, we propose two schemes which are based on the hash chain based scheme [5,7]. We use notation introduced in Table 1 in the rest of this paper.

3.1 Scheme 1: Redundant Hash Approach

The redundant hash approach is designed to minimize the unverified packets. In addition to hash chain, our scheme introduces a redundant hash which is selectively placed within a hash chain. The redundant hash, containing the hash data of the d-th subsequent packet, is placed in every s-th packet starting from pkt_0, which is an advertisement packet. It is desirable that s must be less than d, because: If $s > d$, the coverage of the redundant hash cannot be overlapped. In other words, if a packet loss occurs within the interval of the coverage, subsequent packets of the lost packet cannot be authenticated. If $s = d$, the coverage is overlapped in a single packet. Hence, if this single point of overlap is lost, subsequent packets of the lost packet cannot be authenticated.

In case that $s = 2$ and $d = 4$, the redundant hash scheme is illustrated in Fig. 2. The total number of packets is M with exception of pkt_0.

The trusted source is responsible for preparing update data by constructing a hash chain (with redundant hashing) and computing digital signatures. After the processing at the trusted source, the stream of packet is prepared as follows:

$$pkt_i = \begin{cases} ([H_1|H_d]_{SK}|H_1|H_d) & i = 0 \text{ (advertisement packet)} \\ (D_i|H_{i+1}|H_{i+d}) & i \bmod s = 0 \text{ and } i + d \leqq M \\ (D_i|H_{i+1}) & i \bmod s \neq 0 \text{ or } i + d > M \end{cases}$$

If packets arrived in order, they are checked against the hash data of the immediate previous packet. If packets arrived out of order due to losses or jitters over communications channels, the cached redundant hash is used to authenticate them. Packets which cannot be authenticated by the cached data, are buffered in memory for further authentication.

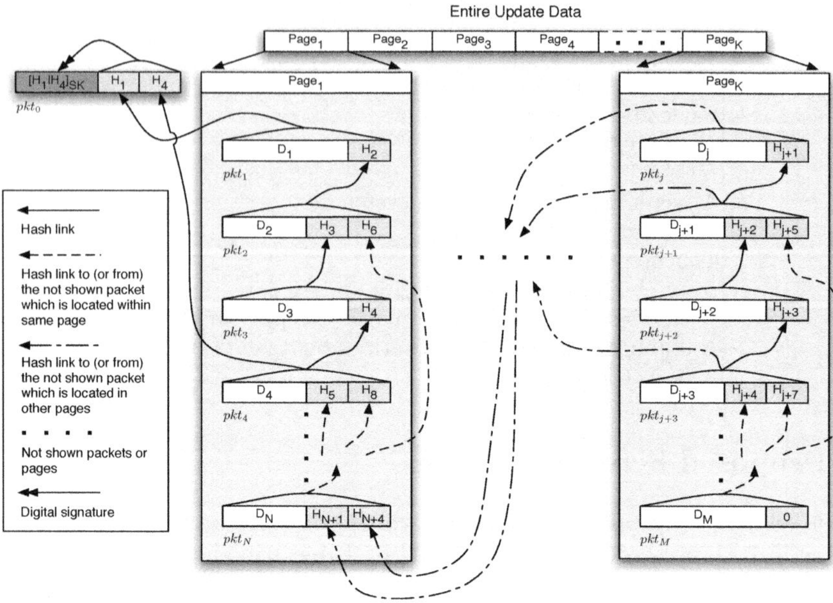

Fig. 2. Redundant Hash scheme ($s = 2$, $d = 4$)

3.2 Scheme 2: Page Digest Approach

The second approach for secure network reprogramming is a page digest scheme. The page digest consist of a set of truncated hash fraction or the digest of the hash data, which is called a "hash slice", for packets in a page. At the end of the page, the page digest for the next page is transmitted by following the data packets. In case of the first page, the page digest is included in the advertisement packet. The size of page digest is determined from the size of hash slice, h_s, and the number of packets in a page, N. For example, when $h_s = 4$ (bytes) and $N = 24$, the overhead of 96 bytes are required per page as a page digest. Fig. 3 illustrates the structure of page digest. In Fig. 3, the page digest consists of hash slices for upcoming packets and hash data of the next packet.

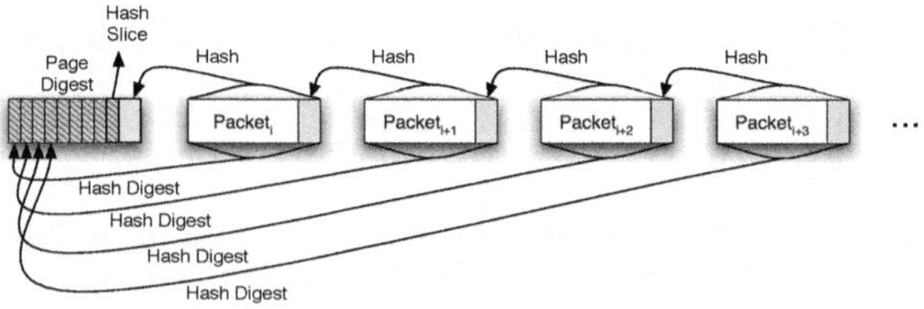

Fig. 3. Page digest scheme

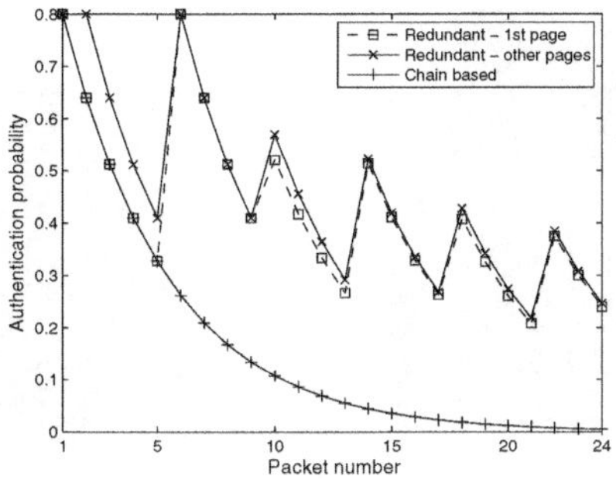

Fig. 4. Authentication probability for each packet

When a packet is lost or out-of-order arrivals happen, the sensor node can verifies subsequent packets with the page digest. But, even if the packet is verified by the hash slice, it is only marked as partially verified. Basically, partially verified packets are not written into the flash memory, but when the buffer occupation grows over a certain threshold, T_{buf}, the sensor node starts to write partially verified packets into the flash memory. When a lost packet is retransmitted, node checks whether partially verified packets can be completely verified using hash chain.

4 Analysis and Performance Evaluation

In order to compare our schemes with the other hash chain based schemes, we define two strategies: *Write At Full (WAF)* and *Drop At Full (DAF)*. When the received packet cannot be verified, it is stored in the node's buffer. Both strategies are the same until the buffer is full or overflowed. However, in WAF, the overflowed packet is written into the flash memory but it is dropped in DAF.

4.1 Authentication Probability

We define the authentication probability for a packet pkt_i as the probability that a packet is received without error and it can be authenticated by the hash value from previous packets. In other words, the authentication probability, P_{auth} can be represented like followings:

$$\begin{aligned} P_{auth} &= Pr[pkt_i \text{ can be authenticated} \wedge pkt_i \text{ is received}] \\ &= Pr[pkt_i \text{ is received}] \cdot (1 - Pr[pkt_i \text{ cannot be authenticated}]). \end{aligned}$$

Let q_i and $t_{j,i}$ be P_{auth} for the hash chain based scheme and the redundant scheme, respectively. From the assumption that the advertisement packet, pkt_0 is successfully received, q_i is defined as following with the initial condition of $q_0 = 1$.

$$q_i = (1-p)q_{i-1} = (1-p)^i \tag{1}$$

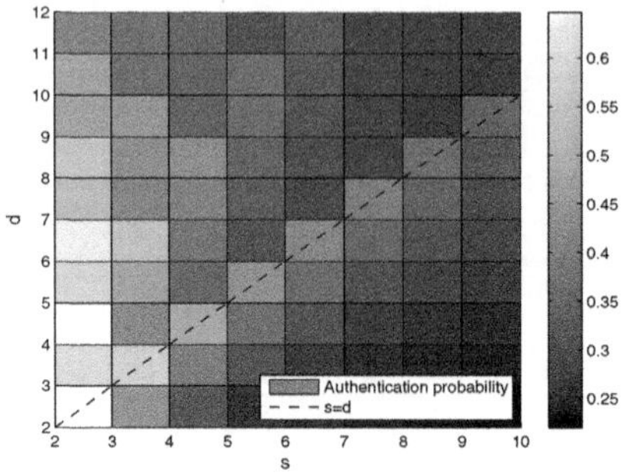

(a) Contour map of the 1st page

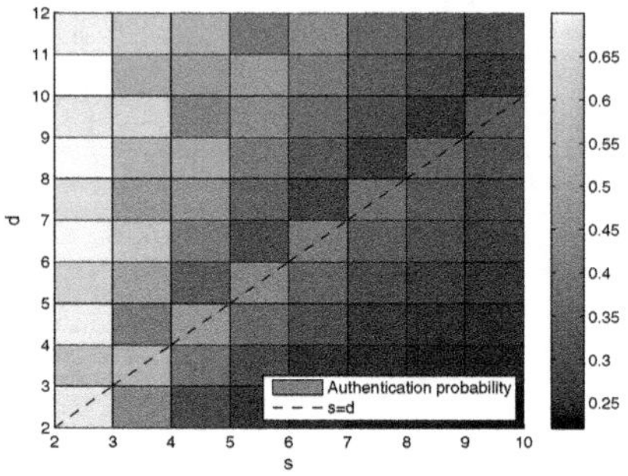

(b) Contour map of the other pages

Fig. 5. Authentication probability with respect to s and d

The $t_{j,i}$ is changed from page to page. At the first page, the first $d-1$ packets cannot utilize the redundant hash (*start-up penalty*) because the redundant hash is placed from pkt_0 with the interval of s. The higher d causes the higher penalty. Considering the start-up penalty, we calculate $t_{j,i}$ for the first page ($j=1$) and the other pages ($j=2$), separately. [2] Additionally, $t_{j,i}$ is determined according to whether the packet is referenced by the redundant hash or not.

Therefore, $t_{1,i}$ for the first page is like following recurrence equation.

$$t_{1,i} = \begin{cases} (1-p)\{1-(1-t_{1,i-1})(1-t_{1,i-d})\} & i-d \mod s = 0 \wedge i >= d \\ (1-p)\{1-(1-t_{1,i-1})\} & i-d \mod s \neq 0 \end{cases} \tag{2}$$

with the initial condition of $t_{1,0}=1$, $t_{1,1}=(1-p)t_{1,0}$ and $t_{1,n}=0$, where $n<0$.

$t_{2,i}$ for the other pages is like following:

$$t_{2,i} = \begin{cases} (1-p)\{1-(1-t_{2,i-1})(1-t_{2,i-d})\} & i-d \mod s = 0 \\ (1-p)\{1-(1-t_{2,i-1})\} & i-d \mod s \neq 0 \end{cases} \tag{3}$$

with the initial condition of $t_{2,0}=1$, $t_{2,1}=(1-p)t_{2,0}$ and $t_{2,n}=1$, where $n<0$.

Due to the complexity of finding solutions for the recurrence equations, we evaluate the equations recursively. Fig. 4 depicts P_{auth} (q_i and $t_{j,i}$) for each packet. In Fig. 4 , q_i and $t_{1,i}$ are the same until pkt_5 which is $d-1$-th packet. This shows the impact of the start-up penalty.

Fig. 5 shows the authentication probability of the first page and other pages. Both results show better authentication probabilities at the lower s because the number of redundant hash is increased as the s grows. In Fig. 5(b), the case of $s<d$ shows higher authentication probability than the case of $s \geqq d$ because the coverage of redundant hash is more overlapped at the higher d, as explained

[2] Actually, the authentication probability can be different among other pages. But, the difference is small enough to be negligible.

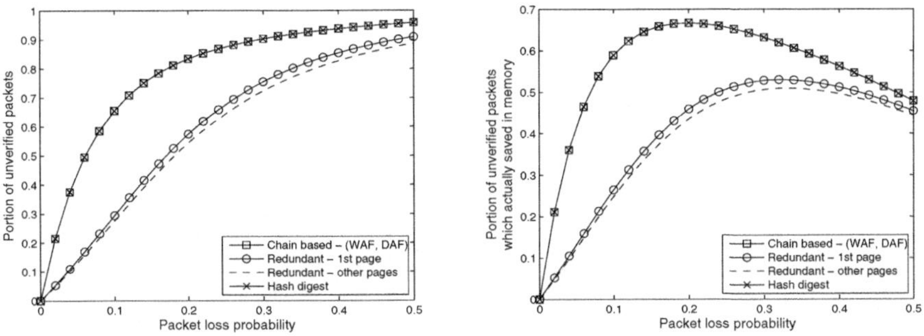

(a) Unverified packets (b) Unverified packets which actually saved in RAM

Fig. 6. Ratio of unverified packets with respect to packet loss probability

in Section 3.1. However, in Fig. 5(a), note that the authentication probability is falling when d increases due to the start-up penalty.

Based on the results and the configuration of [7] and [5], we select the parameters as $s = 4$ and $d = 6$, which are used for the rest of this section.

4.2 Storage Overhead Analysis

Let D be the random variable for the number of unverified packets. The expected value of D is like followings:

$$\begin{aligned} E[D] &= N(1 - \text{Authentication Probability}) \\ &= N(1 - \frac{\sum_1^N q_i}{N}) \end{aligned} \tag{4}$$

From the Eq. 4, the portion of unverified packets in a page will be $\frac{E[D]}{N}$. We can obtain the expected value of unverified packets in the redundant scheme, $E[R]$, with the same way of $E[D]$, $E[R] = N(1 - \frac{\sum_1^N t_{j,i}}{N})$.

The portion of this unverified packets in one page after an initial transmission is depicted in Fig. 6(a). There are no difference between the hash chain based schemes and page digest scheme. However, the redundant hash scheme produces less unverified packets. When the packet loss probability is 0.2, the redundant hash scheme shows only about 62% of that of hash chain based schemes. In the redundant hash scheme, the portion of the first page is slightly higher than other pages, because of its *start-up penalty*.

However, since the unverified packets are also transmitted on the lossy wireless channel, the only $E[D] \times (1 - p)$ and $E[R] \times (1 - p)$ are actually received and stored. In Fig. 6(b), the portion of the unverified packet in a page, which is actually stored in memory, is depicted. Similar to the result of Fig. 6(a), the redundant hash scheme shows the lowest memory requirement for the unverified packets.

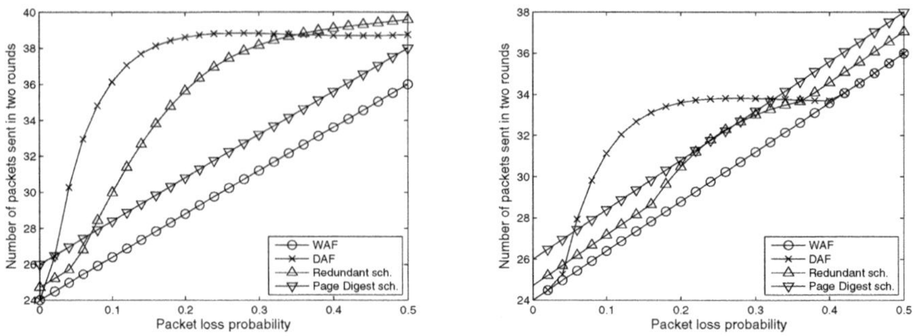

(a) B=3 (b) B=8

Fig. 7. Communication overhead with different buffer sizes

4.3 Communication Overhead Analysis

In Deluge, the sender transmits requested packets of a page and the receiver responses with SNACK, then the retransmission of the lost packet of the page is followed. Each period of transmission is called a *round*. To transmit a whole page, several rounds are required due to lossy wireless channel.

Among sequential rounds for a page, we consider first two rounds. The number of transmitted packet during these two rounds is like the followings:

$$\begin{aligned} \text{WAF} &: N + pN \\ \text{DAF} &: N + pN + ((1-p)E[D] - B) \times u((1-p)E[D] - B) \\ \text{Redundant sch.} &: \{N + pN + ((1-p)E[R] - B) \times u((1-p)E[R] - B)\}\tfrac{sl-sh}{sl-(s+1)h} \\ \text{Page Digest sch.} &: N + pN + O_{PD} \end{aligned} \tag{5}$$

where B is the size of buffer by unit of packets. $u(t)$ is the unit step function which is 1 only $t > 0$ and otherwise 0. Moreover, $\frac{sl-sh}{sl-(s+1)h}$ is a scaling factor for increasing number of packets due to the redundant hash, where l is the size of packet's payload and h is the size of a hash data. In the page digest scheme of Eq. 5, O_{PD} is the number of page digest packets. When we use the 4-byte hash slice and $N = 24$, O_{PD} is 2 with the 56-byte payload.

Fig. 7 depicts the communication overhead with different buffer sizes. Due to the retransmitted packets in the second round, DAF shows the worst communication overhead. Our schemes are next and WAF is best. Also, the sensitivity to buffer size of the redundant hash scheme can be seen in Fig. 7. The redundant hash scheme shows lower overhead when p is lower than the page digest scheme, but it is reversed when p is high. In other words, in the situation of lossy channel and small buffer, the page digest scheme is better than the redundant hash scheme.

4.4 Security Analysis

Using initial public key authentication and packet based hash chain, our schemes have the same level as the hash chain based schemes in the respects of authenticity

Table 2. Security level of written data at buffer overflow

	DAF	WAF	Redundant sch.	Page digest sch.
Before recovery	2^{32}	0	2^{32}	2^{16}
After recovery	2^{32}	0	2^{32}	2^{32}

and integrity. Therefore, we focus on the DoS attack in security analysis. The DoS attack on network reprogramming consists of two stages. At first stage, the adversary makes a packet to be discarded. (e.g., by jamming) Then, at second stage, he or she sends modified packets which can not be authenticated in order to fill node's buffer or drain node's energy by writing unverified packets into flash memory. Moreover, filling the buffer prevents receiving of normal packets.

In DAF and the redundant hash scheme, unverified packets are dropped at the buffer overflow, hence only verified packets resides in flash memory. Contrarily, in WAF, unverified packets are easily written into the flash memory, hence WAF is vulnerable to the DoS attack. In the page digest scheme, at least partially verified packets can be written into the flash memory. Therefore, a certain level of security is always guaranteed according the size of page digest.

From the fact that a birthday attack on a hash of size n-bit produces a collision with a workfactor of approximately $2^{n/2}$ [8], Table 2 shows the security levels (i.e., the number of tries to produce a hash collision) when we assume 64-bit hash and 32-bit page digest are used. Since, in the page digest scheme, the partially verified packets can be completely verified after the recovery of lost packets, the security level of the scheme is different from time to time.

As an example, when we assume that the adversary do the DoS attack with 14 packets, Fig. 8 shows the impact or damage of the DoS attack on the node with 8-packet buffer for unverified packets. In WAF and DAF, the node's buffer is overflowed by the DoS attack. Moreover, energy-expensive flash write is also caused in WAF. In the redundant hash scheme, the impact of DoS attack can not exceed $d-1$ packets. Since packets are immediately authenticated in the page digest scheme, the page digest scheme can protect sensor nodes from the DoS attack. From these fact, the propose schemes are DoS attack resilience.

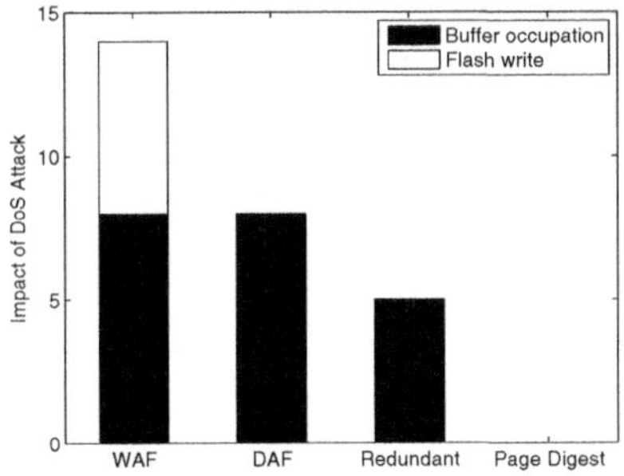

Fig. 8. Impact of DoS attack ($B = 8, d = 6$)

5 Conclusion

In this paper, we propose two distinct schemes such as the redundant hash scheme and the page digest scheme for resolving the problem of delayed authentication caused by lossy wireless channels in WSNs. The redundant hash scheme is similar to DAF strategy but it has the hash chain recovery feature and less storage overhead. In contrast, the page digest scheme uses WAF strategy with security-guaranteed writing by the page digest. In spite that our schemes require slightly more packets in the initial transmission, the total communication overheads are lower than the previous schemes because of the robustness against the packet loss and the DoS attack.

References

1. Hui, J.W., Culler, D.: The Dynamic Behavior of a Data Dissemination Protocol for Network Programming at Scale. In: Proc. of the 2nd International conference on Embedded Networked Sensor Systems (SenSys'04), pp. 81–94 (2004)
2. Kulkarni, S.S., Wang, L.: MNP: Multihop Network Programming for Sensor Networks. In: The 25th International Conference on Distributed Computing Systems (ICDCS'05) (June 2005)
3. Arumugam, M.: Infuse: A TDMA Based Reprogramming Service for Sensor Networks. In: Proc. of the 2nd International Conference on Embedded Networked Sensor Systems (SenSys'04), pp. 281–282 (2004)
4. Xiao, W., Starobinski, D.: Exploiting Multi-Channel Diversity to Speed Up Over-the-Air Programming of Wireless Sensor Networks. In: Proc. of the 3rd International Conference on Embedded Networked Sensor Systems (SenSys'05) (2005)
5. Deng, J., Han, R., Mishra, S.: Secure Code Distribution in Dynamically Programmable Wireless Sensor Networks. In: Proc. of the 5th International Conference on Information Processing in Sensor Networks (IPSN'06) (April 2006)
6. Lanigan, P.E., Gandhi, R., Narasimhan, P.: Sluice: Secure Dissemination of Code Update in Sensor Networks. In: The 26th International Conference of Distributed Computing Systems (ICDCS'06) (July 2006)
7. Dutta, P.K., Hui, J.W., Chu, D.C., Culler, D.E.: Securing the Deluge Network Programming System. In: Proc. of the 5th International Conference on Information Processing in Sensor networks (IPSN'06) (April 2006)
8. Stallings, W.: 11. In: Cryptography and Network Security: Principles and Practice. 3rd edn. Pearson Education, pp. 340–345 (2002)

Self-deployment of Mobile Nodes in Hybrid Sensor Networks by AHP

Xiaoling Wu[1], Jinsung Cho[1], Brian J. d'Auriol[1], Sungyoung Lee[1,*], and Hee Yong Youn[2]

[1] Department of Computer Engineering, Kyung Hee University, Korea
{xiaoling,dauriol,sylee}@oslab.khu.ac.kr,
chojs@khu.ac.kr
[2] School of Information and Communication Engineering,
Sungkyunkwan University, Korea
youn@ece.skku.ac.kr

Abstract. The proper deployment of sensors is very important for the successful completion of the sensing tasks due to the inevitable relation with the physical world. This paper presents a novel method for the redeployment of mobile nodes in a hybrid sensor network consisting of a collection of both static nodes and mobile nodes. In such a sensor network, the locomotion ability of mobile nodes helps the autonomous deployment to enhance the network coverage. An optimal decision of a sensor node moving direction is made based on Analytical Hierarchy Process (AHP). Four factors contributing to the optimal deployment are considered and they are coverage hole, obstacle avoidance, hot spot, and the boundary effect, respectively. The moving style is flip by flip until the stable status is achieved. Simulation results show that our approach can provide high coverage with limited movement distance as well as ensuring connectivity.

1 Introduction

Wireless sensor networks are expected to be widely employed in various applications such as medical care, military, environmental monitoring and industry since they have high flexibility, low production costs, and scalability [1]. Due to the inevitable relation with the physical world, the proper deployment of sensors is very important for the successful completion of the sensing tasks.

Sensor deployment has received considerable attention recently. Some of the work [2], [3], [4] assume that the environment is under control. However, when the environment is inhospitable such as remote inaccessible areas, disaster fields and toxic urban regions, sensor deployment cannot be performed manually. To scatter sensors by aircraft is one possible solution. However, using this scheme, the actual landing position cannot be controlled due to the existence of wind and obstacles such as trees and buildings. Consequently, the coverage may not be able to satisfy the application requirements. Some researchers suggest simply deploying large amount of static

* Corresponding author.

J. Indulska et al. (Eds.): UIC 2007, LNCS 4611, pp. 663–672, 2007.

sensors to increase coverage; however it often ends up harming the performance of the network [5]. In such cases, it is necessary to take advantage of mobile sensor nodes, which can move to the appropriate places to provide the required coverage.

To address this issue, a class of work has recently appeared where sensor nodes with full mobility are utilized to achieve desired deployment [6~11]. Typically in such works, all sensor nodes are fully mobile and they are relocated to maximize the coverage of a given target area with constraints on deployment time, the distance the sensors have to travel and the complexity of the protocol. The sensor network deployment scenario when only some of the sensors are mobile while others are static, that is, hybrid sensor networks [12], has also been under active research, especially in the field of robotics for exploration purposes. The movement capable sensors can help in network maintenance and repair by moving to appropriate locations within the topology to achieve desired level of coverage and connectivity, and to connect a possibly disconnected network.

In [13], Batalin et al. suggest a combined solution for the exploration and coverage of a given target area. The coverage problem is solved with the help of a constantly moving robot in a given target area. The mobile robot first performs the network deployment in the target area as it explores the unknown environment. The deployed static nodes then guide the robot to poorly covered areas. However, the algorithm does not consider the communications between the deployed nodes. All decisions are made by the robot by directly communicating with a neighbor sensor node. In fact, the deployment strategy and network repair policy can also benefit from the multi hop information derived out of a communicating sensor network.

Wang et al. [14] address the single coverage problem by moving the available mobile sensors in a hybrid network to heal coverage holes. The static sensors detect their local coverage holes by using Voronoi diagrams as in [7]. The mobile sensors also calculate coverage holes formed locally if they decide to leave their current position. The static sensors bid for the mobile sensors based on the size of their detected coverage hole. A mobile sensor compares the bids and decides to move if the highest bid received has a coverage hole size greater than the new hole generated in its original location due to its movement. However, the local broadcast may prevent the bid messages reaching mobile sensors if they are located farther than two hops. Moreover, the environment influences are not included in the design.

In [15], a hybrid sensor network is considered and a Voronoi diagram based approach is provided to estimate the amount of coverage holes in a sensing field. They also propose a collaborative algorithm (Coven) to estimate the number of additional mobile nodes to be deployed and relocated to fix the coverage holes. However, their collaborative algorithm doesn't consider any environmental factors such as obstacle and hot spot.

Luo, R.C. et al. [16] propose a mechanism which divides the map into many grids, and sets up weighting fields generated by various environmental effects such that the deployed goal can be determined. Without changing the previous distribution of static nodes, the coverage and uniformity are improved by incrementally placing additional mobile nodes one by one into the monitored environment. Although this "grid method" has inexpensive computation, it provides only approximate result rather than an optimal one.

In this paper, we also solve the coverage problems in hybrid sensor networks by our proposed analytic hierarchy process (AHP) based algorithm. It is different from the previous methods since it not only incorporates various environmental factors such as hot spot and obstacles in the design but also provides the optimal decision for mobile nodes movement. After a random deployment of static sensors, a certain amount of mobile nodes are deployed randomly into the monitored environment without changing the existing deployment of static sensor nodes. In order to increase the network coverage and uniformity, the mobile nodes are relocated according to our proposed scheme. The decision of moving direction of each mobile node is made according to AHP method, in which a set of criteria is evaluated and the optimal alternative is selected.

The rest of the paper is organized as follows. We define the basic assumptions and state the problems in section 2. The third section presents our deployment method. Section 4 evaluates and analyzes the performance of the proposed method. Finally, we draw the conclusion and discuss future work in section 5.

2 Problem Statements

Assume that there have been some static nodes deployed in the monitored region. Then, some mobile nodes are randomly deployed into this system. The problem is how these mobile sensor nodes should be relocated for coverage enhancement under the constraint of environment factors. Fig. 1 is the illustration of our design scenario.

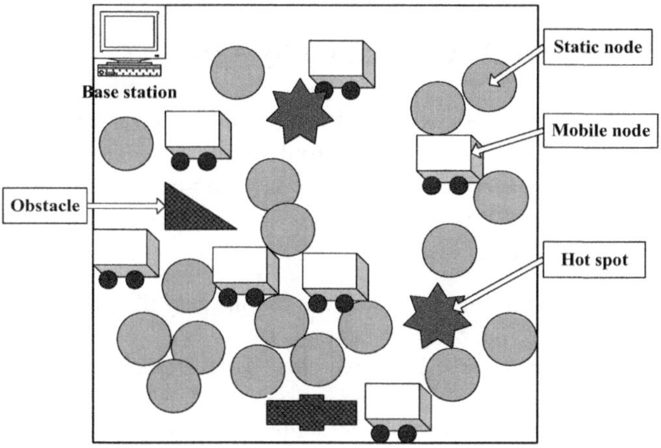

Fig. 1. Illustration of the design scenario

Some basic assumptions are made in our design. First, the networking system is a hybrid sensor network containing both mobile and static nodes. The static nodes must be pre-placed into the environment and the base station records all these locations. All nodes are equipped with the same sensing and communication devices. Second, the map should be well-known in detail including the distribution of obstacles. For example, to monitor a hazardous area suffered from terrible attacking, we need be familiar with the environment pattern and the distribution of static nodes. Third, the mobile nodes have only flip-based mobility as introduced in [17]. This type of model is adopted in most cases and normally trades-off mobility with energy consumption. The object of our proposed relocation scheme is to reduce the coverage holes and improve the network topology in specific environment after redeploying the additional mobile nodes.

To enable desired coverage while satisfying the environment requirements, we move the mobile nodes to proper locations according to their specific situation. In real environment, fours factors influence coverage directly, that is, the location and size of coverage hole in the network, the existence of hot spot and obstacle in the environment, and the boundary effect:

- Coverage hole: Areas not covered by any node. The direction to the nearest and largest coverage hole is preferred to be selected.
- Hot spot: The region in which events happen most frequently. The mobile node should ensure at least single coverage in hot spot. Thus the moving direction towards hot spot is also preferred.
- Obstacle: The mobile nodes need to avoid obstacles on their moving direction.
- Non-boundary: The mobile node is not preferred to move to the boundary since it will cause certain amount of sensing coverage loss.

The optimized next step moving direction determination is a multiple factors optimization problem and can be achieved using the AHP approach which is introduced in the next section.

3 Moving Direction Determination by AHP

The Analytical hierarchy process (AHP) is a multiple criteria decision-making method which decomposes a complex problem into a hierarchy of simple subproblems (or factors), synthesizes their importance to the problem, and finds the best solution. In this paper, AHP is used to determine the moving direction of a mobile node and is carried out in three steps:

Step 1: Collect information and formulate the moving direction selection problem as a decision hierarchy of independent factors.

Step 2: Calculate the relative local weights of decision factors or alternatives of each level.

Step 3: Synthesize the above results to achieve the overall weight of each alternative direction and choose the one with the largest weight as the desired direction.

A. Structuring Hierarchy

The goal of the decision "choosing an appropriate moving direction" is at the top level of the hierarchy as shown in Fig. 2. The next level consists of the decision factors which are called criteria for this goal. At the bottom level there are 8 alternative directions to be evaluated.

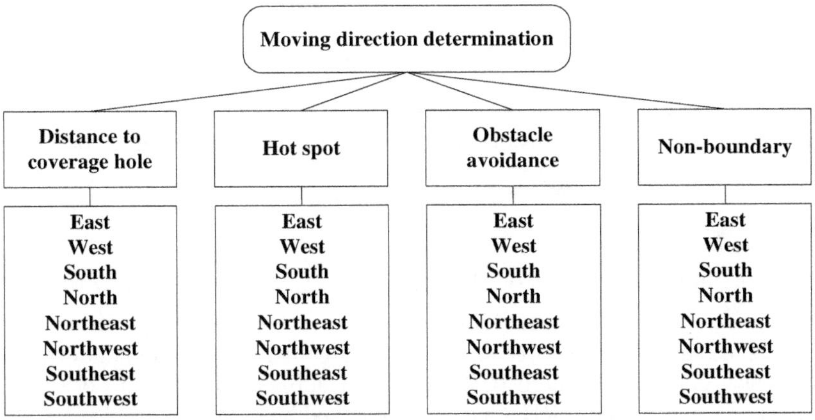

Fig. 2. AHP hierarchy for moving direction selection

B. Calculating Local Weights

Local weights consist of two parts: the weight of each decision factor to the goal and the weight of each nominee to each factor. Both of them are calculated with the same procedure. Taking the former as an example, we describe the procedure as the following three steps.

1) Making Pairwise Comparison

The evaluation matrices are built up through pairwise comparing each decision factor under the topmost goal. The comparison results are implemented by asking the questions: "Which is more important? How much?" and they may be presented in square matrix A as

$$A = \left(a_{ij}\right)_{n\times n} = \begin{pmatrix} a_{11} & a_{12} & \cdots & a_{1n} \\ a_{21} & a_{22} & \cdots & a_{2n} \\ \cdots & \cdots & \cdots & \cdots \\ a_{n1} & a_{n2} & \cdots & a_{nn} \end{pmatrix}, \tag{1}$$

where a_{ij} denotes the ratio of the ith factor weight to the jth factor weight, and n is the number of factors. The fundamental 1 to 9 scale can be used to rank the judgments as shown in Table 1.

Table 1. A fundamental 1 to 9 scale

Number Rating	Verbal Judgment of Preferences
1	Equally
3	Moderately
5	Strongly
7	Very
9	Extremely

2, 4, 6, 8 indicate the medium value of above pairwise comparison.

2) Calculating Weight Vector

For the given matrix A in Eq. (1), we calculate its eigenvalue equation written as AW = $\lambda_{\max}$W, where W is non-zero vector called eigenvector, and $\lambda_{\max}$ is a scalar called eigenvalue. After standardizing the eigenvector W, we regard the vector element of W as the local weight of each decision factor approximately, which can be denoted as:

$$\mathbf{w}_j^T = \{w_1, w_2, \cdots, w_n\} \tag{2}$$

3) Checking for Consistency

If every element in Eq. (1) satisfies the equations $a_{ij} = 1/a_{ji}$ and $a_{ik} \cdot a_{kj} = a_{ij}$, the matrix A is a consistency matrix. Unfortunately, the evaluation matrices are often not perfectly consistent due to people's random judgments. These judgment errors can be detected by a consistency radio (CR), which is defined as the radio of consistency index (CI) to random index (RI). CI can be achieved by

$$CI = (\lambda_{\max} - n)/(n-1)\ , \tag{3}$$

where

$$\lambda_{\max} = (1/n)\sum_{i=1}^{n}(AW)_i / W_i \tag{4}$$

The *RI* is given in Table 2 [18]. When $CR \le 0.1$, the judgment errors are tolerable and the weight coefficients of the global weight matrix W_j are the weights of decision factor under the topmost goal. Otherwise, the pairwise comparisons should be adjusted until matrix A satisfies the consistency check.

Table 2. Random index

n	1	2	3	4	5	6	7	8	9	10	11
RI	0	0	0.58	0.90	1.12	1.24	1.32	1.41	1.45	1.49	1.51

C. Calculating Global Weights

From above steps, we can obtain not merely the weights of decision factors towards the topmost goal from W_j but also the weights of alternative directions towards each factor. It is assumed that there are eight directions. All the eight weight matrixes of alternatives under four factors construct a 8×4 matrix, denoted as $W_{n_i/j}$, i=1, 2, … 8, j=1, 2, 3, 4.

The global weight of each senor node can be achieved through multiplying the local weight by its corresponding parent. So the final weight matrix in the symbol of W_{n_i} is calculated as

$$W_{n_i} = W_{n_i/j} \cdot W_j\ , \tag{5}$$

where the final weight of each alternative is calculated as

$$W_{n_i} = \sum_{j=1}^{4} W_{n_i/j} \cdot W_j \tag{6}$$

The larger the final weight of the direction, the more important it towards enhancing the network topology quality. Thus, the direction with the largest weight is selected as next step moving direction of the mobile node.

4 Performance Evaluations

4.1 Simulation Environment

In order to evaluate the relocation scheme by AHP, we compare it with random deployment case. In our simulation, the 50*m* by 50*m* square monitored area is divided into 100 uniform square grids. Each grid has the same length of 5*m*, and all nodes equip with identical sensors with sensing radius equal to 5*m*. The communication range is set as 10*m* to ensure the network connectivity. The moving style of a mobile node is flip by flip until the stable status is achieved. One flip distance is assumed to be 2*m*.

In AHP modeling, the matrix A is determined as follows according to Section 3:

	Coverage hole	Hot spot	Obstacle	Non-boundary
Coverage hole	1	3 / 1	2 / 1	5 / 1
Hot spot	1 / 3	1	1 / 2	3 / 1
Obstacle	1 / 2	2 / 1	1	4 / 1
Non-boundary	1 / 5	1 / 3	1 / 4	1

$$A = \begin{bmatrix} 1 & 3/1 & 2/1 & 5/1 \\ 1/3 & 1 & 1/2 & 3/1 \\ 1/2 & 2/1 & 1 & 4/1 \\ 1/5 & 1/3 & 1/4 & 1 \end{bmatrix}$$

The computed eigenvector W = [0.4729 0.1699 0.2844 0.0729]. It indicates the local weight of coverage hole, hot spot, obstacle and non-boundary, respectively, so that we can see clearly that coverage hole is the most important criterion, and non-boundary is the least. According to Eq. (4), we can get the eigenvalue $\lambda_{max} = 4.0505$. Consequently, consistency radio can be calculated as $CR = 0.02 < 0.1$, thus matrix A satisfies the consistency check.

Each mobile sensor node determines the weight matrixes of alternatives under four factors[1] and then gets global weight based on its specific location and environment characteristics. Its moving direction can be finally selected by the AHP model.

4.2 Simulation Results

In contrast to random deployment which achieves desired coverage with 70 static sensors deployed, the proposed AHP based scheme can achieve the same amount of coverage (*k* coverage can be guaranteed in hot spot with $k \geqslant 1$) using only a combination of approximate 20 static and 20 mobile sensors.

In Fig. 3, the static node locations and coverage of the initial random deployment before running the algorithms are shown. Tiny points with red numerical label beside represent the positions of 20 static nodes. The 2 red small disks denote the hot spots,

[1] Coverage holes positions and area can be calculated by using Voronoi diagrams as in [7].

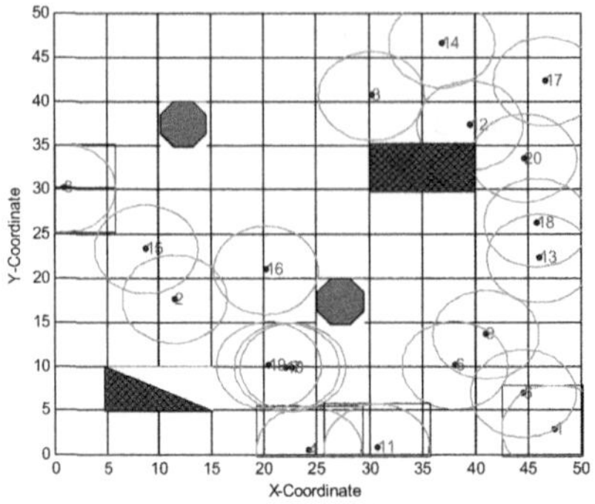

Fig. 3. Initial static sensor nodes placement

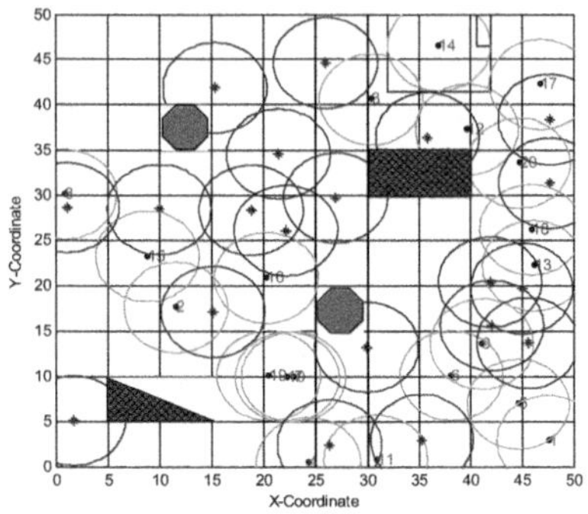

Fig. 4. Random mobile nodes deployment

the rectangle and triangle denote the obstacles in the environment. It's obvious that many uncovered areas exist and the hot spots are not well covered. Fig. 4 shows the random 20 mobile nodes deployment without change of original static sensors placement. The tiny stars denote the mobile node positions, and the green and blue circles represent the sensing range of the static sensor and mobile sensor respectively. The final mobile node positions with desired coverage after executing AHP based algorithm are shown in Fig. 5.

Fig. 6 provides the coverage ratio comparison between proposed AHP based redeployment and random deployment. The proposed scheme is only compared with the random deployment case because of our different assumptions from other existing mobile node relocation schemes. In AHP based redeployment, the coverage is achieved by deploying a hybrid sensor network in which mobile nodes occupy a half and the environment has a 3% obstacle area. The coverage here is defined as the ratio of the union of all sensor nodes' sensing areas to the whole monitored environment excluding obstacles. For the detailed explanation of coverage ratio calculation method, please refer to [10]. Note that, as the number of mobile nodes increases (the total number of nodes also increase), the coverage increases sharply because the sensing field becomes more flexible by movement of sensors.

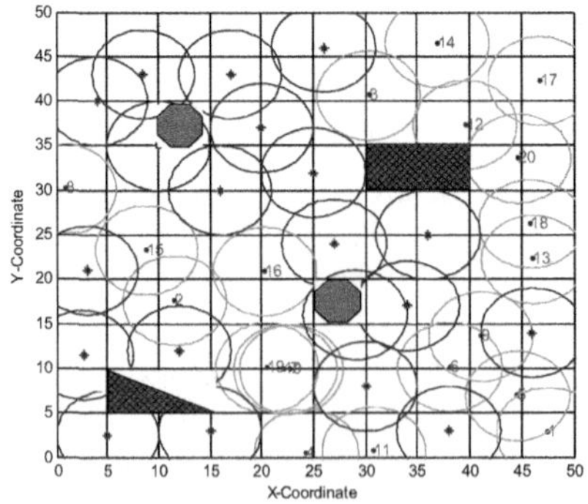

Fig. 5. Mobile nodes relocated

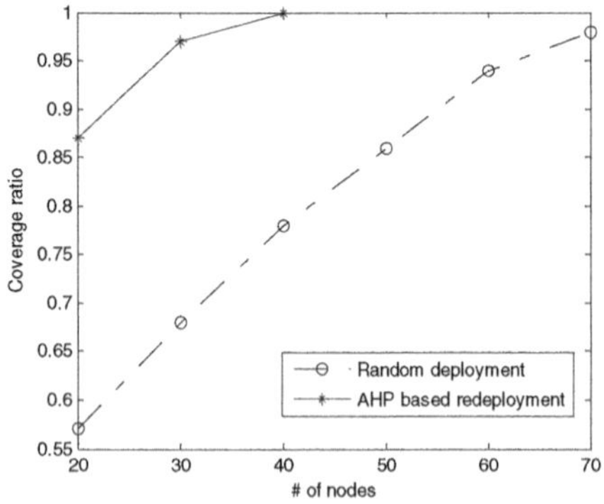

Fig. 6. Coverage vs. total number of nodes

5 Conclusion and Future Work

In this paper, a novel method for the redeployment of mobile nodes in a hybrid sensor network which consists of a collection of both static nodes and mobile nodes were proposed. An optimal decision of the mobile sensor node moving direction is made based on Analytical Hierarchy Process (AHP). Four factors contributing to the optimal deployment are considered which are coverage hole, obstacle avoidance, hot spot, and the boundary effect, respectively. The moving style is flip by flip until the stable status is achieved. Simulation results showed that our approach could provide high coverage with limited movement distance without compromising connectivity.

In the future work, we may consider mobile energy consumption and communication overhead between the sensor nodes and test more realistic sensing and communication range.

Acknowledgments

This research was supported by the MIC (Ministry of Information and Communication), Korea, under the ITRC (Information Technology Research Center) support program supervised by the IITA (Institute of Information Technology Advancement) (IITA-2006-C1090-0602-0002).

References

1. Wu, X., Heo, H., Shaikh, R.A., Cho, J., Chae, O., Lee, S.: Individual Contour Extraction for Robust Wide Area Target Tracking in Visual Sensor Networks. In: Proc. of 9th IEEE International Symposium on Object and component-oriented Real-time distributed Computing (ISORC), Gyeongju, Korea, pp. 179–185 (2006)
2. Meguerdichian, S., Koushanfar, F., Qu, G., Potkonjak, M.: Exposure in Wireless Ad-Hoc Sensor Networks. In: Mobicom, Rome, Italy, pp. 139–150 (2001)
3. Dhillon, S., Chakrabarty, K., Iyengar, S.: Sensor Placement for Grid Coverage under Imprecise Detections. In: Proc. International Conference on Information Fusion, Annapolis, USA, pp. 1581–1587 (2002)
4. Clouqueur, T., Phipatanasuphorn, V., Ramanathan, P., Saluja, K.k.: Sensor Deployment Strategy for Target Detection. In: WSNA, Atlanta, Georgia, USA, pp. 42–48 (2002)
5. Tilak, S., AbuGhazaleh, N.B., Heinzelman, W.: Infrastructure Tradeoffs for Sensor Networks. In: WSNA, Atlanta, Georgia, USA, pp. 49–58 (2002)
6. Wu, J., Wang, S.: Smart: A Scan-based Movement-assisted Deployment Method in Wireless Sensor Networks. In: Proc. IEEE INFOCOM Conference, Miami, pp. 2313–2324. IEEE Computer Society Press, Los Alamitos (2005)
7. Wang, G., Cao, G., La Porta, T.: Movement-assisted Sensor Deployment. IEEE Transactions on Mobile Computing 5(6), 640–652 (2006)
8. Zou, Y., Chakrabarty, K.: Sensor Deployment and Target Localization in Distributed Sensor Networks. ACM Trans. on Embedded Computing Systems 3(1), 61–91 (2004)
9. Heo, N., Varshney, P.K.: Energy-Efficient Deployment of Intelligent Mobile Sensor Networks. IEEE Transactions on Systems, Man, and Cybernetics—Part A: Systems And Humans 35(1), 78–92 (2005)

10. Wu, X., Lei, S., Jie, Y., Hui, X., Cho, J., Lee, S.: Swarm Based Sensor Deployment Optimization in Ad hoc Sensor Networks. In: Proc. of ICESS' 05, Xi'an, China. LNCS, pp. 533–541. Springer, Heidelberg (2005)
11. Wu, X., Niu, Y., Shu, L., Cho, J., Lee, Y.-K., Lee, S.: Relay Shift Based Self-Deployment for Mobility Limited Sensor Networks. In: Ma, J., Jin, H., Yang, L.T., Tsai, J.J.-P. (eds.) UIC 2006. LNCS, vol. 4159, pp. 556–564. Springer, Heidelberg (2006)
12. Ahmed, N., Kanhere, S., Jha, S.: The Holes Problem in Wireless Sensor Networks: A survey. Mobile Computing and Communications Review 9(2), 4–18 (2005)
13. Batalin, M.A., Sukhtame, G.S.: Coverage, Exploration and Deployment by a Mobile Robot and Communication Network. Telecommunication Systems Journal, Special Issue on Wireless Sensor Networks 26(2), 181–196 (2004)
14. Wang, G., Cao, G., La Porta, T., Berman, P.: Bidding Protocols for Sensor Deployment. IEEE Trans. on Mobile Computing 2(5), 563–576 (2007)
15. Ghosh, A.: Estimating Coverage Holes and Enhancing Coverage in Mixed Sensor Networks. In: 29th Annual IEEE International Conference on Local Computer Networks (LCN'04), Tampa, Florida, U.S.A, pp. 68–76 (2004)
16. Luo, R.C., Tu, L.C., Chen, O.: Auto-deployment of Mobile Nodes in Wireless Sensor Networks Using Grid Method. In: IEEE International Conference on Industrial Technology (ICIT'05), 2005, Hong Kong, China, pp. 359–364 (2005)
17. Chellappan, S., Bai, X., Ma, B., Xuan, D.: Sensor Networks Deployment Using Flip-based Sensors. In: Proc. of IEEE International Conference MASS'05 (2005)
18. Song, Q.Y., Jamalipour, A.: A Network Selection Mechanism for Next Generation Networks. IEEE Int. Conf. Communication (ICC) 2, 1418–1422 (2005)

Data Synchronization in Distributed and Constrained Mobile Sensor Networks*

Shuai Hao[1] and Hock Beng Lim[2]

[1] School of Computing, National University of Singapore
haos@comp.nus.edu.sg
[2] Intelligent Systems Center, Nanyang Technological University
limhb@ntu.edu.sg

Abstract. Data fusion in sensor networks involves the processing of data from multiple sources. For distributed settings, the fusion operation has to be executed at individual nodes, which makes data synchronization among nodes a crucial task to ensure consistency. If the sensor nodes are mobile, the communication channel between them can sometimes be broken. When communication is re-established, the snapshots of the nodes may no longer be consistent. The challenge is further made more difficult given limited communication bandwidth.

In this paper, we propose two algorithms for data synchronization in distributed and constrained mobile sensor networks. The first one uses timestamps to locate data records to be transferred between nodes. The second one employs hash digest and index tree to locate the discrepancy set between two sensor nodes. For the hash-based algorithm, we further investigate the cases for complete and rounded data. The evaluation results show that the timestamp-based algorithm is better if complete data are required for fusion, while the hash-based algorithm can outperform the timestamp-based one if the fusion algorithm can tolerate errors within some given threshold.

1 Introduction

Wireless Sensor Networks (WSNs) generally consist of a large number of low-cost and miniaturized sensor nodes, which act autonomously and are equipped with physical sensors, limited processors and memory, and short-range wireless transceivers [1]. While large-scale WSNs make many applications possible, one of the key challenges is to develop efficient algorithms for automatic fusion and interpretation of the information generated. Data fusion in WSN involves the combination of data and information from multiple sources [2]. The motivation behind fusion is to maximize useful information and represent it in more effective ways. Fused information, therefore, generally provides more details with less uncertainty. In addition, the new representation produced by data fusion enables observation of higher-order relationships between respective entities.

* This project was funded in part by DSO National Laboratories, Singapore.

J. Indulska et al. (Eds.): UIC 2007, LNCS 4611, pp. 673–683, 2007.

In a distributed multi-sensor network, each sensor executes data fusion and makes decisions in a distributed manner. To ensure that each sensor has consistent snapshots before fusion, data synchronization among multiple sensor nodes becomes a crucial task. However, if sensor nodes are mobile, the communication channel between them can sometimes be broken. When communication is re-established, the snapshots of the sensor nodes may no longer be consistent. The challenge is further made more difficult given limited communication bandwidth.

As one of the potential applications for data synchronization, let us consider the network formed by sensors installed in Unmanned Aerial Vehicles (UAVs). In this scenario, all nodes (UAVs) are highly mobile, resulting in dynamic behavior of the communication link. Moreover, the communication bandwidth is limited. It is desired that each UAV has consistent snapshot of the environment and thus is able to make consistent decisions locally. Although energy efficiency is important for sensor networks, limited bandwidth plays a more crucial role in these mission-critical UAV networks.

In this paper, we propose two algorithms to efficiently synchronize data among multiple sensor nodes, under dynamic and limited communication bandwidth. The first algorithm is timestamp-based data sync, which makes use of timestamps to keep track of the data records to be transferred between nodes. The second algorithm is based on hash digest and extended B+ tree data structure, through which the discrepancy set between two sensor nodes is located and transferred. For the hash-based algorithm, we further investigate the cases for complete and rounded data. We then compare the two algorithms through simulations. The performance results show that in mobile sensor networks, timestamp-based algorithm is better if complete data are required for fusion, while the hash-based algorithm can outperform timestamp-based one if fusion algorithm can tolerate errors within some given threshold.

The rest of the paper is organized as follows. Section 2 summarizes the related work. Section 3 describes our proposed algorithms. Experimental evaluations are presented in section 4. Finally, section 5 concludes the paper.

2 Related Work

Up to our knowledge, there are few available algorithms for data sync in the field of WSN. However, there exist several that handle data sync between PDAs and PCs as well as those synchronize transactional databases. We will summarize the related papers in these two fields.

Data sync between PDAs and PCs has to deal with similar challenges as present in WSN [3]. Some of the representative algorithms are: HotSync, IntelliSync and SyncML. HotSync [4] provides two operation modes: Fast Sync and Slow Sync. Fast Sync is applicable only when a PDA is being synchronized with the same PC as in its previous sync. Status flag is used to determine the changes occurred since last sync and thus PDA only has to transmit records whose status flags have been changed. In cases where conditions for Fast Sync are not met, Slow Sync is performed. PDA sends all the records to PC and record-by-record comparisons are performed. It is not hard to see that Fast Sync is much more efficient than Slow Sync with respect to latency and bandwidth usage. Fast Sync, however, cannot be used for multiple devices, since status flags could be reset when synchronizing with one device even if they are needed for another device. Slow Sync does not scale with the number of devices.

IntelliSync [5] seeks to make every sync "Fast-Sync-enabled" and relies on a central server. Since each device always synchronizes with the same server, each sync can be characterized as Fast Sync. Moreover, no peer-to-peer connections are needed to synchronize multiple devices. It, however, suffers from the same problems that generally plague centralized architecture, namely a central point of failure, and lack of scalability.

SyncML [6] seeks to provide an open standard for data sync across different platforms and devices. To minimize communication time, the standard assumes that each device stores a modification flag for each record with respect to every other device on the network. Thus modifying a record would entail toggling one set of status flags for each device on the network. After two devices synchronize, only status flags corresponding to these two devices are cleared. In this way, each data sync looks like Fast Sync. However, SyncML requires a device to maintain status flags for each record with respect to all other devices. If there are n nodes and each with r records, each device should have at least $n * r$ unit of memory.

For sync between transactional databases, [7] proposed a two-layer data sync algorithm between two transactional databases by utilizing MD5 summaries of records and B+ tree data structure. The bottom layer, usually implemented in B+ tree, consists of a general purpose database engine, enhanced with capabilities for computing certain kinds of summaries. A typical summary operation on the database would input a key range K and return a short summary of all the records whose keys are within K. The top layer consists of a sync facility, which makes use of the summarizing capabilities of the bottom layer to support range synchronization operation. The algorithm assumes that one side acts as master while the other side as slave and tries to synchronize master with slave.

The algorithm starts at master by calling slave to transfer the summary for key range R of its B+ tree. Then master compares its own summary against the slave's for the key range R. If the summary at master side agrees with that from slave, master will conclude it has already synchronized with slave. Otherwise, it will invoke slave to divide R into several (in this case k) subranges $(R_1, R_2, R_3, ..., R_k)$ and return summaries for each subrange R_i. The key range division and summary computation at slave side continue until the number of keys within range R_i is within some threshold. Then master will invoke slave to transfer all the records whose keys are within range R_i and do the record-by-record comparisons.

While the authors in [7] conclude this algorithm is optimal for links with limited bandwidth, they implicitly have the assumption that the two databases contain large number of records, of which only a small fraction differ. Therefore, for situations where this assumption is not met, the hash-based algorithm may not achieve the performance stated.

3 Proposed Algorithms

In this section, we present the timestamp-based and generic hash-based algorithms. Firstly, we introduce the notions and the motivation to propose these algorithms. Then we describe in detail the algorithms for two nodes, i.e. pairwise data sync. Finally, we extend pairwise data sync to n-node data sync.

3.1 Notions

Data Record: In our algorithms, nodes are assumed to be time-synced and store sensed data locally, which we model as light-weight databases in form of (*key, value*) records. We use "UAV target tracking" as the example application, where n mobile UAVs are used to track k moving targets. The (*key, value*) record is defined as follows:

$$\underline{(\texttt{sense\_t, taget\_id}}\texttt{, target\_x, target\_y)}$$

where `sense_t` is the timestamp for sensing; `target_id` is the target identifier; `target_x` and `target_y` are the observed raw `x,y` coordinates of a target.

Rounded Data: Rounded data are computed based on the raw data and given precision threshold δ. For example, the rounded data for raw data `target_x` is defined as:

$$\texttt{target\_x'} = \lfloor \frac{\texttt{target\_x}}{\delta} \rfloor * \delta$$

Discrepancy Set: The key part in data sync is to locate the discrepancy set of records. We define the "Discrepancy Set" (DS) between database $\mathcal{D}_1$ and $\mathcal{D}_2$ as

$$DS = \mathcal{K}_1 \cup \mathcal{K}_2 \cup \mathcal{K}_{12}$$

where $\mathcal{K}_1$ is the set of records with keys inside $\mathcal{D}_1$ but not $\mathcal{D}_2$; $\mathcal{K}_2$ is the set of records with keys inside $\mathcal{D}_2$ but not $\mathcal{D}_1$; $\mathcal{K}_{12}$ represents the set of records whose keys appear in both $\mathcal{D}_1$ and $\mathcal{D}_2$ but with different values.

3.2 Motivation

From section 2, we find that to utilize the limited bandwidth in data sync, one possible way is to use compressed information, for example, digest rather than the actual data records. As discussed, hash-based algorithm works well under the assumption that only a small portion of the database gets updated or changed. In the case of WSN, for example the "target tracking" application, it is hardly the case that two nodes have identical observations at the same time for the same target. Therefore, hash-based algorithm will eventually have to transfer all the records in both sides with "searching process" as overhead.

To eliminate the searching overhead, we propose timestamp-based algorithm. It uses timestamps to keep track of the data sync process. The only overhead are timestamps exchanged. Another possible solution is to match the assumption of hash-based algorithm. We introduce rounded data, which makes a tradeoff between precision and efficiency. Data records in both nodes are rounded based on agreed precision threshold, resulting that data records within precision threshold become identical while those outside precision threshold remain different.

3.3 Pairwise Data Sync

We first consider data sync for two nodes, i.e. "pairwise data sync". Throughout the process, S_1 and S_2 are used to denote the node at each side, with S_1 acting as server/master and S_2 as client/slave, respectively.

Algorithm 1. Pairwise Timestamp-based Data Sync

```
T: current system time
p: data sync period
τ: data sync duration allowed
t: time elapsed after data sync starts

// initialize when the node is up
S1.lastSync ← 0;
t ← 0;

// it is time to do data sync
if T%p == 0 then
   S1.send(S2, S1.lastSync);
   if S1.lastSync < S2.latestRecord.timestamp then
      while t < τ do
         S2.send(S1, records with timestamp > S1.lastSync.timestamp);
         t ← t + delay;
      end while
      S1.lastSync ← S1.lastReceived.timestamp;
      t ← 0;
   end if
end if
S1 does other scheduled activities;
T ← T + delay;
goto 11;
```

Timestamp-based Data Sync: It uses timestamps for last sync point to locate data records to be transferred. As listed in algorithm 1, it starts at the server side by sending its last sync timestamp to client. Upon receiving, the client will compare against the timestamp of its latest observation record. If the client has newer records, it will start sending those between last sync and current latest timestamp. Otherwise, server side concludes it has already synchronized with client. The process ends either when the data transfer is finished or time is used up for data sync. When the process ends, server side will update the last sync point as timestamp of the last record it received from client.

We can see the only overhead here is the transmission of timestamps to locate data records to be transferred. Therefore, this algorithm is highly efficient in situations where all the records will eventually be transferred.

Generic Hash-based Data Sync: As described in motivation, hash-based data sync may not preform well in WSN. We proposed a generic hash-based algorithm by introducing the concept of rounding based on given precision threshold. Figure 1 shows the basic components in both master and slave side and also the interactions between two sides. There are two components in both sides: the B+ tree index file (digests are based on rounded observation data), and the actual observation records. The first component is used to guide the search for discrepancy set between two sides, while the second one is for actual data records transfer. Algorithm 2 lists the pseudo-code showing how generic hash-based algorithm works. δ_i is the precision threshold used in sensor S_i to round raw observation data.

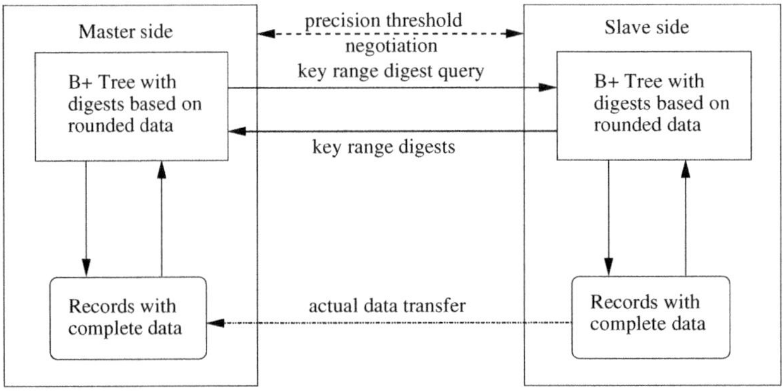

Fig. 1. Basic components and interactions in generic hash-based data sync

There are three phases in the algorithm: building index tree, locating discrepancy set of records, and transferring records in discrepancy set. The first phase starts with precision threshold negotiation. S_1 and S_2 exchange δ_1, δ_2 and decide the common threshold δ_0 to use. Then both sides build the index tree based on the digests of rounded observations. In phase 2, S_1 starts querying S_2 with key range $(-\infty, +\infty)$, equally, the whole database. Then S_1 compares its own digest for the key range against that of S_2. If the two digests are the same, S_1 concludes that its records in this range are synchronized with S_2's records. If the two digests differ, S_1 further checks the number of records in this range. If there are less than $thresh_n$ records, S_1 will ask S_2 to send all the records in this range, do record-by-record comparison, and update discrepancy set. Otherwise, i.e. there are more than $thresh_n$ records, S_1 asks S_2 to divide key range into k subranges and compute respective digests. S_1 will add those subranges with different digests from its own to set of remaining queries. This phase ends when there are no more key range queries in remaining query set. In phase 3, S_1 will ask S_2 to send respective records in discrepancy set.

Algorithm 2. Pairwise Generic Hash-based Data Sync

```
T: current system time
p: data sync period
τ: data sync duration allowed
t: time elapsed after data sync starts
t ← 0;

// it is time to do data sync
if T%p == 0 then
   // Phase 1: Build index tree based on negotiation
   S1.send(S2, δ1);
   S2.send(S1, δ2);
   S1, S2 agree on δ0 as common threshold;
   S1, S2 round respective data records based on δ0, compute digests for rounded
   records, and build index tree;

   // Phase 2: Locate discrepancy set
   querySet ← {(−∞, +∞)}; // set of remaining queries
   discrSet ← {}; // discrepancy set
   while !querySet.isEmpty() do
      query ← querySet.remove();
      S1.send(S2, query);
      dgt2 ← S2.computeDigest(query);
      S2.send(S1, dgt2);
      dgt1 ← S1.computeDigest(query);
      if dgt1! = dgt2 then
         if |query| ≤ thresh_n then
            S2.send(S1, all records with keys in query);
            discrSet ← discrSet ∪ S1.computeDiscSet();
         else
            subq1, subq2, . . . , subqk ← S2.divide(query,k);
            for all subqi s.t. 1 ≤ i ≤ k do
               dgt2i ← S2.computeDigest(subqi);
               S2.send(S1, dgt2i);
               dgt1i ← S1.computeDigest(subqi);
               if dgt1i! = dgt2i then
                  querySet = querySet ∪ subqi;
               end if
            end for
         end if
      end if
   end while

   // Phase 3: Transfer records in discrepancy set
   while t < τ do
      S2.send(S1, records with keys in discrSet);
      t ← t + delay;
   end while
   t ← 0;
end if
S1 does other scheduled activities;
T ← T + delay;
goto 8;
```

Generic hash-based data sync tries to reduce the number of data records to transfer by introducing digests of rounded data. The hash-based algorithm in section 2 can be regarded as a special case of the generic algorithm with $\delta_0 = 0$.

3.4 N-Node Data Sync

To synchronize data among n nodes, the intuitive way may do pairwise data sync for each pair, thus $n * (n-1)$ pairwise data sync in total. This method is inherently 1-hop data sync and thus cannot handle the case when not all sensors are within communication range. Furthermore, the intuitive algorithm is sequential and thus has time complexity $O(n^2)$. To tackle this, we propose an algorithm based on hierarchy tree for n nodes [8] with best-case $O(logn)$ ($logn$ is the height of a balanced tree with n nodes) and worst-case $O(n)$ time complexity. It consists of two phases: tree construction and data sync.

Assumptions: We assume that within the sync interval, link conditions among n nodes are stationary and the link is bi-directional. The assumptions are reasonable if the synchronization interval is relatively short and sensors move in relatively slow speed, compared to the communication range.

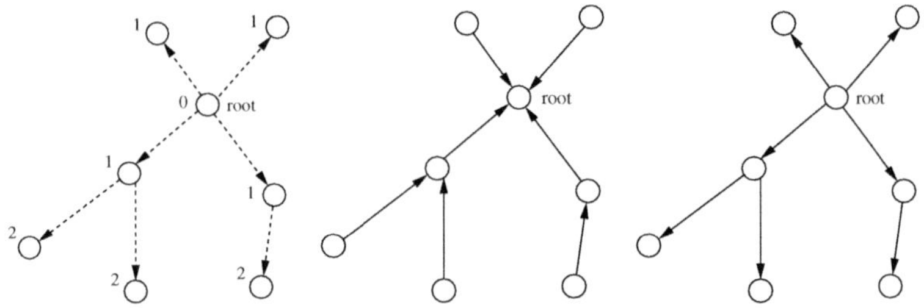

(a) Tree building phase (b) Data sync: 1st pass (c) Data sync: 2nd pass

Fig. 2. Tree construction and data sync phases for n-node data sync algorithm

Tree Construction Phase: As shown in Figure 2(a), circles represent nodes, dotted-line represents level packets broadcasting, and numbers are corresponding level numbers. We first select one sensor as root, which can also be assigned or selected by some election algorithm. The root node is assigned level 0 and broadcasts its level number to neighboring nodes. Upon receiving the level packet, which contains the level number, neighboring nodes assign themselves a level number, one greater than the one received, and then broadcast their level numbers. The process continues and eventually all nodes in the network will be assigned a level number. Upon being assigned, the node neglects all incoming level packets to avoid flooding congestion.

Data Sync Phase: Upon the construction of hierarchy tree, the two-pass data sync starts (see Figure 2(b), where black-lines represent data records transfer). The first pass begins from leaf nodes in the tree. Leaf nodes concurrently do pairwise data sync with their parent nodes (leaf node acts as slave and parent as master). After parent nodes finish sync with their children, they initiate pairwise data sync with their parents. This pass ends at root node, where information from all nodes is stored. The second pass starts from root node (see Figure 2(c)). It initiates pairwise data sync with its neighbors (root node acts as slave). After the neighbors finish pairwise data sync with root, they start data sync with their child nodes. This pass ends at leaf nodes and by then all nodes should have the information from each other.

4 Experimental Evaluations

In this section, we present the experimental evaluation results for proposed algorithms. Since n-node data sync is based on the pairwise algorithm, its complexity has a constant factor of that for pairwise algorithm. We, therefore, only present the results for pairwise data sync. We conducted two sets of experiments. The first set is to compare performance of 2 algorithms for complete data. The second set is to study the effect of different precision thresholds for generic hash-based algorithm. All experiments are conducted in Matlab and Table 1 shows the parameters for simulation.

Table 1. Parameter settings for simulation

Parameter	Value	Remarks
bw	42.8 kbps	communication bandwidth
p	3 second	data sync period
r_1	10 Hz	update rate for node 1
r_2	10 Hz	update rate for node 2
$\#tar$	3	number of targets
T	100 seconds	total simulation time

4.1 Experiment Set 1

In this experiment, the ratio of sync finished is used as performance metric. We vary bandwidth from 0 to 100 kbps and record down the average ratio of sync finished for both algorithms as shown in Figure 3(a).

From Figure 3(a), we can see hash-based data sync is worse than timestamp-based in term of ratio of finished and thus bandwidth usage. For timestamp-based algorithm, as bandwidth increases, the ratio of sync finished increases. However, for the small bandwidth, hash-based cannot even finish the traffic to search discrepancy set (for bandwidth 0-9 kbps) and thus the ratio of sync finished is 0. We can see bandwidth of about 28 kbps can make the two sensors fully synchronized for timestamp-based algorithm while hash-based needs around 50 kbps to become fully synchronized. We can also see there are two increments in the plot for hash-based: 9-24, 33-48 kbps. This is because we do pairwise data sync in asymmetric manner. The 9-24 kbps corresponds to the time when master synchronizes with slave, while 33-48 kbps is for the time spent when slave synchronizes with master.

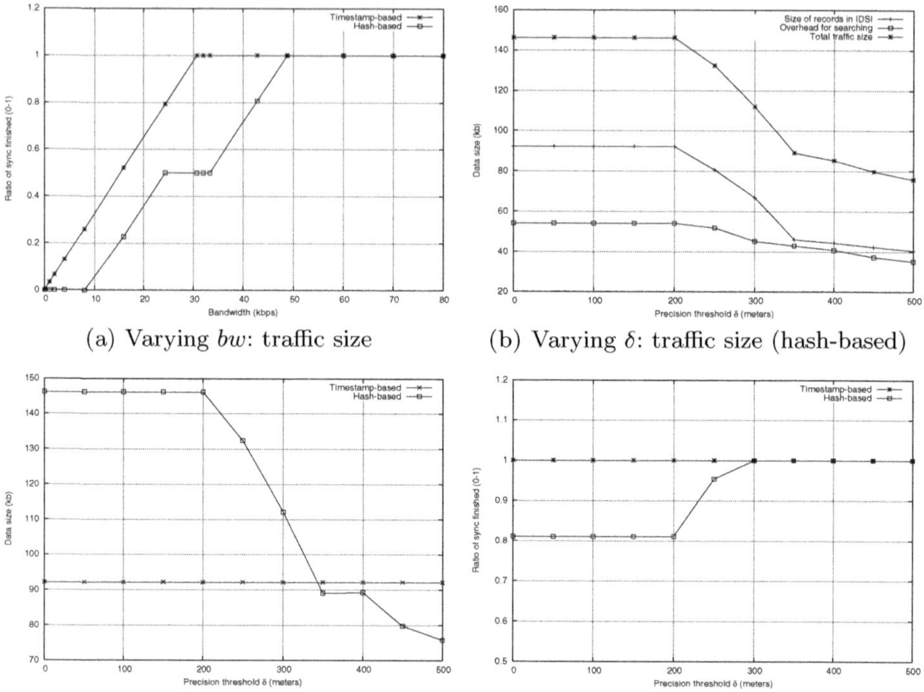

(a) Varying bw: traffic size

(b) Varying δ: traffic size (hash-based)

(c) Varying δ: traffic size

(d) Varying δ: ratio of finished

Fig. 3. Simulation results for experiment set 1 and 2

4.2 Experiment Set 2

In this experiment, we want to see if we make the tradeoff between precision and efficiency, by introducing precision thresholds, how hash-based algorithm will perform, compared to that with complete data. Figure 3(b) shows effects of varying precision threshold for traffic size, size of data to send and size of data sent. Figure 3(c) shows the comparison of bandwidth usage for time-based and hash-based, as the precision threshold changes. Figure 3(d) shows the ratio of sync finished with respect to precision threshold.

From Figure 3(b), we can see that as precision threshold δ increases, the average traffic and size of total data to send decrease. This is due to the precision threshold we introduce. However, it is interesting that for $\delta < 200$ meters, there is no improvement for performance (i.e. total data to send does not decrease accordingly). Only after that point, rounding can help reduce the traffic overhead, total data sent and total data to send.

In Figure 3(c), we can see for timestamp-based algorithm, total data to send remain the same regardless precision threshold δ. For hash-based, the size of total data to send decreases at $\delta = 200$ meters and becomes less than that of timestamp-based (i.e. outperform timestamp-based) at around $\delta = 340$ meters.

Figure 3(d) shows the reduction of traffic and data to send helps improve the ratio of sync finished. The ratio increases at $\delta = 200$ meters and approaches 1 at $\delta = 300$ meters.

The comparisons in Figure 3(c) and 3(d) show that in real applications, if δ is set properly, hash-based algorithm can perform better and thus utilize limited bandwidth to only transfer records that are "most" different (with largest difference) between sensors.

5 Conclusion

In this paper, we proposed two efficient algorithms for data sync among multiple sensors, under dynamic and limited communication bandwidth. The results obtained show that for data sync in WSN, timestamp-based algorithm is better if complete data are required for fusion and hash-based algorithm will outperform timestamp-based algorithm if fusion algorithm can tolerate errors within some given threshold.

However, this is an initial step towards efficient data sync under constrained network environment. There are a few directions that we can follow. Right now, pairwise hash-based algorithm cannot be used in n-node data sync directly. The fusion algorithm can be extended to support this. It will also be desirable to find the mapping function: $f : bw \mapsto \delta_{opt}$, which gives the optimal δ to utilize current available bandwidth.

Acknowledgement

The authors would like to thank Ng Thiam Poh Daniel and Ng Gee Wah at DSO National Laboratories for their help and insightful discussions.

References

1. Akyildiz, I.F., Su, W., Sankarasubramanian, Y., Cayirci, E.: A Survey on Sensor Networks. IEEE Commun. Mag. 40, 102–114 (2002)
2. Ng, G.W.: Intelligent Systems - Fusion. In: Tracking and Control. Research Studies Press (2003)
3. Agarwal, S., Starobinski, D., Trachtenberg, A.: On the Scalability of Data Synchronization Protocols for PDAs and Mobile Devices. IEEE Network (2002)
4. Palm developer knowledge manuals. [Online]. Available: `http://palmos.com/dev/support/docs/palmos/ReferenceTOC.html`
5. Invasion of the data snatchers. [Online]. Available: `http://www.pumatech.com`
6. SyncML specifications. [Online]. Available: `http://www.syncml.org`
7. Khrabrov, A., Sobti, S., Yianilos, P.N.: A Synchronizable Transactional Database. Yianilos Lab Technical Report New Jersey U.S.A (1999)
8. Ganeriwal, S., Kumar, R., Srivastava, M.B.: Timing-sync Protocol for Sensor Networks. ACM SenSys (2003)

Reference Interpolation Protocol for Time Synchronization in Wireless Sensor Networks*

Chongmyung Park, Joahyoung Lee, and Inbum Jung**

Department of Computer Information & Telecommunication Engineering, Kangwon National University, Hyoja-Dong, Chunchon, Kangwon, 200-701, Korea
{cmpark,jhlee,ibjung}@snslab.kangwon.ac.kr

Abstract. Advance in processor, memory and wireless communication technique have led to an increase of economical and small wireless sensor nodes. To provide the right responses quickly for the diverse events, wireless sensor nodes have cooperation with together. For successful cooperation, the time synchronization among sensor nodes is an important requirement for application execution. In wireless sensor networks, message packets are used for the time synchronization. However, the transmission of message packets dissipates the battery energy of wireless sensor nodes. Since wireless sensor nodes works on the limited battery capacity, the excessive use of message packets has a negative impact upon their lifetime. In this paper, reference interpolation protocol is proposed for reducing the number of message packets for the time synchronization. The proposed method performs time interpolation between the time of reference packets and the global time of the base station. The proposed method completes the synchronization operation with only two message packets. Due to the simple synchronization procedure, our method greatly reduces the number of synchronization messages. From the decrease in the transmission of message packets, the convergence time among wireless sensor nodes is shortened and the lifetime of wireless sensor nodes is also prolonged as much as the amount of saved battery energy.

1 Introduction

Based on recently the amazing growth of subminiature, low-cost and low-powered hardware, the wireless sensor network is strongly researched for the various application areas. The wireless sensor nodes have cooperation with together to support the right and quick responses for the diverse events. However, to perform the cooperation between sensor nodes, time synchronization operations between sensor nodes are an important requirement to provide the correct operations. In particular, some spotlight applications performing the functions such as the location search, data collection in mobile sensors, event awareness in the

* This research was financially supported by the Ministry of Commerce, Industry and Energy (MOCIE) and Korea Industrial Technology Foundation (KOTEF) through the Human Resource Training Project for Regional Innovation.

** Corresponding author.

J. Indulska et al. (Eds.): UIC 2007, LNCS 4611, pp. 684–695, 2007.

complex area and highly privileged security are based on the precise time synchronization of wireless sensor nodes. Without time synchronization function, the time-ordering in triggered events cannot be distinguished but also the duplicated data driven from same events cannot be handled.

Research on time synchronization techniques over the last decades has culminated in the distributed computing area. However, since wireless sensor nodes are worked on the low power, mobility, and the lack of computing ability, it is difficult to exploit the existing time synchronization solutions. The methods used in the existing computer network environment have taken the aim at the accurate time synchronization. However, to guarantee the accurate synchronization, many computing resources are required. Since the use of many resources causes the increase of the power consumed, these previous methods have a negative impact upon the lifetime of wireless sensor nodes worked in the isolated battery capacity. In addition, wireless sensor networks are configured based on the multi-hop protocol between neighbor sensor nodes [1,2].

In the case of NTP and GPS method, when the timestamp in messages is broadcasted to exploit as a global time, the sending time and the access time of messages incurs time delay problem for time synchronization[3,4,5]. To solve this problem, the Reference Broadcast Synchronization (RBS) method is proposed. The RBS does not perform time synchronization activities based on the global time value. This method is based on the relative time difference of reference message packets arrived in each wireless sensor node. The RBS has an advantage that it greatly reduces the time period for the message sending and access. However, as the number of sensor nodes is increased, the number of message for time synchronization is highly increased. In wireless sensor nodes, the message transmission via the RF antenna takes a major part of the energy consumption. Therefore, in the RBS method, the increase of messages for time synchronization results in a significant energy waste in wireless sensor nodes.

In this paper, to address the energy waste problem occurred in the previous RBS method, Reference Interpolation Protocol (RIP) method is proposed. The RIP method uses the broadcast messages come from both reference packet transmission nodes and a base station node. In this way, wireless sensor nodes receive two reference packets from two source nodes. After that, each sensor node synchronizes its local time by interpolating the time difference between two packets. The RIP does not use the synchronization message with timestamp values so that it reduces the errors occurred in MAC layer transmission. In addition, since each sensor node receives only two messages within the single-hop range for its own time synchronization, the number of message for total time synchronization is reduced tremendously. The decrease of messages also reduces the amount of energy consumption in the wireless sensor nodes so that their lifetime would be prolonged. In addition, the reduced messages results in greatly shorten the convergence time of all wireless sensor nodes performing the time synchronization. The rest of this paper is organized as follows. Section 2 describes the common errors occurred in the time synchronization methods and the classification of the time synchronization and the existing time synchronization techniques in the wireless sensor networks. In section 3, the Reference Interpolation Protocol is proposed to reduce the number of message transmitted for the timing synchronization. In section 4, the performance of our RIP is measured and evaluated throughout compared to the RBS protocol. Section 5 concludes the paper.

2 Related Work

2.1 Sources of the Inaccurate Time Synchronization

The non-deterministic delay characteristics of the network communication cause the inaccuracy in time synchronization activities. To get accurate time synchronization, these sources should be analyzed and alternative methods should be considered to alleviate the effect of the synchronization error.

Based on this phenomenon, the non-deterministic factors for the network communication are classified as follows [6].

Send Time. It is actually exhausted time when applications send the data over the system operations. This time include the kernel processing time, context switching time and system call processing time. It depends on the amount of current sender system's workloads.

Access Time. It is the time required to access the wireless channel after ready to transmit in the sender node. It depends on the amount of the current network workloads.

Propagation Time. It is the necessary time until the radio signal transmits from the sender to the receiver. It depends on the distance between the sender and receiver. When compared to the send time and the access time, its exhausted time is trivial.

Receive Time. The time it takes for the received data to reach the application level.

2.2 RBS Time Synchronization

The RBS(Reference Broadcast Synchronization) method performs the time synchronization based on the received time of messages. Firstly, the reference packet sender transmits reference packets to its neighbor nodes. For the time synchronization, all sensor nodes receive reference packets and exchange their local times each other.

The Fig. 1 shows that reference packets are broadcasted and the neighbor sensor nodes are stored their relative time from the received referenced packets. Thus, the RBS method performs the time synchronization with the time difference offset values between sensor nodes. The RBS model has several advantages compared to the global time based time synchronization such as NTP, GPS.

Since the RBS method does not perform the time synchronization depending on the global time transmission such as the server-client models, it eliminates the errors from the unexpected sending time and access time. In the global time based time synchronization, these errors usually have occurred in the packet

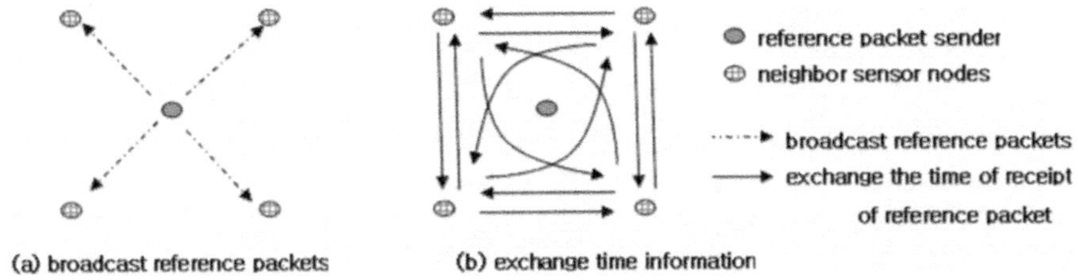

Fig. 1. RBS Operations

transmission procedure. In addition, since the reference packets do not include timestamp values, time synchronization is easily done by the several broadcast methods such as the RTS/CTS. However, the RBS method should keep the clock information of neighboring sensor nodes. In addition, the number of messages exchanged for the time synchronization rises sharply according to increasing the number of sensor nodes. Since RF using takes a major part of energy consumption, the increased messages cause the wireless sensor nodes to exhaust their battery power. As a result, it is inevitable that the lifetime of sensor nodes is shortened.

3 Reference Interpolation Protocol

3.1 Basic Operations in Single Hop

The existing RBS method performs the time synchronization based on reference packets. After received reference packets, sensor nodes broadcast their received time. In this method, as the sensor nodes are added in the sensor network, not only the messages for the time synchronization but also the amount of memory usage for sustaining the received time value of reference packets are highly increased. In addition, since a reference packet sender node does not participated in time synchronization activities and just relative time offsets between sensor nodes are used, the global time value can not exist in the sensor network.

In this paper, we propose the RIP(Reference Interpolation Protocol) to reduce the number of messages for time synchronization in wireless sensor networks. The reduction of messages causes the sensor nodes to prolong their lifetime and also to shorten the convergence time for synchronizing. In our RIP, since all sensor nodes including reference packet sender nodes and a base station node are participated in time synchronization activities, the global time can be sustained in working sensor networks.

The RIP method uses reference packets to synchronize all sensor nodes that are exploited in the previous RBS method. When compared to the previous NTP method based on time stamp packets, the use of reference packets takes advantage of eliminating the synchronization errors due to the nondeterministic characteristics of the send time and the access time occurred in the sender. The factors of inaccuracy in the RIP method are the propagation time and the receive time. However, the propagation time can be ignorable as sensor nodes are deployed densely.

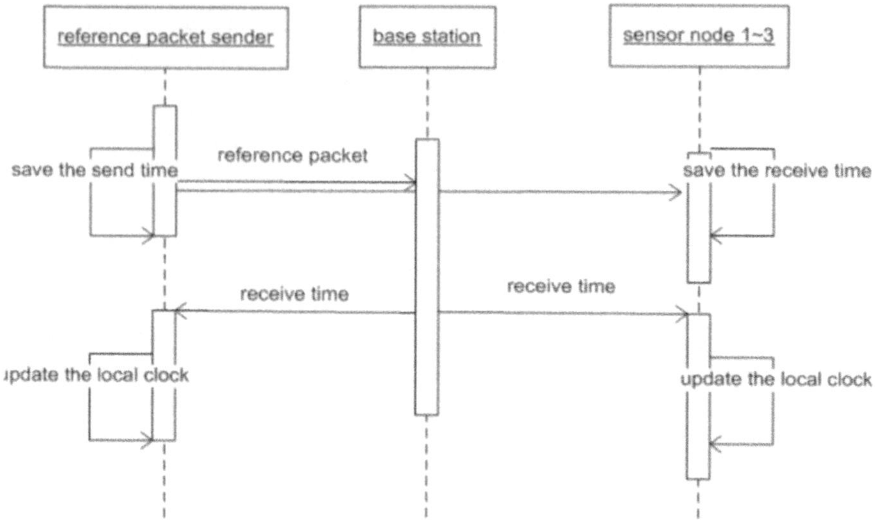

Fig. 2. Sequence Diagram of RIP Method

The Fig. 2 shows the sequence diagram of the RIP method suggested in this paper. From this figure, the reference packet sender broadcasts reference packets. The neighbor sensor nodes 1 3 and the base station node store their local time when they receive reference packets. The reference sender node writes the sending time of reference packets. After the base station receives reference packets, the time of receipt of reference packets is broadcasted. This message is include the global time maintained in the base station. Based on the global time data sent by base station node, adjacent sensor nodes and a reference packet sender node interpolate their local time. By these procedures, the local time of the reference packet sender node and all sensor nodes synchronize with the global time of the base station node.

3.2 Operations in Multiple Hops

The wireless sensor nodes in the sensor network are usually worked on the multiple hop communication features. The Fig. 3 shows the brief diagrams for the topology of the wireless sensor network. As shown in this figure, the A, B and C node represent the reference packet sender node. The node 2 and 3 are the gateway node synchronized by the reference packet sender in either side. For example, if the node 1 is a base station node and our RIP method is worked on the multi-hop mode, the steps for time synchronization are next;

Step 1: The base station send a packet to start the time synchronization
Step 2: The node A broadcast the Reference Packet (RP) after it received the start message from the base station
Step 3: Each node write its local time received the reference packet.

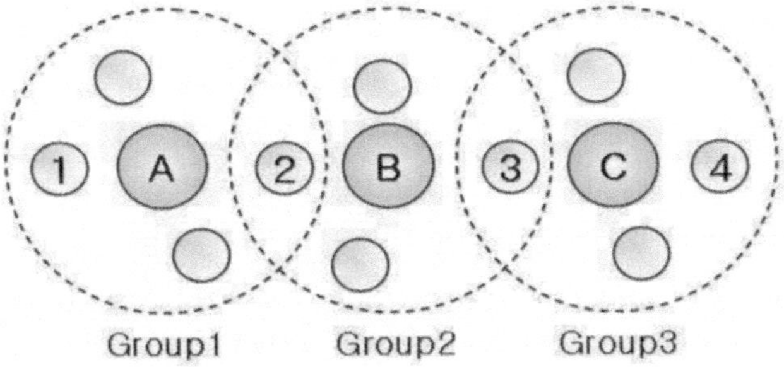

Fig. 3. Interpolation Protocol in Multiple Hops

Step 4: The node 1 as a base station broadcasts the time of receipt of the reference packet.
Step 5: Each node interpolates its local time based on the time information broadcasted by the node 1.
Step 6: The gateway node 2 change its role as a base station and performs the procedure from the step 1 to the step 5.

Based on the Fig. 3 and the above 6 steps, the number of message can be calculated to complete the time synchronization. In the RIP method, only the 2 messages are exchanged each other within one hop group and the 2 x G messages are needed in the multiple hops with G groups. On the other hand, if the number of sensor nodes is n, the RBS method described in the Section 2 takes the n x (n - 1) messages in a single hop. Thus, in the multiple hops composed of the G groups, the n x (n -1) x G messages are come out. As the number of sensor nodes is increased, the RBS method suffers from highly increased messages for time synchronization. Its big-O is $O(n^2)$. Otherwise, the RIP method is O(G).

3.3 Convergence Time for Synchronization

The convergence time means the exhausted period until all sensor nodes complete their time synchronization. Since the RIP method completes the time synchronization by the broadcast of 2 messages, its convergence time is greatly shorter than that of RBS method. In the case of the RIP method using the multiple hops, after finishing the synchronization in upper level groups, lower level groups can perform their time synchronization. However, the RBS method commences the time synchronization as flooding the ignition message from the base station into sensor networks. After that, since a reference packet sender node establishes the random time for the synchronization, all sensor nodes perform the time synchronization after this designated time.

Due to the sequence processing in RIP method, the long convergence time may be supposed. However, since the RIP method uses very fewer messages, the speed of the time synchronization is greatly fast over our expectation. On the other hand, in the RBS method, when sensor nodes are deployed densely, many messages causes the high contention to occupy the network bandwidth between sensor nodes. As a result, the increase of convergence time is inevitable.

4 Performance Evaluation

4.1 Experimental Environment

To evaluate our RIP and the RBS method, the NS2 2.26 combined with the NRLSensorSim Extension function with all other parameters is plugged into the tested methods to obtain quantitative information on the behavior on the different schemes. Our experiments are performed with varying the number of sensor nodes and the size of Grid.

4.2 Performance in the Single Hop

To measure the performance of the RIP and RBS method in the single hop model, firstly we make 500 x 500 Grid map. Base on this Grid map, a reference packet sender node is deployed into the center position and the other sensor nodes are spread across the entire Grid map randomly. As the performance metrics, the number of messages and the convergence time for all sensor nodes are considered. The Fig. 4 shows the number of messages according to the increase in the number of sensor nodes. As shown in this figure, the RBS scheme exchanges 17677 messages between sensor nodes. Otherwise, the RIP scheme just represents 427 message exchanging. When the number of sensor nodes is 30, the RIP method results in 98% less messages than the RBS method.

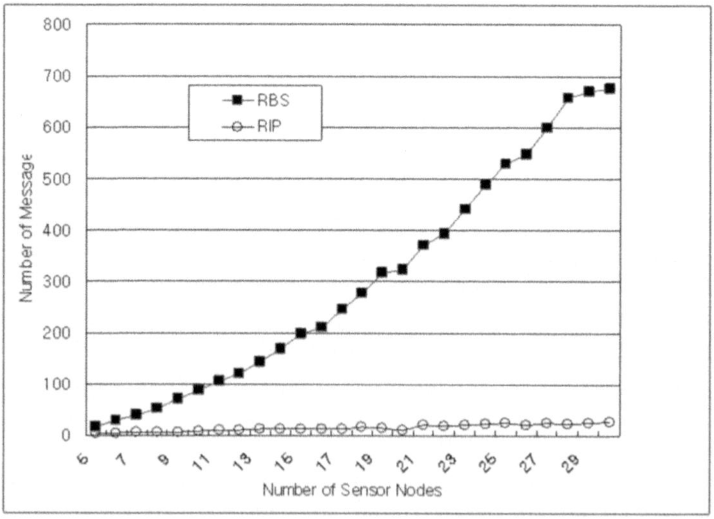

Fig. 4. Number of Messages

In the case of where applications and communication protocols are developed in the basis of wireless sensor networks, the low power consumption is an important requirement to prolong sensors' lifetime. According to the previous researches such as the Mica series [7], the wireless communication operation via the RF took a great amount of power consumption. From our experiments to the RIP and the RBS methods, the RIP method takes not only the small number of messages to synchronize all sensor nodes but also it reduces the amount of overheads introduced by wireless communication. These advantages let the wireless sensor nodes perform their originally required functions well, without the burden of the time synchronization.

The Fig. 5 shows the convergence time until all sensor nodes completed the time synchronization. As shown in this figure, compared to the convergence time of the RBS method, the RBS method rises up abruptly according to the number of sensor nodes. However, the RIP method represents a small quantity in the increment. As described in the Section 3, in the RIP method, the time synchronization is started by a message from a reference sender node and is finished by interpolating the relative time difference to the time of a base station. This method completes the time synchronization by exchanging two messages. Due to the step by step synchronization activities in the RIP method, it appears to need the more time for completing the time synchronization. Contrary to our thinking, since the RIP method requires only two message exchanges to complete the synchronization of one group, the total convergence time is too shortening as shown in this figure.

However, since the RBS method begins to synchronize all sensor nodes simultaneously included in each group, this operational characteristic causes the

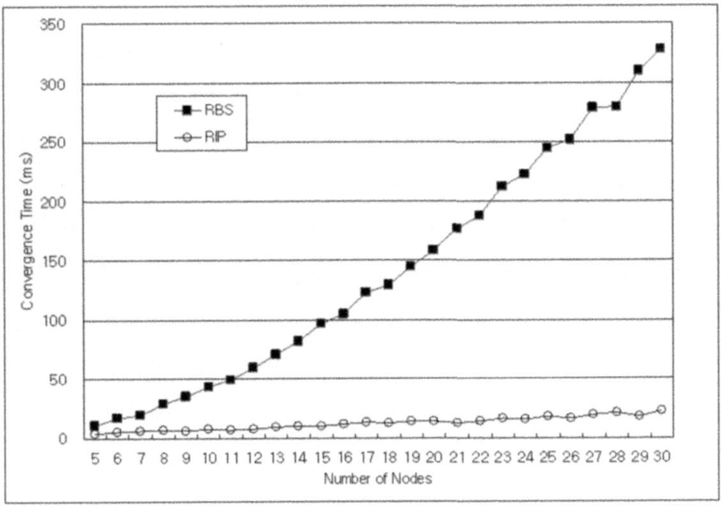

Fig. 5. Convergence Time

conflicted messages across all wireless sensor nodes. From the message conflictions, the RBS results in the relative long convergence time. As shown the Fig. 5, under 30 sensor nodes, the RIP method produces 91% less convergence time than the RBS.

4.3 Performance in the Multiple Hops

For the performance in multiple hops environment, the number of messages and the convergence time are measured across from 2 hops to 5 hops. In our experiment, one group is composed of a base station, a reference packet sender node, general sensor nodes and a gateway node that communicates with the other group. The Fig. 6 shows the number of messages according to increased hop sizes. As calculated in the Section 3, if the number of sensor nodes is n, the RIP method generates 2 messages and the RBS takes n x (n-1) messages. Since the synchronization activities in each hop have not impact upon the other hops, it is natural that the amount of messages in the both is increased linearly as the number of nodes is added. However, as shown in the Fig. 6, the speedup of the RBS scales quite steeply when compared to the RIP method.

The Fig. 7 shows the convergence time in the multiple hop environments. As shown in this figure, the result is similar to that of the number of messages induced in single hop environment. In the RIP method, after the upper groups near to a base station are synchronized firstly, the proceeding of synchronization spreads over the lower groups successively. Otherwise, the RBS method performs

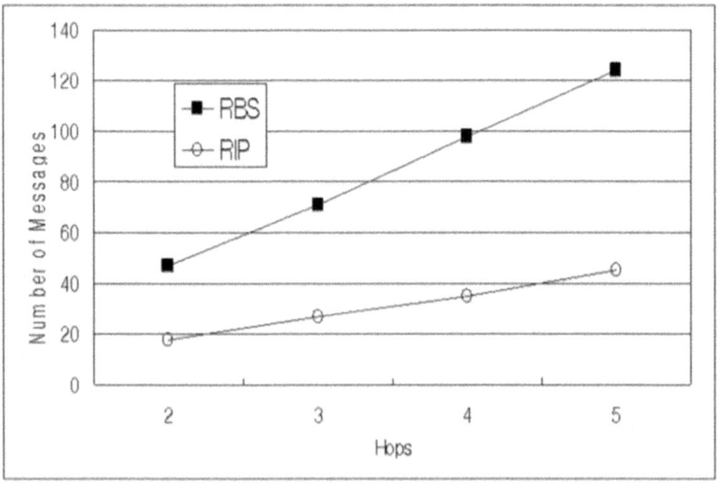

Fig. 6. Number of Messages

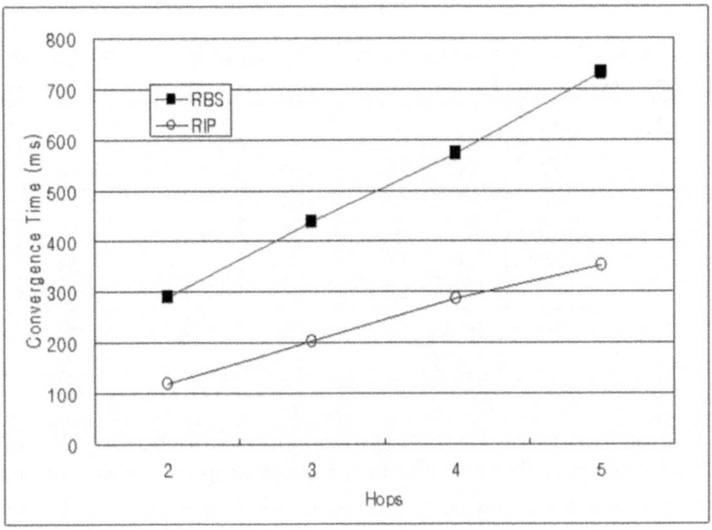

Fig. 7. Convergence Time

the time synchronization at once in all groups after a reference packet sender establishes the random time for synchronizations. However, since the RIP completes the synchronization within short limits in each group, the convergence time is more than two times as fast as that generated in the RBS.

4.4 The Amount of Power Consumption

The reduced messages are helpful to decrease the amount of power consumption. Based on the experiments of the previous Section, we will attempt to compute the impact of our RIP method in the aspect of power consumption. In the Mica2 Mote, the RF receipt requires 29 mW and the transmission needs 42 mW. On the sleep state of micro processors, the small amount of power is exhausted such as the ranges of uW. Thus, by controlling the state of micro processor between the sleep and the active state, the energy of sensor nodes can be saved. However, as shown in this Table, the transmission and the receipt of a message take a great part of energy consumption compared to the amount of power exhausted by doing the data processing in the micro processor. Based on these observations, the energy saving in data communications is more efficient than the controlling of the micro processor's state. In the case of RF communication, the power of antenna can be cut off for non working situation, which is similar to the way with controlling of micro processors' state [8].

In RIP method, each sensor node uses only the two messages for its own time synchronization. The number of message is very smaller than that of RBS method. Since small number of messages let the RF communication use less, the amount of battery energy consumed is also saved. The Table 1 shows the

Table 1. Power Consumption Rate in the RIP and RBS

Num. of Nodes	Num. of Messages		Consumed Power (Tx)		Convergence Time(ms)		Power consumption Rate (W/s)	
	RIP	RBS	RIP	RBS	RIP	RBS	RIP	RBS
5	4	17	0.17	0.71	0.04	0.11	1.56	6.65
10	8	88	0.34	3.7	0.08	0.43	0.78	8.55
15	13	198	0.55	8.32	0.1	0.97	0.57	8.61
20	11	323	0.46	13.57	0.14	1.58	0.29	8.59
25	24	529	1.01	22.22	0.18	2.44	0.41	9.09
30	27	677	1.13	28.43	0.23	3.28	0.35	8.67
Average							0.66	8.36

amount of power consumed by message exchanges in both the RIP and the RBS method. They are based on both the amount of power consumed by the Tx functions described in the Table 1 and the number of messages generated by two methods in single hop environment. As shown in this Table, the RIP results in the 0.66 W/s and the RBS consumes 8.36 W/s. Due to the use of less messages, the RIP method consumes 12.7 times less power than the RBS method.

5 Conclusion and Future Work

In this paper, we proposed a new time synchronization method designated by RIP. The RIP method reduced the number of messages for the time synchronization in wireless sensor network. This effect resulted in the decrease in the amount of power consumption so that the lifetime of sensor nodes could be prolonged. To synchronize all wireless sensor nodes, the RIP method used two messages broadcasted from both the reference packet sender and the base station. Each sensor node has synchronized its local time by interpolating with the time difference achieved from two messages. Instead of synchronizing with the timestamp values of all sensor nodes, since the RIP performed the synchronization based on the reference packets such as doing the RBS method, it eliminated the access time and transmission time that were regarded as the sources of inaccurate time synchronization. In addition, since each sensor node received only the two messages for its own time synchronization, the number of message exchanges fell down tremendously. Since the decrease in the number of messages caused the diminishing the energy consumption, the lifetime of wireless sensor nodes could be extended.

Throughout the detailed experiments for the RIP and the RBS method, we confirmed that the RIP method has greatly decreased the number of messages for synchronizing. In addition, the reduced messages might shorten the convergence time for total time synchronization. When applying these results to the real wireless sensor motes, the RIP method showed the 12.7 times less power consumption than the RBS method. As a result, the saved energy has contributed to the extension of the lifetime of the wireless sensor nodes and the shorten convergence time has guaranteed the quick response to events inadvertently happened. These effects by the RIP method could facilitate the deployment of wireless sensor nodes in isolated working areas.

In our future works, we plan to implement the component libraries to support the RIP method in various sensor network applications. In addition, the periodicity of the time synchronization will be studied to make economies of the energy consumption and to keep the successful cooperation among wireless sensor nodes.

References

1. Mills, D.L.: Internet Time Synchronization: the Network Time Protocol. IEEE Transactions on Communications 39(10), 1482–1493 (1991)
2. Mannermaa, J., Kalliomaki, K., Mansten, T., Turunen, S.: Timing performance of various GPS receivers. In: Proceedings of IEEE International Frequency Control Symposium, IEEE Computer Society Press, Los Alamitos (1999)
3. Lemmon, M., Ganguly, J., Xia, L.: Model-based Clock Synchronization in Networks with Drifting Clocks. In: Proceedings. 2000 Pacific Rim International Symposium on Dependable Computing, pp. 177–184 (2000)
4. Berthaud, J.: Time synchronization over networks using convex closures. IEEE/ACM Transactions on Networking 8(2), 265–277 (2000)
5. Romer, K.: Time Synchronization in Ad Hoc Networks. In: ACM Symposium on Mobile Ad Hoc Networking and Computing (MobiHoc 01), pp. 173–182. ACM Press, New York (2001)
6. Romer, K., Blum, P., Meier, L.: Time Synchronization and Calibration in Wireless Sensor Networks. In: Handbook of Sensor Networks: Algorithms and Architectures, pp. 199–237. Wiley and Sons, Chichester (2005)
7. Hill, J., Szewczyk, R., Woo, A., Hollar, S., Culler, D., Pister, K.: System architecture directions for network sensors. In: Proceedings of the 0th International Conference on Architectural Support for Programming Languages and Operating Systems (ASPLOS-IX) (2000)
8. Polastre, J., Szewczyk, R., Sharp, C., Culler, D.: The Mote Revolution: Low Power Wireless Sensor Network Devices. In: Proceedings of Hot Chips 16: A Symposium on High Performance Chips (2004)

Mesh-Based Sensor Relocation for Coverage Maintenance in Mobile Sensor Networks

Xu Li[1], Nicola Santoro[1], and Ivan Stojmenovic[2]

[1] SCS, Carleton University, Ottawa, Canada
{xlii,santoro}@scs.carleton.ca
[2] EECE, Engineering, University of Birmingham, UK
ivan@site.uottawa.ca

Abstract. Sensor relocation protocols can be employed as fault tolerance approach to offset the coverage loss caused by node failures. We introduce a novel localized structure, *information mesh*, for publishing and retrieving node location information. Based on the structure, we propose a Mesh-based Sensor Relocation Protocol (MSRP) for mobile sensor networks. MSRP maintains a sensor network's sensing coverage by replacing failed sensors with nearby redundant ones using near optimal time delay and balanced energy consumption. Simulation indicates that it guarantees closest node replacement with high probability ($> 96\%$) and with considerably low message overhead. We show that MSRP is superior to the existing sensor relocation schemes for its localized message transmissions and optimal (constant) per node storage load.

1 Introduction

Sensing coverage (or coverage) is an important QoS factor. It is measured by the overall area that a sensor network is currently monitoring. The larger the coverage, the better service the network can provide. In order to maintain quality of service, a sensor network must be able to preserve its coverage in the presence of node failures. In static sensor networks, distributing a large number of redundant sensors is the only way to tolerate node failures. Relevant research [3] concentrates mainly on how to schedule sensor activities to save energy without jeopardizing coverage. However, in mobile sensor networks, node mobility can be exploited to facilitate coverage maintenance. That is, it can be used to deploy a moderate number of redundant sensors and strategically relocate them to fill the position of failed nodes. This type of movement-assisted coverage maintenance approaches are called *sensor relocation* and constitute the focus of this article.

In our work, we consider a connected mobile sensor network deployed in plane, where uncoverable obstacles such as hills and lakes may exist. We assume that the network has achieved a full coverage over the coverable area in the sensor field, through a sensor self-deployment algorithm [4,6], after its initial placement. The nodes that constitute the coverage always remain active and are called *active nodes (or A-nodes)*. We also assume that some predefined *redundant nodes (or R-nodes)* are scattered in the network at random. R-nodes run a sleep/wakeup

J. Indulska et al. (Eds.): UIC 2007, LNCS 4611, pp. 696–708, 2007.

protocol to save energy and do not contribute to network connectivity. Both A-nodes and R-nodes stay static unless they are requested to move. All the nodes are homogeneous. They are aware of their own location (an (x,y) coordinate) by a localization system and know about their neighbors' position through lower level protocols. Their communication radius cR is at least twice as large as their sensing radius sR. Any node may fail at any time.

Our research goal is to develop, based on the above network model, a sensor relocation protocol that can maintain a network's coverage by relocating nearby R-nodes to the position of failed A-nodes. Note that, in a disconnected network, there is no guarantee that failed A-nodes are successfully replaced. For this reason, we additionally assume the network always remains connected in spite of node failures. Further, message collision and transmission errors can also affect the effectiveness of solution protocols. However, since these are MAC layer issues and beyond the scope of this paper, we assume perfect wireless communication channels so that we can concentrate on the sensor relocation problem itself.

In this paper, we propose a mesh-based sensor relocation protocol (MSRP) to solve the sensor relocation problem. With zero pre-knowledge of the sensor field, MSRP accomplishes the following two tasks: finding a nearby redundant sensor for sensor replacement (*replacement discovery task*) and moving the discovered redundant sensor to replace a failed one (*node relocation task*).

MSRP accomplishes the replacement discovery task by a Distance-Sensitive Node Discovery algorithm (DSND). Based on some dynamically determined R-node proxies, DSND constructs a localized *information mesh* with constant per node storage load. Upon an A-node failure, the A-node neighbors of the failed node find a nearby R-node proxy via the information mesh and take the proxy node's nearest delegated R-node as the failed node's replacement. The message complexity of DSND is never larger, in fact much smaller in average case, than that of the node discovery methods of the existing relocation protocols.

MSRP fulfills the node relocation task by a shifted node relocation method. That is, it builds a path between a failed A-node and a discovered R-node and then shifts all the nodes' position along the path toward the failed A-node. This method uses a novel localized relocation path discovery mechanism and generates constant relocation delay and balanced energy consumption. Two shifted relocation methods have been presented in [12,5]. But, they both have weakness in their relocation path discovery part, when compared with MSRP.

In the rest of the paper, we first summarize some related work in Sec. 2. Then, in 3, we present algorithm DSND and evaluate its performance through simulation. Afterward, we propose protocol MSRP in Section 4 and discuss its implementation issues in Sec. 5. Space limitation does not allow to present all details and proofs. Readers can find them in the full version of this article in [7].

2 Related Work

Wang, Cao and Porta [11] presented a proxy-based sensor relocation protocol (referred to as WCP) for the sensor networks composed of both static nodes and

Table 1. Protocol comparison

	MSRP	WCP [11]	WCPZ [12]	ZONER [5]
Protocol Nature	localized	quasi-distributed	quasi-distributed	localized
ZERO Pre-knowledge	yes	yes	no	yes
Guaranteed Node Replacing	yes	no	no	yes
Constant Relocation Latency	yes	no	yes	yes
Constant Per-node Storage Load	yes	no	no	no
Replacement Discovery Method	mesh	flooding	quorum	quorum
Closest Replacement Discovery	no	no	no	yes
Message Complexity	$O(\psi(G))$	$O(n'n)$	$O(n'\sqrt{n})$	$O(n'\sqrt{n})$
Node Relocation Method	shifted	direct	shifted	shifted
Guaranteed Relocation Path Discovery	yes	N/A	no	yes
Energy-aware Relocation Path	yes	N/A	yes	no

n and n' denote the number of A-nodes and the number of R-nodes, respectively; $\nu + \sqrt{n} \leq \psi(G) \leq Min\{\nu\sqrt{n}, n\}$ where $\nu \leq Min\{n', n\}$; $O(\psi(G))$ can be much less than $O(n)$ in terms of order of magnitude when $\nu > \sqrt{n}$.

mobiles. Static nodes construct a Voronoi diagram and bids closest mobiles to fill the sensing holes in their Voronoi polygons. Mobile nodes move to large holes from small ones. WCP relies on flooding for replacement discovery and uses a direct relocation method that can generate inconstant relocation delay.

Wang, Cao, Porta and Zhang [12] presented a grid-quorum-based relocation protocol (referred to as WCPZ) for mobile sensor networks. The network field is partitioned into a 2-D grid. In each grid cell, a node as cell head run the quorum-based location service [9, 8] over the grid to find replacement for local failed sensors. Then the discovered replacement is relocated along a carefully selected path in a cascaded (shifted) way. WCPZ requires pre-knowledge of the sensor field and may fail in the presence of void grid cells.

Li and Santoro [5] presented a zone-based relocation protocol (ZONER) for mobile sensor networks with pre-deployed redundant sensors. Similar to WCPZ, it is also a variant of the quorum-based location service, and it employs the shifted relocation method as well. However, it requires no pre-knowledge of the sensor field and guarantees replacement discovery (by resorting to face routing) and node replacing, and therefore it is superior to WCPZ [12].

To our knowledge, the above three sensor relocation protocols are the only existing ones for coverage maintenance in the literature. Beside the weaknesses stated above, they share a common drawback, i.e., inconstant per node storage load. The properties of these protocols are listed, in comparison with our new protocol MSRP, in Tab. 1. Their detailed analysis can be found in [7].

3 Distance-Sensitive Node Discovery

Each R-node spontaneously takes the nearest neighboring A-node as *proxy*. In case of tie, nodal relative position can be used to help make decisions. A R-node has one and only one proxy, while a proxy may be shared by multiple R-nodes.

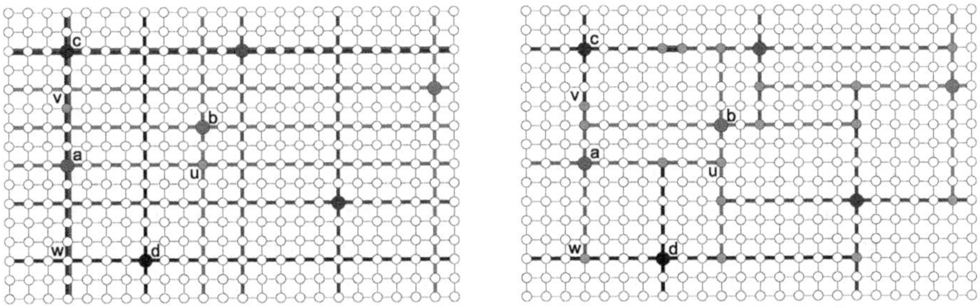

(a) A complete mesh structure (b) An information mesh

Fig. 1. Information mesh construction in a grid sensor network

Proxy nodes record the location of their delegated R-nodes and together construct an information mesh over the network. When a nearby R-node is wanted, an A-node just need to find a proxy node in its vicinity. The core of DSND consists of two parts: *information mesh construction* and *proxy node lookup*. For easy understanding, in the following, we present the two key components first in well-structured grid networks and then in arbitrary network scenarios, ignoring practical impact factors and implementation details.

3.1 Grid Sensor Networks

In a grid sensor network, A-nodes are placed exactly at the intersection points of a grid structure. Any A-node can find out its own role in the grid structure just by counting the number of its A-node neighbors. Consider only the residing rows and columns of the proxy nodes in the network. They intersect each other and form a mesh structure, as illustrated in Fig. 1(a). In this figure, R-nodes are not displayed; proxy nodes are represented by big colorful dots, and their residing rows and columns are highlighted by the corresponding color. If each proxy node distributes its own location information among the A-nodes along its residing row and column, then this mesh structure distributedly stores the location information of all the proxy nodes.

Let us examine the mesh structure shown in Fig. 1(a). Proxy node c is closer to the area above the mid-point A- v between itself and the vertically collinear proxy node a, and thus it (essentially, its delegated R-nodes) has relatively high priority to be discovered by the A-nodes in that area. In addition, proxy node b might be a better choice for the A-nodes located in its right-side area than proxy node a. In these cases, a does not need to distribute its location information in those areas. Similar argument can be made against other proxy nodes. According to this observation, we define the following **blocking rule**:

For an A-node u shared by the residing rows/columns of two different proxy nodes a and b, it stops the further propagation of a's location information, if and only if $(|ua| > |ub|) \vee (|ua| = |ub| \wedge \neg Colline(a,b) \wedge Horizontal(a,b)) \vee (|ua| = |ub| \wedge Colline(a,b))$, *where* $Colline(a,b)$ *and* $Horizontal(a,b)$ *denote the case that a and b are (vertically or horizontally) collinear and the case that the* *involvement of b is along the horizontal direction, respectively. And, when this blocking happens, we say "b blocks a at u".*

The application of above blocking rule can lead to the merger of adjacent mesh cells and result in a pruned mesh structure, i.e., *information mesh*, Figure 1(b), where gray dots represent the A-nodes at which the blocking rule applies, shows the information mesh corresponding to the complete mesh structure in Fig. 1(a). Due to asynchronous execution and proxy-role change, information inconsistency can occur in the information mesh. DSND uses *revocation processes* to eliminate inconsistent information. Please refer to [7] for details.

Consider an arbitrary A-node a. Define the *Home Cell* of a as the mesh cell where a is located in or the aggregation of the mesh cells which it is adjacent by. And, let the *Set of Proxies in Vicinity (SPV)* of a be the set of proxy nodes whose residing grid rows/columns form the home cell of a. Then for a, its objective of proxy lookup is to identify the location of the nearest proxy node, referred to as *target proxy*, in its SPV. Note that there exist examples where a node's target proxy is not a globally closest proxy.

Suppose that a is residing in a cell of the information mesh. When it wants to find its target proxy, it just inquires the A-nodes along its residing row and column in the grid structure in four directions. By this means, a is able to reach all the mesh edges constituting its home cell and get the location of the proxy nodes recorded on those edges. After that, it can find its target proxy simply through a local comparison. If there exist no R-node (i.e., no proxy) in the network, a will be aware after it reaches the border of the network in each of its query directions. Because the query paths form a cross, this type of proxy lookup method is called *cross lookup*. Cross lookup can also be applied when a is located on the information mesh. In this case, a inquires along its residing mesh edges and stops at their farthest ends on its home perimeter.

Let us denote the underlying grid sensor network by G. And, let $\nu(G)$ (or simply ν) represent the number of proxy nodes in G. By definition, $\nu(G) \leq Min\{n, n'\}$ where n and n' are respectively the number of A-nodes and the number of R-nodes. In addition, denote the information mesh constructed on top of G by $\mathcal{IM}(G)$ (or simply by $\mathcal{IM}$), and define the *extension* $\eta(\mathcal{IM})$ (or η for short) of $\mathcal{IM}$ as the length summation of all the edges in $\mathcal{IM}$. Then we have the following lemmas and theorems, whose proofs can be found in [7].

Lemma 1. *In a square G, $\eta \in O(Min\{\nu\sqrt{n}, n\})$.*

Lemma 2. *In a square G, $\eta = \Omega(\nu + \sqrt{n})$.*

Theorem 1. *In a square G, the message complexity of information mesh construction is $O(\psi(G))$ where $\nu + \sqrt{n} \leq \psi(G) \leq Min\{\nu\sqrt{n}, n\}$.*

Theorem 2. *In a square G, the message complexity of cross lookup is $O(\sqrt{n})$.*

Theorem 3. *In an arbitrary G, $\mathcal{IM}$ generates constant per node storage load.*

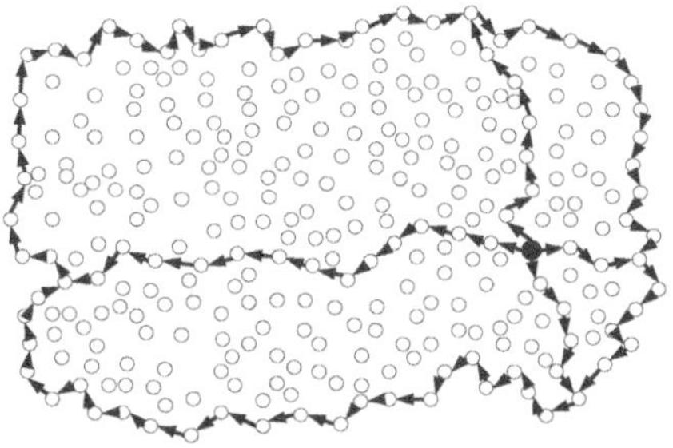

(a) One proxy node

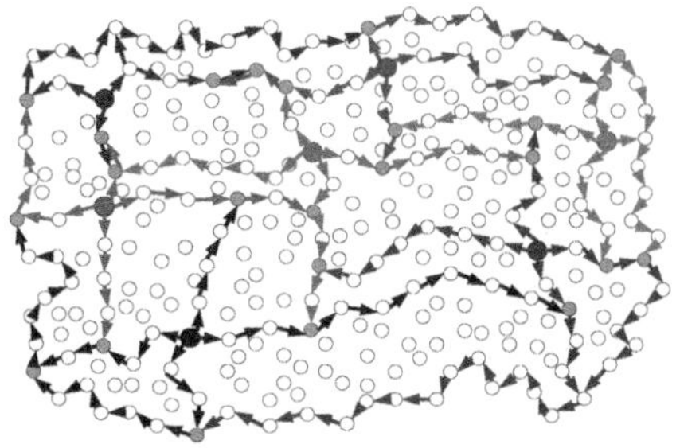

(b) Seven proxy nodes

Fig. 2. Information mesh construction in an arbitrary sensor network

3.2 Arbitrary Sensor Networks

In an arbitrary sensor network, DSND can be implemented by using routing protocol GFG [1], which is known for its guaranteed packet delivery and has been used for quorum formation in the quorum-based location service [9, 8].

An arbitrary proxy node generates four registration messages carrying its location information respectively for the four directions, i.e., the north, the south, the west, and the east. Then it sends them to the corresponding directional foremost A-node neighbors. These registration messages are retransmitted by receiver nodes following protocol GFG. Specifically, upon receiving a registration message, an A-node retrieves the embedded node information from the message, stores the information locally and then greedily forwards the message to its foremost A-node neighbor in the same direction. When a registration message reaches a void area, it is switched to the *face routing* mode and then passed around the void area. Greedy forwarding resumes whenever possible.

If the source is the only proxy node in the network, a registration message will finally stop at the globally foremost A-node in its transmission direction, and its transmission path will include the entire network boundary, as shown in Fig. 2(a) where the registration paths of the only proxy node is highlighted by arrowed colorful lines. In the case that there is more than one proxy node in the network, proxy nodes' registration paths intersect each other inside the network and/or overlap on the network boundary. For two intersecting registration paths, they will be either in a *node-sharing situation* or in a *link-crossing situation*. In the former situation, the two path intersect at a common node, while in the latter situation, they have a pair of crossing links. It can be observed that, a link-crossing intersection can be easily transformed to a node-sharing intersection in a localized way and without extra message transmission. Therefore, for any two different proxy nodes, their registration paths are guaranteed to have some A-node(s) in common. Then these common nodes apply the blocking rule as in the context of grid sensor networks. Finally, an information mesh structure is established as a result. Figure 2(b) shows an information mesh created by 7 proxy nodes in an arbitrary sensor network. In this figure, proxy nodes and their

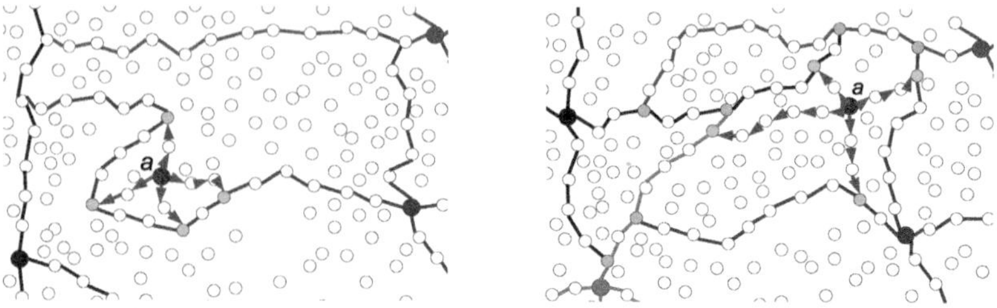

(a) Curly edge (b) Irregular shape

Fig. 3. Cross lookup in an arbitrary sensor network

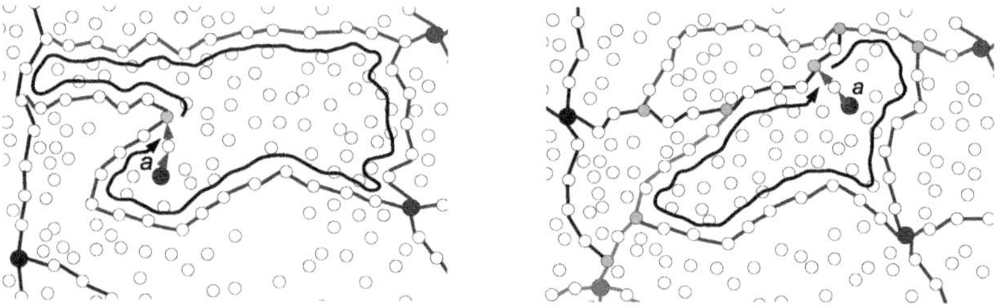

(a) Curly edge (b) Irregular shape

Fig. 4. Perimeter lookup in an arbitrary sensor network

registration paths are differentiated by different colors, and gray dots represent the nodes where the blocking rule applies.

When an A-node a wants to find its target proxy, it sends a query message to its directional foremost neighbors. In each direction, the message is retransmitted through protocol GFG and stops at the first receiver A-node that resides on the information mesh. Then this A-node sends a a positive reply containing its locally stored proxy node information. Node a selects its target proxy from positive replies. However, if there does not exist any proxy node in the network, which is possible when all the R-nodes become unavailable, such a query message will reach a boundary A-node b and then traverse the entire network boundary starting from there, by the property of GFG. In this case, once the query message gets back to b along the network boundary, b sends a a negative reply, indicating the failure of proxy lookup.

Under the assumption of $cR \geq 2sR$, if the sensor field is fully covered, no void area exists in the network topology, and the greedy forwarding part of GFG will never fail [13]. As a result, every cell in the information mesh has a rectangular shape, and the cross lookup method always works. However, if void areas (e.g., due to uncoverable obstacles) do exist in the network topology, messages are routed along the perimeters of the void areas, leading to zigzag message transmissions and thus possible cross lookup failure. Figure 3, where arrowed gray lines indicate query paths, shows two examples. In the first example, the query messages of A-node a all hit the same curly edge of its home cell; in the second example, the home cell of a is composed of five edges, causing that no query message reaches the northmost edge. Apparently, a fails to find its true target proxy in these two cases.

To ensure successful proxy node lookup in such undesired situations, an alternate *perimeter lookup* method can be used. By this method, the requesting A-node a sends a query message to an arbitrarily selected direction through GFG. The query message will hit a's home cell perimeter at certain A-node, called *entry node*, which then retransmits the message along the cell perimeter. The query message picks up the information of the closest proxy node that it have seen during its perimeter traversal. After it travels all the way along the cell perimeter back to the entry node, it has found the target proxy of a. Therefore, upon receiving the query message back, the entry node immediately forwards the message back to a as a reply. This perimeter lookup method is illustrated in Fig. 4 where light blue dots denote the entry nodes that start perimeter traversal.

3.3 Performance Evaluation

We simulate algorithm DSND in a large-scaled sensor network. The network consists of 10, 000 nodes and fully covers the sensor field with average node density of 8 – 9. During our simulation, we run two sets of experiments. In the first set, the network is set to be a synchronous environment with simultaneous execution and unified link delay; in the second set, the network is configured to be an asynchronous environment where nodes start the protocol maximally 30 simulated time units off each other, and each communication link has transmission delay of 10 simulated time units at most. We choose 1%-, 2%-, $\cdots$, 10%-, 20%-, $\cdots$, and 50%-service-provider settings. For each setting, we execute DSND over 100 randomly generated network scenarios in order to get average experimental results, which are given in Fig. 5. Based on these results, we study the performance of DSND, as the Percentage of Proxies (PP) varies, using the following metrics:

- Total Number of Construction Messages (TNCM): the total number of messages transmitted in the network for information mesh construction;
- Number of Construction Messages per Proxy(NCMP): the average number of messages generated in the network by an arbitrary proxy node for information mesh construction;
- Number of Discovery Messages per Requester (NDMR): the average number of node discovery messages generated in the network by a requester node (reply messages are not counted);
- Target over Closest Ratio (TCR): the average ratio of the distance of a requester to its target proxy over its distance to the closest proxy node;
- Probability of $TCR = 1$ (PTCR1): the probability that the $TCR = 1$ for an arbitrary requester in the network.

Figure 5(a) shows TNCM in relation with PP. For reference, mesh extension is also drawn in the figure. As PP grows, the information mesh has a more complex structure, therefore exhibiting an increasing mesh extension and a growing construction message overhead, which correspond to the ascending trend of the

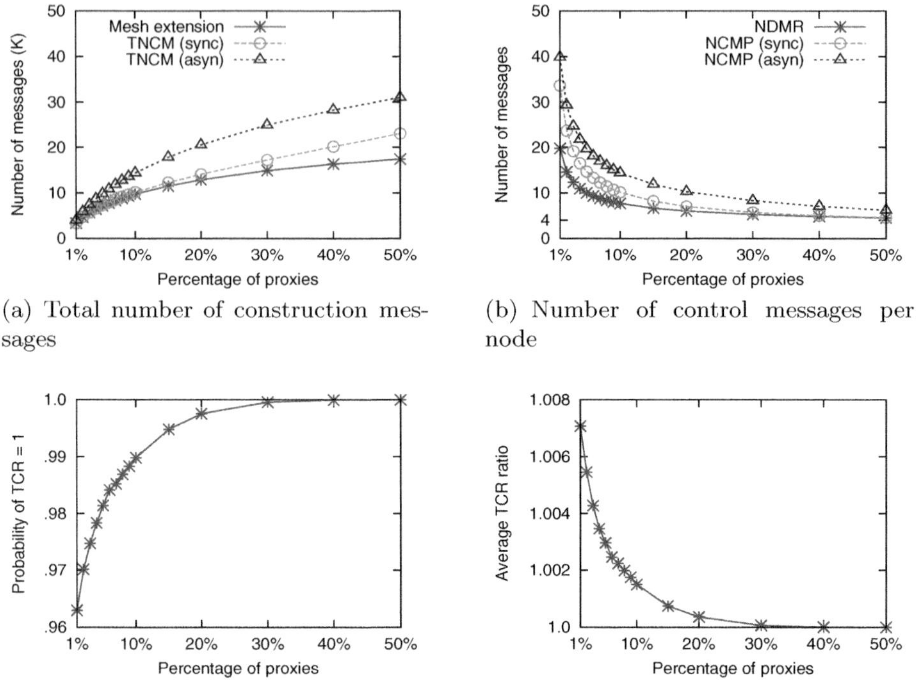

(a) Total number of construction messages

(b) Number of control messages per node

(c) Probability of TCR = 1

(d) Average TCR ratio

Fig. 5. Experimental results based on a sensor network of 10, 000 nodes

curves in the figure. We can find that, in all the PP cases, TNCM in the asynchronous environment is always higher than that in the synchronous environment. This is because of the extra messages used for consistency maintenance. The results shown in this figure clearly indicates that DSND has considerably low message overhead (compared with the size of the network).

Figure 5(b) illustrates NDMR and NCMP in relation with PP. NDMR has only one corresponding curve since it is subject to mesh structure but not synchrony. From the figure, we can see that, as PP goes up, both NCMP and NDMR drop and approach 4. The reason is that, when the density of proxies increases, a requester's node discovery message (or a proxy node's registration message) travels a distance of decreased length (on average) in each direction before finding a proxy (resp., being blocked), and the travel distance can be as low as 1-hop, resulting in merely 4 node discovery messages (resp., registration messages) in the extreme case. It can also be observed that a proxy node uses slightly more construction messages in the asynchronous environment than in the synchronous environment due to the extra cost of consistency maintenance. The results shown in this figure again verify the low message overhead of DSND.

Figures 5(d) and 5(c) respectively show TCR and PTCR1 as a function of PP. The results in the two figures are regardless of the (synchronous or asynchronous) nature of the execution environment. From Fig. 5(d), we can see that PTCR1 is always larger than 96%, and that it actually increases as PP goes up and closely approaches 1.0 after PP reaches 10%. From Fig. 5(d), we observe that, TCR is nearly equal to 1 in all the PP cases. This is because of the low probability of $TCR > 1$ (confirmed by Fig. 5(c)). We also observe that, the two curves decline and approach 1 closer and closer as PP increases. This phenomenon is due to the decreasing probability of $TCR > 1$ in case of increasing PP. The results in the two figures demonstrate the satisfactory distance performance of DSND.

4 The Mesh-Based Relocation Protocol

In this section, we are going to propose the *Mesh-based Sensor Relocation Protocol (MSRP)* to solve the sensor relocation problem defined in Sec. 1, based on algorithm DSND. For simplicity, we will present protocol framework only and leave implementation details for the next section.

At initiation, each R-node spontaneously takes the nearest A-node as proxy, by sending that A-node a delegation request. After being chosen as proxy, an A-node executes algorithm DSND to construct an information mesh. While being awake, a R-node monitors the liveness of its proxy; once it finds that its proxy fails, it moves to replace the proxy node directly. Upon an ordinary (i.e., non-proxy) A-node failure, the A-nodes neighboring the failed A-node cooperate to discover a *replacement*, which is defined as the nearest delegated R-node of the target proxy of the failed A-node, by using DSND. For brevity, the target proxy of a failed A-node is referred to as *replacement proxy*. During the replacement discovery process, the two lookup methods, i.e., cross lookup and perimeter lookup, may be selectively used, depending on requirement. For the cross lookup method, the northmost, the southmost, the eastmost and the westmost neighbors of the failed A-node, as *servers*, send four query messages respectively to the north, the south, the east, and the west direction. After getting replies, they exchange their discovery results through underlaying routing protocol to find the replacement proxy. For the perimeter lookup method, only one neighbor, say the northmost neighbor, acts as the server of the failed A-node. It sends a query message to an arbitrarily selected direction, and later receives a reply that contains the replacement proxy's location. Whichever lookup method is employed, only the server that is closest to the replacement proxy is considered as *replacement discoverer*.

The replacement discoverer issues a relocation request to the replacement proxy, which then grants the request by sending back an ACK message to the discoverer. After receiving the ACK message, the replacement discoverer starts a relocation path discovery process by sending an action message to the replacement proxy through routing protocol GFG [1]. Relocation path discovery is in essence a QoS routing process. Its objective is to establish a path, between a replacement discoverer and a replacement proxy, which yields minimized energy usage and time delay for shifted relocation. Recall that the shifted relocation method requires all the node along a relocation path to shift their position toward a failed A-node. From energy-saving point of view, node relocation should involve shortest total moving distance and a least number of moves. In other words, a relocation path is expected to have both minimized path length and minimized hop count. On the other hand, to reduce relocation latency in the case of simultaneous shifting, longest hop length in a relocation path must be minimized, which is virtually equivalent to maximizing the hop count of the relocation path. Under this contradictory circumstance, MSRP takes COST over PROGRESS ratio [10] as routing criterion and combine it with the greedy forwarding part of GFG. Here, COST is defined as the Euclidean distance from current node to the considered next hop, and PROGRESS is defined as the difference between the Euclidean distance from current node to the destination, i.e., a replacement proxy, and the Euclidean distance from the considered next hop to the destination. More formally, denote by a_0 the source, i.e., a replacement discoverer, and by a_i the i-th hop along the path from a_0 to destination d. Then, the $(i+1)$-th hop a_{i+1} must be closer to d than a_i and meanwhile minimize the following objective function:

$$f(a_{i+1}) = \frac{|a_i a_{i+1}|}{|a_i d| - |a_{i+1} d|} \quad .$$

Normally, the shifted node relocation process starts after a relocation path is constructed. However, in order to save messages and reduce relocation latency, in MSRP, node relocation and relocation path discovery are performed in parallel. More specifically, after sending the action message, the discoverer moves to the failed node's location right away; intermediate nodes move to the position of their priori hop after forwarding the action message. As for the replacement proxy, after receiving the action message, it first informs the replacement node to fill its current position and then itself moves toward the location of its prior hop. In order not to jeopardize the information mesh or the execution of other network protocols, every relocating node transfers all its local data to the newcomer at its original position immediately after.

5 Implementation Details

A straightforward implementation of the basic protocol design is not sufficient in practice. Some mechanisms must be provided to deal with impact factors such as node failures and node contention. Because of page limitation, we will discuss these implementation issues at very short length. Details can be found in [7].

The storage load of an edge intersection node a in the information mesh is bounded by the number of incidental mesh edges of the node, which may however not be constant and can be equal to the degree of the node in the worst case. In order to keep constant per node storage load, MSRP requires an edge intersection node store data pointer (nearly at no cost) instead of actual data. In addition, unlimited R-node delegation could also cause inconstant storage load, which may be as bad as $O(n')$, per A-node in the case that R-nodes are densely distributed. To handle this problem, a limit can be put on the number of an A-node's accepted delegation requests.

Although protocol MSRP is designed to deal with node failures, its execution is not automatically fault-tolerant. The impacts from node failures on MSRP can include loss of proxy information, loss of control messages and replacement failure. In order to make its execution resilient against run-time node failures, MSRP employs the following fault-tolerance techniques: thick message transmissions, transmission retrials, and real-time monitoring and taking over.

Because of the distributed nature of MSRP, node contention is very likely to happen during node relocation processes. There are two types of node contention. Type-I is that multiple A-nodes are attempting to relocate the same R-node to replace different failed A-nodes; type-II is that an A-node appears in multiple relocation paths and is required to shift its position along those paths. MSRP handles the two types of node contention on a first-come-first-serve basis.

Acknowledgments. This research is partially supported by the UK Royal Society Wolfson Research Merit Award, NSERC Collaborative Research and Development grant CRDPJ 319848-04 and NSERC Strategic Grant STPGP 336406.

References

1. Bose, P., Morin, P., Stojmenovic, I., Urrutia, J.: Routing with Guaranteed Delivery in Ad Hoc Wireless Networks. In: Proc. of ACM DIALM, pp. 48–55 (1999)
2. Frey, H., Stojmenovic, I.: On Delivery Guarantees of Face and Combined Greedy-Face Routing Algorithms in Ad Hoc and Sensor Networks. In: Proc. of ACM MobiCom, pp. 390–401 (2006)
3. Gallais, A., Carle, J., Simplot-Ryl, D., Stojmenovic, I.: Localized Sensor Area Coverage with Low Communication Overhead. In: Proc. of IEEE PerCom, pp. 328–337 (2006)
4. Heo, N., Varshney, P.K.: Energy-Efficient Deployment of Intelligent Mobile Sensor Networks. IEEE Tran. on Systems, Man, and CyberNetics - Part A: Systems and Humans 35(1), 78–92 (2005)
5. Li, X., Santoro, N.: ZONER: A ZONE-based Sensor Relocation Protocol for Mobile Sensor Networks. In: Proc. of IEEE LCN/WLN, pp. 923–930. IEEE Computer Society Press, Los Alamitos (2006)
6. Li, X., Santoro, N.: An Integrated Self-Deployment and Coverage Maintenance Scheme for Mobile Sensor Networks. In: Cao, J., Stojmenovic, I., Jia, X., Das, S.K. (eds.) MSN 2006. LNCS, vol. 4325, pp. 847–860. Springer, Heidelberg (2006)
7. Li, X., Santoro, N., Stojmenovic, I.: Mesh-based Sensor Relocation for Coverage Maintenance in Mobile Sensor Networks (Full Version), `http://www.scs.carleton.ca/ xlii/MSRP.pdf`
8. Liu, D., Stojmenovic, I., Jia, X.: A scalable quorum based location service in ad hoc and sensor networks. In: Proc. of IEEE MASS, pp. 489–492. IEEE Computer Society Press, Los Alamitos (2006)
9. Stojmenovic, I.: A scalable quorum based location update scheme for routing in ad hoc wireless networks. Technical Report, TR-99-09. SITE, Univ. of Ottawa (1999)
10. Stojmenovic, I.: Localized network layer protocols in wireless sensor networks based on optimizing cost over progress ratio. IEEE Network 20(1), 21–27 (2006)

11. Wang, G., Cao, G., Porta, T.L.: Proxy-Based Sensor Deployment for Mobile Sensor Networks. In: Proc. of IEEE MASS, pp. 493–502. IEEE Computer Society Press, Los Alamitos (2004)
12. Wang, G., Cao, G., Porta, T.L., Zhang, W.: Sensor Relocation in Mobile Sensor Networks. In: Proc. of IEEE INFOCOM, pp. 2302–2312. IEEE Computer Society Press, Los Alamitos (2005)
13. Xing, G., Lu, C., Pless, R., Huang, Q.: Impact of sensing coverage on greedy geographic routing algorithms. IEEE Tran. on Parallel and Distributed Systems 17(4), 348–360 (2006)

Neighbor Position-Based Localization Algorithm for Wireless Sensor

Yong-Qian Chen, Young-Kyoung Kim, and Sang-Jo Yoo

Multimedia Network Lab, Graduate School of IT&T,
Inha University 253, Yonghyun-Dong, Nam Gu,
Incheon 402-751, Korea
chen.yongqian@gmail.com, miniwalker@naver.com, sjyoo@inha.ac.kr
http://multinet.inha.ac.kr

Abstract. Sensor node localization is an important issue in wireless sensor networks (WSNs) due to the dynamic nature of sensor deployment. Generally, in wireless sensor network localization, the absolute positions of certain anchor nodes are required based on the use of global positioning systems, then all the other nodes are approximately localized using various algorithms based on a coordinate system of the anchors. This paper proposes a neighbor position-based localization algorithm (NPLA) that can greatly enhance the positioning accuracy when compared with current overlapping connectivity localization. The proposed method localizes the sensor nodes using both the anchors' positions and neighbor node information. However, unlike existing overlapping-based methods, the proposed NPLA does not assume the same radio transmission range.

1 Introduction

In many circumstances, low-cost sensor localization is a necessary and important requirement for the deployment of wireless sensor network (WSN) applications. For example, event-detection data is not particularly meaningful if the WSN is unable to provide any information on where an event occurred.

Nodes can be equipped with a global positioning system (GPS) to provide them with absolute positions, yet this is currently infeasible due to the cost and various deployment limitations (e.g. does not work indoors). Techniques to estimate node positions without using a GPS have already been developed and usually rely on measuring the distances between the nodes and the anchors. In this paper, we classifies the various localization approaches into two groups based on whether or not they require an estimation of the distance or angle between nodes during their communication. Therefore, approaches that infer fine grained information, such as the distance to a reference point based on the signal strength or timing measurements, fall into the category of range-aware localization methods, while those that do not estimate the distance or angle are categorized as range-free localization methods.

In a range-aware approach, the representative localization methods are TOA, TDOA, RSSI, and so on. The time of arrival (ToA) exploits the relationship between

J. Indulska et al. (Eds.): UIC 2007, LNCS 4611, pp. 709–719, 2007.

distance and transmission time when the propagation speed is known. Yet, depending on the transmission medium that is used, time of arrival requires very high resolution clocks to produce results of acceptable accuracy. And the wave propagation speed is affected by external factors, such as temperature of humidity.

Thus, to overcome the need for precise synchronization, the time difference of arrival (TDoA) was proposed in [2][3]. In TDoA schemes, the sender transmits two very different propagation speeds wave (e.g. radio waves and ultrasound) simultaneously and calculate the distance according the different arrival time. While the main advantage of TDoA is that it does not require explicit synchronization, the obvious disadvantage is the need for two types of transceiver at each node.

The received signal strength indication (RSSI) is a measurement of the received radio signal strength and is closely related to range. In theory, the energy of a radio signal diminishes with the square of the distance from the sender in free space. As a result, the receiver can use the received signal strength to calculate its distance from the transmitter. However, in practice, RSSI values maybe have ranging errors of ±50% because of multipath fading, mobility, background interference, and irregular signal propagation characteristics[4]. To some degree, this error can be reduced by repeated sampling and filtering out incorrect values using statistical techniques [5]. In [6], the calibration problem is considered based on [5].

Generally, range-free solutions only use regular radio modules as the basis for localization, thereby avoiding additional high hardware costs. Among the existing range-free localization approaches, the approximate point in a triangle (APIT) is perhaps the most well-known [7][8]. APIT uses a novel area-based approach, in which the nodes are assumed to be able to hear a fairly large number of beacons. However, instead of calculating the exact distance to beacon nodes with ranging, each node forms a number of "beacon triangles", where each triangle is formed by three arbitrary beacons. The node then decides whether it is inside or outside each triangle, intersects the beacon triangles within which it lies, and finally chooses the center of this intersection region as its position estimate.

In [1], a simple connectivity-metric method for localization in an outdoor environment is proposed that makes use of the inherent radio-frequency (RF) communication capabilities of nodes. This location system consists of various fixed RF stations with overlapping coverage regions, where each anchor periodically broadcasts its unique ID and position coordinates.

Accordingly, this paper proposes a neighbor position-based localization algorithm (NPLA) that increases the positioning accuracy by gathering certain information from the neighbors and maintaining a neighbor table and their coordinates. Instead of using simple fixed circles for overlapping, NPLA uses crescent overlapping, where the crescent is selected based on optimization principles, resulting in a smaller intersection area. Furthermore, the actual sensor network and wireless channel assumptions used with the proposed algorithm are more realistic than those used in an overlapping circle-based localization algorithm (OCLA).

The rest of this paper is organized as follows. Section 2 describes the proposed neighbor position-based localization algorithm in detail. Section 3 then presents some simulation results under different network conditions. Finally, Section 4 gives some conclusions.

2 Neighbor Position-Based Localization Algorithm

2.1 Problem Statements

Overlapping circle-based localization algorithms usually assume a fixed and predefined transmission range for the anchors. Anchor nodes in wireless sensor networks are either special fixed devices that include a GPS or sensor nodes that already obtained their position information from other anchor nodes. When a sensor node detects a signal from a certain anchor node, it simply draws a predefined circle corresponding to the maximum radio transmission range and concludes that it is inside this circle. But, in a real environment, the transmission range is time varying due to battery energy consumption and changes in the environmental condition (e.g. moving obstacles). This situation is shown in Figure 1. Initially, anchors *A*, *B*, and *C* all have the same transmissions range, the sensor receives signals from all of them, and determines an accurate position, shown by *X*. However, with time, anchor *C*'s transmission range diminishes due to a decreased battery energy, the sensor then only receives messages from anchor *A* and *B*, and can no longer hear anchor *C*. Thus, the estimated position is shown as *X'*.

With overlapping-based localization methods, the positioning error is represented by the overlapping area. Therefore, more overlapping circles make a smaller overlapping area, resulting in more accurate positioning. Thus, based on the positioning error, each sensor node can decide whether the accuracy of the estimated position coordinate is satisfied or not to its application requirement. Figure 2 shows that some sensors can obtain an accurate position, while others can not.

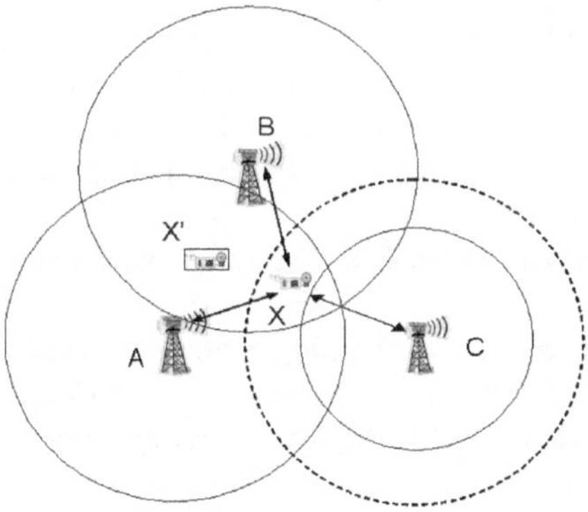

Fig. 1. Inaccurate localization due to decreased transmission range of anchor *C*

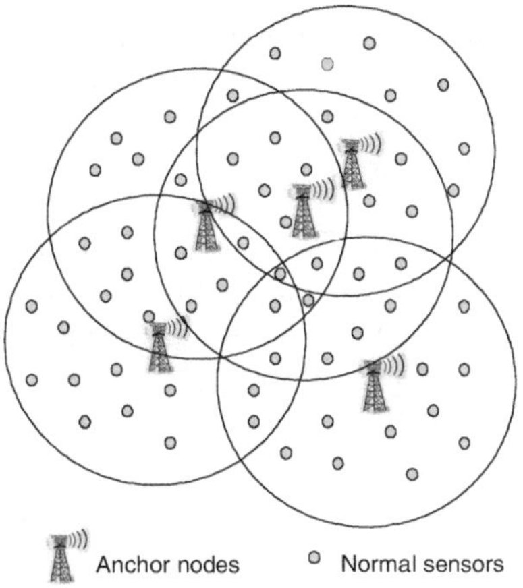

Fig. 2. Different positioning accuracy according to location

2.2 Overlapping Using Crescents

In the proposed neighbor position-based localization algorithm (NPLA), the radio transmission range of each sensor is not assumed to be the same, but rather time varying in accordance with the battery energy and channel characteristics. The basic idea of NPLA is that sensors with highly accurate position information help improve the positioning accuracy of their neighbors. Therefore, when more sensor nodes (i.e., neighbor nodes) are deployed within a given area, the proposed NPLA provides more accurate localization results.

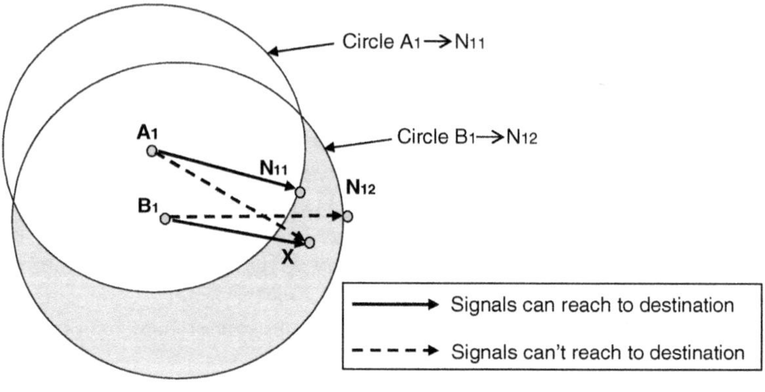

Fig. 3. Overlapping crescent with NPLA

Figure 3 shows the basic model of the proposed method for estimating node positions. In Figure 3, sensor X is the node requiring a position estimate and sensors N_{11}, N_{12}, and B_1 are the neighbors of sensor X. In this paper, neighbors mean they are inside the communication range. As such, A_1 is the neighbor of N_{11}, yet it is not the neighbor of sensor X, as the beacon message from A_1 can reach N_{11}, yet not X, meaning that X is located outside of circle $A_1 \rightarrow N_{11}$. Similarly, since the beacon message from B_1 can reach X, yet not X's neighbor node N_{12}, this means X is located inside of circle $B_1 \rightarrow N_{12}$. Thus, based on the following information: A_1's beacon can reach N_{11}, yet it can not reach X, B_1's beacon message can reach X, yet it can not reach N_{12}; it can be determined that sensor X is located somewhere in the shadow crescent area shown in Figure 3. Therefore, the sensor node set $\{A_1, B_1, N_{11}, N_{12}\}$ that already includes highly accurate position information makes a crescent that contains the location of sensor X.

In OCLAs, the position estimation is based on overlapping several circles, as shown in Figure 1, whereas, in the proposed method, it is based on overlapping several crescents. Essentially, certain sensors with highly accurate position information assist other sensor nodes in estimating their positions. As such, if a sensor node that is trying to estimate its position has many neighbor nodes that already have accurate positions, several crescents can be made $\{A_i, B_i, N_{i1}, N_{i2}\}$, resulting in a smaller overlapping area than with OCLAs. For example, in Figure 4, sensor X finds $\{A_1, B_1, N_{11}, N_{12}\}$ and $\{ A_2, B_2, N_{21}, N_{22} \}$, where sensors N_{21}, N_{22}, and B_2 are the neighbors of sensor X, resulting in two crescents and an overlapping area that is much smaller than the case of a single crescent. The actual node position is then calculated as the center point of the overlapping area.

To obtain a crescent, the following two conditional neighbor relationships for the target sensor node X should be satisfied:

i) At least one neighbor node (N_{i1}) of the sensor node X should have a neighbor (A_i) that cannot reach the sensor node X.
ii) At least one neighbor node (B_i) of the sensor node X should not be able to reach one of the neighbors (N_{i2}) of the sensor node X.

In NPLA, the position overlapping area can be derived using (1). As previously mentioned, when there are many neighbor sets that satisfy the above relationships, the position overlapping area can be reduced. Yet, to reduce the overhead for position estimation, the number of crescents used may need to be limited. For the present simulation study, five crescents were concluded adequate to obtain an accurate positioning result.

$$PositionArea = \bigcap(i = 1,k)[Crecent(A_i,B_i,N_{i1},N_{i2})] \quad (1)$$

where $Crescent(A_i, B_i, N_{i1}, N_{i2})$ denotes the crescent determined by $\{A_i, B_i, N_{i1}, N_{i2}\}$ and $\cap$ denotes the overlapping of the crescents.

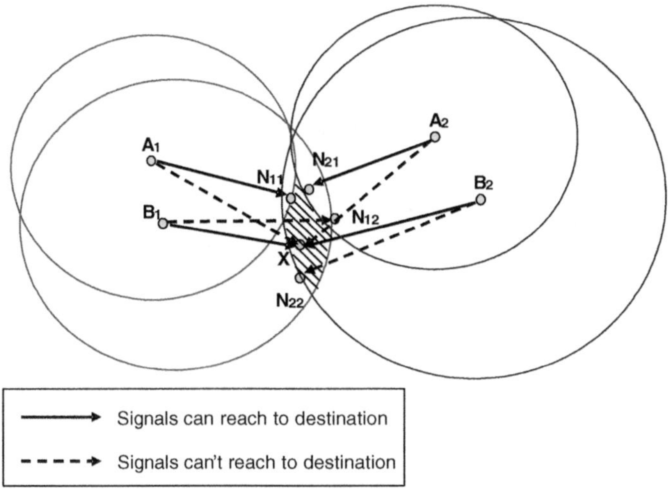

Fig. 4. Overlapping of two crescents with NPLA

Since the position is then estimated based on the center point of the overlapping area, this produces a positioning error compared with the real position, plus the larger overlapping position area, the higher positioning error. Therefore, in this paper, the overlapping area is used as the positioning accuracy measure. For calculation overlapping area, in this paper, we divide the area into many grids and decide whether the grid is in the overlapping area or not. If only two grids are in the overlapping area, then the overlapping area is 2 × S[grid area]. Then we calculate the maximum distance between each two inter-points. Based on this maximum inter-point distance, we represent position estimation error as numerical value.

2.3 Neighbor Table List Request and Positioning Neighbor Selection Method

Making a crescent requires obtaining not only the neighbor's position information but also their neighbor information. When a sensor node does not know it position information or its currently estimated positioning accuracy is low, the sensor node initiates a neighbor table list (NTL) request procedure by broadcasting an NTL Request (NTLR) packet. Each sensor then maintains an NTL that includes the positioning information about itself and its neighbors. The format of the NTL is shown in Figure 5 and contains the node ID, position coordinates, and position estimation error for both the neighbors and their neighbors.

ID		Estimated Position(m)	Position Estimation Error (m^2)
Sensor	Sensor A	(23.83, 55.32)	2.04
Neighbors	Neighbor-1	(12.45, 35.64)	3.79
	Neighbor-2	(29.71, 72.32)	9.52
	Neighbor-3	(76.42, 95.12)	2.13
	Neighbor-4	(55.93, 43.28)	8.19
	Neighbor-5	(32.68, 81.85)	2.12

Fig. 5. Format of NTL for sensor A

If anchor nodes or any neighbor sensor nodes that have already estimated their positions receive an NTLR broadcast message, they send their NTL to the sensor node that sent the NTLR message (request node), allowing a set of $\{A_i, B_i, N_{i1}, N_{i2}\}$ to be created from the neighbor table lists.

In wireless sensor networks, energy consumption is an important issue. Thus, to reduce the energy and process overhead for NTL requests and make the reporting as minimal as possible, an adaptive power control mechanism is proposed for NPLA. As such, any neighbors receiving the request send their NTL to the request node, then the most suitable neighbors for positioning are selected using a new positioning neighbor selection algorithm. If the request node does not identify enough neighbors or the desired positioning accuracy from the reported neighbors is inadequate, the

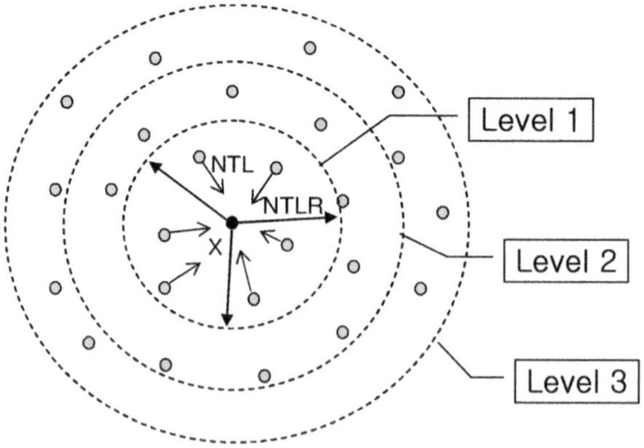

Fig. 6. Adaptive power control for NTLR broadcasting

transmitting power of the NTLR is increased to extend the reply range of the NTL. In Figure 6, when sensor X broadcasts an NTLR with transmitting power Level 1, about 6 sensors send their NTL to sensor X. Yet, when sensor X broadcasts the NTLR with transmitting power Level 2, more than 15 sensors send their NTL to sensor X, thereby increasing the probability of selecting enough or more accurately positioned neighbors than with the Level 1 transmission power.

When a sensor node requests NTLs from its neighbors, it could receive many NTLs, resulting in a large number of position sets, especially in high density wireless sensor networks. The situation can occur where small crescents are fully included within large crescents. In this case, the large crescents are redundant and useless. Thus, selecting the appropriate neighbors for localization is important and significantly decreases the calculation involved. In other words, sensor X needs to determine the best crescents based on the NTLs received.

Accordingly, this paper also presents a method for selecting the optimum neighbor set to minimize the area of a crescent. Thus, the set $\{A_i, B_i, N_{i1}, N_{i2}\}$ is selected that satisfies the following three requirements.

i) maximizes the distance $A_i \rightarrow N_{i1}$;
ii) minimizes the distance $B_i \rightarrow N_{i2}$;
iii) minimizes the distance $A_i \rightarrow B_i$.

This makes the outer and inner boundaries as close as possible, thereby minimizing the overlapping area and providing the best accuracy for the position estimation.

2.4 Accuracy-Based Adaptive NPLA

In a WSN, the application decides the positioning accuracy requirements of each sensor. Therefore, this paper proposes an accuracy-based adaptive neighbor position-based localization algorithm (NPLA). As shown in Figure 7, the position estimation process has three phases. In each phase, if the desired application positioning accuracy is satisfied (as mentioned in Section 2.2, position estimation error is defined as overlapping area), then the estimation process is finished.

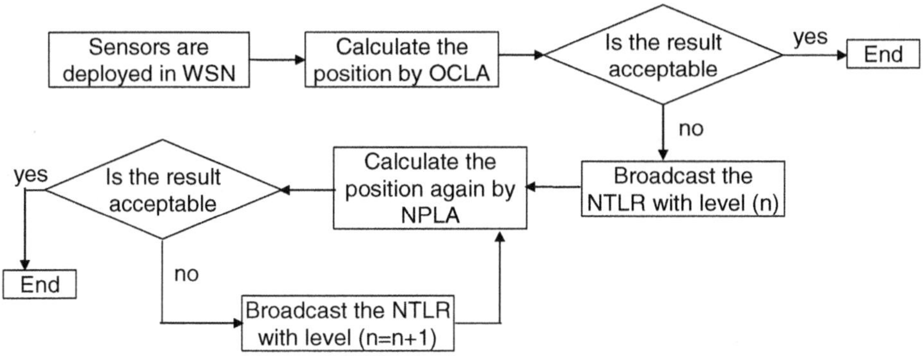

Fig. 7. Accuracy-based adaptive NPLA

In the first phase, a sensor node's position is roughly estimated using a simple overlapping circle-based location algorithm (OCLA) with a predefined maximum transmission range. For example, as shown in Figure 8-(a), the sensor receives signals from anchors *B*, N_{11} and N_{12}, so it can estimates its position as *X'*. The proposed NPLA does not assume the same transmission range, so anchor B's transmission range is decreased due to battery consumption. And it is reflected in the smaller circle ($B_1 \rightarrow N_{12}$) area, as shown in Figure 8-(b). Thus, proposed method can produces a more accurate overlapping area.

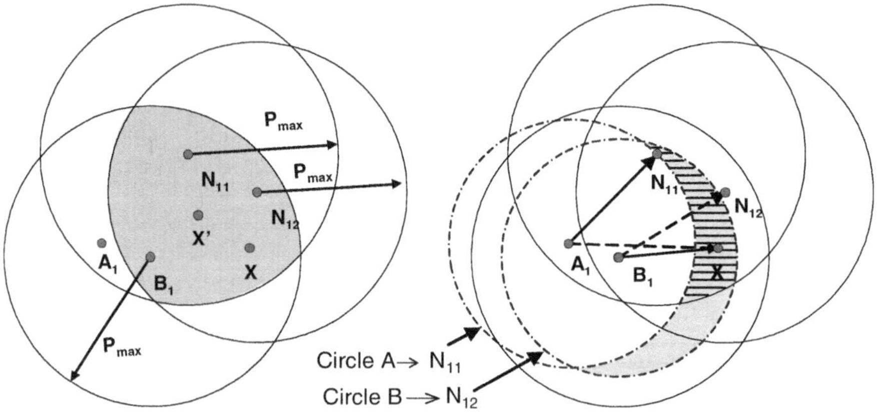

(a) Estimation using overlapping connectivity (b) Estimation with NPLA

Fig. 8. Example of positioning

3 Simulation Study

In this paper, we used the ns-2 simulator to evaluate the performance. In the simulation study, the proposed NPLA was compared with an overlap circle based localization algorithm (OCLA). For the NPLA, the function for NTLR broadcast power control with different levels was not included for a fair positioning error comparison, plus the broadcast overhead was measured in the worst case conditions with a predefined maximum transmission range.

3.1 Simulation Parameters and Evaluation Criteria

In the simulation, 400 wireless sensor nodes with unknown positions and 40 anchors with known positions were randomly deployed in a given area. The parameters for the simulation are shown in Table 1. The positioning accuracy threshold is the minimum required the overlapping area to finish the positioning process with OCLA.

Fifteen different network topologies were made, each with randomly deployed sensor and anchor nodes. The positioning error was computed as the difference between the real position and the estimated position.

Table 1. Simulation parameters

Number of sensor nodes	400
Number of anchor nodes	40
Sensor node radio transmission range	20m
Anchor node radio transmission range	40m
Posititition accuracy threshold	$40m^2$

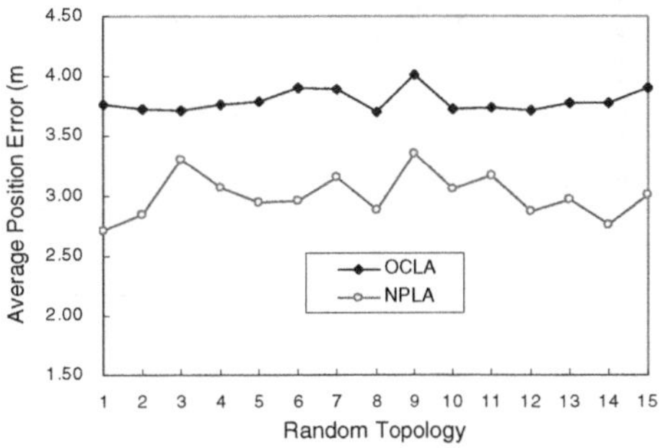

Fig. 9. Average position estimation error for different network topologies

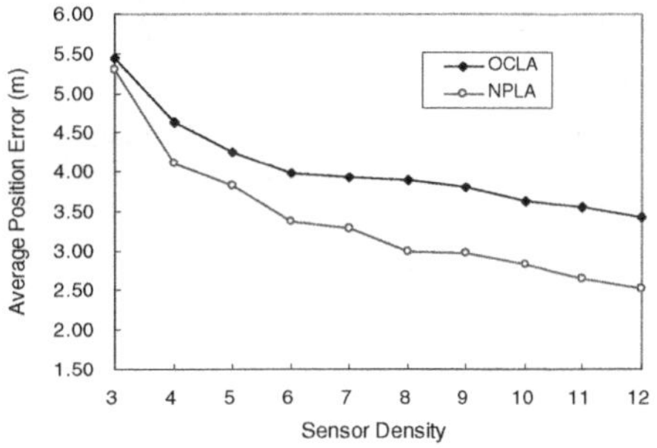

Fig. 10. Average position estimation error with different densities

Figure 9 shows the average position error for the 15 different network topologies. The sensors and anchors were randomly deployed in a 220m x 220m area. Sensor density was 8. In this paper, sensor density means the average number sensors per 1000m2.In most of the topologies, the proposed NPLA improved the accuracy by 30% when compared with the OCLA.

Figure 10 shows the average position error for the OCLA and NPLA with different sensor densities. For the average position error calculation, each sensor's positioning errors were averaged for all the topologies. As the sensor density increased, the positioning accuracies of both the OCLA and NPLA also increased. The NPLA showed a better performance than the OCLA due to the higher probability of finding more crescents in a high density wireless sensor network, and smaller overlapping area than with the OCLA.

Figures 11 and 12 compare the performance of the NPLA with different position accuracy thresholds. In the proposed position accuracy-based adaptive NPLA, a simple OCLA with fixed circles is used first to estimate the sensor node positions. If the overlapping area based measurement is then greater than the threshold, the NPLA method is applied, as shown in Figure 7. As shown in Figure 11, when the accuracy threshold was low, a better positioning performance was achieved, as the OCLA was unable to meet the accuracy requirement in many cases, meaning the NPLA was executed to meet the requirement.

Figure 12 shows the overheads for the NPLA, which mainly consisted of NTL replies in accordance with NTL requests. The number of exchange packets when the NTL request was transmitted with the maximum power was computed as the worst case in terms of the packet overhead. The packet overhead increased with a higher sensor density. Also, when the threshold was decreased with a fixed density, the overhead increased, as many sensors with rough position coordinates will broadcast an NTLR to collect the NTLs. Thus, a suitable threshold (i.e. application requirement) is needed for the NPLA considering the overhead and average error of the position estimation, which is actually a tradeoff problem.

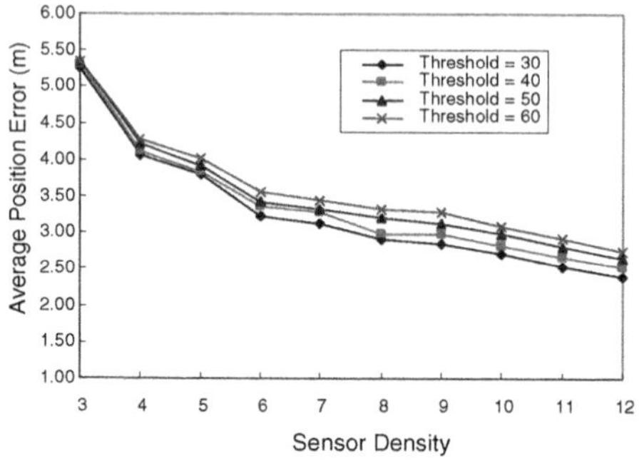

Fig. 11. Average position error with different thresholds in NPLA

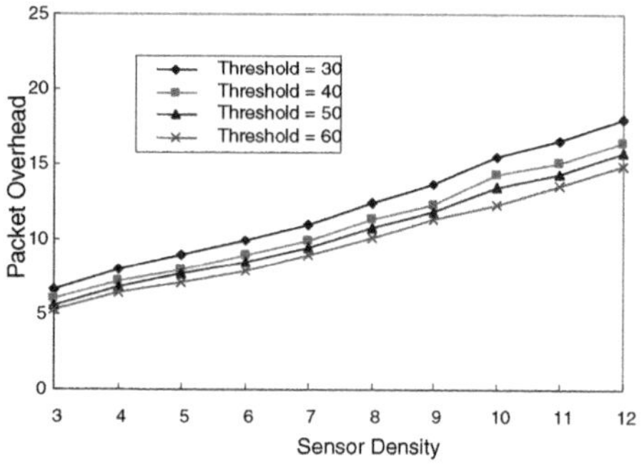

Fig. 12. Average number of exchanged packets with different thresholds in NPLA

4 Conclusion

This paper proposed a neighbor position-based localization algorithm (NPLA) for wireless sensor networks. The proposed method does not require a complex and precise ranging mechanism. Instead, the NPLA estimates the sensor node position using messages received from anchor nodes or neighbor sensor nodes. To eliminate redundant neighbor information, an efficient positioning neighbor selection method and adaptive power control method are proposed to make the smallest crescents. Simulation results show that the NPLA can improved the positioning accuracy.

References

1. Bulusu, N., Heidemann, J., Estrin, D.: GPS-less Low Cost Outdoor Localization for Very Small Devices. IEEE Personal Communications Magazine , 28–34 (2000)
2. Savvides, A., Han, C., Srivastava, M.B.: Dynamic Fine-Grained Localization in Ad-Hoc Networks of Sensors. In: Proceedings of the 7th Annual International Conference on Mobile Computing and Networking, pp. 166–179 (2001)
3. Riyantha, N.B., Chakraborty, A., Balakrishnan, H.: The Cricket Location-Support System. In: 6th International Conference on Mobile Computing and Networking, pp. 32–43 (2000)
4. Savarese, C., Rabaey, J.M., Langemdoen, K.: Robust Positioning Algorithms for Distributed Ad-Hoc Wireless Sensor Networks. In: Proceedings of the Annual USENIX Technical Conference, pp. 317–327 (2002)
5. Ward, A., Jones, A., Hopper, A.: A New Location Technique for the Active Office. IEEE Personal Communications 4(5), 42–47 (1997)

6. Whitehouse, K., Culler, D.: Calibration as Parameter Estimation in Sensor Networks. In: Proceeding of the 1st ACM International WSN and Applications, pp. 59–67. ACM Press, New York (2002)
7. He, T., Huang, C., Blum, B.M., Stankovic, J.A., Abdelzaher, T.: Range-Free Localization Schemes for Large Scale Sensor Networks. In: Proceedings of the ninth annual international conference on Mobile computing and networking, pp. 81–95 (2003)
8. He, T., Huang, C., Blum, B.M., Stankovic, J.A., Abdelzaher, T.: Range-Free Localization and Its Impact on Large Scale Sensor Networks. ACM Transactions on Embedded Computing Systems 4(4), 877–906 (2005)

Location Estimation with Mobile Nodes in Wireless Sensor Networks

Ying-Hong Wang, Chien-Min Lee, Wei-Ting Chen, and Chieh-Hsin Kuo

Department of Computer Science and Information Engineering
TamKang University
Tamsui, Taipei, Taiwan, R.O.C.
inhon@mail.tku.edu.tw, 693191545@s93.tku.edu.tw,
694192419@s94.tku.edu.tw, 695420157@s95.tku.edu.tw

Abstract. The sensor nodes of wireless sensor networks (WSNs) have the following abilities such as: sensing, computation, and wireless communication capabilities. Hence, WSNs can be used for various application domains. In this paper, we propose a location mechanism with mobile reference nodes and Global Positioning System (GPS) to help sensor nodes to calculate the coordinate location information. And then sensor nodes deliver the coordinate location to base station through neighboring sensor nodes. By using this mechanism, we can calculate the coordinate location of the target sensor nodes. And then we can apply this mechanism to track or transfer data packets in the WSNs efficiently.

1 Introduction

In recent years advancements in battery technology miniaturization, and wireless transmission have increased the scope for sensor applications. Sensors are used in Wireless Sensor Networks (WSN) [1] [2]. Sensors are small, cheap, consume little power, and are capable of detecting changes in their environment. Due to their small size however, their energy, computing power and storage capacities are very limited.

Sensors have a wide range of applications such as: 1. Scatter sensors on the battlefield for monitoring or reconnaissance. 2. When a fire occurs, the sensor detects the abnormal increase in temperature and identifies the location of the fire directly, allowing people to be sent to put it out. Research into improving the performance of WSNs can be categorized into the following topics: Routing Protocol, Locating, Data Aggregation, Fault Tolerance and Energy Consumption. The above research topics on WSN [10-11] are described below:

1. Routing Protocol: When sensor nodes further away from the base station sense data that should be transmitted back to the base station, the data must be routed through other sensor nodes. A routing protocol must therefore ensure that the data is sent back to the base station via the shortest route.
2. Locating: In a WSN the sensors are distribution is therefore random and the location of individual sensors is not known in advance. If an event occurs at a certain point within the deployed WSN, we will not know where the event occurred. This study hopes to determine a way to calculate the coordinates of individual sensors.

J. Indulska et al. (Eds.): UIC 2007, LNCS 4611, pp. 720–729, 2007.

3. Data Aggregation: When a sensor node is transmitting data, it consumes energy, meaning that the sensor node would be drained in a short period of time. If there is a data aggregation mechanism to collect all the appropriate data and then transmit it only when needed, this will help to extend the sensor node's service life.
4. Energy Consumption: The question of how to conserve energy is at the moment best answered through the use of a sleep mechanism algorithm. The amount of energy wasted by the sensor while in stand by is thus minimized

When building a WSN, if we can discover the location of the sensor nodes, this will greatly enhance the performance of the WSN. To enhance the performance to the WSN, this paper chooses to focus on the Locating component of the above five research topics and propose a positioning mechanism that utilizes mobile reference points. The paper consists of five sections. In section 2, current WSN positioning methods and the characteristics of wireless radio are introduced. Section 3 proposes a positioning mechanism for the topic of Locating, with explanations on how to move the reference points and transmit data on coordinates. In section 4 we analyze the simulation results generated by this particular positioning mechanism. Section 5 is the conclusion and direction of future research.

2 Related Works

2.1 Radio Waves

Once an antenna transmits a radio signal, the signal travels at the speed of light to be diffracted, refracted or reflected by the ionosphere in order to reach its destination and achieve the purpose of the radio transmission. Radio waves are usually transmitted through an antenna, so the antenna is a very important transmission medium for radio waves. The effective sensory area of an antenna is related to its gain. This can be seen using the formula for antenna gain [3] [6]:

$$A = G\frac{\lambda^2}{4\pi} \tag{1}$$

A: Antenna's effective sensory area.
G: Antenna gain.
λ : Radio signal wavelength

From (Eq.1), the antenna gain formula can be used to determine the antenna's effective sensory area.

2.2 Wireless Sensor Network Locating Method

In recent years the following positioning methods have been developed for Wireless Sensor Networks:

1. Angle of Arrival Detection Method [5] [7]
This method uses the antenna to directly detect the range and bearing of a target. To detect a target's range and bearing, a complicated and expensive antenna is installed

in a fixed location. This antenna rotates, so when the radio waves coming from the target is at peak power, the antenna is able to determine the target's range and bearing. The advantage of using this method is the high level of accuracy it achieves.

2. Time of Arrival Detection Method [5] [7]

In this method, the sender transmits radio signals. After the radio signal reaches the target, the time spent in transit is converted into the distance traveled to find the distance between the sender and target. From this, the target's range and bearing can be determined. However, if this method is used indoors, obstacles may interfere with the radio waves, lowering the method's accuracy.

3. Received Signal Strength Method [4] [5] [7]

In this method the sender transmits a radio signal. When the signal reaches the antenna at the target, the power of the received signal can be converted into distance to give the distance from the sender to the target as well as the target's range and bearing. There is a distance measurement formula used for this method: The Friis Transmission Formula [4]. This formula uses the above method to convert power into distance.

The Friis Transmission Formula is expressed below:

$$\frac{\mathbf{P}_r}{\mathbf{P}_t} = \frac{\mathbf{A}_{er}\mathbf{A}_{et}}{\mathbf{r}^2\lambda^2} \tag{2}$$

$\mathbf{P}_r$: Power at receiver. $\mathbf{P}_t$: Power at sender.

$\mathbf{A}_{er}$: Transmission range of receiver. $\mathbf{A}_{et}$: Transmission range of sender.

λ : Wavelength. $\mathbf{r}$: The range value we want.

4. Frequency of Arrival Detection Method [5]

If the target is moving, in this method the sender transmits a radio signal. When the radio signal arrives at the receiver, it then converts the rate at which signals are received from the sender into frequency. The more signals that arrive at the receiver the more accurately the target's range and bearing can be determined. This will then allow us to work out the target's range, bearing and speed.

5. Mobile Locating Method

The locating method that uses a moving reference point as described in [9] we shall refer to as LWMAP. In LWMAP, by moving within the WSN, the fact that the perpendicular bisector of chords all intersect at a single point results in a simultaneous equation. The equation can then be solved using Gramer's Rule to derive the coordinates of the sensor node.

3 A Location Mechanism with Mobile Reference Nodes in WSNs

3.1 Locating Mechanism

In the locating mechanism described by this paper, a GPS device and the Received Signal Strength Method are used with a mobile reference point to determine the sensor node coordinates of the whole WSN.

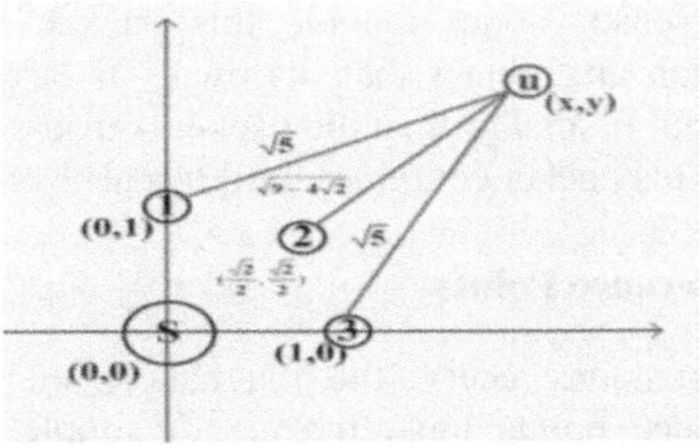

Fig. 1. points 1, 2 and 3 are mobile sensor nodes with GPS while point u is a sensor node with unknown coordinates

3.2 Locating Process - Calculate the Coordinates

Step 1: Define the Parameters

Let us call these 3 GPS equipped sensor nodes G1, G2 and G3. When the 3 nodes are all at distance r from sink, we define this as 1R. When G1, G2 and G3 are 2r away from the sink, we define this as 2R… and so on.

Step 2: When G1, G2 and G3 are on 1R

G1, G2 and G3 begin transmitting signals to all sensor nodes with unknown coordinates within 1R. These sensor nodes with unknown coordinates must receive at least 3 radio signals before using the Friis Transmission Formula to work out their distance to G1, G2 and G3. The Distance Formula is then used to draw up a simultaneous equation that when solved gives the sensor node's own coordinates.

Step 3: Transmission of Coordinate Data

Their own coordinate data is then transmitted back to the base station through neighboring sensor nodes. Sensor nodes with unknown coordinates located outside 1R may not receive 3 or more signals.

Step 4: When G1, G2 and G3 are on 2R

G1, G2 and G3 begin moving on the circumference of 2R. This will enable sensor nodes with unknown coordinates located between 1R and 2R to receive the third signal. Calculate their own coordinates and transmit it back.

Step 5: When G1, G2 and G3 are on 3R or greater than 3R

G1, G2 and G3 move on the circumference of 3R. They will send radio signals to sensor nodes with unknown coordinates located between 2R and 3R to provide them with a third signal. Calculate their own coordinates and transmit it back.

3.3 Transmission of Coordinate Data

1. When a sensor node with unknown coordinates calculates its own coordinates, it broadcasts a packet in the format shown in Table 1

Table 1. Format of Transmitted Coordinate Packet

ID: Numbering of Sensor Nodes
Coordinate: Sensor Node X-axis and Y-axis coordinates.

ID	Coordinate

2. When neighboring sensor nodes receive this packet, they check whether the coordinate information are greater than its own. If larger then it broadcasts the packet and saves it, but if smaller then the packet is discarded.
3. The transmission of this packet continues until it reaches the base station.

3.4 Movement of Reference Points

To make sure all sensor nodes receive three signals so they can calculate their own coordinates, the reference points must move. A simple explanation of how the reference point moves is provided here. Every time G1, G2 and G3 move on 1R, 2R, 3R they will travel 1/8, 1/16, 1/32 of the circumference, and so on. This is to ensure that sensor nodes with unknown coordinates will receive at least 3 radio signals. As shown in Fig.2(a), reference point with fixed distance movement about 1/8 of the circumference on 2R will occur the sensor nodes with unknown coordinates in the green area that only receive 1 or 2 radio signals and be unable to determine their own coordinates. G1, G2 and G3 must therefore move 1/16 of the circumference on 2R as shown in Fig.2(b). This will ensure that sensor nodes with unknown coordinates located between 1R and 2R can receive 3 or more radio signals and can determine their own coordinates. Since we only need 3 mobile reference points to be installed to calculate the coordinates of a sensor node, a maximum of three is needed at most.

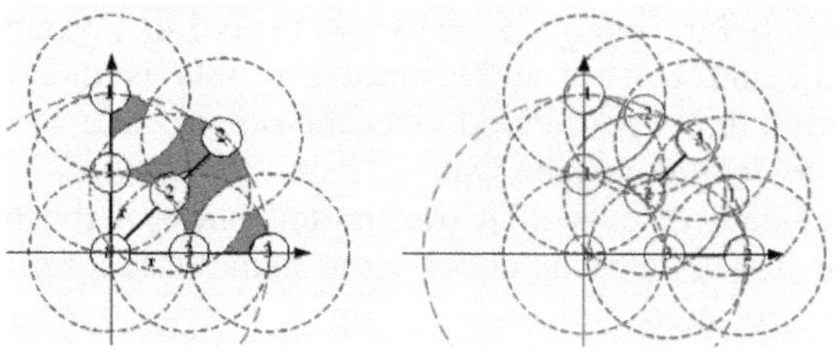

Fig. 2. (a)Fixed Distance Movement(b)Variable Distance Movement

3.5 Movement of Three Reference Points

1. G1, G2 and G3's Tracks

Fig.3(a) shows the tracks left by G1, G2 and G3's movements. At 1R and 3R they moved in a clock-wise direction while at 2R and 4R they moved in a counter-clockwise direction. In Fig.3(b)(c)(d), we give an example about G1, G2 and G3

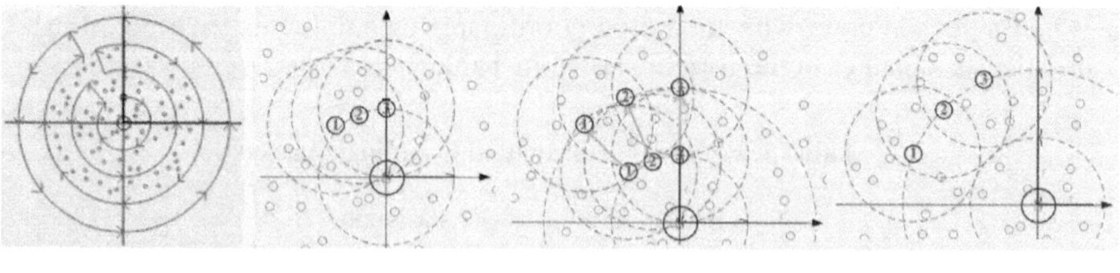

Fig. 3. (a)Tracks of G1,G2,G3 -- G1's Tracks(b)G1, G2 and G3 moving for the 7th time on 1R (c)move in a straight line outwards from 1R by a distance of 1R(d)moving for the 1st on 2R

moving on 2R. Moreover at 4R, G1, G2 and G3 no longer detect any sensor nodes so they stop moving.

2. *Movement Formula*

From the above movement method, we can conclude the following movement principles:

1. The number of times G1, G2 and G3 move for 1R, 2R..., kR,...nR where $1 \leq k \leq n$

When G1, G2 and G3 are at 1R, 2R, and 3R they move 1/8, 1/16, 1/32 of the circumference each time for a total of 7, 15, and 31 times, giving us the result $7 = 2^0 \times 2 \times 4 - 1$, $15 = 2^1 \times 2 \times 4 - 1$, and $31 = 2^2 \times 2 \times 4 - 1$. We can define the formula for the number of times that G1, G2 and G3 move for kR below.

$$2^{r+2} - 1, r = 1,2,3 \ldots\ldots n. \tag{3}$$

But with G1 at 2R, 4R, 6R... (2K)R it will always move one time less, so for odd number circles G1's number of movements is:

$$2^{r+2} - 2, r = 2,4 \ldots\ldots 2k. \tag{4}$$

G3 will also at 1R, 3R, 5R... (2k+1)R moves one time less as well.
The number of times that G3 moves in an odd number circle is:

$$2^{r+2} - 2, r = 1,3 \ldots\ldots 2k+1. \tag{5}$$

2. G1, G2 and G3's Distance Moved Each Time at 1R, 2R.........nR.

G1's movements on 1R divides the circumference into 8 equal sections, so G1, G2 and G3 moves by a distance of $\frac{2\pi r}{8} = \frac{2\pi(1r)}{2^0 \times 2 \times 4}$ on 1R each time. Therefore the formula for G1, G2 and G3's distance moved each time for 1R, 2R... nR can be expressed as:

$$\frac{x\pi r}{2^{x+1}}, x = 1,2,3, \ldots\ldots n. \tag{6}$$

3. The Distance of G2's Last Move on 1R, 2R, 3R...........nR

However, the distance covered by G2's last move on 1R, 2R, 3R......... nR is only half of the previous moves. When G2 is at 1R, 2R... nR the distance it covers in its last move can be expressed as:

$$\frac{y\pi r}{2^{y+2}}, y = 1,2,3, \ldots\ldots, n. \tag{7}$$

3.6 Calculation Method

3.6.1 The Algorithm for Calculating the Coordinates

Parameter Definitions:

(x_i, y_i) : Represents a sensor node with unknown coordinates where i=1, 2, 3, ... , n.
(x_j, y_j) : Represents the current coordinates of G1, G2 and G3 where j=1,2,3.
r_k : Indicates the distance calculated by using the Friis Transmission Formula where k=1,2,3.

Calculation Process:

1. Setting up the simultaneous equations:
   When a sensor node with unknown coordinates receives 3 signals, it calculates the range to G1, G2 and G3 then sets out the following simultaneous equations.

$$\sqrt{(x_i - x_k)^2 + (y_j - y_k)^2} = r_k \quad where \quad k = 1,2,3 \tag{8}$$

2. Solving the simultaneous equations:
   Calculate the value x_i, y_j from equation (8).

$$y_j = \frac{1}{2} \times \frac{[(r_3^2 - r_2^2) - (x_3^2 - x_2^2) - (y_3^2 - y_2^2)] \times (x_1 - x_2) - [(r_2^2 - r_1^2) - (x_2^2 - x_1^2) - (y_2^2 - y_1^2)] \times (x_2 - x_3)}{(x_1 - x_2)(y_2 - y_3) - (x_2 - x_3)(y_1 - y_2)} \tag{9}$$

$$x_i = \frac{\dfrac{(r_3^2 - r_2^2) - (x_3^2 - x_2^2) - (y_3^2 - y_2^2)}{2} - (y_2 - y_3) y_j}{(x_2 - x_3)} \tag{10}$$

3.6.2 Algorithm for Reference Point Movement

Parameter Definitions:

L : Number of sensor nodes with GPS.
mR : Distance from GPS equipped sensor node to the sink, where m=1,2,3…k…n, $1 \le m \le n$

The range of radio signals from the sink and G1, G2, G3 is 1r.

Different Movement Methods Depending on the Number of Reference Points:

1. When L=1:
   G1's total number of movements is: $2^{m+2} - 1$ with the distance covered in each move: $\frac{m\pi R}{2^{m+1}}$
2. When 1<L<=3:
   Place GPS equipped sensor node at 1R (i.e. m=1) with the interval between GPS equipped nodes being $\frac{1\pi R}{4}$ then transmit radio signals to sensor nodes with unknown coordinates. When L=2, G1 and G2 must move twice before transmitting, and when L=3, G1, G2 and G3 must move 3 times before transmitting. When m=1,3,5………,(2k+1), GPS equipped sensor nodes move in a clockwise direction. When m=2,4,6………,2k, GPS equipped sensor nodes move in a counter-clockwise direction.
   When m=1,2,3,………,n. The number of times that the GPS equipped sensor nodes have moved: $2^{m+2} - 1$.The distance that the GPS equipped sensor nodes move: $\frac{m\pi R}{2^{m+1}}$.

When L=2 or 3, the distance covered by the G2 in its last move is: $\frac{m\pi R}{2^{m+2}}$

When L=3, m=2,4,6,… 2k+1, G1 will move one time less.
When L=3, m=1,3,5,… 2k, G3 will move one time less.

3. Because we need at most 3 points to calculate the coordinates of a sensor node, so at most L=3.

4 Simulation Results

4.1 Simulation Environment

1. 300 sensor nodes were set up within a 100 x 100 m^2 area. In this simulation we shall look at what effect the sensor radius of the base station, G1, G2 and G3 may have on the calculation of coordinates. Three scenarios were used with the sensor radius for the base station, G1, G2 and G3 set to 5m, 10m and 15m.
2. Assume that the time taken for G1, G2 and G3 to move **1/4 π R** was t seconds and each sensor node's calculation time was c seconds. The radio frequency as well as the sensor range of the base station, G2, G2 and G3 were then used in the simulation to calculate the average execution time, average distance and average distance error rate.

4.2 Simulation Results

From Table 2 we can see that the greater the sensor radius of the base station, G1, G2 and G3 were, the shorter the average execution time was. The average distance error and average distance error rate also became bigger as well. Therefore to get the coordinates more quickly a large sensor radius should be used. To get more accurate coordinates however a smaller sensor radius should be used instead.

From Fig.4(a) it can be seen that as R increases so does the average error. This means that as G1, G2 and G3 circle outwards, the further they go the higher the average error percentage becomes.

Table 2. Results of Different Sensor Ranges

t:Time taken for G1, G2 and G3 to move 1/4 π R.
c:Each sensor node's calculation time.

Sensor Radius (M)	Average Execution Time (sec)	Average Distance Error (M)	Average Distance Error Rate (%)
5	511.11t+c	0.101	1
10	152.75t+c	0.174	1.03
15	67.5t+c	0.314	1.12

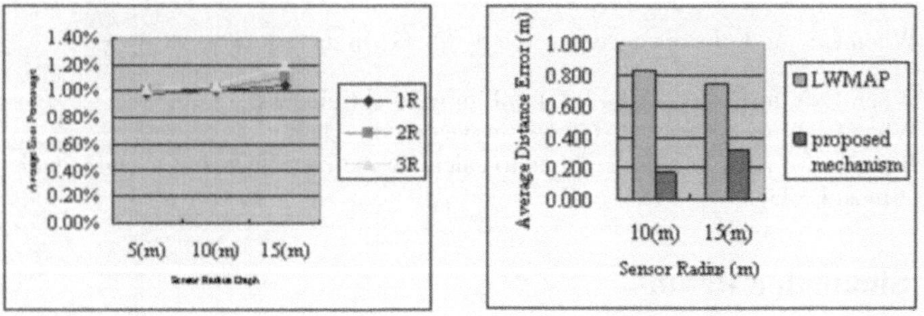

Fig. 4. (a)Average Error Percentage at each R for each sensor radius(b) Comparison of proposed mechanism with LWMAP

From the comparison in Fig.4(b) it can be seen that the positioning mechanism proposed in this paper when the sensor radius is 10(m) and 15(m) results in a calculated average distance error of 0.174(m) and 0.314(m) respectively. When compared to the 0.83(m) and 0.74(m) calculated using LWMAP, it can be seen that the average distance error calculated by the proposed mechanism is lower.

5 Conclusions and Future Work

In the locating mechanism using mobile reference points proposed by this paper, mobile reference points supplemented by GPS is used to let sensor nodes with unknown coordinates determine their own location. Once they have determined the coordinates for their own location, this information is then transmitted back to the base station through neighboring nodes. This allows the base station to be certain about the location of its sensor nodes, improving the data transmission performance of the Wireless Sensor Network. Through a comparison with LWMAP, it can be seen that the mechanism proposed in this paper provides an effective method of calculating the coordinates of sensor nodes, and the calculated results do not deviate seriously from the actual coordinates.

For future research, the "Positioning Mechanism Using a Mobile Reference Point" proposed in this paper can be used to track a moving object. Alternatively, a router protocol can be set up within the WSN so the data collected by the sensors can be transmitted quickly and accurately back to the base station through the use of coordinates.

References

1. Akyildiz, I.F., Su, W., Sankarasubramaniam, Y., Cayirci, E.: A survey on sensor networks. IEEE Communications Magazine 40(8), 102–114 (2002)
2. Hill, J.L., Culler, D.E.: Mica: a wireless platform for deeply embedded networks. IEEE Micro 22(6), 12–24 (2002)
3. Hickman, I.: Practical RF Handbook, 3rd edn. Elsevier Newnes, Amsterdam (2002)

4. Mondinelli, F., Kovacs-Vajna, Z.M.: Self-Localizing Sensor Network Architectures. IEEE Transactions on Instrumentation and Measurement 53(2), 277–283 (2004)
5. Arias, J., Lazaro, J., Astarloa, A., Jimenez, J., Zuloaga, A.: Location algorithm for wireless sensor networks in industrial applications. In: 2004 IEEE International Conference on Industrial Technology, vol. 2(8–10), pp. 757–762 (2004)
6. Hogg, D.C.: Fun with the Friis free-space transmission formula. IEEE Antennas and Propagation Magazine 35(4), 33–35 (1993)
7. Patwari, N., Ash, J.N., Kyperountas, S., III Hero, A.O., Moses, R.L., Correal, N.S.: Locating the Nodes. IEEE Signal Processing Magazine 22(4), 54–69 (2005)
8. Stoleru, R., He, T., Stankovic, J.A.: Walking GPS: A Practical Solution for Localization in Manually Deployed Wireless Sensor Networks. In: 29th Annual IEEE International Conference on Local Computer Networks, pp. 480–489. IEEE Computer Society Press, Los Alamitos (2004)
9. Ssu, K.-F., Ou, C.-H., Jiau, H.C.: Localization With Mobile Anchor Points in Wireless Sensor Networks. IEEE Transactions on Vehicular Technology 54(3), 1187–1197 (2005)

A Novel Architecture for Hierarchically Nested Network Mobility

Hye-Young Kim and Sung Hyun Cho

Department of Game Software, School of Games,
Hongik University, South Korea
{hykim,scho}@hongik.ac.kr

Abstract. We propose an efficient location management scheme based on collaboration of mobile nodes in a mobile network. This proposed scheme integrates Hierarchical Mobile IPv6 with Network Mobility to manage macro mobility and seamless handoff. We address the key functions of the proposed scheme and analyze the performance of our proposed scheme mathematically. We show that our proposed scheme perform much better than Network Mobility, especially when the number of mobile nodes, mobile routers, or correspondent nodes increases in hierarchically nested mobile networks.

1 Introduction

Identification of nodes is necessary for routing inside a network [1]. A network can be virtually recognized as a single node with one address such as a prefix address and some interfaces attached to the node. A mobile router (MR) is a node which manages the mobility of a mobile network, where it is also the default gateway. Network Mobility (NEMO) is generally transparent to mobile nodes inside a mobile network. In a NEMO basic support protocol, a mobile network node (MNN) or an MR is classified into a local mobile node, a local fixed node, or a visiting mobile node[2]. An MNN attaches to a MR, which attaches to a stationary router. This relationship can be expressed as a graph. When an MR or MNN leaves the area its parent manages, the edge linking the mobile node to its parent is broken, and the MR or MNN may attach to another mobile network via a router which becomes its new parent. The graph structure changes dynamically, and it is a tree if loops are avoided. When an MR moves, all nodes in its subtree rooted at itself move together, and create a new hierarchy in a wireless network.

Now we see that there is hierarchical relationship rooted at a stationary router in a mobile network, and the hierarchical mobility management is well applicable. Therefore, we propose a system protocol that integrates Hierarchical Mobile IPv6 (HMIPv6) [3] with NEMO. In order to manage the macro mobility and the seamless handoff in nested NEMO environments, our proposed protocol exploits a multicasting protocol to deliver network prefix scope binding updates.

The organization of this paper is as follows. In section 2, we propose a new model for integrated location management, including a binding update multicast

J. Indulska et al. (Eds.): UIC 2007, LNCS 4611, pp. 730–738, 2007.

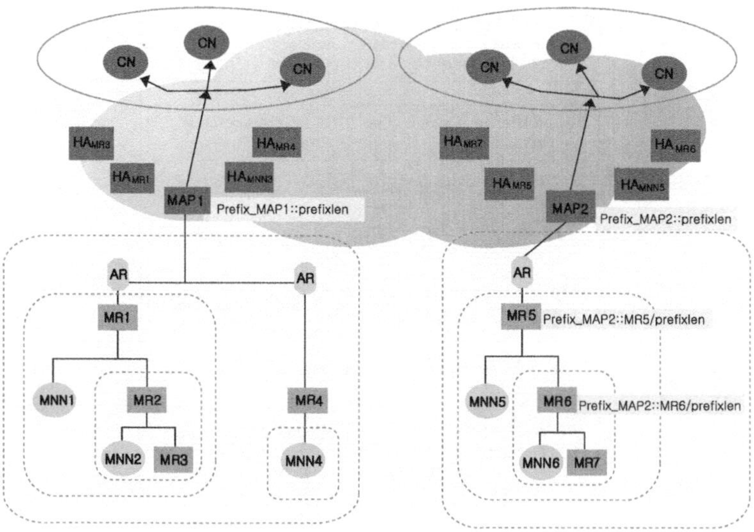

Fig. 1. Proposed System Architecture

routing scheme and its algorithm. We present an analytic model of our proposed scheme, and compare the performance of NEMO and that of our proposed new model in section 3.

2 Proposed System Protocol

2.1 System Architecture

In section 1, we propose a new binding update scheme for nested NEMO environments, and it is based on multicast that integrates HMIPV6 and NEMO to update binding information efficiently. Our proposed system architecture is shown in Figure 1, where an MNN attaches to an MR, and it attaches to a MAP which is newly introduced in HMIPv6. The entire mobile network under the MAP becomes a local MAP domain. The MAP advertises an address of an MR on its subnet, regional care-of-address (RCOA), in an regional area (RA) which is a local MAP domain. The MR adds an address in its subnet to its RA as optional information by using the MAP option field. All MRs and MNNs in a mobile network bind a RCOA based on the mobile network prefix of the MAP and bind on-Link Care-of Address (LCOA) based on the mobile network prefix of its MR [3]. An MNN creates its COA based on the RA, which gives its location in the mobile network. The MNN also creates its own COA_{MNN} with a prefix equal to $PREFIX_{MNN}$.

When an MR or MNN moves to another mobile network, the MR or MNN receives a new MAP option including RA information, and it must send binding update (BU) messages with a new RCOA and a new LCOA. Then, the MR must send BU messages to its new MAP, HA, and CNs. But if the MR or MNN doesn't change its point of attachment and receives a new MAP option, it is

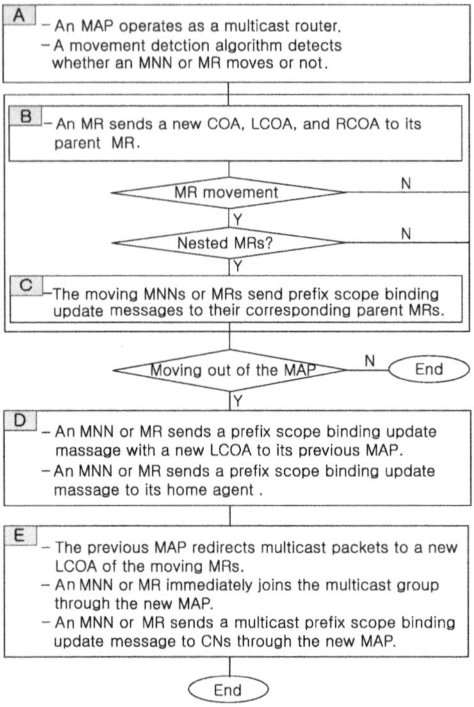

Fig. 2. Proposed Binding Update Procedures

not necessary to send BU messages with a new LCOA and RCOA. Thus, the number of BU messages sent to CNs and HA may be reduced in our proposed scheme. However, HMIPv6 requires that packets be tunnelled from the MAP to the MR or MNN, and this requirement causes QoS to deteriorate in a large scale mobile network, where scalability becomes a very important issue.

2.2 Binding Update Procedures

We will explain the procedure to multicast prefix scope binding update messages when an MR and MNN move in our proposed scheme, assuming a four-layered nested NEMO environment. An MNN attaches to a nested MR, which attaches to its outer MR, which attaches to the MAP which is a stationary router. When an MNN and its ancestor MRs move, Figure 2 shows the proposed binding update procedure in order to manage their locations. The MAP advertises an address of an MR on its subnet, $RCOA_{MR}$'s prefix, in the RA of the MR. The MR and the MNN in a nested NEMO environment add an address in their subnet to their RA as optional information by using the MAP option field. So, the MR and the MNN create their COA based on their RA, which gives their location in the mobile network. The MR creates its own COA_{MR} with a prefix equal to MR_{PREFIX}, and the MNN also creates COA_{MNN} with a prefix equal to MNN_{PREFIX}.

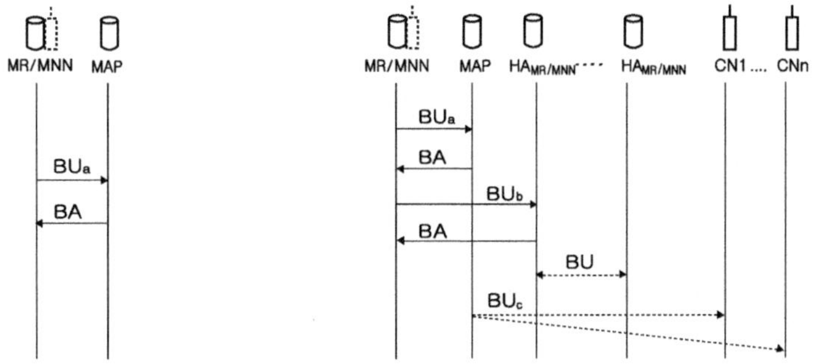

(a) When an MNN (or MR) moves in the MAP

(b) When an MNN (or MR) moves out of the MAP

Fig. 3. Binding Update Procedures of Hierarchically Nested NEMO

3 Performance Analysis

This section presents the performance analysis of our proposed scheme, in which we compute the average binding update costs per unit time for a single MR (or MNN) and nested MRs to examine the effect of the scheme proposed in Section 2. Especially, we derive mathematically the performance of our binding update scheme based on a statistical approach, considering the movement of a MR (or MNN) within a MAP and out of a MAP. The binding update cost in our proposed scheme is evaluated in terms of both the level of the hierarchy in a nested mobile network and the network size.

3.1 Analytic Model of Our Proposed Scheme in a Hierarchically Nested NEMO Environment

Figure 3 shows binding update procedures of a hierarchically nested NEMO environment. We use parameters in Table 1 to calculate the binding update cost of a MR (or MNN). If it moves or expires just before its lifetime within a MAP, it is denoted as C_{within}; if it moves out of the current MAP in a nested NEMO environment, it is denoted as C_{out}. Since the cost of a wireless communication network is usually higher than that of a wire communication network, we denote ρ as the ratio of the former to the latter. Thus, $\rho \geq 1$. If the communication cost of a wire communication network is δ, the transmission cost of a wireless communication is $\delta\rho$. IPv6 multicast routers use the multicast listener discovery (MLD) protocol to learn the existence of multicast group members on their connected links. We exploit multicasting to send binding updates to CNs in this paper, and consider γ as the cost of multicasting in our proposed scheme.

Note that the number of hops or the distance between routers is ignored in this paper because it does not have much influence on the number of BU

Table 1. Binding Update Parameters

Item	Description
C_{mp}	The transmission cost between the MR (or MNN) m and the MAP p .
C_{mhm}	The transmission cost between the MR (or MNN) m and HA hm of the MR (or MNN).
C_{hh}	The transmission cost between the HA h of the MR (or MNN) and the HA h of the parent of the MR (or MNN).
C_{phm}	The transmission cost between the MAP p and the HA hm of the MR (or MNN).
C_{pc}	The transmission cost between the MAP p and the CN c.
C_{phn}	The transmission cost between the MAP p and the HA hn of the MR (or MNN).
C_{mc}	The transmission cost between the MR (or MNN) m and the CN c.
C_{hc}	The transmission cost between the HA h of the MR (or MNN) and the CN c.
C_{hm}	The transmission cost between the HA h of the MR (or MNN) and the MAP p.
U_{mn}	The processing cost of location update at the MR (or MNN) mn.
U_{map}	The processing cost of location update at the MAP map.
U_{hmn}	The processing cost of location update at the MR (or MNN)'s HA hmn.
U_{cn}	The processing cost of location update at the CN cn.

messages [4]. C_{mhm}, C_{pc}, and C_{mc} in Table 1 are the most expensive in a wireless communication network. Then a binding update cost is given as follows.

$$C_{within} = 2 \cdot C_{mp} + U_{mn} + U_{map} = 2 \cdot \delta \cdot \rho + U_{mn} + U_{map} \tag{1}$$

$$\begin{aligned} C_{out} &= 2 \cdot C_{mp} + 2 \cdot C_{mhm} + 1 \cdot C_{pc} + m \cdot C_{hh} + U_{map} + m \cdot U_{hmn} \\ &+ U_{cn} = (4 + \gamma) \cdot \delta \cdot \rho + U_{map} + m \cdot U_{hmn} + U_{cn} + \delta \end{aligned} \tag{2}$$

In this paper, staying time t_c is assumed to be exponentially distributed, and independent and identically exponentially distributed [5,6]. However, field study showed that staying time is not exponentially distributed, and the above exponential assumption will not be valid in general. So, we relax the first assumption as in [7], and introduce the following general conditions. We assume that t_c of an MNN (or MR) is independent of its RA, and $t_1, t_2...$, and t_n are identically distributed with a pdf $f(t)$. Figure 4 illustrates two consecutive periods [T_4,T_1] and [T_1,T_2], and the MR (or MNN) sends a BU message at the end of each period when it moves to another RA. Let T_0 be the time of the last RA boundary crossing before T_1 and T_3 be the time of the first MR (or MNN) RA boundary crossing after T_1. As presented in Figure 4, t_h is the residual time of a parent of the MR (or MNN). Also, period t_M denotes the inter-boundary crossing time, and t_m is the residual time of the MR (or MNN). Let the t_h, t_M, and t_m have the probability density functions f_h^*, f_M^*, and f_m^*, respectively. Let $1/\lambda_M$, $1/\lambda_m$, and $1/\lambda_h$ indicate the expected values of t_M, t_m, and t_h [7]. Let X and Y be

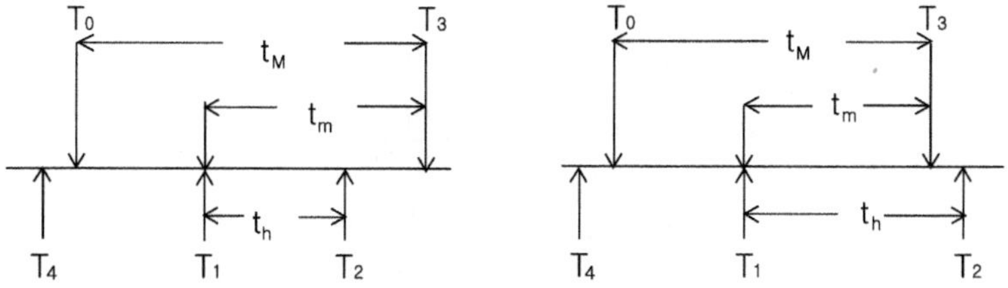

(a) movement of an MR according to its parent

(b) movement of an MR

Fig. 4. Time Diagram

nonnegative random variables, and $F_X(t)$ and $F_Y(t)$ denote probability density functions with Laplace transforms $f_X^*(s)$ and $f_Y^*(s)$, respectively. As referred from [7], we have

$$Pr = \frac{1}{2\pi j}\int_{\sigma-j}^{\sigma+j}\frac{f_X^*}{s}f_X^*(-s)ds = 1 + \sum_{\rho\in\sigma Y} Res_{s=p}\frac{f_X^*(s)}{s}f_Y^*(-s) \tag{3}$$

In order to find the movement probability of the MR (or MNN), we derive equation (4) based on equation (3).

$$f_m^*(s) = \frac{\lambda_M(1 - f_M^*(s))}{s} \tag{4}$$

So, we can apply above equations to obtain the movement probability of the MR (or MNN)'s parent.

$$Pr_h(T_3 > T_2) = 1 + \lambda_M \sum_{\rho\in\sigma Y} \underset{s=p}{RES}\, \frac{1 - f_M^*(s)}{s^2} f_h^*(-s)$$

If t_M is exponentially distributed, we obtain equation (5) according to similar procedures shown above.

$$Pr_M(T_3 > T_2) = f_h^*(\lambda_M) \tag{5}$$

Equation (5) can be translated as follows.

$$Pr_h(T_3 > T_2) = 1 - \frac{\lambda_M}{\lambda_h}(1 - f_M^*(\lambda_h)) \tag{6}$$

In order to relax the exponential assumption, we will use Erlang distribution. The Erlang distribution with parameters (m, η) has been used in many application, and if t_M is Erlamg distributed with parameters (m, λ_M) and its probability density function and Laplace transform are given as follows.

$$f(t) = \frac{\eta^m t^{m-1}}{(m-1)!} e^{(m\eta)^t} \tag{7}$$

$$f^*(s) = (\frac{m\eta}{s+m\eta})^m$$

$$f_M^*(s) = (\frac{m\lambda_M}{s+m\lambda_M})^m$$

Based on equations (4), (5) and (6), we can derive the movement probability of an MR (or MNN) with the ith nesting depth as follows.

$$Pr_m(T_3 > T_2) = \frac{1}{m} \sum_{i=0}^{m-1} \frac{(m-i)(-m\lambda_M)^i}{i!} f_h^{*(i)}(m\lambda_M) \tag{8}$$

Finally, we have the total signaling cost $C(total)$ of our proposed scheme from equations (1), (2), and (8) as follows:

$$C(total) = Pr_m(T_3 > T_2) \cdot C_{within} + (1 - Pr_m(T_3 > T_2)) \cdot C_{out}$$

3.2 Analytic Model of NEMO

Using a method that is similar to section 3.1, we compute the cost of location management in NEMO as follows.

$$C_{NEMO} = c \cdot (U_{cn} + C_{hc}) \cdot m \cdot 2 \cdot \delta \cdot \rho \cdot (U_{mr} + U_{hmn}) \tag{9}$$

c and m represent the number of the MR (or MNN)'s CNs and the number of MRs (or MNNs) within the MR respectively. Let $Pr_{nemo}(T_3 > T_2)$ denote the movement probability of a new MAP. An MR (or MNN) moves at least once if and only if the MR (or MNN)'s lifetime t_c is greater than the MR (or MNN)'s lifetime t_h. Then we have

$$Pr_{nemo}(T_3 > T_2) = -\sum_{\rho \in \sigma Y} Res_{s=p} \frac{f_r^*(s)}{s} f_{t_c}^*(-s) \tag{10}$$

We have the total signaling cost $C(total)_{NEMO}$ of NEMO protocol from equations (9) and (10) as follows:

$$C(total)_{NEMO} = Pr_{memo}(T_3 > T_2) \cdot C_{NEMO}$$

3.3 Performance Comparison

We have analyzed the binding update costs of an MR and MNN depending on the number of CNs and MNNs within the MR, and the binding update cost ratio depending on the nesting depth. The results were computed by MATLAB, and Table 2 lists some of the parameters used in our performance analysis. γ is a

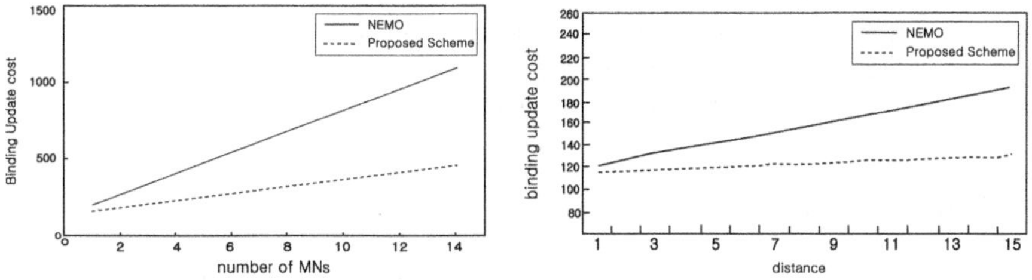

(a) Impact of the number of MNs (b) Impact of the distance between CNs and MAP

Fig. 5. Binding Updates Cost

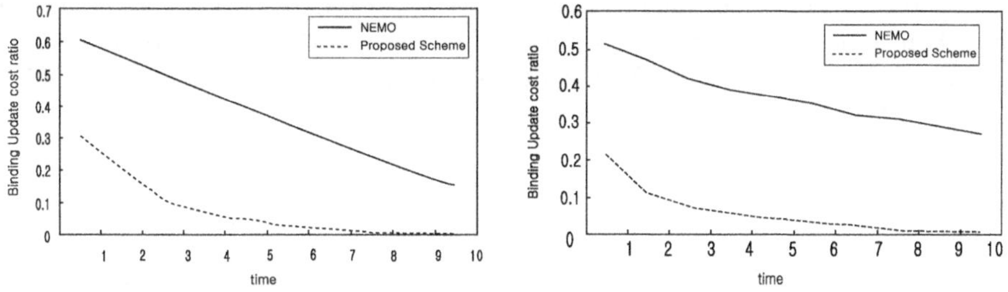

(a) 3 tiers of nesting (b) 4 tiers of nesting

Fig. 6. Binding Update Cost Ratio according to the depth of nested NEMO

variable for multicast costs in a network. We propose a scheme based on multicast routing protocols for delivering a BU message to each CN. There are many multicast routung protocols such as DVMRP, PIM-DM, and CBT [8,9,10,11]. Our proposed scheme is influenced by multicast routing protocols and membership mechanisms such as joining, leaving, and sending data to multicast groups. U_{mrn}, U_{map}, U_{hmr}, U_{hmn} and U_{cn} denote the processing costs of BU message at MR, MAP, MR's HA, MNN's HA, and the CNs respectively. The binding update costs in our proposed scheme and NEMO increase almost linearly, but the cost of our scheme increase much slower than that of NEMO as in Figure 5(a). NEMO protocol has poor performance because the MRs or MNNs sends BU messages whenever they move. On the other hand, our proposed scheme is almost not affected by the distance between CNs and the MAP because they send BU messages only

Table 2. Performance Parameters

U_{mn}	U_{map}	U_{hmn}	U_{cn}	δ	ρ	γ
10	15	25	25	1	10	0.1-1

just when they move out of MAP as shown in Figure 5(b). Figure 6 illustrates the effect of the hierarchical structures of a domain on cost reduction in our proposed scheme. We found that as the depth of the domain is deeper, the cost is less because the parents of the MR or MNN process BU messages.

4 Conclusion

We proposed a scheme which integrates HMIPv6 and NEMO to manage the macro mobility and seamless handoff in a nested NEMO environment. Further presented in this paper is a technique that can minimize binding update costs for MNNs and MRs by multicasting the binding update toward CNs. Finally, we model and analyze binding update costs of NEMO protocol and our proposed scheme. The number of MRs or MNNs or CNs does not have much influence on our proposed scheme. As shown in section 3.3, our scheme is more efficient than NEMO in a nested NEMO environment. Consequently, our proposed scheme perform much better than NEMO protocol, especially when the number of MNNs or MRs or CNs increases.

References

1. Devarapalli, V., Wakikawa, R., Petrescu, A., Thubert, P.: Network Mobility(NEMO) Basic Support Procol, IETF RFC 3963 (January 2005)
2. Ernst, T., Lach, H-Y.: Network Mobility Support Terminology, draft-ietf-nemo-terminology-01.txt, IETF (February 16, 2004)
3. Soliman, H., Castelluccia, C., El-malki, K., Beller, L.: Hierarchical MIPv6 Mobility Management (HMIPv6), dfraft-ietf-mipshop-hmipv6-04.txt, IETF (December 2004)
4. Conta, A., Deering, S.: Generic Packet Tunneling in IPv6 Specification, IETF RFC 2473 (December 1998)
5. Jabbari, B.: Teletraffic Aspects of Evolving and Next-generation Wireless Communication Networks. IEEE Personal Communication Magazine 3(6), 4–9 (1996)
6. Nanda, S.: Teletraffic Models for Urban and Suburban Microcells: Cell Sizes and Handoff Rates. IEEE Transactions on Vechicle Technology 42(4), 673–682 (1993)
7. Fang, Y.: Modeling and Performance Analysis for Wireless Mobile Networks: A New Analytical Approach. IEEE/ACM Transactions on Networking 13(5), 989–1002 (2005)
8. Waitzman, D., Partridge, C., Deering, S. (eds.): Distance Vector Multicast Routing Protocol. RFC1075 (November 1998)
9. Moy, J.: Multicast Routing Extension for OSPF. CACM 37(8), 61–66 (1999)
10. Ballardie, A., Francis, P., Crowcroft, J.: Core Based Trees (CBT): An Architecture for Scalable Inter-domain Multicast Routing. In: ACM SIGCOMM 93, pp. 85–95 (1993)
11. Deering, S., Estrin, D., Farinacci, D., Jacbson, V.: An Architecture for Wide-area Multicast Routing. In: ACM SIGCOMM 94, pp. 126–135 (1994)

Route Optimization Using Scalable Cache Management for Intra-NEMO Communication

Hyemee Park, Moonseong Kim, and Hyunseung Choo*

Intelligent HCI Convergence Research Center
Sungkyunkwan University, Korea
{hyemee,moonseong,choo}@ece.skku.ac.kr

Abstract. In Network Mobility (NEMO) protocol, the traffic for internal routing within the mobile network should be transmitted via external Internet by using a bi-directional MR-HA tunneling. This results in undesirable effects, such as longer route leading to increased delay, increased packet overhead and processing delay. We propose the intra-NEMO Route Optimization (RO) scheme to solve the pinball routing problem in internal routing of nested mobile networks. The proposed scheme employs the routing cache of each nested MR for sharing the route information of the nested mobile network. Each cache entry is composed of simplified routing information by hierarchy architecture of nested mobile networks, enabling scalable and efficient cache maintenance. By using tree routing based on the proposed caching mechanism, the proposed scheme has less packet overhead and improves the latency of the data traffic in intra-NEMO data communications.

1 Introduction

Network Mobility (NEMO) becomes increasingly important to support the movement of a mobile network consisting of several mobile nodes. For the network mobility, the IETF NEMO working group proposed the NEMO basic support protocol [1] extending host mobility support protocol, Mobile IPv6 [2]. The ultimate objective of this solution is to allow all nodes in the mobile network to be reachable via their permanent IP addresses, as well as to maintain ongoing sessions when the Mobile Router (MR) changes its point of attachment within the Internet. It ensures session continuity by using a bi-directional tunnel between the MR and the Home Agent (HA). By using this MR-HA tunneling, it has a pinball routing problem since all packets sent between a source and destination node are forwarded via the HAs of all the MRs. It suffers from increased latency and packet size as an extra IPv6 header is added per level of nesting.

Most research focuses on a Route Optimization (RO) solution to allow packets between two end nodes to be routed along the optimal path. These approaches solve the pinball routing problem in inter-NEMO communication between a mobile network (*e.g.* MNN) and external Internet (*e.g.* CN). However, such problem is generated in intra-NEMO communication between nodes inside the same

* Corresponding author.

J. Indulska et al. (Eds.): UIC 2007, LNCS 4611, pp. 739–747, 2007.

nested mobile network. The traffic for internal routing within the mobile network should be routed via external Internet, all HAs of nested MRs, as shown in Fig. 1. It results undesirable effects such as longer route leading to increased delay, increased packets overhead and processing delay. Since network node does not know whether the destination node belongs inside the same nested mobile network or not, the packet is encapsulated as the nesting levels. To provide efficient internal routing, it requires a caching mechanism for sharing the route information of nested mobile network.

In this paper, we propose a novel route optimization protocol for intra-NEMO communication using scalable caching scheme. The proposed scheme employs the routing cache of each nested MRs to optimize a route to be taken for traffic between MNNs within nested mobile network. Each cache entry is composed of simplified routing information by hierarchy architecture of nested mobile networks, enabling scalable and efficient cache maintenance. Outbound packet from the source node is transmitted based on prefix delegation method without nested tunneling, and inbound packet to the destination node is forwarded using tree routing. As it does not require many levels of encapsulation, it has greater data efficiency with less packet overheads, and improves the latency of the data traffic using an optimal route.

The rest of this paper is organized as follows. In Section 2, related works are introduced with some discussion. Section 3 presents the proposed scheme for intra-NEMO routing optimization. The performance of the proposed scheme is evaluated in Section 4. Finally, we conclude in Section 5.

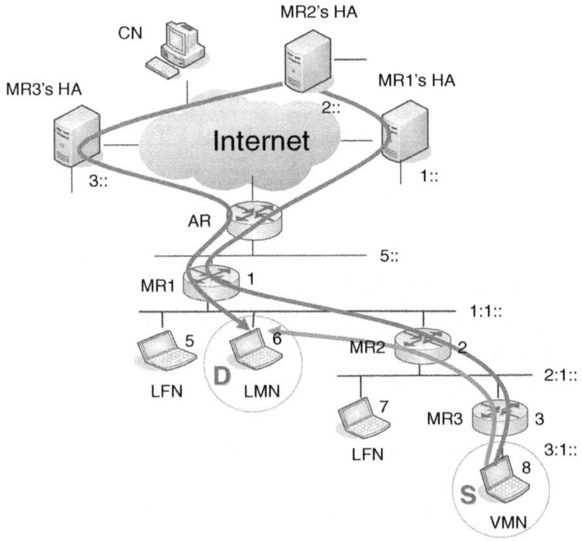

Fig. 1. The pinball routing problem in intra-NEMO communication

2 Related Works

2.1 Inter-NEMO RO Scheme

A number of route optimization protocols have been proposed for inter-NEMO data communication in nested mobile networks [3].

One of the proposals is a Reverse Routing Header (RRH) [4], using a new routing header called RRH. It records the address of intermediate MRs into the extension RH2 with pre-allocated slots, and informs the MR's HA of the nested structure of a mobile network, in order to avoid packet delivery through all HAs of nested MRs. This scheme avoids multiple encapsulations of the packet, and maintains only one tunnel between the first MR and its HA. Therefore, the packet destined for another node located inside the nested mobile network will be transmitted via external Internet by tunnel between the MR and its HA.

The Path Control Header (PCH) [5] scheme constitutes an optimal route through new infrastructure, the Correspondent Router (CR). Although this approach provides routing optimization through tunnel between the MR and CR acting as a gateway at the CN's domain, the first packet should be forwarded via all HAs of nested MRs to piggyback the routing information in the PCH option. Therefore, it requires additional delay and cost for route optimization in intra-NEMO routing.

Prefix Delegation (PD) [6] and Improved Prefix Delegation(IPD) [7] protocols are a solution where the entire mobile network forms a logical multilink subnet in a nested mobile network, and thus eliminates nesting. The BU storm occurs whenever the root-MR changes its point of attachment, since network nodes configure their CoA using the delegated prefix from the AR.

These approaches are the routing optimization solutions for nested NEMO, to allow packets between CN and MNN to be routed along the optimal path. On the other hand, they are not suitable in inter-NEMO data communication between end nodes located within the mobile network. The main reason is that two nodes belonging to different subnets are not aware of each other when mobile networks are nested. Accordingly, each MR should keep the routing information of downstream or upstream networks, to determine whether the destination node belongs or not. It requires a mechanism for sharing the information of nested mobile networks to provide efficient intra-NEMO routing.

2.2 Intra-NEMO RO Scheme

ROTIO [8] is a routing optimization scheme for intra-NEMO based on extended tree information option (xTIO) that contains the CoAs of nested MRs. Each MR appends its CoA in the xTIO suboption of the RA message while the RA is propagated to overall network. Then, the receiving MR can obtain the information of all ancestors MRs from the RA message with this option. The MR sends two BU messages: a normal BU to its HA and local BU to the TLMR. The former informs the HoA of the TLMR as its CoA. The latter appends the xTIO option with the list of CoAs of all ancestor MRs to each binding update message. It is to let the TLMR learn the topology of the nested mobile networks. The binding cache of the TLMR consists of its HoA and the CoAs of intermediate MRs between TLMR and corresponding MR. In ROTIO scheme, when the MR receives the packet from the MNN, it encapsulates the packet as the source address of the outer header is set to the TLMR's HoA. When the TLMR receives that packet, it searches its binding cache to find whether the destination address belongs itself or not. If it exists, the TLMR decapsulates and performs source routing using the list of intermediate MRs in its cache entry. Fig. 2 represents the operation of ROTIO protocol.

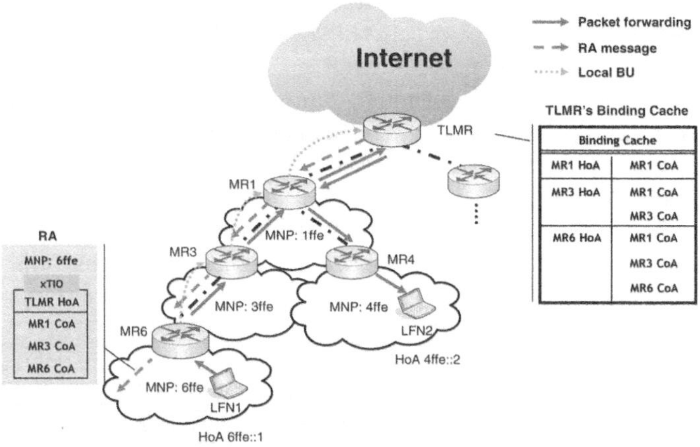

Fig. 2. The operation of ROTIO protocol

Even though ROTIO supports intra-NEMO routing optimization, there are overheads associated with the binding cache formation and maintenance. To maintain the cache in a dynamic large network requires a lot of message exchange between the TLMR and nested MRs. This control message that contains the addresses of intermediate MRs suffers from an increasing overhead as the depth of the MR increases. The binding cache demands memory space of large volumes as it should keep the all ancestor MRs of each nested mobile networks. The more MRs are nested, the more entries need to be made in the cache. In addition, ROTIO has limitation of increased packet size and routing latency. As the number of nested levels increases, it suffers from the overhead due to the increased number of packets for source routing between the TLMR and destination node. The packet should pass through the TLMR since it only keeps the binding cache of entire mobile networks.

3 The Proposed Scheme

Nested mobile networks organize a hierarchy architecture using the prefix delegation method. Prefix delegation is a method where MRs of mobile networks share the prefix of Access Router (AR), to reduce the tunneling overhead according to ingress filtering. Each MR keeps the prefix advertised from AR, called Delegated Prefix (DP), in addition to its original subnet prefix, called Mobile Network Prefix (MNP). DP is disseminated to whole mobile network through extended Router Advertisement (RA) message adding new DP option. Each MR inserts the address of AR received from upstream MR into the DP option and propagates the RA message downwards. The receiving MRs can deduce the DP from this option. When the MRs of each nested mobile network receive the RA message with this option, they allocate the DP to their ingress interface link additionally. They can forward the packet with the source address configured by MNP and DP without nested tunneling by ingress filtering.

Mobile networks form a tree topology from the AR to the MRs of nested mobile networks based on the proposed prefix delegation method. In this paper, we propose to use the MR's Hierarchy ID (HID) as a logical address. The logical HID indicates the location of nodes on the tree topology. This is a routing information to deliver the packets among MNNs within mobile networks. It enables to optimize the route for intra-NEMO data communication and to efficiently manage the routing cache with minimum overhead. In order to configure the HID of the tree topology, each MR establishes a parent-child association with the upper MR using 3-way handshake. After establishing this association, each MR uses the parent as a default route toward the AR. Control packets of the 3-way handshake procedure consist of the RA message disseminated for prefix delegation, ID Request, and Ack. Each MR adds new ID option with its HID to the RA message. When the MR receives Ack message from the parent MR, it concatenates the receiving number and parent's ID, and then propagates the HID with the RA message. Fig. 3 shows the operation of HID configuration in hierarchy architecture of nested mobile networks.

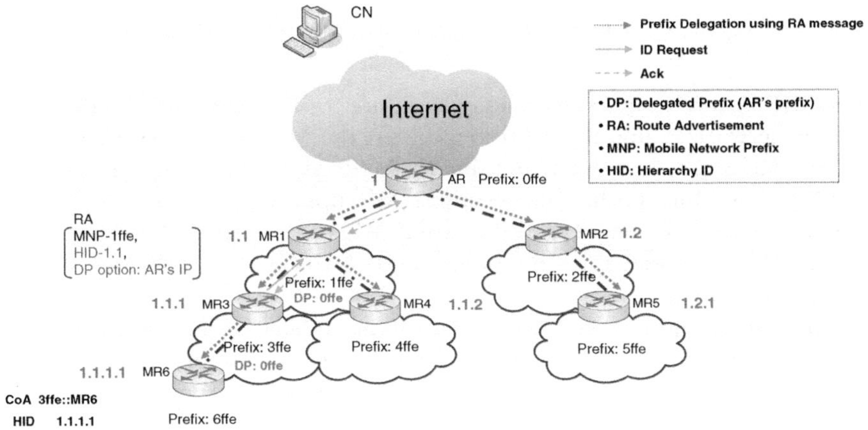

Fig. 3. The HID configuration of the proposed scheme

AR and all MRs have a routing cache that consists of MNP and HID pairs of each nested mobile networks for intra-NEMO routing optimization. In order to construct and maintain the routing cache, the MR performs a Routing Update (RU) procedure for exchanging routing information (MNP, HID) within nested mobile networks. The RU is divided into registration and de-registration phases for cache consistency. These messages are carried by the Hop-by-Hop extension header of IPv6. Hop-by-Hop header includes options that need to be processed by every node along the packet's delivery path (include final receiver) [9]. When the MR transmits the RU message with the destination field set to the AR's address by using this option header, it can register and update the routing cache of the all MRs along the path toward the AR. Consequently, AR keeps the routing information of entire mobile networks, and each MR keeps that of its downstream mobile networks in the routing cache.

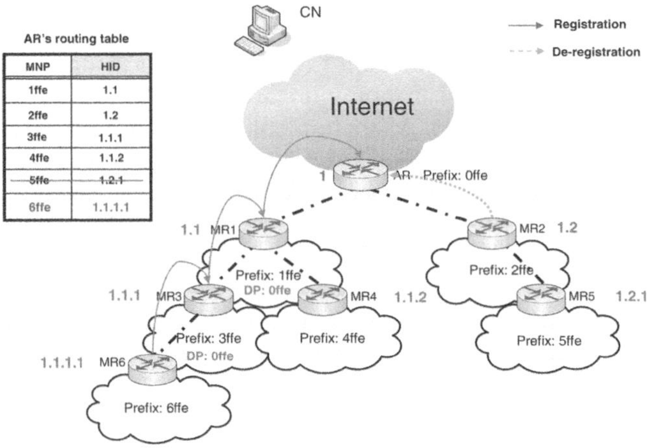

Fig. 4. Routing cache management of the proposed scheme

The MR performs the registration procedure to save new routing information of mobile network in upstream MRs' cache. If the MR detects the movement, it sends the RU message, which contains its MNP and new HID pair, to the AR through parent-child path. The receiving MR updates its routing cache entry and forwards the RU message to its parent MR recursively. When the MR performs the RU, its upstream MRs along the path toward the AR can obtain new information at a time.

In contrast, the de-registration procedure is to report the invalid routing information, and lets the corresponding cache entry delete. If mobile network moves to another network, it results in routing error since the routing information cannot avail any more. Furthermore, it may require additional costs for maintaining the useless information. For these reasons, the MR transmits the RU message for de-registration to upper mobile networks. Each MR periodically monitors its network nodes to perform de-registration on behalf of the MR which does not exist in subnet. If the parent MR does not detect its child, it assumes that the child MR has moved away. It deletes the cache entry, releases the positive integer assigned to the child, and transmits the de-registration message to the AR. Then, the upstream MRs and AR can delete their cache entry.

The cache entry consists of the MNP and HID of each nested mobile network, and the RU message contains the same information as cache. By using the hierarchical ID based on tree topology, the routing information required for mobile network is simplified. Therefore, the routing cache and RU message keep constant size regardless of nesting level of mobile networks. As the volume of them is considerably reduced, the proposed scheme can efficiently manage the routing information for intra-NEMO with the minimum cost.

We support the optimal routing protocol using the routing cache based on hierarchical mobile networks for intra-NEMO data communications. When the MR receives the packet, it first searches its cache for the prefix of destination address in the packet. If it finds the corresponding entry in the cache, the packet is forwarded to the subnet with the destination node. In contrast, if it does not exist, the MR transmits the packet to its parent MR recursively. Finally, if it is not matched in the AR's cache, the destination node does not belong to the mobile network behind the AR. Then, the packet is delivered through the external network (*e.g.* HA).

When the MR receives the packet from MNN, it replaces the prefix of source address with the DP advertised from the AR to avoid nested tunneling by ingress filtering. That is, the source address configured by <MNP || MNN's ID> is changed to <DP || MNN's ID>. After that, the MR inserts the original MNN's address into extended slot. The modified packet is directly forwarded to the AR without tunneling overhead since every MRs keeps the DP in its subnet prefix list. Each MR that receives the packet with the source address configured by DP searches its cache to finds out whether the destination node belongs to downstream mobile networks or not. If the MNP of destination address exists, it obtains the corresponding HID. By using the HID to the packet header, the MR forwards this packet downwards.

Since the proposed scheme performs the tree routing based on the hierarchical ID, it can reduce the routing overhead by eliminating unnecessary flooding to overall network. In addition, it does not need to pass through the top level root node (AR) as every MR keeps the routing information of each nested mobile networks. As a result, it can reduce the routing delay by optimal path between the source and destination node. It keeps low packet overhead in comparison with previous work, because it has no tunneling by prefix delegation and source routing by tree path.

4 Performance Evaluation

We compare the additional cost for intra-NEMO RO in the proposed scheme and previous work, ROTIO. These protocols keep the routing cache to optimize the path between MNNs within nested mobile networks. For this, they require the cost for constructing and maintaining the cache. Cache maintenance represents the total size of cache retaining in the MR. Each MR keeps the cache entry in proportion to the total number of its downstream MRs (represented as |nested MR|). In ROTIO, each entry consists of its HoA and CoAs of intermediate MRs toward the TLMR. The proposed scheme has the prefix and HID with 64-bits each in every entry. Signaling overhead is to measure the size of updating message required to maintain the cache. Increased packet size represents the header size added to original data packet for routing. ROTIO performs one tunneling from the source node to the TLMR and source routing from the TLMR to the destination node. The proposed scheme appends two options with source address and HID. Accordingly, it maintains a constant size of control message and data packet irrespective of level, while that of ROTIO is variable according to the nesting level of MR. In ROTIO, the size of the packets is consistently increasing for source routing as the number of nested levels increases. The proposed scheme remains constant irrespective of the number of nesting levels. As the packet is delivered via the optimal route, the transmission and propagation delays are smaller than other schemes.

Table 1. Additional cost comparison with ROTIO

	Increased packet size		Cache maintenance	Signaling overhead	
	outbound	inbound		RA	LBU/RU
ROTIO	Tunneling + HAO	slot * Nesting Level	$\sum_{i=1}^{\lvert nested\ MR \rvert} (MR_i\_level * CoA + HoA)$	TLMR HoA + CoA * |ancestor MRs|	CoA * |ancestor MRs|
Proposed	Slot	Slot + hopbyhop	(MNP+HID) * |nested MR|	AR HoA + HID	MNP + HID

5 Conclusion

In this paper, we propose the intra-NEMO RO scheme to solve the pinball routing problem in internal routing of nested mobile networks. The proposed scheme provides an adaptive mechanism for efficient cache design and management, and optimizes the route using this cache. As the routing operation is based on prefix delegation method and tree routing, it improves overall QoS characteristics such as latency, bandwidth usage, network load, and data efficiency.

Acknowledgment

This research was supported by MIC, Korea under ITRC IITA-2006-(C1090-0603-0046) and grant No. R01-2006-000-10402-0 from the Basic Research Program Korea Science and Engineering Foundation of Ministry of Science & Technology.

References

1. Devarapalli, V., Wakikawa, R., Petrescu, A., Thubert, P.: Network Mobility (NEMO) Basic Support Protocol, IETF, RFC 3963 (2005)
2. Johnson, D., Perkins, C.E., Arkko, J.: Mobility Support in IPv6, IETF, RFC 3775 (2004)
3. Ng, C., Thubert, P., Ohnishi, H., Paik, E.: Taxonomy of Route Optimization models in the NEMO Context, Internet-draft, draft-thubert-nemo-ro-taxonomy-04.txt (2005)
4. Thubert, P., Molteni, M.: IPv6 Reverse Routing Header and its application to Mobile Networks, Internet-draft, draft-thubert-nemo-reverse-routing-header-05.txt (2005)
5. Na, J., et al.: A Unified Route Optimization Scheme for Network Mobility. In: Niemegeers, I.G.M.M., de Groot, S.H. (eds.) PWC 2004. LNCS, vol. 3260, pp. 29–38. Springer, Heidelberg (2004)
6. Lee, K., et al.: Route Optimization for Mobile Nodes in Mobile Network based on Prefix Delegation. In: IEEE 58th VTC, vol. 3, pp. 2035–2038 (2003)
7. Park, H., Lee, T.-J., Choo, H.: Optimized Path Registration with Prefix Delegation in Nested Mobile Networks. In: Jia, X., Wu, J., He, Y. (eds.) MSN 2005. LNCS, vol. 3794, pp. 327–336. Springer, Heidelberg (2005)
8. Cho, H., Kwon, T., Choi, Y.: Route Optimization Using Tree Information Option for Nested Mobile Networks. IEEE JSAC 24(9), 1717–1724 (2006)
9. Deering, S., Hinden, R.: Internet Protocol Version 6 (IPv6) Specification, IETF, RFC 2460 (1998)

Content Aware Selecting Method for Reducing the Response Time of an Adaptive Mobile Web Service*

Euisun Kang, Daehyuck Park, and Younghwan Lim

Department of Media, Soongsil University, Seoul, Korea
{kanges86,hotdigi}@naver.com
yhlim@ssu.ac.kr

Abstract. One of the particulars to be considered for effective servicing of wireless Internet to mobile terminal is the information of terminal environment. It is because time cost is required in producing mobile contents to suit environment of the connected terminal. In other words, in order to provide mobile web service by considering terminal characteristics, methods to minimize response time and server capacity in accordance with transcoding time in server are required. In this paper, response time to occur in the course of mobile web contents servicing was analyzed and, as a solution for this, Pre-Service method was introduced. Also, this paper suggests two methods in Pre-Service process for selecting optimize content in Cache. One is Device Profile Aware Selection using mobile device information. The other is Content Aware Selection using component information of requested content. Performance level of each method proposed was compared through experiment and the result of analysis was described.

1 Introduction

One of the particulars to be considered in servicing mobile web page is effective contents service to suit the environments of various terminals. Therefore, in order to display mobile web page in mobile terminals of PDA or mobile phone, etc., contents adaptation is required to provide service by considering characteristics of client terminals with different environments. The methods of contents adaptation include the method to transcode the contents into language recognized by mobile terminal [4][5], the method to transcode and service multimedia resources in PC web on real-time basis in mobile terminal [6][7] and the method to provide quick response service by considering terminal characteristics [8], etc. However, from the suppliers' perspective, contents adaptation requires space and time-wise cost. In other words, time-wise cost incurs not only for diversity in environments of the connected terminals, but also for real-time creation of mobile contents in the connected terminal. Furthermore, various versions of the same contents are stored as the contents become transcoded in accordance with the specifications of each mobile terminal. Therefore, repetition of

* This work was supported by the Soongsil University Research Fund.

J. Indulska et al. (Eds.): UIC 2007, LNCS 4611, pp. 748–757, 2007.

contents occurs and server capacity is consumed accordingly. In order to solve this problem, this paper intends to analyze response time of the existing mobile web page service method. Also, as a means to solve the problems raised in the analyzed data, pre-service method is proposed as a plan to enable quicker response time for terminal request.

2 Mobile Web Service

The methods of servicing mobile web pages created to diverse mobile terminals [11] are divided into device-specific service to draw up each content in advance to suit characteristics of terminals and full-automatic service to automatically recreate contents to suit characteristics of terminals when service request is received from client. In order to provide effective wireless Internet service, this paper implemented the 2 methods and has compared response times of each method.

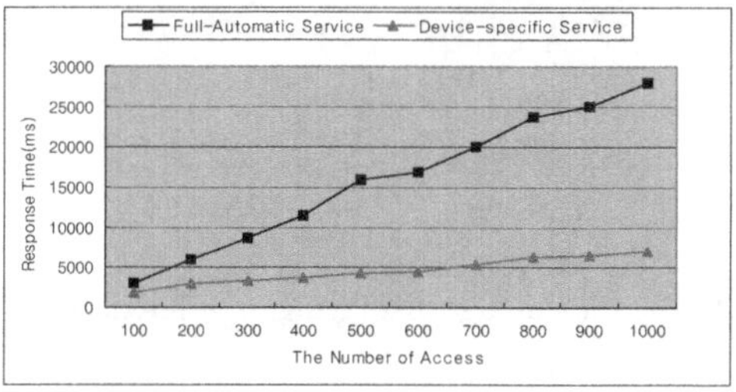

Fig. 1. Response time for Generating Mobile Content

In this paper, test was carried out from 100 to 1000 persons simultaneously logged on to check the response times accordingly. As shown by device-specific service method of [Fig. 1], it does not require the process of multimedia transcoding or contents creation time when contents are transcoded in advance to suit each terminal and are directly serviced. Therefore, naturally, this method produces the quickest response time. However, it results in repetition of version because contents must be transcoded per each version and saved in server according to the count of various terminals. Also, it requires a fixed level of server capacity at all times. In terms of full-automatic service method, it can be observed that response time continuously increases as the number of persons logged on is greater. The reason is because providing high-quality service to users involves time to transcode markup language to suit mobile terminal information. Therefore, time is delayed because of service standby time for the request made. Furthermore, transcoding performance of multimedia data changes per multimedia type and target value. So, it is difficult to predict the transcoding time. Therefore, in order to solve the above problems, this paper proposes the method to reuse contents in cache so that to reduce server capacity, to prevent version repetition and to use the existing web cache. In other words, the objective of this paper is to minimize response time by placing the top priority in servicing contents saved in cache as much as possible even if the quality of contents serviced to mobile terminal may be low.

3 The Pre-service Method for Enhancing the Response Time of Mobile Web Service

3.1 Definition of Pre-service

Despite using cache, creating contents to suit specifications of diverse terminals in mobile web service required the cost of response time because it demanded frequent replacing of the cache due to existence of various versions for the same contents within the limited cache capacity. Here, the frequent replacing of the cache signifies demanding server to administer significant transcoding of contents. In order to improve on such weaknesses, this paper proposes the method of Pre-Service.

120 ×96 176×144

Fig. 2. The same image displaying in different Resolution

As of [Fig. 2], let's assume a mobile phone with resolution of 120×96. The size of maximum image to be displayed in this mobile phone would be 120×96 when vertical and horizontal scroll bars are not had. However, service is possible without any transcoding in terminals to hold the same markup language and resolution (176×144) higher than 120×96. It is only that the image will be viewed smaller in the eyes of user. Pre-Service is the method to select content playable in terminal among a number of contents in cache and to service them first even if contents of the optimal quality cannot be serviced in case the contents to suit the requesting terminal do not exist in cache. Here, the playable mobile page refers to the range in which each object of page is visible in browser of the requesting client even though the selected mobile page may be of low quality. Selecting is based on threshold values, the range of possible service. These threshold values are determined by user or server administrator.

3.2 Process of Pre-service

The objective of Pre-Service is to minimize transcoding time required in contents provision and to reduce response time by decreasing the frequent substitutions in cache. The algorithm of Pre-Service to reduce latency time when request for specific document has been received from a mobile terminal is as of [Algorithm 1]. Firstly, Pre-Service waits for service requirement for specific contents from a mobile terminal. When a specific terminal has logged in, it reads HTTP_USER_AGENT of the

Algorithm 1. Pseudo code of Pre-Service algorithm

```
Pre-Service Algorithm
md : requested content by Device
mc_i : ith content in Cache
T : Threshold
Similarity(mc_i, md) : similar degree between mc_i and md
flag : success flag for searching playable content in Cache

I. Parsing md and Device
 Initialize QoSList and DeviceInfo to NULL
 Read HTTP_USER_AGENT from md
 Get PageID from requested Page
 DeviceInfo = Parshing(HTTP_USER_AGENT)
 QoSNumber = Count(DeviceInfo)
 for i=1 to QosNumber
   begin
     DeviceQoS = Analyze(i, DeviceInfo)
     Set all DeviceQoS to DeviceQosList
   end
  endfor

II. Select and Response a playable mc_i in Cache
 Initialize flag to false
 count = CountContent(Cache)
 for i=1 to count
   begin
     Get ID from mc_i
     if PageID == ID then
        calculate similarity(mc_i, md)
        if similarity(mc_i, md) ≥ T then
           flag = true
           break;
        else
           flag = false
        endif
     endif
   end
 endfor

if flag ≠ true then
 mc_i = TR(mc_i)
   Replace Cache(mc_i, QosList)
endif
   Response(mc_i) to Device
```

terminal to extract terminal information and analyze the contents requested. Secondly, it searches for the mobile contents to suit the service-requesting terminal in cache. Here, in order to compare similarity between contents in cache and contents requested by terminal, calculation is made by using the selection method described in Section 4. In case the contents are the same or contents playable in browser of the connected terminal are included in cache, it services the corresponding contents and waits for the next request from terminal. If not, it provides service after creating mobile contents by using the extracted terminal information.

4 Methods to Select Contents in Cache for Pre-service

Mobile contents create description on the basis of QoS(Quality of Service) information of the connected terminal. Therefore, it is possible to extract essential elements required for displaying from contents. The similarity between contents of service-requesting terminal and those playable in mobile contents within cache can be represented in numerical value. To calculate contents similarity, the following preconditions are required.

$$QoS_i(mc_i) \leq QoS_j(md) \quad (1)$$

For mc_i, 'i' refers to the 'i'th mobile contents saved in cache and *md* is the mobile terminal to request service. QoS_j means the *QoS* information of 'j'. The reason for precondition as shown in (1) is because it is impossible to service contents to hold QoS information greater than QoS information of the service-requesting terminal. Even if it were possible, accurate information delivery would still be unattainable. For example, it is not possible to service image created to suit the resolution of 320×240 in a terminal with resolution of 176×144. Furthermore, even if servicing were to be possible, it requires great network bandwidth and cost in order to transmit the large image.

4.1 Device Profile-Aware Selection Method

In displaying contents in browser of the connected mobile terminal, distinction can be made between the necessary information and unnecessary information in accordance with the expression object. For example, markup language is a necessary element for service. However, text length to be applicable in browser is the secondary information necessary in expressing text. The selection method based on terminal profile is to display similarity between QoS information of the requesting terminal and QoS to be extracted from mobile contents in numeric values through 1:1 mapping. This method

Table 1. Elements of QoS according to the level of importance

Essential Element for Service	MarkUp
Essential elements for playback	Image Format, Audio Format, Video Format
Quality service elements	Sound Poly, Color Depth, Length of Text Resolution(Vertical*horizontal)

classifies QoS elements to determine whether the selected contents can be expressed in terminal according to their importance and gives them weighted values to find satisfaction among the playable contents.

[Table 1] shows classification of QoS according to the level of importance. Here, *essential elements for service* refer to elements essentially required in serving contents to a specific terminal. When this condition is not satisfied, service itself is not possible. *Essential elements for playback* refer to elements, which cannot be checked of information. Service can be provided, but accurate information delivery is not provided. *Quality service elements* refer to the information among those expressed in terminal that is not significantly limited or can be serviced even partially. For example, in terms of text length, it is serviced from the starting point of text to the end of the text length provided by terminal. Also, in terms of the vertical length of resolution, the entire image is not visible in a single screen. However, the full image can be checked by using up-down scroll bar. Using QoS information of the connected terminal, similarity of mobile contents in cache is calculated by using the following (2).

$$\begin{aligned} Similarity(mc_i, md) = {} & Markup(mc_i, md) \\ & \times (W_i \times Data\_Format(I, V, A) \\ & \times (W_j \times Data\_Quality(SP, CL, RES, TL)) \end{aligned} \quad (2)$$

$$W_i + W_j = 1 \quad (But,\ W_i > W_j)$$

Here, *Markup(mc$_i$, md)* refers to markup language of terminal and contents. Markup language provided by terminal and contents is an essential element for service. Therefore, it is expressed as 1 when contents are the same and as 0 when not. *Data_Format(I, V, A)* is an essential element for playback. Image, video and melody types, the essential elements for playback, cannot be expressed in numeric values. Therefore, as of comparison of markup language, they are expressed as 1 or 0. *Data_Quality(SP, CL, RES, TL)* is a quality service element. The quality service elements of sound poly(SP), color depth(CL), resolution(RES) and text length hold information in numeric figures. Therefore, they hold the similarity values between 0 ~ 1. The reason of $W_i > W_j$ is thatl essential elements for playback are more important than quality service elements. *Similarity((mc$_i$, md)*, ultimately with application of W_i and W_j, signifies the calculated similarity of contents. In other words, it indicates the difference between contents selected in the connected terminal and cache in probability values. In detail, it serves as the basis to indicate the degree of quality service enabled when contents are serviced to terminal.

4.2 Content-Aware Selection Method

In general, a single mobile web page consists of a multiple number of objects expressible by markup language. The content-aware selection method is where objects to configure a single mobile web page use the configuration elements. In other words, while terminal profile-aware selection method is where overall information of terminal is used in relations to mobile web contents, content-based selection method is where objects to configure a mobile web page are analyzed, only the information required in expressing the objects is extracted and compared and the result is expressed numerically.

As shown above, [Fig. 3] is the mobile contents consisted of images and texts. To express mobile web contents of [Fig. 3] in mobile terminal, markup language, image type, color depth, resolution and text length of the mobile terminal are required.

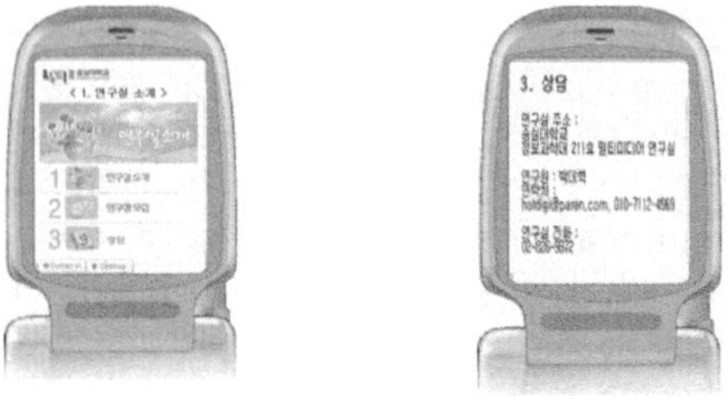

<Content A> < Content B>

Fig. 3. Example of Object Configuration in Mobile Contents

mc_i is the 'i'th mobile contents requested by the connected terminal. O means the group of objects in mobile page. mc_i holds 'n' number of multimedia data objects. Each object in page is obtained by farcing mobile page. O_i signifies each object obtained by farcing mobile page.

$$mc_i \in \mathrm{O}$$

$$O = \{ 0_1, 0_2, 0_3, \ldots, 0_n \}$$

Here, when QoS_f is the essential element for object playback within contents and QoS_q is quality service element to improve service quality of object further, each object consists with essential elements for playback and quality service element.

$$Oi = \{< QoS_f, QoS_q > \mid QoS_f \in Data\_Format, QoS_q \in Data\_Quality\}$$

$$Data\_Format = \{QoS_i, QoS_v, QoS_a\}$$
$$Data\_Quality = \{QoS_{sp}, QoS_{cl}, QoS_{res}, QoS_{tl}\}$$

Here, QoS_f and QoS_q are determined by the types of objects and are given actual values by using QoS information of terminal. QoS information finally selected by multimedia contents is as of the following. QoS_n is the group of all QoS information, which can be included in mc_i. Here, QoS value is used in case the information is required to express multimedia object included in mobile page. If not, it is set as 1.

$$mc_i \in QoS_n = \{ QoS_1, QoS_2, \ldots, QoS_n \}$$

$$QoS_i = \begin{cases} 1 & O \notin QoS_i \\ QoS_i & O \in QoS_i \end{cases}$$

Similarity(mc_i, md) is calculated by applying device profile-aware selection method (2) on the basis of the determined QoS information.

5 Experiments and Evaluation

In general, the process to improve response time by using cache is correlated to cache hit ratio. To find document and service in cache without transcoding contents in the course of service means that the time required in transcoding contents decreases. The objective of this paper is to minimize response time. Therefore, performance evaluation was administered on the basis of cache hit ratio and the result was compared for analysis. The experiment and test were administered in Windows XP Professional with the specifications of 2.66GHz and 1GB memory. In the experiment, 5 cache capacities were used and, as the algorithm to substitute cache, LFU was used to erase mobile contents with the lowest frequency of use. Also, in the course of selecting contents in cache for pre-service, user randomly set threshold value in order to measure service possibility on the basis of specific threshold value and the calculated result and threshold values were compared. 20 random mobile pages were used and the average size of markup language created after farcing mobile pages was 2KB. The following figure displays cache hit ratio according to the number of persons logged on in relations to contents selection method in cache for pre-service. The cache capacity used here is 100KB. In the figure, 100%~60% signifies the threshold values designated by user. As shown by [Fig. 4] and [Fig. 5], cache hit ratio improved by approximately 10% when serving contents of 90 ~ 60% similarity with slightly low level of quality service rather than when servicing contents of 100% similarity. However, when the level was 70 ~ 60%, no significant difference was observed.

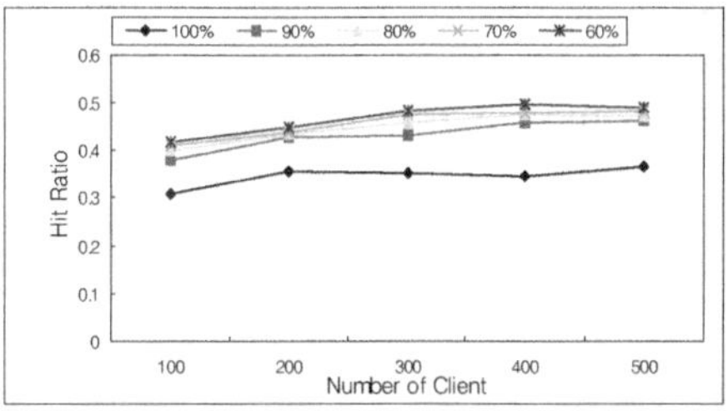

Fig. 4. Device Profile Aware

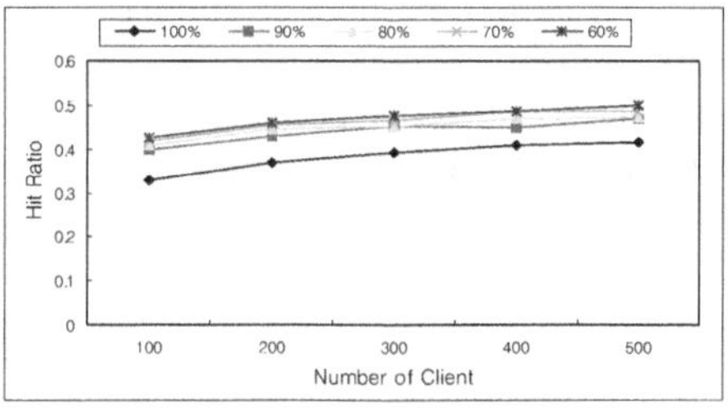

Fig. 5. Content Aware

The [Fig. 6] above shows comparison of hit ratios in relations to terminal profile and content-aware selection methods in case cache capacity is 100KB and number of persons logged on is 300 in [Fig. 4] and [Fig. 5].

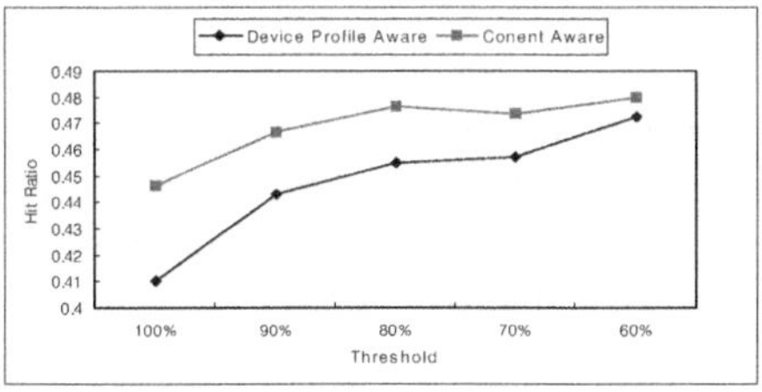

Fig. 6. The Comparison of Hit Ratio between Device Profile and Content Aware

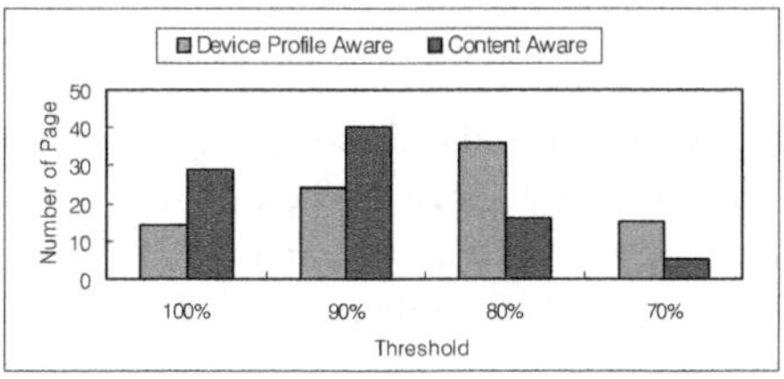

Fig. 7. The Number of Pages according to each Threshold

As shown in the figure, content-aware method displayed higher cache hit ratio than terminal profile-aware selection method. The reason is because, while terminal profile-aware selection method finds the optimal contents by comparing all information on terminal, content-aware selection method compares only the information related to contents type within the page. Therefore, as a whole, content-aware selection method displayed higher performance improvement. To service high-quality contents is to select contents precisely matching for specifications of the requesting terminal in cache. Therefore, in this paper, accuracy of contents was analyzed through the number of contents serviced to be optimal for hardware specifications of the requesting terminal in the course of pre-service. When there are 200 persons simultaneously logged on and cache capacity is 100KB, page count according to threshold value is displayed. Here, when the overall threshold value was set as 70%, page count serviced per each threshold value is displayed. For example, 100% in x axis signifies the case in which similarity of the serviced contents is 100%. 90% means count of contents holding similarity of 100 ~ 90%. In other words, left side of the graph is for serving pages of higher accuracy. As illustrated in [Fig. 7], when using terminal profile-aware selection method, higher number of contents service was distributed in case of the similarity of 90 and 80%. When using content-aware selection method, higher serviced contents count was distributed in case of mainly 100 and 90%. This indicates that content-aware selection method shows higher accuracy because it compares contents on the basis of elements to configure them. It also means that users are provided with services of higher quality. In [Fig. 8] and [Fig. 9] above, response time according to the number of persons logged on is compared against that of full-automatic service.

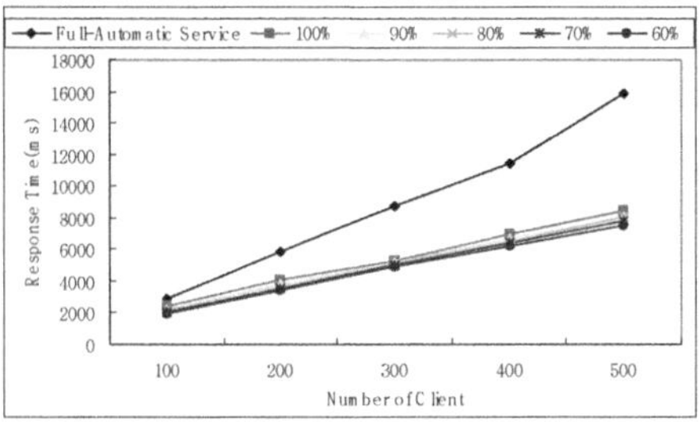

Fig. 8. Device profile Aware

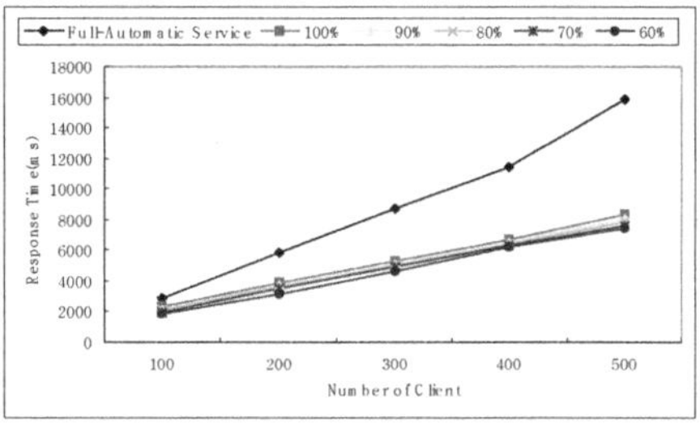

Fig. 9. Content Aware

As shown in the figures, response time displayed overall improvement from that of full-automatic service when using cache. It decreased by 10% when the count of persons logged on was 100 and by 25% when the count was 500. Although it dropped by 25% when the number of persons logged on was 500, improvement of performance can be anticipated in case a more number of people log on to the server. Unlike pre-service, full-automatic service method is where terminal services content after transcoding them at the time of request on real-time basis. Although the time of transcoding contents is short, it indicates importance of cache as the number of persons simultaneously logged on increases. Furthermore, it indicates that the method of transcoding after pre-service produces the superior performance.

6 Conclusions

In ubiquitous environment, wireless Internet is endeavoring to provide users with required information at any time and in any place. However, in order to provide Internet service in diverse environments of mobile communications, it involves difficulty of having to newly create contents to suit such environments. Accordingly, development and maintenance cost becomes an inevitable issue to be considered. As a means to overcome such problems, this paper proposed mobile gate system, with which the general PC web pages can be viewed in mobile communications terminals, such as mobile phone or PDA, etc. Also, to overcome problems in the proposed system, this paper suggested the pre-service method to be provided in the connected mobile terminal. As illustrated by performance evaluation, it was observed that the proposed pre-service method, unlike the existing method, could make improvement in the response time. Pre-service firstly compares information of terminal and contents, then service the contents within serviceable range. Therefore, it is capable of improving client standby time. Also, being able to prepare for service to the same terminal in the future, this method will be able to organically and independently respond to the rapidly changing terminal specifications.

References

1. Goodman, D.J.: The Wireless Internet: Promises and Challenges. IEEE Computer 33(7), 36–41 (2000)
2. Xie, X., Miao1*, G., Song, R., Wen, J.-R., Ma, W.-Y.: Efficient Browsing of Web Search Results on Mobile Devices Based on Block Importance Model. In: 3rd IEEE Intelligent Conferebce on Pervasive Computing and Communications (2005)
3. Hwang, Y., Kim, J., Seo, E.: Structure-Aware Web Transcoding for Mobile Device. IEEE, Seoul National University, pp. 14–21 (September 2003)
4. Kirda, E., Kerer, C., Matzka, G.: Using XML/XSL to build adaptable database interfaces for Web site content management. In: XML in Software Engineering Workshop, 23rd International Conference on Software Engineering, Toronto,Ontario, Canada (2001)
5. WebSpere: http://www-3.ibm.com/software/info1/websphere/index.jsp
6. Hong, M., Park, D., Lim, Y.: Transcoding Pattern Generation for Adaptation of Digital items Containing Multiple Media Streams in Ubiquitous Environment. In: Lau, R.W.H., Li, Q., Cheung, R., Liu, W. (eds.) ICWL 2005. LNCS, vol. 3583, pp. 1036–1045. Springer, Heidelberg (2005)
7. Kang, E., Hong, M., Lim, Y.: A Guided Search method for Real time Transcoding a MPEG2 P frame into H.263 P Frame in a Compressed Domain. In: Miksch, S., Hunter, J., Keravnou, E.T. (eds.) AIME 2005. LNCS (LNAI), vol. 3581, pp. 242–251. Springer, Heidelberg (2005)
8. Pashtan, A., Heusser, A.: Personal Service Areas for Mobile Web Applications. IEEE Internet Computing (2004)
9. Chua, H.N.a., Scott, S.D.b., Choi, Y. W. c., Blanchfield, P.: Web-Page Adaptation Framework for PC & Mobile Device Collaboration. In: 19th International Conference on Advanced Information Networking and Applications(2005)
10. Kim, C.Y., Lee, J.K., Cho, Y.H., Kim, D.H.: VISCORS: A Visual-Content Recommender for the Mobile Web. IEEE Intelligent System (2004)
11. Whang, Y-h., Jung, C., et al.: WebAlchemist: A Web Transcoding System for Mobile WebAccess in Handheld Devices. In: Proc. SPIE, vol. 4534, pp. 37–47 (2001)

A Study of Speech Emotion Recognition and Its Application to Mobile Services

Won-Joong Yoon, Youn-Ho Cho, and Kyu-Sik Park

Dankook University
Division of Information and Computer Science
San 8, Hannam-Dong, Yongsan-Ku, Seoul Korea, 140-714
{helloril,adminmaster,kspark}@dankook.ac.kr

Abstract. In this paper, a speech emotion recognition agent for mobile communication service is proposed. The proposed system can recognize five emotional states - neutral, happiness, sadness, anger, and annoyance from the speech captured by a cellular phone in real time and then it calculates the degree of affection such as love, truthfulness, weariness, trick, friendship of the person who you are interesting to know through the mobile phone. In general, a speech acquired by a cellular phone contains noise due to the mobile network and environmental noise. Thus it can causes serious performance degradation due to the distortion in emotional features of the query speech. In order to alleviate the effect of these noises, we adopt a MA (Moving Average) filter which has relatively simple structure and low computational complexity. Then a feature optimization method is implemented to further improve and stabilize the system performance. For a practical application, we create an agent that can measure the degree of affection from the person who you want to know on the mobile phone. Two pattern classification methods, k-NN and SVM with probability estimates, are compared for estimating the degree of affection. The experimental results indicate that the proposed method provides very stable and successful emotional classification performance as 72.5 % over five emotional states and it shows the feasibility of the agent for mobile communication services.

1 Introduction

Depending on the methods employed for *feature extraction* and *classification,* several speech emotion detection strategies are employed in the literature. Dellaert et al. [1] used 17 features and compared three classifiers: maximum likelihood Bayes classification, kernel regression and k-NN (Nearest Neighbor) with four emotion categories. Scherer [2] extracted 16 features and achieved overall accuracy 40.4% for fourteen emotional states. As a first attempt for emotion recognition in call center application, nonlinear teager energy operator (TEO) feature is used for stressed/neutral classification [3]. Paper [4] focused on distinguishing anger versus neutral speech for call center applications and they achieved a maximum accuracy of 94%. Other good works on general speech emotional classification can be found in [5-7].

J. Indulska et al. (Eds.): UIC 2007, LNCS 4611, pp. 758–766, 2007.

Although many combinations of emotional features and classifiers have been evaluated in those works, little attention has been paid on speech emotion recognition in mobile environment. This paper focuses on the following issues of the emotion recognition problem.

Firstly, the proposed system accepts query sound captured by a cellular phone in real-time using INTEL Dialogic D/4PCI board and an agent can recognize five emotional states - neutral, happiness, sadness, anger, and annoyance with a classification probability about each state.

Secondly, we employ MA (Moving Average) filter in order to minimize the effect of mobile noises and improve the system performance.

Thirdly, a SFS (Sequential Forward Selection) feature optimization method is implemented to further improve and stabilize the system performance. We choose SVM with probability estimate capability [8] as our classification algorithm and compared the performance with simple k-NN algorithm.

Finally, for a practical application, mobile agent was implemented to provide a degree of affection such as love, truthfulness, weariness, trick, friendship by the person who you are interesting to know through the mobile phone. This agent will be quite useful in various mobile applications.

This paper is organized as follows. Section 2 describes proposed mobile-based emotion recognition system. Section 3 explains the methods of noise-robust feature extraction and optimization. Section 4 compares experimental results of the proposed system. Finally, a conclusion is given in section 5.

2 Proposed System

The proposed system consist 3 stages – speech signal acquisition, emotion pattern classification and the calculation of affection index with mobile agent. A query speech signal is first picked up by the single microphone of the cellular phone and then transmitted to the emotion recognition server. The transmitted signal is acquired in real-time by using INTEL dialogic D4PCI-U board in 8 kHz sampling rate, 16 bit, MONO. Then the queried speech is classified with confidence probability (for the case of SVM) and the classification result will be reported and transmitted to the mobile agent. Base on the probability of emotion classification, the mobile agent calculates the index of affection to provide the various barometers about the person who you are interesting to know.

Fig. 1 shows the block diagram of the proposed emotional engine.

Raw speech data set is randomly divided into two sets of data set – training set and test set. At the training phase, feature set as defined in section 3.2 is extracted from pre-processed speeches in training set. Then a SFS feature optimization is applied to select only those features that are most significant in the system classification performance with respect to k-NN and SVM classifier. These feature set is used to build up emotional feature vector DB.

At the testing phase, a test input speech is picked up by a cellular phone and preprocessed as before, and the same indexed feature set from the SFS optimization stage is extracted. Then the 5th order MA (MA(5)) filter is applied to feature vector to

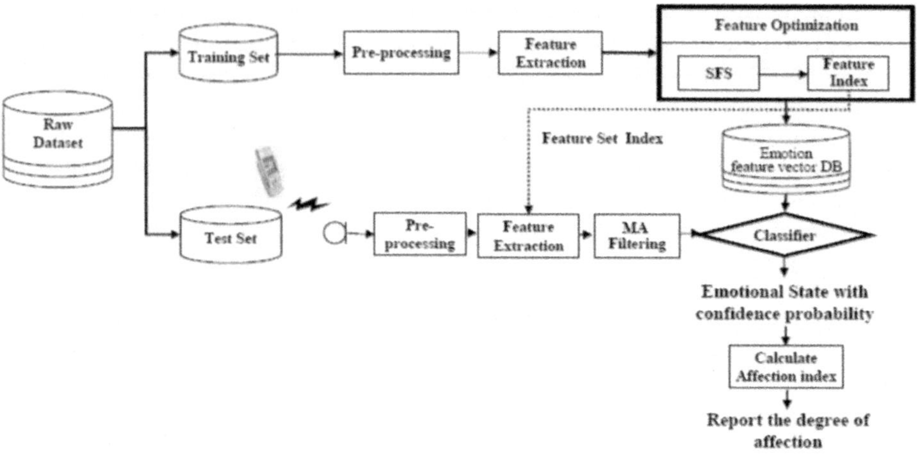

Fig. 1. Proposed emotional engine

minimize the effect of background noise. Finally the k-NN, SVM pattern classifier is tested for the classification of queried speech and the performance of the system is evaluated.

Finally, based upon the confidence probability of each emotional state by SVM pattern classifier, mobile agent calculates the index of affection such as love, truthfulness, weariness, trick, friendship by the person who you are interesting to know through the mobile phone.

3 Emotional Feature Extractions and Optimization

3.1 Pre-processing and Feature Extraction

Speech pre-processing is required to build up the robust emotional features and it consists of a BPF (Band Pass Filtering), 20 ms speech segmentation, hamming windowing, and end-point detection procedure.

The input speech signal is first band-pass filtered with a passband 300Hz – 2500 Hz. The reason for this BPF is clear if we compare the spectrogram of the original clean speech and the speech acquired from the cellular-phone. The speech through the mobile network undergoes the two main distortions – bandwidth reduction to 300Hz - 2500Hz and mobile noise. Here the BPF allows extracting only the meaningful signal portion of the noisy speech.

At the sampling rate of 8 kHz, the filtered signal is divided into 20ms frames with 50% overlapped hamming window at the two adjacent frames. Then the end-point detection algorithm is applied to distinguish voiced and non-voiced segment from the input speech so that the emotional features are extracted only from the voiced portion of speech. In this paper, we used a Li. Gu's [9] end-point detection algorithm.

Two types of emotional features are computed from every 20 ms frame- one is the prosodic features such as pitch and energy, and the other is speech phoneme feature such as mel-frequency cepstral coefficients (MFCC). The means and standard deviations of these original features and their delta values are computed over each frame to form a total of 32-dimensional feature vector. Followings are short descriptions of the features used in this paper.

A few pitch detection algorithms including HPS[10], AMDF[11], SHR[12] are tested and compared in noisy speech environment. Among them, SHR algorithm shows good robust characteristics against mobile noise and so the SHR is used in this paper. SHR (Subharmonic-to-Harmonic Ratio) transforms the speech signal into the FFT domain, and then decides two candidate pitches by detecting the peak magnitude of the log spectrum.

Short time energy of the speech signal provides a convenient representation that reflects amplitude variations.

MFCC is the most widely used feature in speech recognition. It captures short-term perceptual features of human auditory system. In this paper, 6th order MFCC is used.

3.2 Feature Selection Procedure

In order to reduce the computational burden and so speed up the search process, while maintaining a system performance, an efficient feature dimension reduction and selection method is desired. In ref. [13], a sequential forward selection (SFS) method is used to meet these needs. In this paper, we adopt the same SFS method for feature selection to reduce dimensionality of the features and to enhance the classification accuracy. Firstly, the best single feature is selected and then one feature is added at a time which in combination with the previously selected features to maximize the classification accuracy. This process continues until all 32 dimensional features are considered.

3.3 Noise Reduction Using MA Filtering

In order to minimize the effect of these noises we adopt a simple MA (Moving Average) filter that has relatively simple structure and low computational complexity.

The key idea is to apply MA filter to the feature sequences on feature domain to smooth out spikes due to the mobile noises. In order to apply MA filter, we represent feature data by two dimension matrix FM_{td}. Each row of FM_{td} represents a feature vector and each column represents a time sequence. Then the features in column order are normalized to zero mean and unit variance in order to avoid numerical problems caused by small variances of the feature values. This normalized time sequence of features is further processed by MA filter as follows.

$$\widehat{x}_{td} = \frac{1}{M}\sum_{i=0}^{M} x_{(t-i),d}\,, \quad x_{(t-i),d} = \text{feature coefficierts} \tag{1}$$

In this paper, the filter order M=5 was found to yield the best results for our experiments.

4 Experimental Results

4.1 Experimental Setup

A database from the Yonsei University [14] is used for experiment. The data set includes short utterances by fifteen semi-professional actor and actress and it consists of total of 5400 utterances across 5 emotional states, i.e., neutral, happiness, sadness, anger, and annoyance in 8 kHz, 16 bit recording. Among them, 2500 utterances (500 utterances for each emotional state) were chosen as training set to define an optimal feature set by SFS optimization stage and to setup the emotional feature vector DB. Another 500 utterances (100 utterances for each emotional state) are used as the test data set for system evaluation.

Fig. 2 shows a block diagram of experimental setup. In order to compare the system performance, two sets of experiment have been performed.

One is the system (called "proposed system") with a proposed method as in fig. 1 and the other is the system (called "reference system") without any noise reduction technique and the feature optimization method. Here the proposed system works as follows. Firstly, a test speech is acquired through actual cellular phone via INTEL dialogic D4PCI-U board in 8 kHz sampling rate, 16 bit, MONO. Secondly, emotional features are extracted according to the feature index from the SFS feature optimization stage and then MA(5) filter is applied to feature vector in order to minimize the effect of mobile noises. Finally the k-NN, SVM pattern classifier is tested for the classification of queried speech and the performance of the system is evaluated.

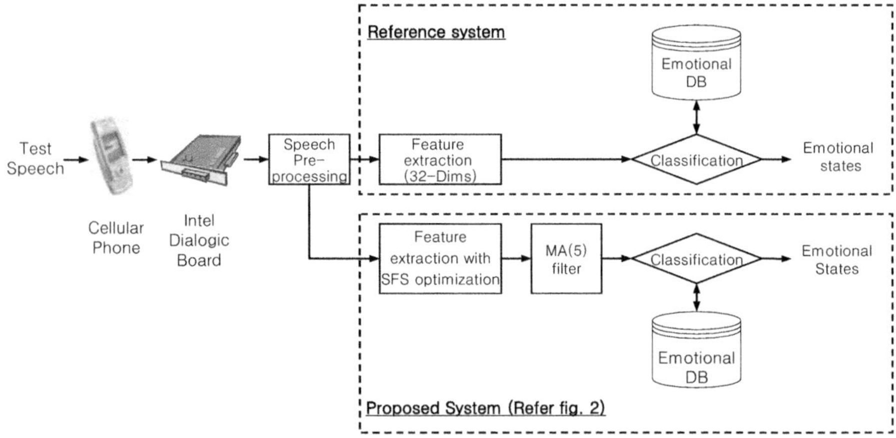

Fig. 2. Experimental setup for performance comparison of the proposed system

4.2 SFS Feature Selection Experiment

From the figure 3, we see that the classification performance increases with the increase of features up to certain number of features, while it remains almost constant after that. Thus based on the observation of this boundary, we can select first 10 features up to the boundary and ignore the rest of them. For both k-NN/SVM classifiers, we observed that pitch and MFCC feature is most significant in the classification result.

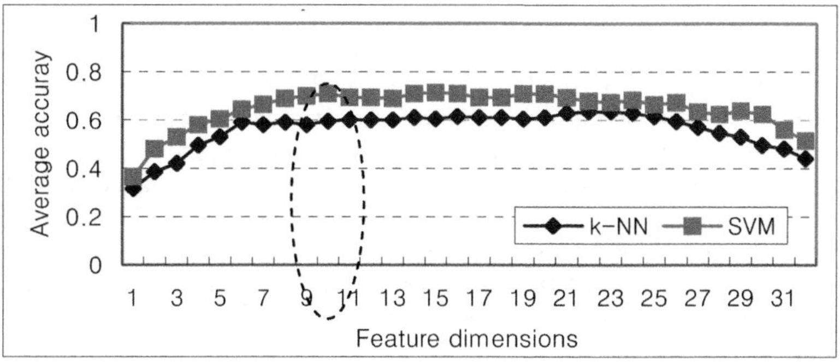

Fig. 3. SFS feature optimization procedure

4.3 Emotional States Classification Results

Table 1 compares the classification results for five emotional states between the proposed system and the reference system under the experimental setup as shown in fig. 3. The classification accuracy for table 1 is measured with the noisy query, so this accuracy is a little bit lower than the ones shown in fig. 6. As seen on the table 1, the proposed method achieves more than 20% higher accuracy than the reference system even with less number of feature dimensions.

Table 1. Average classification results for five emotional states

	k-NN (Feature Dim.)	SVM (Feature Dim.)
Reference system	44.5 % (32)	51.5% (32)
Proposed system	63.5 % (10)	72.5% (10)

Table 2 shows SVM classification performance of the proposed system in a form of a confusion matrix. As a comparison purpose, the classification result of the reference system is included in the table and they are shown in parenthesis. The numbers of correct classification results lie in the diagonal of the confusion matrix.

Table 2. Classification accuracy in a form of confusion matrix (SVM)

Query	Neutral	Happiness	Sadness	Anger	Annoyance
Neutral	37 (40)	0(0)	1(0)	2(0)	0(0)
Happiness	3(11)	24(23)	4(4)	2(0)	7(2)
Sadness	4(14)	2(1)	25(24)	4(0)	5(1)
Anger	2(16)	4(2)	2(5)	25(3)	7(4)
Annoyance	1(5)	4(8)	0(14)	1(0)	34(13)
Average Classification Accuracy 72.5% (51.5%)					

From the table 2, we see much improvement of classification performance with proposed MA filtering and a SFS feature optimization. It actually can achieves more than 20% improvement even with fewer number of feature set. The proposed method works fairly well over the emotional states of neutral and annoyance while the average number of correct classification is little lower in happiness, sadness and anger state. Happiness and anger state is often misclassified as annoyance state. From the confusion matrix, we observe that the proposed method is very efficient especially to the anger and annoyance states where these were quite susceptible to the mobile noise. We note that the SVM [8] classifier used in this paper has a probability estimate capability for each of five emotional states and this feature will be used in mobile agent in next section.

4.4 Application Study - Mobile Emotion Agent

Based upon the confidence probability of each emotional state by previous SVM pattern classifier, we create the mobile agent that can measure a degree of affection in terms of love, truthfulness, weariness, trick, friendship of the person who you are interesting to know through the mobile phone. Fig. 4 describes proposed mobile agent.

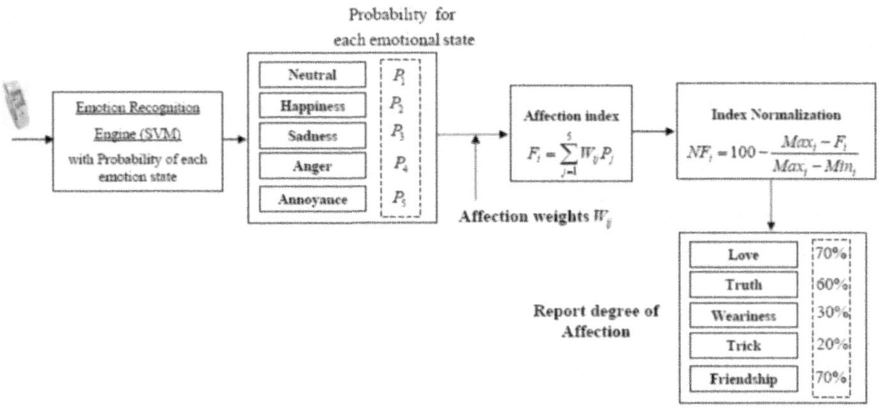

Fig. 4. Proposed mobile agent that can estimate the degree of affection

The decision rule of the agent is follows. Before the agent, the correlation weights W_{ij} of five emotional states j of neutral, happiness, sadness, anger, annoyance corresponding to each affection class i of love, truthfulness, weariness, trick, friendship, are predefined. Then with the emotion classification probability of emotion recognition engine P_i and the predefined weight W_{ij}, we can calculate the affection index for each class as follows.

$$F_i = \sum_{j=1}^{5} W_{ij} P_j = W_{i1} \cdot P_1 + W_{i2} \cdot P_2 + W_{i3} \cdot P_3 + W_{i4} \cdot P_4 + W_{i5} \cdot P_5 \tag{2}$$

where F_i is the calculated affection index regarding $i=1$ (love), $i=2$ (truthfulness), $i=3$ (weariness), $i=4$ (trick), $i=5$ (friendship), and W_{ij} is the predefined weight of emotional states neutral, happiness, sadness, anger, annoyance for each affection class, and P_i is the classification probability of SVM regarding each emotional states. Then the calculated index F_i for each affection class is further normalized as follows to get the standard score from 0 to 100.

$$NF_i = 100 - \frac{Max_i - F_i}{Max_i - Min_i} \tag{3}$$

where $\max_i$ and $\min_i$ are maximum and minimum affection index for each class i.

5 Conclusion

In this paper, we propose a speech emotion recognition agent for mobile communication services. The agent can recognize five emotional states - neutral, happiness, sadness, anger, and annoyance from the speech captured by a cellular-phone in real time. For a practical application, mobile agent was implemented to provide a degree of affection such as love, truthfulness, weariness, trick, friendship, of the person who you are interesting to know through the mobile phone. This agent will be quite useful in various mobile applications. In order to alleviate noise effect due to the mobile network and environment, we adopt a simple MA filter on the feature domain. SFS feature optimization is also utilized to improve and stabilize the system performance. The proposed system has been tested and compared with cellular phones in the real mobile environment and it shows a very stable and successful emotional classification performance as 72.5 % and it shows the feasibility of the agent for mobile communication services. Future work will involve the development of new emotional features and further analysis of the system for practical implementation.

References

1. Dellaert, F., Polzin, T., Waibel, A.: Recognizing emotion in Speech. In: Proc. International Conf. on Spoken Language Processing, pp. 1970–1973 (1996)
2. Scherer, K.R.: Adding the affective dimension-A new look in speech analysis and synthesis. In: Proc. International Conf. on Spoken Language Processing, pp. 1808–1811 (1996)
3. Zhou, G., Hansen, J.H.L., Kaiser, J.F.: Nonlinear Feature Based Classification of Speech Under Stress. IEEE Transactions on speech and audio processing 9(3) (2001)
4. Yacoub, S., Simske, S., Lin, X., Burns, J.: Recognition of emotions in interactive voice response system. In: Eurospeech 2003 Proc. (2003)
5. Kostov, V., Fukuda, S.: Emotion in user interface. Voice Interaction system. no. 2. In: IEEE Intl. Conf. on systems, Man, Cybernetics Representation, pp. 798–803 (2000)
6. Oriyama, T.M, Oazwa.: Emotion recognition and synthesis system on speech. In: IEEE Intl. Conference on Multimedia Computing and Systems, pp. 840–844. IEEE Computer Society Press, Los Alamitos (1999)

7. Lee, C.M., Narayanan, S., Pieraccini, R.: Classifying emotions in human-machine spoken dialogs. In: ICME'02 (2002)
8. Wu, T.-F., Lin, C.-J., Weng, R.C.: Probability Estimates for Multi-class Classification by Pairwise Coupling. Journal of Machine Learning Research (2004)
9. Gu, L., Zahorian, S.A.: A new robust algorithm for isolated word end-point detection. In: ICASSP2002, Orlando, USA (2002)
10. Noll, M.: Pitch determination of human speech by the harmonic product spectrum, the harmonic sum spectrum, and a maximum likelihood estimate. In: Proceedings of the Symposium on Computer Processing Communications, pp. 779–797 (1969)
11. Ross, M.J., Shaer, H.L., Cohen, A., Freudberg, R., Manley, H.J.: Average magnitude difference function pitch extractor. ASSP-22, 353–362 (1974)
12. Sun, X.: A pitch determination algorithm based on subharmonic-to harmonic ratio. In: ICSLP, pp. 676–679 (2000)
13. Liu, M., Wan, C.: A study on content-based classification retrieval of audio database. In: Proc. of the International Database Engineering & Applications Symposium, pp. 339–345 (2001)
14. Bong-Seok, K.: A text-independent emotion recognition algorithm using speech signal. MS Thesis, Yonsei University (2000)

Mobility Driven Vertical Handover for Mobile IPTV Traffic in Hybrid IEEE 802.11e/16e Networks*

Eunjun Choi[1], Wonjun Lee[1], and Joongheon Kim[2]

[1] Division of Computer and Communication Engineering, Korea Univ., Seoul, Korea
wlee@korea.ac.kr
[2] Digital Media Research Lab., LG Electronics, Seoul, Korea

Abstract. This paper addresses a mobility driven vertical handover (M-VHO) scheme to avoid unnecessary handovers for IEEE 802.11e/16e wireless networks. In the M-VHO scheme, the mobility of a mobile station (MS), e.g., an IPTV terminal, can be estimated by the pattern of velocities and directions. As the mobile IPTV traffic strictly needs to be considered for supporting high quality and large scale multimedia services, IEEE 802.11e-based QoS-aware MAC is good to use. Therefore, the proposed M-VHO scheme is operated over IEEE 802.11e/16e networks. Results demonstrate that M-VHO scheme is efficient to supply QoS in various traffic.

1 Introduction

Currently the tremendous development of communications and networks technologies leads the evolution of wireless broadband networks. Among the numerous wireless broadband networks technologies, IEEE 802.16-based fixed WiMAX shows the most positive perspectives. The basic feature of IEEE 802.16-based WiMAX is developed by the IEEE 802.16 standard committee activities [1]. Because IEEE 802.16 fixed WiMAX cannot support the robust mobility in mobile terminals, it is not suitable for mobile computing environments. Therefore, several schemes are proposed in IEEE 802.16e mobile WiMAX to support seamless mobility on mobile stations (MSs). As a mobility support technology, IEEE 802.16e addresses a handover procedure among same kinds of networks. However in upcoming advanced network environments, we must support handover among heterogeneous wireless networks, i.e., vertical handover. Therefore, the research on vertical handover [3] is activated in many research institutes and universities. Under this research trends, this paper addresses the vertical handover scheme for hybrid IEEE 802.11e/16e networks. By the increment of the volume of multimedia resource such as mobile IPTV applications, the proposed scheme in this paper, uses IEEE 802.11e QoS-aware WLAN. Furthermore, to adopt the mobile computing environments, the *mobility* of MSs can be considered as a vertical handover decision factor. Therefore, a *mobility driven vertical handover (M-VHO)* scheme for

* This work was jointly supported by grant from ITRC Project supervised by IITA-2005 [C1090-0501-0019] and KOSEF [R01-2005-000-10267-0].

J. Indulska et al. (Eds.): UIC 2007, LNCS 4611, pp. 767–776, 2007.

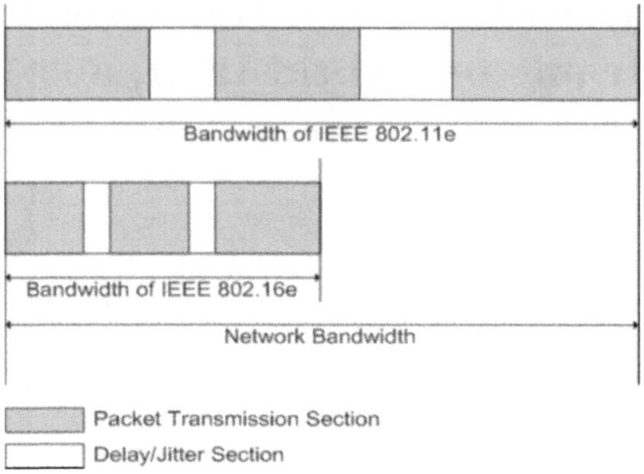

Fig. 1. The Bandwidth of IEEE 802.11e and IEEE 802.16e

mobile IPTV terminals is proposed for hybrid IEEE 802.11e/16e. The proposed M-VHO scheme considers two key factors for QoS provisioning. The first one is 'ping-pong effect' [6]-[8]. The ping-pong effect occurs if vertical handover decision factors are rapidly changed and an MS performs vertical handover as soon as it detects a better BS. It can prevent robust and reliable communications. Our M-VHO scheme uses a dwell timer to alleviate the effect. The second factor is the consideration of delay and jitter for designing a QoS-aware vertical handover decision function. That is to say, the proposed scheme considers the two QoS factors to evaluate the utility of target BS. Real-time traffic such as VoIP and multimedia stream of a mobile IPTV are more sensitive to delay and jitter variations than bandwidth of the target networks. The reason why delay and jitter are more important factors than bandwidth is explained in Fig. 1. Although the bandwidth of 802.11e is larger than that of IEEE 802.16e, IEEE 802.11e wireless network cannot guarantee QoS requirements of real-time traffic because delay and jitter of IEEE 802.11e network is not acceptable to provide QoS for real-time traffic. Bandwidth is less an important factor to support traffic transmissions. Based on these phenomena, we propose an M-VHO scheme.

The remainder of this paper is organized as follows. Section 2 shows the related work of this paper. Section 3 describes the proposed vertical handover scheme between IEEE 802.11e and IEEE 802.16e. In Section 4, the vertical handover algorithm is evaluated through simulation. Finally, the conclusions are drawn in Section 5.

2 Related Work

As an initial step of vertical handover research, radio signal strength (RSS) is used for the main factor of vertical handover decision [6][10]. However, the vertical handover decision needs to consider further diverse factors [6]. Therefore, the proposed policy-enabled vertical handover decision algorithm uses utility functions with various factors. It performs vertical handover to the best target base station (BS). The factors used in vertical handover are service types, monetary cost, network conditions, system performance, mobile node conditions, and etc [9]. Such vertical handover decision algorithms can be used to provide QoS. To achieve more robustness, related research starts to consider a 'ping-pong effect'. The effect is a phenomenon that rapidly repeats vertical handover between two BSs [5]. It occurs if factors for the vertical handover decision are changing rapidly and an MS performs vertical handover as soon as the MS detects the better BS [11]. The dwell timer scheme has been used to avoid such effects [8][9]. It starts to work when the vertical handover condition is first satisfied. If the condition persists during the dwell time, the MS performs vertical handover after the dwell timer is expired. Otherwise the MS resets the dwell timer [12]. Consequently, the MS does not execute vertical handover until the target BS becomes stable. Ping-pong effect can also occur if the speed of an MS is high or the moving direction of the MS is irregular. In [13], the MS remains in the serving BS as long as the serving BS satisfies the QoS requirement of an MS. When the type of the application used is changed or an MS leaves the serving BS, the MS attempts to find the other target BS. The vertical handover decision algorithm in [13] can avoid ping-pong effect since it is based on the need of the application, but not the RSS of the BS. On the other hand, our proposed M-VHO scheme can avoid ping-pong effect as well as select the best target BS among neighbor BSs. Furthermore, almost previous research in vertical handover considers a vertical handover decision for integrated WLAN/3G networks. However, our research considers a vertical handover for supporting QoS to achieve large scale and high quality mobile IPTV multimedia services in integrated IEEE 802.11/16e networks. To the best of our knowledge, our vertical handover scheme is the first trial in integrated IEEE 802.11e/16e. Thus, the M-VHO scheme adjusts the length of the dwell time adaptively according to the ping-pong movement of an MS.

3 Mobility Driven Vertical Handover Scheme

We propose a mobility driven vertical handover (M-VHO) scheme which considers the mobility of mobile IPTV terminals and the traffic category of each service stream to determine when the terminal performs vertical handover. The M-VHO scheme can decrease the number of unbeneficial vertical handovers by estimating the mobility of mobile IPTV terminals. The M-VHO scheme also takes into account delay and jitter for selecting target BS which provides best utilities in the aspect of QoS provisioning.

3.1 Reference Network Model

We consider the interworking architecture of integrated IEEE 802.11e WLAN and IEEE 802.16e mobile WiMAX with mobile IPTV terminals as a reference network model. The vertical handover adaptive mobile station (MS), i.e., a mobile IPTV terminal, has dual interfaces for operating in both WLAN and mobile

Table 1. Notations for describing M-VHO scheme

Notation	Description
ME_t	Mobility estimation time
ME_{ubound}	Lower bound of mobility estimation time
ME_{lbound}	Upper bound of mobility estimation time
$ME_{default}$	Default of mobility estimation time
$E[V]$	Average of velocity until current time
$E[D]$	Average of normalized direction until current time
v_t	Current velocity of an MS
d_t	Current normalized direction of an MS
f_t	The ping-pong flag
α	Exponential smoothing factor
T_{res}	Predictive residence time
$f_{delay}(i)$	Weighting functions of delay
$f_{jitter}(i)$	Weighting functions of jitter
$f_{bandwidth}(i)$	Weighting functions of bandwidth
$U_{network_i}$	The utility that the network provides based on traffic type i

WiMAX. If the WLAN network provides more efficient service for the mobile IPTV terminal, the mobile IPTV terminal uses the WLAN interface to use a WLAN connection link. Otherwise, it uses the mobile WiMAX interface. To interconnect with WLAN or mobile WiMAX, the mobile IPTV terminal connects an access point (AP) of WLAN with a radio access station (RAS) of mobile WiMAX. The AP and RAS provide an interface to communicate with a mobile IPTV terminal. In the subsequent section, the AP and RAS are called as base stations (BSs).

3.2 Algorithm Description

The proposed M-VHO scheme consists of three procedures; (1) mobility estimation procedure, (2)traffic categorization procedure, and (3) M-VHO decision procedure. Mobility estimation procedure predicts the mobility of an MS by considering current position and velocity of the MS. Traffic categorization procedure chooses a target BS which provides the best network utility in the aspects of MS mobility and traffic category.

Mobility Estimation Phase: The estimated mobility of an MS is periodically updated and can be an crucial factor to decide whether the MS performs VHO or not. Period Update is adaptively changed by considering current velocity and average velocity. That is, if current velocity is slower than average velocity, then updating period is modified to be longer. Otherwise, period value will be decreased. By modifying Period Update adaptively, M-VHO estimates mobility pattern of the MS accurately. The adaptive period of update is described in Eq. (1).

$$ME_t = min\left[ME_{ubound}, max\left(ME_{lbound}, \frac{E[V]}{v_t} \times ME_{default}\right)\right] \quad (1)$$

ME_t, ME_{ubound}, ME_{lbound}, and $ME_{default}$ denote the adaptive mobility estimation time, the upper bound and lower bound of mobility estimation time, default of mobility estimation period, respectively. $E[V]$ is the average of velocity until current time. $E[V]$ and current velocity are used to modify the mobility estimation period. ME_t is update time of presuming mobility pattern and average velocity. The average velocity of the MS helps to estimate a T_{res}, is the predictive residence time of the MS. All notations are summarized in Table 1.

$$\begin{aligned} E[V] &= (1-\alpha)v_t + \alpha v_{t-1} \\ &= (1-\alpha)v_t + (1-\alpha)\alpha v_{t-1} + (1-\alpha)\alpha^2 v_{t-2} + \cdots + (1-\alpha)\alpha^{k-1} v_1 \\ &= (1-\alpha)\textstyle\sum_{i=1}^{t} \alpha^{i-1} v_{t-i+1} \end{aligned} \quad (2)$$

$$\begin{aligned} E[D] &= (1-\alpha)d_t + \alpha d_{t-1} \\ &= (1-\alpha)d_t + (1-\alpha)\alpha d_{t-1} + (1-\alpha)\alpha^2 d_{t-2} + \cdots + (1-\alpha)\alpha^{k-1} d_1 \\ &= (1-\alpha)\textstyle\sum_{i=1}^{t} \alpha^{i-1} d_{t-i+1} \end{aligned} \quad (3)$$

We adopt exponential smoothing average to get $E[V]$ and $E[D]$. v_t and d_t in Eq. (2) and Eq. (3) mean the current velocity and normalized direction of the MS. $E[D]$ stands for the average of direction pattern until current time. α is 0.5 and heuristically determined through a number of simulations. To detect the mobility pattern of an MS, the direction at current time t (d_t) is compared to the direction at time $t-1$ (d_{t-1}). If there is significant change of more than 90 degree, the ping-pong flag (f_t) is set to 1.

$$f_t = \begin{cases} 1, \text{ if } \cos^{-1}(d_t \cdot d_{t-1}) > 90^\circ \\ 0, \text{ otherwise} \end{cases} \quad (4)$$

Based on the weighted average of f_t, M-VHO scheme get to know that the mobility pattern of the MS change rapidly and results in ping-pong movement. In case that the weighted average of f_t exceeds a threshold, M-VHO scheme considers that the ping-pong effect is occured. Since this mobility pattern tends to cause the ping-pong effect, the method to address this problem is needed.

Traffic Categorization Phase: The target BS is the BS that provides the maximum utility among detected neighbor BSs. After receiving QoS information from neighbor BSs, the utilities of BSs are calculated according to QoS requirements, mobility support, and so forth. QoS is determined not only by BSs bandwidth, but also by delay and jitter. Eventually, if all neighbor BSs provide minimum bandwidth for communications, delay and jitter must be considered as important factors for QoS provisioning. To provide better service qualities to users, M-VHO scheme differentiates traffic into four categories and calculates the utilities of neighbor BSs differently based on the traffic categories. IEEE 802.11e MAC has a four separate traffic queue in it for differentiating services and each queue acts as a virtual terminal. This means that IEEE 802.11e MAC sets up different QoS parameters such as $AIFS$, CW_{min}, CW_{max}, and so on. M-VHO scheme adopts a differentiation mechanism similar to the IEEE 802.11e

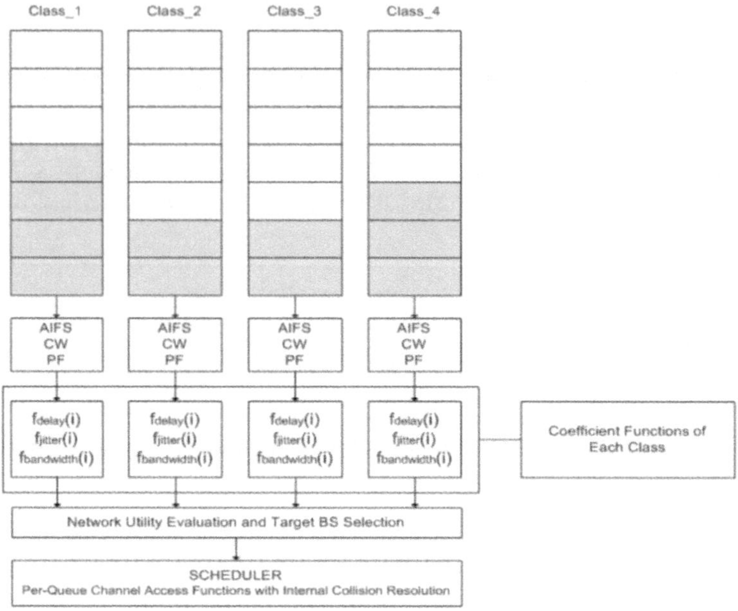

Fig. 2. Differentiated queue management architecture in QoS-aware IEEE 802.11e

QoS provisioning scheme. That is, M-VHO scheme sets up different parameters which are used to calculate the utilities of neighbor BSs based on traffic categories as shown in Fig. 2. Although MS is located in the same network, the utility which can be obtained is different based on traffic categories that the MS transmits or receives. The utility of target BS is calculated by using Eq. (5). The values of $f_{delay}(i)$, $f_{jitter}(i)$, and $f_{bandwidth}(i)$ are weighing factors of delay, jitter, and bandwidth to calculate the utilities of neighbor BSs. In Eq. (5), $U_{network_i}$ denotes the utility that the network provides based on traffic type i.

$$\begin{aligned} U_{network_i} &= f(delay, jitter, bandwidth, traffic\_category) \\ &= f_{delay}(traffic\_category) \cdot (delay)^{-1} \\ &\quad + f_{jitter}(traffic\_category) \cdot (jitter)^{-1} \\ &\quad + f_{bandwidth}(traffic\_category) \cdot (bandwidth) \end{aligned} \tag{5}$$

M-VHO Decision Procedure: The target BS provides a better utility that current serving BS, the handover to the target BS becomes unbeneficial if the predictive residence time in the target BS is smaller than the delay caused by the handover procedure. Therefore, vertical handover has to consider both network utility and predictive residence time. A predictive residence time of an MS can be obtained by using estimated mobility pattern and range of the target BS. If the predictive time exceeds the handover execution time, M-VHO performs vertical handover. On the other hand, although current serving BS provides maximum utility, vertical handover must be performed when the RSS of the current serving

BS is lower than pre-determined threshold. Consequently, handover occurs when one of the following conditions is satisfied until the dwell timer expires.

- $U_{serv.BS} < U_{target.BS}$
- $RSS_{target.BS} > Threshold_{target.BS}$
- $T_{res} > T_{make} + T_{HO}$
- $RSS_{serv.BS} < Threshold_{serv.BS}$

serve.BS and *target.BS* denote a serving BS and a target BS, respectively. $RSS_{targe.BS}$ and $Threshold_{target.BS}$ address the radio signal strength of target BS and the threshold of the signal strength of target BS. T_{make} and T_{HO} denote "make up time" and "handover delay time", respectively. The dwell timer provides smoothing and seamless vertical handover to cope with ping-pong effect. Under this design rationale, we can obtain the value by Eq. (6). It starts working provided one of the above conditions is satisfied. The adaptive dwell timer adjusts duration of mobility estimation of the MS and the utility of target BS. If the utility of target BS is far better than the current serving BS, the dwell timer will be shorter than current dwell timer. If mobility pattern of the MS is irregular, i.e., ping-pong movement, the dwell timer is extended. In consideration of target BS utility and mobility pattern of the MS, Eq. (7) adjusts the dwell timer as follows:

$$T_{dwell\_timer} = min\left[ubound(T_{dwell\_timer}, max\left(lbound(T_{dwell\_timer}), \Omega\right)\right] \quad (6)$$

$$\Omega = \left(1 + \widetilde{f}\right) \frac{U_{serv.BS}}{U_{target.BS}} default(T_{dwell\_timer}) \quad (7)$$

T_{dwell_timer}, $ubound(T_{dwell\_timer})$, $lbound(T_{dwell\_timer})$, and $default(T_{dwell\_timer})$ imply current, upper, lower, and default dwell timer, respectively.

4 Performance Evaluation

We conduct simulation using Qualnet 3.9.5. We observe the performance of M-VHO when the MS receives mobile IPTV service traffic while it moves into an

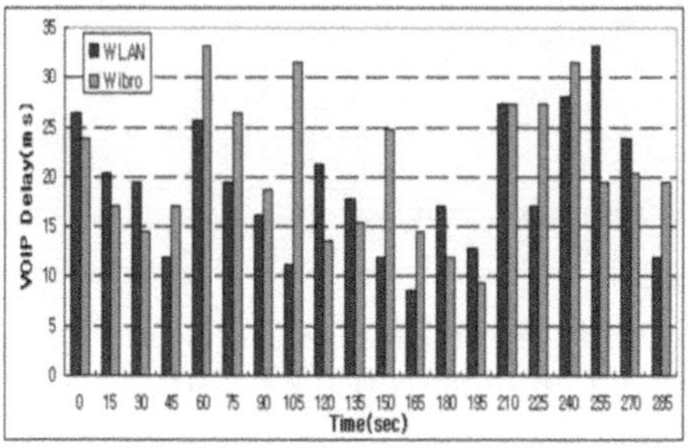

(a)

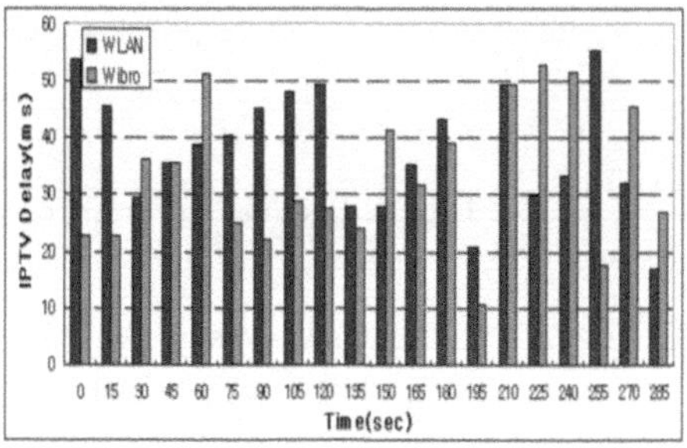

(b)

Fig. 3. Scenario 2: (a) VoIP delay variance vs. simulation time simulation time (b) IPTV delay variance vs. simulation time

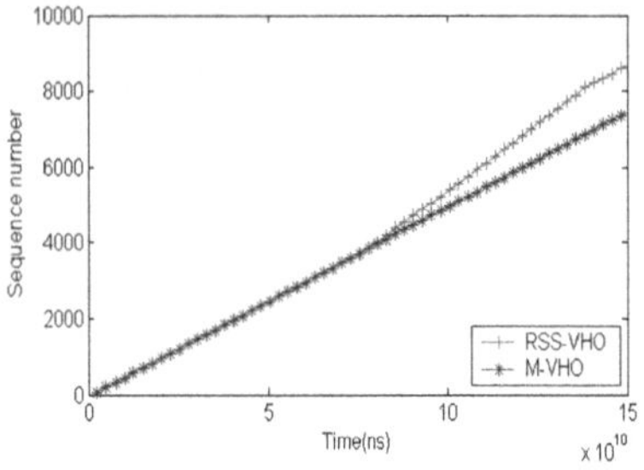

Fig. 4. Scenario 2: packet sequence number vs. simulation time

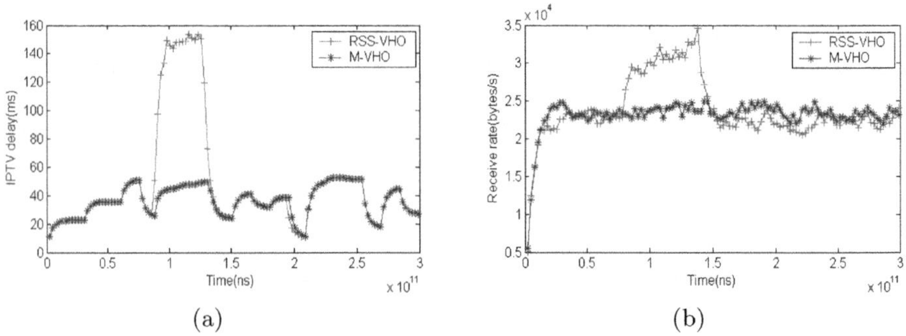

Fig. 5. Scenario 2: (a) IPTV delay variance vs. simulation time simulation time (b) IPTV receive rate variance vs. simulation time

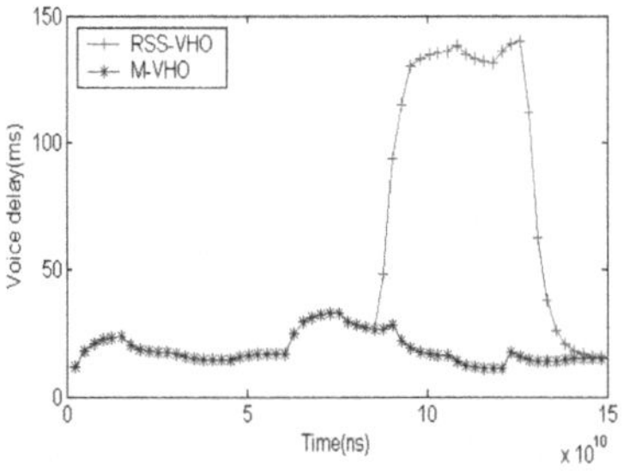

Fig. 6. Scenario 2: VoIP delay variance vs. simulation time

IEEE 802.11e network slowly. An MS move into an IEEE 802.11e network at a slow speed while receiving real-time traffic, i.e., mobile IPTV or VoIP. M-VHO scheme calculates the utilities of target BS and serving BS using delay and jitter. Variations of the delay and jitter of IEEE 802.11e and IEEE 802.16e networks are shown in Fig. 3. The MS arrives in an IEEE 802.11e network at about 60 second. In this network configuration, RSS-based vertical handover scheme performs vertical handover and connects its communication with the IEEE 802.11e network because received signal strength from the IEEE 802.11e increases. Bandwidth-based vertical handover scheme also performs vertical handover. However, the proposed M-VHO scheme does not vertical handover. Between 60 and 120 second when the MS is located in an IEEE 802.11e network, the delay and jitter of the IEEE 802.11e shows unsuitability to provide the MS with appropriate QoS requirements as shown in Fig. 5(a). Although IEEE 802.11e network is better than IEEE 802.16e network in terms of bandwidth and RSS, IEEE 802.16e network is more suitable to provide QoS for mobile IPTV terminals, because the delay and jitter of IEEE 802.16e are lower than those of IEEE 802.11e network. In Fig. 4, we observe that RSS-based vertical handover mechanism performs vertical handover to IEEE 802.11e and increases the receiving rates. However, we figure that RSS-based vertical handover does not provide good QoS according to delay and jitter. On the other hand, the M-VHO scheme selects a target network which has lower delay and jitter. This behavior of the M-VHO scheme results in providing more reliable services. We also analyze the performance of M-VHO scheme when the MS receives different QoS required traffic, i.e., VoIP. Similar to mobile IPTV terminals, voice traffic is well serviced by M-VHO scheme as shown in Fig. 6.

5 Conclusions

This paper addresses a mobility driven vertical handover (M-VHO) scheme for IEEE 802.11e/16e. Efficient VHO schemes can make better performance for robust communications. However, frequent VHO for a short time period causes more loss/delay and decrease the overall throughput. The ping-pong effect results from the short residence time in the preferred network. We have investigated the cause of the short residence time and proposed the M-VHO scheme which is an improved handover decision algorithm that avoids the ping-pong effect. Furthermore, we considers jitter and delay as QoS factors. By using a mobile IPTV terminal as an MS, we need to consider QoS provisioning. Therefore the of jitter and delay is impressive. For more reliability, we have integrated IEEE 802.11e/802.16e. In previously, almost research is for WLAN/3G networks. The co-existence of IEEE 802.11e/16e for mobile IPTV is the first trial in this paper.

References

1. IEEE Stand. for Local and metropolitan area networks, Part 16: Air Interface for Fixed Broadband Wireless Access Systems, IEEE Comittee (2006)
2. IEEE Stand. for Local and metropolitan area networks, Part 16: Air Interface for Fixed and Mobile Broadband Wireless Access Systems Amendment 2, IEEE Committee (2006)
3. Stemm, M., Katz, R.H.: Vertical Handoffs in Wireless Overlay Networks, ACM Mobile Networks and Applications, 335–350 (1998)
4. IEEE Stand. for Local and metropolitan area networks, Part 11: Wireless LAN MAC and PHY specification, IEEE Committee (2001)

5. IEEE Stand. for Local and metropolitan area networks, Part 11: Wireless LAN MAC and PHY specification, IEEE Committee (2001)
6. Pollini, G.P.: Trends in Handover Design. IEEE Communications Magazine, 82–90 (1996)
7. Wang, H.J., Katz, R.H., Giese, J.: Policy-enabled Handoffs Across Heterogeneous Wireless Networks. In: Proc. IEEE Workshop on Mobile Computing Systems and Applications, pp. 51–60 (1999)
8. Ylianttila, M., Pande, M., Makela, J., Mahonen, P.: Optimization Scheme for Mobile Users Performing Vertical Handoffs between IEEE 802.11 and GPRS/EDGE networks. In: Proc. IEEE Global Telecommunications Conference, pp. 3439–3443 (2001)
9. Hsieh, R., Zhou, Z.G., Senevirante, A.: S-MIP: A Seamless Handoff Architecture for Mobile IP. In: Proc. IEEE INFOCOM, 2003, pp. 1774–1784 (2003)
10. McNair, J., Zhu, F.: Vertical Handoffs in Fourth-Generation Multinetwork Environments. IEEE Wireless Communications, 8–15 (2004)
11. Chen, W.T., Liu, J.C., Huang, H.K.: An Adaptive Scheme for Vertical Handoff in Wireless Overlay Networks. In: Proc. IEEE Intl. Conference on Parallel and Distributed Systems, pp. 541–548 (2004)
12. Ye, M.H., Liu, Y., Zhang, H.M.: The Mobile IP Handoff between Hybrid Networks. In: Proc. IEEE Intl. Symposium on Personal, Indoor and Mobile Radio Communications, pp. 265–269 (2002)
13. Chen, W.T., Shu, Y.Y.: Active Application Oriented Vertical Handoff in Next-Generation Wireless Networks. In: Proc. IEEE Wireless Communications and Networking Conference, pp. 1383–1388 (2005)

An Efficient Scheme for Lifetime Setting in the MIPv6

Hye-Young Kim[1] and Jitae Shin[2]

[1] Department of Game Software, School of Games,
Hongik University, South Korea
hykim@hongik.ac.kr
[2] School of Information and Communication Engineering,
Sungkyunkwan University, South Korea
jtshin@skku.edu

Abstract. The role of location management in mobile communication is to make the seamless packet transmission to the correspondent nodes. Most research imposes mainly on how to reduce the frequency of the binding update messages, how to make the level of the signaling constant notwithstanding the increase in the number of the mobile nodes, and how to minimize the packet loss in transmission. This paper addresses these issues and develops a new technique for optimizing location management in mobile communication. Our proposed method adds a server mobile-node to existing Mobile IPv6 protocol and the server node maintains the functioning of mobile communication and has necessary information. Through these schemes, the lifetime of the mobile nodes can be increased. We provide the usefulness of our proposed method using analytical models and compare the results with the previous researches.

1 Introduction

The current mobile communication system carries out location management through two procedures: one is location registration, meaning that mobile node (MN) informs the system of its own location, and the other is paging which is that the system broadcasts for the call setting at the calling time [1].

In order to support user's mobility, MN frequently creates the BU messages which in turn causes network overload because the additional signaling unnecessarily consumes the frequency bandwidth. Therefore the increase in the BU messages has emerged as one of serious barriers to efficient location management. This paper proposes a method to solve the problems mentioned above by adding the Server Mobile-Node (SMN) to the IETF MIPv6 protocol. Since SMN provides a mobile networking function, an information keeping function, and a buffering function for the transmission packets, it can perform the efficient setting of lifetime on the BU messages and minimizes the delay or loss of transmitted packets. This idea can be applied to the transmission of the BU messages in order that the number of the BU messages will not increase more or less despite the increase of MN or CNs,. Our proposed method minimizes

J. Indulska et al. (Eds.): UIC 2007, LNCS 4611, pp. 777–786, 2007.

```
 0 1 2 3 4 5 6 7 8 9 0 1 2 3 4 5 6 7 8 9 0 1 2 3 4 5 6 7 8 9 0 1
                               +-+-+-+-+-+-+-+-+-+-+-+-+-+-+-+-+
                               |           Sequence #          |
+-+-+-+-+-+-+-+-+-+-+-+-+-+-+-+-+-+-+-+-+-+-+-+-+-+-+-+-+-+-+-+-+
|A|H|L|K|R|S|     Reserved      |           Lifetime            |
+-+-+-+-+-+-+-+-+-+-+-+-+-+-+-+-+-+-+-+-+-+-+-+-+-+-+-+-+-+-+-+-+
|                                                               |
.                      Mobility options                         .
+-+-+-+-+-+-+-+-+-+-+-+-+-+-+-+-+-+-+-+-+-+-+-+-+-+-+-+-+-+-+-+-+
```

Fig. 1. BU message formats for proposed system configuration

the signaling due to the minimized addition of the BU messages and due to the expansion of MN.

The organization of this paper is as follows. Next section is the main body of the paper, where we explain a new model for efficient location management including a location management scheme and its algorithm. The Section 3 shows the mathematical modeling and analysis, and the comparison of performance between the existing IETF Mobile IPv6 and the proposed new model. The final section suggests a further study direction.

2 System Configuration

2.1 Proposed System Configuration

Our proposed scheme manages network mobility and maintains binding information on MN by adding SMN governing an area for location registration by the subnet connected with many MNs. The router used on the aircraft, bus, or train has a Server Gateway (SG) that manages the network connection of SMN. HA that is in the home link of SMN will have the home address of SMN acquired upon location registration and will have COA_{SMN} acquired when it moves to another subnet. SMN performs location management through the BU messages like MN does [1]. We add a new flag (S) which is included in the BU message to inform the HA that the BU message is coming from a SMN and not from a MN. If the SMN wishes to act as a mobility server and provide connectivity to mobile nodes, it indicates this to the HA by setting a flag (S) in BU message as same scheme of Network Mobility (NEMO) [7]. The Fig. 1 shows the BU message format in this paper. It sends the BU messages to HA and CN of SMN through SMN's SG right before the expiration of lifetime set in the BU messages and when it moves to another subnet. When the HA receives this BU message, it create a binding cache entry binding the SMN's Home Address to its COA at the current point of attachment. The HA acknowledges the BU by a Binding Acknowledgement (BA) to the SMN through SG. A positive acknowledgement means that HA has set up forwarding for the network. Once the binding process completes, a bi-directional tunnel is established between the HA and SMN. The

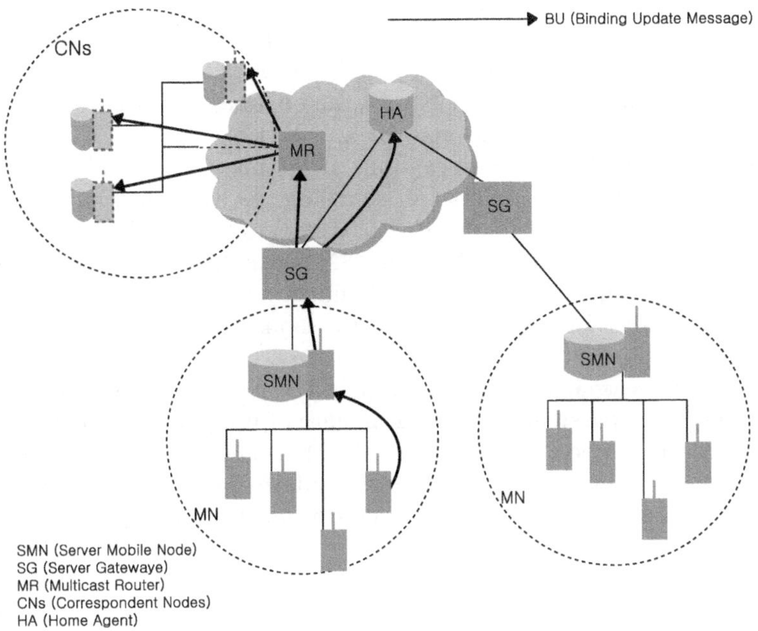

Fig. 2. Proposed System Configuration

tunnel end points are SMN's Address and the HA's address. At that time SMN broadcasts the BU to MNs connected with it.

SMN keeps information about each of MNs for location management of MNs. If a packet with a source address belonging to the SMN's prefix is received from the network, the SMN reverses the packet to the HA through this tunnel. This reverse-tunneling is done by using IP-in-IP encapsulation [9]. The HA decapsulates this packet and forwards it to the CN. For traffic or originated by itself, the SMN can use either reverse tunneling or route optimization as specified in [1]. When a data packet is sent first by a CN to a MN, it gets routed to the HA which currently has the binding for the SMN. When the HA receives a data packet meant for a MN, it tunnels the packet to SMN's current COA. The SMN decapsulates the packet and forwarding to MN. Then the CN can send packets directly to the MN. Fig. 2 shows the system configuration proposed in this paper.

2.2 Proposed Scheme for BU

When MN moves to a new and different subnet, it gets two COAs. One is the SMN's COA (COA_{SMN}) and the other is the MN's COA (COA_{MN}). COA_{MN} is the same COA acquires by a MN in MIPv6 and can be acquired by the MN through the IPv6 Address Auto-Configuration [8]. The COA_{SMN} is the SMN's address that maintains the binding information of a MN which is currently visiting the associated SMN. If a MN moves into a new SMN area, it registers the binding between its HA and the two COAs and informs to its HA and CNs. If MN moves within a domain, it only needs to change its COA_{MN}, and the COA_{SMN} remains the same. Notice that it does not register any binding to its HA. MN has its own lifetime T_m and lifetime T_s of SMN. It is should be noted, however, that the determining of lifetime values and the frequency of binding refresh will also affect the signaling load of a network. If lifetimes have small values and the frequency of binding refresh is high, the signaling bandwidth for updating the COAs of an MN is also high. On the other hand, if the lifetimes have large values and the frequency of binding refresh is low, the signaling bandwidth for updating the COAs is also low. If only lifetime of MN is simply set too long, the chances of having a security problem between MNs and CNs are increased. But in our proposed system configuration, MN's lifetime, T_m, becomes possible to set long in spite of no movement of MN, because BU procedure is happened by lifetime of SMN. These lifetimes are initialized from the lifetime field continued in the BU and are decremented until it reaches zero. At this time, the entry must be deleted from the binding cache of CNs and the BU list of MNs. If the MN requires the binding service from this node to go beyond this period, it must send a new BU to the HA, the SMN, and CNs before the expiration of the period, in order to extend the lifetime. Lifetime of SMN has to be the same as or longer than lifetime of MN. (That is, $T_m \leq T_s$). MN's mobility in this proposed scheme can be classified into three cases and the proposed scheme for its location management is as follows:

Case 1. When MN moves within SMN
If $T_m > T_s$, no BU messages are produced by MN, but BU procedure is happened by Case 3.

Otherwise (that is, $T_m \leq T_s$)

1) MN sends BU_a, BU messages, to SMN. BU_a contains MN's home address, COA, and lifetime in the form of $\{MN_{IP}, COA_{MN}, T_m\}$
2) SMN updates or creates the information list of MN kept as contents of BU_a, $\{MN_{IP}, COA_{MN}, T_m\}$ and sends BA responding to MN.
3) SMN sends the BU_a of the CNs through through SG. The CNs create or update the MN's information.

Case 2. When MN moves to another SMN

1) MN sends BU_a, BU messages, to new SMN in the area it moved to. A BU_a contains $\{MN_{IP}, COA_{MN}, T_m\}$ as information on MN.
2) SMN creates MN's information by using the contents of BU_a, $\{MN_{IP}, COA_{MN}, T_m\}$ and sends BU_b , BU messages, to HA of MN through SG. A BU_b contains $\{MN_{IP}, SMN_{IP}, COA_{SMN}, COA_{MN}, T_s, T_m\}$ as information on SMN.
3) HA updates or creates information as content of BU_b,$\{MN_{IP}, SMN_{IP}, COA_{SMN}, COA_{MN}, T_s, T_m\}$, and sends BA, response to BU_b, to the SMN through the SG.
4) SMN sends a BA, response to BU_b, to the MN.

5) SMN sends a BU_b to the CNs of MN through the SG. The CNs create or update the MN's information as content of BU_b, $\{MN_{IP}, SMN_{IP}, COA_{SMN}, COA_{MN}, T_s, T_m\}$.

Case 3. The expiration just before lifetime T_s of SMN or when SMN moves

1) SMN sends BU_b, BU messages, to the HA of SMN through SG. As described in section 3.2, BU message is included a flag, S.
2) HA updates or creates information as content of BU_b, $\{MN_{IP}, SMN_{IP}, COA_{SMN}, COA_{MN}, T_s, T_m\}$, and sends BA, response to BU_b, to the SMN through the SG.
3) SMN broadcasts information as content of BU_c,$\{SMN_{IP}, COA_{SMN}, T_s\}$ to all connected MNs.
4) MNs of the SMN updates information kept as contents of BU_c.
5) SMN sends BU_b to a CNs of SMN through the SG. The CNs create or update the MN's information as content of BU_b, $\{MN_{IP}, SMN_{IP}, COA_{SMN}, COA_{MN}, T_s, T_m\}$.

Similar to [10], we define the following parameters for location update in the rest of this paper:

C_{ms} : The transmission cost of location between the MN and the SMN.
C_{sh} :The transmission cost of location between the SMN and the HA.
C_{sc} :The transmission cost of location between the SMN and the CN.
U_s : The processing cost of location update at the SMN.
U_h : The processing cost of location update at the HA.
U_c : The processing cost of location update at the CN.

Here, If the MN moves in the SMN, it is referred to $C_{mn\_in\_move}$, and if the MN moves out of the current SMN to another SMN, it is referred to $C_{mm\_out\_move}$, and if the SMN moves, it is referred to C_{smn}. Since usually the costs for a wireless communication network is higher than a wire communication network [6], the ratio is considered by using ρ to distinguish the difference between wire and wireless communication networks. The communication cost for a wire communication network is referred to δ, and the transmission cost for a wireless communication is referred to $\delta\rho$. Because the SMN can be mobile, a communication network between the SMN and the SG is assumed to be a wireless one. Therefore, C_{ms}, C_{sc}, and C_{sh} are the wireless communication networks, which incur most expensive communication costs. Because the number of hops or the distance between routers does not have much influence on the number of the binding update messages [11] or on costs, they are not considered in this paper. The following computations can apply to each case for one time BU cost.

$$C_{mn\_in\_move} = \begin{cases} 0 & if\ T_s < T_m \\ (2 + \sharp\ of\ CNs) \cdot \delta\rho + U_s + \sharp\ of\ CNs \cdot U_c & if\ T_s \geq T_m \end{cases} \quad (1)$$

$$C_{mn\_out\_move} = (4 + \sharp\ of\ CNs) \cdot \delta\rho + U_s + U_h + \sharp\ of\ CNs \cdot U_c \quad (2)$$

$$C_{smn} = (3 + \sharp\ of\ CNs) \cdot \delta\rho + U_s + \sharp\ of\ CNs \cdot U_c \quad (3)$$

3 Performance Analysis

3.1 An Analytical Model of the BU Costs in IETF MIPv6

Costs for the BU of MNs incur when they move to another subnet and right before their lifetime expires. If the number of the CNs is referred to c, the BU process by means of the MIPv6 protocol of IETF. As in the section 2.2, the following variables are used for computing costs for BU.

C_{mh} : The transmission cost of location between the MN and the HA.
C_{mc} :The transmission cost of location between the MN and the CN.

BU costs for location registration when MN leaves its current location or right before expiration of its lifetime can be computed as follows:

$$C_{mn\_in\_move} = C_{mn\_out\_move} = 2\delta\rho + 2 \cdot c \cdot \delta\rho + U_h + c \cdot U_c \tag{4}$$

In this paper, we assume that MN that has lifetime T_m moves on the path R to compute total cost C_{tot_mip} for binding update of MN on the MIPv6 protocol of IETF. The duration of time that MN stays in a location registration area is referred to a random variable, T. If T is assumed to follow the exponential distribution that has the average $\frac{1}{\lambda}$, MN stays in a location registration area is referred to C_{tot_mip}, it is shown as follows:

$$C_{tot\_mip} = (\lceil \frac{\frac{1}{\lambda}}{T_m} \rceil + 1) \cdot 2\delta\rho + 2 \cdot c \cdot \delta\rho + U_h + c \cdot U_c \tag{5}$$

3.2 An Analytical Model of the BU Costs in the Proposed Scheme

To analyze the BU costs of the proposed method in this paper, it is assumed that MN moves on the path R that is divided into as many as n of location registration areas. If the staying time of MN on the ith path, R_i is shown as T_R, staying time of MN, T_{R_i} follows the exponential distribution that has the average $\frac{1}{\lambda}$. $T_{R_1} = 0$ is assumed. T_s represents the binding lifetime of SMN in a location registration area. T_m represents MN's binding lifetime. The relation with T_{R_i}, T_s, T_m is $T_{R_i} \geq T_s \geq T_m (1 \leq i \leq n)$, and in the case of $T_{R_i} < T_s < T_m$, it is excluded from the analytical model because no BU occurs. $T_s = \alpha \cdot T_m$(provided that $\alpha \geq 1$), $T_{R_i} = \beta_i \cdot T_s$(provided that $\beta_i \geq 1$) is assumed. $T_{s_{ij}}$ represents the jth T_s section of SMN in the path R_i.(provided that $j \geq 0$) That leads to $\sum_{i=0}^{n-1} T_{R_i} + T_s \leq T_{s_{ij}} < \sum_{i=0}^{n-1} T_{R_i} + j \cdot T_s$ represents the kth T_m section within $T_{s_{ij}}$, SMN's binding lifetime. That leads to $(k-1) \cdot T_m \leq T_{m_{ijk}} < k \cdot T_m$ within $T_{S_{ij}}$. The formula for time required for MN to move on the path can be shown as Fig. 3.

As shown in Fig. 3, it becomes $T_R = \sum_{i=1}^{n} T_{R_i}$, $T_{R_i} = \sum_{j=1}^{\beta_i} T_{s_{ij}}$, $T_{s_{ij}} = \sum_{k=1}^{\alpha} T_{m_{ijk}}$ assume that the initial state refers to time when MN in possession of binding lifetime T_s stays within a SMN on the path R_i for cost analysis.

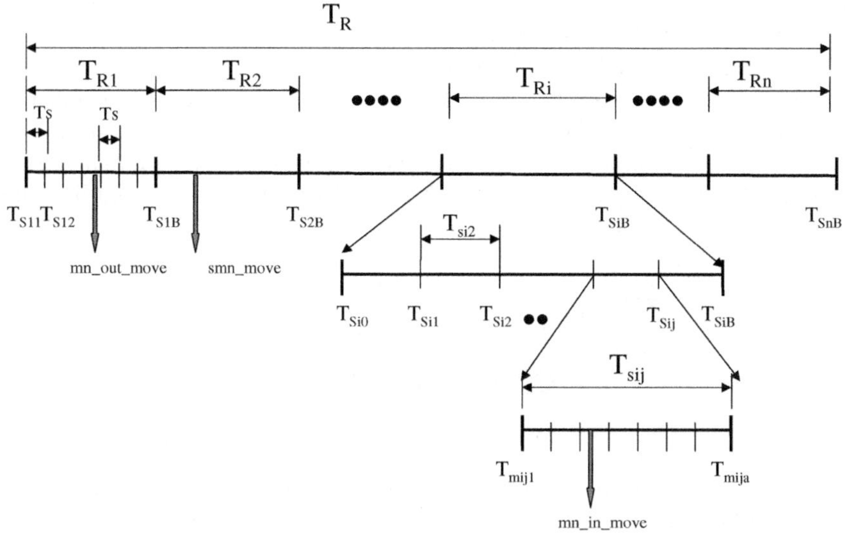

Fig. 3. The Relationship Between T_m, T_s and T_R

An Analysis Model of BU Cost for MN's Movement within the given SMN. If the probability that MN within the jth binding lifetime section of SMN on the path R_i stays in the kth binding lifetime section $(k \geq 1)$ is $P(k-1,k)$. Before MN that stays in the jth binding lifetime section of SMN exceeds the kth binding lifetime section on the path R_i, the frequency of the BU messages caused by MN becomes $k-1$. The average frequency of location update that is caused by MN within the jth binding lifetime section of SMN can be expressed as follows:

$$P(0,1) = P_r[0 \leq X < T_m] = 1 - e^{-\lambda \cdot T_m}$$

$$\begin{aligned}\sum_{k=1}^{\alpha-1} k \cdot P(k-1,k) &= (e^{-\lambda \cdot T_m} + (e^{-\lambda \cdot T_m})^2 + \cdots + (e^{-\lambda \cdot T_m})^{\alpha-1}) \cdot P(0,1) \\ &= e^{-\lambda \cdot T_m} \cdot (1 - (e^{-\lambda \cdot T_m})^{\alpha-2})\end{aligned}$$

The BU costs of the MN's movement only within SMN can be shown as in Formula(1) of 2.2. Therefore, $E_{[mn\_in\_move]}$, the average total costs for MN's location update within only SMN are as follows:

$$\begin{aligned}E_{[mn\_in\_move]} &= \sum_{k=1}^{\alpha-1} k \cdot P(k-1,k) \cdot BU\ cost \\ &= e^{-\lambda \cdot T_m} \cdot (1 - (e^{-\lambda \cdot T_m})^{\alpha-2}) \cdot C_{mn\_in\_move}\end{aligned} \quad (6)$$

An Analytical Model of the BU Costs for moving to another SMN after staying within the given SMN. MN is assumed to be within the jth binding lifetime of SMN on the path R_i. Before MN within the jth binding lifetime section of SMN on the path R_i moves to another SMN that exceeds the kth binding lifetime, the frequency of BU messages caused due to its moving to another SMN becomes $k-1$. Therefore, the average frequency of location update caused by the movement of MN to another SMN within the kth binding lifetime section of the SMN can be expressed as follows:

$$\sum_{k=1}^{\alpha-1} k\cdot Q(j,k-1,k) = \sum_{k=1}^{\alpha-1} k\cdot e^{-\lambda\cdot(k-1)\cdot T_m} \cdot Q(j,k-1,k) = e^{-\lambda\cdot T_s}\cdot(1-(e^{-\lambda\cdot T_m})^{\alpha-2}) \quad (7)$$

When MN in possession of binding lifetime T_m within the jth binding lifetime section of SMN on the path R_i moves to another SMN on the path R_i, if the frequency of its movement is w, the frequency for T_m results in $r = \frac{w}{\frac{T_{R_i}}{T_m}}$ and because the assumption based on Section 2.2 leads to $T_{R_i} = \alpha\cdot\beta_i\cdot T_m$, $r = \frac{w}{\alpha\cdot\beta_i}$, results. The BU costs for MN caused by the movement of MN to another SMN within the kth binding lifetime section of SMN can be shown as in formula (2) of the Section 2.2. The average total costs of location update $E_{[mn\_out\_move]}$ that are incurred because MN within the jth lifetime section of SMN moves to another SMN are as follows:

$$E_{[mn\_out\_move]} = e^{-\lambda\cdot T_s}\cdot(1-(e^{-\lambda\cdot T_m})^{\alpha-2})\cdot\frac{w}{\alpha\cdot\beta_i}C_{mn\_out\_move} \quad (8)$$

An Analytical Model of the MN's BU Costs for SMN's movement. When SMN moves from $j-1$ to j of binding lifetime T_s on the path R_i, the frequency of location update by the binding update messages of MN created in the movement becomes $j-1$. Therefore, the number of location update by the MN's binding update messages are as follows:

$$\sum_{j=0}^{\beta_i-1} j\cdot R(j-1,i) = e^{-\lambda\cdot T_s}\cdot(1-(e^{-\lambda\cdot T_s})^{\beta_i-2}) \quad (9)$$

When SMN moves from $j-1$ to j of binding lifetime T_s on the path R_i, the frequency of location update by the binding update messages of MN created in the movement becomes $j-1$. When SMN moves from $j-1$ to j of binding lifetime T_s on the path R_i, the MN's binding costs incurred in this movement can be shown as in Formula (3) of the section 2.2. Therefore, the average total costs for location update by the MN's BU messages created, $E_{[mn\_out\_move]}$ are as follows:

$$E_{[smn\_move]} = e^{-\lambda\cdot T_s}\cdot(1-(e^{-\lambda\cdot T_s})^{\beta_i-2})\cdot C_{smn\_move} \quad (10)$$

Accordingly, if the total average costs for location registration by the MN's BU messages in the proposed method are referred to $E_{[TOT]}$,

$$\begin{aligned} E_{[TOT]} &= e^{-\lambda \cdot T_m} \cdot (1 - (e^{-\lambda \cdot T_m})^{\alpha - 2}) \cdot C_{mn\_in\_move} \\ &+ \quad e^{-\lambda \cdot T_s} \cdot (1 - (e^{-\lambda \cdot T_m})^{\alpha - 2}) \cdot \frac{\omega}{\alpha \cdot \beta_i} C_{mn\_out\_move} \\ &+ \quad e^{-\lambda \cdot T_s} \cdot (1 - (e^{-\lambda \cdot T_s})^{\beta_i - 2}) \cdot C_{smn\_move} \end{aligned} \tag{11}$$

3.3 MN's Lifetime Setting Model

In our proposed model as explained in the section 2.2, it becomes possible to give long lifetime that is contained in the MN's BU messages by adding SMN. Therefore, MN's lifetime T_m is set to minimize the average total costs $E_{[TOT]}$ for location registration by the BU messages on the path R_i defined in the equation (9). In the formulas (1),(2),(3), if $U_s = U_h = U_c$, and if ψ is included, then $C_{mn\_out\_mov} = C_{mn\_in\_move} + 2 \cdot \delta\rho + \psi$, $C_{smn\_move} = C_{mn\_in\_move} + \delta\rho$. Here, $T_s = \alpha \cdot T_m$(provided $\alpha > 1$), $A = e^{-\lambda \cdot T_m}$ results. Therefore, the equation(10) can be expressed as follows:

$$\begin{aligned} E_{[TOT]} &= A \cdot (1 - A)^{\alpha - 2} \cdot C_{mn\_in\_move} + A^{\alpha} \cdot (1 - A)^{(\alpha - 2)} \cdot \frac{\omega}{\alpha \cdot \beta_i} \\ &\cdot \ (C_{mn\_in\_move} + 2 \cdot \delta\rho + \psi) + A^{\alpha} \cdot (1 - A)^{\alpha \cdot (\beta_i - 2)} \cdot (C_{mn\_in\_move} + \psi) \end{aligned} \tag{12}$$

$C_{mn\_in\_move} \geq 0$, $\delta\rho \geq 0$, $\psi \geq \beta_i \geq 0$, and $w \geq 0$ results and is expressed with constant values. The equation(10) is influenced by and it results in the lowest value when is applied. Then, when $\alpha = 2$ is applied. Then $T_s = 2 \cdot T_m$ is applied, it has the optimal $E_{[TOT]}$ value. Therefore, it can be known that MN's optimal binding lifetime becomes $T_m = \frac{1}{2} \cdot T_s$.

4 Conclusion and Future Work

This paper adds the SMN having mobility upon the IETF MIPv6 protocol with consideration of both MN's and SMN's lifetimes. This paper presents a technique that can minimize costs for MN's binding update by applying the multicast for CNs and adding the SMN. Also we propose the location update methods on different cases which BU of MN happens, we calculate location update costs to be required in each cases and compare the technique of IETF MIPv6 and our proposed method using mathematical analysis. Our proposed method is not influenced more or less with the increased number of MNs. If the staying time of MN follows the exponential distribution that has the average $\frac{1}{\lambda}$, as λ is smaller, MN's mobility becomes frequent. When compared with IETF MIPv6, our proposed method is more efficient for frequent MN's mobility. In general, the mobility model should be included in the changes in both the direction and speed of MNs [12]. Since results of our proposed method can be influenced by the speed of MN in mobility, so it is required that further works for more accurate studies.

Acknowledgements

This work was supported by the Korea Science and Engineering Foundation (KOSEF) grant funded by the Korea government(MOST)(R01-2006-000-10556-0).

References

1. Johnson, D.B., Perkins, C.: Mobility Support in MIPv6, IETF(International Engineering Task Force) Internet Draft, draft-ietf-mobileip-ipv6-24.txt (June 30, 2003)
2. Castelluccia, C.: HMIPv6: A hierachical mobile ipv6 proposal. ACM Mobile Computing and Communication Review 4(1), 48–59 (2000)
3. Castelluccia, C., Beller.: A Hierarchical Mobile IPv6,IETF Internet draft, dfraft-castelluccia-mobileip-hmipv6-00.txt, work in progress (July 2000)
4. Perkins, C.E.: Mobile-IP Local Registration with Hierarchical Foreign Agents, Internet Draft-perkins-mobileip-hierfa-00.txt (February 1996)
5. Yumiba, H., Sasda, K., Yabusaki, M.: Concatenated Location MAnagement. IEICE Transaction Communication E85-B (10), 2083–2089 (2002)
6. Narten, T., Nordmark, E., Simpson, W.A.: Neighbor Discovery for IP version 6(IPv6), IETF Internet draft, rfc2461.txt (December 1998)
7. Devarapalli, V., Wakikawa, R., Petrescu, A., Thubert, P.: Network Mobility(Nemo) BAsic Support Protocol. IETF Internet draft, dfraft-ietf-nemo-basic-support-02.txt (December 2003)
8. RalphDroms, Perkins, C., Bound, J., Carney, M.: Dynamaic Host Configuration Protocol for IPv6, INTERNET-DRAFT, draft-ietf-dhc-dhcpv6-20.txt, (September 2001)
9. Conta, A., Deering, S.: Generic Packet Tunneling in IPv6 Specification, RFC 2473, IETF (December 1998)
10. Xie, J., Akyildiz, L.F.: A Novel Distributed Dynamic Location Management S for Minimizing Signaling Coasts in Mobile IP. IEEE Transaction on Mobile Computing 1(3), 163–175 (2002)
11. Stephane, A., Aghvami, A.H.: Fast Handover Schemes for Future Wireless IP Network:a Proposal and Analysis, pp. 2046–2050
12. Zonoozi, M.M., Dassanayake, P.: "User mobility modeling and characterization of mobility patterns. IEEE J.Sel. Areas Commun. 15(7), 1239–1252 (1997)

Bridging OSGi Islands Through SLP Protocol*

Choonhwa Lee[1], Jongkyu Yi[1], and Wonjun Lee[2,**]

[1] College of Information and Communications,
Hanyang University, Seoul, Republic of Korea
{lee,kaulin}@hanyang.ac.kr
[2] Department of Computer Science and Engineering,
Korea University, Seoul, Republic of Korea
wlee@korea.ac.kr

Abstract. As wireless and mobile computing technologies start to penetrate every corner of our life, highly anticipated smart spaces are becoming a reality. Recently, OSGi has proven quite successful in enabling collaboration and interaction among entities within a single space. However, distributed collaboration over a wider area spanning multiple spaces will be more often required, as more spaces turns intelligent. This paper addresses the need of cross-space service discovery and interaction. Our approach is to utilize SLP protocol as a means to bridge isolated OSGi islands together. We have validated our architectural design through prototype implementations and a comparative evaluation study.

1 Introduction

As wireless communication and mobile computing technologies make their way to our daily life, we are seeing increasingly more spaces turning smart towards the vision of ubiquitous computing. Before getting to the perfection of "the ubiquitous system", as articulated by the Boundary Principle [1], we are early on the evolutionary path with individual ubiquitous systems being deployed and operating on their own. The deployment of individual smart spaces likely isolated at early stages may reflect discreteness in physical environments (e.g., personal spaces, rooms, and homes) as well as other factors such as administrative authority and technology acceptance barrier. However, it is for sure that the smart spaces will get merged together to eventually evolve to "the ubiquitous system."

Primary among the benefits from the smart space integration would be a richer set of qualified services by inter-space service discovery and interaction. As an example, consider your Bluetooth headset and smart-phone serving as a gateway node for your BAN (Body Area Network.) The moment you are back to your house after gardening, your call had better be switched over to your home gateway for a cheaper connection. This is an exemplary case of service discovery and usage beyond a smart space

* This work was supported by the Korea Research Foundation Grant funded by the Korean Government (MOEHRD, Basic Research Promotion Fund) (KRF-2006-003-D00487).
** Corresponding author.

J. Indulska et al. (Eds.): UIC 2007, LNCS 4611, pp. 787–797, 2007.

boundary, involving two entities in different spaces (i.e., the headset belonging to your BAN and the home gateway in your home network.) We can see that the benefit and need of the inter-space service interaction is apparent.

When it comes to the problem of realizing an individual space, OSGi (Open Services Gateway Initiative) [2] can be the solution to ensure dynamic reconfiguration and evolution in response to environmental changes as shown in several leading attempts [3] [4] [5]. It is no doubt that user experiences with ubiquitous systems would improve substantially, if services can be used freely without being constrained within their origin space. However, the need of cross-space interaction has not been addressed by those pilot projects having adopted OSGi. This paper is about enabling dynamic service discovery and use across space boundaries. Such support is provided by IETF SLP protocol [17] that we have chosen to bridge OSGi islands together.

The rest of the paper is organized as follows. Section 2 motivates our research by reviewing the state-of-the-art technologies related to the smart space interconnection. Section 3 explores possible architectural design alternatives for the OSGi-SLP bridge, and then presents internals of the bridge architecture. In Section 4, we show the effectiveness and feasibility of our proposal through experimental prototype implementations along with a comparative performance evaluation study. Finally, Section 5 discusses our future work, and concludes this paper.

2 Related Work

OSGi was originally conceived as a home gateway platform, which has an implication of its limited coverage. Unlike other spontaneous networking technologies such as SLP, UPnP, and Jini, OSGi intends to serves a community of service providers and clients within a clearer, predefined boundary. In other words, the service discovery and interaction is largely confined within an OSGi framework boundary, that is, among those pre-registered services with its service registry. (Of course, it is possible for system administrators to dynamically add services to OSGi systems by means of manual provisioning. However, we argue that it is not considered as a dominant usage scenario from the spontaneous networking scenario standpoint.) This implication that an OSGi-supported community is more or less limited to a certain boundary may not have been a problem in self-sufficing networking scenarios like a home network. However, we believe that things will become quite different in the near future, as spaces are increasingly instrumented with ubiquitous computing technologies. Service interaction across the boundary is expected to be a norm.

The same problem of wider coverage support has already been explored by dynamic service discovery research groups. Wider-area service discovery can be enabled by interconnecting local discovery domains in a hierarchical fashion [6] [7] or by expanding service advertisement range and replicating the advertisements [8] [9]. In addition, DHT-based peer-to-peer systems have attracted much attention as a promising solution to Internet-scale service discovery [10] [11].

Similarly to our approach, flowSGi [12] has used SLP protocol as a means to discover a service residing in a remote, neighboring framework. A proxy object for the service is downloaded into the source framework and executed there. While they have been focused on the discovery of services registered on a remote framework, our goal is set to allow better service propagation across OSGi boundaries. For instance, we allow remote service registration with a local registry, which provides full transparency as to whether it is either a remote or local service. Another important difference is that we support bidirectional service propagation between OSGi and SLP domains. Also, we have considered other possible design alternatives, including the flowSGi case, and compared each of them.

The potential of OSGi bridges with UPnP and Jini has already been seen in [13] [14]. In the case of UPnP, it is UPnP Base Driver that is responsible for mapping services discovered in UPnP networks into corresponding OSGi representations and vice versa. It is an OSGi bundle that understands UPnP protocols and handles interactions among UPnP devices. Although the efforts have the same goal of two-way service discovery from and to OSGi domains, they are concerned more about bridging the two worlds, while we about expanding an OSGi domain's reach using SLP as a connecting medium.

OSGi boundary barrier can also be broken down by empowering an individual bundle with ability to move around on its own [15]. They have extended the OSGi framework to incorporate mobile agent features: agent packaging, migration, and execution. Their efforts are orthogonal to ours, since it would be up to individual services themselves whether they choose to support mobility or not. We remain focused on framework and protocol issues to support the space boundary crossing.

3 OSGi Framework Bridging Architecture

Over the past few years, OSGi has seen remarkable growth in its adoption as a basis on which to build smart space systems. In essence, it provides a managed, extensible framework to connect various services and devices around, which serves as solid grounds for a pervasive space infrastructure. By defining a standard execution environment and service interfaces, and by promoting dynamic discovery and collaboration of devices and services from different sources, the goals of flexible, extensible, and adaptive framework architecture has become more feasible. However, as OSGi positions itself as one of mainstream infrastructure solutions for smart spaces, we now have to consider a previously unaddressed need of inter-space service discovery and interaction.

3.1 Alternative Bridging Schemes

The motivation of our research is that bridging isolated OSGi frameworks together would result in much better user experiences from the standpoint of service availability and quality. It is because a requested service may be found not in the local framework, but in a remote framework. Also, one of more desired quality might be discovered in neighbor frameworks. OSGi frameworks can effectively be merged together by employing a service discovery protocol for the purpose of relaying discovery request and result messages among them. We have chosen SLP as the exchange protocol. But it should be mentioned that our architecture is not dependent on a specific protocol. Therefore, it can be easily replaced with any other protocol.

As depicted in Figure 1, we make use of SLP DAs as an intermediary through which services are exchanged among OSGi frameworks. On the framework side, we have an SLPBridge bundle containing Exporter and Importer modules. The former pushes local OSGi services to SLP domains, while the latter is responsible of pulling services from SLP DAs.

When it comes to the problem of what kind of information regarding services to exchange, we have two alternatives: an OSGi proxy or services themselves. The former option is to push and pull a proxy that represents an OSGi space. The proxy signifies the presence of an OSGi framework. More specifically, OSGi spaces are modeled as a proxy service, and actual services resident in that domain can be discovered and accessed through the proxy. The latter contrasts this proxy approach by directly exchanging real services. Another design choice is whether to register remote services with local OSGi service registries. Services from outside may be registered with the local registry, which allows for the same view on service discovery regardless of their origin: local or remote domains. Alternatively, we can go out to SLP DAs every time we need services. This approach avoids local registration and synchronization overheads, but at the cost of discovery latency. Figure 1 illustrates a possible combination of the two classification criteria: OSGi proxy vs. real services and SLP registration vs. local OSGi registration.

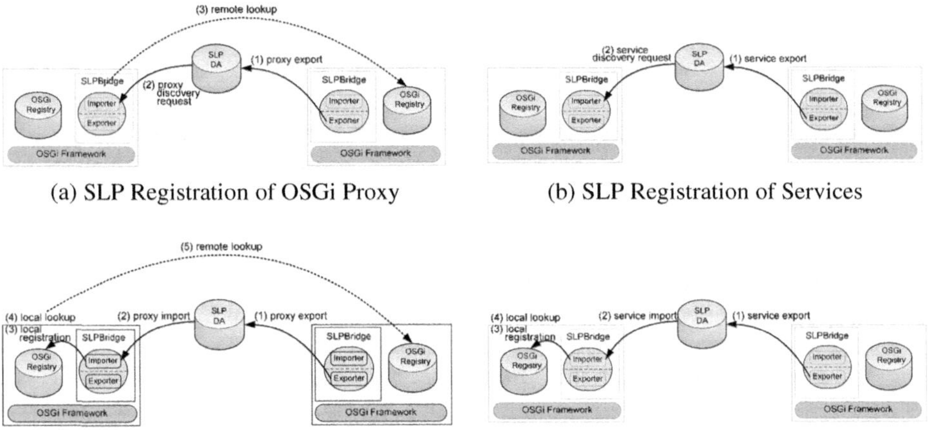

(a) SLP Registration of OSGi Proxy

(b) SLP Registration of Services

(c) Local Registration of OSGi Proxy

(d) Local Registration of Services

Fig. 1. Alternatives to Bridge OSGi Frameworks

First, consider the case of individual service propagation. The Exporter module on a source domain pushes its services towards SLP domains (by registering with SLP DAs.) Then, the Importer module on the other side may fetch them from the SLP DAs and proactively register to its local OSGi registry (Figure 1 (d)). Alternatively, the Importer may reactively query the DAs, when it receives a discovery request (Figure 1 (b)). In the cases of OSGi framework proxy propagation (Figure 1 (a) and (c)), the proxies are first discovered instead of individual services. Then, services belonging to a remote domain are discovered by invoking lookup methods on the obtained proxy.

3.2 Design of SLPBridge Service

SLP serves as an intermediary to advertise service information in between OSGi domains. When being pushed beyond their domain boundary, OSGi service information should be converted to conform to SLP service syntax. Service attribute mapping is necessary as part of this conversion process. We note that the syntax of both OSGi properties and SLP attributes is based on LDAPv3 filter notation, which ensures compatibility between the two service representations and eases the conversion process. Beside the original service attributes, services are annotated with additional meta-information, when they are pushed towards SLP domains. Table 1 summarizes our attribute extension of importance.

The *category* attribute can have either of "osgi" or "slp" as its value, indicating the service's origin domain. The *space* attribute contains the domain name which is typically a symbolic name of OSGi frameworks or SLP DAs (i.e., the machine name hosting the frameworks or DAs in most cases.) The *bundle-location* attribute points to a URL from which the object of discovered services can be downloaded. It may often be the case where we run into a hierarchy of OSGi domains. Imagine that a personal area network is contained within a room network which, in turn, is subsumed by a network covering the entire building. And we assume that each network is represented by a corresponding OSGi domain. How to detect and manage such hierarchical containment relationship is out of the scope of this paper, being left as our further work. In this paper, assuming that such support is readily available, we introduce several attributes to indicate where services are in the hierarchy, including *current*, *containing*, and *contained* for current, child, and parent spaces. For example, consider a hierarchy of the home, room, and desk area. For a service residing in the room network domain, the value of *contained*, *current*, and *containing* attributes can be "home", "room", and "desk", respectively.

Figure 2 zooms into the SLPBridge bundle in Figure 1 (d) case. As briefed earlier in the paper, the bundle takes charge of disseminating local service information to other OSGi domains through intermediate SLP domains. On detecting any changes to the set of services in the local OSGi registry, including service addition, removal, and modification, the Exporter advertises the changes to the SLP world. It tracks service

Table 1. Attribute Extension for OSGi Bridging

Attribute Name	Description
category	It indicates whether a service originates either from an OSGi or SLP domain.
space	It is a symbolic name of the domain, usually the machine name hosting OSGi frameworks or SLP DAs.
bundle-location	A URL from which service objects can be obtained.
contained	It has the name of parent OSGi framework (i.e., the *space* attribute of parent.)
current	It has the name of this OSGi framework (i.e., synonymous with *space* attribute.)
containing	It contains a list of child framework names (i.e., the *space* attribute of children.)

registrations in the framework by extending OSGi's Service Tracker class in order to keep the SLP advertisements up to date. More specifically, the Exporter implements *addingService*, *modifiedService*, and *removedService* methods of *ServiceTracker-Custmizer* class that customize appropriate actions to be taken in the event of such changes. For example, when a new service emerges in the framework, *addingService* method performs OSGi-to-SLP conversion of the service and passes it to the Exporter module which, in turn, uploads the service to SLP DAs. The Exporter is responsible of refreshing the service advertisement (based on its lifetime) and performing its follow-up synchronization between the two domains. Similarly, *modifiedSerice* and *removedService* methods are called to handle service modification and deregistration cases.

The Importer takes care of the other half of the service exchange scenario. It searches for services advertised by neighboring OSGi domains, and registers them with its local service registry. Although the search can be performed either in advance or on demand as mentioned before, Figure 2 depicts the case of service prefetching.

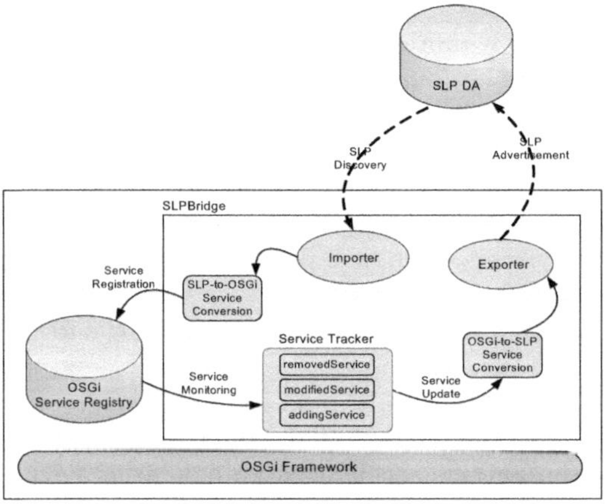

Fig. 2. Design of SLPBridge Bundle

4 Implementation and Evaluation Study

We evaluated the feasibility and effectiveness of our approach by means of prototype experiments, and conducted a basic analytical study to compare the performance and overhead of the bridging alternatives.

4.1 Prototype Implementations

We have developed the SLPBridge bundle on top of Knopflerfish v2.0 [16] and OpenSLP v1.2.1 [18] that are open source implementations of OSGi and SLP, respectively. In addition, we implemented a GUI tool to browser services in an OSGi framework and to retrieve their associated attributes. Two implementations of Swing version on PC platform and AWT version on PDA platform are available as shown in Figure 3.

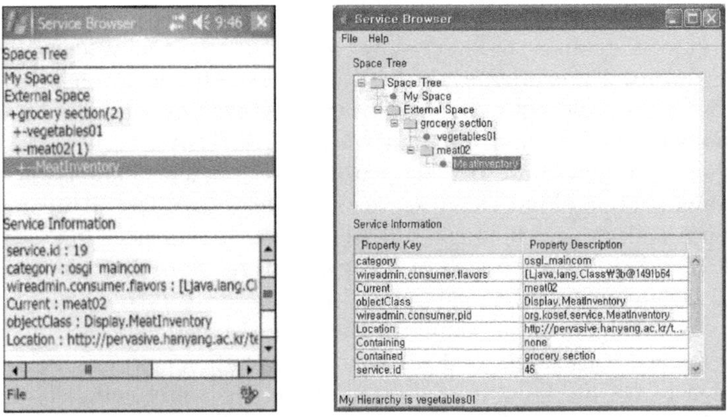

(a) PDA Version (b) Laptop Version

Fig. 3. Screenshots of Service Browser

To demonstrate our system, we have devised an imaginary scenario which involves service discovery across OSGi framework boundaries. The scenario features a shopping aid application running on a PDA that intelligently provides shopping information. Suppose Bob stops by a grocery store on his way home after work. As he walks through the store isles, shopping guide messages on his PDA alert him on his purchasing products. More specifically, when an item matches against his shopping list fetched from his home fridge at the moment he entered the store, the shopping message pops up on this PDA.

Serveral OSGi domains may be deployed in the scenario above. There can be one framework on Bob's PDA that manages a PAN around him. Depending on the size of the store network, there can be one or more frameworks that are assigned to cover a particular area of the store. In our experiment, the store is divided into two sections: vegetable section and meat section that are represented by their own OSGi space. Moreover, we assume that each domain hosts an inventory manager service which keeps inventory information in the area under its jurisdiction.

The shopping aid application will first need discover the inventory service. For example, as Bob approaches the meat section, his PDA detects the OSGi space managing that section and learns about its inventory service. Then, the inventory service will be contacted for further information on the meat items on his purchasing list. Afterwards, the shopping aid application may check with another inventory service in charge of the vegetable section.

Let us take a look at how the shopping aide scenario can be supported by our bridging scheme. First, the Exporter module of the SLPBridge on the shopping center network side, including the meat and vegetable section networks, has to export services stored in the local OSGi service registry. It prepares an SLP counterpart for each OSGi service by performing OSGi-to-SLP attribute mapping and adding additional attributes as discussed in Section 3.2. It then uploads the service information to SLP DAs, and takes care of subsequent periodic refreshes.

On the other hand, the Importer module on his PDA detects the presence of the shopping center framework itself (i.e., the OSGi proxy case) or individual services on it (i.e., the actual service case) by sending SLP discovery requests to DAs. It downloads objects of discovered services, which may be followed by the services' installation and local registration on the framework. This local registration ensures faster discovery later on, but at the cost of the overhead of service information synchronization between the importing framework and SLP DAs.

Screenshots in Figure 3 are our Service Browser implementations for the case of local OSGi registration of individual services (Figure 1 (d)). The GUI displays nearby OSGi domains and services belonging to them. First, "My Space" in the figure represents the PDA OSGi framework. It also shows several store domains organized in a hierarchical fashion under "External Space." We can see that the store grocery section comprises vegetable and meat sections. The figure shows that the Importer on the PDA has fetched, installed, and registered "MeatInventory" service from the "meat02" space. On the bottom of the figure, detailed information on the selected service is being shown.

4.2 Comparison of Bridging Strategies

As illustrated in Figure 1 (a) through (d), we can think of four alternatives of OSGi proxy vs. individual services and SLP DA vs. OSGi registry for service registration. Which of the four will best fit a particular networking environment for inter-space service discovery? To answer this question, we compare each of them from the perspective of service traffic they incur. The service traffic is broken down into bootstrapping messages, discovery request and response messages, and refresh messages for synchronization between SLP DA and OSGi service registry. The bridging schemes are expected to have different compositions of those messages.

Table 2 compares the four cases from the perspective of service traffic. The second and third columns correspond to the SLP DA registrations of OSGi proxy and real services (Figure 1 (a) and (b)), while the fourth and fifth represent the cases in which the proxy and actual services are prefetched and cached in a local OSGi registry (Figure 1 (c) and (d)). We assume that there are o OSGi frameworks and d SLP DAs within discovery range in the network. s is the average number of services registered with each OSGi framework, while s_a indicates the total number of DA-registered services from neighboring OSGi frameworks. Assuming that all services are exported, we know that s_a becomes equal to $s \times o$. In addition, m indicates the number of multicast messages which are sent to discover SLP DAs for the first time. Then table shows service discovery traffic, when the query is looking for any service.

As to service discovery traffic, the case of SLP DA and OSGi proxy needs $d+o \times d$ messages used to contact d SLP DAs and to get back o proxies for OSGi domains. Then, it needs $o+s \times o$ messages to make discovery request calls on each proxy and to receive results from the remote OSGi frameworks. In the case of SLP DA and direct service registration, we will need $d+s_a \times d$ traffic to retrieve service information from d SLP DAs. For the OSGi registry and OSGi proxy case, it will require $o+s \times o$ traffic for service information retrieval from remote OSGi domains through remote discovery requests on proxy objects in the local OSGi framework. Finally, for the case of direction registration of individual services with local OSGi frameworks, no discovery message is necessary, since all we need is to look up the local OSGi registries.

Table 2. Service Traffic of Bridging Alternatives

	SLP DA		OSGi Registry	
	OSGi Proxy	Individual Services	OSGi Proxy	Individual Services
Entry in SLP DA	Presence of neighboring OSGi framework	Service instance	Presence of neighboring OSGi framework	Service instance
Entry in OSGi Registry	None	None	Presence of neighboring OSGi framework	Service instance
Discovery traffic	(d+o×d) + (o+s×o)	$d+s_a \times d$	o+s×o	0
SLPBridge bootstrapping traffic	m+d+d	m+d+d×s	(m+d+d) + (d+o×d)	(m+d+d×s) + $(d+s_a \times d)$
Synchronization traffic	d	d×s	d+o	$d \times s+s_a$

SLPBridge bootstrapping traffic consists of messages to export local services and to import remote services, when the SLPBridge starts out. For example, the SLP DA and OSGi proxy case needs $m+d$ messages to discover SLP DAs using multicast messages and d messages to advertise itself to d SLP domains. Note that there is no import traffic, since the discovery is performed only on an on-demand basis. On the opposite side is the case of direct registration of individual services with OSGi frameworks which consumes $(m+d+d\times s)$ + $(d+s_a\times d)$ traffic; the exporter needs $m+d$ messages for DA discovery, which is followed by $d\times s$ export messages containing service information. In addition, the importer will need to contact d SLP DAs to get back $s_a\times d$ messages. Finally, synchronization traffic is made up of refresh messages between the local OSGi framework and SLP DAs and those of the other side (i.e., SLP DAs and remote OSGi frameworks.) In the case of SLP DA and individual services, the synchronization will require no traffic on the local OSGi framework side (because service information is not cached on this side) and $d\times s$ traffic on the remote side. The OSGi registration of OSGi proxy will need o and d messages for each side.

As we can see in the table, OSGi proxy cases require less overhead traffic for SLPBridge bootstrapping and subsequent synchronization, but at the higher discovery cost in terms of network traffic and discovery latency. Another disadvantage is that, by having to invoke additional remote lookup requests after a local proxy lookup, users should handle the two cases in a different way by themselves.

Next, let us compare the cases of SLP DA registration of discovered services vs. local OSGi registry registration. As expected, the SLP DA cases have to pay higher cost for service discovery (i.e., more traffic and longer query latency) compared to their counterparts of the local registration. But they are opposite in position when we consider SLPBridge bootstrapping overhead and synchronization traffic.

5 Concluding Remarks

Although OSGi has recently proven quite successful as a service framework, it is mostly concerned about fostering service collaboration and interoperability in a single space. We argue that it should be extended to be able to support a new need of cross-space service discovery and interaction. This is because we expect in the near future that distributed collaboration over a wider area spanning multiple spaces will be imperative, as more spaces turns intelligent. Our approach to the space integration problem is to utilize SLP as a means to bridge isolated OSGi islands together. Although the technical solidity, effectiveness, and feasibility of the approach have been evaluated through a prototyping and performance evaluation study, we can think of further enhancements as discussed below.

Keeping OSGi and SLP domains synchronized requires that the Importer check back with DAs, when individual services' lifetime is about to expire. In addition to this lifetime-based checking of cached services, it has to periodically ask the DAs about other changes such as a new service arrival. Our current implementation relies on this polling scheme. However, it might be better to switch over to a push mechanism for medium size networks or larger by which the Importer is notified of changes within SLP domains. We note that SLP standard readily supports this eventing feature [19].

From SLP standpoint, our Exporter and Importer modules are service providers (SAs) and clients (UAs). Up to this point when we present our approach, we have assumed the presence of SLP DAs which caches services in the local network. But SLP actually allows two operation modes: directory-based and directory-less [17]. Without a directory node (DAs) in between them, which is not unusual in a small network, service providers and clients rely on multicasts for service advertisements and discovery. Support for this directory-less mode can be added to our architecture without affecting the rest of it.

As briefly discussed, our architecture partially supports the notion of a space hierarchy. Spaces can be interconnected in a hierarchical fashion, mirroring the containment relationship in the physical world. Our current implementation may be enhanced in such a way that the hierarchy is exploited to resolve user service requests. By default, services from the current space may be preferably returned in response to client discovery requests. Alternatively, the clients may specify additional constraints, e.g., which part of the hierarchy the search should be restricted to and how far the query can travel beyond the space boundary. This enhancement of query specification and resolution in regard to space hierarchy is being left for our future work.

References

1. Kindberg, T., Fox, A.: System Software for Ubiquitous Computing. IEEE Pervasive Computing 1(1), 70–81 (2002)
2. Marples, D., Kriens, P.: The Open Services Gateway Initiative: An Introductory Overview. IEEE Communications Magazines 39(12), 110–114 (2001)
3. Lee, C., Nordstedt, D., Helal, S.: Enabling Smart Spaces with OSGi. IEEE Pervasive Computing 2(3), 89–94 (2003)
4. Gu, T., Pung, H.K., Zhang, D.Q.: Toward an OSGi-Based Infrastructure for Context-Aware Applications. IEEE Pervasive Computing 3(4), 66–74 (2004)
5. Valtchev, D., Frankov, I.: Service Gateway Architecture for a Smart Home. IEEE Communications Magazines 40(4), 126–132 (2002)

6. Czerwinski, S.E., Zhao, B.Y., Hodes, T.D., Joseph, A.D., Katz, R.H.: An Architecture for a Secure Service Discovery Service. In: Proceedings of the 5th Annual ACM/IEEE International Conference on Mobile Computing and Networks (MobiCom'99), IEEE Computer Society Press, Los Alamitos (1999)
7. Jose, R., Vavies, N.: Scalable and Flexible Location-Based Service for Ubiquitous Information Access. In: Proceedings of the 1st International Symposium on Handheld and Ubiquitous Computing (HUC'99) (1999)
8. Rosenberg, J., Schulzrinne, H., Suter, B.: Wide Area Network Service Location. IETF Internet Draft (1997), http://www.globecom.net/ietf/draft/draft-ietf-svrloc-wasrv-01.html
9. Adjie-Winoto, W., Schwartz, E., Balakrishnan, H., Lilley, J.: The Design and Implementation of an Intentioinal Naming System. In: Proceedings of the 17th SCM Symposium on Operating Systems Principles (SOSP) (1999)
10. Balazinska, M., Balakrishnan, H., Karger, D.: INS/Twine: A Scalable Peer-to-Peer Architecture for Intentional Resource Discovery. In: Proceedings of the 1st International Conference on Pervasive Computing (Pervasive'02) (2002)
11. Stoica, I., Morris, R., Karger, D., Kaashoek, M.F., Balakrishnan, H.: Chord: A Scalable Peer-to-peer Lookup Service for Internet Applications. In: Proceedings of the Annual Conference of the Special Interest Group on Data Communication (SIGCOMM 2001) (2001)
12. flowSGi Project, http://flowsgi.inf.ethz.ch
13. Dobrev, P., Famolari, D., Kurzke, C., Miller, B.A.: Device and Service Discovery in Home Networks with OSGi. IEEE Communications Magazine 40(8), 86–92 (2002)
14. The OSGi Alliances: OSGi Service Platform Release 4 (2006)
15. Lee, S., Lee, J.: OSGi Service Mobility Management for Pervasive Computing Environments. In: Proceedings of the 24th IASTED International Conference on Internet and Multimedia Systems and Applications (2006)
16. Knopflerfish - Open Source OSGi http://www.knopflerfish.org
17. Guttman, E., Perkins, C., Veizades, J., Day, M.: Service Location Protocol, Version 2. IETF RFC 2608 (1999)
18. OpenSLP Project, http://www.openslp.org
19. Kempf, J., Goldschmidt, J.: Notification and Subscription for SLP. IETF RFC 3082 (2001)

Selective Grid Access for Energy-Aware Mobile Computing*

Eunjeong Park[1], Heonshik Shin[2], and Seung Jo Kim[3]

[1] BK21 School for Creative Engineering Design of Next Generation Mechanical and Aerospace Systems
ejpark@cslab.snu.ac.kr
[2] School of Computer Science and Engineering
shinhs@cslab.snu.ac.kr
[3] School of Mechanical and Aerospace Engineering,
Seoul National University
sjkim@snu.ac.kr

Abstract. Conservation of battery power is one of the main issues in mobile computing. In this paper, we propose to exploit a grid infrastructure to extend the battery life of mobile devices based on the contexts of mobile applications, devices, and grid systems. In doing so, we present a framework, called SGA (selective grid access), to optimally utilize the limited resources of mobile devices and grids. SGA aims to reconfigure the placement of mobile applications on either the mobile device or grid nodes and to adjust QoS level according to the current context of the residual energy and the resource availability of the grids. Simulation-based experiments show that as the number of applications increases, the SGA-based scheme greatly reduces the energy consumption and response time in comparison with the traditional proxy-based approach.

1 Introduction

Grid computing is used for computationally intensive applications and large problem solving. In this paper, we propose a new way to use a grid infrastructure of fixed hosts as a means of extending the battery life of mobile devices through dynamic software reconfiguration.Our approach is based on an adaptive algorithm that reconfigures mobile applications between the mobile device and grid nodes and adjusts the QoS (quality of service) level to suit the residual energy of the mobile device and the resource availability on the grid. The proposed algorithm uses the context of the mobile applications, the mobile device, and the grid to calculate profit and loss when determining how to use the grid infrastructure. We have developed SGA (selective grid access) middleware, which aims (a) to reduce the energy consumption of the mobile device by utilizing the grid infrastructure; (b) to control the balance between grid access and on-device execution by adapting to changes in the context; (c) to balance the load on the grid so as not to exhaust the available resources; and (d) to adjust the QoS of the applications.

* This work was supported by the Brain Korea 21 Project in 2007.

J. Indulska et al. (Eds.): UIC 2007, LNCS 4611, pp. 798–807, 2007.

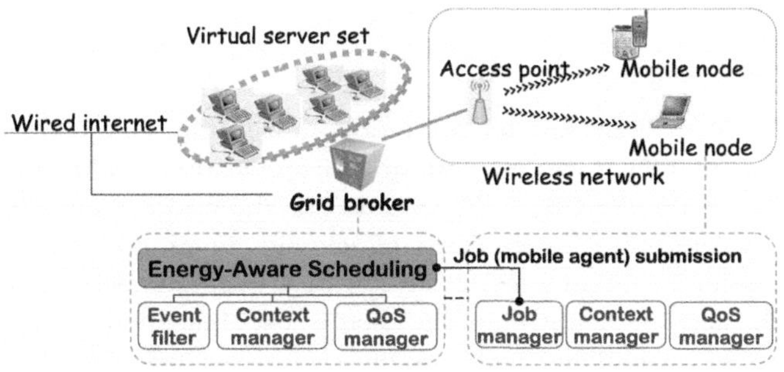

Fig. 1. The SGA (selective grid access) environment

2 Grid Services for Mobile Computing

Most approaches to intermittent connection use ***queueing*** and ***autonomous actions***. Queueing overcomes intermittent network failure by storing temporary copies of processes and data in the queueing server of grid systems. It has various incarnations, such as a SOAP router, a mobile queueing server or keep-alive server [2,13,16]. Stalled processes have to be completed when reconnection occurs, and this involves autonomous behavior by mobile agents. A mobile agent is a software component that has the ability to move from one host to another while preserving its state. Mobile agents have been used within mobile computing environments to achieve adaptation, service customization, autonomy, fault tolerance and load balancing [1]. Recent research shows that the integration of mobile agent technology into grid services is an effective antidote to the inflexibility of current grid services (e.g. OGSI) which are designed to support synchronous, permanently connected networks [18].

Despite the continual growth of system resources in notebooks and PDAs, the short battery time of mobile devices restricts the amount of computation which they can perform. As a result, there have been several efforts to combine grid computing and mobile devices to save power in the mobiles [4]. [14,19] have addressed the problem of selecting components for migration with the aim of minimizing local energy consumption and computational load. These approaches concentrate either on the migration technique itself, or on migration plans for minimizing one mobile resource constraint. None of them support code migration to multiple servers or consider the resource constraints on the servers themselves. In our previous work, we have proposed a power-aware scheduling policy that dynamically adapts to the context of mobile devices [5], supported by the directory service of a grid system with multiple servers. Fig. 2 shows an example specification of a mobile device for power-aware process scheduling. In this paper, we will focus on system resource management and energy-aware scheduling of SGA middleware, while leaving aside other issues such as authentication and authorization.

3 SGA System Model for Energy-Aware Reconfiguration

3.1 Context in Energy-Aware SGA

To minimize the energy consumption of a mobile device, the SGA reconfiguration algorithm decides whether the use of the grid for each application would reduce energy cost compared to on-device execution. We assume that the grid has heterogeneous nodes with different system performance rates and network conditions. This means that the energy consumption of the mobile device can vary with the response time of the application and the network bandwidth. The energy cost of an application, which is composed of the cost of computation and communication, is calculated in the context of the mobile device, the application, and each grid node shown in Table 1.

```
<Service>
 <Node-Context>
        <Network-Context>
                <Wireless-Bandwidth> 802.11b </Wireless-Bandwidth>
                <Disconnection-Rate> 0.1 </Disconnection-Rate>
        </Network-Context>
        <Device-Context>
                <CPU> 1166 MTOPS        </CPU>
                <Available-Memory> 100MB </Available-Memory>
                <Residual-Battery> 30% </Residual-Battery>
        </Device-Context>
        ...
 </Node-Context>
</Service>
```

Fig. 2. Example context specification of a mobile node

Definition 1. Let the mobile device k contain the application set $A = \{a_1, a_2, \ldots, a_{|A|}\}$ and let the grid correspond to the virtual server set $S = \{S_1, S_2, \ldots, S_{|S|}\}$. The total energy consumption of the mobile device is defined as $E_k = \sum_{i=1}^{|A|} energy\_cost_{i,p(i)}$, where $p(i) \in \{\{k(on\text{-}device)\} \bigcap S\}$ and $energy\_cost_{i,p(i)}$ is the energy consumption in device k, that is incurred when application a_i is executed on server $S_{p(i)}$ or on device k.

Each term $energy\_cost_{i,p(i)}$ is the sum of the costs of computation ($energy\_cost_{i,p(i)}^{comp}$) and communication ($energy\_cost_{i,p(i)}^{comm}$). When application a_i is executed on mobile device, $energy\_cost_{i,p(i)}$ is composed of $P_i^{comp} \times T_i$ for computation and $\frac{Size_i^{tx}}{DR_{k,up}} \times P_{k,up} + \frac{Size_i^{rx}}{DR_{k,down}} \times P_{k,down}$ for communication, where T_i is the duration of execution. On the other hand, when a_i is migrated to a grid node $S_{p(i)}$, the incurred energy cost in mobile device is calculated as $P_i^{stub} \times T_i$ for computation and $\frac{Size\_st_i^{tx}}{DR_{k,up}} \times P_{k,up} + \frac{Size\_st_i^{rx}}{DR_{k,down}} \times P_{k,down}$ for communication. P_i^{stub} is power rate for a stub which is executed on the mobile device in place of application a_i, in order to manage the related information and communication.

Definition 2. Let the mobile device k have the resource constraint $Limit_{k,on-device} = w_o \times R_k$. The workload function $W_{k,on-device} = \sum_{i:p(i)=on-device} workload_{k,i,p(i)}$, in which

Table 1. Notation for the description of a context in SGA

Context in mobile application a_i

QoS (quality of service)	$q = FL_i$	Power rate for computation	P_i^{comp}
Power rate for stub	P_i^{stub}	Size of computation	$Size_i^{comp}$
Size of data communication (transmit, receive)	$Size_i^{tx}$, $Size_i^{rx}$	Size of stub communication (transmit, receive)	$Size\_st_i^{tx}$, $Size\_st_i^{rx}$

Context in mobile device k

Residual energy	R_k	Location	L_k
Available memory	AM_k	Available CPU	AC_k
Network bandwidth (uplink, downlink)	$DR_{k,up}$, $DR_{k,down}$	Power rate for communication (uplink, downlink)	$P_{k,up}$, $P_{k,down}$
Disconnection rate	λ_k		

Context in grid node S_j

Number of clients	NC_j	Network bandwidth	DR_j
Available memory	AM_j	Available CPU	AC_j

$workload_{k,i,on-device}$ is then defined as the amount of data traffic or computation incurred when application a_i is executed on mobile device k.

The constraint $Limit_{k,on-device}$ reflects the resource available to mobile device k, in particular, the residual energy R_k and the weighting factor w_0, which controls the desirability of migration to be associated with that residual energy. Additional system resources, such as available memory and CPU, with their own weighting factors, can be included to extend the formulation of $Limit_{k,on-device}$.

Definition 3. Let each host S_j in the grid has the resource quotient $Limit_{k,j} = w_1 \times AM_j/NC_j + w_2 \times AC_j/NC_j$ for mobile device k. We define a workload function $W_{k,j} = \sum_{i:p(i)=j} workload_{k,i,p(i)}$, in which $workload_{k,i,j}$ is the amount of data traffic or computation imposed on node $S_j \in S$ by application a_i.

The constraint $Limit_{k,j}$ reflects the resource availability of S_j for the mobile device k, which consists of available memory and CPU. We assume that NC_j clients share system resource of S_j equally and the residual energy of S_j is not in the consideration since the fixed node is supplied by wall power.

3.2 The Scheduling Problem Description

To reduce the energy consumption of the mobile device, the SGA scheduling policy needs to decide whether an application should be executed on the mobile device ormigrated to a grid node. If migration is chosen, then the algorithm needs to determine which node on the grid should execute the application. We construct this scheduling problem as a network model.

Definition 4. A SGA network of a mobile device k is described by a weighted directed graph $G = (V,E)$, where $V = \{A \bigcap \{on-device\} \bigcap S\}$, and E represents the set of edges (a_i, S_j) and $(a_i, on-device)$ where $1 \leq i \leq |A|$ and $1 \leq j \leq |S|$. Each edge has a weighting factor $(energy\_cost_{i,j}, workload_{i,j})$ or $(energy\_cost_{i,on-device}, workload_{i,on-device})$.

Definition 5. A SGA flow of a mobile device k is defined as $<A,P>$ where P is a set of edges $p(i)$ of each a_i, which represents total energy consumption E_k to be minimized, and the constraints $W_{k,on-device} \leq Limit_{k,on-device}$ and $W_{k,j} \leq Limit_{k,j}$ hold, for where $1 \leq i \leq |A|$ and $1 \leq j \leq |S|$.

If the energy cost of migrating an application is lower than that of on-device execution, the application is offloaded to the grid node with the minimum energy cost. As the residual resource of the mobile device decreases, more applications need to be delegated to grid nodes to save mobile resources. Therefore, the reconfiguration algorithm uses an admission control technique that controls the extent of on-device execution according to the residual resources of the mobile device. More formally, the reconfiguration algorithm schedules applications on the mobile device k with the constraint $W_{k,on-device} \leq Limit_{k,on-device}$.

The extent of reconfiguration is also constrained by the availability of grid resources. Each grid node monitors the consequences of varying the proportion of its resources allocated to applications transferred from each mobile device. If accelerated migrations, due to the decreasing battery power of k, exhaust the resource of a grid node, the algorithm must divert the data traffic to other grid nodes. Accordingly, migrations to each grid node are constrained by the inequality, $W_{k,j} \leq Limit_{k,j}$.

Theorem 1. SGA flow search is NR-hard.

Proof. Energy consumption and workload are the factors that affect migration. To formulate the SGA flow analytically we use these factors to generate a generalized assignment problem in the optimization model with the goal of minimizing a given objective function. More formally, the problem is to

$$\text{Minimize} \sum_{i \in I} \sum_{j \in J} c_{ij} x_{ij} \tag{1}$$

$$\text{subject to} \quad \sum_{i \in I} a_{ij} x_{ij} \leq d_j \quad \text{for all } j \in J, \tag{2}$$

where $\sum_{j \in J} x_{ij} = 1$ for all $i \in I$, and $x_{ij} \geq 0$ for all (i,j) in the adjacency matrix of bipartite graph G with vertex set I and J. We model our objectives as a generalized assignment problem by formulating the energy consumption and workload using Equations (1) and (2) respectively. The value of x_{ij} is 1 if application a_i is scheduled on grid node S_j, where c_{ij} and a_{ij} in (1) and (2) correspond to the energy consumption and workload of that application, and d_j in (2) is the $Limit_{k,j}$. Thus, SGA flow search is identical to the generalized assignment problem, which is known to be NP-hard [6,11]. Consequently, SGA flow search is also NP-hard.

3.3 Enhancement Techniques

We have developed other enhancement techniques for low battery of mobile device and severe contention in grid systems. Since SGA flow search is NP-hard problem, SGA utilizes an approximation algorithm which only guarantees a workload several times the actual limit. We introduce the optional tightening phase for the concrete $Limit_{k,j}$ by relocating applications into less allocated nodes.

QoS control is another technique for the enhancement of SGA flow search. [9,12] analyzed the resource availability resulting from video compression, limited window size and quality-aware transcoding. In addition, recent research [15] addressed that quality of applications affects energy consumption in mobile devices.We embed QoS control in SGA reconfiguration which determines when to trigger QoS control and selects applications for adjusting P_i^{comp}, P_i^{stub}, $Size_i^{comp}$ and $Size_i^{comm}$.

4 SGA Reconfiguration Algorithm

For a SGA network, as described in the previous section, energy-aware reconfiguration involves a scheduling algorithm and the triggering of QoS control, as shown in Fig. 3.

Phase 1. We use an approximation algorithm to perform SGA flow search. Shmoys and Tardos [3] have formulated the best-known solution, which is $(O((|S|+1)|A|^2 log(|A|))$, and Jansen and Porkolab [10] have proposed an algorithm with $O(|A|)$ run-time on a small and fixed number of grid nodes.

Phase 2. Either of these approximation algorithms only guarantees a workload several times the actual data limit, so we use greedy heuristics to tighten the bounds on $Limit_{k,j}$ and $Limit_{k,on-device}$. After initial assignment, each application running on the set of

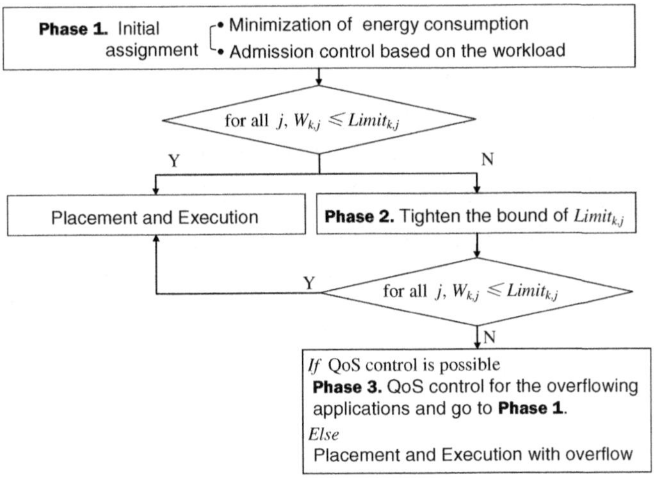

Fig. 3. Diagram of energy-aware reconfiguration using SGA

nodes which have excessive workload is relocated on to a node with spare capacity. Relocation takes account of the required energy consumption of the mobile device and also of the reduced data traffic to the node. Although this phase increases the precision of the workload limit, an additional overhead with $O(|A|(|S|+1)^2)$ is incurred. We suggest that this phase should be optional, and only used when the overflow of data traffic to a specific grid node causes a severe problem.

Phase 3. After applying the generalized assignment algorithm of Phase 1 and the bound-tightening of Phase 2, the workload on some mobile devices may still exceed $Limit_{k,j}$. In this case, QoS control is triggered to reduce the workload represented by the relevant mobile applications. QoS control can be achieved by changing algorithms, as well as by varying control prarameters. Encoding and decoding may be performed at different rates, the quality of compression schemes can be relaxed, and the resolution of image processing can be reduced. The choice of application to be degraded is made in a similar way to the process of Phase 2, by balancing the reduction of energy consumption against the satisfaction of users.

5 Performance Evaluation

We evaluated the proposed scheme using SGA simulator developed for power-aware mobile computing (Fig. 4). It consists of a mobile agent, networking support, a battery model, and a system resource model of CPU and memory. The simulator is based on the *ns-2* network simulator [17], Aglet from IBM [7], and the performance value of a CPU by Intel [8]. The system and battery models that we used were taken from real devices [8,19], and are characterized in Table 2. The number of mobile devices is set to 3, and the mobile applications can utilize only 30% of the memory in the grid nodes for migration.

Fig. 5 shows the result of SGA arrangement with two types of applications. Both are computation-intensive applications such as image processing applications and mpeg players with different ratio of workload on computation and communication. SGA leaves each application on the mobile device or delegates it to a grid node according to the current context of systems and profile of the application. In the case of 30 applications in Fig. 5(a), Node1 and Node2, which are faster than Node3 and Node4, have sufficient resources for all the migrated applications.

Fig. 6 shows the benefit of using a grid system with 4 nodes, in terms of energy consumption, compared with migration on to a single proxy server. We assumed that the proxy server has resources twice as large as those of Node1 in the grid. As shown in the figure, the energy consumption is initially less with a proxy server, because the single proxy server concentrates exclusively on the minimization of energy consumption, whereas SGA algorithm predicts the overflow in Node1 and Node2, and diverts the applications to Node3 and Node4. The initial disparity is caused by the high performance of the proxy server and a difference between the predicted values of $Limit_{k,j}$ and the real threshold values of overflow on to the grid nodes, at which the performance of application decreases by severe contention. However, use of the grid saves more energy than migration to a single proxy as migration continues. Subsequently, SGA reconfiguration outperforms the single proxy server in terms of battery life and scalability, as shown in Fig. 7 (a). Selective grid access and load balancing in grid nodes also enhances

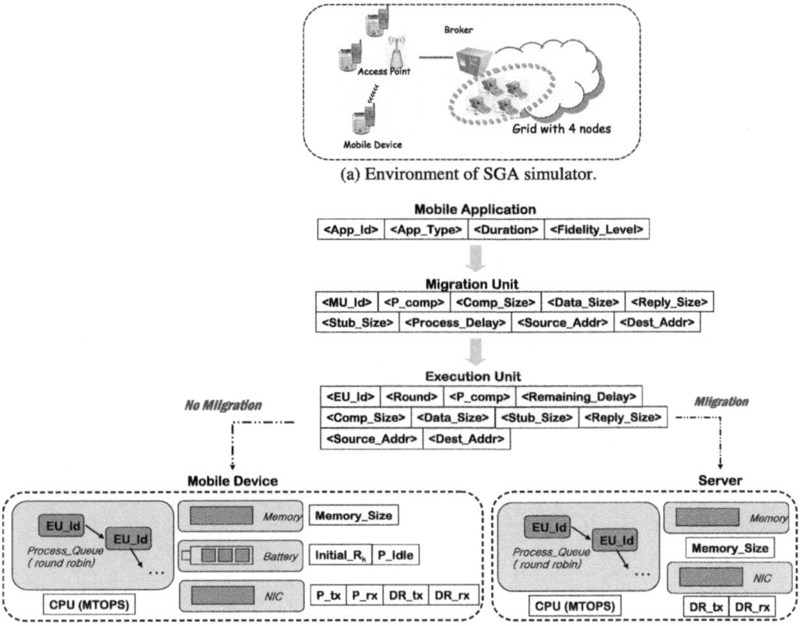

(a) Environment of SGA simulator.

(b) Process of SGA simulator.

Fig. 4. SGA simulator

Table 2. Experimental Parameters

System model

Type	System	CPU	MTOPS	Memory
Mobile Device	iPAQ 3650	Intel StrongArm 206MHz	1166	32MB
Node1	Itanium2	Intel Itanium2 1.3GHz	8450	4GB
Node2	Itanium2	Intel Itanium2 1.3GHz	8450	4GB
Node3	Itanium2	Intel Itanium2 2.4GHz	6400	1.5GB
Node4	Itanium2	Intel Itanium2 2.4GHz	6400	1.5GB

Battery model of a mobile device

(Avg. power rate for application *i* and mobile device *k*)

P_i^{comp}	P_i^{stub}	P_{idle}	$P_{k,up}$	$P_{k,down}$
2.15 Js	1.8 J/s	1.5 J/s	2.05 J/s	1.95 J/s

application performance with respect to the average response time, since it avoids severe contention in the faster nodes as shown in Fig. 7 (b).

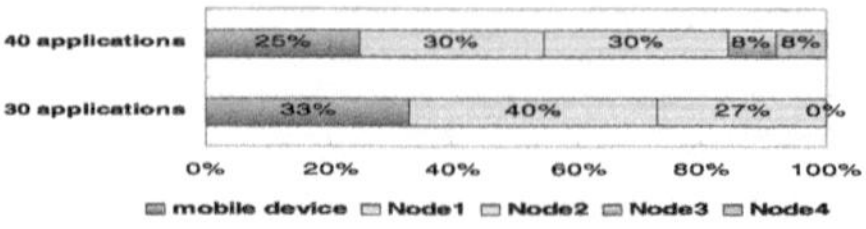

(a) Application1 (computation:communication = 2:1)

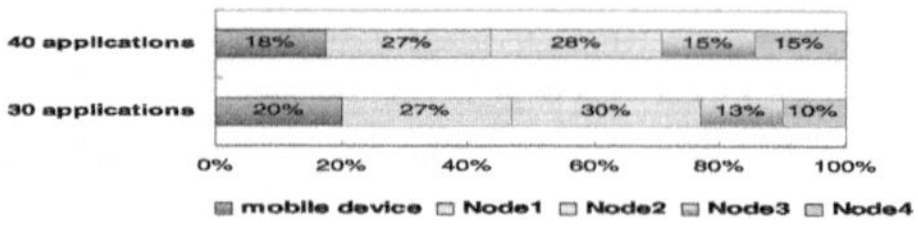

(b) Application2 (computation:communication = 4:1)

Fig. 5. Distribution of applications

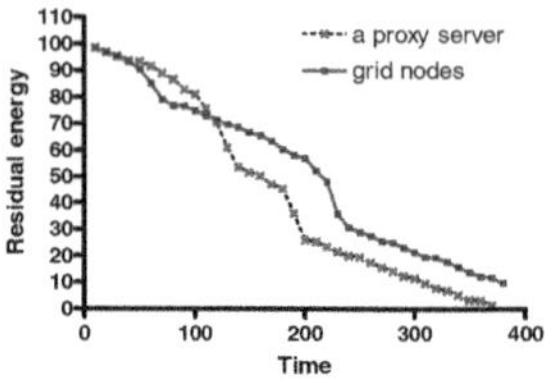

(a) Residual energy (40 applications)

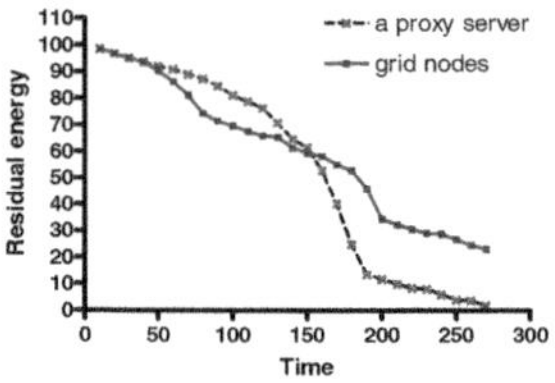

(b) Residual energy (50 applications)

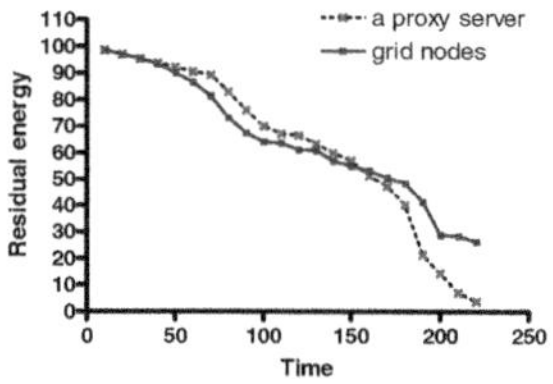

(c) Residual energy (60 applications)

Fig. 6. Performance evaluation : residual energy

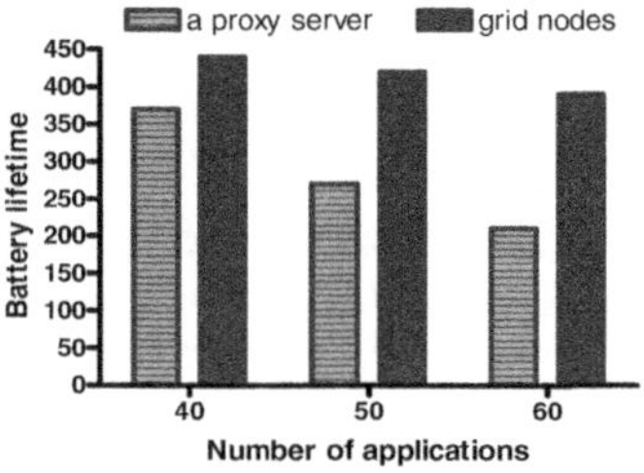

(a) Battery life

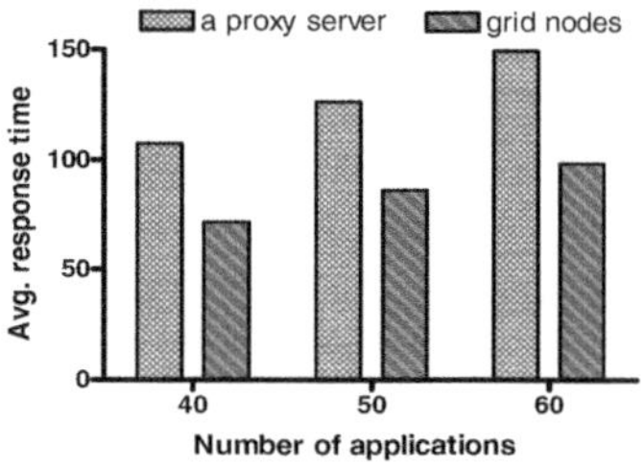

(b) Average response time

Fig. 7. Performance evaluation : battery life & average response time

6 Conclusions

We have shown how the selective grid access can be used to extend the battery life of mobile devices and to enhance the performance of mobile applications. By continuously monitoring the current context of the mobile devices, mobile applications, and grid nodes, SGA reconfiguration reduces energy consumption by migrating applications into an improved arrangement which reduces the energy cost. SGA reconfiguration not only reduces the energy consumption but also bounds the data traffic to specific nodes in grid. This combined optimization results in extended battery life of mobile devices and fast response time of applications. The algorithm also determines when QoS control of applications should be triggered not to conflict with the migration scheme. The cooperative and adaptive characteristics of SGA outperforms the use of single proxy server and absolute grid access.

References

1. Fuggetta, A., Picco, G.P., Vigna, G.: Understanding code mobility. IEEE Transactions on Software Engineering 24(5), 342–361 (1998)
2. Hampshire, A.: Extending the open grid services architecture to intermittently available wireless networks. In: Proceedings of UK eScience All Hands (2004)
3. Shmoys, D.B., Tardos, E.: An approximation algorithm for the generalized assignment problem. Mathematical Programming 62(3), 461–474 (1993)
4. Chu, D., Humphrey, M.: Mobile OGSI.NET: grid computing on mobile devices. In: Proceedings of the IEEE/ACM International Workshop on Grid Computing, pp. 182–191 (2004)
5. Park, E., Shin, H.: Software-migration policy for power-aware mobile computing under network resource constraints. In: Proceedings of the International Workshop on Mobility Aware Technology and Applications, pp. 25–29 (2004)
6. Ross, G.T., Soland, R.M.: A branch and bound algorithm for the generalized assignment problem. Mathematical Programming 8, 91–103 (1975)
7. IBM Tokyo: Research Lab, Aglets: mobile java agents, `http://www.trl.ibm.com/aglets`
8. Intel Corporation, Intel boxed processors (2004), `http://support.intel.com/support/processors/sb/CS-017346.htm`
9. Flinn, J., Satyanarayanan, M.: Energy-aware adaptation for mobile applications. In: Proceedings of the ACM Symposium on Operating Systems Principles, pp. 48–63 (1999)
10. Jansen, K., Porkolab, L.: Improved approximation schemes for scheduling unrelated parallel machines. In: Proceedings of the ACM Symposium on Theory of Computing , 408–417 (1999)
11. Ahuja, R.K., Magnanti, T.L., Orlin, J.B.: Network Flows. Prentice-Hall, Englewood Cliffs (1993)
12. Chandra, S., Gehani, A., Ellis, C.S., Vahdat, A.: Transcoding characteristics of web images. In: Proceedings of the Multimedia Computing and Networking, pp. 135–149 (2001)
13. Kurkovsky, S., Bhagyavati, Ray, A.: Modeling a grid-based problem-solving environment for mobile devices. Journal of Digital Information Management 2(2) (2004)
14. Mohapatra, S., Venkatasubramanian, N.: PARM: power aware reconfigurable middleware. In: Proceedings of the International Conference on Distributed Computer Systems, pp. 312–320 (2003)
15. Mohapatra, S., Cornea, R., Dutt, N., Nicolau, A., Venkatasubramanian, N.: Integrated power management for video streaming to mobile handheld devices. In: Proceedings of the ACM international conference on Multimedia, pp. 582–591 (2003)
16. Park, S., Ko, Y., Kim, J.: Disconnected operation service in mobile grid computing. In: Proceedings of the International Conference on Service Oriented Computing, pp. 499–513 (2003)
17. VINT Project: Network simulator ns-2, `http://www.isi.edu/nsnam/ns/index.html`
18. Zhang, W., Zhang, J., Ma, D., Wang, B., Chen, Y.: Key technique research on grid mobile service. In: Proceedings of the International Conference on Information Technology for Application, pp. 142–150 (2004)
19. Li, Z., Wang, C., Xu, R.: Task allocation for distributed multimedia processing on wirelessly networked handheld devices. In: Proceedings of the International Parallel and Distributed Processing Symposium, pp. 79–81 (2002)

Cognitive Computing Resource Management for a Ubiquitous Wireless Access*

Vuk Marojevic, Nemanja Vucevic, Xavier Revés, and Antoni Gelonch

Dept. of Signal Theory and Communications, Universitat Politècnica de Catalunya,
C/ Jordi Girona 1-3, Modul D4,
08034 Barcelona, Spain
{marojevic,vucevic,xavier.reves,antoni}@tsc.upc.edu

Abstract. In the near future many radio access technologies (RATs) will coexist to offer a vast variety of user services at different quality levels. Software-defined radio (SDR) facilitates to flexibly choose the RAT by means of a software-reconfiguration of the SDR terminal. Cognitive radio automates this process, being an ambient aware, intelligent radio resource management system. We extend its scope in that we introduce the cognitive computing resource management. Our cognitive radio system scans the computing environment, decides whether to reconfigure a candidate SDR mobile terminal or not, and learns from the effects of these decisions. The simulations, which model a simplified though realistic case study, show that two simple computing resource management algorithms outperform an algorithm that is unaware of the present computing environment. The paper concludes that a cognitive computing resource management is necessary for providing a ubiquitous wireless access where the user demands are satisfied as a function of the currently available computing resources of their terminals.

1 Introduction

Today's wireless communications can be described as a heterogeneous mix of radio access technologies (RATs). The emerging 3rd generation (3G) systems, for example, neither pretend to substitute the worldwide available access to 2nd generation (2G) services nor directly compete with wireless local area networks (WLANs). These RATs will rather coexist and complement each other: 2G systems offer worldwide roaming for carrying voice traffic and low-volume data. 3G systems will offer higher data rates for many different classes of multimedia services. WLANs locally offer very high data rates at lower cost. This view of cooperative rather than competitive networks facilitates the ubiquitous wireless access.

An intelligent (radio) resource management system is necessary to fully exploit the heterogeneous and dynamic wireless access networks of today and tomorrow. Such a system should observe the environment and react intelligently upon its changes. This

* This work has been supported by the DURSI of the Catalonian Government and the CYCIT (Spanish National Science Council) under grants TIC2003-08609 and TEC2006-09109, which is partially financed from the European Community through the FEDER program.

J. Indulska et al. (Eds.): UIC 2007, LNCS 4611, pp. 808–818, 2007.

idea is known as *cognitive radio* [1] [2]. Cognitive radio is an ambient aware system that automates the joint radio resource management (JRRM). JRRM refers to the coordination of the spectrum management of the different RATs that are accessible within a certain area.

The cognitive radio concept is an extension of software radio or software-defined radio (SDR) [3]–[5], which was coined in the early 90s. Software radio has led to a conceptual change in radio communications, from inflexible and hardware-centric to software-reconfigurable mobile terminals and network elements. In particular, the signal processing chains for radio communication of SDR platforms are to some extent defined in software and executed on programmable hardware. Then, a simple software switch can change the operational mode of an SDR platform to use a particular radio access technology for establishing a radio link between the communicating entities.

Future SDR platforms will contain some number of programmable processors, such as general-purpose processors (GPPs), digital signal processors (DSPs), or field-programmable gate arrays (FPGAs) [6]. An SDR mobile terminal will comprise a few, an SDR base station many of these processors to provide sufficient processing power for the execution of SDR applications. An SDR base station will execute many SDR applications in parallel, one for each user. Although this paper deals with SDR mobile terminals, the introduced concepts and conclusions can be directly applied to SDR base stations.

In future, the software-defined signal processing chains for many RATs will be available on servers. It is not envisaged that more than one RAT-specific signal processing chain, the active one, will be locally available on an SDR mobile terminal, because of its memory constraints and the steady evolution of RATs. Therefore, before the reconfiguration of an SDR mobile terminal, the new RAT-software is downloaded form the network using a radio link (over the air, or OTA, download) [7].

We consider software radio as an application of general-purpose computing, where the software, or application, defines the hardware functionality: An SDR application represents the signal processing chain that defines the radio functionality of an SDR platform. Hence, software-defined radio is not only about radio but also about computing [8].

In this paper we extend this vision of computing resource management to cognitive radio systems. Our cognitive radio system analyzes the computing environment and takes intelligent decisions from its observations and the accumulated knowledge (section 2). We simulate a real-world scenario to demonstrate the importance of cognitive computing resource management for a ubiquitous wireless access (sections 3–5).

2 Cognitive Computing Resource Management

Cognitive radio, introduced in the late 90s, is an ambient aware system that reacts upon changes in the radio environment. It incorporates a learning mechanism and is, thus, an intelligent system that pretends to optimize the usage of radio resources [9].

We already argued for the importance of computing resource management in software-defined radio [8]. In this paper we correspondingly extend the scope of cognitive radio introducing the *cognitive computing cycle*, which observes and intelligently manages the computing resources of SDR platforms. Some arguments for this extension are the expected commercialization of software-defined radio and the vast variety of SDR platforms.

Fig. 1 shows the cognitive computing cycle. It continuously scans the computing environment and provides any changes to the computing resource management (CRM) entity, which decides upon an appropriate action. The CRM entity is the brain of the system; it reacts upon its inputs and its current knowledge. This knowledge is accumulated during the learning process of the CRM algorithm, which observes the effects of its decisions (*learning-by-observing*). Hence, the cognitive computing cycles has to run continuously.

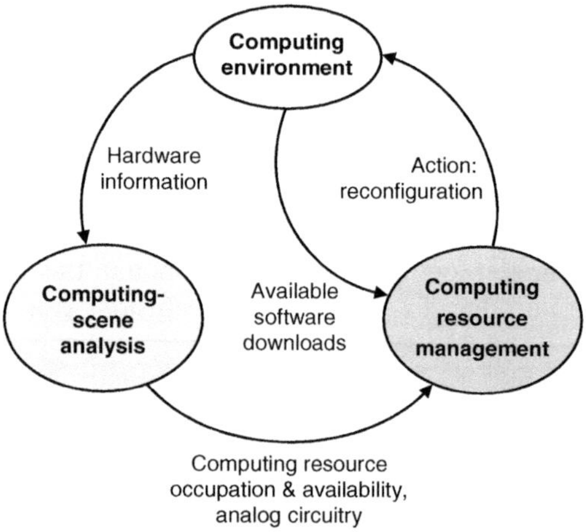

Fig. 1. The cognitive computing cycle

Let us consider a simple example: In a certain area two radio access technologies, RAT *A* and RAT *B*, are supported. If the radio resources of RAT *A* are overused, while those of RAT *B* are not (radio scene analysis, see [9]) and if the network infrastructure, including software downloads, and mobile terminals facilitate a switch to RAT *B* (computing scene analysis, see Fig. 1), the action could be to reconfigure some mobile terminals to access RAT *B*. This paper argues that such a scenario requires a cognitive computing resource management that should be able to initiate the reconfiguration of the appropriate SDR mobile terminals.

The computing resources of emerging SDR platforms are and will be limited. Even though the computing power may once grow faster than its requirement, related issues, such as energy consumption, will not become obsolete even in the far future of radio communications. It is therefore necessary to optimize the usage of SDR computing resources to facilitate an anytime, anywhere, and anyhow wireless access. In particular, we expect that many cognitive computing cycles will be globally distributed and coordinated to intelligently use the available computing resources of SDR platforms and, thus, provide a ubiquitous wireless access where the user is unaware of the RAT that satisfies its service demand.

The computing cycle of Fig. 1, which addresses the intelligent reconfiguration of SDR mobile terminals, can be easily extended to aid the reconfiguration of SDR network elements as well. Although network elements are less critical in terms of computing power, their intelligent management can greatly reduce power consumption and, thus, reduce the operational costs. The rest of the paper does not study these aspects but rather pretends to demonstrate the need for a cognitive computing resources management in future wireless communications. Therefore, we consider a typical case study and evaluate three simple CRM algorithms or policies. Without loss of generality, we focus on the cognitive management of SDR mobile terminals.

3 Case Study

The spectrum scanning at a certain time and area with 2G and 3G coverage shows that the number of GPRS (general packet radio service) sessions is elevated. Some of these terminals should be reconfigured to operate in another mode to increase the network capacity and, thus, potentially satisfy more users. We assume that the UMTS (universal mobile telecommunications system) radio resources are underused and that the necessary infrastructure is available. A reconfiguration of some of the SDR-GPRS terminals to access the UMTS RAT would balance the traffic load between the two standards so that penetrating 2G mobile terminals, as opposed to SDR mobile terminals, could still initiate their GPRS sessions.

This case study considers 15 000 SDR-GPRS mobile terminals of different architectures and computing loads. The objective is to reconfigure any SDR-GPRS mobile terminal that provides the necessary computing capacity for executing the SDR-UMTS signal processing chain instead of the SDR-GPRS application. We assume that additional, non-RAT-specific applications may concurrently run on an SDR mobile terminal. Hence, part of a platform's computing resources may momentarily not be available for the SDR-UMTS application.

The CRM algorithms, which we describe in continuation, evaluate the reconfiguration of each SDR mobile terminal separately, that is one by one; they either initiate the reconfiguration of a particular terminal or not.

3.1 Computing Resource Management Algorithms

Baseline Algorithm (Alg_0). Algorithm 0 is not aware of the SDR mobile terminals' computing capabilities and, thus, initiates the reconfiguration of any candidate SDR terminal. A terminal that does not have sufficient computing capacity to execute the SDR-UMTS signal processing chain fails in applying the requested reconfiguration and, consequently, loses its currently running session. The system chooses the 384 kbps UMTS realization because it offers the best quality of service.

CRM Algorithm 1 (Alg_1). Algorithm 1 uses the supplied hardware information. It reconfigures mobile terminals as a function their hardware capacities and the available reconfiguration information. This information is successively accumulated during the learning process: If a mobile terminal loses its session due to an unsuccessful reconfiguration (*infeasible mapping*, which means that the system's computing or timing requirements are not met), terminals of these characteristics are not considered again for reconfiguration.

The system, furthermore, dynamically chooses the particular UMTS realization as a function of a terminal's processing capacity; it selects the UMTS realization as a function of the terminal's total processing capacity P_T:

- 384 kbps UMTS if $P_T \geq T_{384}$,
- 128 kbps UMTS if $T_{128} \leq P_T < T_{384}$,
- 64 kbps UMTS if $T_{64} \leq P_T < T_{128}$,
- no reconfiguration if $P_T < T_{64}$.

Later we specify the values of the thresholds T_{384}, T_{128}, T_{64}.

Some services may not be maintained at the same quality when implementing a 64 kbps or a 128 kbps instead of a 384 kbps UMTS receiver. Here we assume that the users are willing to accept a possible quality degradation for the sake of a ubiquitous wireless access. Typically, a user prefers a lower QoS than no service at all.

CRM Algorithm 2 (Alg_2). Algorithm 2 is an extension of Algorithm 1. Initially, the same three thresholds are defined. The learning process is, though, slightly different: If a reconfiguration to the 384 kbps (128 kbps) realization has failed, the next terminal of the same characteristics is considered for reconfiguration to 128 kbps (64 kbps) UMTS. Unfeasibly mapping the 64 kbps UMTS processing chain means that this kind of terminal will not be considered for reconfiguration again.

3.2 SDR Platforms

Fig. 2 shows 3 SDR mobile terminal types. Fig. 2a illustrates a full-duplex architecture, where all three processors $\mathbf{P_1}$, $\mathbf{P_2}$, and $\mathbf{P_3}$ are interconnected by dedicated communication lines. The half-duplex architecture of platform II permits a more flexible bandwidth assignment between any two processors. Finally, the bus system of Fig. 2c permits a flexible assignment of the platform's bus bandwidth. The application mapping process (subsection 3.4) implicitly handles the necessary bus scheduling in case of architectures II and III.

These platform types represent a small, though representative, excerpt of the numerous possible SDR mobile terminal architectures. P in Mops (million operations per second) and B in Mbps (mega-bits per second) define a platform's processing and bandwidth capacities after the projected deallocation of the SDR-GPRS transceiver functions. Each terminal's computing capacity then consists of the total processing capacity $P_T = 3 \cdot P$ and the total bandwidth $B_T = 6 \cdot B$.

This case study addresses 5000 SDR mobile terminals of each type. Their computing capacities are randomly obtained, where P and B are uniformly distributed in [2700, 2750, …, 4200] and [200, 250…, 1500]. This way we simulate SDR platforms of different architectures and computing loads.

We assume that the 15 000 SDR-GPRS platforms contain the analog RF circuitry that is necessary to operate in UMTS mode. We address the digital signal processing part at the physical layer of an UMTS downlink receiver (see next subsection) and presume that additional computing resources for implementing the higher protocol layers and the UMTS uplink transmitter are sufficiently available.

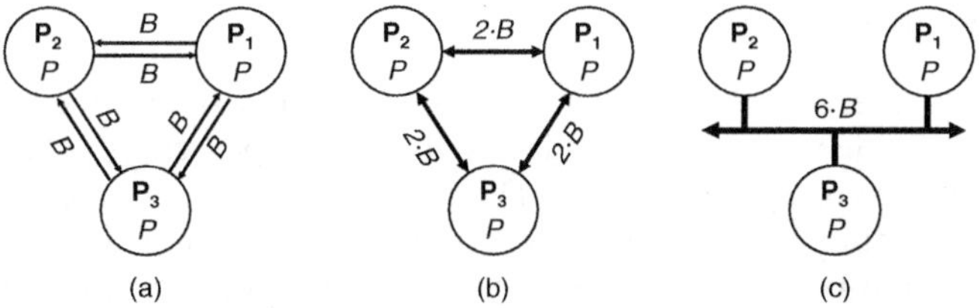

Fig. 2. SDR platform types: I full-duplex (a), II half-duplex (b), and III bus (c) architectures

3.3 SDR Applications

Figs. 3 and 4 show the computing requirements of the chip- and bit-rate processing chains of a UMTS downlink receiver supporting the raw data rates of 64, 128, and 384 kbps. We obtained the processing and bandwidth demands from [10]–[13] and from available implementations, considering that a processing requirement is the number of multiply-accumulate operations times the required processing frequency. Similarly, the bandwidth requirement is the sampling frequency *fs* multiplied by the number of bits per sample.

The three processing chains require a minimum processing capacity of 8133, 8301, and 9403 Mops. Because the total processing capacity $P_T = 3 \cdot P$ of an SDR platform takes the values 8100, 8250, ..., 9300, 9450, ..., 10 350, the CRM entity straightforwardly specifies thresholds T_{64}, T_{128} and T_{384} as 8250, 8400, and 9450 Mops. We introduce $T'_{384} = T_{384} / 3$, $T'_{128} = T_{128} / 3$, and $T'_{64} = T_{64} / 3$ for a simplified notation.

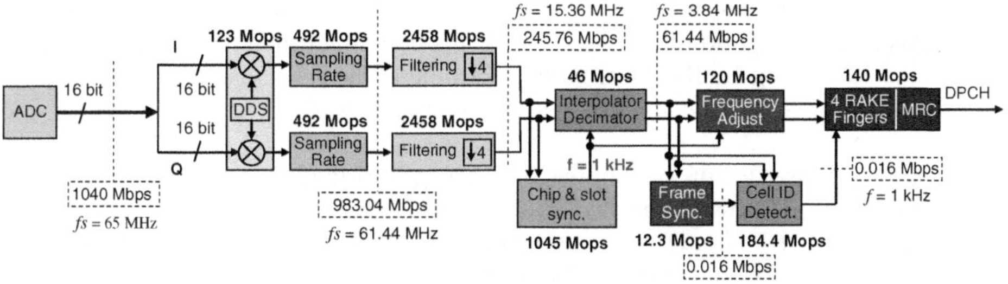

Fig. 3. Chip-rate computing requirements of a UMTS downlink receiver

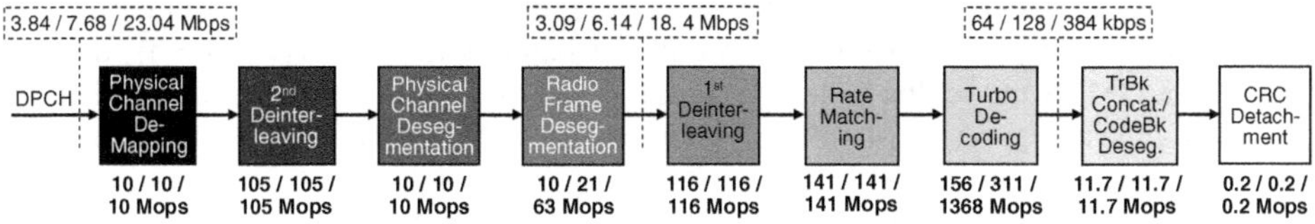

Fig. 4. Bit-rate computing requirements of a 64 / 128 / 384 kbps UMTS downlink receiver

3.4 Application Mapping

The SDR mobile terminals of this case study are equipped with the *t*-mapping algorithm [8], which maps the downloaded SDR-UMTS processing chain to the platform's available computing resources. The SDR functions are mapped one by one to all processors minimizing the sum between the computation and the communication costs. A bandwidth is reserved if two communicating processes are mapped to different processors; otherwise, the data is accessed via shared memory. The mapping of each SDR function to all *N* processors results in *N* different mapping options of the entire processing chain. The algorithm then chooses the least-cost solution.

The low complexity of this mapping approach greatly facilitates its implementation. Since being non-optimal, it does not always find a feasible solution. A feasible solution, or *feasible mapping*, reserves no more than 100% of any computing resource and, hence, meets the RAT-specific computing constraints. In particular, a feasible mapping can meet the timing constrains because our SDR system modeling considers time as an implicit resource [8].

4 Results

Fig. 5 shows the number of lost sessions as a function of the SDR platform index. It shows that the curves corresponding to Alg_1 and Alg_2 saturate, indicating the learning process: Alg_1 and Alg_2 learn which terminals can be feasibly reconfigured and which not. Alg_0, on the other hand, constantly loses user sessions, because lacking any hardware information.

Figs. 6a-c show the evolution of successful reconfigurations as a function of the CRM algorithm and the platform type. Fig. 7 presents the number of operating SDR terminals after the 15 000 test cases and their operational modes. Then, the sum between the remaining SDR-GPRS mobile terminals, the 64 kbps, 128 kbps, and 384 kbps UMTS sessions, and the number of lost sessions due Fig. 5 is 5000 for each platform type.

Figs. 8-10 illustrates the accumulated mapping information, which is obtained during the learning process of the two CRM algorithms. (The complete information, as shown in Figs. 8-10, is only partially obtained during the first 5000 terminals of each type.) The topmost level (level 3 - 384 kbps) indicates that the corresponding (*P*, *B*)-tuples can be feasibly reconfigured to 384, 128, or 64 kbps UMTS. The second level indicates that the corresponding terminals can be feasibly reconfigured to the 128 or the 64 kbps realizations, whereas the first level means a maximum achievable bit-rate of 64 kbps. Any *P*-*B* crossing at the bottom level of Fig. 8, 9, or 10 symbolizes an insufficient computing capacity (processing or bandwidth capacity, or both) for operating in a UMTS mode due to the particular CRM algorithm and application mapping process. These figures explain the results of Figs. 5-7, which we analyze in more detail below.

Fig. 5 shows that the number of lost sessions is the highest for the SDR mobile terminals of type I and the lowest for those of type III. Correspondingly, the number of feasible reconfigurations is the lowest for the terminals of type I and the highest for

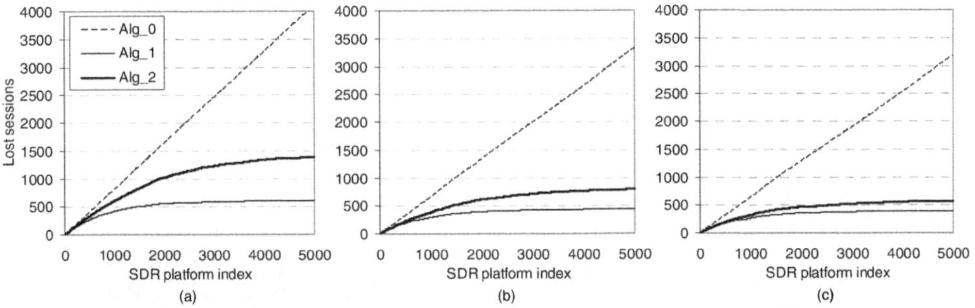

Fig. 5. Number of lost sessions as a function of the CRM algorithm and the SDR platform index for SDR platform types I (a), II (b), and III (c)

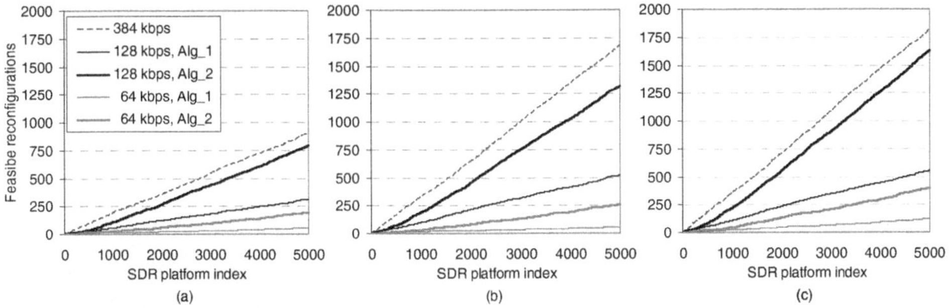

Fig. 6. Number of feasible reconfigurations as a function of the CRM algorithm and the SDR platform index for SDR platform types I (a), II (b), and III (c)

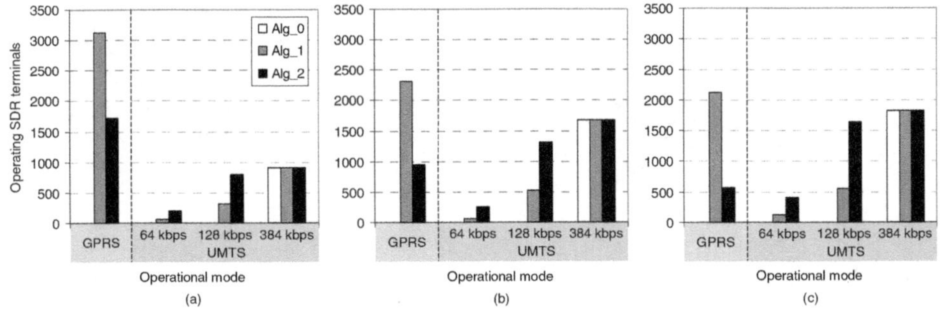

Fig. 7. Final number of non-reconfigured and feasibly reconfigured SDR mobile terminals of platform types I (a), II (b), and III (c)

those of type III (Fig. 6). The inflexibility, the partial flexibility, and the total flexibility in the bandwidth assignment of architectures I, II, and III, as discussed in section 3.2 and reflected in Figs. 8-10, explains this.

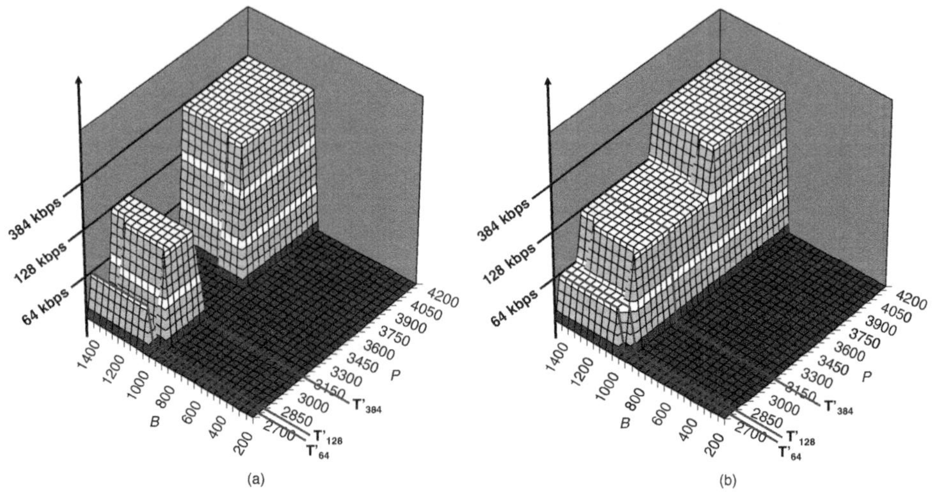

Fig. 8. Accumulated mapping information due to the learning process of Alg_1 (a) and Alg_2 (b) for SDR platform type I

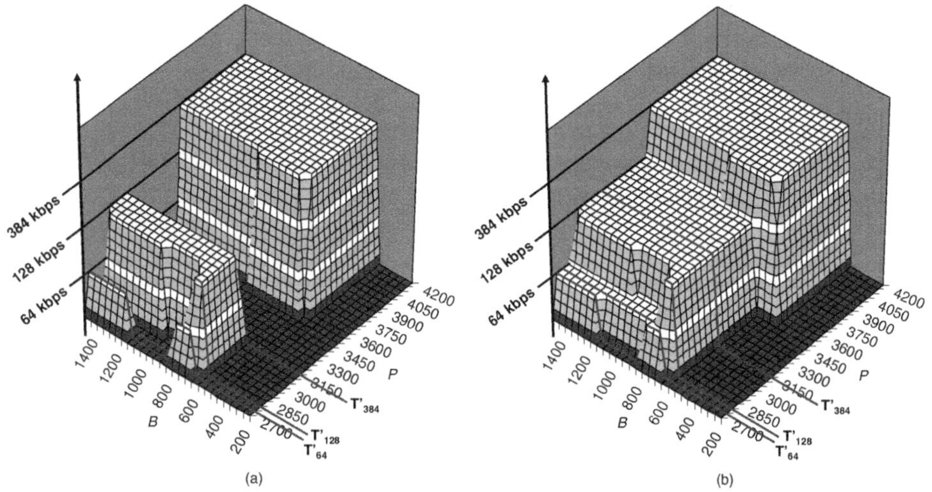

Fig. 9. Accumulated mapping information due to the learning process of Alg_1 (a) and Alg_2 (b) for SDR platform type II

Alg_0 either feasibly reconfigures an SDR-GPRS mobile terminal to the 384 kbps UMTS realization or loses the current user session. Alg_1 and Alg_2 lose much fewer sessions than Alg_0 because they either do not reconfigure those SDR-GPRS terminals that momentarily cannot operate in the 384 kbps UMTS mode or reconfigure them to a lower bit-rate UMTS realization. Alg_2 loses more sessions than Alg_1

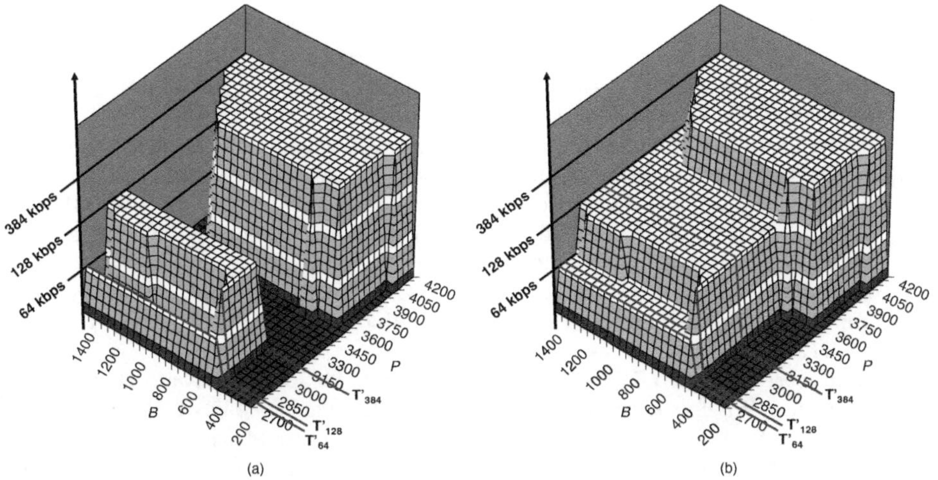

Fig. 10. Accumulated mapping information due to the learning process of Alg_1 (a) and Alg_2 (b) for SDR platform type III

(Fig. 5) but also feasibly reconfigures more terminals (Fig. 6). The shapes of the corresponding curves in Figs. 5 and 6 indicate that Alg_1 behaves better than Alg_2 for a low number of reconfiguration intents, whereas the higher their number the more efficient becomes Alg_2. The algorithm selection finally depends whether the principal objective is to lose less sessions or reconfigure more terminals; it is a trade-off between losing less sessions and reconfiguring more terminals.

Fig. 7 shows that many more of the 5000 SDR mobile terminals of each type remain in operation when applying Alg_1 or Alg_2 instead of Alg_0. In other words, our cognitive computing resource management proposal can satisfy more users in such a heterogeneous wireless scenario.

5 Conclusions

This paper has introduced the concept of computing resource management in cognitive radio. We have coined it *cognitive computing resource management* because it intelligently reconfigures SDR platforms as a function of the current state of the computing environment. A simple case study has demonstrated the importance and the potentials of our proposal in a heterogeneous radio environment.

Similarly to the insight that the problem of radio resource scarcity is actually a problem of an appropriate radio resource management, we argue for the importance of computing resource management in radio communications. In particular, we believe that a cognitive computing resource management may leverage the introduction of SDR platforms and applications, introducing flexibility in accessing a radio service for the sake of a ubiquitous wireless access.

References

1. Mitola, J., Maguire, G.Q.: Cognitive Radio: Making Software Radios More Personal. IEEE Pers. Commun. 6(4), 13–18 (1999)
2. Mitola, J.: Cognitive Radio: An Integrated Agent Architecture for Software Defined Radio. Ph.D. dissertation, Royal Institute of Technology, Stockholm, Sweden (2000)
3. Mitola, J.: The Software Radio Architecture. IEEE Commun. Mag. 33(5), 26–38 (1995)
4. Tuttlebee, W.H.W.: Software Defined Radio: Facets of a Developing Technology. IEEE Personal Commun. 6(2), 38–44 (1999)
5. Buracchini, E.: The software radio concept. IEEE Commun. Mag. 38(9), 138–143 (2000)
6. Cummings, M., Haruyama, S.: FPGA in the Software Radio. IEEE Commun. Mag. 37(2), 108–112 (1999)
7. Hoffmeyer, J., Park, I.-P., Majamundar, M., Blust, S.: Radio Software Download for Commercial Wireless Reconfigurable Devices. IEEE Commun. Mag. 42(3), 26–32 (2004)
8. Marojevic, V., Revés, X., Gelonch, A.: Computing Resource Management for SDR Platforms. In: Proc. 16th IEEE International Symposium on Personal, Indoor and Mobile Radio Communications, Berlin, September 11–14, 2005, pp. 685–689 (2005)
9. Haykin, S.: Cognitive Radio: Brain-empowered Wireless Communications. IEEE JSAC 23(2), 201–220 (2005)
10. Tanner, R., Woodard, J.: WCDMA – Requirements and Practical Design. John Wiley and Sons Inc., Chichester (2004)
11. Faber, T., Schönle, M.: DSP-platform target report. SLATS Consortium, Project no. 27016, Deliverable D23 (1999)
12. Technical Specification Group Radio Access Network (3GPP): TS 25.213 V5.5.0 – Spreading and Modulation (FDD) (2003), http://www.3gpp.org
13. Technical Specification Group Radio Access Network (3GPP): TS 25.212 V6.4.0 – Multiplexing and Channel Coding (FDD) (2005), http://www.3gpp.org

Research of UWB Signal Propagation Attenuation Model in Coal Mine

Fangmin Li, Ping Han, Xuehong Wu, and Wenjun Xu

Information Engineering School, Wuhan University of Technology,
Wuhan, Hubei Province, China, 430070
lifangmin@whut.edu.cn

Abstract. Now, the study of UWB signal's propagation attenuation model concentrates mainly on residential indoor environment. In this paper, the monitor of the personnel and equipments in tunnel of coal mine is regarded as application background, the environment in coal mine is looked as a kind of special indoor environment. On the basis of residential indoor UWB propagation model, the tunnel of coal mine is divided into near-field region and far-field region according to Fresnel theory. The propagation mode of UWB signal is mainly multimode in near-field region and mainly waveguide in far-field region. Considering the additional ullage factors that caused by the factors of tunnel, such as personnel and coal transports and slicers etc at the same time, this paper puts forward the UWB signal propagation attenuation model in coal mine. Aiming at the parameter of symbol BER, comparison and analysis that based on the existing residential indoor propagation attenuation model and the model of this paper is done.

1 Introduction

UWB has extensive application prospect for indoor short distance communication, there have been a large amount of research about residential indoor propagation attenuation model. FCC defines that any signal with it's bandwidth exceeds 500M is UWB signal. UWB can offer the ability of transmitting a great deal of data in short distance (10- 20m), because of its own characteristic. At the same time, it has very high time resolution ratio, which can be precise to ns grade (the corresponding precision of measuring distance can reach 1 inch), so it is very suitable for indoor wireless data transmission and accurate localization. The tunnel's environment in coal mine can be regarded as a kind of special indoor environment. Using UWB to realize the accurate localization in the coalmine is the goal that we want to realize, so it is necessary to research the UWB propagation attenuation models in the coal mine.

The working capability of the wireless propagation system is restricted by the propagation environment, the existence of multipath propagation and propagating delay increase the complexity and time changing characteristic of propagating channels. The LOS path that from transmitter to receiver does not exist in the indoor propagation environment, because there are wall and barriers in the indoor environment, the arrival of signal must pass multi-way. In recent years, there have corresponding research of UWB indoor propagation model. These documents put forward

J. Indulska et al. (Eds.): UIC 2007, LNCS 4611, pp. 819–828, 2007.

a series of UWB indoor propagation model aiming at residence, which draw by experimental measurement or discursion of theory. This paper puts forward UWB propagation model in coal mine based on residential indoor propagation model, considering various kinds of concrete environmental factors in coal mine. The imitation and analyses are done by aiming at the existing residential indoor propagation model and the results are given out.

2 Uwb Indoor Propagation Model

University of Southern California puts forward indoor UWB propagation model for wireless communication[1],This model is build on the basis of the result from a large number of measurements. The measuring people place a UWB transmitter and several UWB receivers among 14 offices and a storeroom and corridor of a modern office block. They measure 49 different positions in every office room, 21 different positions in store, 34 different positions in corridor. The mathematical statistics model of UWB signal in different positions (i, j) is gotten based on the measured data above:

$E_{i,j}$ expresses the magnitude of received signal at the position (i , j)

$$F_{i,j} = 10\log_{10} E_{i,j} - 10\log_{10} E_{ref} . \tag{1}$$

$$E_{i,j} = \int_0^T | r_{i,j}(t) |^2 \, dt . \tag{2}$$

$r_{i,j}(t)$ expresses multipath signal measured in the position (i, j), T expresses the observing time. E_{ref} is the LOS receiver's energy that measured at the position of 1m far from transmitter.

Characteristic of UWB path attenuation in residential environment[2] is got from the data of LOS and NLOS path between transmitter and receiver in 23 rooms, which have been measured 300,000 times. The central frequency of UWB signal is 5GHz, the bandwidth is 1.25GHz. The path attenuation model:

$$PL(d) = [PL_0 + 10\gamma \log_{10}(\frac{d}{d_0})] + S(d); d \ge d_0 . \tag{3}$$

PL0 is the value of path attenuation when d=1m, γ obeys the normal distribution with standard deviation $N[\mu_\gamma, \sigma_\gamma]$. $\gamma = \mu_\gamma + n_1\sigma_\gamma$, n1 is zero-mean Gaussian variant, which obeys the normal distribution with unit standard deviation N[0,1]. $S = n_2\mu_\sigma + n_2 n_3 \sigma_\sigma$, n2 and n3 are zero-mean Gaussian variant, which obey the normal distribution with unit standard deviation N[0,1].

Indoor Wireless channel model[3], which further calculates the relationship between capacity C and distance d on the basis of document[2]:

$$SNR_r(d)|_{dB} = P_t(dB) - 10\lg(N_0 B) - PL(d) - M_{dB} . \tag{4}$$

$$C(d) = B\log_2(1 + SNR_r(d)) . \tag{5}$$

M_{dB} is chain surplus, it's typical value is 6db.

Those 3 kinds of UWB indoor propagation models mentioned above are all aiming at residential environment. But, there is great different between the environment of coal mine and residential indoor environment. So it must design UWB wireless propagation attenuation model according to the concrete environmental factors of coal mine.

3 Uwb Propagation Model in Coalmine

3.1 Theoretical Gist of Dividing Propagation Area in Tunnel

The tunnel can be looked as a kind of non-ideal waveguide, the wave whose frequency is higher than the cut-off frequency can travel in it[4]. The frequency band adopted by UWB signal is above 500MHz. The propagation mode of the signal in this frequency band must be multimode in coal mine. There is a large amount of reflection and dispersion in tunnel at the same time, the multipath effect is obvious. Through a series of tests and measurements, it can be found that the field intensity in tunnel is divided into two different regions. Attenuation coefficient of field intensity is larger in the frontal region, and the amplitude of field intensity declines very quickly, this frontal region is called near-field region. The attenuation coefficient of field intensity is reduced in back region, and the amplitude of field intensity is alleviative too, this back region is called far-field region. Most electric waves travel in near-field region. The guide propagation has not been set up in this region, so the propagation mode of the wave is mainly multimode. In far-field region, the propagation mode of the wave is mainly steady guide propagation. The turning point of two propagation regions can be confirmed by Fresnel[5] theory. Fresnel area is an ellipsoid using transmitting antenna and receiving antenna as focus. If the distance between transmitting antenna and receiving antenna is d, then the difference between the distance that from random point of the ellipsoid to the two antennas and d is a constant $q\lambda/2$, q is positive integer, λ is wavelength of electromagnetic wave in free place. When q = 1, the area that ellipsoid surrounds is called the first Fresnel area. The area that ellipsoid surrounds with q from 1 to 2 is called the second Fresnel area, the rest can be deduced by analogy. Now, it supposes that there is a plane, which is perpendicular to the link line between transmitting antenna and receiving antenna. The crossing lines between the plane and ellipsoid are a series of concentric circles, except the near area of the antenna. The radius of these concentric circles can be shown as:

$$r_q = \sqrt{\frac{q\lambda d_1 d_2}{d_1 + d_2}} . \tag{6}$$

In this formula, d1 and d2 are the distance from transmitting antenna to plane and from receiving antenna to plane separately. Obviously, when it assumes that r_q closes to the transmitting antenna or the receiving antenna, the value of r_q minish. When the position of r_q is between the transmitting and receiving antenna, the value of r_q is maximum $r_{q\max} = \frac{1}{2}\sqrt{q\lambda d}$. If the width of tunnel is w, high is h. It makes $r_{q\max} = \frac{w}{2}$, then $d = \frac{w^2}{q\lambda}$. It makes $r_{q\max} = \frac{h}{2}$, then $d = \frac{h^2}{q\lambda}$. If it defines the distance between the transmitting and receiving antenna as turning point, when the first Fresnel area begin to be interdicted, then the turning point are separately $d = \frac{w^2}{q\lambda}$ or $d = \frac{h^2}{q\lambda}$ when the barriers are left and right wall or upper and nether wall. In tunnel, the boundary between the two propagation areas is the maximal distance from transmitting antenna to turning point:

$$d_{NF} = Maximum(\frac{h^2}{\lambda}, \frac{w^2}{\lambda}). \tag{7}$$

3.2 Propagation Model in Near-Field Region

In this area that propagation distance is smaller than d_{NF}, the propagation mode of electromagnetic wave is mainly multimode. This kind of propagation mode is similar with the propagation mode of electromagnetic wave in free space, the propagation model based on the basic prototype of residential indoor propagation model can be used. UWB signal mentioned in this paper is PPM-TH-UWB signal, which is time hopping UWB signal with pulse position modulation. The signal is defined as follows:

$$v(t) = \sum_{j=1}^{N_s} p(t - jT_s - \eta_j). \tag{8}$$

Its fourier transform is:

$$P_v(f) = P(f)\sum_{m=1}^{N_s} e^{-j(2\pi f(mT_s + \eta_m))}. \tag{9}$$

The repeating rate of UWB pulse signal is given as T_b, and then the double PSD of PPM-TH-UWB is:

$$P_s(f) = \frac{|P_v(f)|^2}{T_b}\left[1 - |w(f)|^2 + \frac{|w(f)|^2}{T_b}\sum_{n=-\infty}^{+\infty}\delta\left(f - \frac{n}{T_b}\right)\right]. \tag{10}$$

In free space, the receiving energy model[6] of narrowband signal at distance d is:

$$P_r(d) = \frac{P_t}{PL(d)}. \tag{11}$$

Path attenuation model in free space is:

$$PL(d) = \frac{(4\pi)^2 d^2 f_c^2}{G_t G_r c^2}. \tag{12}$$

The PSD of UWB signal's pulse is very wide, so the corresponding amendment must be done to make formula 12 suits for wideband signal. The transmitting and receiving energy of UWB can be calculated using integral of PSD in certain frequency band range, transmitting energy must meet the restriction of FCC. The transmitting energy equals the integral of $P_s(f)$ in the range of transmitting frequency band, f_H and f_L are defined as upper limit and lower limit of transmitting frequency band. The transmitting energy is:

$$P_t = \int_{f_L}^{f_H} P_s(f)df \ . \tag{13}$$

The receiving energy at the position of distance d is:

$$P_r(d) = 2\int_{f_L}^{f_H} \frac{P_s(f)}{PL(d)} df = \frac{G_t G_r c^2}{(4\pi)^2 d^2} 2\int_{f_L}^{f_H} \frac{P_s(f)}{f^2} df \ . \tag{14}$$

The UWB signal propagation model in near-field region is:

$$PL(d) = \left[\frac{P_t}{P_r}\right] - L_a = \frac{8\pi^2 d^2 \int_{f_L}^{f_H} P_s(f)df}{G_t G_r c^2 \int_{f_L}^{f_H} \frac{P_s(f)}{f^2} df} - L_a \ . \tag{15}$$

Because the transmitting antenna and receiving antenna are full-direction antenna, so antenna gain G_t and G_r are 1. L_a is additional ullage element[4], it is decided by below factors:

1. The distance attenuation factors of horizontal wave and polarized wave are separately 2.96db and 3.71db in empty tunnel, the attenuation factors add to 3.17db and 5.49db when people crowd in tunnel.
2. The additional ullage caused by coal carrier is 10-13db, caused by slicers is 5-10db, caused by hydraulic pressure pump is 5-8db, caused by transmitting strap is 5.8db.

3.3 Propagation Model in Far-field Region[5]

In far-field region, propagation distance is larger than d_{NF} , the higher-order mode has been almost attenuated. The propagation mode of electromagnetic wave is mainly fundamental mode, which is similar with the propagation mode in waveguide. The propagation ullage in this region can be calculated by waveguide propagation model, the whole ullage is:

$$PL(d) = -(Pl_s + Pl_r + Pl_t) \ . \tag{16}$$

In this formula, $Pl_s = Pl_{sH} + Pl_{sV}$, Pl_r, Pl_t are the ullage caused by refraction of wall and coarseness of surface and wall slope separately.

◆ The horizontal ullage and vertical ullage in tunnel are separately:

$$Pl_{sH} = 5.0\lambda^2\left(\frac{1}{w^3\sqrt{\varepsilon_r - 1}} + \frac{1}{h^3\sqrt{\varepsilon_r - 1}}\right)d\,. \tag{17}$$

$$Pl_{sV} = 4.5\lambda^2\left(\frac{1}{w^3\sqrt{\varepsilon_r - 1}} + \frac{\varepsilon_r}{h^3\sqrt{\varepsilon_r - 1}}\right)d\,. \tag{18}$$

ε_r is the relative dielectric constant.

◆ The fundamental mode ullage caused by surface coarseness is:

$$Pl_r = 4.343\pi^2 r^2 \lambda\left(\frac{1}{w^4} + \frac{1}{h^4}\right)d\,. \tag{19}$$

◆ The slope ullage is:

$$Pl_t = 10\lg C_f(\phi,\theta)\,. \tag{20}$$

$C_f(\phi,\theta) = [C_{f1(\theta)}]^{(\pi d/k_0 w^2)}[C_{f2(\theta)}]^{(\pi d/k_0 h^2)}$, $C_{f1}(\theta)$ and $C_{f2}(\phi)$ are power coupling factors when gradient angle are θ and ϕ separately.

Synthesizing the near-field region model and far-field region model above, the propagation model of UWB signal in tunnel is:

$$PL(d) = \begin{cases} \dfrac{8\pi^2 d^2 \int_{f_L}^{f_H} P_s(f)df}{c^2 \int_{f_L}^{f_H} \frac{P_s(f)}{f^2} df} - L_a & \text{Near-field region} \\ -(Pl_{sH} + Pl_{sV} + Pl_r + Pl_t) & \text{Far-field region} \end{cases}\,. \tag{21}$$

4 Simulation and Analysis

In this paper, emulation and analysis of PSD of PPM-TH-UWB signal and chain budget of the propagation model are done on computer. In the emulation of PSD of PPM-TH-UWB signal, the PSD figures of two kinds of UWB signals, which are one kind without PPM modulation and TH code and another kind with PPM modulation and TH code, are enumerated to be analyzed. The UWB signal without PPM modulation and without TH code is shown in Fig. 1, the UWB signal with PPM modulation and with TH code is shown in Fig. 2.

Comparing with Fig. 1 and Fig. 2, it can be seen that the Gaussian form of power spectrum is made twisted by TH code and PPM modulation. The PSD of PPM-TH-UWB signal is totally included in the envelope of PSD of UWB signal without PPM modulation and TH code, when the pulse with same interval is transmitted in same form and repeating rate.

In the following parts of this paper, all the contrast and emulation and analysis that done toward the parameters of attenuation model are aiming at near-field region. In

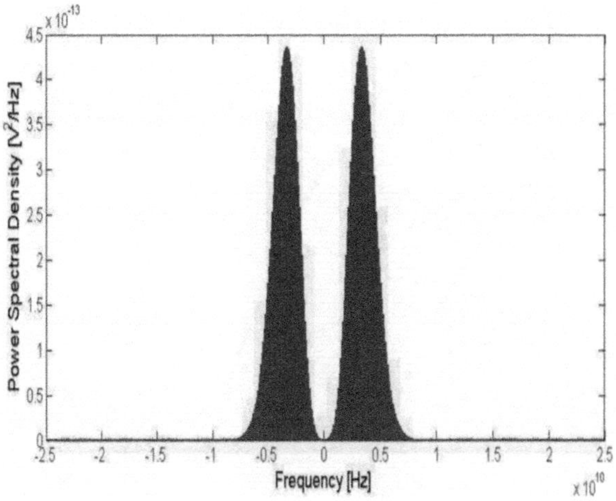

Fig. 1. PSD without PPM modulation and TH code

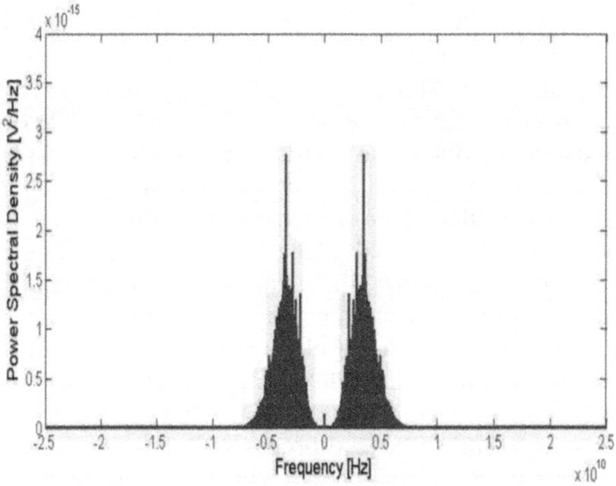

Fig. 2. PSD with PPM modulation and TH code

far-field region, the propagation mode of electric wave has changed, so analysis is not needed. The relative receiving power of horizontal polarization and vertical polarization can be seen in document [5].

In most articles, the symbol BER (Bit Error Rate) $\Pr_e$ is used as criterion for systematic guideline. The relationship between Symbol BER and SNR depends on different mode of signal's modulation. The expressive formula of Symbol BER with the binary PPM modulation is:

$$\Pr_b = \frac{1}{2} erfc(y) \text{Thereinto: } y = \sqrt{\frac{1}{2} SNR_{spec}} = \sqrt{\frac{E_b}{2N_0}} . \tag{22}$$

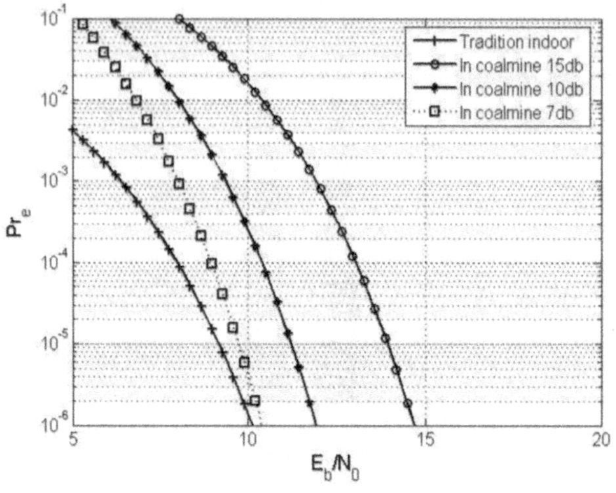

Fig. 3. Compare of symbol CER in two kinds of models

In this paper, symbol BER is analyzed in condition of traditional indoor propagation attenuation model and propagation attenuation model in coal mine, regarding PPM-TH-UWB signal with PPM modulation as target. The result is shown in Fig. 3.

It can be seen from the figure that the symbol BER of UWB signal of indoor propagation attenuation model is obviously smaller than the symbol BER of the model in coal mine. In the propagation attenuation model in coal mine, for the existence of tunnel additional ullage factors that mentioned in section 3.2, the simulation is made when the values of additional ullage factors are separately 7db and 10db and 15db. It can be seen from Fig. 3 that BER is maximal at 15 db and BER is minimal at 7db in the same propagation attenuation mode in coal mine.

Next, the simulation and analysis of chain budget of UWB signal in propagation attenuation model in coal mine will be done. The largest allowable power of propagation is determined by the ultimate value of PSD. When the allowable power is given, the relationship between data speed and propagation distance of UWB signal can be calculated with the condition of BER of the receiver is unchangeable.

To the receiver with system surplus is M_s, in order to meet the request for SNR, what the power of received signal P_r in formula 14 is expressed in the format of energy needs to satisfy:

$$E_r = 0.5kM_s SNR_s Temp_s \,. \tag{23}$$

E_r is receiving energy, $Temp_s$ is temperature of receiving antenna, SNR_s is signal to noise rate. According to the definition of SNR, formula 23 can be rewritten as:

$$M_s SNR_s = \frac{E_r}{E_n} = \frac{P_r T_b}{0.5k(Temp_a + (F(f)-1)Temp_c)} \,. \tag{24}$$

$Temp_a$ and $Temp_c$ delegate separately temperature of receiving antenna and temperature of environment. Considering the real condition in tunnel, these two temperatures can be equal: $Temp_a$=$Temp_c$. Using the narrow noise exponential model[7] at the same time, then formula 23 can be rewritten as:

$$d = \sqrt{\frac{\frac{c^2}{4\pi^2} Tb \int_{f_L}^{f_H} \frac{P_s(f)}{f^2} df}{M_s SNR_s F(f) kTemp_c}}. \tag{25}$$

According to the symbol BER Pr_e that defined in documents [8] and the relationship among Pr_e and SNR and data speed, the relationship between the propagation distance of PPM-TH-UWB signal and data speed in the propagation attenuation model in coal mine is shown in Fig. 3. If the use of omni-directional antenna is considered, then G_t=G_r=1; The chain surplus is set to 4dB; The environment in coal mine is fouler than the residential indoor environment, so BER Pr_e is set to 2×10^{-3}. The value of tunnel additional ullage factors that mentioned in section3.1 is acutely changing with the change of person in tunnel and grabs and transporting equipments. Their effect to propagation of UWB signal is very obviously. The relationship between the propagation distance of PPM-TH-UWB signal and data speed is listed in Fig. 3, when the noise index in coal mine is separately 7dB and 10dB and 15dB. It can be seen from the figure that the propagation distance of UWB signal drops with the increase of noise index. The nearest propagation distance of UWB signals is only 4m, under the condition of 15dB noise.

5 Future Work

On the basis of forefathers' job, combining with the concrete environment of the tunnel in coal mine, this paper puts forward the theory model of UWB signal propagation in coal mine. The wireless signal propagation model used in tunnel is divided into near-field region and far-field region according to Fresnel theory. There are different characteristics of signal propagation in each region. The following work is to carry on the real measurement and validate the theory model using the test data. The model will be made close to the real UWB propagation course furthest through revising further.

Acknowledgement

This paper was supported in part by Support Program for Excellent Talent of New Century (No. NCET-05-0657), Hubei Province Young Talent Foundation Item (No. 2006ABB028) and the Key (Key grant) Project of Chinese Ministry of Education (No. 107130).

References

1. Win, M.Z., Scholtz, R.A.: Ultra-Wide Bandwidth Signal Propagation for Indoor Wireless Communications. University of Southern California, Los Angeles, CA 90089-2565 USA
2. Ghassemzadeh, S.S.: Senior Member, IEEE, Vchid Tarokh, Senior Member, IEEE.: UWB Path Loss Characterizatio. In: Residential Environments. IEEE Radio Frequency Integrated Circuits Symposium, pp. 501–504 (2003)

3. Zhongtang, H., lijun, Z.: Research of UWB indoor propagation model. Joumal of Nanjing University of Posts and Telecommunications 25(5) (2005)
4. yueping, Z., wenmei, Z.: Forecast of propagation attenuation mixed model in tunnel. Acta Electornic Sinica 29(9) (2001)
5. Emslie, A.G., L, R.: Theory of the Propagation of UHF Radio Waves in Coal Mine Tunnels. IEEE Transctions On Antenna And Propagation ap-23(2) (1975)
6. Rappaport, T.S.: Wireless Communications Principles and Practice. Prentice-Hall, Upper Saddle River. NJ (1996)
7. IEEE 802.15.SG3a.: Channel modeling Sub-committee Report Final. IEEE P802. 15-02/490r1-SG3a (February 2003)
8. Guvenc, I., Arslan, H.: On the Modulation Options for UWB Systems. In: IEEE Military Communications Conference, October 2003, pp. 892–897 (2003)

Context Script Language and Processor for Context-Awareness in Ubiquitous Intelligent Environment*

Jae-Woo Chang and Yong-Ki Kim

Dept. of Computer Engineering
Chonbuk National University, Chonju, Chonbuk 561-756, South Korea
jwchang@chonbuk.ac.kr, ykkim@dblab.chonbuk.ac.kr

Abstract. In this paper, we propose a new context script language which can be used for building context-aware systems in an effective manner. The proposed context script language can represent both various decisions on context-awareness and appropriate procedures according to the decision as a standard syntax. Thus, it is regarded as a general purpose language to provide users with functions to define a given context in a clear and precise way. We also design and implement the processor of our context script language, which can automatically execute a series of involved procedures acquired for context-awareness. To show the usefulness of our context script language and its processor, we develop a context-aware application system which can provide users with a music playing service in ubiquitous intelligent environment.

1 Introduction

Ubiquitous computing applications are embedded in the users' physical environments and integrate seamlessly with their everyday tasks [1, 2, 3, 4]. Mark Weiser at Xerox Palo Alto Research Center described ubiquitous computing as being about interconnected hardware and software that are so ubiquitous that no one notices their presence [5]. An effective software infrastructure for running ubiquitous intelligent applications must be capable of finding, adapting, and delivering the appropriate applications to the user's environment based on the user's context. Thus, context-aware systems determine which user tasks are most relevant to a user in a particular context. They may be determined based on history, preferences, or other knowledge of the user's behavior, as well as the environmental conditions. Once the user has selected a task from the list of relevant tasks, an application may have to move seamlessly from one device to another and from one environment to another based on the user's activity. The context-awareness is one of the most important technologies in ubiquitous computing, which can facilitate information acquisition and execution by supporting interoperability between users and devices based on users' context.

* This work is financially supported by the Ministry of Education and Human Resources Development (MOE), the Ministry of Commerce, Industry and Energy (MOCIE) and the Ministry of Labor (MOLAB) though the fostering project of the Lab of Excellency.

J. Indulska et al. (Eds.): UIC 2007, LNCS 4611, pp. 829–838, 2007.

In this paper, we propose a new context script language which can be used for building context-aware systems in an effective manner. The proposed context script language can represent both various decisions on context-awareness and appropriate procedures according to the decision as a standard syntax. Thus, it is regarded as a general purpose language to provide users with functions to define a given context in a clear and precise way. We also design and implement the processor of our context script language, which can automatically execute a series of involved procedures acquired for context-awareness. To show the usefulness of our script language and its processor, we develop a context-aware application system which can provide users with a music playing service in ubiquitous intelligent environment. The remainder of this paper is organized as follows. The next section discusses related work on context-awareness. In section 3 and 4, we describe the design of our context script language and its processor for context-awareness, respectively. In section 5, we present the development of our context-aware application system using them. Finally, we draw our conclusions in section 6.

2 Related Work

In this section, we introduce some related work on context-awareness. First, Arizona State Univ. [6] presented Reconfigurable Context-Sensitive Middleware (RCSM), which made use of the contextual data of a device and its surrounding environment to initiate and manage ad hoc communication with other devices. In addition, they provided a context definition language called CA-IDL (Context-enabled Interface Definition Language). That is, context tuples for defining context can be represented as Context tuple : $< a_1, \ldots , a_n, t_m >$. Here, n means the number of unique context data, a_i means the value of the i-th context data, and t_m means the time for tuple creation. For example, if the context tuple consists of location, direction, and velocity, it can be represented as <(x,y), north, m, t> when its context object is moving toward north. If the context is detected, its corresponding method can be called. Secondly, INRIA in France [7] proposed a general infrastructure based on contextual objects to design adaptive distributed information systems in order to keep the level of the delivered service despite environmental variations. The contextual objects (COs) are mainly motivated by the inadequacy of current paradigms for context-aware systems. The use of COs does not complicate a lot of development of an application, which may be developed as a collection of COs. The COs are defined as CO(id) : <Variant V_x Attribute A_i: value, Attribute A_j: value, ...>. For example, two contextual Web documents can be defined as <V_1; Location:L_1, Language:French, Browser:with frame> and <V_2; Location:L_2, Language:English, Browser:without frame>. The Web documents can be browsed by selecting its appropriate variant according to users' location, users' language, and browser type.

3 Context Script Language for Context-Awareness

A context object is any logical concept that can be used to characterize the situation of any entity [9]. An entity is a person, place, or object that is considered relevant to the interaction between a user and an application, including the user and applications themselves. In order to develop a variety of application software for context-awareness in an effective manner, a context script language is required to describe both various decisions on context-awareness and appropriate procedures according to the decision. Even though the CA-IDL was proposed as a context script language, it is not a general purpose one because of being dependant on a specific system. Thus, we define a new context script language which can represent a given context as a standard syntax in a clear and precise manner as well as can provide users with functions to describe a variety of contexts with a general purpose. Our context script language has such components as context object declaration, context definition & destroy, context instance creation & deletion, and context instance activation & deactivation.

3.1 Context Object Declaration

A context object is a logical concept that can be used to represent any entity or device around application software for context-awareness. Some attribute values for a context can be updated by hardware devices, which can be used in a conditional clause being mentioned in the next. The declaration clause of the context objects is shown as follows. Here object_name and element_name never begin with a numeric or special letter, and they have less than 256 in length. In addition, data_type consists of two types; string data type (i.e., string) and numeric data type (i.e., int, float, long, double, time, date).

```
ContextObject object_name (
    data_type element_name1,
    data_type element_name2,
    data_type element_name3
          :          )
```

3.2 Context Definition and Destroy

A context can define a rule to execute an action when a context satisfies a given condition. It consists of a conditional expression and an action being executed. The context definition represents the template of context table and the values of context table are actually inserted in case of inserting a context instance. The definition clause of the context is shown as follows, where context_name being less than 256 in length cannot begins with a numeric or special letter. Here a condition clause is used to represent a given condition while action and parameter clauses are used to indicate both a function and its parameters being called when satisfying the condition.

```
ContextDefine context_name
Condition   (condition_expression) [during time_value]
Action      function_name
          [before/when/after time_value] or
          [from time_value to time_value]
Param       (param1, param2, ... )
```

First, the conditional expression (i.e., condition_expression) can be composed of N conditional clauses and N-1 logical operators (i.e., AND, OR, NOT). The conditional clause has two operands and one relative operator (i.e., =, >, <, <=, >=). The during time_value clause being optional can be used to represent a condition related with time. The time_value expresses a time interval with s(second), m(minute), and h(hour). For example, if you need a time interval for 1 hour and 12 minutes and 30 seconds, it can be expressed as 1h12m30s. Thus, the condition that a person P locates in A or B place for 1 minute and 30 seconds can be expressed as (((P_person.location = A_place) during 10s) or ((P_person.location = B_place) during 1m30s)). Secondly, the function_name means the name of a function to be executed when a given condition is satisfied. If there is no need to call a function, NULL can be used as the function_name. The optional clauses of [while/when/after time-value] and [from time_value to time_value] can be used to determine when and how long an action should be executed. For the while/when/after time-value, an action should be executed once before, exactly when, and after a given time, respectively. For the from time_value to time_value, an action should be executed continuously during the time (from time_value to time_value). Figure 1 shows time relationship in the action clause.

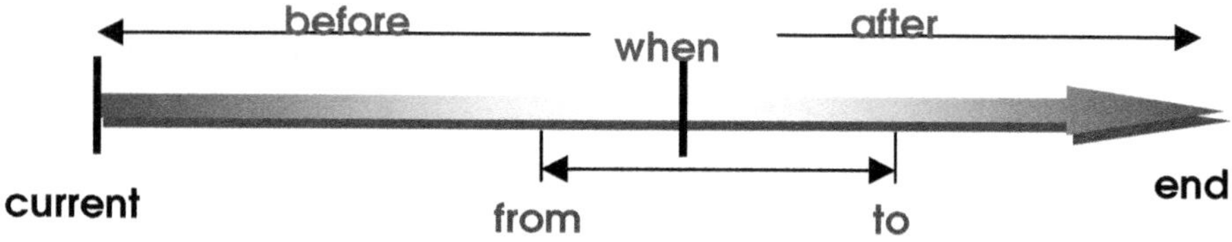

Fig. 1. Time relationship in the action clause

Finally, Param (param1, param2, ..) means a list of parameter names which are used in a function being executed by Action. If there is no parameter, NULL can be used for parameter names. The defined context can be destroyed by the clause of ContextDestroy as follows. When a context is destroyed, all the instances of the context are deleted and a status for checking a condition to activate the context is disabled.

ContextDestroy context_name

3.3 Context Instance Insertion and Deletion

Once a context is defined, it is necessary to add context instances into the context. The clause of context instance insertion is shown as follows, where ContextInsert, Condition, and Param are used. Here the context_name means the name of a context which the instance will be inserted into, while the instance_name means the name of a context instance to be inserted. The condition_value, which has a constant or constant literal, is used to instantiate a variable in the condition_expression for defining a context. Similarly, the param_value has a real value for a parameter of a function being called by Action in the context definition clause.

ContextInsert instance_name Into context_name
Condition (condition_value1, condition_value2, ...)
Param (param_value1, param_value1, ...)

The context instance inserted can be deleted by the clause of ContextDelete as follows. Here the context_name means the name of a context which the instance will be deleted from, while the instance_name means the name of a context instance to be deleted.

ContextDelete instance_name In context_name

3.4 Context Instance Activation and Deactivation

Once a context is defined and its context instances are inserted, the activation of a context instance makes it possible to check a condition and execute an appropriate action when satisfying the condition. On the contrary, the deactivation of a context instance makes it impossible to execute an action by checking its corresponding condition. The clause of context instance activation and deactivation is shown as follows.

ContextActiv instance_name In context_name
ContextDeAct instance_name In context_name

Here the context_name means the name of a context whose instances will be activated or deactivated, while the instance_name means the name of a context instance to be activated or deactivated. In addition, the asterisk symbol (*) can be used when all the instances in a context are activated or deactivated.

4 Context Script Language Processor

A context script language processor is a program to analyze the grammar of a context script file which is made following the BNF specification, as well as to execute it through lexical analysis. The overall architecture of the context script language processor is shown in Figure 2.

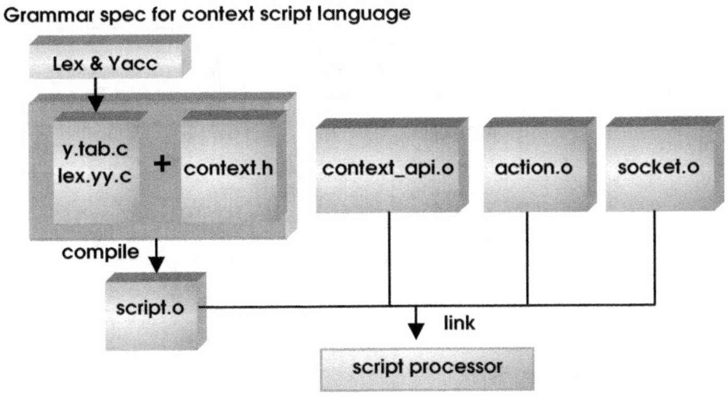

Fig. 2. Overall architecture of our script language processor

Here script.o includes the grammar and syntax rules of the context script language which are created using Lex and Yacc, and it contains some context API calls. The context_api.o describes context APIs to process all the expression of the language while action.o describes the body of functions being called in the context definition clause, which will be executed when a condition is satisfied. Finally socket.o contains context APIs used to deliver contexts to a server after the context script file is processed. The context script language processor is executed as a program to link the above modules. The context script language processor can serves as a middleware in the fixed node. The procedure to process the context script language is the following. First, when the context script language processor interprets a context script file and calls APIs according to the interpreted content. The content of APIs is made as a packet and it is delivered to the server by using a socket. The context server receives and interprets the packet, and then it executes APIs related with DBMS and stores into DBMS the result made by processing the context script file. The procedure to process a context script file in a fixed node and a server is shown in Figure 3. Figure 4 show an example for processing the context script file by using the context script processor.

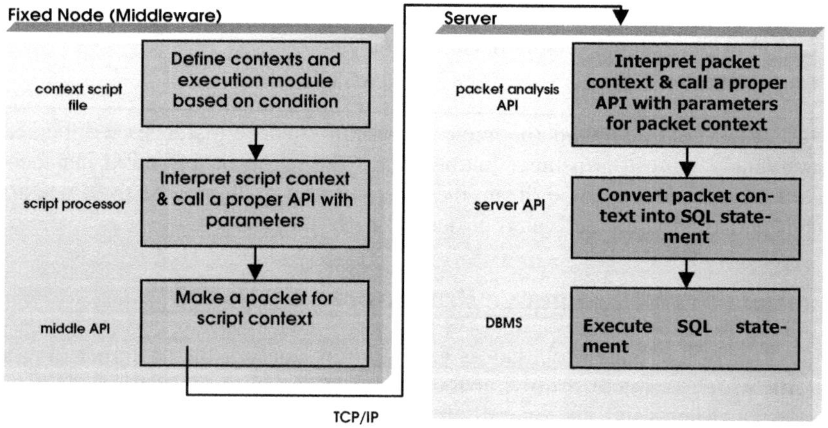

Fig. 3. Procedure for processing a context script file

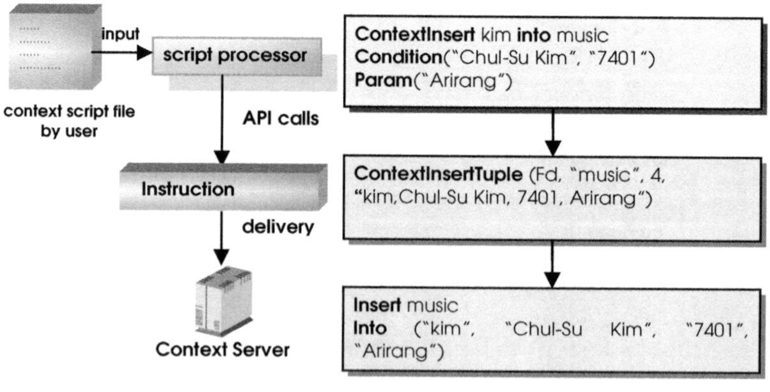

Fig. 4. Example of processing a context script file

5 Context-Aware Application System

To show the efficiency of our context script language and its processor, we develop a context-aware application system which provides users with a music playing service in ubiquitous intelligent environment. Figure 5 shows an overall architecture for supporting our music playing service. When a user belonging to a moving node approaches to a fixed node, the fixed node starts playing the user's music with his (her) preference according to his location. In general, each user has a list of his (her) music with his preference and even a user can have a different list of his (her) popular music depending on time, i.e., morning time, noon time, and night time. For example, when a user hearing his music with his preference in the place A moves to the place B, the fixed node 1 stops playing his music in the place A while the fixed node 2 starts playing his music in the place B.

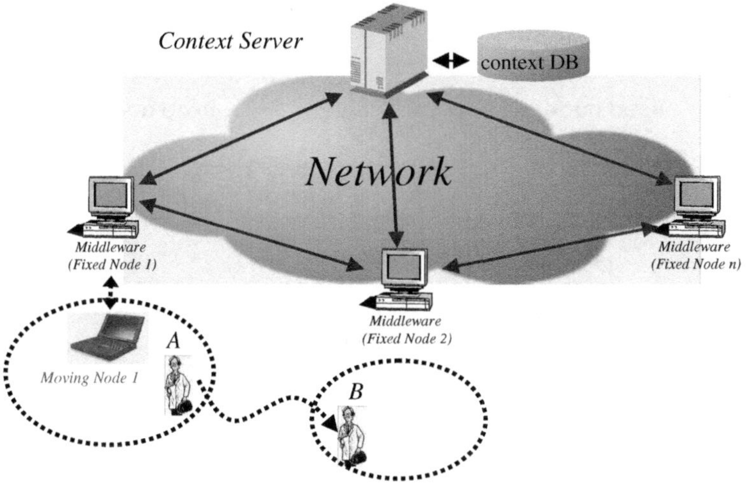

Fig. 5. Overall architecture for supporting context-aware application services

We develop our context-aware application system providing a music playing service by using affix 2.0.2 as a Bluetooth device driver protocol stack [10] and by using GCC 2.95.4 an a compiler, under Redhat Linux 7.3 (kernel version 2.4.20) with 866 MHz Pentium-III CPU and 64 MB main memory. In addition, the Bluetooth device follows the specification of Version1.1/Class1 and makes a connection to PCs using USB interfaces [11]. To develop a context server, we make use of a commercial MySQL DBMS because we can reduce the developing time, compared with using a storage system and can increase the reliability of the developed system. In the context server, a user record for the music playing service has six attributes, such as User_ID, User_Name, Location, Music_M, Music_A, and Music_E. The User_ID serves as a primary key to identify a user uniquely. The User_Name means a user name and the Location means a user's current location which can be changed whenever a fixed node finds the location of a moving object. Finally the Music_M, the Music_A, and the Music_E represent his (her) preferred music file in the morning time, the noon time, and the night time, respectively. The context server manages a list of music files for a user, processes queries given from a fixed node, and delivers the corresponding music file to the fixed node on its request.

We test our context-aware application system by adopting a scenario used in Cricket [12], one of the MIT Oxygen project. For this, we test its execution in the following three cases; the first case when a user covered by a moving node approaches to a fixed node or move apart from it, the second case when two different users approaches to a fixed node, and final case when a user approaches to a fixed node at different times. Among them, because the first case is the most general one, we will explain it in more detail. For our testing environment, we locate two fixed nodes in the database laboratory (DB Lab) and the media communication laboratory (Media Lab) of Chonbuk National University, respectively, where their middleware can detect a moving node by using Bluetooth wireless communication, as shown in Figure 6. There is a corridor between DB Lab and Media Lab and its distance is about 60 meter.

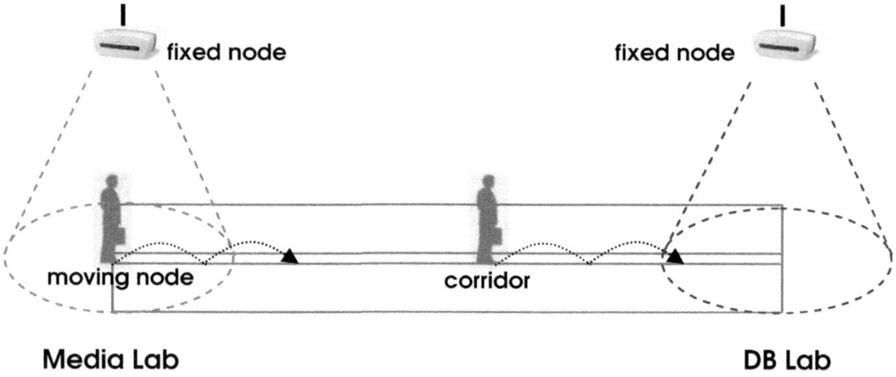

Fig. 6. Testing environment

We test the execution of our middleware in case when a user having a moving node moves from DB Lab to Media Lab or in a reverse direction. When a user having a moving node approaches to a fixed node, the fixed node first receives a user name from the moving node as the moving node is approaching to it. Secondly, the fixed node determines whether the information of the user has already been stored into a server or not. If the information has been there, the context server searches the music file belonging to the user in a current time and downloads the music file from the database. Finally, the fixed node starts playing the downloaded music file using a MP3 player. On the contrary, when a user having a moving node moves apart from a fixed node, the fixed node stops the process to play music and removes the music playing process since it detects that a user is too far from the fixed node to communicate with it. Conclusively, when a user approaches to a fixed node, the fixed node starts playing the user's music while when a user moves apart from the fixed node, the fixed node stops playing the music.

To analyze the performance of our context-aware application system, we measure an average time by adopting a boundary detection of beacons used in Cricket [10]. First, as a moving node is approaching to a middleware, it takes 1.34 second to make a connection between them. It means the time for the fixed node to detect the presence of a moving node when a moving node enters into its communication boundary. The time mainly depends on the specification of Bluetooth wireless communication. Secondly, it takes 0.5 second for the fixed node to start music playing service after making the connection between them. It means the time for the fixed node to search the profile of the corresponding user and to call the module to play music. The searching time for a user's profile is dependant both on the packet transfer time of TCP/IP and on the DBMS performance of the context server. The calling time for the music playing module means the one for an operating system (OS) to load it, which is affected by the available memory of the OS kernel and the speed of a hard disk. Finally, as a moving node is going apart from a fixed node, it takes 1.45 second to make a disconnection between them. It means the time for the fixed node to detect the absence of the moving node. The time is relatively long because the kernel tries to communicate with the moving node even though the moving node is beyond the communication boundary of the fixed node. Therefore, when the kernel is disconnected with the moving object, it is very reasonable for the fixed node to set a time limit to two seconds. If it takes long time for a fixed node to establish a connection to a moving node and to detect a context from it, a user may consider the situation as a fault. Because the detection time for a context is less than two seconds, our context-aware application system is reasonable for the music playing service in ubiquitous computing environment.

6 Conclusions and Future Work

In this paper, we proposed a new context script language as well as designed its processor for context-awareness in ubiquitous intelligent environment. The proposed context script language can be used for building context-aware systems in an effective manner. The proposed context script language can also represent both various decisions on context-awareness and appropriate procedures according to the decision as a standard syntax. Thus, it can be regarded as a general purpose language to provide users with functions to define a given context in a clear and precise way. The designed processor of our context script language can automatically execute a series of involved procedures acquired for context-awareness. To show the usefulness of our script language and its processor, we developed our context-aware application system which can provide users with a music playing service in ubiquitous intelligent environment. We tested our context-aware application system by adopting a scenario used in Cricket, one of the MIT Oxygen projects. It was shown that it took about 1.5 seconds to make a connection (or disconnection) between a fixed node and a moving node, thus being considered reasonable for our music playing service. As future work, it is required to study on a rule description language which can be used to express an inference of a new context from the existing contexts.

References

1. Banavar, G., Bernstein, A.: Issues and challenges in ubiquitous computing: Software infrastructure and design challenges for ubiquitous computing applications. Communication of ACM 45(12), 92–96 (2002)
2. Keays, R., Rakotonirainy, A.: Context-oriented programming. In: Proc. of the 3rd ACM international workshop on Data engineering for wireless and mobile access, pp. 9–16 (2003)
3. Dey, A.K., Hamid, R., Beckmann, C., Li, I., Hsu, D.: CAPpella: Programming by Demonstration of Context-Aware Applications. In: Proc. of ACM Conference on Human Factors in Computing Systems, ACM Press, New York (2004)
4. Henricksen, K., Indulska, J.: Developing context-aware pervasive computing applications: Models and approach. Journal of Pervasive and Mobile Computing 2(1), 37–64 (2006)
5. Weiser, M.: Some Computer Science Issues in Ubiquitous Computing. Communication of the ACM 36(7), 75–84 (1993)
6. Yau, S.S., Karim, F.: Context-sensitive Middleware for Real-time Software in Ubiquitous Computing Environments. In: Proc. of 4th IEEE Symposium on Object-oriented Real-time Distributed Computing, pp. 163–170. IEEE Computer Society Press, Los Alamitos (2001)
7. Couderc, P., Kermarrec, A.M.: Improving Level of Service for Mobile Users Using Context-Awareness. In: Proc. of 18th IEEE Symposium on Reliable Distributed Systems, pp. 24–33. IEEE Computer Society Press, Los Alamitos (1999)
8. Harter, A., Hopper, A., Steggles, P., Ward, A., Webster, P.: The anatomy of a Context-aware application. Wireless Networks 8(2/3), 187–197 (2002)
9. Dey, A.K.: Understanding and Using Context. Personal and Ubiquitous Computing Journal 5(1), 4–7 (2001)
10. Affix: Bluetooth Protocol Stack for Linux, http://affix.sourceforge.net
11. Bluetooth Version 1.1 Profile, http://www.bluetooth.com
12. Priyantha, N.B., Chakraborty, A., Balakrishnan, H.: The Cricket Locaion Support System. In: 6th ACM/IEEE Int'l Conf. on Mobile Computing and Networking(MOBICOM), pp. 32–43 (2000)

A Semantics-Based Framework for Context-Aware Services: Lessons Learned and Challenges

Theodore Patkos, Antonis Bikakis, Grigoris Antoniou, Maria Papadopouli, and Dimitris Plexousakis

Institute of Computer Science, FO.R.T.H.
Vassilika Vouton, P.O. Box 1385, GR 71110
Heraklion, Greece
{patkos,bikakis,antoniou,mgp,dp}@ics.forth.gr

Abstract. Location-based ubiquitous services have evolved significantly during the last years and are reaching a maturity phase, relying primarily on the experience gained and the utilization of recent technologies. This paper proposes a context-aware platform for mobile devices in dynamic environments, which uses Semantic Web technologies to model context information and advanced interactive map-based interfaces for accommodating pedestrians. To test and demonstrate the approach, a prototype has been developed and a number of further extensions are studied. Building and using this system has enabled us to identify the main challenges that need to be addressed for realizing the objectives of next generation semantics-based pervasive information systems.

1 Introduction

Location-based services and mobile ubiquitous applications represent an emerging research paradigm that aims at empowering users through personalized, context-aware and context-adaptive environments. Although mobile guides and navigation systems have come a long way since their first release, certain challenges have yet to be addressed, while new requirements are continuously becoming apparent. Thereby, new methodologies and advanced technologies are being developed that focus on providing flexible and extensible design models, proposing efficient solutions for dynamic environments, structuring solid context-aware infrastructures, as well as promoting openness and interoperability in response to the current highly heterogeneous reality.

Considering recent trends, the present paper proposes a framework for structuring advanced location-based and context-aware services that integrates up-to-date technologies and develops novel mechanisms and interactive interfaces by applying techniques and formalisms from the Semantic Web and Ubiquitous Computing domains. The objective is to explore the intelligent pedestrian navigation by implementing a Context Pedestrian Guiding platform (CG) for users in indoor environments. We focus on modelling and representing context using Semantic Web technologies for efficient processing and dissemination of context-based knowledge,

J. Indulska et al. (Eds.): UIC 2007, LNCS 4611, pp. 839–848, 2007.

in order to develop services for mobile users. Integrating web ontology languages, such as RDF or OWL, with context-aware applications has manifold benefits. These languages offer enough representational capabilities to develop a formal context model that can be shared, reused, extended for the needs of specific domains, but also combined with data originating from other sources, such as the Web or other applications. Moreover, the development of the logic layer of the Semantic Web is resulting in rule languages that will enable reasoning with the user's needs and preferences and with the available ontology knowledge.

During the course of this project, we implemented a prototype that operates in the premises of the FORTH research facilities located in the technological and research park in Heraklion, supporting several of the basic functionalities that have been considered. Based on the experience gained during the development and usage of the platform, we reveal and comment on problems and challenges that must be considered in ubiquitous information systems engineering.

Our overall contribution is twofold. We exploit the expressive capabilities of Semantic Web technologies to develop a formal, shareable and extensible context model and integrate this model with a positioning mechanism and with flexible, interactive map-based interfaces to implement context-aware guiding services. Additionally, from a theoretical standpoint, motivated by our experiences, we raise and discuss numerous research issues and challenges that emerge, when attempting to understand the domain for enabling ubiquitous information systems to operate effectively.

The paper is organized as follows. In Section 2, related work is considered. The system architecture and implementation is presented next, while in Section 4 we describe the supported context-aware services. The paper concludes with a discussion on the main challenges that we encountered while developing and using the system.

2 Related Work

The existing implemented prototypes can be classified based on several criteria, namely the types of services that they provide (simple information guides, navigation systems), the context representation model (semantic vs. non-semantic), the environment they work in (indoor vs. outdoor), the type of the interface (map-based vs. text-based, interactive vs. non-interactive) and their adaptation capabilities. Two of the most prominent early mobile navigation systems were *Cyberguide* [1] and *GUIDE* [6], both of which were designed to provide visitors with up-to-date and context-aware information whilst exploring a city.

Only recently, systems that integrate Semantic Web technologies with navigation services have been developed. Two such systems are *mSpace Mobile* [17] and *COMPASS* [16]. They both use interactive map-based interfaces and aim to provide users with context-aware recommendations and map-based services based on the collection of distributed semantic information from the user's context. Furthermore, *mSpace Mobile* supports the lightweight semantic publication of comments, annotations and recommendations on any map element. *Navio* [13] and *OntoNav* [2] are two typical examples of navigation systems that use profile and context information for shaping routes and semantics-based methods for representing them.

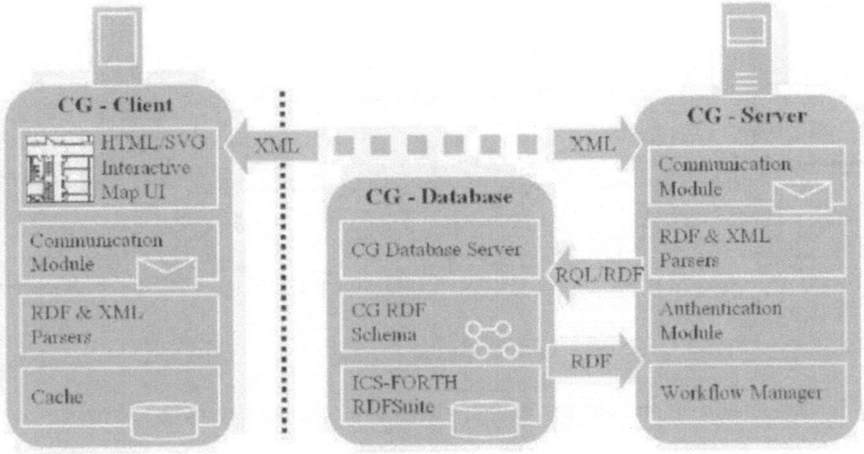

Fig. 1. The system architecture

While the former proposes a pure ontology-based approach (a route modelling ontology), *OntoNav* uses a hybrid context model, which combines geometric with semantic modelling constructs.

Two are the distinct features of the Context Pedestrian Guiding platform, namely the extensible context ontology model and the interactive mechanism. The first includes representations of many aspects of context (such as, people, devices, locations, rooms), and combines spatial with temporal entities to model events. The second enables the users to not only issue queries about their context but also modify it, by updating the knowledge base through an interactive interface. Thus, the system can be used in two different ways: for automatically detecting changes in the user's context, but also as a medium to update the context in certain ways.

3 Context Pedestrian Guiding System Architecture

The platform's architecture, shown in Fig. 1, is designed to support user-centered and device-independent functionality, in order to provide the technical feasibility for building a multitude of context-based services. The framework, intended for indoor environments, is based on a centralized configuration and achieves a high level of transparency in inter-device communication, context management and service deployment.

Various context models have been proposed, but ontology-based are considered the most appropriate ones, as documented in [15], since they permit formal representation, richness of information and interoperability among different applications and devices. An RDF-based context model has been designed for use in the CG platform, aiming at addressing issues concerning semantic context representation, knowledge sharing and context classification. The ontology captures the relevant notions of physical and semantic entities situated in the system and provides a formal vocabulary for structuring location and other context-aware

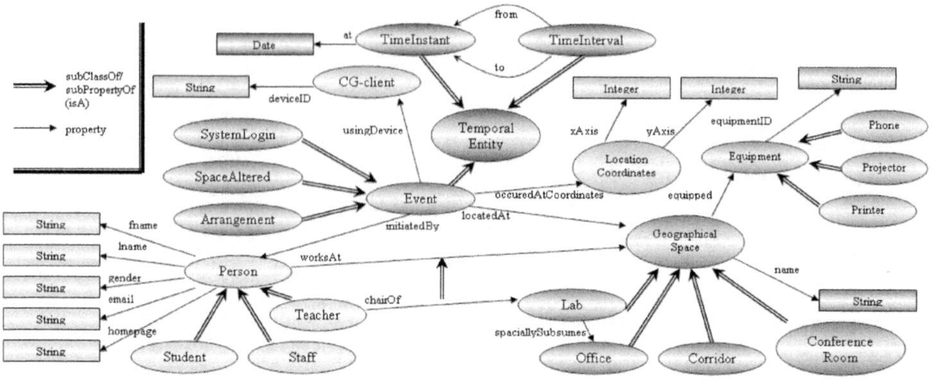

Fig. 2. The schema of the context ontology (different colours denote groupings of distinct concept clusters)

services. The generic CG RDF Schema follows the abstract design principles of other large-scale pervasive computing ontology frameworks, such as the SOUPA project [5], and defines the high-level concepts of Person, Geographical Space, Location Coordinates, CG-Client and Event, as well as the relations among them. The model captures static information (i.e., device ID for CG-Client devices) and dynamic contextual data (events) that have both spatial and temporal extensions, such as user login, change of location in the building and other.

The CG Schema, along with all static and dynamic data, is stored by means of the ICS-FORTH RDFSuite [9]. RDFSuite is a suite of tools for RDF validation, storage and querying, using an object-relational DBMS. The language used for querying the database is RQL [10], a typed language following a functional approach, which supports generalized path expressions featuring variables on both labels for nodes (classes) and edges (properties).

A CG-Client module characterizes the devices with which a user can experience services provided by the CG platform. Different mobile devices can connect as CG-Clients in the system, such as PDAs or laptops, taking advantage of the flexible and portable Web-based model used for its development. CG-Clients connect with the CG-Server, a core component of our centralized architecture that acts as a middleware for processing, managing and transforming stored and inferred knowledge preserved in the CG-Database, while also offering the medium for synthesizing and publishing the desired services.

Implementation. For the CG platform to be adaptive to the complexity of context-aware scenarios, a number of up-to-date technologies and systems have been integrated that collaborate through a set of primitive methods (java api). An important component of location-based systems is the positioning mechanism that locates a mobile device or user in the environment, using some tracking technology. The CG prototype uses the IEEE802.11 infrastructure for both communication and positioning. Specifically, it employs the Collaborative Location Sensing (CLS) [8] system that exploits the IEEE802.11 for positioning. The wide popularity of the IEEE802.11 network, low cost, and complexity advantages of using it for both communication and positioning make it an attractive choice. Typically, location-sensing systems that use an infrastructure of APs, employ a *signal-strength signature* or *map* of the physical space and contrast the run-time measurements with the map ([3], [11]).

The core functionalities of the CG-components, such as remote communication, multithreaded design and caching, have been implemented in Java. The CG-client user interface is composed of numerous Scalable Vector Graphics (SVG 1.2) files augmented by Javascript 1.2 functions for accessing the underlying Java procedures. This choice was not arbitrary. SVG is a vector graphics format suitable for the implementation of maps on the web, as well as on mobile devices [13]. These files are imported in HTML templates to allow familiarity with web-enabled interactions. Finally, all data is stored in RDF format using the ICS-FORTH RDFSuite semantic DBMS and exchanged using XML messages, while queries, expressed in RQL, are automatically generated, validated and manipulated.

4 Deployed Services

The system implements several services that enable users to obtain information about their context, to transparently utilize this information for supporting their everyday activity in their working environment and, also, to interact with the flexible map-based interfaces, by selecting or superimposing data objects on the map. Typical services that are included in the platform involve:

Semantic-based services. Users can have access to information stored in the platform's knowledge base regarding other users, such as their name, occupation, e-mail, homepage, current location in the institute, or regarding geographical spaces, such as room names, room equipment and other supported features. The client application automatically creates queries in a semantic language to retrieve static and dynamic data for performing the requested tasks. In addition, users can engage in interaction with entities appearing on their interface; for example they can send instant messages, publish semantically and contextually annotated notes, arrange presentations in conference rooms, check upcoming events etc.

Personalized services. Users that interact with a context-aware system are expected to experience independencies not only from the application and location perspectives, but also from the device perspective. Adapting content to the users' preferences and tailored to the capabilities of the device used is a priority for the CG system. We can use the user's profile information to support a variety of personalized services, such as message exchange among user groups, context sharing, group note creation etc. We also plan to augment the user's profile with privacy preferences that the system must take into account whenever it tries to retrieve a user's personal information.

Navigation / Route Finding. Using path planning algorithms, the context model, and the available information from the user's profile, we are developing services that help users navigate in the premises. These services will take into account not only the start and end point of the user's route, but also the user's special needs and characteristics, i.e., the authorization to pass through specific areas, potential corporal disabilities etc.

Calendar services. The integration of a calendaring application with the room reservation service is a valuable aspect of the CG system. We plan to employ a web calendar application that supports semantic descriptions of the calendar entries, in order to combine these entries with the room reservation semantic descriptions, but also with data originating from other semantic-based applications and sources.

A more detailed description of the supported services, along with a use-case scenario that demonstrates the ways that the system can be used as a valuable tool for the accomplishment of various everyday activities performed by people working in FO.R.T.H. are available in [4].

5 Challenges in Ubiquitous and Context-Aware Implementations

Motivated by the experience and knowledge gained during the development of the CG platform, this section investigates certain problems that emerge and fundamental issues that must be addressed, during the implementation of ubiquitous, context-aware systems. We discuss the practical limitations and theoretical challenges of many fields of AI research, when applied to highly demanding realistic environments.

5.1 Distributed Planning and Multi-agent Coordination Techniques

Extending our platform with new services has made evident the importance of seamless collaboration between numerous devices (or respectively the agents representing them) that must work together to achieve common objectives. Even the more ordinary services like the management of a presentation in a meeting room may involve continuous cooperation between devices, as diverse as the room's projector, the lighting dimmer, the lecturer's laptop and many others. More complicated services require more sophisticated models of teamwork between devices, which differ in capabilities, characteristics and resource limitations. The establishment of common objectives among them entails a comprehensive understanding of the problem domain between participating entities and a desire to distribute their knowledge and to contribute their capabilities, in order to generate plans for achieving these objectives. Moreover, the assumption that the availability of devices is known beforehand is not valid in our platform, and, therefore, we have to come up with ways to arrange the formation of coalitions at execution time.

A sensor and device-rich environment along with software capable of fully leveraging their capabilities is, in fact, the domain of ubiquitous computing applications. If all the agents in the system were omniscient of the goals, actions and interaction of their fellow community members and could also have unlimited computational resources, it would be possible to know exactly the present and future actions and intentions of each agent and systems could be perfectly combined. Obviously, this in not the case in most real-world systems and in ubiquitous IS, in particular. Despite the fact that our platform currently utilizes a centralized knowledge base, there are many situations where services would benefit by distributing reasoning and planning tasks among different devices. A typical example is when a user's connectivity with the network is undermined due to coverage range limitations or bandwidth restrictions, while he can still engage in ad hoc communication with other mobile devices in its vicinity, which can contribute resources and services. The self-organization and autonomy of devices are important design goals in several mobile computing environments, especially due to the very dynamic characteristics of the environment, frequent disconnections, and frequent interactions with other peer-devices. This decentralized self-organizing infrastructure is a nontrivial challenge for the realization of the ubiquitous computing vision.

Coordination does not imply either cooperation or reciprocation. desJardins et al. in [7] recognize two directions of research in approaching the problem of coordinating the actions of multiple agents in a distributed environment. *Cooperative Distributed Planning* is carried out by agents that have been endowed with shared objectives and representations, with the purpose to jointly develop and execute a plan in a coherent and effective manner. On the other hand, *Negotiated Distributed Planning* concerns agents engaging in negotiations over planned activities not to form good collective plans, but to try to influence each other to accommodate their individual preferences and ensure their local objectives will be met when viewed in a global context. Both directions have attracted significant research interest in an attempt to develop algorithms that perform efficiently considering a variety of metrics and at different environmental configurations. In the vast majority of situations, the ubiquitous computing domain involves agents engaging in Cooperative Distributed Planning, since it is assumed that personal devices of different users and appliances in a smart space will be willing to collaborate in achieving common objectives, when a particular level of trustfulness has been established.

5.2 Complex, Dynamic and Uncertain Environments

The majority of services provided by our platform requires a certain degree of reasoning and plan management skills by the participating agents. For instance, an agent wishing to print a document deliberates on whether to use the slow inkjet printer located near the user or the faster high resolution laser printer of the next room. While trying to enhance our platform with more aspects of context, the complexity of the planning task becomes computationally intractable. Planning and reasoning about action are well studied branches of AI, but have not yet been fully integrated in the ubiquitous computing domain. When research on planning within the AI community established the *classical planning problem* for the development of techniques for agents to generate courses of action to reach a desirable world state, it adopted a number of simplifying assumptions to delimit the domain. Some of these assumptions were very restrictive; the planning agent was considered omniscient, its actions deterministic, atomic and simultaneous, the environment static and the only source of change in the environment was the agent itself, while no other exogenous event occurring. Of course, these simplifications do not persist in realistic planning situations and must be relaxed or completely eliminated when adapting planners to ubiquitous information systems.

Therefore, in studying the ubiquitous computing domain under the planning context, it is important to understand the classes of problems that planning methods face and the challenges that these problems introduce. The ubiquitous computing environment is an open and highly dynamic environment. Mobile devices connect and disconnect to the network, contributing services with durations that vary according to their expected presence in the environment and the availability of their resources. In fact, even actions, goals and sensor observations have a temporal dimension, whose duration may only be partially known in advance. The assumption of complete world knowledge can no longer persist; agents do not know *a priori* all other entities that are present at a specific time instance nor can they communicate directly with all of them. As a consequence, they have limited perception to acquire knowledge about the world they live in and have to generate plans preserving a level of uncertainty on both the state of the world, the available actions to achieve certain state of affairs and the outcome of those actions. Even the fact of committing different agents to certain tasks cannot be guaranteed to persist, since agents might disconnect before plan generation completes or new and more beneficial opportunities might arise, underscoring the importance of monitoring plan execution and replanning in opportunistic ways. The nondeterministic nature of the environment is emphasized by the recognition that not only agents, but also exogenous events occur in unpredictable and concurrent manner, affecting the state of the world. These observations essentially sketch a very challenging dynamic and uncertain environment with increased planning complexity. It remains questionable whether current efforts can attack this problem and provide computationally efficient and scalable solutions under these conditions.

5.3 Plan Representation and Sharing

The overall implementation of our context-aware platform was structured around a number of observations that specify the basic motivations of the domain, such as the desire to provide context-aware services to users that operate on a variety of mobile devices. In order for our architecture to support this scheme, we seek ways to represent the capabilities of these devices so that services can be adapted according to them. Profiles of devices must be flexible enough to capture both the complex actions that they can perform, but also decompositions of them to more lower-level actions, so that planning agents can understand and combine these actions to distribute responsibilities during service execution. There are problems that need to be overcome for achieving this type of interactions in our framework, since we assume that the existence of visitors possessing unknown mobile devices is going to be a common situation for the system. We also wish to exploit all the appropriate aspects of contextual information and to integrate them in the planning process, but also to dynamically associate with plan evaluation other dimensions, such as resource preservation, importance of execution, trust and privacy issues.

In order for any ubiquitous computing framework to support the challenges discussed so far, we also need to seek ways to represent device and service profiles, plans and goals in a manner that is mutually understood and correctly interpreted by all participating entities. Instead of exclusively focussing on improving our planners, other facets of the problem should also come into consideration that can refine the planning task. Recent studies suggest that it is not enough to just build better planners, which can generate plans for dynamic, uncertain, multi-agent environments ([12]). Autonomous agents also need to recognize which planning problems and opportunities to consider in the first place. They need to be able to weight alternative incomplete plans and to decide among competing alternatives. They need to be able to function intelligently in a ubiquitous environment in a way that comports with the inherent bounds on their computational resources. They need to share a common plan representation or a common ontology for describing their plans, goals and actions. And, they need to be able to exchange freely their plans and describe their action behaviors, privacy policies and authenticity certificates, in terms of expressive planning languages.

In order to attain the goal of planning in partially known environments with incomplete information, we have to endow agents with cognitive capabilities. When agents weight alternative subplans to reach a certain state of affairs, it is often useful to interleave reasoning in the process. We indeed believe that the ubiquitous computing domain raises many opportunities for exploiting reasoning to influence the efficiency of planning and reduce the search space. The most important leverage is to exploit the context in which an agent is situated, affecting its plan-generation capabilities. Context awareness has become one of the hot topics in recent computing research and reasoning on context can be an important source of information. It will enable them to constraint and better prioritize their goals, leading to computationally more efficient planning solutions in real world conditions.

6 Conclusions

The Contextual Pedestrian Guiding framework is a first effort to exploit the representational capabilities of the Semantic Web formalisms for the needs of a context-aware guiding application for the Institute of Computer Science of FORTH in Crete. The development and operation of a system prototype, and the study for the integration of more complex ubiquitous services have revealed us new research challenges, which require more effective solutions from the field of AI. The need for distributed, continual, and context-aware planning in a highly dynamic and demanding ambient environment dictates abandoning some strong assumptions of current methods and techniques, and inquiring new models that will enable the implementation of more efficient ubiquitous information systems. The study and integration of such models are part of our ongoing work on designing the extensions for our system.

References

1. Abowd, D.A., Atkeson, C.G., Hong, J., Long, S., Kooper, R., Pinkerton, M.: Cyperguide: A Mobile Context-Aware Tour Guide. Wireless Networks 3(5), 421–433 (1996)
2. Anagnostopoulos, C., Tsetsos, V., Kikiras, P., Hadjiefthymiades, S.: OntoNav: A Semantic Indoor Navigation System. In: Proceedings of the 1st Workshop on Semantics in Mobile Environments (SME), MDM'05, Cyprus (2005)
3. Bahl, P., Padmanabhan, V.N.: RADAR: An In-Building RF-based User Location and Tracking System. IEEE Infocom'00, Tel Aviv (2000)
4. Bikakis, A., Patkos, T., Antoniou, G., Papadopouli, M., Plexousakis, D.: A Semantic-based Framework for Context-Aware Pedestrian Guiding Services. In: Second International Workshop on Semantic Web Technology For Ubiquitous and Mobile Applications, Riva del Garda, Trentino, Italy (2006)

5. Chen, H., Finin, T., Joshi, A.: The SOUPA Ontology for Pervasive Computing. In: Tamma, V., Cranefield, S., Finin, T. (eds.) Ontologies for Agents: Theory and Experiences, Springer, Heidelberg (2005)
6. Cheverst, K., Davies, N., Mitchell, K., Friday, A., Efstratiou, C.: Developing a Context-aware Electronic Tourist Guide: Some Issues and Experiences. In: Proceedings of the 2000 Conf. on Human Factors in Computing Systems (CHI-00), pp. 17–24. ACM Press, New York (2000)
7. desJardins, M.E., Durfee, E.H., Ortiz, C.L., Wolverton, M.J.: A Survey of Research in Distributed, Continual Planning. AI Magazine 20(4), 13–22 (1999)
8. Fretzagias, C., Papadopouli, M.: Cooperative location-sensing for wireless networks. In: Second IEEE International conference on Pervasive Computing and Communications, Orlando, Florida (2004)
9. ICS-FORTH, The ICS-Forth RDFSuite web site, http://139.91.183.30:9090/RDF (2006)
10. Karvounarakis, G., Alexaki, S., Christophides, V., Plexousakis, D., Schol, M.: RQL: A Declarative Query Language for RDF. In: Proceedings of the Eleventh International World Wide Web Conference (WWW'02), Honolulu, Hawaii, USA (2002)
11. Ladd, A.M., Bekris, K.E., Rudys, A., Marceau, G., Kavraki, L.E., Wallach, D.S.: Robotics-Based Location Sensing using Wireless Ethernet. In: The Eighth ACM International Conference on Mobile Computing and Networking (MOBICOM), Atlanta (2002)
12. Pollack, M., Horty, J.F.: There's More to Life than Making Plans. The AI Magazine 20(4), 71–84 (1999)
13. Reichenbacher, T.: SVG for adaptive visualisations in mobile situations. In: SVG Open Conference, Zürich (2002)
14. Retscher, G., Thienelt, M.: NAVIO - A Navigation and Guidance Service for Pedestrians. In: Papers presented at the GNSS Sydney 2004 Conference, Sydney, Australia (2004)
15. Strang, T., Linnhoff-Popien, C.: A Context Modeling Survey. Workshop on Advanced Context Modelling. In: Reasoning and Management as part of UbiComp 2004 - The Sixth International Conference on Ubiquitous Computing, Nottingham, England (2004)
16. van Setten, M., Pokraev, S., Koolwaaij, J.: Context-aware Recommendations in the Mobile Tourist Application COMPASS. In: Nejdl, W., De Bra, P. (eds.) AH 2004. LNCS, vol. 3137, pp. 235–244. Springer, Heidelberg (2004)
17. Wilson, M.L., Russell, A., Smith, D.A., Owens, A., Schraefel, M.C.: mSpace Mobile: A Mobile Application for the Semantic Web. In: Proceedings of End User Semantic Web Workshop, ISWC2005, Galway, Ireland (2005)

Devising a Context Selection-Based Reasoning Engine for Context-Aware Ubiquitous Computing Middleware

Donghai Guan, Weiwei Yuan, Seong Jin Cho, Andrey Gavrilov, Young-Koo Lee, and Sungyoung Lee*

Department of Computer Engineering, Kyung Hee University, Korea
{donghai,weiwei,babebear,avg,sylee}@oslab.khu.ac.kr, yklee@khu.ac.kr

Abstract. We propose a novel reasoning engine for context-aware ubiquitous computing middleware in this paper. Our reasoning engine supports both rule-based reasoning and machine learning reasoning. Our main contribution is to utilize feature selection method to filter the low-level contexts which are not useful for certain special high-level context reasoning. As a result, rules and learning models in the reasoning engine's knowledge base are refined since useless context have been filtered. The merits of our proposed reasoning engine are described in details in this paper.

1 Introduction

By gathering context data and adapting systems behaviors accordingly, context-aware systems offer entirely new opportunities for application developers and end users. Especially when combined with mobile devices, these systems are of high value and are able to increase usability tremendously.

In order to adapt applications to different situations and be more receptive to users' needs, a number of works have been done in trying to make applications context aware in ubiquitous computing environments [1][2][3][4][5]. The design of these applications needs to take account of heterogeneous devices, mobile users and rapidly changing contexts. Hence, ubiquitous computing environments must provide middleware support for context-awareness.

The role of middleware is to ease the task of designing, programming and managing distributed applications by providing a simple, consistent and integrated distributed programming environment; such middleware-based approach is quite appealing in context-aware ubiquitous computing [2].

In last several years, we have developed our own context-aware ubiquitous computing middleware (CAMUS) [6]. In the process of analyzing existing middleware and devising our own middleware, we have identified a set of necessary functional elements that a context-aware system needs to support essential context aware mechanisms. These functional elements are shown in Table 1.

* Corresponding author.

J. Indulska et al. (Eds.): UIC 2007, LNCS 4611, pp. 849–857, 2007.

Table 1. Necessary functional elements in context-aware middleware

Context Sensing	Obtain the context data from diverse context sources
Context Modeling	Foundation for expressive context representation and high-level context interpretation
Context Repository	Provide a persistent storage for distributed context
Context Reasoning/Inferring	Interpret low-level information and derive additional, high-level context
Context Discovery/Delivery	Searching appropriate context aggregators and delivering them to the applications.

Instead of describing all the elements in Table 1, in this paper, we focus on context reasoning. We argue that context reasoning plays an important role in a context-aware ubiquitous system. To truly understand the importance of context reasoning, first of all, we need to know what is context.

Context is defined as any information that can be used to characterize the situation of an entity. And entity could be the person, place, or object that is considered relevant to the interaction between a user and an application, including the user and applications themselves [7]. Context can be divided into low-level context and high-level context. In general, low-level context is simple and can be directly got from sensors or other sources. While, high-level context is abstract and need to be inferred from a piece of low-level context. This can be as simple as taking in a name and returning the corresponding email address. It could be more complex and take in the number of people in a room, the relative gaze directions, the audio level, and the time of day, and return whether or not a meeting was occurring.

Most applications show more interest in high-level context. For example, many smart spaces [8][9][10] would like to know the information about user's activity, which is a typical high-level context. Some adaptations will be made based on activity.

After understanding what is high-level context and why it is so important. Now we would like to present the reason why we should do the high-level context reasoning task in the middleware. Why not in application? There are two main reasons. One reason is that in ubiquitous environment, many applications are installed in mobile devices (mobile phone, PDA). Due to the constrained nature of small mobile computers in terms of processing power, memory and persistent storage, it is very difficult for them to do the reasoning task. Context reusability is the other reason to put the reasoning engine in middleware, not applications themselves.

This paper is organized as follows: in section 2, by introducing the related works about the reasoning engines adopted by other ubiquitous middleware, we conclude that all of them utilize rule-based reasoning and/or machine learning methods. This drives us to propose multiple reasoning mechanisms in our middleware's reasoning engine. In section 3, we present the main characters of our reasoning engine: multiple reasoning mechanisms, pluggable reasoning modules and ontology reasoning module. Section 4 gives our proposed method on how to improve reasoning engine based on our existing one. We propose to use feature selection method to filter the irrelevant low-level context for a given high-level context. At last, we present conclusions and future works in section 5.

2 Related Work

In this section, we will cover context reasoning mechanisms adopted by some well-known ubiquitous computing middleware.

In Context Toolkit [1], Context Interpreters are responsible for interpreting or converting context from one form to another. They maintain no state but simply take context in and output new context information. While the Context Toolkit does provide a starting point for applications to make use of contextual information, it does not provide any generic mechanism for writing rules about contexts, inferring high-level contexts or organizing the wide range of possible contexts in a structured format.

In Gaia [11], Context Synthesizer takes charge of reasoning. Context Synthesizers are agents that provide high-level contexts based on simpler sensed contexts. A Context Synthesizer gets source contexts from various Context Providers, applies some sort of logic to them and generates a new type of context. Agents can reason about context using rules written in different types of logic like first order logic, temporal logic, description logic, higher order logic, fuzzy logic, etc. Instead of using rules written in some form of logic to reason about context, agents can also use various machine learning techniques to deal with context. Learning techniques that can be used include Bayesian learning, neural networks, reinforcement learning, etc.

In SOCAM [12], the Context Reasoning Engine reasons over the knowledge base. Multiple logic reasoners can be incorporated into the Context Reasoning Engine to support various kinds of reasoning tasks. Currently RDFS reasoner, OWL reasoner and a general rule-based reasoner are built in to SOCAM. Different inference rules can be specified and preloaded into various logic reasoners. The interpreters is implemented by using Jena2 [13], a semantic Web toolkit. The Context Interpreter also acts as a context provider as it provides high-level contexts by interpreting low-level contexts. It consists of a context reasoner and a context KB.

In CASS [14], deriving of high-level context is also based on an inference engine and a knowledge base. The knowledge base contains rules queried by the inference engine to find goals using the so-called forward chaining techniques. As these rules are stored in a database separated from the interpreter neither recompiling nor restarting of components is necessary when rules change. In Cobra [15], the reasoning engine is responsible for reasoning with ontology knowledge and contextual knowledge in the knowledge base. In addition, the inference engine will apply learning algorithms and pattern recognition mechanisms to learn about high-level context. In ECA [16], the reasoning engine determines when the left-hand-side (LHS) of user specified rules are matched by the current set of facts stored in the knowledge base of the engine. As a result of this process, the engine initiates the actions specified in the right-hand-side (RHS) of rules.

By analyzing above context reasoning engines, we can see that although their detailed implementation parts are different, the main reasoning methods they applied are almost the same: rule-based reasoning and/or machine learning methods. Rule based reasoning is the most common form of knowledge processing nowadays. User predefined rules written in some form of logic are used to infer different contexts. However, most developers find that building the rules is the most difficult task in ubiquitous computing systems. Also rule-based reasoning is not flexible and can not adapt to changing circumstances. Making use of machine learning techniques to deduce the higher-level context enables us to get around this problem. In addition to multiple reasoning methods, knowledge base is also needed. The knowledge base is composed of two parts. One part is user-defined rules for rule-base reasoning. The other part is learning models. These learning models are inferred by utilizing inductive methods to analyze context history. In the next section, we will describe the detailed structure and important characters involved in our reasoning engine.

3 Our Existing Reasoning Engine

3.1 Overview

Our context reasoning engine includes one to many reasoners which handle the facts present in the repository as well as to produce composite contexts. The reasoners can provide the entailed knowledge not formally present in the repository using various kinds of logics to support inference; description logic, first order logic, temporal logic and spatial logic to name a few. Moreover, many kinds of reasoning over uncertainty such as Bayesian inference or fuzzy logic can also be applied.

The reasoning service is used by some context mapping services and context aggregators. They invoke the reasoners through a fixed API, providing the reasoners with a context data which can be considered as a knowledge base containing all the facts needed for inference. All new inferred facts will be inserted into that context data for later queries. The use of a fixed interface for all kinds of reasoning engine makes it possible to add and handle different reasoners. The developers can then use any kind of reasoning they want.

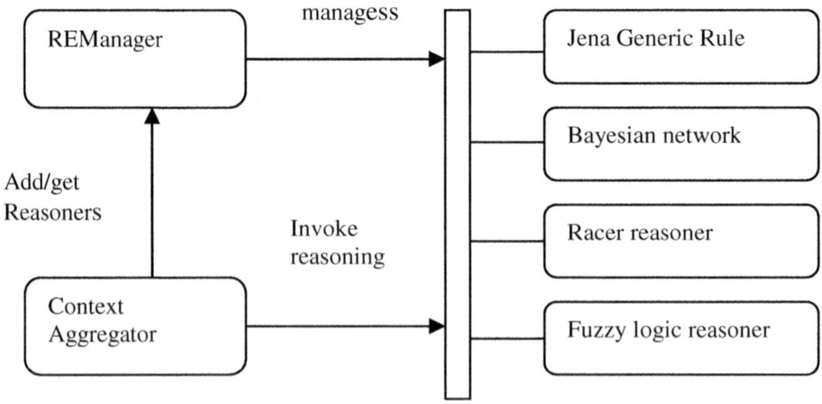

Fig. 1. Reasoning engine in our middleware

3.2 Main Characters of Our Reasoning Engine

(1) **Multiple Reasoning Mechanism.** Considering different upper applications' different reasoning requirements, multiple reasoning mechanisms are proposed. Agents can reason about context using rules written in different types of logic like first order logic, temporal logic, description logic (DL), higher order logic, fuzzy logic, etc. Different agents have different logic requirements. Agents that are concerned with the temporal sequence in which various events occur would need to use some form of temporal logic to express the rules. Agents that need to express generic conditions using existential or universal quantifiers would need to use some form of first order logic (FOL). Agents that need more expressive power (like characterizing the transitive closure of relations) would need higher order logics. Agents that deal with specifying terminological hierarchies may need description logic. Agents that need to handle uncertainties may require some form of fuzzy logic.

Instead of using rules written in some form of logic to reason about context, agents can also use various machine learning techniques to deal with context. Learning techniques that can be used include Bayesian learning, neural networks, reinforcement learning, etc. Depending on the kind of concept to be learned, different learning mechanisms can be used. If an agent wants to learn the appropriate action to perform in different states in an online, interactive manner, it could use reinforcement learning or neural networks. If an agent wants to learn the conditional probabilities of different events, Bayesian learning is appropriate.

(2) **Pluggable Reasoning Modules.** To provide more help to developers so that they can concentrate on developing rules or networks for reasoning and not be burdened with the low-level details, our middleware defines wrappers for each reasoner type. For example, a wrapper of Jena generic rule reasoner allows the developer to easily add a new reasoner just by declaring the rule file name and some namespace abbreviations. The following piece of code illustrates how to add and invoke a rule-based reasoner.

```
/* add a new reasoner providing the rule file*/
ContextReasonerManager.addReasoner("Location",ReasonerType.GENERIC_REASONER,
"etc/contel.rules") ;
/*declare some statements*/
sms=new ContextStatement[ ] {PastLocationDescription, hasLocation};
/*invoke the reasoner to do reasoning, providing the reasoner name, the context data name and the re-
quired statements*/
cdm.invokeReasoning("Location", "Data", sms);
```

(3) **Ontology Reasoning Mechanisms.** Ontology reasoning helps us to find subsumption relationships (between subconcept-superconcept), instance relationships (an individual i is an instance of concept C), and consistency of context knowledge base, provided by Racer Server. In the design phase of formalizing the context entities, OWL reasoning services (such as satisfiability and subsumption) can test whether concepts are non-contradictory and can derive implied relations between concepts.

Let us take an example to see how ontology reasoning can help deducing implied context. In location ontology, the property locatedIn is a TransitiveProperty, and isPartOf is subProperty of locatedIn. So when knowing that Bilbo is locatedIn Bed, and Bed is a part of BedRoom which is part of Home, the system can deduce that Bilbo is locatedIn BedRoom and Home.

4 Improvement on Our Reasoning Engine

In this section, we will present our idea on how to improve our existing reasoning engine described in last section.

Knowledge base is an indispensable part of our reasoning engine. For rule-based reasoning, the knowledge base provides many user-made rules. As for machine learning reasoning, many learning models are required to be loaded into the knowledge base. These learning models are deduced by analyzing context history using machine learning methods. Since both rule-based and machine learning reasoning are supported by our reasoning engine, the knowledge base of our system includes two parts: user-defined rules and learning models. The process to construct a knowledge base is shown in Fig. 2.

Knowledge base plays an important role in knowledge-based reasoning systems. The content quality in knowledge base directly influences the reasoning result. So improving the quality of rules and models in our knowledge base is urgently needed. Currently, there are some potential problems with our knowledge base.

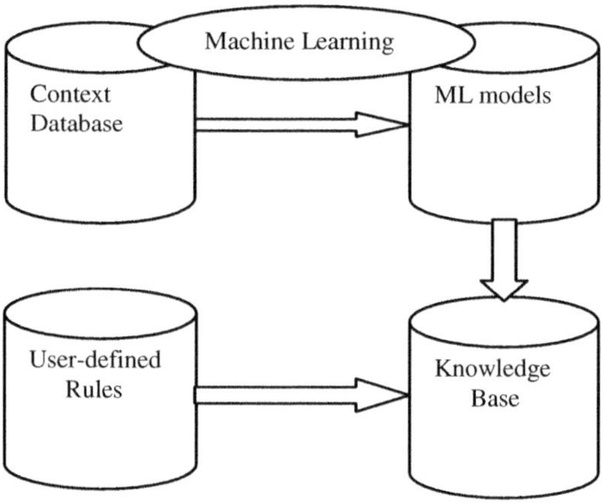

Fig. 2. Knowledge base of our reasoning engine

4.1 User-Defined Rules in Knowledge Base

Rule-based reasoning has proved itself effective decision makers for many types of problems. However, the accuracy of such systems is highly dependent upon the accuracy of the user's domain theory. When users learn or create a set of rules, they are subject to a number of hindrances. As a result, the user-defined rules are always incomplete or erroneous. In ubiquitous environment, the rules for high-level context reasoning usually follow this format: if $lc_1 = x_1$ and/or $lc_2 = x_2$ ....and/or $lc_n = x_n$, then $hc = M$, in which lc_i (i=1,2,...n) represents low-level context and hc represents high-level context. It is easy to see that hc is determined by the value of lc_i. In ubiquitous environment, the number of different types of low-level context is huge. In some simple cases, it is feasible for users to manually choose which low-level context should be used to deduce a given high-level context. However, as for some complex high-level context reasoning, such as activity and mood reasoning, users are not able to exactly determine which low-level context should be selected. As a result, many useless low-level contexts are mistakenly selected to deduce a given high-level context, which makes the rules used for some high-level context reasoning is not correct.

To solve the above problem, rules refinement is urgently needed. In this paper, we propose to use feature selection method to analyze context history, so that those low-level context, which has more weight to deduce a give high-level context, could be figured out. Then, these extracted low-level contexts could be used to compare with those provided by users to improve user-defined rules' quality.

4.2 Learning Models

We got learning models by utilizing machine learning methods to analyze context history. Compared with user-defined rules, the accuracy of learning models is improved. However, one potential problem still exits.

Here, we take user activity as an example of high-level context. In general, activity could be divided into several classes. Hence, this high-level context deduction could be treated as a classification problem.

Classification systems depend upon having the best set of input features from which a classification decision can then be made. This is true both for the classifiers themselves and for the learning models might be used to classify. This drives us to select the "relevant" low-level contexts for training, instead of all the low-level contexts.

To achieve this function, firstly, we still utilize feature selection method to find the most relevant low-level context for a given high-level context. Then, different inductive learning methods could be used to deduce the learning models. Many work [17][18] showed that the learning models deduced from relevant features (low-level context) could be much improved. Now the process to build a knowledge base for reasoning engine can be depicted by Fig. 3.

In addition to refine rules and learning models, other advantages using feature selection method include:

1) Saving sensors. Since useless low-level contexts could be detected by using feature selection method. So in real ubiquitous environment, only those useful sensors need to be deployed. As a result, the cost to build a smart environment is reduced.
2) Reducing human's burden. Now many experiments are based on the sensors attached to human. Human's burden could be reduced by filtering those useless sensors.
3) Saving context database size. Most algorithms in reasoning engine are supervised learning method, which need to analyze historical context data to design an accordingly model. In a ubiquitous environment, effectively mining useful low-level context can avoid data explosion.

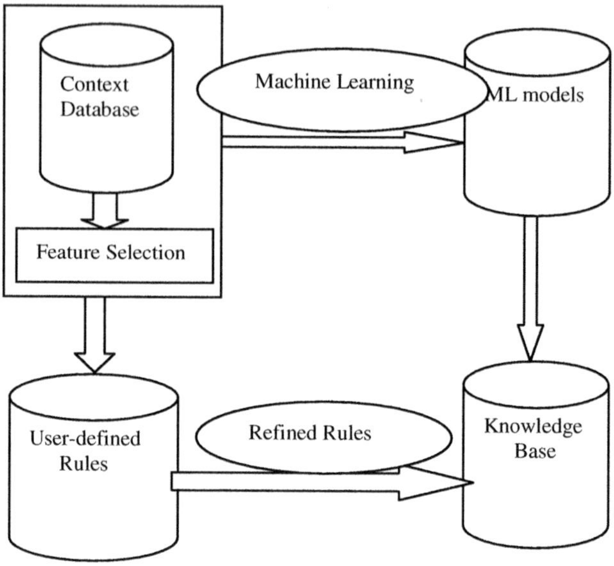

Fig. 3. Knowledge base construction based on feature selection

4) Easy to see the relationship between low-level context and high-level context. Since most irrelevant features have been filtered by feature selection, it is easy to make human-understandable rules.
5) Reducing reasoning uncertainty. As we all know that sensors have their inherent uncertainty. The more sensors used for reasoning, the more uncertainty will arise.

5 Conclusions

In this paper, we propose to utilize feature selection method in our context-aware middleware reasoning engine. Our reasoning engine supports both rule-based reasoning and machine learning reasoning. The main advantages using this engine are described in our paper.

Feature selection method is used to filter those low-level contexts which do not contribute a lot for a given high-level context reasoning. The direct effect is that fewer sensors are required. As a result, context database occupation is reduced.

Our plan for future work is to assess our reasoning engine in our smart office. We are currently deploying different sensors in our office and will use them for collecting empirical data. Finally more high-level contexts will be inferred to further prove the feasibility of our reasoning engine.

Acknowledgement

This research was supported by the MIC (Ministry of Information and Communication), Korea, under the ITRC (Information Technology Research Center) Support program supervised by the IITA (Institute of Information Technology Advancement) (IITA-2006-(C1090-0602-0002)).

References

1. Dey, A.K., Abowd, G.D., Salber, D.: A Conceptual Framework and a Toolkit for Supporting the Rapid Prototyping of Context-Aware Applications. J. of Human-Computer Interaction (HCI) 16, 97–166 (2001)
2. Hong, J.I., Landay, J.A.: An Infrastructure Approach to Context-Aware Computing. J. Human-Computer Interaction (HCI), London, UK, 287–303 (2001)
3. Shafer, S.A.N., Brumitt, B., Cadiz,J.J.: Interaction Issues in Context-Aware Interactive Environments. J. Human-Computer Interaction (HCI), London, UK, 363–378 (2001)
4. Pascoe, J., et al.: Issues in Developing Context-Aware Computing. In: Proc. of the International Symposium on Handheld and Ubiquitous Computing, pp. 208–221. Springer, Heidelberg (1999)
5. Schilit, W.N.: A Context-Aware System Architecture for Mobile Distributed Computing. PhD Thesis. Columbia University (1995)
6. Hung, N.Q., Shehzad, A., Kiani, S.L., Riaz, M., Lee, S.: A Unified Middleware Framework for Context Aware Ubiquitous Computing. In: The 2004 IFIP International Conference on Embedded And Ubiquitous Computing. EUC2004, Japan, pp. 672–681 (2004)
7. Dey, A.K.: Understanding and Using Context. Personal and Ubiquitous Computing 4–7 (2001)
8. Kulkarni, A.: A Reactive Behavioral System for the Intelligent Room. Master's Thesis in Computer Science and Engineering at the Massachusetts Institute of Technology. Cambridge, MA (2002)
9. Brumitt, B.L., Meyers, B., Krumm, J.: EasyLiving: Technologies for Intelligent Environments. In: Proc. of Handheld and Ubiquitous Computing, pp. 12–27 (2000)
10. Elrod, S., Hall, G., Costanza, R., Dixon, M., Des Rivieres, J.: Responsive Office Environments. Proc. of ACM Communications , 84–85 (1993)
11. Gaia Project (2005), http://gaia.cu.uiuc.edu/
12. Gu, T., Pung, H.K., Zhang, D.Q.: A middleware for building context-aware mobile services. In: Proc. of IEEE Vehicular Technology Conference (VTC 2004), Italy, pp. 2656–2660. IEEE Computer Society Press, Los Alamitos (2004)
13. Jena: A Semantic Web Framework for Java, http://jena.sourceforge.net/
14. Fahy, P., Clarke, S.: CASS – a middleware for mobile context-aware applications. In: Proc. of the Workshop on Context Awareness, MobiSys (2004)
15. Chen, H., Finin, T., Joshi, A.: An ontology for context-aware pervasive computing environments. In: Proceedings of the Workshop on Ontologies in Agent Systems, pp. 197–207 (2003)
16. Ipina, D., Katsiri, E.: An ECA Rule-Matching Service for Simpler Development of Reactive Applications. In: Proc. of Middleware 2001 at IEEE Distributed Systems Online 2(7) (2001)
17. Liu, H., Yu, L.: Toward Integrating Feature Selection Algorithms for Classification and Clustering. IEEE Transactions on Knowledge and Data Engineering 1–12 (2005)
18. Kwak, N., Choi, C.-H.: Input Feature Selection for Classification Problems. IEEE Transactions on Neural Networks, 143–159 (2002)

The u-Class Based on Context-Awareness*

Jae-Hyun Lim, Chi-Su Kim, and Yong-Woo Lee

Department of Computer Engineering, Kongju National University
{defacto,cskim,ericlee}@kongju.ac.kr

Abstract. In this paper, we present design and implementation of u-Class supporting intelligent services. Checking the attendance automatically and providing assistance for the lecture procedure in according with intentions of lecturer intelligently are supported by the middleware that has architecture of context-aware interpretation in circumstance of the u-Class. Implemented u-Class with context-aware technology, subsequently it has tested and evaluated whether it is possible controlling of assistant equipments for lecture and serving intelligent services for the lecture depending on various situations and circumstances of lecture room.

1 Introduction

Today's campus has evolved to the u-Campus adapting ubiquitous technologies. Ubiquitous campus is focused on two factors concerning the 'Portable' and 'Pervasive'. Those are m-Campus based on wireless/mobile network infrastructure and u-Campus that leads to automate and intellectualize campus facilities such as library and a lecture room using RFID/USN technologies. The m-Campus is emphasis on information's flows that makes it possible sharing information and building an online community among residents in campus life using the wireless and mobile network infrastructure. The u-Campus, however, is focused on context-aware technology recognizing a user and deciding how the states around the user are. Researches about context-awareness in ubiquitous environment have been dynamically explored worldwide, yet it has not been defined what the "context" means exactly. Schilit refer to context as location, identities of nearby people and objects, and changes to those objects[1][2], Dey defines context as the user's emotional state, focus of attention, location and orientation, date and time, objects, and people in the user's environment[3]. And Pascoe defines context to be the subset of physical and conceptual states of interest to a particular entity [4]. These definitions are useful to create a context required by an application service. But those are not fit for various application services in common. It could be used of diverse sensors and applications under the ubiquitous environment, and it definitely needs core program which could control and communicate with various sensors. This core program has to be coped with sensors and applications in a flexible way. Also, it can be minimizing changes of

* This work was supported by grant No. (R01-2006-000-10555-0) from the Basic Research Program of the Korea Science & Engineering Foundation.

J. Indulska et al. (Eds.): UIC 2007, LNCS 4611, pp. 858–867, 2007.

established system and must carry on a service through proper context-aware interpreting architecture.

Many campuses have been set up wireless internet networking circumstance since a quite long time ago, and these are getting combined electronic space with the campus based on new technologies, especially recognizing user's intentions. Those technologies such as checking the attendance automatically using u-ID card with a RFID tag and with a smart chip are already being used in the class room among a few campuses. Today, lecture rooms are also providing a lecture with many kinds of assistant equipments, and this environment helps to make progress for the multimedia and visual driven lecture. Professors could get some burdens to prepare a lecture due to lack unity of lecturing equipment and poor knowledge about manipulating complicated devices. And there are some problems to make it happen delay of lecture progress caused by malfunction of the equipment and inefficient procedure of the lecture.

It has designed and implemented u-Class based on context-awareness that enables intelligent service to solve the problems which mentioned the above. The u-Class is to let professor only concentrates on the lecture by providing intelligent services that are recognizing professor's intentions and tastes in a natural way. To provide those intelligent services, we have implemented it using Ubi-Core [5]. The Ubi-Core is a middleware that integrates two types of contexts those are information collected by sensors and record of user's history so as to perceive the user's intentions, and it provides intelligent services.

This paper consists of as follows. Chapter 2 will introduce Ubi-Core as a middleware of context-awareness, and it will be designed and implemented a lecture model supported by intelligent service in chapter 3. Chapter 4 analyzes the results of test about the lecture model according with interpretation of context-awareness. Also chapter 5 describes about subsequent working of the research in future.

2 The Context-Aware Middleware: Ubi-Core

The u-Class provides suitable services for a lecturer during lecture. It is using context-aware middleware so called Ubi-Core to achieve of it [5].

The Ubi-Core has designed to make it possible using an application dealing with a context-awareness that can minimize correction times, and it also has a role as an intermediate between sensors unit and services interface. The Ubi-Core mainly consists of 5 structures. The collectors of both internal and external contexts are related with physical sensors and contexts database with user's records and are being collected raw information. The external contexts are collected via external sensors to create context information enabling apply to various context-aware environments. The internal contexts are records of history and user's data on contexts DB such as a list of previous served services, user's ID data and data of user's taste. Integrated message controller is to integrate messages that are raw information collected through internal and external contexts collector, and context interpreter finds out what user's intention is. Service retriever searches appropriate services referring to the user's intention, meanwhile Service executor executes the retrieved service and manages computing resources for execution. Figure 1 shows architecture of Ubi-Core that is context-aware middleware.

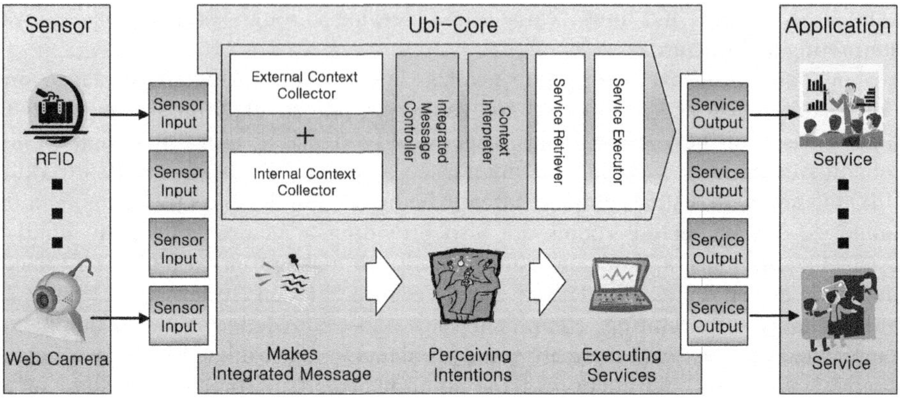

Fig. 1. Shows architecture of Ubi-Core that is context-aware middleware

3 The Context-Aware Lecture Room: u-Class

The model of lecture room supporting intelligent service has focused on ordinary college lecture room. In the lecture room, checking the attendance is carried on automatically and it provides proper service according to what the lecturer's status is such as coming in and out of and positioning of professor among lecture rooms. These services are collecting external contexts from various sensors and are making the circumstance of lecture room fitting for lecturer's taste which has already referred to context database.

3.1 Scenario of u-Class

Basically, u-Class scenario is as same as a procedure of traditional lecture. Students enter the lecture room holding a student's ID card with a built-in RFID tag before getting starts a lecture. Once a student passes through the entrance installed a RFID reader, it would read a student's ID and write its information to the column and assign to electronic roll book of database. A lecturer passes through the same entrance holding a RFID card in order to give a lecture as well. At the moment lecturer passes through the entrance, the Ubi-Core recognizes the context of "Lecture is started". The system retrieves service concerning about lecturer's tastes from context database and customizes environment of current class. At this time, various devices are running as a service according with lecturer's taste, for example "An electric screen is downed", "A beam projector" and "Lights". And there are some basic services triggered automatically when lecture is started such as "be powered on lecturer's PC", "run an electronic roll book" and " execute presentation of the lecture note". The lecturer, first of all, should be seated before the PC for the lecture as soon as the above services are served. After lecturer seated, PC is waiting for lecturer's command while u-Class controller is running on the display. The lecturer can check the attendances via electronic roll book that has already been running. Positioning of lecturer is being kept tracking by web camera. As long as the lecturer is positioning on the lecture platform, the lecture is practically going on. When lecturer has finished the lecture and stepped out of lecture room, the system automatically recognizes "Lecturer is gone" by tagging of its ID card through the RFID reader and triggers "Lecture is completed".

The Ubi-Core perceives current contexts based on various contexts information those are external contexts, user's ID data, and record of history collected from external sensors deployed around lecture room. In u-Class, the system collects external contexts using four external sensors such as a RFID, a Web camera, lights and a pressuring sensor. Internal contexts use context information that is fitted for lecturer's ID record and tastes. Changes of environmental context for the lecture are depending on lecturer's tastes. Predefined contexts in u-Class are "Lecturer is in", "Lecture is started", "Lecture is completed" and "Lecturer is seated". These contexts interpreted by the Ubi-Core have made more two cubed of combinations of the external contexts and internal contexts than predefined contexts. But only 4 combinations could be served for appropriate service because there are non-executable combinations made in real progress of the lecture. And others than those are error status which couldn't give a service. Table 1 show various combinations that could be made and used as a context in practical progress. According to following table 1, the case of second to third won't make usable contexts. Because of that web camera or pressuring sensor couldn't be worked in condition of not being identified lecturer's entrance through RFID, the system will call the "Error context". The status of the eighth is to be "Error context" because the lecturer couldn't be occupied the lecture platform and chair at the same time.

Table 1. Predefined Contexts

Data of External Sensor				Analysis of Context	Intention Code
	RFID	Web Camera	Pressuring Sensor		
1	**x**	**x**	**x**	**Lecture is complete**	**000000**
2	x	x	o	Error Status	000001
3	x	o	x	Error Status	000100
4	x	o	o	Error Status	000101
5	**o**	**x**	**x**	**Lecturer is in**	**010000**
6	**o**	**x**	**o**	**Lecturer is seated**	**010001**
7	**o**	**o**	**x**	**Lecture is started**	**010100**
8	o	o	o	Error Status	010101

- The shading cells shows services that are being served in real.

The RFID reader installed on the gate recognizes the lecturer with a RFID card. When the lecturer passes through the entrance by upon the scheduled lecture time, the Ubi-Core recognizes as "Lecture is started" and serves the service for that in a row. This service makes lecture's environment for the lecturer's tastes and executes the presentation of lecture notes. The services include works of beam projector, electronic screen and lights. When lecturer is seating on the chair before PC, the system basically executes a electronic roll book for enabling check the attendances at the moment. Also, controller of the Ubi-Core is executed and waited for the other command. As soon as lecturer is unseated, controller of Ubi-Core is quitted automatically. Web camera helps to decide whether lecturer wants to give the lecture more or not as it is photographing of the lecture platform during the class. The system could perceive the progressing of current lecture as lecturer moves around the lecture platform therefore it keeps executing itself for the environment of lecture. System will declare momentary "Break" when lecturer is positioned onto another spot from the lecture platform and passes through entrance. If lecturer wouldn't come back to the lecture room through entrance and it comes to about time for quitting the lecture after the laps of prescribes break time, system will declare "lecture is completed" and change the lecture room to be set various equipments back to the waiting state.

3.2 A Model of Lecture Room

Various sensors are used in u-Class and each sensor is selected for collecting its proper contexts.

Each of sensors performs its different job but it might collect the contexts for same purpose. Keeping tracks of lecturer's position which carried by web camera, RFID and pressuring sensor has made it restrictively. Table 2 shows what each sensor's doing. It has made up of hardware structure to implement the u-Class as you see Figure 2. It consists of hardware being served the services and sensors that is in basis of the server with Ubi-Core. Lighting and pressuring sensors are not communicating with the server directly but communicating with it through the Input-Controller. When a signal transmitted to the Input-Controller from a sensor, Input-Controller interprets the signal and assigns it to the server via RS-232C as the value "1" for the signal of "On" and the value "0" for the signal of "Off". Each of hardware providing context-aware services those are electronic screen, beam projector, PC and lights is connected to the Output-Controller just the same as sensors do. Values from services are transmitted to the Ubi-Core through the Output-Controller.

Table 2. Sensors of the u-Class

Sensors	Functions	Transmitted Values
RFID tag	Identification, trace for positioning	RFID Tag's own individual Serial No.
Web camera	trace for positioning	A Photographed still Image
Pressure sensor	trace for positioning and actions	On/Off
Lighting sensor	Check that lights are on	On/Off

3.3 Progress of Interpreting Contexts in u-Class

The core classes and methods, roles of each class and method are described on Table 3. Making the integrated message in u-Class doesn't need to be fulfill of every fields and it is depends on the context.

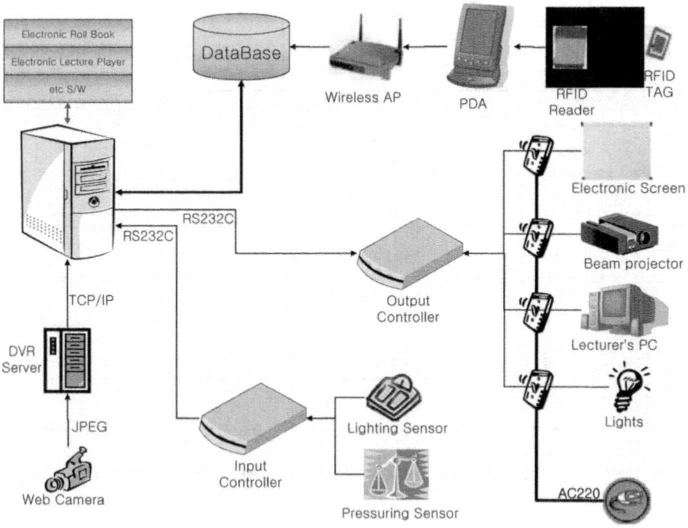

Fig. 2. The basic structure of u-Class

Table 3. Core Classes and Methods of Ubi-Core

Role	Class	Method	Description
Collecting of Contexts	InInfor	loadicontext()	Collecting internal contexts from DB
	OutInfor	colsdata()	Collecting external contexts from external sensors
Making integrated message & Reasoning of intention	CTMessage	inssection()	Inputting data referring by contexts collected on massage section
		cmessage()	Making integrated message from message section
	PIntention	prointention()	Grasping a intention
		pservice()	Transmitting intention to the service retriever
Retrieve services	FindService	loadservice()	Searching a service for the intention from DB
	CreateList	clist()	Listing
Sevice Execute	ExecService	exeservice()	Having a hardware to run a service on the list
Service End	ProgInit	chistory()	Making a history for executed service
		inshist()	Saving the history onto DB as a record
		pinit()	Initializing of the Ubi-Core

The point of time making the integrated message is mainly when the event is occurred in case of transmitting sensing data to the Ubi-Core or changing of data existed in DB.

You can see how it has made the integrated message using both internal and external contexts on Figure 4. Current user's position and the time of event that has occurred are transmitted to the Ubi-Core via RFID system and it inquires about RFID card and records of history to get user's ID information from DB. There's no data for entrance of lecturer therefore it transmit a context of that lecturer entered the lecture room.

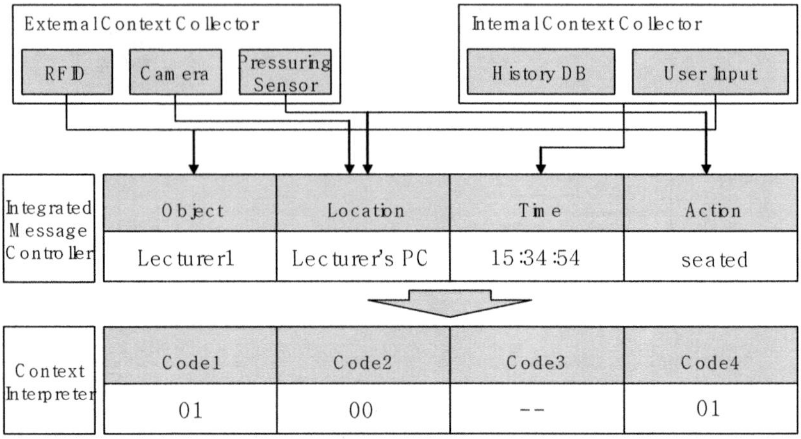

Fig. 3. Interpreting of the intention and integrated message when lecturer is seated on the chair

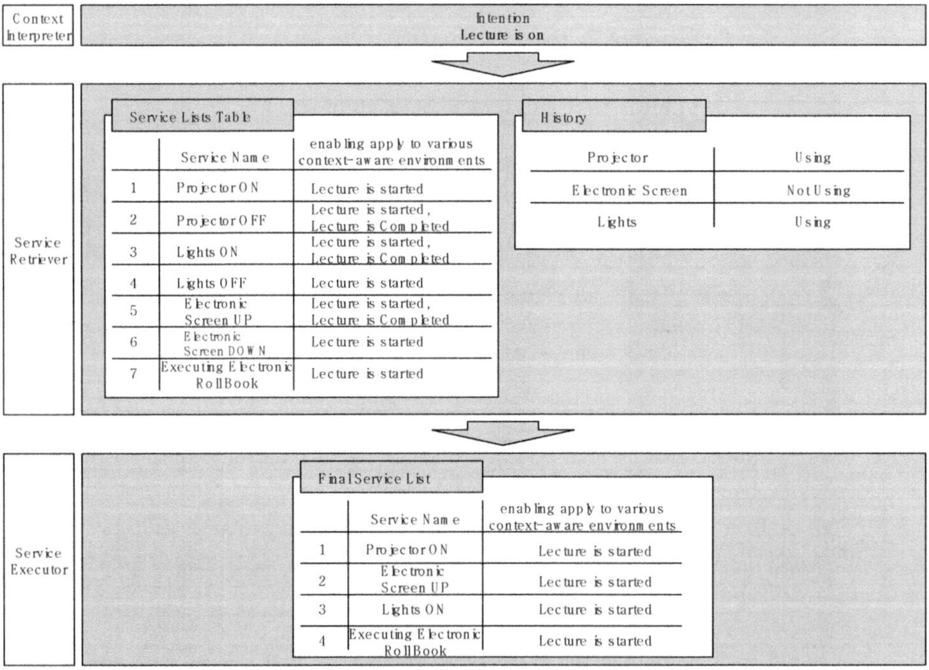

Fig. 4. Running of the service retriever and service executor in the progress of lecture

Figure 3 shows that are to make the integrated message when lecturer gives a lecture on the lecture platform and the architecture of context-aware interpreter. A time is not a factor that doesn't affect to context interpreter a quite well so it has not been included. The lecturer is in the state that has already been in lecture room so value "01" should be inputted to the Code 1 that is meant by Object, value "01" inputted to Code 2 for value of Location to keep track of lecturer's position and value "00" inputted to Code 3 for value of Action which meant by lecturer's seating. The Value "010100" of "intention Code" is meant by user's intention that is "Lecture is started". Service retrieval has made it by these user's intentions. Service retrieval searches every service that is being served in current state. The following Figure 4 shows that searching the service for intention of "Lecture is started" and selecting the service executor.

The service retriever, first of all, searches every service to be executed for the context of "Lecture is started". And it searches the record of lecturer's history and figures out what lecturer's tastes are. The lecturer uses "Beam projector" and not uses "Electronic screen" also he has tastes of turning on the light during the class as shown in Figure 5. As a result, it reorganizes the service list for lecturer's intentions. And it transmits final service list to the service executor in order to serve the service. You can see via

4 Test and Evaluation

We have implemented test bed for u-Class to verify practical use and effectiveness of the proposal addressed in this paper.

Figure 6 shows the integrated messages and intentions that analogized from the Ubi-Core as the sate of that lecturer is on the platform. You can see interpreting of contexts from the basis of a status of sensors by the hour and data collected from internal/external context collector according to the scenario.

Fig. 5. Status windows of u-Class

Table 4. The result of quantitative evaluation

Item	Lecture with u-Class	Traditional lecture
Number of times of inputting entire contexts	1time	6times
Input time for entire running	1sec.	9 sec.
Average running time of entire system	2 min. and 56 sec.	3min. 5sec
Average complete time for readiness(including check the roll book)	2min. and 57 sec.	6min. and 4 sec.

Test has done by scale-downed volume upon the scenario due to a real lecture is too big to have an experiment upon Ubi-Class. It has demonstrated the states of "lecturer is seated" after students are attended, "Lecture is started", execution of several intentions and "Lecture is completed" according to the basic scenario in a row. As a result, we have proved to that the u-Class provided automated services grasping the lecturer's intentions exactly.

To approach exact result of the test, it has used of the quantitative evaluation that checked the number of times and runtime for equipment's manipulation, execution time of the assistant equipment for lecture and time of spending for checking the attendance in the lecture room. Table 4 shows the result of quantitative evaluation. This simulation shows that complete set up time for the lecture has also reduced of more 50% than classic lecture room. The duration of testing is not the period of time for every lecturers but the average. Time and inputted quantity are might be changed due to the various valuables in that are lecturer's tastes, age and healthy condition. Errors could happen to be generated as sudden change of lecturer's intentions or malfunction of system in u-Class

5 Conclusion and Future Work

Educational environment has continually been changed and evolved to the e-Class enabling multimedia-driven education using such as a white board, a beam project and TV from classic chalkboard. Ubiquitous technology, definitely, is being gives many effects to these educational background. The lecture room has been changed itself to the cyberspace as another paradigm of lecture room that recognizing professor and student, which provides and serves intelligent services for their demands. This type of lecture room is requiring context-aware technology to support intelligent services. In this work, we have designed and implemented context-aware lecture room so-called "u-Class". The u-Class is able to check the attendance automatically and is providing intelligent services to make environment of lecture room according with professor's intentions and tastes. We have tested and proved that is being served intelligent services in basis of context-aware through an experiment.

Context-aware in ubiquitous environment is using many sensors and executing various services for many users. It might be conflicted among various user's intentions. It could happen to conflict professor's intention with that of student, this paper has dealt with context-aware only for the professor. In future work, it has to be progressed of researching about context-aware technology that is to grasp not only professor's intentions but also among student's intentions respectively. The important points on study are to avoid and correct conflicts with among different user's intention effectively. Also, context-aware technology for multi-user should be a technology that is able to be applied in the lecture room as well as various places for many users.

References

1. Pascoe.: Adding generic contextual capabilities to wearable computers. In: Proceedings of 2nd International Symposium on Wearable Computers, pp. 92–99 (1998)
2. Nishibe, Y., et al.: Mobile digital assistants for community support. AAAI Magazine 19(2), 31–49 (1998)
3. Dey, A.K.: Providing Architectural Support for Building Context-Aware Applications. PhD thesis, College of Computing, Georgia Institute of Technology (2000)
4. Pascoe.: Adding generic contextual capabilities to wearable computers. In: Proceedings of 2nd International Symposium on Wearable Computers, pp. 92–99 (1998)
5. Lim, J.: Design and Implementation of Context-awareness Interpretation Structure for Intelligent Service. Journal of Korean Society for Internet Information (2006)
6. Dey, A.K., Salber, D., Abowed, G.D.: A conceptual framework and a toolkit for supporting the rapid prototyping of context-aware applications (Anchor article of special triple issue on Context-Aware Computing). The Human-Computer Interaction (HCI) Journal 16 (2001)
7. Schilt, B.N., LaMarca, A., Borriello, G., Griswold, W., McDonald, D., Lazowska, E., Balachandran, A., Hong, J., Iverson, V.: Ubiquitous Location-Aware Computing and the Place Lab Initiative. In: The First ACM International Workshop on Wireless Mobile Applications and Services on WLAN(WMASH) (2003)
8. Dey, A.K.: Providing Architectural Support for Building Context-Aware Applications. PhD thesis. College of Computing, Georgia Institute of Technology (2000)

Audio-Visual Fused Online Context Analysis Toward Smart Meeting Room

Peng Dai, Linmi Tao, and Guangyou Xu

Tsinghua National Lab on Information Science & Technology, Tsinghua University, 100084 Beijing, China
daip02@mails.tsinghua.edu.cn, {linmi,xgy-dcs}@tsinghua.edu.cn

Abstract. Context-aware systems incorporate multimodal information to analyze contextual information in users' environment and provide various proactive services according to dynamic context. In this paper, a novel online context analysis framework is proposed to support context-aware computing in smart meeting room. A novel dynamic context model is presented to model human group interactions. Robust audio and visual modules are integrated for the effective processing of multimodal signals from various sensors, based on which a multi-level dynamic context reasoning mechanism is adopted for the online understanding of group interactions in meeting scenarios. Experimental results show the effectiveness of our framework.

1 Introduction

Computer understanding of human actions and interactions has recently gained much attention from researchers in the field of human-computer interaction and ubiquitous computing. In real-life situations such as meeting scenarios, context has to be considered in the reasoning of human actions and interactions. In the light of context-awareness, computer systems analyze users' actions and intentions based on multi-modal sensor data, and further provide attentive services to users without drawing their attention away from their current tasks. Therefore a computer applicable context model has to be defined to guide the reasoning procedures.

Greenberg defined context as a dynamic construct [1], which is in accordance with the dynamic nature of group interactions in meetings. In this paper, the human subjects and the physical and information environments are considered in a whole framework, and the whole context is divided into two types: "*interaction context*" and "*environment context*", among which "*interaction context*" is defined to represent the interactive situations among human. As is shown in Fig. 1, the "*interaction context*" of meetings is of hierarchy and can be expressed as a tree structure. Since most of the current context models mainly deal with the problems such as context storage, sharing and management [2], which are not capable to handle the multi-level context reasoning problem we face in this paper, we present a novel dynamic context model to serve as a reasoning framework for group interaction analysis in meetings.

There have been some works on automatic recognition of group actions in meeting scenarios. The well-known examples are EU research project M4 and its follow-up

J. Indulska et al. (Eds.): UIC 2007, LNCS 4611, pp. 868–877, 2007.

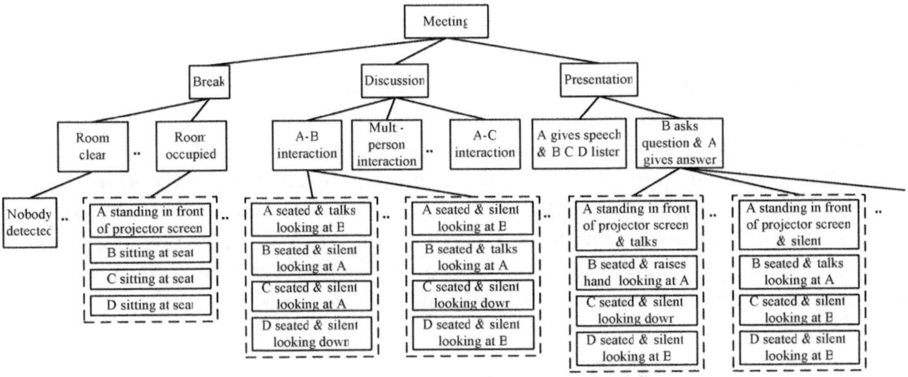

Fig. 1. Context hierarchy in meetings

project AMI [3], [4], [5]. Some researches only made use of features from single-module. In [6] personal states and meeting states were inferred through Finite State Machines (FSM) separately, where only visual cues were used and only users' standing-sitting states were analyzed. Brdiczka et al. [7] adopted speech features for the automatic detection of interaction group configurations. McCowan et al. [3] employed Hidden Markov Models (HMM) for the recognition of group actions in meeting scenarios based on audio-visual information. Zhang et al. [4] extended the above work and proposed a two-level HMM framework to model individual and group actions simultaneously. More recently new types of multimodal features such as prosody, speaker turns etc. were added to classify meeting scenarios and Multistream Dynamic Bayesian Model (DBN) was adopted in [5]. However, most of the related works mentioned above were constrained to the offline framework, which means holistic analysis was performed based on the overall audio-visual sequences only after the meetings had finished. Recently some efforts have been made for the research issue of dynamic context in smart environment. Trivedi et al [8] presented a distributed system paradigm for dynamic context capture in indoor environment, where dynamic context means changes of user's location and face orientation. Crowley [9] proposed a framework for context-aware observation of human activity. However the context model in these literatures did not deal with such composite group interactions which consist of multiple abstract levels as in this paper.

In this paper, we propose a novel context aware engine to analyze group interactions in meetings online. Multi-level events are defined within the context aware engine, based on which a bottom-up and top-down integrated framework is presented to analyze current context. Through online analysis of current context, proactive services such as active control of sensors and context-dependent archiving of meeting data can be performed.

The rest of the paper is organized as follows. In Section 2 On-the-Spot Archiving System (OSAS) is introduced as our research platform. Section 3 presents our dynamic context model and online context analysis approach. Experimental results are presented in Section 4 and conclusions are drawn in Section 5.

2 Research Platform

An intelligent multimedia archiving system named On-the-Spot Archiving System (OSAS) is adopted as the research platform of our context-aware group interaction analysis. The objective is to extract low level features automatically from multimodal sensor data, based on which hierarchical semantic representation of group interactions can be derived through a context-aware reasoning framework, which is capable of handling dynamic context situations. Proactive services can be provided as meeting support in our system, including active control of PTZ camera and microphone arrays, and automatic archiving of meeting data during the interaction.

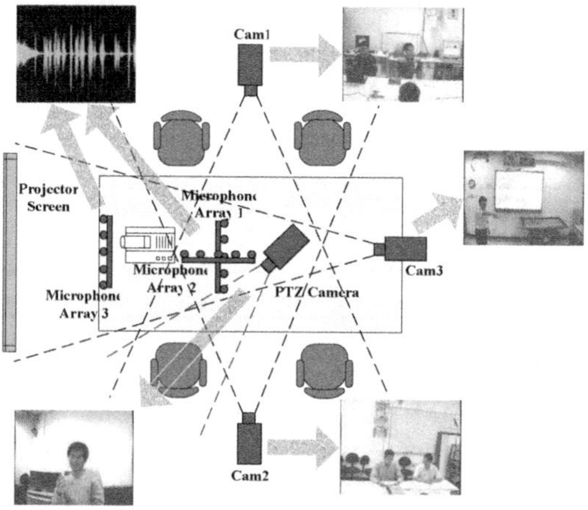

Fig. 2. Sensor setting in smart meeting room

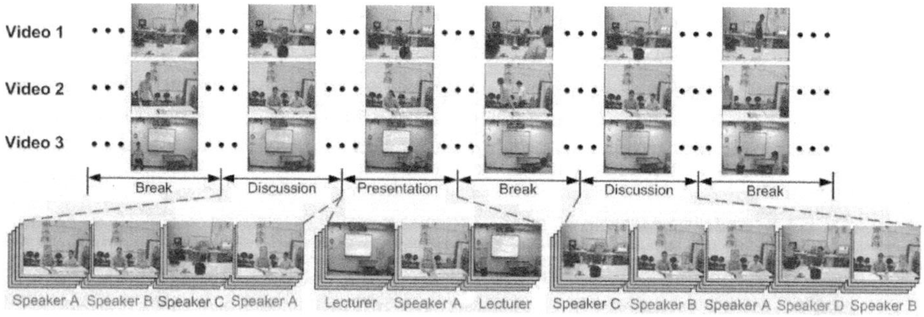

Fig. 3. Context-dependent online archiving of meeting data

A smart meeting room environment is set up for the OSAS project. Hardware setting is shown in Fig. 2. Three fixed cameras are deployed to monitor the meeting room from distinct perspectives. A Pan-Tilt-Zoom (PTZ) camera is placed on the table to focus on any specific target. Three linear microphone arrays are installed on the table to collect speech information from various participants. As for the network and software infrastructure, a flexible multi-server platform has been developed to support distributed multimedia information processing [10].

In our system, two major types of proactive services are addressed: (1) active control of sensors, i.e. PTZ camera and microphone array can both be steered to focus on specific directions; (2) automatic archiving of meeting semantics based on current context analysis result as the meeting proceeds. Eventually audio-video meeting streams can be segmented into a sequence of group situations online, which can be dissected into sequential sub-scenarios simultaneously, as is illustrated in Fig. 3.

3 Online Context Analysis

The underlying challenge of context-aware system is to make computers sense current context. In group interactions, context cannot be determined simply by collecting the multimodal sensor data; on the contrary, context has to be inferred based on detected events, which convey semantic meanings at different abstract levels. Therefore online event detection in dynamic context is our research focus.

3.1 Context Aware Engine

In this paper, a novel dynamic context model is introduced, which is comprised of context hierarchy, event hierarchy, context aware engine, and context guiding engine. Context hierarchy has been introduced in Section 1, and current context is sensed through multi-level event detection, therefore event hierarchy is defined. Different from Crowley's definition of events in [9], we define two types of events in our system: one represents the switching of situations, and the other denotes meaningful actions or states that characterize current situation. Events are defined at individual, interactive and group levels corresponding to the multi-level context hierarchy.

Based on the context and event hierarchy, online detection of multi-level events constitutes the core of context aware engine, as is illustrated in Fig. 4. In our framework, context reasoning and audio-visual processing are tightly integrated and affect each other in a bidirectional way. Lower level events and bottom level sensor data can be used as cues for higher level event inference. Those inferred higher level events can be used as the context in detection of lower level events and in guiding sensor data processing.

At the beginning, no "*interaction context*" is available except for the "*environment context*" such as meeting room settings. During this stage, a coarse level visual processing task is completed, based on which overall group scenarios can be recognized as contextual information in a bottom-up way. The coarse level context can be employed as the top-down guidance of a refined level context analysis task.

3.2 Online Analysis of Group Scenarios

Group interactive patterns are dynamically changing during meetings, and the computer system might not get exact contextual information at the starting point. In order to start the context analysis in meeting scenarios, a coarse level bottom-up reasoning method is presented to analyze group scenarios based on the visual information extracted from the three fixed cameras.

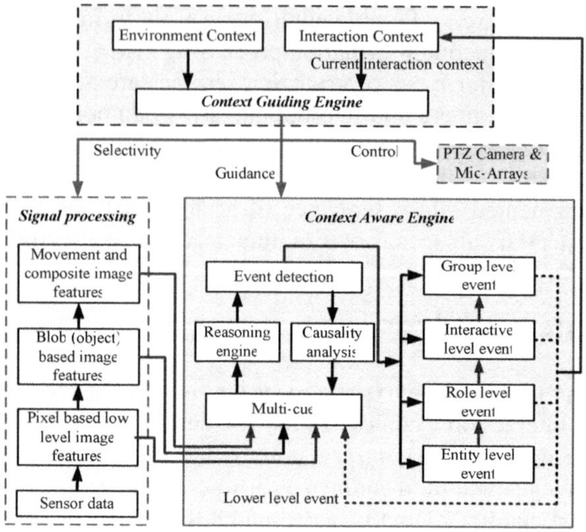

Fig. 4. Dynamic context model for online analysis of group interaction

Group scenarios are categorized as the top level semantic information in our context model, which can be a top most guidance for the lower level event reasoning and sensor signal processing tasks. Visual information of human head and body is utilized as significant cues of group situation understanding. An effectively integrated human detection and tracking system is created to detect human presence and track human head and body positions in the three camera views [11].

Fig. 5. Visual detection, tracking and verification

In our vision system, multiple visual cues such as motion, color, gradient and facial gray features are adopted [11]. Firstly foreground objects are generated through a robust foreground detection method. Skin area detection is performed as the second step based on an HSV skin color model. Head ellipses are generated according to gradient information around those top most skin areas inside foreground objects, based on which body blobs are further segmented according to anthropometric knowledge. Those potential human heads and bodies are tracked and updated through video sequences by a multi-cue Condensation tracker. Furthermore, an AdaBoost face detector is applied to verify human objects during tracking procedures. The entire visual processing flow is illustrated in Fig. 5.

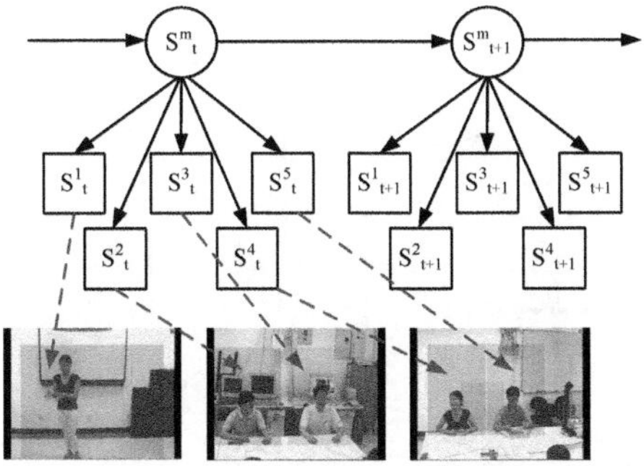

Fig. 6. DBN for group scenario analysis

Due to our meeting room settings, five interest locations are defined in the three camera views, where participants stay most of the time during meetings. Dynamic Bayesian Network (DBN) is applied here to infer group scenarios from visual observation at the five interest areas. By combining the human detection and tracking results, we might get the human presence states S_t^i $(i = 1, \cdots, 5)$ in each interest area, which can be enumerated as nobody, standing person and sitting person. Group scenario state S_t^m (i.e. *presentation*, *discussion* or *break*) can be inferred from previous scenario states and current observations. DBN model is illustrated in Fig. 6, and online filtering tasks are performed instead of offline sequence processing, which means group scenario estimation S_t^m is generated at each time step during meetings.

3.3 Online Analysis of Interactive Scenarios

Although group scenarios are recognized above, contextual information is still not sufficient for proactive services. Thus context at lower levels needs to be analyzed further. Meaningful individual actions, states and interactive states of meeting participants are to be detected and taken as lower level context in the top-down guidance of higher level group scenarios. At the same time, these detected individual and interactive events can be regarded as meeting sub-scenarios, which could be archived sequentially as the semantic description of the current meeting.

In meeting situations, speaking, head gestures and meaningful hand actions (e.g. raising hand for QA, pointing to a specific direction) can be significant events and contain most of the semantic information. Thus appropriate audio and visual information should be adopted for the detection of these events. Mean-shift tracker is applied for visual hand tracking in our system, which generates hand trajectories along video sequences [11]. A Finite State Machine (FSM) framework is introduced to classify meaningful participants' hand actions such as raising hand or pointing.

Another significant class of event is speech related event, which indicates interactive patterns among various participants. Since major functionality of meetings is to exchange ideas about specific topics, speech content and corresponding speaker might contain the majority of information about meeting content.

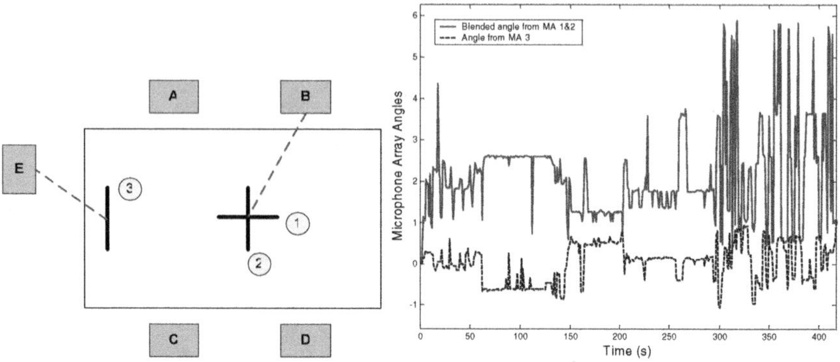

Fig. 7. Microphone array based speaker localization

In this paper, three microphone arrays are utilized for the recording of audio information in meeting situation, among which two microphone arrays are combined to detect speaker locations around the table during *discussion*, and another one is placed near the projector screen to determine lecturer's locations during *presentation*, as is illustrated in Fig. 7. Each microphone array not only records audio signals from speakers in the meeting room, but also offers estimated speaker direction angles.

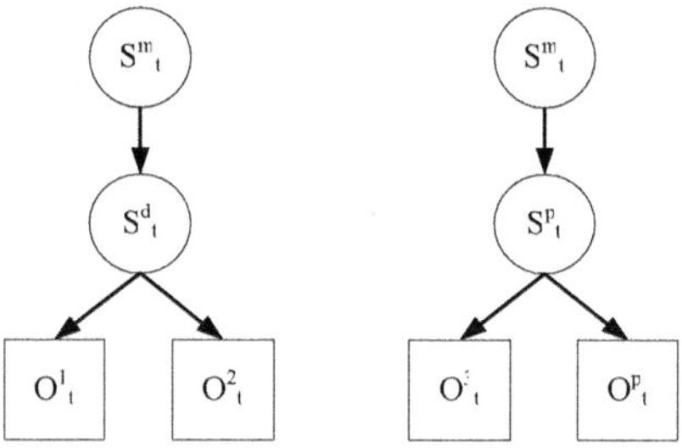

Fig. 8. BN for speech event analysis

Microphone array based speech event analysis is guided by current group scenario, i.e. during *discussion*, signals from microphone array 1 and 2 are taken as valid, and during *presentation*, microphone array 3 is regarded to be effective. Bayesian Network (BN) is employed to infer current speaker's location. As is shown in Fig. 8, the left model is for the inference of speakers around table, and the right one is for inferring lecturer locations in front of the projector screen. S_t^m denotes current group event, O_t^1, O_t^2 and O_t^3 are audio source angles extracted from the microphone arrays, and O_t^p is the visual feature regarding human presence in front of the projector screen.

Within this level of context analysis, meaningful events related to human hand and speech are detected online. Such events can be used for the detection of interactive sub-situations, such as *lecturing* or *QA* during *presentation*, *two-person discussion* or *four-person discussion* during *discussion* scenarios.

4 Experimental Results

Our online context analysis approach has been tested in our smart meeting room environment. Audio and visual signals are captured synchronously from the three fixed cameras and three microphone arrays. Each of the meetings lasts about 5 minutes to 12 minutes. Based on the extracted features, multi-level event detection can be performed at the speed of 50 fps in Intel Xeon CPU of 2.40 GHz.

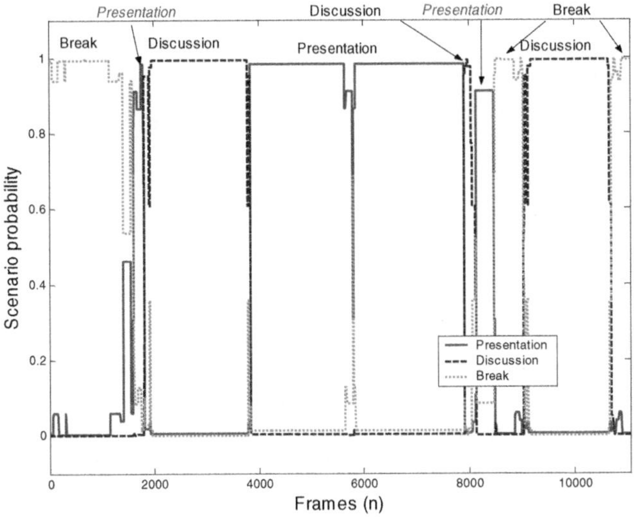

Fig. 9. Result of group scenario analysis

Fig. 9 shows the result of group scenario analysis based on a test meeting sample. The Y-axis denotes the output probability of current group scenario analysis. The extracted meeting in this case lasts about 5 minutes and contains three possible states, *break*, *presentation* and *discussion*. The first and the last *break* means meeting starts and ends respectively. The two italic-marked *presentation* scenarios between *break* and *discussion* are false detected, during which one person is walking in front of the projector screen while the others are seated. The situation is actually *break* scenario and similar to *presentation*. Within our current reasoning model, such kind of situation is false classified due to its deficiency of other visual cues. Such type of problems can be handled by considering visual features indicating projector usage.

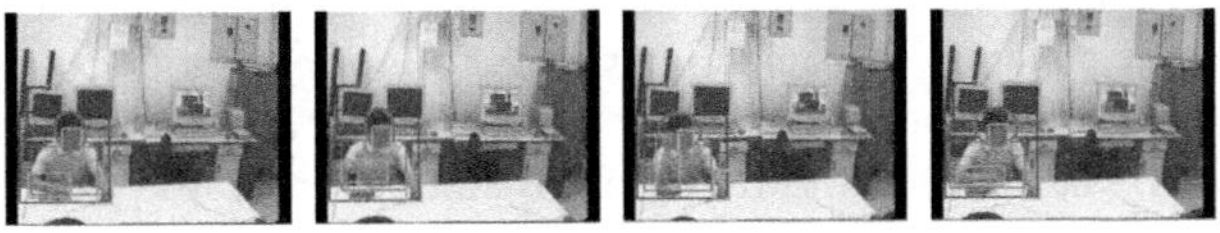

Fig. 10. Visual detection of raising hand actions

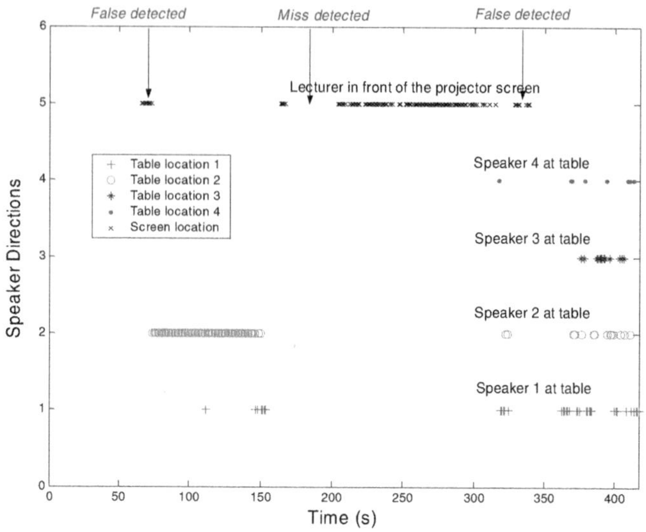

Fig. 11. Result of speech event analysis

Fig. 10 shows the samples from a detected raising hand action sequence. There might be hysteretic effects during the detection of hand actions, and it is determined by the characteristics of our method. In our approach, a raising hand action is detected only after an expected sequence is completed (i.e. hand is put up and kept still over a certain threshold). Therefore the hysteresis interval might be several seconds.

The result of speech event analysis is presented in Fig. 11, from which we can see different speakers are separated clearly such as lecturer in front of the screen and speakers at table, corresponding to the five locations depicted in Fig. 7. Turn takings among the four participants formulate the sequential structure of group interactive patterns during meetings, based on which we can further classify *two-person interaction* and *four-person interaction* during *discussion* scenarios in the future work. However, there are also false detected lecturers due to the false detection of group scenarios depicted in Fig. 9. Besides, during *presentation* lecturer is miss-detected sometimes due to the low intensity of speech signals when lecturer turns to the screen.

5 Conclusion

In this paper, the problem of context-aware computing is addressed in smart meeting room environment. A novel dynamic context model is proposed to model group interactions. As a significant part of the dynamic context model, the context aware engine is presented in this paper, which characterizes a bottom-up and top-down integrated reasoning mechanism for the online understanding of meeting scenarios at multiple levels. Effective visual and audio processing methods are employed to generate multimodal cues for our context analysis model. Preliminary experiments in our smart meeting room have demonstrated the effectiveness of our framework.

Future work includes model improvement, using more features, detection of interactive events, and integration of more sensors and proactive services.

References

1. Greenberg, S.: Context as a Dynamic Construct. Human-Computer Interaction 16, 257–268 (2001)
2. Baldauf, M., Dustdar, S., Rosenberg, F.: A Survey on Context-Aware Systems. Intl. Journal of Ad Hoc and Ubiquitous Computing (2006)
3. McCowan, I., Gatica-Perez, D., Bengio, S., Lathoud, G., Barnard, M., Zhang, D.: Automatic Analysis of Multimodal Group Actions in Meetings. IEEE Trans. on Pattern Analysis and Machine Intelligence 27(3), 305–317 (2005)
4. Zhang, D., Gatica-Perez, D., Bengio, S., McCowan, I.: Modeling individual and group actions in meetings with layered HMMs. IEEE Trans. on Multimedia 8(3), 509–520 (2006)
5. Dielmann, A., Renals, S.: Automatic Meeting Segmentation Using Dynamic Bayesian Networks. IEEE Transactions on Multimedia 9(1), 25–36 (2007)
6. Rybski, P.E., De la Torre, F., Patil, R., Vallespi, C., Veloso, M., Browning, B.: CAMEO: Camera Assisted Meeting Event Observer. In: Proc. Int. Conf. on Robotics and Automation, vol. 2, pp. 1634–1639 (2004)
7. Brdiczka, O., Maisonnasse, J., Reignier, P.: Automatic Detection of Interaction Groups. In: Proc. 7th Intl. Conf. on Multimodal Interfaces (2005)
8. Trivedi, M.M., Huang, K.S., Mikic, I.: Dynamic Context Capture and Distributed Video Arrays for Intelligent Spaces. IEEE Trans. on Systems, Man, and Cybernetics—PART A: Systems and Humans 35(1), 145–163 (2005)
9. Crowley, J.L.: Context Driven Observation of Human Activity. In: Proc. European Symposium on Ambient Intelligence (2003)
10. Wang, Y., Tao, L., Liu, Q., Zhao, Y., Xu, G.: A Flexible Multi-Server Platform for Distributed Video Information Processing. In: Proc. 5th Intl. Conf. on Computer Vision Systems (2007)
11. Dai, P., Tao, L., Xu, G.: Dynamic Context Driven Human Detection and Tracking in Meeting Scenarios. In: Proc. 2nd Intl. Conf. on Computer Vision Theory and Applications (2007)

An Offset Algorithm for Conflict Resolution in Context-Aware Computing

Min Xi[1], Jizhong Zhao[1], Yong Qi[1], Hui He[1], and Liang Liu[2]

[1] Institute of Computer Software and Theory
Xi'an Jiaotong University
Xi'an 710049, China
{ximin,zjz,qiy,huihe}@mail.xjtu.edu.cn
[2] IBM China Research Lab
Beijing, 100094, China
liuliang@cn.ibm.com

Abstract. In context-aware system, applications should adjust their execution policies in the light of context information of equipment, such as equipment's position, electric power, network bandwidth, and so on. In various context-aware systems, an important solution is to isolate executable codes in different context into a number of program segments and to select different execution policies according to the context in the process of operation, thus increasing the programming flexibility. Since not all possible contexts can be taken into consideration in the definition of policies, several policies might meet the current context simultaneously in some given environments, thus resulting in policy conflict. This paper proposes a kind of conflict solution algorithm, which, through defining the context center of each execution policy, computes the offset between the current context and the center and selects the one closest to the current context as the execution policy in the case of conflict. Experiments testify that the algorithm can effectively eliminate conflicts of policy selection and well manifest the intention of policy definition, making policy selection more reasonable.

1 Introduction

With the continuous appearance of new mobile devices, people's demand for obtaining information or services is becoming stronger and stronger, and pervasive computing system gradually becomes an important research area. To make users concentrate on problems themselves, application program and service should be able to automatically adjust their behaviors in terms of the context environment so as to meet users' demands. Therefore, context-awareness becomes a significant technology in pervasive computing. Context-aware applications should obtain context information of users at any moment and decide the corresponding execution policy in the light of the information, such as Active Badge Location System[1], context toolkit[2], Gaia[3], and so on.

In the process of establishing context applications, it is required to isolate executable codes in different circumstances into a number of program segments

J. Indulska et al. (Eds.): UIC 2007, LNCS 4611, pp. 878–887, 2007.

and dynamically select executed code segments in program operation according to the current context. The research result including COP[4] and Olympas[5]. We call the codes executed in terms of different contexts as different execution policies. The method can effectively lift the flexibility of application development, thus reaching the purpose of adapting to environment changes. Studies have presented the method for isolating codes. In the process of defining the context environment of execution policy, however, several policies may satisfy the current context at the same time because of the different starting points of definition[6]. We call the situation as conflict. Once a conflict occurs, the system will be unable to select correct execution codes to complete operation according to needs of users. Therefore, the selection of algorithm in conflicts becomes a problem that should be solved.

This paper introduces possible cases of conflict through the analysis of an actual case. After the formalized description of conflicts, it brings forth a method solving conflicts through the calculation of policy and context offset degree. In terms of the selection center of each entry of context environment factor and its scope, the method computes the offset value. In the event of conflicts, the system will select the execution policy with the smallest offset value to complete operation. Experiments show that the algorithm can effectively solve conflicts and avoid frequent switches of policy selection.

2 A Case Study

We have such a scenario in mind: Bob is reading a novel through his PDA on a running train. Since the novel is extremely long, he needs to continuously connect the context-aware server to read it through the designated service. The contents of the novel include both character information and colored picture information. Although being not obligatory, the pictures can make the novel more vivid. The wireless connection bandwidth on the train fluctuates greatly, and the power of PDA is limited. To make Bob read the novel uninterruptedly, the service offering him novel should carry out dynamic adjustment in the light of context information without his interference(**Scenario1**).

In the process of development, service falls into three different operation ways according to users' context information. We call them three policies of configurations, namely transmitting characters only, transmitting characters and black and white pictures, and transmitting characters and colored pictures. Table 1 reveals contexts corresponded by different configurations.

In terms of the explanation of Table 1, if the bandwidth is less than 10K, or the power is less than 40%, the service only offers character information to users; if the bandwidth is bigger than 10K and smaller than 30K, and the power is between 40% and 80%, the service will offer character information and black and white pictures to users; and if the bandwidth is bigger than 30K, and the power exceeds 80%, the service will offer character and colored pictures to users.

Table 1. the protocol of the reflection operation

	Character (P1)	Character (P1)	Character black & white picture (P2)	Character colored picture P(3)
Bandwidth	<10K		≥10K	>30K
Power		<40%		>80%

Problems arise from this as well. In terms of the explanation of Table 1, conflicts will occur in the following two cases:

1. Bandwidth is bigger than 10K, and the power is smaller than 40%
2. Bandwidth is bigger than 30K, and the power is bigger than 80%

In the first case, the current context environment meets policies P1 and P2 at the same time; in the second case, the context environment meets policies P2 and P3. If there is a devoid of suitable algorithms, the system will be unable to send suitable information to users.

3 Conflict Description

In our previous studies, we brought forth the Isotope Programming Model. This model is the expansion of the current object-oriented model. In IPM, the object includes not only property statement but also a group of isotope factors (execution policy). Each isotope factor represents the object's behavior in the given context environment. Isotope factor contains a context environment statement and an execution code in the environment statement. The environment statement consists of several context entries. Utilizing the model can effectively enhance the flexibility of program, reduce influence degree of environment changes to programs, and offer application for application development better than the object-oriented model. However, execution policies may conflict with each other in program operation.

To illustrate conflict problems, we offer part of definition and formalized description.

sign: Environmental information obtained in the system is called system environmental information. The aggregate of names of environmental information is called *EName*. The aggregate of all possible environmental values is E, and the aggregate of the value of each environmental information is V; the environmental value of the current environment is $e^0 (e^0 \in E)$. The aggregate of services is called S. The aggregate of all service configurations is called C. The set of all policies of service S named *P(S)*.

service: Service is the functional entity dynamically adjusting itself behaviors in terms of users' context environment to offer information to users in the context-aware system. Service includes service implement and configuration document.

Configuration document is the set of policies, and each policy is corresponding with an context statement and an execution segment. Context statement is used to designate the context environment that the policy can come into effect, and the execution identity instructs the service to adjust its service mode in the light of the context environment. Execution identity, in terms of varied realization mechanisms, may represent a method name, a parameter value, or an attribute value.

$$\begin{aligned} service &::= serviceImplement\ \ configuration \\ configuration &::= policySet \\ policySet &::= policy\ \ policySet \mid policy \\ policy &::= context\ \ identity \end{aligned}$$

context statement: Context statement in a policy is used to define the context environment that the policy can come into effect. Each context statement includes a group of statement entries, and each entry is used to define a kind of environmental information. For example, "temperature between $10°C$ and $20°C$" is the character description of the environmental information restriction entry of temperature.

$$\begin{aligned} context &::= contextEntrySet \\ contextEntrySet &::= contextEntry\ \ contextEntrySet \mid contextEntry \\ contextEntry &::= name\ \ operator\ \ value\ \ bound \\ bound &::= min\ \ max\ \ defaultMin\ \ defaultMax \end{aligned}$$

evaluate function: $EName * E \rightarrow V$, obtaining the context information value of a designated name. *operator* and *value* in context statement entry e constitute the defining condition of environmental information. $e.operator(e.value,$ $evaluate(e^0, e.name) = true$ indicates that the entry meets the current context environment.

fit function: $P * E \rightarrow Boolean$, if a policy match the current context environment, the function *fit* will return *true*, and vise verse return false.

$$\begin{aligned} fit(p, e) &= fit(entry(1), e) \wedge fit(entry(2), e) \wedge \ldots \wedge fit(entry(n), e) \\ fit(entry(k), e) &= fit(entry(k), evaluate(e, entry(k).name)) \\ fit(entry(k), v) &= entry.operator(entry(k).value, v) \end{aligned}$$

adaptSet function the set of policies which satisfied the context environment $C * E \rightarrow 2^P$

$$\begin{aligned} adaptSet(c, e) &= adaptSet(p1, e) \cup adaptSet(policySet/p1, e) \\ adaptSet(p, e) &= if\ \ fit(p, e)\ \ then\ \ p\ \ else\ \ \emptyset \end{aligned}$$

conflict: If $\|adaptSet(C, e^0)\| = 0$, this indicates that there are no policies in the configuration meeting the current environment; =1, there is only one meeting the current environment, system use this policy to execute; >1, there are above two policies meeting the current environment. We call the case conflict. Therefore, the system should select policies according to conflict solutions.

4 Conflict Solutions

When a conflict takes places, we need to define a policy through a kind of algorithm as the basis for system execution. The normal solution is to define a priority level for each policy, and in case of conflict, the policy enjoying the high priority can be taken as the execution policy[7,8,9]. The method is of low flexibility. In terms of characters of environment definition, we put forward the offset calculation method, selecting the corresponding execution policy according to the value of offset. The method can well manifest the intention of policy definition, making policy selection more reasonable.

Generally speaking, an environment information can be defined as a scope. For example, the temperature can be between $10°C$ and $20°C$, and the power of battery is bigger than 80%. The policy has a selection center corresponding to the environment. For instance, if the temperature is between $10°C$ and $20\ °C$, the selection center can be considered $15°C$. The closer the value of the same environmental variable in two policies is to the selection center, the smaller its offset of selection is. We define the offset range as offset. Smaller offset indicates higher adaptability of the current environment and policies. Therefore, the policy with the lowest offset should be the result of the selection.

Offset not only related to the selection center, but also related to the selection scope. We assume that smaller scope of environmental indicate more precise of the policy. Therefore, the lower value should be obtained in the calculation of offset. Please think about the following cases:

Example1: a policy defines that the environmental temperature should be between $0°C$ and $50°C$, and another policy defines that the temperature be between $20°C$ and $30°C$. The current temperature should be $25°C$.

In this case, if the current environment should meet definitions of two policies at the same time, the selection center will be same as well. But based on the principle of smaller scope, more precise the definition and smaller the offset value, the calculation result of offset should be in direct proportion to the scope.

Therefore, we make the following definition:

Offset function: $offset : P * E \rightarrow R^+$

Offset is equal to the mean value of offsets of all context statement entries in the policy. Higher offset indicates that the current environment has bigger difference with the context environment defined in the policy.

$$offset(i) = \frac{|evaluate(e^0, entry(i).name) - \frac{entry(i).max+entry(i).min}{2}|}{|entry(i).defaultMax - entry(i).defaultMin|} \times \frac{|entry(i).max - entry(i).min|}{|entry(i).defaultMax - entry(i).defaultMin|} \quad (1)$$

$$offset(P_i) = \sum_{i=1}^{m} offset(i)/m \quad (2)$$

In formula(1), $\frac{entry(i).max+entry(i).min}{2}$ is used to calculate the selection center of environmental entry, and denominator to calculate the selection scope of entry. Offset of the policy can be obtained through all entry's mean offset values.

It deserves attention that we discovered the calculation results of the two policies were both 0 in calculating the description in **Example1** through the formula, making system difficult to selection. The reason is that the current environmental value is at the selection center of its entry in both of the two policies, so the offset is 0. Therefore, we introduced the constant C, and the modified formula is:

$$offset(i) = \left(\frac{\left|evaluate(e^0, entry(i).name) - \frac{entry(i).max+entry(i).min}{2}\right|}{|entry(i).defaultMax - entry(i).defaultMin|} + C \right) \times \frac{|entry(i).max - entry(i).min|}{|entry(i).defaultMax - entry(i).defaultMin|} \quad (3)$$

C is a constant bigger than 0. Its value will not affect the final offset computed, thus being unable to change the result of policy selection. Therefore, its value can be any positive number. We usually take it as 1.

Formual(3) can get the different value of the policies in **Example1**, so the system can make decision of which policy to use.

Although the case is unlikely to take place, it is possible that offsets of two policies are completely the same in some special cases. This indicates the two policies have the same offset degree to the current environment, and we can select one as the result at random.

5 Experiment Result and Analysis

Through the offset calculation result of **Scenario1** under various environments, we explain the applicability of the algorithm.

Consider matching policy in the following circumstances:

Table 2. match policy aggregate of the given context environment

Power \ Bandwidth	5K	15K	50K
20%	P1	P1 & P2	P2
60%	P1	P2	P2
90%	P1	P2	P2 & P3

From Table 2 we may see that when the bandwidth is 15K and the power 20%, policies P1 and P2 meet the defined conditions at the same time; when the bandwidth is 50K and the power 90%, policies P2 and P3 meet the defined conditions at the same time. But conflict may take place at the time, so it is required to select policies in the circumstance.

Table 3. offset of the given policy

policy / Context	15K,20%	50K,90%
P1	0.875	
P2	1.28	1.1725
P3		0.5025

In calculating the offset of a policy under the current environment, we can obtain the following results:

From Table 3 we may see that although the bandwidth is 15K and power 20%, which meet P2 conditions, compared with P1, it is far from the selection center. Therefore, the offset is big, and the policy selection result is P1. Compared with P2, P3 has even smaller defined region, so in the case of power is 90% and bandwidth is 50K, P3 may have lower offset. Therefore, the policy selection result is P3. This is consistent with our intuition.

To better illustrate the problem, we simulate the continuous changes of bandwidth and power to calculate the impact on policy selection by environmental changes in a bigger scope.

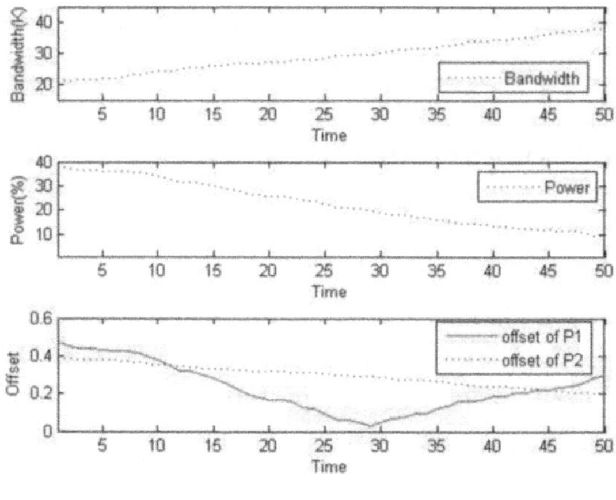

Fig. 1. offset value of the given context environment

In Fig. 1 we can see that bandwidth and power change persistently within a certain scope. In the initial stage of environment, the offset of policy P2 is low, so the system selects P2 as the execution policy. With the increase of bandwidth and the drop of power, the offset of policy P1 gradually declines, and the difference between P1 and P2 is narrowing down. When t=11 (bandwidth = 24K and power =32%), the offsets of P1 and P2 are equal. Later, the offset of P1 is smaller than that of P2, and the system selects P1 as the execution policy. In the final stage

($47 \leq t \leq 50$), the offset of P2 is smaller than P1, so the system will choose P2 as the execution policy again.

6 Related Works

In recent years, most research has been done to resolve conflicts. Reactive Behavioral System(ReBa) [10] supports conflict resolution among devices in office environment such as electric lamps, display devices and so on. [shin] proposed the Conflict Manager to resolve conflicts for context-aware applications in smart home environments. The Conflict Manager assigns priority to each user so that the user with the highest priority can be selected by exploiting conflict history of users. In addition, it detects and resolves conflicts among applications by utilizing references of users and properties of the services.

CRISMA [6] uses reflection to build the system. When the context changed, the policy in the context will be changed to adapt the environment. To resolve the conflict, it classify the different types of conflicts that may arise and argue that conflicts need to be resolved at execution time. It proposed the method uses a micro-economic approach that relies on a particular type of sealed-bid auction. Chisel's [11] framework is as same as CRISMA, but it doesn't give the solution of resolving conflicts.

[7] propose a framework for allowing everyone to easily describe scenarios for context-aware computing systems including various information appliances and sensors. They defined a rule-based language called CADEL and defined the check module to judge the conflicts among the rules. When a conflict detected, system told the user to give the priority to the rule.

[12] proposed behavior coordination mechanism using action selection mechanism for intelligent home environments. It compare to the high level applications as a robot, since task applications generally have activity scenarios to achieve their own objectives. In order to avoid multiple objective behavior conflict, it proposed the Subsumption architecture as an action section mechanism, and also introduces service management techniques for seamless services at an intelligent home.

[8]proposed a priority-based mechanism, behaviors with higher priorities are allowed to suppress the output of behaviors with lower priorities. Gaia [9] deals with conflicts that occur among simultaneously triggered rules in the same application . It also use priority to resolve a conflict.

[13] proposed three layers of abstractions: the runtime infrastructure, the context middleware and the user applications to decrease the adaptation complexity of self-adaptable context-aware systems. If one layer wishes to self-adapt but requests assistance from another self-adapting layer, it marks its new reconfiguration as tentative and waits for approval of the other layer. This approval ensures that its own self-adaptation does not conflict with the self-adaptation of the layer on which it depends.

[14] proposed scheme can detect semantic conflicts without explicit descriptions of the conflicts between different applications. Conflicts are resolved by

a dynamically generated adaptation policy based on the weight value of user preference on each service.

7 Conclusion

In context-aware computing, applications need to select different execution policies in terms of different context environments. The policies may conflict with each other. The paper brings forward a kind of offset algorithm. When conflict takes places, the algorithm can calculate the selection center of each conflicting policy and the offset of the current context environment, and select the policy with the lowest offset as the execution policy. Experiments show that offset algorithm can effectively solve the problem of policy conflict.

Acknowledgments. This work is supported by National Natural Science Foundation of China (No. 60573119), National 863 plan(2006AA01Z101), National Key Technology R&D Program of China(2006BAH02A01), IBM China Research Lab Joint Project and Nature Science Fund Project of Shaanxi Province(2005F14).

References

1. Want, R., Hopper, A., Falcao, V., Gibbons, J.: The active badge location system. ACM Transactions on Information Systems 10(1), 91–102 (1992)
2. Salber, D., Dey, A.K., Abowd, G.: The context toolkit: Aiding the development of context-enabled applications. In: ACM SIGCHI Conf. Human Factors in Computing Systems (CHI 99), New York, pp. 434–441. ACM Press, New York (1999)
3. Romn, M., Hess, C.K., Cerqueira, R., Ranganathan, A., Campbell, R.H., Nahrstedt, K.: Gaia: A middleware infrastructure to enable active spaces. IEEE Pervasive Computing, 74–83 (2002)
4. Keays, R., Rakotonirainy, A.: Context-oriented programming. In: MobiDe '03: Proceedings of the 3rd ACM international workshop on Data engineering for wireless and mobile access, New York, NY, USA, pp. 9–16. ACM Press, New York (2003)
5. Ranganathan, A., Chetan, S., Al-Muhtadi, J., Campbell, R.H., Mickunas, M.D.: Olympus: A high-level programming model for pervasive computing environments. In: Third IEEE International Conference on Pervasive Computing and Communications, 2005. PerCom 2005, pp. 7–16. IEEE Computer Society Press, Los Alamitos (2005)
6. Mascolo, L.C., Emmerich, W., Cecilia: Carisma: Context-aware reflective middleware system for mobile applications. IEEE Transactions on Software Engineering 29, 929–944 (2003)
7. Nishigaki, K., Yasumoto, K., Shibata, N., Ito, M., Higashino, T.: Framework and rule-based language for facilitating context-aware computing using information appliances. In: Proceedings of the First International Workshop on Services and Infrastructure for the Ubiquitous and Mobile Internet (SIUMI) (ICDCSW'05), vol. 3, pp. 345–351 (2005)
8. Pirjanian, P.: Behavior coordination mechanisms – state-of-the-art. Technical Report IRIS-99-375, Institute of Robotics and Intelligent Systems, School of Engineering, University of Southern California (October 1999)

9. Ranganathan, A., Campbell, R.H.: An infrastructure for context-awareness based on first order logic. Journal of Personal and Ubiquitous Computing 7(6), 353–364 (2003)
10. Hanssens, N., Kulkarni, A., Tuchinda, R., Horton, T.: Building agent-based intelligent workspaces. In: Proceedings of ABA Conference (2002)
11. Keeney, J.: Chisel: A policy-driven, context-aware, dynamic adaptation framework. In: Proceedings of the Fourth IEEE International Workshop on Policies for Distributed Systems and Networks (POLICY 2003), pp. 3–14. IEEE Computer Society Press, Los Alamitos (2003)
12. Minkyoung, K., Hyun, K.: Behavior coordination mechanism for intelligent home. In: ICIS-COMSAR 2006, pp. 452–457 (2006)
13. Preuveneers, D., Berbers, Y.: Multi-dimensional dependency and conflict resolution for self-adaptable context-aware systems. In: International Conference on Autonomic and Autonomous Systems, 2006. ICAS '06, p. 36 (2006)
14. Insuk, P., Lee, D., Hyun, S.J.: A dynamic context-conflict management scheme for group-aware ubiquitous computing environments. In: 29th Annual International Computer Software and Applications Conference, 2005. COMPSAC 2005, vol. 1, pp. 359–364 (2005)

UCIPE: Ubiquitous Context-Based Image Processing Engine for Medical Image Grid*

Aobing Sun, Hai Jin, Ran Zheng, Ruhan He, Qin Zhang, Wei Guo, and Song Wu

Services Computing Technology and System Lab
Cluster and Grid Computing Lab
School of Computer Science and Technology
Huazhong University of Science and Technology, Wuhan, 430074, China
hjin@hust.edu.cn

Abstract. Medical diagnosis and intervention increasingly rely upon medical image processing tools that are bound with high-cost hardware, designed for special diseases, and incapable of being shared by common medical terminals. In this paper, we present our *Ubiquitous Context-based Image Processing Engine* (UCIPE) for MedImGrid (*Medical Image Grid*). It encapsulates image processing algorithms as WS (*Web Services*), and creates virtual algorithm barn to store their metadata. The user contexts are captured by UCIPE clients and used as clues to search the optimal WS from the algorithm barn. UCIPE supports all-weather accesses (anytime, anywhere, with any means) of numerous multiple terminals to guarantee the algorithm resources be accessed transparently. The UCIPE prototype for MedImGrid is based on CERNET2. The performances of UCIPE-based 3D reconstruction verify the feasibility of UCIPE and prove the improvement of IPv6 network to medical gird applications.

1 Introduction

In the last decades, new digital imaging systems such as computer tomography, ultrasound imaging, digital radiography, magnetic resonance imaging, and tomographic radioisotope imaging, have revolutionized medical diagnosis to provide the clinicians with new information about the interior of human body unavailable before. Therefore medical image processing has become an extremely active domain in the fields of computer vision and imaging in recent years [1].

Medical images, which present the visual healthy or diseased features, are very important to assist doctors' diagnosis. But under current conditions, the tomography images captured by different devices (such as CT, PET and MRI) can not be read easily. Only experienced clinicians can find out abnormal images from mass cases. Some rare details of medical images that go beyond of the clinicians' cognizing space

* This paper is supported by the National High Technology Research and Development Program of China (863 Program) under grant No.2006AA02Z347, and National Nature Science Foundation of China under grant No.60673174.

J. Indulska et al. (Eds.): UIC 2007, LNCS 4611, pp. 888–897, 2007.

will be ignored regrettably. Medical image processing technology (such as 3D reconstruction, images merging and surgical operation simulation) strengthens the feature details of images or transforms them to the forms that people can observe conveniently. But related tools are bound with high-cost hardware and software, and are special for fixed diseases and image types. That restricts them from being used widely. With the popularity of various terminals (such as PDA, mobile terminals and PC) in hospitals, it has become the new demand to share the medical image processing services with ubiquitous, intelligent and all-weather means [2].

The combination of medical image processing and grid technology will arouse new approaches to solve the bottleneck of medical image processing. MedImGrid is a grid prototype, which aims to make full use of grid's superiorities to support medical researches, collaborations and services widely [3]. In this paper, we present our MedImGrid UCIPE, which provides an ubiquitous image processing scheme for intricate healthcare environments. It encapsulates medical image processing algorithms as web services, and enables various terminals to access them transparently. User contexts are captured by UCIPE client and used as clues to select the optimal WS from algorithm barn, or as parameters to determine result quality and return means of image processing.

The rest of this paper is organized as follows: the next section introduces the related works. Section 3 presents the overview of MedImGrid UCIPE. The 3D reconstruction algorithm for UCIPE is briefly described in section 4. Experiments of UCIPE-based 3D reconstruction are discussed in section 5. Finally, we draw conclusions and give out future works in section 6.

2 Related Works

Many researchers have addressed at the combination of medical image processing and gird technology to create more efficient and economical plans for actual medical applications. MedIGrid [4], one component of European HealthGrid [5], is an application that enables doctors to transparently use high-performance computers and storage systems for PET *(Positron Emission Tomography)* image processing, management and visualization analysis. Telescience [6] is a project devoted to the investigation of tomographic applications, which provides a complete solution that will connect scientists' desktops to distributed databases and high-performance analysis environments. The product of Telescience, GTOMO, is based on Globus Toolkit and being used by *NASA Information Power Grid*. DISMEDI's architecture is very close to grid [7]. It uses a distributed computing architecture to provide a parallel computing environment for image processing to support the standard computers connected to network. Different from these projects, we aim to realize one ubiquitous and intelligent scheme for medical image processing in hospitals. It enables various common terminals to share more high-performance image processing algorithms to facilitate the daily operations of clinicians in healthcare units.

3 Overview of MedImGrid UCIPE

The healthcare environments, which are involved with numerous digital medical devices, information systems and terminal devices, are so complicated that the image processing software can only be bounded with special workstations. MedImGrid UCIPE aims to break through the limits and provides one robust scheme to support the demands of different medical occasions.

3.1 The Work Environment of MedImGrid UCIPE

Even in one hospital, there are many resources needed to be linked and integrated seamlessly. Within MedImGrid, every healthcare unit or the interconnected areas can construct one *Domain Management Center* (DMC) to manage and schedule the available resources shown in Fig.1.

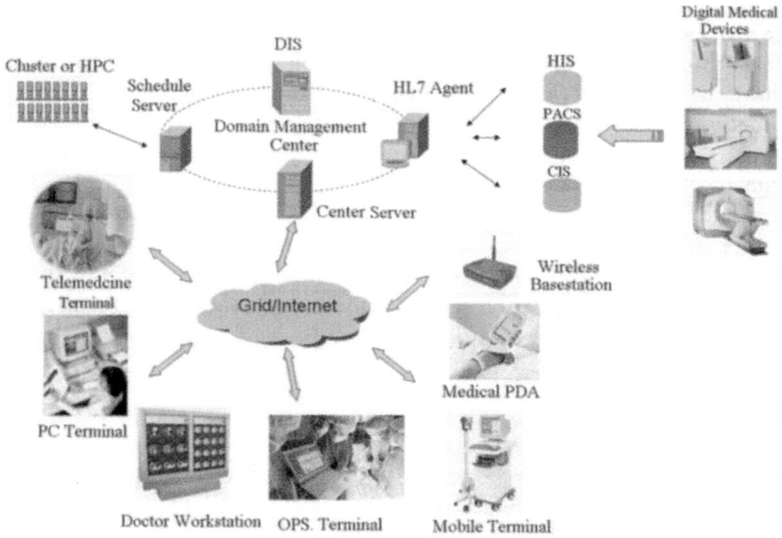

Fig. 1. The Typical Work Environment of MedImGrid UCIPE

DMC is mainly composed of *Center Server*, *Domain Information Server* (DIS), *HL7 Agent* (data agent server) and *Scheduling Server*. *Center Server* is the responder and executant of user demands submitted through the GUI (*Graphic User Interface*) of UCIPE terminal clients. DIS stores and manages the metadata of all kinds of resources including medical data sources and image processing web services. *HL7 Agent* is a data agent to bridge the gap between different data models and access heterogeneous medical information systems. *Scheduling Server* is connected with high-performance computing resources such as cluster and HPC (*High Performance Computer*) where image processing algorithms are deployed. DMCs of different areas can be linked together to expand their available resources through metadata exchange.

3.2 The Framework of MedImGrid UCIPE

The framework of MedImGrid UCIPE is shown in Fig.2, which can be separated into 2 main parts: *MedImGrid UCIPE DMC* and *UCIPE Terminal Client*.

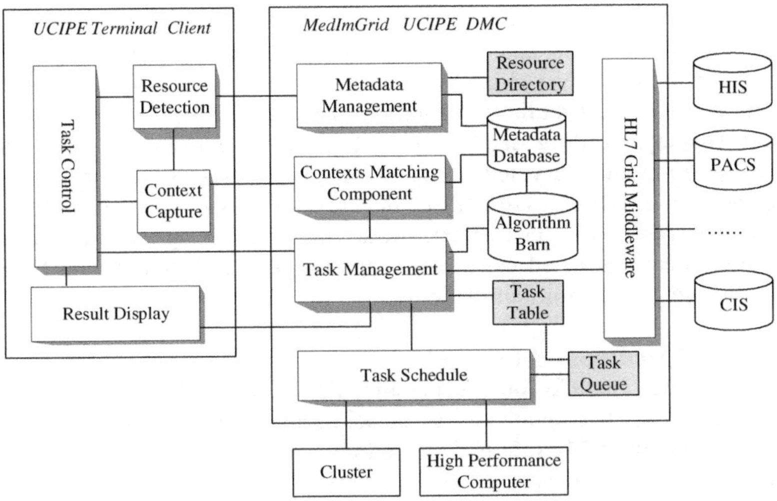

Fig. 2. The Framework of MedImGrid UCIPE

3.2.1 UCIPE Terminal Client

To support low-configuration terminals, UCIPE terminal clients have different versions, which respond to user requests, capture user contexts and display various results of image processing.

Task Control Module is the core of UCIPE terminal client which can identify the task types of user requests and inform DMC to choose the suitable image processing algorithms and parameters. The module manages the flow of task execution when multitasks are executed at the same time, and controls the process of resource detection, context capture, task submission and result retrieval. DMC returns a deadline for every task and entitles the client to cease the overdue tasks.

Resource Detection Module enables the terminal user to know which kinds of resources are available to create UCIPE projects through the GUI. It communicates with *Metadata Management Module* of DMC to acquire available resources (web services) directory that is composed of the metadata of image processing algorithms and medical information systems. The necessary information submitted through the GUI is also recorded in the metadata of corresponding resources such as parameters of image processing or access password used to login medical information systems.

Context Capture Module helps DMC to capture user contexts, such as hardware configuration, network speed, terminal mode (PC, PDA and etc), access means (wireless or wired) and access location (within or out of creditable areas). They are used to determine the parameters of image processing to guarantee safe data transfer and the optimal display of results. We use one autotest program to evaluate the integrated capabilities of a terminal at different aspects when the client is initialized. The benchmark given out by the autotest program is a set E ($E=\{\delta, \varepsilon, \varphi, \gamma\}$). δ ($\delta \geq 0$) is a floating point number that denotes the benchmark of one terminal's computing ability. ε ($\varepsilon=\{\varepsilon_1, \varepsilon_2\}$) is a set related with the display ability of terminals. ε_1 ($\varepsilon_1 \geq 0$) denotes the benchmark of the client's display performance and ε_2 is a Boolean value to represent whether 3D mode is enabled on current terminal. φ ($\varphi \geq 0$) indicates the average network transfer speed between current terminal and DMC. γ ($\gamma \in N$) represents the security level related with user authority, access location and terminal mode, and is used to restrict the precision of image processing.

Result Display Module displays UCIPE processing results on terminal client, which have different encrypted formats, image formats (static or dynamic) and compressed format (MPEG, GIF, JPEG and etc). The module must be able to identify the formats according to user context, extract the actual image data out, and display them on the client supported by graphic engines (such as OpenGL and DirectX) for 2D or 3D images, animations and videos.

3.2.2 DMC of MedImGrid UCIPE

The works of DMC include contexts parsing, algorithm matching, web service calling and result returning. Its components are detached and installed on different servers.

Task Management Module is deployed on *Center Server*. It responds to the user requests, returns their deadline (i.e. maximum waiting time) and appends task information in *Task Table*. Then the module calls *Context Matching Module* to find the optimal WS for the task and updates its state in *Task Table*. The task then is submitted to *Task Scheduling Module* and waits for being processed. When one task is finished, the module informs the client to retrieve result from *Scheduling Server*. It can force the tasks exit whose execution time is out of the maximum waiting time.

Task Scheduling Module is deployed on *Scheduling Server*. It creates a queue for every available WS and monitors their loads. The module acquires parameters from *Context Matching Module* and appends them into *Task Queue* of corresponding WS. It controls the order of task execution and retrieves the task from the top of *Task Queue* to be processed by corresponding WS. When one task is finished, it returns the result to the terminal client under the control of *Task Management Module*.

Algorithm Barn is a virtual component. It uses a metadata table to record the description information of image processing WS deployed on local or remote computing resources. The image processing algorithms are all encapsulated as *Web Services* and can be called by *Task Scheduling Module*. The web services metadata is used by *Context Matching Module* to find the optimal WS for one task. The metadata of some image processing web services are shown in Table 1.

Metadata Management Module is deployed on DIS. It records the metadata of medical data and algorithm resources registered in MedImGrid, which creates *Resources Directory* and *Algorithm barn* to manage them respectively. The medical

Table 1. Metadata of Image Processing Web Services in Algorithm Barn

ID	WS Type	Image Type	Organ/Position	Output Format
3D1	3D Reconstruction	CT	Head	3D Raw File
3D2	3D Reconstruction	ALL	Chest	3D Raw File
I1	Images Merging	CR, CT	Lung	JPEG, GIF
S1	Operation Simulation	ALL	Heart, Blood	AVI

information systems submit their metadata to the component to support the access of *HL7 Agent*. The module sends out handshake signals to computing and data resources. If feedback signals can not be acquired, it modifies the available flag of corresponding resources to prohibit them from being called again. A mistaken calling can also update the available flag when its resource is proven unusable.

Context Matching Module is deployed on *Center Server*. It accepts user context of set D, which is composed of content context ($T=\{T_i | 1 \le i \le n,\ i \in N\}$) and terminal benchmark context ($E=\{\delta, \varepsilon, \varphi, \gamma\}$). T is composed of the parsing result of user request as image URL, processing type and parameters. Some context information of T needs to be extracted by the module from medical image files with normal DICOM (*Digital Imaging and Communications in Medicine*) format as shown in Table 2.

Table 2. Extracted Contexts from DICOM File

DICOM Element Tag	Semantic Meaning	Sample Values
0008,0000	Identified Group Length	558
0008,0005	Specific Character Set	ISO.IR.100
0008,0008	Image Type	DERIVED
0008,0060	Modality	CR
0018,0015	Body Part Examined	CHEST
0018,1164	Image Pixel Spacing	0.168\0.168
0018,1402	Cassette Orientation	PORTRAIT
0018,1403	Cassette Size	35cm x 43cm
0018,5101	View Position	PA

T is used to discover available algorithm resources from *Algorithm Barn* according to metadata set C ($C=\{C_i | 1 \le i \le n,\ i \in N\}$) of web services. T can be processed by the web service corresponding with C only when ($T_i \in C_i$, $\forall i \in [1, n]$). Function L counts the correlation degree between C and T with a return value within [0, 1]. The rule of L is that the priority of special algorithm surpasses that of universal algorithms. F is one function that returns the element amount of one item (T_i or C_i). If one web service is universal (tagged with "all"), F will return a given maximum value. The module will choose one WS from algorithm barn according to the correlation degree K shown in Eq.(2). When C_i does not match with T_i, the correlation degree will be zero (i.e. K=0). We can also take the hardware load into account and select one WS with minimal hardware load from several available resources.

$$L(T_i, C_i) = \begin{cases} F(T_i)/F(C_i) & T_i \in C_i \\ 0 & T_i \notin C_i \end{cases} \tag{1}$$

$$K(T, C) = \sum_{i=1}^{n} L(T_i, C_i) \times \left\lceil \prod_{i=1}^{n} L(T_i, C_i) \right\rceil \tag{2}$$

Some parameters of WS are acquired from E ($E=\{\delta, \varepsilon, \varphi, \gamma\}$) to determine the size and precision of result. For example, it can be a 3D model file or only its 2D projections with different resolution. The result size is an important value to determine the computing scale. Function f_1, f_2, f_3 and f_4 will return the permitted maximum result size corresponding to computing ability (δ), display ability (ε_1), network speed (φ) and security level (γ) within E. Then the result size will be restricted by P shown in Eq.(3). Function *Min* returns the minimum of its involved parameters.

$$P=Min(f_1(\delta), f_2(\varepsilon_1), f_3(\varphi), f_4(\gamma)) \tag{3}$$

HL7 Grid Middleware is one component deployed on *HL7 Agent* to support UCIPE-based access to heterogeneous data resources as HIS (*Hospital Information Systems*), PACS (*Picture Archiving and Communication System*) and CIS (*Clinical Information System*). The HL7 protocol is widely accepted by healthcare industries to provide a comprehensive framework and related references for retrieval, integration, and exchange of electronic health information [4]. Within MedImGrid, we encapsulate HL7 v.3.0 protocol as HL7 grid middleware, which uses HL7 standard as an efficient middle format to realize protocol adaptation and data transformation among different information systems. DMC registers its medical information systems as web services to *Metadata Manage Component* to enable *HL7 Grid Middleware*'s access through HL7 or compatible protocols. Supported by the middleware, *HL7 agent* can retrieve images from medical information systems directly.

4 UCIPE Based 3D Reconstruction Algorithm

3D reconstruction can create 3D surface models based on tomography images. The algorithm makes it possible that the clinicians can observe medical images with an approximate view angle resembled with human knowledge [7]. The reconstruction algorithm reads DICOM files to acquire the serial number of every image in one image group and combines them to create the 3D volume. The UCIPE parameters are used to evaluate the time cost and result size of the algorithm that can decrease the amount or resolution of involved images according to needs. MC (*Marching Cubes*) algorithm is the core of our 3D reconstruction algorithm. It constructs the 3D surface by scanning through all voxels in the 3D volume. Each voxel is a cube created from 8 pixels. The algorithm uses one lookup table to record 256 possible on-off combinations of the cube vertex referring to one grayscale threshold. After initializing the lookup table, the algorithm scans through the whole volume to produce triangle surface for every cube and composes them to create a 3D surface model [8].

5 Experiments

The implementation of MedImGrid UCIPE prototype is based on CGSP2 (*ChinaGrid Support Platform 2.0*) [9]. It utilizes China first IPv6 backbone network (CERNET2) to establish the experimental environment. The experimental data server storing real clinical images (80GB) locates in Wuhan Tongji Hospital. MedImGrid UCIPE utilizes a cluster with 16 nodes as computing resources, and uses PostgeSQL [10] database to store metadata and create the algorithm barn. The servers in MedImGrid own approximate configurations (PIV 1.2GHz XEON/512MB/Red Hat Linux 9.0).

We create a 3D reconstruction project from one mobile terminal (AMD Sempron 2200+/256MB/Windows XP) and confirm which 3D surface will be reconstructed through giving a grayscale threshold, then submit the IDs of a group of serial Head CTs in PACS to DMC. The reconstruction result is shown in Fig.3. We can find directly from the 3D model that the patient has a lacuna at his right above teethridge, but which can not be judged easily through observing mass CTs. To support low-configuration terminals, UCIPE can create 2D snapshots of a 3D model with different resolution, angle and reconstruction surface as shown in Fig.4.

UCIPE depends on network speed heavily, which determines whether the waiting time of terminal clients can be restricted in an acceptable range. We use one terminal to submit 3D reconstruction demands with different amount of CT images to MedImGrid UCIPE and compare the performances of UCIPE within IPv4 and IPv6 network environment. The performance comparison is shown in Fig.5. The computing

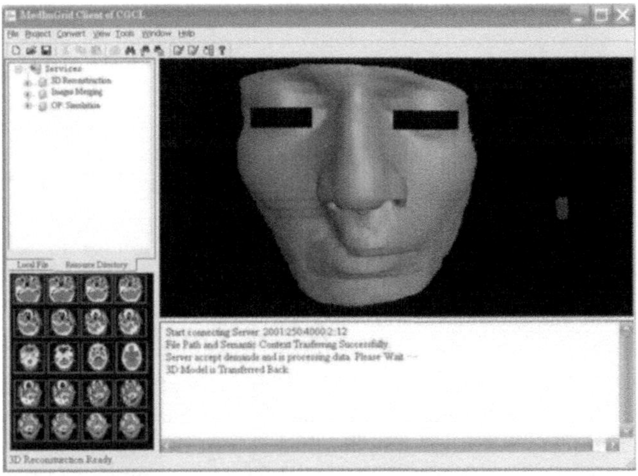

Fig. 3. The GUI of MedImGrid UCIPE Client

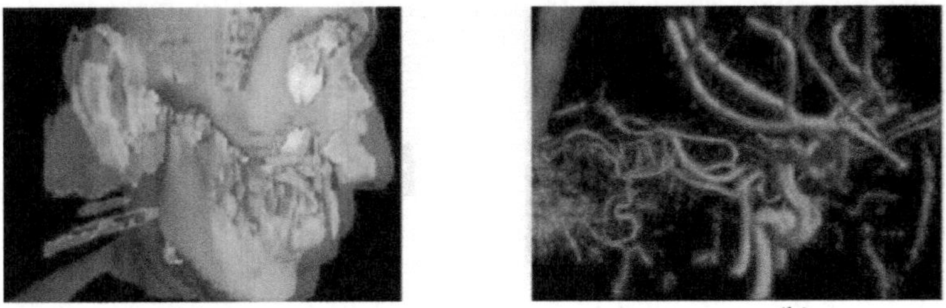

(a) (b)

Fig. 4. 2D Snapshots of UCIPE-based 3D Reconstruction for Low Configuration Terminal (a) Skull Perspective of 3D Head. (b) Partial Artery View in 3D Head.

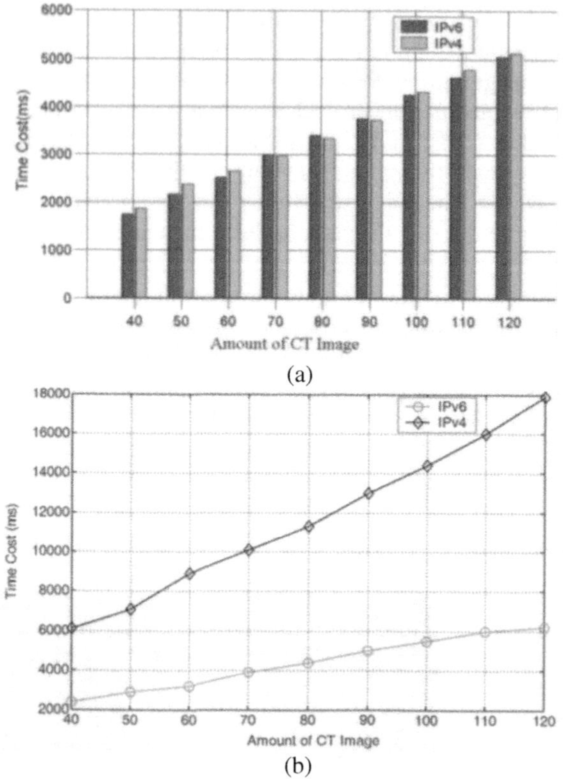

Fig. 5. Time Cost Comparison of UCIPE-based 3D Reconstruction with Different CT Amount in IPv4 and IPv6 Environment (a) Computing Time Comparison (b) Total Time Comparison

time cost of UCIPE within IPv4 and IPv6 network will increase (but keep approximate) with the increasing of CT amount. But the total time cost of UCIPE in IPv4 environment increases more quickly than that in IPv6 environment. The network speed becomes the bottleneck for UCIPE in IPv4 environment. The performance may be seen as incomparable because IPv4 environment (CERNET) and IPv6 environment (CERNET2) perhaps have different loads or random bandwidth conflicts during experiments. But even excluding these factors, we can also make sure that IPv6 network will accelerate the approach of UCIPE.

6 Conclusions and Future Works

Supported by UCIPE, various terminals can access the medical information systems and images processing algorithms transparently. Our UCIPE-based 3D reconstruction instance verifies the feasibility of our approach to support various terminals, and proves the improvement of IPv6 network to medical grid applications. In the future, we will improve our algorithm barn model, security control model and context matching components of MedImGrid UCIPE to guarantee image processing more efficiently and safely. MedImGrid UCIPE breaks through the limits of existing medical image processing systems to hardware and software. Its success will help to simplify the operations of clinical doctors and decrease the hardware cost of healthcare units.

References

1. Antonelli, L., Ceccarelli, M., Carracciuolo, L., Amore, L.D., Murli, A.: Total Variation Regularization for Edge Preserving 3D SPECT Imaging in High Performance Computing Environments. In: Sloot, P.M.A., Tan, C.J.K., Dongarra, J.J., Hoekstra, A.G. (eds.) Computational Science - ICCS 2002. LNCS, vol. 2330, pp. 171–180. Springer, Heidelberg (2002)
2. Ding, H., Wang, G., Hong, B., Zhou, Y., Meng, M., Gao, S.: Construction of a Knowledge Center for Medical Image. In: Proceedings of Engineering in Medicine and Biology Society (EMBC'05), September 2005, Shanghai, China, pp. 82–85 (2005)
3. Jin, H., Sun, A., Zhang, Q., Zheng, R., He, R.: MIGP: Medical Image Grid Platform Based on HL7 Grid Middleware. In: Yakhno, T., Neuhold, E.J. (eds.) ADVIS 2006. LNCS, vol. 4243, pp. 254–263. Springer, Heidelberg (2006)
4. Bertero, M., Bonetto, P.: MedIGrid: a Medical Imaging Application for Computational Grids. In: Proceeding of International Parallel and Distributed Processing Symposium (IPDPS '03), April 2003, Nice, France, pp.22–26 (2003)
5. Vision of a HealthGrid, http://www.healthgrid.org/
6. http://www.npaci.edu/Alpha/telescience.html
7. Mayer, A.: Providing with High Performance 3D Medical Image Processing on a Distributed Environment. Journal of Computer Methods and Programs in Biomedicine 58(3), 207–217 (2005)
8. Yang, S.N., Wu, T.S.: Compressing Isosurfaces Generated with Marching Cubes. The Visual Computer Journal 18(1), 54–67 (2004)
9. ChinaGrid Support Platform, http://www.chinagrid.edu.cn/cgsp
10. PostgreSQL: The World's Most Advanced Open Source Database, http://www.postgresql.org/

Ontology-Based Semantic Recommendation for Context-Aware E-Learning

Zhiwen Yu[1,2], Yuichi Nakamura[1], Seiie Jang[2], Shoji Kajita[2], and Kenji Mase[2]

[1] Academic Center for Computing and Media Studies, Kyoto University, Japan
yu@ccm.media.kyoto-u.ac.jp, yuichi@media.kyoto-u.ac.jp
[2] Information Technology Center, Nagoya University, Japan
jang@itc.nagoya-u.ac.jp, kajita@nagoya-u.jp, mase@nagoya-u.jp

Abstract. Nowadays, e-learning systems are widely used for education and training in universities and companies because of their electronic course content access and virtual classroom participation. However, with the rapid increase of learning content on the Web, it will be time-consuming for learners to find contents they really want to and need to study. Aiming at enhancing the efficiency and effectiveness of learning, we propose an ontology-based approach for semantic content recommendation towards context-aware e-learning. The recommender takes knowledge about the learner (user context), knowledge about content, and knowledge about the domain being learned into consideration. Ontology is utilized to model and represent such kinds of knowledge. The recommendation consists of four steps: semantic relevance calculation, recommendation refining, learning path generation, and recommendation augmentation. As a result, a personalized, complete, and augmented learning program is suggested for the learner.

1 Introduction

E-learning allows learners to access electronic course contents through the network and study them in virtual classrooms. It brings many benefits in comparison with conventional learning paradigm, e.g., learning can be taken at any time, at any place (e.g., campus, home, and train station). However, with the rapid increase of learning content on the Web, it will be time-consuming for learners to find contents they really want to and need to study. The challenge in an information-rich world is not only to make information available to people at any time, at any place, and in any form, but to offer the right thing to the right person in the right way [1][2]. Therefore, e-learning systems should not only provide flexible content delivery, but support adaptive content recommendation.

For better learning experience and effect, the recommendation of learning content should take into account the contextual information of learners, e.g., prior knowledge, goal, learning style, available learning time, location and interests. This new learning paradigm is called context-aware e-learning [3]. In this paper, we propose an ontology-based approach for semantic recommendation to realize context-awareness in learning content provisioning. We aim to make recommendation by exploiting

J. Indulska et al. (Eds.): UIC 2007, LNCS 4611, pp. 898–907, 2007.

knowledge about the learner (user context), knowledge about the content, and knowledge about the learning domain. The recommendation approach is characterized with semantic relevance calculation, recommendation refining, learning path generation, and recommendation augmentation. The knowledge modeling and the whole recommendation process are performed based on ontology. In the current system, we mainly consider two kinds of the most important contexts in learning, i.e., the learner's prior knowledge and his learning goal.

The paper is structured as follows. Section 2 discusses previous work relevant to this paper. In Section 3, we present the ontology model to express knowledge about the learner, content, and the domain being learned. Section 4 describes the ontology-based semantic recommendation in detail. The prototype implementation and preliminary results are described in Section 5. Finally, Section 6 concludes the paper and points out directions for future work.

2 Related Work

There has been much work done in the area of recommendation over the past decade. The interest in developing various recommender systems still remains high because of the abundance of practical applications that help users to deal with information overload and provide personalized service [4]. The objects manipulated by recommender systems include a broad spectrum of artefacts, such as documents, books, CDs, movies, and television programs. Compared with these fields, learning content recommendation is a new topic with the emergence of e-learning. It has only been investigated in several systems in the past few years.

The EU project, LIP [3] aims to provide immediate learning on demand for knowledge intensive organizations through incorporating context into the design of e-learning systems. A matching procedure is presented to suggest personalized learning programs based on user's current competency gap.

COLDEX [5] considers the learner's preferences and hardware/software characteristics in serving learning materials. Collaborative filtering technique is utilized for content recommendation.

The authors of [6] present learning content recommendation based on ontology, which utilizes sequencing rules to connect learning objects. The rules are formed from the knowledge base and competency gap analysis.

The Elena project [7] ranks learning resources according to text filter (a weight is calculated between the specified text and each document), category filter (the distances from the specified classifications in the ontology to the entries specified in the subject field from each resource are evaluated), and the combination of the weight and the distance in the ontology.

Bomsdorf [8] introduces a concept of "plasticity of digital learning spaces" for the adaptation of learning spaces to different contexts of use. A rule-based ascertainment engine is used to identify learning resources according to learner's situation.

Paraskakis [9] proposes a paradigm of ambient learning aiming at providing access to high quality e-learning material at a time, place, pace and context that best suits the individual learner.

K-InCA [10] is an agent-based system supporting personalized, active and socially aware e-learning. The personal agent is aware of the user's characteristics and cooperates with a set of expert cognitive agents.

Our work differs from previous work in several aspects. First, we provide content recommendation through knowledge-based semantic approach. LIP project [3] retrieves objects by matching rather than through semantic relevance. COLDEX [5] recommends learning materials based on collaborative filtering not knowledge-based technique. Second, besides learning content ranking, we also support recommendation refining, learning path generation, and recommendation augmentation. The learning content recommendation presented in [6] is based on ontology and connects learning objects. However, it did not support recommendation refining and recommendation augmentation. Elena [7] provides content ranking and aggregation, while learning path recommendation and results refining are not supported. Third, as for content recommendation, we mainly consider user's personal learning context, e.g. learning goal and prior knowledge. The rule-based recommendation strategy proposed by Bomsdorf [8] mainly considers device and network context rather than personal context. Although [9] and [10] claim to provide personalized learning material access, the approach of recommendation has not been described.

3 Ontology Model

We use ontologies to model knowledge about the learner (user context), knowledge about the content, and the domain knowledge (the taxonomy of the domain being learned). Within the domain of knowledge representation, the term *ontology* refers to the formal and explicit description of domain concepts, which are often conceived as a set of entities, relations, instances, functions, and axioms [11]. By allowing learners or contents to share a common understanding of knowledge structure, the ontologies enable applications to interpret learner context and content features based on their semantics. Furthermore, ontologies' hierarchical structure lets developers reuse domain ontologies (e.g., of computer science, mathematics, etc.) in describing learning fields and build a practical model without starting from scratch.

In our system, we have designed three ontologies: Learner Ontology, Learning Content Ontology, and Domain Ontology. The Learner Ontology shown in Fig. 1 depicts contexts about a learner, e.g., subject or particular content already mastered, learning goal, available learning time, current location, desired learning style, and learning interests. The learning goal may be an abstract subject or a particular content. *lco* and *do* stand for Learning Content Ontology and Domain Ontology, respectively. Properties of contents as well as relationships between them are defined by the Learning Content Ontology (see Fig. 2). The relation *hasPrerequisite* describes content dependency information, i.e., content needs to be taken before the target content. Actually, nowadays most of the departments in university provide a course dependency chart when issuing their courses. The Domain Ontology is proposed to integrate existing consensus domain ontologies such as computer science, mathematics, chemistry, etc. The domain ontologies are organized as hierarchy to demonstrate topic classification. For instance, the hierarchical ontology of computer science domain is presented in Fig. 3. It derives from the well-known ACM taxonomy (http://www.acm.org/class/1998/).

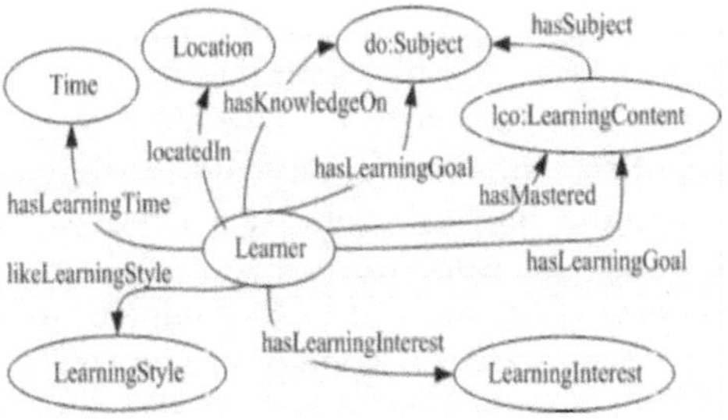

Fig. 1. Learner ontology

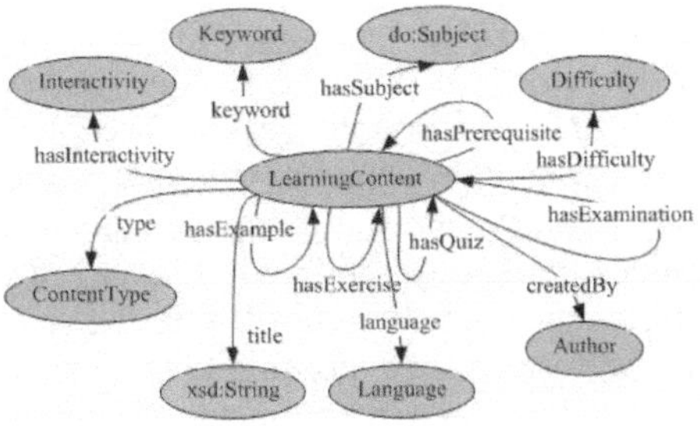

Fig. 2. Learning content ontology

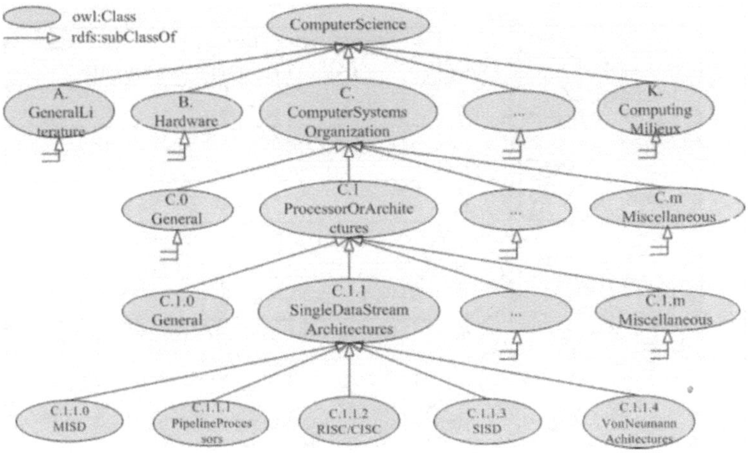

Fig. 3. Computer science domain ontology

We adopt OWL (Web Ontology Language) [12] to express ontology enabling expressive knowledge description and data interoperability of knowledge. It basically includes ontology class definition and ontology instance markups. According to the aforementioned learner ontology, the following OWL based markup segment describes the learning contexts about **Harry**.

```
<Learner rdf:about="Harry">
<hasLearningGoal>Distributed Compuing</hasLearningGoal>
<hasMastered>CS100</hasMastered>
<hasLearningTime>20:00:00-22:00:00</hasLearningTime>
...
</Learner>
```

4 Semantic Content Recommendation

The learning content recommendation consists of four steps as shown in Fig. 4. First, the Semantic Relevance Calculation computes the semantic similarity between the learner and the learning contents, and then generates a recommendation list accordingly. Second, the Recommendation Refining provides an interactive way to adjust the result until several acceptable options are achieved. When the learner selects one item from the candidates, the Learning Path Generation builds a studying route composed of prerequisite contents and the target learning contents, which guides the learning process. Finally, the Recommendation Augmentation aggregates appendant contents related with the main course. Each step of the recommendation are performed by exploiting knowledge about the learner (goal and prior knowledge), knowledge about the contents (features and relations among them), or the domain knowledge. The Ontology Base provides persistent storage and efficient retrieval of such knowledge.

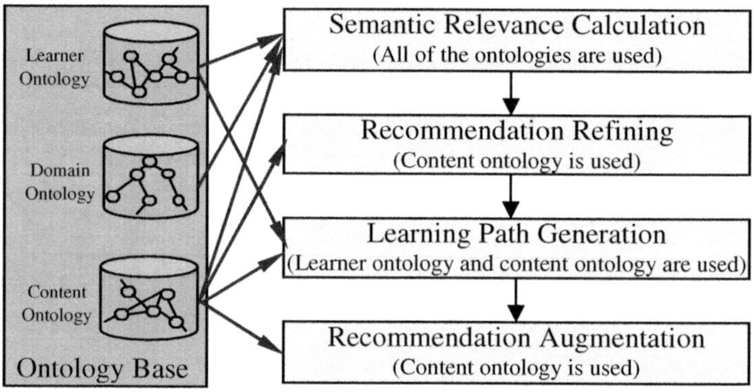

Fig. 4. Content recommendation procedure

4.1 Semantic Relevance Calculation

For recommendation, we first need to rank the learning contents with respect to how much the content satisfies the learner's context. Here we mainly consider the learning goal context. Our system uses the semantic relevance between the learner's goal and learning content as the ranking criteria.

The semantic relevance is inspired by category theory and conceptual graph [13]. It is intuitive that objects in the same domain or related domain may have some similarity within each other. In other words, instances in a category hierarchy have some commonality. Similarity between two objects in the category hierarchy can be measured according to their correlation in the hierarchy model. This is done through analyzing the positions of the objects in the hierarchy model. The closer two objects are, the larger similarity between them will be.

The semantic relevance is calculated through the following steps:

1. *Map the user's goal to the domain ontology*
2. *Locate the subject of the learning content in the domain ontology*
3. *Estimate the conceptual proximity between the mapped element and the subject node of the learning content*

The conceptual proximity ($S(e1, e2)$) is formally defined and determined according to the following rules ('e1' and 'e2' are two elements in the hierarchical domain ontology):

Rule (1): The conceptual proximity is always a positive number, that is,

$$S(e1, e2) > 0 \tag{1}$$

Rule (2): The conceptual proximity has the property of symmetry, that is,

$$S(e1, e2) = S(e2, e1) \tag{2}$$

Rule (3): If 'e1' is the same as 'e2',

$$S(e1, e2) = Dep(e1) / M \tag{3}$$

Rule (4): If 'e1' is the ancestor or descendant node of 'e2',

$$S(e1, e2) = Dep(e) / M \qquad e = \begin{cases} e1 & e1 \textit{ is the ancestor node of } e2 \\ e2 & e1 \textit{ is the descendant node of } e2 \end{cases} \tag{4}$$

Rule (5): If 'e1' is different from 'e2' and there is no ancestor-descendant relationship between them,

$$S(e1,e2) = Dep(LCA(e1, e2)) / M \tag{5}$$

In equations (3), (4) and (5), *M* denotes the total depth of the domain hierarchy ontology; *Dep(e)* is the depth of node 'e' in the hierarchy (the root node always has the least depth, say 1); *LCA(x, y)* means the Least Common Ancestor node for node 'x' and 'y'.

With the above definitions and the domain hierarchy structure given in Fig. 3, we can infer that M=5; LCA(MISD, SISD)= SingleDataStreamArchitecture; Dep(LCA(MISD, SISD))=4; hence S(MISD, SISD)= Dep(LCA(MISD, SISD))=4/5=0.8.

The semantic relevance is based on the intuitive notion that the amount of relevance between the learning goal and content subject increases as they are nearer and more is known about them. For example, two contents of "SingleDataStreamArchitecture" are known to be more similar than two contents of "ProcessorOrArchitecture".

With semantic relevance calculated, we can recommend those contents whose semantic relevance is larger than a preset threshold.

4.2 Recommendation Refining

A recommendation list can be provided to the learner with respect to semantic relevance. However, it may still include overwhelming contents or those contents that are not satisfactory according to the learner's preferences, e.g., difficulty level. Our system offers interactive recommendation refining [14], through which the learner can interact with the system critiquing its recommendation and interactively refining the results until several acceptable options are achieved. The recommendation result can be refined according to the following features: speciality, difficulty, and interactivity.

Speciality. If the result contains very few items and the learner wants to get more generalized contents, the system can give all contents whose subject falls one upper level of LCA (here we define LCA as the least common ancestor of the current recommendation items, which may contains subclass or not) in the hierarchy. Similarly, if the result includes a lot of items and the learner wants to get more specialized contents, the system can return those contents whose subject is one lower level of LCA in the hierarchy. When "More specialized" refining action is triggered, a dialog will pop up to ask the learner to choose one subclass of the LCA.

Difficulty. The learner can refine the result to choose easier or more difficult contents. This can be achieved through the property of *hasDifficulty* of the contents. Each content are assigned a difficulty level when authored, which includes "very easy", "easy", "medium", "difficult", and "very difficult". The difficulty critiquing is made to a particular candidate in the recommendation list. For example, if the learner wants to obtain easier contents with item X as reference, the system will put forward the contents whose difficulty level is lower than that of X while the other features are the same.

Interactivity. Similar to difficulty, the learner can get contents with preferred interactivity by increasing or decreasing the interactivity level of a particular item. The critiquing can be accomplished through the property of *hasInteractivity* of the contents. When created, the content is given an interactivity level according to its presentation method and layout. The interactivity level ranges from "very low", "low", "medium", "high", to "very high".

4.3 Learning Path Generation

Usually a single learning content will not be practicable for the learner to meet his goal, because learning contents themselves may have prerequisites that the user has not mastered yet. Therefore we need to provide the learner with a learning path to guide the learning process and suggest the user to obtain some preliminary knowledge before immersing in the target content.

When the learner selects one item from the recommendation list, the system can generate a learning path connecting with prerequisite contents and the target learning content. This is accomplished by recursively adding prerequisite contents of the learning content into the path until it reaches the basic contents that have no prerequisites, and then pruning it based on the learner's prior knowledge. The prerequisite course information is provided by the *hasPrerequisite* relation of a particular content. The learning path should be a DAG (Directed Acyclic Graph). We therefore detect and eliminate cyclic graph in building the path.

The following algorithm outlines the executions taking place during learning path generation. For each content C^i in the current learning path, first extract the prerequisite list from its XML description file xml_C^i (line 10). Then for each content C^j in the prerequisite list, if it does not belong to the user's prior learned course list and the current learning path, add it into the learning path and revise C^j's direct subsequence list, offspring list, and number of steps to the target learning content (line 14-18). If C^j already exists in the learning path, but does not belong to the user's prior learned course list and the offspring list of C^i, it is not necessary to add again, but need to update its direct subsequence list, offspring list, and number of steps to the target learning content (line 19-24).

Algorithm. Generating the learning path for the specified learning content ***LC***.

```
Input: LC, user's prior learned course list PC_List
Output: LC's learning path LP
Procedure: Generate_Learning_Path
Begin
LP = NULL
LC_Offspring_List = NULL
LC_JumpsToGoal = 0
LP ← LP+LC
For each C^i ∈ LP
    C^i_Prerequisite_List ← Get_Prerequisite(xml_C^i)
    For each C^j ∈ C^i_Prerequisite_List
      C^j_DirectSubsequence_List = NULL
      C^j_Offspring_List = NULL
      If C^j ∉ PC_List AND C^j ∉ LP then
          LP ← LP + C^j
          C^j_ DirectSubsequence_List ← C^j_ DirectSubsequence_List + C^i
          C^j_Offspring_List ← C^j_Offspring_List + C^i + C^i_Offspring_List
          C^j_JumpsToGoal = C^i_JumpsToGoal + 1
      Else If C^j ∉ PC_List AND C^j ∈ LP AND C^j ∉ C^i_Offspring_List then
          C^j_ DirectSubsequence_List ← C^j_ DirectSubsequence_List + C^i
          C^j_Offspring_List ← C^j_Offspring_List + C^i + C^i_Offspring_List
          If C^j_JumpsToGoal < C^i_JumpsToGoal + 1 then
            For each C^k ∈ LP_After_C^j
              C^k_JumpsToGoal = Max(C^k_DirectSubsequence_JumpsToGoal) + 1
Return LP
End
```

4.4 Recommendation Augmentation

While studying the main course, the learner usually needs to refer to some appendant contents within the course. For instance, when given a concept, the learner hopes to see some examples about it so as to strengthen his understanding, and after a section finishes, the learner may want to take a quiz to verify whether he has mastered the knowledge in the section. In our system, we provide recommendation augmentation with references to examples, exercises, quizzes, and examination related with the main course that the user is currently studying. This is accomplished by aggregating the contents through the properties of "hasExample", "hasExercise", "hasQuiz", and "hasExamination". Then the system provides links for such appendant contents along the main course. With the recommendation augmented, the learner needs merely to click on a button rather than looking up such contents in a large space by himself.

5 Prototype Implementation and Experiment

With the proposed recommendation approach, we built a semantic learning content recommender system. It was developed with Java (JDK1.5).

Fig. 5 shows several client-side interfaces for the semantic content recommendation. Fig. 5a is the main interface. It mainly consists of four parts. The top part provides interface for the learner to input learning goal and select the courses already learned. To ease the learning goal input, we provide a subject tree for the learner to choose one. Here the subject tree is automatically generated from ACM taxonomy (see Fig. 5b). Then, the recommendation list is presented below. Here the learner can refine the result through 6 options (i.e., "Easier", "More difficult", "More interactive", "Less interactive", "More generalized", and "More specialized", see Fig. 5c). The learning path is generated and shown in the left bottom column, while the recommendation package for the content selected from the path is presented in the right bottom column.

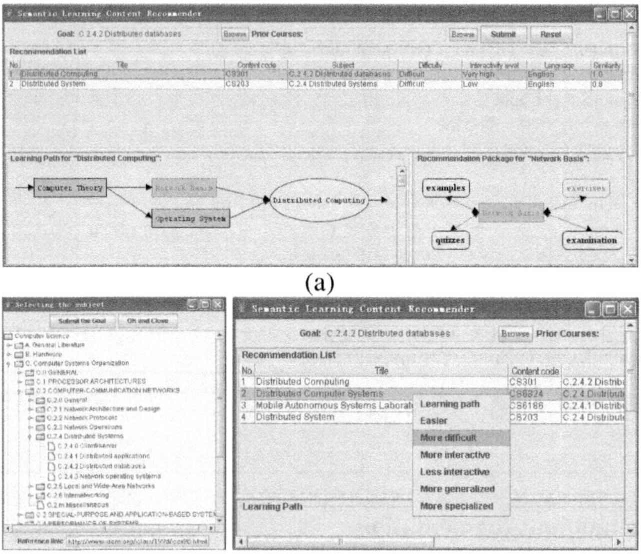

(b) (c)

Fig. 5. Client-side interfaces for the semantic content recommendation

We tested the overhead of the semantic content recommendation in terms of response time. The experiment was deployed on a PC with 1.60GHz Pentium 4 CPU and 1GB memory running Windows XP. The running time for each step, i.e., content recommendation list generation, recommendation refining, learning path generation and package generating, was an average value of 10 runs. We observed that the time for content recommendation list generating was the largest, say 78 ms; the learning path generation took 16ms; both of the refining and package generating cost less than 1 ms. The total time for semantic recommendation is therefore less than 100ms. Through this experiment, we could conclude that our approach is light-weight and feasible to be deployed.

6 Conclusion and Future Work

As the amount of electronic course content becomes very large, providing adaptive and personalized content recommendation is significant for today's e-learning systems. In this paper, we present a semantic recommendation approach for learning content based on ontology. For future work, we plan to incorporate additional learner contexts, e.g., available learning time, location, learning style, and learning interests into the recommendation process in order to make the system more comprehensive and intelligent. We also plan to consider the shared-knowledge among group members so as to recommend content to a group of learners [15].

Acknowledgement

This work was partially supported by the Ministry of Education, Culture, Sports, Science and Technology, Japan under the projects of "Development of Fundamental Software Technologies for Digital Archives" and "Cyber Infrastructure for the Information-explosion Era".

References

1. Fischer, G.: User Modeling in Human-Computer Interaction. User Modeling and User-Adapted Interaction 11(1/2), 65–86 (2001)
2. Yu, Z., et al.: Supporting Context-Aware Media Recommendations for Smart Phones. IEEE Pervasive Computing 5(3), 68–75 (2006)
3. Schmidt, A.: User Context Aware Delivery of E-Learning Material: Approach and Architecture. Journal of Universal Computer Science 10(1), 28–36 (2004)
4. Adomavicius, G., Tuzhilin, A.: Toward the Next Generation of Recommender Systems: A Survey of the State-of-the-Art and Possible Extensions. IEEE Transactions on Knowledge and Data Engineering 17(6), 734–749 (2005)
5. Baloian, N., et al.: A Model for a Collaborative Recommender System for Multimedia Learning Material. In: de Vreede, G.-J., Guerrero, L.A., Marín Raventós, G. (eds.) CRIWG 2004. LNCS, vol. 3198, pp. 281–288. Springer, Heidelberg (2004)
6. Shen, L., Shen, R.: Ontology-Based Learning Content Recommendation. International Journal of Continuing Engineering Education and Life-Long Learning 15(3/4/5/6), 308–317 (2005)
7. Simon, B., Mikls, Z., Nejdl, W., Sintek, M., Salvachua, J.: Smart Space for Learning: A Mediation Infrastructure for Learning Services. In: WWW 2003, May 2003, Hungary (2003)
8. Bomsdorf, B.: Adaptation of Learning Spaces: Supporting Ubiquitous Learning in Higher Distance Education. In: Dagstuhl Seminar Proceedings 05181, Mobile Computing and Ambient Intelligence: The Challenge of Multimedia (2005)
9. Paraskakis, I.: Ambient Learning: a new paradigm for e-learning, m-ICTE2005, Spain, pp. 26–30 (2005)
10. Nabeth, T., et al.: InCA: A Cognitive Multi-Agents Architecture for Designing Intelligent & Adaptive Learning Systems. ComSIS Journal 2(2), 99–114 (2005)
11. Gruber, T.: A Translation Approach to Portable Ontology Specification. Knowledge Acquisition 5(2), 199–220 (1993)
12. McGuinness, D.L., Harmelen, F.: OWL Web Ontology Language Overview, W3C Recommendation (2004)
13. Sowa, J.F.: Conceptual Structures. Addison-Wesley, Reading, MA (1984)
14. Burke, R.: Hybrid Recommender Systems: Survey and Experiments. User Modeling and User-Adapted Interaction 12(4), 331–370 (2002)
15. Yu, Z., et al.: TV Program Recommendation for Multiple Viewers Based on User Profile Merging. User Modeling and User-Adapted Interaction 16(1), 63–82 (2006)

Deployment of Context-Aware Component-Based Applications Based on Middleware

Di Zheng, Jun Wang, Yan Jia, Wei-Hong Han, and Peng Zou

School of Computer Science,
National University of Defence Technology,
Changsha, Hunan, China 410073
dizheng@nudt.edu.cn

Abstract. Ubiquitous computing allows application developers to build a large and complex distributed system that can transform physical spaces into computationally active and intelligent environments. Ubiquitous applications need a middleware that can detect and act upon any context changes created by the result of any interactions between users, applications, and surrounding computing environment for applications without users' interventions. The context-awareness has become the one of core technologies for application services in ubiquitous computing environment and been considered as the indispensable function for ubiquitous computing applications. The need for high quality context management is evident to the component-based middleware for it forms the basis of the component adaptation and the component deployment in the pervasive computing. Adaptive deployment is a key factor for the deployment in mobile environments and deployed applications have to be suited to different contexts such as the user requirements, the resources of his terminal and the surrounding environment. Therefore, we put forward a middleware based deployment approach for the context-aware component-based applications so as to make these applications can be adapted more easily than traditional applications by simply adding and deleting components.

1 Introduction

With the technical evolution of wireless networks, mobile and sensor technology, the vision of pervasive computing is becoming a reality. The paradigm for pervasive computing aims at enabling people to contact anyone at anytime and anywhere in a convenient way. And it also brings the new challenges to traditional applications [1, 2]. In this environment, the applications should become context aware for the reason that the resources (e.g. memory, battery, CPU) of the mobile devices may be limited and the application execution context (e.g. user location, device screen size) is variable[3].Therefore, the applications need adapt their behaviors basing on corresponding context information. The context-awareness has become the one of core technologies for application services in ubiquitous computing environment and been considered as the indispensable function for ubiquitous computing applications.

J. Indulska et al. (Eds.): UIC 2007, LNCS 4611, pp. 908–918, 2007.

At the same time, middleware is a widely used term to denote generic infrastructure services above operating system and protocol stack. The role of the middleware is to ease the task of designing, programming and managing distributed applications by providing a simple, consistent and integrated distributed programming environment. Therefore, ubiquitous applications need a middleware that can detect and act upon any context changes created by the result of any interactions between users, applications, and surrounding computing environment for applications without users' interventions.

Furthermore, deployment refers to all activities performed after the development of the software which make it available to its users. These activities consist essentially in installing and configuring the software but can also include software reconfiguration, updates and even un-installation. With the continuous growth of wireless communication, mobile hand-held devices such as PDAs and mobile phones are becoming powerful platforms that allow users to utilize a whole range of entertainment and business applications. Hand-held devices have scarce resources, such as low battery power, slow CPU speed and limited memory. They rarely have a secondary memory. The specificity of mobile users is that they undergo constant changes in their context, such as a high variability of network bandwidth, location and physical environment. A mobile user needs to be able to deploy the same application on different execution environments and in different contexts. Hence, the deployment needs to be processed differently according to the environment and the user's situation. The resource limitation of hand-held devices and the high variability of contexts lead mobile users to perform several repetitive deployment activities.

For all these reasons, mobile environments require the deployment process to be context-aware and entirely automated. Context-awareness will satisfy the user's requirements, which are constantly changing according to the context, and automation will relieve the user of repetitive deployment tasks. Several component-based deployment solutions have been specified, such as the CCM (CORBA Component Model) component packaging and deployment model [12], the EJB deployment solution [4], the .Net deployment solution [5] and the J2EE deployment API [6]. The deployment process of these solutions is not context-aware and is not completely automated. It requires the user's intervention in the placement of the components. OSGi [7] is an open specification for a component model that allows services to be deployed and managed. OSGi is a good starting point for developing flexible applications that are easily manageable but the specification does not describe anything about the adaptation of the deployment process to the context. [8] describes a deployment approach which supports software deployment into networks of distributed, mobile, highly resource constrained devices. This approach is based on the principles of software architecture, which allow the description of a software assembly. However, the application architecture is not able to vary according to the context. Therefore, we put forward a middleware based deployment approach for the context-aware component-based applications so as to make these applications can be adapted more easily than traditional applications by simply adding and deleting components based on different types of context and is not limited either to the target environment or to the user preferences.

2 Context-Aware Applications

In context-aware computing, a number of definitions of context have been proposed, usually based on enumerations of context information that can be sensed by applications. Dey [9] provides a widely accepted definition which is as follows: "any information that can be used to characterize the situation of an entity. An entity is a person, place, or object that is considered relevant to the interaction between a user and an application, including the user and applications themselves".

In mobile and ubiquitous computing, interaction with computers is inevitably in context. The user's expectations about a system and their anticipation of the reaction of a system [10] that they are interacting with, is highly dependent on the situation and environment, as well as on prior experience. Therefore, context is essential for building usable ubiquitous computing systems that respond in a way that is anticipated by the user.

A system is context-aware if it can extract, interpret and use context information and adapt its functionality to the current context of use. The challenge for such systems lies in the complexity of capturing, representing and processing contextual data [11]. To capture context information generally some additional sensors and/or programs are required. To transfer the context information to applications and for different applications to be able to use the same context information a common representation format for such information should exist. In addition to being able to obtain the context-information, applications must include some "intelligence" to process the information and to deduce the meaning. This is probably the most challenging issue, since context is often indirect or deducible by combining different pieces of context information.

3 Architecture of the Context-Aware Middleware for the Component-Based Pervasive Computing

3.1 Component Based Middleware StarCCM

In terms of middleware, lots of emphasis has been given to enterprise (or server-side) component technologies, such as Enterprise Java Beans or the CORBA Component Model. As depicted in figure 1, in previous work we have developed a component based middleware StarCCM which conform to the CORBA Component Model. The components execute inside a container, which provides implicit support for distribution in terms of support for transactions, security, persistence and resource management. This offers an important separation of concerns in the development of business applications; i.e. the application programmer can focus on the development and potential re-use of components to provide the necessary business logic, and a more "distribution-aware" developer can provide a container with the necessary non-functional properties. Containers also provide additional functionality including life-cycle management and component discovery.

The OMG Specification of the Deployment and Configuration presents a data model for the description of a deployment plan which contains information about artifacts that are part of the deployment, how to create component instances from

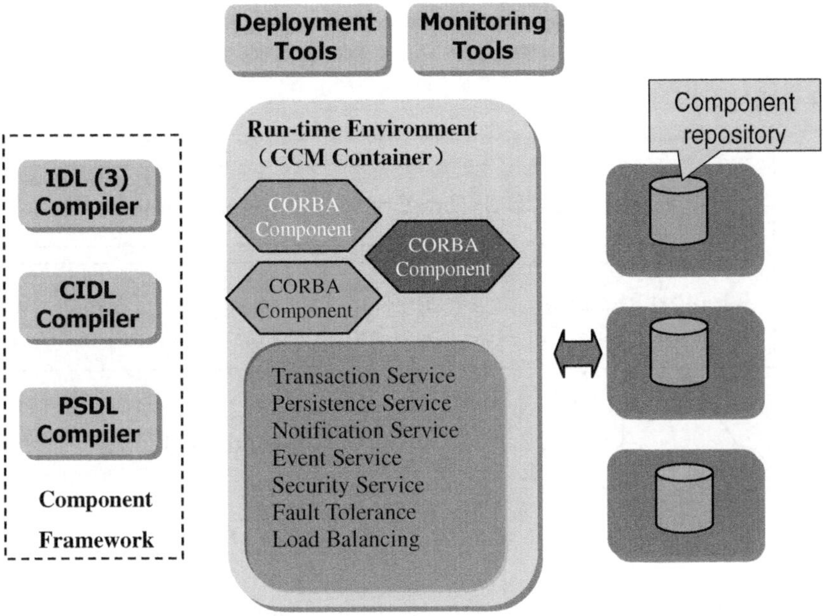

Fig. 1. The Architecture of the StarCCM

artifacts, where to instantiate them, and information about connections between them. This specification also presents a data model for the description of the domain into which applications can be deployed as a set of inter-connected nodes with bridges routing between inter-connects. However, these data models are still insufficient for the context of the mobile devices and do not support a description of the rules achieving the adaptation of the deployment.

3.2 Architecture of the Middleware Based Context Management

The overall middleware architecture is shown in the figure 2. The core provides the fundamental platform-independent services for the management of applications, components and component instances. The core relies on the basic mechanisms for instantiation, deployment and communication provided by the distributed computing environment. StarCCM Core Component Management provides platform-independent services for the management of the component based applications, components and component instances as depicted in the figure 1. It also provides uniform platform-independent access to the execution platform resources. Furthermore, the middleware offers the other three core services:

- The Context manager which monitors the user and the execution context for detection of relevant changes.
- The Adaptation Manager which reasons about the impact of the changes and decides about appropriate adaptations based on architectural description of component properties.

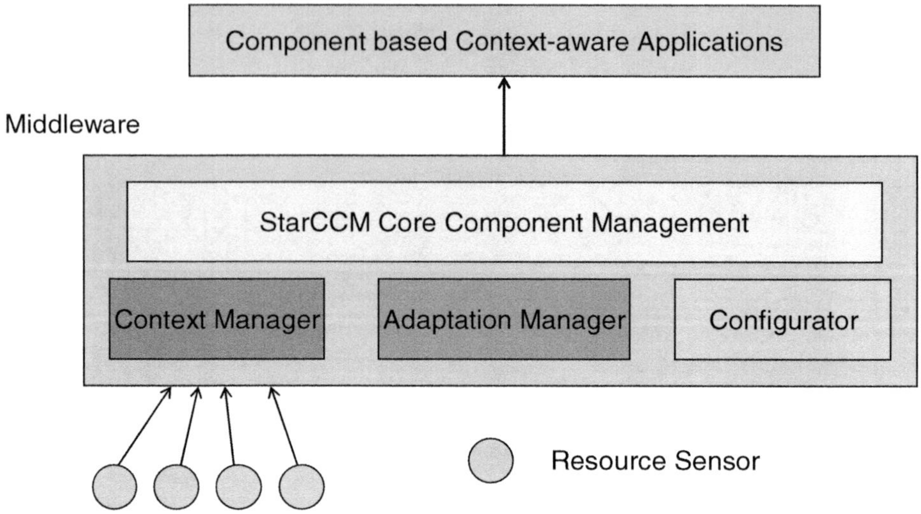

Fig. 2. Architecture of the Context-Aware Middleware

- The Configurator which reconfigures the application variant to put the decided adaptations into effect.

Context Manager is responsible for sensing and capturing context information and changes, providing access to context information (pull) and notifying context changes (push) to the Adaptation Manager. The Context Manager is also responsible for storing user needs and preferences on application services. The Context Manager should provide flexible context sensing. We recommend the Context Manager to be developed as a Component Framework where new context sensor components can be plugged in. The Context Manager may provide advanced reasoning operations on context. For example, it may aggregate complex context elements from elementary context elements or derive user needs from context. The Context Manager may also keep track of context change history.

Adaptation Manager is responsible for reasoning on the impact of context changes on the application(s), and for planning and selecting the application variant or the device configuration that best fits the current context. As part of reasoning, the Adaptation Manager needs to assess the utility of these variants in the current context. The Adaptation Manager produces dynamically a model of the application variant that best fits the context. We use the term "configuration template" to denote a model of an application variant where all variation points have been resolved.

Configurator is responsible for coordinating the initial instantiation of an application and the reconfiguration of an application or a device. When reconfiguring an application, the Configurator proceeds according to the configuration template for the variant selected by the Adaptation Manager. Thus, the Configurator carries out the adaptations decided by the Adaptation Manager by applying the configuration template. The Adaptation Manager and the Configurator are tightly coupled as they operate on a common information element: the configuration template.

4 Context-Aware Deployment for the Component-Based Applications

4.1 Deployment of the Component Based Applications

The objective of the component-based software technology is to take elements from a collection of reusable software components (i.e. off-the shelf components) and build applications by simply plugging them together. This allows the applications to be adapted more easily than through traditional approaches involving the reconfiguration of components, the adaptation of existing components, or the introduction of new components.

The deployment of component-based applications in distributed systems requires the description of an application deployment plan. The deployment plan is meta-data that describes the following four deployment parameters of the application:

(A) The application architecture. This parameter describes the components making up the application and the connections between them.
(B) The placement of each component on the nodes of the deployment domain.
(C) The component implementation version
(D) The property values that the components will be instantiated with.

The deployment plan is used by the deployment tool during the deployment process to instantiate the application components where they are expected to be placed and to configure them by using the information supplied about the property setting. Once all of the components are instantiated, they are connected. This deployment process, which is used by several deployment services provided by component-based middleware [12, 13, 14] is static. The structure of the application is fixed for any context and the placement of the components must either be defined before the deployment of the application without studying the node capacity or else it must be fixed by the user manually at the deployment time.

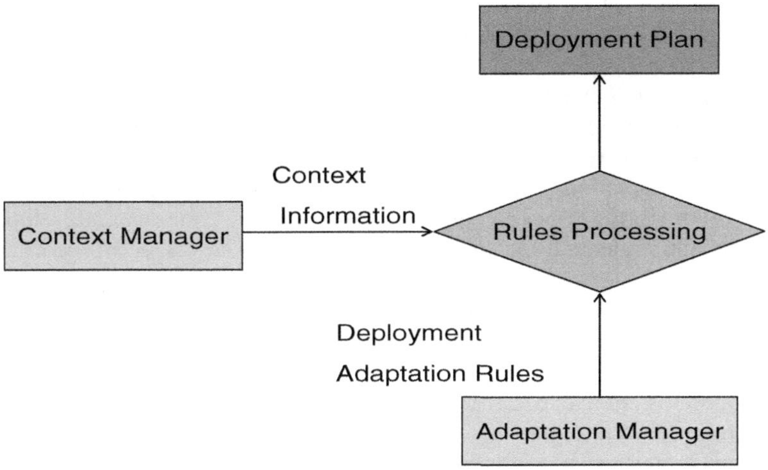

Fig. 3. The Principle of the Context-aware Deployment

In order to adapt the deployment of component-based applications, we propose to adapt the four different deployment parameters that we identified according to the context. To adapt the four deployment parameters to the context, we propose to dynamically generate the deployment plan according to the context. For this purpose, we define and develop a set of adaptation rules and adaptation algorithms which are stored in the adaptation manager and can be replaced dynamically. These algorithms process the rules for dynamically creating a deployment plan after studying the current context state (cf. Figure 3).

4.2 Deployment Adaptation Rules

We define an adaptation rule of a deployment parameter as an association between a context constraint and a value of this parameter. It can also be defined as an association between a context constraint and a context mapping which maps the value of the parameter to a given context. It is generally written as follows:

$$constraint \Rightarrow parameter \Rightarrow value \text{ , or}$$
$$constraint \Rightarrow parameter \Rightarrow ContextMapping$$

Each deployment parameter is associated with a set of adaptation rules that specify the different values that it can take. A context constraint represents a particular state of the context. A context constraint can be a composition (conjunction and/or disjunction) of several context states.

As an application is an assembly of components, we define two levels of rules: The component level rules and the application level rules:

The component level rules are the adaptation rules that are specific to a given component. The component developer who does not know in which application the component will be deployed, specifies these types of rules. This is why these rules take into account the component semantics without considering the application semantics in which they will be deployed.

The application level rules are the adaptation rules that are specific to an application to be deployed. The application assembler who takes into account the application semantics specifies them.

The component developer can specify the component level rules of two deployment parameters at the component level: the adaptation of the properties according to the context and the choice of the implementation versions.

Properties Adaptation Rules: A component can have several functional configuration properties. For each of these properties, the component developer has to specify a default value, and the values that the property can take on, according to the context.

Rules of Choice of Implementation Versions: A component can have several implementation versions dedicated to various execution contexts. The developer has to specify the context constraints required by each of these versions. An implementation version can have two types of constraints: strong constraints and weak constraints. An implementation version cannot be selected during deployment if its strong constraints are not satisfied. Satisfaction of low constraints is not obligatory though it is preferable.

A placement algorithm processes these rules. It checks whether the context satisfies the implementations constraints and it chooses the implementation suited to the context.

The application level rules specify essentially the adaptation of the application architecture according to the context. But they can also complete the component level rules that depend on the application semantics. They do that by specifying the placement site and the configuration of the properties of the components making up the application.

Architecture Adaptation Rules: When the application assembler writes the architecture adaptation rules of the application, he distinguishes between two types of components: the obligatory components, which are deployed whatever the context state, and the optional components, whose existence in the final deployment plan depends on the context. The application assembler specifies for each component of the application if it is obligatory or optional and for each optional component he specifies a condition which determines its existence. This condition represents a disjunction of several context constraints. The application assembler also distinguishes between two types of connections: the obligatory connections, which are deployed whatever the context state, and the optional connections, whose existence in the final deployment plan depends on the context. Optional components also require the specification of a condition that determines their existence. This condition has the same structure as the optional component. The establishment of an optional connection is possible only if the existence condition of the connection is satisfied and the component that it will connect to is deployed i.e. the components that it will connect to are either obligatory, or else they are optional but their existence condition is satisfied.

Complement of the component level rules: Besides the architecture of the application, the adaptation rules of the application level can specify the placement site and the properties adaptation of the components making up the application. The rules described at this level are prior to those described at the component level, since they take into account the semantics of the application. The description of the properties adaptation rules at the application level is specified in the same manner as the component level. The placement of a component is performed by the specification of one or several logical node names associated with a context constraint as follows:

$$constraint \Rightarrow ComponentDestination \Rightarrow logicalNode_i$$
$$(i = 1..n, n \textit{ is the number of possible placements})$$

A logical node represents a description of a set of node properties. A physical node corresponding to the logical node is determined at the deployment time through a discovery service [15]. The placement specification of a component completes the rules of choice of the implementation versions of the component level. If no placement rule is specified for a given component at the application level, the placement algorithm will automatically perform the component placement by using the rules of choice of implementation versions at the component level.

The placement algorithm processes the placement rules at the application level then it determines the placement site and the implementation version of all the component instances for which a site has not been specified at the level of the application rules. To perform the second stage, the placement algorithm starts by finding the valid implementations/nodes assignments for each component instance. As we can have several valid assignments for the same component, the algorithm selects the best one. The best assignment can be chosen according to several different criteria such as maximizing the number of satisfied weak constraints or optimizing the resources consumption. We use the A* algorithm [5] in order to explore all the possible assignments and approach the best one.

5 Performance Results

During the deployment tests, the middleware was run on Red Hat Linux 9.0 powered by a 2.4GHz Pentium Intel with 512MB of RAM. The PDAs used are iPAQ with Microsoft Pocket PC 4.20.0 powered by a TI OMAP1510 processor and 56MB of Memory. Besides the PDAs, we have four nodes which can contain the components when the users' terminals do not have enough resources. These nodes play the role of the component servers offered by the deployment providers. We have performed experiments in order to study the additional delays caused by the adaptation rules processing. Figure 4 shows the average deployment time with and without adaptation according to the number of deployed components. Each test was executed 30 times in order to obtain meaningful averages.

The results show that the adaptation time increases linearly with the application size at an average of 0.21%. The processing of the adaptation to the context represents an average of 5.48% of the total average deployment time. Since we have a number of adaptation rules associated with each component to deploy at the application and the component level, the number of rules increases with the number of components involved in the application. This explains the delay increase corresponding to the increasing number of components.

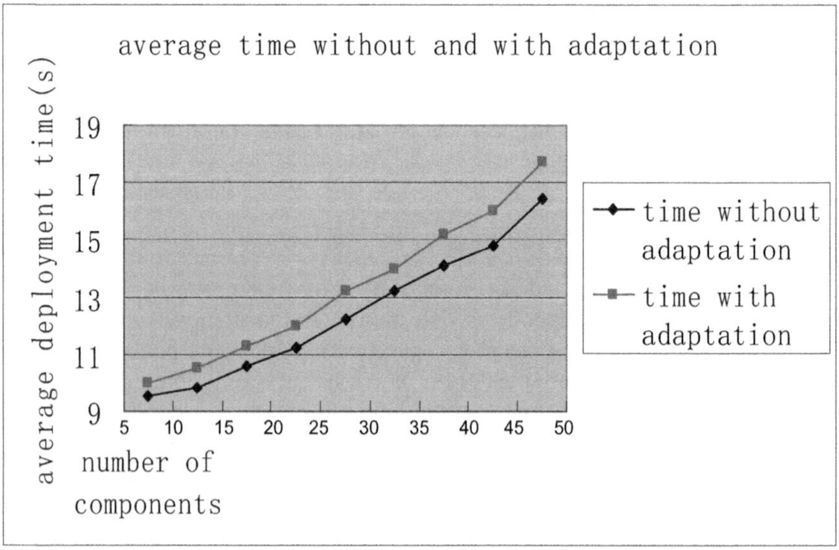

Fig. 4. Average Deployment Time According to the Number of Deployed Components

6 Conclusions

Ubiquitous computing allows application developers to build a large and complex distributed system that can transform physical spaces into computationally active and intelligent environments. Ubiquitous applications need a middleware that can detect and act upon any context changes created by the result of any interactions between users, applications, and surrounding computing environment for applications without users' interventions. The context-awareness has become the one of core technologies for application services in ubiquitous computing environment and been considered as the indispensable function for ubiquitous computing applications. The need for high quality context management is evident to the component-based middleware for it forms the basis of the component adaptation and the component deployment in the pervasive computing. Adaptive deployment is a key factor for the deployment in mobile environments and deployed applications have to be suited to different contexts such as the user requirements, the resources of his terminal and the surrounding environment. Therefore, we put forward a middleware based deployment approach for the context-aware component-based applications so as to make these applications can be adapted more easily than traditional applications by simply adding and deleting components.

Acknowledgements. This work was funded by the National Grand Fundamental Research 973 Program of China under Grant No.2005cb321804 and the National Natural Science Foundation of China under Grant No.60603063.

References

1. Weiser, M.: Some Computer Science Problems in Ubiquitous Computing. Communications of the ACM, 75–84 (July 1993)
2. Roy, W., Trevor, P.: System Challenges for Ubiquitous & Pervasive Computing. In: Proceedings of the 27th International Conference on Software Engineering, pp. 9–14 (May 2005)
3. Dey, A.K.: Understanding and Using Context. Personal and Ubiquitous Computing 5, 4–7 (2001)
4. Enterprise JavaBeans Specification 2.0, Sun Microsystems (2002)
5. Scott, S.: Structuring a .net application for easy deployment. In: Technical Article of Microsoft Corporation (2000). [Online]. Available: http://msdn.microsoft.com/library/
6. Searls, R.: Java 2 Enterprise Edition Deployment API Specification. Version 1.1, (August 2003) http://java.sun.com/j2ee/tools/deployment/
7. Open Services Gateway Initiative, OSGi services platform specification, Release3 (March 2003), http://www.osgi.org
8. Mikic-Rakic, M., Medvidovic, N.: Architecture-Level Support for Software Component Deployment in Resource Constrained Environments. In: The first International IFIP/ACM Working Conference on Component Deployment, Berlin, Germany, June 2002, pp. 31–50 (2002)
9. Dey, A.: Providing Architectural Support for Building Context-Aware Applications. Ph.D. Thesis Dissertation, College of Computing, Georgia Tech (December 2000)

10. Dey, A., Abowd, G.D.: Towards a Better Understanding of Context and Context Awareness. Technical Report, GITGVU-99-22, Georgia Institute of Technology (1999)
11. Schmidt, A.: Ubiquitous Computing- Computing in Context. Ph.D. Thesis, Lancaster University, UK (2002)
12. CORBA Components Version 3.0: An adopted Specification of the Object Management Group, OMG (June 2002)
13. Bruneton, T.C.E., Stefani, J.: The fractal component model (2004)
14. OMG, Specification for Deployment and Configuration of Component Based Distributed Applications (March 2003)
15. Information technology - open distributed computing - odp trading function. ISO/IEC JTC1/SC21.59 Draft, ITU-TS-SG 7 Q16 report (November 1993)

Identifying a Generic Model of Context for Context-Aware Multi-services

Tae Hwan Park and Ohbyung Kwon

School of International Management, Kyunghee University
Seochun-Dong, Ghyheung-Gu, Yongin, 449-701, South Korea
{serveLord,obkwon}@khu.ac.kr

Abstract. Context-aware systems aim to provide users with proactive services based on the users'context, which is collected in a quick and exact manner. To build a context-aware service in a real setting, a model of context is needed which is generic enough to allow for new service plugins. Since the context-aware system is used for multi-services in a specific domain, it is desirable that it utilizes more generic context models than previously used domain dependent context models. Hence, the purpose of this study is to propose a methodology for assessing the quality of context models to select a model type that is appropriate for the communication of the agents that reside in the context-aware systems.

1 Introduction

A model of context is crucial for the robust development of context-aware services. Collecting context data has been regarded as essential in building context-aware systems. Moreover, selection of the context constructs to be used in the context-aware system development projects is also crucial for successful system development and maintenance. These considerations are more important when the system contains multi-services and allows for new service plugins. In this case, the underlying model of context needs to be generic so that the model is extensible enough to support heterogeneous context-aware services. Although the legacy context-aware services tend to be domain specific, the system developers ultimately need to design a generic model of context for multi-services in certain physical spaces such as a marketplace, car or home.

Therefore, domain dependent context models with various modeling methods have been proposed and implemented in context-aware systems. Among those, Strang and Linnhoff-Popien[20] have classified the context models into six types: the key value, entity relationship, markup scheme, object-oriented, logic based-, and ontology-based models. They compared and evaluated the models of context. However, the evaluation efforts so far are not systematic. Moreover, to what extent the models of context are generic enough for building multi-services has rarely been assessed.

Hence, the purpose of this study is to analyze the legacy model types of context and to develop an assessment methodology with two evaluation criteria: model simplicity and model representation power. To do so, the classification criterion of

J. Indulska et al. (Eds.): UIC 2007, LNCS 4611, pp. 919–928, 2007.

Strang and Linnhoff-Popien[20] was utilized. The quality of context models is evaluated using the perspectives of three user types, novice, expert and the agent system, and then an assessment methodology is suggested and applied to select a model type of context. Next, a generic model of context is generated as OWL-DL format for the agents working in the context-aware services.

2 Literature Review: Models of Context

Until now, frequently suggested models of context are composed of six types, which are used to share contextual information with the services in a domain, as listed in Table 1 [20].

Table 1. Classification table of context models

Model type	Description
Key Value (KV) models	Key value models represent simple data structure for modeling context. [16, 17]
Markup Scheme (MS) models	Most markup scheme models are modeled as a hierarchical data structure by using markup tags for the attributes. [8]
Entity Relationship (ER) models	Entity relationship models represent context data as Unified Modeling Language that has UML diagrams. [1, 3, 7, 9, 11, 14]
Object-Oriented (OO) models	Object-oriented models primarily use the features of object-orientation: encapsulation, reusability, inheritance. [4, 10, 18,19]
Logic-Based (LB) models	Logic-based models represent contextual knowledge and facts with a high degree of formality. [6]
Ontology-Based (OB) models	Ontology-Based models describe the concepts and their relationships of each context entity, as it is possible to reason with ontologies. [5, 13, 15, 20, 21]

3 The Assessment Methodology of Context Models

3.1 The Scenarios for the Evaluation

In order to demonstrate the feasibility and validity of the methodology proposed in this study, six typical scenarios were considered in evaluating the model representation power and simplicity of the candidate models of context. The scenarios were extracted from the literature of the last ten years.

The six scenarios are then abstracted with the competing six models of context. Using the scenarios with conceptual models, the models of context are assessed in terms of model simplicity and representation power.

3.2 Conceptual Framework

Our methodology of assessing models of context is based on the general model assessment approach. The general approach to the assessment of the quality of the

Table 2. Scenarios for the evaluation

Scenarios	Descriptions of the Scenario	References
Scenario #1	When a user is sleeping in the bedroom or taking a shower in the bathroom, incoming calls are forwarded to the voicemail box.....	Wang X. H. et al., 2004 [21]
Scenario #2	After a long-haul flight, Maria lands at an airport in a Far Eastern country. The immigration officer in this country has been replaced by a device....	Dogac A. et al., 2004 [5]
Scenario #3	Bob has finished reviewing a paper for Alice, and wishes to share his comments with her. He instructs his communication agent to initiate a discussion with Alice ...	Henricksen K. et al., 2002 [9]
Scenario #4	The assistant is an agent that interacts with visitors at the office door and manages the office owner's schedule. The assistant is activated when a visitor approaches....	Chen G. et al., 2000 [2]
Scenario #5	Patrick enters his living room carrying his PDA. The room is equipped with a plasma display, a sound system and a digital picture frame. Patrick turns on his PDA	Preuveneers, D. et al., 2003 [15]
Scenario #6	Robert (Maria's and Jerry's son) is waiting for his best friend so that they may play video games. Robert's friend arrives bringing his new portable DVD player. ...	Mokhtar S. B. et al.,2005 [12]

models considers two conflicting criteria according to model complexity: model simplicity and representation power.

The quality of the models is simply the summation of the degree of model simplicity and model representation power. However, ultimate model selection is performed by the model users, rather than picking a model which is ranked as the highest in terms of the simple summation of the evaluation results with two criteria. For example, a model novice would prefer simpler models, while the model experts would be more concerned with representation power. Under the context-aware system context, since the agent program will be in charge of collecting and administrating the context data set, model simplicity can be extremely succinct if the agent program can parse the context data file.

3.3 Model Representation Power

Model representation power is important in that the model of context should sufficiently describe a user's context in an explicit manner. We regard the following requirements as included in model representation power:

- To what extent the model can describe the user's current context in detail
- To what extent the model can describe the relationships among the context entities and/or attributes.
- To what extent the model can describe the logics and hierarchies among the context entities.
- To what extent the model can describe the behavior or functions of the context entities.

Based on these requirements, we have developed a comparison sheet. Experts in context models were selected from faculty members and project managers, who are

Table 3. Comparison of model representaion power

Measures \ Models of Context	KV	MS	ER	OO	LB	OB
Objects	○	○	○	○	○	○
Attributes	○	○	○	○	○	○
Relationships among objects		○	○○	○	○	○○
Relationships among attributes		○○			○	○○
Logics		△		△	○○	○
Hierarchies		○	△(ECR)	○○		○○
Behavior/ Functions			△(EER)	○○	○	○

engaged in the context-aware system development projects, to perform Focus Group Interview (FGI). During the interviews, some extensible models were gradually added such as the Entity Category Relationship (ECR) and Extensible Entity Relationship (EER) models. The other extensions, such as the object-relationship model, however, were excluded in the assessment simply because they have not been considered in the models of context nor in Strang and Linnhoff-Popien's studies. The results are listed in Table 3.

First, the KV model focuses on representing objects and attributes for simplicity. Second, using the MS model, one could represent relationships among objects and attributes, hierarchies and partial logics, as well as objects and attributes. And logic could be represented weakly. The MS model is excellent in showing the relationships among attributes, as is the ontology-based model. Third, the basic form of the ER model basically expresses objects, attributes and relationships. Beyond these, some extended model such as the ECR and EER models could cope with hierarchies and functions, respectively. Fourth, the OO model could not only deal with expressing object, attributes, the relationships among objects, hierarchy and behaviors, but also represent logics within a behavior. The OO model is appropriate in the hierarchical structure of a system domain using an inheritance feature, and easily extended to the implementation phase since the object-oriented development methodology already contains some excellent sub-models that represent behavioral aspects very well. Next, one can use the LB model for representing objects, attributes, and relationships among objects, as well as relationships among attributes, logics and functions. The LB model is superior to the other models of logical representations in that linguistic representation is acceptable in the LB model. Last, the OB model represents context with concepts and facts, which correspond to classes and instances in an object-oriented paradigm. Moreover, directions and linguistic representations in the OB model are superior to the competing models in showing hierarchies and logics. Consequently, the OB model is best in terms of model representation power. The MS, OO and LB models also are relatively more competitive than the KV and ER models.

3.4 Model Simplicity

As the second evaluation criteria, model simplicity is developed based on the number of concepts and values used in a specific context model of scenarios [2,5,9,12,15,21].

Table 4. A comparison summary of Nc and Nv of the six scenarios

		KV	MS	ER	OO	LB	OB
Number of Concepts (Nc)	Scenario 1	3	29	18	19	22	27
	Scenario 2	3	17	15	11.5	15	16
	Scenario 3	3	17	17.5	11	16	18
	Scenario 4	3	18	17.5	10.5	10	17
	Scenario 5	3	24	30	18	13	31
	Scenario 6	3	24	31	18	10	30
Number of Values (Nv)	Scenario 1	15	16	9	22	20	16
	Scenario 2	9	10	6	14	9	10
	Scenario 3	9	10	11	13	12	12
	Scenario 4	6	11	11	12	4	11
	Scenario 5	9	13	14	18	8	17
	Scenario 6	6	14	16	18	4	17

Concepts are the elements considered to systematically organize and represent the context data. In practice, they are any elements such as objects, relationships and links. Meanwhile, in the case of links, half weights were given to the simple links which have no direction. As a result, the number of concepts (Nc) and that of values (Nv) are summarized in Table 4.

To determine model simplicity, two basic performance measures are proposed: the degree of relative model grasp and that of model lightness. The degree of relative model grasp (DRMG) of model i is formalized as shown in (1):

$$DRMG_i = DMG_i / Max_{\forall i}\{DMG_i\} \tag{1}$$

where DMG indicates the degree of model grasp, which is a function of Nc and Nv as shown in (2):

$$DMG_i = 1/(\alpha * N_C(i) + (1-\alpha) * N_V(i)) \tag{2}$$

where α, $0 \le \alpha \le 1$ is a weight which shows to what extent concepts are more important than values in understanding a model of context.

Meanwhile, the degree of model lightness (DML) describes how many concepts are brought to the model of context per value as shown in (3):

$$DML_i = N_V(i) / N_C(i) \tag{3}$$

where DML is the reciprocal number of overhead, N_c/N_v. Using DML, the degree of relative model lightness (DRML) is simply derived as (4):

$$DRML_i = DML_i / Max_{\forall i}\{DML_i\} \tag{4}$$

Based on these two measures, model simplicity (MS) is represented as the weighted average of DRMG and DML as shown in (5):

$$MS_i = \beta * DRMG_i + (1-\beta) * DML_i \tag{5}$$

where β, $0 \le \beta \le 1$ is the weighted importance of DRMG.

Using the above formulae, model simplicity of each context of models in the context of the six scenarios are derived as shown in Table 5. α and β were set to 0.5.

Table 5. A comparison summary of model simplicity (**α=0.5, β=0.5**)

	KV	MS	ER	OO	LB	OB
α*Nc+(1-α)Nv	6	16.916	16.333	15.416	11.916	18.5
DMG:1/{α*Nc+(1-α)Nv}	0.166	0.0591	0.061	0.064	0.083	0.054
DRMG-①	1	0.354	0.367	0.389	0.503	0.324
Overhead	0.333	1.743	1.925	0.907	1.508	1.674
DML (=1/overhead)	3	0.573	0.519	1.102	0.662	0.597
DRML-②	1	0.191	0.173	0.367	0.220	0.199
MS{β*①+(1- β)*②}	1	0.272	0.270	0.378	0.154	0.261

Meanwhile, to identify how the change of the weight value α affects the model simplicity, the value of the relative model grasp was observed by increasing the value of α from 0.0 to 1.0. As a result, Table 6 could be obtained which shows the α sensitivity for each model of context. The MS and LB models turn out to be more sensitive than the other models of context. This implies that the models are more affected by the determinations of the relative importance of concepts compared with that of values. On the other hand, the KV, OO and OB models turn out to be more stably evaluated.

Table 6. α sensitivity test

α	KV	MS	ER	OO	LB	OB
0.1	1.0000	0.6554	0.6783	0.5490	0.8796	0.6109
0.3	1.0000	0.4983	0.5618	0.5307	0.6761	0.5301
0.5	1.0000	0.3731	0.4528	0.5070	0.5106	0.4472
0.7	1.0000	0.2709	0.3508	0.4752	0.3735	0.3623
0.9	1.0000	0.1860	0.2550	0.4303	0.2581	0.2752
α sensitivity	0.0000	0.1166	0.1058	0.0293	0.1546	0.0839

3.5 Context Model Selection

Based on the context model assessment in terms of the two criteria, model representation power and model simplicity, a synthetic evaluation of each model of context is performed. The evaluation results are plotted in Figure 7. Curve ① indicates the utility to the model novice. Since the novice would be more focused on the simplicity of the models rather than representation power, the KV model is more likely to be selected by the novice. Curve ② indicates the utility function for model experts. The experts would concentrate more on the representation power than the novice. Therefore, the OO model has a better chance for selection by the expert group. Lastly, curve ③ indicates the utility function of the agent program in the context-aware services. If the model of context can be parsed, then the agent system is more likely to neglect the model simplicity simply because of a more powerful model

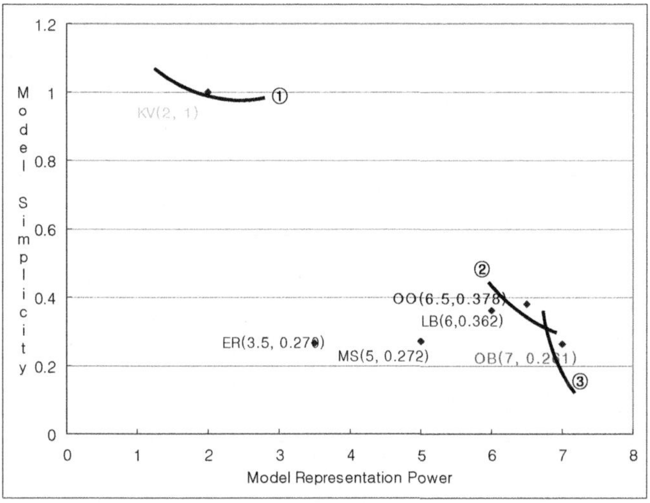

Fig. 7. Synthetic model assessment

processing capability. In this case, model representation power would dominate model simplicity in selecting an appropriate model of context. Hence, the OB model will be selected as the most appropriate model type and is considered as a generic model of context used in the context-aware multi-service development project. Note that the selected model of context is not the optimal choice for each situation, implying that selecting a model of context depends on how the model fits to the purpose of usage and to the users.

4 Generic Model of Context

To obtain the generic model of context based on the ontology-based model, representative projects on mobile computing or ubiquitous computing are investigated which have appeared in the literature from the past ten years. The union set of context found in the literature is identified as the constructs in our generic model of context. The BNF format context constructs are shown in Table 7.

Since the set of constructs appearing in Table 7 contained the constructs considered in the context models of the literature listed in Appendix A, the model of context could be regarded as sufficiently generic and the model therefore was adopted for the u-Market service development project. The generic model of context is represented as an ontology-based model. The generic model of context represents the user's context by using 15 entities listed in Table 7. All entities as classes could have a sort of relationships with one another and the relationships are described as object properties. Also each entity has its own attributes and their relationships are described as data type properties. Practically, some entities or properties could be omitted from the original generic model of context according to the characteristics of the applications to be implemented.

Table 7. Main constructs of generic model of context

Context Entities	Context Definition
Intention	*user's intention *
Identity	*user or person*
Task	*tasks the user is now conducting or will conduct in the future *
Agenda	*reserved or already planned*
Activity	*user's activity or behavior *
Application	*what end-user uses*
Role	*user's roles: what the user is going to do in a certain zone *
Time	*(ss/mm/hh) or day, week, month, season*
CompEntity	*ubiquitous sensor network infra in a certain place*
Device	*devices which a user is carrying *
Location	*user's location*
Zone	*the place that a user is located *
Service	*what applications use*
Environment	*environment factors around user*
Privacy Access	*used to determine a user's access right *

Moreover, the proposed generic model of context is used in the actual u-Market system development as an OWL-DL formatted file.

5 Conclusion

This study attempts to analyze and assess legacy models of context which could be good alternatives as generic context models used in developing multiple context-aware services in a specific physical area. To do so, the current models of context were investigated. Two evaluation criteria were developed for this study, model simplicity and representation power, with corresponding performance measures. Through applying the evaluation methodology to the representative scenarios which come from actual context-aware system development projects, the ontology-based model is identified as more competitive as a generic context model than any other type. Based on the ontology type, development of a u-Market service system is underway for transforming a traditional marketplace based in Seoul, South Korea. The generic context model is very useful in making the system extensive when incorporating new services, and hence increases the productivity of system development and maintenance.

We will improve our evaluation method to cope with some unconsidered issues. First, our method should be extended enough to take complexity of reasoning into account to give more strength to our work. Second, the metrics proposed in this paper tend to focus on subjective evaluations of what is important and how to measure it. Despite these limitations, however, we believe that the proposed method could inspire productive debates on the related issues.

Acknowledgments. This research was partially supported by the Seoul R&BD Program (Developing u-Market for revitalizing the traditional market in Seoul) in Korea and IBM Ubiquitous Computing Lab funded by the Institute of Information Technology Assessment in Korea.

References

1. Bauer, J.: Identification and Modeling of Contexts for Different Information Scenarios in Air Traffic. Diplomarbeit (2003)
2. Chen, G., Kotz, D.: A survey of context-aware mobile computing research. Tech. Rep. TR2000-381, Dartmouth (2000)
3. Chtcherbina, E., Franz, M.: Peer-to-peer coordination framework (P2Pc): Enabler of mobile ad-hoc networking for medicine, business, and entertainment. In: Proceedings of International Conference on Advances in Infrastructure for Electronic Business, Education, Science, Medicine, and Mobile Technologies on the Internet (2003)
4. Cheverst, K., Mitchell, K., Davies, N.: Design of an object model for a context sensitive tourist GUIDE. Computers and Graphics 23, 883–891 (1999)
5. Dogac, A., Laleci, G.B., Kabak, Y.A.: Context Framework for Ambient Intelligence. In: Proceedings of the Fourth IEEE International Workshop on Distributed Auto-adaptive and Reconfigurable Systems, IEEE Computer Society Press, Los Alamitos (2004)
6. Gray, P., Salber, D.: Modeling and Using Sensed Context Information in the design of Interactive Applications. In: Proceedings of 8th IFIP International Conference on Engineering for Human-Computer Interaction, vol. 2254, pp. 317–335 (2001)
7. Halpin, T.A.: Information Modeling and Relational Databases: From Conceptual Analysis to Logical Design. Morgan Kaufman Publishers, San Francisco (2001)
8. Held, A., Buchholz, S., Schill, A.: Modeling of context information for pervasive computing applications. In: Proceedings of SCI (2002)
9. Henricksen, K., Indulska, J., Rakotonirainy, A.: Modeling context information in pervasive computing systems. In: Proceedings of 1st International Conference on Pervasive Computing, vol. 2414, pp. 167–180 (2002)
10. Hofer, T., Schwinger, W., Pichler, M., Leonhartsberger, G., Altmann, J.: Context-Awareness on Mobile Devices - the Hydrogen Approach. In: Proceedings of the 36th Annual Hawaii International Conference on System Sciences, Track 9, vol. 9 (2003)
11. Indulska, J., Robinsona, R., Rakotonirainy, A., Henricksen, K.: Experiences in using cc/pp in context-aware systems. In: Proceedings of the 4th International Conference on Mobile Data Management, vol. 2574, pp. 247–261 (2003)
12. Mokhtar, S.B., Kaul, A., Georgantas, N., Issarny, V.: Context-aware Service Composition in Pervasive Computing Environments. In: Proceedings of the 2nd International Workshop on Rapid Intergration of Software Engineering techniques, vol. 3943 (2005)
13. Ötztürk, P., Aamodt, A.: Towards a model of context for case-based diagnostic problem solving. In: Context-97. Proceedings of the interdisciplinary conference on modeling and using context, Rio de Janeiro, pp. 198–208 (1997)
14. Pascoe, J.: Adding Generic Contextual Capabilities to Wearable Computers. In: Proceedings of the 2nd International Symposium on Wearable Computers, pp. 92–99. IEEE Computer Society, Los Alamitos (1998)
15. Preuveneers, D., Bergh, J.V., Wagelaar, D., Georges, A., Rigole, P., Clerckx, T., Berbers, Y., Coninx, K., Jonckers, V., Bosschere, K.D.: Towards an extensible context ontology for Ambient Intelligence. In: 2nd European Symposium, Ambient Intelligence, pp. 148–159 (2004)
16. Samulowitz, M., Michahelles, F., Linnhoff-Popien, C.: Capeus: An architecture for context-aware selection and execution of services. In: New developments in distributed applications and interoperable systems, pp. 23–39. Kluwer Academic Publishers, Dordrecht (2001)

17. Schilit, B.N., Adams, N.L., Want, R.: Context-aware computing applications. In: Workshop on Mobile Computing Systems and Applications, pp. 85–90. IEEE Computer Society Press, Los Alamitos (1994)
18. Schmidt, A., Aidoo, K.A., Takaluoma, A., Tuomela, U., Laerhoven, K.V., Velde, W.V.: Advanced interaction in context. In: Proceedings of First International Symposium on Handheld and Ubiquitous Computing, pp. 89–101 (1999)
19. Schmidt, A., Beigl, M., Gellersen, H.W.: There is more to Context than Location. Computers & Graphics Journal 23, 893–901 (1999)
20. Strang, T., Linnhoff-Popien, C., Frank, K., Stefani, J.B., Demeure, I., Hagimont, D.: CoOL: A Context Ontology Language to enable Contextual Interoperability. IFIP International Federation for Information 2893, 236–247 (2003)
21. Wang, X.H., Zhang, D., Gu, T., Pung, H.: Ontology based context modeling and reasoning using OWL. In: Workshop on Context Modeling and Reasoning at 2nd IEEE International Conference on Pervasive Computing and Communication, pp. 18–22 (2004)

Context Privacy and Obfuscation Supported by Dynamic Context Source Discovery and Processing in a Context Management System

Ryan Wishart[1,2], Karen Henricksen[2], and Jadwiga Indulska[1,2]

[1] School of Information Technology and Electrical Engineering,
The University of Queensland
[2] NICTA*
{wishart,jaga}@itee.uq.edu.au, Karen.Henricksen@nicta.com.au

Abstract. The extensive context information collection abilities of ubiquitous computing environments represent a significant threat to user privacy. In this paper we address this threat by introducing a context information privacy mechanism. Our approach relies on context-dependent ownership definitions and context owner-specified privacy preferences to control context disclosure to third-parties. These privacy preferences enable context owners to stipulate not only to whom their context information can be disclosed and the conditions of disclosure, but also the level of detail at which the context information can be disclosed. Context information that cannot be disclosed at its existing level of detail is obfuscated to meet detail level requirements stipulated by its owner. To achieve this obfuscation of context information we introduce a new approach based on dynamic discovery and processing of context sources. Our new approach is demonstrated in a Context Management System in which context source discovery and processing is facilitated by the SensorML sensor description standard being developed by the Open Geospatial Consortium.

1 Introduction

Potential users of ubiquitous computing environments frequently cite privacy as a major concern [1] in their adoption of the technology. These user privacy concerns arise from both the degree and the sensitivity of the context information collected by the ubiquitous computing environment.

To address these concerns it is necessary to provide a context information privacy mechanism that can (1) determine the owner of particular context

* NICTA is funded by the Australian Government's Department of Communications, Information Technology, and the Arts; the Australian Research Council through Backing Australia's Ability and the ICT Research Centre of Excellence programs; and the Queensland Government.

J. Indulska et al. (Eds.): UIC 2007, LNCS 4611, pp. 929–940, 2007.

information, and (2) dynamically handle the disclosure of the context information according to that owner's preferences.

Here we consider the owner of context information to be the person, or organisation, that determines how that context information should be used and when it can be disclosed to other parties.

With regard to the first of the requirements, existing work in the field either does not explicitly address the issue of ownership or, if it does, ownership is statically allocated to a particular entity (often the producer of the context information). This does not correlate with ownership in ubiquitous computing environments which may be context-dependent and involve multiple parties [2].

In addressing the second requirement, context-dependent privacy preferences can be used to capture the context information owner's disclosure preferences. While several systems supporting such preferences exist (such as PawS [3] and the Semantic e-Wallet [4]) they provide only limited control over the level of detail/granularity at which context is disclosed. To meet disclosure detail level requirements for context information, obfuscation mechanisms are required. In existing systems these obfuscation mechanisms are restricted to obfuscating particular types of context information (e.g., location), returning preset values as the result of obfuscation, or supporting a set number of levels of detail for all types of context information.

To address the deficiencies in existing work, we present a context information privacy mechanism that (1) supports context-dependent, multi-party ownership of context information, (2) enables context information owners to control to whom and the level of detail with which their context information is disclosed and (3) provides a general obfuscation mechanism that can dynamically adjust the detail level of context information to meet the disclosure requirements of the context information's owners.

A Context Management System (CMS) is used to demonstrate our general obfuscation mechanism. This CMS is able to automatically discover new context sources, or perform processing of stored sensor output, to fulfil the detail level required by any preferences the context information owner may have specified. The CMS's ability to perform this automatic discovery leverages off the Open Geospatial Consortium's SensorML sensor description specification [5].

The remainder of the paper is structured as follows. We first motivate our research with an overview of related work in the field (given in Section 2). In Section 3 we present background information on the SensorML specification, as well as our context modelling approach and privacy preference mechanism. Obfuscation of context information is discussed in Section 4 before we then present an architecture for a CMS capable of dynamic context source discovery and processing in Section 5. An explanation of how this CMS can be used to support our context information privacy and obfuscation approach is given in Section 6. Concluding remarks for the paper are then made in Section 7.

2 Related Work

In this related work section we provide an overview of the context information privacy literature focusing on support for context information obfuscation.

The Confab toolkit, developed by Hong and Landay [1], enables the expression of complex, context-dependent privacy policies for context information in a ubiquitous computing environment. In addition, a built-in obfuscation mechanism allows the release of this context information at different levels of detail. A significant shortcoming of the approach is that the system operates on the tacit assumption that producers of context information are its owners. This is not always the case with ubiquitous computing environments where ownership may be multi-party and context-dependent [6].

Lederer at al. [7] present an approach to context information privacy which allows users to define sets of disclosure preferences in terms of a few predefined types of context information. The system provides limited obfuscation of context information to a maximum of four levels of detail (precise, approximate, vague and undisclosed). However, these four levels are not appropriate for all types of context information; some types of context cannot be obfuscated at all (as in the case of simple boolean or on/off values), while other types can be meaningfully disclosed at more than four levels of detail.

A different approach to context information privacy in ubiquitous computing environments was developed by Gandon and Sadeh [4] for their Semantic eWallet privacy management system. The approach supports detailed, context-dependent preference specification. Obfuscation of context information is also provided. However, the obfuscation is extremely static in the sense that users predefine the values disclosed by the system in a case-by-case fashion. Unfortunately, if the environment changes, the statically-defined values may become meaningless or unusable.

Rather than actively protect context information using a rule-based approach, the pawS system [3] seeks to make the user aware of the context gathering infrastructure available within a particular location. The system operates by notifying users using a privacy beacon wherever context information is collected. This privacy beacon transmits data usage policies that explain which context information will be collected and how the collector intends to use that information. The pawS system is capable of providing information at different levels of detail but cannot obfuscate a particular item of context to a lower level of detail. The concept of ownership is also not directly addressed as there is no mechanism for specifying which context information belongs to a user.

From this review of the related work it is clear that existing privacy mechanisms (1) do not support context-dependent, multi-party ownership as is found in real ubiquitous computing scenarios, and (2) lack or provide only limited support for obfuscation of context information. Those that do support obfuscation of context information support obfuscation on a limited number of context types or restrict the number of levels of obfuscation that can be applied.

3 Background Information

3.1 SensorML for Automated Sensor Discovery and Configuration

In recognition of the growing heterogeneity of sensor networks, the Open Geospatial Consortium (OGC) is developing a common format for describing sensor functionality, their outputs (referred to as observations) and how to process these observations. It is intended that such descriptions would be made available online along with sensor observations, allowing applications to automatically discover and use remote sensors.

The XML syntax and semantics for sensor descriptions are covered in the SensorML specification [5], while mapping sensor output to SensorML Observations is discussed in the Observations and Measurements proposal of the OGC[8]. SensorML also supports Process Chains, a mechanism for describing the inputs, outputs and parameters of executable programs that can be used to transform sensor data into more meaningful results. As with the SensorML descriptions of sensors and sensor data that can be dynamically discovered online, Process Chains can also be found and loaded at runtime, enabling dynamic processing of sensor data.

As discussed in [9], the wide-spread adoption of emerging standards like SensorML would enable a ubiquitous computing environment to automatically locate new sensors, interpret their output (observations) and, by applying SensorML Process Chains, automatically perform any processing of the sensor observations necessary to make them compatible with the context information required by applications in the ubiquitous computing environment.

3.2 Context Modelling and Ownership

Our context information privacy mechanism requires a context model of the ubiquitous computing environment to operate. In the Context Modelling Language (CML) [10] we use to construct our context model, major entities in the environment are captured as object types (e.g., Employee, Location, Activity). Instances of the object types, such as the employee Alice, or the location Brisbane, are referred to as objects. Relationships between object types are modeled as fact types, while relationships between objects are represented as facts.

An example context model, depicted using the graphical notation for CML, is given in Figure 1. This model has several object types: Employee, Company, Location, Device (representing wireless computing devices) and Activity.

In the example context model, companies assign wireless computing devices to their employees. Both the wireless computing devices and the employees have a location, while the employees also have an activity (such as "meeting clients", or "using the computer"). In the context model, the location of employees can be derived from the location of devices according to the derivation rule specified in Figure 1. Within this rule "workingHours()" is a situation that returns true if the current time is within working hours and false otherwise. More information on situations can be found in [10].

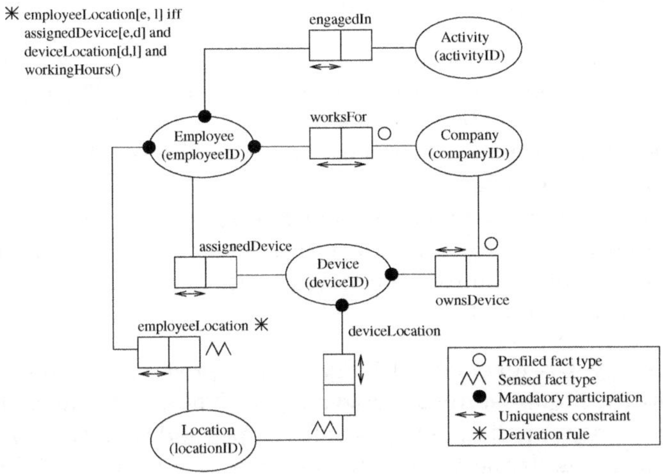

Fig. 1. An example context model for a company that tracks the location of its employees using wireless computing devices that it assigns to each employee

The context model is mapped onto database schema such that fact types are represented as relations. Context information in the database is stored as context facts, which express assertions about one or more objects. An example context fact is **worksFor[Alice, MiracleMart]**. The fact type in this example is "worksFor", while Alice is an instance of the Employee object type, and MiracleMart an instance of the Company object type.

To make the context model ownership-aware, we introduced an ownership modelling approach in [2]. Our approach recognises that some of the object types in the context model (referred to as *first class* object types) have the capacity to act as owners of the context information related to them. Examples of this type include Employee and Company object types.

Other objects types, such as computing devices and physical places, fall under the ownership of various first class object types. These are *second class* object types. The associations between first and second class objects types can be context-dependent; therefore, we state their ownership using one or more fact types. A detailed discussion of the vocabulary used for declaring this ownership is outside the scope of this paper, but more information can be found in [2].

The ownership model also supports *third class* object types, which are any object types that require no owners.

Our approach also supports ownership specification at the level of the fact type. This enables each fact type to have its own rules for assigning ownership. These rules associate each fact (i.e. an instance of a fact type) with zero, one or multiple owners. Facts that have zero owners are *public* and can be freely disclosed to anyone.

3.3 Privacy Preference Language

In our approach, context information owners are able to express their privacy requirements using context-dependent privacy preferences. These preferences can be defined for certain contexts, and then combined to form a comprehensive privacy policy. Due to space restrictions, we provide only a brief overview of the privacy preference language.

Our privacy preference language supports two preference types: binary privacy preferences that allow disclosure to be either granted or denied, and granularity preferences that enable context owners to specify detail level restrictions on the disclosure of their context facts.

Binary Privacy Preferences. Binary privacy preferences are structured as a unique identifier, a scope statement and a rating. The scope defines the context in which the preference applies, in terms of fact types and conditions on parameters of the current access request (most importantly, the identity of the *requester*). The rating indicates whether the preference is to allow or deny the disclosure of the context information.

```
alice_preference_1 = when NOT worksFor[requester, MiracleMart]
                          rate deny
```

An example binary preference is given above that denies access to all Alice's context information if the requester does not work for MiracleMart.

Granularity Preferences. Granularity preferences enable context information owners to control the obfuscation of their context information. These preferences are linked to object types in the context model, and apply to context facts containing instances of the linked object type.

To support the obfuscation process, we rely on predefined ontologies for each object type, which we refer to as obfuscation ontologies. These consist of *ontology values* arranged by relative detail into a hierarchy such that parent nodes in the hierarchy are more general than their children. Simplified obfuscation ontologies for the Activity and Location object types are shown in Figure 2.

Granularity preferences contain a scope statement, the object type to which the granularity preference is linked, and a detail limit that context facts containing the instances of the linked object type must meet before those context facts can be disclosed. This limit is expressed as a level number in the obfuscation ontology of the linked object type (e.g., detail level 1). An example granularity preference is given below for the employee Alice:

```
alice_preference_2 = when equals(requester, Bob) AND workingHours()
                          on Activity
                          limit level 1
```

This preference stipulates that any context information disclosed to the requester Bob during working hours 'that contains instances of Activity should be at most detail level 1. In this example **equals** and **workingHours** are *situations* as discussed briefly in Section 3.2.

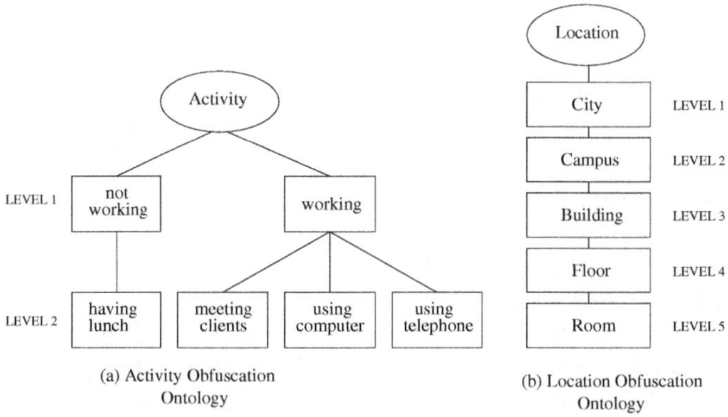

Fig. 2. Simplified obfuscation ontologies for the Activity and Location object types

```
City:
    Brisbane
    Campus:
            Brisbane Campus
            Building:
                    MiracleMart Main Office
                    Floor:
                          floor 6
                          Room:
                               78-633
                               78-625
                               78-621
                          floor 4
                          ...
```

Fig. 3. An excerpt from a taxonomy for the Location object type that shows how valid Location objects are related in terms of detail level

4 A General Obfuscation Mechanism for Context Information

Our obfuscation mechanism is activated when a context owner's granularity preferences require a context fact to be reduced in detail. This detail reduction process is performed on objects within the context fact using obfuscation ontologies. Two kinds of obfuscation ontologies are recognised by the mechanism: Class 1, and Class 2.

We address obfuscation of objects whose object types have a Class 1 obfuscation ontology first, using the context fact **engagedIn[Alice, using computer]** as an example. For this context fact, we assume "using computer" must be obfuscated to a lower detail level. As we are dealing with a Class 1 obfuscation ontology, the ontology values in the obfuscation ontology are themselves valid object instances [6].

To generate a new context fact the obfuscation mechanism needs to (1) locate the current ontology value ("using computer") in the obfuscation ontology and then (2) traverse up the hierarchy until an ontology value of the required detail level is reached. For example, if the required detail level is level 1, and "using computer" has detail level 2 (based on Figure 2), the obfuscation mechanism would traverse up the hierarchy of ontology values to reach the detail level 1 ontology value "working".

The obfuscation mechanism is then able to generate the new context fact **engagedIn[Alice, working]**.

To demonstrate the obfuscation of objects with a Class 2 obfuscation ontology we use the example context fact **employeeLocation[Alice, 78-633]**. In this example the "78-633" object is an instance of the Location object type, and is of detail level 5 ("78-633" corresponds to the ontology value "Room" in the taxonomy shown in Figure 3. "Room" is of level 5 detail according to the obfuscation ontology for Location in Figure 2).

To obfuscate objects using a Class 2 obfuscation ontology requires that the obfuscation mechanism understand how each object instance is related (i.e. the system must know that 78-633 is on floor six within the MiracleMart Main Office in Brisbane). This can be achieved using a top-down approach in which a knowledgeable system designer specifies detailed taxonomies describing how particular object instances are related (such as the taxonomy given in Figure 3).

An alternative approach to using a large, detailed taxonomy of object instances is to split up the knowledge in the taxonomy into a large number of rules (e.g., one of these rules could be 'all rooms with room numbers matching "78-6.." are located on the 6th floor').

The taxonomy approach to obfuscation of context facts, which we discussed first, suffers from scalability issues as the relationship between object instances for each object type must be pre-specified. As the ubiquitous computing environment is highly dynamic, generating an exhaustive taxonomy for all possible object instances of each object type in the context model is infeasible. This means that non-exhaustive taxonomies must be used. However, if the ubiquitous computing environment changes, the non-exhaustive taxonomy must be re-specified.

In comparison, the bottom-up rule-based approach does not require large, detailed taxonomies to be specified by a knowledgeable designer. Rather, the system dynamically discovers rules (potentially implemented as declarative rules or as data processing programs) to process the context facts to the desired level of detail. This gives it the ability to adjust to significant changes in the ubiquitous computing environment (such as when a user moves location) that a non-exhaustive taxonomy of object instances cannot handle. In the following section we describe a Context Management System that performs obfuscation using this bottom-up rule-based approach (implemented using executable programs accompanied by SensorML Process Chain descriptions).

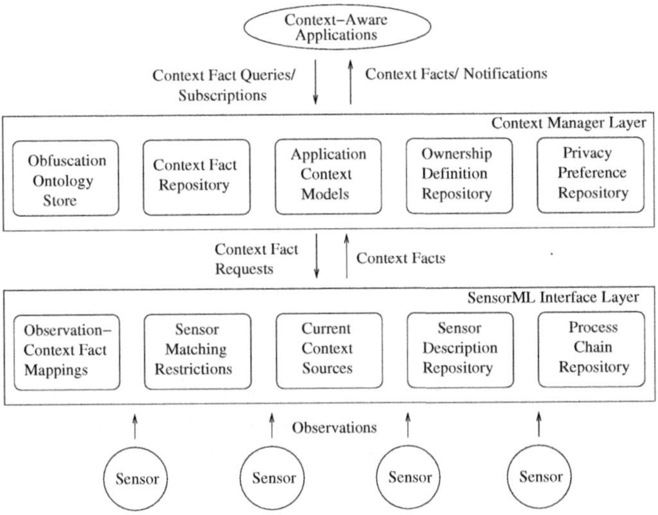

Fig. 4. An example layered architecture for a Context Management System implementing our context information privacy mechanism

5 Architecture of the Context Management System

To demonstrate our privacy approach, including our obfuscation mechanism, we introduce a layered Context Management System (CMS) based on that of Indulska et al. [9]. Figure 4 shows the layered structure of the CMS.

The architecture is composed of three layers: a Sensor Layer, a SensorML Interface Layer and a Context Manager Layer.

The Sensor Layer represents the software and hardware sensors within the ubiquitous computing environment that emit SensorML Observations. These observations are fed into the SensorML Interface Layer.

The SensorML Interface Layer (SIL) performs two important tasks. Firstly, it processes observations from the Sensor Layer before converting them into context facts using the Observation-Context Fact Mappings. Secondly, it locates new sources of context information by searching the Sensor Description Repository for sensors using the Sensor Matching Restrictions. The Sensor Description Repository is where SensorML descriptions of active sensors are stored. The Sensor Matching Restrictions are selection rules for choosing new sensors (such as sensor type or accuracy) as well as restrictions on where the sensor is (e.g., geographical location). A Process Chain Repository is also maintained that stores currently used Process Chains and their associated executable programs.

In the Context Manager Layer context facts provided by the SensorML Interface Layer are stored in a Context Fact Repository. Application Context Models for context-aware applications in the ubiquitous computing environment are also stored. These are used to interpret the stored context facts on a per application basis. The Obfuscation Ontology Store, the Ownership Definition Repository and the Privacy Preference Repository are also located in the Context Manager Layer. The Obfuscation Ontology Store houses the obfuscation ontologies used by the obfuscation mechanism. The Ownership Definition Repository and the Privacy Preference Repository hold the ownership definitions and the privacy preferences for our context information privacy mechanism, respectively.

6 The Privacy and Obfuscation Mechanism

The privacy functionality of the Context Management System operates as follows. Context-aware applications issue context fact queries (or requests for notification of context changes) to the Context Manager Layer. Each query (or request) is first evaluated to determine (1) the owner of the requested context fact, (2) whether or not the requested context fact is present in the Context Fact Repository, and (3) if the owner has preferences pertaining to the disclosure of the requested context fact.

If the requested context fact is public (i.e. it has no owner), then the request is permitted. Should the requested context fact be owned (as per the ownership definitions), then the identity of the requester is checked to see if it is one of the owners. If it is an owner, then the request is permitted as our ownership mechanism guarantees access to all owners of a context fact. If the requester is not an owner, then the preferences of the owners are evaluated to determine whether or not the context fact should be disclosed. Provided the disclosure is permitted, any relevant granularity preferences are then evaluated. If the granularity preferences require obfuscation of the context fact prior to disclosure this obfuscation process occurs.

Obfuscation of context facts associated with Class 1 obfuscation ontologies occurs as described in Section 4.

When the obfuscation of an object associated with a Class 2 obfuscation ontology is required (such as when the context fact **employeeLocation[Alice, 78-633]** must be obfuscated to detail level 1) the following occurs.

The Context Manager Layer first checks the context model for any additional information about the context fact. In our example, **employeeLocation[Alice, 78-633]** is marked as derived from the location of WirelessDevice1 (the device assigned to Alice). To obfuscate the location of Alice requires the location of the device be obfuscated. To achieve this, the Context Manager Layer issues an obfuscation request to the SIL for **deviceLocation[WirelessDevice1, 78-633]**, with the Location object obfuscated to detail level 1 (i.e. city level).

The SIL notes that the current Observation to context fact mappings produce deviceLocation context facts of detail level 5. The SIL re-examines its mappings to determine if an alternative context source is available that provides SensorML Observations which can be mapped to a context fact with the required detail level. If the SIL fails to find an alternative context source, it locates the SensorML Observation that produced the context fact **deviceLocation[WirelessDevice1, 78-633]**. This SensorML Observation, a location report for "WirelessDevice1", is shown in Figure 5.

```
<om:Observation gml:id="Observation1">
...
  <om:featureOfInterest
     xlink:href="http://MiracleMart.org/Devices/instances/WirelessDevice1"/>
  <om:observedProperty
     xlink:href="http://MiracleMart.org/DeviceLocation"/>
  <om:result xsi:type="swe:ScopedNameType"
     codeSpace="http://MiracleMart.org/Offices/">
          78-633
  </om:result>
...
</om:Observation>
```

Fig. 5. Excerpt from a SensorML Observation giving the location of WirelessDevice1 as office *78-633*

The SIL then searches through the Process Chain descriptions in the Process Chain Repository looking for a program capable of converting the SensorML Observation in Figure 5 to a SensorML Observation of the required city-level detail. It is assumed that each Process Chain description includes information (such as the format and detail level) on the inputs and outputs of the associated program.

If no single program is able to do the conversion, the SIL attempts to chain multiple programs together to obtain a SensorML Observation with the required detail level. If this also fails, the SIL then conducts an online search for suitable programs. If this search also fails, the SIL cannot proceed further and the obfuscation process is aborted. This means that the context information cannot be disclosed.

For this example we assume that the SIL is successful in its search, and uses the program(s) it found to convert the SensorML Observation in Figure 5 to the required detail level.

This new SensorML Observation is then mapped using the Observation to Context Fact Mappings maintained by the SIL to produce a new context fact **deviceLocation[WirelessDevice1, Brisbane]**. This is returned to the Context Manager Layer, where the derivation rule "During working hours, Alice's location is that of the device that she is assigned" (defined in Figure 1) is applied to obtain the context fact **employeeLocation[Alice, Brisbane]**. The Context Manager Layer then releases the context fact to the context-aware application that queried (or requested) it.

7 Conclusion

In this paper we presented a context information privacy mechanism designed to protect the privacy of context information owners in the ubiquitous computing environment. Unlike existing approaches, our solution provides explicit support for context-dependent, multi-party ownership. In our approach owners of context information are able to specify the conditions under which their context information is disclosed, including the detail level at which disclosure may take place. We presented a context obfuscation mechanism able to dynamically adjust the level of detail of context information to meet any detail level disclosure requirements specified by the context owner(s). Unlike existing approaches to obfuscation of context information, our approach is not restricted to particular context types (such as location), does not return pre-specified values as the result of obfuscation, and does not restrict obfuscation to a static number of detail levels for all context types. Two schemes for implementing our obfuscation mechanism were discussed: using taxonomies, and using a bottom-up rule-based approach in which the data processing rules used for obfuscation of context facts can be implemented as dynamically discoverable programs. We then described a Context Management System incorporating our context information privacy mechanism's functionality. This Context Management System is able to dynamically discover new sources of context information, and new executable programs (which are accompanied by SensorML Process Chain descriptions) to process the information from context sources, enabling it to obfuscate context information without the need for detailed taxonomies.

References

1. Hong, J., Landay, J.: An architecture for privacy-sensitive ubiquitous computing. In: 2nd International Conference on Mobile Systems, Applications, and Services, pp. 177–189. ACM Press, New York (2004)
2. Henricksen, K., Wishart, R., McFadden, T., Indulska, J.: Extending context models for privacy in pervasive computing environments. In: 2nd International Workshop on Context Modelling and Reasoning (CoMoRea), PerCom'05 Workshop proceedings, IEEE Computer Society Press, Los Alamitos (2005)
3. Langheinrich, M.: A privacy awareness system for ubiquitous computing. In: Proceedings of the 4th International Conference on Ubiquitous Computing (Ubicomp 2002) (2002)
4. Gandon, F., Sadeh, N.: Semantic Web Technologies to Reconcile Privacy and Context Awareness. Web Semantics Journal 1 (2004)
5. Open Geospatial Consortium: OpenGIS Sensor Model Language (SensorML) Implementation Specification. OpenGIS Implementation Specification (Draft proposed version) 06C 05-086r2 (2006)
6. Wishart, R., Henricksen, K., Indulska, J.: Context obfuscation via ontological descriptions. In: Strang, T., Linnhoff-Popien, C. (eds.) LoCA 2005. LNCS, vol. 3479, pp. 276–288. Springer, Heidelberg (2005)
7. Lederer, S., Beckmann, C., Dey, A., Mankoff, J.: Managing Personal Information Disclosure in Ubiquitous Computing Environments. Technical Report IRB-TR-03-015, Intel Research Berkley (2003)
8. Open Geospatial Consortium: Observation and Measurements. OGC Best Practices Document (Draft) 06C 05-087r4 (2006)
9. Indulska, J., Henricksen, K., Hu, P.: Towards a standards-based autonomic context management system. In: Yang, L.T., Jin, H., Ma, J., Ungerer, T. (eds.) ATC 2006. LNCS, vol. 4158, pp. 26–37. Springer, Heidelberg (2006)
10. Henricksen, K.: A Framework for Context-Aware Pervasive Computing Applications. PhD thesis, University of Queensland, Information Technology and Electrical Engineering Department (2003)

Context-Aware Service Composition for Mobile Network Environments*

Choonhwa Lee[1], Sunghoon Ko[1], Seungjae Lee[1], Wonjun Lee[2,**], and Sumi Helal[3]

[1] College of Information and Communications,
Hanyang University, Seoul, Republic of Korea
{lee,archit01,mixxer}@hanyang.ac.kr

[2] Dept. of Computer Science and Engineering,
Korea University, Seoul, Republic of Korea
wlee@korea.ac.kr

[3] Dept. of Computer and Information Science and Engineering
University of Florida, FL, U.S.A.
helal@cise.ufl.edu

Abstract. Recent advances in wireless and mobile networking technology pose a new set of requirements and challenges that are not previously thought of, when it comes to smart space middleware design. Leading the list is how to embrace diversity and unpredictability inherent in mobile computing environments. Service-oriented computing is being recognized as one of viable solutions to the problem. According to the paradigm, dynamic service discovery and composition should be able to handle the dynamism and diversity in the environments. However, most current service frameworks do not provide sufficient support to mask the complexity from having to deal with the uncertainty by ourselves. Therefore, building an application via qualified service composition still remains a cumbersome and daunting task. In this paper, we present a smart space middleware architecture designed to hide the complexity involved with context-aware, automated service composition. We also report our prototype implementations as an effort to validate the effectiveness and feasibility of the architecture.

1 Introduction

Service-Oriented Computing (SOC) has widely been recognized as a viable solution to cope with the dynamics inherent in mobile and pervasive computing environments. Embracing unpredictable changes requires that the computing system be open and extensible to ensure its evolution, adaptive to environmental changes, and flexible enough to allow its reconfiguration. It has been shown that these crucial properties of the ubiquitous computing middleware can be enabled, in essence, by the concept of services [1] [2] [3] [4]. According to the service paradigm, everything is modeled as a service, including hardware devices, network resources, a piece of computation, and

---

* This work was supported by grant No. R01-2005-000-10267-0 from the Basic Research Program of the Korea Science & Engineering Foundation.

** Corresponding author.

J. Indulska et al. (Eds.): UIC 2007, LNCS 4611, pp. 941–952, 2007.

even a human being. A value-added, composite service can also be formed by interconnecting those component services that provide limited functionality. Being based on the service concept implies dynamic service discovery and late binding whereby desired application functionality is mapped to appropriate module(s) available in the environment at the moment. Moreover, this mapping may be replaced with what is considered a more desired one later on. This concept of services renders the architecture effective in dealing with the future unpredictability.

Originally introduced as a home gateway platform, OSGi Service Platform [5] provides a managed service execution environment on which services can dynamically be installed, invoked, and then uninstalled. Being similar, in spirit, to the micro-kernel approach, it allows for extendable, flexible system configuration, to which OSGi's wide acceptance might be attributed. Although OSGi specification underwent rapid growth over the past few years, some advanced features related to service use and management remain yet to be further developed to date. Especially, we notice that service composition is one of such desired features.

This paper presents our work on an OSGi-based smart space middleware architecture with its emphasis on context-aware service composition. We first discuss our design principles and overall architecture of the smart space middleware, before delving into the main issues of service discovery and composition assisted by context awareness.

2 Architectural Design of Smart Space Middleware

Recent advances in wireless and mobile networking technologies for small-sized networks [6] [7] pose a new set of requirements and challenges that are not previously thought of, when it comes to smart space middleware design. The examples of small networks we consider include PAN (Personal Area Network), VAN (Vehicle Area Network), and home networks. Their size constraint is inevitably passed on the middleware that likely resides on a gateway node in the networks. Therefore, the requirement of being lightweight middleware is one of the most critical. At the same time, the middleware architecture should be flexible and extensible enough to accommodate a range of applications over various network configurations. While designing the middleware architecture, its configuration flexibility was regarded as a key feature to facilitate interactions and collaboration among middleware components. Our smart space middleware has been designed on top of OSGi Service Platform to address those primary requirements. It is worthwhile to note that the OSGi Alliance has also established Mobile Expert Group and Vehicle Expert Group to explore the possibility of OSGi for mobile devices and in-vehicle environments [8].

This paper focuses on the issue of context-aware, automated service composition in a mobile network environment. By introducing an OSGi system service, named as Plumber Service, to support automatic service composition, a composite service can be embodied by a combination of best qualified instances available at the moment. After then, during service runtime, any broken and deteriorated composition can automatically be recovered and replaced, respectively. Context awareness (i.e., service quality) enabled by our proposal of dynamic service ranking helps Plumber Service in providing this failure resilient service composition.

Figure 1 illustrates the overall architecture of our mobile space middleware. At the bottom are OSGi framework and system services. Our additions of network access services (Space Gateway, WiBro, WPAN, etc) and service composition services (Plumber) are positioned on top of them. All communication need is served by Space Gateway service that passes communication requests on to appropriate network modules such as WiBro service, WPAN service, or others. When building up a composite service as described by a service composition graph, Plumber Service figures out what would be the best combination by the help of the dynamic service ranking. At the top are shown applications such as Service Browser & Composer, Space Monitor, Preference & Capability Policy Manager, healthcare application, and so on.

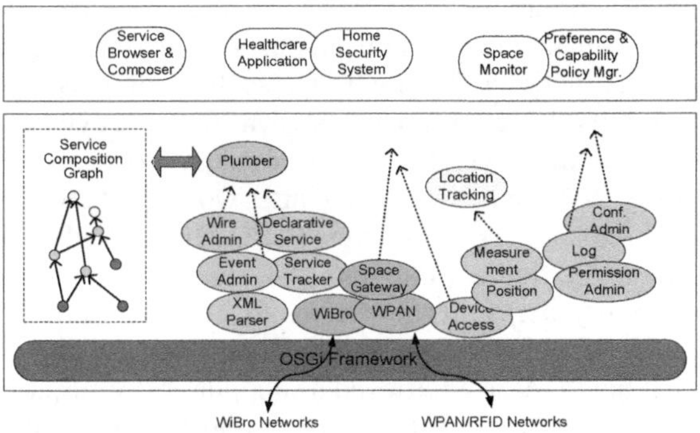

Fig. 1. Overall Architecture of Smart Space Middleware

3 Automated Service Composition Support in OSGi Environments

The latest OSGi specification [5] offers some advanced features related to service monitoring and composition: Wire Admin Service, Service Tracker, and Declarative Service. First, Wire Admin Service defines a set of APIs that can be used to wire a pair of services, providing support for the producer-consumer design pattern. Service Tracker offers assistance for service availability tracking beyond the low-level event mechanism of OSGi Service Platform that notifies which bundle has become available, unavailable, or modified. Declarative Service is a new addition to OSGi specification release 4.0 that helps to manage service dependency [5] [9]. Basically, it provides system support for automatic service dependency management. According to the scheme, service dependencies are described in a declarative way, i.e., separate from service logic itself. In other words, by filling in the callbacks of a component's bind and unbind, developers can program actions that are taken to automatically handle changes to service availability the module depends on.

Despite those handy features for service availability checking and composition by the current OSGi specification, one missing piece we see is system support for automated service composition. As we will see below, a composite service is described as an interconnection of component services. Plumbing the components is a complex task, involving several issues such as service discovery, selection based on availability and quality, and continuous monitoring. For example, any component turning out unavailable in the middle of composition process will require that the half composed services be unwired. Imagine, also, what to do if one link of initially optimal composition is clogged up later. In this paper, we propose Plumber Service that takes care of much of the intricacy involved in service composition and maintenance.

3.1 Shopping Aid Scenario: A Case of Service Composition

Before getting into the details of our Plumber Service, let us first consider an exemplary scenario of shopping aid application. The application is constructed by assembling several component modules as shown in Figure 2 (a). The graph shows information processing and flows over an interconnection graph of component services that provides basic functionality. Each node in the graph represents a component module, and information being passed to its successor node is shown over an edge between the two. The information is abstracted and aggregated, as it propagates over the graph. Suppose that Bob stops by a grocery store on his way home after work. As he walks through the store isles, shopping guide messages pop up on his PDA. This is made possible by a service composition depicted in the figure. First, his PDA equipped with a RFID reader reads in the UPC codes of grocery items on the shelves that he passes by. The codes are then translated into product information retrieved by URLMapper from manufacturer's Web sites. We assume that his PDA also retrieved a shopping list via SpaceGateway from the home fridge the moment he entered the store. ProductBrowser compares the product information and shopping list, and alerts Bob on the matches between the two by providing shopping information through Display.

To foster service composition, we have developed an XML-based service composition graph editor, called Service Composer, along with our Plumber Service. It is a GUI tool to guide us to walk through the service composition process from a graph

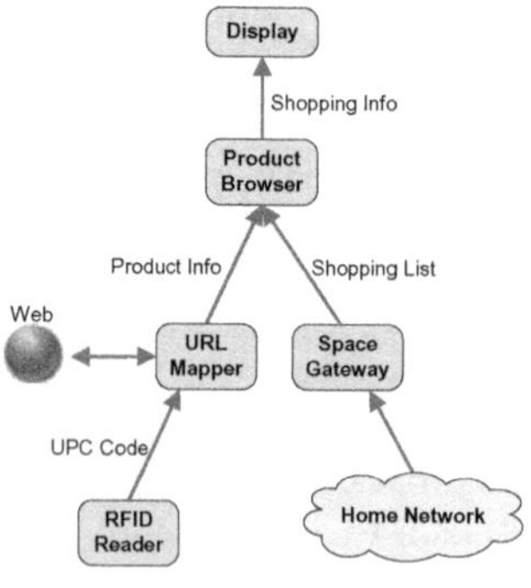

(a) Service composition graph

```
<?xml version="1.0" encoding="UTF-8"?>
<composite name="shopping-aid" adaptation="yes" ... >
    <!-- adaptation attribute can be either yes or no. -->
    <comment>A shopping aid scenario</comment>
    <pipe name="p1" replacement="better">
    <!-- replacement attribute can be one of fixed, any, and better. --
>
        <producer>
                <name>org.kosef.service.ProductBrowser</name>
                <properties> language="en" </properties>
        </producer>
        <consumer> org.kosef.service.Display
                <properties>
                        language="en"
                        location=Harry's
                </properties>
        </consumer>
    </pipe>
    <pipe name="p2" replacement="fixed" sharing="permitted">
        <producer>
                <name>URLMapper</name>
                ......
        </producer>
        <consumer>org.kosef.service.ProductBrower</consumer>
    </pipe>
```

(b) Corresponding XML description

Fig. 2. Shopping Aid Scenario

specification to its plumbing to runtime management. More specifically, it helps to describe a composition by providing visual information about component services and a library of composite services currently available in the framework. It also performs compatibility checking of the producer and consumer service on both ends of a link on our behalf. Once the composer generates the graph in XML, actual instantiation of it is taken care of by Plumber Service. Without these supports, we will end up having to hard-code the graph construction by adding links leg by leg. Although the current OSGi specification provides some help with service composition as mentioned earlier, more can be done to relieve the burden of the composition complexity and unpredictability in mobile computing environments. It is important to know that the composed service is put back into the framework service registry, so that others can see and make use of the composite. Simplified part of the XML description corresponding to the graph in Figure 2 (a) is shown in Figure 2 (b). The important fields of the graph are explained below.

3.2 Plumber Service

Given a service graph specification, Plumber Service first makes sure that all necessary component services are readily available and there is no dependency problem by utilizing OSGi's support for service tracking and events. It, then, makes use of OSGi Wire Admin Service to interconnect the graph nodes, which implies that each graph edge is represented by an OSGi Wire object. Figure 3 shows Plumber interface that the Plumber Service implements. The interface defines *compose*() and *decompose*() methods for the purpose of building up and dismantling a graph. If a client wants to be notified of any change to the wiring, it should register callback methods for those events by calling *addPlumberListener*() method. It means that the client must implement PlumberListener interface as well.

```
public interface org.kosef.service.Plumber {
    String compose(String xml-graph-description);
    void decompose(String graph-name);

    void addPlumberListener(String graph-name, PlumberListener appl);
}

public interface org.kosef.service.PlumberListener {
    // Callback functions to be when the wiring has been
    // completed, a failure occurs, and the graph has been
    // recovered or part of it has been replace.

    String constructed();
    String broken();
    String reconstructed();
}
```

Fig. 3. Class Definition of Plumber Service

On system startup, Plumber Service registers itself with OSGi service registry to join the framework. After getting the handle of Plumber Service from the framework registry, a client calls *compose*() method on it by providing a service graph. The client is notified through *constructed*() callback method in PlumberListener interface, when the graph instantiation is completed.

As shown in Figure 2 (b), *composite* element has *adaptation* attribute of which value can be either *yes* or *no*. It indicates whether a composite service should try to adapt itself to environmental changes during service runtime. The latter means that, once constructed, a component replacement with an equivalent is not permitted in the event of failures. Consequently, the breakdown of any part of the graph results in the composite service being flagged as down and unavailable. The former case mandates that the system service performs automatic recovery of the broken service graph. Problematic components should be replaced with an equivalent one or a substitute with better quality. (Service suitability can effectively be dealt with by the concept of our dynamic service ranking whose details are discussed below). An alternative can be substituted for a current yet still working participant that was the best choice at the time of service plumbing. In either case, the client application is informed of the changes in the graph via *broken*() and *reconstructed*() callbacks.

The *replacement* attribute of a *pipe* element specifies its replacement policy at the grain of an individual link: *fixed*, *any*, or *better*. The case of *fixed* says that the pipe must not be replaced even in case of the component failure, which leaves no choice but to dismantle the entire graph. The value of *any* means that the problematic link can be switched over to any other alternative. The *better* case allows only better replacements in terms of service quality. By the way, this *replacement* attribute precedes the graph-wise *adaptation* policy, in case there's a conflict between them.

3.3 Dynamic Service Ranking

Dynamic service ranking is our approach to the service selection problem that is about choosing the best when there are more than one qualified candidates. It is common that service property is indicated by service attributes attached to it. One can think of two types of static and dynamic attributes. For instance, a stationary service's location information is a static attribute which remains unchanged during the service lifetime, whereas frequently changing load on the service can be viewed as a dynamic attribute. We propose that contextual information be attached as an attribute to service instances, and the contextual property be dynamically updated to keep up with changes in the environments. Dynamically changing context information often plays a crucial role in avoiding unnecessary distraction in ubiquitous computing environments. Think about the distance between a moving person and display devices in surroundings. Perhaps, the best display may be determined by a combination of dynamic attributes (e.g., the display's location and orientation) and static attributes like the display size. In other words, we can narrow candidate display devices down to a few more qualified by evaluating the dynamic attributes at the time of service selection.

Like other service discovery frameworks, OSGi supports static attributes only. It defines SERVICE_RANKING as one of service registration properties that indicates service quality. The higher ranking value of the attribute, the better service quality it can provide. Therefore, a service with the highest ranking tends to be returned as OSGi's service lookup results, in case of more than one matches. While it should prove useful to some extent, it will not be capable of capturing the endless changes of mobile computing environments. This is because it remains the same throughout service lifetime, once the value of static attributes is initially set by service providers. Consequently, an instance recommended by the service ranking may not be the best any more. This limitation can be overcome by our idea of dynamic service ranking that represents dynamically changing contextual aspects. The ranking property is dynamically evaluated either on demand or periodically. Code snippet in Figure 4 shows dynamic service ranking extension to OSGi specification. A service will provide its own implementation of DynamicRanker interface, if dynamic service ranking is supported by that. A Java thread may be dedicated to periodically re-evaluate the service quality every *refreshInterval* interval specified as an argument.

```
public static final String DYNAMIC_RANKING = “service.dynamicRanking”;

public interface org.kosef.service.DynamicRanker {
    Integer evaluate(int refreshInterval); // returns service quality index
}

public class DynamicService implements DynamicRanker, BundleActivator {
    public void start(BundleContext context) {
        Hashtable properties = new Hashtable();
        properties.put(SERVICE_DESCRIPTION, “sample service”);
        properties.put(DYNAMIC_RANKING, evaluate(0));

        ...

        context.registerService(this.class.getName(), this, properties);
    }

    Integer evaluate(int refreshInterval) {
        // It dynamically determines its rank by considering
        // any contextual information relevant to the service.
        return dranking;
    }

    public void stop(BundleContext context) {
        // stop the context evaluation thread
    }
}
```

Fig. 4. Dynamic Service Ranking Example

With the help of dynamic service ranking attributes, failure resilient service composition is now made possible. In the event of a fault or significant service quality degradation, the problematic component can be replaced with a better equivalent. It is on the value of the dynamic ranking attributes that our Plumber Service bases its recovery decision.

3.4 Service Composition Support Subsystem

Putting together those ingredients we discussed to this point, we have come up with an architecture of service composition subsystem. The architecture is illustrated in Figure 5, and it has been designed to make use of, whenever and wherever possible, existing OSGi features in support of service composition and management. The subsystem provides a visual service composition editing and management environment.

Service Composer on the top is an application program that produces a service composition graph specified in XML. The graph description is then passed to Plumber Service which orchestrates all the interactions for service composition and maintenance. Particularly, Plumber Service uses Wire Admin APIs to perform actual service wiring as directed in the graph. Once the wiring has been done, the availability and quality changes of participating component services are monitored through Event Admin service. Either periodically or on demand, whichever way is appropriate for the service in question, Dynamic Ranking Evaluator evaluates its dynamic ranking attribute to determine the value of the attribute. If the evaluation results in a new value, it is communicated to Plumber Service via Event Admin service. Also, the service's property in OSGi framework registry is accordingly updated. Being notified of any topological changes through Event Admin, Plumber Service may take recovery actions by issuing necessary wiring commands to Wire Admin service.

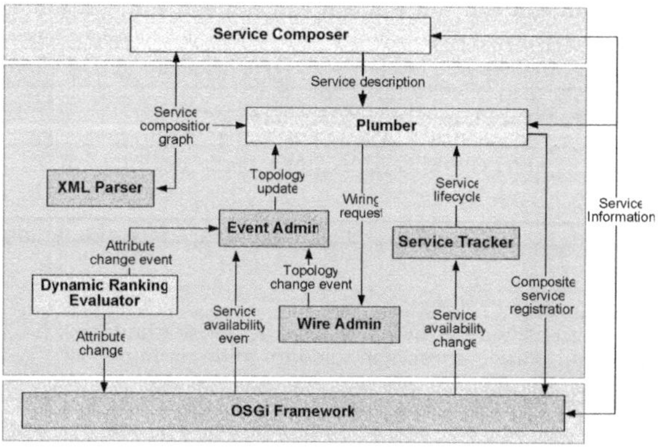

Fig. 5. Service Composition Subsystem Architecture

4 Prototype Implementation

To validate the effectiveness and feasibility of our smart space middleware architecture, we have developed two versions of its prototype for PC and PDA platforms, respectively. The former corresponds to the middleware being hosted on a gateway node in home/office environments, while the latter on a personal gateway node in a PAN/BAN. Both implementations are based on Knopflerfish v2.0 on top of JVM (J2SE 1.4.2 in the case of PC and IBM J9 CDC + Personal Profile v1.0 for PDA). Figure 6 shows some screenshots of them, while composing the shopping aid application depicted in Figure 2. The menu provides functionalities to retrieve and monitor system status with regard to individual services and their compositions and to change the configuration. Using the GUI, users can list up available services, including either of component and composite services, compose a new service, or change existing service attributes and compositions. It also provides the service management facility of service start and termination.

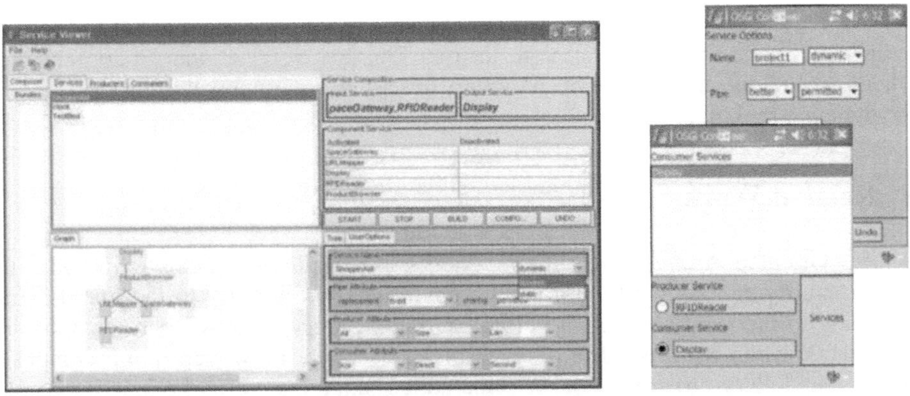

(a) PC version (b) PDA version

Fig. 6. Screenshots of Service Composer

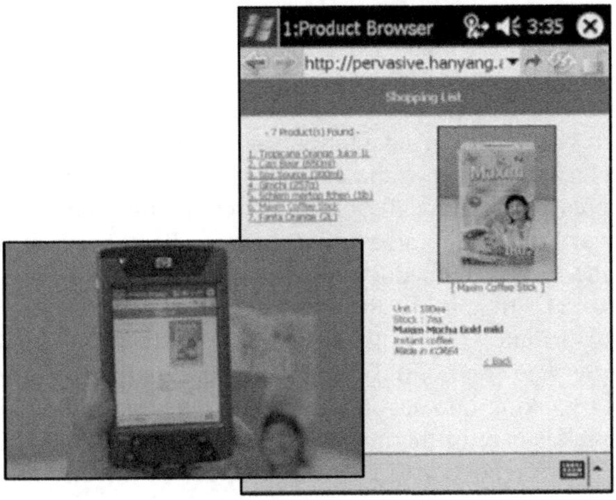

Fig. 7. Shopping Aid Scenario Demonstration

Figure 7 shows the shopping aid application running on Bob's PDA. As we can see in the figure, the purchasing list is being displayed on the left. As Bob passes by a product of the list in a grocery store, shopping information is cropping up on the right-hand side. He will be able to make a decision on whether to buy it or not at a glance. According to the service composition graph presented in Figure 2, Product Browser is linked to Display with a dynamic ranking attribute attached to it. The attribute evaluation ends up with a quality index indicative of how good the service is. The index value may be determined based largely on the distance between Bob and display devices. Suppose that Display service is embodied by PDA's display on entering the store. As Bob moves around, the mapping can be changed to a bigger display mounted on a wall or shelf in the store. In other words, Bob's movement affects the dynamic rankings of candidate display devices in the store, which leads to Plumber

Service replacing a failed or inferior component. The composition graph in Figure 2 includes all necessary information to instruct Plumber Service what to do, including whether to allow this adaptation based on observed environmental changes through the dynamic ranking.

5 Related Work

Service-Oriented Architecture (SOA) benefits us by allowing flexible and adaptive system configurations befitting a certain environment. Similarly to the micro-kernel approach, component services are discovered and plugged into the base composition framework when required. The plugged-in services can be woven into a composite service capable of providing a new, value-added functionality on the individual component's own. This composition problem has been explored under different context [3] [4] [10] [11] [12] [13]. Among recent salient efforts, in particular, in pervasive computing environments, are the exploitation of semantic service descriptions [14] [15] [16] and opportunistic combination/chaining of component services [17] [18] [19] beyond the previous, naive I/O matching scheme. Other research on the composition programming model and methodology [15] [20] is also worthy of notice.

Our work differs in that it addresses the need of service composition support especially for OSGi-based SOA framework. More specifically, an emphasis is placed on automated service composition, adaptation, and failure recovery made possible by being aware of relevant context to the composition. It is the dynamic service ranking attribute that expresses dynamically-changing contextual information in our case, while other noteworthy ones are also found. In fact, the concept of the dynamic ranking is similar to the idea of embedding context capturing modules into a service discovery framework [21]. In spirit, it may also be viewed as close to the dynamic URL [22] and dynamic attribute [13]. With the help of the dynamic service ranking attribute, our Plumber Service can not only provide an optimal composition solution under a given condition by taking into account relevant contextual properties. Once successfully built, it also takes care of the maintenance need of the composite such as partial replacements or failure recovery to adapt to changes to the environment. In sum, by providing system support for automatic service composition and maintenance, it eases the development process and operation of autonomous, complicated applications in pervasive computing environments.

Current OSGi specification [5] offers some level of supports for service availability monitoring and composition. They include Service Tracker (to be notified of changes to service availability), Declarative Service (to manage dependencies among services), and Wire Admin Service (to wire a producer-consumer pair together.) Although Service Tracker already provides basic assistance for tracking service availability, it has been shown that such support can be furthered in [23]. OSGi's Declarative Service has its root in Gravity project [9] where the problem of service dependency management is overcome by separating service logic itself from service management logic handled by the execution environment. A component description, including its dependency on other services it requires, is defined in XML documents (i.e., in a declarative way.) The execution environment manages bindings between the component and required services. Whenever it sees changes to its dependent service availability, the execution environment invokes bind and unbind callback methods (which is part of the component description), so that the application can act on the changes. The project also addresses the need of service composition management support, which makes it similar to our work from the perspective of the level of service composition and automatic dependency management. Unlike Gravity project, however, our approach enables better adaptation to service availability by supporting mechanisms both for proactive actions (through the dynamic service ranking attribute) and for reactive responses as with in Gravity project.

6 Conclusion

This paper presents a service framework, especially designed for small-sized mobile networks, that can automate context-aware service composition. The two major contributions of our work are summarized as an architectural middleware design and its evaluation via prototype implementations. At the heart of the middleware architecture is Plumber Service that enables the best qualified service composition. After then, it keeps the composition optimal with the help of the dynamic ranking attributes that reflect the quality of the component service. The architecture has been designed to make use of, wherever possible, OSGi features to support service composition and management. Through the prototypes, we have demonstrated that the architecture achieves its main design goals of lightweight, flexible, failure resilient service composition middleware.

References

1. Curbera, F., Duftler, M., Khalaf, R., Nagy, W., Mukhi, N., Weerawarana, S.: Unraveling the Web Services Web: An Introduction to SOAP, WSDL, and UDDI. IEEE Internet Computing 6(2), 86–93 (2002)
2. Sun Microsystems: Jini Network Technology, http://www.sun.com/jini
3. Gribble, S.D., Welsh, M., von Behren, R., Brewer, E.A., Culler, D., Borisov, N., Czerwinski, S., Gummadi, R., Hill, J., Joseph, A., Katz, R.H., Mao, Z.M., Ross, S., Zhao, B.: The Ninja Architecture for Robust Internet-scale Systems and Services. Computer Networks 35(4), 473–497 (2001)
4. Deelman, E., Blythe, J., Gil, Y., Kesselman, C., Mehta, G., Vahi, K.: Mapping Abstract Complex Workflows onto Grid Environments. Journal of Grid Computing 1(1), 25–39 (2003)
5. The OSGi Alliances: OSGi Service Platform Release 4 (2006)
6. IEEE 802.15 Working Group: IEEE 802.15 WPAN, http://www.ieee802.org/15
7. Devarapalli, V., Wakikawa, R., Petrescu, A., Thubert, P.: Network Mobility (NEMO) Basic Support Protocol. IETF RFC 3963 (2005)
8. Giuli, T., Watson, D., Prasad, K.V.: The Last Inch at 70 Miles Per Hour. IEEE Pervasive Computing 5(4), 20–27 (2006)
9. Cervantes, H., Hall, R.S.: Autonomous Adaptation to Dynamic Availability Using a Service-Oriented Component Model. In: Proceedings of the 26th International Conference on Software Engineering (ICSE'04), pp. 614–623 (2004)

10. Fu, X., Shi, W., Akkerman, A., Karamcheti, V.: CANS: Composable, Adaptive Network Services Infrastructure. In: Proceedings of USENIX Symposium on Internet Technologies and Systems (USITS'01) (2001)
11. Andrews, T., Curbera, F., Dholakia, H., Goland, Y., Klein, J., Leymann, F., Liu, K., Roller, D., Smith, D., Thatte, S., Trickovic, I., Weerawarana, S.: Business Process Execution Language for Web Services Version 1.1 (2003), http://www-128.ibm.com/ developerworks/library/specification/ws-bpel/
12. Dey, A., Futakawa, M., Salber, D., Abowd, G.: The Conference Assistant: Combining Context-Awareness with Wearable Computing. In: Proceedings of the 3rd International Symposium on Wearable Computers (ISWC '99), pp. 21–28 (1999)
13. Chen, C., Li, M., Kotz, D.: Design and Implementation of a Large-Scale Context Fusion Network. In: Proceedings of the 1st Annual International Conference on Mobile and Ubiquitous Systems: Networking and Services (MobiQuitous'04), pp. 246–255 (2004)
14. Fujii, K., Suda, T.: Dynamic Service Composition Using Semantic Information. In: Proceedings of the 2nd International Conference on Service Oriented Computing (ICSOC'04) (2004)
15. Ranganathan, A., Chetan, S., Al-Muhtadi, J., Campbell, R.H., Mickunas, M.D.: Olympus: A High-Level Programming Model for Pervasive Computing Environments. In: Proceedings of the 3rd IEEE International Conference on Pervasive Computing and Communications (PerCom'05), pp. 7–16. IEEE Computer Society Press, Los Alamitos (2005)
16. Song, Z., Labrou, Y., Masuoka, R.: Dynamic Service Discovery and Management in Task Computing. In: Proceedings of the 1st Annual International Conferences on Mobile and Ubiquitous Systems: Networking and Services (MobiQuitous'04), pp. 310–318 (2004)
17. Kalasapur, S., Kumar, M., Shirazi, B.: Personalized Service Composition for Ubiquitous Multimedia Delivery. In: Proceedings of the 6th IEEE International Symposium on a World of Wireless Mobile and Multimedia Networks (WoWMoM'05), IEEE Computer Society Press, Los Alamitos (2005)
18. Karastoyanova, D., Leymann, F., Buchmann, A.P.: An Approach to Parameterizing Web Service Flows. In: Proceedings of the 4th International Conference on Service Oriented Computing, pp. 533–538 (2005)
19. Ponnekanti, S.R., Fox, A.: Application-Service Interoperation without Standardized Service Interfaces. In: Proceedings of the 1st IEEE International Conference on Pervasive Computing and Communications (PerCom'03), IEEE Computer Society Press, Los Alamitos (2003)
20. Kaabi, R.S., Souveyet, C., Rolland, C.: Eliciting Service Composition in a Goal Driven Manner. In: Proceedings of the 2nd International Conference on Service Oriented Computing (ICSOC'04) (2004)
21. Lee, C., Helal, A.: Context Attributes: An Approach to Enable Context-awareness for Service Discovery. In: Proceedings of the 3rd IEEE/IPSJ Symposium on Applications and the Internet (SAINT 2003), pp. 22–30 (2003)
22. Voelker, G.M., Bershad, B.N.: Mobisaic: An Information System for a Mobile Wireless Computing Environment. In: Proceedings of IEEE Workshop on Mobile Computing Systems and Applications, pp. 185–190. IEEE Computer Society Press, Los Alamitos (1994)
23. Offermans, M.: Automatically Managing Service Dependencies in OSGi (2003), http://www.osgi.org/documents/osgi_technology/AutoManageServiceDependencies_byMOffermans.pdf

A Context-Awareness Middleware Based on Service-Oriented Architecture

Eunhoe Kim and Jaeyoung Choi

School of Computing, Soongsil University,
1-1 Sangdo-dong, Dongjak-gu, Seoul 156-743, Korea
ehkim@ss.ssu.ac.kr, choi@ssu.ac.kr

Abstract. This paper presents a middleware based on SOA (Service-Oriented Architecture) for context-awareness in a home network with ubiquitous computing. The context-awareness middleware addresses design issues such as heterogeneity, dynamicity, and extensibility issues of ubiquitous computing environment. We also suggest a context model supporting semantic level interoperability of context. In this paper, first we model context metadata ontology as well as context information ontology for the context-awareness middleware. Then we explain a service-oriented context-awareness middleware based on the context model which is introduced in this paper.

1 Introduction

The more embedded computing devices and wireless networking technologies are advanced, the more we attend to ubiquitous computing environment; miniaturized computers are embedded in our everyday physical world, wirelessly interconnected with each other, and providing suitable services for users. To realize ubiquitous computing environment context-awareness is essential because behavior of the services is determined by the context. Context is defined as situational information of entities such as a person, place, or object that is considered relevant to the interaction between a user and an application, including the user and applications themselves [1]. A ubiquitous computing system consists of various components that acquire, interpret, process, transfer, or use the context. Therefore we need a context-awareness middleware which is shared by ubiquitous computing services and is responsible for acquiring, interpreting, processing, and transferring the context.

This paper suggests a context-awareness middleware for ubiquitous computing in a home domain. Especially since the context-awareness middleware is built on heterogeneous platforms such as sensors, smart appliances, and mobile devices, it has to be enabling interoperability of context and interoperable interaction between these platforms. To address this problem we apply a service-oriented approach to the context-awareness middleware so as to achieve interoperable interaction. For interoperability of context we design and develop the context-awareness middleware based on ontology [2], which is a formal explicit specification of a shared conceptualization. We use OWL which is a web ontology language for modeling the context.

Ubiquitous computing environment is also dynamic, for example the users can move rapidly and the positions of many portable devices can be changed. Therefore

J. Indulska et al. (Eds.): UIC 2007, LNCS 4611, pp. 953–962, 2007.

associations between them are variable in runtime. Ubiquitous computing environment has to be extensible because new sensors and devices are able to participate in it seamlessly. In this paper, we explore a service oriented architecture [3] approach to address these issues.

This paper consists of 6 sections. Section 2 discusses the related works for this area. Section 3 explains an ontology based context model which consists of context information ontology and context metadata ontology. Section 4 suggests a context-awareness middleware based on SOA and shows how to use the context model in it. In this section, we also explain context reasoning. In Section 5, we evaluate the performance of the context-awareness middleware. Section 6 describes the conclusion and suggests future work.

2 Related Works

Recently many researches for context-awareness middleware in ubiquitous computing environment have progressed. ContextToolkit [4] introduces context widgets that mediate between the environment and application in the same way graphical widgets mediate between the user and the application. While a context widget hides the complexity of sensors used from the application, it doesn't provide any context model for interoperability of the context.

GAIA [5] suggested a middleware based on First-order-logic context model. It provides powerful expressiveness of context and ways to perform the various operations defined in the context model. It used CORBA to enable distributed computing. While GAIA uses service-oriented architecture such as CORBA, it needs to be more loosely coupled for heterogeneity and dynamicity in ubiquitous computing environment. GAIA also has a weakness for semantic interoperability of context, it has to translate first-order-logic-based context to ontology such as DAML+OIL.

SOCAM (A Service-Oriented Context-Aware middleware) [6] provides the building and the rapid prototyping of context-aware services. It is based on CONON (OWL Encoded Context Ontology) but it models context information only. We model context metadata used in context-awareness middleware for evaluation of qualities of context. CoBrA (Context Broker Architecture) [7] uses an agent-based approach to build context-aware applications for ubiquitous domains. While CoBrA models good context ontology, it is a centralized system, so it isn't extensible.

In this paper, we suggest a context-awareness middleware to overcome the above shortcomings. Ontology-based context information and metadata model provide the context-awareness middleware with semantic interoperability and effective maintenance of the context. Our service oriented context-awareness middleware achieves extensibility, and solves heterogeneity and dynamicity for smart home services.

3 The Context Model

3.1 Context Information Ontology

Context information consists of Entities, contextTypes, and Values in our context model. Entity represents an element of context, such as person, schedule, activity, TV, bed, and curtain. ContextType describes an attribute of the entity, such as location, power status, current activity, weather, and lighting. Value includes real data value of the contextType. For example, if we want to describe the information of a TV's power status, we can define the entity as "TV", the contextType as "powerStatus" of the TV, and the value of the power status as "On" or "Off". We describe entities as owl:class constructs, and describe contextTypes as owl:datatype-Property or owl:objectProperty constructs. In some cases, context value might contain an absolute numerical value (25.5, 0) or feature describing context (on/off, hot/neutral/cold). In addition, we define that 'locatedIn' and 'contains' are transitive, 'nearbyPerson' and 'atTheSameTime' are symmetric, 'locatedIn' is the inverse of 'contains', and 'uses' is the inverse of 'user'.

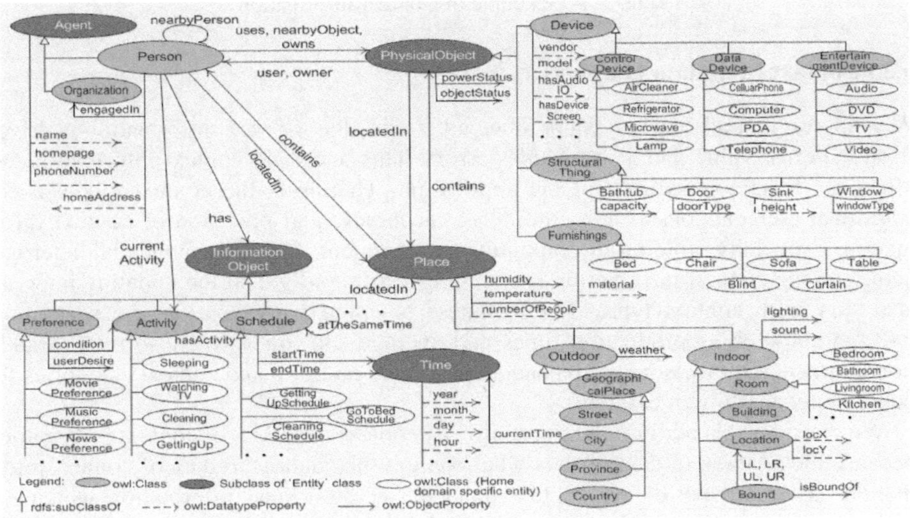

Fig. 1. Entities and ContextTypes in a Home Domain

Fig. 1 shows the structure of context information in a home domain. We define the highest level class, 'Entity', and it has subclasses (child nodes): 'Agent', 'PhysicalObject', 'InformationObject', 'Place', and 'Time'. 'PhysicalObject' class has three subclasses: 'Device', 'StructuralObject', and 'Furnishing'. In 'Place' class, there are three contextTypes: 'humidity', 'temperature', and 'numberOfPeople'. We define super property, 'contextType', and the other contextTypes as sub properties of this 'contextType'. These names of properties are shown on the arrow.

Fig. 2 shows an example of context information ontology used in the application which checks Mr. Kim's wake up schedule and provides adequate services such as alarm service, light service, and TV service depending on his current activity. For example, Kim's name is 'ChulSu Kim', Kim's location is bedroom, and its lighting status is very dark. This context information is shared between applications and context-awareness middleware services.

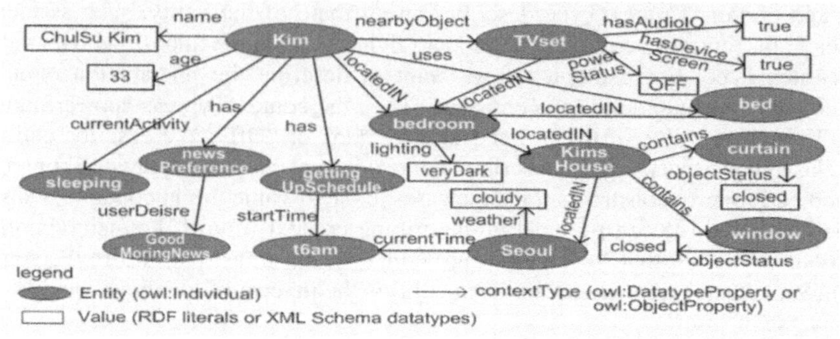

Fig. 2. An example of Context Information

3.2 Context Metadata Ontology

We suppose that all sensors can produce an error value. Context information is driven from the error value and also includes errors. This uncertain context information can affect the behavior decision of the application. Therefore, the context model needs additional elements describing confidence, accuracy, and precision of context information. Especially, ubiquitous computing environment is very dynamic and heterogeneous, so the context information is changing very rapidly, and the updating intervals also vary with context types. For freshness of context information, we need more information such as production times and average life times. We also require additional information for context dependency, context sources, and context categories for better understanding of context.

We consider this additional information as context metadata of context information because metadata is to data of data what context metadata is to data of context information. After all, we define context metadata as additional information which explains context information to improve certainty, freshness, and understanding of the context information. Therefore we describe context metadata using owl:annotationProperties which allow annotations on classes, properties, individuals and ontology headers. We define eight owl:annotationProperties: 'hasConfidence', 'hasAccuracy', 'hasPrecision', 'productionTime', 'averageLifeTime', 'hasSource', 'classifiedAs', and 'beDependentOn' to describe context metadata. Owl:annotationProperties are not interpreted nor used in OWL DL reasoning process, then the context metadata doesn't increase the reasoning time. This information is delivered to the context-awareness middleware for context management. The context-awareness middleware generally uses these metadata to maintain qualities of context. We describe it in Section 4 for details.

Fig. 3 shows a part of 'locatedIn' context metadata such as 'beClassifiedAs', 'hasSource', 'hasPrecision', and 'hasAccuracy'. An annotated contextType such as 'locatedIn' contextType, is classified as 'sensed' context, the source of 'locatedIn' context is 'RFID', the precision of RFID is 95%, and the accuracy of RFID is 9 centimeters.

The metadata of 'bedroom lighting' is mentioned in Fig. 4. For example, when the value of 'bedroom lighting' context information is very dark, the creation time of the context information is 5:50 a.m. and 'averageLifeTime' value is 15 minutes.

```
<owl:ObjectProperty rdf:ID="locatedIn">
  <beClassifiedAs>
    <SensedContextType rdf:ID="Sensed"/>
  </beClassifiedAs>
  <hasSource>
    <Source rdf:ID="RFID"/>
  </hasSource>
  <hasPrecision>
    <Precision rdf:ID="LocatedInPrecision">
      <unit rdf:datatype="http://www.w3.org/2001/XMLSchema#string">percent</unit>
      <value rdf:datatype="http://www.w3.org/2001/XMLSchema#float">95.0</value>
    </Precision>
  </hasPrecision>
  <hasAccuracy>
    <Accuracy rdf:ID="LocatedInAccuracy">
      <value rdf:datatype="http://www.w3.org/2001/XMLSchema#float">9</value>
      <unit rdf:datatype="http://www.w3.org/2001/XMLSchema#string">centimeter</unit>
    </Accuracy>
  </hasAccuracy>
  ......
</owl:ObjectProperty>
```

Fig. 3. The 'locatedIn' Context Metadata Encoding

```
<Bedroom rdf:ID="bedroom">
  <lighting rdf:resource="#veryDark"/>
  <averageLifeTime>
    <Time rdf:ID="bedroom_lighting_averageLifeTime">
      <minute rdf:datatype="http://www.w3.org/2001/XMLSchema#int">15</minute>
    </Time>
  </averageLifeTime>
  <productionTime>
    <Time rdf:ID="bedroom_lighting_productionTime">
      <minute rdf:datatype="http://www.w3.org/2001/XMLSchema#int">50</minute>
      <hour rdf:datatype="http://www.w3.org/2001/XMLSchema#int">5</hour>
    </Time>
  </productionTime>
</Bedroom>
```

Fig. 4. The 'bedroom lighting' Context Metadata Encoding

4 Context-Awareness Middleware

4.1 Architecture

In this section we explain the structure of our service-oriented context-awareness middleware which manages context information and context metadata ontology. It consists of Context provider services, Context aggregator service, Context observer service, Context discovery service, Context ontology reasoner service, and Context query service. Fig. 5 shows the structure in detail. In Fig. 6, we represent an interaction scenario from context providers to an application in order to get context.

Context provider service. This service registers itself to Context discovery service, and obtains raw context information from various sources such as sensors and translates them into low level context information based on the context model. Context provider service also annotates productionTime, averageLifeTime, and confidence of the context.

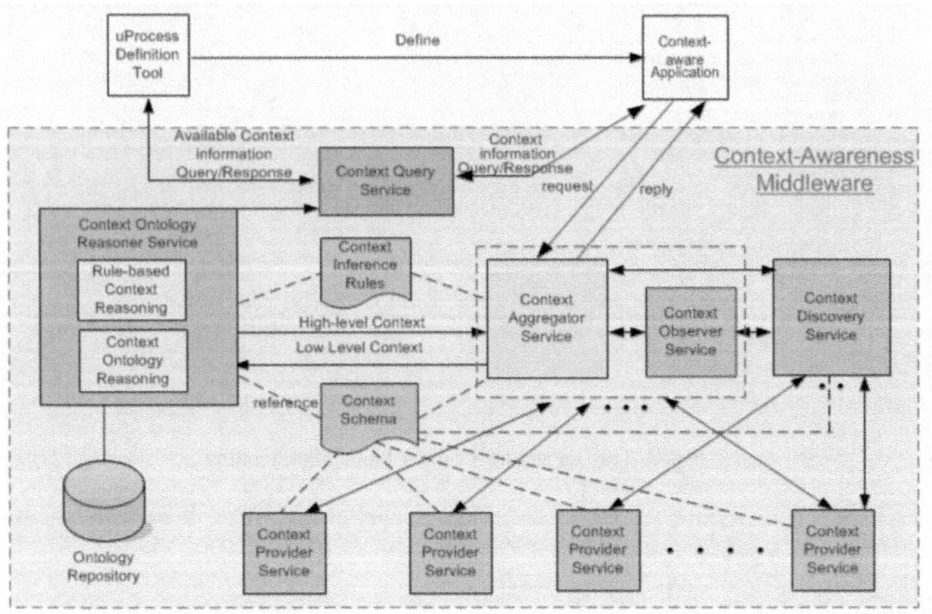

Fig. 5. The Service-oriented Context-Awareness Middleware

Context aggregator service. This service asks Context discovery service what context provider services can offer the context which is required by the application, then gathers current context information from Context provider services. Context aggregator service uses context metadata such as beClassifiedAs and hasSource for the effective collecting of the context. Context aggregator service also checks availability of context using validationCheck() method based on productionTime and averageLifeTime context metadata.

Context observer service. This service is in charge of context event requests. When an application wants to be notified of the changes of some context, context aggregator service delegates this request to Context observer service. Context observer executes publish-subscribe mechanism to processing context event.

Context ontology reasoner service. This service consists of two modules: Context ontology reasoning module and Rule-based context reasoning module. Context ontology reasoning module reasons using context schema and current context information. Context schema is an XML representation of context model which is suggested in Section 3. Rule-based context reasoning module has facilities to deduce derived contexts.

Context discovery service. This service maintains information which maps between Context provider services and context information. It provides two interfaces: register interface for Context provider services and context discovery interface for the Context aggregation service and Context observer service.

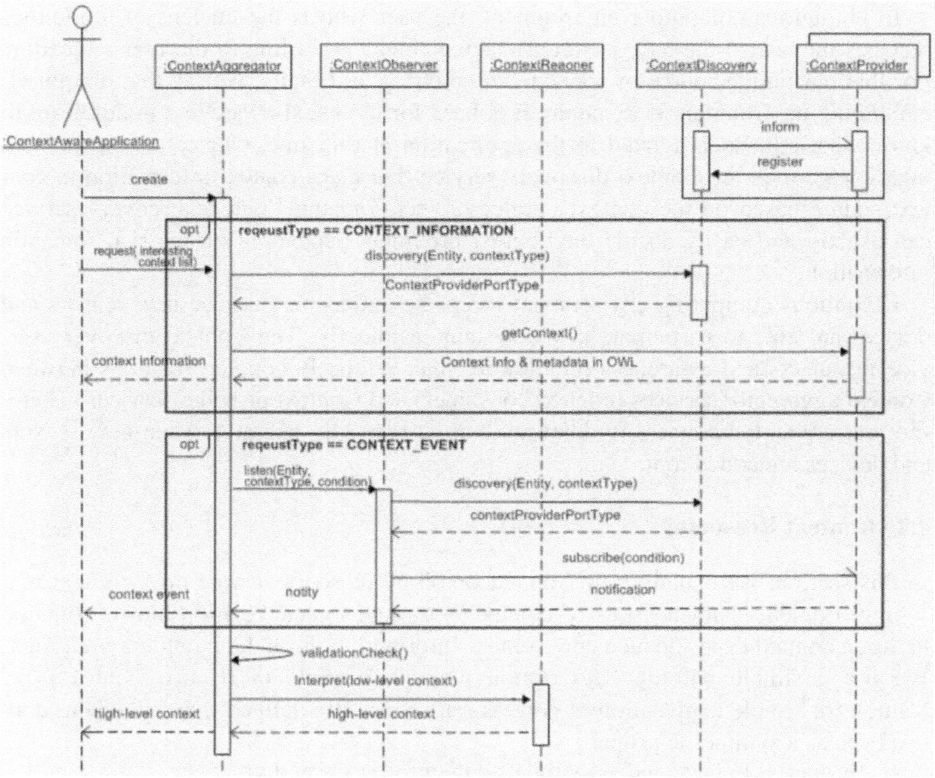

Fig. 6. Service-oriented Context-Awareness Middleware

Context query service is an additional query engine service and it provides context retrieval services requested by applications and the uProcess definition tool. Context query service is also used when a user wants to search context information or context metadata. To search for context information, it provides users with SPARQL which is a query language for RDF. uProcess definition tool is an application to describe the flow of services in ubiquitous applications. The execution, termination, and transition of services depend on the context information. Therefore uProcess definition tool requests available context to Context query service for describing pre-condition, post-condition, and transition condition of the services.

In a home domain various devices exist, for example sensors, bio sensors, embedded appliances, traditional computing devices, and communication devices. These devices have different platforms, and a context-awareness middleware can collect context information from these heterogeneous devices. Since our context-awareness middleware is based on SOA (Service-Oriented Architecture) [3], all elements are services which highly abstract the middleware operations, and provide consistent interfaces and uniform protocol with standardization manners. Therefore we overcome heterogeneity in ubiquitous computing environment.

In ubiquitous computing environment, the user who is the nucleus of ubiquitous services moves, so the user's circumstance changes according to the user's location. For that reason the source of context can be changed. Finally, we say that ubiquitous computing environment is dynamic. It is hard for a context-awareness middleware to know what context is related to the application at run time. Our context-awareness middleware uses the Context discovery service that maps context information to context source based on the context ontology. Therefore the Context discovery service can exactly and easily decide the context providers depending on the rich semantic information.

Ubiquitous computing environment has to be extensible because new sensors and devices are able to participate in the system seamlessly. The Context discovery service in our context-awareness middleware makes loosely coupled relations between Context aggregator services (context consumer) and Context provider services. Therefore our context-awareness middleware can be normally operated when new sensors and devices are added to it.

4.2 Context Reasoning

In this section, we explain how Context ontology reasoner service does context reasoning. Logical characteristics of contextTypes and logical relationship information between contextTypes deduce new context information through an ontology reasoner. We use a simple ontology description method, a triple of (Entity, contextType, Value), for simple explanation of context reasoning. We defined 'nearbyPerson' contextType as a symmetric property.

If a property, P, is tagged as symmetric then for any x and y:

$$(x, P, y) \text{ iff } (y, P, x)$$

For example, context information (Kim, nearbyPerson, Lee), which includes symmetric property 'nearbyPerson', can deduce another information (Lee, nearbyPerson, Kim) using an ontology reasoner. Besides symmetric characteristic properties like 'nearbyPerson' and 'atTheSameTime', transitivity and inverseOf properties are used.

We use a rule-based inference reasoner to produce derived context from context ontologies. Fig. 7 shows three inference rules to derive high-level context from a lot of low-level context. For example, context-awareness middleware decides if someone is watching TV, if he is located in the living room and the power status of television is ON. 'beDependentOn' metadata, described in the derived contextType, provides a hint for dependency between contexts to users who define rules. Besides the metadata, 'confidence' metadata of context can be used for reasoners which use probabilistic or fuzzy logic mechanism.

Our context-awareness middleware is implemented by using Java and Jena 2.4 ontology API which was developed by HP. We implemented the Rule-based context reasoning module using GeneralRuleReasoner which includes RETE engine or one tabled engine supported by Jena, and Context ontology reasoning module using Racer which is a well-known OWL DL reasoner. We used SOAP for interaction protocol between components.

```
#From Low-level context to High-level context
@prefix ct: <http://ss.ssu.ac.kr/ontology/Home.owl#>.
[rule1: (?a ct:locatedIn ct:livingroom) (ct:television ct:powerStatus ct:ON)
        → (?a ct:currentActivity ct:watchingTV)]
[rule2: (?a ct:locatedIn ct:bedroom) (ct:bedroom ct:lighting ct:Dark)
        (?a ct:uses ct:bed) (ct:bed ct:locatedIn ct:bedroom)
        (?tv ct:powerStatus ct:OFF) (?tv ct:locatedIn ct:bedroom)
        (?tv rdfs:subClassOf ct:TV)
        → (?a ct:currentActivity ct:sleeping)]
[rule3: (?a ct:locatedIn ct:studyroom) (ct:deskLamp ct:powerStatus ct:ON)
        (ct:computer03, ct:locatedIn ct:studyroom)
        (ct:computer03 ct:powserStatus ct:ON)
        → (?a ct:currentAcitivity  ct:working)]
```

Fig. 7. Inference rules: from low-level context to high-level context

5 Performance Evaluation

The service-oriented context-awareness middleware suggested in this paper is based on the context ontology model described in Section 3. In particular the context-awareness middleware uses not only context metadata ontology, but also context information ontology to evaluate qualities of context. However, ontology processing needs a lot of computing resources, especially ontology reasoning performs poorly according to the weight of the ontology. Therefore we measured the context ontology reasoning performance as the number of triples of context ontology increased for each case of context information only and with context metadata included.

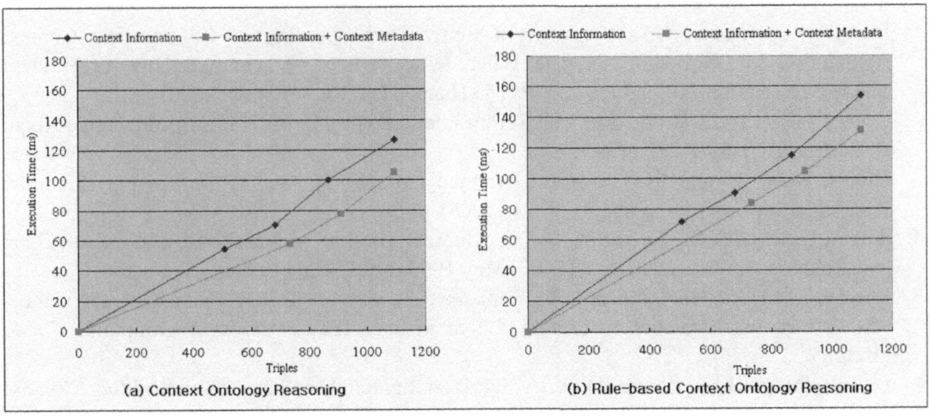

Fig. 8. The Performance of Context Reasoning

Fig. 8 shows the performance of context ontology reasoning and rule-based context ontology reasoning. For example, in the context ontology reasoning experiment, we got 54.5ms when the context information consisted of 507 triples, but we obtained 57.8ms when 228 triples context metadata were added to 507 triples context information. The difference of execution time was just 3.3ms. After all, although context metadata increased the size of ontology, it didn't seriously influence the reasoning performance. Because we described context metadata using owl:annotationProperties which are not interpreted nor used in OWL DL reasoning process, the context metadata didn't increase the reasoning time. This information is delivered to the context-awareness middleware for effective context management.

6 Conclusion

This paper presents a context-awareness middleware based on service-oriented architecture for acquiring, interpreting, processing, and transferring the context. The context-awareness middleware provides semantic interoperability and effective maintenance of the context, because we modeled context metadata ontology, but also context information ontology using OWL. The context-awareness middleware is based on service oriented architecture, so it achieved interoperability, adaptation, and extensibility in ubiquitous computing environment. In the future, we will model application service ontology, and then develop a context-aware application framework based on the model using our context-awareness middleware. The goal of the context-aware application framework is intelligent and automatic service execution according to the context in ubiquitous computing environment.

Acknowledgement. This work was supported by Korea Research Foundation Grant (KRF-2006-005-J03803).

References

1. Dey, A.K., Abowd, G.D.: Towards a Better Understanding of Context and Context-Awareness. In: Workshop on The What, Who, Where, When, and How of Context-Awareness (CHI 2000), April 3, 2000, The Hague, The Netherlands (2000)
2. Gruber, T.: A Translation Approach to Portable Ontology Specification. Knowledge Acquisition Journal 5, 199–220 (1993)
3. Huhns, M.N., Singh, M.P.: Service-Oriented Computing: Key Concepts and Principles. IEEE Internet Computing 09(1), 75–81 (2005)
4. Salber, D., Dey, A.K., Abowd, G.D.: The Context Toolkit: Aiding the Development of Context-Enabled Applications. In: CHI'99, May 1999, pp. 15–20 (1999)
5. Roman, M., Hess, C., Cerqueira, R., Ranganat, A., Campbell, R.H., Nahrstedt, K.: Gaia: A Middleware Infrastructure to Enable Active Spaces. IEEE Pervasive Computing, 74–83 (2002)
6. Gu, T., Pung, H.K., Zhang, D.Q.: A Service-Oriented Middleware for Building Context-Aware Services. Elsevier Journal of Network and Computer Applications (JNCA) 28(1), 1–18 (2005)
7. Chen, H.: An Intelligent Broker Architecture for Pervasive Context-Aware Systems, Ph.D. Dissertation, University of Maryland, Baltimore Country (December 2004)

On the Design, Deployment and Use of Ubiquitous Systems

R.S. Sohan and R.K. Harle

Computer Laboratory, University of Cambridge, UK
firstname.lastname@cl.cam.ac.uk

Abstract. Increasingly advanced ubiquitous systems are becoming possible through advances in technology. This paper reviews the design and deployment of two technologies across an office space of 550m^2 to form a pervasive smart environment. The first technology provides ubiquitous location awareness, using ultrasonic tags, and the second provides a pervasive input/output device in the form of an advanced, networked telephone. The paper identifies issues within both deployments and looks at the subsequent usage of both systems. The need for especially high dependability in pervasive smart environments is noted, alongside the need to design with affordances and to include novel feedback channels to the user. The issue of how to select a deployment site is raised, together with the need for maximal logging of events, faults and usage.

In analysing usage, we find repetitive trends including novelty periods when users court new applications and smart devices, group-based adoption of services, and an advantage in deploying with a large number of diverse applications. Users take to the technologies well, but must expend great effort in customising them and interest wanes.

1 Introduction

The Ubiquitous Computing paradigm [1] lends itself to a world of pervasive devices and systems, working in harmony to create smart environments. Research into relevant technologies continues apace, but tends to concentrate on specific technical issues, providing proof-of-concept devices and prototypes that are shown to have the *potential* to achieve the goals rather than actually realising them. It is rare to find smart devices deployed into a wide-area environment that is used by people external to their development. Such deployments are difficult and expensive to achieve, but necessary to define the requirements of this computing paradigm—it is difficult, for example, to predict just how users will respond to and interact with innovative pervasive systems that are so different from their traditional counterparts. To progress, there is a need to produce studies that better approximate the life cycle of a ubiquitous system: its design, its deployment, and its use over time.

This paper looks at the design, deployment and subsequent usage of two components of a smart office. The first is a high-accuracy ultrasonic location system (the "Bat system") that provides real-time location-awareness within the smart space. The second is a series of networked communication devices ("broadband phones") that provide ubiquitous inputs and outputs. Both have been deployed within an office environment of

J. Indulska et al. (Eds.): UIC 2007, LNCS 4611, pp. 963–972, 2007.

approximately $550m^2$ and have undergone iterative developments both in design and deployment. The systems have been available to users of the space for many months and their usage has been monitored. The goal is to document experiences and highlight those aspects where designers of smart environment should concentrate their efforts.

The remainder of this paper is structured as follows: Section 2 introduces the components in greater detail, Section 3 looks at issues of their design and deployment before generalising to a series of design criteria, Section 4 examines the usage of the systems since deployment and Section 5 concludes.

2 The Technologies

2.1 The Bat System: Location Awareness

The Bat system is a real-time location system for wearable, active tags known as 'Bats'. Bats use a combination of ultrasound and narrow-band radio to create an indoor time-of-flight system capable of locating to within 3cm 95% of the time [2].

The system uses a dense distribution of ultrasonic receivers embedded throughout the ceiling of the space. A Bat is worn on a necklace and emits ultrasonic pulses towards the ceiling when so instructed by a centralised component over a 433MHz radio channel. The radio signals (moving at the speed of light) are assumed to travel instantaneously relative to the ultrasonic pulses (travelling at the speed of sound, 330m/s). Thus the ceiling receivers are able to estimate the time delay between sending the radio signal and receiving ultrasonic pulses to a high precision. The quoted accuracy of the system is achieved through a high density distribution that ensures redundancy within the time-of-flight data sets.

The system uses arrays of precisely-located receivers installed in the ceiling. The deployment of the system in 2002 consisted of 409 receivers distributed across approximately $550m^2$. Receivers were tested on a room-by-room basis before being integrated into the connection fabric and at every stage regression tests were run against the server and middleware to ensure location sightings were correct and the system was functioning as specified.

The system feeds time-of-flight data collected by the ceiling receivers into a centralised server that coalesces, records and updates the Bat locations. This data is further input to an event-based middleware known as SPIRIT [3, 4] that provides common functionality such as spatial indexing. Applications interact with the data interface using CORBA [5].

2.2 The Broadband Phones: Ubiquitous Output/Input

The broadband phone system refers to a hardware-software coupling consisting of a number of phone-like devices connected via a network to a centralised software server running on a conventional computer.

The hardware was prototyped by AT&T Laboratories Research, Cambridge and was designed as a communications platform that could take advantage of the increasing ubiquity of broadband data connections to businesses and consumers [6]. Each Broadband Phone uses a Strong-ARM 1100 with 8MB of flash, 32MB of RAM, a colour touchscreen, 10Mbps Ethernet and a sound card—an image is shown in Figure 1. This hardware forms a *thin-client*—the phone is used purely as an input/output device, with all state and processing performed elsewhere on the network. The display, for example, simply shows a VNC [7] session (i.e. the session runs on a server with the graphics exported as a bitmap, so the phone need only know how to display an image and to forward control events).

When deployed within the University of Cambridge the hardware was adopted as a ubiquitous input/output device, and a custom software architecture, TiCL [8], was developed to handle loosely coupled thin-client networks of differing size and disparate technologies such as a broadband phone network. The TiCL architecture allows for interconnection between heterogeneous networks without sacrificing performance or autonomy of serviced clients, and has been designed to suit large scale smart environments. Its design was based on three principles:

Network Locality. Clients are assumed to be connected to servers via high-bandwidth, low-latency links (e.g. a LAN) whilst servers are interconnected via lower-bandwidth, higher-latency links (e.g. a WAN).

Abstraction. Smart environments will contain a variety of inputs and outputs and any architecture must be able to adapt. By abstracting components of the architecture we avoid technology 'lock in'.

Modularity. Smart spaces can ill afford downtime and yet must adapt over time. By keeping the architecture modular, we ensure easy extensibility and system management *without* affecting currently connected clients.

The core of the design is a single-level, loosely coupled message-passing infrastructure consisting of five basic functional units (*modules*) connected by *communication channels*, as shown in Figure 1. It is sufficient to recognise that the system is a thin-client system, but the interested reader can find more details in [8].

With respect to deployment in a large scale smart space, the use of thin-client technology and TiCL ensures that the broadband phones are resilient to common failure

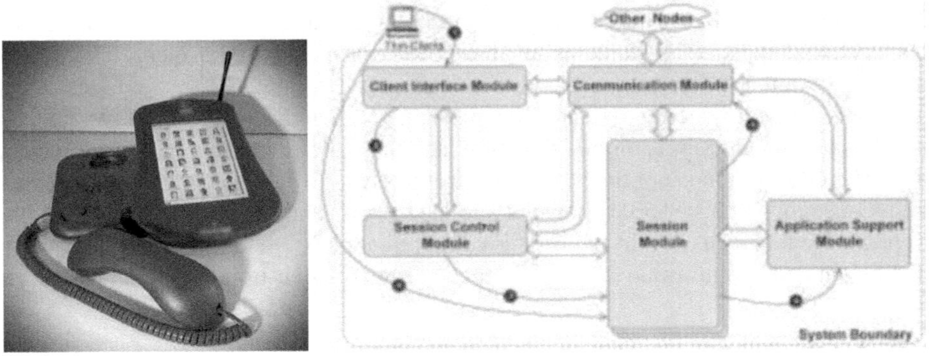

(a) A Broadband Phone (b) Core Architecture

Fig. 1.

such as network outages or application crashes. All important session data is stored on a server that is secured within the environment and properly maintained. This also decouples the physical location of the interactive device from the associated user session, allowing sessions to move from device to device.

The current deployment of 53 broadband phones and a single TiCL server took place in late 2003. Each broadband phone on the network can contact any other, allowing internal Voice-over-IP (VoIP) phone calls and data interaction between group members. However, external phone calls are not possible since the local telephony network is not VoIP-based.

In terms of applications, the phones display VNC framebuffers to a custom interface based on the QTopia [9] application platform. As such, they provide standard PDA applications (contacts, calendar, text editor, calculator, games etc) alongside custom applications used to present sensed data in the smart environment. These applications include an interface to a real-time weather station (Figure 4(a)), visual (head-shot based) user dialling, and location data derived from the deployed tracking systems.

3 Design and Deployment Issues

Since the initial deployment of the smart space there have been a variety of design changes and deployment issues. Whilst many of these are individual to the systems, generalisations can be made; in this Section we review the challenges presented and attempt to define a set of criteria to consider before deploying a smart space.

3.1 The Bat System

Deployment of the Bat system was completed before users and furniture moved into the smart space. This eased installation and configuration, but has had an unforeseen consequence: the usage of a space rarely changes and not adapting to that usage incurs a performance penalty. Here, installing receivers to give a uniform positioning coverage throughout a room resulted in an unnecessary density of receivers in areas of low use (for example, areas inaccessible because they contained large furniture or specialist machinery). Receivers in these areas would have been better deployed to increase coverage in areas of high activity.

Following deployment, it became apparent that knowledge of the system state was problematic: the system is mobile in nature, and there are few visual clues to inform a user when the system is not functioning correctly. This is a fundamental issue with pervasive systems—if a system truly melts into the background, it may not always be able to find a feedback channel to the user. Finding a feedback mode that is not needlessly distracting and yet informative remains an open research question.

3.2 The Broadband Phones

Following deployment, The broadband phones act as a portal into the world of location-awareness for the user: they describe what is happening and what conclusions the system has reached. There are few comparable modes of output for a fundamentally mobile system, and thus reliability is key. The broadband phone system caters for this requirement in a variety of ways: the server has built-in load-balancing and fail-over characteristics—the loss of a host from the server cluster allows seamless transfer of existing phone session state to alternative servers. In the extreme case of system failure, phones are programmed to minimise effects on users—for example phone conversations remain uninterrupted until termination. On the device themselves, a watchdog timer ensures instantaneous reboot and reconnection to the server in case of transient software or hardware error. The use of VNC means the phones are stateless and can be unplugged or rebooted without loss.

This design ensures that the Broadband Phone infrastructure is very dependable, but a subtlety soon emerged after deployment: the *perceived* dependability of the system was linked to the Bat system. To prevent faults within the closely-tied Bat system affecting the phone system it was necessary modify the phone system to allow degraded functionality (for example by using cached location data). This increases system complexity, but prevents cascade failure through the components of the smart environment.

The phone deployment also highlighted the degree to which affordances (used within product design to refer to whether a user *perceives* an action to be possible) are important in a large scale roll-out. The broadband phone units have affordance in their shape: the use of a phone-like casing encouraged their immediate perception as a communications device and assisted in educating new users since they felt happy to explore. Unfamiliar applications seep into users' consciousness over time as they experiment with them. The device does not look out of place in an office and this helps the smart aspect of the environment disappear into the tapestry.

With both systems, the choice of deployment site is, with hindsight, critical. A research environment, with its ill-constrained working hours and tendency to discourage large collaboration groups, is not an ideal deployment candidate. Users work independently to a large extent, and invariably a proportion of them are involved in the development of the smart system, or at least represent very technical users. Similarly, deployment scale is important: location-aware applications and communication devices excel in environments where space is sufficiently great to deter direct person-to-person meetings; a 550m^2 contiguous space on one floor is not sufficient to achieve this. Careful choice of deployment site should allow testing of scalability claims, access to a wide range of users at different technical levels, and may encourage novel applications.

3.3 Summary of Major Design and Deployment Criteria

To assist the construction of future systems, we highlight the major considerations in the design of a smart environment component, derived from the previous discussion. Whilst many of these criteria apply equally well to any general system engineering, we have found their consideration to be a prerequisite for smart environments, rather than optional.

Build for dependability. Service outages and unpredictable reliability encourage users away from the system (permanently!). User confidence in a complex pervasive system is very important and their perception of the dependability dictates whether or not the system remains used and therefore useful. There is also a requirement for associated systems to handle faults equally seamlessly.

Design for space usage rather than physical space. If the usage of a particular space is known, it is best to design for that usage rather than a generic usage. The loss in flexibility is compensated for by the increase in performance and irregularity of significant change.

Centralisation is acceptable. Most of the processing done in pervasive systems consists of simple data aggregation, manipulation, distribution and storage. Coupling the comparatively few resource requirements of such systems with the ever increasing speed and throughput capabilities of commodity hardware makes centralised designs a viable option.

Maximise the feedback channels. Our experiences with both the location and broadband phone systems have emphasised the importance of including as many feedback paths to users as possible. Smart environments cannot guarantee standard input/output devices (computer displays, keyboards, etc), but must be able to provide feedback at any moment and in any circumstance.

Following design, ideals for deployment are readily identifiable:

Choose the site carefully. What is the demographic of users in the space? Is it large enough to test scalability? How easy is it to access? Will the aesthetics be impacted?

Deploy Incrementally. An incremental deployment allows for better validation with thorough testing at a series of scales. The scalability of the system may be more accurately measured, validated and tuned in accordance with the incremental load increase. This approach also produces better error tolerance since users recognise the system may not be fully functional and often react favourably to their choice as a test candidate

Deploy to Redeploy. No matter how well-thought the design, it is likely that the system will have to be rebuilt in the future to address new, unanticipated uses or to integrate new technologies.

4 Usage

Figure 2(a) shows the usage of the Bat system for typical users over 27 months; usage is represented by averaging the number of sightings within a 24-hour period across each month. Traces such as these clearly show novelty periods: each time a major new application was rolled out, a corresponding rise in location use was registered, before usage fell back to prior levels. The major peaks in 2(a) can be attributed to the initial system roll-out (01/2003), the initial phone deployment (11/2003) and a major software update for the phones (10/2004). For designers of smart environments, this has an important consequence: users will court new applications, but long-term adoption is not guaranteed. Applications can be used to attract users and encourage exploration of the system and therefore the greater the diversity of applications available from the initial roll-out, the greater the system adoption.

Figure 2(b) presents a histogram of the number of unique users seen daily in the smart space across three months in 2004, chosen to come after any novelty period. It clearly shows high variability in the long term adoption of Bats. In response to a survey, 42.1% of those issued with a Bat indicated that they wear their Bat daily, whilst 31.5% hardly

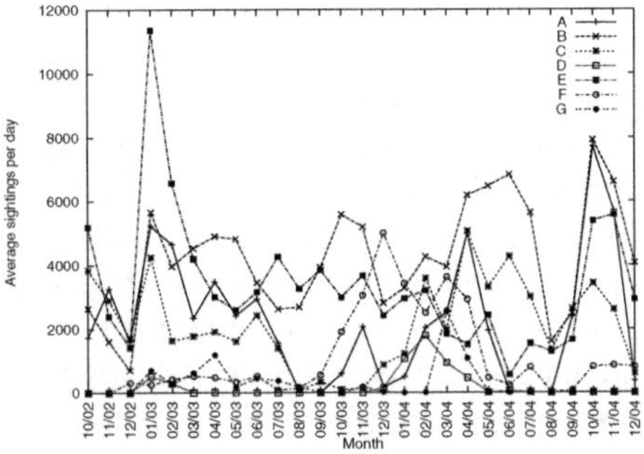

(a) Logged system usage over 27 months

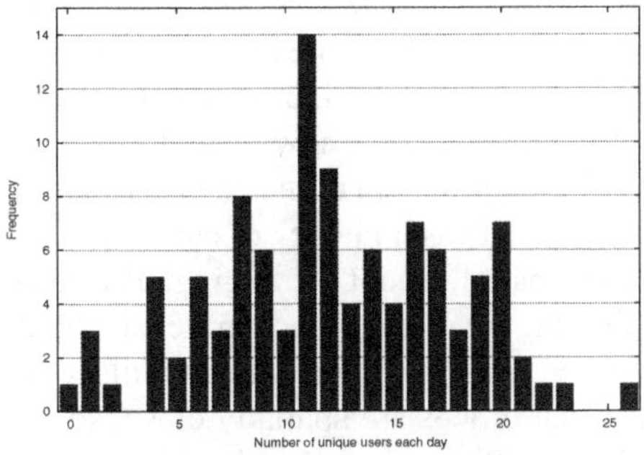

(b) Unique daily users in 2004

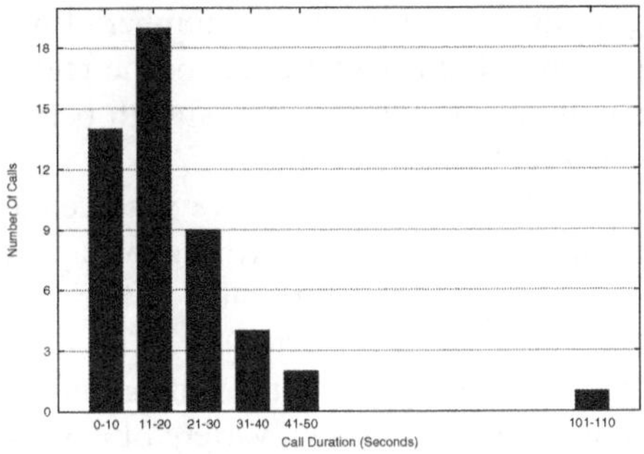

(c) Phone call durations

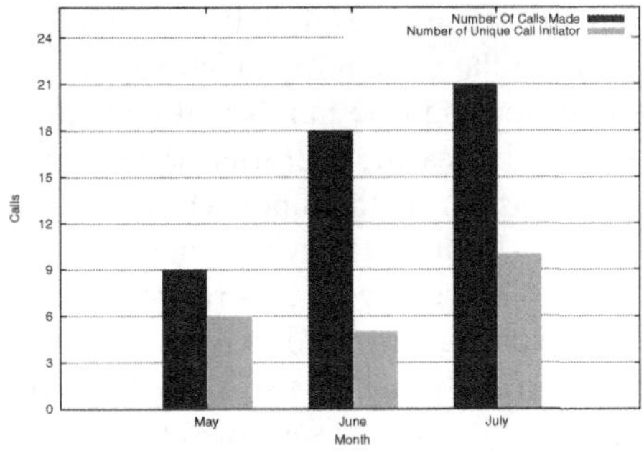

(d) Total calls made vs. number of unique callers

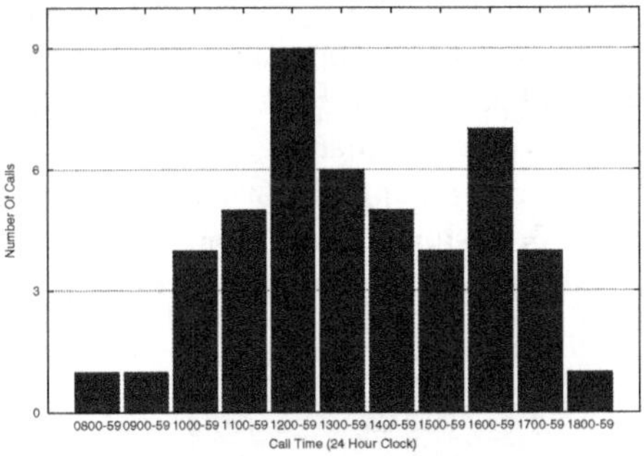

(e) Call time-of-day

Fig. 2.

ever. When asked what would encourage adoption, users cited more applications and a need for their colleagues to wear their Bat more —this is an example of a pervasive application vicious cycle [10], whereby pervasive applications are devalued by reduced system usage, and this devaluation itself encourages abandonment of the system and hence further devaluation for remaining users.

The broadband phones have tended to be adopted by small groups for the purposes of audio communications. The lack of external call capability undoubtedly weakened the use of the phones, but since the laboratory has a policy of one telephone per room rather than per desk, the broadband phones offer direct person-to-person contact within the research group. Figure 2(c) illustrates the call durations observed over the recorded period. The results show virtually all calls are concluded within a minute, hinting toward use for information and confirmation rather than discussion. Also of interest is the result that a vast majority of calls are between 0-20 seconds, showing similar behaviour to text-based instant messaging. The relatively small number of people initiating voice calls (Figure 2(d)) demonstrates the tendency for specific people to adopt the technology for direct communication, whilst others do not. We attribute this empirically to the fact that offices are spatially close, so many users default to physically moving to the relevant office to communicate. A similar barrier was also observed for the location-aware system, hinting that a truly grand-scale deployment may encourage greater use of both system types. Finally, it is interesting to note that although the number of people using the system remained approximately constant, the actual usage of the phones was increasing (the number of calls more than doubled over the three month period) showing increasing user trust and utility with respect to the system.

In considering the times when calls were made (Figure 2(e)), we have observed the tendency for usage to peak at lunchtimes and at the end of a typical day, suggesting that people use the device to arrange social gatherings rather than for collaborative work (for which we have informally observed physical presence is preferred).

When analysing the use of the broadband phones for non-telephony applications, we have found a greater sustained usage. The phones make available a variety of applications which we have classified into five areas: *Information* applications display information and are typically not interactive (e.g. a clock, weather status); *Location-based* applications use location data from the Bat system (e.g. searchable graphical map); *PIM* applications are standard organisational applications (a to-do list etc); *Gaming* applications include simple graphical games; whilst the *Miscellaneous* application category is used for all other applications (e.g. calculator).

Figure 3(a) shows the usage of all applications that were executed at least once over the analysis period. Figure 3(b) shows the number of invocations for each recorded application over the analysis period. As indicated by the graph, usage is fairly constant

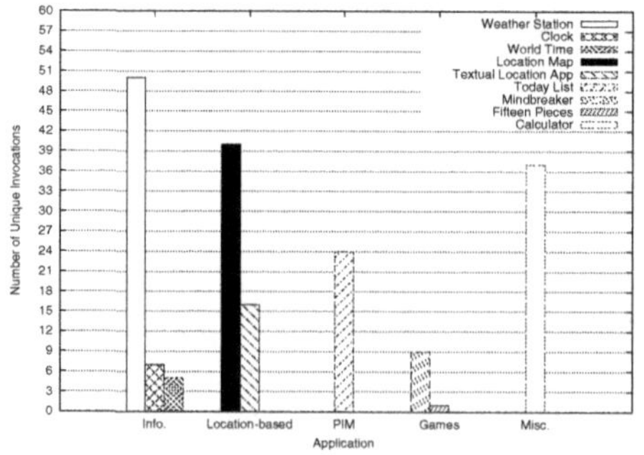

(a) Applications run over three month period, organised by category

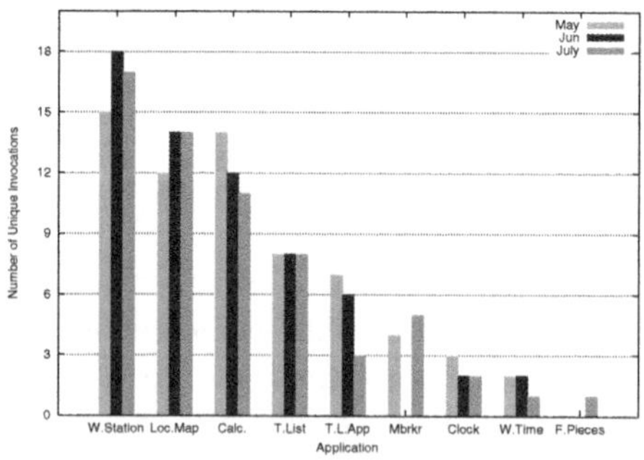

(b) Monthly breakdown of application usage

Fig. 3.

over the same period, demonstrating that users form preferences for certain applications. It is interesting to note that out of the total 31 applications available on the system, just 9 were used over the analysis period. This highlights user behaviour in preferring applications from which they perceive they will draw utility—other applications were not even investigated. From those applications that were run, the most common were those acting as passive information displays, notably a weather map (Figure 4(a)) which converts the weather statistics collected by the weather station [11] into a graphical format and the location map (Figure 4(b)) which integrates with the location system to provide real-time tracking of all users wearing Bats.

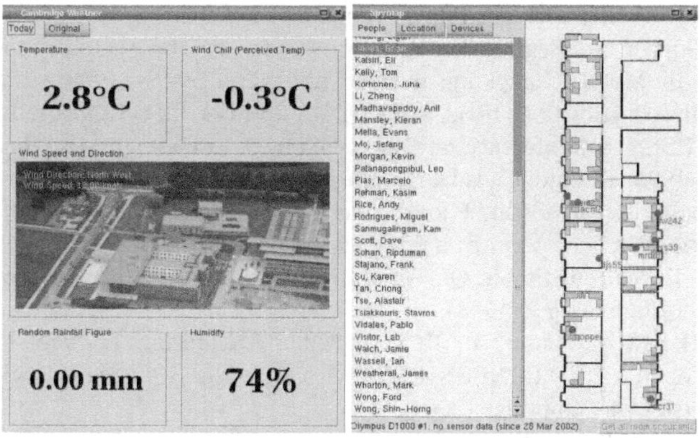

(a) Weather Station (b) Location Map

Fig. 4.

5 Conclusions

Research into smart environments is often highly innovative and challenges the traditional concepts of computing. However, this novelty complicates the validation of any system design: just how will users react to a ubiquitous system deployment? How will they use the smart services, and for how long?

This paper has looked at the issues in design and deployment of two mature systems that contribute to a smart space in daily use. It has drawn on practical experience gained in designing and deploying both systems to emphasise the challenges concerning the design, deployment and use of such systems across a multitude of users. The design phase of a smart component should: consider affordances in physical design; analyse usage of the deployment space to define requirements; be centralised where appropriate; maximise feedback to the user.

Similarly, the deployment should: use a carefully chosen site to best evaluate the design; be deployed incrementally; deploy to redeploy; take detailed logs.

The experiences presented here highlight that smart spaces demand dependability and tight integration, with easy system extension from the outset of the design process. Long term usage is hard to predict, whilst short term usage tends to dissipate following an explosion of interest. Technology, then, is only part of the story in designing a smart space: user studies will be important and the involvement of users in the design process seems invaluable.

References

1. Weiser, M.: The Computer for the 21st Century. Scientific American (1991)
2. Addlesee, M., Curwen, R., Hodges, S., Newman, J., Steggles, P., Ward, A., Hopper, A.: Implementing A Sentient Computing System. IEEE Computer 34 (2001)
3. Adly, N., Steggles, P., Harter, A.: SPIRIT: a Resource Database for Mobile Users. In: Proceedings of ACM CHI'97 Workshop on Ubiquitous Computing (1997)
4. Harter, A., Hopper, A., Steggles, P., Ward, A., Webster, P.: The Anatomy of a Context-Aware Application. In: Mobile Computing and Networking, pp. 59–68 (1999)
5. Martin, B.: Introduction to CORBA and CORBA services. In: USENIX (ed.) Proceedings of the Second USENIX Conference on Object-Oriented Technologies and Systems (COOTS), June 17–21, 1996, Toronto, Canada, Berkeley, CA, USA (USENIX) (1996)
6. AT&T Laboratories, Broadband Phone Project, `http://www.uk.research.att.com/bbphone`
7. Richardson, T., Stafford-Fraser, Q., Wood, K.R., Hopper, A.: Virtual Network Computing. IEEE Internet Computing 2 (1998)
8. Sohan, R., Harter, A., Harter, A.: TiCL: A Server Architecture For Thin-Client Networks. Technical Report CUED.F-INFENG.TR-493, Cambridge University Engineering Department, University Of Cambridge (2004)
9. Incorporated, T.: QTopia (WhitePaper)
10. Harle, R.K., Hopper, A.: Deploying and Evaluating a Location-Aware System. In: MobiSys 2005 (2005)
11. AT&T Laboratories, Cambridge Weather Station, `http://www.uk.research.att.com/cgi-bin/weathergauges-html-cgi`

Performance Evaluation of 3-Hierarchical Resource Management Model with Grid Service Architecture

Eun-Ha Song[1], Laurence T. Yang[2], Sung-Kook Han[1], and Young-Sik Jeong[1,*]

[1] Department of Computer Engineering, Wonkwang University
344-2 Shinyong-Dong, Iksan, 570-749, Korea
{ehsong,skhan,ysjeong}@wku.ac.kr
[2] Department of Computer Science, St. Francis Xavier University
Antigonish, NS, B2G 2W5, Canada
lyang@stfx.ca

Abstract. The paper constructs a 3–hierarchical resource management model (3-HRMM) in order to adapt to variability of grid resources. We propose resource brokering strategy and adaptive performance task allocation algorithm on 3-HRMM. Resource brokering strategy improves performance through brokering of the application and LRM(Local Resource Manager), a component of 3-HRMM, by *performance index* and resolves a fault caused by virtual organization by using LRM *virtual observer*. Under performance evaluation through real-time resource monitoring, adaptive performance task allocation algorithm supports load balancing and fault tolerance. This paper proves feasibility of grid service through the implementation of 3-hierarchical resource management model(3-HRMM), and it shows some results of performance evaluation based on its by using two applications such as image rendering and fractal image processing.

1 Introduction

Grid computing environment must be able to use grid resource that users request; it should also, if an user submits a certain job specification, provides resource sharing regardless of a position and the type of the resource as if the environment is run on a single system. Combining heterogeneous and variable resources, grid efficiently manages information for resource management[1,2].

Among structure models for grid resource management, hierarchical model has interdependent relationship between resource provider and resource requester[3]. Currently, many grid systems like Globus[4], Legion Ninf, NetSolve and GridIMF[5] are based on such model. Globus is one of the well known grid related researches. Globus is not an inseparable single system, but is a system that provides various services which grid requires as an independent element. Elements of Globus may be similar to this paper constructs in terms of providing a function that integrates systems that differ from both hardware and software point of view, minimizing performance degradation, However, Globus is ineffective from metadata management point of view in

* Corresponding author.

J. Indulska et al. (Eds.): UIC 2007, LNCS 4611, pp. 973–982, 2007.

that it has uniform transforming and transmitting period regardless of distinct characteristics of data, thus impeding overall grid performance[6,7].

This paper reconfigures passive and active hierarchical model components into 3-hierarchical resource management model(3-HRMM) in terms of their function and management. 3-HRMM provides an active combination of grid resource and grid application. Optimal virtual organization selection mechanism provides performance improvement and executability of applications. LRM auto-recovery mechanism supports availability of a service when fault or error of resource occurs. Adaptive performance task allocation algorithm's performance is improved due to load balancing. Virtual observer periodically receives metadata information included in a certain local resource and considers replicated computation due to certain fault by running a scheduler. Real-time resource monitoring and resource visualization intuitively interprets the flow and status sensor of resource. Having minimum code debugging and minimal relationship with its infrastructure, application proxy replies requests from certain applications. Finally, this paper analyzes adaptability and executability of grid resource by applying two applications on 3-HRMM.

2 3-Hierarchical Resource Management Model(3-HRMM)

3-HRMM categorized into Resource Provider(RP), Local Resource Manager(LRM), and Global Resource Manger(GRM) depending on the intention and objectives of participation. A following fig. 1 shows structure of 3-HRMM and its control flow[5].

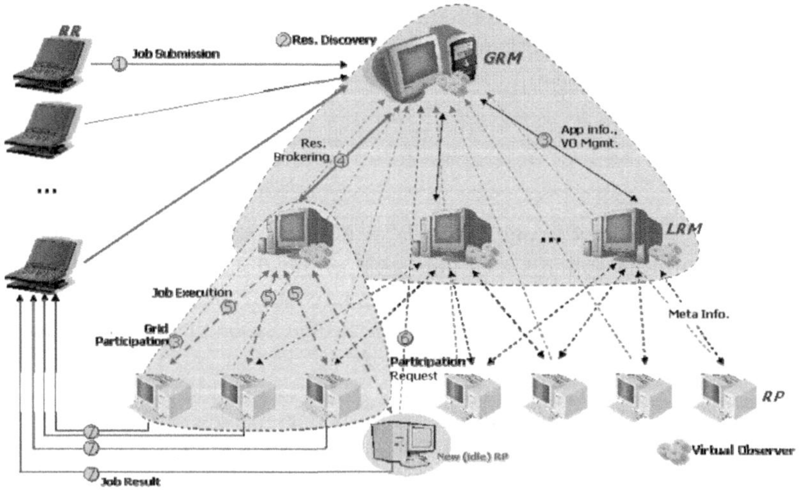

Fig. 1. 3-HRMM framework and control flow

RR is the end user of grid computing environment, requesting a solution to grand challenge problem by sharing distributed resources. It is capable of requesting multiple grid applications simultaneously, and for each job it sends network positioning information and job specification in the form of a parameter. RR provides a

Table 1. Cockpit functions of an adaptive resource management

Component	Module	Remark
RR	RR UI	-Downloading an applet for interactive with GRM -Registering to grid system through RMI
	App. UI	-Interface exhibiting application running result -Interface includes job specification of an application
	App. Information Provider	-Provides task unit (application specification)
	RR Protocol Data Maker/Parser	-Alteration to enable reading command, event, and query and analysis of a protocol able
	Task Information	-Boolean-type task table that shows application's total task size and task results
	Task Results Gathering/Verify	-Gathering job results from RPs, and sending Application UI -Visualization of progress rate and running time
GRM	GRM UI	-User event and visualization module -GRM State Transition Frame, LRM/RP Hierarchical View, LRM/RR Join View
	Connection Brokering	-Brokering components' initial connection -Creating RR Entry, LRM Entry in vector-table-formed and managing in the form of a list -Sending LRM list to RP
	RR/LRM Join Brokering	-Connection brokering between RR and optimized executable LRM
	LRM Virtual Observer	-A proxy for transferring status information and updated information of LRM
	GRM Protocol Data Maker/Parser	-Alteration to enable reading command, event, and query and analysis of a protocol able
LRM	LRM UI	-Management frame for connection and binding status, event and protocol, Monitoring information visualization
	Process Connection	-Connecting RR and RP
	Resource Factor	-Performance examination of RP by recording its metadata information
	Scheduler Manager	-Requesting scheduler
	Scheduler	-Control task job allocation and re-allocation
	RP Virtual Observer	-Managing updated information of RP -Sensing LRM's performance and status
	LRM Protocol Data Maker/Parser	-Alteration to enable reading command, event, and query and analysis of a protocol able
RR	Resource Info DLL	-Extracting RP's metadata -Performance Data Helper(PDH) library
	Resource Broker	-Declaring a native method at JIN to use Resource Info DLL
	Resource Register	-Extracting resource information -Separating static resource information from dynamic resource information
	Processor Manager	-Mediating scheduling method -Creating process (dynamic/static)
	Process Proxy	-Mediating processor for task processing
	RP Protocol Data Maker/Parser	-Alteration to enable reading command, event, and query and analysis of a protocol able

transparency, that is, a submission of jobs regardless of position of computational resource, availability, and access method. Being a super manager on 3-HRMM, GRM is also a resource brokering proxy, connecting grid users and remote resource. GRM manages the connection between components by providing their common interfaces; moreover, it also authorizes a maximum level of usage. GRM periodically responds to the availability of the entire system and its fault tolerance through monitoring LRM's status information. LRM manages RPs from each site, and is delegated to perform a job allocation and to mine necessary information in order to carry out various job requests from RR to GRM. LRM also selects RPs based on resource discovery, mediates connections between RPs and RR, and performs core scheduling between remote resources. RP is a set, of which function contains three following modules: collecting metadata information, transferring executable resource, and computing, sending the final results. These functions of four components of adaptive resource management framework in grid service architecture were shown the table 1 as followed;

3 Adaptive Resource Management on 3-HRMM

3.1 Resource Brokering

Resource Brokering connects between grid users and resources and controls the connection; it can be categorized into either connection brokering rule or job brokering rule.

Connection brokering rule has four major functions: user access control, user authorization, and job submission and monitoring. RR entry is automatically created by RR's connection request, and includes additional information such as image files or data files according to an application specification included in RR. GRM searches LRM by RR entry information and name of the application. GRM implements a job brokering service when suitable LRM is found, and registers on the RR waiting list when such LRM does not exist. RP is disconnected after sending a DLL file for gaining LRM list and system hardware property information through GRM. LRM creates LRM entry by outside connection requests, and LRM virtual observer is dynamically created in order to monitor LRM itself. GRM manages to a fault that is originated from unexpected or intentional system error by saving LRM's updated information and status information and tracing a log file.

Job brokering rule follows four factors when selecting virtual organization.

- Step 1 : Filter about can provide Application
- Step 2 : Filter about idle state
- Step 3 : Get Application power
- Step 4 : LRM Performance Index

Grid computing environment is a virtual space where connection and disconnection of resource can be done with great latitude[7]. This paper refers to adaptability of LRM that operates as a mediator between requested job and resource provider. LRM auto-recovery strategy guarantees availability of a service by detecting LRM fault in real-time and receiving substitute resource from other virtual organization. Fig. 2 is a demonstration of a LRM_0 fault where RR finishes rest of the request task with new LRM_n.

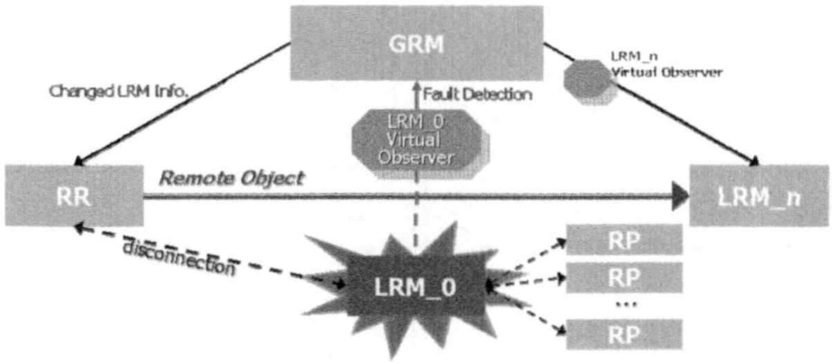

Fig. 2. LRM auto-recovery strategy

RR must maintain continuous usage of resource until the manual disconnection from grid system. Also RR should be able to use resource connected to LRM despite the change in application specification. GRM detects faults with LRM sensor and information recording LRM virtual observer. When a fault of a certain LRM is detected, GRM searches LRM in idle state. RR sends remote reference object, an address referenced to a new LRM, and task table, thus adaptively initiating a computation by the new LRM. If new LRM search should be failed, RR goes into wait state, and it is put up on a waiting list. RR's task table and remote object reference do not carry on replicated computation even when LRM fault occurs.

3.2 Task Allocation Algorithms

Task allocation algorithm of 3-HRMM can be categorized into either static, dynamic or adaptive according to resource management.

Table 2. Task Allocation Algorithms of 3-HRMM

Classification	Task Allocation Algorithms	Performance and Reallocation Factor	Num. of RP
Static	UTA(Uniform Task Allocation)		Fixed
	CPTA(CPU Performance Task Allocation)	-MFLOPS	
	SPTA(Static Performance Task Allocation)	-MFLOPS	
Dynamic	DPTA(Dynamic Performance Task Allocation)	-CPU Speed -Job History	Variable
Adaptive	APTA(Adaptive Performance Task Allocation)	-CPU Speed -CPU Usage -Proportional Factor -Realtime State Monitoring	

UTA is an algorithm that uniformly allocates tasks regardless of RP's performance. It does not consider RP's status and reallocation does not take place. CPTA reallocates tasks according to the result of Linpack benchmarking RP performance. It shows faster running time than UTA does; however, RP's performance is static while the task is running. SPTA has RP performance-based reallocation; it reallocates a task that has been allocated a low-performance RP to an RP that has already completed a

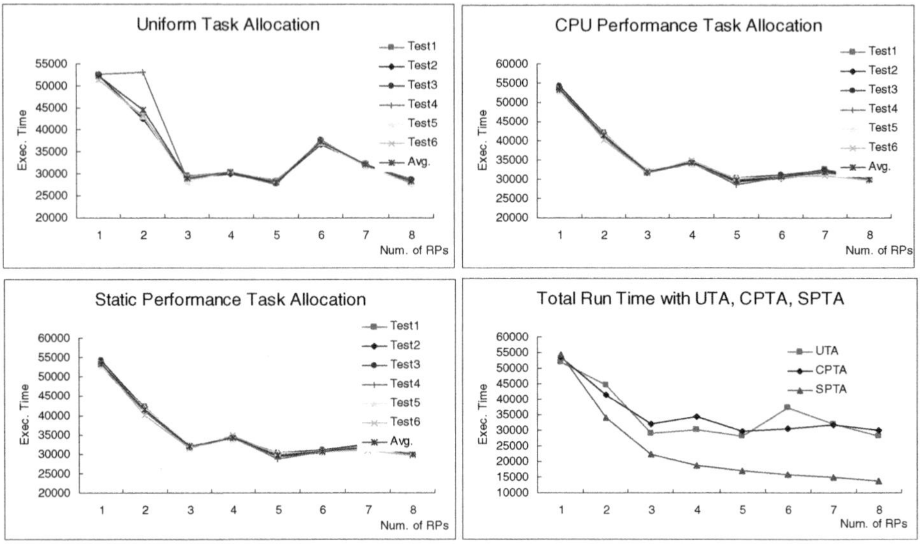

Fig. 3. Performance evaluation is accomplished by averaging six measurements of the capacity of static task allocation algorithms

task, thus exhibiting fast processing ability. Performance evaluation shown in fig. 3 is a comparison between static task allocation algorithms.

However, SPTA makes a decision based on the initial result of RP performance benchmarking during reallocation; therefore, it cannot respond to the varying RP performance or status.

DPTA while processing a task takes performance variation of RP and its participation and disconnection into consideration; it reallocates tasks based on CPU speed and job history. Fig. 4 shows the capacity results in regards to the cases where a certain RP cannot execute tasks due to system fault of its where new RP participate in the task processing.

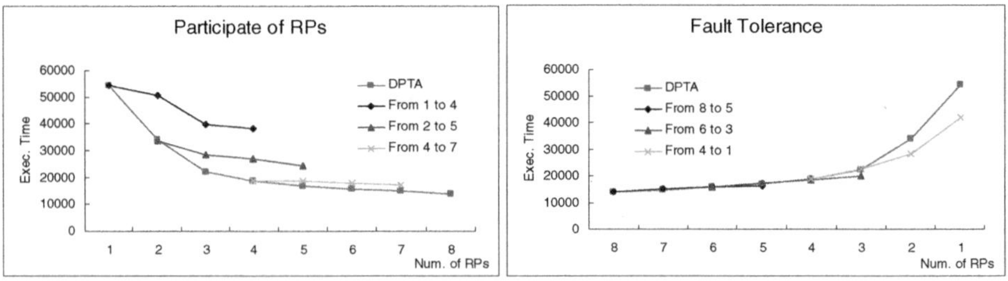

Fig. 4. Performance evaluation according to participation and disconnection of RPs

APTA is not based on simple physical number, but based on real-time monitoring information when determining RP's performance. Since the effect of CPU usage by users and internal system on total processing time can vary, the standard value that measures RP's performance is applied by defining a PF(Proportional Factor). PF can be obtained by calculating RP's task processing time based on its CPU usage, while two identical tasks are run on two identical RPs. If CPU speed of RP is defined as $\{sRP_0, sRP_1, \cdots sRP_{NumRP-1}\}$, expected value of total CPU usage as $cpuUsageAvg$ during reallocation, and the expected value of job processor usage as, a performance value of RP_i can be calculated from the following equation:

$$RP_i Performance = (100 - (cpuUsageAvg - jobUsageAvg)) \times PF \times sRP_i \times 0.01$$

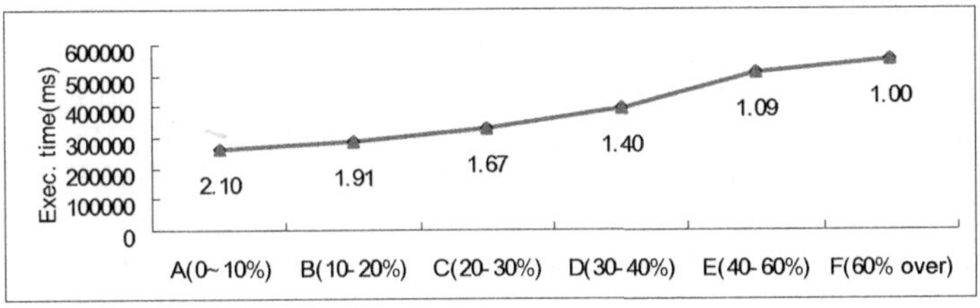

Fig. 5. Segmented proportional factor

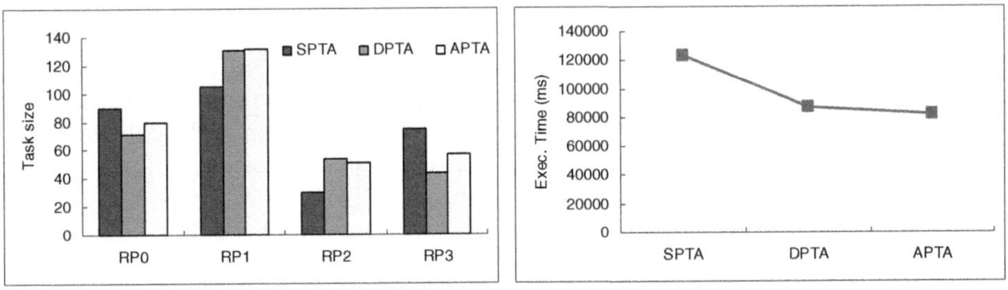

Fig. 6. Performance evaluation between task allocation algorithm of 3-HRMM

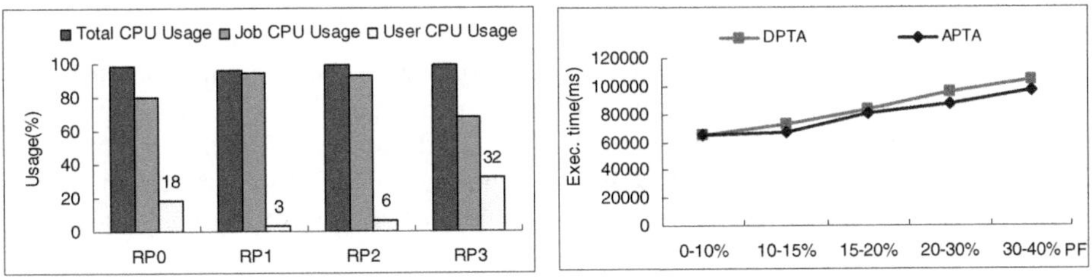

Fig. 7. Comparison of RPs' CPU usage and task allocation algorithm according to user CPU usage

Performance evaluation shown in fig. 6 is a comparison between task allocation algorithms of 3-HRMM which constructs virtual organization with four RPs that has different performance levels. In a case of DPTA and APTA, there exists an improvement in performance and a change in task size. APTA decreases the total execution time by efficient reallocation based on RP's performance variation. Fig. 7 shows the result of calculating, based on the total CPU usage, expected value of a Job CPU usage used in processing a task and a user CPU usage independently used by the users measured periodically. Because of the relative decrease in job CPU usage among total CPU usage, the higher the user CPU usage is the greater effect on the total running time it will have. And, Fig. 8 shows the result of user CPU usage randomly imposed and applied on a task allocation algorithm.

3.3 Resource Monitoring and Visualization

3-HRMM provides visualization in multiple forms through real-time monitoring of a manager and a system designer. Monitoring information visualization is provided in terms of GRM and LRM. Monitoring element of GRM is that LRM entry and RR entry information is transmitted to the view. GRM provides LRM/RR Join View and LRM/RP Hierarchical View. LRM/RR Join View provides a relationship between RR and LRM as a table component, and specific information on selected row of the table is printed as a text component. LRM/RR Hierarchical View provides node structure of the entire grid system according to its hierarchy. RR monitoring affects on LRM scheduling and task allocation algorithm, and responds to the computation fault and its efficiency by measuring status change. If RP metadata were updated, it accepts status information through RP virtual observer and sends the metadata to RP Entry. LRM provides five views. RP Information View shows selected RP metadata information in the forms of a progress bar and a text component, analyzes extracted hardware information, and applies to the RP performance evaluation. RP Real-time Table View shows information of every RP that is updated periodically in a form of table. RP State Graph View shows CPU usage and user CPU usage of every RP as a real-time graph. Connection Graph View observes RP task process status connected to LRM. RP Network Information View shows total length of running time of RP tasks and a ratio between network transferring times in the form of a bar graph.

4 Application Implementation

Grid resource management system requires structure separation in order to obtain minimum relations between various grid application specifications. Containing core functions of 3-HRMM, application proxy is a fixed common API that provides grid service to a certain application. It defines a plug-in, which is to approach to a certain application, by application-name, while application template dynamically creates an object.

This paper uses an application that requires an absence of relations between the tasks which also require greater number of computations for small amount of data. Fig. 8–(a) is an example of Mandelbrot fractal image processing which follows LSM coloring method. Faults occurred in two RPs out of four RPs during the process, but reallocation occurred by APTA method, finishing the task. Fig. 8–(b) is an example of rendering image generation. During the task that has been run by two RPs, performance change and new RP participation occurred, thus initiating reallocation.

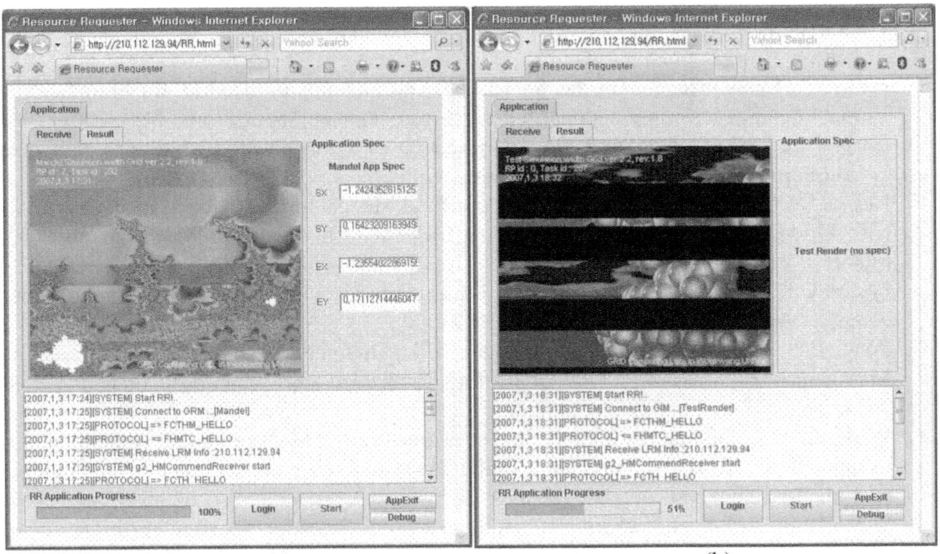

(a) (b)

Fig. 8. Examples of grid application

5 Conclusions

This paper defines 3-HRMM in order to enable efficient sharing, extensibility of grid resource, and systematic management of resource usage. Due to characteristics of grid resource, the components are functionally categorized into GRM, LRM, RP, and RR. Resource brokering exhibits a performance improvement by optimal virtual organization selection based on performance index of an application, and decreases in communication overhead and fault in virtual organization were responded with LRM auto-recovery method by LRM virtual observer. APTA also exhibits in terms of resource variability a performance improvement by task allocation algorithm which is applied with PR performance value based on resource monitoring–APTA supports load balancing and fault tolerance. Resource monitoring provides reliability of resource information collection through metadata extraction and analysis, and resource discovery that satisfies users' requests. Feasibility of the proposed grid service is proven through two different example applications.

Acknowledgement

"This work was supported by the Korea Research Foundation Grant funded by the Korean Government(MOEHRD)" (KRF-2006-521-D00387), in which main calculations were performed by using the supercomputing resource of the Korea Institute of Science and Technology Information(KISTI).

References

1. Foster, C., Kesselman, S., Tueche, S.: Tueche: The Anatomy of the Grid: Enabling Scalable Virtual Organizations. International Journal Supercomputer Applications 15(3) (2001)
2. Chapin, S., Clement, M., Snell, Q.: A Grid Resource Management Architecture. Strawman 1, Grid Forum Scheduling Working Group (1999)
3. Buyya, R., Chapin, S., DiNucci, D.: Architectural Models for Resource Management in the Grid. Grid Computing GIRD 2000. In: First IEEE/ACM International Workshop, pp. 20–33 (2000)
4. Foster, C.K.: Globus: A Metacomputing Infrastructure Toolkit. International Journal supercomputer Applications 11(2), 115–128 (1997)
5. Song, E.H., Jeon, Y.S., Han, S.K., Jeong, Y.S.: Hierarchical and Dynamic Information Management Framework on Grid Computing. Embedded and Ubiquitous Computing 151–161 (2006)
6. Waheed, W.S., George, J., Yan, J.: An Infrastructure for Monitoring and Management in Computational Grids. In: Proceedings of the 2000 Conference on Languages, Compiles, and Runtime Systems (2000)
7. Subhlok, J., Lieu, P., Lowekamp, B.: Automatic Node Selection for High Performance Applications on Networks. In: Proceedings of the Seventh ACM SIGPLAN Symposium on Principles and Practice of Parallel Programming, pp. 163–172. ACM Press, New York (1999)

A Study on Ubiquitous Intelligent Healthcare Systems in Home Service Aggregation Business Model

Mun-Suck Jang[1], Kwang-Sik Shin[1], Eung-Huyk Lee[2], and Sang-Bang Choi[1]

[1] Dept. of Electronic Engineering, Inha Univ., Incheon, Korea
sirius93@paran.com, {KwangSik,sangbang}@inha.ac.kr
http://can.inha.ac.kr/index1.html
[2] Dept. of Electronic Engineering, Korea Polytechnic Univ., Gyeonggi-Do, Korea
ehlee@kpu.ac.kr
http://www.roboticslab.co.kr

Abstract. This study proposes a ubiquitous intelligent healthcare system that can be applied to a Home Service Aggregation business model. This system consists of a wireless network system to collect data and a sensor module, which measures body fat, blood pressure, quantity of exercise, and SPO2. In addition, an HSA server is configured to integrate user certification and security, VOD, and power usage information. A healthcare server collects user health information and sends the data in case of emergency to a doctor or guardian in order to achieve a ubiquitous intelligent healthcare system.

1 Introduction

A Ubiquitous Intelligent Healthcare (UI-Healthcare) system allows users to check their health conditions freely using wireless internet without limitations in time and place in order to cope rapidly with emergencies. In order to achieve this, it is necessary to measure patient conditions precisely using multiple sensors located on the patient's body rather than using a single sensor. In addition, the data measured using sensors is integrated and filtered to identify a patient's condition. A mobile diagnosing device produced by a single sensor is used as a personal sensor module to monitor health conditions in the home or office and to assess and report these conditions. Furthermore, a mobile diagnosing device can be applied as a rescue device in a state of emergency. This study investigated a mobile diagnosing device to measure user health and diagnosis information by establishing a wireless sensor network system with a protocol to interface the measured data with mobile terminals or personal home servers. In addition, an HSA(Home Service Aggregation) server is used to integrate data with other services, such as user certification and security, VOD, and power usage information. Finally, a healthcare server was interfaced with an HSA server to collect user data in order to send data in the case of an emergency to a doctor or guardian thus realizing a ubiquitous intelligent healthcare system.

J. Indulska et al. (Eds.): UIC 2007, LNCS 4611, pp. 983–992, 2007.

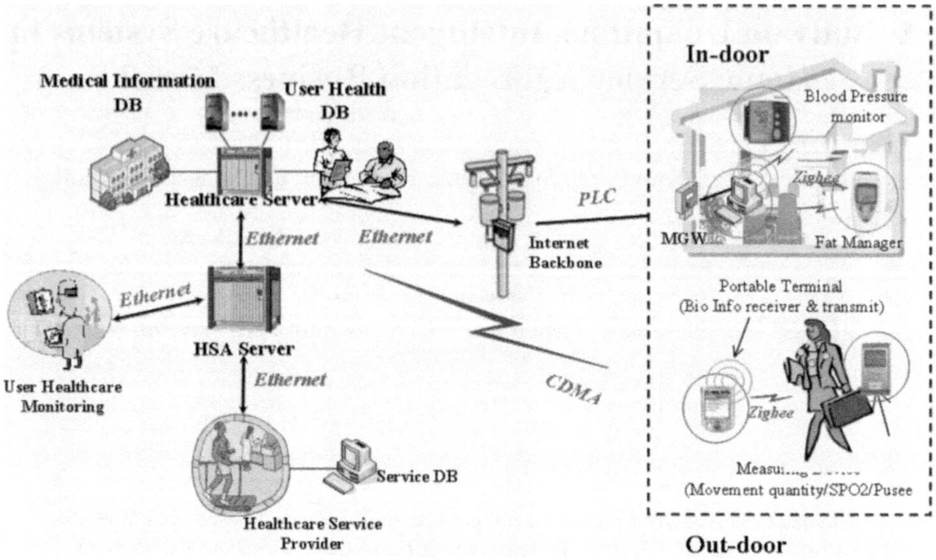

Fig. 1. Architecture of a UI-Healthcare System

2 Architecture of a UI-Healthcare System

Yoon proposed an art therapy service that provided data on the physical and mental conditions of a patient in order to implement a healthcare system. This service sensed physical and mental conditions of a patient using a device, which consisted of various sensors, and provided information such as music or a painting to the user [1]. Ali proposed a ubiquitous kitchen environment to implement a home network system [2], and Choi introduced an environment monitoring system to sense user ECG, weight, snoring, insomnia, and changes in temperature during sleep [3]. These monitoring systems verify user health conditions only in specific places and are therefore only part of the implementation of a ubiquitous healthcare system. In addition, these systems cannot be directly applied to treat patients by transferring user data measured from biomedical modules to a doctor or specialist. This paper developed a mobile biomedical module to verify user conditions during movement and proposed a ubiquitous healthcare system that can be applied to treat patients by transferring user data to a doctor or specialist.

Fig. 1 illustrates the architecture of the ubiquitous intelligent healthcare system proposed in this paper. A sensor module measured user health information such as blood pressure, body fat, quantity of exercise, and SPO2 modules. In addition, a PC and mobile terminal were used to collect data inside and outside a user's home. Communication between devices was performed using a zigbee wireless sensor network that conformed to an IEEE 802.15.4 protocol in real time [4-9]. In the configuration of a network inside the home, a PLC network was used to integrate security, VOD, education, and power loading service as a single unit. Furthermore, an internet backbone was used to communicate between the MGW (Meter Gateway) inside the home, a device outside the home, and the internet. Data measured outside the home was transmitted from a mobile terminal to a healthcare server through a CDMA network. A healthcare server managed user medical information transmitted from a data acquisition device according to the type and date of the information. When an abnormal level of data was received, it was forwarded to a user's guardian or doctor via an SMS text message. A service aggregation server (HSA server) provided not only user certification and healthcare, but also integrated other services.

3 Details of a UI-Healthcare System

3.1 Sensor Network System

A wireless network is an interfacing technology that connects detected environmental data to application servers using various sensing devices in order to recognize conditions in wire and wireless network infrastructure widely installed due to the increased use of ubiquitous computers. Fig. 2 shows the wireless sensor network system used in this paper. A sensor module consisted of a body fat, quantity of exercise, SPO2, and blood pressure measuring modules. In addition, each module included a miniaturized zigbee module [10] and transmitted health information using a data acquisition device connected to a server through a wireless network. The sensor module was used as an

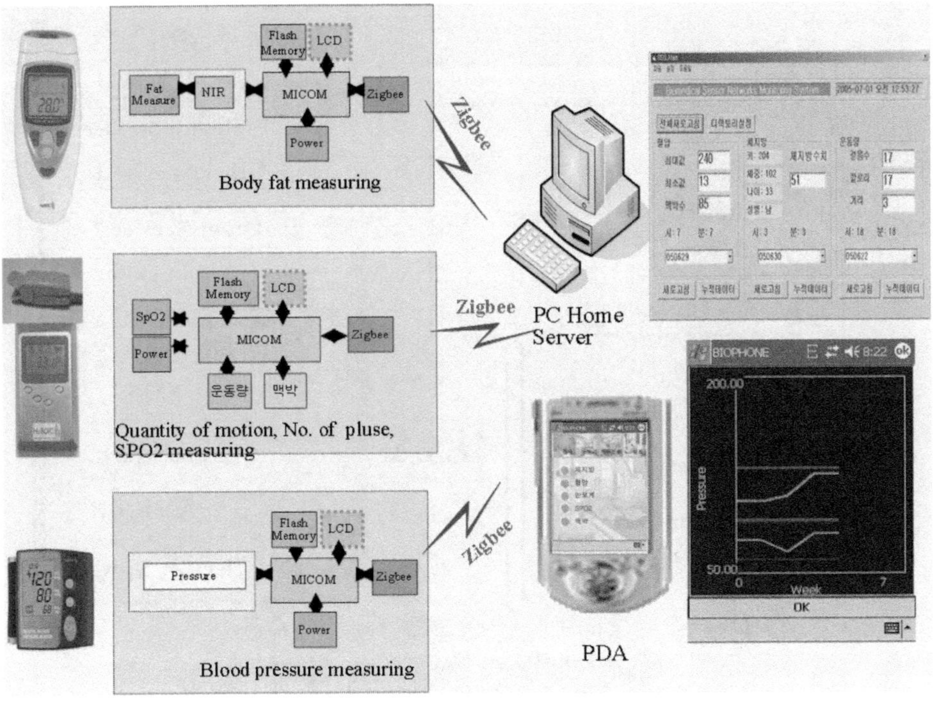

Fig. 2. Architecture of a wireless sensor network system

end-device of the zigbee and a data acquisition device was used as a coordinator. In addition, network topology was based on a mesh in which the coordinator was directly connected to the end-device.

A data acquisition device has four different functions: Connection, DB View, Data Trans, and Setup. Connection verifies the connection of sensor modules in which the measured data is transmitted by clicking on the sensor module of the data to be sent to a server. DB View verifies the transmitted data through a mobile terminal and is identified as a list by date, time, and graphical images. Data Trans transmits biomedical data stored in a data acquisition device to a healthcare server. Setup inputs user certification numbers and physical information. Diagnosis can be performed by analyzing the input physical information and data measured by sensor modules.

3.2 HAS Server and Healthcare Server

To realize a ubiquitous intelligent healthcare system, a service that transmits an SMS text message regarding user health conditions or emergencies to a doctor or guardian by sending biomedical information measured by a mobile terminal to a healthcare server must be implemented. The server used in this system consisted of an aggregation server that integrated user certification and security, VOD, power usage information, and a service server that provided these services. The aggregation server used in this paper was an HSA server and a healthcare server was used as a service server.

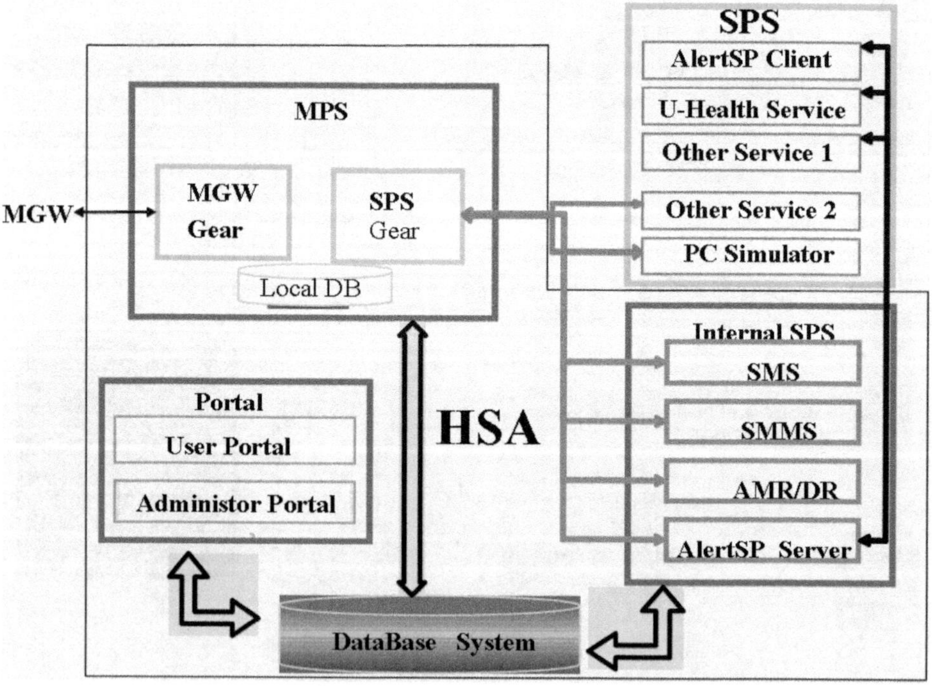

Fig. 3. Architecture of an HAS System

Fig. 3 illustrates the system architecture of an HSA server. The connection of the entire system can be defined as the messages transmitted between each system and configured using a protocol that transmitted these messages. General message flow was accomplished using the MGW to a SPS (Service Propulsion System) via the HSA. An MPS (Message Passing System) is a module that connected the MGW to service providers and managed multiple connections in this process. An SMS (State Management System) periodically reflected the state of information for all MGW registered in an HSA server to the DB and represented their states as a module that transmitted detailed state values for a specific MGW. The AMR/DR (Automatic Meter Reading/Demand Response) was a module that recorded periodical data obtained from the MGW registered in an HSA server and implemented DR control based on this record. An AlertSP server recorded all MGW registered in an HSA server including events and collected information in a device, which recognized all registered MGW and transmitted this information to users. In addition, this module supported multiple connections of users. A portal consisted of a Web Portal and HSA manager Web Portal. The SPS was connected to various services, such as an AlertSP Server System, UI-Healthcare Service, VOD (Video on Demand), and Security Service. The AlertSP Client was a GUI program that could be read by a manager by receiving the data collected by the AlertSP Server and the UI-Healthcare Service was the Healthcare Server program applied in this study. The UI existed in a manager portal for the entire server program.

A healthcare server included various functions, such as login, storing measurements, searching last measurement results, and checking doctor lists. The health information measured by a user was transmitted using a data acquisition device to a server, and then the server verified biomedical data and sent an SMS text message to a doctor or guardian in the case of an emergency. Next, the server saved data in the DB. A healthcare server can be classified in three different modes. First, it receives user data and manages the data. Second, it applies a doctor mode by analyzing personal data to treat patients and describes the patient's condition. Third, it manages servers as a manager mode. Access in the user and doctor mode was configured as *http://healthcare address/index.htm* and the manager mode was determined as *http://healthcare address/Admin/index.html.*

4 Healthcare System Protocol

4.1 Sensor Network Protocol

The zigbee module (end-device) was connected to and installed in the biomedical module used in this study. The zigbee module (coordinator) was connected to a data acquisition device using an RS-232C. A communication packet was divided into a Header section that included packet information, such as type of transmission device, commands, and data section (Fig. 4 (a)). In a packet, the Header represented sensor modules, CMD showed commands, INFO represented the effectiveness of data, DL represented the length of data, FM showed the frame number, MA represented the address of a zigbee module, and CRC represented the checksum code. For data, body fat was represented by measured time, height, weight, age, sex, and level of body fat.

Blood pressure was represented by measured time, height, maximum blood pressure (hypertension), minimum blood pressure (hypotension), and pulse. Quantity of exercise was represented by measured time, number of steps, caloric intake, and distance. Finally, SPO2 was represented by measured time, SPO2 data, and pulse. User physical information was used to produce actual data based on this physical information stored in a personal or home server.

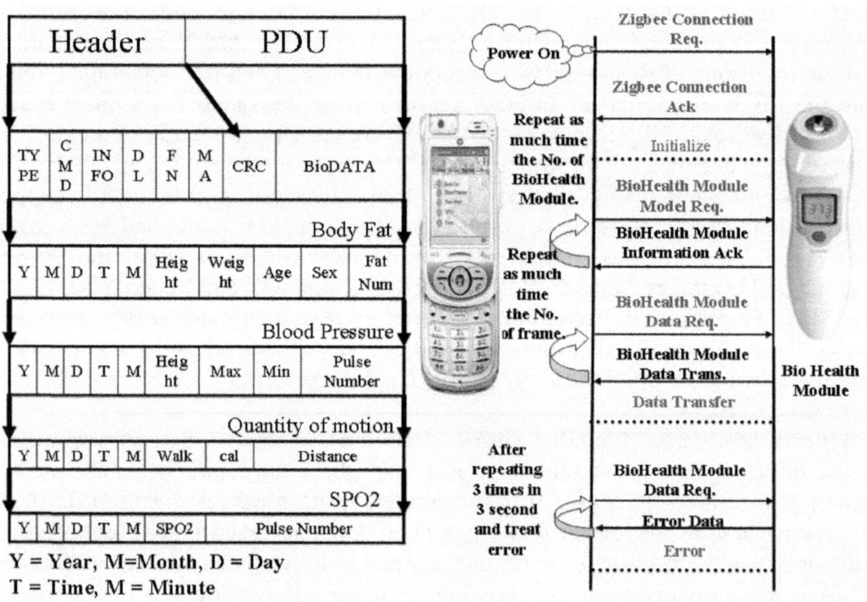

(a) Packet (b)Protocol

Fig. 4. Packet & Protocol of a sensor network

Fig. 4 (b) illustrates a communication protocol used in a sensor network. This protocol consisted of a biomedical module (end-device), connection check command for a data acquisition device (between coordinators), data transmission command, and error handling command. The connection check command managed an initialization process for the zigbee when the power of a mobile terminal or biomedical module was on. The data transmission command transmitted user health information measured in a biomedical module to a data acquisition device. The error handling command required data retransmission when errors in data transmission occurred.

4.2 Server Protocol

After acquiring data using the body fat module, blood pressure module, quantity of exercise module, and SPO2 module, the acquired data was transmitted to a data acquisition device using a sensor network, and this data was transmitted to a healthcare server. Data transmission to a healthcare server was performed using a CDMA communication method. Power cable communication was used to transmit data from a home PC to a Gateway and an Internet backbone was applied to transmit data to a healthcare server.

Communication between a mobile terminal and a healthcare server was facilitated using a Get method. The Get method transmitted data that included information on parameters in the URL window of a Web browser. In other words, it transmitted data using a URL name. In order to transmit data for a single packet to a healthcare server regardless of the measured item, an integrated communication method that aggregated packets as a single packet was applied. The packet definition that was transmitted from a mobile terminal to a healthcare server is as follows:

Italics: represent the applied parameter
Bold: represent the value of data

*http://healthcareaddress/MeaRawRegister.aspx?MEADATE=*__Date__*&USERNUM=*__UserNum__*&SENDDEVCODE=*__PDA__*&DEVCODE=*__KPU1__*&NBP1=*__Oxidized hemoglobin__*&NBP2=*__DeoxidizedHemoglobin__*&ECR1=*__Pulse__*&HIGT=*__Height__*&HBBF=*__BodyFat__*&WHGT=*__Weight__*&AGE1=*__Old__*&GEND=*__Sex__*&WNUM=*__NumberofStep__*&CAL1=*__Caloric intake__*&DIST=*__Distance__*&SOR1=*__SPO2.__

5 Experiment of a UI-Healthcare System

A mobile diagnosing device was configured to measure body fat, quantity of exercise, SPO2, and blood pressure. Measurements in the quantity of exercising and SPO2 were integrated into a single module. An NIR sensor with light receiving and emitting

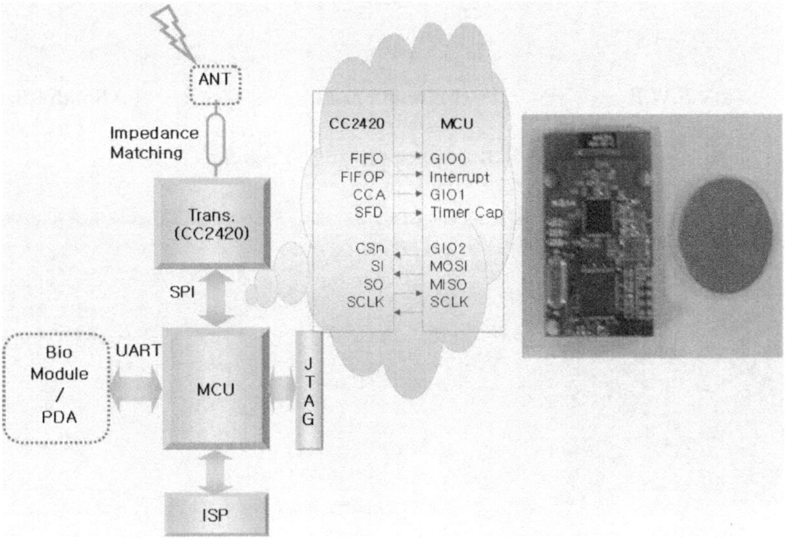

(a) H/W Architecture (b) Zigbee Module

Fig. 5. Architecture & Picture of a Zigbee Module

elements was used to measure body fat. The light emitting element was CQX15 with a 940nm wavelength by FAIRCHILD and the light receiving element was an L14C2 phototransistor by FAIRCHILD. In order to measure the quantity of exercise, a walking sensor that recorded in increments of 1 for every step by sensing the up and down movement of an arm sensor stabilized by a GND pin was used to count the number of steps. To measure SPO2, 660nm of red light and 940nm of infrared that analyzed the absorbance of the wavelength between oxidized hemoglobin and deoxidized hemoglobin were used to measure oxygen saturation. Finally, a bellows pressure sensor was used to measure both systolic and diastolic blood pressure.

This paper established system hardware as illustrated in Fig. 5 in order to configure a zigbee network module. The controller for zigbee wireless communication was a CC2420 [11] by ChipCon. In addition, a chip antenna was developed and installed inside a mobile diagnosing device with a zigbee module. Reflection caused by the difference in impedances in the chip antenna was minimized by introducing impedance matching (50ohm) between the CC2420 and the antenna (Fig. 5 (b)) in which performance was enhanced using an FR4 material with lower conductivity than that of ceramic (Fig. 6(a), Fig. 6(b)). Fig. 6(c) illustrates a Smith chart regarding VSWR and Return Loss. The maximum communication distance in a zigbee communication module was 70m.

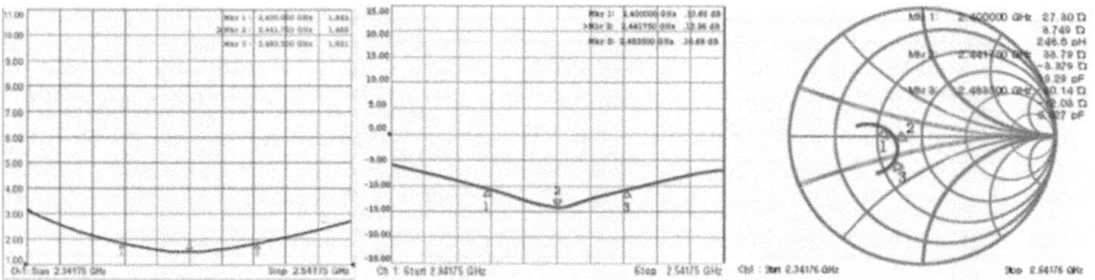

(a)V.S.W.R (b) Return Loss (c) Smith Chart

Fig. 6. Performance of wireless Antenna

(a) Server (b) Homepage (c) Data Analysis

Fig. 7. HAS & Healthcare Server

Fig. 7 shows the server and healthcare UI. A Dell (TM) Power Edge (TM) SC1425 Server was used to develop the server and healthcare UI and development was performed using Microsoft Visual Studio .Net under the .Net Frame Work 1.1.4322 environment. A Momo Short Message Service (msms) [12] was used to implement the SMS text transmission in a server program.

6 Conclusion

This paper designed and implemented a ubiquitous intelligent healthcare system to collect and manage user health information both in and outside the home. In addition, this study developed a mobile health-diagnosing device, which measured user health information (body fat, blood pressure, quantity of exercising, and SPO2) and a mobile terminal and home server program to collect health information. Furthermore, a wireless sensor network with a zigbee module, which adhered to communication protocol IEEE 802.15.4, was applied as an interface to communicate between these devices.

In order to store user health information in a healthcare server system, the mobile terminal used a CDMA network to transmit data. Moreover, a personal home server was configured using a PLC and Ethernet. The major functions of a healthcare server can be classified as three different modes. First, a user mode verifies data transmission and management. Second, a doctor mode analyzes personal data to treat patients and assess a patient's condition. Third, a manager mode manages servers. In addition, this system was configured to interface with the HSA system to connect other services (VOD, power loading management, and security) including user certification.

It is evident that this system provided not only healthcare services regardless of location, such as in the home, hospital, or on the street, but also a new medical system of daily living based disease prevention as an alternative to hospital care.

References

1. Yoon, S.-I., Ha, J.I., bae, J.S., Kim, S.-H.: The Implementation of Art Therapy Service asan Ubiquitous Health-care Service. In: TENCON 2004, 2004 IEEE Region 10 Conference, vol. C, pp. 200–203. IEEE Computer Society Press, Los Alamitos (2004)
2. Ali, J.A., Yoon, W.-S., Kim, J.-H., Cho, W.-D.: U-Kitchen: Application Scenario. In: Software Technologies for Future Embedded and Ubiquitous Systems, 2004 Second IEEE Workshop, pp. 169–171 (2004)
3. Choi, J.M., Choi, B.H., Seo, J.W., Sohn, R.H., Ryu, M.S., Yi, W., Park, K.S.: A System ofr Ubiquitous Health Monitoring in the Bedroom via a Bluetooth Network and Wireless LAN. In: Proceeding of the 26th Annual International Conference of the IEEE EMBS, 2005, San Franciso, CA, USA, pp. 1–5 (2004)
4. Kahn, J., Katz, R., Pister, K.: Next Century Challenges:Mobile Networking for Smart Dust. In: Progrceedings of the ACM/IEEE International Conference on Mobile Computing and Networking, Seattle, USA, pp. 271–278 (1999)
5. Heinzelman, W., Kulik, J., Balakrishnan, H.: Adaptive Protocols for Information Dissemination in Wireless Sensor Networks. In: Proceedings of the ACM/IEEE International Conference on Mobile Computing and Networking, Seattle, USA, pp. 174–185 (1999)

6. Heinzelman, W., Chandrakasan, A., Balakrishnan, H.: Energyefficient communication protocol for wireless micro sensor networks. In: Proceedings of the Hawaii International Conference on System Sciences, Maui, USA, pp. 4–7 (2000)
7. Intanagonwiwat, C., Govindan, R., Estrin, D.: Directed diffusion: A scalable and robust communication paradigm for sensor networks. In: Proceedings of the ACM/IEEE International Conference on Mobile Computing and Networking, Boston, USA, pp. 56–67 (2000)
8. Chen, B., Jamieson, K., Balakrishnan, H., Morris, R.: Span: An Energy-Efficient Coordination Algorithm for Topology Maintenance in Ad Hoc Wireless Networks. In: Proceedings of the ACM/IEEE International Conference on Mobile Computing and Networking, Rome, Italy, pp. 70–84 (2001)
9. Ye, W., Heidemann, J., Estrin, D.: An Energy-Efficient MAC Protocol for Wireless Sensor Networks. In: Proceedings of the 21st International Annual Joint Conference oft he IEEE Computer and Communications Societies, New York, USA (2002)
10. Zigbee Web Site: http://www.zigbee.com
11. ChipCon Web Site: http://www.chipcon.com
12. Momo Web Site: http://www.momoweb.co.kr

Implementation and Quantitative Evaluation of UbiMDR Framework*

Jeong-Dong Kim[1], Dongwon Jeong[2], Jinhyung Kim[1], Yixin Jing[1], and Doo-Kwon Baik[1]

[1] Dept. of Computer Science and Engineering, Korea University, 1, 5-ga, Anam-dong, Sungbuk-gu, Seoul, 136-701 Republic of Korea
{kjd,koolmania,jing,baik}@software.korea.ac.kr
[2] Dept. of Informatics and Statistics, Kunsan National University, San 68, Miryong-dong, Kunsan, Jollabuk-do, 573-701 Republic of Korea
djeong@kunsan.ac.kr

Abstract. This paper describes an implementation and quantitative evaluation of the UbiMDR framework. The UbiMDR framework has been proposed for consistent semantics management between ubiquitous applications. This framework enables an application field-independent information exchanging sharing and maxmize the usability of ubiquitous applications and data in devices (tags or smart cards). In the previous study, we just proposed the framework at the conceptual level including description of key components. In other words, the previous proposal has no implementation and evaluation. In this paper, we present a prototype implementation of the UbiMDR framework for semantic interoperability on the ubiquitous environment. To show the merits of the framework, we describe comparative evaluations between the conventional ubiquitous framework and the UbiMDR framework.

1 Introduction

Ubiquitous computing is recognized as a new paradigm and can be defined as the anytime/anywhere/any device [1]. Under ubiquitous environment, applications can gather and utilize various sensing information. It allows the applications to provide high quality services with context, sensing information from sensors. Although current applications use sensing information, they are dependent and restricted to a specific boundary, i.e. a correspondent application field (sensor field). In other words, current frameworks are not suitable for the ubiquitous environment allowing applications to use the context at anytime, anywhere, and with any devices.

There are many issues such as energy management, protocol standardization, independency on application fields, and security to be resolved for the complete ubiquitous computing. In addition many researchers have been studying to define and develop frameworks (middleware) for ubiquitous computing [13,14,15]. However, most of researches do not consider the semantic interoperability between data in various and different sensor fields. Especially, the application field-independent information access

* This research is supported by BK (Brain Korea) 21.

J. Indulska et al. (Eds.): UIC 2007, LNCS 4611, pp. 993–1002, 2007.

is one of the most important issues to maximize the usability of sensors in various sensor fields [2, 3].

The UbiMDR is a framework for semantic interoperability in ubiquitous computing environments. Therefore, the UbiMDR allows us to develop ubiquitous applications that are semantically independent on application fields. It also enables high quality services, enhanced context-aware applications. The MDR is a framework for interoperability of databases and is the international standard developed by ISO/IEC JTC 1/SC 32 [4]. The MDR has been used to implement applications in various domains [5,6,7,8,9,10,11] and develop frameworks to facilitate sharing and exchanging of data in such as e-Commerce [12]. Most applications in ubiquitous computing environment require real-time data processing and precise semantic interpretation of gathered information from many sensors. The MDR is much suitable to achieve both of them because the goal of the MDR is to prevent from the inconsistent semantic creation and eliminate cost for integrating built-in semantics. However, the original MDR is too complicated and heavy for ubiquitous application. Therefore, the definition of an optimized MDR is needed for ubiquitous computing environment. The UMDR is a modified and optimized version of MDR [16].

In [16], we already proposed the UbiMDR, a MDR-based framework to provide application fields-independent semantic interoperability in ubiquitous computing environment. However, the implementation and comparative evaluation of UbiMDR framework is not enough to validate outstanding characteristics. Therefore, we define formal model for comparison and execute comparative evaluation for verifying the superiority of UbiMDR framework.

2 Prototype Implementation

In this section, we describe a prototype implementation of UbiMDR. An evaluation results present comparison between the existing framework (application) and the UbiMDR. The chosen application is about the agricultural product history management.

The UbiMDR has three key processes for ubiquitous applications. The first process is to record data to a tag. In the writing process, semantics of data is defined according to the UMDR. The other process is creation process. If there is no proper semantic in the UMDR, the creator suggests the corresponding semantic. The new semantic can be used to define the meaning of data. Another process is the interpretation to recognize tags, read information from the tags, and use the achieved data for providing services to the applications. In this process, the ubiquitous applications also should follow the definitions in the UMDR.

2.1 Scenario and Implementation Environment

In this section, we describe restrictions of existing framework clearly show the goal of UbiMDR and its motivation. A scenario is assumed to help your understanding as follows.

- ✓ **Scenario***: An object (e.g. RFID tag) exist in the sensor field-I, a cellular phone. The object can freely within the sensor field-I, as well as move to the other sensor fields, such as II and III. All these sensor fields, I, II and III, can access the RFID tag, read and utilize the tag data, such as object name, manufactory etc.*

With this scenario, if the RFID tag is designed the sensor field-I, the device can interpret and utilize the data in the RFID tag. However, the devices (sensor field-II, III system) in different fields cannot interpret and use data of the RFID tag, because of data heterogeneity between devices and applications. That is, the remainder except for the first device cannot use and interpret the RFID tag information.

We use two RF systems a product of ECO company [17] for the prototype implementation. However, the tags of the current RF systems do not support the function of sensors for the emerging ubiquitous environment. Hence, we define and implement a virtual tags-based system with current tags. The virtual tag is an in-memory data structure to provide additional functions including the functions the physical tag.

2.2 Prototype Implementation

Under the above implementation environment and scenario, the UbiMDR prototype is implemented based on following steps:

- ✓ *Step1*: Recognizing tag ID: First, the physical ID (0100000006E71D5C) of the detected tag, which is attached to an object, is identified and delivered.
- ✓ *Step2*: Writing information: Before writing data (values), proper semantics should be selected by retrieving data elements which is managed in UMDR. Once a proper semantic is selected, a corresponding value is input. The Fig. 2 (Left) shows the definition result of in the list box.
- ✓ *Step3*: The final information written into the tag is viewed Fig. 2 (Right) in the list box "Update Object Information".

The Fig. 1 (Left) shows the snapshot for the initial step 1 which is the step 1 to add (write) both of semantics (semantic list) and data (value) into the tag according to the data elements in UMDR. Where "Write Info" button open to the Fig. 2 (Left).

Fig. 2 (Left) shows the implementation result of the step 2. In this figure, after recognizing the tag and reading information, additional information is recorded by the application. The additional written information is shown the right hand side list box "Update Object Information" in Fig.2. "Semantic List" creates in compliance with the designer "Checking Processor" and "Creation Processor" process "Condition" shows the condition of the element which it defines in UMDR; "M" is Mandatory, "O" is Optional, "I" is Indicative, and "C" mean Contingent [4].

Fig. 3 shows an application query result. In the Fig. 2 (Right), "View Application" button open to the Fig. 3. "Semantic List" has creation and extinction cycle; creation cycle: Incomplete, Candidate, Recorded, Qualified, and Standard. Extinction cycle: Preferred standard, Retired, and superseded. Creation and extinction cycle condition of UMDR is same process of MDR conditions [4].

The UbiMDR provides several advantages compared the existing approaches. Most previous frameworks do not consider the semantic interoperability between sensors and applications in different fields. Previous frameworks have many restrictions to facilitate data usability in the ubiquitous environment. The proposed framework, the UbiMDR is proposed to resolve these issues. Sensor information in the existing frameworks is designed and used for the applications in the same field. Therefore the sensor information depends on a specific sensor field/application. The UbiMDR enables the independency on every sensor field/application.

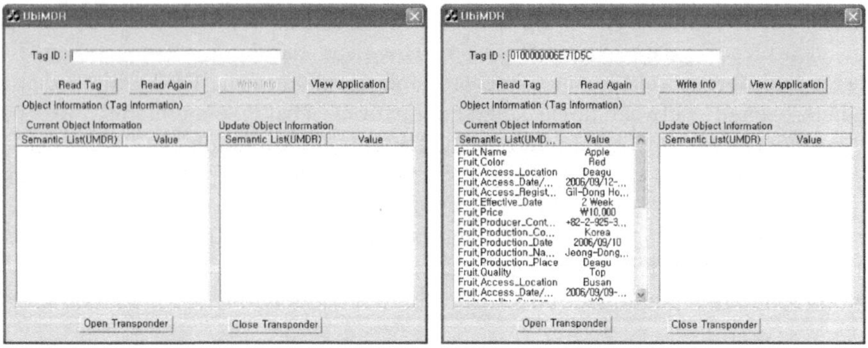

Fig. 1. The before read Tag ID (*Left*) and the read the Tag ID (*Right*)

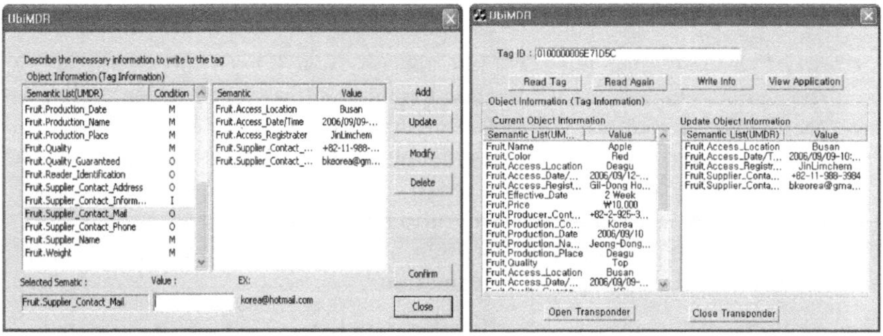

Fig. 2. The data input (*Left*) and the snapshot of data input result (*Right*)

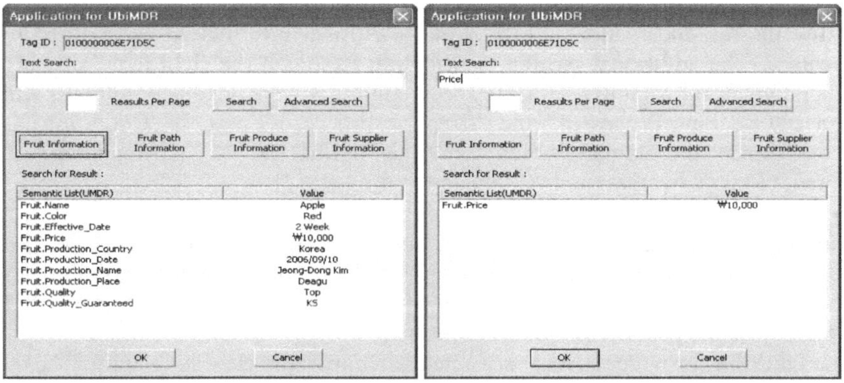

Fig. 3. The group query result (*Left*) and the single query result (*Right*)

3 Comparative Evaluation

This section describes preliminary constraints, notations, and symbols models. In addition, we describe comparative evaluation between conventional ubiquitous computing framework and the UbiMDR framework with data consistency of interoperability. This section considers the evaluation model for comparing cost of adding a new sensor field(s) of sensor fields for interoperability.

3.1 Notations and Symbols

Notations and symbols are used to describe evaluation models. Table 1 shows their description.

Table 1. Summary of Notations and Symbols

Notations & Symbols	Description
SenFN	# of sensor fields (the number of sensor fields.)
SemN	# of semantic per each sensor fields
SF	a set of sensor fields; SF={SF1, SF2, …, SFn}
s_i	a set of semantics
S_{ij}	a semantic sj in SFi
UMDR	the UMDR including standardized semantics; SFu
SF_u	the UMDR; defined to describe the relevant calculation formula consistently
$AanT_{ij}$	time for interpreting the meaning of a semantic, sj in SFi
InterpretSem()	interpreting time of semantic in Sensor Fields
MapN	# the number of mapping number or mapping table number
LSenFN	# of existing sensor fields (the number of existing(local) sensor fields)
NSenFN	# of new sensor fields (the number of new sensor fields)

3.2 Assumptions

For effective comparative evaluation, we need several assumptions. Assumptions are defined to support the evaluation models about the mapping cost and the cost of adding a new sensor field.

- ✓ *Each sensor field has the same number of semantics data.*
- ✓ *Each semantic data of sensor field has 1:1[n(SF-I):n'(SF-II)] mapping.*
- ✓ *The semantic analysis time of sensor field (or UMDR) is generated by random number generator (0sec< analysis time ≤1sec).*
- ✓ *The number of Sensor Fields is rather than 1 (sensor field >1).*

3.3 Cost Evaluation for Integrating Initial Built-In Semantics

Fig. 4 describes the model for comparing cost of the mapping among sensor fields.

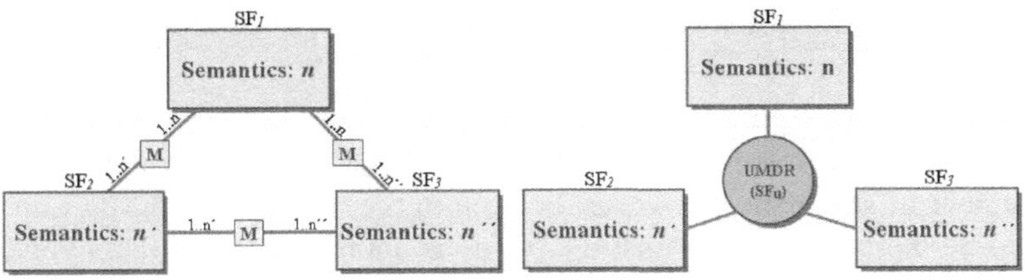

Fig. 4. Evaluation for comparing mapping cost in the previous approach (*Left*) and the UbiMDR approach (*Right*)

The calculation formula for estimating the mapping cost of the previous approach is as follows:

Formula 1: Previous approach

$$Cost(MSF_{PREV})$$

$$= \sum_{i=1}^{SenFN-1} \cdot \left[\sum_{j=i+1}^{SenFN} \left\{ \sum_{k=1}^{SemN_{SF_i}} InterpretSem(SF_i.s_k) + \sum_{l=1}^{SemN_{SF_j}} InterpretSem(SF_j.s_l) \right\} \right]$$

$$= \sum_{i=1}^{SenFN-1} \cdot \left[\sum_{j=i+1}^{SenFN} \left\{ \sum_{k=1}^{SemN_{SF_i}} InterpretSem(S_{ik}) + \sum_{l=1}^{SemN_{SF_j}} InterpretSem(S_{jl}) \right\} \right]$$

$$= \sum_{i=1}^{SenFN-1} \cdot \left\{ \sum_{j=i+1}^{SenFN} \left(\sum_{k=1}^{SemN_{SF_i}} AanT_{ik} + \sum_{l=1}^{SemN_{SF_j}} AnaT_{jl} \right) \right\}$$

InterpretSem($SF_i.s_k$) is the time for analyzing and describing a $SF_i.s_k$ and its semantic data set, in the *InterpretSem(S_{ik})* is a random number generator that is Interpretation time of semantic data between sensor fields (0< Interpretation time$\leq$1), *AnaT* is semantic analysis which value is randomly generated (0< Analysis time$\leq$1).

By contrast, the UbiMDR approach only uses a mapping table (UMDR) to gather semantic data from the sensor fields. Therefore, the development cost of UbiMDR approach is independent of the number of sensor fields. The UMDR of UbiMDR contains predefined semantics (data elements) commonly used in the sensor fields. Therefore, this UbiMDR framework does not map sensor fields to other sensor fields and its calculation model is Formular 2. In this formular, *InterpretSem(UMDRs_k)* is the time for analyzing and describing semantics in the UMDR including standardized semantics.

Formula 2: UbiMDR approach

$$Cost(UbiMDR_{UMDR})$$

$$= \sum_{i=1}^{SenFN} \cdot \left[\sum_{j=1}^{SemN_{SF_i}} \left\{ InterpretSem(SF_i.s_j) + \sum_{k=1}^{SemN_{UMDR}} InterpretSem(UMDR.s_k) \right\} \right]$$

$$= \sum_{i=1}^{SenFN} \cdot \left[\sum_{j=1}^{SemN_{SF_i}} \left\{ InterpretSem(SF_i.s_j) + \sum_{k=1}^{SemN_{UMDR}} InterpretSem(SF_u.s_k) \right\} \right]$$

$$= \sum_{i=1}^{SenFN} \cdot \left[\sum_{j=1}^{SemN_{SF_i}} \left\{ InterpretSem(S_{ij}) + \sum_{k=1}^{SemN_{UMDR}} InterpretSem(S_{uk}) \right\} \right]$$

$$= \sum_{i=1}^{SenFN} \cdot \left\{ \sum_{j=1}^{SemN_{SF_i}} \left(AnaT_{il} + \sum_{k=1}^{SemN_{UMDR}} AnaT_{uk} \right) \right\}$$

Fig. 5 shows the evaluation results of comparing cost for the mapping among sensor fields between previous approach and the UbiMDR approach. In this case, a factor is the number of sensor fields. As can be seen in the result, the UbiMDR approach is proven to be more efficient against the previous approach. When the number of sensor fields is 6, UbiMDR : Previous = 13.38 : 736.275 (that is, about 1: 55).

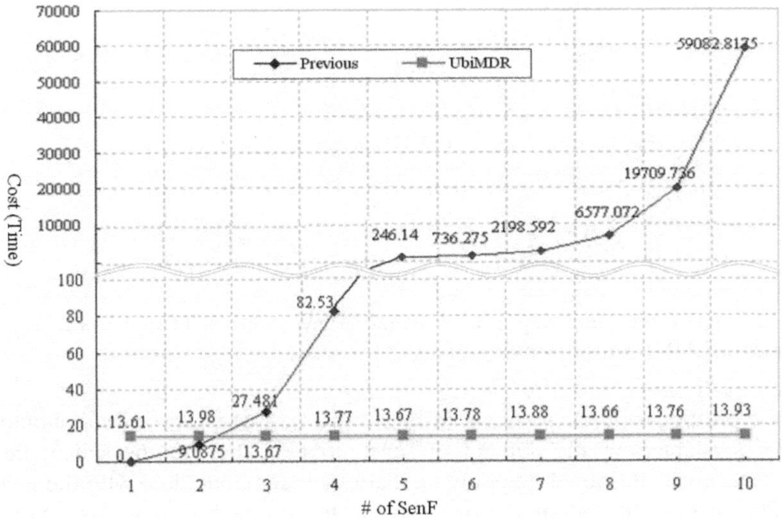

Fig. 5. Integration cost of initial built-in semantics

3.4 Cost Evaluation for Adding New Sensor Fields

The model for calculate the number of required mapping tables by adding new sensor fields, *MapN* is defined as Fomular 3. Fig. 6 illustrates the relationship between the number of mapping tables and the number of sensor fields for integrating new sensor fields.

Formula 3:

$$MapN = \frac{SenFN \cdot (SenFN - 1)}{2} = \frac{(SenFN^2 - SenFN)}{2}$$

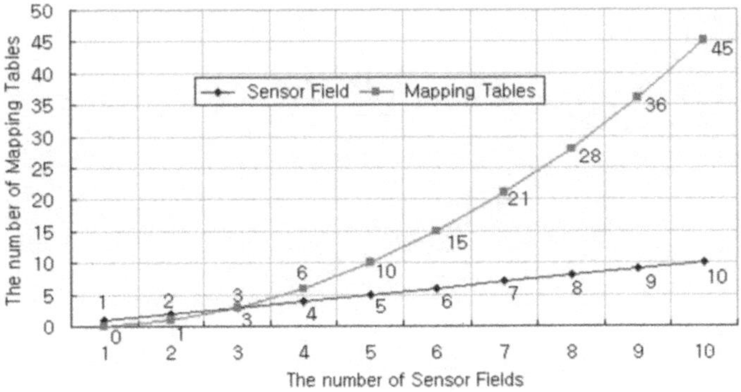

Fig. 6. Relation between sensor fields and mapping tables

Fig. 7 illustrates the evaluation models for adding new sensor fields to the existing sensor fields.

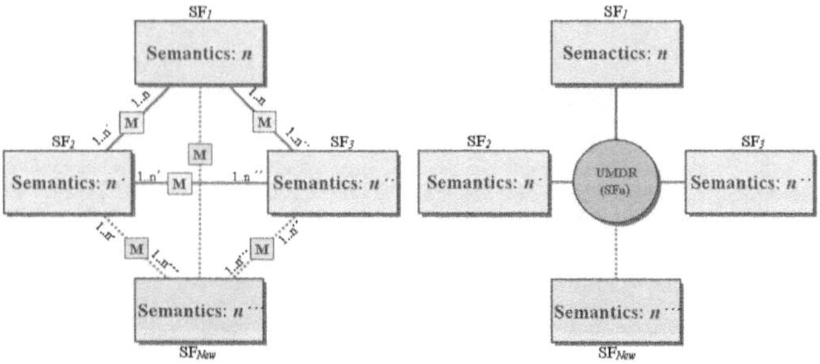

Fig. 7. Evaluation for comparing cost of adding a new sensor field in the previous approach (*Left*) and the UbiMDR approach (*Right*)

As the previous approach shown in Fig. 7 (Left), a new sensor field should creates and shares adapters as the number of sensor fields. The existing sensor fields also need to create an additional mapping to share their semantic data with the new sensor field. The cost calculation model of the previous approach is as follows and *LSenFN* is the number of local (existing) sensor fields.

Formula 4:

$$
\begin{aligned}
&Cost(NewADD_{PREV}) \\
&= C_{PREV} \cdot \left\{ \frac{(NSenFN + LSenFN)\cdot(NSenFN + LSenFN - 1)}{2} - \frac{LSenFN(LSenFN-1)}{2} \right\} \\
&= C_{PREV} \cdot \left\{ \frac{(NSenFN + LSenFN)\cdot(NSenFN + LSenFN - 1) - (LSenFN^2 - LSenFN)}{2} \right\}
\end{aligned}
$$

In case of the UbiMDR approach in Fig. 7 (Right), only new sensor field requires one adapter, and thus the calculation formula of the UbiMDR approach is defined as Formular 5.

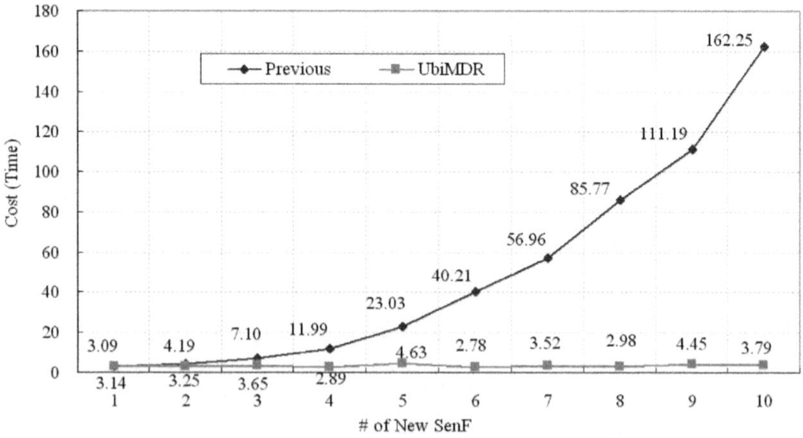

Fig. 8. Cost of adding new sensor field

Formula 5:

$$Cost(NewADD_{UbiMDR}) = C_{UMDR} \cdot NSenFN$$

Fig. 8 shows the evaluation result for adding new sensor fields. As shown in the result, the UbiMDR approach is more efficient than the previous approach. When the numbers of sensor fields and new sensor field are 5 and 1 respectively, UbiMDR: Previous = 2.22 : 40.21 (that is, about 1: 18).

4 Conclusion and Future Works

In this paper, we proposed the implementation of the Metadata Registry-based framework (UbiMDR) in the ubiquitous environment regarding semantic issue. This framework can provide the semantic interoperability among ubiquitous applications or various sensor fields. The UbiMDR framework solves the semantic inconsistency occurred by the diversity of consistency sensor field. In addition, we described comparative evaluation between the conventional framework and the UbiMDR framework on the cost for integrating initial built-in semantics and cost for adding new sensor fields.

As future work, we will focus on the deployment of UbiMDR to encourage its flexible utilization in a larger scale. The UbiMDR will be extended to support the situation awareness concept [14]. This work can provide higher quality services with context information. Finally, security issue will be studied and added to the UbiMDR.

References

1. Weiser, M.: http://www.ubiq.com/hypertext/weiser/Ubi- Home.html
2. Ilyas, M., Mahgoub, I.: Handbood of Sensor Networks: Compact Wireless and Wired Sensing Systems. CRC Press (2004)
3. Jeong, D., Lee, L.: A New MDR-based RFID System Architecture for Ubiquitous Computing Environment. Journal of Korea Society for Simulation (The Korea Society for Simulation) 14(4), 43–53 (2005)
4. ISO/IEC JTC 1/SC 32, ISO/IEC 11179: Information Technology - Metadata Registries (MDR) - Part 1 Part 6 (2004)
5. Jeong, D., In, P., Jarnjak, F., Kim, Y., Baik, D.-K.: A Message Conversion System, XML-based Metadata Semantics Description Language, and Metadata Repository. Journal of Information Science (JIS) 31(5), 394–406 (2005)
6. Environmental Protection Agency (EPA), Environmental Data Registry (EDR) (2004), http://www.epa.gov/edr/
7. Australian Institute of Health and Welfare, Australian National Health Information Knowledgebase (2004), http://www.aihw.gov.au/
8. U.S. Department of Transportation, U.S. Intelligent Transportation System (ITS) (2004), http://www.dot.gov/
9. Environmental Protection Agency, Data Standards Publications and Guidances: (2003) http://oaspub.epa.gov/edr/ stddoc$document_type_vw.actionquery
10. Australian National Health Data Committee, National Health Data Dictionary (2003), http://www.aihw.gov.au/

11. ITS Architecture Development Team, ITS Logical Architecture: vol. I, vol. II: Process Specifications. vol. III: Data Dictionary (2003), http://www.itsa.org/
12. OASIS, ebXML Registry Information Model: http://www.oasis-open.org/specs/index.php (April 2002)
13. Traub, K., et al.: The EPCglobal Architecture Framework (EPCglobal Final Version) (2005) EPCglobal Network, http://www.epcglobalinc.org/
14. Jeong, D., Kim, Y., In, H.: New RFID System Architectures Supporting Situation Awareness under Ubiquitous Environments. Journal of Computer Science 1(2), 114–120 (2005)
15. Kim, Y., Park, J., Cheong, T.: Study of RFID Middleware Framework for Ubiquitous Computing Environment. In: International Conference on Advanced Communication Technology (ICACT 2005), February 2005, Phoenix Park, South Korea, pp. 825–830 (2005)
16. Kim, J.-D., Jeong, D., Jing, H., Baik, D.-K.: UbiMDR: Supporting Application-Independent Semantic Interoperability for Ubiquitous Applications. In: International Conference on Computational Intelligence and Security (CIS 2006), November 2006, China Guangzhou, pp. 1155–1158 (2006)
17. ECO Inc., ER200: http://www.eco.co.kr/newhp/english/submenu/sub02_1c.php

A Key-Index Based Distributed Mechanism for Component Registration

Ming Zhong, Yaoxue Zhang, Pengwei Tian, Yuezhi Zhou, and Cunhao Fang

Department of Computer Science and Technology, Tsinghua University,
Beijing 100084, China
zhong-m@mails.tsinghua.edu.cn

Abstract. Component registration and organization is the base of component discovery and reuse. With the development of service-oriented architecture (SOA) and component-based software engineering (CBSE), the number of various heterogeneous service components increases rapidly, bringing challenges on component registration and organization, especially the problems of overload both on network and registries for traditional centralized and UDDI registration mechanism. In this paper, a Key-Index (KI) based distributed registration mechanism is introduced. It focuses on reducing the unnecessary but shared information of registered components, by defining a key index tree which extracts key features from original component description, and maintaining the key index trees on all the distributed registry servers, keeping them consistent after each successful registration, without replication of the registered component itself. Experimental evaluation on average registration time, average response time and total traffic cost gives us positive support.

1 Introduction

With the rapid development of software reuse theories and techniques, component-based and service-oriented software architectures are widely used in comprehensive system development, providing intelligent and personalized services, and satisfying various user requirements. In order to ensure sufficient and valid service components in the process of software reuse, it is necessary to specify component registration and organize an efficient platform for heterogeneous components. The quality of service component registration mechanism will directly influence the reuse of components.

Generally, service component registration performs three essential activities [1]. *Description Specification* concentrates on unifying the description of heterogeneous components with ontology or facet mediation methods. *Component Storage* focuses mainly on automatically storing the available component into an organized repository based on its description. *Information Publication* is the task of publishing component onto the network for browsing and invoking. The kernel of these steps is formulating a reasonable mechanism to classify, store and manage the registering components, to reduce the registration spending and raise the efficiency of component discovery.

Many centralized registries have been implemented to support storing, indexing and querying service components, such as ComponentSource [7], RDFDB [8], Inkling [9], RDFStore [10] and Jena [11]. These centralized repositories typically use

J. Indulska et al. (Eds.): UIC 2007, LNCS 4611, pp. 1003–1013, 2007.

in-memory or database-supported processing, and files or a relational database as the back-end store. Centralized registries are very fast and can scale up to thousands of components. However, they have the same bottlenecks as other centralized approaches, such as a single processing bottleneck and a single point of failure. And they also have limitations both in their failure tolerance and scalability [4]. Recent years, there are more and more attention changed to the distributed framework [5, 6] for scalability and flexibility. UDDI [3] (Universal Description, Discovery and Integration) specifications have been brought to the registration and publish of service components [1], whose initial focus was geared to defining a master universal directory for all public service components and providing unified registration in a distributed architecture. UDDI mechanism for service component registration provides an effective extensibility on flexible resource discovery and management. However, some tough problems are still in the way. For example, it has to replicate all service component publications in all server nodes [12], and thus becomes impractical when managing a large number of service components. The information stored in each server node and transferred between nodes will both expand on a large scale, but lots of them are not used for search, so the result is that the utility of such resources is low and maintenance of server node is not guaranteed.

In this paper, we propose a key-index based distributed mechanism for component registration in the precondition of unified component description. The key index tree stores only a small portion of component description, which will be directly used for search. We create and maintain a key index tree on each of the distributed registration hosts and keep all the trees consistent after every successful registration, without replication and transfer of the component itself. Then we evaluate the proposed mechanism by comprehensive simulations on average registration time, average response time and total traffic cost. The experimental results show that it outperforms existing approaches significantly.

The rest of this paper is organized as follows. Section 2 presents an overview of the KI based distributed component registration framework. Section 3 introduces the unified component description and the design of key index tree based on it. Section 4 illustrates the process of KI based distributed registration. We show our experimental results in Section 5 and conclude this work in Section 6.

2 KI Based Distributed Component Registration Framework

KI based distributed component registration takes as input a packet of component description and entity formulated and returns a message of success or failure. The local registration process determines whether to accept the coming component or deny it according to its provided information. A framework for KI based distributed component registration is illustrated in Figure 1. There are several server hosts that can both store components and provide the service of registration, arranged in a network. Each server host should maintain not only a repository that contains components locally registered, but also a key index tree which is always kept consistent with those on other servers by transfer module.

A local component registration process performs three steps in order to check for the quality of the received component and store it into the repository according to the unified methods of component classification and organizing (Fig. 2). In the first

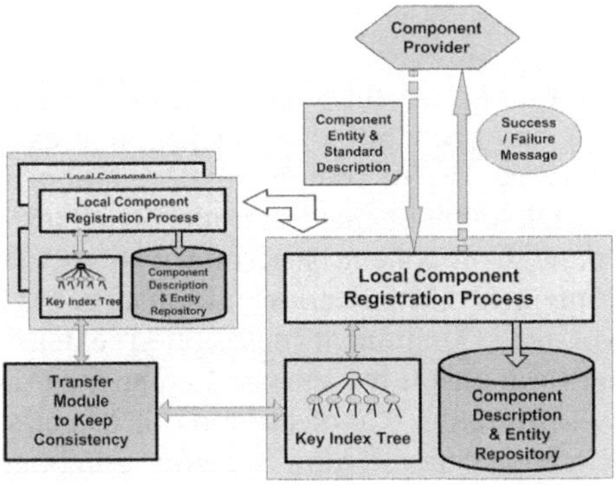

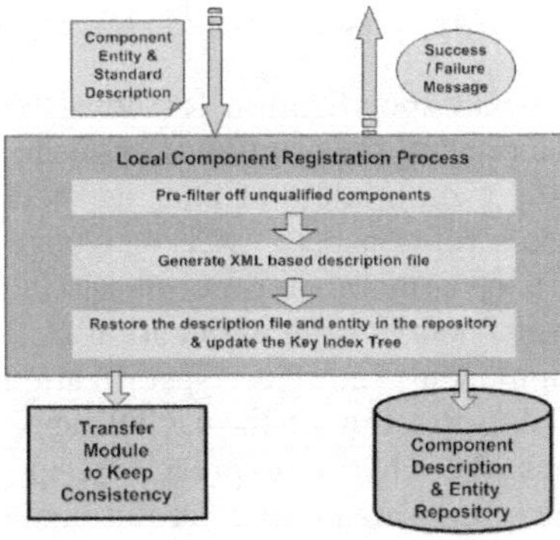

Fig. 1. KI Based Component Registration Framework **Fig. 2.** Local Component Registration Process

optional step a "standard pre-filtering" holds up the unqualified components from entering the repository. The filtering procedures applied in first step must guarantee that all the components with distinct or potential defects, such as information lack or inaccuracy, are filtered out. In the second step, an XML based component description file is created and filled with whole description of the component according to its submitted information. The third pivotal step makes the packet of description file and entity stored into the local repository and extracts key information in order to add new nodes to the local key index tree. The key information is also packed and sent around to keep the indexes on all the distributed servers consistent.

Once a registering component is accepted and ready to be stored in the distributed architecture of network, two key technologies are needed to achieve registration.

1) Unified component description and key index tree based on it. The unified component description makes standard description for components of various formats, which guarantees that all kinds of component be specifically managed. Further more, a key index is created and maintained on every server to provide the service of global search without mass of data transported on the network.
2) Distributed component registration process. This is an essential operating mechanism to accomplish the procedure of how to update the key index tree and communicate among the servers to keep KI trees on all the servers consistent.

These two pivotal points of the KI based distributed component registration will be elaborated further in the next two sections.

3 Component Description and Key-Index Tree

Manufacturers have developed many heterogeneous components of diversified formats. These components offer various functions respectively. But it often happens that users need to organize heterogeneous components to complete their required functions. So in order to consistently register components of all kinds, it is necessary to provide unified access interface for heterogeneous components, screen difference among various components and give users well-organized component resources.

3.1 XML Based Unified Description

A useful specification for consistent description and management, called Universal Component Description Language (UCDL) has been proposed in [2]. It uses the component model in Catalysis specification as the base of component description, and makes reference to OCL language and WSDL component description language to classify component descriptions into five parts, Component basic information (CBI), Component resources location (CRL), Component classification information (CCI), Component interface specification (CIS), and Component description extension (CED). We inherit the UCDL specification to description registered component and select the XML to express descriptors after settling the composition of all its parts in order to satisfy the requirements of independence from specific component technologies and openness to extension.

Regarding the first three parts of UCDL descriptor, we may directly define corresponding XML tag for each descriptor, such as <ID></ID>, <Name></Name> and <Author></Author>. As for the descriptor of interface specifications, we may first apply OCL expression to define interface operation and event and then envelop the expressions in XML tags. Since the OCL expression is also recorded in the form of ASCII code, it is easy to read and analyze and validate with OCL Parser.

3.2 Key Information Tree

The main purpose of defining a key index tree is to maintain a tidy architecture on each distributed server to manage and publish the pivotal information of all the local and remote components, so as to reduce the consistent data transported among the network while registering. The design goals of key index tree are as follows:

1) Define a tree-structured architecture to manage all local and remote components and embody the information for each component as reduced as possible.
2) Provide sufficient information on component classification so as to facilitate establishing relations between user service requirements and components.
3) Support the traditional key-based and facet-based component searching.
4) Provide the information on component location and resources, supporting the component locating and dynamic loading under the network environment.

According to the design goals, unified component description and statistical analysis of user queries, we propose the model of key index tree in which eight key values are extracted from XML based unified component description. First three of them are basic information while the latter five are actually for classification (Fig. 3.).

Component ID. It is the unique identification of component descriptors on the whole range. The component ID is composed of two parts, host number and inner number. Each server has a unique host number such as 001, and each component will be assigned a sorted inner number such as 123456, so the component ID is defined 001123456. This method avoids the repetition of all assigned component IDs.

Component Name. It is the most distinct description of a component that can semantically point out the essential.

Storage Location. It gives the URL link pointing to the storage location of a component, maybe local or remote, and helps connecting to the detailed information and dynamically loading a component.

Application Domain. It indicates the domain of component applications, where the component has been or will be applied, including E-Commerce, E-Government, etc.

Component Function. It indicates the software functions furnished by the component in the original or possible software systems, including user interface design, network functions, file operation etc. Each function may have its own sub-functions. For example, transfer and CGI belong to the main function of network.

Running Platform. It refers to the software and hardware environment that must be offered when using the component, including the operating system for component running and supporting platform software etc.

Component Model. It describes component formats set according to various existing component types, including JavaBeans, EJB and ActiveX etc.

Programming Language. It points out programming languages for component implementation, including Java, Visual C# etc.

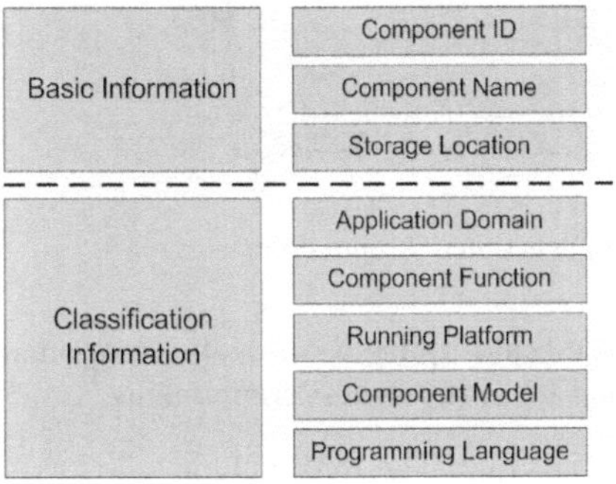

Fig. 3. Composition of Key Information

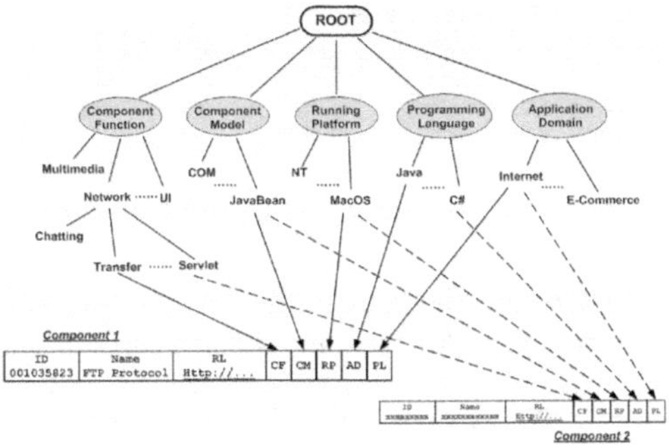

Fig. 4. KI Tree with Two Example Components

These eight items of information are orthogonal and can be systematically organized into a tree-structured architecture, called key index tree, shown as Figure 4. The branches of tree are composed of terminologies of the five classification fields and their subfields. All the terminologies have been specified by the unified component description. Each component is regarded as a leaf node, with component ID, name and research location packed in it, hanging on the related five twigs, which reflect the five values of the component under the five classification fields.

4 KI Based Distributed Registration Process

Figure 5 highlights an example of architecture for the distributed registration. Each component has its detailed description and entity on one of the servers and disperses its key information on all the servers. In this section, we will expatiate on the distributed architecture and procedure of operating the registration mechanism.

4.1 Distributed Architecture

The network is composed of several component servers and one management server, among which the distributed structure is founded and all of the servers are connected

(Fig. 5). Every Server is both a component repository and a registration host. It performs the procedure of receiving a registration request, validating and storing the component, as well as communicating with other servers to keep the component information consistent. The structure and safety manager do not store any information of components or provide the registration service, but has the responsibility to watch all the component servers and adjust their component storage structure, safety degree and other parameters, in order to keep the framework running well.

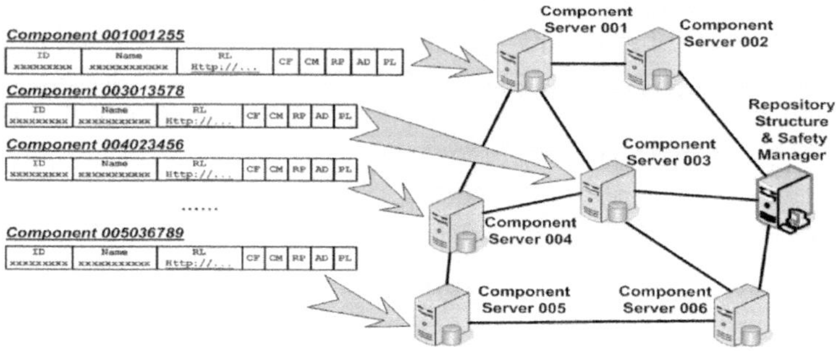

Fig. 5. Composition of an Example Distributed Architecture

There are three essential types of data recorded and updated on every component server, key index tree, neighbor address table, and local-registered components:

- The key index trees on all the servers are the same. The tree includes the key information of components that are stored not only on local server but also on other servers. That is, the key index trees of all the servers should dynamically update after any one of the servers stores a component.
- The neighbor address table is used to communicate between servers. When a new server is added into the network or a server stops working, related servers will detect the change and rewrite the address table of neighbor servers.
- The local-registered components include description files and entities. They are stored only at the server where they are registered and never be transferred to other servers except when manager dispatched them for optimization.

4.2 Sequence of Operations

In this section, we demonstrate what the sequence of operations should be for the standard component registration. Figure 6 shows the sequence of adding a new component to the distributed repository. It can be divided into four pivotal steps.

1) When a registration server receives a component packet submitted from a component provider, it then checks the component description and entity first, in order to guarantee availability, integrality and security of the registering component. If there is any problem with the component, the process will be stopped and a failure report will soon be sent to the component provider.

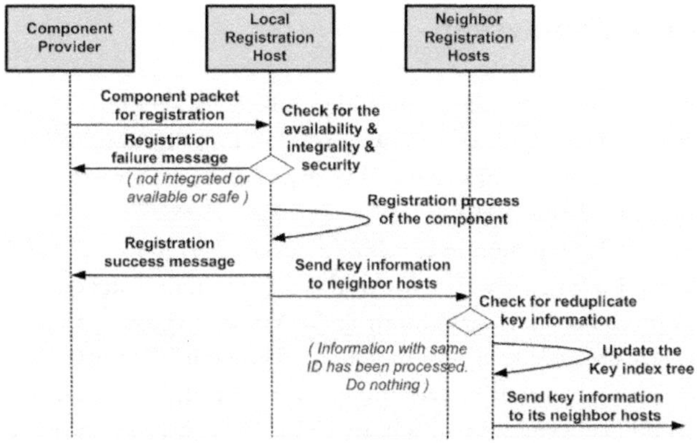

Fig. 6. Sequence of Operations on distributed registration

2) The registration process has been introduced in section 2. The server stores eligible components into the local repository, and updates the local key index tree according to the information of their descriptions.
3) After successfully handling the registering operation, the very server should generate an XML based key information packet, including all the terminologies that depict the registering component in the KI tree. The host then broadcasts the key information packet to its neighbor hosts with XML-based message mechanism and checks for receipt.
4) As soon as a registration server receives a packet of key information, three crucial scenarios are triggered to ensure the key information consistency:
   - Unfold the key information packet to get the component ID, and scan the local KI tree to check whether the component has been already registered on the server earlier. That is, for the same key information, all the servers will send it to its neighbors for consistency, so that several packets can arrive at a host, causing the updating of local key index tree. However, only one packet will get the local KI tree updated and there is no need to deal with all the others. So once the ID is found to be existed in the KI tree, the server just discards the packet and does nothing else.
   - Update the local key index tree with the key information in the packet. As introduced in the section 3, the key information contains component ID, name, storage location, and five classification facet values. The server accordingly extracts the key information, creates a new node to record it, matches the corresponding nodes of the local KI tree, and links the component under the corresponding nodes in the key index tree.
   - Broadcast the key information packet, which was received from one of its neighbors and has been processed to update the local key index tree, to its other neighbors and checks for receipt. Every server just broadcasts the processed packet to its neighbors. So the communication between two servers that are directly connected is absolutely only once. After the flood routing finished, all the server hosts in the network will receive and process the key information packet, so that the key index trees on all the servers are the same, and it can be consistently published on every server.

5 Performance Evaluation

To evaluate the performance of the key-index based distributed registration approach, we coded a simulator using C++, in which a certain number of registration hosts, service component providers and requestors are connected to form a mesh network to simulate the situation of Internet.

We use BRITE [13] to generate topologies up to 200 nodes in random connection. The network delay between every two nodes is calculated according to the shortest path along the physical network topology. We configure some of the nodes as registration servers and create a key index tree on each of them. The other nodes are regarded as service component providers and we randomly deploy among them 1,000 standard diversified components, which are definitely described with UCDL.

In each run, every server is able to process registration, store the components and update local key index tree, while the client nodes have the responsibility to request for registering or searching components. On the other hand, we also simulate the mechanism of UDDI and centralized registry to make comparison. In this section, we introduce our performance metrics, and then the analysis of the simulation results.

5.1 Performance Metrics

The basic function of the KI based distributed registration is to rationally store and manage the registered components in distributed environment, with the purpose of effectively reducing the data transferred in the network and raising the available rate of service components. To better evaluate the new registration mechanism design, we use the following metrics: average registration time, average response time and total traffic cost.

The Average Registration Time is defined as the average time measured from sending registration request of a component, to the moment that all the servers have consistent information of the component.

The Average Response Time is defined as is defined as the average time elapsed from the issuance of a search query till a desired and available service component is found, beginning to be downloaded or invoked.

The Total Traffic Cost is defined as the traffic of messages incurred when processing registration by queries and responses. The traffic of transferring service components to the hosts, flooding key information packets and are all considered.

5.2 Simulation Results

In the first simulation, we in turn configure N (N=10, 20, 30, 40, 50) nodes of the generated topologies as registration servers and randomly disperse 1,000 different standard components over the other (200-N) client nodes. These 1,000 components are registered to the servers and each registration time is recorded. The results in Fig. 7 show that the KI based distributed registration mechanism makes the registration time shorter than that of UDDI and it makes little difference when the number of registration servers changes.

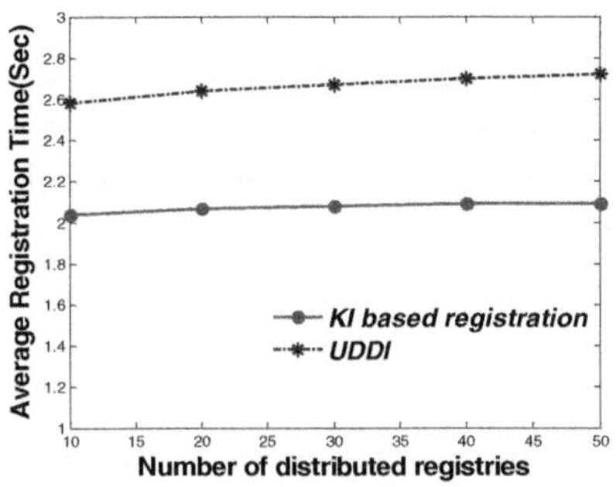

Fig. 7. Average Registration Time V.S. Number of Registry

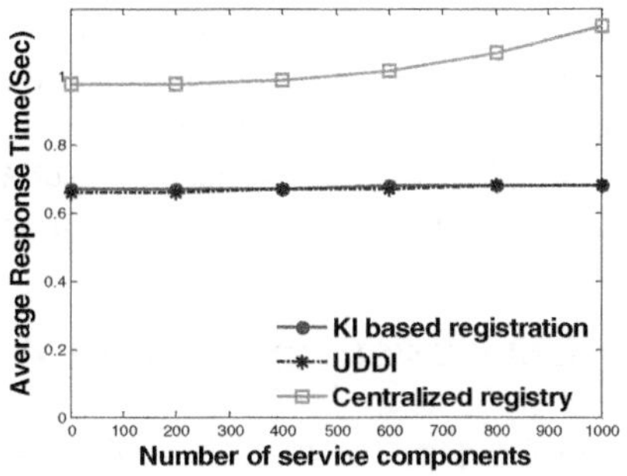

Fig. 8. Average Response Time V.S. Number of Component

We implement the second simulation to analyze the average response time of the requests. The topologies are the same as those in the first simulation with 10 registries and a given number of components M (M=200, 400, 600, 800, 1000) have been registered on the servers after the first simulation. We randomly disperse 10,000 requests from clients searching a component and record their response time. Figure 8 plots the response time against number of components, indicating that the response time will not visibly change with the increase of registered components. And we can see that there is nearly no difference between KI based distributed registration mechanism and UDDI, but lower than the centralized registry. It means that only storing key information on distributed servers is enough to satisfy user requests. The results also show the great scalability of KI based distributed registration mechanism when the number of components increases.

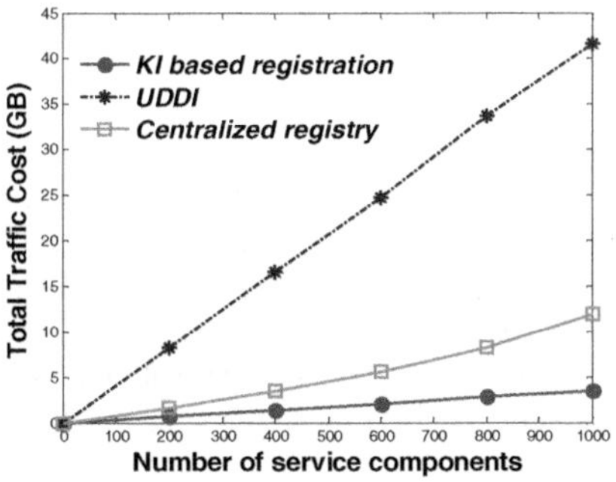

Fig. 9. Total Traffic Cost V.S. Number of Component

We then explore the total traffic cost with different registering component numbers. Traffic of each node in the network will be recorded to calculate the total value. The registering component number, client number and server number are the same as those in the first simulation. According to Figure 9, the total traffic cost is linearly increased with larger number of registering components. With the same number of registering components, the total network traffic with KI based registration mechanism is much smaller than UDDI and centralized registry. An obvious reason for the phenomenon is that KI based distributed registration mechanism reduces both the transfer data among servers and network hops between servers and clients.

6 Conclusions and Future Work

In this paper, we have described a new registering and managing mechanism in distributed component repositories. In the designed architecture, every server creates its local key index tree, and dynamically updates it after each successful registration, to ensure consistent with all the other trees. Based on the result comparison and analysis of experiments, we believe that the KI based distributed registration can effectively abate the overload of network, lighten the burden of each registry server, and raise the utility of component resource. This mechanism can be directly used to create and maintain distributed large-scale repositories for component discovery, in the fields of finance, education, etc. Our future work focuses on integrating ontology and redundancy into the architecture to enhance robustness, and improving efficiency and veracity of component discovery based on the proposed registering mechanism.

Acknowledgement

The author would like to thank anonymous referees for useful comments. This paper is supported by the Natural Science Foundation of China under Grants No. 90604027.

References

1. Yaoxue, Z., Cunhao, F.: Active Service: Concept, Architecture and Implementation. Thomson Learning (2005) ISBN: 7030145763
2. Yuhong, D., Yaoxue, Z., Xing, L.: An XML-based Software Component Description Method for Program Mining. Chinese Journal of Electronics 13(1), 100–104 (2004)
3. Clement, L., Hately, A., Riegen, C.v., Rogers, T.: Universal Description Discovery & Integration (UDDI) 3.0.2 (2004), http://uddi.org/pubs/uddi_v3.htm
4. Cai, M., Frank, M.: RDFPeers: A Scalable Distributed RDF Repository based on A Structured Peer-to-Peer Network. In: Proceedings of the 13th International Conference on World Wide Web, WWW'04 (2004)
5. Hong, W., Lim, M., Kim, E., Lee, J., Park, H.: GAIS: Grid Advanced Information Service based on P2P Mechanism. In: Proceedings of IEEE International Symposium on High Performance Distributed Computing, HPDC'04 (2004)
6. Xiao, L., et al.: On Reliable and Scalable Peer-to-Peer Web Document Sharing. In: Proceedings of the 16th International Parallel and Distributed Processing Symposium, IPDPS (2002)
7. http://www.ComponentSource.com
8. Guha, R.V.: rdfDB: An RDF database, http://guha.com/rdfdb
9. Miller, L.: Inkling: RDF query using SquishQL, http://swordfish.rdfweb.org/rdfquery

10. RDFStore, http://rdfstore.sourceforge.net
11. McBride, B.: Jena: Implementing the RDF Model and Syntax specification. In: 2nd Int'l Semantic Web Workshop (2001)
12. Huai, J., Zhang, Y., Li, X., Liu, Y.: Distributed Access Control in CROWN Groups. In: ICPP, pp. 435–442 (2005)
13. Medina, A., Lakhina, A., Matta, I., Byers, J.W.: BRITE: An Approach to Universal Topology Generation. In: Proceedings of the 9th International Workshop on Modeling, Analysis, and Simulation of Computer and Telecommunication Systems (2001)

BASCA: A Business Area-Oriented Service Component Adaptation Approach Suitable for Ubiquitous Environment

Pengwei Tian, Yaoxue Zhang, Ming Zhong, Yuezhi Zhou, and Cunhao Fang

Department of Computer Science and Technology, Tsinghua University, Beijing, 100084, P.R. China
tpw04@mails.tsinghua.edu.cn

Abstract. Service customization always plays an important role in ubiquitous environment, in which the adaptation of service component according to user requirement is a key problem. Component adaptation is a traditional topic in Component-Based Software Development (CBSD) and Service-Oriented Architecture (SOA) research fields. But most of the existing approaches employ high level abstraction to achieve the adaptation process and usually make it a computation-intensive task, which can hardly be utilized in the ubiquitous environment. In addition, the high level abstraction-based approach is always difficult to understand for normal users. In this paper, based on the analysis of existing approaches, a business area-oriented service component adaptation approach is proposed. The approach employs basic functions of the business area to represent user requirement and service components. Three control structures are introduced to model the interconnection of the functions. Then the adaptation is performed based on the functionality relationships between service components and user requirement. The approach usually causes low computation cost and is easy to be utilized in ubiquitous environment.

1 Introduction

With the development of computing devices, more and more services are available in the ubiquitous environment. As the existing services are rare to always have the identical functions with user requirement, how to select and adapt the services according to user requirement has been an important problem in ubiquitous computing [1][2].

From a user's point of view, each service provided by a single device is a service component, and the service he needs is usually a composition of adapted service components. A service component is usually a computing unit with contractually specified interfaces and can be regarded as a software component [3][4]. Then the experiences in the Component-Based Software Development (CBSD) and Service-Oriented Architecture (SOA) research fields can be borrowed to conduct the service component adaptation issues in ubiquitous environment.

Component adaptation is an active topic in CBSD and SOA research fields, and many works have been done to address the issue. Case-Based Reasoning [5][6] has

J. Indulska et al. (Eds.): UIC 2007, LNCS 4611, pp. 1014–1023, 2007.

long been used in the research of component adaptation, in which existing cases or scenarios are used in the knowledge reasoning process for component adaptation. SPARTACAS [7][8] aims to achieve component adaptation at the specification level, in which both the components and user requirement are defined as axiomatic structure-based specifications. And theorem proving is employed to perform component adaptation. ABC [9] and XSADL [10] achieve software components adaptation based on the software architecture (SA) theory. The two frameworks respectively introduce their own Architecture Description Language (ADL) to model the adaptation architecture. IRules [11] proposes execution rules, named active rules, to adapt and integrate black-box components. Active rules are expressed as event-condition-action structure, in which when an event happens, if the condition holds, the action will be executed. The component functions are invoked by the actions, via which the component adaptation is achieved.

Most of the existing works focus on the functionality relationships between components and user requirement to perform component adaptation, which could also be introduced into the service component adaptation in ubiquitous environment. But most of the existing approaches are originally designed for the computer-centric environment and usually use high level abstraction to represent the functions and functionality relationships, such as knowledge-based cases [5], axiomatic structure-based specification [7], ADL description [9][10] and active rules [11], which makes the component adaptation a computation-intensive task. We know that, in ubiquitous environment, users usually need real-time services while the computing devices may be small and with limited computing ability, then the computation-intensive approaches can hardly work well in the ubiquitous environment. In addition, we all want to build a human-centric ubiquitous environment, in which users are the central roles. However, it is always difficult for normal users to understand the high level abstraction and input their requirement accurately.

Based on the discussions above, in this paper, we propose a Business Area-oriented Service Component Adaptation (BASCA) approach. The approach also focuses on the functionality relationships between service components and user requirement. Basic functions of the business area related to the service environment are introduced as functionality elements to describe user requirement and service component functions, which are called business function units. Three control structures are employed to model the combination of the function units. And functionality relationships are resolved via the comparison between function unit combinations. Then a basic adaptation operation is defined based on the control structures to perform the service component adaptation via the functionality relationships. Users are usually familiar with the business area they focus on and the business process they need, then they can input the requirement conveniently and accurately with BASCA approach.

The rest of the paper is organized as follows: Section 2 gives an overview of the BASCA approach, several basic concepts included; Section 3 detailedly introduces the adaptation process of BASCA approach; Section 4 discusses the representation of the adaptation result and the utilization issues of BASCA approach in a practical service environment. Finally, the conclusion is drawn in Section 5.

2 The BASCA Approach Overview

The BASCA approach is proposed to adapt the service components in ubiquitous environment according to user requirement. In the paper, the service components are mainly the functionality services or the third-party services described in [11].

2.1 BASCA Framework

Fig.1 gives the framework of BASCA approach in a typical application environment. In a ubiquitous environment, there are always various distributed computing devices connected with the wire or wireless networks. Each of the computing devices provides certain services, called service components. All the service components can be registered into the service directory of the environment. Then users can employ certain personal computing devices, such as PDA, smart phone and laptop computer, to obtain the services they need. As shown in Fig.1, the BASCA approach can be utilized to help achieve service customization for users.

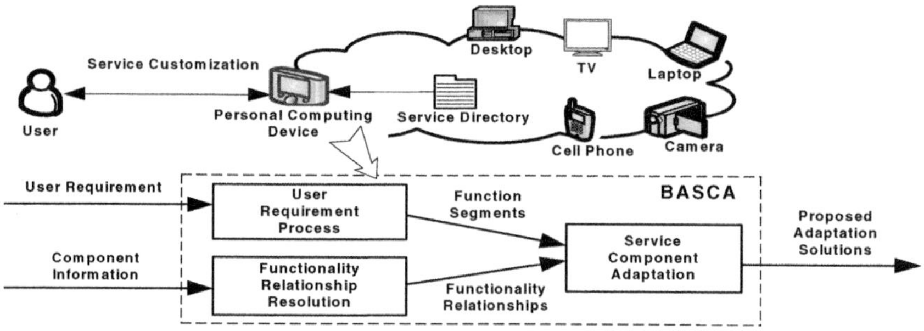

Fig. 1. BASCA framework and application environment

The approach comprises three parts: user requirement process, functionality relationship resolution and service component adaptation. User requirement process module parses user requirement into function segments. Functionality relationship resolution module performs function comparison between service components and user requirement and returns the functionality relationships. Collaborating with other modules, service component adaptation module produces the adaptation solutions.

In the following sections, we will give several basic concepts in BASCA approach.

2.2 Business Area and Function Unit

A service requirement always focuses on a business area which is usually known well by the user. Meanwhile, the services provided in a service environment always belong to a specific business area. Then it is an intuitive way to use the basic functions of the business area as functionality elements to represent both user requirement and service components, which can be called business function units. A business area can be defined as a tuple:

BA={BAName, FunDesc, DataType, BFunUnit}, where:

— BAName gives the name of the business area;
— FunDesc briefly introduces the function of the business area;
— DataType gives the basic data types, in which the relationship between data types is included. A data type EXT can be represented as EXT:{SubEXT1...SubEXTn}, which means the data type EXT comprises other types: SubEXT1,..., SubEXTn;
— BFunUnit is a set of business function units of the business area. A business function unit is expressed as a function signature with input and output;

An example of business area description is shown in Fig.2, which focuses on the business area of a railway station and provides the basic functions frequently used.

BAName: Railway Station Business Area
FunDesc: A set of typical services provided in the environment of a railway station.
DataType: Null:{}, City:{}, TrainNum:{}, Station:{}, Time:{}
BerthTicket:{}, SeatTicket:{}, Ticket:{BerthTicket,SeatTicket}
BFunUnit: StationQuery: {<i1:City>,<o1:Station>, o1= StationQuery (i1)}
StationBrowsing: {<i1:Station>,<o1:Null>, o1= StationBrowsing (i1)}
TrainQuery: {<i1:Station>,<o1:TrainNum,o2:Ticket>, <o1,o2>= TrainQuery (i1)}
TicketBuying: {<i1:TrainNum,i2:Ticket,i3:Time>,<o1:Null>, o1= TicketBuying (i1,i2,i3)}

Fig. 2. The description of a railway station business area

2.3 Control Structures

Control structures are used to organize the business function units. In BASCA approach, three structures from [3][5] are employed as control structures, which are sequential, alternative and parallel structure, as shown in Fig.3.

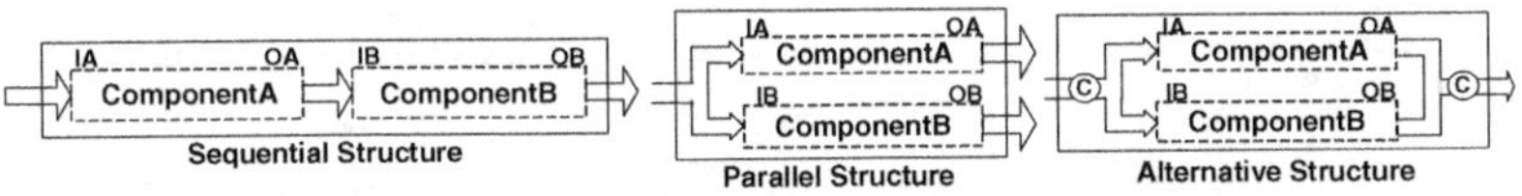

Fig. 3. Three control structures from SPARTACAS

The sequential structure is an interconnection of two components where the output of one component serves as the input of the other. In the parallel structure, given their own input, two independent components can work simultaneously to generate their own output respectively. In the alternative structure, each component can only accept a subset of the input. Given an input, the control condition will be used to decide which component to use and generate the output.

2.4 Service Component Description

A service component is a service provided by a single device. Business function unit combination modeled by control structures is used to represent service components.

The structure of a service component can be various. A component with complex structure, such as the alternative structure, always has low reusability and causes high adaptation cost, which is not considered in BASCA. If a service component with alternative structure is a frequently used service, it can be defined as a function unit of the business area to reuse. In addition, if a service component is in parallel structure, it can be described as several independent service components based on the parallel branches. The paper just focuses on the components with sequential structure as shown in Fig.4, which can be represented as a tuple:

SC= {SCInput, SCOutput, $<SCF_1,SCF_2,\ldots,SCF_i,\ldots,SCF_n>$}, where

— SCInput is the input domain of the service component;

— SCOutput is the output range of the service component;

— $SCF_1 \ldots SCF_n$ is the business function unit series;

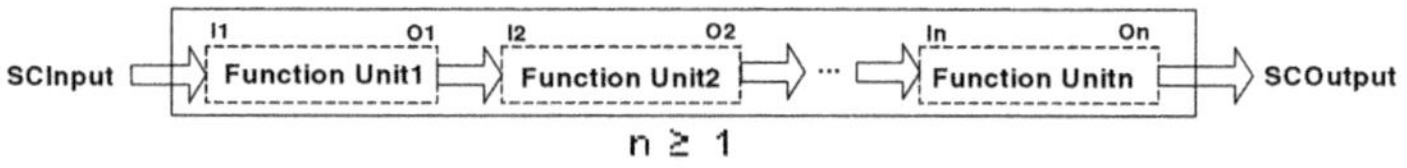

Fig. 4. Service component with sequential structure

As an example, a set of service components belonging to the railway station business area is shown in Fig.5.

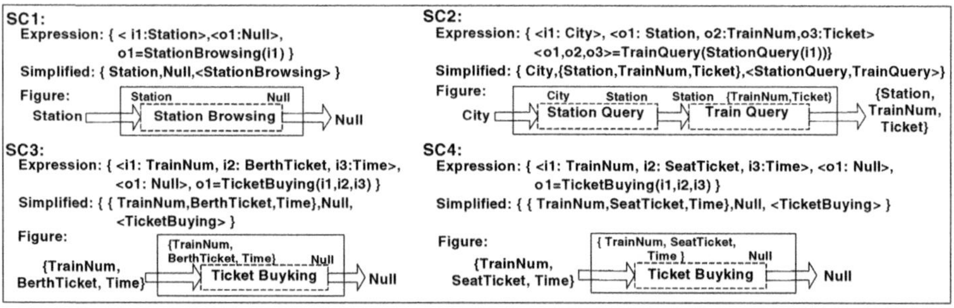

Fig. 5. Service components of the railway station business area

2.5 User Requirement Representation

As shown in Fig.6, user requirement is represented with business function units organized by control structures. URInput is the input of the service requirement and UROutput is the output. As an example, a specific user requirement of the railway station business area is shown in Fig.7, which is represented based on the business function units in Fig.2. From Fig.7, we can see that the user wants to buy a ticket to a city at the given time and meanwhile get some information of the destination station.

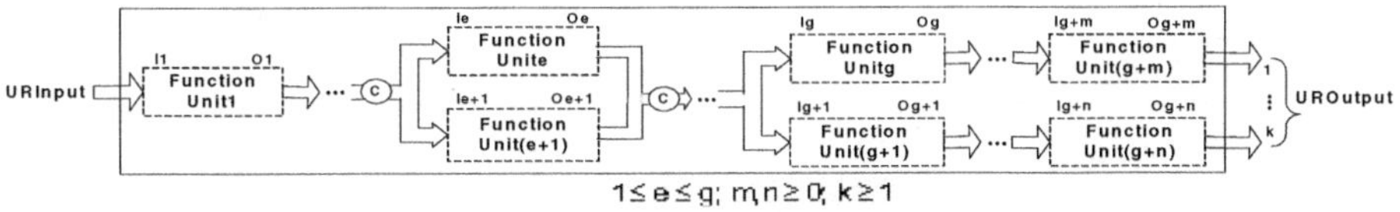

Fig. 6. User requirement representation

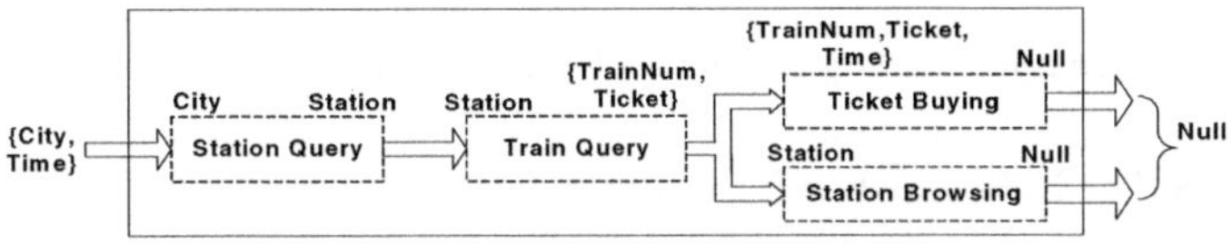

Fig. 7. A user requirement related to the rail way station business area

3 Service Component Adaptation Approach

Based on the representation of service components and user requirement, the service component adaptation can be performed, which comprises three parts: user requirement process, functionality relationship resolution and service component adaptation.

3.1 User Requirement Process

User requirement process is to simplify and parse the user requirement into function segments. Two simplification operations are proposed as shown in Fig.8. The first operation achieves the simplification on the alternative structure, in which the control condition is divided into alternative branches and operates on the input and output to decide which to work. And the alternative structure is simplified into a parallel-like structure. The second operation performs simplification on the parallel structure. The input is passed to the parallel branches independently, which collectively produce the output. Then a parallel structure is simplified to be a set of sequential structures.

With the two simplification operations, all the control structures can be transformed into sequential structures. The user requirement can be transformed into a set of sequential structure-based business function unit combination, each of them called a function segment. A simplified user requirement representation can be given as:

UR={ URInput, UROutput, {I_1,O_1, <URF_1,…,URF_e>},…,
{I_i,O_i,< URF_j,…,URF_k>},…, {I_n,O_n, < URF_m,…,URF_t>}}, where

- URInput is the input of the user requirement;
- UROuput is the output of the user requirement;
- {I_i,O_i,< URF_j,…,URF_k>}is a function segment, in which I_i and O_i are the input and output and < URF_j,…,URF_k> are the business function units;

Then the user requirement shown in Fig.7 can be expressed in the simplified form: UR={{City,Time},Null,{City,{Station,TrainNum,Ticket},<StationQuery,TrainQuery>},{{TrainNum,Ticket,Time},Null,<TicketBuying>},{Station,Null,<SationBrowsing>}}, in which three function segments are included.

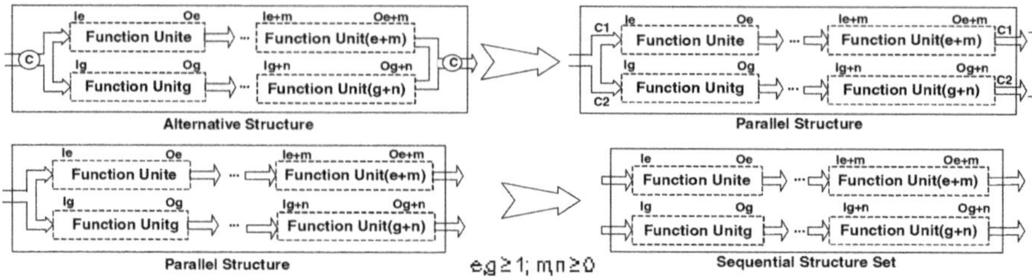

Fig. 8. Simplification operations on the alternative and parallel structures

3.2 Functionality Relationship Resolution

Functionality relationship between service components and user requirement is the focus of BASCA approach. Given the user requirement $UR=\{URInput, UROutput, \{I_1,O_1, <URF_1,\ldots,URFe>\},\ldots,\{I_n,O_n, <URF_m,\ldots,URF_t>\}\}$ and a service component $SC=\{SCInput, SCOutput, <SCF_1,\ldots,SCF_n>\}$, the functionality relationship between SC and UR is performed based on each function segment $URFS=\{IU,OU, <URF_1,\ldots,URFi>\}$ and can be defined as FR(SC,URFS) ={Num, Dom}. Num is the number of common function units contained at the beginning of both SC and URFS. Dom denotes whether the input of SC covers the input of URFS and holds the value of "C" or "N" which means "covering" or "not covering" respectively.

```
SC={SCInput, SCOutput, <SCF1,...,SCFn>}
URFS= {IU, OU, <URF1,...,URFi>}
if (i ≤ n) { FR(SC,URFS)=Null; }
Else if (<URF1...URFj> = <SCF1...SCFj>)
{ if (IU ⊆ SCInput) { FR(SC,URFS)=<j,C> ;}
  Else { FR(SC,URFS)=<j,N> ;} }
Else { FR(SC,URFS)=Null}
```

Fig. 9. Functionality relationship assigning rules

FR(SC,URFS) can be assigned with the rules shown in Fig.9. With the assigning rules, the functionality relationships between the user requirement and service components of the railway station business area are shown in table 1.

Table 1. Functionality relationships of railway station business area

Function Segment \ Service Components	SC1	SC2	SC3	SC4
{City,{Station,TrainNum,Ticket},<StationQuery,TrainQuery>}	Null	<2,C>	Null	Null
{{TrainNum,Ticket,Time},Null,<TicketBuying>}	Null	Null	<1,N>	<1,N>
{Station,Null,<SationBrowsing>}	<1,C>	Null	Null	Null

3.3 Service Component Adaptation

Service component adaptation is to adapt the service components according to user requirement and generate service component composition solution. In BASCA approach, service component adaptation is achieved based on the functionality relationships and performed based on each function segment of user requirement.

First, a basic adaptation operation is defined. Given a service component SC={SCInput, SCOutput, $<SCF_1,\ldots,SCF_n>$}, a function segment URFS={IU,OU, $<URF_1,\ldots,URF_e>$} and the functionality relationship FR(SC,URFS), the adaptation operation can be denoted as URFS_R=Adaptation(SC,URFS), in which URFS_R is the result returned. If FR(SC, URFS) is Null, SC can not be adapted and URFS_R is Null. Otherwise, SC will be adapted and return a new function segment URFS_R as shown in Fig.10. If FR(SC, URFS)=<j,C>, SC replaces the matching function units and links the mismatching function units in sequential structure to generate URFS_R. If FR(SC, URFS)=<j,N>, SC just replaces the matching function units for a subset of the input based on the alternative structure. And the mismatching function units are interconnected sequentially to generate URFS_R.

With the adaptation operation, a part of the function segment is replaced with the service component. With an iterative adaptation process, shown in Fig.11, the whole function segment will be transformed into a service component composition finally.

For the whole user requirement UR= {URInput, UROutput, URFS1,..., URFSi,...,URFSn}, when each function segment has been adapted successfully, the whole requirement will be transformed to be a service component composition, which serves as the adaptation solution.

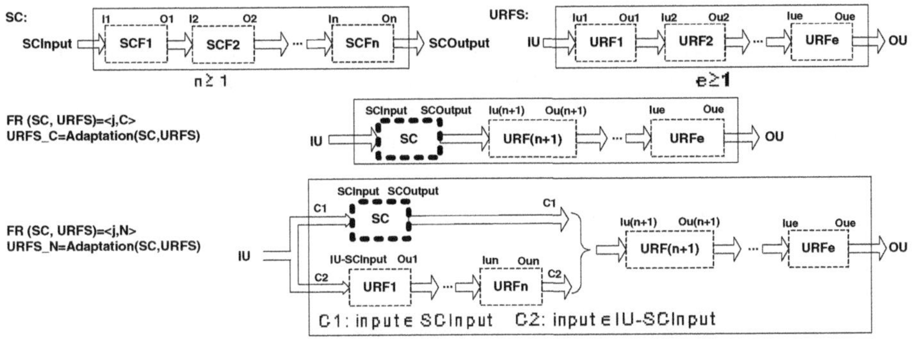

Fig. 10. Adaptation operation description

```
Function Segment Adapation_Result;
Bool Adapt_FS(Function Segment URFS)
{ if (URFS comprises only service components)
   { Adaptation_Result=URFS;
     return true; }
  for (int =1;i<n;i++)
  { Funcition Segment URFS_R=Adaptation(SCi,URFS) ;
     if (URFS_R is Null) break;
     else
     { if (Adapt_FS(URFS_R) is true) return true;
       else break;} }
  return false ;}
```

Fig. 11. Adaptation process for function segment

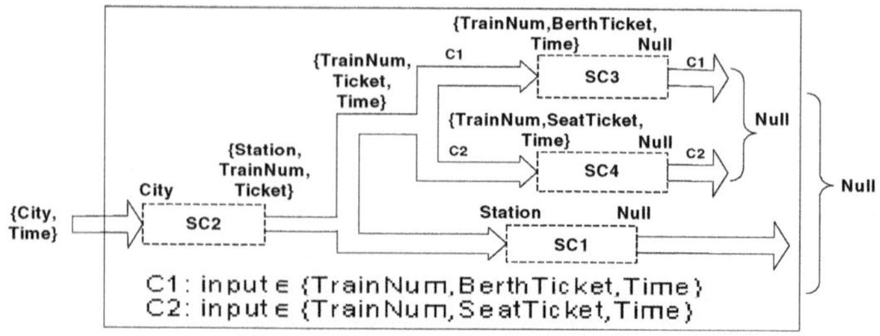

Fig. 12. The adaptation solution of railway station business area

With the functionality relationships in table 1, when the adaptation completes, the user requirement of railway station business area can be finally adapted as shown in Fig.12, which serves as the adaptation solution proposed by BASCA approach.

4 The Adaptation Result and Application Discussions

In practical use, the adaptation result can be in various formats for use purpose, such as plain text, XML script, and so on. As shown in Fig.13, the pseudocode for the adaptation solution in Fig.12 is given, in which a class is defined for the adaptation solution and each service component is imported as an object.

In service environments, the BASCA approach is relatively easy to utilize. The description for the business area can be post in public. Each service provided in the service environment can be described with the basic functions of the business area and registered into the service directory of the environment.

```
public class RailWay_Service_Adaptation
{public City Input1;
 public Time Input2;
 public SC1 cSC1; // Service Component Declaration
 public SC2 cSC2;
 public SC3 cSC3;
 public SC4 cSC4;
 public void Service(City iCity, Time iTime)
 {   iCity=this.Input1;
     iTime=this.Input2;
     Station pStation; //Service Component SC2
     TrainNum pTrainNum;
     Ticket pTicket;
     {pStation,pTrainNum,pTicket}=cSC2.Service(iCity);
     Thread pNewthread; //Service Component SC1 in New Thread
     pNewthread.Start(cSC1.Service(pStation));
     if(pTicket is BerthTicket) //Service Component SC3 and SC4
     { cSC3.Service(pTrainNum,pTicket,iTime); }
     else if(pTicket is SeatTicket)
     { cSC4.Service(pTrainNum,pTicket,iTime);}
     Wait(pNewthread); //Synchronous Operation
     Return Null; } }
```

Fig. 13. Pseudocode for the adaptation example

For users, after reading the service description posted, they can use the basic business functions to express the service requirements. A graphic user interface can provided for users to input the requirement with visual operations, such as drag and drop.

Then the BASCA approach can achieve the adaptation for user requirement and generate the service component composition solution on demand.

5 Conclusions

We propose a business area-oriented service component adaptation approach suitable for ubiquitous environment. The approach employs the basic functions of the business area related to the service environment to represent user requirement and service components. And three control structures are introduced to organize the functions. Then the functionality relationships between service components and user requirement are resolved to achieve the adaptation process. The approach is easy to utilize and causes relatively low computation cost in practice.

The future work includes the optimization on the adaptation algorithm and performance evaluation of the approach.

References

1. Lewis, D., O'Donnell, T., et al.: Managing User-Centric Adaptive Services for Pervasive Computing. In: Proceedings of International Conference on Automatic Computing, ICAC-04, pp. 248–255 (2004)
2. Kantor, P.B., Boros, E., et al.: Capturing Human Intelligence in the Net. Communications of the ACM 43(8), 112–115 (2000)
3. Szyperski, C., Pfister, C.: Summary, workshop on Component-Oriented Programming. In: ECOOP-96 (1996)
4. Szyperski, C.: Component Software: Beyond Object-Oriented Programming, ACM Press, Addison-Wesley, New York (1998)
5. Kinley, D.B.L.A., Wilson, D.: Learning to Improve Case Adaptation by Introspective Reasoning and CBR. In: Case-Based Reasoning: Experiences, Lessons, and Future Directions, AAAI Press/MIT Press, Massachusetts (1996)
6. Smyth, B., Keane, M.T.: Experiments on Adaptation-Guided Retrieval in Case-Based Design.Technical Report TCD-CS-94-17, Trinity College, Dublin (1994)
7. Morel, B., Alexander, P.: SPARTACAS: Automating Component Reuse and Adaptation. IEEE Transaction on Software Engineering 30(9), 587–600 (2004)
8. Penix, J., Alexander, P.: Toward automated component adaptation. In: Proceedings of 9th International Conference on Software Engineering and Knowledge Engineering, pp. 535–542 (1997)
9. Mei, H., Chen, F., Feng, Y.D., Yang, J.: ABC: An architecture based,component oriented approach to software development. Journal of Software 14(14), 721–732 (2003)
10. Zhang, S., Goddard, S.: xSADL: an architecture description language to specify compnent-based systems. In: Proceedings of 6th International Conference on Information Technology: Coding and Computing, pp. 443–448 (2005)
11. Urban, S.D., Dietrich, S.W., Na, Y., Jin, Y., Sundermier, A.: The IRules Project: Using Active Rules for the Integration of Distributed Software Components. In: Proceedings of 9th IFIP 2.6 Working Conference on Database Semantics: Semantic Issues in E-Commerce System, pp. 265–286 (2001)

A Pervasive Service Framework for Pervasive Computing Applications

Yong Zhang, Shensheng Zhang, and Songqiao Han

Department of Computer Science and Engineering, Shanghai Jiao Tong University
No. 800, Dong Chuan Road, Shanghai, 200240, China
zycs926@sjtu.edu.cn

Abstract. Currently, the growth of pervasive computing has introduced an increasing number of services in daily life. There is an urgent need for service provision framework of pervasive computing applications. In this paper, we propose a pervasive service framework that includes a component-based service model and a user-oriented Quality of Service (QoS) model. The fuzzy expression of user preference is covered in our design. Moreover, we reduce the kernel of the service selection problem to Multiple Attribute Decision Making (MADM) problem with incomplete preference, which can be solved by classic methods. The result of experiments on current implementation justifies our design.

1 Introduction

In pervasive computing scenarios, intelligent spaces or smart rooms are full of mobile, wireless and embedded devices. With the popularity of portable devices, the demand of people is surging to access information services beyond personal information management. People equipped with portable device that can connect multiple wireless networks ask for access many kind of information services easily just like using desktop computers. Currently, the growth of pervasive computing has introduced an increasing number of services in daily life[1], which are provided by third-party software vendors, commonly termed value-added service providers, instead of traditional network operators and equipment vendors[2]. There is an urgent need for service provision framework of pervasive computing applications.

Unlike previous applications on the desktop, pervasive computing applications are user-centric, mobile and resource constrained. Moreover, the new user interfaces and interactions on portable devices may cause incomplete and imprecise context information such as use preference. All these characteristics need to be considered in the design of service provision framework. In this paper, we design and evaluate a pervasive service framework which can process fuzzy and incomplete user preference, compute user-oriented Quality of Service (QoS) values and select satisfying services for the user. The rest of the paper is organized as follows: firstly, we describe the problem of service provisioning. A component-based service model and a user-oriented QoS model are presented respectively. We also discuss the expression of user preference to quality criteria based on fuzzy set theory. Then, we reduce the service selection problem to Multiple Attribute Decision Making (MADM) and present the

J. Indulska et al. (Eds.): UIC 2007, LNCS 4611, pp. 1024–1033, 2007.

solution. Finally, we perform several experiments to evaluate our design and come to the conclusion of this paper.

2 Problem Formalization

The problem of service provisioning can be denoted by a tuple $\langle R, Q, S, F(S), \Gamma \rangle$, where:

- R is the collection of context information such as user preference, device capability and network status, etc;
- $S = \{s_1, s_2, ..., s_m\}$ represents a nonempty service set;
- $Q = \langle q, f \rangle$ is a QoS model, where $q = \{q_1, q_2, ..., q_n\}$ is a set of quality criteria, $f = \{f_{q1}, f_{q2}, ..., f_{qn}\}$ is a set of corresponding quality evaluation functions;
- $F(S) = \{S' \mid S' \subseteq S\}$ is the collection of all subsets of S;
- $\Gamma : R \times (S \times Q.f) \to F(S)$ is a function that can evaluate services through $Q.f$ and select a appropriate subset of S, which is the most satisfying to the user in current context.

3 Component-Based Service Model

In our design, a service can be implemented as the composition of service components rather than a monolithic program. The service model is defined as follows:

Definition 1 (Component-Based Service). $\forall s \in S$, s can be formalized as an acyclic graph: $\langle v, e \rangle$, where $v = \{c_1, c_2, ..., c_n\}$ is the set of service components that act as nodes in a graph. e is the set of edges which indicates the sequence of service components in service chain. Usually, s can be written as $\langle c_1, c_2, ..., c_n \rangle$.

Definition 2 (Service Partition). $\forall s \in S$, $s = \langle c_1, c_2 .., c_n \rangle$, in the runtime, $\exists j \in [1, n]$, $s_{ME} = \{\langle c_1, c_2, .., c_j \rangle \mid \forall i \in [1, j], c_i$ runs in mobile-end$\}$, $s_{BE} = \{\langle c_{j+1}, c_{j+2}, .., c_n \rangle \mid \forall i \in [j+1, n]$ c_i runs in back-end.$\}$. So s can also be denoted as: $s = s_{ME} \oplus s_{BE}$.

Except the most common service proxy, the components running in mobile-end (portable devices) include those that can transform the format of data/message, render the result of service to fit the color depth and screen size of portable devices, encrypt or decrypt data/message and buffer data/message to tackle unstable network connection. The components in back-end are those that are deployed and running in the servers distributed in Intranet or Internet. For example, two media playing services are implemented as shown in Fig.1.

Although our service model is similar to the model presented in[3], service partition in our model focusing on the deployment of components will facilitate the quality

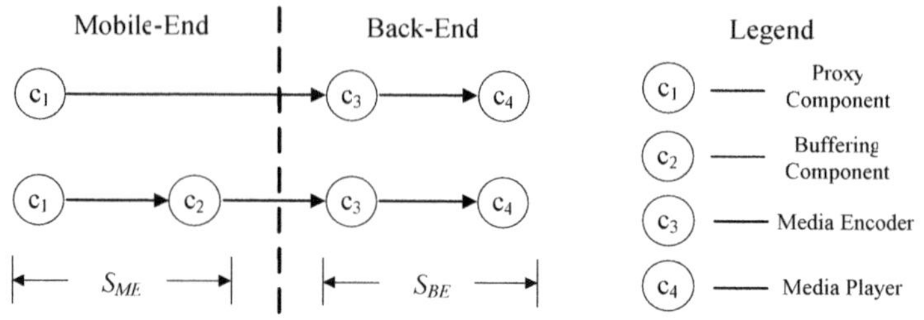

Fig. 1. Two media playing services: one with buffering component and the other without buffering component

evaluation in pervasive computing (see Section 4.). Moreover, for the simplity, we assume that there is no conditional branching in the service model compared with [3].

4 User-Oriented QoS Model

In pervasive computing, the user is the center of computation. Hence, the quality criteria associated with human's perception (e.g. price and latency) need to be covered so as to achieve maximal degree of satisfaction for the user. As mentioned above, the impact of resource-limitedness also must be considered in QoS model. In our design, a user-oriented QoS model is given as follows:

$Q.q = \{$ *price, latency, memory, screen size, color depth, battery life* $\}$,

$Q.f = \{f_{price}, f_{latency}, f_{memory}, f_{screen}, f_{color}, f_{battery}\}$.

Here, the QoS model contains a limited number of quality criteria. However, with good scalability, the QoS model can add or delete quality criteria without influencing service selection method based on the model. For each service s, $s = s_{ME} \oplus s_{BE}$. According to the service model defined in Section 3, the quality evaluation functions can be defined as follows:

- f_{price}. The function is calculating the sum of price of all components contained in the s, denoted as:

$$f_{price}(s) = \sum_{c \in s.v} price(c),$$

Where *price*() is the price of components. Generally, the price of components is assigned by the VASPs and published in the profile of the service component.

- f_{memory}. The function is calculating the sum of memory used by components in mobile-end, denoted as: $f_{memory}(s) = \sum_{c \in s_{ME}.v} memory(c)$,

Where *memory*()can calculate the memory used by a component which equals to the variation of memory after the system loads the component. The *memory*() can be implemented by system performance APIs that can monitor the memory. Usually, the memory used by a component in runtime is not a constant value due to multiple execution paths in the component. The memory can be calculated based on past data, i.e.,

$$memory(c)=\frac{\sum_{i=1}^{n} memory_i(c)}{n}.$$

Where $memory_i()$ is a past value of the used memory, and n is the number of execution times in the past.

- $f_{latency}$. The function is calculating the sum of latency of all components and the time of downloading components to mobile-end, i.e.,

$$f_{latency}(s)=\sum_{c\in s.v} latency(c)+\frac{\sum_{c\in s_{ME}.v} memory(c)}{bandwidth}.$$

The latency of a component is the duration between the moment that the component is invoked and the moment the result is received. Similar to the memory, the latency is also calculated based on past data: $latency(c)=\frac{\sum_{i=1}^{n} latency_i(c)}{n}$, where $latency_i()$ is a past latency of the component and n is the number of execution times in the past.

- $f_{battery}$. The function is calculating the sum of battery consumption of components in mobile-end, which includes downloading and executing the components, denoted as:

$$f_{battery}(s)=\sum_{c\in s_{ME}.v} battery(c)+p_k\cdot\frac{\sum_{c\in s_{ME}.v} memory(c)}{bandwidth}.$$

Where the *battery*() can be implemented by system APIs and the battery consumption is also a value of arithmetical average based on the past execution. p_k is a ratio coefficient of downloading components to battery consumption. p_k can be obtained by a simple experiment which investigates the relationship between downloading components and battery consumption.

- f_{screen} and f_{color}. Executing a service has requirements for screen size and color depth, which are similar to the requirement for memory. We firstly define two functions as:

$$I_1 : S\rightarrow RS,\ and\ I_2 : S\rightarrow RC.$$

Here, RS={"640*480 pixels", "640*320 pixels","96*128 pixels"} is a collection of screen sizes for portable devices. RC={"2 color","8 color",…,"64M color"} is a collection of color depths. Generally, the requirements are published in the profile of the service. I_1 *and* I_2 are the functions that can get the requirements from the service profile. Then we can define the evaluation function of screen size and color depth as:

$$f_{screen} : RS\rightarrow[0,1],\ and\ f_{color} : RC\rightarrow[0,1].$$

For a service s, the quality evaluation on the two quality criteria can be denoted as $f_{screen}(I_1(s))$ and $f_{color}(I_2(s))$ respectively. f_{screen} and f_{color} can be modeled by *first order* and *second order* curve that presented in [4]. Here, we adopt *second order* curve to denote f_{screen} and f_{color}. An example of f_{color} is shown in Table.1.

Table 1. Evaluation function of color depth

Color Depth	2	8	16	256	4096	65536
f_{color}	0.10	0.21	0.40	0.69	0.95	1

5 User Preference Model

It is difficult for a user to depict his/her preference to quality criteria in numeric scale precisely. The concept of linguistic variable is very useful in dealing with the situations which are too complex or too ill-defined to be reasonably described in conventional quantitative expressions. The values of a linguistic variable are not numbers but words or sentences in a natural or artificial language [5]. To facilitate the expression of user preference to quality criteria with natural language, we define a set of linguistic terms as:

T ={t_1=very unimportant, t_2=rather unimportant, t_3=important, t_4=rather important, t_5=very important}.

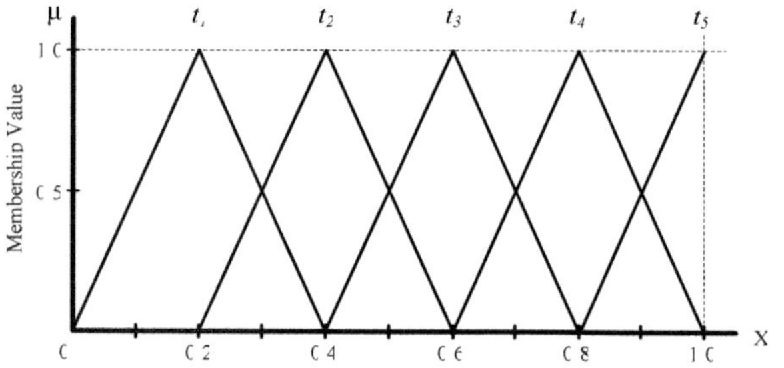

Fig. 2. Membership functions for linguistic terms

Such linguistic terms can be represented by triangular fuzzy numbers as shown in Fig.2. When a user assigns his/her preference with linguistic terms, the corresponding weights of quality criteria can be calculated as:

$$\omega = \mu(t_i) = \frac{\int x \cdot \mu_{t_i}(x)dx}{\int \mu_{t_i}(x)dx}, \quad i \in [1,5]. \tag{1}$$

The formula (**1**) provides the center of area that is covered by the fuzzy number to represent the transformation from the linguistic scale into the numeric scale. For example, if a user expresses his/her preference to battery life as "t_3 = important", we can obtain the weight of battery life:

$$\omega_{battery} = \frac{\int_{0.4}^{0.6} x\cdot(5x-2)+\int_{0.6}^{0.8} x\cdot(4-5x)}{\int_{0.4}^{0.6}(5x-2)+\int_{0.6}^{0.8}(4-5x)} = 0.5995.$$

6 Service Selection

The goal of service selection is to rank the values of service evaluation and select appropriate services, which can not only meet the resource constraints, but also achieve the maximal QoS value. The service selection function can be formalized as:

$$\Gamma(S) = [\![\psi(S)]\!] \text{ and } \psi(S) = (\psi(s_1), \psi(s_2), ..., \psi(s_m)) ,$$

Where $\psi(S)$ is a function evaluating the services on resource constrains and quality criteria. Hence, the $\psi(s_i)$ can be denoted as:

$$\psi(s_i) = E(s_i)\cdot H(s_i), i \in [1,m] , \tag{2}$$

Where $E(s_i)$ is a function calculating the quality value, which aggregates the evaluation on quality criteria. Furthermore, $H(s_i)$ can be written as:

$$H(s_i) = \prod_{r_k\in R} h_k(s_i), and\ \ h_k : S \rightarrow \{0,1\} , \tag{3}$$

Where $R = \zeta(C\times V)$ is the set of all resource constraints. C and V are the name and the value of a resource constraint respectively. $k \in [1,l]$ and l is the number of current resource constraints. r_k may be the memory available in a portable device or the price a user can afford, which can be collected as context data. For example, $R = \{ r_1 = (memory,$ 600KB$),\ r_2 = (price,$ 0.5 dollars$)\}$. The h_k is used to check the kth resource constraint through comparing the quality value (e.g. memory or price) with the value of the kth resource constraint:

$$h_k(s_i) = \begin{cases} 0, f_{q_k}(s_i) > r_k.value \\ 1, f_{q_k}(s_i) \le r_k.value \end{cases} . \tag{4}$$

According to the formula (**2**), (**3**) and (**4**), we can obtain an optimal strategy to compute $\Gamma(S)$:

$$\text{Let } L(S) = \{s_i \mid H(s_i) = 1 \wedge s_i \in S\} , \tag{5}$$

If $s_j \notin L(S)$, according to the formula (**2**) and (**5**), we can obtain $\psi(s_i)=0$. Hence, we just calculate $\Gamma(L(S)) = [\![\psi(L(S))]\!]$. Here, $\psi(s_i)=E(s_i),\ s_i \in L(S)$.

Definition 3 (Service Evaluation Problem Mapping to MADM with Incomplete Preference). MADM problem can be denoted as a tuple $\langle X, U, \omega, A\rangle$, Here, $X=\{x_1,x_2,...,x_m\}$ is an alternative set; $U=\{u_1,u_2,...,u_n\}$ is an attribute set; ω is a weight vector which suggests the importance of attributes; $A=(a_{ij})_{m\times n}$ is a decision matrix, where a_{ij} is a value of alternative $x_i\,(i\in[1,m])$ on the attribute $u_j\,(j\in[1,n])$. Service selection function $\Gamma(S)$ can be mapped to MADM, where $X=L(S), U=Q.q,\ A=L(S)\times Q.f$ and $\omega=\mu(T)$ which has been discussed in section 5. It should be noted that most of users may provide incomplete preference information, as described earlier.

The classic solutions of MADM problem include Simple Additive Weighting Method (SAW), Analytical Hierarchical Process (AHP) and Technique for Order Preference by Similarity to Ideal Solution (TOPSIS). For the simplity, we adopt SAW in service selection which consists of the following steps:

Step 1: Create a decision matrix.
$A=L(S)\times Q.f=(a_{ij})_{m\times n}$, where $a_{ij}=f_{q_j}(s_i)$, and $i\in[1,m], j\in[1,n]$. m is the number of services in $L(S)$. n is the number of quality criteria in $Q.f$.

Step 2: Normalize the decision matrix. $B=(b_{ij})_{m\times n}$.
Here, $b_{ij}=\dfrac{a_{i\max}-a_{ij}}{a_{i\max}-a_{i\min}}$ *or* $b_{ij}=\dfrac{a_{ij}-a_{i\min}}{a_{i\max}-a_{i\min}}$ which depends on that q_j is cost type or benefit type, and $a_{i\max}=\max\{a_{ij}\}$, $a_{i\min}=\min\{a_{ij}\}, 1\le j\le n$.

Step 3: Calculate the unknown weights.
Suppose the known weights are $\omega_j\,(j\in[l+1,n])$, the unknown weights are $\omega_j\,(j\in[1,l])$ and $\sum_{j=1}^{n}\omega_j=1$. The unknown weights can be calculated by average weighted programming[6]:

$$\omega_j=\frac{(1-\sum_{j=l+1}^{n}\omega_j)\sum_{i=1}^{m}b_{ij}}{\sum_{j=1}^{l}(\sum_{i=1}^{m}b_{ij})},\ j=1,2,...,l.$$

Step 4: Calculate the quality value of services with SAW:

$$E(S)=A\times\omega=\{E(s_1),E(s_2),...,E(s_m)\}.$$

Here, $E(s_i)=\sum_{j=1}^{n}b_{ij}\omega_j,\ j=1,2,...,n.$

Step 5: Rank the values of $E(s_j)$ order by decreasing, and select services by setting a threshold value: $\Gamma(L(S))=[\![\psi(L(S))]\!]_\lambda=\{s_i\in S\mid E(s_i)>\lambda\wedge\lambda\in[0,1]\}$.

7 Experiments Evaluation

In order to evaluate our design, we have conducted several experiments based on current implementation and configuration: with Eclipse 3.01[7], we have implemented a prototype of pervasive service framework in java, which includes a package of computing quality value and user preference, a service evaluation package as well as a MIDlet[8] server supporting downloading components. All packages host on a COMPAQ ML350 as back-end, equipped with one Intel Pentium III process, rated at 600MHz, 256MB RAM. The operating system is Microsoft Windows 2000 server, and the Java Virtual Machine version is 1.4.1. A PC machine installed Nokia Developer's Suit 3.0 for J2ME[9] enables us to emulate multiple Nokia's terminals as mobile-end. A machine runs NIST net[10] as a router, which can emulate complex status of wireless network connection between mobile-end and back-end.

We perform the experiments depending on the process of service provisioning: firstly, a portable device launches a request of service provisioning, then the services will be evaluated and selected. Finally, the data of selected services is delivered to the portable device. The data includes the names of the services, quality values and places in the quality evaluation, etc, which is displayed to the user and help the use invoke the services. The overhead is the time of service provisioning that consists of two parts:

1. interaction part: a) establishing a TCP socket between the mobile-end and back-end; b) the latency in the exchange of data/messages; c) the time for delivering the data of selected services to mobile-end as the result of service provisioning;
2. calculation part: a) transforming fuzzy user preferences to numeric weights; b) calculating the unknown weights; c) solving service selection problem with MADM.

We evaluate the performance and scalability in terms of bandwidth, data size of selected services and the number of services for selection. Every experiment has been conducted 50 times, and arithmetical average of the result is used for analysis. With NIST, we set Round Trip Time (RTT) to 200ms as the latency between mobile-end to back-end, and set bandwidth to 10kbps, 50kbps, 200kbps, 1Mbps and 10Mbps to test the framework.

In the first experiment, we fix the other components of overhead, and set the data size of selected services to 5KB, 10KB and 15KB so as to investigate its effect on the

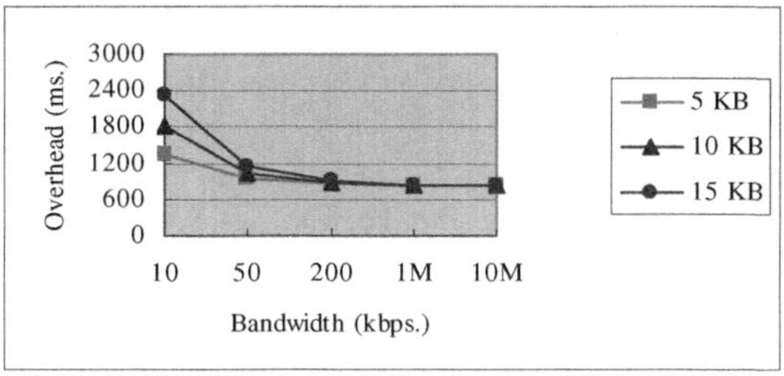

Fig. 3. Impact of the data size

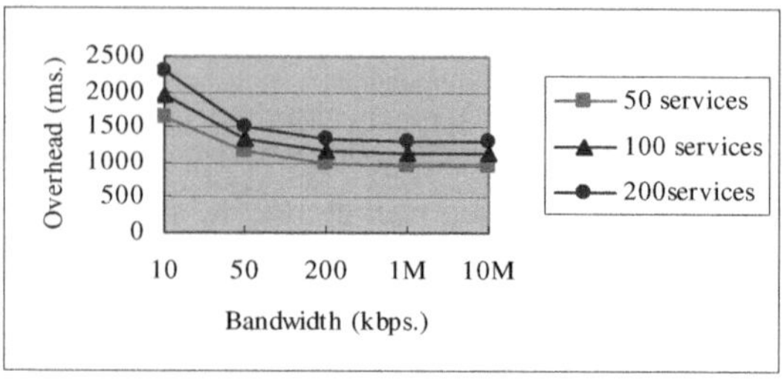

Fig. 4. Impact of the number of services

performance. In Fig 3, we can see the relationship between bandwidth and performance under different information size. Except the section of low bandwidth (10kbps-50kbps), the overhead is insensible to the variation of the data size. Moreover, the overhead is near to a constant value (826 ms) as the bandwidth increases.

In the second experiment, we use the data size of selected service as 10KB. Fig 4 shows the impact of the number of services on the performance. The augmented overhead is introduced by calculation part to calculate weights and solve MADM, as the number of services increases. The amplitudes of augment are not obvious (12 percent-19 percent) due to the little contribution of calculation part to all overhead. However, the overhead ranges from 2309ms to 950ms that is acceptable for the user in practical applications.

The experiments have proved that with the application of our framework, service provision is of better scalability and performance.

8 Conclusion

In this paper, we propose a service provision framework for pervasive applications, which includes the component-based service model and the user-oriented QoS model. To support the expression of user preference with natural language, we design the user preference model on the basic of fuzzy set theory. Moreover, we map the service selection problem to a MADM with incomplete preference which can be solved by classic methods. We have performed the experiments on the current implementation of our design. The experiments testify the validity of our model. We believe the model can facilitate the development of pervasive computing applications.

Acknowledgements

Our work is supported by the Science and Technology Commission of Zhejiang Province (Key Project, 2003C11029), National Research Council of Canada and the Shanghai Science and Technology Commission of China (International Cooperation Project, 05SN07114).

References

1. Riekki, J., Salminen, T., Alakarppa, I.: Requesting pervasive services by touching RFID tags. IEEE Pervasive Computing 5, 40–46 (2006)
2. Zhu, F., Mutka, M.W., Ni, L.M.: Service Discovery in Pervasive Computing Environments. IEEE Pervasive Computing 4, 81–90 (2005)
3. Zeng, L., Benatallah, B.: QoS-Aware Middleware for Web Services Composition. IEEE Transactions on Software Engineering 30, 311–327 (2004)
4. Lum, W.Y., Lau, F.C.M.: User-Centric Content Negotiation for Effective Adaptation Service in Mobile Computing. IEEE Transactions on Software Engineering 29, 1100–1111 (2003)
5. Zimmermann, H.J.: Fuzzy Set Theory and its Applications, 2nd edn. Kluwer Academic Publishers, Dordrecht (1991)
6. Li, D.: Fuzzy multiattribute decision-making models and methods with incomplete preference information. Fuzzy Sets and Systems 106, 113–119 (1999)
7. Eclipse Home Pages, http://www.eclipse.org
8. Java 2 Platform, Micro Edition, http://java.sun.com/javame
9. Nokia Developer's Suite for J2ME^{TM}, http://www.forum.nokia.com
10. National Institution of Standards and Technology, NIST Net Home Page, http://snad.ncsl.nist.gov/itg/nistnet

Symbiotic Computing: Concept, Architecture and Its Applications

Takuo Suganuma[1], Kenji Sugawara[2], and Norio Shiratori[1]

[1] Tohoku University, 2-1-1 Katahira, Aoba-ku, Sendai, 980-5877, Japan
[2] Chiba Institute of Technology, 2-17-1, Tsudanuma, Narashino, 275-0016, Japan
suganuma@shiratori.riec.tohoku.ac.jp

Abstract. Aiming towards the next generation ubiquitous stage we have been pursuing a research on information and communication paradigm, called "Symbiotic computing." Here, we first describe a basic concept and an architecture of the Symbiotic computing, and through several applications such as watch-over system for elderly people and adhoc communication support, we show and discuss the effectiveness of the Symbiotic computing. We first define the traditional ubiquitous computing environment that consists of two computing aspects: mobile computing and pervasive computing. Then, we define the advanced ubiquitous computing that consists of two computing axes: the traditional ubiquitous computing and web computing. In addition to these two axes, we introduced a third new axis (creation of new value) and by integrated these three axes, we created the Symbiotic computing paradigm. Based on the concept of the Symbiotic computing, symbiotic society will be realized, where human and ubiquitous information environment can cooperatively co-exist.

1 Introduction

Aiming towards the next generation ubiquitous stage we have been pursuing a research on information and communication paradigm, called "Symbiotic computing." [1,2,3] We first define traditional ubiquitous computing environment that consists of two computing aspects: mobile computing and pervasive computing. The traditional ubiquitous computing enhances accessibility to services using wireless network and embedded device technologies [4,5,6,7]. On the other hand, web computing is emerging to extend availability and usability of information that has a wide distribution in the world [8]. Here we define advanced ubiquitous computing by integrating the two axes of computing: traditional ubiquitous computing and the web computing. The advanced ubiquitous computing technologies contribute to enhance the IT environment, however, human and social aspects are expected to be sufficiently considered. To overcome this issue and to enhance the advanced ubiquitous computing environment, we introduced a third new axis to create a new value, and by integrated these three axes, we created the Symbiotic computing paradigm. Based on the concept of the Symbiotic computing, symbiotic society will be realized, where human and ubiquitous information environment can cooperatively co-exist.

J. Indulska et al. (Eds.): UIC 2007, LNCS 4611, pp. 1034–1045, 2007.

Regarding the Symbiotic computing, we have been promoting the following researches and developments since 1994 [9,10,11]:

(a) SOTTO: A GIS-based watch-over system for children based on region-wise information.
(b) uEyes: A real-time, multimedia, watch-over system for elderly people, based on environmental information and social knowledge.
(c) Symbiotic group learning: An application to CAI. This group learning support system reinforces the knowledge flow to improve the learning process of the students.
(d) AMACS: An ad-hoc, autonomous network configuration mechanism for wireless networks and application systems.
(e) Ubiquitous multimedia communication system: A real-time multimedia communication system in ubiquitous network environment based on circulation of QoS control knowledge in the network.

In this paper, we first describe the basic concept and architecture of the Symbiotic computing, and through the above mentioned applications, we show and discuss the effectiveness of the Symbiotic computing.

2 Symbiotic Computing: The Concept

2.1 Basic Concept

Symbiotic computing is realized by integrating three axes of computing: ubiquitous computing, web computing, and "P/S (Perceptual/Social) computing," which is newly added, as shown in Figure 1.

Conventional ubiquitous computing consists of two aspects: mobile and pervasive computing. Mobile computing is a technology to realize an environment which enables us to communicate with anyone, anytime and anywhere, using advanced networks and down-sized communication terminals. On the other hand, pervasive computing is a technology, sometimes called as Invisible/Ambient/Disappearing/Calm computing, to realize an environment in which services are embedded onto anything pervasively. In addition, web computing is an emerging technology to provide users in the real space (RS) with information and service in the digital space (DS) simply and readily. Here, we define the advanced ubiquitous computing by integrating the two axes: conventional ubiquitous computing and the web computing. In the concept of Symbiotic computing, as shown in Figure 1, we introduce "P/S computing" as a new third axis. P/S computing is a computing to introduce humanity and sociality of real society into the DS, and to realize providing people with proper information and service.

2.2 Mutual Understanding Between Real Space and Digital Space

To address problems in recent IT society and to realize the Symbiotic computing, it is important to understand situations on the other side, specifically, to realize

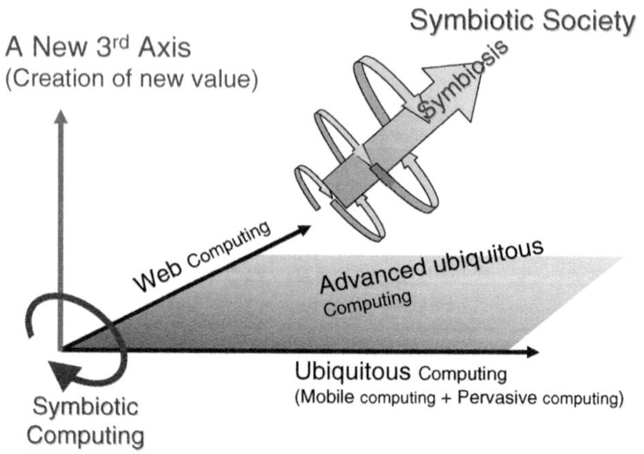

Fig. 1. Basic concept of Symbiotic computing

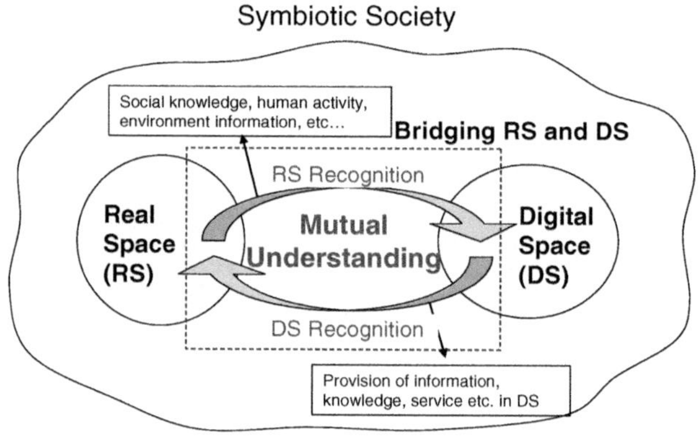

Fig. 2. Mutual understanding between real space and digital space

"Mutual Understanding" between real space (RS) and digital space (DS). This mutual understanding consists of RS recognition and DS recognition as shown in Figure 2. RS recognition is a notion that the DS acquires social intelligence, individual characteristics, and environment information of the RS autonomously. This recognition is accelerated by the ubiquitous computing. DS recognition is a notion that the DS presents and offers information, knowledge, and service of the DS to the RS properly and intelligibly. This recognition is enhanced by web computing. As mentioned above, mutual understanding is a state where the RS and DS can recognize each other.

For example, the DS acquires information of the RS from computer, sensor network, and mobile devices in the RS autonomously and recognizes human activities in the RS. After understanding the requirements and intentions of such activities, the DS actively provides the RS with information, service, and knowledge, those which are appropriate for the RS. Such a mutual understanding between the RS and DS is critical to address the problems in recent IT society. The DS has been passive so far, compared to the RS which has been active. To renew the relationship between the DS and RS, Symbiotic computing effectively works to create autonomy in the DS by the mutual understanding.

3 Basic Architecture of Symbiotic Computing

3.1 Basic Architecture

Here, we show a basic architecture to realize Symbiotic computing in Figure 3. This architecture consists of three parts, that is, Perceptual-ware, Social-ware, and Network-ware. The details are as follows:

(1) Perceptual-ware: This software realizes a sense of perceptual reality in order to understand service offered by DS. Based on signals and data from some ubiquitous devices in RS, this software perceives actions of humans and groups, conditions of environment, and so on, and provides the DS with such information. Furthermore, this software provides, with reflecting people's situations and preferences, RS with information which offered by DS, in the form of enhancing the sense of perceptual reality in order to enhance the users' degree of perception towards the information.

(2) Social-ware: This software realizes a sense of social reality of service offered by the digital space, the service which supports social activities. Combining the information provided by Perceptual-ware with social structure, norms, and common sense, Social-ware understands human's intentions and mental states to provide DS with the information. Furthermore, this software gives the sense of social reality to the information offered by DS in order to enhance the users' senses of ease and safety towards such information.

(3) Network-ware: This software is to support and improve communication between real society and digital society. Network-ware offers functions to distribute the information, knowledge, and service between RS and DS, effectively. This also includes flexible networking technology and ubiquitous networking technology.

3.2 Basic Model

Figure 4 shows a model of Symbiotic computing which realizes mutual understanding to make up a bridge to realize synthesis of the RS and the DS based on the ubiquitous, web, and P/S computing. Here, P/S computing consists of Perceptual computing for perceptual reality and Social computing for social reality. These computings are based on the perceptual-ware and social-ware described in the previous section, respectively. Perceptual computing acquires signals and

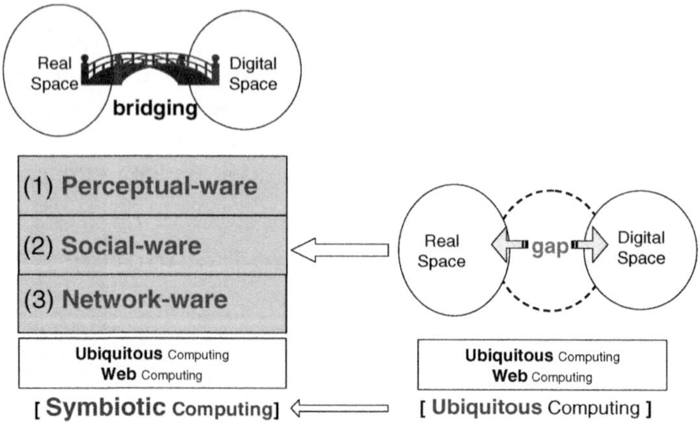

Fig. 3. Basic architecture of Symbiotic computing

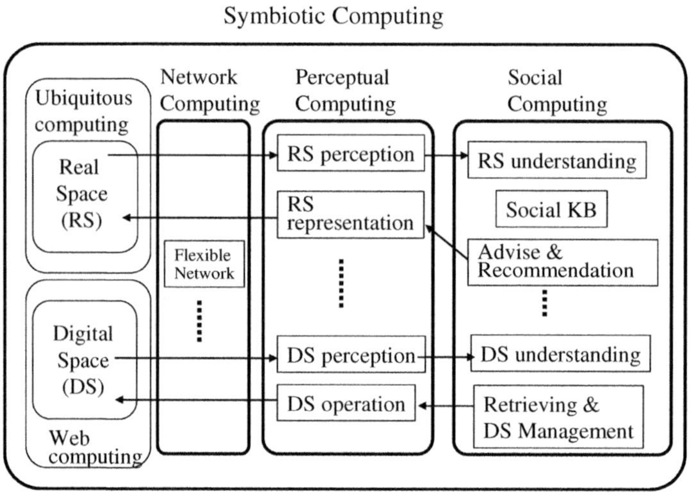

Fig. 4. Model of Symbiotic computing

data from the RS and DS through the Network computing, and processes (identify, express, and operate) them by functions described in the box of Perceptual computing in Figure 4. Then it sends them to Social computing. Using such signal and data, Social computing recognizes users' activities in society based on social intelligence and individual model, using some of the functions and technologies shown in the box of Social computing in Figure 4, in order to provide such activities with some appropriate advice and information.

4 Applications

4.1 SOTTO

We have been developing a novel information system called RUIS: Regional Ubiquitous Information System, and an application of RUIS, called "SOTTO", as a watch over system for children [13]. RUIS is an information infrastructure that supports various applications such as the bargain sell and the watch-over system. Design of these support applications is based on RUIS's "region-oriented social-ware", where the concept of symbiotic computing can be applied effectively. RUIS can obtain and store regional information from network, realize robust security mechanism of personal/private information protection, and provide information to residents of the community that matches to their contexts. Using RUIS features we can realize "smart watch over" for children, senior, and handicapped. And we are working on the implementation of this application based on RUIS prototype.

In our proposed RUIS system there are two distinguishing features:

1) Social-ware for security and safety:
It provides seamless interface to community residents based on "social intelligence". It provides 'smart' and secure access to private information of community residents.
2) Regional information infrastructure based on the social-ware:
It has safety method of utilizing private information by applications. Information providers do not have to take the risk of exposing personal information.

Figure 5 shows the overview of the experimental system of SOTTO that realizes smart support for watch over based on RUIS. The child who is watched over has a ubiquitous terminal that is consisting of PDA device, GPS function, and wireless communication function. Location information of the child is obtained from GPS and sent through wireless device to RUIS that is constructed inside the RUIS Service Subnet. Regional information terminals cast over the region store eventful information that occurs inside the region. In this experimental system, we generate experimental eventful information through the terminal. Server of watch-over service is also placed inside RUIS Service Subnet, and monitors child's activities using location information stored in RUIS. If it judges as emergency (for example, some abnormal activity and no credible person around him), it sends alerts to the home PC of that child's parents.

4.2 uEyes

Real-time multimedia watch-over system is one of the important care-support systems that can be used for watching over children and elderly people from remote site connected by wide-area network.

Researches are at their initial stage to apply this system to the ubiquitous computing environment. The contribution of existing works is to make the system easy-to-use. However, when the watched person wants to keep privacy, or

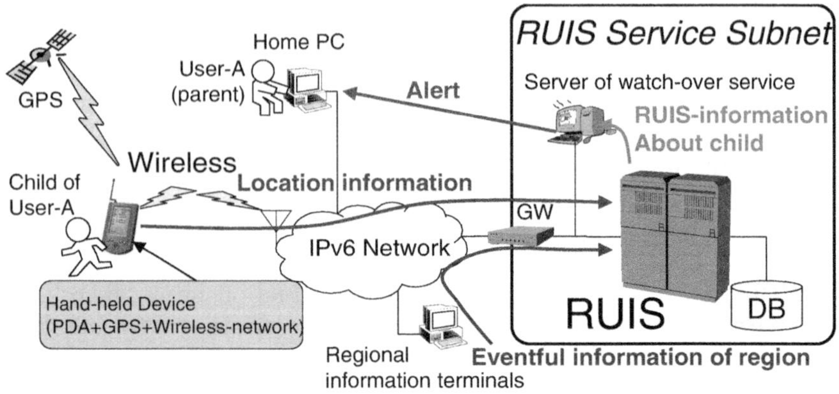

Fig. 5. SOTTO: An experimental system of smart support for children's watch over

when some emergency situation such as the sudden worsening of his/her health condition, they are expected to reflect these conditions for watching-over without any user interactions to the system. To fulfil the above requirement, sophisticated mechanism is needed to infer the situations and requirements of users from detailed analysis of their location information.

In order to achieve a gentle and safe watching-over, we proposed and have been developing a ubiquitous watching over system called "uEyes", a Ubiquitous communication Environment for *Yasashiku* (in Japanese it means "gently" or "kindly") Eyeing Services to solve the above issues.

In uEyes we introduce some distinguished features for watching: Network computing, Perceptual computing and Social computing, based on the concept of Symbiotic computing as shown in Figure 6. We design and implement the features of uEyes by effectively combining the environmental information acquired from real world and knowledge on social activities of people. The knowledge on social context such as human relationship, general behavior of elderly people, life style of the watched person, structure of house, etc., is introduced and effectively used to infer the situation of the users. These features enhance the social awareness of the system to make it gentle and safe to the users. Based on the advanced features, live video streaming system is autonomously constructed according to the users' situation in runtime. As a results, watch-over service that fulfils the detailed users' requirements can be effectively provided.

We implemented a prototype of uEyes for watching over elderly people and performed some experiments based on several real-life scenarios. For instance, we assumed a scenario where an elderly person is watched by his family and his neighbours in the local community. We confirmed that, when the elderly person is in his bedroom, a live video streaming system with low quality was configured to keep his privacy. When it is an emergency, the privacy level was lowered and the situation was autonomously informed to the members of the local community with high quality video. From the results of these case studies, it was confirmed

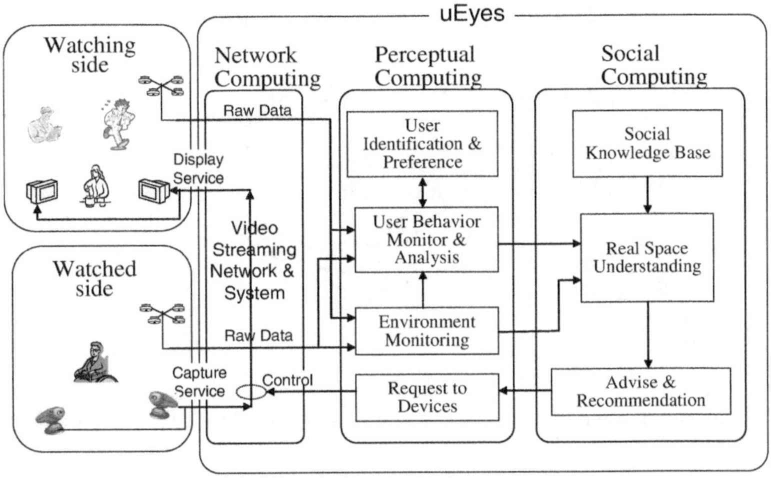

Fig. 6. A model of uEyes based on Symbiotic computing architecture

that uEyes can provide real-time multimedia watching service for elderly people, with reasonable QoS and privacy that meets the users' requirements.

4.3 Symbiotic Group Learning

Many kinds of networked cooperative work support systems, by which users can share information resources and related tasks on network environment, have been developed so far. The objective of these systems is to accelerate process of cooperative work among group members who physically separated from each other.

Here let us reconsider the recent cooperative work support systems in accordance with the basic concept of Symbiotic computing. Information and environmental data needed for the cooperative work in RS, can be effectively acquired using many kinds of sensor technologies. On the other hand, information in DS can be provided to users in RS by employing web computing technologies. The required information for cooperation is systematically accumulated in DS to increase the accessibility. However, flows of data/information from RS to DS and from DS to RS are independent, and mutual relationship between the flows is not strong. Therefore, flow control of data/information according to activities of users in RS does not work, and required information for cooperative work would not be provided to group members in RS when the need arises.

To address the above problem, we propose a new knowledge sharing scheme to effectively support the cooperative works by controlling information flows from RS to DS and the opposite direction. This scheme is based on the concept of mutual understanding between RS and DS in Symbiotic computing. In practice, we control availability of shared workspace for cooperative works in DS, according to the situation of tasks and workers in RS, in order to accelerate proceeding of

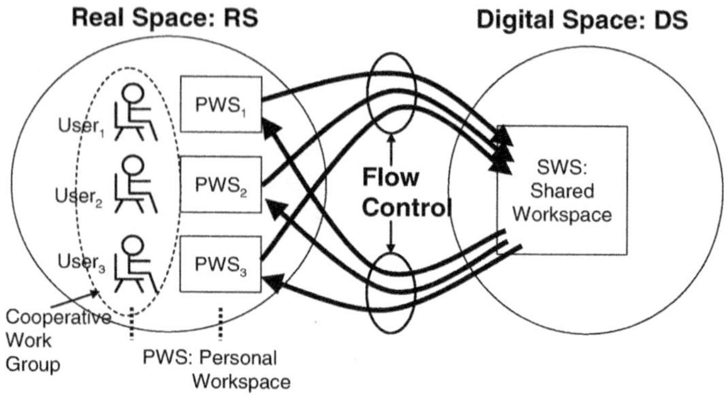

Fig. 7. Effective knowledge sharing by controlling availability of shared workspaces

the cooperative works as shown in Figure 7. When the shared workspace is not available, workers can concentrate on their own tasks to increase their personal ability. After that the shared workspace becomes available, the given task will be proceeded by cooperative work of group members. By switching these phases alternately in right timing, information on shared workspace in DS is reinforced. Then the information would be actively fed back to RS as "Knowledge", and advanced support to increase quality of intellectual cooperative works can be realized.

We applied our proposed knowledge sharing scheme to group learning domain that is one of the intellectual cooperative works. The group learning is an educational activity domain with group members including a teacher and several students. The students cooperatively solve the given problems according to the teacher's advice. Applying to this domain, we show that the proposed scheme, i.e., suitable availability control of shared workspace in DS, can accelerate the cooperative works. From experiment results, we found that the cooperative problem solving by teacher and students were accelerated. We also confirmed that the learning outcomes were improved, by controlling availability of the shared workspace, according to the progress of the group learning process. From these results we evaluated the effectiveness of our proposal.

4.4 AMACS

IEEE 802.11 is a de facto standard of wireless network device. It has two communication modes: infrastructure mode and Ad-hoc mode. Ad-hoc network is a hot topic and several middlewares are proposed in existing works. These existing middlewares support application development for Ad-hoc network in various aspects. However, in general, only the infrastructure mode is mostly used, in which wireless nodes are connected to the Net via base stations and users can use many applications and services in the same manner as wired network. Compare to the infrastructure mode, the Ad-hoc mode is rarely used because it lacks usability,

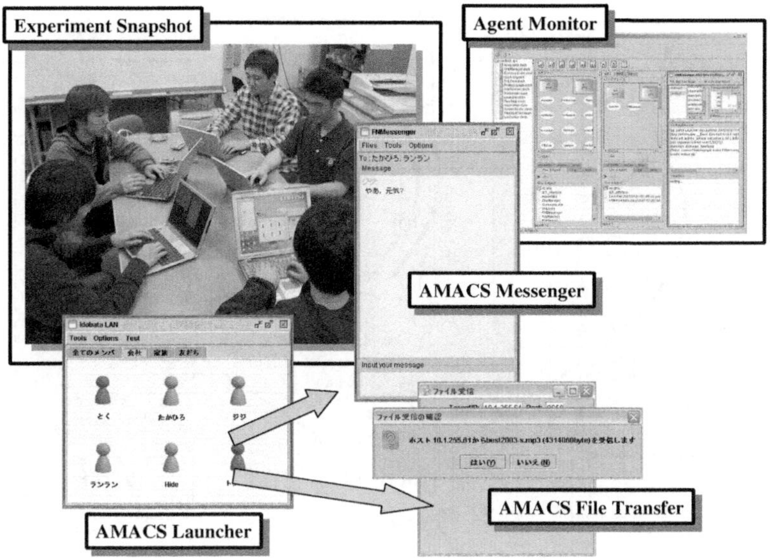

Fig. 8. A meeting on AMACS-based communication environment

which results from temporality of Ad-hoc network, not from application developers' point of view but from users' one. Due to the lacks of usability from user's view point, it is difficult for users to communicate with each other because they cannot find out which computer is owned by whom.

To overcome this issue, that is to improve the usability for users when they want to communicate with others on Ad-hoc network, we propose an agent-based mobile ad-hoc service construction system named AMACS based on the concept of the Symbiotic computing. AMACS is an agent based middleware which makes it possible for users to use several communication services such as messaging or file transferring at a conference or a meeting in a simple and easy-to-use way. The users can use the services by simply selecting target person's name and a certain service name on Ad-hoc network which constructed with participants' computers with wireless LAN interfaces.

Traditionally, typical communication services have used quasi-static identifier such as URL or host name to specify target host. However, assuming on the Ad-hoc network environment, existing name server such as DNS server is not available, users have to correlate target person with IP address of computer which the target person is using in one way or the other. This has been a crucial burden for users to use communication services on the Ad-hoc network.

Correspondingly, AMACS provides user oriented addressing method, i.e. mechanism to address the communication target by using target user's name, utilizing high-level communication unit of Network computing which has been proposed, and reduce the burden. To be specific, by just clicking target user name

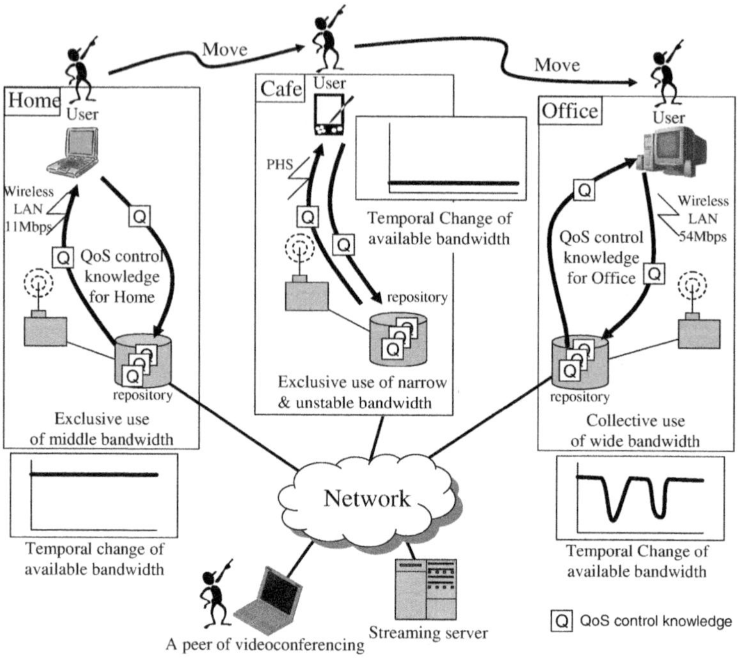

Fig. 9. Concept of Knowledge Circulation Framework for ubiquitous service provisioning

displayed on an user interface which represents presences of other neighbouring users, and choosing an available communication service from pop-up menu, then agents are organized on both local computer and remote computer, and users can use a communication service immediately as shown in Figure 8.

4.5 Ubiquitous Multimedia Communication System

In ubiquitous information environments, service provisioning ability of a system is significantly limited due to the lack of computational power of small devices and sensors, and the lack of availability and stability of wireless network. In this environment, it is a big hurdle to give mechanisms to strategically control the ubiquitous services by monitoring node statuses and network conditions in appropriate manner. Many kinds of the knowledge concerning diverse services and intricately changing environment in ubiquitous information environments would be a challenging research topic.

To resolve these issues, we have proposed a Knowledge Circulation Framework (KCF) that enables sharing the operational knowledge for effective service provisioning, based on the concept of Symbiotic computing, as shown in Figure 9. According to KCF, the operational knowledge is acquired during service provisioning in DS. The evaluation knowledge on the provided services is also acquired from users in RS. The knowledge is stored in operational knowledge repositories and is circulated in DS to be reused. We applied KCF to the ubiquitous videoconference system (VCS), one of the multimedia communication services, and evaluated it by conducting some relevant experiments. We evaluated our proposed system from a viewpoint of QoS to the user. From the experimental results, we confirmed that our system can provide better and more stable QoS, improving the adaptability to the various environments.

5 Conclusion

In this paper, we introduced a research on a new information and communication paradigm, called "Symbiotic computing." We described a basic concept and an architecture of the Symbiotic computing, and through several applications, we showed and discussed the effectiveness of the Symbiotic computing. Based on the concept of the Symbiotic computing, symbiotic society will be realized, where human and ubiquitous information environment can cooperatively co-exist. In future works, we will continuously develop other kinds of applications including health-care support and 3-D symbiotic space for intelligent cooperative works.

References

1. Shiratori, N.: Towards Future Development of Ubiquitous information Society - Symbiotic Computing (Keynote Speech). In: Proc. of 2005 NEC TECHNOLOGY FORUM: Symbiotic Computing for Ubiquitous Information Society, pp. 5–20 (2005)
2. Symbiotic Computing Home Page, `http://symbiotic.agent-town.com/`
3. Suganuma, T., et al.: Bridging the E-Gaps: Towards Post-Ubiquitous Computing. In: The 1st International Symposium on Frontiers in Networking with Applications (FINA 2006), pp. 780–784 (2006)
4. Weiser, M.: Ubiquitous computing, `http://www.ubiq.com/hypertext/weiser/UbiHome.html`
5. Ubiquitous Networking Forum, `http://www.ubiquitous-forum.jp/`
6. Disappearing Computer Project, `http://www.disappearing-computer.net/`
7. Russell, D.M., Streitz, N.A., Winograd, T.: Building Disappearing Computers. Communications of ACM 48(3), 42–48 (2005)
8. Hepp, M.: Semantic Web and semantic Web services: father and son or indivisible twins? IEEE Internet Computing 10(2), 85–88 (2006)
9. Shiratori, N.: Post Modern Distributed Systems (Keynote Speech). In: Proc. of IPSJ Symposium, pp. 1–7 (1994)
10. Shiratori, N.: Post Modern Distributed Systems. IPSJ Maganize 36(9), 811–814 (1995)
11. Shiratori, N., Suganuma, T., Sugiura, S., Chakraborty, G., Sugawara, K., Kinoshita, T., Lee, E.S.: Framework of a flexible computer communication network. Computer Communications 19, 1268–1275 (1996)
12. Fujita, S., Hara, H., Sugawara, K., Kinoshita, T., Shiratori, N.: Agent-based design model of adaptive distributed systems. Applied Intelligence 9, 57–70 (1998)
13. Konno, S., et al.: Development of Regional Ubiquitous Information System and its Applications -Towards a Universal Ubiquitous Information Society. In: Ma, J., Jin, H., Yang, L.T., Tsai, J.J.-P. (eds.) UIC 2006. LNCS, vol. 4159, pp. 200–208. Springer, Heidelberg (2006)

Multi-agent Software Control System with Hybrid Intelligence for Ubiquitous Intelligent Environments

Kevin I-Kai Wang, Waleed H. Abdulla, and Zoran Salcic

Department of Electrical and Computer Engineering, University of Auckland. Private Bag 92019, Auckland, New Zealand
{kevin.wang,w.abdulla,z.salcic}@auckland.ac.nz

Abstract. In this paper, a novel ubiquitous intelligent environment platform and its multi-agent control system are presented. The platform named Distributed Embedded Intelligence Room (DEIR) has been constructed with embedded sensors, actuators and computing devices. All the devices are interconnected using five different physical networks. This platform aims to facilitate realistic data collection and online system performance evaluation. The multi-agent control system incorporating two machine learning algorithms, fuzzy inference and decision tree, has been designed to conform to DEIR architecture. Devices to be controlled are classified based on their possible output states and modelled separately by fuzzy inference agents and decision tree agents in the system. The multi-agent control system with hybrid intelligence shows 11% improvements on overall control accuracy and 84% improvements on learning time compared to its predecessor control system. The vast improvement on computational time shows suitability of the approach towards real-time, embedded applications.

1 Introduction

With the improvement of embedded and communication technologies, the possibility of ubiquitous intelligent environments starts to emerge. In order to achieve such an environment, vast numbers of devices, which are interconnected with each other, are embedded into ordinary living or working spaces. In general, intelligent environments are developed and are expected to be able to adapt, to predict and to have high level of autonomy [1]. Different levels of automation and intelligence can be realised through different hardware architectures, control paradigms and application services to assist human activities. Ultimately, ubiquitous intelligent environments should be aware of the environment context, be able to model and adapt to user's behaviour and respond on user's behalf [2].

There have been a number of academic projects mainly on modelling, controlling and service-providing aspects of ubiquitous intelligent environments. The AIRE (Agent-based Intelligent Reactive Environments) of MIT CSAIL (Computer Science and Artificial Intelligence Laboratory) has been designed to carry a number of ubiquitous computing projects, such as the multi-agent framework - Metaglue [3], resource manager [4], and the recent Hyperglue [5]. The University of Essex uses embedded agents with Fuzzy Inference System (FIS) to model occupant's behaviours

J. Indulska et al. (Eds.): UIC 2007, LNCS 4611, pp. 1046–1055, 2007.

[6]. In the University of Colorado, Artificial Neural Networks (ANNs) are used to control the lighting and heating services of residential environments involving different types of living spaces such dining room, living room and bathroom [7]. Industrial research efforts such as Microsoft Smart House [8] and Amigo project [9] are more concentrated on providing integrated working behaviours, device automation, and integrated network infrastructure.

In this paper, a novel intelligent control system using Multi-Agent System (MAS) approach with hybrid machine learning algorithms is presented. User control behaviours on different physical devices within the environment are modelled with two types of algorithms, namely FIS and decision tree. FIS and decision tree have been applied separately or jointly in other research applications such as activity classification [10] and medical decision making [11]. In our project, FIS and decision tree have been built into agents and incorporated in the multi-agent control system. In order to perform realistic data collection and online system performance evaluation, a ubiquitous intelligent environment platform named DEIR (Distributed Embedded Intelligence Room) has been constructed.

The rest of the paper is organised as follows. Section 2 introduces DEIR platform and its system architecture. Section 3 explains the hybrid modelling techniques. Section 4 evaluates the system performance by comparing learning time and control accuracy with the previous version of multi-agent control system. Section 5 provides future directions of the project and section 6 concludes the paper.

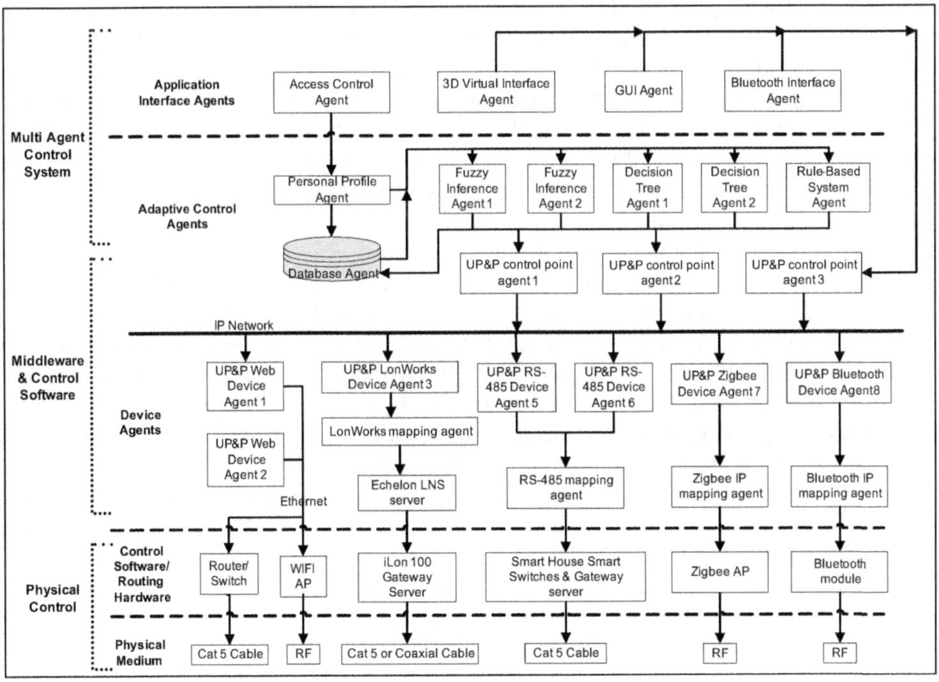

Fig. 1. DEIR System Architecture

2 Distributed Embedded Intelligence Room (DEIR)

To realise a ubiquitous intelligent environment, DEIR has been constructed with a number of sensors, actuators and computing devices [12, 13]. Embedded sensors such as light intensity, temperature, pressure and motion sensors are spread within the environment to monitor occupant's activities and environmental contexts. Embedded actuators are implemented to automate windows, curtains, dimmable lights and other appliances. The overall DEIR system architecture can be considered in 3 parts: the physical layer, middleware layer and multi-agent control layer, as depicted in Fig. 1. The physical layer consists of various physical communication media and routing devices that physically link all the embedded devices. The middleware layer contains middleware agents and control software for certain commercialised network. The middleware is introduced to integrate hybrid device networks and to provide unique portal between high level MAS and low level device networks. The multi-agent control layer includes high level modelling agents and user interface agents which model user activities for proactive device automation and provide integrated control interfaces.

2.1 Device Networks and Middleware

In the current DEIR system architecture, five different device networks, RS-485, LonWorks network [14], Ethernet/WIFI, Bluetooth and Zigbee have been considered and implemented. RS-485 network links most of the actuators for windows, curtains and dimmable lights. RS-485 devices are managed by a smart switch device that resembles traditional switch interface. The smart switch contains a M16C micro-controller that enables RS-485 communication and certain low level automation. LonWorks network connects part of the embedded sensors and the connected devices are managed by an iLon100 gateway server. Ethernet/WIFI and Bluetooth form the backbone communication for all the embedded and mobile devices. Zigbee is employed as the communication protocol for some embedded sensors, such as pressure sensors, and commercial office appliances.

Hybrid device networks improve the system flexibility in terms of incorporating different ranges of hardware devices. However, it adds a burden to the high level multi-agent control system to communicate with different devices. Furthermore, it is even more difficult, in terms of the system architecture, to replace an existing network or to introduce new network technologies. In order to integrate hybrid device networks and provide common portal to the high level control, a middleware level is introduced. In DEIR, Universal Plug and Play (UPnP) is used as the middleware. In general, UPnP is an IP-based device discovery protocol which enables automatic device discovery, configuration and management [12, 13]. Hence, each individual device network is mapped onto IP network and controlled as one integrated network. To enable UPnP communication, two UPnP components, UPnP device agents and UPnP control point agents, need to be implemented. The UPnP device agent is responsible for communicating with the physical devices. It is essentially the software replica of the underlying hardware. UPnP control point agents communicate with the device agent and pass necessary information to the high level modelling and/or interface agents.

2.2 Multi-agent Control System

In DEIR, a well known agent platform, JADE (Java Agent DEvelopment Framework), has been employed as the underlying framework of the high level multi-agent control system [13]. Since both JADE and UPnP are provided in Java, middleware components can be easily integrated as low level agents in the control system. Apart from the system management agents provided by JADE, high level MAS mainly consists of three types of agents: Utility agents, Modelling agents and Interface agents. Utility agents handle things such as access control, user personal profile management and user activities data deposition. Modelling agents involve three types of intelligent agents, namely fuzzy inference agents, decision tree agents and rule-based system agents. The first two agents are data-driven and will perform a series of learning steps to reach the final model of user behaviours. In comparison, the rule-based system agent contains directly hard-coded IF-THEN rules to realise reactive responses of the system. These agents provide the system the ability to model user activities and provide automatic controls to the environment. The modelling techniques will be explained in detail in the next section. Interface agents communicate with user control interfaces such as mobile interface and GUI interface.

3 Hybrid Learning

According to our past research outcomes, it has been found that different devices exhibit different control behaviours [12, 13]. That implies single modelling technique may only be suitable for some control behaviours but not for all of them. The multi-agent architecture provides our control system the ability to apply different machine learning techniques to model different device control behaviours. In the current multi-agent control system, two types of machine learning algorithms, Fuzzy Inference System (FIS) and decision tree, are used. Both algorithms have high tolerance to uncertainties, which are more suitable for modelling human behaviours. The algorithms are incorporated as agents in the control system. The fuzzy inference and decision tree agents acquire necessary user activities data through database agent and perform required data processing and learning steps. Once the learning steps are completed, both techniques will present the modelling results in terms of IF-THEN rules, which coincide with the rule-based system agent and allow a more coherent automatic control rule base. The developed control system is called Multi-Agent Hybrid Intelligence control System (MAHIS).

3.1 Device Grouping and Classification

In our experiments, ten output devices including four dimmable lights, curtain, heater, non-dimmable bed light, non-dimmable desk light, MS Word, MS Media Player are to be controlled by the system. Seven input sensor devices including internal light intensity, external light intensity, internal temperature, external temperature, chair pressure, bed pressure and time of the day are recorded by the system as context information when output devices change status. However, it is important to note that not all the input devices provide useful context information towards controlling the output device. Therefore, modelling agents only acquire data of relevant input devices. Currently, the relevant input devices for each output device are defined by the designer. Fig. 2 shows each output device with its relevant input devices.

In order to apply different modelling techniques to different output devices, output devices need to be classified in certain ways. In our current experiments, simple classification has been made based on the possible number of output states. That means, whether the device has two (binary) or more than two output states. The classification is also shown in Fig. 2. The reasons of using such simple classification method are as follows:

1. Binary output devices are generally easier to be classified by decision tree than devices with multiple output states or even continuous valued output states.
2. The number of relevant input devices is small and hence the learning of decision tree will be efficient. The resultant tree structure is also not complicated.
3. Binary devices tend to contain fewer uncertainties in their control behaviours, possibly due to the limited number of output states. Based on the past experience, fuzzy inference does not work well with modelling behaviours with low uncertainties [12]. Nevertheless, fuzzy inference has been proven to work well with continuous valued output devices with high uncertainties [12].

Output devices	Dimmable lights	Bed light (non-dimmable)	Desk light (non-dimmable)	Curtain	Heater	MS Word	MS Media Player
No. of possible states	>2	2	2	2	2	2	2
Modelling techniques	Fuzzy Inference	Decision Tree	Decision Tree	Decision Tree	Decision Tree	DecisionTree	Decision Tree
No. of relevant input device	5	5	2	5	2	2	3
Relevant input device	Int. Light Ext. Light Chair Press. Bed Press. Time	Int. Light Ext. Light Int. Temp Ext. Temp Bed Press.	Ext. Light Chair Press.	Int. Light Ext. Light Chair Press. Bed Press. Time	Int. Light Time	Ext. Light Chair Press.	Int. Light Ext. Light Chair Press.

Fig. 2. MAHIS device grouping and classification

3.2 Decision Tree Learning

The decision tree learning algorithm implemented in the current decision tree agents is the traditional ID3 algorithm [15]. The learning process of ID3 is shown in Fig. 3(a). It should be noted in Fig. 3(a) that before feeding data into the ID3 algorithm, certain pre-processing is required. Due to the fact that decision tree classification does not handle continuous valued data well, continuous valued input device data needs to be discretised. For simplicity and efficiency, the dynamic range of a particular input device data is divided into arbitrary numbers of even divisions and each division is assigned with a specific linguistic label that denotes the value range.

ID3 algorithm construct the decision tree based on the information gain provided by a specific input attribute towards classifying the target output attribute. To evaluate the most suitable input attribute for a particular node of the tree, the information gain

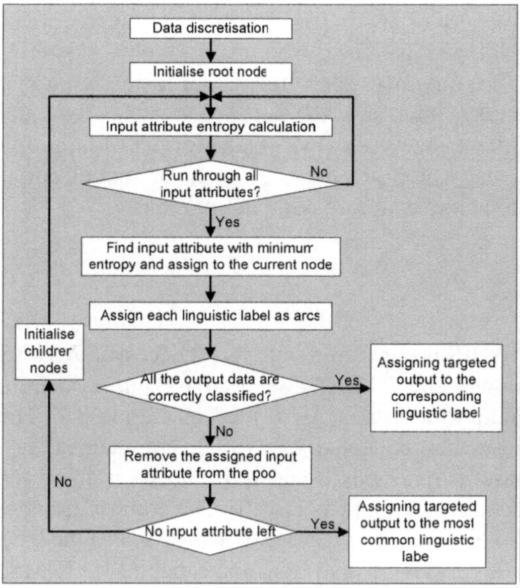

(a)

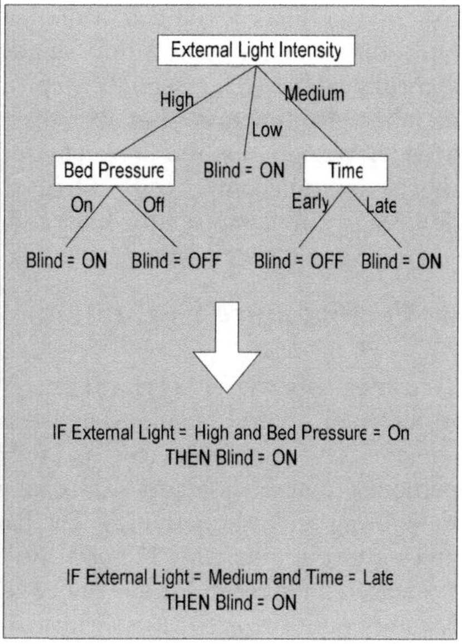

(b)

Fig. 3. (a) Decision tree learning (b) IF-THEN rule conversion

of each available input attribute is calculated according to Eq.(1). The selected attribute is one that generates the maximum information gain at that particular node:

$$Info.Gain(S, A) \equiv Entropy(S) - \sum_{v \in Values(A)} \frac{|S_v|}{|S|} Entropy(S_v) \tag{1}$$

where S is the total population, A is the input attribute, Sv is a subset of population when A has value v.

However, refer to Eq.(1), Entropy(S) is common to all the input attributes and hence can be ignored in the actual implementation to improve algorithm efficiency. The algorithm terminates when all the output data is correctly classified or each path has reached its leaf node, which means it used all the available input attributes.

In order to use the resultant decision tree in the control system, the decision tree is converted into IF-THEN rules. Each path from the root node to leaf node is a unique "multiple inputs, single output" IF-THEN rule as shown in Fig. 3(b).

3.3 Fuzzy Inference Learning

FIS is the first machine learning technique introduced into DEIR's multi-agent control system, named Multi-Agent Fuzzy Inference System (MAFIS) [12]. Due to its tolerance to uncertainty, it has been recognised as one of the best modelling techniques for human behaviours. The learning algorithm used in current fuzzy inference agents and MAFIS is adopted from the Adaptive Online Fuzzy Inference

System (AOFIS) developed at the University of Essex [6]. The first step is to convert multi-dimensional dataset into single dimensional fuzzy sets using double clustering algorithm [16]. The second step is to quantify each fuzzy set using Gaussian membership function. Finally, the fuzzy rules are extracted using the extended Mendel Wang's method [17]. The resultant fuzzy rules will be in format of "multiple inputs, multiple outputs" IF-THEN rules, which are more efficient to model output devices of similar type altogether and to achieve a more compact rule base.

4 Performance Evaluation

To evaluate the system performance, MAHIS is compared with its predecessor, MAFIS, in terms of control accuracy and learning time. The dataset used for this evaluation contains seven input devices and ten output devices as described in section 3.1. This particular dataset contains 408 data instances collected over three consecutive days monitoring real user activities. The dataset is randomised and split into six training sets and six testing sets with 272 and 136 data instances, respectively. The control accuracy is measured based on Scaled Root Mean Square Error (SRMSE) which scales the Root Mean Square Error (RMSE) with the output device data dynamic range [13]. SRMSE ensures fair comparison of control accuracy among different types of output devices. In MAFIS, similar types of output devices are grouped together with their relevant input devices and each device group is modelled by an independent fuzzy inference agent [12]. The same fuzzy inference technique as in MAFIS is implemented in the current control system, MAHIS, but incorporated with the decision tree algorithm.

Fig. 4 (a) and (b) show the control accuracy and learning time results of MAFIS for each device group with different numbers of fuzzy sets [12]. The optimum control accuracy and corresponding learning time are highlighted. The overall system control accuracy and average learning time are calculated by taking averages of the optimum control accuracies and corresponding learning time of each device group. Fig. 5 shows the control accuracy and learning time of each device in MAHIS according to the group division shown in Fig. 2. The number of features shown in Fig. 4 and Fig. 5 indicates the number of relevant input and output attributes used in each modelling process. Fig. 5 shows clearly that the decision tree algorithm generally requires fewer features in the modelling process to achieve comparable control accuracy. The learning process of decision tree is also much faster than fuzzy inference technique.

Fig. 6 shows the performance comparison of MAHIS and MAFIS. The simulation results of MAHIS are further processed by taking averages to fit into the device grouping of MAFIS. For instances, the control accuracy of group 3 is the average control accuracy of curtain and heater shown in Fig. 5. The overall control accuracy and average learning time calculated in Fig. 4 and Fig. 5 are used to estimate the performance improvements of MAHIS. As shown in Fig. 6, MAHIS has achieved 11% improvements on overall control accuracy and 84% improvements on average learning time. The substantial improvement on learning time indicates that MAHIS is far more suitable for real-time, embedded applications such as ubiquitous intelligent environments.

MAFIS Scaled Root Mean Squared Error (SRMSE)				
No. of Fuzzy Sets	Group 1 (9 features)	Group 2 (9 features)	Group 3 (6 features)	Group 4 (7 features)
2	0.6726	0.7963	0.6608	0.5415
3	0.2102	0.2406	0.3157	0.1390
4	0.1798	0.2057	0.3127	0.1094
5	0.1389	0.1775	0.2687	0.0819
6	0.1204	0.1705	0.2199	0.0853
7	0.0979	0.1739	0.2220	0.1047
8	0.0931	0.1911	0.1536	0.0735
9	0.0893	0.1496	0.1249	0.0665
10	0.0974	0.1354	0.1004	0.0652
11	0.0835	0.1290	0.0972	0.0697
12	0.0865	0.1335	0.1330	0.0735
13	0.0716	0.1126	0.1566	0.0912
14	0.0731	0.1140	0.1404	0.0866
15	0.0742	0.0976	0.0735	0.0735
16	0.0807	0.1080	0.0891	0.0547
17	0.0792	0.1154	0.0976	0.0773
18	0.0780	0.1258	0.0857	0.0676
19	0.0900	0.1080	0.0819	0.0971
20	0.0783	0.1349	0.0949	0.0488
Overall accuracy	(0.0716+0.0976+0.0735+0.0488)/4 = 0.0729			

(a)

MAFIS learning time in seconds				
No. of Fuzzy Sets	Group 1 (9 features)	Group 2 (9 features)	Group 3 (6 features)	Group 4 (7 features)
2	21.46	19.3	10.61	17.14
3	15.80	21.2	15.64	15.92
4	15.80	18.6	14.67	16.95
5	18.71	22.0	12.29	14.49
6	22.40	17.5	14.53	16.06
7	17.20	16.8	13.43	14.63
8	18.10	18.8	15.69	15.31
9	17.18	15.3	12.39	12.08
10	24.43	17.0	13.46	12.73
11	18.39	17.3	13.96	15.90
12	16.75	20.0	12.10	14.52
13	17.32	25.0	13.79	14.18
14	18.95	23.0	15.86	13.54
15	15.85	16.2	12.76	15.52
16	16.18	20.3	15.62	15.55
17	15.48	15.6	14.93	13.18
18	17.25	16.3	13.85	20.27
19	15.45	18.4	13.19	18.71
20	16.94	23.6	14.40	19.07
Average learning time	(17.32+16.2+12.76+19.07)/4 = 16.33			

(b)

Fig. 4. (a) MAFIS control accuracy (b) MAFIS learning time

Output device	Modelling techniques	No. of features	Control accuracy (SRMSE)	Learning time (secs)
Dimmable Light 1-4	Fuzzy Inference	9	0.0716	17.32
Curtain	Decision tree	6	0.0286	0.09
Heater	Decision tree	3	0.0948	0.186
Bed Light	Decision tree	6	0.032	0.09
Desk Light	Decision tree	3	0.0572	0.0186
MS Word	Decision tree	3	0.0948	0.0186
MS Media Player	Decision tree	4	0.0756	0.096
Overall control accuracy			(0.0716+0.0286+0.0948+0.032+0.0572+0.0948+0.0756)/7 = 0.0649	
Average learning time			(17.32+0.09+0.0186+0.09+0.0186+0.0186+0.096)/7 = 2.546	

Fig. 5. MAHIS control accuracy and learning time

Device Groups	Devices	Control accuracy		Learning time	
		MAHIS	MAFIS	MAHIS	MAFIS
Group 1	Dimmable Light 1-4	0.0716	0.0716	17.32	17.32
Group 2	MS Word MS Media Player	0.0852	0.0976	0.141	16.2
Group 3	Curtain Heater	0.0617	0.0735	0.138	12.76
Group 4	Bed Light Desk Light	0.0446	0.0488	0.138	19.07
Overall control accuracy & average learning time		0.0649	0.0729	2.55	16.33
% of improvement		11%		84%	

Fig. 6. Performance comparison of MAHIS and MAFIS

In previous experiments, the adopted fuzzy inference technique AOFIS has been proved to generate comparable or better control accuracy compared with the other techniques including Genetic Programming (GP), Adaptive-Network-Based Fuzzy Inference System (ANFIS) and Multi-Layer Perceptron (MLP) [6]. Later, MAFIS has been evaluated to outperform AOFIS by applying the technique in the multi-agent architecture [12, 13]. Accordingly, MAHIS shows better control accuracy and faster learning than MAFIS should also perform better than those offline control systems.

5 Future Works

Based on the current findings, some aspects of the project can be further investigated.. In MAHIS, data division and linguistic mapping for decision tree learning use even scales. Different data division method involving statistically sound distribution such as Gaussian distribution should be discovered. Algorithms for automatic device classification and grouping should also be implemented. Online update function which adapts the IF-THEN rule base should be incorporated into the system to better suit the user from time to time and hence achieve a real-time unsupervised control system.

6 Conclusions

In this paper, we presented a novel ubiquitous intelligent environment platform, DEIR, and its multi-agent control system, MAHIS. DEIR contains a number of embedded sensors, actuators and computing devices. Contemporary network technologies such as WIFI, Zigbee and Bluetooth are employed as device networks to interconnect all the devices. UPnP is incorporated as middleware which integrates various device networks and provides a unique control interface to the high level multi-agent system. In order to model human control behaviours over different devices, two types of machine learning techniques, namely fuzzy inference and decision tree, are used in MAHIS. The modelling results are presented as IF-THEN rules for the system to apply automatic controls according to the environmental context. The system performance has been evaluated in terms of control accuracy and learning time. MAHIS achieves 11% improvements on control accuracy and 84% improvements on learning time. The results show that MAHIS outperforms many contemporary offline control systems including MAFIS, AOFIS, ANFIS, GP and MLP and is more suitable for real-time, embedded applications due to high computation efficiency.

Acknowledgement

The authors would like to thank Dr. Faiyaz Doctor, Prof. Victor Callaghan and Prof. Hani Hagras for their kind contribution of providing the dataset for comparative analysis and various helps regarding to the use of their AOFIS learning technique.

References

1. Augusto, J.C., Nugent, C.D. (eds.): Designing Smart Homes. LNCS (LNAI), vol. 4008. Springer, Heidelberg (2006)
2. Ducatel, K., Bogdanowicz, M., Scapolo, F., Burgelman, J.-C.: Scenarios for Ambient Intelligence in 2010. Information Soc. Technol., Advisory Group (ISTAG), Inst. Prospective Technol. Studies (IPTS), Seville (2001)
3. Philips, B.A.: Metaglue: A Programming Language for Multi-Agent Systems. In: M.Eng. thesis, MIT, Cambridge, MA, USA (1999)

4. Gajos, K.: A Knowledge-Based Resource Management System For The Intelligent Room. In: M.Eng. thesis, MIT, Cambridge, MA, USA (2000)
5. Peters, L.S.: Hyperglue: An Infrastructure for Human-Centred Computing in Distributed, Pervasive, Intelligent Environments. In: PhD thesis, MIT, Cambridge, MA, USA (2006)
6. Doctor, F., Hagras, H., Callaghan, V.: A Fuzzy Embedded Agent-Based Approach for Realizing Ambient Intelligence in Intelligent Inhabited Environment. IEEE Trans. Sys. Man Cybern. 35(1), 55–65 (2005)
7. Mozer, M.: The neural network house: An environment that adapts to its inhabitants. In: Proc. Amer. Assoc. Artif. Intell. Spring Symp. Intell. Environ., pp. 110–114 (1998)
8. Brumitt, B., Cadiz, J.J.: Let There Be Light! Comparing Interfaces for Homes of the Future. Microsoft Research, Redmond, WA 98052, MSR-TR-2000-92 (2000)
9. Ambient intelligence for the networked home environment (Amigo) (January 2007), http://www.hitech-projects.com/euprojects/amigo/index.htm
10. Parkka, J., Ermes, M., Korpipaa, P., Mantyjarvi, J., Peltola, J., Korhonen, I.: Activity Classification Using Realistic Data From Wearable Sensors. IEEE Trans. Info. Tech. in Biomedicine 10(1), 119–128 (2006)
11. Papageorgiou, E., Stylios, C., Groumpos, P.: A Combined Fuzzy Cognitive Map and Decision Trees Model for Medical Decision Making. In: Proc. of the 28th IEEE EMBS Annual Int. Conf, pp. 6117–6120. IEEE Computer Society Press, Los Alamitos (2006)
12. Wang, K.I., Abdulla, W.H., Salcic, Z.: Distributed Embedded Intelligence Room with Multi-agent Cooperative Learning. In: Ma, J., Jin, H., Yang, L.T., Tsai, J.J.-P. (eds.) UIC 2006. LNCS, vol. 4159, pp. 147–156. Springer, Heidelberg (2006)
13. Wang, K.I., Abdulla, W.H., Salcic, Z.: Multi-agent fuzzy inference control system for intelligent environments using JADE. In: Proc. of 2nd IET Int. Conf. on Intel. Environ., pp. 285–294 (2006)
14. Echelon Corporation: LonWorks Overview (February 2006) http://www.echelon.com/solutions/overview/default.htm
15. Mitchell, T.M.: Machine Learning. McGraw-Hill, New York (1997)
16. Castellano, G., Fanelli, A.M., Mencar, C.: Generation of interpretable fuzzy granules by a double clustering technique. Arch. Contr. Sci. 12(4), 397–410 (2002)
17. Wang, L.X.: The MW method completed: A flexible system approach to data minig. IEEE Trans. Fuzzy Syst. 11(6), 678–782 (2003)

IUMELA: A Lightweight Multi-Agent Systems Based Mobile Learning Assistant Using the ABITS Messaging Service

Elaine McGovern, Bernard J. Roche, Eleni Mangina, and Rem Collier

School of Computer Science & Informatics University College Dublin,
Belfield, Dublin 4, Ireland
{elaine.a.mcgovern,bernard.roche,rem.collier,
eleni.mangina}@ucd.ie

Abstract. University College Dublin has made an unprecedented transition from its once traditional educational metaphor to a modularised education framework, the first of its kind in Ireland. Queries have been raised regarding whether students who are unfamiliar with the concepts of modularisation, are capable of making informed decisions, ensuring success from specifically tailored module combinations. IUMELA is an intelligent modular-education learning assistant designed, using multi-agent systems (MAS), in order to assist students in their decision-making process. This paper introduces an alternative IUMELA MAS architecture that uses a significantly more lightweight mobile assistant.

1 Introduction

"Just as technology can be used to strengthen different forms of intelligence, so too it can target different learning styles." [1] IUMELA, Intelligent Ubiquitous Modular Education Learning Assistant, uses multi-agent systems (MAS) technologies to create an intelligent learning assistant that is capable of supporting students in their choice of modules based on their learning preferences, academic abilities and personal preferences. A wireless device can support the functionality of the Managed Learning Environment (MLE) and IUMELA has been designed to run on the XDA Mini S. Unfortunately, PDA's and Smart Phone are still unable to compete with desktop and laptop computers based on screen real estate, computational and processing power. This paper considers a more lightweight alternative to the original IUMELA MAS architecture. The remainder of this paper is structured as follows: Section 2 provides a description of current research in the area. Section 3 presents the internal structure of IUMELA. Section 4 enters into a debate regarding whether adoption of an ultra lightweight client side results in an enhanced communicative capacity. Finally, the conclusions are drawn and future developments are discussed in Section 5.

2 Related Work

A wireless device is any form of networked hardware that can communicate with other devices without being physically attached to them [2]. IUMELA has been

J. Indulska et al. (Eds.): UIC 2007, LNCS 4611, pp. 1056–1065, 2007.

designed to run, exploiting smart phone technologies available on the XDA Mini S. Colour screens with high resolution tend to require more power than the older monochrome equivalents. This results in an increase in battery weight or a reduction usage [3]. A smart phone can be considered to be any handheld device that has integrated personal information management facilities as well as mobile phone capabilities [4]. Furthermore, according to recent finding, while over 83% of third level students have mobile phones; only 23% have access to another form of mobile computing device. Of that 23% of students, less than one fifth would regularly bring this device with them into university. This contrasts with 90% of students who regularly bring their mobile phones with them [4] and IUMELA findings that suggests that providing third level students with access to modularised education learning assistant via smart phone technologies ensures that the resources are being provided in an on-demand, ubiquitous manner. Significant research into the area of mobile computing devices have suggested that PDA's provide enhanced performance to the third level student when used as a mobile learning tool and can ensure further collaboration and sharing of information and software [5].

IUMELA was installed on the XDA MINI S smart phone. It provides an array of smart phone technologies, combined with traditional mobile phone functionality in a lightweight and portable device. Microsoft Windows Mobile 5.0 drives the XDA Mini. Simply integrated with the MLE installed at the University, it can assist in the significant reduction of administrative overheads within a university [3].

In past research, it was evident that students were using mobile devices as a graphing calculator, word processor, database, test prep tool, and as a means of accessing resource. These devices have afforded students with "opportunities to connect questions and investigations to the data in a real time setting that enhances "systematic investigations, critical thinking and cooperation" [5] Additional research suggests that PDA's facilitate group work, the immediate analysis of data particularly during laboratory exercises or when conducting scientific investigations in the field [6]. Collaboration and sharing of information and software is enhanced by PDAs also. According to Wallace et al [7], this sharing and commenting on other's work leads to an improved finished product.

UCD Horizons is the flagship of modularised education in Ireland. Modular education in UCD has provided a structured modular and credit-based taught degree programme. UCD Horizons is student-centric, allowing students to have a greater choice in degree content. They are required to undertake some core modules and have the opportunity to elect some optional and free choice modules also. This, in theory, enables them to adapt their degree programme based on their own study preferences and strengths [8]. IUMELA was developed because although there is enhanced freedom of choice in a modularised education, students entering UCD are often poorly equipped to deal with such freedom. They subsequently make misinformed module choices, frequently resorting to poor decision-making metrics.

Learning styles are considered to be preferences for dealing with intellectual tasks [1]. Psychologists agree that a learning style can be considered a consistent preference over time for perceiving, thinking about and organising information in a particular way [9]. Witken [10] theorised that individuals can be influenced by their surrounding context and that there are two groups of learners: field dependent and field independent. Sternberg's [9] styles of mental self –government theory describes thirteen styles that fall into one of five categories. This concept supports the belief that IUMELA would assist students by suggesting appropriate modules based on their preferred learning styles.

Teachers often use various instructional methodologies to engage any number of styles of learning at one time or another. They are required to use various test formats to measure accurately what students have learned. IUMELA measures those classes in which students consistently participate well, through the inclusion of an expert agent. IUMELA's expert agent defines each teachers style based on one of several well-documented behavioural approaches; constructivist, humanistic and social. [11] theorised that the cognitive taxonomy consists of six hierarchal levels of instructional outcomes. A bottom up approach that indicates that evaluation can only occur after the prior mastery of knowledge or facts.

The behavioural approach to teaching involves arranging and implementing those conditions that make it highly likely that a desired response will occur in the presence of a particular stimulus. [12] has documented one popular behavioural approach known as direct instruction. This style is most frequently used and is used in IUMELA. Two cognitive approaches considered for IUMELA's expert agent are that of information processing and constructivism. The information processing methodology involves the implementation of those conditions that assist students to effectively assimilate course material into their psyche. The constructivist approach focuses on the provision of opportunities to students that enable them to create their own meaningful views of learned materials [13]. A social constructivist orientation applies a greater weight to the role of social interaction during knowledge acquisition. IUMELA lends itself to these cognitive teaching strategies. A humanistic approach strives to help students better understand themselves and to create a supportive classroom atmosphere that activates the inherent desire all human beings have to learn and fulfil their potential [14].

Historically, assessment involves measuring how much knowledge and skills a student has and its acceptability based on the teacher's eventual goals. The summative and formative techniques are two popular methods of evaluation. These methodologies are frequently used by the lectures in UCD and so have been incorporated into IUMELA expert agents reasoning abilities and knowledge base. 2.7.

Software systems are becoming increasingly more complex and online information spaces are growing exponentially. Kay [15] highlights how the use of MAS has resulted in a transition from the traditional direct manipulation of a system to indirect human-intelligent agent interactions. Agents have enabled the delegation of the mundane and tedious tasks. Shneiderman [16] considered user confidence and agent autonomy as areas that required consideration. MAS based MLE's along with MAS currently under development allow users to delegate tasks such as meeting scheduling, email filtering and reminder notification. MAS should have the overall effect of reducing the users workload [17]. In order to develop a working IUMELA application, it was necessary that an understanding be obtained of how a student interacts with a generic multi-agent system. Agent Factory and Agent Factory Lite [20] were studied as these were used in the development of the IUMELA multi-agent architecture.

3 IUMELA – The Agent Architecture

The IUMELA application conforms to FIPA specifications [18]. The multi-agent system (MAS) was developed using Agent Factory [17] toolkit, using Java as the programming language. In particular, the Assistant Agent runs on a XDA Mini S. The high-level communication protocols have been implemented using ACL messages, whose content refers to the IUMELA ontology. IUMELA uses a FIPA compliant MAS architecture, displayed in fig 1, to fulfil the task of an intelligent application capable of autonomous human computer interaction for communication, event monitoring and the performance of higher order cognitive tasks. IUMELA consists of a community of five agent types: assistant, moderator, learning agent, expert agent and analysis agent. They co-operate in order analyse the students learning patterns and make an accurate module recommendation in an on demand manner, at a time and location appropriate to the student.

The assistant agent resides on the student's client device and is responsible for the seamless interaction between IUMELA's MAS and the student. As an interface technology, it is the assistant's task to be aware of the current student and by which device the student is currently accessing the application. The application makes use of the XDA Mini S in a mobile context and is implemented using java-based servlet technology. The assistant agent provides a mechanism by which the user can interact with the resources offered by the multi-agent system in a ubiquitous manner. Adaptive personalization was considered as the mechanism that would best assist students based on the belief that a simple interface is not the best way to provide assistance to heterogeneous user groups. The assistant agent performs best when it receives

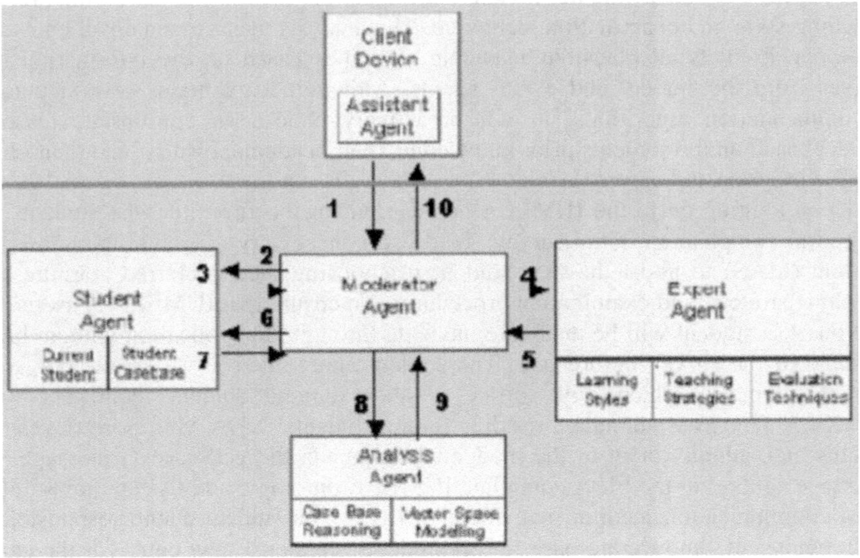

Fig. 1. The Agent Architecture of IUMELA

guidance and insight through the examination of student's interactions with the interface. These observations thus enable it to draw complex, higher level inferences [19] and are acted upon through its internal reasoning and machine learning strategies.

The mediator agent family is composed of three basic agent patterns: the broker, the matchmaker, and the mediator. They act as intermediaries between any number of other agent types. It is their task to provide access to services and communication channels in accordance with agreed upon agent communication language, via the IUMELA ontology. Analysis of their differences [3] however, indicated that the application of the mediator design pattern is most appropriate to the task of agent communications in the IUMELA MAS. The moderator arbitrates interactions between the other agent types. In addition to this, it also maintains an acquaintance model based on past interactions. The moderator agent acts as a liaison between the other agent types in IUMELA. Assistant and expert agents inform each other of actions preformed via the moderator agent, see fig. 1.

The student agent enables all other agents in IUMELA to connect to the student case base and to access the administrative data of the analysed student. It provides a single, generic method by which other agents can interact with the student data while, simultaneously, ensuring student confidentiality. IUMELA aims to help students in their attempts to achieve their ultimate academic goals by assisting them in devising competent and obtainable academic goals while traversing through a specially tailored module schema. The student agent enables students to envision, at the click of a button, a potential overview of their academic journey based on the student's current academic profile and previous academic achievements.

The role of the expert agent is to depict the teaching strategies of the module lecturers in an accurate and current manner. It is the task of the expert agent to maintain this directory of all available modules, the lecturer directing it, and their preferred teaching style and examination technique. The analysis agent maintains a knowledge base that predicts all plausible academic outcomes based on the information it receives from the student and expert agents. Although it maintains several potential recommendation algorithms, it will proactively choose an appropriate reasoning model based on the students prior knowledge, their academic history, and their chosen degree program and current level.

Upon logging on to the IUMELA application for the first time, the student is required to complete an initial survey. To do so is necessary to enable the multi-agent system (MAS) to assist the new student in choosing their preferred learning style, teaching strategy and examination procedures. To ensure that IUMELA is useful from the onset, a student will be unable to navigate through the application without having completed the survey beforehand. The student enters their UCD email address and student number, which will suffice as their unique student identifiers within IUMELA. The assistant agent, residing on the students' XDA Mini S, retrieves these details and submits them to the moderator agent via the getSurvey() message. This message adheres to the FIPA compliant IUMELA ontology, and its generic usefulness as a communication medium is evident in fig 2. The student agent, responsible for maintaining the knowledge base for all students, creates a new entry for the student using their student ID and email address as their unique identifier. The task of posing each new question is an iterative process that is complete only when all questions have been answered.

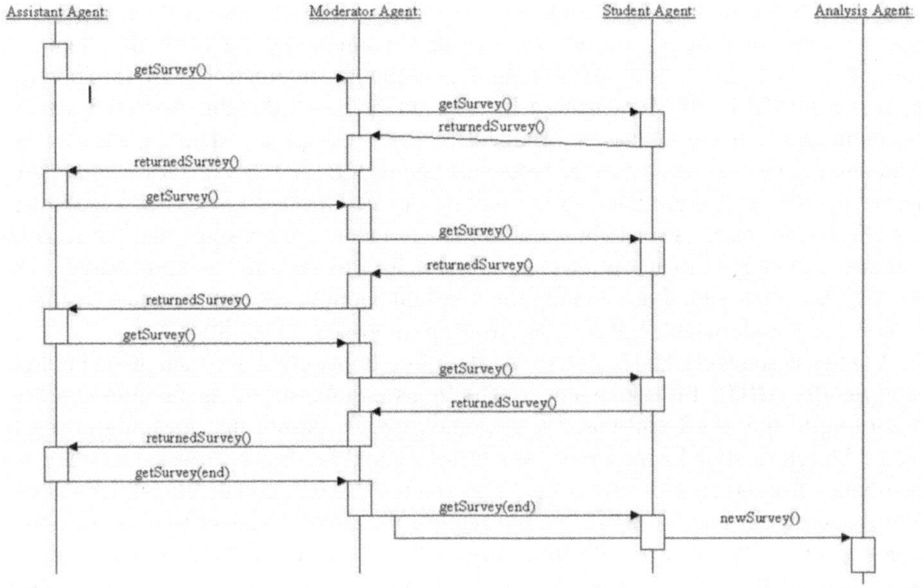

Fig. 2. Sample Agent Interactions within the IUMELA MAS

The task of the expert agent is similar to that of the student agent in that it maintains a registry of the user information. It stores all information relating to the modules available at the university. Including, but not limited to, the current lecturer, their preferred teaching strategies and examination procedures. It is the task of the analysis agent to analyse all information received from the assistant agent via the moderator agent and stored by either the student or expert agents. The analysis agent retrieves the results from the student agent and combines these with past student histories to predict all plausible academic outcomes based on the possible module combinations currently available.

4 Evaluation

It was the aim of this study to determine whether the optimal number of concurrent agent interactions occurring within the IUMELA multi-agent system (MAS) would be different based on the FIPA compliant messaging service used; that incorporated within the Agent Factory Toolkit or the ABITS FIPA Messenger. Because IUMELA is a mobile application, this study would be undertaken using a lightweight client side, where the personalized and adaptive assistant agent is located, and the more computationally expensive server side where the remainder of the MAS agents resides. IUMELA makes use of the XDA Mini S. It harnesses the power of the TI OMP 850 200 MHZ processor and is equipped with a 64k colour touch screen and 240*320 backlit LCD screen. The server-side is maintained on a Dell Dimension E521 with 4GB Dual-Channel DDR2 SDRAM 533MHz processor. The Moodle MLE is maintained on the server-side.

Although Agent Factory maintains a messenger service that enables inter agent communications, past studies have shown that maintaining a lightweight client side can ensure faster and more efficient human-computer interactions (HCI). Therefore by using ABITS FIPA Messenger, a lightweight Java API that enables unidirectional communication from a Java environment to FIPA compliant MAS, processing and communicative overheads may be reduced. The IUMELA MAS resides within client-server based architecture. Due to the mobile devices limited processing capabilities, the client side maintains a lightweight assistant agent. This ensures that the learning assistant can operate to an optimal level. It was for this reason that a pull based architecture was employed, thus enabling the assistant agent to request resources or logs in a "lazy" or "on-demand" manner and ensuring improved scalability.

A study was undertaken to determine if a more lightweight assistant agent could be used via the ABITS FIPA messenger. The lightweight assistant agent, communicates according to the MAS pull-based agent ontology. To ensure that meaningful results would be returned and appropriate conclusions could be drawn, it was necessary that two types of interaction would occur. The control IUMELA interactions, typical of a traditional Agent Factory MAS, would require the assistant agent to have an understanding of all request and inform messages specific to the IUMELA ontology. The second set of IUMELA interactions undertaken merely require the assistant agent to obtain messages from the moderator agent and does not require it to submit processed information as these messages would be relayed via the ABITS FIPA Messenger service.

The initial IUMELA survey was used as part of this study. The assistant agent is informed of each subsequent question each time a request is made until the survey is completed. In the control scenario, each time a student completes a question the assistant agent informs the moderator and the results are passed to the student agent for analysis. In the test scenario, each time a student completes a question the assistant agent passes it to a queue of messages to be sent to the moderator agent and the completed messages are sent via the ABITS FIPA Messenger service.

In order that the optimal number of concurrent message interactions could be determined, it was necessary that several key time codes were retrieved. For each message interaction, regardless of the mechanism: the time at which the first inform message interaction occurs, the time at which the message is received from the sender, the time at which a second inform message is returned to the sender, the time at which the message interaction is completed, and finally the overall duration of the message interaction

On average, around 144 message interactions are required in order for each initial IUMELA survey to be completed by a student. The results obtained are evident in fig 3. The time codes retrieved enable the multi-agent system to determine if and when a bottleneck is occurring within the IUMELA MAS architecture due to the moderator agents message interactions having surpassed its optimal level. While undertaking the survey, the bottleneck occurred mid-way through completion, at the sixty-first interaction.

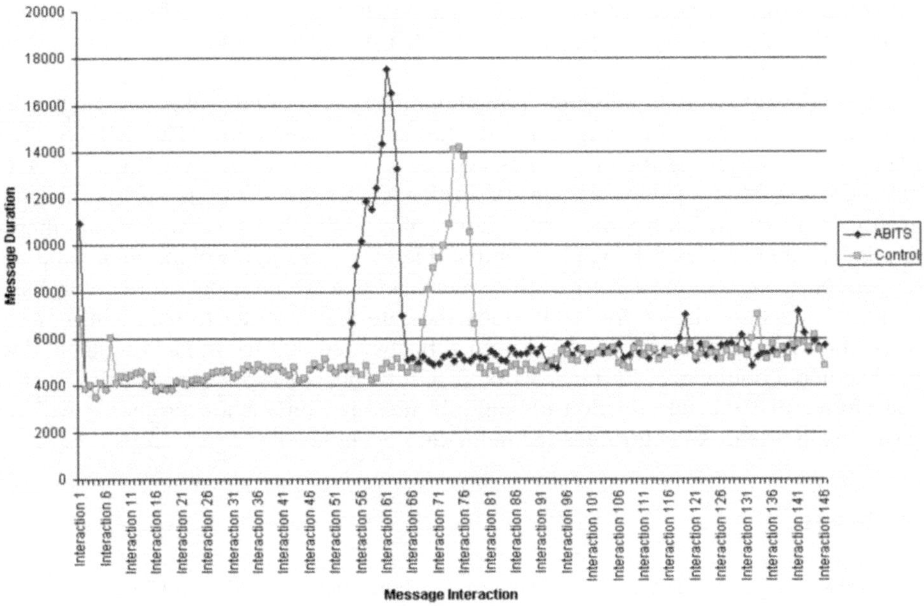

Fig. 3. ABITS FIPA Messenger Message Interaction Duration

Using the ABITS FIPA Messenger, the optimal number of concurrent message interactions occurs at interaction forty-seven. This does not occur until interaction seventy-eight within the control scenario and is attributed to the assistant agent maintaining a full ontology and undertaking more complicated inter-agent communications. The results indicate that a bottleneck occurred mid-way through completion of the survey because it is at this time that the greatest number of message interactions is occurring between the assistant and moderator agents. The ABITS FIPA Messenger achieved optimality of message interactions at a faster rate than the control scenario due to the inclusion of a java class that maintained a separate queue of completed surveys to be returned to the server side moderator for processing. This had the effect of reducing the size of the assistant agents ontology.

5 Discussion and Future Work

IUMELA makes use of MAS technologies to create an intelligent learning assistant that can support students in their choice of modules based on their learning preferences, academic abilities and personal preferences. The learning assistant uses expert systems analysis functionality to recommend and predict potential outcomes through the investigation of the students' learning styles and comparative analysis of similar past student's achievements. Its conclusions and recommendations are displayed to the student via the XDA Mini S client interface. Because the mobile devices currently available to the average student are still unable to compete with desktop and laptop computers, this paper considered the use of a lightweight client-side using ABITS

FIPA Messenger. An evaluation of such an adaptation was achieved by undertaking a comparative study between the original IUMELA MAS and that incorporating the ABITS FIPA Messenger.

Several results were highlighted throughout the course of this study; the first is that a bottleneck occurred mid-way through the survey completion. The ABITS FIPA Messenger achieved optimality of message interactions at a faster rate than the original IUMELA MAS. This results in the further reduction of the size of the assistant agents ontology, which has the further effect of reducing its processing requirements. An unexpected result of the study was that due to a more lightweight client-side, the moderator agent became a bottleneck sooner than that which occurred in control scenario. Conclusions drawn from this study indicate that in order to maintain message interaction levels at an optimal level it must be ensured that the moderator agent does not become a bottleneck. In future work, it will be necessary that the IUMELA MAS can ensure that the introduction of multiple message interaction protocols will not result in a bottleneck occurring at the moderator agent level.

References

1. Snowman, et al.: Psychology Applied to Teaching, Houghton Mifflin Company, Boston (2006)
2. Tarasewich, P.: Wireless Devices for Mobile Commerce: User Interface Design and Usability. In: Mennecke, Straden (eds.) Mobile (2002)
3. McGovern, E.: A Comparative Study of Multi-Agent and Object Oriented Methodologies for Mobile Managed Learning Environments, MSc. Thesis, Department of Computer Science, University College Dublin (2005)
4. Ballagas, R., et al.: The Smart Phone: A Ubiquitous Input Device [NJ]. Merrill Prentice Hall, Englewood Cliffs (2006)
5. Staudt, C.: Probing untested ground: Young Students Learn to Use Handheld computers (1999) Retrieved from http://concord.org
6. Belanger, Y.: Laptop Computers in the K-12 Classroom Retrieved from ERIC DIGEST: Notebooksystems.com (2000)
7. Wallace, R.M., Kupperman, J., Krajcik, J., Soloway, E.: Science on the Web: Students online in a sixth-grade classroom. Journal of the Learning Sciences 9(1), 75–104 (2000)
8. Nolan, P.: UCD Horizons, UCD Press, University College Dublin (2006)
9. Sternberg, R.J., Grigorienko, E.L.: A capsule history of theory and research on styles. In: Sternberg, R.J., Zhang, L.F. (eds.) Perspectives on Thinking, Learning and Cognitive Styles, pp. 1–21. Lawrence Erlbaum, Mahwah, NJ, London (2001)
10. Witkin, H., Moore, C., Goodenough, D., Cox, P.: Field-dependent and field-independent cognitive styles and their educational implications. Review of Educational Research 1–64 (1977)
11. Bloom, B.S., et al.: Taxonomy of Educational Objectives. The Classification of Educational Goals. Handbook I, cognitive Domain (1956)
12. Adams, G.L, Engelmann, S.: Research on Direct Instruction: 25 Years beyond DISTAR. [WA] Educational Achievement System (1996)
13. Metzger, M.: Maintaining a Life. Phi Delta Kappan. January 1996. NCTM (1996)
14. Rogers, C.R.: Freedom to Learn for the 80's. [OH]. Merril Prentice Hall, Englewood Cliffs (1983)

15. Kay, A,: User Interfaces: A Personal View. The art of Human Computer Interface Design. Addison-Wesley 1990 Shneiderman, S. Human Factors Experiments in Designing Interactive Systems. Computer 12 (12) (1979)
16. Mayer, Shneiderman Mayer, R., Shneiderman, B.: Syntactic/Semantic Interactions in Programmer Behavior: a Model and Experimental Results. International Journal of Computer and Information Sciences 8(3), 219–238 (1979)
17. Collier, R.: The Realisation of Agent Factory: An Environment for the Rapid Prototyping of Intelligent Agents, UMIST, Manchester, UK (M.Phil. Thesis) (1995)
18. Foundation for Intelligent Physical Agents, FIPA 97 Specification Part 2: Agent Communication Language, pp. 101–124 (1997)
19. O'Hare, G.M.P.: The Agent Factory: An Environment for the Fabrication of Distributed Artificial, Systems. In: O'Hare, G.M.P., Jennings, N.R (eds.) Foundations of Distributed Artificial Intelligence, Sixth Generation Computer Series, pp. 449–484. Wiley Interscience Publishers, New York (1996)

Towards Intuitive Spatiotemporal Communication Between Human and Ubiquitous Intelligence Based on Mental Image Directed Semantic Theory --- A General Theory of Tempo-logical Connectives ---

Masao Yokota

Department of System Management, Faculty of Information Engineering,
Fukuoka Institute of Technology,
3-30-1, Wajiro-higashi, Higashi-ku, Fukuoka-shi, 811-0295 Japan
yokota@fit.ac.jp
http://www.fit.ac.jp

Abstract. The Mental Image Directed Semantic Theory (MIDST) has proposed the knowledge representation language L_{md} for facilitating intuitive human-system interaction in the real world. The L_{md} has employed the 'tempo-logical connectives (TLCs)' to represent both temporal and logical relations between two events, and the 'temporal conjunctions', a subset of TLCs, have already been applied to formulating natural event concepts, namely, those represented in natural language. This paper presents the theory of TLCs extended for formalizing natural spatiotemporal knowledge in general in order to facilitate intuitive human-system interaction such as comprehensible communication in natural language between ordinary people and home robots.

1 Introduction

Towards more human-friendly ubiquitous intelligence, the author has proposed the idea of distributed intelligent robot network (DIRN [8,10,11]) shown in Fig.1, consisting of one brain node and numerous distributed sensor and actor nodes with human-friendly interfaces.

In a DIRN, it is assumed that the sensors and actuators collaborate autonomously to perform appropriate actions just like reflexive actions in humans and that the brain node works exclusively for complicated computation based on profound knowledge in order to control the other kinds of nodes, to communicate with ordinary people, etc. Therefore, the 'ubiquitous intelligence' on a DIRN is assumed to work based on a certain systematically computable knowledge representation language [11] as well as efficient networking technologies [15]. This type of language is indispensable to knowledge-based processing such as understanding sensory events, planning appropriate actions and knowledgeable communication even with ordinary people, and therefore it needs to have at least a good capability of representing spatiotemporal events that correspond to human/robotic sensations and actions in the real world.

There have been several theories about formalization and computation of spatial or temporal relations and a considerable number of their applications [1-5,14]. They, however, do not necessarily keep tight correspondence with spatiotemporal

J. Indulska et al. (Eds.): UIC 2007, LNCS 4611, pp. 1066–1078, 2007.

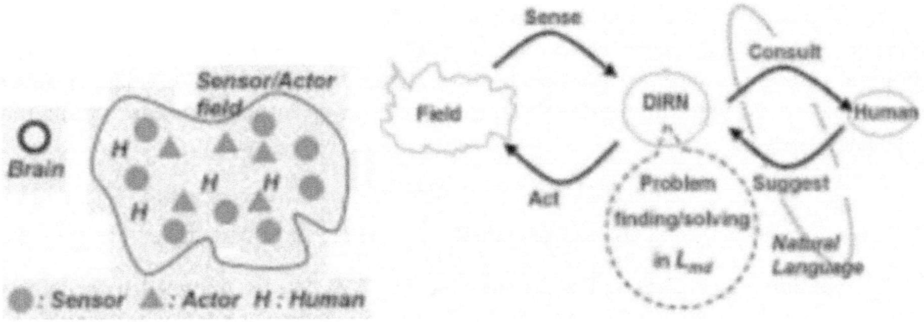

Fig. 1. Configuration (Left) and function (Right) of DIRN

expressions in natural language reflecting human cognitive processes strongly [6, 7]. For example, consider such expressions as S1 and S1′.

(S1) It got cloudy ***and*** it rained.

(S1′) It rained ***and*** it got cloudy.

It is very natural for people to understand each one by synthesizing the mental images evoked by the two clauses into an intuitively plausible one where spatiotemporal relations of the matters involved do not conflict with their empirical knowledge of the real world. In this case, people would make a special effort to arrange the two events, namely, 'getting cloudy' and 'raining' on the time axis adequately because the temporal relation between them is not explicit in either expression. According to the results of our psycholinguistic experiments [6], people are apt to interpret the construction 'A happened ***and*** B happened' in spatiotemporal expressions as a specific event, namely, as 'A happened ***before*** B happened' (c.f., S3′). That is, people usually do not understand such expressions as S1 and S1′ in the same meaning as 'A $\wedge$ B' equivalent to 'B $\wedge$ A' in pure logic.

For another example, consider such an expression as S2.

(S2) It gets cloudy ***before*** it rains.

People usually interpret the construction '*A* happens *before B* happens' as a general causality, namely, as 'If *B* happens, *A* happens in advance.' This is easily understood by the fact that S2 and S2′ are not semantically identical while S3 and S3′ can refer to the same compound event as S1. That is, it is not always the case that cloudiness is followed by rain.

(S2′) It rains ***after*** it gets cloudy.

(S3) It got cloudy ***before*** it rained.

(S3′) It rained ***after*** it got cloudy.

The point-based time theories can formalize the constructions of S1 and S2 as (1) and (2), respectively, where the events *A* and *B* are somewhat unnaturally but inevitably to be provided with the time points and their relations. Here and after, a time point 't_i' is represented as a real number (i.e., $t_i \in \boldsymbol{R}$).

$$(\exists t_1,t_2)\ A(t_1)\wedge B(t_2)\wedge t_1<t_2 \tag{1}$$

$$(\exists t_1)(\forall t_2)(B(t_2) \supset A(t_1))\wedge t_1<t_2 \tag{2}$$

On the other hand, the interval-based time theories can provide a counterpart for (1) as (3), possibly more naturally, but not for (2) because such a predicate as *'after'*, *'contains'* or so is intrinsically a conjunction (i.e., '∧') furnished with a certain ***purely*** temporal relation. That is, (3) could be formalized otherwise as (4), where *A* and *B* are parameterized with time-intervals $[t_{11},t_{12}]$ and $[t_{21},t_{22}]$, respectively, presuming that $t_{11}<t_{12}$ and $t_{21}<t_{22}$.

$$\textit{before}(A,B)(\equiv \textit{after}(B,A)) \tag{3}$$

$$(\exists t_{11},t_{12},t_{21},t_{22})A([t_{11},t_{12}])\wedge B([t_{21},t_{22}])\wedge t_{12}<t_{21} \tag{4}$$

The Mental Image Directed Semantic Theory (MIDST) is intended to provide a formal system for natural semantics and general knowledge of space and time [7, 8]. This formal system is one kind of applied predicate logic consisting of definitions and postulates subject to human perceptive processes of space and time while other similar systems [e.g., 1-5] in Artificial Intelligence are objective, namely, independent of human perception and do not necessarily keep tight correspondences with natural language.

The MIDST has proposed a systematic method to model natural event concepts as 'loci in attribute spaces', so called, and describe them in a formal language $\boldsymbol{L_{md}}$. This language is employed for many-sorted predicate logic provided with 'tempo-logical connectives (TLCs)' with which to represent both temporal and logical relations between two loci over certain time-intervals.

Therefore, TLCs are for interval-based time theories but are generalized for all the binary logical connectives (i.e., conjunction '∧', disjunction '∨', implication '⊃' and equivalence '≡') unlike the conventional ones exclusively for the conjunction. This is intended for facilitating formulation and computation of people's empirical (i.e., natural) knowledge pieces such as S1 and S2 that are possibly formalized as (1)-(4) in the conventional schemes. This paper presents a brief sketch of $\boldsymbol{L_{md}}$, a general theory of TLCs and its application to formulating human empirical knowledge expressed in spatiotemporal language.

2 The Formal Language $\boldsymbol{L_{md}}$

2.1 Omnisensory Image Model

The MIDST treats word meanings in association with mental images, not limited to visual but omnisensory, modeled as "Loci in Attribute Spaces". An attribute space corresponds with a certain measuring instrument just like a barometer, thermometer or so and the loci represent the movements of its indicator. Such a locus is to be articulated by "Atomic Locus" over an ***absolute*** time-interval, which is in turn to be formulated as (5) with its interval suppressed. This formula is called 'Atomic Locus Formula' whose first two arguments are often referred to as 'Event Causer (EC)' and 'Attribute Carrier (AC)', respectively. A logical combination of atomic locus formulas defined as a well-formed formula (i.e., wff) in predicate logic is called simply 'Locus Formula'.

$$L(x,y,p,q,a,g,k) \tag{5}$$

The intuitive interpretation of (5) is given as follows.
"Matter 'x' causes Attribute 'a' of Matter 'y' to keep (p=q) or change (p ≠ q) its values temporally ($g=G_t$) or spatially ($g=G_s$) over a time-interval, where the values 'p' and 'q' are relative to the standard 'k'."

When $g=G_t$ and $g=G_s$, the locus indicates monotonic change or constancy of the attribute in time domain and that in space domain, respectively. The former is called 'temporal event' and the latter, 'spatial event'.

For example, the motion of the 'bus' represented by S4 is a temporal event and the ranging or extension of the 'road' by S4´ is a spatial event whose meanings are formulated as (6) and (7), respectively, where 'A_{12}' denotes the attribute 'Physical Location'. These two formulas are different only at the term 'Event Type (i.e., g)'.

(S4) The bus runs from Tokyo to Osaka.

$$(\exists x,y,k)L(x,y,Tokyo,Osaka,A_{12},\mathbf{G_t},k)\wedge bus(y) \quad (6)$$

(S4´) The road runs from Tokyo to Osaka.

$$(\exists x,y,k)L(x,y,Tokyo,Osaka,A_{12},\mathbf{G_s},k)\wedge road(y) \quad (7)$$

The author has hypothesized that the difference between temporal and spatial event concepts can be attributed to the relationship between the Attribute Carrier (AC) and the Focus of the Attention of the Observer (FAO) [8]. To be brief, it is assumed that the FAO is fixed on the whole AC in a temporal event but *runs* about on the AC in a spatial event. According to this assumption, the *bus* and the FAO move together in the case of S4 while the FAO solely moves along the *road* in the case of S4´.

The duration of an atomic locus corresponds to the absolute time-interval over which the FAO is put on the corresponding phenomenon outside and which is suppressed in the atomic locus formula. The MIDST has introduced 'tempo-logical connectives (TLCs)' in order to represent both logical and temporal relations between two loci. This is more natural and economical than explicit indication of time-intervals, considering that people do neither be conscious of absolute time nor consult chronometers all the time in their daily lives.

The definition of a tempo-logical connective K_i is given by **D1**, where τ_i, χ and K refer to one of ***purely*** temporal relations indexed by an integer 'i', a locus, and an ordinary binary logical connective such as the conjunction '$\wedge$', respectively.

The definition of each τ_i is provided with Table 1 implying the theorem **T1,** where the durations of χ_1 and χ_2 are $[t_{11}, t_{12}]$ and $[t_{21}, t_{22}]$, respectively. This table shows the complete list of temporal relations between two intervals, where 13 types of relations are discriminated by the suffix 'i' ($-6\leq i \leq 6$). This is in accordance with the conventional notation [1] which, to be strict, is for 'temporal conjunctions ($=\wedge_i$)' but not for pure 'temporal relations ($=\tau_i$)'.

D1. $\chi_1\ K_i\ \chi_2 \leftrightarrow (\chi_1\ K\ \chi_2) \wedge \tau_i(\chi_1, \chi_2)$

T1. $\tau_{-i}(\chi_2, \chi_1) \equiv \tau_i(\chi_1, \chi_2)$ $(\forall i\in \{0,\pm1,\pm2,\pm3,\pm4,\pm5, \pm6\})$
(Proof) Trivial in Table1. [**Q.E.D.**]

The TLCs used most frequently are 'SAND ($\wedge_0$)' and 'CAND ($\wedge_1$)', standing for 'Simultaneous AND' and 'Consecutive AND', conventionally denoted by 'Π' and '•', respectively. As easily proven, Associative and Commutative Laws hold among

Table 1. List of temporal relations

Definition of τ_i		Allen's notation
$t_{11}=t_{21} \wedge t_{12}=t_{22}$	$\tau_0(\chi_1, \chi_2)$	equals(χ_1,χ_2)
	$\tau_0(\chi_2, \chi_1)$	equals(χ_2, χ_1)
$t_{12}=t_{21}$	$\tau_1(\chi_1, \chi_2)$	meets(χ_1, χ_2)
	$\tau_{-1}(\chi_2, \chi_1)$	met-by(χ_2, χ_1)
$t_{11}=t_{21} \wedge t_{12}<t_{22}$	$\tau_2(\chi_1, \chi_2)$	starts(χ_1, χ_2)
	$\tau_{-2}(\chi_2, \chi_1)$	started-by(χ_2, χ_1)
$t_{11}>t_{21} \wedge t_{12}<t_{22}$	$\tau_3(\chi_1, \chi_2)$	during(χ_1, χ_2)
	$\tau_{-3}(\chi_2, \chi_1)$	contains(χ_2, χ_1)
$t_{11}>t_{21} \wedge t_{12}=t_{22}$	$\tau_4(\chi_1, \chi_2)$	finishes(χ_1, χ_2)
	$\tau_{-4}(\chi_2, \chi_1)$	finished-by(χ_2, χ_1)
$t_{12}<t_{21}$	$\tau_5(\chi_1, \chi_2)$	before(χ_1, χ_2)
	$\tau_{-5}(\chi_2, \chi_1)$	after(χ_2, χ_1)
$t_{11}<t_{21} \wedge t_{21}<t_{12} \wedge t_{12}<t_{22}$	$\tau_6(\chi_1, \chi_2)$	overlaps(χ_1, χ_2)
	$\tau_{-6}(\chi_2, \chi_1)$	overlapped-by(χ_2, χ_1)

SANDs but the latter does not among CANDs. As easily imagined, (3) or (4) is represented as (8) in MIDST.

$$A \wedge_5 B \ (\equiv B \wedge_{-5} A). \qquad (8)$$

2.2 Empty Event

An 'Empty Event (EE)', denoted by 'ε', stands for nothing but for ***absolute*** time elapsing and is explicitly defined as **D2** with the attribute 'Time Point (A_{34})' and the Standard of absolute time 'T_a'. Usually people can know only a certain ***relative*** time point by a clock that is seldom exact and that is to be denoted by another Standard in the $\boldsymbol{L_{md}}$. Hereafter, Δ denotes the total set of absolute time intervals. According to this scheme, the suppressed absolute time-interval $[t_a, t_b]$ of a locus χ can be indicated as (9).

$$\mathbf{D2}.\varepsilon([t_i,t_j]) \leftrightarrow (\exists x,y,g) L(x,y,t_i,t_j,A_{34},g,T_a),$$
$$\textit{where } [t_i, t_j] \in \Delta \ (=\{[t_1, t_2] \mid t_1<t_2 \ (t_1, t_2 \in \boldsymbol{R})\}).$$

$$\chi \Pi \varepsilon([t_a,t_b]) \qquad (9)$$

2.3 TLCs Extended for Conceptual Loci

A locus corresponding directly to the live image of a specific phenomenon outside is called 'Perceptual Locus' and can be formulated with atomic locus formulas and temporal conjunctions (TCs) such as SAND and CAND. This is not necessarily the case for the other type of locus, so called, 'Conceptual Locus' that does not correspond directly to such a live image but to such a generalized mental image or knowledge piece as is conventionally represented by (2) with logical connectives other than conjunctions also involved. This is essentially due to no interpreting a negated atomic locus formula as a locus with ***a unique time-interval***. That is, **D1** is exclusively for perceptual loci so far as it is.

Whereas, such theses as '$A \vee B. \equiv .\sim(\sim A \wedge \sim B)$' and '$A \supset B. \equiv .\sim A \vee B$' in pure logic can imply identity of a locus formula with its negative in absolute time-interval, that is, negation-freeness of absolute time passing under a locus referred to by its suppressed absolute time-interval. Therefore, to make **D1** valid also for conceptual loci, the absolute time-interval of a general locus formula is defined as **D3**, where δ is a meta-function for extracting the ***suppressed*** absolute time-interval of a locus formula χ.

D3. $\delta(\chi) \in \Delta$,

where if χ consists of a single atomic locus formula with a ***suppressed*** *absolute time-interval $[t_i, t_f]$ or its negative,*

then $\delta(\chi)=[t_i, t_f]$,

otherwise $\delta(\chi)=[t_{min}, t_{max}]$,

where t_{min} *and* t_{max} *are respectively the minimum among the* t_is *and the maximum among the* t_fs *of the atomic locus formulas, either positive or negative, within χ.*

This definition leads to **T2** (Theorem of negation-freeness of a suppressed absolute time-interval) below.

T2. $\delta(\sim\chi)=\delta(\chi)$

(Proof) The time-interval of each atomic locus formula involved in $\sim\chi$ is negation-free and therefore so are t_{min} and t_{max} in $\delta(\sim\chi)$. **[Q.E.D.]**

The counterpart of the contraposition in pure logic (i.e., $A \supset B. \equiv .\sim B \supset \sim A$) is given as **T3** (Tempo-logical Contraposition) whose rough proof is as follows immediately below, where the left hand of ':' refers to the theses (e.g., **PL** is a subset of those in pure predicate logic) employed at the process indicated by the meta-symbol ('$\Rightarrow$' or) '$\Leftrightarrow$'.

T3. $\chi_1 \supset_i \chi_2. \equiv .\sim\chi_2 \supset_{-i} \sim\chi_1$

(Proof)

D1: $\chi_1 \supset_i \chi_2 \Leftrightarrow (\chi_1 \supset \chi_2) \wedge \tau_i(\chi_1, \chi_2)$

PL: $\Leftrightarrow (\sim\chi_2 \supset \sim\chi_1) \wedge \tau_i(\chi_1, \chi_2)$

T2: $\Leftrightarrow (\sim\chi_2 \supset \sim\chi_1) \wedge \tau_i(\sim\chi_1, \sim\chi_2)$

D1: $\Leftrightarrow (\sim\chi_2 \supset \sim\chi_1) \wedge \tau_{-i}(\sim\chi_2, \sim\chi_1)$

D1: $\Leftrightarrow \sim\chi_2 \supset_{-i} \sim\chi_1$ **[Q.E.D.]**

3 Formulation of Natural Event Concepts

3.1 Temporal Event Concepts

The temporal event concepts of the English verbs 'carry', 'return', 'fetch', and 'hand/receive' are to be defined as (10)-(13), respectively. These formulas can refer to such loci as depicted in Fig.3(a)-(d), respectively.

$$(\lambda x,y)carry(x,y) \leftrightarrow (\lambda x,y)(\exists p,q,k)L(x,x,p,q,A_{12},G_t,k)\Pi L(x,y,p,q,A_{12},G_t,k) \wedge x \neq y \wedge p \neq q \quad (10)$$

$$(\lambda x)return(x) \leftrightarrow (\lambda x)(\exists p,q,k)L(x,x,p,q,A_{12},G_t,k) \bullet L(x,x,p,q,A_{12},G_t,k) \wedge x \neq y \wedge p \neq q \quad (11)$$

$$(\lambda x,y)\mathrm{fetch}(x,y)\leftrightarrow(\lambda x,y)(\exists p_1,p_2,k)L(x,x,p_1,p_2,A_{12},G_t,k)\bullet$$
$$((\underline{L(x,x,p_2,p_1,A_{12},G_t,k)\Pi L(x,y,p_2,p_1,A_{12},G_t,k)})$$
$$\wedge x\neq y\wedge p_1\neq p_2 \quad (12)$$

$$(\lambda x,y,z)\mathrm{hand}(x,y,z)\leftrightarrow(\lambda x,y,z)\mathrm{receive}(z,y,x)$$
$$\leftrightarrow(\lambda x,y,z)(\exists k)L(x,y,x,z,A_{12},G_t,k)\Pi L(z,y,x,z,A_{12},G_t,k)\ \wedge x\neq y\wedge y\neq z\wedge z\neq x \quad (13)$$

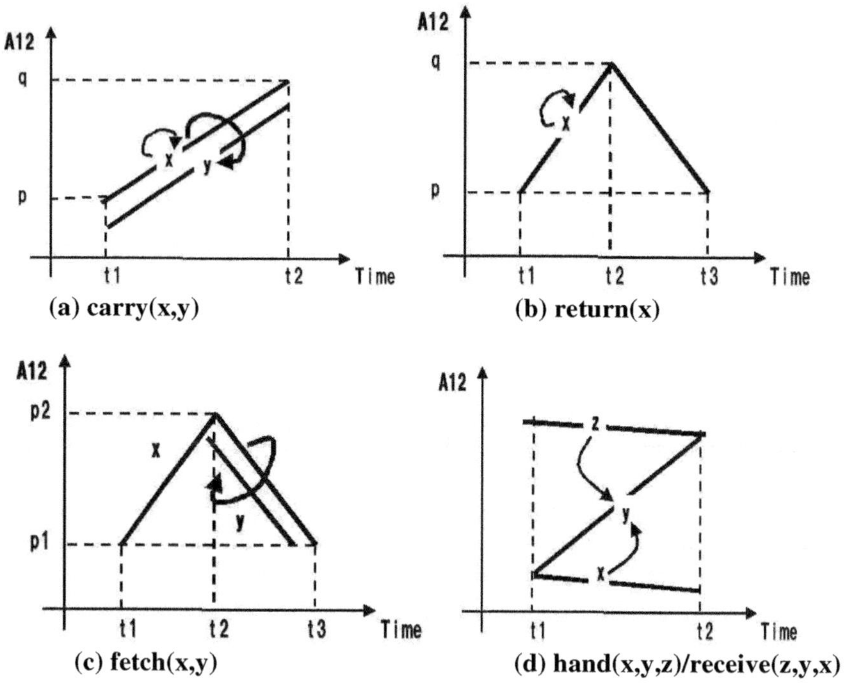

Fig. 3. Loci of temporal event concepts

Such locus formulas as correspond with natural event concepts are called 'Event Patterns' and about 40 kinds of event patterns have been found concerning the attribute 'Physical Location (A_{12})', for example, *start*, *stop*, *meet*, *separate*, *carry*, *return*, etc [7].

3.2 Spatial Event Concepts

As already mentioned in Section 2, all loci in attribute spaces are assumed to correspond one to one with movements or, more generally, ***temporal events*** of the FAO. And this is why S5 and S6 can refer to the same scene in spite of their appearances, where what 'sinks' or 'rises' is the FAO and whose conceptual descriptions are given as (14) and (15), respectively, where 'A_{13}', '↑' and '↓' refer to the attribute 'Direction' and its values 'upward' and 'downward', respectively.

(S5) The path *sinks* to the brook.
(S6) The path *rises* from the brook.

$$(\exists x,y,p,z,k,k_1)L(x,y,p,z,A_{12},G_s,k)\Pi L(x,y,\downarrow,\downarrow,A_{13},G_s,k_1)\wedge path(y)\wedge brook(z)\wedge p\neq z \quad (14)$$

$$(\exists x,y,p,z,k,k_1)L(x,y,z,p,A_{12},G_s,k)\Pi L(x,y,\uparrow,\uparrow,A_{13},G_s,k_1)\wedge path(y)\wedge brook(z)\wedge p\neq z \quad (15)$$

Such a fact is generalized as '***Postulate of Reversibility of a Spatial Event*** (PRS)', to be formalized as **P1** in the next section, that can be one of the principal theses belonging to people's common-sense knowledge about geography. This postulation is also valid for such a pair of S7 and S8 as interpreted approximately into (16) and (17), respectively. These pairs of conceptual descriptions are called ***equivalent in PRS***, and the paired sentences are treated as ***paraphrases*** each other.

(S7) Route A and Route B meet at the city.
(S8) Route A and Route B separate at the city.

$$(\exists x,p,y,q,k)L(x,Route\_A,p,y,A_{12},G_s,k)\Pi L(x,Route\_B,q,y,A_{12},G_s,k)\wedge city(y)\wedge p\neq q \quad (16)$$

$$(\exists x,p,y,q,k)L(x,Route\_A,y,p,A_{12},G_s,k)\Pi L(x,Route\_B,y,q,A_{12},G_s,k)\wedge city(y)\wedge p\neq q \quad (17)$$

For another example of spatial event, Fig.4 concerns the perception of formation of multiple objects, where FAO runs along an imaginary object so called 'Imaginary Space Region (ISR)'. This spatial event can be verbalized as S9 using the preposition 'between' and formulated as (18), corresponding also to such concepts as 'row', 'line-up', etc.

(S9) □ is between Δ and ○.

$$(\exists x,y,p,k,k_1)(L(x,y,\Delta,\square,A_{12},G_s,k)\bullet L(x,y,\square,\circ,A_{12},G_s,k)\Pi L(x,y,p,p,A_{13},G_s,k_1)\wedge ISR(y) \quad (18)$$

At last of this section, consider such somewhat complicated sentences as S10 and S11. The underlined parts are deemed to refer to some events neglected in time and in space, respectively. These events correspond with skipping of FAOs and are called 'Temporal Empty Event' and 'Spatial Empty Event', denoted by 'ε_t' and 'ε_s' as EEs with $g=G_t$ and $g=G_s$ at **D2**, respectively. The concepts of S10 and S11 are given by (19) and (20), where 'A_{15}' and 'A_{17}' represent the attribute 'Trajectory' and 'Mileage', respectively.

(S10) The *bus* runs 10km straight east from A to B, and <u>*after a while*</u>, at C it meets the street with the sidewalk.

$$(\exists x_1,x,y,z,p,q,k,k_1,k_2,k_3)\ (L(x_1,x,A,B,A_{12},G_t,k)\ \Pi\ L(x_1,x,0,10km,A_{17},G_t,k_1)\Pi\ L(x_1,x,Point,Line,A_{15},G_t,k_2)\ \Pi\ L(x_1,x,East,East,A_{13},G_t,k_3))\bullet\ \varepsilon_t \bullet\ L(x_1,x,p,C,A_{12},G_t,k)\ \Pi\ L(x_1,y,q,C,A_{12},G_s,k)\Pi\ L(x_1,z,y,y,A_{12},G_s,k))\wedge bus(x)\wedge street(y)\wedge sidewalk(z)\wedge p\neq q \quad (19)$$

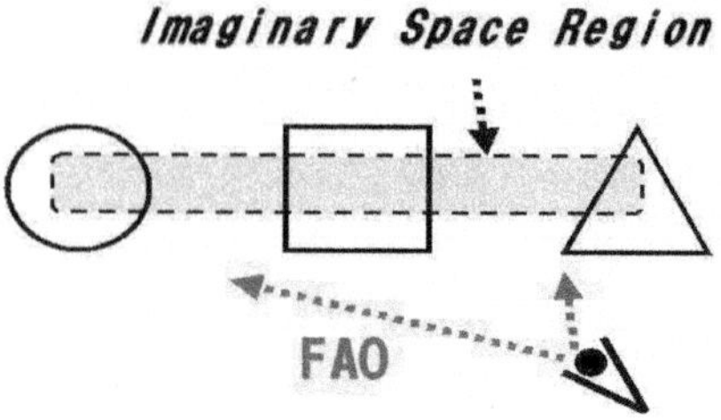

Fig. 4. Spatial event for the word 'row'

(S11) The *road* runs 10km straight east from *A* to *B*, and <u>*after a while*</u>, at *C* it meets the street with the sidewalk.

$$(\exists x_1,x,y,z,p,q,k,k_1,k_2)(L(x_1,x,A,B,A_{12},G_s,k)\Pi L(x_1,x,0,10km,A_{17},G_s,k_1)\Pi L(x_1,x,Point,Line,A_{15},G_s,k_2) \Pi L(x_1,x,East,East,A_{13},G_s,k_3))\bullet\varepsilon_s\bullet L(x_1,x,p,C,A_{12},G_s,k) \Pi L(x_1,y,q,C,A_{12},G_s,k)\Pi L(x_1,z,y,y,A_{12},G_s,k)) \wedge road(x)\wedge street(y)\wedge sidewalk(z)\wedge p\neq q \quad (20)$$

4 Formulation of More General Knowledge

4.1 Utilization of Temporal Implications

The knowledge piece of the causality represented by (2) can be formulated as (21) by employing the temporal implication '$\supset_5$' or as its equivalent (22) with '$\supset_{-5}$'. As easily understood, these formulas are equivalent to such ones using temporal disjunctions as parenthesized. By the way, (22) can be verbalized as S12 although it might sound somewhat unusual.

$$A.\supset_5.B \ (\equiv \sim A\vee_5 B) \quad (21)$$

$$\sim B.\supset_{-5}.\sim A \ (\equiv B\vee_{-5} \sim A) \quad (22)$$

(S12) It does not rain ***after*** it does not get cloudy.

Temporal implications are often employed for formalizing miscellaneous tempo-logical relations between event concepts as knowledge pieces without explicit indication of time-intervals. For example, an event 'fetch(x,y)' is necessarily *finished by* an event 'carry(x,y)' as indicated by the underline at (12). This fact can be formulated as (23), which is not an axiom but a theorem deducible from the definitions of event concepts here. Similarly, the tempo-logical relation between 'fetch(x,y)' and 'return(x)' can be theorematized as (24). Furthermore, if necessary, these can be temporally quantified as (25) and (26), respectively, where $d_1, d_2 \in \Delta$.

$$(\forall x,y)fetch(x,y)\supset_{-4} carry(x,y) \quad (23)$$

$$(\forall x,y)fetch(x,y)\supset_0 return(x) \quad (24)$$

$$(\exists d_2)(\forall d_1)(\forall x,y)\ fetch(x,y)\Pi\varepsilon(d_1).\supset_{-4}.carry(x,y)\Pi\varepsilon(d_2) \quad (25)$$

$$(\exists d_2)(\forall d_1)(\forall x,y)\ fetch(x,y)\Pi\varepsilon(d_1).\supset_0.\ return(x)\Pi\varepsilon(d_2) \quad (26)$$

4.2 Utilization of Temporal Equivalences

For example, the postulate PRS can be formulated as **P1** using '$\equiv_0$', where χ and χ^R is a perceptual locus and its 'reversal' for a certain spatial event, respectively. These loci are substitutable with each other due to the property of '$\equiv_0$'.

P1. $\chi^R .\equiv_0 .\chi$

The recursive operations to transform χ into χ^R are defined by **D4**, where the reversed values p^R and q^R depend on the properties of the attribute values p and q. For example, at (27), p^R=p, q^R=q for A_{12}; p^R=-p, q^R=-q for A_{13}.

D4. $(\chi_1 \bullet \chi_2)^R \leftrightarrow \chi_2^R \bullet \chi_1^R$
$(\chi_1 \Pi \chi_2)^R \leftrightarrow \chi_1^R \Pi \chi_2^R$
$(L(x,y,p,q,a,G_s,k))^R \leftrightarrow L(x,y,q^R,p^R,a,G_s,k)$

According to **D4**, (20) is transformed into (27) as its reversal and equivalent in PRS to be verbalized as S13.

$$(\exists x_1,x,y,z,p,q,k,k_1,k_2,k_3)(L(x_1,x,C,p,A_{12},G_s,k)\Pi L(x_1,y,C,q,A_{12},G_s,k)\Pi L(x_1,z,y,y,A_{12},G_s,k)) \bullet \varepsilon_s \bullet (L(x_1,x,B,A,A_{12},G_s,k)\Pi L(x_1,x,0,10km,A_{17},G_s,k_1) \Pi L(x_1,x,Point,Line,A_{15},G_s,k_2) \Pi L(x_1,x,West,West,A_{13},G_s,k_3)) \wedge road(x) \wedge street(y) \wedge sidewalk(z) \wedge p \neq q \quad (27)$$

(S13) The road separates at *C* from the street with the sidewalk and, after a while, runs 10km straight west from *B* to *A*.

4.3 Definition of Natural Object Concepts

An object concept is to be defined as an integration of the potential events on its properties and its relations with others involved (e.g., functions) [9,16]. For example, the conceptual descriptions of 'danger', 'bullet' and 'shield' can be intuitively given as (28), (29) and (30), reading 'Danger makes a human less alive', 'Bullet is a danger, sent from a gun, …,' and 'A human puts a shield in line between a danger and himself/herself in order not to get less alive, …' respectively, where A_{39} is the attribute of 'Vitality'. These analytical definitions of word concepts can be helpful for artificial and ubiquitous intelligence to compute about security of human societies.

$$(\lambda x)danger(x) \leftrightarrow (\lambda x)(\exists x_1,q_1,q_2)L(x,x_1,q_1,q_2,A_{39},G_t,\_) \wedge human(x_1) \wedge q_1>q_2 \quad (28)$$

$$(\lambda x)bullet(x) \leftrightarrow (\lambda x)(\exists x_1,q_1,q_2)danger(x) \wedge L(x_1,x,q_1,q_2,A_{12},G_t,\_) \wedge gun(x_1) \wedge q_1 \neq q_2 \ldots \quad (29)$$

$$(\lambda x)shield(x) \leftrightarrow (\lambda x)(\exists x,x_1,x_2,y,p,q_1,q_2,\ldots)L(\_,x_1,p,p,A_{13},G_t,\_)\Pi (L(x_2,y,x_1,x,A_{12},G_s,\_) \bullet L(x_2,y,x,x_2,A_{12},G_s,\_))\Pi L(x_2,y,p,p,A_{13},G_s,\_)\Pi L(x_1,x_2,q_1,q_2,A_{39},G_t,\_) \wedge ISR(y) \wedge danger(x_1) \wedge human(x_2) \wedge \sim(q_1>q_2) \ldots \quad (30)$$

5 Discussions and Conclusions

The theory of tempo-logical connectives was extended for general natural spatiotemporal knowledge in order to realize more intuitive human-system interaction. This extension was concentrated on providing the theory with tempo-logical connectives other than tempo-logical conjunctions, where the principal definitions and postulates have been induced from several psycholinguistic experiments [6]. To remark reversely, the theses deduced from them have been already psycholinguistically validated.

The semantic description of an event in L_{md} is compared to a movie film recorded through a floating camera because it is necessarily grounded in FAO's movement over the event. At my best knowledge, there is no other theory or method that can provide spatiotemporal expressions with semantic interpretation in such a systematic way as ours where both temporal and spatial events are simply and adequately formulated by controlling the term of Event Type of the atomic locus formula. These simplicity and adequacy are due to its medium-freeness and its good correspondence with the performances of human sensory systems in both spatial and temporal extents.

The author has analyzed a considerable number of spatial terms over various kinds of English words such as prepositions, verbs, adverbs, etc. categorized as 'Dimensions', 'Form' and 'Motion' in the class 'SPACE' of the Roget's thesaurus [10], and found that the greater part of the concepts of spatial terms can be defined in exclusive use of five kinds of attributes for FAOs, namely, 'Physical location (A12)', 'Direction (A13)', 'Trajectory (A15)', 'Mileage (A17)' and 'Topology (A44)'. Most of computations on L_{md} are simply for unifying (or identifying) atomic loci and evaluating arithmetic expressions such as 'p=q', and therefore we believe that our formalism can reduce the computational complexities of the traditional ones when applied to the same kinds of problems described here.

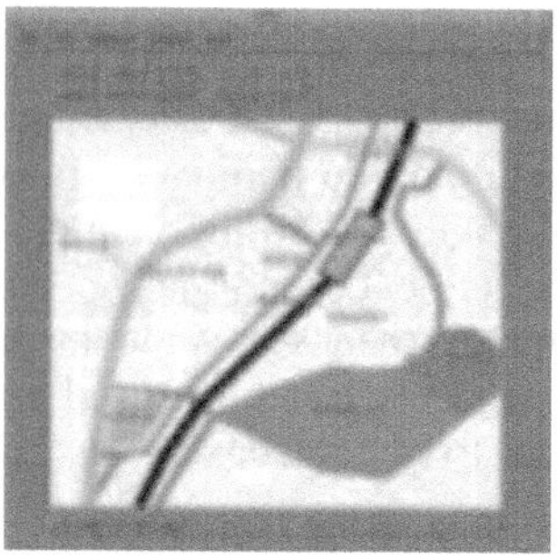

H: How does the national road run?
S: It extends between Pref. A and Pref. C via Pref. B.
H: Where does the bus go from the rail way station A?
S: It reaches the town D.
H: Where do the street A and the road B meet?
S: At the crossing C.
H: Where do the street A and the road B separate?
S: At the crossing C.

Fig. 5. Q-A on a map between a human (H) and IMAGES-M (S)

Fig. 6. Text-to-Action translation by IMAGES-M: 'Stand up *AND* turn right' was interpreted as 'Turn right *AFTER* standing up'

Some parts of the spatiotemporal terms have already been provided with semantic descriptions in $\boldsymbol{L_{md}}$ and implemented on the integrated multimedia understanding system IMAGES-M. This system can perform cross-media operations between texts in several languages and pictorial patterns like maps or robot actions [8-11], where such postulates as PRS are effectively utilized in order to allow people intuitive access. Figures 5 and 6 show examples of Q-A on a map and text-to-action translation by IMAGES-M, respectively, where the semantic contents of maps, texts and actions are represented in $\boldsymbol{L_{md}}$, and distinction between temporal and spatial events is crucially important. In this research area, it is most conventional that conceptual contents conveyed by information media such as language, picture, robot action, etc. are represented in computable forms independent of each other and translated via 'transfer' processes which are often specific to task domains [e.g., 12, 13]. That is, there is no other system that can perform cross-media operation in such a seamless way as described here.

Most of computations on $\boldsymbol{L_{md}}$ are simply for unifying (or identifying) atomic locus formulas and for evaluating arithmetic expressions such as '$p=q$', and therefore we believe that our formalism can reduce the computational complexities of the traditional ones when applied to the same kinds of problems described here.

Our future work will include further elaboration and validation of the formal system, automatic acquisition of word concepts from sensory data and text data, and distributed intelligent robot networking under real environments.

Acknowledgements

This work was partially funded by the Grants from Computer Science Laboratory, Fukuoka Institute of Technology and Ministry of Education, Culture, Sports, Science and Technology, Japanese Government, numbered 14580436 and 17500132.

References

1. Allen, J.F.: Towards a general theory of action and time. Artificial Intelligence 23(2), 123–154 (1984)
2. Beek, P.: Reasoning about qualitative temporal information. Artificial Intelligence 58, 297–326 (1992)
3. Haddawy, P.: A logic of time, chance, and action or repesenting plans. Artificial Intelligence 80, 243–308 (1996)
4. McDermott, D.V.: A temporal logic for reasoning about processes and plans. Cognitive Science 101–155 (1982)
5. Shoham, Y.: Time for actions: on the relationship between time, knowledge, and action. In: Proc. of IJCAI 89, Detroit, MI, pp. 954–959 (1989)
6. Yokota, M.: A psychological experiment on human understanding process of natural language. Trans. of IEICE Japan J71D-10, 2120–2127 (1988)
7. Yokota,M.: An approach to natural language understanding based on a mental image model. In: Proc. of the 2nd International Workshop on Natural Language Understanding and Cognitive Science, pp. 22–31 (2005)

8. Yokota, M.: Integrated Multimedia Understanding for Ubiquitous Intelligence Based on Mental Image Directed Semantic Theory. In: IFIP EUC'05 UISW 2005, Nagasaki, pp. 538–546 (2005)
9. Yokota, M.: An Approach to Integrated Spatial Language Understanding Based on Mental Image Directed Semantic Theory. In: Proc. of the 5th Workshop on Language and Space, Octoer 2005, Bremen, Germany (2005)
10. Yokota, M.: Towards a Universal Knowledge Representation Language for Ubiquitous Intelligence Based on Mental Image Directed Semantic Theory. In: Proc. of the 3rd International Conference on Ubiquitous Intelligence and Computing, Wuhan and Three Gorges, September 2006, China (2006)
11. Yokota, M.: Towards a Universal Language for Distributed Intelligent Robot Networking. In: Proc. of 2006 IEEE International Conference on Systems, Man and Cybernetics, October 2006, Taipei, Taiwan (2006)
12. Adorni, G., Di Manzo, M., Giunchiglia, F.: Natural Language Driven Image Generation. In: Proc. of COLING 84, pp. 495–500 (1984)
13. Coradeschi, S., Saffiotti, A.: An Introduction to the Anchoring Problem. Robotics and Autonomous Systems 43, 85–96 (2003)
14. Egenhofer, M., Khaled, K.: Reasoning about Gradual Changes of Topological Relations. In: Proc. of International Conference GIS—From Space to Territory: Theories and Methods of Spatio-Temporal Reasoning, Pisa, Italy, pp. 196–219 (1992)
15. Akyildiz, I.F., Kasimoglu, I.H.: Wireless Sensor and Actor Networks: Research Challenges. Ad Hoc Networks 2, 351–367 (2004)

Graph-Based Semantic Description in Medical Knowledge Representation and 3D Coronary Vessels Recognition

Marek R. Ogiela, Ryszard Tadeusiewicz, and Mirosław Trzupek

AGH University of Science and Technology, Institute of Automatics,
Bio-Cybernetics Laboratory, 30 Mickiewicza Ave,
30-059 Krakow, Poland
{mogiela,rtad,mtrzupek}@agh.edu.pl

Abstract. The work presents the new opportunity for making semantic descriptions of medical structures with the use of AI graph-based linguistic formalisms and especially graph grammar of edNLC type. In the paper there will be discussed in detail the manners of applying methods of computational intelligence to the development of a syntactic semantic description of spatial visualizations of the heart's coronary vessels. Thanks to these, the analysis conducted allows fast and – to a great degree – automated interpretation of the semantics of various morphological changes in the coronary vascular tree, and especially makes it possible to detect these stenoses in the lumen of the vessels that can cause critical decrease of blood supply to the heart muscle. Presented methodology of analysis can furthermore be used for attaining other goals related performance of computer-assisted semantic interpretation of selected elements and/or the entire 3D structure of the coronary vascular tree.

1 Introduction

The subject of automatic understanding (and not only analysis and recognition) of images medical is very important because the ultimate goal of interpretation in the case of medical images is always the understanding of the essence of the pathological process troubling the organ examined and the definition of appropriate therapy. To attain this goal, it is not enough to classify and recognize (automatically or manually), as recognition means only assigning names to diseases, while treatment is performed not on the name but on the diseased organ or, to be more precise: on the human being. Clinical practice proves that, despite the frequent use of major computer-assisted diagnostic equipment, the obtained visualizations which include the spatial reconstructions of specific body parts, later undergo only a rough qualitative assessment by the physician diagnostician, with no in-depth semantic analysis. This results from a number of circumstances.

Firstly, the entire system of education of physicians still makes predominant use of flat images: they are presented in lectures and books as 2D and not 3D. Physicians have become accustomed to such images and can provide their diagnostic

J. Indulska et al. (Eds.): UIC 2007, LNCS 4611, pp. 1079–1088, 2007.

interpretations, while finding the 3D renderings – in fact closer to the actual anatomic or pathomorphological condition – less known if not 'exotic' and, consequently, harder to interpret.

Secondly, the progress in IT, electronics, and the development of research in the field of Medical Imaging make the evolution of visualisation method very fast: in fact, much faster than the process of gathering experience by the physicians who should expertly interpret those new visualisations. For that reason, it is often the case that a new method of medical visualisation does present the essence of a medical problem, but the physician watching such a new visualisation is unable to interpret it properly because, in simple words, there are so many things shown that he or she does not know what to look at. To make matters even worse, the progress in the visualisation technology mentioned still accelerates at greater and greater speeds, which means that by the time today's alumni become experienced masters in the filed of interpreting certain state-of-the-art forms of medical visualisation, these forms of visualisation will have become dated and replaced by successive, even finer, yet again not in line with the experience acquired by the physicians.

Thirdly and lastly, there is something known as spatial imagination. Some posses it, others do not. The mutual relations between elements on a flat image can be interpreted correctly by anyone, while making correct conclusions referring to the interdependencies and relative placement of spatially perceived elements requires those special abilities. This means that a certain proportion of physicians, and there are good reasons to believe that quite a large proportion this can be, would never be able to understand and interpret correctly the spatial co-dependences of the elements viewed. This deficiency will always limit the efficacy of their diagnostic reasoning, however suggestive and effective the images are displayed on the screens of ever finer 3D visualisation systems: an effect that has to be borne in mind.

These remarks prove that the actual progress in the practical application of 3D visualizations in medicine may depend on the progress in developing smart diagnostics support systems, making use of automatic analysis and understanding of medical 3D images.

2 Description of the Problem

The problem tackled in this work is the semantic interpretation and an attempt at automatic understanding of a 3D structure of spatially visualized coronary vessels. At the stage of the initial analysis, it was found that the problem is subject to numerous important limitations. These limitations result, among other things from the serious obstacles encountered in the development of a universal standard, defining the model shape of the healthy or diseased organ that could possibly undergo typical recognition. Such difficulties were encountered already in the case of analyzing 2D images of various organs, however, the additional degree of freedom given by the transition from 2D to 3D visualization makes this question exceptionally intricate.

The path to finding appropriate languages, necessary for the description of the semantic aspect of the 3D medical visualization is long and complex. Description of important semantic aspects of the image may not be burdened with the detail that – from the point of view of understanding the content of the image – are of secondary importance. This is why, besides the development of methods for linguistic description of 3D images and development of intelligent methods of using the experts' experience and knowledge for acquiring the effect of cognitive resonance [10], of key importance for image understanding is the application of pre-processing methods and analysis of 3D medical visualizations adjusted to the specific features of this task. Hence, this work will also include finding such methods of extraction and description of medical image features that would ignore individual distinctive features characteristic for a given patient, being at the same time focused on the exposition and appropriate representation of morphological properties crucial for the understanding of pathologies presented in the visualizations.

The problem embarked upon in this work may be considered significant due to the frequency of practical use of identification of location of stenoses in coronary vessels in ischemia, being one of the most burning medical problems of the early 21st century. The technical solutions proposed do not aim at the elimination of the physician from the diagnostic process; on the contrary, they should provide the physician with additional information to provide him or her with higher efficiency in discrimination between obvious cases from ones that may require a more thorough consideration. A system for understanding 3D medical images may also facilitate interpretation of especially complex and atypical cases, when even the physician's knowledge combined with experience may be insufficient for diagnosing and defining treatment strategy. Here, a system that offers automatic semantic case assessment based on its 3D image may come in very handy, as it may, for example, make up for the spatial imagination that the given physician may lack. Furthermore, such an approach may also be applied for context-sensitive and semantic searches in databases of medical spatial models showing changes in the morphology of coronary arteries in the semantic sense (i.e. the nature of the pathology and the treatment required) analogically to the currently examined case that, from the point of view of superficial semblances of images, may be highly dissimilar.

3 Functional Analysis of Coronary Arteries

The automatic understanding of 3D images of coronary arteries is the subject of AI research, and as such it is present in the article. However, to speak of the understanding of morphological changes in an organ, one must first become acquainted with the organ as such. Obviously, the comments made here are no more than an abstract of an abstract of the vast repository of medical knowledge on coronary arteries that has been gathered. Let the facts that the oxygen and nutrient supply for the heart muscle as well as the removal of final products of metabolism and carbon dioxide is performed through coronary circulation [5, 7] testify to the high importance of the correct functioning of the coronary system – and the advisability of analysis of these anatomic structures in a system of 3D presentation – for the life and well-being of patients. The individual branches of the coronary arteries are situated coil-like on the heart's surface so as not to cause increased flow resistance during the contraction and relaxation phases; they supply blood to defined areas of the heart, taking only minor branches to the aorta and the pulmonary trunk [5, 7]. As the layout of the arteries on the diaphragmatic surface of the heart muscle may differ in its form, three basic types of distribution of these arteries may distinguished. The first type is most widespread, and in 60–70% of cases it features a balanced distribution of arteries, with none being dominant. In the second type, the circumflex branch of the left coronary artery is highly retarded while the right coronary artery is highly developed and is the main supplier of blood to the posterior surface of the left chamber. Such situation is present in on average 20–24% of cases, with a variety of intermediate forms possible. In the third type, present in 10–14% cases, the right coronary artery is strongly retarded, while the posterior surface of the right chamber is vascularised by the left coronary artery, whose anterior interventricular branch may additionally reach the diaphragmatic surface [7]. This shows what difficulties resulting from the lack of universal standards to allow unambiguous representations of such vessels may arise.

In the case of the sternocostal surface, there are no significant variations of coronary arteries, with the exception being the variations in the anterior interventricular branches, which may be divided into two branches of similar thickness, both in its initial and final section [5].

The key element of the diagnostic examinations of the heart performed with methods including the angiography of coronary arteries, helical CT scanning, and IVUS are a number of complex algorithms focused on acquisition and pre-processing of such images [1, 3, 6]. All these examinations are complementary, which provides the diagnostician with vast amounts of information that allows formulating the proposals of appropriate diagnosis and reconstruction of information concerning the structure of coronary vessels. As concerns computer-assisted methods of 3D structure rendering, it is possible to perform visualization of the 3D spatial structure [1, 2, 4]. Application of such methods makes it possible to obtain diagnostic material containing crucial information on the presence and/or advancement of pathologic changes characteristic for certain medical conditions. Most unfortunately, no computer-assisted systems offering automatic interpretation comparable to that conducted by the specialist's keen eye have as yet been built. For that reason, the article in its further part describes the manner of developing linguistic semantic representation of spatial structure of coronary vessels showing certain pathological changes and their analysis with the use of cognitive methods of image understanding.

4 Semantic Description of Coronary Vessels with the Use of Graph-Based Formalisms

This chapter presents the manner of developing semantic models for spatial reconstruction of the heart's coronary vessels.

4.1 Characteristics of the Image Data

To allow the introduction of linguistic formalisms in the form of graph-based image grammar that allows finding the stenoses in main arteries or their ramifications and, at the same time, quantification of the pathological changes discovered, several visualization sequences were performed for the arteries in the DICOM format. Such sequences were obtained for various patients during diagnostic examinations of the heart conducted with a helical CT scanner with 64 detectors. Such visualizations present in a very clear manner all morphologic changes of individual sections of arteries in any plane. Furthermore, they allow performing spatial rendering of coronary vessels. Shown in the Fig. 1 examples of spatial reconstruction of the heart's coronary vessels, presenting the vessels without the accompanying muscle tissue of the heart. It presents the main arteries together with the main minor vessels and a stenosis in the initial section of both left and right coronary arteries and in the posterior interventricular branch of right coronary artery. The structures made visible in this manner will be described with the use of graph-based grammars – constituents of the graph-based language defining their proper, spatial topology.

4.2 Graph-Based Description of Coronary Arteries

The proper graph-based grammar describing these structures was defined so that the individual branches of the graph in the description provided identify all start and end points of coronary vessels and all bifurcations or transitions of main vessels into lower-level ones. Thus developed, the graph-based structure will constitute the elements of the language for defining spatial topology and correct vascularisation of the heart muscle together with the potential morphological changes (Fig. 1).

In practice, the mutual spatial relations that may occur between elements of the vascular structure represented in the form of a graph describing the set of edge labels. Elements of the set are defined by the introduction of appropriate spatial relations: vertical $\{\alpha, \beta, \ldots, \pi\}$ and horizontal $\{1, 2, \ldots, 24\}$, defined by the set of labels which designate individual sections, each with the angular span of 15° on the hypothetical sphere surrounding the heart muscle which represents the 'geographical' spatial relations of the graph representing the vascular structure. Next, for labels defined in this manner, edge terminal labels are assigned to each of the bifurcations marked by the

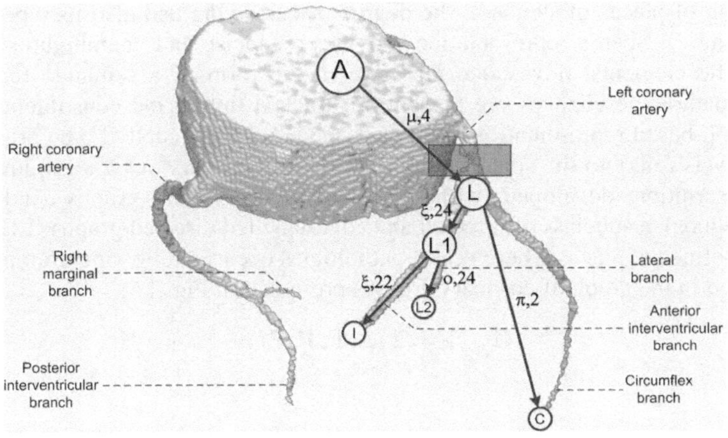

Fig. 1A. Spatial labelling of coronary arteries and defining relations occurring between them for the left coronary artery. The grey rectangle marks the place of a major stenosis in a coronary artery.

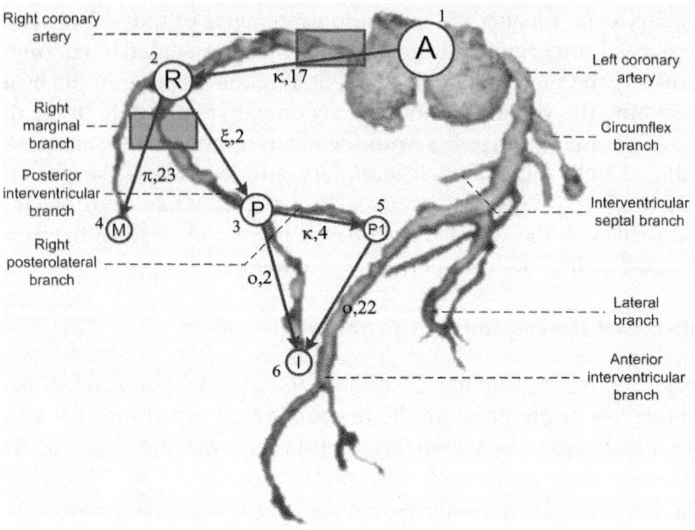

Fig. 1B. Spatial labelling of coronary arteries and defining relations occurring between them for the right coronary artery. The grey rectangle marks the place of a major stenosis in a coronary artery.

start and end points of appropriate coronary artery sections, depending on the situation of sections of the arteries. Once these relations have been taken into account and node labels of the artery-spanning graph have been entered, it is possible to develop a linguistic description for the needs of defining the semantics of the changes sought after and the recognition of pathologic stenoses. This inter alia allows for conducting a computer-supported analysis of the rendered structure, oriented on the automatic detection of places of stenoses, the degree of narrowing and also its type (concentric or eccentric). Such a representation provides a concise and unambiguous description of all the elements of vascular structure in the form of a semantic record. Places where pathologic changes are present are tracked during the constituent analysis of the graph-based representations analyzed, made with the edNLC type grammar. Such an analysis refers to the spatial representation of coronary vessels acquired thanks to the description developed with the application of IE graphs (indexed egde-unambiguos), a subclass of directed and edge-labelled directed graphs (EDG) [9].

To define the places where vessel pathologies occur, a following grammar has been proposed in the graph of coronary arteries presented in Fig. 1A.

$$G_{edNLC} = (\Sigma, \Delta, \Gamma, P, Z) . \tag{1}$$

where

$\Sigma = \Sigma_N \cup \Sigma_T$ is a set of both terminal and non-terminal node labels describing the examined graphs and defined as follows.

$\Delta = \Sigma_T =$ {left coronary artery, anterior interventricular branch, circumflex branch, lateral branch}

. $\Sigma_N = \{A, B, C, I, L, L1, L2\}$

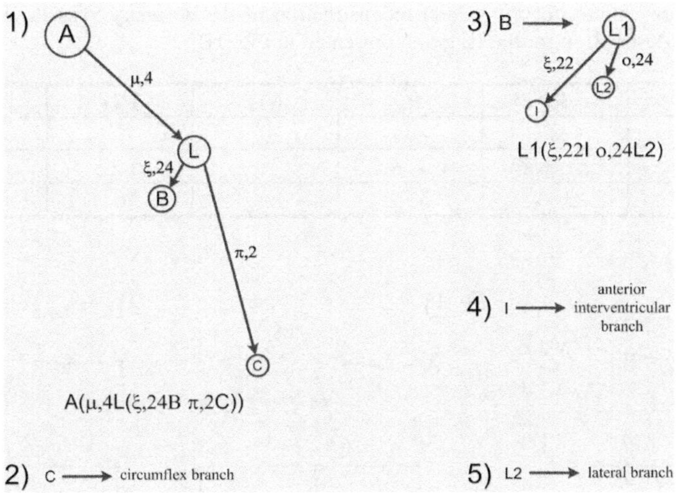

Fig. 2. Production set for the G_{edNLC} grammar

$\Gamma = \{\mu,4; \xi,22; \xi,24; o,24; \pi,2\}$ is a set of labels describing edges of the graph
$Z = \{A\}$ is the original starting graph
P is a finite set of productions recorded in paranthesis-based form and with the use of diagrammatic graph-based notation (Fig. 2).

To define the location where the vessel pathology is present in the graph of coronary arteries in Fig. 1B., the following grammar is proposed.

$$G_{edNLC} = (\Sigma, \Delta, \Gamma, P, Z) . \quad (2)$$

where

$\Sigma = \Sigma_N \cup \Sigma_T$ and is a set of both terminal and non-terminal node labels describing the examined graphs and defined as follows.
$\Delta = \Sigma_T =$ {right coronary artery, right marginal branch, posterior interventricular branch, right posterolateral branch}
$\Sigma_N = \{A, I, M, P, P1, R, X, Y\}$
$\Gamma = \{\kappa,4; \kappa,17; \xi,2; o,2; o,22; \pi,23\}$ is a set of labels describing edges of the graph
$Z = \{A\}$ is the original starting graph
P – is a finite set of productions recorded in the graph-based form and presented in Fig. 3

The IE graph presented in Fig. 1B together with the characteristic description of the nodes present therein (Table 1) may be used to describe the selected sections of the coronary vessels.

For the graph-based grammar introduced earlier, the set of deriving rules in the form of IE graphs, which allow for deriving spatial representation for the right coronary artery described in Fig. 1.B is presented in Fig. 3.

Table 1. Representation of the spatial reconstruction of the coronary vessels with the vertex characteristic description for the IE graph presented in Fig. 1B

A_1	R_2	P_3	M_4	$P1_5$	I_6
1	2	2	0	1	0
κ,17	ξ,2 π,23	κ,4 o,2	-	o,22	-
2	3 4	5 6	-	6	-

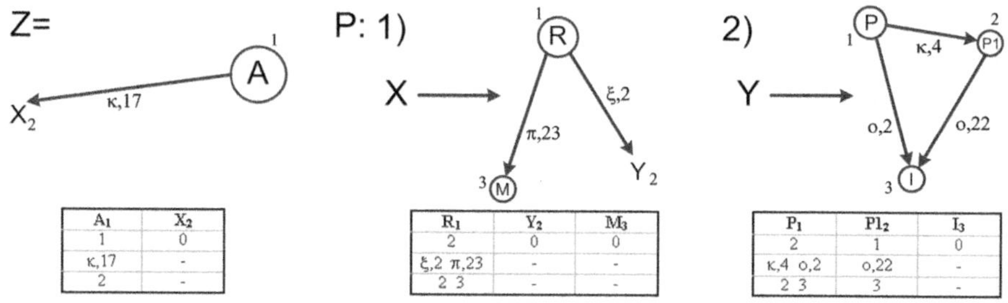

Fig. 3. The set of productions in the form of IE graphs deriving the structure of coronary vessels together with the vertex characteristic description

5 Results

Through the application of the formalisms of the graph-based grammars presented in this work we have shown that it is possible to develop semantic descriptions and spatially model the morphology of coronary vessels as well as discover in them the symptoms of ischemia. Thanks to the application of the described type of grammar, allowing semantic interpretation of spatial reconstruction of coronary vessels, it is possible to analyze the correct morphology of individual sections of arteries and their branches. The discovery of such changes is performed by determining the place of their occurrence i.e. the definition of the position of the vessel and the degree of the stenoses of the artery lumen, and by the designation of morphometric parameters defining its scope and type (eccentric or concentric). The proper element of the syntactic and semantic analysis is parsing that, in the case of structural analysis of the representations developed, provides automatically (thanks to the use of semantic actions and procedures) full information defining the spatial topology of the graph in question, describing the coronary vessels together with the individual constituents. Subsequently, such information is used for the structural and semantic analysis of individual sections of the arteries, which are defined by terminal node and edge labels. This allows for precise definition of morphological irregularities in the vessels examined that may be present in the form of various stenoses [8]. All the information mentioned here makes it possible to develop a semantic record containing the semantic description of the structure in question. Such descriptions may provide a certain type of indexing keys that allow archiving and finding of data (in the form of 3D visualizations) based on information concerning pathological conditions present. Due to the small set of test data (covering several elements) the results achieved are highly promising. Such efficiency, however, is also the result of high generalization properties of the formalisms applied.

In the research conducted, unsolved have remained certain questions, namely the question of the automatic selection of the proper projection of the coronary vessels in the manner allowing the most unambiguous visualization of the pathologies present. Another problem is the question of automation of the process of generating new grammars for the cases not accounted for in the existent language. These problems are another subject followed by the authors.

Results of conducted examinations confirmed that the use of graph-based image formalisms based on IE graphs generating grammars allow discovering and automatic semantic interpretation of irregularities visualized on the images obtained during diagnostic examinations of the heart muscle. A practical application of these methods allows to diagnose states of ischaemic heart disease.

6 Conclusions

The IT methodology described in this work makes it possible to find, for each biological 3D structure considered, its semantic description whose elements make reference to the medical significance of the entire structure described, while at the same time refrain from the formal differences (i.e. appearance and shape) of individual visualizations. Application of such formalisms provides vast opportunities to focus interpretation tasks on the performance of automatic analysis and detection of actual morphological irregularities in a perceptive manner, which inspires the development of cognitive information systems based on graph-based image languages.

The methodology can furthermore be used for attaining other goals related performance of computer-assisted semantic interpretation of selected elements and/or the entire 3D structure of the coronary vascular tree. The obtained semantic information makes it possible to make a description of the structure focused on the semantics of various morphological forms of the visualized vessels from the point of view of the operation of coronary circulation and the blood supply of the heart muscle. Thanks to these, the analysis conducted allows fast and – to a great degree – automated interpretation of the semantics of various morphological changes in the coronary vascular tree, and especially makes it possible to detect these stenoses in the lumen of the vessels that can cause critical decrease of blood supply to extensive or especially important fragments of the heart muscle.

Such methods are of profound significance as they allow not only for the discovery of pathologic changes but also for the definition of their semantics, which – in the case of medical diagnostic images – may lead to computer-assisted ‘understanding’ of their medical significance and in future also to fine-tune the optimum therapeutic options.

Acknowledgement. This work was supported by the Polish State Committee Research under Grant No. N519 007 32/0978.

References

1. Bankman, I. (ed.): Handbook of Medical Imaging: Processing and Analysis. Academic Press, London (2002)
2. Higgins, W.E., Karwoski, R.A., Ritman, E.L., Spyra, W.J.T.: System for analyzing true three-dimensional angiograms. IEEE Trans. Med. Imag. 15, 377–385 (1996)
3. Higgins, W.E., Reinhardt, J.M.: Cardiac image processing. In: Bovik, A.I. (ed.) Handbook of Video and Image Processing, pp. 789–804. Academic Press, London (2000)
4. Hoffman, K.R., Sen, A., Li, L., Kok-Gee, C., Esthappan, J., Mazzucco, M.: A system for determination of 3D vessel tree centerlines from biplane images. The International Journal of Cardiac Imaging 16, 315–330 (2000)
5. Khan, M.G.: Heart Disease Diagnosis and Therapy. Williams & Wilkins, Baltimore (1996)
6. Meyer-Baese, A.: Pattern Recognition in Medical Imaging. Elsevier–Academic Press, Amsterdam, London (2003)
7. Netter, F.H., Colacino, S.: Atlas of Human Anatomy. Novartis Medical Education (1998)
8. Ogiela, M.R., Tadeusiewicz, R.: Nonlinear Processing and Semantic Content Analysis in Medical Imaging - A Cognitive Approach. IEEE Trans. on Instrumentation and Measurement 54(6), 2149–2155 (2005)
9. Skomorowski, M.: A Syntactic-Statistical Approach to Recognition of Distorted Patterns. Jagiellonian University, Krakow (2000)
10. Tadeusiewicz, R., Ogiela, M.R.: Medical Image Understanding Technology. Springer, Heidelberg (2004)

Persistent Storage System for Efficient Management of OWL Web Ontology*

Dongwon Jeong[1], Myounghoi Choi[1], Yang-Seung Jeon[2], Youn-Hee Han[3], Laurence T. Yang[4], Young-Sik Jeong[2], and Sung-Kook Han[2]

[1] Department of Informatics and Statistics, Kunsan National University, Gunsan, Jeollabuk-do, 573-701, Korea
{djeong,cmh775}@kunsan.ac.kr

[2] Department of Computer Engineering, Wonkwang University, Iksan, Jeollabuk-do, 570-749, Korea
{globaljeon,ysjeong,skhan}@wku.ac.kr

[3] School of Internet-Media, Korea University of Technology and Education, Cheonan, Chungnam, 330-708, Korea
yhhan@kut.ac.kr

[4] Department of Computer Science, St. Francis Xavier University, Antigonish, NS, B2G 2W5, Canada
lyang@stfx.ca

Abstract. This paper proposes a new persistent storage to efficiently manage OWL Web ontologies. The Semantic Web is recognized as a next direction for progress of the current Web. To realize the Semantic Web, various technologies have been developed. Especially, OWL (Web Ontology Language) is the most important and state-of-the-art technology toward the ideal Semantic Web. However, most of research is being focused on designing and building OWL documents (OWL Ontology). One of the most important issues is how to efficiently and persistently store a very large OWL data into database management systems. In this paper, we propose a persistent storage system to achieve the purpose. This paper describes the performance evaluation result on the load time. The experiment result explicitly shows that our proposal provides more enhanced performance comparing with the existing systems.

1 Introduction

OWL (Web Ontology Language) is recognized as a next technology for the Semantic Web. Even though various technologies (For example, XML, RDF, RDF Schema, OIL, and DAML) have been developed [1, 2, 3, 4], we are faced with several issues such as no reasoning function and high implementation complexity. For resolving these problems, OWL has been proposed as an international standard of W3C [5]. Much research is concentrated on OWL-based Web ontology tools or systems for building, editing, displaying, and so on.

One of the most important issues is to efficiently load OWL ontologies into a specific permanent management system such as relational database management systems.

---

* This work was supported in part by MIC & IITA through IT Leading R&D Support Project.

J. Indulska et al. (Eds.): UIC 2007, LNCS 4611, pp. 1089–1097, 2007.

Generally, we can store OWL data using file systems or database management systems. In case of the file system, an OWL document is stored as a plain text. However, this approach has many disadvantages in management and performance aspects. The other approach is to use databases such as the relational database or object-oriented database. Especially, most OWL storage systems are based on the relational database, because it is widely used for data management and is stable through improvement over several decades.

Permanent OWL ontology storage systems (including APIs) using relational databases have been developed and the representative storage system includes Sesame-DB, DLDB-OWL, and Jena [6, 7, 8, 9, 10]. However, these systems have several issues to deal with very large OWL data sets (OWL ontologies). Most systems are based on the triple (3-tuple) model. In other words, their load processing is time-consuming and requires high response time. Therefore, we cannot fully use many advantages of the relational database model.

In this paper, we propose a new enhanced persistent storage model to efficiently load a very large OWL ontology. To show prominence of our proposal, comparative evaluations are described.

2 Definition of Persistent Storage System

2.1 Framework

Fig. 1 depicts the framework for the persistent storage system.

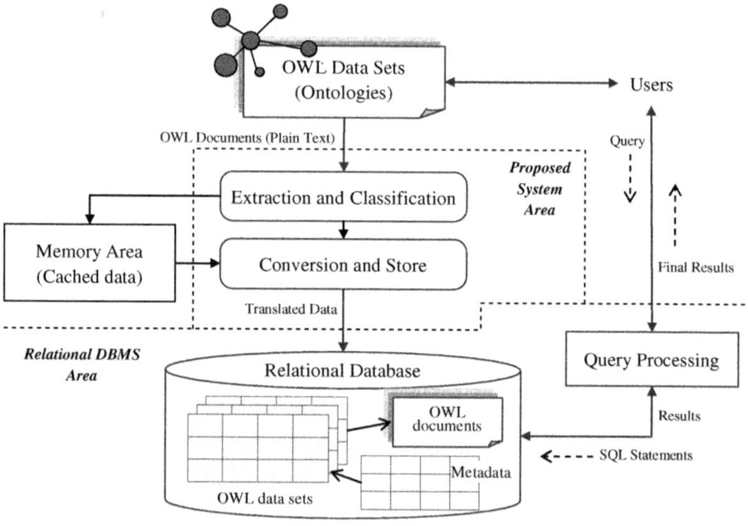

Fig. 1. Framework of the proposed storage system

2.2 Permanent Storage System Model Definition

PSSM denotes the persistent storage system proposed in this paper and is defined as Definition 1.

Definition 1

PSSM = (I, OP, MDM, PDM),

where
- I: OWL ontology (Plain text files)
- OP: Operations for extraction, classification, mapping and store
- MDM: Memory data structure for the classified OWL elements
- PDM: Persistent data model

Our system conceptually consists of five components: Input OWL documents, operations, memory data structure, and relational data model. More details are described in Section 3.

Definition 2. PDM, denoting the relational database model, is defined as follows.

PDM = (RDM, Meta, Plain),

where
- RDM means the defined relational data model for OWL data (i.e., classes and instances)
- Meta indicates meta-information such as ontology type
- Plain is the set of original OWL documents

To manage OWL ontologies, the relational database needs to accept actual ontology (classes and instances), metadata such as ontology type and its source file, and original OWL files (plain text type).

Fig. 2 illustrates a metamodel to store OWL data sets into relational databases. The defined relational database model is composed of three parts. The first part is to store classes and instances. OWL specification names both Class and Individual respectively. The meta-information part is to manage header information, full prefix names, and relevant OWL sources. The final part is the set of OWL document files.

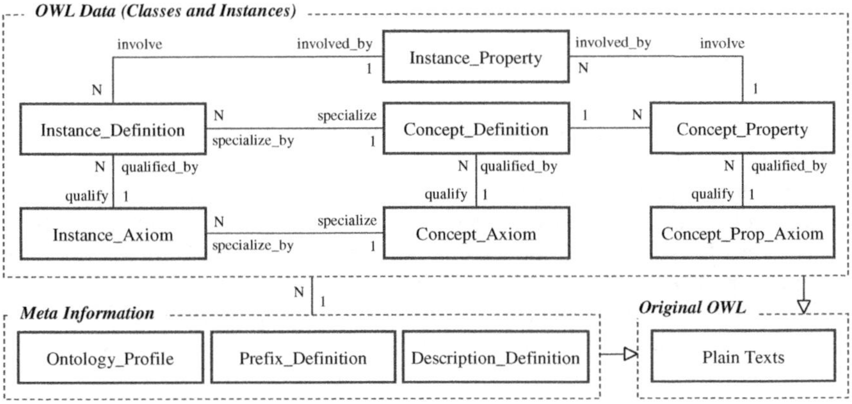

Fig. 2. Metamodel for the relational schema structure

3 System Design for Implementation

This section describes the system architecture for implementation of the persistent storage system including algorithms of key operations.

3.1 System Architecture

The system architecture for implementation of the proposed storage system is illustrated in Fig. 3. The system consists of two layers: Storage system layer and DBMS layer. The storage layer is also composed of OWL Ontology Loader and Result Manager. The ontology loader is the core of our proposal and the result manager is designed to show the persistent store result.

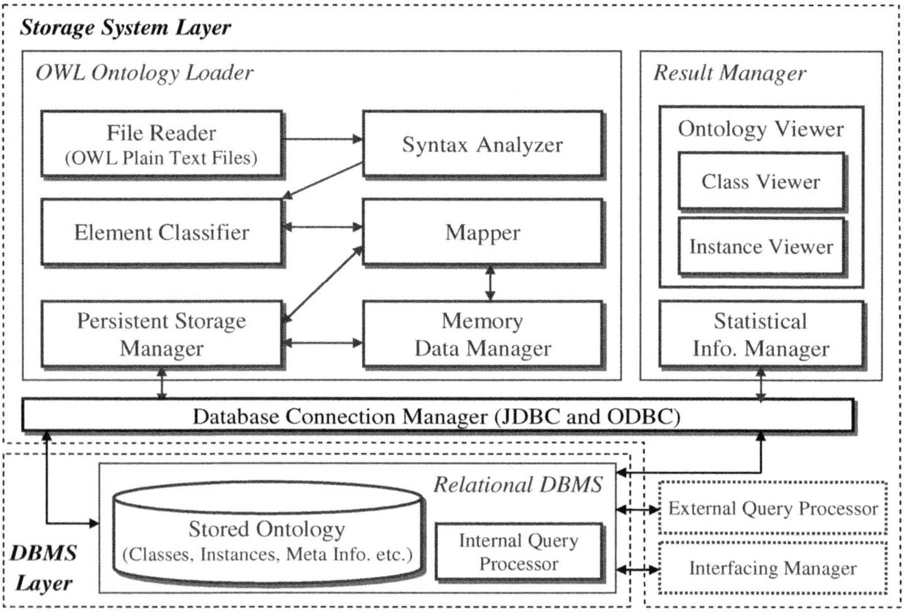

Fig. 3. System architecture for implementation of the proposed system model

The OWL ontology loader has six components: File Reader, Syntax Analyzer, Element Classifier, Mapper, Memory Data Manager, and Persistent Storage Manager. The file reader plays a role to read OWL documents (plain text format) and the syntax analyzer checks the validation of OWL data. The element classifier extracts OWL elements from the valid OWL documents and then classifies them into each correspondent group. The classified OWL elements are used as input data of Mapper. The mapper first sends each element to Persistent Storage Manager and Memory Data Manager to load them on memory and into a persistent database. The persistent storage manager and the memory data manager load the elements into a database and on memory respectively.

The result manager has three components: Class viewer, Instance Viewer and Statistical Information Manager. The class viewer and instance viewer show the stored data (OWL data) to users. The statistical information manager has a displaying role of statistical information such as the number of stored instances or classes, the size of ontology, and so on.

Finally, additional two functions (query processing function and interfacing function to other systems or APIs) could be added to the system. The query processing function is to accept other query language for OWL ontology and to provide query language independent access to users. Relational database management systems have their query processor and they can understand and execute just SQL query statements. However, user queries could be composed in KIF, RQL, or SPARQL style including SQL [11, 12, 13]. In fact, in our prototyping system, only queries by SQL are available. It means that users should compose their queries using SQL. The external query processor should be realized for this function in future.

As aforementioned, various similar systems, APIs, and tools to our proposal have been developed. Also there are diverse ontology models. For interoperation between heterogeneous systems, an interfacing module is required to support the interoperation. This function remains as a further work.

3.2 Overall Loading Algorithm

The loading process mainly consists of two steps: (Step-1) Classification (Analysis and Extraction) step and (Step-2) Conversion (Mapping and Storing) step. The overall algorithm is described as follows:

Overall algorithm for OWL ontology loading

```
INPUT: I          /** OWL ontology (OWL documents) */
OUTPUT: R         /** R indicates PDM in the definition 1 */
START Algorithm {
  /** Reading a specific OWL document */                                   /** Step-1 */
  owlText = read(I);   //owlText: Stream object for the OWL document
  boolean vr = validator.check(owlText);

  if (!vr) {// if the OWL document is not valid, then return an error message
     ExceptionHandler.show(INVALID_ERROR);
     return;
  }

  /** Extracting and classifying OWL elements */
  EClassifier classifier new EClassifier(owlText);
  Mapper mapper = classifier.createMapper();  //Creating a Mapper object

  /** Loading OWL data on memory and into the persistent database */      /** Step-2 */
  if (MEM_TAG) {
     memManager.load(mapper);
     persistentManager.load(memManager); // Creating the final output, R
  }
  else {  // Loading OWL data into only persistent database
     persistentManager.load(memManager); // Creating the final output, R
  }

  /** Generating statistical information of the loading result */
  StatisticalManager.createInfo(persistentManager);
}END Algorithm
```

4 Performance Evaluation

This section describes the experiment environment and performance result, and the performance evaluation is presented to show prominence of the proposed system.

4.1 Target Systems and Experiment Environment

This section includes the descriptions on the target systems for comparison, experiment data sets (Ontology sets), and system environment for experiment.

Target Systems
The target system for this comparative evaluation includes Sesame-DB and DLDB-OWL. Jena also provides a method to store OWL data into relational databases. However, Jena is one of APIs for development of systems or tools such as storage, viewer, editor, and so on. Hence, Jena is excluded from the target systems.

Data Sets for Experiment
For experiment, this paper uses data sets generated from UBA (Univ-Bench Artificial Data Generator), which is provided by Lehigh University. The OWL data generator has been developed for SWAT project evaluation [15]. There are two reasons why we use the OWL data sets by UBA as follows: (1) Even though we gathered several OWL ontologies, its ontology size is not acceptable for our experiment on performance evaluation; (2) The SWAT project team already published their evaluations using an ontology set by UBA [16, 17].

We can also generate the same ontology set through using the UBA and the generated data is five OWL ontology sets: LUBM(1,0), LUBM(5,0), LUBM(10,0), LUBM(20,0), and LUBM(50,0). In the notations LUBM(N,S), N and S denote the number of universities and the seed value respectively [16, 17].

System Environment
System environment is as follows:

(1) CPU: Pentium 4 (1.60 GHz);
(2) Memory size (RAM): 256MB;
(3) Heap memory size: 512MB;
(4) Hard disk size: 80GB;
(5) Platform: Windows XP Professional OS;
(6) Java SDK version: Java SDK 1.5.0;
(7) DBMS: Access.

The system requirement is similar to the setting environment in [17]. Our evaluation result is based on the result of Guo's proposal [16, 17]. Thus we prepare for the almost same system setting. In Guo's experiments, the CPU capability is 1.8GHz and it is more powerful than our setting. It means our experiment result is reliable.

4.2 Experiment Result and Discussion

The experiment result is summarized in Table 1. The table presents the load times of each system for four OWL data sets, i.e., {LUBM(1,0), LUBM(5,0), LUBM(10,0), LUBM(20,0)}, except LUBM(50,0).

For LUBM(50,0), Sesame-DB and our system cannot load because of heap memory error. Therefore, this paper finally shows the experiment result with four OWL data sets. We thought the reason of this error is the ontology size in memory. Memory size is also one of important comparative items, but this paper remains it as one of further study issues. For exact estimation of our experiment, the experiment result with our system for each data set has been done two times. Hence, the result in Table 1 describes the average values of both experiment results.

Table 1. Experiment results

(Unit: Second)

Data Set	DLDB-OWL	Sesame-DB	Proposed (Avg)
LUBM(1,0)	343	542	270
LUBM(5,0)	3,117	10,811	1,691
LUBM(10,0)	6,881	44,870	3,341
LUBM(20,0)	15,773	167,753	7,546

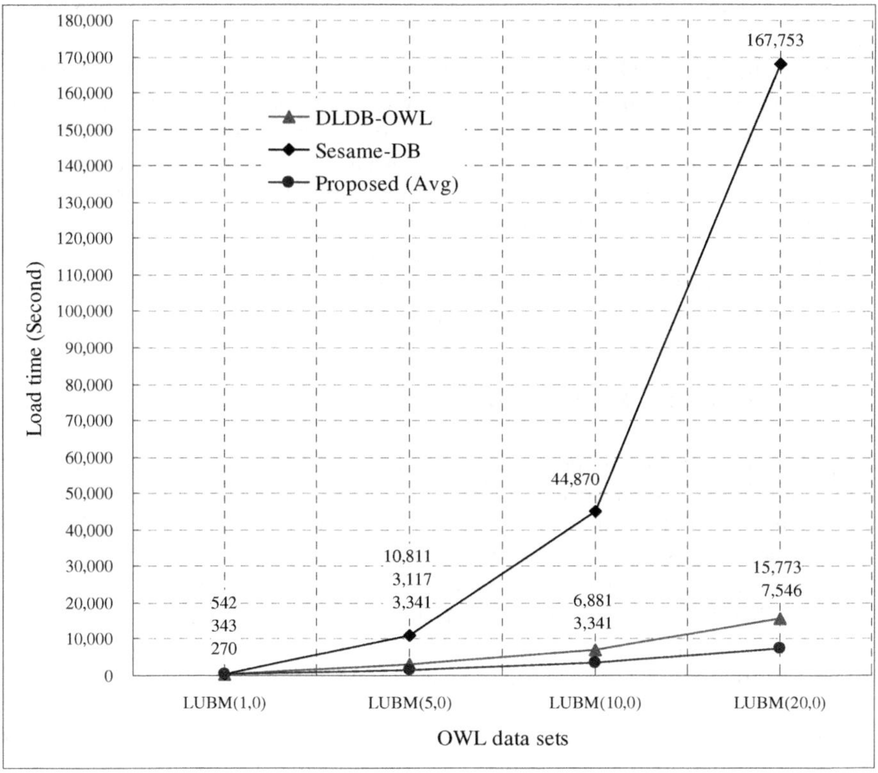

Fig. 4. Graph model-based experiment result

Table 2. Performance analysis: Ratio (Pivot model: The proposed)

Data Set	DLDB-OWL	Sesame-DB	Proposed (Avg)
LUBM(1,0)	1.27	2.00	1.00
LUBM(5,0)	1.84	6.39	1.00
LUBM(10,0)	2.06	13.43	1.00
LUBM(20,0)	2.09	22.23	1.00

With LUBM(1,0) data set, Sesame-DB requires 542 seconds to load it. On the other hand, DLDB-OWL and our system take 343 seconds and 270 seconds respectively. For LUBM(5,0), Sesame-DB:DLDB-OWL:Proposed = 10,811:3,117:1,691.

Fig. 4 graphically depicts the experiment result in Table 1. This figure shows intuitively how the loading time grows as the OWL set size increases. Our system's performance is more efficient than the others.

Table 2 shows the performance ratio. In this table, in case of the first data set, DLDB-OWL and Sesame-DB require much cost (load time) than our system (1.27 times and 2.00 times). For LUBM(20,0), both systems consume much more time (2.09 times and 22.23 times). Especially, Sesame-DB's load time exponentially increases.

In addition, we carried out an experiment on the load time for comparison with the Jena persistent storage model and our proposal. Jena provides two storage models-Jena1 version and Jena2 version. Jena2 changed the Jena1 storage model for performance improvement and provides an abnormalized database structure. In our experiment result, our system showed the efficient performance comparing with Jena. However, this comparative evaluation has no critical meaning, because Jena is an API developed for general purpose. Even though this experiment is not useful, we can use the evaluation result when we try to design and develop a Jena plug-in for enhanced management under the Jena development environment.

5 Conclusion and Further Study

This paper proposed a new persistent storage system. To achieve our goal, we first defined a relational data structure for permanently storing OWL ontologies. The structure has been defined considering its usability and performance. Second, we designed the processing system to check OWL files, extract and classify elements, and store OWL data (Classes and Individuals) into a specific relational database. And the system has been implemented under the following environment: (1)Java SDK: JDK 1.5; and (2)RDBMS: MS Access. Finally, we conducted the performance experiment. In the performance result, our persistent storage system is better than the target systems, Sesame-DB and DLDB-OWL.

There still remain several considerations. First, the performance is dependent on data characteristics, database servers, and so on. We have a research plan to define the relationships between the variable factors. Second, for applying storage systems to real applications, query response time is one the most important key factors. This paper didn't deal with this issue. It is a critical further study and should be handled to show the usability of storing systems including our proposal.

References

1. Yergeau, F., Cowan, J., Bray, T., Paoli, J., Sperberg-McQueen, C.M., Maler, E.: Extensible Markup Language (XML) 1.1, W3C Recommendation (February 2004)
2. Resource Description Framework (RDF), http://www.w3.org/RDF/
3. Bechett, D.: RDF/XML Syntax Specification (Revised), W3C Recommendation (10 February, 2004)
4. Connolly, D., Harmelen, F.V., Horrocks, I., McGuinness, D.L., Patel-Schneider, P.F., Stein, L.A.: DAML+OIL Reference Description, W3C Note (18 December, 2001)
5. Smith, M.K., Welty, C., McGuinness, D.L.: OWL Web Ontology Language Guide, W3C Recommendation (10 February 2004), http://www.w3c.org/TR/2004/REC-owl-guide-20040210/
6. Roldan-Garcia, M.M., Aldana-Montes, J.F.: A Tool for Storing OWL Using Database Technology (November 2005)
7. Pan, Z., Heflin, J.: DLDB: Extending Relational Databases to Support Semantic Web Queries. In: Workshop on Practical and Scaleable Semantic Web Systems, The 2nd International Semantic Web Conference (ISWC2003) (2003)
8. Broekstra, J., Kampman, A.: Sesame: A Generic Architecture for Storing and Querying RDF and RDF Schema. In: The 1st International Semantic Web Conference (ISWC2002) (2002)
9. SourceForge.net, Jena2 Database Interface - Database Layout (November 2004) http://jena.sourceforge.net/DB/layout.html
10. Jena, A.: Semantic Web Framework for Java, http://jena.sourceforge.net/
11. Gensereth, M., Fikes, R.: Knowledge Interchange Format, Stanford Logic Report Logic, Stanford University, http://logic.stanford.edu/kif/kif.html
12. Karvounarakis, G., Magkanaraki, A., Alexaki, S., Christophides, V., Plexousakis, D., Scholl, M., Tolle, K.: Querying the Semantic Web with RQL, Elsevier Science. Computer Networks and ISDN Systems Journal 42(5), 617–640 (2003)
13. Prud'hommeaux, E., Seaborne, A.: SPARQL Query Language for RDF, W3C Candidate Recommendation (6 April, 2006)
14. Carroll, J.J., Roo, J.D.: OWL Web Ontology Language Test Cases, W3C Recommendation (10 February, 2004)
15. Guo, Y.: Data Generator(UBA): UBA1.7, http://swat.cse.lehigh.edu/projects/lubm/
16. Guo, Y., Pan, Z., Heflin, J.: An Evaluation of Knowledge Base Systems for Large OWL Datasets. In: McIlraith, S.A., Plexousakis, D., van Harmelen, F. (eds.) ISWC 2004. LNCS, vol. 3298, Springer, Heidelberg (2004)
17. Guo, Y., Pan, Z., Heflin, J.: LUBM: A Benchmark for OWL Knowledge Base Systems. Journal of Web Semantics (2005)

Prediction-Based Dynamic Thread Pool Management of Agent Platform for Ubiquitous Computing*

Ji Hoon Kim, Seungwok Han, Hyun Ko, and Hee Yong Youn**

School of Information and Communication Engineering
Sungkyunkwan University, 440-746, Suwon, Korea
{ji_hoon,lovedonny,osthein,youn}@ece.skku.ac.kr

Abstract. The applications for ubiquitous system require to effectively utilize the resources distributed in the environment to provide intelligent services to the users. In order to satisfy the requirement, the applications need to be developed using intelligent agents based on multi-thread model. In this paper we propose the prediction-based dynamic thread pool management scheme for maximizing the resource utilization. In the proposed scheme the number of threads in the pool is predicted by modeling the rate change in the requested number of threads using the Gaussian distribution. An experiment shows that the proposed scheme outperforms the existing representative models in terms of response time for thread generation in practical operational environment.

1 Introduction

Recently, advanced technologies in the wireless communication, mobile computing, intelligent agent, and real-time system have enabled a new class of applications requiring ubiquitous access to the information anywhere and anytime. The applications for ubiquitous system need not only to effectively utilize the resources distributed in the environment but also provide intelligent services to the users. In order to satisfy such requirement, the applications require a high degree of flexibility and adaptability in order to deal with heterogeneous platforms and dynamic ubiquitous environments. Also, they are preferred to be implemented using intelligent agents and agent platform providing customized services to each user [1].

The agent platform usually employs the multi-thread model supporting concurrent services to multiple agents. The agent platform creates a thread whenever an agent requests it. If many agents request a thread for a short task, the response time can become very large. In this situation the agent platform needs to employ an approach for allowing small response time. This is an important issue especially for the application providing interactive services to a number of users. Numerous methods reducing the overload of thread management have been reported in the literature [2].

* This research was supported by the Ubiquitous Autonomic Computing and Network Project, 21st Century Frontier R&D Program in Korea and R01-2006-000-10954-0, Basic Research Program of the Korea Science & Engineering Foundation.

** Corresponding author.

J. Indulska et al. (Eds.): UIC 2007, LNCS 4611, pp. 1098–1107, 2007.

In this paper we propose the prediction-based dynamic thread pool management scheme for maximizing the resource utilization. In the proposed scheme the number of threads in the pool is predicted by modeling the rate change in the requested number of threads using the Gaussian distribution. An experiment shows that the proposed scheme outperforms the existing representative bounded thread pool models in terms of response time for thread generation in practical operational environment.

The rest of the paper is organized as follows. Section 2 describes an overview of agent platform and the strategies for multi-threading. Section 3 presents the proposed scheme, and Section 4 evaluates it. Section 5 concludes the paper with some remarks.

2 The Related Work

Agents can be defined to be autonomous problem solving computational entities capable of effective operation in dynamic and open environments [6]. The main characteristics of the agents are autonomy, intelligence, mobility, and social ability. Additional characteristics are reactivity against the change in the environment, veracity for prohibiting wrong information, and rationality for supporting rational method. The agents can be classified into multi-agent and mobile-agent. The multi-agent system is used for handling complex operations requiring collaboration between the agents. The mobile-agent moves through the network to process the tasks.

The agent platforms have to support agent communication language such as ACL (Agent Communication Language) and KQML (Knowledge Query Manipulation Language) to allow collaboration between the agents residing in different agent platforms. The agents provide the designers and developers with a way of structuring an application around autonomous, communicative elements and lead to the construction of software tools and infrastructure supporting the design metaphor [7]. The widely recognized agent platforms are JADE [8] and Aglet [9].

The FIPA (Foundation for Intelligent Physical Agents) [10] agent management specifications identify the roles of the key agents required for managing the platform, and describe the language and ontology of agent management. The main modules of a standard agent platform are AMS (Agent Management System), ANS (Agent Name Server), and DF (Directory Facilitator). The AMS is the agent that exerts supervisory control over access to and use of the platform. It is responsible for maintaining the directory of resident agents and handling their life cycle. The ANS is a server acting as a registry or white pages of agents, storing agent names, host machines, and port numbers in its cache. It helps the platform inter-agent communication by providing a mechanism for locating the agents. The DF is the agent providing yellow page services to the agent platform. It supports a way to find an agent existing in the network.

Various thread models have been proposed. The thread-per-request model [3] creates a worker thread for each request, and destroys it after finishing the request. This model handles each request from a client in a separate thread of control. Its main advantage is that it is straightforward to implement. This model is useful for the servers handling the requests of long duration such as database queries from multiple clients. The disadvantage is, however, that it can consume a large amount of resources if many clients generate the requests simultaneously. Moreover, it is inefficient for short-duration requests causing excessive thread creation overhead. In addition, it is not suitable for real-time applications since the overhead of spawning a thread for each request is non-deterministic.

The worker thread pool model [4] is a variation of the thread-per-request model that amortizes the thread creation costs by pre-spawning a pool of threads. This model is useful for the servers wanting to bind the resources they consume. The client requests can be executed concurrently until the number of simultaneous requests exceeds the number of threads in the pool. At this point, additional requests must be queued until a thread becomes available.

When the watermark thread pool model [5] is used, it spawns a pre-established number of threads instead of creating one new thread each time a connection request arrives. This model has been designed in such a way that it can be easily customized with low and high watermark used for the decision of the moment of thread regeneration and elimination, respectively.

3 The Proposed Scheme

3.1 The Dynamic Thread Pool

The number of threads needs to be dynamically controlled to maximize the performance and utilization of the system resource. The basic approach here is to create and delete the threads in advance. When the number of agent requests increases, threads are created in advance properly. When the number of agent requests decreases, it does not reduce the number of threads quickly. This is to avoid unnecessary overhead of thread creation/deletion occurring when the number of threads increases shortly. Also, if the variation in the thread increment/decrement is low, the control frequency is reduced. Otherwise, it is increased for timely adjustment. Fig. 1 shows the number of threads, n, as time moves. Here variable n_t is defined as follows.

$$n_t = \{x \mid x \text{ is the number of threads in the system at time } t\} \tag{1}$$

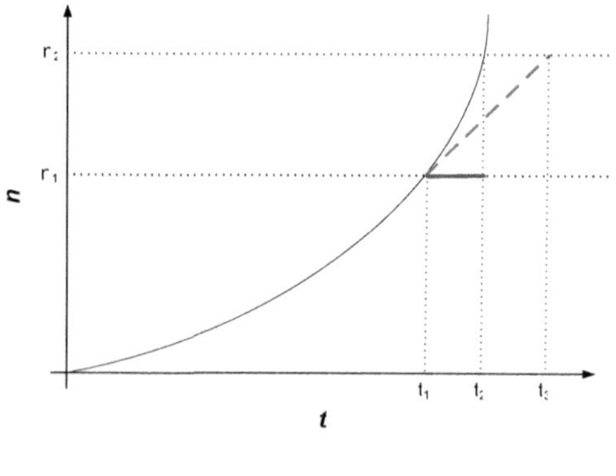

Fig. 1. The number of threads as time moves

The variant (slant) of the thread number at time t, a^t,and set A of a^t are defined as follows.

$$a^t = \{x \mid x \text{ is the variant at time } t\} = \frac{n_t - n_{t-\Delta t}}{t - \Delta t} \tag{2}$$

$$A = \{x \mid x \text{ is the set of } a^t \text{ under coverage}\} \tag{3}$$

$f_{expected}(t_2, t_1)$ is the number of threads at time t_2 predicted at time t_1.

$$\begin{aligned} f_{\text{expected}}(t_2, t_1) &= \{x \mid x \text{ is the expected } n_{t_2} \text{ at time } t_1\} \\ &= a_{t_1} \cdot t_2 \end{aligned} \tag{4}$$

Δt_{delay} decides the prediction frequency, and one thread is created in $\Delta t_{\min}$. The observation error function, f_{error}, and the resource exhaustion in system k, $resource_k$, are defined as follows.

$$\begin{aligned} &\Delta t_{delay} = \{x \mid x \text{ is the time delay between two consequtive predictions}\} \\ &\Delta t_{\min} = \{x \mid x \text{ is the time taken to generate one thread}\} \\ &k \subset Z, \forall \Delta t_{delay} \qquad \Delta t_{delay} = k \cdot \Delta t_{\min} \end{aligned} \tag{5}$$

$$\begin{aligned} f_{error}(t) &= \{x \mid x \text{ is the expected value of error at time } t\} \\ &= \left| f_{\text{expected}}(t, \Delta t_{delay}) - n^t \right| \end{aligned} \tag{6}$$

The value of f_{error} gets bigger when the predicted value obtained by Expression (4) is varied from t_1 to t_2 and t_3 as shown in Fig. 1. The error decreases as the prediction frequency is reduced. However, the overhead gets larger if the prediction frequency increases. This relationship can be expressed as follows.

$$f_{error} \propto \Delta t_{delay}, \quad resource_k \propto \frac{1}{\Delta t_{delay}} \tag{7}$$

The prediction frequency needs to be properly adjusted according to the rate of the change in the number of threads. First, we need to define the variable representing the sampling rate.

$$\Delta t_{\text{coverage}} : \text{the number of samplings} \tag{8}$$

In this paper $\Delta t_{\text{coverage}}$ is set to 40, which was obtained by experiment. It sets average and dispersion of the slant a^t to 40 per hour. Using this parameter, the Gaussian irregularity variable on variant value a^t is obtained as follows.

$$f_{A_{\Delta t_{\text{coverage}}}}(x) = \frac{e^{-(x-m)^2/2\sigma^2}}{\sqrt{2\pi\sigma^2}} \tag{9}$$

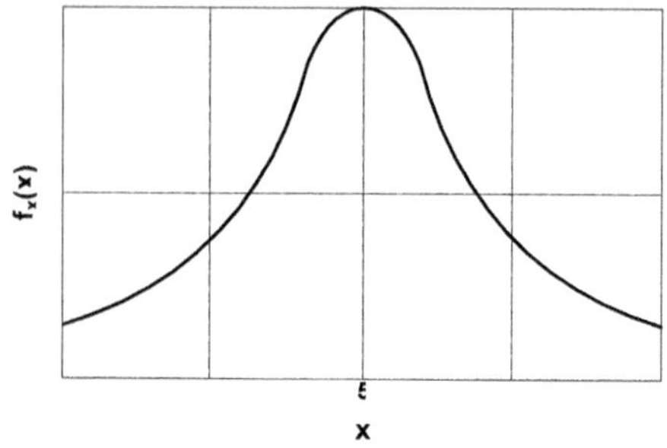

Fig. 2. The graph of Gaussian probability density function with m = 5 and σ= 5

With the average and dispersion of variant a^t of m = 5 and σ= 5, the graph looks as follows.

If the change of the slant value a^t is within 70% of the calculated value through the Q-function from center spot (below 3 or over 7 in the graph above), we decrease or increase Δt_{delay} by one, respectively. The process is formalized as follows.

$$m_{A_{\Delta t_{\text{coverage}}}} : \text{average of } A_{\Delta t_{\text{coverage}}},\ \sigma_{A_{\Delta t_{\text{coverage}}}} : \text{standard deviation of } A_{\Delta t_{\text{coverage}}}$$

$$\begin{aligned} &if\ \forall a_t,\ 2Q\left(\frac{a_t - m_{A_{\Delta t_{\text{coverage}}}}}{\sigma_{A_{\Delta t_{\text{coverage}}}}}\right) \geq 0.7 \text{ then } \Delta t_{\text{delay}} = \Delta t_{\text{delay}} - \Delta t_{\min} \\ &if\ \forall a_t,\ 2Q\left(\frac{a_t - m_{A_{\Delta t_{\text{coverage}}}}}{\sigma_{A_{\Delta t_{\text{coverage}}}}}\right) < 0.7 \text{ then } \Delta t_{\text{delay}} = \Delta t_{\text{delay}} + \Delta t_{\min} \end{aligned} \tag{10}$$

A waiting thread in the thread pool becomes active when a request arrives. An active thread becomes a waiting thread after the operation finishes. If a waiting thread has been waiting more than one idle timeout period, it deletes itself.

3.2 The Agent Platform

When the agent platform starts to operate, it creates a thread pool. The size of the pool can be dynamically controlled by a request of an agent. In the developed agent platform [1], a thread pool controller exists. It applies the prediction value calculated by the $f_{expected}(t_2, t_1)$ function and controls the size of the thread pool accordingly. Fig. 3 shows the agent platform architecture where the proposed scheme is employed.

The agent platform consists of the MTP (Message Transport Protocol) and the agent platform core module. The MTP is in charge of the event-based communication, and the agent platform core module is in charge of the management of platform and agents. The MTP layer contains HTTP Communication module built for the communication between the agents. An agent has a HTTP server and client module in itself. When a message is received, the HTTP server processes it. When a message is sent, the HTTP client is used for the communication. It also contains the ACL Parser

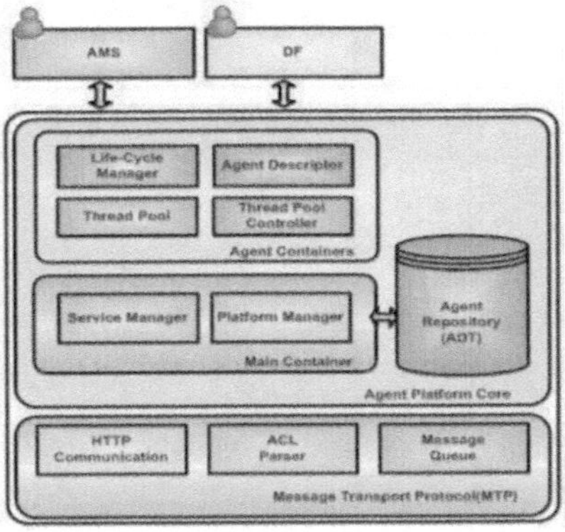

Fig. 3. The architecture of the agent platform [1][11][12][13]

module encoding and decoding the ACL messages. An agent can simultaneously send a message to several agents through the process of ACL. The Message queue module supports ordering and queuing of messages for receiving/sending the messages.

The agent platform core consists of Main Container, Agent Container, and ADT(Agent Description Table). The Main Container is the main module managing the agent platform. It contains Platform Manager handling the initialization of the agent platform and delivery of messages from the MTP layer to the agent processing module and Service Manager that registers and manages additional services such as reflection module. The Agent Container manages groups of agents having similar roles or functions hierarchically. It contains Life-Cycle Manager that manages the actions of an agent as a thread and Agent Descriptor that manages the information of agent description such as id, address, roles, etc. The ADT is a hash table that manages the reference information of the agents' description using the hash key of the agent's id.

The agent platform core uses MTP library, and it consists of one main container and several agent containers. An agent container manages groups of agent descriptions, where the agent description contains the information required for connection and management of the agent, and status information required for life cycle management. The agent platform monitors and manages agents as threads. The threads take actions such as start, stop, resume, and running dynamically with the agent's present state.

The agent platform core consists of the parts allowing interactions among the agents and managing the execution of agent platform. It governs the relationships between the modules and services through the main action flow. Fig. 4 shows the sequence among the principal modules of the agent platform core in case of initializing the agent platform, registering and releasing an agent, and delivery of message.

When the agent platform begins to operate, it creates Main Container firstly. Main Container reads the setting file of XML format for initialization. The setting file has the version information of the platform besides the name, address, port, and resource information. It also creates ADT to directly access the agent description information and Main Thread Group Table that manages the Agent Container's reference values. Then, it finishes the initialization to receive ACL messages by initializing the communication server module of MTP.

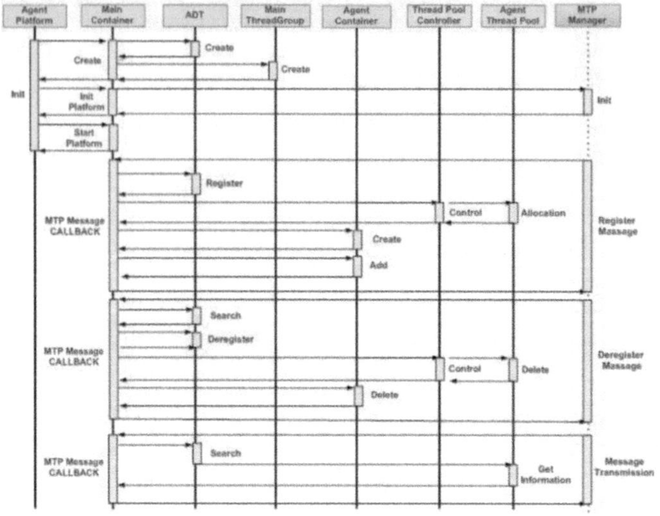

Fig. 4. The main operational sequence of agent platform core

Each agent sends an ACL message to register to the agent platform. Then, the agent platform core receives a callback message from the MTP. It confirms if it is a message sent by the agent platform through the receiver part of ACL. After checking the content of ACL if it is a registration message, it extracts the agent's name, address, port, description information, container information from the message. Then, it examines the Agent ID from the ADT using the hash key if it has been already registered of not. If it was already registered, the platform sends a failure message indicating 'already registered' to the agent. After the agent is registered to the ADT, the agent platform allocates an agent thread from the agent thread pool. The allocated agent thread has the agent description information, and it dynamically monitors the agent according to its state. It checks if there already exists a relevant agent container. If not, it makes a one. Otherwise, it adds it to the existing container. Then the registration process is complete, and it sends the agent the result of the process.

When an agent sends a destroy message, the agent platform core receives an ACL message through message callback. Then it confirms that the receiver part of that is agent platform and the content is for deletion. It searches the ADT using the hash key of the Agent ID, and then deletes the reference value of the relevant agent information from the ADT. Also, it destroys the relevant agent thread from the agent thread pool and deletes a reference of the thread from the table of agent container.

The agent platform core delivers messages to the relevant agent in case the receiver of the ACL message entering through message callback is not the agent platform. The sender agent does not know the receiver agent's IP Address and Port information but only the receiver's name. Therefore, it requests a transmission to the agent platform. The agent platform core searches the ADT to find the address information corresponding to the receiver agent's name. After searching the ADT, the agent platform core receives necessary information from the agent thread module managing the agent description information. It also talks to the relevant agent after changing the receiver's name and attribute value of the address, and so on. The principal sequence of operations of agent platform core is supported by the MTP, and it processes the messages at once. Also, the platform core collects the information of management obtained by the thread monitoring the system.

4 Performance Evaluation

In this section the proposed algorithm dynamically managing the size of thread pool is evaluated by computer simulation and compared with the existing representative algorithm in term of memory usage and response time. The agent platform and agent are implemented in a PC of a Pentium-4 processor and 1 GB main memory.

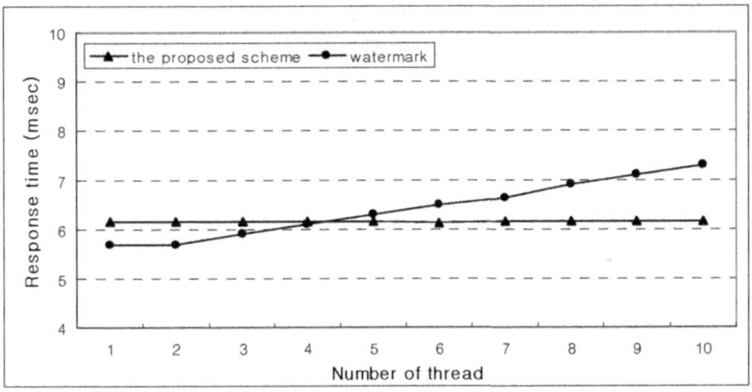

Fig. 5. The response times when the load is high

Fig. 5 shows the response times when the load is high. Here one agent request is generated in every 0.1 second. The thread pool controller predicts the pool size, while the maximum idle timeout before deleting a thread is set to 0.3 second. Observe from Fig. 5 that the proposed scheme outperforms the existing representative algorithms when the number of thread is larger than 4. The proposed scheme requires to use about 0.5% more memory space than the other models (7450KB vs 7330KB). If agent request increases, the number of threads scheduled also increases. Therefore, the

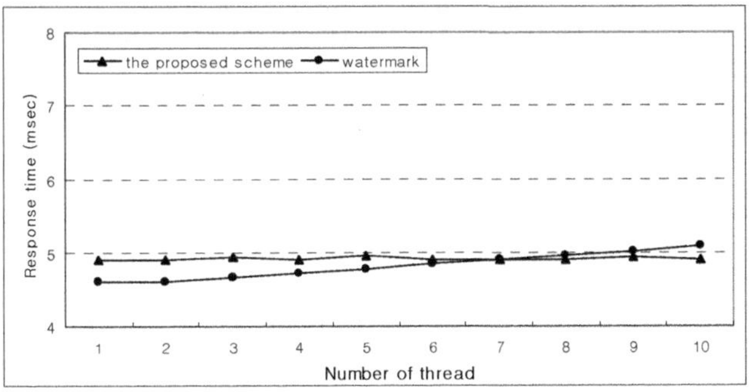

Fig. 6. The response times when the load is low

response time will also increase. In this case the agent platform uses more system resource, and reduces the response time.

Fig. 6 shows the response times when the load is low such that one agent request is generated in every 5 seconds. In this case the watermark thread pool model uses low watermark, and thus it acts like the worker thread pool model. Notice from the figure that we get similar results as with high load. For memory usage, however, the proposed scheme requires slightly smaller space than the watermark scheme (6300KB vs 7300KB).

5 Conclusion

The applications for ubiquitous system require to effectively utilize the resources distributed in the environment and provide intelligent services to the users. In order to satisfy such requirement, the applications need to be developed using intelligent agents providing optimized services to each user. Furthermore, the platform itself needs to be able to support platform-level service optimization.

In this paper we have proposed a prediction-based dynamic thread pool management scheme using Gaussian distribution for maximizing the utilization of resources. From the experiments, we showed that the proposed scheme outperforms the existing representative thread pool models. We have also introduced a new architecture of agent platform that provides an interactive environment between intelligent agents, along with the operation sequence flow of registration, removal, and transmission of agents with the proposed agent platform core. It allows both the group management and individual management of the agents for efficiency.

As the future work, we will further optimize the dynamic thread pool management scheme by properly adjusting the parameters used in the prediction.

References

1. Han, S., Youn, H.Y.: A Middleware Architecture for Community Computing with Intelligent agents. Ubiquitous Computing & Networking System (2005)
2. Schmidt, D., Pyarali, I., Spivak, M., Cytron, R.: Evaluating and Optimizing Thread Pool Strategies for Real-Time Cobra. ACM Sigplan Notices 36(8), 214–222 (2001)
3. Schmidt, D., Vinoski, S.: Object Interconnection: Comparing Alternative Programming Techniques for Multi-Threaded Servers-the Thread Per-Request Concurrency Model. C++ Report, SIGS, 801(2) (1996)
4. Schmidt, D.: Evaluating Architectures for Multi-thread CORBA Object Request Brokers. In: Seetharaman, K. (ed.) Communication of the ACM, Special Issue on CORBA 41(10) (1998)
5. Dynamic TAO Documentation, http://choices.cs.uiuc.edu/2k/dynamicTAO/doc/
6. Luck, M., McBurney, P., Preist, C.: Agent Technology: Enabling Next Generation Computing. AgentLink community (2003)
7. Jennings, N.R.: An agent-based approach for buildingcomplex software systems. Communications of the ACM 44(4), 35–41 (2001)
8. JADE, Java Agent Development framework, http://jade.cselt.it
9. IBM Japan Research Group: Aglets Workbench, http://www.trl.ibm.com/aglets

10. FIPA-Foundation for Intelligent Physical Agents, http://www.fipa.org
11. Park, A.H., Park, S.H., Youn, H.Y.: A Flexible and Scalable Agent Platform for Multi-Agent Systems. Enformatika Transactions on Engineering, Computing and Technology 19, 1–6 (2007)
12. Ko, H., Youn, H.Y.: Adaptive Bridging with Portable Interceptor for Efficient Integration of Reflective Middleware. In: Ma, J., Jin, H., Yang, L.T., Tsai, J.J.-P. (eds.) UIC 2006. LNCS, vol. 4159, pp. 669–678. Springer, Heidelberg (2006)
13. Park, S.Y., Youn, H.Y.: Message Transport Interface for Efficient Communication Between Agent Framework and Event Service. In: Gavrilova, M., Gervasi, O., Kumar, V., Tan, C.J.K., Taniar, D., Laganà, A., Mun, Y., Choo, H. (eds.) ICCSA 2006. LNCS, vol. 3983, pp. 1–10. Springer, Heidelberg (2006)

A Ubiquitous Watch-Over System Based on Environmental Information and Social Knowledge

Takuo Suganuma[1], Kazuhiro Yamanaka[1], Yoshikazu Tokairin[1], Hideyuki Takahashi[1], Kenji Sugawara[2], and Norio Shiratori[1]

[1] Tohoku University, 2-1-1 Katahira, Aoba-ku, Sendai, 980-5877 Japan
[2] Chiba Institute of Technology, 2-17-1, Tsudanuma, Narashino, 275-0016 Japan
suganuma@shiratori.riec.tohoku.ac.jp

Abstract. In this paper we propose a gentle watching over system that considers users' situations and quality/privacy requirements, in ubiquitous information environment. To realize a gentle and safe watching-over, we have to cope with real situation of a watched person. Moreover, social relationships between observers and the watched person should be considered to give adequate privacy level to the services. To do this, we propose a ubiquitous watch-over system "uEyes". In uEyes we introduce a distinguished feature for watching: Social awareness. To realize the feature, environmental information acquired from real world and knowledge on social activities of people are effectively combined. Based on the advanced feature, live video streaming system is dynamically constructed according to the users' situation in runtime. We implemented a prototype of uEyes for watching over elderly people, and performed some experiments based on several scenarios. From the experimental results, we confirmed effectiveness of our proposed system.

1 Introduction

Recently, real-time multimedia watching system is widespread as a care-support system that watches over children and elderly people from remote site connected by wide-area network. Researches are at their initial stage to apply this system to the ubiquitous computing environment. There are some researches on delivering video streaming from the selected camera closest to the target people, by using physical positional information of the target [1]. Also, there exist works on flexible displaying that plays the video seamlessly from the nearest display device to the observer based on the location of the watcher [2,3].

However, in these existing works, when the watched person wants to keep privacy, or when some emergency situation such as the condition of his/her health worsens, it is expected to reflect these conditions in watching-over without any user interactions to the system. This is because, in these previous systems, the location information of a user is utilised only for specifying the user's physical location. To fulfill the above requirement, sophisticated mechanism is needed

J. Indulska et al. (Eds.): UIC 2007, LNCS 4611, pp. 1108–1120, 2007.

to infer the situations and requirements of users from detailed analysis of their location information.

To realize the gentle and safe watching-over, we have to cope with real life situation of a watched person. Moreover, social relationships between observers and the watched person should be considered to give adequate privacy to the services. To do this, we propose a ubiquitous watching over system "uEyes", a Ubiquitous communication Environment for Yasashiku (in Japanese it means "gently" or "kindly") Eyeing Services to solve the above issues. In uEyes we introduce a distinguished feature for watching: Social awareness. The Social awareness is a capability of the system that can recognize/understand actual situation of users and social relationship between users.

To achieve the points mentioned above, we build uEyes based on the concept of Symbiotic Computing [4,5,6]. We design and implement the feature of uEyes by effectively combining environmental information acquired from real world and knowledge on social activities of people. Social knowledge on human relationship, life style of the watched person, structure of house, etc., is introduced and effectively used to infer the situation of the users. Based on the advanced feature, live video streaming system is dynamically constructed according to the users' situation in runtime. As a results, gentle watching-over service that fulfils the detailed users' requirements can be effectively provided.

We implemented a prototype of uEyes for watching over elderly people, and performed some experiments based on several scenarios. For instance, we assumed a scenario where an elderly father is watched by his family and his neighbours in the local community. We confirmed that, in case when the elderly father is in his bedroom, a live video streaming system with low quality was dynamically configured to keep his privacy. Also in case when it is an emergency, the privacy level was lowered and the situation was informed to the members of the local community with high quality video. From the results of these case studies, it was confirmed that uEyes can provide real-time multimedia watching service for elderly people, with reasonable QoS and privacy that meets the users' requirements.

2 uEyes: The Concept and Model

2.1 Concept of uEyes

Our target watching task is as shown in Figure 1(a). In this figure, community of watching persons cooperatively watches over a target person. We call this kind of watching task as "Community-based watching-over" task. The purpose of uEyes is to solve the problem described in Sec.1 in this watching-over task. To achieve this, it is necessary to introduce mechanism where entire system configuration that consists of various system elements is dynamically selected and organized according to the states of the system, users, situation around the users and social aspects, as shown in Figure 1(b).

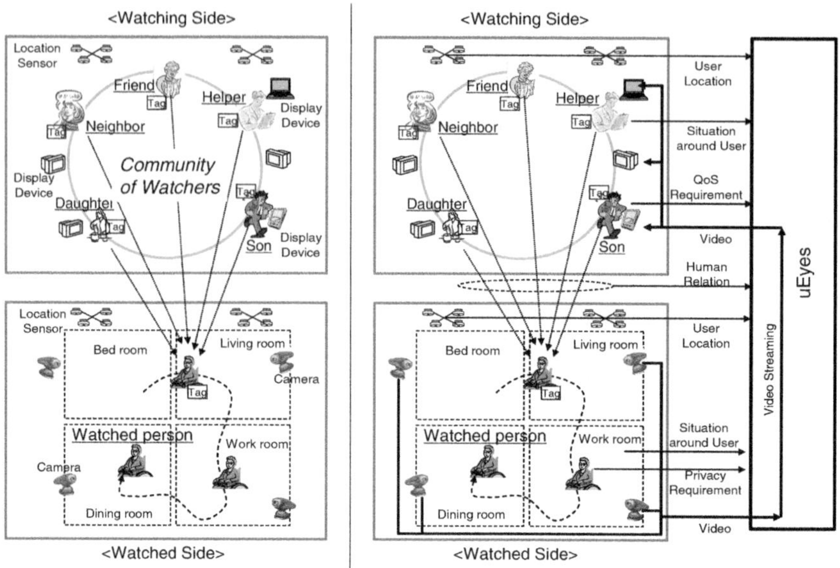

(a) Concept of our watching task: Community-based watching-over

(b) Support of community-based watching-over by uEyes

Fig. 1. Concept of uEyes

Following three characteristics are newly introduced:

(S1) Device awareness: uEyes effectively handles and coordinates multiple contexts of ubiquitous devices for provisioning of appropriate QoS of watching systems. The contexts involve not only user location, but also status of display/camera device, available resources of PCs and hand-held devices, available network access and bandwidth, etc.

(S2) User awareness: uEyes closely associates with user's requirement for watching tasks in the best possible way. For example, where a watcher requires the video streaming so that he can vividly view the facial color of the watched person, high quality and zoomed picture should also be appeared in the nearest display.

(S3) Social awareness: uEyes deeply considers social relationship between watched person and watchers, and keeps adequate privacy according to the situation. For instance, in case of normal situation, watched person's privacy should be protected, however in case of emergency, the privacy level would moderately be lowered.

(S1) and (S2) are discussed in our previous works [10,11] and we omit the details of them here. In this paper we focus on (S3) Social Awareness of uEyes.

2.2 Functional Model of uEyes

A functional model of uEyes is shown in Figure 2. The uEyes mainly consists of three functional mechanisms: Device Awareness, User Awareness and Social

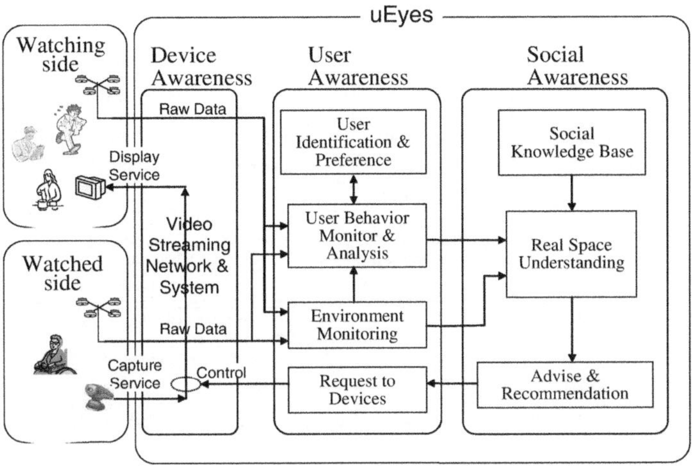

Fig. 2. Functional model of uEyes

Awareness. Device Awareness consists of a set of components for video streaming system and sensor devices for capturing raw data from real world. User Awareness is for capturing user's behavior and conditions around the user. Moreover Social Awareness is for recognizing social relationship between watched and watching person. It also understands the current presence and situation of the user. The three mechanisms have some functional modules as shown in Figure 2, and these modules cooperatively work to support the watching task described in the previous section.

3 Real Space Understanding Mechanism Based on Social Knowledge

3.1 Real Space Understanding Mechanism

The objective of this work is to realize safe and convenient watch-over system that autonomously provides users with services that fulfill user's requirement on its quality and privacy. To do this, the system should recognise user's actual requirements from "situation of users" and "human relationship" without any burden of users in system operation. To obtain the users' situations, available sensing data is limited due to its installation condition. Moreover to get the human relationship, users do not want to open all their personal information to keep their privacy. Therefore, it is difficult to judge the situation and relationship of users from the limited information from real space.

To resolve this problem, we introduce "Social Knowledge" to perform inference to recognize the situation of users and human relationship. Moreover we propose a method to create quality/privacy request to video streaming system from the recognized information.

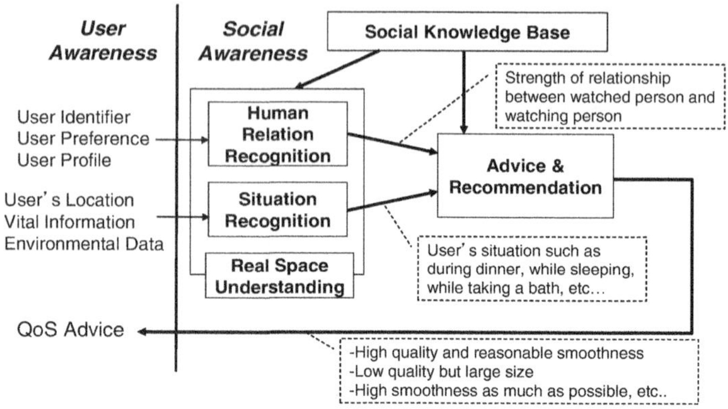

Fig. 3. Relationships among mechanisms in Social Awareness

We propose "Real Space Understanding Mechanism" in this paper, to infer the situation and relationship of users by combining sensing information and Social Knowledge. The sensing information is the data of environment acquired from real space. It includes user's physical location and temporal change of the location. On the other hand, the Social Knowledge involves common knowledge on human relation, human behavior, structure of house, etc. The Real Space Understanding Mechanism consists of "Human Relation Recognition" function and "Situation Recognition" function as shown in Figure 3. The Human Relation Recognition gets user's identifier, preference, profile, etc. and puts the strength of relationship between watched person and watching person. The Situation Recognition gets user's location, environmental data, etc. and derives the user's situation such as "during dinner", "while sleeping", "while taking a bath", etc.

These recognized information is utilized to create QoS advice in "Advice & Recommendation" mechanism. This mechanism produces user-oriented QoS requirement to video streaming system based on the acquired recognized information. For example, when the user requirement of high quality of video is derived in the situation where the watcher is worrying about the watched person's health condition; the mechanism creates request of high quality in video encoding. In case when it requires to keep high privacy level, it issues request to degrade the quality of the video. Moreover, in case of emergency of the watched person, it produce request the reasonable quality of video that is delivered to as many watchers as possible.

In this paper we use ontology as knowledge description scheme to represent Social Knowledge and environmental information. T. Gu et al. define context ontology in [7]. The context ontology is an ontology to express knowledge for ubiquitous computing. The authors insist that the ontology consists of User, Location, Activity and Computational Entity. These elements have relations as shown in Figure 4. In our system, we define the properties, subclasses and individuals (instances) to each basic element, focusing on the watching system domain.

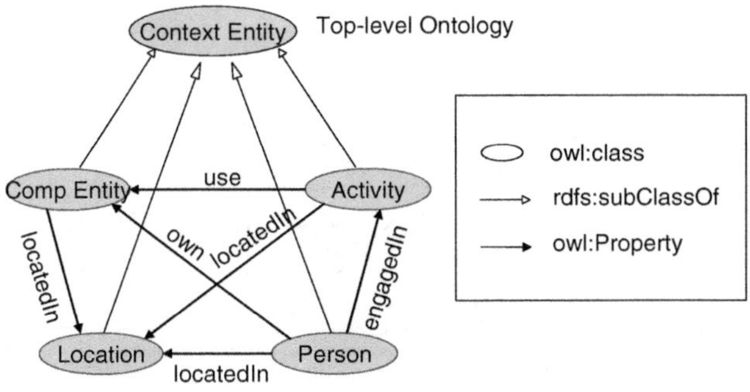

Fig. 4. Context ontology for uEyes

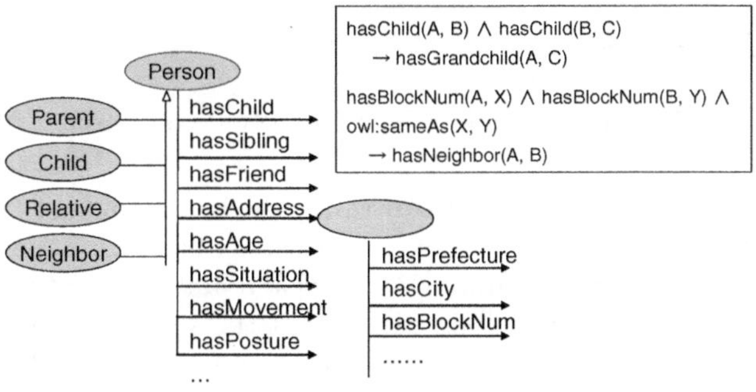

Fig. 5. Human relationship ontology

3.2 Human Relation Recognition Function

In this section we describe the details of Human Relation Recognition function. It derives human relationship between watching person and watched person, such as family relation, friendship and block association relation. To conduct these relations, knowledge, as shown in Figure 5 is introduced in the system. Here the "Person" in this Figure corresponds to the "Person" in Figure 4.

The block association relation can be acquired from address given to each user. The family relation can be derived from each user's information of sex, partner, and children. All the blood relations can be complemented from the above three information, using ontology [8]. In the current version of this function, only the direct friendship is given statically, however it can be dynamically changed through the socialization in the local community activities.

3.3 Situation Recognition Function

In this section we explain the design policy of "Situation Recognition" function. This function infers the situation of users, especially in watched person side, in detail, by combining sensing data on real space such as user's location, current

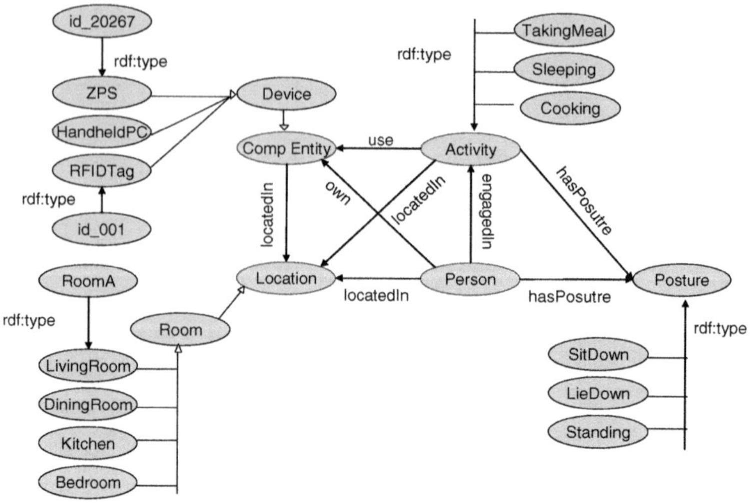

Fig. 6. Ontology to represent situation of users

time, etc, and social knowledge. For instance the situations are "during lunch", "sleeping", "watching TV", etc. In some cases, conflict will arise between inference results. This conflict is an important decision making point to judge whether the situation is normal or not. This means that the system autonomously recognizes the situation that departs from the usual status. This policy is natural to this kind of problem solving, because it is impractical to describe all the abnormal situation in real world. We represent the unusual situation by inferencing from finite knowledge of common-sense.

Figure 6 shows a part of ontology used in the "Situation Recognition" function. We added some essential knowledge for watch-over to the basic four elements on the context ontology described in Section 3.1.

3.4 Behavior

Previous section describes the design policy of "Situation Recognition" function. Here we explain a behavioral example that is shown in Figure 7.

Suppose that a rule described in top-left text box fires. It has six conditions. If all the conditions match, the rule fires and then an situation is derived. In this case, the situation where the elderly person X is taking lunch is inferred.

In the similar way, from a rule described in bottom-left text box, the situation "the height up to the chest of the elderly person X will be around 100 cm high, and it will be slightly moving" is conducted.

However, this inferred situation has a conflict with the situation expressed in top-right text box. This is acquired from environmental information. It says that the tag with ID=3 is actually staying in the same position for five minutes. Therefore, a conflict exists in terms of height and temporary movement of the tag. In this situation, this function recognizes that some abnormal might have happened.

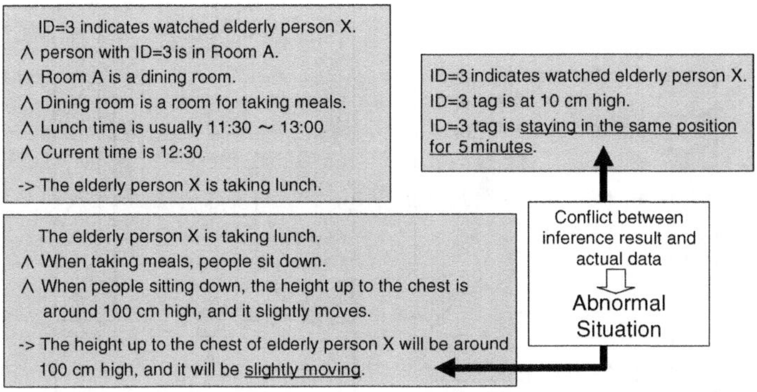

Fig. 7. An example of behaviour of Real Space Understanding Mechanism

4 Application: A Watching System for Elderly People

4.1 Implementation

We are developing an application of uEyes to watch over elderly people at home. We use some USB cameras and DV cameras for capturing live video of the watched people. For the watchers, PC displays and televisions are used to play the live video. The live streaming is realized by an application of Java Media Framework. We use a sensor system to obtain location information of users in the room. We use Furukawa Sanki's ZPS (Zone Positioning System) [12] for ultra sonic sensors.

In the implementation, we employed DASH, an agent-based programming environment based on ADIPS [9]. Each agent in ADIPS has its own knowledge base and inference engine. To implement the ontology we describe in OWL (Web Ontology Language) and then convert it to Jess (Java Expert System Shell). This conversion is needed due to performance concerns.

4.2 Knowledge Representation

We show an example of knowledge representation. When describing "LivingRoom" class as a subclass of "Room" class, it is represented as "`(deftemplate LivingRoom Extends Room)`" in Jess. As an example of individual (instance) of a class, when "UserX" is represented as an instance of "Person" class, it is expressed as "`assert (Person (name UserX))`" in Jess.

Here is an example of rule description. For example, a rule "a person has a tag, and the tag is in a room, the person is in the room" is represented in SWRL as:

`own(?user, ?tag)` ∧ `locatedIn(?tag, ?room)`
→ `locatedIn(?user, ?room).`

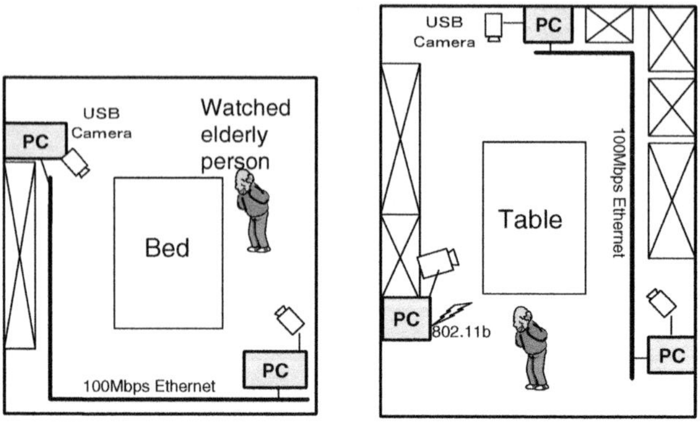

(a) Bed room (b) Dining room

Fig. 8. Experimental room settings

However in Jess syntax, it is implemented as follows:

```
  (defrule Def-1-userRoom (owns ?user ?tag) (putOn ?tag ?room)
=> (assert (locatedIn ?user ?room)) ).
```

4.3 Experimental Environment

We introduce application scenarios to evaluate feasibility and effectiveness of our system. We consider a situation where the elderly father is watched over by his son, a relative, a neighbor and a friend living in the same block. We have two experimental rooms; a bed room and a dining room in watched site. Figure 8 shows the room setting. In terms of the location sensor, ZPS ultra-sonic sensor is used in both rooms.

Here, suppose that the elderly father is in bed room. In this situation, our system will select the most appropriate camera and PC with reasonable network connection in the room. Then suitable quality of live streaming video is captured and displayed to a PC on the watching side.

We will perform two kinds of experiments. The first experiment (Exp.1) is for evaluating effectiveness of the Real Space Understanding Mechanism. The second experiment (Exp.2) is to confirm the effect of overall Social Awareness including the Real Space Understanding Mechanism in uEyes.

5 Experiments

5.1 Exp.1: Effect of Real Space Understanding Function

In Exp.1, we evaluate the effect of "Real Space Understanding" function. To verify the behavior and effectiveness of the proposed function, we perform the experiments by inputing test data of real space and confirm the output of the

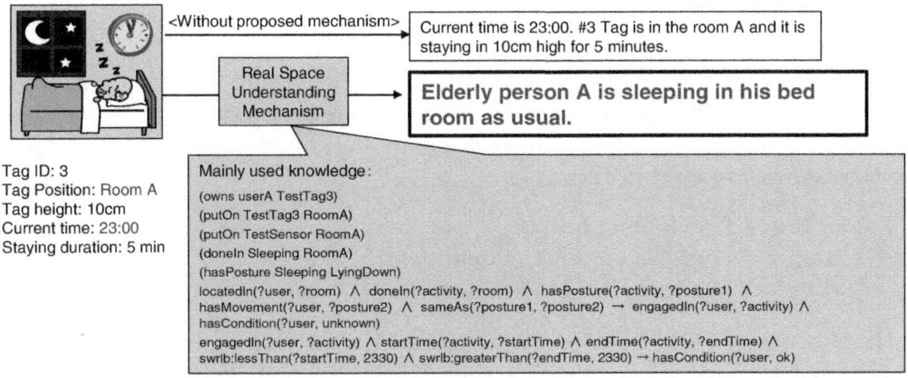

Fig. 9. Experiment result of Exp.1(1): A normal situation

inference result. We give two patterns of the test data, considering real situation of elderly watched person. The given data consists of tag ID, room ID where the tag is located, height of the tag from floor, current time and staying duration.

(1)Exp.1(1)
Considering a situation where the watched person is sleeping at midnight, we give the following data as an input of the function; Tag-ID:3, Tag-Position:RoomA, Tag-height: 10cm, Current-time: 23:00, Staying-duration: 5min. The result is shown in Figure 9.

Without the function, the given data is pass through to the output as it is. This means that the recognition results was "the current time is 23:00. A tag with #3 is in the room A and it is staying in 10cm high for five minutes." On the other hand, with this function, "Elderly father A is sleeping in his bed room as usual" was obtained as a result.

To recognize this situation, the following knowledge is used.

- The elderly father has #3 tag.
- The room A is a bed room.
- A bed room is a room for sleeping.
- During sleep, people lie in the bed.
- People sleep at night.
- A people is making an action, and the action is normally performed in a specific time period, and if the current time is within the time period, the action is usual.

This result shows that Social Knowledge such as common-sense of human behavior and house structure are used to create meaning on the environmental information obtained from read space.

(2)Exp.1(2)
Next, we assume the emergency situation where the elderly father is lying in the dinning room. We give following data as an input of the function; Tag-ID:3,

Tag-Possition:RoomB, Tag-height: 10cm, Current-time: 11:00, Staying-duration: 5min.

Using this function, we could obtain the inference result of "The elderly father A is lying in the dining room and he is in a emergency situation."

We used the following Social Knowledge in our actual experiment, in addition to the knowledge used in Exp.1(1).

- The Room B is a dining room.
- A dining room is a room for taking meals.
- During taking meals, people are in sitting position.

In this pattern the room is different from the pattern in Exp.1(1). Thus the speculated activity of the elderly father is also different. From the three Social Knowledge described above, the function induces the result of "he is sitting down". However the tag location from real space indicates that he is lying. This is an example of conflict. As a result, the function concluded that "he is in an emergency situation."

5.2 Exp.2: Effects of Proposed Function on uEyes

Subsequently, we have performed experiments to verify the effect when Social Awareness is introduced. It is expected that it achieves the watching by community of two or more people, because understanding of the interpersonal relationship and recognition of the situation can be done by the Social Awareness.

Here, we show an example of watching by (a) watched person's son, (b) his relatives, (c) his neighbor with a good relation, and (d) a person living in his same block. In a situation when the watched person's privacy is considered, for example, he is in his bed room, the raw video with high quality was delivered to the son. The image of lower quality to understand only movement was delivered to the relatives. The others did not receive the video because the privacy concerns reflect to the video quality.

Figure 10 shows the example of the display in the emergency situation when the watched person falls in the fit. The "Situation Recognition" function judges it as a state of emergency due to the fall etc., using elderly person's location information obtained from real space, and the "Social Knowledge" concerning the structure of the house. The display is changed so that many people may know the situation by lowering the privacy level. Concretely, an untouched video image is delivered to the son and the relative, the neighbor with a good relation receives a low quality video that tells only the appearance, and the person in the same block is notified by the emergency message without any video image.

5.3 Evaluation

(1)Effect of Real Space Understanding Mechanism: From the experiments described in previous sections, we confirmed the effectiveness of our proposal. The results show that we can create meaningful conclusions from environmental information got from real space by introducing the Social Knowledge. Therefore,

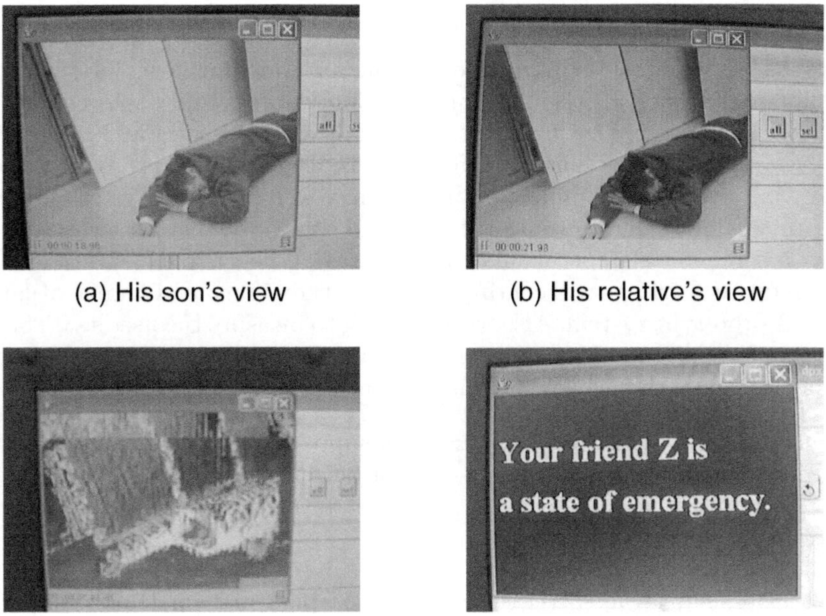

(a) His son's view

(b) His relative's view

(c) His neighbor's view

(d) View of his friend living in the same block

Fig. 10. Result of Exp.2: Effect of Social Awareness in case of watched person in emergency

we can infer many types of situations that is hard to recognize only from analysis of environmental data.

More general knowledge such as common-sense can be employed not only in watching-over application domain, but also in other domains. Namely, by accumulating and managing the general knowledge, design and implementation of other type of application system based on the Social Knowledge can be effectively supported. In addition, increasing the general knowledge, situation dependent knowledge can be expected to be reduced. This would greatly contribute to increase the development efficiency by decreasing burden in knowledge description that is one of the bottlenecks of this kind of systems.

(2)Effect of Social Awareness in uEyes: From the experiments in previous sections, we confirmed the effect of Social Awareness. By employing the function, uEyes can recognize relationship between people in real world and detailed situation of the watched person. Based on the information uEyes can autonomously handle QoS parameter and privacy level in an adequate level. The significant point of this system is its automatic acquisition of user requirement. It would be very difficult for elderly people to manipulate the system. Moreover, in the emergency situation, the watched person cannot do anything. This feature would enable secure and safe watching-over services to especially help non-expert users.

6 Conclusion

In this paper we proposed a gentle system for watching over for ubiquitous care-support services. In this system, situation of users and environmental information around him/her are effectively handled to provide watching services. Social awareness such as human relationship is also considered to increase sense of safety in watching. We build an application of watching over system supposed to be provided for elderly people at home, and confirmed the effectiveness of the idea with some initial experiments with the prototype system.

In the future work, we will continue the case study in many different situations using this prototype system. Also we are trying to measure the user's satisfaction in quantitative manner. Moreover, we will enhance studies on the social-ware to give much more social aspects to this system.

Acknowledgement. This work was partially supported by the Japan Society for the Promotion of Science, Grants-in-Aid for Scientific Research, 19200005.

References

1. Takemoto, M., et al.: Service-composition Method and Its Implementation in Service-provision Architecture for Ubiquitous Computing Environments. IPSJ Journal 46(2), 418–433 (2005)
2. Cui, Y., Nahrstedt, K., Xu, D.: Seamless User-level Handoff in Ubiquitous Multimedia Service Delivery. Multimedia Tools and Applications Journal, Special Issue on MobileMultimedia and Communications and m-Commerce 22, 137–170 (2004)
3. Lohse, M., Repplinger, M., Slusallek, P.: Dynamic Media Routing in Multi-User Home Entertainment Systems. In: The Eleventh International Conference on Distributed Multimedia Systems(DMS'2005) (2005)
4. Shiratori, N., et al.: Framework of a flexible computer communication network. Computer Communications 19, 1268–1275 (1996)
5. Symbiotic Computing Home Page, `http://symbiotic.agent-town.com/`
6. Suganuma, T., et al.: Bridging the E-Gaps: Towards Post-Ubiquitous Computing. In: The 1st International Symposium on Frontiers in Networking with Applications (FINA 2006), pp. 780–784 (2006)
7. Gu, T., et al.: A service-oriented middleware for building context-aware services. Journal of Network and Computer Applications 28, 1–18 (2005)
8. Golbreich, C.: Combining Rule and Ontology Reasoners for the Semantic Web. In: Antoniou, G., Boley, H. (eds.) RuleML 2004. LNCS, vol. 3323, pp. 6–22. Springer, Heidelberg (2004)
9. Fujita, S., Hara, H., Sugawara, K., Kinoshita, T., Shiratori, N.: Agent-based design model of adaptive distributed systems. Applied Intelligence 9, 57–70 (1998)
10. Takahashi, H., et al.: Design and Implementation of An Agent-based middleware for Context-aware Ubiquitous Services. Frontiers in Artificial Intelligence and Applications, New Trends in Software Methodologies, Tools and Techniques 129, 330–350 (2005)
11. Takahashi, H., et, a.: AMUSE: An Agent-based Middleware for Context-aware Ubiquitous Services. In: The International Conference on Parallel and Distributed Systems (ICPADS2005), pp. 743–749 (2005)
12. Zone Positioning System (in Japanese), `http://www.furukawakk.jp/products/`

Ubiquitous Intelligent Information Push-Delivery for Personalized Content Recommendation

Ranzhe Jing[1,2], Xun Qiu[2], Yiyi Tao[2], Caifen Guo[2], and Zhiyun Xin[1]

[1] Department of Computer Science and Technology, Tsinghua University, Beijing, 100084, China
[2] National Engineering Research Center for Enterprise Information Software, Suzhou Manufacturing Industry Information Research Center, Suzhou, 215104, China
Jrz@tsinghua.edu.cn

Abstract. In this paper, an adaptive information push delivery method for time series data recommendation in ubiquitous environment is proposed for personalized information service, in which complicated financial data time series prediction method based on LS-SVM is adopted to learn to user's preference in a fairly good way, experiments of the method showed good forecasting performance for time series content recommendation.

1 Introduction

Along with the quick development of Internet, the Internet has become a huge information space, and provides a great deal of data information for various customers. Everyday a great deal of data will be produced especially in the financial information realm, The process that the financial data produce is random, part decided, and affected by many factors such as economy, politics, investor's personal mental situation etc. , its internal regulation is very complicated; there is noise in most of the financial data. Usually there will be some abrupt affairs, which will not make the construction of the financial data change a lot, only make the data deviate temporarily; the financial data is more non-linear. A notable characteristic that shows in the data of the financial information realm is effectiveness for a period of time. How to base the accurate inquisition statistics data and financial information, set out from the history, present condition and regulation of the financial data, use the scientific method, carry on forecasting to the change regulation of the financial data, instruct the customer's problems such as economic decision and investment direction etc. according to the actual need of the financial customer, is a hot problem researched in financial information domain.

2 The Search Present Condition and Scarcity of Time Series in the Financial Realm

The time series is a special form of data existence. Currently a lot of searches have taken to predict the financial time series, including the neural network method, the

J. Indulska et al. (Eds.): UIC 2007, LNCS 4611, pp. 1121–1129, 2007.

association rule method, such as Fu-Lai Chung proposed an evolutionary approach to pattern-based time series segmentation[1].Z. Struzik, A. Sibes measured time series similarity through large singular revealed with wavelet transformation[2].E. Keogh. S. Kasetty studied needs for time series data mining benchmarks[3].G.Das's research group studied rule discovery from time series[4], R. Agrawal proposed an efficient similarity search insequence databases[5]. CAO studied financial forecasting using support vector machines[6-8]. In paper [9], an adaptive information retrieval method based on support vector machine is proposed for timely information recommendation.

Vapnik proposed a kind of new statistics theories study method the support vector machines (SVM) in 1995[8]. The support vector machine have perfect statistics learning theory foundation and outstanding study performance, having already become the newly hot search focus in the machine learning field. And it has already been applied successfully in many domains such as person face identification, the handwritten form digit identification, the text automatic classification. The support vector machines adopts quadratic programming method, and applies to the pattern recognition and the nonlinear function reckon, obtain better result, have advantages such as operation simple, convergence velocity quick, the precision high etc.. This article is going to adopt the support vector machine to steer analysis anticipation and search to the financial time series data.

In this paper, an adaptive information push delivery method for time series data recommendation in ubiquitous environment is proposed for personalized information service, in which complicated financial data time series prediction method based on LS-SVM is adopted to learn to user's preference in a fairly good way, experiments of the method showed good forecasting performance for time series content recommendation.

3 Financial Time Series Forecast Analysis Based on the SVM

3.1 Support Vector Machines Theoretical Foundation

SVM made rapid development and improvement in field of how to solve the small sample, nonlinear high-dimensional pattern recognition and display and also show many unique advantages. The method can also be applied to other machine learning problems.

Linear Classifier attempt to separate different types of samples use classification hyperplane, in R_n classification hyperplane can express as :

$$f(x) = \langle w, \quad x \rangle + b = 0 \tag{1}$$

$x \in R_n, w \in R_n, b \in R, w$, was the classification hyperplane normal vectors. The hyperplane corresponding to the classifier:

$$f(x, w, b) = \mathrm{sign}(\langle w, x \rangle + b) \tag{2}$$

The classification hyperplane f (x) which shape as (1) of can express with point (w, b), (2w,2b). To make a hyperplane only corresponding with one point, can make restrictions to point with the following:

$$\mathrm{Min}|\langle w, x \rangle + b| = 1 \tag{3}$$

Under the restraint of (4) type, classification hyperplane change into:

$$Yi(<w, xi>+b) \geq 1 \tag{4}$$

The main idea of SVM is to construct a largest partition classification hyperplane, make various kinds of samples from the distance between the recent classification hyperplane the largest. By (3) - we can see that the separation distance $\frac{2}{\|w\|}$ between the separating hyperplane. Classification interval $\frac{2}{\|w\|}$ largest, in essence, is to make the smallest value of $\| w \|$.

$$\text{Min } \| w \| = \min<x,w>^{\frac{1}{2}} \tag{5}$$

If $\| w \|^2$ with the smallest value, in classification hyperplane the upper bound of the VC dimension h will be minimal, separating hyperplane the generalization ability of the strongest classification counterparts. So the optimal classification hyperplane meet (4) Type 2 also stepped $\frac{\|w\|^2}{2}$ smallest classification hyperplane. The problem of solving optimal classification hyperplane change into solving the optimization problem:

$$\begin{cases} \min_{w,b} \frac{1}{2}\|w\|^2 \\ s.t.\ y_i(<w, x_i>) + b \geq 1 \end{cases} \tag{7}$$

Among them, C is the constant, as the penalties factor of wrong imposed sub-samples, or called the penalty factor. In the circumstances data can be linear classification, we can use formula (7) - to achieve the optimal classification hyperplane and their counterparts' classifier. Formula (7) can be transformed into convex quadratic programming problems as the following:

$$\begin{cases} \max_a \sum_{i=1}^{n} a_i - \frac{1}{2} \sum_{i,j=1}^{n} a_i a_j y_i y_j < x_i, x_j > \\ \sum_{i=1}^{n} a_i y_i = 0 \\ a_i \geq 0, i = 1,2,..., n. \end{cases} \tag{8}$$

Among them, a_i is the Lagrange multipliers factor. Solving the optimization problems can have a classifier:

$$f(x,w,b)=\text{sign}(<w,x>+b)=\text{sign}(\sum_{i=1}^{1} a_i y_i<x_i,x>+b) \tag{9}$$

This is the embryonic form of SVM, the x we called support vector.

3.2 Time Series Forecasting Model Based on the Support Vector Machine

In the financial information realm, the quantity of information is enormous, and the kind of data is various with many yawp data, so for the sake of processing and predicting rationally time series data of many fields, we preprocess the collected data firstly, removing some redundant data and divide the inputted time series into training model sample and pending predicted time series data sample. Depending on time series prediction model based on support vector machines, train and mend the model through the training sample firstly, and then predict the time series data and output the result of prediction. Essentially time series prediction is seeking mapping f: R_m->R_n according to old data sequence, approaching data connotative nonlinear mechanism F, so as to make use of the mapping to predict the time series.

Usually, the noise in the original sequence can influence the accuracy of the model prediction directly. For raising the accuracy of the prediction model , preprocess the collected data, carrying on annihilator process and normalization process, getting the new time series Y={x 1, x 2, x 3, ... , xn}, suppose original time series Y(t) is constituted with the normal trend Z(t) and the noise signal N(t). Namely:

$$Y(t)= Z(t)+ N(t) \tag{10}$$

The purpose of the data preprocessing is to hope by the noise percolation producing a signal Z(t) reflecting general trend.

Using the standard support vector machine to foretelling the financial time series data, the training speed sometimes may be slow. As for the problem of consuming large amount of memory, this article try to adopting the least square support vector machine (LS-SVM) to steer anticipation search to the financial time series, to steer prediction model training and to steer foretelling approximation of function. The training thought is described in brief as follows:

Suppose the training sample set T={(x_k,y_k)|k=1,2,3,...,n},x_k□R_n,y_k□R,x_k is the input, y_k is the output. Then the optimization subject of the original space(ω space) can be described as :

$$\min_{\omega,b,e} J(\omega,e) = \frac{1}{2}\omega^T\omega + \frac{1}{2}\gamma\sum_{k=1}^{N} e_k^2 \tag{11}$$

Constraint condition:

$$y_k = \omega^T\varphi(x_k) + b + e_k, k = 1,2,\ldots,N \tag{12}$$

There into, $\varphi(.) : R^n \to R^m$ is mapping function of the core space, the weight vector $\omega \in R^m$, the error variable $e_k \in R$, the b is the offset vector, the loss function J is the sum of SSE error and regularize quantity, γ is an adjustable constant. The purpose of the core space mapping function is to extract character from the original space, mapping a sample in the original space into a vector in the high dimension space, resolving impartibly linear problem of the original space.

According to the optimization formulation (11), the Lagrange function defined as:

$$L(\omega,b,e;\alpha) = J(\omega,e) - \sum_{k=1}^{N} \alpha_k\{\omega^T\varphi(x_k) + b + e_k - y_k\} \tag{13}$$

Thereinto the Lagrange multiply factor $\alpha_k \in R$, the above formulation can be optimized:

$$\begin{cases} \dfrac{\partial L}{\partial \omega} = 0 \rightarrow \omega = \sum_{k=1}^{N} \alpha_k \varphi(x_k) \\ \dfrac{\partial L}{\partial b} = 0 \rightarrow \sum_{k=1}^{N} \alpha_k = 0 \\ \dfrac{\partial L}{\partial e_k} = 0 \rightarrow \alpha_k = \gamma e_k \\ \dfrac{\partial L}{\partial \alpha_k} = 0 \rightarrow \omega^T \varphi(x_k) + b + e_k - y_k = 0 \end{cases} \tag{14}$$

Thereinto, k=1,2,3, …, N. Eliminate the variable ω, e, can get the following matrix square equation :

$$\begin{bmatrix} 0 & l_v^T \\ l_v & \Omega + \frac{1}{\gamma} l \end{bmatrix} \begin{bmatrix} b \\ a \end{bmatrix} = \begin{bmatrix} 0 \\ y \end{bmatrix} \tag{15}$$

Thereinto, y=[y 1, y 2, … , y_n], l_v=[1,2, … , l], α =[α 1, α 2, … , α n], $\Omega_{kl} = \varphi(x_k)^T \varphi(x_l)$, k, l=1,2,3, … , N. According to the mercer condition, existence a mapping function φ and the core function k (•,•), make

$$K(x_k,x_l)= \varphi(x_k)T\varphi(x_l) \tag{16}$$

The LS-SVM function reckon up:

$$y(x) = \sum_{k=1}^{N} \alpha_k K(x, x_k) + b \tag{17}$$

Thereinto, the α ,b is from formulation (4). The core function K(xk, xl) of this article is: the Gaussian radial basis Function:

$$K(x_k, x_l) = \exp(-\frac{\|x_k - x_l\|^2}{2\sigma^2}) \tag{18}$$

Formulation (17) is affected by the reckon precision and the selection of convergence rate. Select a suitable training sample, training the prediction model based on SVM time series, and examine the foretelling data. If the data error is comparatively greatly, can re-select the training sample, until find out a comparatively suitable model, and the task training the model is completed.

3.3 Prediction Algorithm Description Based on Time Series of Support Vector Machine

Algorithm Time series prediction algorithm based LS-SVM

Input. The financial time series data（training sample and prediction time series data）:Y={$x_1,x_2,x_3,\ldots,x_t$},1≤t≤n。
Output. Time series data forecasting result: $\hat{Y}^{(t)}$ ={ $x_1,x_2,x_3,\ldots,x_t,\ldots$ }。

Step1: Obtain the financial data, including stock data, stock certificate data, futures data, the bank interest rate data, etc. A certain data of forecasting is been the forecasting importation;
Step2: It can carry on zero turn a processing and normalization processing to time series data Y={x1,x2,x3,...,x_n}, get time series Y(t)= Z(t)+ N(t). N(t) means some noise data in time series;
Step3: The data prepare for processing, which carry on the discrete Fourier transformation to the original time series Y(t) and get Y(Z), filter the noise data, then carry on Fourier reverse transformation to get a new time series $\hat{Y}(t)$, $\hat{Y}(t)$ can reflect accurately the general trend of the data;
Step4: Choice suitable training sample, set an error variable e_k , warp b and adjustable constant γ ;
Step5: Select RBF core function □with Formulation (18).Then on the basis of training sample, it can carry on the model training by adopting the least square support vector machine, get estimate of function (Formulation(17)),and complete model training;
Step6: The importation need time series data with forecasting, carrying on time series forecasting based on LS-SVM, Do: Get input sequence data $\hat{Y}(t)$ ={x1,x2,...,x_t,...}, Get forecast parameter e_k ,b and γ σ^2 ,For t=0 to n, Output Y_l based the L step forecast model:

$$Y_l = \sum_{k=1}^{N+l} \alpha_k K(x, x_l) + b \tag{19}$$

End For ,End Do, output the forecasting result。
Step7: Using root-mean-square error(RMSE Formulation(20)), and mean absolute percentage error(MAPE Formulation(21)) carry on evaluation to have got the forecasting result, estimate the effect of forecasting, if it is not satisfied (RMSE&MAPE< e_k),jumping to the Step4 to retrain model;
Step8: Finished。

4 The Evaluation and the Experiment Analysis of Algorithm

4.1 The Environment of the Experiment and the Evaluation Index

The experiment data come from stock market-Chinese stock certificate net (http://www.cnstock.com/stock/), we adopted 198 piece bases of Shanghai and Shenzhen 300 whole income index from 2006 September 18th to 2007 January 8th in the experiment, it will estimate the closing price of the day by the closing price of the period of time before some day, namely the system importation is the stock closing price time series data k before t day, output the closing price index of the t day.

To the valuation of the experiment data, we will carry on valuation by adoption before algorithm evaluation index-mean absolute percentage error (MAPE) and root-mean-square error (RMSE) .The data before 184 days use for the establishment of forecasting model, the data after 15 days use for the model forecasting result examination. The evaluation index mainly includes MAPE、RMSE and MAE.

1) root-mean-square error :

$$RMSE = \sqrt{\frac{1}{n}\sum_{t=1}^{n}(y_t - \hat{y}_t)^2} \quad (20)$$

2) mean absolute percentage error :

$$MAPE = \frac{1}{n}\sum_{t=1}^{n}\frac{|y_t - \hat{y}_t|}{|y_t|} \quad (21)$$

3) mean absolute error :

$$MAE = \frac{1}{n}\sum_{t=1}^{n}|y_t - \hat{y}_t| \quad (22)$$

The diagram is the time series of the original training sample, as follows:

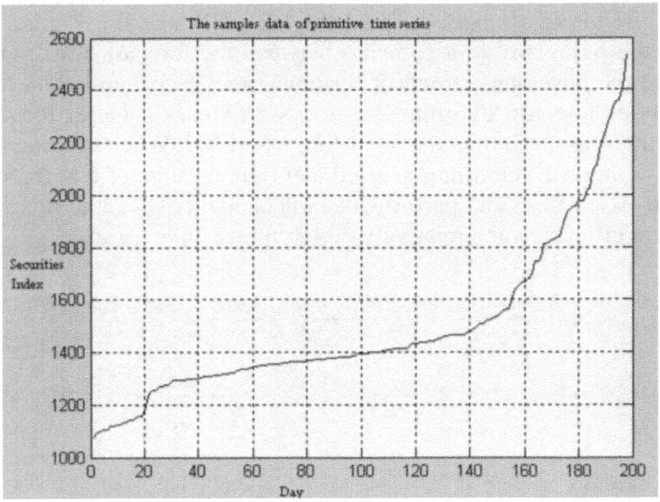

Fig. 1. original training sample time series diagram

4.2 Experimental Result and Analysis

By several times training to forecast model, we choose different training swatch, engender more appropriate training model, and then we forecast the data in several other days. We have got the following forecast effect by forecasting the last 25 AAA in the experiment(using Gauss core σ =2.75, e_k =0.001, γ =10)and have compared with the former forecast effect. From the forecast effect Table and we can see clearly that the time series forecast effect based on LS-SVM can approach actual index more exactly, from which we achieved comparatively approving forecast effect and less forecast error. But at the same time there are many complex factors influencing the actual securities index, so the forecast effect in some points are still far away from actual index. But all in one word, the time series forecast model based LS-SVM has more rapid speed and less training times, compared with traditional time series forecast

Table 1. Change of forecast error along with number of forecast days

Number of forecast days	3	5	10	15
MAPE	0.00795	0.00681	0.00372	0.00398
RMSE	0.00573	0.00603	0.00491	0.00447

methods the efficiency and precision of which are all have a farther improvement. The following figure is the contrast of forecast effect and factual conditions in last 15 days, the table lists the change of average error along with number of forecast days. We can see that forecast model had a good performance in long-term forecast.

In addition, for analyzing the validity of algorithm and model forecast, in experiment, we processed a contrast test with the time series forecast method based NN. Inside, the NN forecast model adopted the RBF NN to train. Figure 2 is gained as follows. In the figure we do a compare between the forecast effects of two forecast methods and the developing trend of Shanghai and Shenzhen index. It's easy to see that time series forecast algorithm based LS-SVM has a better forecast effect and more rapid training speed than the algorithm based NN. When training swatch is large in quantity or number, the training speed and training time of NN forecast are larger. The forecast based LS-SVM performed some characteristics like more rapid training speed, greater efficiency and relatively higher forecast precision.

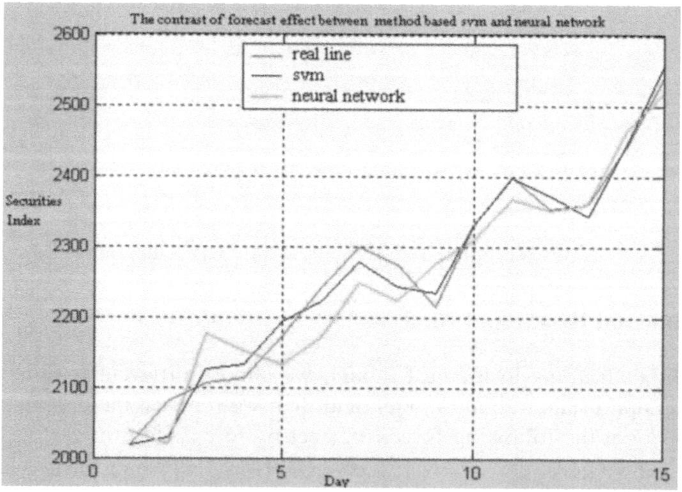

Fig. 2. Comparison of forecast effect between LS-SVM and NN

5 Summary

According to the time series prediction model based on the least squares support vector machines, LS-SVM changes the inequality constraint which is the traditional support vector machines to equality constraints, and the loss function of error square as a experience function of the training set, so the problem of the quadratic programming transforms the solution of linear equations, improving the speed and accuracy of convergence of solving the problem. Selecting the most appropriate samples makes the time series prediction of the stock index, analyzing the experimental results and data, the prediction algorithm has been more improved than other methods in training time and accuracy of forecast. it has carried on the contrast experiment with the forecast based on the nerve network in the experiment, and improved in training time, training speed, training errors, forecasting error and so on. So it fully proved the advantage of the support vector machine in the time prediction.

However, the data of securities stocks is a complex time-series, it affected by many factors, displaying nonlinear, high-noise and so on, the effect of forecasting may well describe the development of a longer-term trend. How to create dynamic forecasting model combining the various actual impact factors, better approach and fitting the actual development tendency, and provide the quite accurate forecast information for the financial user, it is still an important research topic.

Acknowledgement

The research is supported by the Science & Technology Development Projects of Suzhou (the Project No. ZXR0603).

References

1. Chung, F.-L., Fu, T.-C., Ng, V., Luk, R.W.P.: An evolutionary approach to pattern-based time series segmentation. IEEE Transactions on Evolutionary Computation 8, 471–489 (2004)
2. Struzik, Z., Sibes, A.: Measuring Time Series Similarity Through Large Singular Revealed with Wavelet Transformation. In: Proc Of the 10th Intl. Workshop on Database and Expert Systems Application, pp. 162–166 (1999)
3. Keogh, E., Kasetty, S.: On the Need for Time Series Data Mining Benchmarks: A Survey and Empirical Demonstration. In: Proceedings of the 8th ACM SIGKDD International Conference on Knowledge Discovery and Data Mining, ACM Press, New York (2002)
4. Das, G., Lin, K., Mannila, H.: Rule Discovery from Time Series. In: KDD'98, pp. 16–22 (1998)
5. Agrawal, R., Faloutsos, C., Swami, A.: Efficient similarity search insequence databases. In: Procs. Of the Fourth International Conference on Foundations of Data Organization and Algorithms (1993)
6. Breiman, L.: Classification and regression trees. Wadsworth Statistical Press, CA (1984)
7. Cao, L.J., Tay Francis, E.H.: Financial forecasting using support vector machines. Neural Computing & Applications 10, 184–192 (2001)
8. Vapnik, V.N.: Statistical Learning Theory NewYork. Springer, Heidelberg (1998)
9. Ma, Z.F., Feng, B.Q.: Support Vector Machines Learning for Adaptive and Active Information Retrieval. In: Yu, J.X., Lin, X., Lu, H., Zhang, Y. (eds.) APWeb 2004. LNCS, vol. 3007, pp. 89–99. Springer, Heidelberg (2004)

Location-Based Recommendation System Using Bayesian User's Preference Model in Mobile Devices

Moon-Hee Park, Jin-Hyuk Hong, and Sung-Bae Cho

Dept. of Computer Science, Yonsei University
Shinchon-dong, Seodaemun-ku,
Seoul 120-749, Korea
{moonypark,hjinh}@sclab.yonsei.ac.kr, sbcho@cs.yonsei.ac.kr

Abstract. As wireless communication advances, research on location-based services using mobile devices has attracted interest, which provides information and services related to user's physical location. As increasing information and services, it becomes difficult to find a proper service that reflects the individual preference at proper time. Due to the small screen of mobile devices and insufficiency of resources, personalized services and convenient user interface might be useful. In this paper, we propose a map-based personalized recommendation system which reflects user's preference modeled by Bayesian Networks (BN). The structure of BN is built by an expert while the parameter is learned from the dataset. The proposed system collects context information, location, time, weather, and user request from the mobile device and infers the most preferred item to provide an appropriate service by displaying onto the mini map.

1 Introduction

Recently, personalized techniques have been widely studied to automatically recommend or find customized information [1]. Personalized recommendation systems recommend an item to which a user prefers by using automatic information filtering method. Moreover, as mobile computing progresses, various resources can be available to model user preference. A Mobile device provides a user with information and services related to the physical location based on user's location. Since there are lots of information and services, it is difficult to find a proper service to one's preference at proper time.

In particular, such research has focused on user interface and location. The "MovieLens Unplugged" project [2] explores the usability of such recommender systems on devices with limited display and intermittent connectivity to the backend data store. Their focus is on improving the recommender interface for the mobile user. In this paper, we build a map-based recommendation system to overcome the limitation with mobile device such as small-size screen and interface.

2 Related Works

2.1 The Context and Recommendation in Mobile Environment

The context means information which can be a feature of environment such as time and a location. In context-aware computing restaurant recommendation [3,4], tour

J. Indulska et al. (Eds.): UIC 2007, LNCS 4611, pp. 1130–1139, 2007.

guide [5] and commercial recommendation[6] are serviced by using context information (location, ID and time). Geographical location represents where mobile device user stays [7]. Time is information related to system or service request [8]. ID means a current user of device. Due to the limitation of mobile device such as latency, users request a personalized service recommendation at proper situation. Mobile phone provides user with more direct recommendation through 'push' service using SMS or other interaction channel [9]. Recommendation and personalization in the mobile web have interest in the user preference based recommendation method [6]. Many researches define context in the mobile web and apply context information to recommend service and contents. The some of service recommendation system are summarized in Table 1.

Table 1. Context-aware recommendation systems

	MIT Media Lab	National Tsing Hua Univ.	Telematica Institute	Fu-Jen Univ.
Recommendation type	Restaurant	Restaurant	Travel information	Commercial
Context information	Location	Location, Time, Weather	Location, Time, Weather, Shopping list, Schedule	Location, Time, Fare, Contents
Recommendation method	Interaction between 2 agents	Search after requesting	Variable prediction strategy	Neural network learning
Device	PDA, GPS	Pocket PC, GPS	Mobile phone, GPS	Mobile phone

2.2 Recommendation Systems

Traditional recommendation systems use collaborative filtering to predict the rating of a product to a particular user. The general idea behind collaborative filtering is that similar users vote similarly on similar items. There are two major flavors of collaborative filtering [10]. Memory-based collaborative filtering, known as user-based collaborative filtering, these algorithms try to establish a correlation between users based on their voting pattern. Such correlation is dynamically computed among different groups of users whoever prediction is made. This puts big computational and memory loads on the system if the prediction is to be delivered in real time. For that reason, such systems do not scale particularly well for large datasets and are not popular in real applications [10]. Model-based collaborative filtering, known as item-based collaborative filtering, these algorithms are widely popular today and are used primarily because of their scalability with huge datasets. Instead of focusing on similarity between users, such systems compute the similarity between voted items [10].

Microsoft (MS) evaluated the algorithm for three separate datasets as follows [11]:

1. MS Web: individual visit to various areas of the MS web sites (visited or not).
2. Television: Neilsen network television view data for individuals for a two-week period (watched or not).
3. EachMovie: Collaborative filtering site deployed by Digital Equipment Research Center during 2 years (ranged in value from 0 to 5).

The dataset is applied to Bayesian networks, the correlation, Bayesian cluster and vector similarity, respectively. Bayesian networks and the correlation techniques showed the best performance [11]. In this paper, we implement BN-based recommendation system suitable for mobile environment that requires data processing in real time.

3 BN-Based Personalized Recommendation System

3.1 Overview

The proposed method consists of 3 parts as shown in Figure 1: context log collection, recommendation module and system mapping module. User profile and context information are collected by using mobile device. The collected context information is preprocessed to train the parameters of BN. We obtain CPT (conditional probability table) by EM algorithm with preprocessed context data. When a user requests a new demand, we select the highest probability parameter of each attribute the learned BN-model. We find the real information in accordance with the high-order data set through search of contents database. The proposed method is implemented for mobile devices to collect information and to provide a service.

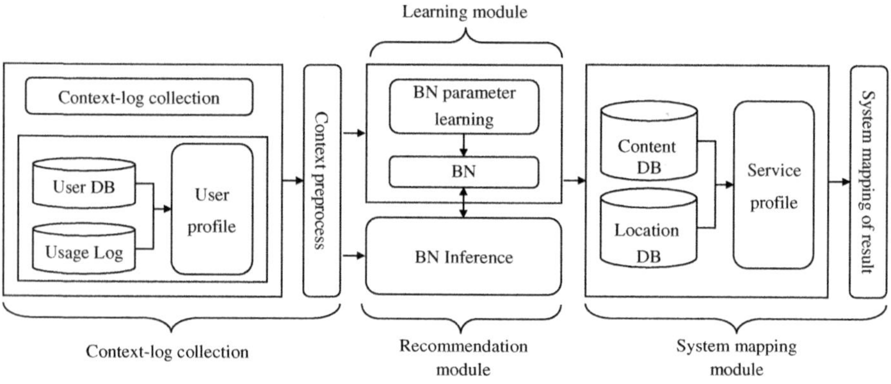

Fig. 1. The overview of the proposed system

3.2 Context Information

As shown in Figure 2, various kinds of context log information are used, including weather information, temperature and weather from web sites, and season, time of day, periods and user location collected from mobile devices. Some information such as user requests are collected directly from users through a mobile application implemented as shown in Figure 3. After preprocessing the context information collected by each device, we integrate each data file on the basis of the time.

3.3 Bayesian Network Based User Preference Model

BN were built by an expert as shown in Figure 4. In addition, Bayesian networks built by an expert cannot reflect a change of environment. To overcome this problem, we

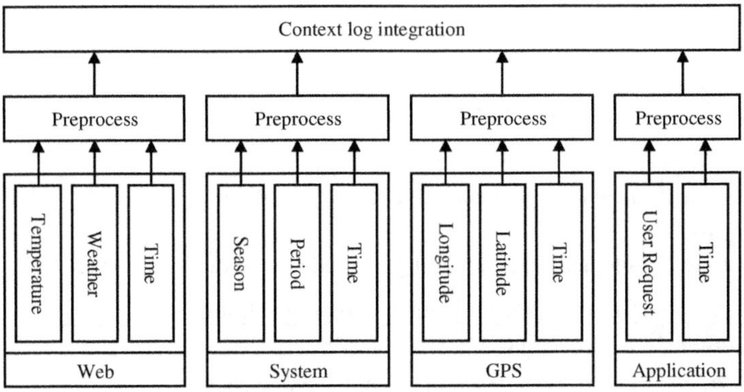

Fig. 2. Context log information

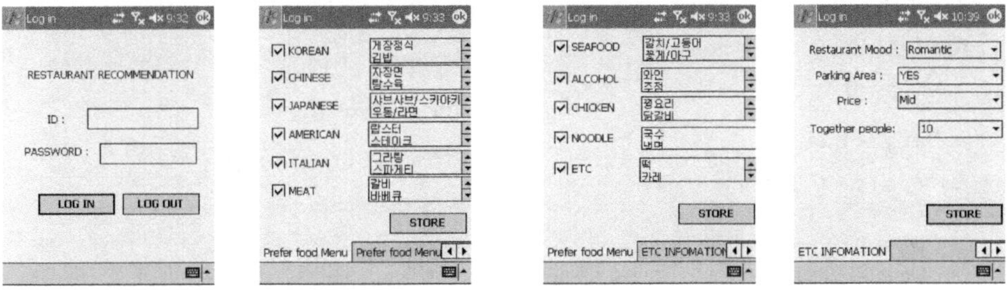

Fig. 3. Mobile application to collect context log information

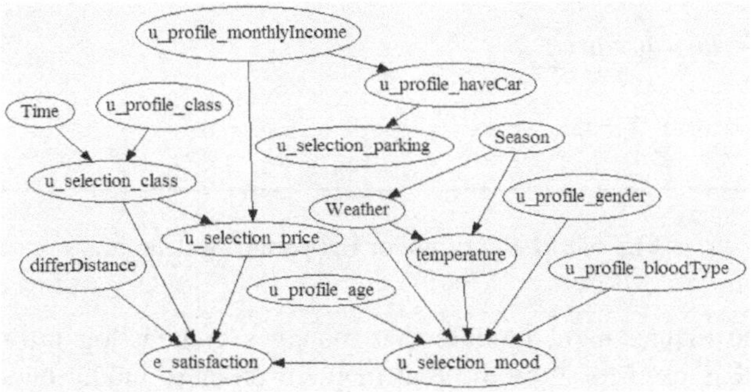

Fig. 4. BN structure for inferring user preference

apply a parameter learning technique. Based on collected data, CPTs are learned by using EM (Expectation Maximization) algorithm as shown in Figure 5.

3.4 Restaurant Recommendation

To overcome the limitation of display and resource of mobile devices, we have implemented map-based interface which is intuitive to user as shown in Figure 6. The implemented system consists of the user-input module that stores user's personal

Input:

k : # of clusters,

$Y=\{y_1, y_2, \cdots, y_n\}$: set of n p - *dimensional* points,

$\in$: a tolerance for loglikelihood,

max-iterations, maximum number of iterations.

Output:

C, R, W : the matrices containing the updated mixture parameters.

X : a matrix with cluster membership probabilities.

1.***Initialization***: Set initial values for C, R and W

2.***While:*** $\delta(llh) \rangle \in$ and *max-iteration* has not been reached

DO E and M steps

E step:

$C'=R'=W'=llh=0$

for $i=1$ **to** n

$\sum p_i = 0$

for $j=1$ **to** k

$\delta_{ij} = (y_i - C_j)^t R^{-1} (y_i - C_j)$

$$p_{ij} = \frac{w_j}{(2\pi)^{\frac{p}{2}} |R|^{\frac{1}{2}}} \exp(-\frac{1}{2}\delta_{ij})$$

$\sum p_i = \sum p_i + p_{ij}$

end-for

$x_i = \frac{p_i}{\sum p_i}$, $llh = llh + \ln(\sum p_i)$

$C' = C + y_i x_i^t$, $W' = W + x_i$

end-for

M step:

for $i=1$ **to** k

$C_j = \frac{C_j}{W_j}$

for $j=1$ **to** n

$R' = R' + (y_i - C_i) x_{ij} (y_i - C_j)^t$

end-for

end-for

$R = \frac{R'}{n}$, $W = \frac{W'}{n}$

Fig. 5. EM algorithm for BN parameter learning

profiles and the management module that manages content log information. Naver Map Open API is used to show the real map. In order to model personal traits, we collect user's general information such as name, gender, age, birthday, blood type, possesses of car and monthly income, and user's prefer food information. The management module embodies the ability to search, delete and update restaurant information so as to directly input through the map. Inference results are used to find proper restaurants and they are mapped on the map so that users can intuitively obtain information through the map.

In order to find proper restaurants, in this paper, we calculate the preference on restaurants based on the inference results of BN. A restaurant consists of three attributes

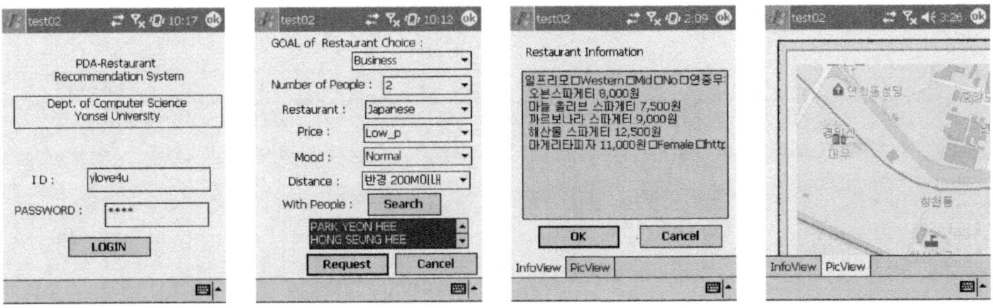

Fig. 6. The personalized recommendation system

such as class, price, and mood. The preference on a restaurant is calculated as the following formula.

$$X_{ijk} = (c_i \times w_{class}) + (p_j \times w_{price}) + (m_k \times w_{mood})$$
$$RecommendValue = \max_{i=1\cdots l,\, j=1\cdots m,\, k=1\cdots n}(X_{ijk}) \tag{1}$$

$Class = \{c_1, c_2, \cdots, c_l\}$, $Price = \{p_1, p_2, \cdots, p_m\}$, and $Mood = \{m_1, m_2, \cdots, m_n\}$ means the restaurant class probability, the price probability, and the mood probability, respectively, where $Weight = \{w_{class}, w_{price}, w_{mood}\}$ is the weight for the corresponding node. According to the results, several restaurants of high value are displayed on the map of the mobile application.

4 Experimental Results

4.1 Experimental Environment

In this paper, we used about the information of 50 restaurants [12] in the Shinchon area (870×500 ㎡). Current data were collected by 4 registered users for 7 days (11/1~11/7). We conducted the parameter learning through 7-fold cross validation. As shown in Table 2, user profile consists of age, gender, blood-type, possession of car, monthly income and food preference. Generally researches about preferences of food include traits of subjects for an experiment such as age, gender, occupation, economic strength and educational level [13]. We collected a possession of car to know parking area of recommended restaurants.

Table 3 shows the preprocessed data set which consists of context information such as time, user request, user profile, location and weather. Time is composed of season and period: the former includes with spring (March ~ May), summer (June ~ August), fall (September ~ November), and winter (December ~ February), and the latter includes with breakfast (3:00~11:00), lunch (11:00 ~18:00), and dinner (18:00~3:00). User requests are obtained from direct inputs which include restaurant class, mood, price and parking area. Location has three attributes such as Near (in 100m), Mid (in 200m), and Far (in 300m) according to user's current location. Weather represents Sunny, Rain, Cloudy and Snow according to the weather service on web. Temperature is categorized into Warm(13~20℃), Hot(20~30℃), Cool(7~13℃), and Cold(-5~7℃) [14].

Table 2. User profile information (K: Korean, J: Japanese, C: Chinese, A: American)

	user1	user2	user3	user4
Age	Mid-20	Early 30	Late 20	Early 30
Gender	Female	Female	Male	Male
Blood Type	B	AB	B	O
Own Car	No	Yes	No	Yes
Income (1,000won)	150~200	250~300	100~150	250~300
Prefer Food	K, J, C, A	K, J, A	K, J, C	K, J, C, A

Table 3. Collected log dataset

		Node	Value
Time		Season	Spring, Summer, Fall, Winter
		Time	Breakfast, Lunch, Dinner
User Request	Restaurant	Class	Korean, Japanese, Chinese, American, Italian, Etc
		Mood	Romantic, Tidy, Exotic, Normal
		Price	Low, Mid-Low, Mid, Mid-High, High
		Parking Area	Yes, No
User Profile		Preference	Korean, Japanese, Chinese, American, Italian, Etc
		Gender	Male, Female
		Age	10~19, 20~29, 30~39
		Own Car	Yes, No
		Income	100~150, 150~200, 200~250, 250~300
		Blood Type	A, B, AB, O
Location		DifferDistance	Near, Mid, Far
Weather		Weather	Sunny, Rain, Cloudy, Snow
		Temperature	Warm, Hot, Cool, Cold

4.2 Experimental Results

User-preference restaurant class, price and mood were inferred by the BN-model. Attribute probability distributions of nodes of time, user profiles, system information and weather are represented in Figure 7, which shows probability distributions about restaurant class, price and mood, respectively. Accordingly the system consists of probability distributions of are the highest attribute dataset, and then it recommends the most similar real data. For instance, user1 prefers Japanese class, Low-Mid price and Tidy mood in breakfast, Korean class, Low-Mid price and Romantic mood in lunch and American class, Low price and Romantic mood in dinner as showing Figure 7.

User1 prefers Japanese class, Low-Mid price and Tidy mood in breakfast, Korean class, Low-Mid price and Romantic mood in lunch and American class, Low price and Romantic mood in dinner. Table 4 shows the highest probability distribution set of each node in accordance with the user through calculation. Table 5 shows restaurants recommended to the user. In comparison with the result of Table 4 and Table 5, restaurant class items faithfully implemented for BN probability to infer correct

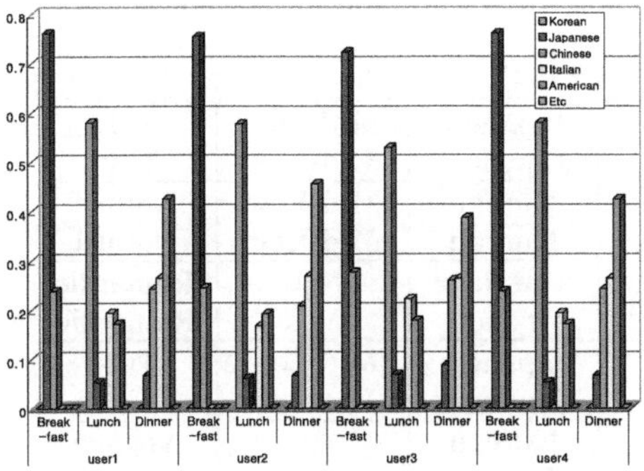

(a) recommended classes

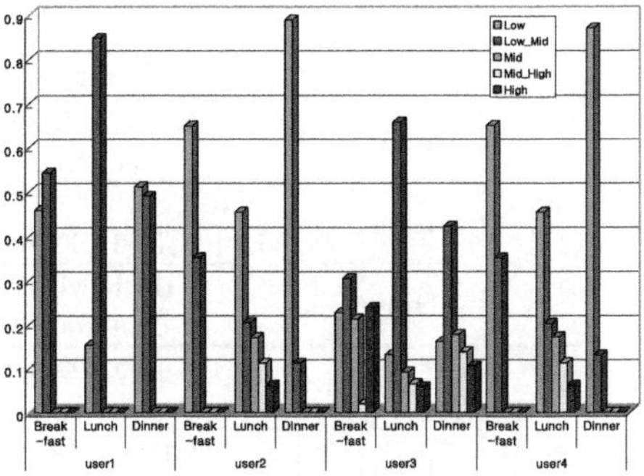

(b) recommended prices

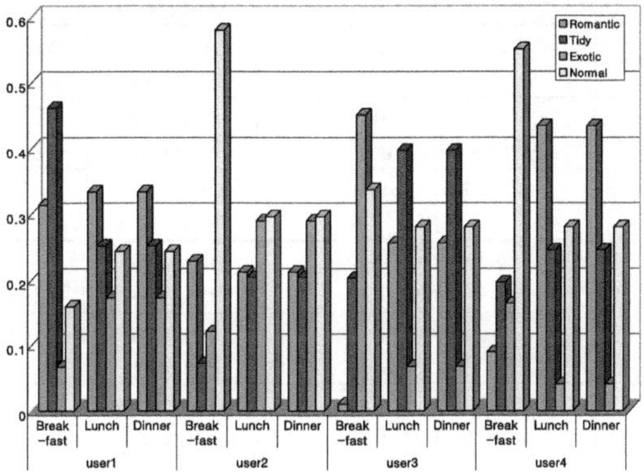

(c) recommended moods

Fig. 7. The probability distribution

Table 4. An example of recommended attributes to each user

		Restaurant class	R_price	R_mood
user 1	Breakfast	Japanese	Mid-Low	Tidy
	Lunch	Korean	Mid-Low	Romantic
	Dinner	American	Low	Romantic
user 2	Breakfast	Japanese	Low	Normal
	Lunch	Korean	Low	Normal
	Dinner	American	Low	Normal
user 3	Breakfast	Japanese	Mid-Low	Exotic
	Lunch	Korean	Mid-Low	Tidy
	Dinner	American	Mid-Low	Tidy
user 4	Breakfast	Japanese	Low	Normal
	Lunch	Korean	Low	Romantic
	Dinner	American	Low	Romantic

results. However, the price and mood are often the different from these of inferred data. Since the amount of content data accorded with the recommended attributes is few.

Table 5. The result of actual recommended restaurants (Upper 2 Ranking)

		R-Name	R-Class	R-Price	R-Mood
user 1	Breakfast	Kuma ZZang	**Japanese**	**Mid-Low**	**Tidy**
		Yoisis	**Japanese**	**Mid-Low**	**Tidy**
	Lunch	Nolbu BudeaZZiGe	**Korean**	**Mid-Low**	Normal
		HongCho Hot Chicken	**Korean**	**Mid-Low**	Normal
	Dinner	ILPRIMO	**American**	Mid	**Romantic**
		Net-Bar	Italian	Mid	**Romantic**
user 2	Breakfast	Kuma ZZang	**Japanese**	Mid-Low	Tidy
		Yoisis	**Japanese**	Mid-Low	Tidy
	Lunch	One Chicken	**Korean**	Mid	**Normal**
		GumTer	**Korean**	Mid-Low	**Normal**
	Dinner	Outback Steak	**American**	Mid	Exotic
		Uno	**American**	Mid	Exotic
user 3	Breakfast	Kuma ZZang	**Japanese**	**Mid-Low**	Tidy
		Yoisis	**Japanese**	**Mid-Low**	Tidy
	Lunch	Pumpkin	**Korean**	**Mid-Low**	**Tidy**
		Nolbu BudeaZZiGe	**Korean**	**Mid-Low**	Normal
	Dinner	Outback Steak	**American**	Mid	Exotic
		Uno	**America**	Mid	Exotic
user 4	Breakfast	Kuma ZZang	**Japanese**	Mid-Low	Tidy
		Yoisis	**Japanese**	Mid-Low	Tidy
	Lunch	GumTer	**Korean**	Mid-Low	Normal
		Pumpkin	**Korean**	Mid-Low	Tidy
	Dinner	ILPRIMO	**American**	Mid	**Romantic**
		Net-Bar	Italian	Mid	**Romantic**

5 Concluding Remarks

To overcome the limitation of display and resource of mobile devices, we implemented a map-based interface which is familiar to user. We proposed BN-based recommendation system reflecting user's preference using user profile and context information which can obtain from mobile devices.

For future works, we will verify the usefulness from usability tests, and enlarge the data set including the number of case samples as well as restaurants to confirm the stability.

Acknowledgement

This research was supported by MIC, Korea under ITRC IITA-2006-(C1090-0603-0046).

References

1. Sarwar, B.: Item-based collaborative filtering recommendation algorithms. In: WWW10 Conference, pp. 285–295 (2001)
2. Miller, B., Albert, I., Lam, S., Konstan, J., Riedl, J.: MovieLens unplugged: Experiences with a recommender system on four mobile devices. ACM Intelligent User Interfaces (IUI 03) (2003)

3. Tewari, G., Youll, J., Maes, P.: Personalized location-based brokering using an agent-based intermediary architecture. Decision Support Systems 34, 127–137 (2003)
4. Tung, H., Soo, V.: A personalized restaurant recommender agent for mobile e-service. In: IEEE International Conference on e-Technology. e-Commerce and e-Service (EEE'04), pp. 259–262 (2004)
5. Setten, M., Pokraev, S., Koolwaaij, J.: Context-aware recommendations in the mobile tourist application COMPASS. In: AH2004, pp. 235–244 (2004)
6. Yuan, S., Tsao, Y.: A recommendation mechanism for contextualized mobile advertising. Expert Systems with Applications 24, 399–414 (2003)
7. Lee, I., Kim, J., Kim, J.: Use contexts for the mobile internet: A longitudinal study monitoring actual use of mobile internet services. International Journal of Human-Computer Interaction 18, 269–292 (2005)
8. Hofer, T., Schwinger, W., Pichler, M., Leonhartsberger, G., Altmann, J.: Context-awareness on mobile devices: The hydrogen approach. In: The 36th Hawaii International Conference on System Sciences, vol. 9, pp. 292–301 (2003)
9. Ho, S., Kwok, S.: The attraction of personalized service for users in mobile commerce: An empirical study. ACM SIGecom Exchanges, 310–318 (2003)
10. Horozov, T., Narasimhan, N., Vasudevan, V.: Using location for personalized POI recommendations in mobile environments. In: SAINT 2006, pp. 124–129 (2006)
11. Breese, J., Heckerman, D., Kadie, C.: Empirical analysis of predictive algorithms for collaborative fitering. In: Poc. of the 14th UAI (1998)
12. http://www.cocofun.co.kr/
13. Cho, K.: A study on the relationship between lipid intake style and cardiovascular disease of the elderly. KHEA 40, 1–14 (2002)
14. http://www.kma.go.kr/intro.html

Fuzzy-Smith Control for QoS-Adaptive Notification Service

Yuying Wang and Xingshe Zhou

College of Computer Science, Northwestern Polytechnical University,
Xi'an 710072, P.R. China
wangyy@nwpu.edu.cn

Abstract. In this paper, a QoS-Adaptive Notification Service (QANS) scheme is proposed to prevent system overload, in which the Fuzzy-Smith control approach is applied. Different with traditional admission control, QANS adaptively adjusts the QoS level of task to control the service frequency of service provider by real-time monitoring the event channel. As a result, the system load is controlled and the performance of notification service is guaranteed. QANS is independent of the mathematical model of event channel and provides a non-linear control action, which eliminate the control error caused by inaccurate system model and linear assumption. Experimental results show that the proposed QANS scheme outperforms traditional event channel controllers in terms of system load control, response delay, and task miss-rate.

Keywords: Notification Service, QoS, Event Channel, Fuzzy control.

1 Introduction

Notification service [1,2], a kind of CORBA service defined by OMG, is widely used in distributed computing systems, such as web servers, e-commerce system, and so on, to provide interaction between consumer and service provider. Fig 1 shows a general logistic diagram of CORBA notification service.

The performance of notification service is very sensitive to event channel overload. When too many requests are sent to the server at the same time and cause event channel overload, not all requests can be served in a timely manner and some tasks are even postponed over their deadline. Therefore, overload avoiding mechanisms that prevent overload situation automatically while guarantee good service to consumer's requests when mass requests burst are major importance.

Admission control mechanism with PI controller [3] is a popular method to avoid event channel overload, which rejects the requests that can not be served before their deadline to reduce the burden of event channel. But system non-linearity and modeling inaccuracy are inherent problems of PI controller. To solve this problem, admission controller based on queuing-theoretic prediction [4,5] was used to deal with incoming requests. However, since predictions from queuing theory apply only long term averages, they do not handle transient behavior very well. In wide distributed computing systems, traditional PI controller

J. Indulska et al. (Eds.): UIC 2007, LNCS 4611, pp. 1140–1147, 2007.

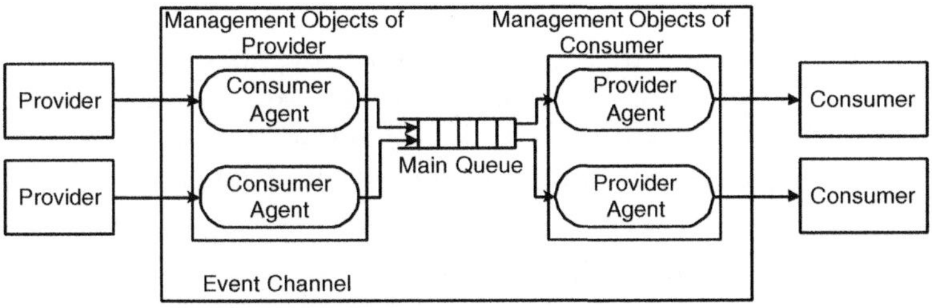

Fig. 1. Diagram of notification service

meets another problem, named large feedback delay, caused by large distance between consumer and service provider [6]. The performance of PI controller is damaged seriously when the information of consumer can not be feedback quickly. To solve this problem, Smith-PI controller [7] is applied, which uses Smith predictor to compensate the system feedback delay. All these approaches try to accommodate non-linearity and establish accurate mathematical model, but they can not solve this problem perfectly. Another disadvantage of admission control is that the requests of consumers maybe rejected when system is overload, which is not allowable in many computing systems, such as military control system, e-commerce.

This paper presents a new notification service scheme, called *QoS-adaptive notification service*(QANS), to prevent the event channel overload issue by applying a Fuzzy-Smith nonlinear controller. Different with traditional admission control, the QANS adjusts the QoS levels of requests to control the service frequency of service provider adaptively by real-time monitoring the data flow of event channel. As a result, the event channel load is controlled and the notification server could still provide its service for consumers though QoS levels of some tasks are reduced. Our approach provides the following benefits:

a) It is independent of the accurate model of event channel, which makes it very adequate for notification servers because of it's inherently nonlinearity.
b) The QoS of event services are adaptively adjusted according to the load of event channel to ensure the basic function of notification server.
c) The performance of our proposed Fuzzy-Smith controller is superior to the classical PI controller.

The rest of the paper is organized as follows. In Section 2, QoS-adaptive notification service approach is presented. The Fuzzy-Smith controller is designed in Section 3. The simulation results are documented and discussed in Section 4. In Section 5, conclusions are drawn.

2 QoS-Adaptive Notification Service

The key novelty of our QoS-adaptive event channel control lies on adjusting the QoS of requests dynamically according to the load of event channel to reduce the service frequency of service providers, and accordingly reduce the data flow of event channel. As a result, the event channel overload is avoided effectively and the basic service performance of notification server is guaranteed. In the proposed QANS system, a flexible task scheduling model and a Fuzzy-Smith controller are designed to control the load of event channel.

2.1 Flexible Task Scheduling Model

Our flexible task scheduling model is as follows. Let each task has n discrete job cycles, which could be adjusted with some degrees in period of system running. Task i denoted as $W_i(n, P_{i1}, P_{i2}, \ldots, P_{in})$, where n is the number of job cycles, P_{ij} is the No. j level of the job. Each job cycle corresponds to a QoS level of W_i. Small cycle period means high QoS level, while long cycle period means low QoS level. When the notification server receives too many tasks and can not process them in timely, it will degrade the QoS levels of tasks to ensure its basic service function. In this way, the load of event channel could be kept in safety state. On the other hand, if the event load is low, the QoS levels of tasks will be upgraded to enhance the service quality for consumer.

2.2 QoS-Adaptive Event Channel Feedback Control Framework

Fig 2 shows our QoS-adaptive event channel feedback control framework. It includes service provider, event channel, monitor, and Fuzzy-Smith controller modules.

- Event Channel

Event channel provides the interaction between consumer and service provider. It receives the requests of consumer and transmits them to the queue of service provider, while it sends back the service to consumers. Event channel separate the consumer and server such that the server is transparent to consumers.

- Service Provider

Service provider could provide differential services for consumers according to their requests. Only the requests in the service queue could be responded.

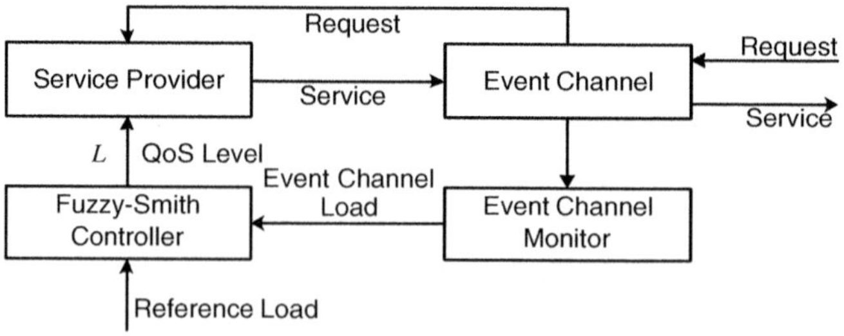

Fig. 2. QoS-adaptive event channel control framework

– Monitor

The monitor carries out the measurements of the data flow of event channel, and reports the event channel load to Fuzzy-Smith controller to control the service rate of server.

– Fuzzy-Smith Controller

The fuzzy-smith controller controls the QoS level L of tasks to reduce the request arrive-rate of service provider according to the difference between measured event channel load and the reference load.

3 Fuzzy-Smith Controller

3.1 Fuzzy-Smith Controller Architecture

Based on the mathematical model of a system, traditional controllers, such as PI controller and Smith-PI controller, use inputs to design control actions or analyze their effectiveness. These methods meet difficulties in event channel load control, since the accurate model of notification service system can not be established. Fuzzy control, introduced by Mamdani for control complex process [8], does not need an accurate mathematical model as PI controllers do. Instead, Fuzzy controllers facilitate incorporation of human expert knowledge on server tuning [9].

By integrating the benefits of Fuzzy control and Smith predictor, we obtain the Fuzzy-Smith controller for event channel load control, which does not need accurate system model and linearity assumption, and also overcomes the large feedback delay difficulty. Fig 3 shows the Fuzzy-Smith controller, where $G(s) = G_p(s)e^{-\tau s}$ is the trans-function of control object, $G_p(s)$ is the non-delay part of control object, and $G_\tau(s) = G_p(s)(1 - e^{-\tau s})$ is the Smith predictor.

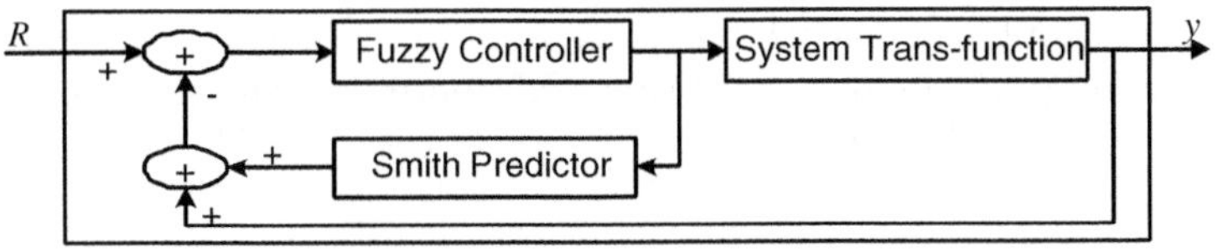

Fig. 3. Fuzzy-Smith Controller

3.2 Fuzzy-Smith Controller Design

Our proposed Fuzzy-Smith controller has two inputs: the difference between system load ρ and the reference load ρ_{ref} , denoted as E_U, and the change of E_U, denoted as EC_U. The output is the QoS level adjusting value of tasks, denoted as E_A.

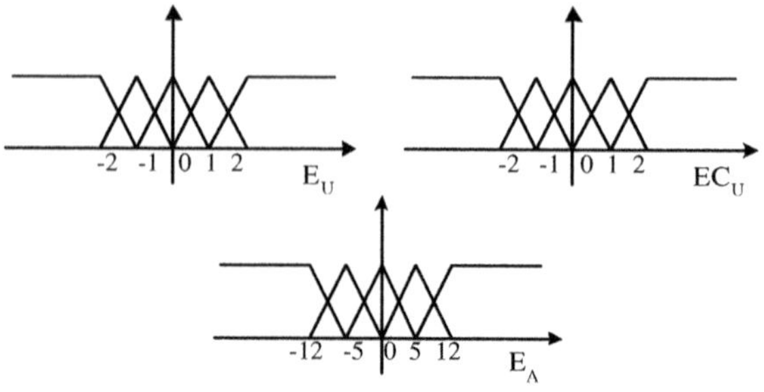

Fig. 4. Membership functions

The actions of the Fuzzy-Smith controller are guided by a rule set with linguistic **IF-THEN** rules, so called fuzzy rules. For example, 'IF A is NB and B is PB, THEN C is NB', where A and B are input linguistics variables, C is output linguistics variable, NB and PB are linguistic values. Linguistics variables take on a 'degree of truth' for each possible linguistic value. This is represented as a continuous value between 0 and 1, where 0 is FALSE, 1 is TRUE, and 0.5 indicates we are halfway certain. We use membership functions as Fig.4 to convert the value of numeric variables into linguistic values of linguistic variables, and do the reverse as well.

The model of the Fuzzy-Smith controller, comprising the control rules and the terms of the variables with their related fuzzy sets, was obtained through a tuning process that started from a set of initial insight consideration. Then we progressively modify the parameters of the system until it reaches level of performance considered to be adequate. Fig 4 shows our membership functions designed for the Fuzzy-Smith controller. For all E_U, EC_U and E_A, we have chosen seven term sets, which are negative big (NB), negative medium (NM), negative small (NS), zero (Z), positive big (PB), positive medium (PM), and positive small (PS). Table 1 describes all the 45 possible control rules. To design these rules, we apply the expert heuristics about our specific experiment system to produce good performance. Note that "X" represents the situation which will not occur (called dead area).

3.3 QoS Level Adjusting

When mass of requests arrive and the load of notification service system is heavy, the Fuzzy-Smith controller degrades the QoS levels of tasks with high QoS requirement in the queue at first to reduce the system load. If the server load is still higher than expected value, the Fuzzy-Smith controller will reduce the QoS levels of tasks with middle/low QoS requirement. These steps are repeated until the system load is in the safety value. Fuzzy-Smith controller not only prevents system overload, but also avoids tasks losing, since the deadline of task is postponed by reducing its QoS level.

Table 1. Fuzzy control rules

E_U \ EC_U	NB	NM	NS	Z	PS	PM	PB
PB	PB	PM	NM	NM	NB	NB	**X**
PM	PB	PM	NM	NM	NS	NS	**X**
PS	PB	PM	NS	NS	NS	NM	NB
Z	PB	PM	PS	Z	NS	NM	NB
NS	PB	PM	PS	PS	PS	NM	NB
NM	**X**	PB	PS	PS	PM	NM	NB
NB	**X**	PB	PB	PM	PM	NM	NB

4 Experiments and Discussions

In this section, the performance of the proposed QoS-adaptive notification service system is evaluated and compared with two traditional notification service systems with PI and Smith-PI admission controller respectively, in terms of system load, service delay, and target miss-rate.

The event channel is simulated with the RTSMT discrete event simulator (M/M/1 queue, EDF scheduling method). Fig 5 is the model of our event channel, including four parts: S-RPC (the RPC time in the service end), C-RPC (the RPC time in the consumer end), S-Filter (the filters in the service end), C-Filter (the filters in the consumer end). The event filters open door only for the qualified requests, but holds back the unwarranted events. When EDF schedule method is applied, the delay time of each part in event channel model is described in Table 2. The total time delay of a task in the event channel is the summation of S-filter and C-filter processing time.

To evaluate the overload control capability of the proposed Fuzzy-Smith controller, burst requests is created during normal notification service state, which tries to push the system into overload situation. In the first 39 time unit, we create

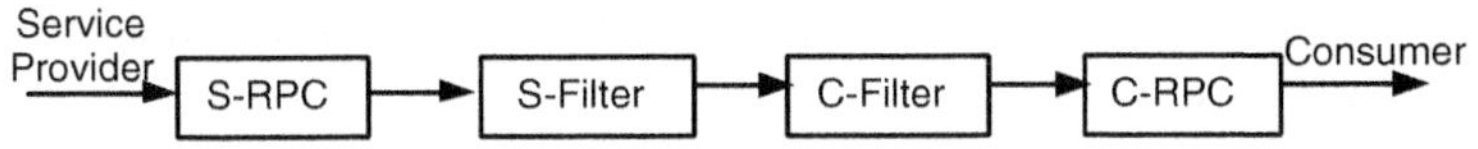

Fig. 5. Event channel model

Table 2. Parameters of event channel

Item	S-RPC	S-filter	C-filter	C-RPC
Time	0.98s	1/143.9s	1/66.9s	0.98s

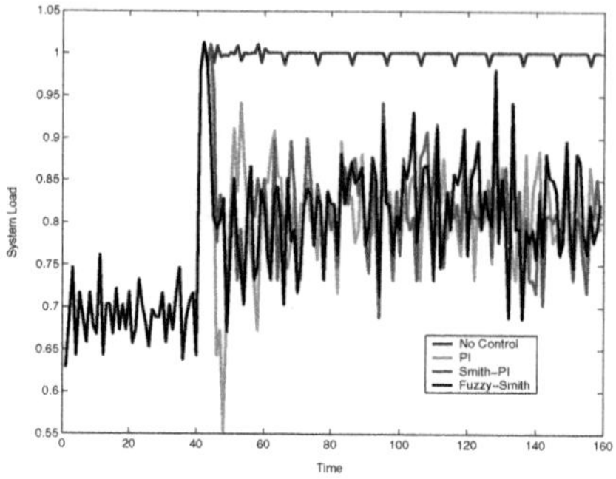

Fig. 6. System load comparing

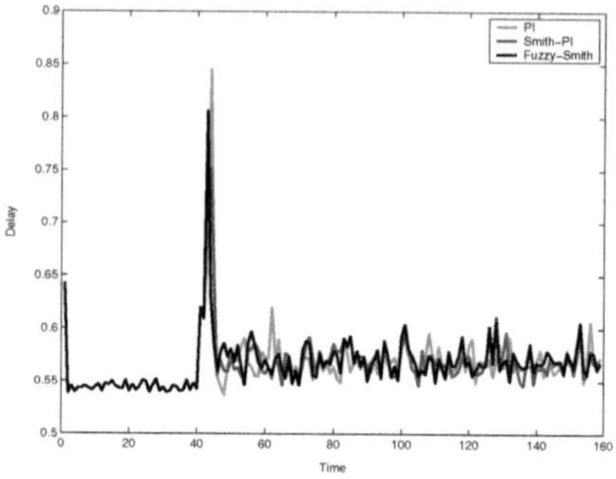

Fig. 7. Response delay comparing

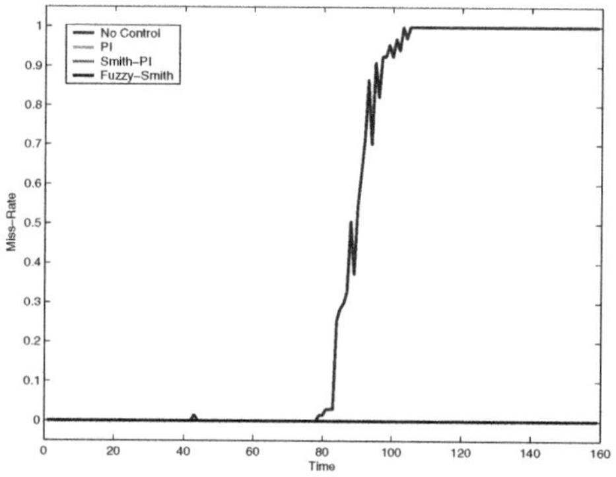

Fig. 8. System miss-rate comparing

50 periodical tasks with the periods 0.42, 0.44, 0.46 . . . , respectively. Their initial QoS levels are set as 3. After 40 time unit, we create 10 periodical tasks with 0.4 periods. Their initial QoS level is 2. The reference load $\rho_{ref} = 0.8$. By using Ziegler-Nichols method, we obtain the control parameters for PI and Smith-PI controller: $K_p = 0.9037$, $K_I = 0.0813$, sampling periods is $1s$, time delay $T_d = 0.98s$.

Four kinds of notification service systems, including no admission controller, PI controller, Smith-PI controller, and Fuzzy-Smith controller, respectively, are compared in our experiments.

Fig 6 compares the load control capability of the four notification service systems. We can see that the notification server without any admission control mechanism suffers overload after 40 time unit, while the systems with PI, Smith-PI, and Fuzzy-Smith controllers could keep the system load around the reference load 0.8. Comparing with the PI and Smith-PI controllers, the Fuzzy-Smith controller produces smaller load variation around the reference value.

Fig 7 compares the delay time of the PI, Smith-PI, and Fuzzy-Smith controllers. Fuzzy-Smith controller outputs the smallest delay time on 40 time unit, when burst requests arrive. Since the notification service system without any admission controller is overload after 40 time unit, it is too busy to provide any service for new requests. Therefore, its delay time is increasing very fast and is much greater than the other three servers.

Fig 8 compares the task miss-rate of the four systems. It is clear that the system without controller lost more and more tasks after 40 time unit. The system without controller does not response any request nearly after 100 time unit. Since the notification service systems with PI, Smith-PI and Fuzzy-Smith controller could prevent system overload successfully, the three systems do not lost any tasks even events burst.

5 Conclusion

We have developed a novel QoS-adaptive notification service system, which applies a Fuzzy-Smith controller to monitor the system load and adjust QoS level of tasks adaptively to control system load. Different with traditional admission control, our approach prevent system overload by reducing the QoS level of tasks, but not reject consumer's requests. The other advantage of the method is that it is independent of the mathematical model and provides a non-linear control action, which eliminates the control error caused by inaccurate system model. This benefit comes from fuzzy control algorithm. Experimental results show that the Fuzzy-Smith controller could prevent system overload efficiently.

References

1. PrismTech: Openfusion notification service: Performance evaluation. Website (2001), `http://www.prismtechnologies.com`
2. Gore, P., Schmidt, D., Gill, C., Pyarali, I.: The design and performance of a real-time notification service. In: Proceedings of the 10th IEEE Real-Time and Embedded Technology and Applications Symposium, pp. 112–120. IEEE Computer Society Press, Los Alamitos (2004)
3. O'Ryan, C., Schmidt, D.C.: The design and performance of real-time CORBA event and notification services. In: OMG Second Workshop on Real-time and Embedded Distributed Object Computing (2001)
4. Lee, W., Sabata, B.: Admission control and QoS negotiations for soft-real time applications. In: ICMCS, vol. 1, pp. 147–152 (1999)
5. Abdelzaher, T.F., Shin, K.G., Bhatti, N.: Performance guarantees for Web server end-systems: A control-theoretical approach. IEEE Transactions on Parallel and Distributed Systems 13, 80–96 (2002)
6. Lu, C., Abdelzaher, T.F., Stankovic, J.A., Son, S.H.: A feedback control architecture and design methodology for service delay guarantees in web servers. Technical report, Charlottesville, VA, USA (2001)
7. Xiaoan, S.: Control Theory-based Adaptive Real-Time Resource Management. PhD thesis, Northwestern Polytechnical University, Xi'an, PRC (2005)
8. Mamdani, E.H.: Application of fuzzy algorithm for control of simple dynamic plant. Proc. IEEE 12(12), 1585–1588 (1974)
9. Fatta, G.D., Re, G.L., Urso, A.: A fuzzy approach for the network congestion problem. In: ICCS 2002. LNCS, pp. 286–295. Springer, Heidelberg (2002)

Petri Nets for the Verification of Ubiquitous Systems with Transient Secure Association*

Fernando Rosa-Velardo

Dpto. de Sistemas Informáticos y Computación
Universidad Complutense de Madrid
fernandorosa@sip.ucm.es

Abstract. *Transient Secure Association* has been widely accepted as a possible alternative to traditional authentication in the context of Ubiquitous Computing. We develop a formal model for the *Resurrecting Duckling Policy* that implements it, called TSA systems, which is based on Petri Nets, thus obtaining amenable graphical representations of our systems. We prove that TSA specifications have the same expressive power as P/T nets, so that coverability, that can be used to specify security properties, is decidable for TSA systems. Then we address the problem of implementing TSA systems with a lower level model that only relies on the secure exchange of keys. If we view these systems as closed then our implementation is still equivalent to P/T nets. However, if we consider an open framework then we need a mechanism of fresh name creation to get a correct implementation. This last model is not equivalent to P/T nets, but the coverability problem is still decidable for them.

1 Introduction

The term *Ubiquitous Computing* was coined by Mark Weiser [18] to describe environments full of devices that compute and communicate with its surrounding context and, furthermore, interact with it in a highly distributed but pervasive way. This paradigm gives rise to new problems, in the context of mobility, coordination and security, among others [8]. The new framework of ubiquitous computing affects traditional security assumptions. Authentication is probably the major security problem for ubiquitous systems, since it is a precondition for other properties as confidentiality or integrity. But in this new context, we can no longer rely on an always online policy, due to the unreliable nature of ad hoc nets. Thus, we cannot approach the problem of authentication by assuming the existence of an online server that verifies in real time the (global) identity of principals, nor the existence of public key repositories.

In order to solve this problem, several weak forms of authentication that substitute global identity-based authentication have been proposed. One of the proposals is that of *Transient Secure Association*, implemented by the *Resurrecting Duckling Policy* [16]. This policy is based on the fact that sometimes a

* Work partially supported by the Spanish projects DESAFIOS TIN2006-15660-C02-02, WEST TIN2006-15578-C02-01 and PROMESAS-CAM S-0505/TIC/0407.

J. Indulska et al. (Eds.): UIC 2007, LNCS 4611, pp. 1148–1158, 2007.

principal may not know anything at all about some concrete device (e.g., when a user has just bought a PDA), but still it wants to be the only one to use it (e.g., because she is the first one who gets to push the button). In this case, even if they have no prior knowledge of each other, they can still become associated, so that from then on they share an asymmetric relation, one being a slave and the other becoming its master. Other proposals are based on the notion of *trust* [2].

Another issue of great importance in the field of ubiquitous computing is that of Coordination. Indeed, inherent to ubiquitous computing is the continuous change of state of the different components that form a system, that need to coordinate to achieve their goals. This fact, together with the unreliable nature of ad hoc nets and the heterogeneity of the components make the orchestration approach unrealistic and little robust, so that a choreographic coordination is more advisable. Therefore, a key technology is service discovery, which nowadays is based on a heavy standardization [10] (as in Sun's Jini or in Microsoft's UPnP).

In this paper we develop a formal model for choreographic coordination in ubiquitous systems, with primitives implementing the resurrecting duckling policy. The model, called TSA, is based on Petri nets. By using Petri Nets we obtain an amenable graphical representation of our systems, together with a number of theoretical results for their analysis, which would not hold in other more expressive models. In particular, we will prove that TSA specifications can be seen as a syntactic sugar formalism for P/T nets. Moreover, we will see that we can implement TSA systems by means of Mobile Synchronizing Petri Nets, which can be seen as a class of Coloured Petri Nets [6] with a single colour of pure names, and syntactic sugar for mobility, except for the fact that they can create fresh names, in a way borrowed from π-calculus [7]. We have proved several useful decidability results for them, which are inherited by TSA systems, even though TSA systems may represent infinite state systems. In particular, decidability of coverability in MSPN system implies that all the properties of TSA systems which can be stated in terms of coverability are decidable. For an extended version of this work see [15].

2 The Resurrecting Duckling Policy

Let us briefly describe Transient Secure association and the Resurrecting Duckling security policy model. Transient secure association is about creating a link between two components, that establishes a master-slave relationship (typically between a controller and a peripheral). This link needs to be secure, so that no other principal can play the role of either the master or the slave. This produces a tree topology of master-slave relationships between components. The association must also be transient, in the sense that the topology can change if desired (by the master) along the execution of the system.

The Resurrecting Duckling policy model implements transient secure association with the following metaphor: *A duckling that emerges from its egg recognizes as its mother the first moving object that emits a sound.* From then on, the duckling obeys its mother duck until its death. Similarly, a peripheral can recognize as its mother duck the first entity that sends it a secret key, called *imprinting key*, which it will use to recognize its master. In order to make this association transient, we assume that the duckling can die and resurrect, and then it can recognize as its mother duck a different entity, to which it will be faithful from that point on. The policy can be described as a list of four principles:

1. **Two State principle.** Entities can be either *imprintable* (dead) or *imprinted* (alive). Imprintable entities can be imprinted by anyone and imprinted entities only obey their mother duck.
2. **Imprinting principle.** The step from imprintable to imprinted is called *imprinting*, and happens when an entity, from now on the mother duck, sends a key to the duckling.
3. **Death principle.** The step from imprinted to imprintable is called *death*. The default cause of death is the mother duck's order to its duckling to commit *seppuku*, though other causes are envisaged.
4. **Assassination principle.** It must be uneconomical for an attacker to kill a duckling (to cause its death).

3 TSA Systems

Our aim is to define a model for ubiquitous systems, that we call TSA, based on Petri Nets and with primitives implementing the Resurrecting Duckling policy. It will be a variation of the one developed in [4]. A TSA system is essentially a set of localized nets that can move between locations and can imprint other nets, give orders to the nets they have previously imprinted, kill those nets, and been imprinted or receive orders from its master when imprinted.

We assume that the different components of a system have a type, taken from a set $\mathcal{O}$. We use a special type $\top \in \mathcal{O}$ for the type of components that need not be imprinted to be alive (e.g., users). Components can be dead or alive. Top or imprinted components are alive, otherwise they are dead. Alive components can imprint dead ones, thus creating an unique and asymmetrical link between them. From then on the imprinted component becomes a slave of the other, doing everything its master orders to it. However, when executing its code, the slave component can as well imprint other components, thus creating a hierarchical relation between components. Therefore, not only the component been killed becomes death, but also all of its slaves and so on, recursively.

We assume that components can only be imprinted within a certain range, that depends on the imprinting method being used (e.g., physical contact). We abstract from those particular methods and simply assume that the imprinting can take place whenever both components are in the same location. In particular, we assume that the key exchange that takes place when imprinting a component is done in a secure way. Besides, a component can only give orders to those slave components that are currently co-located with it.

Dually, a slave component can be killed by its owner only when they are co-located. Thus, we are implementing the default variant of the death principle, in which the death of the duckling is caused by the mother duck.

We will use the set $\mathcal{L}$, a set of location names. $\mathcal{O}$ is a set of component types, with a special element $\top \in \mathcal{O}$. We use a set S for the syntactic primitives of the standard used for coordination and $\mathcal{A}$ to denote autonomous actions. $\mathcal{A}$ contains among others the labels *go* k for every $k \in \mathcal{L}$. We denote $S? = \{s? \mid s \in S\}$ and $S! = \{s! \mid s \in S\}$. For $m > 0$, we denote by $Labels(m)$ the set $\mathcal{A} \cup S? \cup \bigcup_{i=1}^{m}(\{i\} \times Labels_{Auth})$, where $Labels_{Auth} = S! \cup \{imprint(o) \mid o \in \mathcal{O} \setminus \{\top\}\} \cup \{kill\}$.

Definition 1. *A TSA component is a tuple* $N = (P_N, T_N, F_N, \lambda_N, o_N)$ *such that* P_N *and* T_N *are disjoint finite set of places and transitions, respectively,* $F_N \subseteq (P_N \times T_N) \cup (T_N \times P_N)$, $\lambda_N : T_N \to Labels(m)$ *for some* $m > 0$ *and* $o_N \in \mathcal{O}$. *We say that* N *has type* o_N, *that* m *is the capacity of* N, *and we denote by* $cap(N)$ *the set* $\{1, \ldots, m\}$.

A TSA component is a typed-labelled Petri net. The capacity of a component represents the number of slaves it can have simultaneously imprinted. Its type o is just a syntactic category, which can be intuitively understood as the type of device it is (e.g., PDA, electronic note,...), as the imprinting protocol it uses when been imprinted or both simultaneously. The labelling of the transitions of the net establishes a partition in its transition set: Those transitions t with $\lambda(t) \in \mathcal{A}$ are autonomous transitions, that is, those that can be executed in an autonomous way, without needing to synchronize with others; If $\lambda(t) \in S?$ the transition is used to receive orders from their masters, when imprinted; Otherwise, we have that $\lambda(t) \in \{i\} \times Labels_{Auth}$. In this case the transition is used to *communicate* with its i-slave. If some net fires t with $\lambda(t) = (i, imprint(o))$ then some component of type o is henceforth a i-slave of it. If $\lambda(t) = (i, s!)$ then the firing of t instructs the corresponding slave to perform action $s?$. Finally, if $\lambda(t) = (i, kill)$ then its i-slave is instructed to commit seppuku. Given a transition t we will denote by ${}^\bullet t = \{p \mid (p, t) \in F\}$, the set of preconditions of t and by $t^\bullet = \{p \mid (t, p) \in F\}$, its set of postconditions. If $cap(N) = \{1\}$ and $\lambda(t) = (1, \ell)$ we simply write $\lambda(t) = \ell$.

Definition 2. *A TSA system* $\mathcal{N}$ *is a set of pairwise disjoint TSA components.*

Intuitively, the nets N with $o_N = \top$ are components that need not be imprinted in order to execute their actions. We will denote by $P_{\mathcal{N}}$ the set of all places in $\mathcal{N}$ and by $T_{\mathcal{N}}$ the set of all transitions in $\mathcal{N}$, or just P and T when there is no confusion. Next we define the part of the state of the system regarding the dependency relations between its components.

Definition 3. *Given a TSA system* $\mathcal{N}$, *a dependency function of* $\mathcal{N}$ *is a partial mapping* $R : \{(N, j) \mid N \in \mathcal{N}, j \in cap(N)\} \to \mathcal{N}$. *A dependency function* R *induces a dependency graph* $G(R)$ *with set of nodes* $\mathcal{N}$ *and an arc from* N *to* N' *labelled by* j *if* $R(N, j) = N'$, *and we say that* N' *is a* j*-slave of* N *in* R.

We will call *directed tree* to any directed graph in which there is a node, that we call *root* of the tree, so that for every node in the graph there is a single path from the root to it. Therefore, a *directed forest* is a set of directed trees. Given two nodes s and s' of a directed forest, we will say s' is a descendant of s if there is a path in the forest from s to s'. Moreover, given a set A we will denote by $\mathcal{MS}(A)$ the set of multisets with elements in A.

Definition 4. *A marking of a TSA* $\mathcal{N}$ *is a tuple* $\mathcal{M} = (M, loc, R)$, *where* $M \in \mathcal{MS}(P_{\mathcal{N}})$, $loc : \mathcal{N} \to \mathcal{L}$ *and* R *is a dependency function of* $\mathcal{N}$ *such that* $G(R)$ *is a directed forest and for every* $N \in \mathcal{N}$, *if* $o_N = \top$ *then* N *is not a slave in* R.

Therefore, a marking is composed by an ordinary marking for Petri nets, a function specifying the locality of each component, and a dependency function. We say N is alive in R if $o_N = \top$ or it is a slave in R. Otherwise, we say it is dead. The components N and N' are co-located if $loc(N) = loc(N')$.

Now let us define the behaviour of TSA systems. In general, only alive components can fire transitions. Next we define the firing of autonomous transitions, that are as ordinary transitions in P/T nets, that remove tokens from precondition and add them in postconditions, except that they are restricted to alive components and can cause the movement of the executing net. We will denote by $+$ and $-$ the multiset union and the multiset difference, respectively.

Definition 5. *Let* $\mathcal{N}$ *be a TSA system,* $\mathcal{M} = (M, loc, R)$ *a marking of* $\mathcal{N}$, N *an alive component in* R, *and* $t \in T_N$ *such that* $\lambda(t) \in \mathcal{A}$. *We say that* t *is enabled in* $\mathcal{M}$ *if* ${}^\bullet t \subseteq M$. *In that case we say that* t *can be fired and then the marking* (M', loc', R) *is reached, where* $M' = M - {}^\bullet t + t^\bullet$. *If* $\lambda(t) = go\ k$ *then* $loc'(N) = k$ *and* $loc'(N) = loc(N)$ *for every* $N' \neq N$. *Otherwise,* $loc' = loc$.

Now we define the firing of imprinting transitions. The net firing any of them specifies the type it wants to imprint.

Definition 6. *Let* $\mathcal{N}$ *be a TSA system,* $\mathcal{M} = (M, loc, R)$ *a marking of* $\mathcal{N}$, N *and* N' *an alive and a dead component in* R, *respectively, both co-located, and* $t \in T_N$ *such that* $\lambda(t) = (i, imprint(o_{N'}))$. *We say that* t *is enabled in* $\mathcal{M}$ *if* ${}^\bullet t \subseteq M$ *and* $(N, i) \notin Dom(R)$. *Then* t *can be fired, to reach the marking* (M', loc, R'), *where* $M' = M - {}^\bullet t + t^\bullet$ *and* R' *extends* R *with* $R'(N, i) = N'$.

The imprinted net must be dead in order to be imprinted, and of the type required by the imprinting component. Moreover, the imprinting net must not already have an i-slave net. Now we define orders from masters to slaves.

Definition 7. *Let* $\mathcal{N}$ *be a TSA system,* $\mathcal{M} = (M, loc, R)$ *a marking of* $\mathcal{N}$, N *and* N' *two co-located alive components such that* N' *is a* i*-slave of* N *in* R. *Let us also consider* $t \in T_N$ *such* $\lambda(t) = (i, s!)$ *and* $t' \in T_{N'}$ *such that* $\lambda(t') = s?$. *We say that the pair of transitions* (t, t') *is enabled in* $\mathcal{M}$ *if* ${}^\bullet t + {}^\bullet t' \subseteq M$. *Then the pair* (t, t') *can be fired, getting* (M', loc, R) *where* $M' = M - {}^\bullet t - {}^\bullet t' + t^\bullet + t'^\bullet$.

Therefore, if N' is an i-slave of N then N can give orders to N', which is formalized by a synchronous firing of two transitions. Finally, let us define how a master can kill one of its slaves.

Definition 8. *Let* $\mathcal{N}$ *be a TSA system,* $\mathcal{M} = (M, loc, R)$ *a marking of* $\mathcal{N}$, N *and* N' *two co-located alive components such that* N' *is a* i*-slave of* N, *and* $t \in T_N$

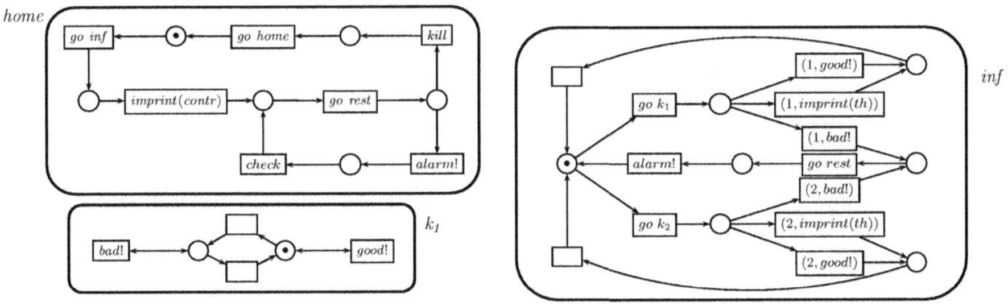

Fig. 1. Nurse (up left), thermometer controllers (right) and patients (down left)

such $\lambda(t) = (i, kill)$. *We say that* t *is enabled in* $\mathcal{M}$ *if* ${}^\bullet t \subseteq M$. *Then* t *can be fired, getting* (M', loc, R') *where* $M' = M - {}^\bullet t + t^\bullet$ *and* R' *is the result of removing* (N, i) *from the domain of* R*, and removing* $(\overline{N}, j)$ *from the domain of* R*, for every* $\overline{N}$ *descendant of* N' *in* $G(R)$ *and every* j.

Reachability for TSA systems is defined as expected. We say a marking (M, loc, R) can be covered if there is a reachable marking (M', loc', R') such that $M \subseteq M'$, $loc = loc'$, $Dom(R) \subseteq Dom(R')$ and for every $(N, i) \in Dom(R)$, $R(N, i) = R'(N, i)$. The coverability problem consists on deciding if a given marking can be covered.

4 An Application Example

In this section we present a simple application example to illustrate the definitions in the previous section. Let us consider a scenario with several patients in two rooms of a hospital, called k_1 and k_2. Each of the patients has an electronic thermometer [17] that reads the temperature every once in a while, and willing to send (e.g., using RFID) a message stating whether everything is all right or not. We assume that these thermometers are inactive (that is, dead according to our terminology), except when a thermometer controller takes over them. Intuitively, we assume that every room has one of these controllers, that reads the messages output by thermometers, and sends an alarm message to a nurse whenever the temperature is not correct. For simplicity, we assume that all these controllers are in fact part of a single component that moves between rooms in the hospital and that it can only simultaneously control two thermometers, so that it has capacity two. Finally, there is a night shift nurse, that must check the temperature of the patients. For that purpose, it may imprint a controller, so that she is the only one to receive alarm messages from it. Therefore, the life cycle of a night-shift nurse consists on going from her home to the infirmary, imprinting a thermometer controller, going to rest, checking the patient in case she receives an alarm message, or killing the controller and going back home.

We model this scenario by means of a TSA system with several components (see Fig. 1). The first one represents the nurse, that we assume has type $\top$. Initially, it is located in location *home*. Then it can fire *go inf*, thus moving to

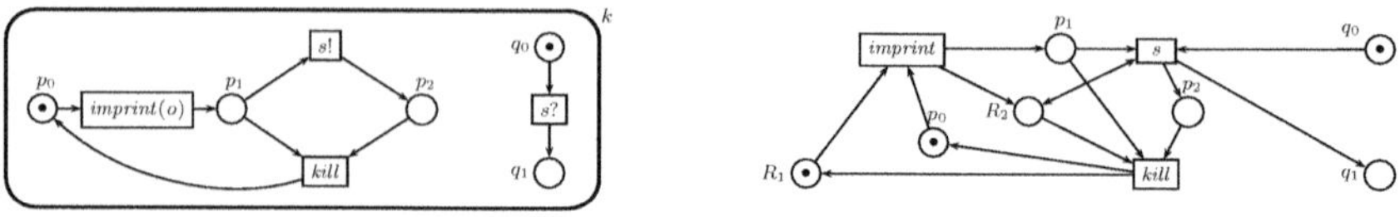

Fig. 2. Example of TSA system (left) and P/T net that simulates it (right)

the infirmary, where it can imprint the thermometer controller and then go to rest. Notice that, since the nurse has capacity one, we use simple names as labels of its synchronizing transitions, such as *kill*, instead of $(1, \mathit{kill})$.

The thermometer controller, with type *contr*, is initially in location *inf*. The controller, however, does not have a $\top$ type, so that it must wait to be imprinted to perform any action. After been imprinted, it can go either to location k_1 or to k_2. In these locations there are patients. Now the controller has a choice between *good*!, *bad*! or *imprint*(th). However, since the patient thermometers are still dead (in our sense), all the controller can do at the present time is imprinting them. Then it can again choose between any of the locations. If it goes back again to the same place then it can read the thermometer and, if it reads *bad*, that is, if it synchronizes with the thermometer in transition *bad*!, then it goes to the resting room and sends an alarm message to the nurse.

Eventually, the system will reach a dependency state in which both thermometers are imprinted by the controller. At any point, the nurse can fire its *kill* transition, thus killing the controller (and, recursively, the controller killing its thermometers). Notice that the controller does not have any killing transition, so that it only kills its thermometers when the nurse kills it.

5 Verification of TSA Systems

In the previous sections we have presented a model that allows us to specify systems using primitives that implement the resurrecting duckling policy, which are correct by definition. In this section we will see how we can use the known decidability results for the verification of the obtained TSA systems.

First of all, we will prove that the locality component of TSAs is not essential in the model. More precisely, we will say a TSA system is centralized if none of its components have movement transitions and all of them are initially located in the same location. Under these assumptions, we can ignore the locality component of centralized TSA systems, thus writing just (M, R) instead of (M, loc, R).

Lemma 1. *Every TSA system can be simulated by a centralized TSA system.*

Therefore, in the following we can assume that every TSA system is centralized. Now, we prove that every TSA system can be simulated by a P/T net.

Proposition 1. *Every TSA system can be simulated by a P/T net.*

The proof is based on the fact that, since the TSA system is considered as closed, the number of components is fixed in the initial state and, therefore, the

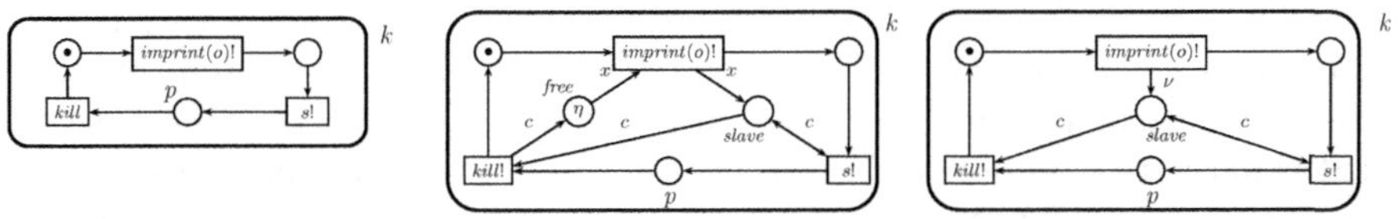

Fig. 3. TSA system (left), implementation (center) and open implementation (right)

number of dependency functions is finite. Figure 2 shows the P/T net (right) that simulates the TSA system in the left.

By applying this result, we can use all the existing machinery for ordinary P/T nets in the analysis of our systems. For instance, coverability and home state problems are known to be decidable for P/T nets (for a survey see [3]). Then, in principle, we could algorithmically check any property that can be stated in terms of them. For example, regarding the example in the previous section, we could check that, whenever a thermometer is imprinted by a doctor, then whenever needed it eventually raises the alarm, and only to the right doctor, since that is a home state property. Another property that could be interesting to analyze, and can be stated in terms of coverability (adding a control point to the specification), is checking that it is not possible for a controller to (for example) send out an alarm message without first been imprinted. Assuming that we have several nurses and controllers, we could also specify in terms of coverability the property that says that any nurse has at most one controller.

So far, we are regarding our TSA systems as the specification of systems using the resurrecting duckling policy, since our primitives assume that the imprinting and killing mechanisms are always correct. However, it is also desirable to perform a lower level analysis, with weaker assumptions. For that purpose, we will prove that every TSA system can be implemented by an MSPN system. An MSPN system intuitively consists on a set of Petri nets, each of them at some location. Those nets can move between location and, synchronize between them. Moreover, and this is more important, they can manage pure names, that we call *identifiers*, and use them for authentication purposes, that is, as imprinting keys. Therefore, apart from ordinary tokens, MSPN components can have identifiers as tokens. For instance, a component could offer a synchronization only to components exhibiting a determined identifier. This is formalized by using variables as labels on arcs. MSPN components can also create fresh identifiers by means of a special variable ν, which can only be instantiated to fresh identifiers. However, they do not need to use this variable to implement TSA systems.

Proposition 2. *Every TSA system can be simulated by a MSPN system without name creation.*

Figure 3 (center) shows the implementation of the TSA system in the left of that figure. MSPN systems without name-creation are still equivalent to P/T nets, so that we can take advantage of all the existing analysis methods for P/T nets even in the implementation of TSA systems as closed systems. The previous proof profits from the fact that we are regarding TSA systems as closed systems, so that we can extensively and statically analyze all of their participants. In particular, we can check (and force) that the components being imprinted, that is, receiving their masters imprinting key, throw away those keys when they are killed. Therefore, components can reuse those keys in a new imprinting.

However, it is not very realistic to deal with closed systems in the context of ubiquitous computing. Here we want our services to be offered in a global and uniform way, so that some of the principals that imprint or some of the devices that are imprinted may not be part of the system, but part of the *environment* of the system. In this case, we can no longer check that they erase the imprinting keys after been killed so that, if we reuse them, then the principals of the environment could use old keys to illegitimately interact with a component.

Proposition 3. *Every TSA system can be simulated by an open MSPN system.*

This result can be proved similarly to the previous one, with one crucial difference: Instead of having a predefined set of identifiers to imprint other components, each component will create a fresh identifier for every imprinting. The right of Fig. 3 shows the open implementation of the TSA system in its left, which is similar to that in the center, but it does not have a place *free* for free identifiers and it has the special variable ν labelling the arc to the place called *slave*. As we have proved in [12,14], the general class of MSPN system (in which we allow name creation) is not equivalent to P/T nets anymore, but are not Turing-complete either. In particular, we have proved that coverability is still decidable, even in the open case.

6 Conclusions and Future Work

In this paper we have defined a model based on Petri Nets that addresses the problem of Secure Transient Association in ubiquitous systems. The fact of using Petri Nets gives us an amenable and easy to grasp model.

Then we study whether we can approach the problem of the verification the properties of these systems. As a first step, we prove that TSA systems, seen as specification of systems using the primitives of the Resurrecting Duckling Policy, are equivalent to P/T nets, so that we have many decidable properties for them as reachability, coverability or home state. Then we show how these primitives can be implemented solely relying on a mechanism that manages pure names, that can be seen as imprinting keys. These implementations can be studied from two different points of view: first assuming that our systems work in a closed environment, and then without this assumption. In the first case, we have proved that this implementation is still equivalent to P/T nets. However, this is no longer true in the second case, because we need to allow the creation of fresh identifiers, but even so we can approach the verification of their properties.

As future work, we plan to study in a more systematic way the kind of properties of TSA systems that can be studied. It would also be interesting to follow a dual approach, namely that in which we want to verify that a given system does indeed implement the resurrecting duckling policy, which would certainly lead us to approaches like proof carrying code [9] or dynamic typing [5]. We also plan to consider the studies about transactions in the context of Petri nets [1], to apply them to killing of slaves in our model, which are clearly transactions, though we do not treat them explicitly as such in the open implementation.

In [13] we presented a tool for the verification of MSPN system. We are currently extending this prototype to make it cope with the primitives presented in this paper, so that it automatically performs the translations we have described and checks the properties that we have proved to be decidable.

References

1. Bruni, R., Montanari, U.: Executing Transactions in Zero-Safe Nets. In: Nielsen, M., Simpson, D. (eds.) ICATPN 2000. LNCS, vol. 1825, Springer, Heidelberg (2000)
2. Carbone, M., Nielsen, M., Sassone, V.: A Calculus for Trust Management. In: Lodaya, K., Mahajan, M. (eds.) FSTTCS 2004. LNCS, vol. 3328, Springer, Heidelberg (2004)
3. Esparza, J., Nielsen, M.: Decidability issues for Petri Nets - a survey. Bulletin of the EATCS 52, 244–262 (1994)
4. Frutos-Escrig, D., Marroquín-Alonso, O., Rosa-Velardo, F.: Ubiquitous Systems and Petri Nets. Ubiquitous Web Systems and Intelligence. In: Zhou, X., Li, J., Shen, H.T., Kitsuregawa, M., Zhang, Y. (eds.) APWeb 2006. LNCS, vol. 3841, Springer, Heidelberg (2006)
5. Hennessy, M., Riely, J.: Resource Access Control in Systems of Mobile Agents. In: High-Level Concurrent Languages. ENTCS, vol. 16, pp. 3–17. Elsevier, Amsterdam (1998)
6. Jensen, K.: Coloured Petri Nets. Basic Concepts. In: Analysis Methods and Practical Use. Basic Concepts. Monographs in TCS, vol. 1, Springer, Heidelberg (1997)
7. Milner, R., Parrow, J., Walker, D.: A calculus of mobile processes I. Information and Computation 100(1), 1–40 (1992)
8. Milner, R.: Theories for the Global Ubiquitous Computer. In: Walukiewicz, I. (ed.) FOSSACS 2004. LNCS, vol. 2987, Springer, Heidelberg (2004)
9. Necula, G.C., Lee, P.: Safe, Untrusted Agents Using Proof-Carrying Code. In: Vigna, G. (ed.) Mobile Agents and Security. LNCS, vol. 1419, Springer, Heidelberg (1998)
10. Richard, G.G.: Service Advertisement and Discovery: Enabling Universal Device Cooperation. In: Richard, G.G. (ed.) IEEE Internet Computing archive. IEEE Educational Activities Department, vol. 4(5), pp. 18–26 (2000)
11. Rosa-Velardo, F., Marroquín-Alonso, O., Frutos-Escrig, D.: Mobile Synchronizing Petri Nets: a choreographic approach for coordination in Ubiquitous Systems. In: MTCoord'05. ENTCS, vol. 150(1), pp. 103–126. Elsevier, Amsterdam (2006)
12. Rosa-Velardo, F., Frutos-Escrig, D., Marroquín-Alonso, O.: On the expressiveness of Mobile Synchronizing Petri Nets. In: 3rd Int. Workshop on Security Issues in Concurrency. ENTCS (to appear)
13. Rosa-Velardo, F.: Coding Mobile Synchronizing Petri Nets into Rewriting Logic. In: 7th Int. Workshop on Rule-based Programming. ENTCS (to appear)
14. Rosa-Velardo, F., Frutos-Escrig, D.: Symbolic Semantics for the Verification of Security Properties of Mobile Petri Nets. In: Graf, S., Zhang, W. (eds.) ATVA 2006. LNCS, vol. 4218, Springer, Heidelberg (2006)

15. Rosa-Velardo, F.: Petri nets for the verification of Ubiquitous Systems with Transient Secure Association. Technical Report 2/07, Dept. Sistemas Informáticos y Computación, Universidad Complutense de Madrid (2007)
16. Stajano, F.: Security for Ubiquitous Computing. In: Wiley Series in Communications Networking & Distributed Systems, John Wiley & Sons, Chichester (2002)
17. Want, R.: Enabling Ubiquitous Sensing with RFID. Computer 37(4), 84–86 (2004)
18. Weiser, M.: The Computer for the 21st Century. In: Human-computer Interaction: Toward the Year 2000, pp. 933–940. Morgan Kaufmann Publishers Inc, San Francisco (1995)

An Approach of Trusted Program Generation for User-Responsible Privacy

Ken'ichi Takahashi[1], Zhaoyu Liu[2], Kouichi Sakurai[1,3], and Makoto Amamiya[3]

[1] Institute of Systems & Information Technologies/KYUSHU,
2-1-22 Momochihama, Sawara-ku, Fukuoka, 814-0001, Japan
{takahashi,sakurai}@isit.or.jp

[2] University of North Carolina at Charlotte,
9201 University City Boulevard, Charlotte, NC 28223, USA
zhliu@uncc.edu

[3] Faculty of Information Science and Electrical Engineering, Kyushu University,
744 Motooka, Nishi-ku, Fukuoka, 819-0395, Japan
amamiya@al.is.kyushu-u.ac.jp

Abstract. Presently, one can use services on the Internet. These services require user's sensitive information such as name, address, credit card number, etc. However, various privacy problems such as information leakage cases are becoming serious social concern. Therefore, we propose a framework to protect user's sensitive information. It allows a user to specify the usage of his/her sensitive information and restricts the use of information by an information recipient.

The main concept of the framework is that an information recipient can use sensitive information only in the manner considered safe by the information owner. This is realized by a *trusted program* that implements the manner of information usage trusted by the information owner. The user offers his/her trusted program to an information recipient and requires to make use of the user's sensitive information through the trusted program. In this paper, we propose the approach for trusted program generation.

1 Introduction

Recently, we can access the Internet through not only personal computers but also cellular phones, PDAs, and household appliances such as A/V appliances. The Internet is increasingly an essential tool for our business and daily life. However various instances of information leakage such as the ones pertaining to Yahoo! BB and CardSystems Solutions have occurred and are becoming a serious threat.

Not all these problems are caused by the defects in cryptographic algorithms, illegal accesses, and/or software bugs; rather, they are caused by the carelessness and/or malicious intent of the human beings accessing this information. For example, notebook thefts and illegal carrying of a USB device storing the information [4]. These problems can be solved by providing sufficient training to the

J. Indulska et al. (Eds.): UIC 2007, LNCS 4611, pp. 1159–1170, 2007.

employees, using PCs which are unable to connect to external storage devices, etc. Therefore, if a user wishes to protect his sensitive information, he needs to ensure that the information recipient takes the appropriate measures to avoid these problems. However, there exist no good ways to achieve this, even if the information recipient takes countermeasures against these problems. Therefore, a user has to devise ways to protect sensitive information and prevent illegally using it.

Therefore we propose a framework [12,13] to protect sensitive information. The core concept of our framework is that a user should be responsible for the way in which his/her sensitive information is used. That is, not only an information recipient but also the information owner should be able to decide the way the information is used and a protocol for transmitting the information. In other words, a user should be able to devise countermeasures for protecting his/her information.

In our framework, a user defines a usage policy that specifies the way the information is used, which the user considers safe. A service provider, who is the information recipient, has a program referred to as the *original program* to handle user information. When the service provider requests sensitive information from a user, the user creates a program referred to as the *trusted program* from the original program according to his/her usage policy. The trusted program restricts ways of information use according to his/her usage policy. The user sends it back to the service provider. The service provider accesses the information through the trusted program. Since a service provider makes use of the information through the trusted program that implements the way specified in the user's usage policy, the use of information by the service provider is restricted to within the trusted program capability. Moreover, since a trusted program is created from the original program, it imitates the behavior of the original program. Consequently, the user prevents the service provider from an illegal use of the information. Moreover, the responsibility of the information recipient will be mitigated, because the user also has its responsibility. However, there exist some challenges in the realization of our framework. In this paper, we propose a way for generating a trusted program.

The remainder of this paper is structured as follows. Sect. 2 describes related works. Sect. 3 introduces our framework. Sect. 4 proposes a way of generating a trusted program and provides examples of trusted program generation. Finally, Sect. 5 discusses other challenges for the framework and Sect. 6 concludes the paper.

2 Related Works

Cryptographic algorithms such as symmetric and public-key algorithms and technologies based on them such as digital signatures and public key infrastructure (PKI) have been proposed [11]. These algorithms and technologies aim at preventing message interception or identification of communication partners. Therefore, we can ensure message confidentiality, integrity, and availability against malicious exploitation by third parties; however, these are difficult to prevent the illegal uses of released information.

At the bottom of homepages, we often find a link concerning privacy, shown as "Privacy Policy" at Yahoo!, "Privacy" at IBM, etc. The page describes how the company treats users' personal information that it collects. However, the users cannot confirm whether the company actually abides by its privacy page or not. Consequently, one has no choice but to believe that the company complies with its privacy policy.

The Platform for Private Preferences (P3P) [9] enables Web sites to express their privacy policies in a standard format that can be interpreted automatically by user agents. Thus, a user agent can automate decision-making by the comparing a company defined privacy policy and user-specified privacy preferences. P3P, however, does not provide technical assurance that the sites abide by their respective privacy policies.

The Enterprise Privacy Authorization Language (EPAL) [3] is a formal language to specify fine-grained enterprise privacy policies. It defines formal privacy authorization rules. Employees within an organization are required to comply with EPAL policies. Thus, EPAL prevents the illegal use of information by the employees within the organization. However, EPAL does not assure the users of how the organization protects their personal information. Consequently, users cannot know whether the organization manages personal information securely or not.

Various researchers have attempted to provide the right of information access or services based on trustworthiness [2,14]. These researchers aim to develop trust relationships among users. However, it is difficult to define a general method for developing trust relationships; this is because trustworthiness depends on users' conditions and/or situations. Moreover, a user simply trusts an information recipient to not use his/her personal information illegally. Therefore, the information recipient can use user's information in any manner, even for an illegal purpose.

Some researchers propose to protect user information by employing a mediator support [5,8]. Here, we have to provide a mediator(s) which both side of a communication can trust. However, it seems difficult in real situations with countless users and service providers. Otherwise, a computational load will be centralized at the mediator end.

Encapsulated Mobile Agent-based Privacy Protection (EMAPP) [15] protects user's sensitive information by not showing the information to outside of a user. In EMAPP, each user is assigned an *encapsulated space* that manages his/her information. A service provider has a *mobile agent* that checks user's sensitive information. When a user requests a service, the mobile agent migrates into the user's encapsulated space, checks the user's sensitive information, and sends only its result, permitted by the user, to the service provider. Since sensitive information is not released to outside the encapsulated space, the information is protected. However a user may alter the result of a mobile agent. Consequently, the service provider cannot trust the result provided by the mobile agent.

3 Information Protection Framework

Some services are offered only to particular users, who provide specific information such as an ID and password pair, the right to use a service, address, age, etc. Service providers intend to use users' information as the inputs for a programs for processing service requests. For example, a liquor vending machine provides service only to adults, so that, it has a program for checking the customer's age. Therefore, we need to check users' information by a program service providers have. On the other hand, users want to protect their sensitive information.

3.1 Approaches for Checking Information

The first approach for checking user information (Fig. 1(a)) is that a user checks his/her information by himself. A user gets a program from the service provider and replies the results of the program execution. Hence, the user does not face the risks of information release, since the user does not release the information to the service provider. However, it is difficult to apply this method to situations where the service provider needs a foolproof authentication of user information since the user may forge the result. Consequently, this method is inappropriate in the situation that requires the exact confirmation such as user's password, right to use the service, etc.

The second approach (Fig. 1(b)) is to provide a trusted third party. A user reveals his/her information only to the trusted third party. A service provider commits the confirmation of the user's information to the trusted third party. Subsequently, the trusted third party confirms user's information instead of the service provider. The service provider receives only the result of the check from the trusted third party without actually receiving the user information. Then the user need not worry about the risks of information leakage from the service provider. However, we must provide a third party that any pair of users and service providers can trust. This seems difficult in actual situations, especially ubiquitous computing environment, because there are countless users and service providers. Furthermore the fact that the responsibility and computational load are centralized at the third parties cannot be ignored.

In the third approach (Fig. 1(c)), the service provider checks user information. Almost all Web services employ this approach. However, once a user releases his information to a service provider, he/she cannot control its use anymore. Therefore, the service provider can use this information for any purpose, even an illegal one. If the service provider is reliable, the user does not worry about the risk. However, the numerous information leakage cases are making it increasingly difficult for users to trust service providers.

Hence, we require a new approach that enables a service provider to confirm user information and also enables users to prevent the illegal use of their information. Therefore, we propose a framework in which a user requires a service provider to access his/her information through a program which the user relies on.

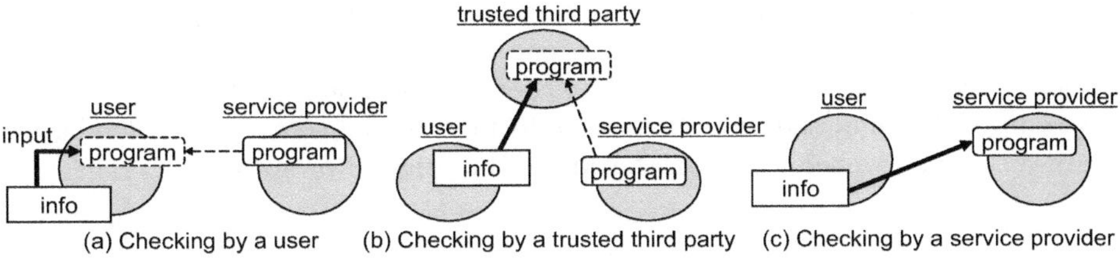

Fig. 1. Approaches for Checking Information

3.2 Information Protection Framework

We propose a framework to protect users' sensitive information. In our framework, service providers intend to employ user's sensitive information, therefore, they have a program, named *original program*, to handle user information. The original program consists of *client* and *service program*, which are executed at the user and the service provider end, respectively. The task of the client program is mainly to obtain user information and send it to the service provider. The service program receives the information from the client program and processes it. Based on the results of the execution of the client and the service program, the service provider provides the requested service to the user. Thus, the information use and providing service will be realized by the communication between the client and the service program, i.e. communication between the user and the service provider (Fig. 2). Moreover, the service provider has a *usage policy* that defines what information the service provider needs, for what purpose, and how the service provider uses the information for providing the service. The user has a *protection policy* that defines the way the information is used, which he/she considers safe. The protection policy contains a *program conversion rule*; it converts an original program to a *trusted program.*

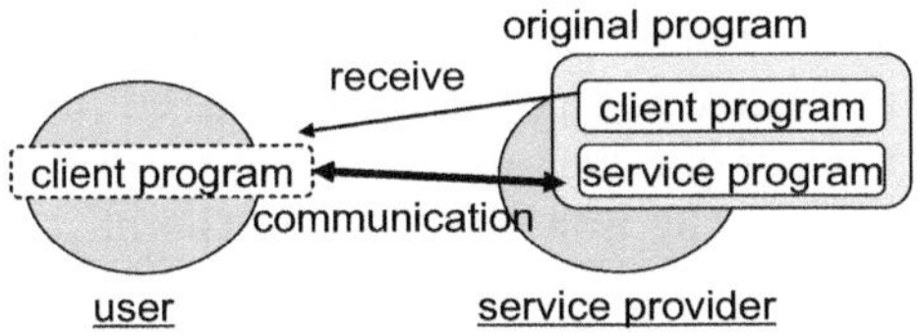

Fig. 2. Service Realization using the Client and Service Program

When a user utilizes a service, he/she receives the usage policy and original program from the service provider. Then, the user creates a trusted program (which includes a *trusted client program* and a *trusted service program*) from the original program and the usage policy according to his/her protection policy (Fig. 3) and sends the trusted service program back to the service provider. The service provider employs the user information through the trusted service program. Here, the service is realized by the trusted program instead of the original program. Therefore, the information use of the service provider is restricted to within the trusted program capability. Thus, the user prevents the service provider from an illegal use of his/her information. Moreover, the trusted program implements the way of using information the service provider hopes, because the base of the trusted program is the original program.

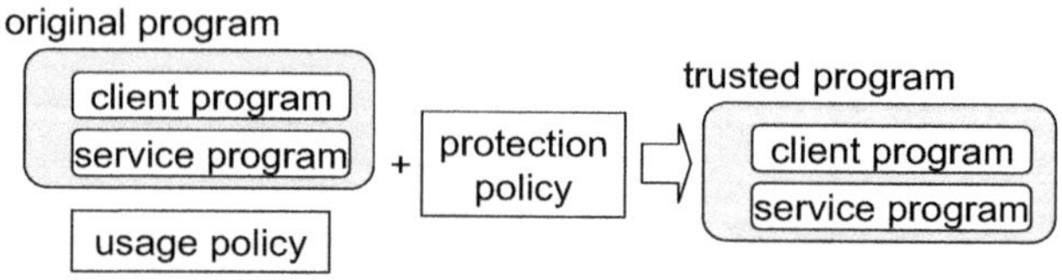

Fig. 3. Trusted Program Generation

3.3 Challenges for the Framework

We have provided an overview of the proposed framework to protect sensitive information. However, there are some challenges in its realization.

The first challenge is the generation of the trusted program: In the framework, a user creates a trusted program from an original program and usage policy according to his/her protection policy. Therefore, we need to define the usage and protection policy for generating a trusted program from an original program.

The second challenge is to protect a trusted service program from a service provider: A trusted service program is executed at the service provider end. Therefore, the service provider can access and rewrite it and thus acquire sensitive information. Therefore, it is necessary to protect the trusted service program from the illegal access and modification by the service provider.

The third challenge is to confirm trusted program behaviour: A service provider utilizes user's sensitive information through a trusted program which is created by the user. However, the trusted program will be of no use to the service provider, if it fails to imitate the behaviour of the original program. Therefore, the service provider wishes to verify certain aspects of the trusted program, such as its behaviour, the trustworthiness of its creator (user), etc.

In this paper, we address the first challenge in the next section.

4 Usage and Protection Policy

In this section, we define the usage policy and the protection policy and provide examples of a trusted program.

4.1 The Usage and Protection Policy

The usage policy specifies what information the service provider needs, its purpose, and how the service provider uses this information for providing the requested service. Therefore, we define the usage policy as shown in Fig. 4. `<info>`

specifies the information required by the service provider. `<purpose>` specifies the purpose of using `<info>`. `<operation>` specifies an operation performed on `<info>` in order to achieve `<purpose>`. `<placement>` has `<op-place>` and `<va-place>`. `<op-place>` specifies the line number of `<operation>` in the original program. `<va-place>` specifies the line number on which the value used in `<operation>` appears. Further, `<va-place>` has an attribute of the value: `"owned"` represents the owner of the value: user or service provider. `"received from <line>"` represents the user/service provider receives the value at `<line>` from the service provider/user, `"created from <names>"` represents the value is created from the values of `<names>`.

```
<usage policy> ::= <info><purpose><operation><placement>
<info>         ::= information necessary for providing the service
<purpose>      ::= P3P policy
<operation>    ::= "equal" | "greatherthan" | "lessthan" | ...
<placement>    ::= <op-place><va-places>
<op-place>     ::= <name><line>
<va-place>     ::= <name><attribute><line>
<name>         ::= the name of the instruction for <operation> or of the value
<line>         ::= a line number in the original program
<attribute>    ::= "owned" | "received from "<line> | "created from "<names>
```

Fig. 4. Usage Policy

The protection policy defines the way the information is used which the user considers safe; so, we define the protection policy as shown in Fig. 5. `<info>` specifies the information to which this protection policy is applied. `<preference>` specifies the permitted purposes as the purposes of `<info>` use. `<operation>` specifies the permitted operation that can be applied to `<info>`. `<conversion-rule>` is a program conversion rule that converts an original program to a trusted program that implements the way the user considers safe. The details of the program conversion rule are presented in the next section.

```
<protection policy> ::= <info><preference><operation><conversion-rule>
<info>              ::= information this policy applies
<preference>        ::= P3P preference
<operation>         ::= "equal" | "greatherthan" | "lessthan" | ...
<conversion-rule>   ::= described in Sect. 4.2
```

Fig. 5. Protection Policy

For example, only the equality operation is required by a service provider to confirm a password for user authentication. Therefore, the service provider will define a usage policy as follows: a password is required for user authentication, the password is used in an equality operation, and the line numbers in the original program where the password and equality operation appear. On the other hand, if a user wants to protect the password, he will define a protection policy as follows: permit the password to be used only for authentication, only the equality operation is permitted, and the program conversion rule for the equality operation is defined.

4.2 The Program Conversion Rule

A trusted program is created from an original program according to a program conversion rule. Since a trusted program aims to restrict the use of information by a service provider, the program conversion rule needs to convert some instruction in the original program to other instructions that complies with the user's protection policy. For this purpose, the program conversion rule consists of the following elements:

`<exe-side>`: specifies the entity (user or service provider) that initiates the trusted program.

`<operation-rule>`: defines the manner in which the result of `<operation>` are obtained. This rule is defined as follows:

```
<operation-rule> ::= <function>"->"<function>[<append-func>]
<append-func> ::= <operator><function>[<append-func>]
<operator> ::= "&&" | "||" | "xor" | ...
```

For example, if a rule is "f1(x) -> f2(y) && f3(z)," f1(x) is true if and only if both f2(y) and f3(z) are true.

`<value-rule>`: defines the values necessary for the implementation of `<operation>` and the method of its creation. This rule is defined as follows:

```
<value-rule> ::= <values>"from"<values>"by"<function>"at"<side>
<side> ::= "user" | "service provider"
```

For example, if a rule is "x from y, z by plus(y, z) at user," then the user creates value x from y and z by implementing the plus(y, z) method.

`<value-attribute>`: defines whether it is permitted to send the value to other entities or not. This rule is defined as follows:

```
<value-attribute> ::= <name><sendable>[<condition><to>]
<sendable> ::= true | false
```

`<condition>` and `<to>` are optional. The default value of `<to>` is `user` or `service provider`. If `<sendable>` is true and `<condition>` is satisfied, the value of `<name>` is sent to `<to>`.

`<function-rule>`: connects `<function>` defined in `<operation-rule>` and `<value-rule>` with the real function such as a Java method.

The user will create a trusted program by converting an original program according to the abovementioned program conversion rule.

4.3 Examples of the Trusted Program Generation

We provide examples of creating a trusted program for user authentication and for confirming of user's age.

```
<exe-side> = user
<operation-rule> = equal(password, y) -> equal(hash-password, hash-y)
<operation-rule> = equal(y, password) -> equal(hash-y, hash-password)
<value-rule> = hash-password from password, r by hash(password,r) at user
<value-rule> = r from NONE by generateRandomString() at user
<value-rule> = hash-y from y, r by hash(y,r) at service provider
<value-attribute> = password, false
<value-attribute> = hash-password, true
<value-attribute> = r, true
<value-attribute> = y, false
<value-attribute> = hash-y, false
```

Fig. 6. Example of a Program Conversion Rule for Protecting Passwords

Example of the Password Protection. A user considers it safe to use the password in a hashed form for user authentication[1]. Therefore, the program conversion rule will be defined as shown in Fig. 6[2].

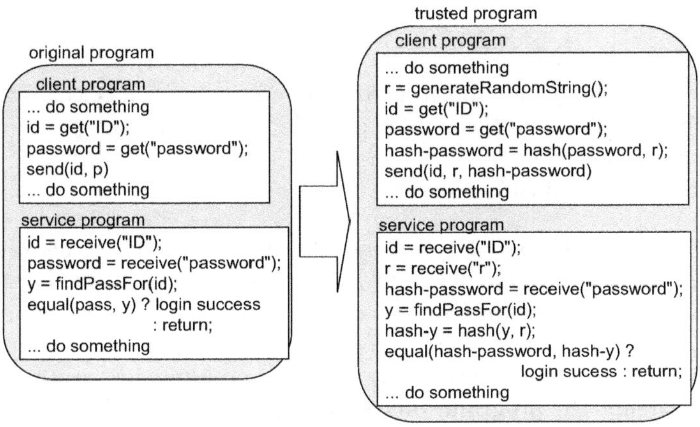

Fig. 7. Example of a Trusted Program for Protecting Passwords

We assume the original program as the left in Fig. 7. Then, according to the program conversion rule, the user converts password and y in the original program to hash-password and hash-y, respectively. Simply equal(password, y) is converted to equal(hash-password, hash-y). Further, since the `<value-attribute>` for hash-password and r are true, hash-password is sent from the client program to the service program, i.e. from the user to the service provider. As a result, the trusted program shown on the right in Fig. 7 is created from the original program.

---

[1] If the user wishes to protect the password in other way, for example, the Caesar cipher encryption, the program conversion rule will be defined accordingly.

[2] Actually, this rule is insufficient, because it does not prevent a man-in-the-middle attack.

```
<exe-side> = user
<operation-rule> = greaterthan(age, y) -> equal(w[y], wy)
<value-rule> = Pa, Sa from NONE by generateKey() at user
<value-rule> = r fron NONE by generateRandomNumber() at service provider
<value-rule> = z from Pa, r, y by E_Pa(r) - y at service provider
<value-rule> = w[i=1..age] from Sa, z, age by hash(D_Sa(z + i)) at user
<value-rule> = w[i=age+1..100] from Sa, z, age by hash(D_Sa(z + i)) + 1 at user
<value-rule> = wy from r by hash(r) at service provider
<value-attribute> = {y, Pa, z, z[i=1..100]}, true
<value-attribute> = age, false
<value-attribute> = y, true
<value-attribute> = Pa, true
<value-attribute> = Sa, false
<value-attribute> = r, false
<value-attribute> = z, true
<value-attribute> = w[i=1..100], true
<value-attribute> = wy, false
```

Fig. 8. Example of a Program Conversion Rule for the Protocol for the Millionaire Problem

The service provider authenticates the user through the trusted program received from him/her. Since the trusted program uses the hash-password instead of the plaintext password, the service provider cannot use the password illegally. Thus, the user can safeguard the password against an illegal use, even if the service provider is a phishing site.

Example of Protection of Age Information. Some services, such as a cigarette machine and a liquor vending machine, need to confirm user's age. Therefore, when a user uses these services, he/she is required to inform the service provider that he/she is an adult. However, the user does not wish to disclose his exact age. Therefore, the user considers using the protocol for the millionaire problem [16]. Then the user will define the program conversion rule as shown in Fig. 8.

The parts for the confirmation of user's age in the original program are replaced with the protocol for the millionaire problem as per the program conversion (Fig. 9). As the result, the user can prove that he/she is an adult without disclosing the exact age.

5 Discussions for Other Challenges

We defined the program conversion rule and presented examples of the trusted program generation. Now, we consider the other challenges described in Sect. 3.3.

Protection of a trusted service program. A service provider may access and acquire sensitive information from the trusted service program. Therefore, we must protect a trusted service program from the service provider. Although the examples in Sect. 4.3 are free from this threat, it potentially exists in this

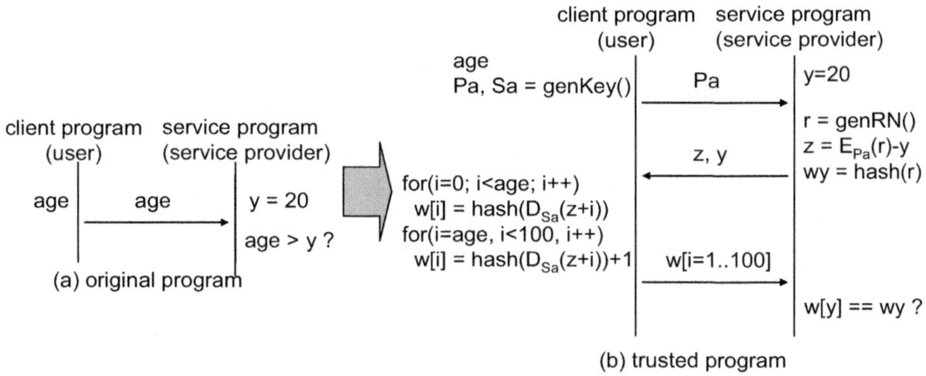

Fig. 9. Conversion of the Operation for the Confirmation of User's Age

framework. We believe that this threat will be eliminated by mobile cryptography technique [10], software obfuscation techniques [1,7] and/or the use of a tamper-proof device.

Confirmation of trusted program behavior. When the trusted program behaves in a way that a service provider does not expect, the program has no value for the service provider. Therefore, the service provider wants to confirm that the trusted program is created from the original program and a legitimate protection policy. We believe that this challenge will be solved by attaching a certificate issued by legitimate authorities to the program conversion rule. The proof carrying code (PCC) [6] is also useful for addressing this challenge.

6 Conclusion

We introduced the framework that a user can devise countermeasures for protecting his/her information. In this framework, a user creates a trusted program that implements the way the user considers safe. Then, a service provider utilizes user's sensitive information through the trusted program. Thus, the user prevents the service provider from illegally using his/her information.

In this paper, we defined usage policy, protection policy and program conversion rule for a trusted program generation. Further, we provided examples of a trusted program. The user can protect his/her other information in the same manner. Future works shall consider more complex cases of trusted program generation, give their formal definitions and solve challenges discussed in Sect. 5.

Acknowledgments

This research was supported by Strategic International Cooperative Program, Japan Science and Technology Agency (JST); Strategic Information and Communications R&D Promotion Programme (under grant 052310008). And the first author is supported by a Grant-in-Aid for Young Scientists (B), 18700076.

References

1. Aucsmith, D., Fraunke, G.: Tamper Resistant Software: An Implementation. In: Proc. of International Workshop on Information Hiding, pp. 317–333 (1996)
2. English, C., Nixon, P., Terzis, S., McGettrick, A., Lowe, H.: Dynamic Trust Models for Ubiquitous Computing Environments. In: Borriello, G., Holmquist, L.E. (eds.) UbiComp 2002. LNCS, vol. 2498, Springer, Heidelberg (2002)
3. The EPAL 1.1. `http://www.zurich.ibm.com/security/enterpriseprivacy/epal/`
4. Japan Network Security Association. Information Security Incident Survey Report ver.1.0, `http://www.jnsa.org/result/index.html`
5. Karabulut, Y.: Towards a Next-Generation Trust Management Infrastructure for Open Computing Systems. In: SPPC04 (2004)
6. Necula, G.C.: Proof-Carrying Code. In: POPL'97, pp. 106–119 (1997)
7. Ogiso, T., Sakabe, Y., Soshi, M., Miyaji, A.: Software Obfuscation on a Theoretical Basis and its Implementation. IEICE Trans. on Fundamentals E86-A (1), 176–186 (2003)
8. Pearce, C., Bertok, P., Schyndel, R.: Protecting Consumer Data in Composite Web Services. IFIP/SEC 2005 (2005)
9. P3P project, `http://www.w3.org/P3P`
10. Sander, T., Tschudin, C.: Protecting Mobile Agents Against Malicious Hosts. In: Vigna, G. (ed.) Mobile Agents and Security. LNCS, vol. 1419, pp. 44–60. Springer, Heidelberg (1998)
11. Stinson, D.R. (ed.): Cryptography: Theory and Practice. Crc Pr I Llc (1995)
12. Takahashi, K., Sakurai, K., Amamiya, M.: A Framework for Protecting Private Information through User-Trusted-Program and its Realizability. In: UISW 2005. LNCS, vol. 3823, pp. 433–442. Springer, Heidelberg (2005)
13. Takahashi, K., Sakurai, K.: A Framework for the User-Oriented Personal Information Protection. In: Gotzhein, R., Reed, R. (eds.) SAM 2006. LNCS, vol. 4320, pp. 12–18. Springer, Heidelberg (2006)
14. Theodorakopoulos, G., Baras, J.: Trust Evaluation in Ad-Hoc Networks. In: Zhou, X., Su, S., Papazoglou, M.M.P., Orlowska, M.E., Jeffery, K.G. (eds.) WISE 2004. LNCS, vol. 3306, pp. 1–10. Springer, Heidelberg (2004)
15. Yamada, S., Kamioka, E.: Access Control for Security and Privacy in Ubiquitous Computing Environments. IEICE Trans. on Comm. E88-B (3), 846–856 (2005)
16. Yao, A.C.: Protocols for Secure Computations. In: FOCS82, pp. 160–164 (1982)

Self-updating: Strong Privacy Protection Protocol for RFID-Tagged Banknotes*

Eun Young Choi[1], Su Mi Lee[1], and Dong Hoon Lee[2]

Center for Information Security Technologies(CIST),
Korea University, 1, 5-Ka, Anam-dong, Sungbuk-ku, Seoul, 136-701, Korea
{bluecey,smlee}@cist.korea.ac.kr, donghlee@korea.ac.kr

Abstract. RFID systems have already used in less sensitive application such as manufacturing since the use of RFID technology increases the efficiency of a work. According as researchers are interested in RFID systems gradually, RFID systems will be applied to various fields than before. One of RFID application fields, a bank system uses RFID tagged banknotes(tagged banknotes) in order to prevent illegal transactions such as counterfeiting banknotes and money laundering. Several researchers have proposed RFID schemes which are able to apply in RFID-based bank systems [2,5,10]. Unfortunately, the proposed schemes did not provide privacy protection of individuals since sensitive information about individuals' location is revealed by an adversary despite one of basic requirements in RFID systems. We propose a RFID scheme for protecting location privacy of a banknote holder in RFID-based bank systems.

Keywords: RFID-tagged Banknotes, Privacy protection, Self-updating.

1 Introduction

A Radio Frequency Identification (RFID) tag were developed as a small and low-priced device, which is capable of transmitting a unique serial number and other additional data through Radio Frequency (RF) signals. As an advantage of RFID systems is to be able to identify objects remotely by embedding tags into the objects, the systems have applied to various fields such as manufacturing, supply chain management, and inventory control.

Besides these fields, people of the financial world are attracted by RFID system's characteristic recognizing objects based on RF signal. In the concrete, we use banknotes to purchase objects or utilize various facilities in daily life. Sometimes malicious consumers may counterfeit banknotes to satisfy their selfish interest or perform money laundering to use one in black market. In particular, the European Central Bank (ECB) has decided to apply a RFID system into Euro banknotes in order to prevent illegal transactions. Although physical security property already may be provided by Euro banknotes, it does not imply that the physical property completely provides anti-counterfeit in RFID-based bank systems.

* This work was supported by the Korea Science and Engineering Foundation(KOSEF) grant funded by the Korea government(MOST) (No.R01 − 2004 − 000 − 10704 − 0).

J. Indulska et al. (Eds.): UIC 2007, LNCS 4611, pp. 1171–1180, 2007.

Although a tagged banknote can prevent RFID-based bank systems from illegal transactions, it can bring about a problem about invasion of privacy which is to reveal sensitive information about individuals' location history, e.g., attending a political rally. Namely, a malicious adversary is able to eavesdrop on messages between a reader and a tagged banknote, and may try to distinguish whether the messages are transmitted by the target tagged banknote or not. Once a link is established the messages and the target tagged banknote, the adversary who wants to know the person's location may achieve her goal. Hence a RFID scheme in RFID-based bank system should also satisfy a requirement protecting location history of an individual. Unfortunately, no RFID schemes for protecting completely individual's privacy in RFID-based bank systems have been proposed in the literature. The goal of our work is to strongly protect individual's privacy in RFID-based bank systems.

1.1 Related Works and Our Contribution

Researchers have already recognized security requirements in RFID systems and have devised better approaches prevent systems from various threats such as eavesdropping, traffic analysis. In result, many schemes are proposed to satisfy security requirements of RFID systems [1,2,4,5,3,7,6,8,9,10]. Among of previously proposed schemes, several papers [1,5,2,10] dealt with schemes related to Euro banknotes. ECB first has disclosed plans to embed tags in Euro banknotes by 2005 and Juels et al. proposed the scheme used within tagged banknotes in the paper [5].

Now, we briefly describe Juels et al. scheme as follows ; Juels et al. scheme, a RFID-based bank system applied a re-encryption method for messages stored in tagged banknotes to protect privacy of a person. The re-encryption process is performed by a reader of a merchant. Also, the RFID-based bank system use the mechanism of privilege separation on tagged banknotes to prevent an adversary from extracting information of tagged banknotes. Namely, a reader who has a right to read about information in predefined parts only performs re-encryption process and then write re-encrypted message on predefined part. The authors claimed that the proposed scheme provides privacy of a person by using the mechanism of privilege separation. However, in the paper [1], Avoine showed that an adversary is able to obtain an authorized key by eavesdropping between a tagged banknote and a reader of a merchant. The attack method shown by Avoine is as follows ; an adversary is able to obtain an authorized key by eavesdropping between a tagged banknote and a reader of a merchant, and then she has a right to read a secret message. Thus, the adversary is able to extract a serial number of a specified banknote and can trace a person carrying banknotes by the serial number. I.e., the adversary can obtain the person's location history.

Recently, Zhang proposed an improved scheme for RFID tagged banknotes [10]. Ateniese et al. [2] proposed an untraceable scheme which allows authorized readers to write an encrypted message. In the Ateniese et al.'s scheme, a legal reader stores a tag with a dummy encryption if the tag's information is not a valid. Then, although the tag passes the verification which checks whether the tag's information is a valid or not, the tag is not identified by legal readers correctly. As mentioned above, in the paper [10], Zhang proposed an improved scheme to protect a bank system from insider adversaries who may be merchants. Such as the attack is carried out by inserting fake messages into banknotes. For example, an adversary obtains messages of two tagged banknotes and swaps messages of tagged banknotes each other. Then, honest merchants are able to detect invalid messages sent from a tagged banknote and report incorrect data in the tagged banknote. In that case, a law enforcement is unable to correctly trace the illegal banknote. To resolve the problem, Zhang proposed an improved scheme to provide lawful tracing [10]. However, the improved scheme is able to be attacked by Avoine's method since the scheme is not constructed considering Avoine's attack method. In result, by eavesdropping on between readers of merchants and tagged banknotes, the adversary can track a person carrying banknotes and obtain the person's location history. Therefore, by granting the write/read capabilities in banknotes, the scheme of the ECB is not able to protect location privacy of a person. Besides, if a person who carries tagged banknotes does not meet merchants for a long time, the tag which is embedded in banknotes maintains a static value. In this case, an adversary is able to trace the person using the static value.

In this paper, we study a scheme which provides a person's privacy protection for tagged banknotes. The previously proposed schemes have been considered that tagged banknotes only stored secret values and had to be updated values of a tag by external agencies, readers. The schemes using external agencies are vulnerable against a attack method stated in the paper [1]. After all, we conclude on that a tag updates values by itself. In this paper, we use a self-updating method that a tag makes the best of a low-cost function. In our scheme, whenever a tag receives a query from a reader, the tag responds with a updated value by itself. Our scheme enhances location privacy by self-updating on every session and is secure against various attacks such as eavesdropping, replay and counterfeiting.

Organization of the paper. This paper is organized as follows: In Section 2, we describe briefly a RFID-based bank system, security and privacy risks in the systems. We describe our scheme to protect location privacy of a person in Section 3. In Section 4, we analyze our scheme in security. Finally, we conclude in Section 5.

2 RFID-Based Bank System

In this section, we describe components, security and privacy risks in RFID-based bank systems.

2.1 Components

A RFID-based bank system is composed of four components, law enforcement, central bank, merchant, and consumer. Characteristics of each component are as follows.

- **Law Enforcement** ($\mathcal{L}$): This entity $\mathcal{L}$ consists of one or more agencies and plays a pivotal role in tracing serials of illegal banknotes. We assume that the entity is a trust third party.

- **Central Bank** ($\mathcal{B}$): The role of a entity $\mathcal{B}$ is to issue banknotes to consumer. $\mathcal{B}$ performs digital signatures to prevent an adversary from counterfeiting banknotes and then injects digital signatures into banknotes. $\mathcal{B}$ holds and manages a database including information about each tagged banknote e.g., a serial number, a signature of a banknote, and so on.
- **Merchant** ($\mathcal{M}$): This entity $\mathcal{M}$ handles banknotes using a reader which should be tamper-resistant to prevent an adversary from getting secret information of banknotes. A reader, used by $\mathcal{M}$, communicates with tagged banknotes. Whenever a consumer pays by banknotes, $\mathcal{M}$ should check if the banknote is a legal. If illegal banknotes occurs in transaction process, $\mathcal{M}$ will report information of illegal banknote to Law Enforcement.
- **Consumer** $\mathcal{C}$: This entity $\mathcal{C}$ is the bearer of tagged banknotes. A tag embedded in a banknote is composed of an antenna and a microchip for storage and logical operations. In our RFID-based bank system, memory of a tag imbedded in a banknote is separated into three parts as illustrated in Figure 2 : RF, internal and optical. These parties have properties as follows.
  - Internal part: The internal part is no-access range. Secret values of a banknote are securely stored in the part.
  - RF part: A reader can read the values of the RF part through RF signals. The values of the RF part can be read by anyone able to communicate through RF signals. Also, the value of the RF part is updated by a tag itself using secret values stored in the internal part.
  - Optical part: We assume that the value of the optical part can be read by only a corresponding reader and it is impossible for an adversary to eavesdrop the values of the optical part. The values of the optical part may be encoded in human readable or machine-readable form.

2.2 Security and Privacy Risks

In RFID-based bank systems, an adversary can monitor all messages transmitted in wireless communication between readers of merchants and tagged banknotes of consumers. So, the adversary can infringe upon a consumer's privacy using various methods such as eavesdropping, traffic analysis,and counterfeiting (e.g., replay and spoofing attacks): an adversary obtains sensitive information about a consumer and is able to track some consumer by establishing a link between a consumer and a tagged banknote. We describe these threats in detail below.

· *Information Leakage*: A consumer is prone to carrying tagged banknotes in every life. In store, a tagged banknote emits information of its banknote in response to a query from a nearby reader of a merchant. If an adversary know the information, e.g., denomination of tagged banknotes by eavesdropping on messages transmitted in wireless communication between the reader and the tagged banknote, she may extract banknotes from the consumer by threats.

· *Traceability*: When a tagged banknote of a target consumer transmits a response to a nearby reader of a merchant, an adversary can record the transmitted messages and can establish a link between the response and the target consumer. Once a link established, the adversary is able to know the consumer's location history.

· *Counterfeiting*: Although an adversary can not easily access tagged banknotes physically, she is able to interfere in wireless communication of RFID-based bank systems. By eavesdropping messages transmitted in wireless communication, the adversary can collect the information sent by the tag, and then the adversary can try a spoofing or reply attack to counterfeit a target banknote's tag. Thus the adversary may counterfeit tagged banknotes by using the information.

3 Our Scheme: Self-updating Protocol

In this section, we describe our scheme for RFID tagged banknotes. The architecture of our scheme is as shown Figure. 1, and our scheme consists of set-up, banknotes issue, verification and updating, and tracing phases.

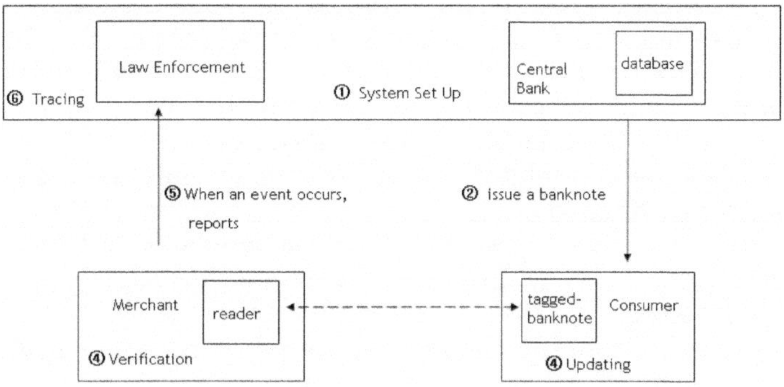

Fig. 1. The architecture of a RFID-based bank system

3.1 System Set-Up

In the set-up phase, we choose three systems and publish security parameters. We use three cryptographic systems, a public encryption system CS, a digital signature system Σ, a one-way hash function H in our scheme.

1. Encryption system : we let $CS = (\mathcal{K}, E, D)$ denote a public key encryption system, where $\mathcal{K}$, E and D are *key generation*, *encryption* and *decryption* algorithms. CS is set up by the following parameters.
   – We choose two primes p, q $(q|p-1)$ and generates G $(\in \mathbf{Z}_p^*)$, a subgroup of prime order q, where g is a generator of G.
2. Signature system : we use a digital signature system $\Sigma = (K, S, V)$ where K, S and V are *key generation*, *signing* and *verification* algorithms. Σ is a secure against existential forgery under a chosen message attack.
3. One way hash function : we make use of $H : \{0,1\}^* \rightarrow \{0,1\}^{k_1}$, where a hash value space belongs to $\{0,1\}^{k_1}$ for a security parameter k_1.

In order to use these systems, law enforcement generates a public encryption key pair $(PK_{\mathcal{L}}, SK_{\mathcal{L}})$. To be concrete, $\mathcal{L}$ chooses a private key x randomly in $\mathbf{Z}_q$ and computes $y = g^x \ mod \ p$. $\mathcal{L}$ publishes $PK_{\mathcal{L}} = y$ as a public key.

3.2 Banknotes Issue

In Banknote issue phase, Central bank $\mathcal{B}$ creates banknotes. To prevent an adversary from counterfeiting attack, $\mathcal{B}$ generates a signature and stores each tagged banknote' information used to check if the banknote is a legal. The detailed process is as follows:

1. $\mathcal{B}$ generates a digital signing key pair $(PK_{\mathcal{B}}, SK_{\mathcal{B}})$.
2. For each banknote i, $\mathcal{B}$ selects a unique serial number S_i and computes a signature $\Sigma_i = S(SK_{\mathcal{B}}, [S_i||D_i])$, where D_i is the banknote denomination, $||$ denotes bitstring concatenation. By including a banknote denomination in the signature, our scheme prevent attacks including forgery of alternation of a banknote denomination. In addition, we use serval values to protect a privacy of a person who possesses banknotes. Also, these values are used as inputs of a one way hash function H to provide randomness of banknotes' values.
   - TC_i^j : this value is a j-th counter of a banknote i and is initialized to an arbitrary value. Whenever a banknote receives a query from a reader, the tag in the banknotes increases the counter.
   - R_i : it is a random value of a banknote i and is initialized to an arbitrary value for each banknote i.
3. $\mathcal{B}$ generates a ciphertext message C_i^0 for each banknote i where a ciphertext is used to prevent an unauthorized party from extracting information of tagged banknotes.
   - For each banknote i, $\mathcal{B}$ chooses a secret key k_i randomly in $\mathbf{Z}_q$ and computes a ciphertext C_i according to following formula.

$$C_i = [\alpha_i^0, \beta_i^0] = [m_i y^{k_i}, g^{k_i}], \ m_i = S_i||\Sigma_i||D_i$$

   - Using published public key $PK_{\mathcal{L}}(= y)$ and a secret k_i, $\mathcal{B}$ computes $T_i = y^{k_i}(= g^{xk_i}) \ mod \ p$ used to verify whether banknotes' information is counterfeited by an adversary or not.
   - Then $\mathcal{B}$ generates a cipertext C_i^0 stored in a banknote i. The cipertext C_i^0 is generated using a one way hash function H as like following formula. The exclusive-or (xor) operation of bits is denoted by $\oplus$.

$$C_i^0 = C_i \oplus H(TC_i^0 \oplus R_i)$$

4. $\mathcal{B}$ prints a serial number S_i, a signature Σ_i and secret values R_i, T_i on optical part of a tag embedded in a banknote i. Then, $\mathcal{B}$ embeds R_i, H into internal part of the tag and stores C_i^0, TC_i^0 in RF part of a tag (embedded in a banknote i) as shown in Figure 2. Note that A_i^j and B_i denotes j-th value A of the banknote i and value B of the banknote i, respectively.
5. When a consumer $\mathcal{C}$ withdraws her savings from the bank $\mathcal{B}$, $\mathcal{B}$ sends banknotes corresponding to amount demanded.

RF	Internal
C_i^0, TC_i^0	R_i, H

Optical		
Serial	Secrets	Signature
S_i	R_i , T_i	$\sum_i = S(SK_B, [S_i \vert\vert D_i])$

Fig. 2. The internal configuration of a banknote i

3.3 Verification and Updating

Verification. Whenever a merchant $\mathcal{M}$ receives a banknote i for payment, the $\mathcal{M}$ verifies the correctness of the exiting contents with the following. Verification and Updating process is generally shown in Figure 3 (we assume that the banknote i communicates with readers of merchants j times).

1. $\mathcal{M}$ optically reads S_i, Σ_i, R_i and T_i in the optical part of a banknote i.
2. $\mathcal{M}$ reads C_i^j, TC_i^j from a RF part and obtains an original ciphertext C_i using H, C_i^j and TC_i^j as the following formula.
   - computes $A = H(TC_i^j \oplus R_i)$ using C_i^j and TC_i^j.
   - then, computes $C_i^j \oplus A = C_i (= [\alpha_i^0, \beta_i^0] = [m_i y^{k_i}, g^{k_i}]$, $m_i = S_i||\Sigma_i||D_i)$.
   - checks if α_i^0/T_i is equal to the received $S_i||\Sigma_i||D_i$. If it is not, $\mathcal{M}$ reports the invalid ciphertext C_i^j, the counter TC_i^j and the random value R_i to Law enforcement $\mathcal{L}$ and halts.
3. $\mathcal{M}$ checks if Σ_i is a valid signature using $V(PK_{\mathcal{B}}, \Sigma_i, [S_i||D_i]) = 1$, where $V(-,-,-)$ is a verification algorithm and '1' means that it is a valid signature. If it is not, $\mathcal{M}$ halts and sends these values to law enforcement $\mathcal{L}$.

Updating. After transmitting the contents of the banknote i, the tag of the banknote i updates its contents by itself. The tag performs as follows:

1. increases the counter TC_i^j into TC_i^{j+1}.
2. computes a fresh hashed value $H(TC_i^{j+1} \oplus R_i)$ using two values TC_i^{j+1}, R_i.
3. updates an original ciphertext C_i using the computed values $H(TC_i^{j+1} \oplus R_i)$. The updated value C_i^{j+1} is replaced by $C_i \oplus H(TC_i^{j+1} \oplus R_i)$ and is used in next $j+1$-th communication.

3.4 Tracing

When a law enforcement $\mathcal{L}$ wants to know a particular banknote or receives a report of a invalid banknote from merchants $\mathcal{M}$, the law enforcement $\mathcal{L}$ performs the tracing phase as follows:

1. Using the received values C_i^j, TC_i^j and R_i, $\mathcal{L}$ obtains C_i by performing as follows:
   - computes the hashed value $H(TC_i^j \oplus R_i)$.
   - obtains C_i by computing $C_i^j \oplus H(TC_i^j \oplus R_i)$ $(=[\alpha_i^0, \beta_i^0] = [m_i y^{k_i}, g^{k_i}])$.

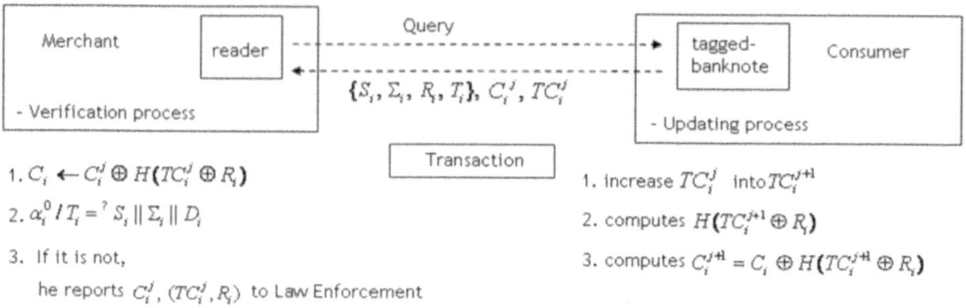

Fig. 3. Verification and Updating Processes

2. $\mathcal{L}$ computes $\alpha_i^0/(\beta_i^0)^x = S_i||\Sigma_i||D_i$ using a private key x, α_i^0, β_i^0 included in the obtained C_i. Then, $\mathcal{L}$ checks if Σ_i is a valid signature using a signature of verification algorithm $V(PK_{\mathcal{B}}, \Sigma_i, [S_i||D_i]) = 1$. If it is a valid, $\mathcal{L}$ indeed obtains the serial number S_i, the signature Σ_i and the denomination D_i of the invalid banknote i.

4 Security Analysis

In this section, we analyze our protocol, Self-updating protocol in security. We analyze the security of our protocol against the threats introduced in section 2.2; *information leakage*, *traceability* and *counterfeiting*.

Information Leakage. In our scheme, memory of a tag imbedded in a banknote is divided into three parts, internal, RF and optical. While RF part transmits a response from a query by a reader, e.g., a reader of a merchant through radio frequency signals, optical part is only read by a reader at a short distance. Even if an adversary is remotely able to eavesdrop on communication between a reader of a merchant and a target tagged banknote, she receives only the encrypted message of the RF part through RF signals. The encrypted message is encrypted by Law enforcement's private key $SK_{\mathcal{L}}$. In order to extract the information of the banknote, the adversary should know a private key $SK_{\mathcal{L}}$ of Law enforcement. It is impossible for the adversary to know a private key of Law enforcement even if a public key $PK_{\mathcal{L}}$ is published in the system. Therefore, the adversary is unable to extract any information of the target banknote such as a banknote's denominate.

Traceability. Our scheme guarantees location privacy of an individual against eavesdropping by using self-updating method. Generally, eavesdropping method is divided into two sorts, a long distance and a short distance. First, we describe about a long distance attack. In our self-updating method, whenever a reader of a merchant transmits a query, a tagged banknote generates a blinding value to transmit always a randomized value to a reader in each communication. In our scheme, the blinding value is to a fresh hashed value $H(TC \oplus R)$ where TC is increased by a tag embedded in a banknote in each communication. By using the randomized blinding value in self-updating method, an adversary cannot distinguish whether the message is transmitted by a target tagged banknote or not. To perform a short-distance attack, an adversary will try to scan on communication between a reader and a specific tagged banknote at a close range. However, since such as the scanning attack requires a short distance to gain the useful information of banknotes, we can easily detect by monitoring communication between readers and tagged banknotes. So, an adversary is not able to obtain information of tagged banknotes at a short-distance and track some banknote of a target person. I.e., an adversary never know location history of an individual who hold banknotes.

Counterfeiting. In our scheme, central bank $\mathcal{B}$ signs serial numbers of banknotes using a signing private key $SK_{\mathcal{B}}$. Our scheme uses a signature system that is secure against existential forgery under a chosen message attack. In particular, an adversary does not obtain optical part's information of tagged banknotes but gets RF part's information since a reader is tamper-resistant. To counterfeit a tagged banknotes, the adversary should generate a signature of the tagged banknote. However, using the signature algorithm in our scheme, it is impossible for an adversary to generate the signature of the tagged banknote. Therefore, a malicious adversary is not able to counterfeit tagged banknotes which contains valid signatures. In the worst case, a special adversary who has a powerful machine may be able to generate a signature with a serial number which was not even issued by central bank. In this case, since the difficulty of creating tagged banknotes is supported by the physical security property of banknotes, it is hard to counterfeit tagged banknotes.

5 Conclusion

We have proposed secure protocol to protect a user privacy, especially for RFID tagged Banknotes. By using the self-updating method, our scheme enhances location privacy by updating the transmitting value to a reader on every session. As the results, our scheme completely provides privacy protection of individuals since it is impossible for an adversary to obtain location history of an individual as well as banknotes information in RFID-based bank systems. In other word, our scheme is secure against the threats such as *information leakage*, *Traceability* and *counterfeiting*.

References

1. Avoine, G.: Privacy issues in RFID banknote protection schemes. In: international Conference on Smart Card Research and Advanced Applications - CARDIS, IFIP, pp. 22–27 (2004)
2. Ateniese, G., Camenisch, J., de Medeiros, B.: Untraceable RFID Tags via Insubvertible Encryption. In: 12th ACM Conference on Computer and Communications Security-CCS'05, pp. 92–101. ACM Press, New York (2005)

3. Henrici, D., Muller, P.: Hash-based Enhancement of Location Privacy for Radio-Frequency Identification Devices using Varying Identifiers. In: PerSec'04 at IEEE PerCom, pp. 149–153. IEEE Computer Society Press, Los Alamitos (2004)
4. Juels, A., Molnar, D., Wagner, D.: Security Issues in E-Passports. In: SecureComm'05, pp. 74–88 (2005)
5. Juels, A., Pappu, R.: Squealing euros: Privacy protection in RFID-enabled banknotes. In: Wright, R.N. (ed.) FC 2003. LNCS, vol. 2742, pp. 103–121. Springer, Heidelberg (2003)
6. Junichiro, S., Jae-Cheol, R., Kouichi, S.: Enhancing privacy of Universal Re-encryption scheme for RFID Tags. In: Yang, L.T., Guo, M., Gao, G.R., Jha, N.K. (eds.) EUC 2004. LNCS, vol. 3207, pp. 879–890. Springer, Heidelberg (2004)
7. Ohkubo, M., Suxuki, K., Kinoshita, S.: Efficient Hash-Chain Based RFID Privacy Protection Scheme. In: Ubcomp 2004 workshop (2004)
8. Sarma, S.E., Weis, S.A., Engels, D.W.: Radio-frequency identification systems. In: Kaliski Jr., B.S., Koç, Ç.K., Paar, C. (eds.) CHES 2002. LNCS, vol. 2523, pp. 454–469. Springer, Heidelberg (2003)
9. Weis, S.A., Sarma, S.E., Weis, S.A., Engels, D.W.: Security and privacy Aspects of Low-Cost Radio Frequency Identification Systems. In: Hutter, D., Müller, G., Stephan, W., Ullmann, M. (eds.) Security in Pervasive Computing. LNCS, vol. 2802, pp. 202–212. Springer, Heidelberg (2004)
10. Zhang, X., King, B.: Integrity Improvements to an RFID Privacy Protection Protocol for Anti-counterfeiting. In: Zhou, J., Lopez, J., Deng, R.H., Bao, F. (eds.) ISC 2005. LNCS, vol. 3650, pp. 474–481. Springer, Heidelberg (2005)

Intelligent Detection Computer Viruses Based on Multiple Classifiers

Boyun Zhang[1,2], Jianping Yin[1], and Jingbo Hao[1]

[1] School of Computer Science, National University of Defense Technology, Changsha 410073, P.R. China
hnjxzby@yahoo.com.cn
[2] Department of Computer Science, Hunan Public Security College, Changsha 410138, P.R. China

Abstract. In this paper, we generalize the problem of multi-classifiers combination by using modified bagging method to detect previously unknown viruses. The detection engine applies two algorithms, Support Vector Machine and BP neural network to virus detection. For SVM classifier, we extract the feature vector from the API function calls by monitor the programs. And the static feature of program, n-gram, is used in the BP neural network classifier. Finally, the D-S theory of evidence is used to combine the contribution of each individual classifier to give the final decision. Our extensive experiments have shown that the combination approach improves the performance of the individual classifier significantly. It shows that the present method could effectively be used to discriminate normal and abnormal programs.

1 Introduction

Since the appearance of the first computer virus, computer viruses have been one of the most serious threats to information security due to the significant damage [1]. Excellent technology exists for detecting known viruses. Programs such as Norton and MacAfee's Anti-virus tools are ubiquitous. These programs search executable code for known patterns. The drawback of this method is that we must obtain a copy of a malicious program before extracting the pattern necessary for its detection. It is crucial to develop new methods for defending viruses.

Then there have been few attempts to use data mining for the purpose of identifying new or unknown malicious code. In an early attempt, Lo et al. [2] conducted an analysis of several programs evidently by hand and identified tell-tale signs, which they subsequently used to filter new programs. Researchers at IBM's T.J.Watson Research Center have investigated neural networks for virus's detection and have incorporated a similar approach for detecting boot-sector viruses into IBM's Anti-Virus software [3]. More recently, instead of focusing on boot-sector viruses, Kolter et al [4] used data mining methods, such as Naive Bayes, J48 and SVM to detect malicious codes. There are other methods of guarding against malicious codes, such as object reconciliation, which involves comparing current files and directories to past copies. One can also compare cryptographic hashes. These approaches are not based on data mining.

J. Indulska et al. (Eds.): UIC 2007, LNCS 4611, pp. 1181–1190, 2007.

In this paper, we propose a method to detect new computer virus through multi-classifiers [5]. The detection engine combines static code analysis with dynamic behavior monitoring to identify whether a program is malicious or benign. The present detection engine currently detects new malicious codes without removing any obfuscation.

In the following section, we first illustrate the procedure of the detection model. Then, the details of the methods of extraction feature from Win32 PE format program are introduced. Following the describing of D-S Bagging algorithm, the multiple classification fusion method is stated. Section 3 shows the experiment results. We state our conclusion in Section 4.

2 Viruses Detection Engine

2.1 Model Frame

It is well known that a combination of many different predictors can improve predictions. In the neural networks community ensembles of neural networks has been investigated by several authors [6][7]. Combining the outputs of several neural networks into an aggregate output often gives improved accuracy over any individual output. The set of networks is known as an ensemble or committee. Analogously, the multiple support vector machine decision models are also proposed in Ref [8] to improve the performance of classification.

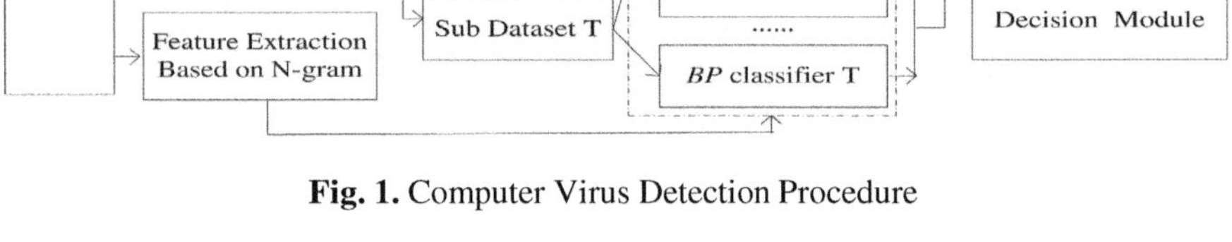

Fig. 1. Computer Virus Detection Procedure

In this paper, we apply two algorithms, such as Support Vector Machine (SVM) and Back-propagation (BP) neural network to virus detection. The detection engine uses two types of features to represent and recognize pattern. For SVM classifier, we extract the feature vector from the API function calls by monitor the programs in a virtual computer. And the static feature of program, n-gram, is used in the BP neural network classifier. We construct individual classifier by using modified Bagging method. Finally, the D-S theory is used to combine the contribution of each individual classifier to give the final decision. Our proposed scheme is shown in Figure.1.

2.2 Feature Extraction

2.2.1 API Call Tracing

Now our intuition into the problem is to extract information from the PE executables that would dictate its behavior. In our experiments, we choose the Windows API function calls as the main feature. We could obtain lots of API function calls by tracing the programs in the train set .It is surely that each API calls play different role on detecting malicious code. When an API call often appears in the malicious codes but seldom in the benign codes, so it play more important role in detection. So we use 'mean square deviation' as the main parameter to select API function calls as program's feature. The mean square deviation between classes is calculated as follow:

Step 1. Tracing each sample program in the training set to obtain it API calls sequence $A=\{A_1,A_2,...,A_p\},(1\le i\le p)$, count each API function (A_i) frequency A_{ij}^V in every malicious executables V_j . And count its frequency A_{ij}^N in every benign executables N_j ;

Step 2. Compute average frequency $E(A_i^V)$ and $E(A_i^N)$ of each API function (A_i) in malicious executables set and benign executables set as:

$$E(A_i^V)=\frac{1}{s}\sum_{j=1}^{s}A_{ij}^V \text{，} E(A_i^N)=\frac{1}{n}\sum_{j=1}^{n}A_{ij}^N \tag{1}$$

where s is the number of malicious executables, n is the number of benign executables.

Step 3. Compute total mean frequency $E(A_i)$ of each API function A_i as:

$$E(A_i)=\frac{E(A_i^V)+E(A_i^N)}{2} \tag{2}$$

Step 4. Compute mean square deviation $D(A_i)$ of each API function A_i as:

$$D(A_i)=\sqrt{(E(A_i)-E(A_i^V))^2+(E(A_i)-E(A_i^N))^2} \tag{3}$$

At the last stage, we sorted the API function call sequence on $D(A_i)$, and choose the first t-th API functions as the feature vector. An example of feature vector is shown in table 1.

Table 1. API Calls List

No.	Program's behavior	API Function Calls	DLLS reference
1	File Execute	WinExec; CreateProcess	KERNEL32.dll
2	Read File	CreateFileA; ReadFile; OpenFile	KERNEL32.dll
3	Write File	WriteFile; WriteFileEx	KERNEL32.dll
4	Delete File	DeleteFileA	KERNEL32.dll
5	Move File	MoveFileA; MoveFileExA;	KERNEL32.dll
6	Change Attribute	SetFileAttributesA; SetFileTime	KERNEL32.dll
7	Search File	FindClose; FindFirstFileA; FindNextFileA; FindResourceA	KERNEL32.dll
8	Search Directory	GetWindowsDirectoryA; GetSystemDirectoryA; SetCurrentDirectoryA; CreateDirectoryA	KERNEL32.dll
...	...	...	...

2.2.2 N-Gram Analysis

An n-gram [9] is a subsequence of n consecutive tokens in a stream of tokens. N-gram analysis has been applied in many tasks, and is well understood and efficient to implement. By converting a string of data to n-grams, it can be embedded in a vector space to efficiently compare two or more streams of data. Alternatively, we may compare the distributions of n-grams contained in a set of data to determine how consistent some new data may be with the set of data in question. An n-gram distribution is computed by sliding a fixed size window through the set of data and counting the number of occurrences of each 'gram'.

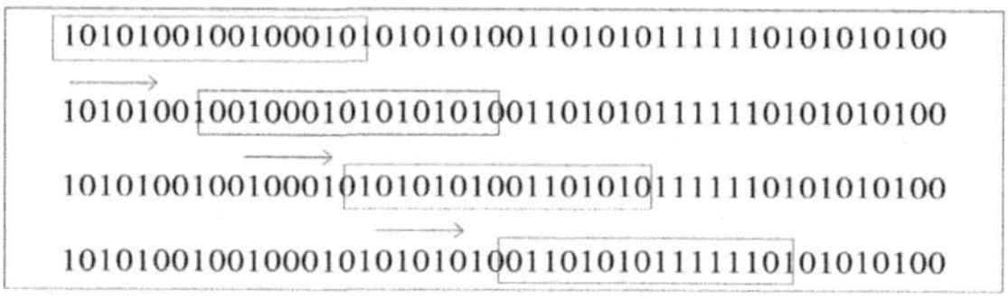

Fig. 2. Sliding Window (window size=2 Byte)

Figure 2 displays an example of a 2-byte window sliding right one byte at a time to generate each 2-gram. Each 2-gram is displayed in the highlighted "window". The choice of the window size depends on the application. In this work, we focus initially on 2-gram analysis of binary values of PE format file. After the preliminary processing, the frequency matrix of data set is obtained. An example of frequency matrix is shown in table 2 of our experiment.

Table 2. Feature Frequency Matrix. (n=2)

Samples	Features					
	0080	61C3	638D	9090	E020	...
Win32.Alcaul.a	2	4	21	8	79	
Win32.Alcaul.b	45	6	40	7	20	
Win32.Alcaul.c	11	11	18	8	14	...
Win32.Alcaul.e	7	0	12	6	25	
...	...	...	...	...	...	

For feature selection in our approach we adopt correlation measures based on the information theoretical concept of entropy, a measure of the uncertainty of a random variable. The distinguishing power of each feature is derived by computing its information gain (IG) based on its frequencies of appearances in the malicious class and benign class. Features with negligible information gain can then be removed to reduce the number of features and speed the classification process.

The entropy of a variable X is defined as:

$$H(X) = -\sum_{i} P(x_i)\log_2(P(x_i)) . \tag{4}$$

And the entropy of *X* after observing values of another variable *Y* is defined as:

$$H(X \mid Y) = -\sum_j P(y_j) \sum_i P(x_i \mid y_j) \log_2 (P(x_i \mid y_j)) . \tag{5}$$

where $P(x_i)$ are the prior probabilities for all values of X, and $P(x_i \mid y_j)$ is the posterior probabilities of x_i given the values of y_j. The amount by which the entropy of X decreases reflects additional information about X provided by Y is called information gain, given by

$$IG(X \mid Y) = H(X) - H(X \mid Y) . \tag{6}$$

Information gain tends to favor variables with more values and can be normalized by their corresponding entropy.

For our problem, the expected entropy calculated as:

$$H(X) = -[P(x\ is\ normal) \cdot \log_2 P(x\ is\ normal) + P(x\ is\ abnormal) \cdot \log_2 P(x\ is\ abnormal)] . \tag{7}$$

If the data set is further partitioned by feature y_i, the conditional entropy $H(X \mid y_i)$ is calculated as:

$$\begin{aligned} H(X \mid y_i) = & -P(y_i = 0) \cdot [P(x\ is\ normal \mid y_i = 0) \cdot \log_2 P(x\ is\ normal \mid y_i = 0) \\ & + P(x\ is\ abnormal \mid y_i = 0) \cdot \log_2 P(x\ is\ abnormal \mid y_i = 0)\ ] \\ & - P(y_i = 1) \cdot [\ P(x\ is\ normal \mid y_i = 1) \cdot \log_2 P(x\ is\ normal \mid y_i = 1) \\ & + P(x\ is\ abnormal \mid y_i = 1) \cdot \log_2 P(x\ is\ abnormal \mid y_i = 1)\ ] . \end{aligned} \tag{8}$$

where $y_i = 0$ denotes that the feature y_i do not appear in the samples, $y_i = 1$ denotes that the feature y_i appears in the samples.

The information gains for each feature are detailed in table 3.

Table 3. The Information Gain of Features (n=2)

Feature	Benign Sample Set		Malicious Sample Set		Information Gain
	y_i=1	y_i=0	y_i=1	y_i=0	
FF84	98	11	92	0	0.000954615
4508	106	3	85	7	0.000387123
FDFF	109	0	89	3	0.001103624
…	…	…	…	…	…

2.3 Detection Method

2.3.1 Heterogeneous Classifiers Ensemble

The methods for producing ensemble classifiers, such as Bagging and Boosting, have been investigated and shown helpful for improving the performance of classifiers [10].

We construct individual classifier by using modified Bagging method, shown in Alg.1. The multiple versions, formed by making bootstrap replicates of the training set and using these as new training sets. Given an original training set S of size N, a training set $S_t, t = 1,2,...,T$ is sampled with replacement from the original dataset S. Then the individual BP Neural Network classifier C_t^{BP} and SVM classifier C_t^{SVM} are trained for each training dataset S_t. To classify an unknown instance x, each BP classifier and SVM classifier returns its class prediction. Then the classification evidences are combined by using D-S theory of evidence to make a final decision. The detailed procedure of fusion method is stated in the next section.

```
1. Given: a training set S = (x_1, y_1),...,(x_n, y_n) where x_i ∈ X
   and y_i ∈ Y = {1,2,...,K} , T is the number of individual
   classifier.
2. For t = 1,2,...,T :
   (1) Generate a new training set S'=bootstrap sample
       from S (sample with replacement).
   (2) Apply the base BP NN classifier on S', C_t^BP : X → Y
   (3) Apply the base SVM classifier on S', C_t^SVM : X → Y
3. Output the aggregated classifier Based on D-S theory
   of evidence:
                  E(x) = arg max_{i∈K} Bel(θ_i)
```

Alg 1. The Ensemble Algorithm

2.3.2 Combination of the Multiple Classifiers Based on D-S Theory

2.3.2.1 Preliminary. In order to take into account uncertainties in classification, the D-S theory of evidence is used in the paper to combine the classification results. In this section, we first briefly describe D-S theory [11], and then generalize the problem of multi-classifier combination based on D-S theory.

Let Θ be a finite set of mutually exclusive and exhaustive propositions about some problem domain and 2^Θ be its power set. A basic probability assignment (BPA), $m: 2^\Theta \to [0,1]$, is used to quantize the belief committed exactly to a subset of the frame of discernment Θ given a certain of evidence. Whenever $m(\varnothing) = 0$, $\sum_{A \subseteq \Theta} m(A) = 1$. The summary of $m(B)$ for all subsets $B \subseteq A$ becomes the total belief in A, i.e.,

$$Bel(A) = \sum_{B \subseteq A} m(B). \tag{9}$$

$Bel(A)$ is a measure of the total belief committed to A.

Two independent evidences expressed as two BPAs m_1 and m_2 can be combined into a single joined basic assignment $m = m_1 \oplus m_2$ by Dempster's rule of combination:

$$m(A) = m_1(A) \oplus m_2(A) = \begin{cases} k \sum_{B \cap C = A} m_1(B) m_2(C) & A \neq \varnothing \\ 0 & A = \varnothing \end{cases} \tag{10}$$

where $k^{-1} = 1 - \sum_{B \cap C = \varnothing} m_1(B) m_2(C) = \sum_{B \cap C \neq \varnothing} m_1(B) m_2(C)$.

2.3.2.2 Combining the Results of Individual Classifiers. In D-S theory, BPA is the degree of the belief of truth induced by a certainty of evidence. Xu et al [12] had proposed a method to calculate the belief. In that approach, the recognition, substitution and rejection rates were used to measure the belief of each classifier. When tested experimentally, this method was found to be quite robust, and was shown to outperform majority voting. However, the way the belief was measured in [12] is not optimal, as it does not take into consideration the accuracy with respect to each class label, and hence does not resolve conflicts between classifiers in an optimal way. This had an impact on the performance of this combination method. So we propose a method that the beliefs calculated from the different class performance of each individual classifier in this paper.

Let there be T classifiers $e^{(1)}, e^{(2)}, ..., e^{(T)}$ used for a K class problem, such that each class is denoted as θ_k, $k = 1, 2, ..., K$. For malicious code detection, there are only two type classes, normal and abnormal. Thus under Dempster-shafer framework we have a frame of discernment denoted as: $\Theta = \{\theta_1, \overline{\theta_1}, \theta_2, \overline{\theta_2}\} = \{N, \overline{N}, A, \overline{A}\}$, where N denotes normal, A denotes abnormal, $N \cap A = \varnothing$. The BBA is defined as:

$$m: 2^{\{N, \overline{N}, A, \overline{A}\}} \rightarrow [0,1],\ m(\varnothing) = 0,\ m(\{N, \overline{N}, A, \overline{A}\}) = 1 - m(N) - m(\overline{N}) - m(A) - m(\overline{A}).$$

Given a test sample x, the related $BPAs$ for the evidence from a classifier $e^{(i)}$ are obtained from the global performance of $e^{(i)}$ as:

$$m_i(N) = TP\ rate/2,\ m_i(\overline{N}) = FP\ rate/2,$$
$$m_i(A) = TN\ rate/2,\ m_i(\overline{A}) = FN\ rate/2.$$

where TP, FP, TN, FN are true positive, false positive, true negative and false negative of classifier $e^{(i)}$ respectively.

At the next stage, the final BPA is calculated as $m = m_{e^{(1)}} \oplus m_{e^{(2)}} \oplus ... \oplus m_{e^{(T)}}$.

As we know that the Dempster's rule of combination is P-complete[13]. However, following Barnett's methods, we can arrive at a computing time cost $O(T)$ [14], where T is the number of total classes.

Now we can finally define the combined classifier E by the following rules:

$$E(x) = \theta_j \text{ if } bel(\theta_j) = \arg\max_{i \in K} Bel(\theta_i). \tag{11}$$

3 Experiment Results

There is no benchmark data set available for the detection of malicious executables unlike intrusion detection. The malicious executables were downloaded from the website VX Heavens [15] were used by [4]. The data used here composed of 423 benign programs and 209 malicious executable codes. All the executables were in Windows PE format. The clean programs were gathered from a freshly installed Windows 2000 server machine and labeled by a commercial virus scanner with the correct class label for our method.

During the experiment, we build byte n-gram profiles with parameter $8bit \leq n \leq 16bit$ and $20 \leq L \leq 4000$, where L is the number of n-gram. For SVM classifier there are some common kernels mentioned in SVM, we must decide which one to try first. Then the penalty parameter C and kernel parameters are chosen. After comparing with the other kernels, we choose Radial Basic Function $K(x, y) = \exp(-\|x - y\|^2 / \sigma^2)$. There are two parameters while using RBF kernel: $1/\sigma^2$ and C. It is not known beforehand which C and $1/\sigma^2$ is the best for one problem. Consequently some kind of parameter search must be done. So we try some variable group value of ($1/\sigma^2$, C) to test the classification performance of each SVM. Parameter used in BP neural network shows in table 4. All input variables are normalized to [0,1].

Table 4. Parameter of BP Neural Network

Number of layers	3
Number of neurons in layer 1	80
Hidden units in each individual network	10
Number of neurons in layer 3	1
Number of training epochs	200
Training function	TRAINGDA
Performance function	MSE
Transfer Function of Layer 1	LOGSIG
Transfer Function of Layer 2	PURELIN

In Data Mining, Receiver Operating Characteristics (ROC) curves are used to compare classification capability of different algorithms. The more the area under the ROC curve of an algorithm, the more robust and better it is in classification. Figure 3 gives the results that compare multi-classifier with single SVM and BP neural network. From the visual inspection of the ROC graph and taking area under the ROC curves into consideration, it is clear that multi-classifier approach outperforms that of single classifier such as SVM and BP neural network.

In literature [4], the authors obtained good results (shows in Fig.4.) in the context of using n-grams for detecting malicious executables. When compare our work with that of [4], we can observe the same conclusion that ensemble method is do improve the performance of classification. When it comes to polymorphic viruses, static analysis methods do not work. To tackle these malicious codes, we combine the static analysis methods with dynamic analysis methods for efficient detection in this paper. It shows that the present method could effectively be used to discriminate normal and abnormal programs.

4 Conclusion

In this paper, we generalize the problem of multi-classifier combination based on Dempster-Shafer theory of evidence for detecting previously unknown malicious codes. The way to derive initial basic probability assignments takes into consideration each classifier's performance with respect to each class label. Our extensive experiments have shown that the combination approach improves the performance of the individual classifier significantly. It shows that the present method could effectively be used to discriminate normal and abnormal programs.

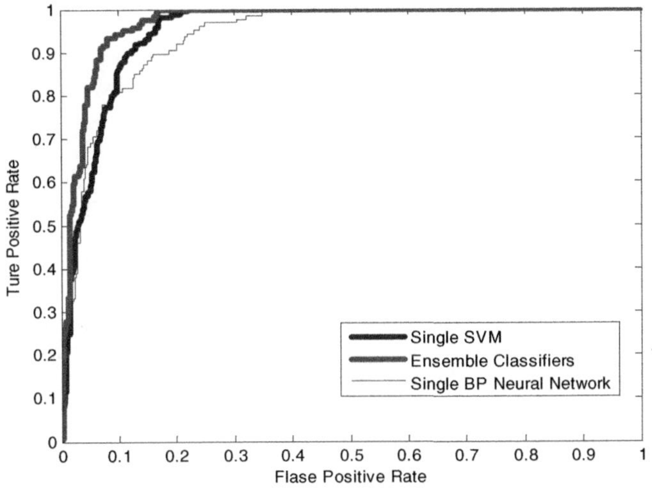

Fig. 3. The ROC graph of ensemble classifier, Single SVM and single BP neural network

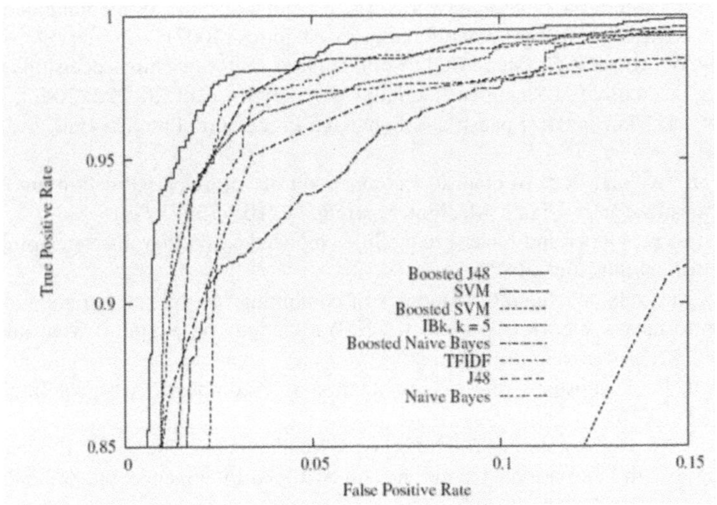

Fig. 4. ROC graph of Ref. [4]

Future work involves extending our learning algorithms to better utilize API function calls and n-gram. We are planning on testing this method over a larger set of malicious and benign executables for a fully evaluation of this method. In addition with a larger data set, we plan to evaluate this method on different types of malicious executables such as Macros and Visual Basic scripts.

Acknowledgment

This work was supported in part by the Scientific Research Fund of Hunan Provincial Education Department of China under Grant No.05B072.

References

1. Kephart, J., Arnold, W.: Automatic Extraction of Computer Virus Signatures. In: Proceedings of the 4th Virus Bulletin International Conference, Abingdon, pp. 178–184 (1994)
2. Lo, R., Levitt, K., Olsson, R.: MCF: A Malicious Code Filter. Computers and Security 14, 541–566 (1995)
3. Tesauro, G., Kephart, J., Sorkin, G.: Neural networks for computer virus recognition. IEEE Expert 8, 5–6 (1996)
4. Kolter, J.Z., Maloof, M.A.: Learning to detect malicious executables in the wild. In: proceedings of the 10th ACM SIGKDD international conference on knowledge discovery and data mining, pp. 470–478. ACM Press, New York (2004)
5. Giacinto, G., Roli, F.: An approach to the automatic design of multiple classifier systems. Pattern Recognition Letters 1, 25–33 (2001)
6. Zhou, Z.H., Wu, J.X., Tang, W.: Ensembling Neural Networks: Many Could be Better than All. Artificial Intelligence 137, 239–263 (2002)
7. Granitto, P.M., Verdes, P.F., Navone, H.D., Ceccatto, H.A.: Aggregation Algorithms for Neural Network Ensemble Construction. In: Werner, B. (ed.) Proceedings of the VII Brazilian Symposium on Neural Networks, IEEE Computer Society, Pernambuco, Brazil, pp. 178–183. IEEE Computer Society Press, Los Alamitos (2002)
8. Yan, W.W., Chen, Z.G., Shao, H.H.: Multi support vector machines decision model and its application. Journal of Shanghai Jiaotong University E-7(2), 220–222 (2002)
9. Jurafsky, D., James, H.: Speech and Language Processing. Prentice-Hall, Inc., New York (2000)
10. Bauer, E., Kohavi, R.: An empirical comparison of voting classification algorithms: bagging, boosting, and variants. Machine Learning 36, 105–139 (1999)
11. Dempster, A.: Upper and lower probabilities induced by multi-valued mapping. Annals of Mathematical Statistics 2, 325–339 (1967)
12. Xu, L., Krzyzak, A., Suen, C.: Methods of combining multiple classifiers and their applications to handwritten recognition. IEEE Transactions on Systems, Man and Cybernetics SMC 22(3), 418–435 (1992)
13. Orponen, P.: Dempster's rule of combination is P-complete. Artificial Intelligence 1-2, 245–253 (1990)
14. Barnet, J.A.: Computational Methods for a Mathematical Theory of Evidence. In: Proceedings of 7th International Conference on Artificial Intelligence, pp. 868–875 (1981)
15. Vx heavens, http://www.vx.netlux.org

Designated Verifier Signature: Definition, Framework and New Constructions

Yong Li[1], Willy Susilo[2], Yi Mu[2], and Dingyi Pei[1,3]

[1] State Key Laboratory of Information Security
Graduate School of Chinese Academy of Sciences,
Beijing 100049, P.R. China
li.yong9@gmail.com
[2] School of Information Technology and Computer Science
University of Wollongong, Wollongong NSW 2522, Australia
{wsusilo,ymu}@uow.edu.au
[3] Guangzhou University, Guangzhou 510400, P.R. China

Abstract. To date, there are numerous variants of designated verifier signatures (DVS), including the notion of strong DVS, multi DVS, universal DVS, etc. In this paper, *for the first time*, we present a *generic definition* of DVS model. We also explore the related security notions in DVS, including unforgeability, non-transferability and non-delegatability, and study the relationship of these notions against variants of DVS. Furthermore, we classify the multi designated verifier signature schemes into four categories depending on the way the verification and simulation is performed. We also point out some drawbacks on the existing DVS schemes, and finally present a new and efficient *constant size* multi DVS scheme that produces a constant size signature regardless the size of the receivers' group. Our scheme is proven secure in the standard model.

1 Introduction

Digital signatures, one of fundamental authentication methods, allow a signer who is equipped with a secret key to sign messages such that anyone can verify the authenticity of the messages with respect to the published public key. The publicly verifiable or self-authenticating property of conventional digital signature is not necessarily desirable in some real scenarios when user's privacy must be taken into account. For example, sometimes it is desirable that a verifier should not present the signatures to other parties, such as certificates for personal health records, income summary, negotiatory price between bidder and tenderee in e-auction system, etc. Designated verifier signature schemes (or DVS schemes, for short) are mainly constructed to address such signer privacy issue by *preventing* the signature from being arbitrarily disseminated [6]. Only a nominated party, called the designated verifier, will trust the authenticity of the message signed via DVS schemes. The intuition behind these schemes is to stop the verifier from transferring his conviction about validity of the signature to any third party, using the fact that the verifier himself can generate such a signature that is indistinguishable from the real signature generated by the signer. Thus, DVS do not provide non-repudiation property of traditional digital signatures.

To date, a number of DVS schemes and their variants have been proposed in the literature, such as universal DVS (UDVS) [12,18,17,5], strong DVS (SDVS) [13,15,16],

J. Indulska et al. (Eds.): UIC 2007, LNCS 4611, pp. 1191–1200, 2007.

multi-DVS (MDVS) [9,11,3], etc. Unfortunately, these abundance have distinct characteristics and addressing different security notions and hence, it has deviated from its original goal and motivation. Therefore, we are motivated to investigate these notions closely and classify them accordingly, so that the resulting framework can be used to analyze the security of DVS schemes and their variants.

Our Contributions. In this paper, we provide a generic definition of DVS model that captures its three variants, i.e. strong DVS, multi DVS and universal DVS, together with its security properties. Based on our framework, we classify the existing DVS variants to enable us to study the characteristics of these schemes.

On non-delegatability notion, we show that one of Zhang et al.'s ID-based UDVS schemes is delegatable. Our new analysis provides an alternative non-transferability proof for the scheme, although such delegation "attack" has been addressed recently in Susilo et al. [14].

On multi-designated verifier signature (MDVS), we analyze Chow's ID-based strong MDVS scheme [3] and show its security problem. The scheme is *fragile* under a forgery attack if the verifier behaves as described in their verification algorithm. Furthermore, we refine the classification of MDVS models. Specifically, there are four types of MDVS schemes according to the number of verifiers participating in the verification and simulation process. Subsequently, we point out that the three MDVS models [9,11,3] actually have subtle differences. Particularly, the two MDVS models [11,3] are different from the first MDVS model in [9] in the sense that the verification and simulation algorithms can *only* be performed by the *coalition* of *all* designated verifiers. Meanwhile, in the model [9], the verification can be performed by every verifier *independently* and simulation can be performed by *coalition* of all designated verifiers.

Finally, we present a new and novel construction of constant-size MDVS scheme which signature length does not grow linearly with the size of the verifiers. Furthermore, it's the first scheme that consistent with type of MDVS [9] and secure in the standard model.

Roadmap. The rest of this paper is organized as follows. In Section 2, we provide formal definition of DVS and its variants. In Section 3, we present the non-delegatability analysis on Zhang et al.'s ID-based UDVS scheme. In Section 4, we present the refined classification of multi DVS schemes, together with presenting the security weakness of Chow's ID-based strong MDVS scheme. In Section 5, we construct a new and efficient constant-size MDVS scheme. Section 6 concludes the paper.

2 DVS and Its Variants

In this section, we present a generic definition of designated verifier signature (DVS) and their variants that could be derived from it. Let S be the signer, and D be the designated verifier. Let $\mathcal{M}$ be the message space. A *designated verifier signature* (DVS) scheme is defined by the following algorithms:

- $\mathsf{Setup}(k)$ is a probabilistic algorithm that outputs the public parameter *param*, where k is the security parameter.
- $\mathsf{KeyGen}(\mathit{param}, k)$ is a probabilistic algorithm that takes the public parameters as an input and outputs a secret/public key-pair $(\mathsf{SK}, \mathsf{PK})$;

– $\mathsf{Sign}_{\mathsf{SK}_S,\mathsf{PK}_D}(m)$ takes as input signer's secret key, designated verifiers' public key, a message $m \in \mathcal{M}$ and a possible random string, and outputs a signature σ;
– $\mathsf{Verify}_{\mathsf{PK}_S,\mathsf{PK}_D}(m,\sigma)$ is a deterministic algorithm that takes as input a signing public key PK_S, public key of designated verifier D, a message $m \in \mathcal{M}$ and a candidate signature σ, and returns accept or reject;

We say that a signature σ on m is valid if $\mathsf{Verify}_{\mathsf{PK}_S,\mathsf{PK}_D}(m,\sigma) = \mathsf{accept}$. As usually, we require that an DVS scheme is correct, that is, for all $(\mathsf{SK}_S, \mathsf{PK}_S)$ and $(\mathsf{SK}_D, \mathsf{PK}_D)$ output by KeyGen, for $m \in \mathcal{M}$, we have

$$\mathsf{Verify}_{\mathsf{PK}_S,\mathsf{PK}_D}(\mathsf{Sign}_{\mathsf{SK}_S,\mathsf{PK}_D}(m)) = \mathsf{accept}.$$

Generally, a secure DVS scheme must satisfy the following two basic properties:

- ***unforgeability***, which is consistent with classical security notion for signature, namely, existential unforgeable against adaptive chosen message attack (EUF-CMA) [4]. More formally, it is defined using the following game between an adversary $\mathcal{A}$ and a challenger $\mathcal{C}$:
  - Let $\mathcal{A}$ be the EUF-CMA adversary. In the startup of the game, $\mathcal{C}$ provides the common scheme parameter *cp* to $\mathcal{A}$, where $cp \leftarrow \mathsf{Setup}(k)$ and k is the security parameter.
  - $\mathcal{C}$ provides the signer's public key PK_S and verifiers' public key PK_D to $\mathcal{A}$.
  - At any time, $\mathcal{A}$ can query the signing oracle for the signature on any message m_i of his choice up to q_S times (which is polynomial in k). $\mathcal{C}$ will answer $\mathcal{A}$'s queries by providing the value $\sigma = \mathsf{Sign}(cp, \mathsf{SK}_S, m_i, \mathsf{PK}_D)$ where SK_S is the corresponding secret key of the specified user queried by $\mathcal{A}$ for m_i.
  - Eventually, $\mathcal{A}$ will output a new DVS σ^* for a message m^*. $\mathcal{A}$ wins the game if $\mathsf{Verify}_{\mathsf{PK}_S,\mathsf{PK}_D}(m^*,\sigma^*) = \mathsf{accept}$, and m^* has never been queried to the signing oracle before, for the designated verifier with public key PK_D.

  The success probability of an adversary to win the game is defined by $Succ_{DVS,\mathcal{A}}^{EUF-CMA}(k)$.

  Definition 1. *(Unforgeability) We say that a DVS scheme is existentially unforgeable under a chosen message attack, or (t,ε)-EUF-CMA secure, if no polynomially bounded adversary $\mathcal{A}$ running in time t has a success probability $Succ_{DVS,\mathcal{A}}^{EUF-CMA}(k) \geq \varepsilon$.*

- ***non-transferability.*** Formally, non-transferability is defined through the following game involving $\mathcal{D}$ and $\mathcal{C}$. Challenger $\mathcal{C}$ can simulate attack environment for $\mathcal{D}$ by running Sign and Simulation algorithm. $\mathcal{D}$ is a distinguisher that tries to distinguish whether a given output is generated by signer or designated verifier.
  - The challenger $\mathcal{C}$ takes as input a security parameter k and executes $cp \leftarrow \mathsf{Setup}(k)$, $(\mathsf{SK}_S, \mathsf{PK}_S) \leftarrow \mathsf{KeyGen}(k, cp)$, $(\mathsf{SK}_D, \mathsf{PK}_D) \leftarrow \mathsf{KeyGen}(k, cp)$. $\mathcal{C}$ provides $\mathsf{PK}_S, \mathsf{PK}_D$ to $\mathcal{D}$ and keeps $\mathsf{SK}_S, \mathsf{SK}_D$ secret.
  - The distinguisher $\mathcal{D}$ issues signing queries on any message m_i. $\mathcal{C}$ responds with $\sigma = \mathsf{Sign}(cp, \mathsf{SK}_S, m_i, \mathsf{PK}_D)$.

- $\mathcal{D}$ submits new message m^* to $\mathcal{C}$. $\mathcal{C}$ then flips a fair coin $b \xleftarrow{R} \{0,1\}$, generates a signature σ^* and returns it to $\mathcal{D}$. For example, if b=0, $\mathcal{C}$ runs Sign algorithm and returns $\sigma^* = \mathsf{Sign}(cp, \mathsf{SK}_S, m_i, \mathsf{PK}_D)$; Otherwise, $\mathcal{C}$ runs Simulation and returns $\sigma^* = \mathsf{Simulation}(cp, \mathsf{SK}_D, m_i, \mathsf{PK}_D)$.
- On receiving the challenging signature, $\mathcal{D}$ can issues new queries with the restriction of not querying m^*.
- Eventually, $\mathcal{D}$ outputs a bit b' and wins if $b' = b$.

The advantage of an adaptively chosen message distinguisher $\mathcal{D}$ is defined as $Adv\mathcal{D}_{DVS}^{CMA} = |Pr[b' = b] - 1/2|$.

Definition 2. *(Non-transferability) We say that a DVS scheme is non-transferability against a (t, q_S) adaptively chosen message distinguisher $\mathcal{D}$ if $Adv\mathcal{D}_{DVS}^{CMA}$ is negligible after making at most q_S signing queries in time t.*

2.1 Differences from Former Definitions

There are several differences between the new definition above and the previously adopted definitions [13,8,10,7]. The new definition is more versatile and extendable because other DVS variants could be derived from it easily. The three main variations of DVS in the literature were unfolded as follows.

A DVS scheme is called to be

- *strong* DVS (SDVS), if the verification algorithm also takes SK_D as an input. Moreover, the verification without SK_D is computationally infeasible.
- *Multi-* DVS (MDVS), if the signature is intended for n verifiers, $n > 1$.
- *Universal* DVS (UDVS), if it contains a conventional signing algorithm (w.r.t. no designated verifier) and an arbitrary signature holder (designator) can convert the conventional signature to a designated signature w.r.t. an arbitrary designated verifier.

We note that we do not further differentiate the DVS variants that are public key based from the identity-based setting. Our view is to capture the variants that are distinct and not only in the view of public key setting.

The three DVS variants were proposed respectively from a different angle. Multi-DVS can be treated as an extended DVS with multiple designated verifiers. Universal DVS allows multiple signature designators (from a signer to any signature holder). The strong DVS notion was proposed to enhance the DVS security for a more hostile environment [6,13,8]. Generally, to make a strong designated verifier signature, one will use the public key of the intended verifier to encrypt the signature, and this implies that only the specific verifier can verify the signature by using his/her private key.

Another difference is that we treat the simulation function (which mainly guarantees non-transferability) as one security requisites instead of as a component of signature algorithms like in [7]. Commonly, non-transferability is guaranteed by a signature *simulation* algorithm that is run by the designated verifier to produce an identically distributed signature that is indistinguishable from the original signature. Such a particular property differentiates DVS from conventional digital signatures. Finally, we treat another security notion of DVS, non-delegatability [10,7,14], as an *enhanced* security option.

3 Delegatability Analysis of ID-Based UDVS Scheme

In this section, we firstly analyze delegatability property on one of Zhang et al.'s ID-based UDVS schemes [19], according to Lipmaa et al.'s original non-delegatability definition in [10]. Furthermore, we interpret the delegatability analysis from new angle of view, inspired by the new refined non-delegatability notion in [14]. The brief review of ZSMC05 scheme [19] is omitted due to page limitation.

3.1 Delegatability Analysis

(Negative aspect) If signer leaks $d = e(SK_S, PK_D)$ or verifier leaks $d = e(PK_S, SK_D)$ to third party T, then T can compute the simulated designated verifier signature as follows.

- Compute $U = rPK_S$, where $r \in_R Z_q^*$, $h = H_1(U||m)$.
- Compute $\sigma' = d^{(r+h)}$.
- Output the designated verifier signature on m as (U, σ').

Clearly,

$$\begin{aligned} e(U + H_1(U||m)PK_S, SK_D) &= e(rPK_S + H_1(U||m)PK_S, SK_D) \\ &= e(PK_S, SK_D)^{r+H_1(U||m)} = e(SK_S, PK_D)^{r+h} \\ &= d^{(r+h)} = \sigma'. \end{aligned}$$

Thus, designated verification equation is satisfied. It means that the scheme has delegatability weakness according to Lipmaa et al.'s definition in [10]. The above "delegation attack" allows us to delegate the signing rights of a fixed signer with respect to a *fixed designated verifier*.

(Positive aspect) The above scheme is indeed a strong DVS scheme and the $d = e(SK_S, PK_D) = e(PK_S, SK_D)$ is a crucial *common key* in the scheme, with which anyone can perform simulation algorithm. According to the new refined non-delegatability notion in strong DVS [14], such an essential key should not be released. This makes the above delegatability analysis no longer significant.

Note that in proof for non-transferability ([19], Theorem 2), the simulation algorithm is actually the *same* as the designated verification algorithm. Interestingly, the computations in delegatability analysis could serve as the simulation algorithm for this scheme if verifier firstly uses his/her secret key to compute $d = e(PK_S, SK_D)$, which provides an alternative non-transferability proof for the scheme. That is, the analysis makes the scheme have different simulation and designated verification algorithm.

4 MDVS Model

To date, to the best of our knowledge, there is only a few MDVS schemes proposed in the literature (i.e. [9,11,3]). Interestingly, we found there is subtle distinction between the above three MDVS models, which has not been pointed out explicitly in the literature. Meanwhile, we also analyze some potential vulnerability of Chow's MDVS scheme [3], that will be presented in the next section.

4.1 Analysis of Chow's MDVS Scheme [3]

Due to page limitation, the brief review of Chow's scheme [3] is omitted.

Vulnerability Analysis
Suppose that an attacker intercepts a signature $\{U_1, U_2, V, Y, Z_1, Z_2, \cdots, Z_n\}$, and he tampers it with $\sigma' = \{U_1, U_2, V, Y, *, *, \cdots, Z_i, \cdots, *\}$. That is, he fills the fragment $\{Z_1, Z_2, \cdots, Z_n\}$ with random values except Z_i. We note that the forged signature σ' still satisfies V_i's verification equations. In fact, verifier V_i only checks the validity of the signature segment $\{U_1, U_2, V, Y, Z_i\}$ in the Verify algorithm.

However, other verifiers $V_j (j \neq i)$ could detect the invalidity of σ'. Unfortunately, since there is no correspondence or cooperation between n verifiers in their MDVS model, V_i will be cheated in this situation, by believing that the signature is indeed valid. Furthermore, the direct countermeasure that all verifiers cooperatively perform Verify algorithm will invalidate the above attack. Unfortunately, $4n$ costly pairing operations are required to perform this operation.

In short, if only one V_i participates in the verification (as the author claimed in [3] that there are only 4 pairing operations in Verify algorithm), the scheme is *fragile* under the above forgery attack. If the scheme is being adjusted to the case where every verifier cooperatively performs the verification steps, then it becomes very inefficient, and hence, we have a paradox.

Amendment of Chow's scheme. We present an alternative scheme to avoid the above attack. The Setup, Extract, Sign and Step 1,2 in Verify algorithm is the same as original scheme. Step 3 in the Verify algorithm is revised as follows.

Return true if the following equations

1. $e(P_{pub}, U_1 + h_1 H_1(ID_S) + U_2 + h_2 P_V) = e(P, V)$;
2. For each $Z_j (j \neq i)$, $e(Z_j, P) = e(H_1(ID_{V_j}) + Q, Y)$.

hold and $\perp$ otherwise.

This improvement fixes the flaw in Chow's scheme. There is totally $4 + 2 * (n - 1) = 2 * (n + 1)$ paring operations in the Verify algorithm. Moreover, the revised Verify algorithm could be performed by every verifier independently.

4.2 Refined Classification

In this section, we present a refined definition of MDVS scheme.

According to number of verifiers required in the Verify algorithm, there are two types of MDVS schemes:

(a) the Verify algorithm can be performed by every verifier *independently*;
(b) the Verify algorithm can be performed only by the *coalition* of all designated verifiers.

Analogously, there are other two kinds of MDVS if the number of verifiers in the signature simulation algorithm is taken into account.

(c) the simulation can be performed by every verifier *independently*;
(d) the simulation can be performed only by the *coalition* of all designated verifiers.

Table 1. Classification of MDVS schemes

Verify\Simulation	(c)	(d)
(a)	n/a	[9]
(b)	n/a	[11] [3]

Therefore, by combining the above categories, we classify four kinds of MDVS schemes. Furthermore, we classify the three existing MDVS schemes [9,11,3] using this classification as shown in Table 1. (The detail description of schemes refer to [9,11,3].)

We stress that the functionality of the simulation algorithm which guarantees non-transferability is *inherent* in DVS schemes. Unfortunately, it was not explicitly stated as a necessary ingredient in [9,3]. (In [11], such simulation capability of verifier was demonstrated in the proof of non-transferability.) According to Li, Lipmaa and Pei's analysis in [7], it needs all verifiers to work cooperatively to accomplish the simulation in [9]. The scheme in [3] also does not provide any simulation algorithm to ensure the non-transferability property. However, the construction is consistent with the generic MDVS construction mechanism from ring signatures from [9] and the author indicated that *signer ambiguity* is directly obtained from the underlying ID-based ring signature.

In conclusion, based on the above analysis and the table, the three MDVS models (all are strong MDVS) have subtle differences. Particularly, the subsequent two MDVS models [11,3] are different from the first MDVS model [9], with respect to the number of verifiers participating in the verification and simulation algorithms.

4.3 Transfer Mode in MDVS

The MDVS model is treated as a generalized DVS in a multi-user setting, in which the signature is intended to a specific set of different verifiers. In such a scenario, there is another question that should be considered in implementing practical MDVS scheme: "How does the signature propagate to all the verifiers?" We refer the signature propagation as the *signature transfer* in DVS schemes.

Essentially, there are two signature transfer modes, namely *sequential mode* and *broadcast mode*. In sequential mode, the signer delivers her signature from verifier V_1 to V_n in a step-by-step manner, while in broadcast mode, the signer broadcasts the signature to all verifiers simultaneously.

In sequential mode, if each verifier could simulate the signature independently, then successor V_j *cannot* distinguish whether σ was generated by the signer or simulated by his/her predecessor V_i $(i < j)$. Such case *breaches* the basic requirement of MDVS and actually it degenerates into DVS, namely, only one specific recipient V_1 can be convinced that "signer has signed on a message". However, if the simulation must be performed by every verifier cooperatively, then V_j can identify the source of signature since he knows that he does not participate in the simulation algorithm.

In broadcast mode, supposing the simulation must be done by all verifiers collaboratively, if a verifier V_i is corrupted or captured/controlled by a hostile third party and hence becomes unavailable, then the simulation cannot be accomplished. In this case, all parties, including the designated verifier and any other third party, can be convinced with the authenticity of the signature, which deviates the purpose of having a designated verifier scheme. Hence, the non-transferability property is no longer satisfied by the scheme. We note that in a normal situation, non-transferability is always guaranteed by the signature simulation algorithm. Additionally, if each verifier can simulate the signature independently, then this case will not influence the characteristic of MDVS schemes.

According to the refined classification in section 4.2 and the above analysis, the secure implemental approach for [9,11,3] is to adopt sequential mode when transferring signature to multiple intended recipients. Furthermore, in [11,3] schemes, every verifier need to be well protected to guarantee their availability, otherwise, no verifier could check the validity of the signature. Simultaneously, to the best of our knowledge, there is no MDVS scheme adapted for broadcast mode, of which the simulation algorithm could be independently executed by each verifier. We leave it as an open problem to explore such scheme.

Therefore, the signature transfer mode is an important issue in implementing a practical MDVS scheme. Unfortunately, the distinction on verification/simulation mode (independently or cooperatively) and correlative problem of signature transfer mode in MDVS was overlooked in the three MDVS models [9,11,3].

5 An Efficient and Constant-Size MDVS

Another shortcoming in Chow's scheme [3] (including our revised scheme) is that signature length is proportional to number of verifiers. For a large set of verifiers, the length of a multi-designated verifier signature (growing linearly with the size) will be impractical. In this section, we propose a new constant-size MDVS scheme. Our scheme is based on Boneh-Boyen short signature scheme [1]. Furthermore, our scheme does not rely on the random oracle model for its proof of security. The description of our new construction is as follows.

- Setup: Let $(\mathbb{G}_1, \mathbb{G}_2)$ be a bilinear groups where $|\mathbb{G}_1| = |\mathbb{G}_2| = p$, k be the system security parameter and g be the generator of $\mathbb{G}_1$. e denotes the bilinear pairing $\mathbb{G}_1 \times \mathbb{G}_1 \rightarrow \mathbb{G}_2$. The system parameter $cp = \{\mathbb{G}_1, \mathbb{G}_2, p, k, e, g\}$ which is shared by all the users in the system.
- KeyGen: Given cp, Signer picks two secret numbers $u_a, v_a \in_R Z_p^*$ and set secret key $sk_s = (u_a, v_a)$. Signer's public key is $pk_s = (U_a, V_a) = (g^{u_a}, g^{v_a})$. Similarly, for $i = 1, \cdots, n$, the verifier V_i's secret/public key pair is $sk_{v_i} = u_i$, $pk_{v_i} = g^{u_i}$.
- Sign: Given a message m, signer's secret key sk_s and verifiers' public keys pk_{v_i}, signer chooses $r, s \in Z_p^*$ and computes $Q_1 = g^{\frac{s}{u_a + m + v_a r}}$, $Q_2 = (\prod_{i=1}^{n} pk_{v_i})^s$, $Q_3 = g^s$. The designated verifier signature of m is $\sigma = (r, Q_1, Q_2, Q_3)$.
- Verify: Given message-signature pair (m, σ), the signer's public key pk_s, verifier's public key pk_{v_i}, the verifier checks whether
  1. $e(Q_1, U_a \cdot g^m \cdot V_a^r) = e(Q_3, g)$;
  2. $e(\prod_{i=1}^{n} pk_{v_i}, Q_3) = e(Q_2, g)$.

  If all the equalities hold, output Accept, otherwise Reject.

The correctness of the scheme is straightforward. The non-transferability property is established by the following theorem.

Theorem 1. *The new scheme satisfies non-transferability.*

Similar to theorem in [18,17], the next theorem shows the unforgeability of the scheme under the strong Diffie-Hellman assumption (SDH)[1] and the knowledge-of-exponent (KEA) assumption [2].

Theorem 2. *The MDVS scheme achieves existential unforgeable against adaptive chosen message attack (EUF-CMA) security under strong Diffie-Hellman assumption and knowledge-of-exponent assumption.*

Due to page limitation, the details of formal security proof and some remarks are provided in the full version.

6 Conclusions

In this paper, we presented a generic definition of designated verifier signature (DVS) and examined several security notions in DVS and its three main variants, namely strong DVS, multi-DVS and universal DVS. Two concrete DVS schemes (UDVS and MDVS) was respectively analyzed from delegatability and forgeability. We proposed the refined classification of MDVS models and indicated that the three MDVS models [9,11,3] are unique. Finally, we also presented a new and efficient constant-size MDVS scheme, which is proven secure without incorporating the random oracle model.

Acknowledgements. We thank Helger Lipmaa and Raylin Tso for helpful and inspired discussions on DVS, as well as the anonymous referees for useful comments.

References

1. Boneh, D., Boyen, X.: Short Signatures Without Random Oracles. In: Cachin, C., Camenisch, J.L. (eds.) EUROCRYPT 2004. LNCS, vol. 3027, pp. 56–73. Springer, Heidelberg (2004)
2. Bellare, M., Palacio, A.: The Knowledge-of-Exponent Assumptions and 3-Round Zero-Knowledge Protocols. In: Franklin, M. (ed.) CRYPTO 2004. LNCS, vol. 3152, pp. 273–289. Springer, Heidelberg (2004)
3. Chow, S.S.M.: Identity-based Strong Multi-Designated Verifiers Signatures. In: Atzeni, A.S., Lioy, A. (eds.) EuroPKI 2006. LNCS, vol. 4043, pp. 257–259. Springer, Heidelberg (2006)
4. Goldwasser, S., Micali, S., Rivest, R.L.: A Digital Signature Scheme Secure Against Adaptive Chosen Message Attacks. SIAM Journal on Computing 17(2), 281–308 (1988)
5. Huang, X., Susilo, W., Mu, Y., Zhang, F.: Restricted Universal Designated Verifier Signature. In: Ma, J., Jin, H., Yang, L.T., Tsai, J.J.-P. (eds.) UIC 2006. LNCS, vol. 4159, pp. 874–882. Springer, Heidelberg (2006)
6. Jakobsson, M., Sako, K., Impagliazzo, R.: Designated Verifier Proofs and Their Applications. In: Maurer, U.M. (ed.) EUROCRYPT 1996. LNCS, vol. 1070, pp. 143–154. Springer, Heidelberg (1996)
7. Li, Y., Lipmaa, H., Pei, D.: On Delegatability of Four Designated Verifier Signatures. In: Qing, S., Mao, W., Lopez, J., Wang, G. (eds.) ICICS 2005. LNCS, vol. 3783, pp. 61–71. Springer, Heidelberg (2005)

8. Laguillaumie, F., Vergnaud, D.: Designated Verifier Signatures: Anonymity and Efficient Construction from Any Bilinear Map. In: Blundo, C., Cimato, S. (eds.) SCN 2004. LNCS, vol. 3352, pp. 105–119. Springer, Heidelberg (2005)
9. Laguillaumie, F., Vergnaud, D.: Multi-designated Verifiers Signatures. In: Lopez, J., Qing, S., Okamoto, E. (eds.) ICICS 2004. LNCS, vol. 3269, pp. 495–507. Springer, Heidelberg (2004)
10. Lipmaa, H., Wang, G., Bao, F.: Designated Verifier Signature Schemes: Attacks, New Security Notions and A New Construction. In: Caires, L., Italiano, G.F., Monteiro, L., Palamidessi, C., Yung, M. (eds.) ICALP 2005. LNCS, vol. 3580, pp. 459–471. Springer, Heidelberg (2005)
11. Ng, C.Y., Susilo, W., Mu, Y.: Universal Designated Multi Verifier Signature Schemes. In: SNDS 2000, pp. 305–309. IEEE Press, NJ, New York (2005)
12. Steinfeld, R., Bull, L., Wang, H., Pieprzyk, J.: Universal Designated-Verifier Signatures. In: Laih, C.-S. (ed.) ASIACRYPT 2003. LNCS, vol. 2894, pp. 523–542. Springer, Heidelberg (2003)
13. Saeednia, S., Kremer, S., Markowitch, O.: An Efficient Strong Designated Verifier Signature Scheme. In: Lim, J.-I., Lee, D.-H. (eds.) ICISC 2003. LNCS, vol. 2971, pp. 40–54. Springer, Heidelberg (2004)
14. Susilo, W., Wu, W., Mu, Y., Huang, X.: On the "Non-Delegatability" Notion of Designated Verifier Signature Schemes. In: IWAP 2006, Springer-Verlag, Heidelberg (to appear, 2006)
15. Susilo, W., Zhang, F., Mu, Y.: Identity-Based Strong Designated Verifier Signature Schemes. In: Wang, H., Pieprzyk, J., Varadharajan, V. (eds.) ACISP 2004. LNCS, vol. 3108, pp. 313–324. Springer, Heidelberg (2004)
16. Tso, R., Okamoto, T., Okamoto, E.: Practical Strong Designated Verifier Signature Schemes Based on Double Discrete Logarithms. In: Feng, D., Lin, D., Yung, M. (eds.) CISC 2005. LNCS, vol. 3822, pp. 113–127. Springer, Heidelberg (2005)
17. Vergnaud, D.: New Extensions of Pairing-based Signatures into Universal Designated Verifier Signatures. In: Bugliesi, M., Preneel, B., Sassone, V., Wegener, I. (eds.) ICALP 2006. LNCS, vol. 4052, pp. 58–69. Springer, Heidelberg (2006)
18. Zhang, R., Furukawa, J., Imai, H.: Short Signature and Universal Designated Verifier Signature Without Random Oracles. In: Ioannidis, J., Keromytis, A.D., Yung, M. (eds.) ACNS 2005. LNCS, vol. 3531, pp. 483–498. Springer, Heidelberg (2005)
19. Zhang, F., Susilo, W., Mu, Y., Chen, X.: Identity-based Universal Designated Verifier Signatures. In: Enokido, T., Yan, L., Xiao, B., Kim, D., Dai, Y., Yang, L.T. (eds.) Embedded and Ubiquitous Computing – EUC 2005 Workshops. LNCS, vol. 3823, pp. 825–834. Springer, Heidelberg (2005)

Towards Secure Agent Computing for Ubiquitous Computing and Ambient Intelligence*

Antonio Maña, Antonio Muñoz, and Daniel Serrano

Departamento de Lenguajes y Ciencias de la Computación
Universidad de Málaga. España
{amg,amunoz,serrano}@lcc.uma.es

Abstract. After a first phase of great activity in the field of multi-agent systems, researchers seemed to lose interest in the paradigm, mainly due to the lack of scenarios where the highly distributed nature of these systems could be appropriate. However, recent computing models such as ubiquitous computing and ambient intelligence have introduced the need for this type of highly distributed, autonomous and asynchronous computing mechanisms. The agent paradigm can play an important role and can suit the needs of many applications in these scenarios. In this paper we argue that the main obstacle for the practical application of multi-agent systems is the lack of appropriate security mechanisms. Moreover, we show that as a result of recent advances in security technologies, it is now possible to solve the most important security problems of agent-based systems.

1 Introduction

Mobile agents are software entities with the ability to migrate from node to node in a network acting autonomously and in cooperation with other agents in order to accomplish a variety of tasks. Currently there are different agent-based applications in numerous computer environments such as peer-to-peer networks, Web crawlers, and surveillance of local area networks, just to mention a few.

Agent-systems, and in particular multi-agent systems (MAS), can bring important benefits especially in application scenarios where highly distributed, autonomous, intelligent, self organizing and robust systems are required. Furthermore, the high levels of autonomy and self-organization of agent systems provide excellent support for the development of systems in which dependability is essential. Ubiquitous Computing and Ambient Intelligence scenarios belong to this category.

However, despite the attention given to the field by the research community, the agent technology has failed to gain a wide acceptance and has been applied only in a few specific real world scenarios. Security issues play an important role in the development of multi-agent systems and are considered one of the main issues to solve for agent technology to be widely used outside the research community.

* Work partially supported by E.U. through projects SERENITY (IST-027587) and GREDIA (IST-034363) and by Junta de Castilla la Mancha through MISTICO-MECHANICS project (PBC06-0082).

J. Indulska et al. (Eds.): UIC 2007, LNCS 4611, pp. 1201–1212, 2007.

But for the provision of appropriate security in the context of multiagent systems it is not enough that the agent platform provides a set of standard security mechanisms such as sandboxing, encryption and digital signatures. It is necessary to design the whole infrastructure with security in mind. Furthermore, the security of an agent platform needs to be tailored to the specific characteristics of these systems.

This paper describes some current technologies that can be used to build secure agent systems suitable for applications in ubiquitous computing and ambient intelligence scenarios. We must note that in these scenarios the computational infrastructure is composed of a very large number of computing devices with heterogeneous capabilities and under the control of different owners. This heterogeneity introduces the need for agents and agencies to learn about the capabilities and needs of each other.

This problem was addressed in a previous paper [2] based on the use of agent profiles, where we also introduced a protection approach based on the Trusted Computing paradigm. We introduced the application of the Protected Computing paradigm to agents in [3]. In this paper we further develop this latter approach. In particular we describe in detail the development of agent systems using the protected computing approach, including the use of different automated tools to support it.

The organization of the paper is as follows. Section 2 describes the background on the security (or lack of) in current and past agent platforms. Section 3 describes two different ways to apply our approach, called Protected Computing, focusing on the development cycle and the tools used. In order for the paper to be self contained, Section 4 describes briefly two other technologies (Trusted Computing and Proof-Carrying Code) that can be used for the implementation of secure agent systems. Finally, Section 5 summarizes conclusions and describes some ongoing work.

2 The Road Behind

We have mentioned that the focus of our paper is the description of suitable mechanisms for the security of agent systems in ubiquitous computing and ambient intelligence scenarios. The purpose of this section is to provide a view about the main agent-based systems and agent oriented tools, focusing on their security mechanisms. This review covers a wide range of applications from the first applications to the more recent ones. The objective of this analysis is to draw attention to the fact that these systems have traditionally neglected the need of a secure underlying infrastructure.

The first MAS applications appeared in the middle 80s. These pioneer systems covered a variety of environments (manufacturing systems, air traffic control, information management ...), but almost all of them were built upon non secure infrastructures [4-6]. At that time, agent technology developers assumed that the underlying infrastructure was secure, but now it is obvious that it is not. Other agent-based applications lacking a security infrastructure were even proposed for nuclear plants [7] and aircraft control [8] applications.

If we focus not on the applications, but on the infrastructures for agent-based systems, the situation is quite similar. Unfortunately, most of the platforms for agents, like Aglet [9], Cougaar [10], JACK™ [11], JADE [12], JAVACT [13], and AgentSpeak [14], share a negative common point, which is their insufficient security.

3 The Road Ahead

The fact that the current situation is far from satisfactory does not mean that the problems do not have a solution. In fact, the goal of this paper, and in particular of this section, is to present several viable technologies that can be used in multi-agent systems in order to provide a secure infrastructure. Three different existing technologies, namely Protected Computing [3], Trusted Computing [16] and Proof Carrying Code [17], are described in this section focusing on the role they can play in securing agent systems and the technical details of their application to this scenario.

Protected Computing approaches are based on the remote execution of part of the code of an application (an agent, in our case). We present two schemes for providing security on multi-agent systems based on the Protected Computing paradigm. The Trusted Computing paradigm uses a specific hardware architecture containing trusted hardware elements. We show how this paradigm can enhance the trust on the configuration of the agencies. Finally, this section is closed by presenting the Proof-Carrying Code technology and showing how this technology contributes to the protection against malicious agents.

3.1 Protected Computing

The Protected Computing approach is based on the partitioning of the software elements into two or more parts. The basic idea is to divide the application code into two or more mutually dependent parts. Some of these parts (which we will call private parts) are executed in a secure processor, while others (public parts) are executed in any processor even if it is not trusted. A detailed description of this technology is presented in reference [3].

As mentioned, the approach uses a trusted processor to enforce the correct execution of the private parts of the program. Therefore, these parts must be carefully selected in order to obtain the best protection. In general, the Protected Computing model requires the use of secure coprocessors that have asymmetric cryptography capabilities; secure storage to contain a key pair generated inside the coprocessor and ensure that the private key never leaves it. Depending on the scenario some of these requirements may be relaxed. An important advantage of this scheme is the fact that different types of coprocessors can be used for different applications, as well as for different partitions of the same application.

It is possible to apply the protected computing model in order to protect agent societies in a multi-agent setting, where several agents are sent to different (untrusted) agencies in order to perform some collaborative task. Because agents run in potentially malicious hosts, the goal in this scenario is to protect agents from the hosts. The basic idea is to make agents collaborate, not only in the specific tasks they are designed to perform, but also in the protection of other agents. In this way each agent acts as secure coprocessor for other agents.

Therefore, using the protected computing model, the code of each agent is divided into public and private parts. For the sake of simplicity, and without loss of generality, we will consider the simplest case where the code of each agent is divided in two parts: a public one and a protected one. From this description, it is easy to derive the possibilities that the division of the code into more parts opens. In particular the inclusion of multiple private parts, which could even be designed to be executed in different coprocessors, is especially relevant for the scenarios that we are considering. In the general case, the private part of each agent must be executed by some other agent running in a different host. This scheme is suitable for protecting a set of several mutually dependent agents. Consequently, in this general case, a conspiracy of all hosts is necessary in order to attack the system.

Fig. 1 depicts the development cycle of the protection of a multi-agent system following this approach. We have divided the complete development cycle into two phases, development and deployment. This section will concentrate on the development phase. Next sections will review the deployment aspects.

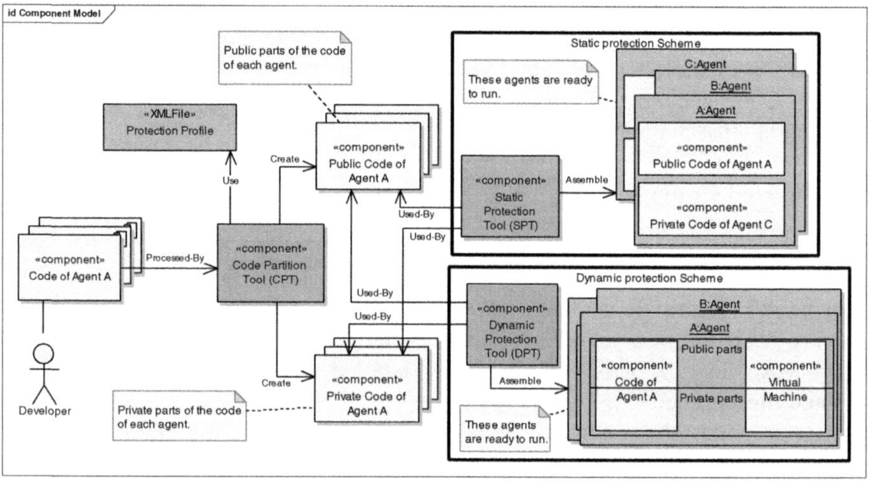

Fig. 1. Development time of a multi-agent system using a protected computing approach

The development phase begins as usual with the coding of the complete multi-agent system by the developer. Then, the developer uses the *"Code Partitioning Tool"* (CPT) in order to divide the code into public and private parts. Since the code partition is a difficult task, and specialized expertise is required for performing it, this tool is responsible for carrying out this process according to a set of predefined rules that we call *"protection profiles"*. The product of the operation of this tool is a set of public parts and a set of private parts. At runtime, these parts will be used in a different way depending on the mutual protection scheme applied (see sections 3.1.1 and 3.1.2). Note also in Fig.1 that there are two different approaches for protecting the agents, namely *Static Mutual Protection* and *Dynamic Mutual Protection*. A detailed description of these approaches is presented in the subsequent subsections.

A key element in this scheme is the *protection profile*. A protection profile consists on a set of rules used to tailor the application of the protected computing approach. These rules describe the way in which the partitioning is carried out. They establish the number of partitions, the kind of instructions to be protected, the sizes of these partitions, etc. Fig. 2 shows a simple example of protection profile defining how the partition method is to be applied and described my means of a set of rules coded in XML. These rules have parameters which can be set from the CPT. The use of protection profiles makes the application of the protection mechanism to a multi-agent system easy for developers. The process is indeed easy to use since developers are aided by a tool that allows them to set up the values to establish a concrete partitioning method, which is then applied automatically to the agents' code.

```
<?xml version="1.0" encoding="iso-8859-1"?>
<agent xmlns:xsi="http://www.w3.org/2001/XMLSchema-instance"
xsi:noNamespaceSchemaLocation="D:\informacion\ProtectionProfile.xsd">
    <settings>
        <MaxNumberOfPartitions> Number </MaxNumberOfPartitions>
        <SetOfProtectedIns>
            <Ins> ControlFlow </Ins>
            <Ins> Load&Store </Ins>
            <Ins> MethodInvocations </Ins>
        </SetOfProtectedIns>
        <MaxPartitionSize> Size</MaxPartitionSize>
        <PriorityOrder>
            <Instructions>
                <Ins> Load&Store </Ins>
                <Ins> MethodInvocations </Ins>
                <Ins> ControlFlow </Ins>
            </Instructions>
            <Data> key </Data>
        </PriorityOrder>
    </settings>
</agent>
```

Fig. 2. Protection profile coded in XML

The XML-based protection profile shown in Fig. 2 describes how a developer configures the tool to protect a multi-agent system, under a set of restrictions. This specific profile establishes a higher priority level to instructions than data, as well as an order for prioritizing several types of instructions according to the requirements of the target system. If the highest priority is efficiency, then the protected profile will be defined so that the protected part of this system will be as small as possible. Of course, this means that this protection profile will provide a lower security level. Conversely, in the case that the developer needs a highly secure system, then he will define a protection profile that instructs the tool to generate a system with larger protected parts, which in turn means a higher workload for the trusted processors.

Additionally, the implementation of these protection mechanisms can be done using two strategies. We can protect agent by protecting its data. For this purpose the tool will select the instructions to protect, taking into account the instruction operands and their associated java labels (such as final, static, etc). The data-based Protection must be done by the developer according to the code and context restrictions.

On the other hand, an agent can be protected on the basis of the types of instructions. With this strategy the profile refers to classes of instructions that will be performed by the trusted coprocessor. For this purpose a classification of instructions has been developed. In general, the instruction-based protection strategy is better for automated processing than the data-based one. In the specific case of our Java-based agents, the byte code instruction set currently consists of 212 instructions. The instruction set can be roughly grouped as follows:

- *Stack operations*: In this category we group operations for storing and retrieving data from the stack. Constants can be pushed onto the stack either by loading them from the constant pool with the *ldc* instruction or with special "*short-cut*" instructions where the operand is encoded into the instructions, e.g. *iconst* or *bipush* (push byte value).
- *Arithmetic operations*: This category contains all arithmetic operations. The Java Virtual Machine uses different instructions to operate on values of different types. Arithmetic operations starting with *i*, for example, denote an integer operation. E.g., *iadd* that adds two integers and pushes the result back on the stack. The Java types *boolean*, *byte*, *short*, and *char* are handled as integers by the *JVM*.
- *Control flow*: These are branch instructions like *goto and if icmpeq*, which compares two integers for equality. Also in this category we include the *jsr* (jump sub-routine) and *ret* pair of instructions , and those related to the management of exceptions, such as the *athrow* instruction.
- *Load and store*: These are operations for dealind with local variables like *iload* and *istore*, and also array operations like *iastore* which stores an integer into an array.
- *Field access*: The instructions in this category deal with fields. The value of an instance field may be retrieved with *getfield* and written with *putfield*. For static fields, the operations are *getstatic* and *putstatic*.
- *Method invocation*: These instructions are used to access (call) methods. Methods may either be called via static references with *invokestatic* or be bound virtually with the *invokevirtual* instruction. Super class methods and private methods are invoked with *invokespecial*.
- *Object allocation*: These instructions are used to create objects. Class instances are allocated with the *new* instruction; arrays of basic types like *int*[] with *newarray*; and arrays of references like *String*[][] with *anewarray* or *multianewarray*.
- *Conversion and type checking*: These operations are related to casting and type conversion. For stack operands of basic types there are casting operations like *f2i* which converts a float value into an integer. The validity of a type cast may be checked with *checkcast* and the *instanceof* operator can be directly mapped to the equally named instruction.

Alternatively, developers can also mark the code to be protected manually during the code production, in order to achieve a very specific protection scheme. Essentially this approach consists on selecting parts of code to be protected. Then the Java compiler marks the byte-code operations corresponding to the selected instructions. This approach can be used to protect instructions, data or any combination of these.

Regarding the assignment of private parts to secure coprocessors, we can distinguish two different strategies. In the simplest case the collaboration between agents is predefined. This means that every agent has private parts of the code of one or more of the other agents that are collaborating. We call this strategy *Static Mutual Protection*. In contrast, the *Dynamic Mutual Protection* strategy makes it possible for any of the collaborating agents to serve as secure coprocessor to any other agent. Therefore, in this case, the interactions between the agents are not predefined. This strategy is more powerful and flexible, but it also entails more complexity and reduced performance. Finally, a combination of both techniques can be implemented.

3.1.1 Static Mutual Protection

The Protected Computing scheme can be applied in order to protect a society of collaborating agents by making every agent collaborate with one or more remote agents running in different hosts. These agents act as secure coprocessors for the first one. Likewise, these agents are in turn protected by other agents as shown in Fig. 3. In this setting, an attack requires the cooperation of all hosts.

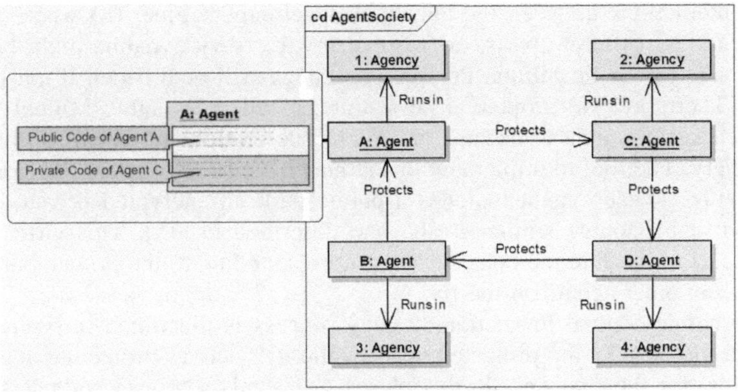

Fig. 3. Mutual Static Protection between four agents

For this specific strategy, it is possible that the protected parts of an agent are directly included in other agents as shown in Fig. 3. This strategy increases the performance by avoiding the transmission of the protected code sections over the network. In contrast, it is only suitable in those scenarios where the set of agents to be protected is static and can be determined before their actual execution.

Two tools are used to implement these strategies as shown in Fig. 1. The Static Protection Tool (SPT) receives as input two different sets of agent codes. The first set contains the public parts of the agents, while the second set corresponds to the private parts. Both sets are generated by the CPT. The SPT will mix these parts according to the static mutual protection strategy.

An example of the possible applications of this strategy is that of a competitive bidding. In this scenario a client requests bids from several contractors to provide a good or a service. It is important that the bidding takes place simultaneously, so that none of the contractors can access the offer from the other contractors, because this would represent an advantage over the others. The client can use several single-hop agents to collect the offers from the contractors [3]. Each agent will be protected, using the Static Protection strategy, by other agents. This is possible since the client generates the whole set of agents, which is static and known a priori. We can also safely assume that a coalition of all contractors is will not happen. In fact, no technological solution can prevent all contractors to reach an external agreement. Because each agent is protected by other agents running in the hosts of the competitors, and because the protected computing model ensures that it is neither possible to discover nor to alter the function that the agents perform and it is also impossible to impersonate the agents, we know that all agents will be able to safely collect the bids, guaranteeing the fairness of the process. One drawback of this strategy is that the failure of an agent affects the whole set of agents. However, if one agent fails, this strategy allows the client to identify the responsible host.

3.1.2 Dynamic Mutual Protection

The Static Mutual Protection strategy can be successfully applied to many different scenarios. However, there will be scenarios where (i) it is not possible to foresee the possible interactions between the agents at development time, (ii) where the agents are generated by different parts, or (iii) that involve very dynamic multi-hop agents. In these cases the Static Mutual Protection strategy will be difficult if not impossible to apply. Therefore, we propose a new strategy called Dynamic Mutual Protection where each agent is able to execute arbitrary code sections on behalf of other agents in the society. The tool to implement this strategy is currently under development. As shown in Fig. 4, each agent includes a public part, an encrypted private part and a specific virtual machine similar to the one described in [15]. This virtual machine allows agents to execute the code sections (corresponding to the private parts) will be received from other agents on-the-fly.

The Dynamic Mutual Protection strategy process is illustrated in figure 4. In the first phase *ag1* acts as the protected agent while *ag2* acts as protecting agent (secure coprocessor) for the first one. In this phase, *ag1* sends a private code section to the virtual machine of *ag2*. This virtual machine processes the private section and returns some results (*results1*). In the second phase *ag3* acts as protecting agent for *ag2* (in this case protected agent), and finally *ag1* provides protection to *ag3*. The scalability of this scheme is very good since only a few agents (one in most cases) is involved in the protection of any other agent.

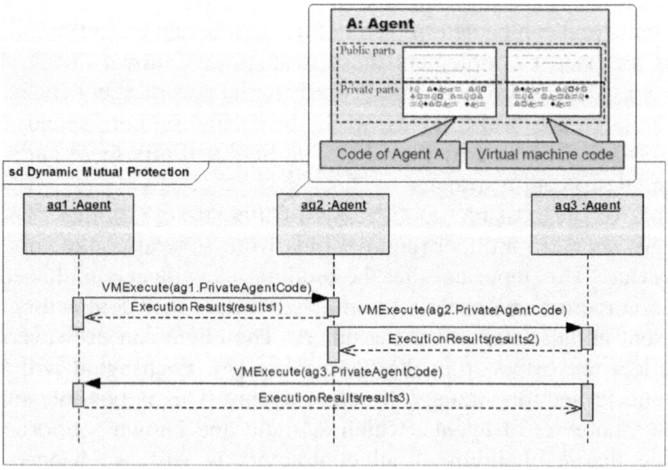

Fig. 4. Sequence diagram showing a Mutual Dynamic Protection between three agents

Despite of the advantages of this strategy, some problems are also introduced. In particular, agents need to be able to recognise other trusted agents and to decrypt the private code sections of other agents when they are received from them for execution. For these reasons a mutual authentication mechanism is required. In principle, we can make all agents in the society share a symmetric key. Again this approach presents advantages (simplicity and efficiency) and also drawbacks (low resilience to successful attacks to one agent). In this case all private sections will be encrypted using this key. In a more complex setting, each agent will have an asymmetric key pair, a certificate of the public key issued by an appropriate authority and the public key of all trusted authorities. In this case, agents are mutually authenticate themselves by means of digital signatures and are able to receive specific licenses for the execution of the protected sections of other agents. In the simplest case the license is the symmetric key used to encrypt the private part of the protected agent encrypted with the public key of the protecting agent.

It is important to remark that regardless of the complexity of the desired protection scheme, this deployment can be done automatically. As in the previous scenario we plan to have a *Dynamic Protection Tool* (DPT). That is responsible for creating the agents and integrating in their code a small virtual machine to allocate into every agent a little virtual machine code. This virtual machine will allow the agent to execute the agent private parts from other agents on the fly.

4 Other Approaches

4.1 Trusted Computing Platform for Secure Agent-Based Environment

Trusted Computing Platforms take the advantage of the use of a hardware element in order to provide a secure environment. These hardware elements are called TPM (Trusted Platform Modules). A TPM is a microprocessor with some special security features. The key idea behind the Trusted Computing Platform is to build a trusted environment starting from the TPM and extending the trust to the rest of the system elements. At the beginning of the execution the only trusted element in the system is the TPM. The TPM contains measurements of each element in the system (hardware or software) that are compared before executing it. TPM stores these measurements in secure internal records.

The boot sequence of a Trusted Computing Platform is modified in order to extend the trust to all elements in the platform (this process is called trusted boot). By this way, the chain of trust starts with in the TPM, which analyses whether the computer BIOS is trusted, in such case the platform will execute it. This process will be repeated for the master boot record, the OS loader, the OS and the hardware devices and finally the applications. Once the OS is in the trusted part of the system, the applications are measured before they begin its execution. In a Trusted Computing scenario an application runs exclusively on top of trusted and pre-approved software and hardware configuration.

The Trusted Computing technology can be applied to protect agent systems. Concretely we can execute the agencies in trusted computing platforms. In this way we achieve a basic security level, by assuring that our agencies are correctly executed. However we need a bidirectional protection in order to obtain a robust system. For this purpose we take advantage of the Remote Attestation feature [16]. This feature allows a system to obtain a security measurement from a remote system before establishing a communication with it. This security measurement is realized as a cryptographic hash of the configuration of the target system.

Thanks to the remote attestation mechanism trust between agencies can be established. In this way a source agency is able to attest that destination agency is trusted before allowing an agent to migrate to it.

In a multi-agent system scenario, we use the remote attestation mechanism between the platforms where each agency runs in order to verify that the agency software has not been tampered with and that it is running over appropriate software, firmware, and hardware configurations. Agencies where agents run (source agencies) are responsible for using remote attestation procedures in order to verify that the next agency in the agent itinerary (destination agency) is also trustworthy. Doing this we create a trusted chain between the agencies (we assume that the first agency is trusted), and we can be sure that all agencies used by the agent are trusted.

In order to verify that an agency if trustworthy before migrating to it, an agent (ag1) informs to the agency where it currently runs (A1), that it plans to migrate to another agency (A2). A2 has to fulfil some requirements (A2req). When an agency (in this case A1) receives this kind of request it uses the TPM (tmp1) in order to perform a remote attestation of the destination agency (A2). The remote attestation done by tpm1 is supported by the TPM of agency A2 (tpm2). After the process, tpm1 has a measure of the configuration of the agency A2 (A2conf). If this configuration (A2conf) fulfils the requirements imposed by ag1 (A2req). The migration is allowed.

The scenario above depicted assumes that the TPM is able to compare if a configuration fulfils some requirements. However this situation will not be always the case. Sometimes the comparison between requirements and configurations can not be done by the TPM due to the complexity of the operation. In this case the source agency (A1, in our scenario) will be the responsible for this compatibility assessment. Semantic attestation [16] represents an advance in this sense, because it provides enhanced flexibility to the attestation mechanism at the expense of more complex processing.

However, it is important to take into account the limitations of this solution. One of the main limitations is that this solution is designed for TPM-enabled devices. Because of this, it is not easy to apply this solution in ubiquitous environments, where there is a high level of device heterogeneity due to the different physical requirements of these devices. Other limitations concern the predefined certificates used by the TPM technology. These certificates are not well suited for dynamic environments, because they cannot be changed. As in the previous limitation, this one is especially relevant for heterogeneous ubiquitous environments and ambient intelligence scenarios

4.2 Proof-Carrying-Code

The technique called proof-carrying code (PCC) is a general mechanism for verifying that a software element can be executed in a secure way [6]. For this purpose, every code fragment includes a detailed proof called code certificate (not to be confused with cryptographic certificates) that in our case can be used to determine whether the security policy of the host is satisfied by the agent. Therefore, hosts just need to verify that the proof is correct (i.e. it corresponds to the code) and that it is compatible with the local security policy. In a variant of this technique, called proof-referencing code, the agents do not contain the proof, but just a reference to it [7]. The potential impact of this paradigm is high, as proved by the growing interest of different researchers in its application. In particular, it is worth to mention some important cooperative projects such as MOBIUS[1] and S3MS[2] that are centred on this paradigm.

As a technique designed for general mobile code, it is not difficult to apply it in agent-based technology. The use of this technique in agent systems allows agencies to verify the code certificates (containing the information related to the tasks that the agent intends to carry out in this agency) before executing agents in order to guarantee that they fulfil the agency policy. If the certificate is successfully verified, the agency will only allow the agent to perform the tasks declared in the certificate.

In our context, one of the main limitations of the PCC approach is that it is only suitable for protecting platforms from malicious mobile code and not for protecting the code from malicious agencies. However, this technique can be very useful in cooperation with the other two aforementioned proposals.

5 Conclusions

We have shown in this paper the potential for agent systems in ubiquitous computing and ambient intelligence scenarios. We have described some current technologies that can be used to build secure agent systems suitable for applications in these scenarios, where the computational infrastructure is composed of a very large number of computing devices with heterogeneous capabilities and under the control of different owners. In this paper we have extended and detailed our preliminary work on the application of the Protected Computing paradigm to agent systems. Finally, we have described in detail the development process of agent systems using the protected computing approach, including the use of different automated tools to support it.

Our ongoing work is focused on two lines. On one hand, we are working on the development of the automatic tools that support the development process. Currently, we have a working prototype of the SPT that works with a predefined protection profile. The DPT is only at the design stage. We are working on the flexibility and adaptability of those tools to different parameters in the policies. This first line also includes the description of such profiles. On the other hand, we are working on the dynamic mutual protection approach. The main task here is to identify and solve problems that can appear such as deadlocks or other synchronization problems.

References

[1] Mouratidis, H., Kolp, M., Faulkner, S., Giorgini, P.: A Secure Architectural Description Language for Agent Systems. AAMAS '05, Utrecht, Netherlands (2005)

[2] López, J., Maña, A., Muñoz, A.: A Secure and Auto-configurable Environment for Mobile Agents in Ubiquitous Computing Scenarios. In: Proc. Of Ubiquitous Intelligence and Computing, Springer-Verlag, Wuhan (China) (2006)

---

[1] http://mobius.inria.fr/

[2] http://www.s3ms.org

[3] Maña, A., Muñoz, A.: Mutual Protection for Multiagent Systems. In: Proceedings of the Third International 3rd International Workshop on Safety and Security in Multiagent Systems (SASEMAS '06)

[4] Jennings, N., Sycara, K., Wooldridge, M.: A Roadmap for Agent Research and Development. Autonomous Agents and Multiagent Systems 1(1) (1998)

[5] Chaib-draa, B.: Industrial Applications of Distributed AI. Communications of the ACM. 38(11), 49–53 (1995)

[6] Jennings, N.R., Corera, J.M., Laresgoiti, I.: Developing Industrial Multiagent Systems. In: Proceedings of the First International Conference on Multiagent Systems, pp. 423–430. AAAI Press, Menlo Park, Calif (1995)

[7] Wang, H., Wang, C.: Intelligent Agents in the Nuclear Industry. IEEE Computer 30(11), 28–34 (1997)

[8] Schwuttke, U.M., Quan, A.G.: Enhancing Performance of Cooperating Agents in Real-Time Diagnostic Systems. In: Proceedings of the Thirteenth International Joint Conference on Artificial Intelligence (IJCAI-93), pp. 332–337. Menlo Park, Calif.: International Joint Conferences on Artificial Intelligence (1993)

[9] Clements, P., Papaioannou, T., Edwards, J.: Aglets: Enabling the Virtual Enterprise. In: the Proc. Of 'Managing Enterprises - Stakeholders, Engineering, Logistics and Achievement' (ME-SELA '97), p. 425 (1997)

[10] Cougaar Project, http://cougaar.org/

[11] Shepherdson, D.: The JACK Usage Report. In: the Proc Of. Autonomous Agents and Multi Agents Systems (AAMAS 03) (2003)

[12] Jade Project, http://jade.tilab.com/

[13] JavaAct Project, http://www.irit.fr/recherches/ISPR/IAM/JavAct.html

[14] Alechina, N., Alechina, R., Hübner, J., Jago, M., Logan, B.: Belief revision for AgentSpeak agents. In: the Proc Of Autonomous Agents and Multi Agents Systems. Hakodate, Japan pp. 1288–1290 (2006)

[15] Maña, A., López, J., Ortega, J., Pimentel, E., Troya, J.M.: A Framework for Secure Execution of Software. International Journal of Information Security, 3(2) (2004)

[16] Trusted Computing Group: TCG Specifications (2005) Available online at, https://www.trustedcomputinggroup.org/specs/

[17] Necula, G.: Proof-Carrying Code. In: Proceedings of 24th Annual Symposium on Principles of Programming Languages (1997)

On the Analysis and Design of a Family Tree of Smart Card Based User Authentication Schemes

Raphael C.-W. Phan[1] and Bok-Min Goi[2,*]

[1] LASEC, EPFL, Switzerland
raphael.phan@epfl.ch
[2] Centre for Cryptography and Information Security (CCIS)
Faculty of Engineering, Multimedia University, Cyberjaya, Malaysia
bmgoi@mmu.edu.my

Abstract. A family (tree) of 2-party password-based authentication protocols based on smart cards abounds in security literature, more popularly known as remote user authentication schemes using smart cards. In this paper, we give a generic treatment to the security and analyses of such protocols, tracing back to the original versions due to Hwang et al. and Hwang-Li from which many variants have been derived. Our work here highlights the security implications of taking the break-and-tweak approach to protocol design.

1 Introduction

In literature we see numerous variants of a particular family (tree) of password-based authentication protocols that rely on the use of a tamper-resistant smart card, between two parties namely a user and a server. These protocols, popularly known as "*(remote) user authentication scheme using/with smart cards*", at times culminate in established session keys too. We simply call them RUA protocols from here on.

These types of RUA protocols are commonly attributed to a protocol by Hwang and Li [8] in 2000, said to overcome the limitation of a scheme by Lamport [10] in 1981 which requires to store password-verifier tables. Nevertheless, tracing this further back, an earlier RUA by Hwang et al. [9][1] in 1990 predates the Hwang-Li protocol.

Throughout the years, researchers discovered different attacks on variants and suggested tweaks to counter these specific attacks. In fact, literature now contains an almost exhaustive list of these variants which can be viewed as independent branches derived from the original protocols in [9,8] because it is most often the case that a variant is tweaked from one predecessor without consideration of other predecessors in other branches, so variations exponentially increase in difference.

* The second author acknowledges the Malaysia IRPA grant (04-99-01-00003-EAR).
[1] Not the same Hwang.

J. Indulska et al. (Eds.): UIC 2007, LNCS 4611, pp. 1213–1221, 2007.

1.1 This Paper

In this paper, we return to the root of all these variants, in particular [9,8] to emphasize the generic structure that the original authors had in mind in the first place. We discuss how later variants differ from the original design structure and subsequently led to weaknesses being exploited in attacks. Clearly, our work here is not meant to be exhaustive as it would be a computationally infeasible task to analyze the security problems of all variants in literature. Instead, we hope that our results here will draw lessons from past mistakes and highlight that newer variants need not necessarily be more secure, and at all stages the design of a protocol should be based on sound rigorous models, e.g. provable security [20].

2 Remote User Authentication (RUA) Schemes

We describe the original RUA schemes in [9,8]. These serve as reference templates, and further discussions of any variants will thus only require to mention the differences from these reference schemes.

2.1 The Hwang et al. Scheme

This scheme basically involves any new user, U_i registering with the authentication server, AS, and being issued a smart card, S_i and subsequently logging in with the smart card to be authenticated by AS. Denote h as a secure one-way hash function, e and d as the public and private key respectively of AS, ID_i the identity of U_i and PW_i his password, p as a large prime number, r is a random number, T as the current time stamp, $\Longrightarrow$ as a secure channel and $\longrightarrow$ denotes the communication of a message via an insecure (unencrypted) channel. Then, all steps of the scheme are described as below:

Registration:

$U_i \Longrightarrow AS$: ID_i

$AS \Longrightarrow U_i$: $PW_i = ID_i^d \bmod p$

$AS \Longrightarrow SC_i$: h, e, p

Login:

$U_i \Longrightarrow SC_i$: ID_i, PW_i

SC_i:

1. Generate a random number r
2. Compute $C_1 = r^e \bmod p$
3. Compute $t = h(C_1, T) \bmod p$
4. Compute $C_2 = PW_i \times r^t \bmod p$

$SC_i \longrightarrow AS$: ID_i, C_1, C_2, T

Authentication:

AS:

1. If ID_i invalid, reject login request
2. If T expired, reject login request
3. Check if $C_2^e = ID_i \times C_1^{h(C_1,T)} \bmod p$
   If YES, U_i is authenticated. Else, reject login request

2.2 The Hwang-Li Scheme

Denote x as the secret key of AS. Then, all steps of the scheme are described as below:

Registration:

$U_i \longrightarrow AS$: ID_i
$AS \longrightarrow U_i$: $PW_i = ID_i^x \bmod p$
$AS \longrightarrow SC_i$: h, p

Login:

$U_i \longrightarrow SC_i$: ID_i, PW_i

SC_i:

1. Generate r
2. Compute $C_1 = ID_i^r \bmod p$
3. Compute $t = h(PW_i \oplus T) \bmod (p-1)$
4. Compute $C_2 = ID_i^t \times PW_i^r \bmod p$

$SC_i \longrightarrow AS$: ID_i, C_1, C_2, T

Authentication:

AS:

1. If ID_i invalid, reject login request
2. If T expired, reject login request
3. Check if $C_2 \times (C_1^x)^{-1} = ID_i^{h(T \oplus PW_i)} \bmod p$
   If YES, U_i is authenticated. Else, reject login request

3 Generic Perspective of Attacks on RUA Schemes

Basic security requirements for any 2-party authentication protocol and key establishment can be referred to e.g. in [3]. Here, we describe with a generic flavour the attacks that have been successfully mounted on RUA type schemes in literature, and the problems that caused them.

3.1 Attacks Due to Distributivity

The Hwang et al. and Hwang-Li protocols have the password PW_i of user U_i generated from U_i's identity raised to a secret exponent known only to the server.

Since exponentiation is distributive over multiplication, attacks apply on both that exploit this property.

In particular, Chan and Cheng [4] proposed the following attack on Hwang-Li: A malicious insider user, U_i wishes to impersonate as another user. He does so by computing a new ID_v as:

$$ID_v = (ID_i \times ID_i) \bmod p. \tag{1}$$

Since U_i does not know the secret key, x, he cannot compute the corresponding password, PW_v of ID_v directly. However, he could use the alternative way as

$$\begin{aligned} PW_v &= ID_v^x \bmod p \\ &= (ID_i^x \times ID_i^x) \bmod p \\ &= (PW_i \times PW_i) \bmod p. \end{aligned} \tag{2}$$

This means that PW_v can be computed by using the attacker's own password, PW_i. Therefore, he can freely use the pair (ID_v, PW_v) to login to the remote system by impersonating as a different user having the identity ID_v.

Later, Chang and Hwang [5] commented that a problem exists with the above attack, namely that the ID_v newly generated by the attacker by squaring his own ID_i may not exist in the scheme. Chang and Hwang further proposed two variants of the attack.

The first variant replaces equation (1) with

$$ID_v = (ID_i^r) \bmod p, \tag{3}$$

for an arbitrary integer r, thus the password is computed as

$$PW_v = (PW_i^r) \bmod p. \tag{4}$$

The second variant considers a group of malicious insiders U_i colluding with each other to generate the new ID_v as

$$ID_v = \prod ID_i \bmod p. \tag{5}$$

thus the password is computed as

$$PW_v = \prod PW_i \bmod p. \tag{6}$$

We remark here that if the Chan-Cheng attack has the problem that squaring an identity may not lead to another valid ID, then the second attack variant would suffer from the same problem since it is a generalization of Chan-Cheng attack applied to multiple attackers, i.e. the newly generated ID_v computed as the product of all colluding identities may not exist in the scheme.

As an aside, it is ironic to observe that Shen et al. [19] presented a reversed version of Chang-Hwang attack 1 of equation (3), i.e.

$$ID_v = (ID_i^{-r}) \bmod p, \tag{7}$$

$$PW_v = (PW_i^{-r}) \bmod p, \tag{8}$$

on the Hwang-Li protocol and suggested a slightly tweaked variant by replacing IDs of users with shadowed IDs [7]. Obviously, it was shown not too long afterwards [12] that the variant equally falls to the Chan-Cheng and Chang-Hwang attacks.

Finally, although never reported before in literature, we note here that the Hwang et al. scheme equally falls to this type of attack since the user's password is generated in the similar exponentiation way from his identity.

To preclude many future papers that propose similar attacks on RUA variants, we state here that all RUA variants where the user password is derived from the user ID in a way similar to Hwang et al. and Hwang-Li, will fall to these attacks.

3.2 Oracle Attacks Due to Symmetry

Although not explicitly formalized in literature, this *symmetry* problem is well known and has been applied to protocols time and again [14,15,16,13]. The basic idea is that if at least two messages within a protocol have the same structure, then one message could be replayed as the other. This is especially useful to an attacker if he is not able to generate the latter message himself since it requires knowledge of some secret to do so. This is a form of replay but then again almost any attack on a protocl uses replays. Others call it reflection, or parallel-session or interleaving, but the gist of it is that an insider party (one of the two involved in the protocol session) is exploited as an oracle to generate a message that the attacker can replay, that the attacker would not have been able to generate himself.

[13] gave such an attack on the RUA variant of Lee et al. [11]. The Lee et al. variant differs from the original Hwang et al. and Hwang-Li protocols by using a nonce instead of a timestamp, and provides mutual authentication i.e. both the user and server authenticate each other. In contrast, the Hwang et al. and Hwang-Li protocols only provide authentication of the user to the server. Nevertheless, it was this extra provision of mutual authentication that required an additional message flow from the server back to the user, that caused the Lee et al. protocol to fall to oracle attacks because the message authenticating the user to the server and the message in reverse direction had symmetry: they had the same form. Thus a message generated by the server to challenge the user for authentication, was replayed by the attacker as a response to answer to the server's own challenge query.

Note that besides a server as illustrated above, in fact any party could potentially be exploited as an oracle, i.e. the user or even his smart card.

The original Hwang et al. and Hwang-Li protocols do not exhibit this weakness because there is only one message over an insecure channel in a session. Here, inclusion of the extra feature of mutual authentication has caused a later variant [11] to fall to attacks not applicable to the originals.

3.3 Dictionary Attacks Due to Verifiers

RUA protocols are password based, and by construction, passwords have low entropy so that they are easily memorizable by humans. Thus, one understood threat for password-based authentication schemes is that they are inherently susceptible to dictionary attacks where an attacker simply brute forces the entire password space. This is possible when values are transmitted over the insecure channel (part of any of the protocol messages) that depend on secrets that are also based on the password and no other secret value. Such values can be used by the attacker as verifiers to check his guesses.

A distinction is made between online and offline dictionary attacks. A dictionary attack is online if to verify a password guess, the attacker needs to be actively interacting with a party in actual protocol sessions. Otherwise, the attack is offline. Online dictionary attacks are less interesting because they can be prevented by limiting the number of times that a party unsuccessfully fails to authenticate itself online. Having said that, a variant of this that cannot be detected is described in [6]. Note that the original Hwang et al. and Hwang-Li protocols do not exhibit this weakness because messages of the protocol that include functions of the password are masked with other secret values.

As a final remark, we note that in contrast to traditional password-based authenticated key exchange (PAKE) protocols where the password is indeed chosen by a user (thus expected to be low entropy), the original RUA protocols in [9,8] use passwords that seemingly are not of low entropy since they are computed as functions of the user ID and the server's secret, thus should be more appropriately viewed as random bit strings of non-low entropy. Then again this raises the issue of whether the original RUA protocols are really password-based in the first place, when password based authentication protocols typically expect passwords to have low entropy so as to be easily memorizable by human users.

3.4 Issues Due to Long-Term Key Compromise

Security protocol literature also considers the case when long-term secrets e.g. private key d or secret key x in the case of Hwang et al. and Hwang-Li protocols, are leaked due to compromise of the server. This needs to be addressed because such long-term secrets could potentially be in use throughout the lifetime of a server, thus in the case of compromise, some form of security guarantee is still desirable.

These guarantees are captured by the notion of perfect forward secrecy and key compromise impersonation [3].

Perfect forward secrecy (PFS) means that even if a long-term secret is compromised, then previously generated session secrets e.g. session key or short-term passwords should remain secure.

The established session key is computed as

$$sk = h(ID_i||K||r||r') \tag{9}$$

where $K = h(x||ID_i||n)$ for n a session counter, and r, r' are respectively ephemeral nonces chosen by the user and server respectively and sent as part of the protocol messages. Now once the server's long-term secret x is compromised, sk can be computed by an attacker.

An RUA variant in [2] was designed specifically to provide forward secrecy, i.e. the user password should remain secure even if the server's long-term secret is compromised. It is very similar to the Hwang-Li protocol, except in the registration phase and login phase, where an extra time stamp, T' is used. The registration phase and login phase are defined as follows:

Registration:

$U_i \Longrightarrow AS$: ID_i
$AS \Longrightarrow U_i$: $PW_i = h(ID_i \oplus T')^x \bmod p$
$AS \Longrightarrow SC_i$: h, p, T'

Login:

$U_i \Longrightarrow SC_i$: ID_i, PW_i
SC_i:
1. Generate r
2. Compute $C_1 = h(ID_i \oplus T')^r \bmod p$
3. Compute $t = h(PW_i \oplus T) \bmod (p-1)$
4. Compute $C_2 = ID_i^t \times (PW_i)^r \bmod p$

$SC_i \longrightarrow AS$: ID_i, C_1, C_2, T

The argument for forward secrecy is that the password generation depends on a post-dated (old) timestamp, T'. Note that care has to be taken here when implementing the T', because in general timestamps should be integrity-protected since they indicate message freshness, but they are typically understood to be in the clear, as is common to the basic RUA structure.

Even when the post-dated timestamp T' is not available to the attacker, note that at the end of the login phase a slightly later version of the timestamp, T is transmitted from the smart card to AS. Again, it is an implementation-dependent argument how many possible values of T' exist that satisfy $T' < T$.

On the other hand, key compromise impersonation (KCI) [3] means that if a party A long-term secret is compromised, then it is trivial for an attacker to impersonate that party to others. However, it should still not be possible for the attacker to impersonate other parties to A; after all, it was A's secret that was compromised, not the other parties.

To preclude future KCI attacks on RUA schemes, we note here that RUA schemes by construction do not provide resilience to KCI attacks. In particular, consider the Hwang et al. protocol. Once the server AS's long-term secret d is compromised, any user U_i's password PW_i can be computed. Since authentication of a user to the server is based only on this secret password, then an attacker can easily impersonate U_i to AS. The same applies to Hwang-Li and many other RUA variants e.g. [11,13].

4 Concluding Remarks

We have attempted to give an overall view of the security of RUA protocols. Tracing back to the original RUA protocols [9,8], one can see how later variants differed, and that inclusion of extra features does not necessarily make the variant more secure. To this end, we described known attacks and other security issues from a generic perspective so that the security analysis of any RUA variant can be done in a more orderly manner rather than following a break-and-tweak approach.

To elaborate, the only difference between the variant in [19] and the Hwang-Li protocol is that the variant appends a nonce generated by the user to his ID_i during registration phase. All other phases and steps are identical. And the only difference between the variant in [2] and the Hwang-Li protocol is that the variant uses an extra timestamp, T' when generating the password during the registration phase. All other phases and steps are identical. These tweaks are not significantly novel, and furthermore minor tweaks should not be seriously considered without rigorous security analysis e.g. using the provable security approach [20]. Otherwise, the same square wheels [1] would be reinvented time and again, repeating the same mistakes of other designers. Instead, increased effort is better spent in studying more novel security constructions and provably secure protocols.

References

1. Anderson, R. (ed.): Security Engineering: A Guide to Building Dependable Distributed Systems. Wiley Publishing, Chichester (2001)
2. Awasthi, A.K., Lal, S.: A Remote User Authentication Scheme using Smart Cards with Forward Secrecy. IEEE Trans. on Consumer Electronics 49(4), 1246–1248 (2003)
3. Boyd, C., Mathuria, A. (eds.): Protocols for Authentication and Key Establishment. Springer, Heidelberg (2003)
4. Chan, C.K., Cheng, L.M.: Cryptanalysis of a Remote User Authentication Scheme using Smart Cards. IEEE Trans. on Consumer Electronics 46(4), 992–993 (2000)
5. Chang, C.C., Hwang, K.F.: Some Forgery Attacks on a Remote User Authentication Scheme using Smart Cards. Informatics 14(3), 289–294 (2003)
6. Ding, Y., Horster, P.: Undetectable On-line Password Guessing Attacks. ACM Operating Systems Review 29(4), 77–86 (1995)
7. Guillou, L.C., Quisquater, J.-J.: Efficient Digital Public-Key Signature with Shadow (Abstract). In: Pomerance, C. (ed.) CRYPTO 1987. LNCS, vol. 293, Springer, Heidelberg (1988)
8. Hwang, M.S., Li, L.H.: A New Remote User Authentication Scheme using Smart Cards. IEEE Trans. on Consumer Electronics 46(1), 28–30 (2000)
9. Hwang, T., Chen, Y., Laih, C.S.: Non-Interactive Password Authentications without Password Tables. In: IEEE Region 10 Conference on Computer and Communication Systems '90, pp. 429–431 (1990)
10. Lamport, L.: Password Authentication with Insecure Communication. Communications of the ACM 24(11), 770–772 (1981)
11. Lee, S.-W., Kim, H.-S., Yoo, K.-Y.: Efficient Nonce-based Remote User Authentication Scheme using Smart Cards. Applied Mathematics and Computation 167(1), 355–361 (2005)
12. Leung, K.-C., Cheng, L.M., Fong, A.S., Chan, C.-K.: Cryptanalysis of a Modified Remote User Authentication Scheme using Smart Cards. IEEE Trans. on Consumer Electronics 49(4), 1243–1245 (2003)

13. Nam, J., Kim, S., Park, S., Won, D.: Security Analysis of a Nonce-based User Authentication Scheme using Smart Cards. IEICE Trans. Fundamentals E90A(1), 299–302 (2007)
14. Phan, R.C.-W., Goi, B.-M.: Cryptanalysis of an Improved Client-to-Client Password-Authenticated Key Exchange (C2C-PAKE) Scheme. In: Ioannidis, J., Keromytis, A.D., Yung, M. (eds.) ACNS 2005. LNCS, vol. 3531, pp. 33–39. Springer, Heidelberg (2005)
15. Phan, R.C.-W., Goi, B.-M.: Cryptanalysis of the N-Party Encrypted Diffie-Hellman Key Exchange Using Different Passwords. In: Zhou, J., Yung, M., Bao, F. (eds.) ACNS 2006. LNCS, vol. 3989, pp. 226–238. Springer, Heidelberg (2006)
16. Phan, R.C.-W., Goi, B.-M.: Cryptanalysis of Two Provably Secure Cross-Realm C2C-PAKE Protocols. In: Barua, R., Lange, T. (eds.) INDOCRYPT 2006. LNCS, vol. 4329, pp. 104–117. Springer, Heidelberg (2006)
17. Schneier, B. (ed.): Applied Cryptography, 2nd edn. John Wiley & Sons, Chichester (1996)
18. Schneier, B., Shostack, A.: Breaking up is Hard to do: Modeling Security Threats for Smart Cards. USENIX Workshop on Smart Card Technology, USENIX PRESS, pp. 175–185 (1999)
19. Shen, J.J., Lin, C.W., Hwang, M.S.: A Modified Remote User Authentication Scheme using Smart Cards. IEEE Trans. on Consumer Electronics 49(2), 414–416 (2003)
20. Stern, J.: Why Provable Security Matters? Advances in Cryptology - Eurocrypt '03. In: Biham, E. (ed.) Advances in Cryptology – EUROCRPYT 2003. LNCS, vol. 2656, pp. 449–461. Springer, Heidelberg (2003)

Secret Key Revocation in Sensor Networks*

YoungJae Maeng, Abedelaziz Mohaisen, and DaeHun Nyang

Information Security Research Laboratory
Graduate School of IT & Telecommunication - INHA University
253 YongHyun-dong, Nam-gu, Incheon 402-751, Korea
{brendig,asm}@seclab.inha.ac.kr, nyang@inha.ac.kr
http://seclab.inha.ac.kr

Abstract. Many challenging security-related issues have been studied in wireless sensor networks to provide a demanded quality and security for deliverable data. Yet, one of these issues which are not handled is the secret key revocation. In a semi-dynamic, resource-constrained and long-living sensor network with self organization features, traditional revocation methods are not desirable and somehow impractical. Through this paper, we discuss the rising issue of key revocation due to the pre-distribution and provide several techniques, structures and algorithms for several network and security conditions and requirements. In addition to the saving of the resources represented by the communication, computation and memory, we provide an extension for special-case networks in which our work can provide a higher performance.

1 Introduction

Wireless sensor networks have received a wide attention of research due to its promising variety of applications that include both the civilian and military purposes. Civilian applications include environmental and habitat monitoring, acoustic and seismic detection, medical and process monitoring and smart spaces. The military applications include battlefield surveillance, location determination and others [4,11]. Though the lifetime maximization, self configuration and mobility are critical issues of the study, the security is still one of the hottest issues to be researched. In the security regard, due to its computational feasibility and resources consumption, the secret key cryptography using the same key for both the sender and receiver of the data is mainly used on the sensor nodes with limited resources. As these nodes construct a network without a pre-dedicated infrastructure and with limited self-resources, the key pre-distribution received a big interest of research [3,6,7,9].

Most of the key pre-distribution schemes consider the distribution itself and did not handle uprising security issues such like the key revocation [3,6,7,9].

* This research was supported by the MIC (Ministry of Information and Communication), Korea, under the ITRC (Information Technology Research Center) support program supervised by the IITA (Institute of Information Technology Advancement)(IITA-2006-C1090-0603-0028).

J. Indulska et al. (Eds.): UIC 2007, LNCS 4611, pp. 1222–1232, 2007.

Upon the compromise of a secret key, the revocation is required to cancel a key or even to replace it with another one which is still secret for the attacker. The problem of the key revocation in sensor network is represented by the resources (specially, the communication and memory) required for exchanging (or even distributing) the list of revoked keys indicted by their identifiers. One of the solutions that are typically used is to publish the identifiers of the keys to be revoked as it is. That is to say, for a network of size N and r number of keys to be revoked, $k \times \lg N$ bits are required as a memory and communication overhead. Given that a single Kilo bit transmission over a 100 link requires an equivalent energy of performing 3 Mega instructions on a typical sensor network [14], this type of representation is not an efficient to be used on the sensor networks the early mentioned limited resources.

In this paper, we introduce the researches performed on the key pre-distribution to determine the required element to be revoked followed by our contributions. On the side of the paper structure, §2 background works, §3 lists our contributions and definitions, §4 presents our contributions in details, §5 is on the analysis and evaluation, §6 extends our work for further applications and §7 includes the conclusion and future works.

2 Basic and Relying Schemes

Two of the early works in [1,2] are widely known for its novelty. For network of N nodes, in the first work by Blom *et al.* [1] a symmetric matrix of size $N \times N$ is required to store the different N^2 keys of the entire network. Node $s_i \in N$ has row and column in the matrix. If two nodes s_i, s_j would like to communicate, they use the entries $\mathbf{E_{ij}}$ in s_i side and $\mathbf{E_{ji}}$ in s_j side which are equal. To reduce the memory requirements, a slight modification is introduced by Du *et al.* in [6]. The following are defined, a public matrix $\mathbf{G}$ of size $(\lambda + 1) \times N$ and a private symmetric matrix $\mathbf{D}$ of size $(\lambda+1) \times (\lambda+1)$ where $\mathbf{D}$ entries are randomly generated. Also, $\mathbf{A} = (\mathbf{D} \cdot \mathbf{G})^{\mathbf{T}}$ of size $N \times (\lambda+1)$ is defined. For a node s_i, row $\mathbf{R_i}$ in $\mathbf{A}$ and column $\mathbf{C_i}$ in $\mathbf{G}$ are dedicated. When two nodes s_i, s_j would eventually communication securely, they exchange their $\mathbf{C_i}, \mathbf{Cj}$ and $k_{ij} = \mathbf{R_i} \cdot \mathbf{C_j}$ is computed by s_i and $k_{ji} = \mathbf{R_j} \cdot \mathbf{C_i}$ by s_j and used as shared key. The second work by Blundo *et al.* [2], a Symmetric Bivariate Polynomial (SBP) is used to distribute keys for N nodes. The SBP is in the form of $f(x, y) = \sum_{i,j=0}^{t} a_{ij} x^i y^j, (a_{ij} = a_{ji})$ of degree $t \leq N$. For a node s_i with identifier i, the share $g^i(y) = f(i, y)$ is calculated and loaded to its memory generate secure keys. Similarly, for two nodes s_i, s_j, $k_{ij} = g^i(j), k_{ji} = g^j(i)$ are are evaluated locally and used respectively.

The early scheme of key pre-distribution specifically for WSN is introduced by ESCHENAUER-GLIGOR (EG) [7]. Each node is let to randomly pick a key ring S_k of size k from big keys pool of size P guaranteeing a probabilistic connectivity $p_{actual} = 1 - \frac{((P-k)!)^2}{(P-2k)!P!}$. If two nodes s_i, s_j share a key $k : k \in S_{k_i} \cap S_{k_j}$ they use it a secret key. Otherwise, a path discovery phase via intermediate nodes is performed. To improve the resiliency, Chan *et al.* proposed the Q-COMPOSITE scheme [3]. Using the same procedure of EG, a key between two nodes s_i, s_j is available

iff $S_{k_i} \cap S_{k_j}$ is a set of q keys. If $\{k_1, \ldots, k_q\} \in \{S_{k_i} \cap S_{k_j}\}$, $\mathbf{hash}(\mathbf{k_1}||\mathbf{k_2}, \ldots, ||\mathbf{k_q})$ is used as k_{ij}, k_{ji}. Otherwise, intermediate node(s) are used.

In addition to [1], Du *et al.* proposed two schemes in [6,5]. In the first work they introduced a location based scheme by avoiding the unnecessary memory, communication, and computation with reasonable connectivity [5]. In [6], a multi-space matrix scheme based on [1,7] is introduced. A τ number of private matrices $\mathbf{D}$ is selected randomly out of ω pre-constructed matrices providing connectivity of $p_{actual} = 1 - \frac{((\omega-\tau)!)^2}{(\omega-2\tau)!)\omega!}$. Different $\mathbf{A}$'s are created using the different $\mathbf{D}$s. τ rows of the different $\mathbf{A}$s are selected and assigned for each node. For (s_i, s_j), If they have a common space $\tau_{i,j} : \tau_{i,j} \in \tau_i, \tau_j$, the rest of Blom's is performed, else, an intermediate space is used to construct a key path. At the same time, Liu *et al.* proposed several schemes [9,10] for key distribution and mainly based on [2]. In [9], Blundo's scheme is used by assigning more than polynomial for each node similar to EG scheme [7]. In [10], a two dimensional grid deployment structure is used where nodes are deployed on different intersection points of the grid and different polynomials are assigned for the different rows and columns of the grid. Two nodes establish direct key if $R_i = R_j$ or $C_i = C_j$. Else, an intermediate node is used in indirect key establishment phase.

Since we interested in the item to be revoked and not the keying material itself, based on [12] which ideally matches with other schemes in [3,6,7,9] in this regard, the identifier which is used to identify the node itself is also used as an associated identity for the corresponding keying material. Given that, once the identifier of the a given node, the secret key associated with the node in [7,3] is revoked, the polynomial share associated with a node [9,10,12] is revoked, and the matrix's row or column associated with a node [6,5] is revoked. To make the above survey clear, the conclusive comparison in Table 1

Table 1. Resources usage vs. a provided connectivity and revocation capabilities

Scheme	Comm.	Com.	Memory	Conn.	Revocation
GBS [10]	c	SBP Evaluation	ID+2 SBP	$\frac{2}{N^{1/2}-1}$	NO
EG [7]	$C \lg(S_k)$	$\frac{(2C+p-p_k)}{2} \lg C$	S_k keys	$1 - \frac{((P-k)!)^2}{(P-2k)!P!}$	NO
CPS [3]	Constant	c	S_k keys	$\frac{m}{N}$	NO
DDHV [6]	$C \lg(n \times \tau)$	2 vectors mult.	$\tau + 1$ vectors	$1 - \frac{((\omega-\tau)!)^2}{(\omega-2\tau)!\omega!}$	NO
HGBS[12]	c	SBP Evaluation	ID+n SBP	1	NO

3 Contribution, Definitions and Terms Elucidation

3.1 Contributions

In this paper, our contribution is as follows:

- Introducing the concept of the symmetric key revocation in sensor networks and the hurdle of the revocation resulting from the representation of the nodes or keys identifiers' representation.

- Introducing the Bit Vector Scheme as an efficient mechanism for symmetric key representation in a key revocation list.
- Employing the Complete Subtree Cover [13,8] for groups representation as a possible method for reducing the revocation list's size.
- Study the impact of simple and dynamic encoding such like the run length encoding on the representation in a simplified version of bit-compression.
- Conclude our contributions by a comparison between our work and the only possible representation method which is the naïve scheme.

3.2 Definitions and Terms Elucidation

In this section, we introduce two definitions that our work relies on. The first one is the complete subtree (CS) [13,8]. In our work, we don't use the key derivation of CS but we just use the representation method to reduce the overhead of set of identifiers representation. In addition, other broadcast encryption method which is the subtree difference (SD) can be used. In CS, we consider a complete binary tree $\mathcal{T}$ with leaves that represent the different network nodes (in this case, the key's/keying material's identifier) $\mathcal{N} : |\mathcal{N}| = N$. The different path from the root to the leaf represents a corresponding leaf identifier (ID). The path itself is represented as left of zero and right of one (relatively from the parent). The set of node's identifiers (that represents the corresponding keying material) to be revoked is $\mathcal{R} = \{v_1, v_2 \ldots v_r\} : |\mathcal{R}| = r$. In definition 2, we are interested in the COVER which is the set of reduced IDs which are required to represent a set of revoked identifiers.

Definition 1 (Naïve Method for Revoked Identifiers Representation). For a space S that permits $2^{|S|}$ possible identifiers, the naïve method for the identifiers representation is by listing these identifiers of at same length resulting that the size of the list is the length of the list multiplied by S.

Definition 2 (Complete Subtree Cover for Representation Reduction). In the above tree, the CS cover of a group of leaves $\mathcal{R} \subset \mathcal{T}$ is the mechanism of finding the set of nodes $V_1 \ldots V_t \subset \mathcal{T}$ (represented by its ID's beginning from the root) such that the group of nodes $v_{i1} \ldots v_{it}$ that represent a complete subtree are rooted at V_i for all i such that $0 < i < t$, $V_i \cap V_j = \phi$ for any $i \neq j$ and $V_1 \cup V_2 \ldots \cup V_t = \mathcal{R}$ considering that V_i is a representative group for the set of nodes rooted at V_i. Here, the set ID of V_i is the binary string constructed by concatenating bits assigned to each branch from the root to the V_i. Note that the length of ID is always less than or equal to $\lg N$.

Definition 3 (Bit Vector for Efficient Representation). The Bit Vector Scheme which is a relative representation mechanism for sequential identifiers including those to be revoked and mainly used to reduce the CRL length. In BVS, for a network of N nodes, a bit vector S of length N is constructed. In S, the $i^{\mathbf{th}}$ bit indicates the validity of a key associated with the identifier i. Also, a '0' valued location in S represents valid (un-revoked) key and '1' represents the revoked key. In the node's side, the keys' identifiers to be revoked can be extracted from offset of the 1's occurrences.

Definition 4 (Run-length encoding RLE). Data encoding algorithm that maps a plain binary string $\mathcal{P} : \mathcal{P} = p_1p_2p_3 \dots p_a$ into an encoded binary string $\mathcal{C} : \mathcal{C} = c_1c_2c_3 \dots c_b$. Considering the instances $\xi_i, \xi_j \in \mathcal{C}$ and $\varphi_i, \varphi_j \in \mathcal{P}$, $\xi_i = \xi_j$ if and only if $\varphi_i = \varphi_j$. The notation h-RLE-l determines both h and l as the header and the length where h expresses the input plain string's header bit and l determines the length of the input and the output as follows: maximum length of input length is 2^{l-1}, length of the encoded output is l and the plain input's header is h and other bits before it (if any) are equal to h's binary compliment.

4 Putting It All Together: Symmetric Key Revocation

4.1 On Symmetric Key Revocation

As we early mentioned, the symmetric key pre-distribution process uses immediate cryptographic secret key [3,7] or secret key's generation material in what so called keying material. This material can be a share of polynomial [2,9,10] or a vector from a matrix [1,6]. In this paper, we are interest in the identifier of the any type of the secret information and not the key itself. As early mentioned, fortunately in most of key pre-distribution mechanisms, the keying material or the key itself are associated with a node with a unique identifier. If we would like to revoke a given key or keying material, then it is enough to publish the identifier of the associated node in the revocation list to be revoked. In the following subsections, we show how the early definition of the BVS, CS and the RLE encoding are used in this revocation process. In the remaining part of this paper, we use the expression key or key to express the key itself or the keying material as well.

4.2 BVS for Symmetric Key Revocation

Scenario I: Static Revocation: The Bit Vector Scheme (BVS) which is a relative representation mechanism for the different keys including those to be revoked can be used for revocation list's reduction. Based on definition 3, it is enough to make a given position of the bit vector string as zero to indelicate a non-revoked identifier that has the offset value of the bit. In the same way, it is enough to make a given position of the bit vector as one to indicate a revoked identifier of the offset of the valued bit. In the node's side, the key's identifiers to be revoked can be extracted from offset of the 1's occurrences. Since this type of substitution considers only one chance for each identifier to be represent as revoked or not, we denote this initial representation as a static scheme (BVS-S). This type of revocation is good for static networks with almost same age and almost same compromise chances. An example of how this scheme works is shown in Fig. 1❶.

Obviously, Not all of the networks follows the same policy of the above one. In a more dynamic network that permits a frequent join-disjoin activities, if a key is revoked another key with other ID will replace it (or might be with the same

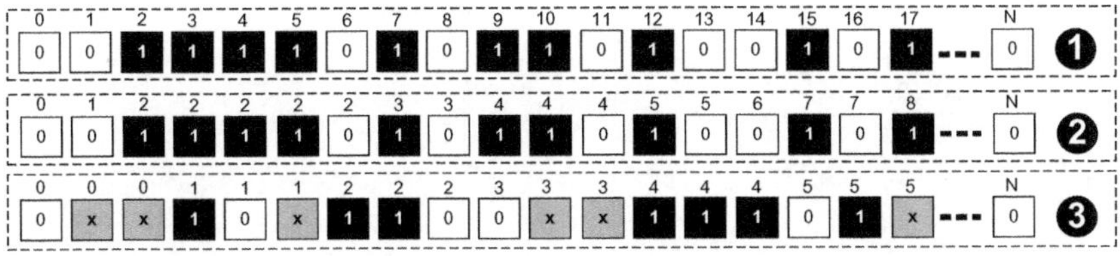

Fig. 1. Different Scenarios of the Bit Vector Scheme for Key Revocation

ID and different parameters). Thus, possibly we would like to extend the BVS-S to cover the multi-revocation case. In the following, we provide two extensions with scalability/memory requirements trade-off.

Scenario II: Dynamic Revocation

Dynamic with Pre-defined Length (BVS-D-I): In the first approach, we provide each sensor node's key with a pre-dedicated (say 10) number of bits to handle a number of revocations for each. The equal number of bits for each sensor node will provide an auto-discrimination mechanism. However, it provides a low efficiency especially when the number of revoked keys is small (in what we call a loosely representation). An example of how does this scheme works is shown in Fig. 1❸.

Dynamic with Expendable Length (BVS-D-II): To overcome this problem, let's consider the BVS-S with some modification. Initially, the bit vector is initialized by 0's when no keys are revoked. Once a key is revoked, a '1' is attached immediately before the corresponding key's '0' offset.

Thus, one revocation adds only one bit to the bit vector. When a check of whether $i^{\mathbf{th}}$ certificate is valid or not is required, first find out the ith block that represent sensor node i and count the number of '1' (say, n) which means that the $(n+1)^{\mathbf{th}}$ issued key for node i is valid. The $i^{\mathbf{th}}$ block for node i is composed of the $i^{\mathbf{th}}$ '0' in the bit vector and proceeding '1's after the $(i-1)^{\mathbf{th}}$ '0'. As in the first scenario, each node can have a limited and pre-defined number of revocation chances (say 10 as before) which can be overflowed. An example that shows how this scheme works is shown in Fig. 1❷. Unlike the other scenarios, BVS-D-II is fully dynamic in that it can support (relatively) infinite times of revocation where the list cost is typically as much as the number of revoked keys plus an additional initial overhead. For the naïve CRL, a bigger range of IDs is provided to permit a 10 revocation chances for each key. While 14 bits are enough to represent 10,000 keys, 18 bits are dedicated to provide 10 revocations for each. In BVS-D-I, an extended number of bits per node is required even they are not used.

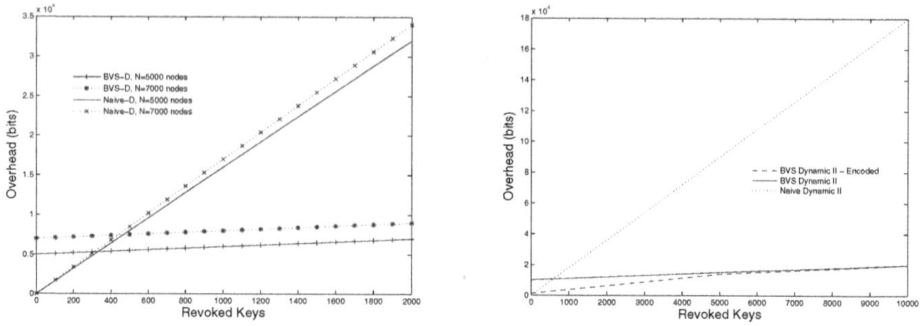

(a) Dynamic I: BVS vs. Naïve

(b) Dynamic II: BVS vs. Naïve

Fig. 2. Communication overhead in bit using (a) Naïve solution vs. BVS-D-I with different network size (b) naïve vs. encoded and un-encoded BVS-D-II

4.3 CS Cover for Symmetric Key Revocation

The Complete Subtree (CS) of definition 2 can be used directly to reduce the the representation size for the list of the key's to be revoked. As an example, if the set of IDs to be revoked r is $\{0011, 0100, 0101, 0110, 0111, 1011, 1101 \text{ and } 1110\}$, the final list representation of the reduced list is $\{0011,10,101,1101,1110\}$ which includes all of the required IDs. From the simulation results, CS probably reduce the overhead when r is about 5% of the network size but it greatly reduces the overhead when r is large enough (say, $r > 20\%$). This efficeincy of reduction is shown in Fig. 3(a).

4.4 On the Encoding

Technically, the in advance knowledge of multiple occurrences of same bits in BVS (for the basic BVS, BVS-D-I, BVS-D-II and even in CS) makes it possible to use the encoding mechanism (RLE) in definition 4 for an efficient compression. The compression efficiency is due to that the long bit vector's fraction of the same bits (consequent ones or zeros) can be eventually represented in a shorter encoded string. The heading and the length parameters of the RLE encoding algorithms determines the structure of the input and the length of the input and output as well. Table 2 shows the two possible heading (i.e. 1 or zero) with two different length (2 and 4).

To get a desired performance of the encoding algorithm, we apply a dynamic encoding using different parameters for h and l at different points (i.e. a, b, c, d in Fig. 3(b))[1]. For the relatively small number of revoked keys (e.g. $r < 40\%$ of the network size or the number of all possible keys in the network), both 1RLE-4b and 1RLE-2b can be used since it's highly probable for long consequent zeros to occur. For a number of revoked certificates r such $40\% < r < 60\%$, the number

[1] The values of these parameters and its percentages are driven from the simulation as shown in Fig. 3(b).

Table 2. RLE with different parameters

1RLE4				0RLE4				1RLE2		0RLE2	
P	C	P	C	P	C	P	C	P	C	P	C
1	0000	000001	0101	0	0000	111110	0101	1	00	0	00
01	0001	0000001	0110	10	0001	1111110	0110	01	01	10	01
001	0010	0000001	0111	110	0010	11111110	0111	00	1	11	1
0001	0011	0000000	1	1110	0011	11111111	1				
00001	0100			11110	0100						

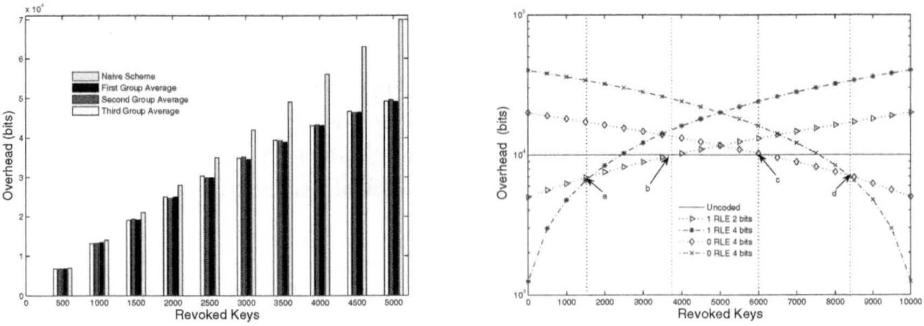

(a) Several CS vs Naïve

(b) Dynamic Encoding

Fig. 3. Overhead in bit using (a) The CS cover using different random generation rounds vs naïve solution (b) Dynamic encoding that considers alternation points for the RLE parameters

of the zeros and ones has the same occurrence probability. Thus, we use the non-encoded vector (i.e full use of N bits. For the remaining part, when $60\% < r < 100\%$ of the number of the nodes' certificates, a reverse encoding can be used (i.e. 0RLE-2b,0RLE-4b). To find out the exact percents where the dynamic encoding parameters should be changed, we encode the same string represent different r percents using the different possible parameters and manually calibrate the points at which the encoding algorithm's alternation points. Fig. 3(b) shows the encoded string using different parameters where the intersections that relies below N (i.e a, b, c, d) are used.

5 Analysis and Evaluation

To justify the performance of the proposed scheme, simulating the following schemes was carried out: naïve, naïve Encoded, CS, BVS-S, BVS-D, BVS-S encoded and BVS-D encoded for the both dynamic scenarios. To handle the revocation randomness, we use a random identifier selector that indicates the current compromised ID from the non-compromised pool (which is the worst case). $N = 10,000$ sensor nodes (the same certificates of the static) and $c = 10$. We noticed the following from the simulation results:

Note 1: the CS scheme to reduce the overhead of the communication and the representation does not follow a constant form. While a 24,917 bits are enough when the number of revoked keys is 2000 from a network size of 10000 nodes which is corresponding to 28000 bits in the naïve scheme, 49140 bits are required when the revoked keys are 5000 at which 70000 bits are required for the naïve scheme. From that we get that the reduction rate at the first case is $\frac{28000-24917}{28000} \times 100\% = 11.012\%$ while it is for the second case as $\frac{70000-49140}{70000} \times 100\% = 29.8\%$. This result is based on the average driven from figure 3(a) however as discussed earlier, this percentage has a range of random variation based on Table 3.

Note 2: the dynamic encoding is achievable through a pre-deployment obtained parameters which permits the node to flip the parameters for different length and headings as shown in Fig. 3(b). Note that, the final overhead of the compressed encoded pattern is always less than the original plain representation of the BVS or any other used scheme.

Note 3: a comparison between our dynamic BVS's two different scenarios and the naïve scheme are shown in Fig. 2. Fig. 2(a) shows that the growth of the overhead is almost constant due to the growth of the network size once it is given and mainly depends on the number of revoked keys in BVS-D-I (where the overhead is typically equal to $d \times N$ where d is the number of revocation chances given for each key) while the naïve scheme depends on both the number of revoked keys and the network size with a linear increment based on the number of revoked keys with a higher slop (which is equal to $\lg N$.) based on the network size which means that the overhead is typically equal to $r \times \lg(d \times N)$ bits.

Note 4: the encoding has parameters which are pre-defined before the installation of the system by considering the size of the network and the algorithm to be used which are dedicated in advance. The RLE dynamic encoding algorithm provides best performance when used with our proposed BVS since it is highly possible to find out the probability of a given pattern to occur in the bit vector with higher probability than others given the number of revoked keys. Based on Fig. 2(b), the overhead using BVS-D-II is equal to $r + N$ which is the best possible reduced overhead that ever achieved for a dynamic revocation. The same as with the BVS-D-I, the naïve solution requires $r \times \lg(d \times N)$ bits.

6 Application: Key Establishment

One of the interesting applications for the BVS in sensor networks is the key establishment. Most of the key establishment procedures relies on exchanging a list of identifiers for keying material or the identifiers of the keys itself as in [3,6,7,9]. For example, in [7] if two nodes would like to establish a key, they

Table 3. The communication overhead in bit for revoking percents of network size using different revocation schemes. $N = 10000$ nodes, r is a percent of the overall network size, **-C** indicates the usage of dynamic RLE.

Scheme	$r = 01\%$	$r = 05\%$	$r = 10\%$	$r = 20\%$	$r = 40\%$	$r = 50\%$
Naïve	1,400	7,000	14,000	28,000	56,000	70,000
Naïve-C	2,595	12,876	26,132	52,104	103,403	130,070
CS	1,355	6,805	13,310	25,004	42,850	49,408
Naïve-D-I	1,800	9,000	18,000	36,000	72,000	90,000
Naïve-D-II	18,000	90,000	180,000	360,000	720,000	900,000
BVS-S	10,000	10,000	10,000	10,000	10,000	10,000
BVS-S-C	1,597	2,994	4,753	7,569	10,000	10,000
BVS-D	10,100	10,500	11,000	12,000	14,000	15,000
BVS-D-II	11,000	15,000	20,000	30,000	50,000	60,000
BVS-D-II-C	3,756	13,778	20,000	27,508	37,498	41,320

Table 4. Overhead comparison between naïve revocation and BVS-based

Scheme	**Original**	**BVS**	**Advantageous**
EG scheme [7]	$k\lceil \lg P \rceil$	P	$k \geq \frac{P}{\lceil \lg P \rceil}$
Liu-Ning-EG [9]	$n' \lceil \lg n \rceil$	n	$n' \geq \frac{n}{\lceil \lg n \rceil}$
DDHV-EG[6]	$\tau \lceil \lg \omega \rceil$	ω	$\tau \geq \frac{\omega}{\lceil \lg \omega \rceil}$
Chan Scheme[3]	m	m	-

first exchange their keys' identifiers list to determine whether they own a common key or not. Similarly, in [9,6] identifiers of the polynomial or the matrix are exchanged respectively (refer to section 2 for the technical details). To show our schemes let us consider [6] where other schemes follow the same way. For the original method, τ matrices are selected from ω number of different matrices for each node. The communication overhead to exchange the identifiers is typically $\tau \lceil \lg \omega \rceil$, however, in BVS ω bits are required. Therefore, our representation will provide better performance as long as $\tau \geq \frac{\omega}{\lceil \lg \omega \rceil}$. For [9], our performance is better when $n' \geq \frac{n}{\lceil \lg n \rceil}$ and so on. Table 4 shows a comparison for the storage/communication overhead between our BVS and the original used mechanisms in key establishment for several schemes.

7 Conclusion and Future Work

In this paper we discussed the uprising problem of key revocation in sensor networks. The main problem is mainly in the required communication overhead for the representation of the different keys to be revoked. We introduced a set of schemes for the efficient revocation based on both the bit vector and the complete subtree cover. Our introduced work provided a reasonable resources saving. We tested different conditions of the dynamic revocation and the impact of encoding which provided an efficient dynamic compression based on the status of the bit vector and the number of revoked keys. On the other side, we consider the general case of a plat network; however, possible deployment knowledge structures and schemes will be considered in future works. It will be interesting to find and apply different compression algorithms on our specific structured bit vector. As well, several applications will be studied for the BVS.

References

1. Blom, R.: An optimal class of symmetric key generation systems. In: Proc. of the EUROCRYPT 84 workshop on Advances in cryptology: theory and application of cryptographic techniques, New York, NY, USA, pp. 335–338. Springer-Verlag, New York, Inc. (1985)
2. Blundo, C., Santis, A.D., Herzberg, A., Kutten, S., Vaccaro, U., Yung, M.: Perfectly-secure key distribution for dynamic conferences. In: CRYPTO, pp. 471–486 (1992)
3. Chan, H., Perrig, A., Song, D.X.: Random key predistribution schemes for sensor networks. In: IEEE Symposium on Security and Privacy, p. 197 (2003)
4. Culler, D., Estrin, D., Srivastava, M.B.: Overview of sensor networks. In: IEEE Computer Society, pp. 41–49 (2004)
5. Du, W., Deng, J., Han, Y.S., Chen, S., Varshney, P.K.: A key management scheme for wireless sensor networks using deployment knowledge. In: INFOCOM (2004)
6. Du, W., Deng, J., Han, Y.S, Varshney, P.K., Katz, J., Khalili, A.: A pairwise key predistribution scheme for wireless sensor networks. ACM Trans. Inf. Syst. Secur. 8(2), 228–258 (2005)
7. Eschenauer, L., Gligor, V.D.: A key-management scheme for distributed sensor networks. In: ACM CCS, pp. 41–47 (2002)
8. Fiat, A., Naor, M.: Broadcast encryption. In: CRYPTO, pp. 480–491 (1993)
9. Liu, D., Ning, P.: Establishing pairwise keys in distributed sensor networks. In: ACM CCS, pp. 52–61 (2003)
10. Liu, D., Ning, P., Zhu, S., Jajodia, S.: Practical broadcast authentication in sensor networks. In: MobiQuitous, pp. 118–132 (2005)
11. Mainwaring, A.M., Culler, D.E., Polastre, J., Szewczyk, R., Anderson, J.: Wireless sensor networks for habitat monitoring. In: WSNA, pp. 88–97 (2002)
12. Mohaisen, A., Nyang, D.: Hierarchical grid-based pairwise key pre-distribution scheme for wireless sensor networks. In: EWSN, pp. 83–98 (2006)
13. Naor, D., Naor, M., Lotspiech, J.: Revocation and tracing schemes for stateless receivers. In: CRYPTO, pp. 41–62 (2001)
14. Pottie, G.J., Kaiser, W.J.: Wireless integrated network sensors. Commun. ACM 43(5), 51–58 (2000)

Hybrid Key Establishment Protocol Based on ECC for Wireless Sensor Network

Yoon-Su Jeong[1] and Sang-Ho Lee[2,*]

[1] Department of Computer Science, Chungbuk National University, Cheongju, Chungbuk, Korea
bukmunro@gmail.com
[2] School of Electrical & Computer Engineering, Chungbuk National University, Cheongju, Chungbuk, Korea
shlee@chungbuk.ac.kr

Abstract. Efficient communication with maintenance of stability between sensor nodes is one of the most important factors in WSN. Recent studies suggest various group key management protocols for maintaining stability between sensors in spite of somewhat lower efficiency of protocol operating in WSN. This paper proposes efficient hybrid key establishment protocol for sensor network self-organized with equal distribution between sensor nodes. The proposed protocol is applicable to distributed environment with expansional aspect without control of base station, combining with elliptic curve Diffie-Hellman key establishment with implicated certificate and symmetric key encryption technology. For performance evaluation of the proposed protocol, this study dividedly evaluated storage cost, communication complexity and computation complexity and showed computation cost 1.3% lower than that of Kotzanikolaou technique.

1 Introduction

Recent development of communication technology has facilitated expansion of WSN(Wireless Sensor Network). The applicable area of WSN includes military sensing & tracking, environmental monitoring, patient monitoring and smart environment, etc. When a sensor node is installed in a dangerous area, its security is very important. WSN has such limitations as lower computing power, smaller storage devices, narrower network bandwidth and very lower battery power, compared with general PC computing environment. Although public key encryption cost is not suitable for sensor node, the studies till now chiefly conducted research on application of limited public key encryption [6] to sensor node through ECC(Elliptic Curve Cryptography) [4.11].

The reason for applying elliptic curve algorithm to WSN is that it has more advantages than RSA or DSA. Since ECC has lower energy consumption, smaller key size and shorter length of signature, it can be applicable to IC card or wireless terminal that has high power limitation. In particular, the problem of discrete

* Corresponding author.

J. Indulska et al. (Eds.): UIC 2007, LNCS 4611, pp. 1233–1242, 2007.

logarithm on an elliptic curve is much more difficult than that defined in general military forces. Therefore, it is widely used because it can maintain higher degree of confidentiality with smaller key than RSA. Recent studies are conducting research on establishing secure communication channel between nodes of DSN(Distributed Sensor Network) not dependant on fixed infrastructure or centralized manager [2,3,7,8,12]. These DSN is known as self-organized model without infrastructure. In DSN, the nodes of not uniformly self-organized model can be divided into full functional device and restricted functional device types; those of uniformly self-organized model exist as restricted functional device type. Since the uniformly self-organized model depends on the sensor with lower security level performance, it is more difficult to perform security level in uniform model. In [12], use of some full functional devices was proposed to save lots of cryptographic burden. The cost of sensor node limited for establishment of each key reduces one scalar product with random point and one scalar product with fixed point. Since it is hypothesized that full functional devices exist, this cost is suitable for security critical DSN. Although use of ECC can conquer security of symmetric technology use, hypothesis of [12] is not suitable for uniformly self-organized DSN, since existence of full functional devices is hypothesized.

This paper proposes a hybrid key establishment protocol for receiving authentication key from cluster head and mutually authenticating with the nodes existing in other cluster when clustering is performed with uniformly self-organized sensor nodes in sensor network. The proposed protocol is combined with standard elliptic curve Diffie-Hellman (ECDH), along with symmetric encryption technology. Computation at cost of ECC performed in the sensor node of the proposed protocol reduces two more key hash functions and one more hash function than that of [8] through authentication process between sensors in cluster after clustering is performed. In addition, since the number and size of keys are not changed irrespective of the size of network, it is possible to expand network.

The remainder of this paper is organized as follows. In section 2 analyzes various prior key agreement protocols. Section 3 proposes efficient hybrid key agreement protocol for WSN. Section 4 describes the results of security and performance evaluation for the proposed protocol. Finally, Section 5 draws the conclusions.

2 Related Works

For establishment of symmetric key, a variety of public key-based establishment protocols have been used such as Shamir's three-pass protocol, Diffie-Hellman public key protocol and Aziz-Diffie protocol [9]. These symmetric key establishment protocols are more suitable for DSN because of limited resources.

The symmetric key methods proposed in [2,3] suggest the technique of multiphase arrangement stable between sensor nodes. In this technique, all nodes included in specifically generated node i are priorly arranged through symmetric key setup used for key establishment. These protocols perform efficient and stable key establishment in various application areas of DSN. This is suitable for DSN of military forces or disaster recovery, but it is strongly hypothesized that the nodes cannot be attacked during key bootstrapping syntax. The reason for this is that the sensor nodes should be protected so that sensor's physical limitations should not become tamper-resistant. In addition, after symmetric encryption technology is used, it cannot be proved that the nodes are taking part in generation of specific nodes. In this case, the protocols in [2,3] prevent fake generation attack and prevent compromised node other than authentication node from participating in other node generation. In [5,6,7], the researchers developed hybrid key establishment protocol using ECC among public key cryptography limited for prevention of fake generation attack. Huang et al. [7] suggest hybrid key establishment protocol for pairwise key establishment in DSN, combining ECC with symmetric key cryptography. For reduction of the number of expensive scalar product, the authors of [7] suggested use of some full-functional devices to decrease lots of cryptographic burdens. For key establishment, [7] reduces one scalar product with random point and one scalar product with fixed point in each limited sensor cost. Although use of EC cryptography can conquer security issue of symmetric technology during multi-phase arrangement, it is not suitable for uniformly self-organized DSN. In particular, [7] was designed for single-phase node arrangement.

For multi-phase node arrangement, [8] suggested hybrid key establishment protocol for sensor network. This protocol combines standard ECDH key establishment with symmetric key encryption technology. Authentication of EC keys is based on implicated certificate spread by off-line certificate authorities. Computation cost of ECC performance for each session reduced one scalar product on fixed point and one scalar product on random point. However, since stability of inner node was strongly hypothesized in [8], the possibility of inner node's compromise is excluded. For expansion of network, it is necessary to verify stability according to whether inner node is compromised.

The hybrid key establishment protocols for sensor network [2,3,7,8] studied till now advanced symmetric key-based techniques so that a compromised node may not generate other sensors in the same group or personalize the nodes in other group. In addition, [2,3] provide forward secrecy that can influence on some nodes, such as node generation. In particular, [2,3] does not hypothesize bootstrapping period although protocol security is enhanced. Further, since this protocol supports multi-phase arrangement and does not provide full functional devices, its performance was enhanced more than that of the hybrid technique in [8].

3 A Hybrid Key Establishment Protocol for WSN

In WSN environment, many nodes are divided into several groups, which are harmonized with the use of key agreement or distribution protocol. The proposed key establishment protocol combined symmetric encryption technology with ECC to support multiphase arrangement stable for uniform self-organized model. The sensors are randomly arranged at sensor network and cannot recognize neighbor nodes until they are arranged. After network initialization, the sensor nodes are priorly arranged with consistent generation keys and can participate in network during operation.

3.1 Notation

Let E be a suitably chosen elliptic curve defined over finite field F_q. The number of points in E can be represented by #E(F_q)=q+1-t(provided |t| $\leq 2\sqrt{x}$), which is called order of E. If q is a decimal, E is cyclic and generator P, a point on E which can be represented by E(F_q) =kP: k $\in$ Z, exists. The method to compute the additive group of the two points can be divided into the cases P=Q and P$\neq$Q. The discrete algorithm problem on the elliptic curve E(F_q) can be defined like this: "If a natural number m, which can satisfy Q=mP for given points P, Q$\in$E(F_q), exists, m is sought for." This m is called discrete logarithm of Q whose base is P, and is determined only by modular Ord(P). Ord(P), the order of P, is a minimum natural number in which mP=0. The $q_{CA} \in$ [2,n-2] is a random integer selected by CA(Certification Authority), and Q_{CA}=q_{CA}×P. The fixed secret/public key pairs are q_{CA} and Q_{CA}. CA generates a symmetric key K that will be used in the range of network, and is used as initial authenticator to prevent error of hello message and individual DoS attack. CA generates an independent symmetric encryption key, which is needed when $\forall$ $S_{k_m} \in$ N(S_i) nodes are generated. N(S_i) is a node set of sensor node. ID_{X_i} is a unique identifier for the node X_i. t_{X_i} is the expiration time of the certificate.

3.2 Key Pre-deployment Phase

This section describes prior key arrangement syntax of node X_i having adequate keying information of CA. The role of CA is different from that of traditional PKI model. CA performs prior arrangement of adequate key at offline node and exerts reliable authority for generated nodes. In the other hand, node X_i computes or verifies integrity of CA keys. After initial process of network, CA no longer participate in key establishment, playing a passive role. CA only performs generation and prior arrangement of the nodes that will be generated from then. Prior key arrangement processes are divided into three steps like this:

• step 1 : CA select a random number $g_{x_i} \in$ [2,n-2] and computes static public key pair(q_{CA},Q_{CA}).

Compute :

- static public key pair: q_{CA}, Q_{CA}=q_{CA} × P

Select :

- Selection of initial network authentication key : K, $g_{x_i} \in$ R and ID_{X_i}

• step 2: After computation of public/private pairwise keys of the node X_i, CA computes the value of secret symmetric key of node.

Compute :

- $Q_{X_i} = d_{X_i} \cdot \mathrm{G} = (\alpha_{X_i}, \beta_{X_i})$
- $\mathrm{M} = ID_{X_i}, t_{X_i}$
- $IC_{X_i} = (Q_{X_i}, \mathrm{M})$
- $e_{X_i} \leftarrow \mathrm{h}(IC_{X_i})$
- $q_{X_i} = q_{X_i} + e_{X_i} \cdot Q_{CA}$
- $Q_{X_i} = q_{X_i} \times \mathrm{G}$

- step 3: CA uses a stable channel to send the generated value to X_i.

- q_{x_i}, IC_{X_i}, Q_{CA}, P, K

3.3 Cluster Formation

When a new node X is going to participate in network, it listens to beacon of cluster head. All cluster heads are responsible for sending CH beacon to cluster to get information on member sensor and cluster head (ID_{X_i},IC_{X_i},Q_{CA_i}) existing in a cluster. If can receive CH beacon from a specific cluster, it can participate in cluster. If not, node should form a new cluster.

When a New Node Receives Beacon. A new node X_i, receiving CH beacon from a specific area C_{X_i}, should be proved to be reliable in area C_{X_i}. If the node X_i has digital signal CA certificate of area C_{X_i}, node S_i submits its own public key. Area C_{X_i}, having the public key of CA, should verify CA and determine whether S_i is reliable. After C_{X_i} verified reliability of X_i, it performs encryption with the public key of X_i and sends CERT(X_i,C_{X_i}) to X_i.

When a New Node does not Receive Beacon. Since a new node X_i, which wants to participate in network but does not receive specific CH beacon, does not exist in cluster, it is necessary to form network. Therefore, node X_i performs initialization process to form network. In that process, node X_i announces itself to CH by sending CH beacon to CH, and X_i's integrity in area C_i gets confirmed through certificate provided by CA. If not, X_i starts to send CH beacon to member sensor Y_j to become a member node of network. A new node X_i, receiving Y_j's beacon, joins in network. If not receiving CH beacon, it waits till CH beacon arrives.

3.4 Key Establishment Between Nodes in Cluster

In key establishment syntax, the two nodes X_i and Y_j use pre-deployed key K to perform authenticated pairwise key establishment. When the two nodes X_i and Y_j mutually communicate, using the secret key generation algorithm, the nodes generate various secret keys in which their own information is included. Authentication provided by this section is known only by the nodes X_i and Y_j. And authentication key is generated by the secret key and random number authentication key generation algorithm generated by the nodes X_i and Y_j. In this section,X_i and Y_j are generated in the range of 1≤i≤j≤m, and m is defined as total numbers of nodes. The nodes are generated in the same range (i=j) or not in the same range (i<j). Among many nodes, the two nodes X_i and Y_j possess j^{th} generated key or instance of key. If i=j, the keys possessed by the two nodes are K_i=K_j. And $Z_{X_iY_j}$ key is possessed by the two nodes according to the process in Figure 1. If i<j, i^{th} generated X_i does not possess j^{th} generated K_j key and cannot deal with Y_j node. Instead, X_i is priorly arranged with $K_j(ID_{X_i})$, the instance of the jth generated key K_j.

For preventing random value from eavesdropper in Figure 1, the node X_i generates temporary key $Z'_{X_iY_j}$, which is encrypted with r_{CA}. For providing key performance for q_{X_i}, the secret key of X_i, the node X_i computes MAC that has $Z'_{X_iY_j}$ key and sends it to Y_j. After verification of the transmitted value, the two nodes X_i and Y_j delete temporary key K, fixed key $Z_{X_iY_j}$ and random values r_{X_i} and r_{Y_i}. Though the process like this, the two nodes X_i and Y_j can infer

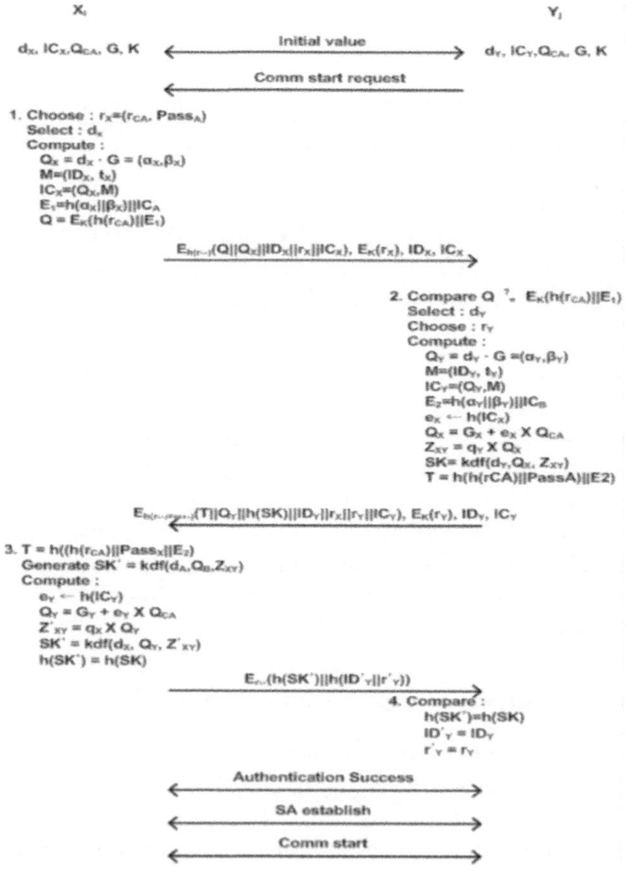

Fig. 1. Authenticated key establishment between the sensor in Cluster

from $Z_{X_iY_j}$ a different key, a key for encryption and a key for authentication. For key freshness, the nodes X_i and Y_j periodically updates pairwise keys. This is because operation time span of the sensor nodes depends on data traffic volume as well as on the length based on cryptographic primitive.

4 Analysis

4.1 Security Analysis

The proposed protocol expands standard ECDH key agreement with random key generation for strengthening prevention of security attack. In addition, for supporting authenticated key agreement along with obvious key performance of nodes, it is based on initial reliability between sensor nodes. The sibling of the node X_i that participated in network generates a new secret key and performs hash action to modify the keys generated before. The newly generated keys are encrypted into the keys of anonymous node in the same group before transmitted to a group. Since all keys in a group are modified when key agreement is made in it, newly added node cannot access the keys already used before. In addition, the node extracted as an infamous one cannot access newly generated encrypted keys because of key information shortage of anonymous node and generation of a new key. In the proposed protocol, the method is simple to prevent invasion node that are going to insert fake data into a group and can be performed without delay. For prevention of those attack, CA examines all transmitted data including MAC and detects fake transmission when temporary sensor node key is revealed. The first method to detect is to make invasion node be recognized within the distance of transmission; the second method is to stop a specific message that receives it from being surrounded. If the fixed key q_{X_i} of the node X_i is compromised and generation key K is safe, an attacker can get $Z_{X_iY_j}$, the specific fixed pairwise key of a node. However, the attacker cannot get random values r_{X_i} and r_{Y_i} that can be used for key outflow because of the size of provided random values. For participation in a group, the reliable secret key q_X has to be possessed for new node Y_j. The new node Y_j sends request to a specific node of CA. The node in cluster sends random value r_{X_i} to the new node Y_j. The new node Y_j can compute $P^{'}$, using one-way function as SK=kdf(r_{X_i},r_{Y_j},$Z_{X_iY_j}$). Then Y_j has fixed pairwise key SK. The new node Y_j obtains present key SK and becomes a member of a cluster.

4.2 Performance Analysis

Environment. For performance analysis of the proposed protocol, parameter and storage space requested for sensor node can be defined like this: In FLASH memory, a total of 96 bytes are needed to save fixed public/private pairwise keys of sensor node and implicated certificate. In ROM's saving space, 200 bytes for generation and verification of ECC implicated certificate, 630 bytes for modular p integer library, 790 bytes for general library, 510 bytes for SHA-1, 1 Kbytes for

Table 1. Energy numbers for AES and SHA-1

Algorithm	Energy
SHA-1	5.9 uJ/byte
AES-128 Enc/Dec	1.62/2.49 uJ/byte

Table 2. Energy consumed by the entire process based on ECC

Algorithm	Sensor	Server
ECC	93.7	93.9

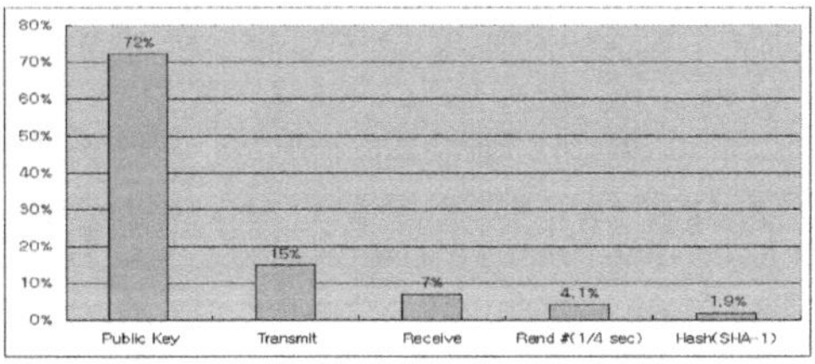

Fig. 2. Decomposition of energy for mutual authentication and key exchange on the sensor side

AES symmetric key algorithm, 1,400 bytes for priorly computed data, 20 bytes for base p phase and 20bytes for elliptic order n are saved.

Energy Cost of Symmetric-key and Hash Algorithms. In this section, in order to obtain energy cost for symmetric key and hash algorithm, the amount of energy for AES with 128 bit key and SHA used for hash is shown as Table 1 and 2 with the same method as in [1, 10].

Figure 2 shows the ratio of energy consumption, in which energy, consumed by sensor for mutual authentication and key exchange, is divided into those for public key, transmission, receiving, random, hash, etc. As can be seen in Figure 2, the public key used in ECC share 72% of total energy consumption and communication cost consumes 22% of energy. Random number generation and hash cost share 4.1% and 1.9%, respectively, which are the values that can be ignored in the aspect of total energy consumption.

Storage Cost. Performance evaluation in section 4.2 is based on cryptographic operation complexity, time for performance, number of message, total number of message transmitted for operation of each protocol, requirement of memory, etc. In this paper, like rekeying cost in communication operation, storage cost for CA and sensor node is computed as follows: n is the number of sensor node, and r is the range of sensor. Storage of sensor key is nr of keys per user:

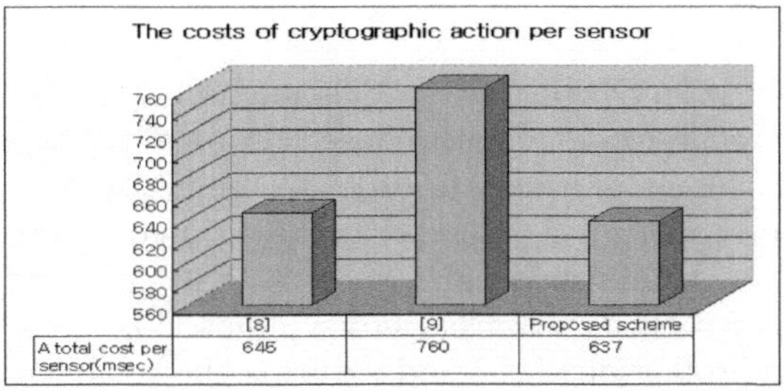

Fig. 3. The costs of cryptographic action per sensor

$log_2\frac{N}{M}$+log_2M =log_2N. Storage of CA key is nr of keys: $(2\times\frac{N}{M})+\frac{N}{M}\times(2\times log_2 M)$ $= 2\times\frac{N}{M}(log_2 M+1)-1$. Communication cost for rekeying is $2\times log_2\frac{N}{M}+log_2 M = 2 \times log_2 N - log_2 M$. The highest value of M is the lowest value of rekeying cost and CA key storage. The non-volatile (FLASH) memory required for sensor needs 96 bytes, including the public/private pairwise keys (q_s,Q_S) and the implicated certificate. In addition, program ROM needs 4.8 Kbytes for code and data, including priorly computed table, order and prime number of the elliptic curve, AES symmetric key algorithm, SHA-A, integer library, modular operation, generation of ECC's implicated certificate, etc.

Communication Complexity. In the proposed protocol, a total of three messages, such as mutual authentication, exchange of random number and key confirmation, are exchanged in relation with key establishment. If the size of device ID used in this experiment is 64 bits, authentication expiration time and random number K also become 64 bits. If elliptic curve module is 160 bits and random number is 64 bits, communication cost in the proposed protocol has 1,453 bits or 183 bytes of communication complexity almost as same as 180 bytes required for [8,10].

Computation Complexity. In order to determine computation complexity, this study uses metrics of [7] in relation with cost of each cryptographic operation. The sensor of the proposed protocol needs computation cost such as one EC scalar product of random point, one EC scalar product of fixed point, two symmetric encryption and decryption, four key hash functions, one hash function, one random number generation. SHA-1 needs only 2ms to decrease 128 bits in the binary string on M16C alone. For symmetric encryption and decryption, AES block cipher is hypothesized as 256 bits of text block as same as in [8] and used for making keyed-hash function. In the results of Fugure 3, the same metrics as in [7,8] was used to obtain computation complexity of total cost per sensor. The proposed protocol, having 637ms of computation complexity, shows 16.2% and 1.3% lower than [7](760ms) and [8](645ms), respectively.

5 Conclusion

This paper is presented a hybrid key establishment protocol, suitable for uniform self-organized sensor networks. The proposed protocol is based on the standard ECDH key establishment protocol. In order to minimize the cost of scalar multiplications, the protocol uses a temporary encrypted channel to protect the randomization of the established pairwise keys. The proposed protocol is more secure to known-key security attacks than symmetric-key based protocols since it does not assume protection of the nodes during the key bootstrapping periods. Moreover, corrupted or captured nodes cannot perform impersonation, sybil or fake generation attacks to any node, other than the corrupted one. A total cost per sensor in our protocol shows about 1.3% lower than the cost of the hybrid protocol of pre-proposed protocol such as [8].

References

1. Carman, D.W., Kruus, P.S., Matt, B.J.: Constraints and Approaches for Distributed Sensor Security. Network Associates Labs Tech, Rep (2000)
2. Dutertre, B., Cheung, S., Levy, J.: Lightweight Key Management in Wireless Sensor Networks by Leveraging Initial Trust. TR SRI-SDL-04-02 (2004)
3. Zhu, S., Setia, S., Jajodia, S.: LEAP: Efficient Security Mechanisms for Large-Scale Distributed Sensor Networks. In: Proceedings of the Seventh IEEE International Symposium on Multimedia, 0-7695-2489-3/05 (2005)
4. Certicom Research: Standard for efficient cryptography. SEC 4: EC Cryptography. Ver. 1.1r1 (2006)
5. Malan, D., Welsh, M., Smith, M.: A Public-Key Infrastructure for Key Distribution in TinyOS Based on Elliptic Curve Cryptography. In: Proceedings of 1st SACN Conference, IEEE SECON, pp. 71–80 (2004)
6. Gaubatz, G., Kaps, J.P., Sunar, B.: Public key cryptography in sensor networks - revisited. In: Proceedings of 1st ESAS Conference (2004)
7. Huang, Q., Cukier, J., Kobayashi, H., Liu, B., Zhang, J.: Fast authenticated key establishment protocols for self-organizing sensor networks. In: Proceedings of 2nd ACM WSNA Conference, pp. 141–150 (2003)
8. Kotzanikolaou, P., Magkos, E., Douligeris, C., Chrissikopoulos, V.: Hybrid Key Establishment for Multiphase Self-Organized Sensor Networks. In: Proceedings of the First IEEE International Workshop on Trust, Security and Privacy for Ubiquitous Computing, pp. 581–587 (2005)
9. Huang, Q., Cukier, J., Kobayashi, H., Liu, B., Zhang, J.: Fast authenticated key establishment protocols for self-organizing sensor networks. In: Proc. of 2nd ACM WSNA Conference, pp. 133–150 (2003)
10. Potlapally, N., Ravi, S., Ranghunathan, A., Jha, N.K.: Analyzing the Energy Consumption of Security Protocols. ISLPED, pp. 30–35 (2003)
11. Williams, H.C.: A modification of the RSA public-key encryption procedure. IEEE Transactions on Information Theory, 726–729 (1980)
12. McGrew, D.A., Sherman, A.T.: Key establishment in large dynamic groups using one-way function trees. Technical Report No. 0755, TIS Labs at Network Associates, Inc., Glenwood, MD (1998)

A Secure Pairwise Key Establishment Scheme in Wireless Ad Hoc Networks*

TaeYeon Kim[1], HeeMan Park[2], and HyungHyo Lee[3]

[1] Dept. of CS and Information Communications, Seonam University, Namwon, Korea
tykim@tiger.seonam.ac.kr
[2] Dept. of Information Security, Chonnam National University, Gwangju, Korea
hareup@lsrc.jnu.ac.kr
[3] Div. of Information and EC, Wonkwang University, Iksan, Korea
hlee@wonkwang.ac.kr

Abstract. Ad hoc networks are exposed to numerous security threats that can adversely affect the success of important applications. Security services such as authentication and key management are important to secure the communication between two nodes in the networks. In the existing key pre-distribution schemes, each node is equipped with a weak authentication mechanism to identify neighboring nodes. During the secret key discovery phase, when any two nodes share at least one key information, one node considers the other side to be worthy of confidence and discloses all the shared information to it without a doubt. These schemes are vulnerable to active attack from authorized nodes as well as unauthorized nodes. This paper proposes a novel key management scheme: each node reduces the disclosure of the shared key information and the network provides strong authentication and privacy. Performance and security analyses have proven that our scheme is suitable for ad hoc networks in terms of availability and security aspects.

1 Introduction

Ad hoc wireless networks require no centralized center or fixed network infrastructure. They consist of low-end nodes such as cellular phones, PDAs and embedded devices. In many cases, the nodes of ad hoc networks suffer from limited resources: battery, memory, processor, network bandwidth, and so on. And these nodes are mobile and the topology of the network may change frequently.

To ensure establishing secure link between any two nodes in distributed sensor networks, Eschenauer et al. [1] first proposed a probabilistic key pre-distribution scheme. Chan et al. [2], Du et al. [3], and Zhu et al. [4] also extended this scheme to further improve the security and the efficiency. There are, however, two shortcomings in terms of security. First, during the shared-key discovery phase, any node which has

* This research was supported by the MIC, Korea, under the ITRC(Information Technology Research Center) support program supervised by the IITA(Institute of Information Technology Assessment).

J. Indulska et al. (Eds.): UIC 2007, LNCS 4611, pp. 1243–1252, 2007.

shared key can forge data and impersonate other authorized nodes. Second, their schemes are not fully resilient against node capture.

To reduce the second problem, Chan [5] recently, proposed a symmetric key management scheme which each node can find secret keys shared with a communicating node without revealing the unshared keys. His scheme has four security problems. First, before completing the shared-key discovery, any malicious node can know how many keys on the key chain are shared with the other side, without receiving a response. Second, it can guess some of the keys held by the other side due to the weakness of encrypted values received from the other side. Third, though its scheme can hide the keys unshared with other nodes, each pair of nodes can know all the shared keys. Lastly, his scheme also does not support user authentication.

To solve user authentication problem and to improve the resilience against node capture, Du et al. [6] and Liu et al. [7] proposed a new key pre-distribution scheme, which combined the basic scheme with Blom's scheme [8]. Under their scheme, multiple key spaces are randomly assigned to all the nodes in the network, and any two nodes are able to calculate a new session key if and only if both nodes share a common key space. However, as long as no more than λ nodes are compromised, the network is perfectly secure (referred to as the λ-secure property). But their scheme [6] causes two important problems. First, when an adversary compromises more than λ nodes among all nodes having the rows of any matrix, e.g. A_c, he can still calculate secret pairwise keys, called secret keys, of all the nodes which he wants to communicate with. Second, to intentionally mount an exhaustive key discovery for a meaningless key establishment with his neighboring nodes, an adversary can broadcast messages containing any legitimate node's ID and false information. This increases the communication overhead because his neighboring nodes, on receiving the message, send response messages to the adversary without ascertaining the identity of the node that it is communicating with.

Accordingly, in this paper, we will present on a new key management scheme having the following merits. First, it supports authentication services. Second, it improves resilience against node capture. Lastly, it can reduce the communication and computation overhead which are caused by any attackers.

The rest of the paper is organized as follows. Section 2 and 3 present the modified Rivest's scheme and the Du's scheme, and our pairwise key establishment protocol. In section 4, Performance results and security analyses are described. Finally, section 5 concludes this paper.

2 Background

2.1 Chan's Scheme

Before describing our scheme, we will briefly review Chan's scheme, called Modified Rivest's Scheme (MRS). The detailed protocol descriptions are described in [5]. In his key pre-distribution scheme, all the nodes are assigned a random subset of keys from a key pool before deployment. And, during the shared-key discovery phase, each node attempts to discover whether it shares any key(s) with the other side node. Unlike the former schemes, when the MRS scheme is used in the shared-key discovery, any two nodes make use of a polynomial expression. That is, the source node forms a polynomial expression using its key sets, encrypts the coefficients with a secret key which he has only, and then broadcasts the encrypted coefficients to its neighbors. The destination node forms the new polynomial expression using the received message, generates a list of modified encrypted values and then sends them to the source node. The source node, on receiving the modified encrypted coefficients, decrypts them so as to discovery how many keys on the key chain held by itself are shared with the other side. Consequently, it does not disclose any information about the keys that the other side does not have.

2.2 Du et al.'s Scheme

In Du et al.'s scheme, during key pre-distribution phase, multiple key spaces generated from Blom's scheme [8] are randomly assigned to all the nodes in the networks. That is, the base station creates a matrix G of size $(\lambda+1)\times N$, ω symmetric matrices (i.e., $D_1, D_2, \ldots, D_\omega$ of size $(\lambda+1)\times(\lambda+1)$) and matrices $A_i = (D_i \bullet G)_c^T(i)$, where $i = 1, \ldots, \omega$. A tuple A_i is defined as a key space. And then each node randomly selects m from the ω key spaces. That is, for matrix A_i selected for node x, the base station assigns the xth row of A_i to its node. After deployment, if any two nodes have a common key space, each node can establish a secret pairwise key directly using a message which contains its unique node ID and the indices of the key spaces it carries. In this case, the indices are disclosed to adversaries as well as authorized nodes. Therefore, this method is not secure because any adversary can mount an exhaustive process in order to increase the communication and computational overhead of the network, and even if each node makes use of m ($<\omega$) distinct key spaces, any adversary can still find the $\lambda+1$ nodes having rows of any matrix $A_c (= (D_c \bullet G)^T)$ as usual. To protect these indices, all nodes may challenge the other party to solve puzzles instead of disclosing the indices in clear text. Though their scheme does not reduce the above security problems, the pairwise key establishment problem is still not fully solved, because their scheme is vulnerable to active attack from authorized nodes as well as unauthorized nodes.

2.3 Notation

In the rest of this paper, we use the following notations.

- N, m, ω, λ : the size of network, the size of key chain, the number of the key spaces, and a security parameter respectively
- G, D, A : a $(\lambda+1)\times N$ matrix, a $(\lambda+1)\times(\lambda+1)$ symmetric matrix, a matrix $A = (D \bullet G)^T$, respectively
- P_{actual} : probability that each node can share at least one key space with its neighbors during key agreement phase
- KA, KB : node A's and B's secret key which remains private, respectively
- $E^K(M), D^K(M)$: encrypted and decrypted message M with key K

$-V_c(=v_{xk})$: the element values of matrix A_c for node x, $k = 0, \dots, \lambda$

$-p, q$: prime numbers

3 Our Pairwise Key Establishment Protocol

In this section, we present our pairwise key establishment scheme in detail. The proposed scheme leverages Eschenauer and Gligor's scheme [1], MRS[5] and Du et al.'s scheme [6]. The path-key establishment phase will not be described since it is assumed that our scheme can employ the same protocol that of Eschenauer and Gligor's scheme.

3.1 Modified Multiple Key Space Generation Phase

To improve the Du et al.'s scheme in terms of security, we propose the following modified multiple-space generation procedure: in the first place, the base station generates a matrix G of $(\lambda+1)\times N$ over a finite field $GF(q)$ and ω symmetric matrices (i.e., $D_1,\dots,D_\omega$) of $(\lambda+1)\times(\lambda+1)$, and generates matrices $A_i=(D_i\bullet G)^T$, $i=1,\dots,\omega$, where q is an element within the finite field and G is considered as public information.

Unlike the Du et al.'s scheme, in our scheme, we construct a key pool with which any two nodes can calculate their secret key using the Blom's scheme, with some probability P_{actual} (i.e., the actual probability that each node can share at least a common key space with its neighbors using their key information). That is, to minimize the possibility that a matrix D_c is computed by any adversary, we control the number of rows of the matrix A_c, called size(A_c), that belong to the key pool. Therefore, the total size of the key pool is size(A_c) $\times\ \omega$. And we randomly select m distinct key information called *key chain* from the key pool and assign them to each node, where the key chain is associated with m randomly selected key spaces $(2\le m\le\omega)$. This is similar to Eschenauer et al.'s assignment of randomly generated keys from a large key pool. We can construct a random graph $G(N, P_{actual})$, which is a graph of N nodes for which the probability that a link exists between any two nodes is P_{actual}.

The key information consists of the following values: the index of a key space S_i, a one-way hash function h_i, the seed of the column of G and the row of matrix A_i for node x, i.e., $(S_i^{index}, h_i, G^{seed}, v_{xk})$, where $1\le i\le\omega$, $k=0,\dots,\lambda$. During shared-key discovery phase, the hash function is used by each node to verify the identity of the other side node. It is for the sake of detecting that a malicious node impersonates any authorized node. However, even if an adversary has any matrix D_c, as long as he does not know the hash function h_c on matrix A_c, he cannot broadcast messages containing any legitimate node's ID and false information, and cannot calculate secret keys of all the nodes that he wants to communicate with.

3.2 Pairwise Key Generation Phase

3.2.1 Negotiatory Keys

After deployment, each node needs to establish a pairwise key with its neighbors. To do this, each node generally generates m non-linear equations with the indices of the key spaces (i.e., $s_1, s_2, ..., s_m$) it carries as expression (1) and (2), and broadcasts the message containing the encrypted coefficients of $f_A(x)$ (i.e., $E^{KA}(A_0), E^{KA}(A_1)$, ..., $E^{KA}(A_{m-1})$), where KA is the secret key of the node A.

$$f_A(x) = (x - s_1)(x - s_2)...(x - s_m) = x^m + A_{m-1}x^{m-1} + ... + A_1 x + A_0 \quad (1)$$

$$f_A'(x) = x^m + E^{KA}(A_{m-1})x^{m-1} + ... + E^{KA}(A_0) \quad (2)$$

But in this paper, we make use of negotiatory keys instead of the indices of the key spaces. The generation of negotiatory keys is as follows. For example, let node A, id_a, has the indices $\{s_1(= a_{11} \parallel a_{12}), s_2\ (= a_{21} \parallel a_{22}), ..., s_m(= a_{m1} \parallel a_{m2})\}$ and node B, id_b, has the indices $\{t_1(= b_{11} \parallel b_{12}), t_2(= b_{21} \parallel b_{22}), ..., t_m(= b_{m1} \parallel b_{m2})\}$, where a_{i1} and b_{j1} are the first half of the indices, and a_{i2} and b_{j2} are the second half of the indices respectively, $1 \le i, j \le m$. We yield a negotiatory key by concatenating the first half of an index and a hash function's value, and in reverse. That is, the half set of node A's negotiatory keys is $\{s_{11}(= a_{11} \parallel h_{i'}(a_{11})), s_{21}(= a_{21} \parallel h_{j'}(a_{21}))$, ..., $s_{m1}(= a_{m1} \parallel h_{k'}(a_{m1}))\}$. The other half set are $\{s_{12}(= h_{i'}(a_{12}) \parallel a_{12})$, $s_{22}(= h_{j'}(a_{22}) \parallel a_{22}), ..., s_{m12}(= h_{k'}(a_{m2}) \parallel a_{m2})\}$, where $1 \le i' \ne j' \ne k' \le \omega$. Similarly, the first half set of B's negotiatory keys consists of the following elements: $\{t_{11}(= b_{11} \parallel h_{i''}(b_{11})),\ t_{21}(= b_{21} \parallel h_{j''}(b_{21})), ..., t_{m1}(= b_{m1} \parallel h_{k''}(b_{m1}))\}$. Also, the second half set of Bob's keys is $\{t_{12}(= h_{i''}(b_{12}) \parallel b_{12}), t_{22}(= h_{j''}(b_{22}) \parallel b_{22}), ..., t_{m2}(= h_{k''}(b_{m2}) \parallel b_{m2})\}$, where $1 \le i'' \ne j'' \ne k'' \le \omega$.

3.2.2 Pairwise Key Generation

In this section, we describe the way how two nodes calculate a pairwise key. The detailed description is as follows. Suppose node A wants to find out a common space with node B. The node A generates its negotiatory keys, i.e., $s_{11}, s_{21}, ..., s_{m1}$, and applys them to expression (1). Then node A encrypts coefficients of $f_A(x)$ with its secret key AK, i.e., $E^{AK}(A_0), E^{AK}(A_1), ..., E^{AK}(A_{m-1})$, and broadcasts them to neighboring nodes. In reverse, when node A receives a requesting message from the other side (i.e., node B), the node applies its negotiatory keys, $s_{12}, s_{22}, ..., s_{m2}$, to expression (4) in order to generate a list of encrypted values, i.e. $r_0 f_B'(s_{12}), r_1 f_B'(s_{22}), ..., r_{l-1} f_B'(s_{m2})$, and sends back them to B, where r_i s are different and nonzero values.

$$f_B(x) = (x - t_{12})(x - t_{22})...(x - t_{m2}) = x^m + B_{m-1}x^{m-1} + ... + B_0 \tag{3}$$

$$f'_B(x) = x^m + E^{KB}(B_{m-1})x^{m-1} + ... + E^{KB}(B_0) \tag{4}$$

The node B also generates negotiatory keys and applys them to expression (3). Then he encrypts coefficients of $f_B(x)$ with its secret key BK (i.e., $E^{BK}(B_0), E^{BK}(B_1), ..., E^{BK}(B_{m-1})$) and broadcasts them to neighboring nodes. In reverse, when he receives a requesting message from other side (i.e., A), he applies his keys to expression (2) in order to generate a list of encrypted values (i.e. $r'_0 f'_A(t_{12}), r'_1 f'_A(t_{22}), ..., r'_{m-1} f'_A(t_{m2})$) and sends them to the node A. Also, r'_i s are different and nonzero values.

[Step 1] $A \rightarrow$ Neighbors: $E^{KA}(A_0), E^{KA}(A_1), ..., E^{KA}(A_{m-1})$, $B \in$ Neighbors
[Step 2] $B \rightarrow A$:
$M' = \{r'_1 f'_A(t_{11}), r'_2 f'_A(t_{21}), ..., r'_m f'_A(t_{m1})\}$ and $E^{KB}(B_0), E^{KB}(B_1), ..., E^{KB}(B_{m-1})$,
where $1 \le i \le m$ and r'_i are different values and nonzero.
[Step 3] $A \rightarrow B$: m-bit bitmap and $M = \{r_1 f'_B(s_{12}), r_2 f'_B(s_{22}), ..., r_m f'_B(s_{m2})\}$
[Step 4] $B \rightarrow A$: m'-bit bitmap
[Step 5] $A \rightarrow B$: R(random number) and $h_c(id_b \| SK \| R)$,
Where $K_j = A_c(B) \bullet G\ (A)$, $SK = h_1(K_1 \| K_2 \| ... \| K_j)$, $1 \le c \le \omega$, $1 \le j \le w'$
[Step 6] $B \rightarrow A$: $h_1(id_a \| SK \| R+1)$, where $K_j = A_c(A) \bullet G\ (B)$

Fig. 1. The pairwise key generation protocol

Fig. 1 shows the node B can check which the indices of the key spaces he has are in common with the node A's and vice versa. The node A broadcasts the encrypted coefficients of $f_A(x)$ to its neighbor nodes (see expression (2)). In the step 2, the node B cannot decrypt them because he does not know the secret key, KA, of the node A. The node B sends M' and the encrypted coefficients of $f_B(x)$ to the node A (see expression (4)). In the step 3, the node A decrypts $D^{KA}(r'_i f'_A(t_{i1}))$ and calculates an m-bit bitmap with 1 at bits where $D^{KA}(r'_i f'_A(t_{i1}))$ is 0 and with 0 otherwise. Where a 1 at the i-th bit indicates to the node B that she also has t_{i1} . But since he has no knowledge about r'_i , he does not know what t_{i1} is, $1 \le i \le m$. And to enhance security, if the number of bits with 1 in m-bit bitmap (i.e. W) is more than 1, she randomly adjusts it to w ($= \left\lceil \frac{W}{2} \right\rceil < m$). The node A sends M and an m-bit bitmap to the other side.

In the step 4, the node B can know that some t_{i1} are associated with 1 in m-bit bitmap are in common with the node A's, and decrypts $D^{KB}(r_i f_B'(s_{i2}))$. The node B also does not know what s_{i2} is. The node B calculates an m'-bit bitmap with 1 at bits where $D^{KB}(r_i f_B'(s_{i2}))$ is 0 and 0 elsewhere. To enhance security, if the number of bits with 1 in m'-bit bitmap (i.e. W') is more than 1, he randomly adjusts it to w' $(= \left\lceil \frac{W'}{2} \right\rceil < m)$. The node B sends the m'-bit bitmap, $r' f_A'(t_{i1})$ associated with 1 in m-bit bitmap and r' to A, where r' is the plaintext. Finally, each node generates a session key using both m-bit, m'-bit bitmap and $r' f_A'(t_{i1})$. That is, a new session key SK is generated as the hashed value of the concatenation of pairwise keys (i.e., $SK = h_1(K_1 \| K_2 \| \ldots \| K_j)$).

4 Performance and Security Analysis

In this section, we analyze the performance and the security property of our proposed scheme. Our approach is compared with the scheme proposed by Du et al. [6]. In our simulations, we induced two metrics to evaluate the availability and the security of the proposed scheme. One metric is the actual probability that any two neighboring nodes share at least one key space during the key discovery phase. The other metric is the probability of the indices of the shared key spaces being disclosed. For the sake of presentation, our scheme and Du et al.'s scheme are hereafter referred to as SPK (Secure Pairwise Key establishment scheme) and Du respectively.

The network model for our simulation assumed as follows: (a) 1000 nodes were randomly placed in a 100m × 100m area, (b) the memory usage is set to 200, (c) the value of λ for each space is 49, (d) the number (ω) of key spaces varied in 20, 50 and 90, (e) the size (m) of the key chain varied in 3, 5 and 7.

4.1 Performance Analysis

We do not consider the computational complexity because this process only uses a few inexpensive symmetric cryptographic algorithms. But we will evaluate the communication overhead because the energy consumption largely depends on it.

4.1.1 Probability of Sharing at Least One Key Space

The actual local connectivity usually is determined by the number of the key spaces or the size of the key chain. When they are fixed, its connectivity is determined by the number of key information (i.e., rows) generated from a key space. In both schemes,

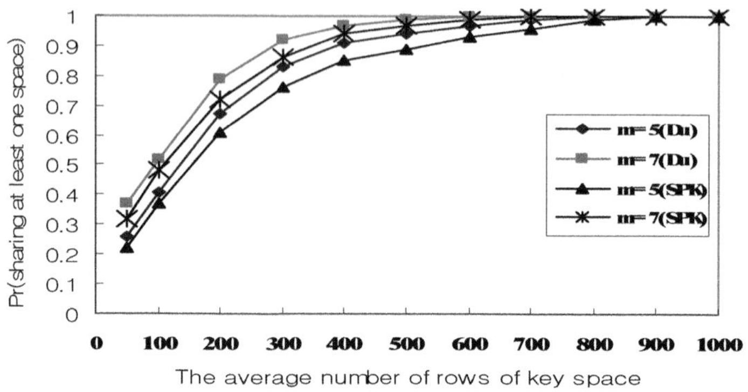

Fig. 2. Key sharing probability vs. # of the rows of key space

the values of P_{actual} have been shown in Fig. 2 when $\omega = 50$, the average number of rows of key space, size (A_c), varies from 50 to 1000, and m = 5 and 7. As shown Fig. 2, as the size (A_c) increases, the probability also increases. The results make a little difference between two schemes, although very little. The size of the key chain determines memory size and security about resilience against node capture. Therefore, for fixed $\omega = 50$ and $m = 5$, to satisfy $P_{actual} \geq 0.45$, the average number of rows of key spaces which we can choose is 100.

4.1.2 Communication Overhead

The communication overhead is mainly due to the transmission and reception of the messages. In random key pre-distribution schemes, to find the shared spaces with its neighbors, each node exchanges all of its key information with its neighbors. In Eschenauer et al. [1], when the source node needs to find a shared key with the destination node, it sends the destination an encryption list, (á , E^{Kv}(á)), $v = 1, \ldots, m$, where á is a challenge and Kv are secret keys it carries. Similar to the Eschenauer et al. [1], in Du et al.'s scheme, to protect the indices of the matrices $A_k (= (D_k \bullet G)^T)$, the source node may challenge the other node to solve trivial puzzles instead of disclosing the indices of the matrices it have, in clear text. But in our scheme, the communication and computational overhead of the messages sent by two nodes will be slightly increase because our scheme made use of negotiatory keys instead of the identifier of the keys or indices of matrices that used in the existing schemes. But in order to mount an exhaustive discovery for key information held by its neighboring nodes, if any malicious node may encrypt some randomly generated information and broadcast them to its neighbors, the communication and computational overhead may be considerably increase. However, our scheme is extremely suitable for ad hoc networks because most applications require enough security level.

4.2 Security Analysis

4.2.1 Probability of One Key Space Being Broken

Unlike the Blom's scheme, in the multiple-space key pre-distribution scheme, each node shares one key space or more than two key spaces with its neighbors. Therefore, during the key space discovery phase, each node needs to find out a common space to improve resilience against node capture without revealing the unshared spaces to its corresponding node while reducing the number of the shared spaces.

After finishing the pairwise key generation in the Du's scheme, each pair of nodes can know all the indices of shared key spaces even if they cannot know unshared key spaces. Therefore, if one node of them is compromised by adversaries, the other side also is easy to suffer from attacks by them later. However, when an adversary compromises more than λ nodes among all nodes that have the rows of any matrix, e.g. A_c, he can still calculate secret pairwise keys of all the nodes which he wants to communicate with. To overcome this problem, we made use of negotiatory keys instead of the method that are generally used by the existing schemes, and mechanism which restricts the number of disclosed shared keys. Fig. 3 shows the relation between size(A_c) and the exposure rate of the indices of the shared key spaces for the fixed $\lambda = 50$ and ω =50. As shown in Fig. 3, the result makes much difference between both schemes.

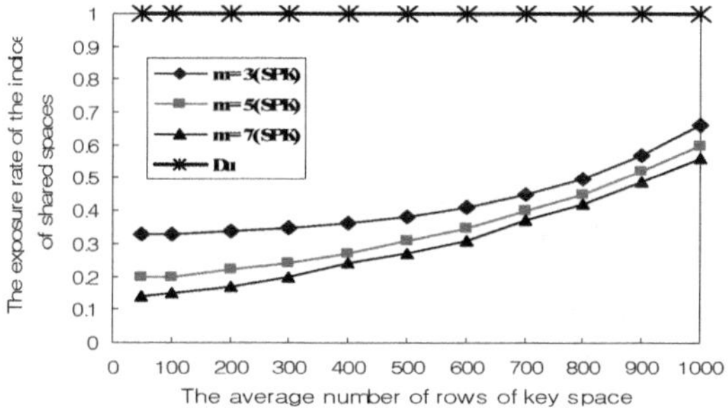

Fig. 3. Information exposure vs. # of the rows of key space

4.2.2 Key Authentication and Impersonator's Notification

Under Du et al.'s scheme and Chan's scheme, the mechanisms which any legitimate node notifies the identity of impersonator are not considered. Upon and after network initialization, in order to increase the communication and computation overhead of networks, a malicious node can broadcast a random key chain falsified by itself to neighboring nodes. In this case, even if indices of some spaces on the falsified key chain are common with any legitimate node, he cannot establish a secure link with the other side. This is because it cannot know xth row of the corresponding space (e.g. for node x) and in addition has no corresponding one-way hash function.

Consequently, even if an adversary compromises more than λ nodes among all nodes, our scheme provides a high confidence communication link with the others (i.e. exclusive of $(\lambda+1)$ nodes), and also cannot masquerade as a legitimate node unless any node of the $(\lambda+1)$ nodes disclose the corresponding one-way hash functions to the adversary. And if any node detects a misbehaving node, it broadcasts the misbehaved node's identifier to the neighboring nodes before the adversary launches a significant attack.

5 Conclusions

In this paper, we proposed a secure pairwise key pre-distribution scheme for wireless ad hoc networks. To enhance security, we made use of the modified multiple-space generation mechanisms and the negotiatory keys instead of the identifier of the keys or indices of matrices used in the existing schemes. Also, the proposed scheme complements the weakness of the cryptographic algorithm by exploiting multiple random numbers during the key discovery phase. Consequently, the proposed scheme guarantees that two nodes discovery a session key in a secure method and provides the robustness against node capture. Simulation results showed that the proposed scheme is more secure than the simple Du et al.'s scheme. That is, judging from the security of the proposed scheme, our protocol is suitable for ad hoc networks. And the implementation of these techniques on real ad hoc platforms may serve to be the subject of future studies.

References

1. Eschenauer, L., Gligor, V.D.: A Key-management Scheme for Distributed Sensor Networks. In: Proc. of the 9th ACM Conference on Computer and Communications Security, pp. 41–47. ACM Press, New York (2002)
2. Chan, H., Perrig, A., Song, D.: Random Key Pre-distribution Schemes for Sensor Networks. In: IEEE Symposium on Research in Security and Privacy, May 11-14, 2003 pp. 197–213 (2003)
3. Du, W., Deng, J., Han, Y.S., Varshney, P.K.: A Key Management Scheme for Wireless Sensor Networks Using Deployment Knowledge. IEEE INFOCOM, 586–597 (2004)
4. Zhu, S., Xu, S., Setia, S., Jajodia, S.: Establishing Pairwise Keys for Secure Communication in Ad Hoc Networks: A probabilistic Approach. In: Proceedings of the 11th IEEE International Conference on Network Protocols (ICNP'03), pp. 1–10. IEEE Computer Society Press, Los Alamitos (2003)
5. Chan, A.C-F.: Distributed Symmetric Key Management for Mobile Ad hoc Networks. IEEE INFOCOM, 2414–2424 (2004)
6. Du, W., Deng, J., Han, Y.S., Varshney, P.K.: A Pairwise Key Pre-distribution Scheme for Wireless Sensor Networks. In: Proc. of ACM Conference on Computer and Communications Security (CCS'03), pp. 42–51 (2003)
7. Liu, D., Ning, P.: Establishing Pairwise Keys in Distributed Sensor Networks. In: 10th ACM Conference on Computer and Communications Security (CCS'03), pp. 52–61. ACM Press, New York (2003)
8. Blom, R.: An Optimal Class of Symmetric Key Generation System. In: Beth, T., Cot, N., Ingemarsson, I. (eds.) Advances in Cryptology EUROCRYPT 84. LNCS, vol. 209, pp. 335–338. Springer, Heidelberg (1985)

Author Index

Abdulla, Waleed H. 1046
Ahn, SungHo 205
Amamiya, Makoto 1159
Antoniou, Grigoris 839

Baik, Doo-Kwon 993
Bikakis, Antonis 839
Bodhuin, Thierry 225

Cao, Jiannong 103, 579
Cha, Woosuk 454
Chan, Hsuan-Hao 331
Chang, Hsiao-Nung 545
Chang, Jae-Woo 829
Chang, Wei-Li 331, 350
Chen, Bo 103
Chen, Chun-Wei 350
Chen, Daoxu 503, 524
Chen, Guihai 579
Chen, Huifang 475
Chen, Lijun 503, 524
Chen, Wei-Ting 720
Chen, Yong-Qian 709
Chen, Zhe 495
Cho, Gihwan 454
Cho, Il-Yeon 43
Cho, Jinsung 285, 663
Cho, Seong-Rak 392
Cho, Seong Jin 849
Cho, Sung-Bae 1130
Cho, Sung Hyun 730
Cho, Tae Ho 535
Cho, Youn-Ho 758
Choi, Byung-Uk 63
Choi, Eunjun 767
Choi, Eun Young 1171
Choi, Jaeyoung 953
Choi, Myounghoi 1089
Choi, Sang-Bang 983
Choi, Yanghee 632
Choo, Hyunseung 739
Chun, Jonghun 13
Collier, Rem 1056
Cong, Lanlan 235

d'Auriol, Brian J. 285, 663
Dai, Peng 868
Dow, Chyi-Ren 545

Eom, Doo-seop 412

Fang, Cunhao 1003, 1014
Feng, Dan 258
Fu, Zhen 434

Gao, Zhenguo 370
Gavrilov, Andrey 849
Gelonch, Antoni 808
Goi, Bok-Min 1213
Gong, Haigang 579
Goumopoulos, Christos 214
Gu, Nam 709
Guan, Donghai 849
Guo, Caifen 1121
Guo, Wei 888

Han, Ping 819
Han, Seungwok 1098
Han, Songqiao 1024
Han, Sung-Kook 973, 1089
Han, Wang Won 163
Han, Wei-Hong 908
Han, Youn-Hee 1089
Hao, Jingbo 1181
Hao, Shuai 673
Harle, R.K. 963
He, Hui 878
He, Ruhan 888
Helal, Sumi 941
Henricksen, Karen 929
He, Xingui 360
Hong, Jin-Hyuk 1130
Hong, Kwang-Seok 113
Hori, Yoshiaki 382
Hsu, Kevin Chihcheng 350
Hu, Xianghua 557
Hua, Yu 258
Huang, Benxiong 402
Huang, Junkai 632
Hwang, Kwang-il 412
Hwang, Shiow-Fen 545

Indrawan, Maria 184
Indulska, Jadwiga 929

Jang, Mun-Suck 983
Jang, Seiie 898
Janlert, Lars-Erik 246
Jeon, Dongwoon 123
Jeon, Yang-Seung 1089
Jeong, Dongwon 993, 1089
Jeong, Yoon-Su 1233
Jeong, Young-Sik 973, 1089
Jia, Yan 908
Jiang, Minghui 33
Jiang, Yingtao 295
Jiao, Xianlong 340
Jin, Beihong 235
Jin, Hai 888
Jin, Jiang 622
Jing, Ranzhe 1121
Jing, Yixin 993
Joseph, Vinod Cherian 205
Joung, Uhjin 309
Jung, Inbum 684
Jung, Kyunghoon 83

Kajita, Shoji 898
Kameas, Achilles 214
Kang, Euisun 748
Kim, Byounghoon 83
Kim, Byung-Seo 276
Kim, Changsoo 83
Kim, Chi-Su 858
Kim, Dongkyun 309
Kim, Doo-Hyun 123, 205
Kim, Eun-Mi 454
Kim, Eunhoe 953
Kim, Hye-Young 730, 777
Kim, Jae-Hyun 53
Kim, Jai-Hoon 444
Kim, Jeong-Dong 993
Kim, Ji Hoon 1098
Kim, Jihoon 143
Kim, Jinhyung 993
Kim, Joongheon 767
Kim, Jung-Hwan 434
Kim, Jung-Hyun 113
Kim, Junu 422
Kim, Kyungkyu 23
Kim, Lila 123
Kim, Moonseong 739
Kim, Sang-Sik 641
Kim, Seung Jo 798
Kim, Sung Won 276
Kim, TaeYeon 1243
Kim, Tea-young 412
Kim, Yong-Ki 829
Kim, Young-Kyoung 709
Kim, Young Man 163
Kim, Young Yong 464
Ko, Hyun 1098
Ko, Sunghoon 941
Ko, Young-Bae 444
Kokogawa, Tomohiro 475
Krishnamurthy, Sudha 610
Krishnaswamy, Shonali 153
Kulyukin, Vladimir 33
Kunii, Tosiyasu L. 1
Kuo, Chieh-Hsin 720
Kutiyanawala, Aliasgar 33
Kwon, Hwasun 123
Kwon, Hyuntaek 422
Kwon, Ohbyung 143, 919
Kwon, Taekyoung 632, 653

Lagriffoul, Fabien 246
Lange, Lajos 610
Lee, Bae-Ho 454
Lee, Byoung-Hoon 444
Lee, Cheol-Hoon 43
Lee, Chien-Min 720
Lee, Choong-Hee 53
Lee, Choonhwa 787, 941
Lee, Danny 567
Lee, Dong-Kon 392
Lee, Dongeun 422
Lee, Dong Hoon 1171
Lee, Donghwan 23
Lee, Eung-Huyk 983
Lee, Hae Young 535
Lee, HyungHyo 1243
Lee, Joahyoung 684
Lee, JongHyup 653
Lee, Joonho 422
Lee, Keunsoo 123
Lee, Kyunghee 205
Lee, Sang-Ho 1233
Lee, Sang-Yun 63
Lee, Seungjae 941
Lee, Su Mi 1171
Lee, Sungyoung 663, 849

Lee, Sungyung 285
Lee, Wonjun 23, 767, 787, 941
Lee, Yong-Woo 858
Lee, Young-Koo 849
Li, Fangmin 485, 819
Li, Jing 103
Li, Shan-shan 514
Li, Xu 696
Li, Yong 1191
Lim, Brian Y. 173
Lim, Hock Beng 567, 673
Lim, Jae-Hyun 858
Lim, Younghwan 748
Lim, Yunjae 93
Lin, Yaping 495
Ling, Sea 184
Linhares, Fernando D. 589
Liu, Liang 878
Liu, Ming 579
Liu, Weiping 632
Liu, Wenyu 622
Liu, Zhaoyu 1159
Loke, Seng Wai 153, 184
Lopes, Carlos Eduardo R. 589
Lou, Wei 579
Lu, Kun-Hsien 545

Maeng, YoungJae 1222
Malik, Muhammad Ali 444
Maña, Antonio 1201
Mangina, Eleni 1056
Mao, Yingchi 524
Marojevic, Vuk 808
Mase, Kenji 898
McGovern, Elaine 1056
Meng, Min 285
Mineno, Hiroshi 475
Mizuno, Tadanori 475
Mo, Yijun 622
Moh, Sangman 267
Mohaisen, Abedelaziz 1222
Mokhtari, Mounir 173
Mu, Yi 1191
Muñoz, Antonio 1201

Nakamura, Yuichi 898
Nam, Young Jin 93
Noh, Donggeon 422
Nyang, DaeHun 1222

O'Flynn, Brendan 214
Obashi, Yoshitsugu 475
Ogiela, Marek R. 1079
Oh, Myoung-Hwan 43
Oh, Seong-Hwan 53

Paik, Bu-Geun 392
Papadopouli, Maria 839
Park, Ae-Soon 641
Park, Beom-Jin 392
Park, Chongmyung 684
Park, Daehyuck 748
Park, Eunjeong 798
Park, HeeMan 1243
Park, Hongjae 163
Park, Hyemee 739
Park, Jongan 13
Park, Kwangkyu 653
Park, Kyu-Sik 758
Park, Moon-Hee 1130
Park, Myong-Soon 434
Park, Tae Hwan 919
Park, Young-Ha 392
Patkos, Theodore 839
Pederson, Thomas 246
Pei, Dingyi 1191
Peng, Shao-liang 514
Peng, Yu-xing 514
Phan, Raphael C.-W. 1213
Plexousakis, Dimitris 839
Preziosi, Rosa 225

Qi, Yong 878
Qiu, Xun 1121
Quan, Shan Guo 464

Rakotonirainy, Andry 153
Revés, Xavier 808
Rhee, Seunghak 13
Roche, Bernard J. 1056
Rosa-Velardo, Fernando 1148
Roy, Abhishek 133
Ruiz, Linnyer B. 589

Sakurai, Kouichi 382, 1159
Salcic, Zoran 1046
Salim, Flora Dilys 153
Santoro, Nicola 696
Santos, Michele M. 589
Saxena, Navrati 133

Seo, Dae-Wha 93
Serrano, Daniel 1201
Shen, Haowei 495
Shi, Jinglun 632
Shi, Ke 321
Shi, Yuanchun 195
Shin, Heonshik 422, 798
Shin, Jitae 133, 777
Shin, Kwang-Sik 983
Shiratori, Norio 1034, 1108
Sjölie, Daniel 246
Sohan, R.S. 963
Son, Yong-Ki 43
Song, Eun-Ha 973
Song, Jooseok 653
Stojmenovic, Ivan 696
Suganuma, Takuo 1034, 1108
Sugawara, Kenji 1034, 1108
Sun, Aobing 888
Sunwoo, John 43
Surie, Dipak 246
Susilo, Willy 1191

Tadeusiewicz, Ryszard 1079
Tak, Sungwoo 83
Takahashi, Hideyuki 1108
Takahashi, Ken'ichi 1159
Tang, Wen-sheng 514
Tao, Linmi 868
Tao, Yiyi 1121
Tian, Chen 622
Tian, Pengwei 1003, 1014
Tokairin, Yoshikazu 1108
Tortorella, Maria 225
Trzupek, Mirosław 1079
Tu, Lai 402

Vucevic, Nemanja 808

Wang, Jianping 295, 370
Wang, Jun 908
Wang, Kevin I-Kai 1046
Wang, Lei 495
Wang, Ling 370
Wang, Miaomiao 103
Wang, Qinqi 360
Wang, Shupeng 295
Wang, Xiaodong 340
Wang, Yi 622
Wang, Ying-Hong 720
Wang, Yufeng 382
Wang, Yuying 1140
Watfa, Mohamed Khalil 599
Wen, Yuanfeng 235
Wishart, Ryan 929
Wu, Eric Hsiao-Kuang 331, 350
Wu, Song 888
Wu, Xiaoling 663
Wu, Xuehong 485, 819

Xi, Min 878
Xiao, Nong 514
Xiao, Xin 195
Xie, Lei 503
Xie, Li 503
Xin, Zhiyun 1121
Xu, Guangyou 868
Xu, Hui 285
Xu, Wenjun 485, 819
Xu, Youlin 103
Xu, Ming 360

Yamanaka, Kazuhiro 1108
Yang, Laurence T. 973, 1089
Yang, Mei 295, 370
Yang, Wen-Cheng 434
Yang, Xuejun 557
Yang, Yuan 434
Yeom, Gwyduk 73
Yi, Jongkyu 787
Yin, Jianping 1181
Yokota, Masao 1066
Yoo, Geel-Sang 93
Yoo, Jae-Hoon 392
Yoo, Sang-Jo 709
Yoon, Won-Joong 758
Youn, Hee Yong 663, 1098
Yu, Zhiwen 898
Yuan, Weiwei 849
Yun, Xiaochun 295

Zhang, Baopeng 195
Zhang, Boyun 1181
Zhang, Daqing 173
Zhang, Fan 402
Zhang, Jian 402
Zhang, Liang 235
Zhang, Qin 888
Zhang, Shensheng 1024
Zhang, Yaoxue 1003, 1014

Zhang, Ying 235
Zhang, Yong 1024
Zhao, Jizhong 878
Zheng, Di 908
Zheng, Ran 888
Zheng, Song 173
Zheng, Yuan 579
Zhong, Ming 1003, 1014
Zhou, Xingming 340
Zhou, Xingshe 1140
Zhou, Yuezhi 1003, 1014
Zhou, Zude 485
Zhu, Manli 173
Zou, Peng 908

Lecture Notes in Computer Science

For information about Vols. 1–4504

please contact your bookseller or Springer

Vol. 4611: J. Indulska, J. Ma, L.T. Yang, T. Ungerer, J. Cao (Eds.), Ubiquitous Intelligence and Computing. XXIII, 1257 pages. 2007.

Vol. 4610: B. Xiao, L.T. Yang, J. Ma, C. Muller-Schloer, Y. Hua (Eds.), Autonomic and Trusted Computing. XVIII, 571 pages. 2007.

Vol. 4605: D. Papadias, D. Zhang, G. Kollios (Eds.), Advances in Spatial and Temporal Databases. X, 479 pages. 2007.

Vol. 4602: S. Barker, G.-J. Ahn (Eds.), Data and Applications Security XXI. X, 291 pages. 2007.

Vol. 4600: H. Comon-Lundh, C. Kirchner, H. Kirchner, Rewriting, Computation and Proof. XVI, 273 pages. 2007.

Vol. 4598: G. Lin (Ed.), Computing and Combinatorics. XII, 570 pages. 2007.

Vol. 4597: P. Perner (Ed.), Advances in Data Mining. XI, 353 pages. 2007. (Sublibrary LNAI).

Vol. 4596: L. Arge, C. Cachin, T. Jurdzinski, A. Tarlecki (Eds.), Automata, Languages and Programming. XVII, 953 pages. 2007.

Vol. 4595: D. Bošnački, S. Edelkamp (Eds.), Model Checking Software. X, 285 pages. 2007.

Vol. 4592: Z. Kedad, N. Lammari, E. Métais, F. Meziane, Y. Rezgui (Eds.), Natural Language Processing and Information Systems. XIV, 442 pages. 2007.

Vol. 4591: J. Davies, J. Gibbons (Eds.), Integrated Formal Methods. IX, 660 pages. 2007.

Vol. 4590: W. Damm, H. Hermanns (Eds.), Computer Aided Verification. XV, 562 pages. 2007.

Vol. 4589: J. Münch, P. Abrahamsson (Eds.), Product-Focused Software Process Improvement. XII, 414 pages. 2007.

Vol. 4588: T. Harju, J. Karhumäki, A. Lepistö (Eds.), Developments in Language Theory. XI, 423 pages. 2007.

Vol. 4587: R. Cooper, J. Kennedy (Eds.), Data Management. XIII, 259 pages. 2007.

Vol. 4586: J. Pieprzyk, H. Ghodosi, E. Dawson (Eds.), Information Security and Privacy. XIV, 476 pages. 2007.

Vol. 4585: M. Kryszkiewicz, J.F. Peters, H. Rybinski, A. Skowron (Eds.), Rough Sets and Intelligent Systems Paradigms. XIX, 836 pages. 2007. (Sublibrary LNAI).

Vol. 4584: N. Karssemeijer, B. Lelieveldt (Eds.), Information Processing in Medical Imaging. XX, 777 pages. 2007.

Vol. 4583: S.R. Della Rocca (Ed.), Typed Lambda Calculi and Applications. X, 397 pages. 2007.

Vol. 4582: J. Lopez, P. Samarati, J.L. Ferrer (Eds.), Public Key Infrastructure. XI, 375 pages. 2007.

Vol. 4581: A. Petrenko, M. Veanes, J. Tretmans, W. Grieskamp (Eds.), Testing of Software and Communicating Systems. XII, 379 pages. 2007.

Vol. 4580: B. Ma, K. Zhang (Eds.), Combinatorial Pattern Matching. XII, 366 pages. 2007.

Vol. 4578: F. Masulli, S. Mitra, G. Pasi (Eds.), Applications of Fuzzy Sets Theory. XVIII, 693 pages. 2007. (Sublibrary LNAI).

Vol. 4577: N. Sebe, Y. Liu, Y. Zhuang (Eds.), Multimedia Content Analysis and Mining. XIII, 513 pages. 2007.

Vol. 4576: D. Leivant, R. de Queiroz (Eds.), Logic, Language, Information, and Computation. X, 363 pages. 2007.

Vol. 4575: T. Takagi, T. Okamoto, E. Okamoto, T. Okamoto (Eds.), Pairing-Based Cryptography. XI, 408 pages. 2007.

Vol. 4574: J. Derrick, J. Vain (Eds.), Formal Techniques for Networked and Distributed Systems – FORTE 2007. XI, 375 pages. 2007.

Vol. 4573: M. Kauers, M. Kerber, R. Miner, W. Windsteiger (Eds.), Towards Mechanized Mathematical Assistants. XIII, 407 pages. 2007. (Sublibrary LNAI).

Vol. 4572: F. Stajano, C. Meadows, S. Capkun, T. Moore (Eds.), Security and Privacy in Ad-hoc and Sensor Networks. X, 247 pages. 2007.

Vol. 4570: H.G. Okuno, M. Ali (Eds.), New Trends in Applied Artificial Intelligence. XXI, 1194 pages. 2007. (Sublibrary LNAI).

Vol. 4569: A. Butz, B. Fisher, A. Krüger, P. Olivier, S. Owada (Eds.), Smart Graphics. IX, 237 pages. 2007.

Vol. 4566: M.J. Dainoff (Ed.), Ergonomics and Health Aspects of Work with Computers. XVIII, 390 pages. 2007.

Vol. 4565: D.D. Schmorrow, L.M. Reeves (Eds.), Foundations of Augmented Cognition. XIX, 450 pages. 2007. (Sublibrary LNAI).

Vol. 4564: D. Schuler (Ed.), Online Communities and Social Computing. XVII, 520 pages. 2007.

Vol. 4563: R. Shumaker (Ed.), Virtual Reality. XXII, 762 pages. 2007.

Vol. 4562: D. Harris (Ed.), Engineering Psychology and Cognitive Ergonomics. XXIII, 879 pages. 2007. (Sublibrary LNAI).

Vol. 4561: V.G. Duffy (Ed.), Digital Human Modeling. XXIII, 1068 pages. 2007.

Vol. 4560: N. Aykin (Ed.), Usability and Internationalization, Part II. XVIII, 576 pages. 2007.

Vol. 4559: N. Aykin (Ed.), Usability and Internationalization, Part I. XVIII, 661 pages. 2007.

Vol. 4551: J.A. Jacko (Ed.), Human-Computer Interaction, Part II. XXIII, 1253 pages. 2007.

Vol. 4550: J.A. Jacko (Ed.), Human-Computer Interaction, Part I. XXIII, 1240 pages. 2007.

Vol. 4549: J. Aspnes, C. Scheideler, A. Arora, S. Madden (Eds.), Distributed Computing in Sensor Systems. XIII, 417 pages. 2007.

Vol. 4548: N. Olivetti (Ed.), Automated Reasoning with Analytic Tableaux and Related Methods. X, 245 pages. 2007. (Sublibrary LNAI).

Vol. 4547: C. Carlet, B. Sunar (Eds.), Arithmetic of Finite Fields. XI, 355 pages. 2007.

Vol. 4546: J. Kleijn, A. Yakovlev (Eds.), Petri Nets and Other Models of Concurrency – ICATPN 2007. XI, 515 pages. 2007.

Vol. 4545: H. Anai, K. Horimoto, T. Kutsia (Eds.), Algebraic Biology. XIII, 379 pages. 2007.

Vol. 4544: S. Cohen-Boulakia, V. Tannen (Eds.), Data Integration in the Life Sciences. XI, 282 pages. 2007. (Sublibrary LNBI).

Vol. 4543: A.K. Bandara, M. Burgess (Eds.), Inter-Domain Management. XII, 237 pages. 2007.

Vol. 4542: P. Sawyer, B. Paech, P. Heymans (Eds.), Requirements Engineering: Foundation for Software Quality. IX, 384 pages. 2007.

Vol. 4541: T. Okadome, T. Yamazaki, M. Makhtari (Eds.), Pervasive Computing for Quality of Life Enhancement. IX, 248 pages. 2007.

Vol. 4539: N.H. Bshouty, C. Gentile (Eds.), Learning Theory. XII, 634 pages. 2007. (Sublibrary LNAI).

Vol. 4538: F. Escolano, M. Vento (Eds.), Graph-Based Representations in Pattern Recognition. XII, 416 pages. 2007.

Vol. 4537: K.C.-C. Chang, W. Wang, L. Chen, C.A. Ellis, C.-H. Hsu, A.C. Tsoi, H. Wang (Eds.), Advances in Web and Network Technologies, and Information Management. XXIII, 707 pages. 2007.

Vol. 4536: G. Concas, E. Damiani, M. Scotto, G. Succi (Eds.), Agile Processes in Software Engineering and Extreme Programming. XV, 276 pages. 2007.

Vol. 4534: I. Tomkos, F. Neri, J. Solé Pareta, X. Masip Bruin, S. Sánchez Lopez (Eds.), Optical Network Design and Modeling. XI, 460 pages. 2007.

Vol. 4533: F. Baader (Ed.), Term Rewriting and Applications. XII, 419 pages. 2007.

Vol. 4531: J. Indulska, K. Raymond (Eds.), Distributed Applications and Interoperable Systems. XI, 337 pages. 2007.

Vol. 4530: D.H. Akehurst, R. Vogel, R.F. Paige (Eds.), Model Driven Architecture- Foundations and Applications. X, 219 pages. 2007.

Vol. 4529: P. Melin, O. Castillo, L.T. Aguilar, J. Kacprzyk, W. Pedrycz (Eds.), Foundations of Fuzzy Logic and Soft Computing. XIX, 830 pages. 2007. (Sublibrary LNAI).

Vol. 4528: J. Mira, J.R. Álvarez (Eds.), Nature Inspired Problem-Solving Methods in Knowledge Engineering, Part II. XXII, 650 pages. 2007.

Vol. 4527: J. Mira, J.R. Álvarez (Eds.), Bio-inspired Modeling of Cognitive Tasks, Part I. XXII, 630 pages. 2007.

Vol. 4526: M. Malek, M. Reitenspieß, A. van Moorsel (Eds.), Service Availability. X, 155 pages. 2007.

Vol. 4525: C. Demetrescu (Ed.), Experimental Algorithms. XIII, 448 pages. 2007.

Vol. 4524: M. Marchiori, J.Z. Pan, C.d.S. Marie (Eds.), Web Reasoning and Rule Systems. XI, 382 pages. 2007.

Vol. 4523: Y.-H. Lee, H.-N. Kim, J. Kim, Y. Park, L.T. Yang, S.W. Kim (Eds.), Embedded Software and Systems. XIX, 829 pages. 2007.

Vol. 4522: B.K. Ersbøll, K.S. Pedersen (Eds.), Image Analysis. XVIII, 989 pages. 2007.

Vol. 4521: J. Katz, M. Yung (Eds.), Applied Cryptography and Network Security. XIII, 498 pages. 2007.

Vol. 4519: E. Franconi, M. Kifer, W. May (Eds.), The Semantic Web: Research and Applications. XVIII, 830 pages. 2007.

Vol. 4517: F. Boavida, E. Monteiro, S. Mascolo, Y. Koucheryavy (Eds.), Wired/Wireless Internet Communications. XIV, 382 pages. 2007.

Vol. 4516: L. Mason, T. Drwiega, J. Yan (Eds.), Managing Traffic Performance in Converged Networks. XXIII, 1191 pages. 2007.

Vol. 4515: M. Naor (Ed.), Advances in Cryptology - EUROCRYPT 2007. XIII, 591 pages. 2007.

Vol. 4514: S.N. Artemov, A. Nerode (Eds.), Logical Foundations of Computer Science. XI, 513 pages. 2007.

Vol. 4513: M. Fischetti, D.P. Williamson (Eds.), Integer Programming and Combinatorial Optimization. IX, 500 pages. 2007.

Vol. 4511: C. Conati, K. McCoy, G. Paliouras (Eds.), User Modeling 2007. XVI, 487 pages. 2007. (Sublibrary LNAI).

Vol. 4510: P. Van Hentenryck, L. Wolsey (Eds.), Integration of AI and OR Techniques in Constraint Programming for Combinatorial Optimization Problems. X, 391 pages. 2007.

Vol. 4509: Z. Kobti, D. Wu (Eds.), Advances in Artificial Intelligence. XII, 552 pages. 2007. (Sublibrary LNAI).

Vol. 4508: M.-Y. Kao, X.-Y. Li (Eds.), Algorithmic Aspects in Information and Management. VIII, 428 pages. 2007.

Vol. 4507: F. Sandoval, A. Prieto, J. Cabestany, M. Graña (Eds.), Computational and Ambient Intelligence. XXVI, 1167 pages. 2007.

Vol. 4506: D. Zeng, I. Gotham, K. Komatsu, C. Lynch, M. Thurmond, D. Madigan, B. Lober, J. Kvach, H. Chen (Eds.), Intelligence and Security Informatics: Biosurveillance. XI, 234 pages. 2007.

Vol. 4505: G. Dong, X. Lin, W. Wang, Y. Yang, J.X. Yu (Eds.), Advances in Data and Web Management. XXII, 896 pages. 2007.

GPSR Compliance

The European Union's (EU) General Product Safety Regulation (GPSR) is a set of rules that requires consumer products to be safe and our obligations to ensure this.

If you have any concerns about our products, you can contact us on ProductSafety@springernature.com

In case Publisher is established outside the EU, the EU authorized representative is:

Springer Nature Customer Service Center GmbH
Europaplatz 3
69115 Heidelberg, Germany

Batch number: 10844661

Printed by Printforce, the Netherlands